HANDGUNS 2004

16th Annual Edition

Edited by
Dave Arnold

Manuscripts, contributions and inquiries, including first class return postage, should be sent to the HANDGUNS Editorial Offices, Krause Publications, 700 E. State Street, Iola, WI 54990-0001. All materials received will receive reasonable care, but we will not be responsible for their safe return. Material accepted is subject to our requirements for editing and revisions. Author payment covers all rights and title to the accepted material, including photos, drawings and other illustrations. Payment is at our current rates.

CAUTION: Technical data presented here, particularly technical data on the handloading and on firearms adjustment and alteration, inevitably reflects individual experience with particular equipment and components under specific circumstances the reader cannot duplicate exactly. Such data presentations therefore should be used for guidance only and with caution. Krause Publications, Inc., accepts no responsibility for results obtained using this data.

Published by

kp krause publications
An F&W Publications Company

700 East State Street • Iola, WI 54990-0001
715-445-2214 • 888-457-2873
www.krause.com

Please call or write for our free catalog of publications.
Our toll-free number to place an order or obtain a free catalog is 800-258-0929
or please use our regular business telephone, 715-445-2214.

Library of Congress Catalog Number: 88-72115
ISBN: 0-87349-649-3

Edited by Ken Ramage
Designed by Ethel Thulien, Patsy Howell, and Tom Nelsen

— HANDGUNS STAFF —

Dave Arnold, Editor

Ken Ramage, Editor
Firearms & DBI Books

Editorial Comments and Suggestions

We're always looking for feedback on our books. Please let us know what you like about this edition. If you have suggestions for articles you'd like to see in future editions, please contact.

Ken Ramage/Handguns
700 East State St.
Iola, WI 54990
email: ramagek@krause.com

About Our Covers...

Colt Firearms, Doug Turnbull Restoration and Adams & Adams Engraving have teamed to produce the Charlton Heston Commemorative Peacemaker. Offered in two grades, Standard and Custom, these limited-edition revolvers commemorate Heston's contribution to the NRA and the American shooting sportsman.

Front Cover: The Custom Grade issue includes the Colt Model P Single Action Army revolver numbered 001CH to 026CH. Each SAA has been reworked to duplicate guns of the 1st Generation. This includes enlarging cylinder flutes & beveling the cylinder's leading edge; beveling the trigger guard and flush-fitting the hammer and backstrap. This issue, like the Standard Grade, has been specially polished in the manner and degree of SAAs produced circa 1913. There the resemblance ends. Each Custom SAA receives B-Master engraving plus a single gold ring at both the front and rear of the barrel, and two gold rings around the rear of the cylinder. Grips are one-piece ivory, with carved "CH" monogram and "NRA" lettering on the left and right grip panels, respectively. The backstrap and butt carry the same gold-plated signature and dates of presidency as found on the Standard Grade. Each Custom SAA is delivered with a presentation–grade walnut case and a leather-bound book, *Charlton Heston*, embossed in gold.

Back Cover: The Standard Grade revolvers, numbered 101CH to 999CH, have been specially polished in the manner and degree of SAAs produced circa 1913. Each revolver receives B+ engraving and a unique rollmark of the NRA banner on the barrel, plus a gold-plated Heston signature on the backstrap as well as dates of his presidency on the butt. The Standard Grade SAA comes with Colt factory hard rubber grips and is delivered with a presentation–grade walnut case patterned after an early Colt case.

Both grades include traditional SAA finishes: color case frame, loading gate and hammer; the balance in the charcoal blue finish. Also included are six cartridges and a copy of the Bill of Rights signed by Charlton Heston.

For more details on this offering, call (866-999-4867) or Doug Turnbull Restoration (585-657-6338).
A portion of all proceeds will go to Charleton Heston's endowment for the NRA.

Handguns 2004

∽ Handguns for Sport and Personal Protection ∽

CONTENTS

Page 60

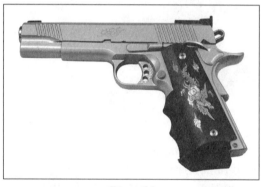

Page 65

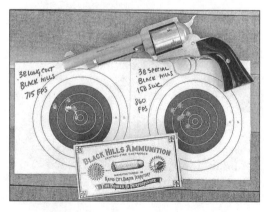

Page 114

CATALOG OF TODAY'S HANDGUNS

SEMI-CUSTOM HANDGUNS

COMMERCIAL HANDGUNS

CENTERFIRE & RIMFIRE

BLACKPOWDER

AIRGUNS

ACCESSORIES

REFERENCE

Page 123

Page 142

Page 205

Page 227

HANDGUN NEWS

AUTOLOADERS

by John Malloy

THERE IS SO much going on that it is difficult to quickly summarize the situation as it pertains to autoloading handguns. At the February 2003 SHOT Show, a surprising number of prototypes and pre-production specimens were exhibited. Although there was a great variety of new pistols, the largest number of recent new model introductions have been for the 45 ACP, and most were based on the 1911 design.

It is hard to believe that the 45 ACP (Automatic Colt Pistol) cartridge, introduced in 1905, and the Colt/Browning 1911 pistol design are just a short time shy of their 100th birthdays. Yet, they remain among the most popular cartridge and pistol choices available today.

The big-bore spotlight does not belong exclusively to the 45 ACP, however. Two other new 45-caliber cartridges have been recently introduced. In addition, smaller-caliber bottleneck centerfire pistol cartridges have entered the scene and are gaining recognition. The 22 Long Rifle (22 LR) remains ever popular, and new pistols—and conversion kits to adapt existing centerfire pistols to 22—are offered. The 17-caliber rimfire made an amazing debut in the rifle field last year, and a new 17-caliber cartridge—and new 17-caliber semiautomatic pistols adapted for it—are now being offered.

Autoloading handguns are acquired by ordinary people for personal protection, for competition, for hunting, for plinking and fun and relaxation; and to some degree, for collecting—or just pride of ownership. With the threat of terrorism now never far from our minds, perhaps defense of our families and ourselves plays an even larger role than before. The personal protection aspect is important, and most of the autoloading pistols offered are suitable for such use.

Politics continues to influence the world of autoloading handguns. The

elections of November 2002 were encouraging, but did not stanch the flow of anti-gun efforts. Some firearms manufacturers have gone out of business, due in part to restrictive legislation, or to litigation. States such as California, Maryland, Massachusetts and New Jersey make their own rules as to what handguns can and cannot be sold within their borders. Gunmakers must decide whether or not to redesign and retool to conform to these rules. Substantial expense is required to change a pistol design, with no guarantee it will be approved. Some companies just resign themselves to not selling in restrictive states. Nevertheless, more manufacturers are incorporating lock and safety mechanisms into their pistols in an effort to comply with at least some of these restrictions.

Guns have been prominent in the news in the past year or so. The "DC Sniper" killings of October 2002 brought predictable calls for more gun control. However, many people saw, instead, the advantage of ordinary citizens being armed. After a

series of murders of women in the Baton Rouge area of Louisiana, the Governor of that state made a public statement that people should become licensed and then carry pistols for personal protection. Airline pilots, after a long uphill fight, were finally authorized by Congress to carry firearms. Or were they? Bureaucratic restrictions were so onerous that at the time of this writing, not a single pilot has been legally armed.

In early 2003, as pressure mounted for war against Iraq, new threats of terrorist activities increased, and the country was put on Orange Alert. Government officials made announcements concerning preparations for a terrorist attack. Although such advice never mentioned firearms (but recommended duct tape), many people read between the lines. They realized they were ultimately responsible for their safety, and that of their loved ones. Another firearm (or a first firearm, for some) seemed like a good idea. Pistols, especially, were favored to be available in case of an emergency.

Stainless-steel firearms made under the AMT name are no longer available. Galena Industries, the manufacturer, went out of business in 2002. AMT handguns tended to be innovative trend eye-catching. Here, Malloy shoots an AMT Long Slide Hardballer, a 1911-style pistol with an impressive 7-inch barrel.

The 22-caliber Beretta U22 Neos pistol is now in production and several variants are available. Malloy tries out one that is equipped with a red-dot sight.

A deluxe version of the 22-caliber NEOS pistol has been added, with optional grip frames and sights. 7 1/2-inch barrels and Inox (stainless) finishes are also available.

The new "Special Duty" specimens of the Beretta 92 and 96 pistols have an integral accessory rail, a heavier "Brigadier" slide and other features.

The new Beretta 92G-SD is an updated version of the original Beretta 92. Here, the new 9mm is fired by Clo Malloy, the writer's sister-in-law.

High-capacity pistols are still being introduced, even though they are limited to 10-round magazines unless sold to police or military. There is a logical reason for this continued interest in high-capacity handguns by people who cannot acquire the high-capacity magazines. Just a short distance down the road lies September 2004. At that time, the so-called "Assault Weapons" law of September 1994 is due to expire. One provision that affected autoloading pistol shooters was the ban on magazines that hold more than 10 rounds. It will be good when this restriction is gone. This provision has created two classes of citizens in the United States—ordinary people who could not be "trusted" with more than 10 shots, and agents of the government who could have more than 10. This provision has

driven a wedge between law enforcement and the armed citizen, who is traditionally the greatest ally of the police. This situation should not be allowed to continue. However, anti-gun forces are campaigning to extend the law past its end time.

These are some of the factors influencing the world of autoloading handguns. With all this in mind, let's take a look at what the companies are doing:

AMT

The innovative stainless-steel pistols made under the AMT name are no longer available. The AMT trademark appeared on a number of "firsts" in the firearms industry. The company was the first to make an all-stainless 1911-type pistol, and first to offer a subcompact 380. They marketed semiautomatic pistols in

calibers from 22 Long Rifle (22 LR) to 50 Action Express (50 AE). In 1998, Galena Industries acquired the right to produce most of the AMT-developed firearms. Within a few years, the company moved from restrictive California to Sturgis, South Dakota, for a new start. Somehow, it did not work out. The final remaining assets of the company were sold at auction in August 2002. Parts are still available from Numrich Gun Parts and Jack First, but shooters will miss the variety of pistols offered under the AMT name.

Arms Moravia

The on-again, off-again importation of the striking-looking Arms Moravia CZ-G2000 seems to have stabilized. Anderson Arms of Fort Worth, TX will import the pistol. Introduced in 1999, the polymer-frame pistol is now available in all-black or two-tone (nickel slide and black frame) variants. Chambering options are 9mm and 40 S&W. Arms Moravia also makes a nifty little miniature 380 pistol, the ZP 98, which uses a gas-delayed blow-back system. However, it is too small to be imported into the United States under the restrictions of the Gun Control Act of 1968 (GCA 68).

Beretta

The new 22-caliber pistol, the U22 Neos, introduced last year, is now in production. It is the first Beretta pistol 100-percent designed and manufactured in the United States. In case you were wondering, "Neos" is from the Greek, meaning "new." This new Beretta has a replaceable polymer grip frame and comes in 4 1/2-inch and 6-inch barrel lengths.

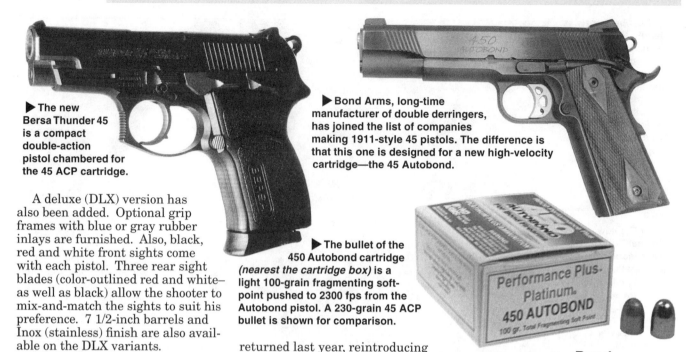

▶ The new Bersa Thunder 45 is a compact double-action pistol chambered for the 45 ACP cartridge.

▶ Bond Arms, long-time manufacturer of double derringers, has joined the list of companies making 1911-style 45 pistols. The difference is that this one is designed for a new high-velocity cartridge—the 45 Autobond.

▶ The bullet of the 450 Autobond cartridge *(nearest the cartridge box)* is a light 100-grain fragmenting soft-point pushed to 2300 fps from the Autobond pistol. A 230-grain 45 ACP bullet is shown for comparison.

A deluxe (DLX) version has also been added. Optional grip frames with blue or gray rubber inlays are furnished. Also, black, red and white front sights come with each pistol. Three rear sight blades (color-outlined red and white–as well as black) allow the shooter to mix-and-match the sights to suit his preference. 7 1/2-inch barrels and Inox (stainless) finish are also available on the DLX variants.

All the Neos pistols have their sights set into a mounting rib that allows easy installation of optical or electronic sights.

The modular construction of the U22 pistol has led to speculation that a light carbine, based on the same operating mechanism, might be introduced. Such a carbine is under development, but is not now available.

In the centerfire line, the new models 92- and 96G-SD (92 indicates 9mm, 96 indicates 40-caliber) have been introduced. To further break the code, **G** denotes a de-cocker mechanism, and SD represents "Special Duty." The pistols might be seen as a modernized alternative to the original 92. The new SD guns have an accessory rail integral with the frame, a "Brigadier" heavy reinforced slide, and 3-dot tritium night sights. The frame is checkered front and back, and the magazine well is beveled.

Your writer had the opportunity to shoot a new 9mm 92G-SD. Standing at the short-range line of a police range, I faced a standard silhouette target that had been liberally sprinkled by other shooters. Looking for an untouched spot, I chose the left ear. The pistol put nine shots in a cluster on the ear, with only one slightly out of the group. I think it is safe to say that shooters will find the Beretta SD pistols acceptably accurate.

The Beretta B-LOK locking device is being phased in on pistols in the company's line.

Bernardelli

Gone from the handgun scene for some time, the Bernardelli name

returned last year, reintroducing much of its previous pistol line. Since then, the company has also added a series of pistols based on the CZ-75 design.

Now, a new design has entered the Bernardelli line. The new pistols are polymer-frame guns using the basic CZ-75 mechanism. To say this is a colorful line is something of an understatement. Frames are available in black, blue, yellow, red, white and purple. Should that array not offer enough choices, slides are available in black or silver finish. The new polymer-frame Bernardelli pistols are designated Model 2000. They entered production in early 2003.

Bersa

The Argentine Bersa firm is noted for their compact blowback pocket pistols. A departure for the company was the introduction of a double-action locked-breech 45-caliber arm in 2003.

The new Bersa, designated the Thunder 45 Ultra Compact, is a nice-looking pistol that feels good in the hand. It has a conventional double-action trigger mechanism, that is, double-action for the first shot, single-action for succeeding shots. The barrel length is 3.6 inches. The pistol measures 4.9 inches high by 6.7 inches long, which neatly puts it into the compact category (5x7). Weight is 27 ounces. The magazine holds 7 rounds, giving the pistol a 7+1 capacity. Finishes are offered as matte black, Duo-tone and satin nickel. Availability of the Thunder 45 was scheduled for Spring 2003, from Eagle Imports.

Bond

Bond Arms, a long-time maker of double derringers, has entered the semi-auto field with their own 1911-style pistol. The Bond pistol has many of the features in vogue with today's shooters. It is not just a newcomer to the pack, however, as it is designed for its own unique cartridge—the 450 Autobond.

The 450 Autobond round is an interesting concept. Externally of about the same dimensions as the 45 ACP, the Autobond cartridge uses a very light 100-grain bullet pushed to the impressive speed of 2300 feet per second (fps) from a 5-inch barrel. Not since the 1904 appearance of the Danish Schouboe pistol has this approach been tried for a 45-caliber pistol. The Schouboe cartridge used an extremely light 63-grain bullet pushed to 1600 fps, an impressive speed for a handgun of those days. The Schouboe, however, used the light bullet to keep pressures within the capabilities of its blowback action. The Bond pistol was designed for very different circumstances.

The Bond uses the traditional tilting-barrel locking system of the 1911 design. The cartridge case is a reinforced version of the 45 ACP case, and is designed to be used in a fully-supported chamber. Thus, the cartridge is not recommended for use in pistols other than the Bond. The bullet is a frangible one that, in Bond's words, "resists over-penetration." Recoil is reported to be only slightly greater than that of a standard 45 ACP 230-grain load. Those who choose the Bond pistol can make

Browning has introduced a new polymer-frame double-action pistol in 9mm and 40 S&W calibers. This is the Pro-9, in 9mm, with a dual-tone finish.

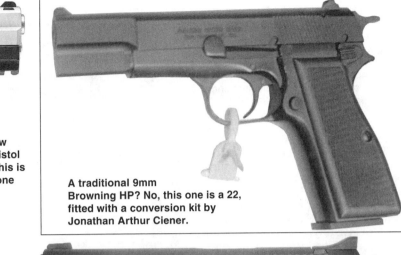

A traditional 9mm Browning HP? No, this one is a 22, fitted with a conversion kit by Jonathan Arthur Ciener.

the recoil comparison for themselves. The Autobond can use standard 45 ACP cartridges as well as the special 450 round.

Browning

New for Browning are polymer-frame pistols in 9mm and 40 S&W. The frames of the new PRO-9 and PRO-40 pistols have integral accessory rails and interchangeable backstrap inserts.

Trigger action is conventional double action, with single-action shots after the first. A cocked hammer can be lowered by a decocking lever. In this case, from either side, as the ambidextrous design has a decocking lever on both sides of the frame. The plugged magazines hold, for ordinary Americans, ten rounds of either cartridge.

Browning celebrated its 125th anniversary in 2003, taking the company's history back to 1878, when John M. Browning introduced his famous single-shot rifle. In commemoration, four famous firearms that have carried the Browning name were made as limited editions. The four guns were the Single-Shot, the 22 autoloading rifle, the Superposed shotgun, and—representing the Browning pistols—the 9mm Hi-Power. Only 125 of the Belgian-made commemorative 9mm pistols were to be made. They will have scroll engraving, gold highlights and select walnut grips.

The standard Hi-Power is mysteriously absent from the 2003 Browning master catalog. This situation has led to rumors that Browning has—or plans to—discontinue the Hi-Power. A Browning representative told your writer that this was not so, but was at a loss to explain the absence.

Century

Century International Arms' line of 1911-style 45 pistols, introduced in 2001, has been well-received. The guns are made in the Philip-

pines by SAM (Shooters Arms Manufacturing, Inc.) and include traditional and enhanced variants.

Introduced in 2003 were several new models. The Blue Thunder Commodore is a 4 1/4-inch barrel version of the original striking-looking full-size Blue Thunder. The Commodore 1911 is a 4 1/4-inch enhanced pistol without the distinctive trigger guard and sculptured grip of the Blue Thunder.

The SAM Chief is mechanically the same as the original Blue Thunder, but has a matte finish rather than the original's polished blue. The SAM GI is a more-or-less traditional 1911 design, but with a 4 1/4-inch barrel.

Perhaps the most interesting is the Falcon pistol—a full-size high-capacity pistol *(which now comes with a 10-round magazine)*. It is built with a steel, rather than polymer, frame. Small separate grip panels are attached. The Falcon has a squared trigger guard and extended controls, including an extended magazine release.

Charles Daly

Charles Daly / KBI has discontinued its line of double-action polymer-frame pistols to concentrate on its single-action line. New are the Daly M-5 polymer-frame high-capacity 1911 pistols. Built by BUL in Israel, the pistols feature beavertail grip safeties and ambidextrous manual safeties. Variants are Government, Commander and IPSC models,

Charles Daly is offering the new M-5 high-capacity polymer-frame 1911-style pistols, in several variants. Shown here is the Commander version.

scheduled for Spring 2003, and the smaller M-5 Ultra-X, coming later.

The newest pistol in the Charles Daly lineup is the Daly HP. Not surprisingly, it is basically a copy of the original Browning HP ("Hi-Power") pistol, a 9mm single-action design. It has the early burr-type hammer spur, but some modern niceties—extended safety lever, ball & bar type express sights, and Uncle Mike's rubber grip panels—have been added. Availability was scheduled for the first quarter of 2003.

Ciener

The 22 Long Rifle (22 LR) conversions of Jonathan Arthur Ciener are especially popular in localities that limit the number of handguns a person may possess. They are not additional firearms, but are kits that may be quickly installed or removed by the shooter. Even without such restrictions, shooters can save ammunition money, get in more practice, and get one gun to serve several purposes. The pistol conversion kits have been available for 1911-type pistols, Beretta and Taurus models, and various Glocks.

Newly introduced is a conversion kit for the Browning Hi-Power and

It looks like a brand new Colt Model 1911—because it really is. Colt is bringing back the original 1911 design of the World War I period, complete with original markings. This prototype is serial number *1002X*.

derivative pistols. Availability was scheduled for May 2003.

The kits are available with fixed or adjustable sights, and in matte, high polish or silver finishes. This variety lets shooters match the conversion to the gun's original finish, or create a two-tone effect. Says Ciener, "I don't want to give anyone an excuse to not get a conversion kit."

Cobra

Cobra Enterprises, which took over the defunct Republic, Talon and Davis pistol designs last year, has made improvements and has also added a new line.

Here is a key to the Cobra line: Pistols in the Patriot series are double-action-only (DAO) and have black polymer frames and stainless-steel slide. Chamberings are 45, 9mm and 380. The 45 is the former Republic 45. The 9mm and 380 are improved Talon designs.

The Freedom series comprises 32- and 38-caliber metal-frame pistols. The CA32 and CA380 are modified Davis pistols. New this year are modifications of the old Lorcin design in 32 and 380. Many people liked the Lorcins, and the company sold a lot of guns in years gone by; the design gives Cobra an addition to their line of larger pistols in 32- and 38-calibers.

Many shooters did not like the situation in which misguided legislation and litigation were able to drive legitimate manufacturers out of business. It is good that updates of these affordable designs are again available.

Colt

Colt continues to explore the roots of its semi-auto pistol line. Recall that about two years ago, the company brought out its recreation of the Model 1911A1 as produced at the beginning of World War II. Now it will offer the original Model 1911 as made in the 1918 period. A prototype, serial number 1002X, was displayed at the February 2003 SHOT Show. This will be an authentic 1911, complete to the unrelieved frame, lanyard loop, narrow-slot grip screws and original markings. All required "modern" markings will be on the frame under the grips.

About 3000 of the 1911A1 recreations were made, and it is no longer in production. Note that the serial numbers had a "WMK" prefix *(for Colt's head, Lt. Gen. William M. Keys, who authorized the project)*. The new 1911 pistols will use "WMK" as a serial number suffix. Availability was scheduled for May 2003.

Colt also offers the reproduction of the Series 70 Government Model—a recreation of the pistol produced during the 1970s. The only difference I could spot is the "big diamond" rosewood grips, which the original pistols did not have.

To prove they do not dwell in the past, Colt also has introduced its Gunsite pistol. The pistol was built incorporating ideas from Colt and the Gunsite training facility in Arizona. Features include a "palm swell" beavertail grip safety, Heinie front and Novak rear sights, Wilson extended safety lever, McCormick hammer and sear, and two 8-round Wilson magazines. The gun comes with a $100 coupon good toward training at Gunsite. The Gunsite pistol will be available in blue or stainless-steel finishes.

CZ

Two new CZ pistols are being offered.

The CZ P-01 was accepted last year by the Czech National Police. It has also been rated as a NATO-classified pistol. During testing, the number of stoppages was seven during a total of 15,000 rounds fired. The pistol can probably be considered reliable. The P-01 is chambered for the 9mm Parabellum cartridge. It has an aluminum frame with an integral accessory rail and a lanyard loop. It features a decocker, checkered rubber grips and front-and-rear slide serrations. With a 3.8-inch barrel, the pistol mea-

sures 5.3 x 7.2 inches, just a hair over the traditional 5 x 7 measurement for the compact pistol category.

Also new is the CZ 75 Tactical pistol sold with a CZ-logo folding knife. The pistol is a CZ 75B with low-profile sights, checkered rubber grips, a lanyard loop and a green poly-coated frame. Only 1000 Tactical combos were scheduled for production in 2003.

Dan Wesson

The Dan Wesson "Patriot" pistol, introduced last year, is now in full production. Recall that the Patriot is a modification of the 1911 design that uses an external extractor.

In the year 2000, Dan Wesson changed from being a revolver-only company to one that produces revolvers and 45-caliber 1911-type autoloaders. Their line has expanded to cover a number of niches. A special limited-quantity run of 10mm semiautos was scheduled for production in 2003.

DPMS / Panther Arms

Last year, DPMS (Defense Procurement Manufacturing Services) introduced a prototype 1911-type 45 pistol, and production was tentatively scheduled for November 2002.

Latest information from a DPMS representative is that the project has been put on hold. DPMS is a maker of AR-15 style rifles and accessories, and at this time will not add the 45-caliber pistol to their line.

EAA

EAA (European American Armory) is offering two new models in its Witness line.

A polymer-frame Witness will be available with a full-size frame and compact slide. The high-

The NATO-classified CZ P-01 pistol was adopted by the Czech National Police and is now offered for commercial sales.

Mike Lott of FNH USA *(left)* points out the operation of the new Hi-Power SFS (Safe Fast Shooting) system to Malloy.

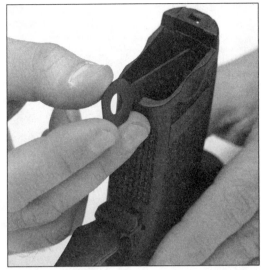

Heckler & Koch is adding a new lockout device to all production pistols.

capacity frame will provide a capacity of 10+1. A bull barrel is fitted to this short slide, which carries low-profile sights. The pistol was so new it had not yet been given a name at the February 2003 SHOT Show.

Some localities permit a 45-caliber or 10mm pistol for big-game hunting if it is equipped with a barrel of six inches or longer. To fill this niche, the Witness Hunter is made with a 6-inch barrel chambered in 45 ACP and 10mm. It is offered with blue or camo finishes, and a scope rail is available.

All right, EAA also has an item that really isn't a semi-auto pistol, but it is related, and so interesting I must mention it. The "Thor" is a conversion unit that can be mounted on a 1911 frame to form a breakopen single-shot hunting pistol. It is offered in 45-70 only now, with other calibers planned for later.

FNH

Recall that FNH USA is the American subsidiary arm of FN Herstal in Belgium. They offer the HP series, commonly thought of as the "Browning Hi-Power." One new HP pistol has been introduced, the HP-SFS. The last three letters stand for "Safe Fast Shooting" and the mechanism combines features of both single-action and double-action systems. When the hammer is cocked and a shot is not to be made, the hammer can simply be pushed forward. This action engages the manual safety, locks the sear and locks the slide. When the safety is pushed down, the hammer rises to its cocked position, and the pistol is ready to fire again.

A new polymer-frame hammer-fired pistol is the FNP 9. The trigger mechanism is conventional double-action, that is, double-action (DA) for the first shot, then single-action (SA) for succeeding shots. Introduced first in 9mm, a 40-caliber version was also scheduled for late in 2003. With a 4-inch barrel, the pistol is 7 inches long and weighs 25 ounces. Magazine capacity for the 9mm is 16 for law enforcement, 10 for us common folk.

The unusual Five-seveN pistol, introduced last year for the special 5.7 x 28mm cartridge, now has an adjustable-sight model added to the line. The new version has a 10-round magazine and a magazine safety. It will be marketed to individual active-duty police officers. Now that there are two versions, the original version has to be called something to differentiate it, so it is now the "Tactical" version.

Glock

Glock has introduced the new Glock 37, a 45-caliber pistol, but not a 45 ACP. The company's previous offering of the Model 21 gave the market a big Glock 45 ACP pistol, and it was subsequently shortened into the 30 and the single-column 36.

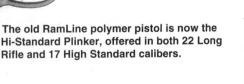

The old RamLine polymer pistol is now the Hi-Standard Plinker, offered in both 22 Long Rifle and 17 High Standard calibers.

The new 17 High Standard *(left)* will work in 22 LR Hi-Standard pistols by simply replacing the barrel. For comparison, the 17 Hornady Magnum Rimfire *(with its parent, the 22 Winchester Magnum Rimfire)* was introduced last year in rifles and the Volquartsen Cheetah pistol.

Near a modest-size enlargement of the new 17 High Standard cartridge, Alan Aronstein of High Standard *(left)* points out to Malloy that only a barrel change was necessary to convert this Hi-Standard Citation to the new 17-caliber cartridge.

The new Hi-Point 45 pistol has adjustable sights, last round hold-open and an accessory rail on a new contoured polymer frame that has separate polymer grips. A similar 40-caliber version is also offered.

Ah—Glock engineers apparently reasoned—it would be possible to produce a full-capacity 45 in the smaller frame size—if only the 45 cartridge were smaller. Accordingly, they created their own cartridge. The new 45 Glock round is smaller than the 45 ACP, with an overall length of 1.10 inches. *(The 45 ACP OAL is 1.28 inches)*. Two 45 Glock loads are planned—a 185-grain bullet at 1100 fps, and a 200-grain bullet at 984 fps.

The Glock 37 pistol has a 4-inch barrel, is 1.18 inches wide and weighs 22 ounces (without magazine). The capacity is 10 + 1.

Heckler & Koch

HK has introduced two new pistols. The P 2000 GPM (German Police Model) is a compact (5x7 inches) polymer-frame 9mm pistol designed for the German Police. The trigger mechanism is HK's LEM (Law Enforcement Modification), in which part of the mechanism is pre-cocked by the slide, allowing a light DA pull for most of the trigger motion, then a short pull

of about 7 pounds to fire. In case of a misfire, the trigger has "second snap" capabilities, but the pull is heavy all the way through. The pistol has a 3.62-inch barrel and features ambidextrous slide releases. Interchangeable rear grip inserts are provided to allow the shooter to fit the pistol to his hand. Magazine capacity is 10 rounds, with larger-capacity magazines now available for law enforcement and military users. A 40 S&W variant is also being planned.

The USP Elite is a new longer variant of the popular USP pistol. Chambered for 9mm and 45 ACP, the Elite has a substantially longer 6.2-inch barrel and elongated 9 1/2-inch slide to match. It has the HK O-ring barrel-positioning system and adjustable target sights. The trigger mechanism is conventional DA, and the trigger has a trigger stop. It has a decocker, but can also be carried cocked-and-locked.

A Lock-Out device is being added to all HK production pistols now.

HIGH STANDARD

High Standard's big news is the 17 caliber. Last year, the 17-rimfire cartridge caught on like wildfire, and a number of companies chambered rifles for the new 17 Hornady Magnum Rimfire (17 HMR) cartridge. Only one semi-auto handgun, however, the Volquartsen Cheetah, was able to handle the 17.

Now, that has changed. High Standard Manufacturing Company

now has several Hi-Standard semi-automatic pistols chambered for a new 17-rimfire cartridge—the 17 High Standard!

A similar cartridge was introduced a year or so ago—at least in concept—as the 17 Aguila. Reportedly, no specimens were actually available at the time of introduction. The 17 Aguila was to be based on the 22 LR case necked down to 17 caliber. The concept interested High Standard as a possibility for use in pistols designed for the 22 LR cartridge. Digging into old company history, High Standard's Alan Aronstein was surprised to learn the company had actually developed a 17-caliber cartridge based on the 22 LR back in 1940, and had made at least one pistol in that chambering. World War II apparently stopped developmental work, and the project lay forgotten.

With this background, High Standard and Aguila got together on the project. Reportedly, the 1940 round was only slightly different in dimension from the specifications of the 17 Aguila. Slight modifications were made, and the cartridge was introduced in January 2003 as the 17 High Standard. With a 20-grain bullet, the pressure is balanced to that of the 22 LR, so that any Hi-Standard pistol can be converted to 17 by simply changing the barrel. This swap also works for removable-barrel rifles, such as the AR-7 Explorer.

High Standard now offers all its target pistols in 17 High Standard as well as 22 LR. From an 18-inch test barrel, the cartridge produced a muzzle velocity of 1830 fps. The 10-inch barrel Hi-Standard Citation pistol reportedly tops 1700 fps.

High Standard has also acquired the rights to the discontinued polymer RamLine pistol, and is also planning to offer it—in 22 LR and 17 High Standard—as the Hi-Standard Plinker. Delivery was scheduled for Fall 2003. The new pistol will resurrect the "Plinker" name and will expand the company's offerings.

Kahr Arms' Randall Casseday displays a prototype of the new Thompson Custom 1911 pistol, an enhanced version of the Auto-Ordnance line of 1911-style pistols. This specimen carries serial number 0002.

Lest someone think I am not consistent, let me mention that the new 17 cartridge was introduced on January 20, 2003 as the "17 High Standard," and I have used that nomenclature. However, at the February 2003 SHOT Show, the round was advertised at the Aguila display as "17 Hi-Standard." Both spellings have long been appropriate in different contexts. The company has always been called "High Standard," and the pistol models have been "Hi-Standard." With the predicted popularity of the new 17 cartridge, the terminology should soon become, shall we say, "standardized."

Also, recall that High Standard introduced its own 45-caliber 1911 pistol line in 2000, and offers variants with 4 1/2-, 5- and 6-inch barrels. In 2003, the company introduced a new Custom line of 1911 pistols.

Hi-Point

Without much fanfare, Hi-Point has introduced two new big-bore pistols. The new polymer-frame handguns are a new 45, and a new 40 S&W. In keeping with Hi-Point's concept of phasing in features, the new guns have push-button magazine release, last round hold-open, 3-dot adjustable sights and frame accessory rails. Magazine safeties *(the gun won't fire with the magazine out)* have also been added. A trigger lock comes with each gun.

Kahr's new little 9mm, the polymer-frame PM9, was introduced last year with a two-tone finish. Now the pistol is in full production, and a new all-black variant has been added.

The new guns have 4 1/2-inch barrels and weigh 32 ounces. The contoured polymer frame feels good in the hand and, unlike most polymer-frame pistols, the grip panels are separate pieces. The 45 uses a 9-shot magazine, and the 40 variant has a 10-rounder. The magazines are different than those previously used in Hi-Point pistols, and are similar in construction to those used in the company's popular 9mm carbine. It is probably not overly speculative to surmise that Hi-Point, looking to the future, plans 40- and 45-caliber carbines and wants magazines to interchange between their pistols and carbines.

The Hi-Points are simple blowbacks, but are "+P" rated, and have a good reputation for functioning. Repair policy is lifetime, with no questions asked. With a suggested retail price of $169, the new Hi-Points are the least expensive big-bore pistols available.

Kahr

The Kahr PM 9, introduced last year, is in full production, and a new variant has been added. The new Kahr has a blackened stainless-steel slide on a black polymer frame. Availability for this variant is scheduled for May 2003. The PM 9 is Kahr's smallest and lightest 9mm pistol, sporting a 3-inch barrel and weighing less than a pound. Small as it is, it is rated for +P and +P+ ammunition. Two magazines—a six-rounder with a flush base and a 7-round version with a grip extension—are furnished.

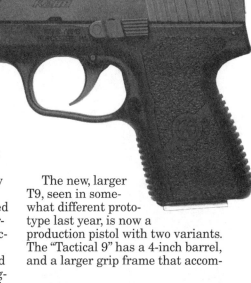

The new, larger T9, seen in somewhat different prototype last year, is now a production pistol with two variants. The "Tactical 9" has a 4-inch barrel, and a larger grip frame that accom-

Kel-Tec's Renee Goldman displays the small size of the company's new 38 ACP pistol, the P-3AT. Diagrams showing the pistol's operation are in the background.

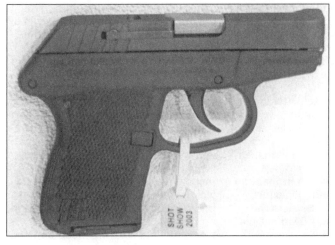

Kel-Tec's new offering is the 380 ACP polymer-frame P-3AT. There are very slight dimensional differences, but the little gun is visually indistinguishable from the firm's 32-caliber P-32.

TRENDS

Here is a first peek at Kimber's new 1911 rimfire pistol, introduced at the February 2003 SHOT Show.

▲ The Kimber TLE (Tactical Law Enforcement) pistol is identical, except for markings, to the sidearm chosen by the Los Angeles Police Department's SWAT Team.

Kimber is now offering 1911 pistols in 22 Long Rifle.

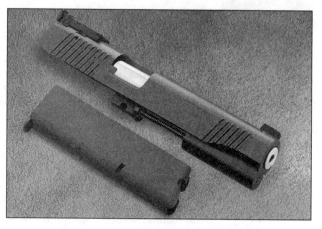

Kimber is also offering a conversion kit to make 1911-type pistols into 22 Long Rifle conversions.

modates checkered wood grips and an 8-round single-column magazine. The construction of frame and slide is matte-finish stainless steel. The pistol measures about 6 1/2 inches by 5 inches and weighs 28 ounces. Sights are Novak low-profile, with tritium night-sight inserts. The "Target 9" is basically the same pistol with an MMC adjustable rear sight.

Also, a TP 9 was introduced, as a polymer-frame pistol with a 4-inch barrel. This new Kahr did not make it in to the company's 2003 catalog, but has a slightly shorter grip frame than the T9, using a 7-round magazine.

Recall that Kahr also offers the Auto-Ordnance line of 45-caliber pistols, in Standard, Deluxe and WWII

Parkerized versions. Now, Kahr is offering a custom 1911. The new Custom pistol will be in stainless steel, with extended safety lever, beveled magazine well, "big diamond" grips, and Chip McCormick trigger and sights.

Kel-Tec

The Florida firm of Kel-Tec comes up with some innovative firearms, both rifles and pistols. The big pistol news is the introduction of their little P-3AT pistol. Sound it out and the name tells its caliber—38. I had to chuckle out loud when I first read the model number.

The new 380 was developed from the popular P-32 (32 ACP) pistol. The clever design makes the P-3AT almost visually indistinguishable from the P-32. It is only about .080-inch longer, and weighs about a half-ounce more.

Thus, the new 380 is about 3.5 inches high by 5.2 inches long, and weighs about 7.2 ounces. Amazingly, the new gun is still only 3/4 of an inch wide. Mechanically, the internal slide stop has been omitted

in the P-3AT, *and (because of the larger-diameter cartridge)* the magazine capacity is reduced to 6 rounds. The nifty little 380 has created a lot of interest, and availability was scheduled for May 2003.

The P-40 pistol has been out of production for a couple of years, and I missed reporting that. A Kel-Tec representative said the pistol worked fine, but the light weight of the gun and the relatively high power of the 40 S&W round could lead to problems when the gun was "limp-wristed" by the shooter.

Kimber

Kimber has been busy in the handgun field. Let's start with the 45-caliber 1911 USA Shooting Team pistol. The distinctive pistol will be used for practice shooting by our rapid-fire pistol team. The gun is offered to the shooting public as the Kimber Team Match II, and for each pistol sold, Kimber is donating $100 to the shooting team. By mid-February 2003, over $50,000 had been raised.

Korth has developed a new 45-caliber version of its semiautomatic pistol. Here is a look at prototype 001.

Korth's Silke Musik demonstrates the new Korth 45 ACP prototype to Malloy.

loaded chamber indicator are now standard on Ten II pistols.

The greatest departure from the traditional Kimber line is the new 1911 in 22 LR. The blowback 22s will be offered in variants of two models—the Rimfire Target (adjustable sights) and the Rimfire Custom (fixed sights). Each model will be available in black or silver finishes. Frames and slides of the rimfire pistols are of aluminum alloy. A conversion kit to convert existing 45-caliber pistols will also be offered.

Korth

The Korth semiautomatic pistol was introduced in 1989 for the 9mm Parabellum cartridge. Since then, it has also been offered in 9x21, 40 S&W and 357 SIG.

At the February 2003 SHOT Show, a new prototype of a Korth pistol in 45 ACP was exhibited. It uses the same basic Korth mechanism, enlarged to handle the dimensions of the 45 cartridge. The magazine is of single-column type and holds 8 rounds. A silenced version of the 45 will be available to law enforcement. As with other Korth pistols, the price is high, but the materials and the workmanship are unsurpassed.

Les Baer

Les Baer Custom was approached by Clint Smith, head of the Thunder Ranch training center in Texas, about a pistol built to his specifications. The result was the Baer 1911 Thunder Ranch Special, a "working" 45 that has features thought desirable by Smith and other shooters. The pistol comes with night sights, extended safety lever and checkered front strap and mainspring housing. The Thunder Ranch logo appears on the slide and grips. For those who like to look at their pistols a lot, a special engraved model with ivory grips is available.

Lone Star

A new series of 1911 pistols has been introduced by Lone Star Armament of Stephenville, Texas.

The TLE (Tactical Law Enforcement) pistol is identical to the full-size pistol chosen by the Los Angeles Police Department SWAT team. The Tactical series is a modified 1911 design with an external extractor. Tactical pistols come in custom (5"), Pro (4") and Ultra (3") variants. A Kimber representative said that, in the future, all Kimber pistols may use the external extractor of the Tactical series.

The Ultra Ten CDP II is a polymer-frame 45 with a machined aluminum insert in the frame. Capacity is 10+1. Kimber Custom Shop features include a "meltdown" treatment *(edges rounded)* and night sights. The new Tactical series extractor and

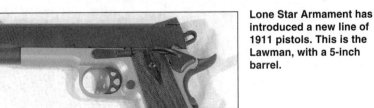

Lone Star Armament has introduced a new line of 1911 pistols. This is the Lawman, with a 5-inch barrel.

Wes Ripley proudly exhibits a specimen of Lone Star Armament's new line of 1911-style pistols.

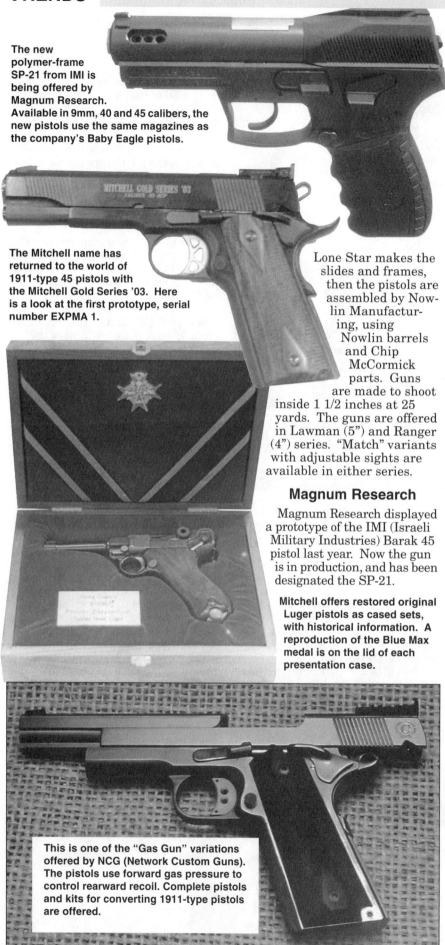

The new polymer-frame SP-21 from IMI is being offered by Magnum Research. Available in 9mm, 40 and 45 calibers, the new pistols use the same magazines as the company's Baby Eagle pistols.

The Mitchell name has returned to the world of 1911-type 45 pistols with the Mitchell Gold Series '03. Here is a look at the first prototype, serial number EXPMA 1.

Mitchell offers restored original Luger pistols as cased sets, with historical information. A reproduction of the Blue Max medal is on the lid of each presentation case.

This is one of the "Gas Gun" variations offered by NCG (Network Custom Guns). The pistols use forward gas pressure to control rearward recoil. Complete pistols and kits for converting 1911-type pistols are offered.

Lone Star makes the slides and frames, then the pistols are assembled by Nowlin Manufacturing, using Nowlin barrels and Chip McCormick parts. Guns are made to shoot inside 1 1/2 inches at 25 yards. The guns are offered in Lawman (5") and Ranger (4") series. "Match" variants with adjustable sights are available in either series.

Magnum Research

Magnum Research displayed a prototype of the IMI (Israeli Military Industries) Barak 45 pistol last year. Now the gun is in production, and has been designated the SP-21.

The pistol has a polymer frame with an integral accessory rail, and the trigger mechanism is conventional double-action. The gun is hammer-fired, and the locking system is tilting-barrel. The barrel has polygonal rifling. Controls comprise an ambidextrous manual safety, a slide release and a decocker on the top of the slide. An internal locking mechanism for times of non-use is included.

The magazine release is reversible for right- or left-hand shooters. The magazines themselves are interchangeable with those of Magnum Research's Baby Eagle pistols—a nice touch. The SP-21 is now offered in 9mm and 40 S&W as well as 45 ACP.

The rear sight is shielded within the raised panel at the rear of the slide. Night sights and adjustable sights are options. A small but important point: there are plenty of grooves at the rear of the slide, and they cover a lot of area. This arrangement makes operating the slide easier, especially under adverse conditions.

Mitchell

It has been a number of years since the Mitchell name has appeared on a 45 automatic. At the February 2003 SHOT Show, three prototypes of a new Mitchell Arms 1911 pistol were exhibited. Pistols numbered EXPMA-1, EXPMA-2 and EXPMA-3 arrived just in time for the opening of the show. Called the Mitchell Gold Series '03 pistols, they are full-size arms with 5-inch barrels. They include some of the niceties today's shooters seem to prefer, such as extended manual safety, beavertail grip safety, skeletonized hammer and trigger and front-and-rear slide serrations. They are cataloged in 40 S&W and 9mm, as well as 45 ACP. Reportedly, the guns will be built by Dan Wesson for Mitchell. Commercial availability was scheduled for Spring 2003.

Mitchell has been doing business as Mitchell's Mausers, and the company has offered rebuilt historical arms. Artisans in Germany are now rebuilding and refinishing original Luger (Parabellum) pistols. Mitchell is offering them, cased, along with the book, *The P08 Luger Pistol* and a History Channel videotape concerning the Luger. Models offered are the Army (4" barrel), Navy (6" barrel) and Artillery (8" barrel) versions.

NCG

NCG (Network Custom Guns) came into our consciousness as a part of KG Industries. KG makes a line of lubrication and cleaning products for firearms owners. Late

◄ North American Arms has made a big splash with its small Guardian pistol in its powerful new chambering, the 32 NAA. The new cartridge pushes a bullet at over 1200 fps from its 2 1/2-inch barrel.

▲ Here is a left view of the new North American Arms 32 NAA pistol.

◄ The new high-velocity 32 NAA cartridge has now been standardized by the SAAMI.

in 2001, KG became associated with NCG for the purpose of producing a gas-operated recoil control system for the 1911 design. The design was from NCG's John Adkins, who developed a system that could be added to an existing 1911 pistols. It uses an under-barrel gas piston to retard the rearward movement of the slide. The company now offers conversion kits and complete pistols under the "Gas Gun" tradename.

North American

North American Arms' new Guardian 32 NAA Guardian, introduced last year, has become a hot item in the world of small pocket pistols. Recall that the cartridge case is basically formed by necking a 380 case to 32-caliber. The new cartridge, called appropriately enough the 32 NAA, has been approved by the Sporting Arms & Ammunition Manufacturers Institute (SAAMI). Now that standards have been set, any ammunition manufacturer may decide to produce the cartridges. At present, Cor-Bon makes the ammunition, which pushes a 60-grain bullet out at over 1200 fps from the Guardian's 2 1/2-inch barrel. Consider that the 2-1/2 inches includes the chamber, so the bullet has less than two inches of bore in which to get up to speed. Pretty impressive.

North American never hesitates to hook up with the good ideas of other companies. They have added the Taurus-design key-locking system to the Guardian 32 and 380 pistols. Now the little pocket pistols are California-compliant, as this device is acceptable as a manual safety.

Olympic

Olympic Arms has introduced an eye-catching addition to its 45-caliber 1911 line. The new "Westerner" features a case-color finish on both frame and slide. Various types of grips can be fitted, but the light-colored ones show the "Westerner" logo well. It is an attractive combination of an Old-West appearance on an up-to-date self-loading pistol.

Para-Ordnance

Para-Ordnance Manufacturing, Inc. has been using the shorter name "Para" more and more lately. Because it uses fewer letters, let's use it here.

The company created quite a stir when it introduced its innovative LDA (Light Double Action) trigger system a few years ago, in 1999. Now, almost all of the Para pistols use this trigger. In February 2003,

three new variants were introduced, all in 45 ACP.

The Para CCW pistol (4 1/4-inch barrel) and the Para Companion – Carry Option (3 1/2-inch barrel) are similar except for barrel length and related slide length. They are stainless-steel guns with spurless hammers and the LDA trigger. Capacity is 7+1, and "big diamond" cocobolo grips are fitted. Tritium night sights are standard.

The new Tac-Four is a high-capacity pistol similar to the Para CCW, but with a staggered-column magazine that allows 13+1 capacity. Where legal, the Tac-Four will be shipped with two pre-ban 13-round magazines.

All three of these pistols have traditional (non-extended) safety and slide release levers, and also have a short-tang grip safety—shorter even than the original 1911 Colt part. Para calls this a "bobbed beavertail", reversing the trend to larger and longer beavertail tangs. The result is a more compact, more concealable package to carry for personal protection. It is a small thing, but Para still cuts slide grooves straight up-and-down, as on the original Colt 1911 and 1911A1 models. Most other companies angle the grooves for appearance. They all

Here is a pre-production specimen of the new Rohrbaugh R-9, a 12-ounce locked-breech 9mm pistol. Type of sights had not been determined when this specimen was exhibited.

Here is a first look at the new Sarsilmaz pistol, which is based on the CZ-75 mechanism. This specimen is serial number 1.

seem to work just fine, but the reality of physics is that the more they are slanted, the less purchase the grooves provide for retracting the slide. It is nice that Para is employing the original configuration.

Pardini

The Italian Pardini firm has produced a 45-caliber competition pistol, the Pardini GT 45. The new pistol is available with either a 5- or 6-inch barrel. With a 5-incher, the gun weighs 39 ounces; the 6-inch version tips the scales at 42 ounces. The magazine holds 10 rounds, and the Pardini is suited for IPSC or Practical pistol shooting. Extras, such as a frame-mounted scope base and a German red-dot sight, are also available from the importer, Nygord Precision Products.

Rohrbaugh

Introduced last year, the Rohrbaugh R-9 9mm pistol had its own production facility by February

2003, and deliveries were scheduled for June 2003. Some changes in final production specifications were to be made. Edges will be rounded, and exact types of sights were yet to be determined.

The little Rohrbaugh pistol claims to be the smallest and lightest 9mm pistol available. There is good evidence for this claim. At 3.6 x 4.9 inches, the pistol will almost hide under a 3x5 index card. Grip choices are polymer, carbon fiber or aluminum. Depending on type of grips, the weight ranges from 12 to 12.7 ounces. The Rohrbaugh pistol uses standard 9mm ammunition, and the capacity is 6+1.

The new company is already looking down the road.

S&W has entered the 1911 market with its new SW1911 pistol. For now, the new pistol is offered only in a 5-inch, stainless steel version.

S&W's polymer-frame SW99, previously available in 9mm and 40 S&W, is now offered in 45 ACP.

Within about 1 1/2 years, they hope to offer a laser-sight option and introduce a 40-caliber version.

Ruger

Sturm, Ruger & Company offered nothing new in their semiauto pistol lines this year. However, developments may be coming soon, as the company is evaluating the need to conform to the requirements of certain restrictive states.

Sarsilmaz

Sarsilmaz, the Turkish company noted for its shotguns, is definitely in the pistol business. Founded in 1880, the company is the only private Turkish armsmaker. Last year, the pistol line was announced, but the pistols themselves were held up in customs. They became available early in 2003. Specimens numbered 01 and 02 were displayed at the 2003 SHOT Show. The Sarsilmaz pistols are based on the CZ-75, and are available in 9mm. Variants are Kilinc (full-size) and Hancer (compact) models.

SIGARMS

Only small changes in the pistol line for SIGARMS, apparently all to their 45-caliber pistols. The full-size P 220 now is available with an accessory rail in the stainless version. Both 7- and 8-shot magazines are available for the P 220.

The downsized P 245 comes with a 6-round magazine, but now an "ErgoGrip" extender can be added to let the smaller pistol use the 8-round magazine. The extender simply snaps over the 8-round magazine. I suspect P 245 owners may want to continue to carry the pistol with the original 6-round magazine, but if a spare is carried, it makes sense to choose the optional 8-rounder.

Smith & Wesson

S&W really introduced a lot of new things at the February 2002 SHOT Show. Without much doubt, the star of their show was a revolver—the big 500 Magnum. That said, you'll have to read about it in the proper place. Here, let us go over the interesting new autoloaders that were almost upstaged by the big revolver.

After years of contending that S&W 45 autos were as good or better than the 1911 design, the company finally entered the fray, and has introduced its own 1911 pistol. The new SW1911 has a few modifications to the original, such as an external extractor. It has an internal drop safety that is disengaged by the grip safety, not the trigger. Other parts interchange, allowing use of 1911 aftermarket parts. However, there may be few that S&W has not already included. The SW1911 uses Wolff springs, Chip McCormick hammer and safety, Wilson beavertail and magazines, Novak sights and Briley barrel bushing. The pistol is offered now in only one version, with a 5-inch barrel, and in stainless steel only.

The polymer-frame SW99 is now available in a new chambering—45 ACP. Barrel length of the new, big SW99 is 4 1/4 inches, with a weight of 25.6 ounces. Capacity is 9+1. A more compact variant of the original 9mm and 40-caliber SW99 is now available with a shortened grip frame. Magazine capacity is still 10 rounds for the 9mm, but reduced to 8 for the 40 S&W.

The new Smith & Wesson Model 4040PD is the first scandium-frame semiautomatic pistol. Caliber is 40 S&W. The pistol uses a single-column magazine that holds 7 rounds. With a 3 1/2-inch barrel, the pistol weighs 25.6 ounces.

S&W's Performance Center handguns are now available to all distributors. Thus, limited-edition products such as the Model 945 *(still considered by S&W as the top-of-the-line 45 single-action auto)*

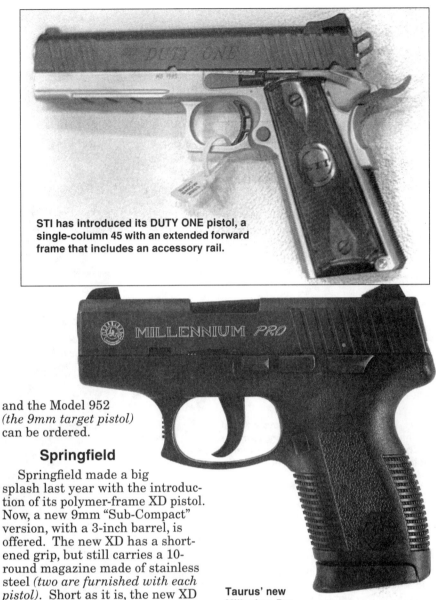

STI has introduced its DUTY ONE pistol, a single-column 45 with an extended forward frame that includes an accessory rail.

and the Model 952 *(the 9mm target pistol)* can be ordered.

Springfield

Springfield made a big splash last year with the introduction of its polymer-frame XD pistol. Now, a new 9mm "Sub-Compact" version, with a 3-inch barrel, is offered. The new XD has a shortened grip, but still carries a 10-round magazine made of stainless steel *(two are furnished with each pistol)*. Short as it is, the new XD has a stubby accessory rail at the forward part of its frame, and Springfield has a special XML light to fit. Weight of the small XD is 20-1/2 ounces, and the sights are 3-dot, dovetailed front and rear.

In just a year, the XD has expanded into an entire line of pistols. They are now available with 3-, 4-, and 5-inch barrels, in 9mm, 40S&W and 357 SIG. Frames are black or OD green, and slides are black or silver. Sights may be white dot, several choices of night sights, or fiber optic type. All this presents a lot of possibilities for mixing or matching.

A number of new variants have also been introduced in the 1911-A1 line. One is a 3-inch barrel version with an accessory rail, which will also take the XML light. Two striking-looking pistols are 3-inch and 5-inch pistols made of stainless steel,

Taurus' new Millenium Pro series is an updated version of the original Millenium design. This PT 145 has an all-black finish.

blackened, then with the sides polished bright. Springfield calls this treatment "Black Stainless."

Steyr

Last year, I reported that Steyr firearms were scheduled to be imported by Dynamit Nobel RWS. Well, that is half-true. The Nobel firm will import Steyr long guns, but not pistols. By press time, I was unable to learn about the status of the Steyr pistols.

STI

STI International is introducing their "Duty One" pistol, a single-column 45 with an extended frame "dust cover" that carries an acces-

Springfield has introduced a 3-inch barrel version of its new XD polymer-frame pistol. Springfield's Terra Davis displays a specimen in 9mm.

More finish options are offered for Taurus pistols. Here is a dual-tone version of the new Millenium Pro 45-caliber pistol.

Taurus' PT 922, introduced in prototype last year, has already undergone changes in design and appearance. It is now a polymer-frame 22 pistol that is shaped just a bit like the old Colt Woodsman.

Linda Moore, Wildey's president, holds one of the big Wildey gas-operated pistols, now available in 44 Auto Mag chambering. The 44 Auto Mag cartridge started the trend to magnum autoloaders.

sory rail. The 5-inch bull barrel is ramped, and the chamber fully supported. Delivery was scheduled for third quarter 2003. Finish was planned as flat blue metal, with rosewood grips.

Taurus

The 22-caliber PT 922 introduced last year has changed considerably. The prototype of 2002 had a metal frame and looked just a bit like a Walther P38. The 2003 version had a polymer frame and looked just a bit like a Colt Woodsman. Even though it was included in the 2003 catalog, Taurus' Eddy Fernandez said it is still under development. This version looked and felt good, and it would be nice to see it finalized.

In the polymer-frame Millenium line, the Millenium "Pro" series has been introduced. This is an updating of the original Millenium design, with pronounced grip checkering, enlarged and smoother-working controls, easier takedown and 3-dot sights. These are some of the subtle, but visible changes. Internally, a captive recoil spring has been added, and the magazine release, trigger pull and internal firing pin lock have been improved.

Tired of all polymer-frame guns having flat black grips? Apparently some people are, for Taurus has brought out the Millenium Deluxe. The new pistols have wood or "pearl" grip inserts added to spruce up the polymer frames.

Valtro

Valtro has added a hard-chrome version to its line of Italian-made 1911-style pistols. The basic pistol is their 1998A1, with many variations made on a custom and semi-custom basis. All Valtro pistols have many of the niceties that modern shooters seem to prefer. The company claims the pistols are machined to the tightest standards in the industry, resulting in accuracy of less than three inches at 50 yards. A Valtro representative said some guns achieve groups of about one inch at that distance, fired from a stationary fixture.

Vektor

Vektor USA, the United States subsidiary of the South African Vektor firm, no longer exists. The only remnant in America is a Vektor Special Projects Office, formed to han-

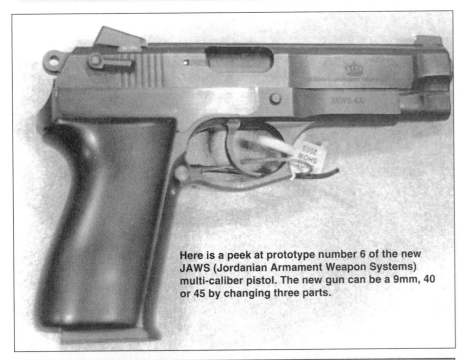

Here is a peek at prototype number 6 of the new JAWS (Jordanian Armament Weapon Systems) multi-caliber pistol. The new gun can be a 9mm, 40 or 45 by changing three parts.

Wildey is now handling the JAWS service pistol, made in Jordan.

chambering, the 45 Winchester Magnum, and the subsequent 45 and 475 Wildey Magnum offerings.

There are lots of hunters who believe that big pistol cartridges are plenty good as ammunition for a handy carbine. For them, Wildey has introduced the Wildey Carbine, based on the pistol mechanism. It has an 18-inch barrel and a skeletonized stock and forearm, both made of walnut. The Wildey Carbine is offered in the same four chamberings as the Wildey pistols.

The company is adding a new line, a big departure for them. Wildey will now also handle a new service-type pistol, chambered for 45 ACP, 40 S&W and 9mm cartridges. The pistol is manufactured in Jordan by Jordanian Armament Weapons Systems, and will be marketed under the logical *(and catchy)* acronym, "JAWS." It is of tilting-barrel locking system, with a conventional double-action trigger mechanism. A special feature is its ability to change calibers simply by changing the barrel, a breechblock in the slide, and an insert in the magazine. JAWS prototype number 6 was exhibited at the February 2003 SHOT Show.

Wilson

Wilson Combat has introduced a Tactical Super Grade Compact pistol. The new handgun is similar to their top-of-the-line 1911-style "Super Grade," but is made with a 4.1-inch barrel. It has many of the features desired today, such as an ambidextrous extended-lever safety, beavertail grip safety and tactical combat sights. Each pistol comes with six magazines *(a nice touch)* and an instructional video, along with other extras. The new pistol has an accuracy guarantee of one inch at 25 yards.

In 2003, Wilson celebrated its 25th year in the custom firearms business. Congratulations!

POSTSCRIPT

It is well to be reminded that anti-gun forces do not want Americans to possess autoloading handguns. They welcomed the passage of the federal "Assault Weapons" bill of 1994 in part because it also restricted pistol magazine capacity. Now, the law is due to expire in September 2004. There is political agitation to continue the restrictions past the sunset date. It would be wise to contact our Senators and Representatives; we should ask for their support in letting this misguided legislation die at the appointed time. •

dle a recall for the Vektor CP-1 series of pistols. The recall was scheduled to end in 2003, so owners of such pistols should call 877-831-8313 as soon as possible.

Volquartsen

The Volquartsen Cheetah, the first *(and apparently still the only)* semiautomatic pistol chambered for the 17 HMR (17 Hornady Magnum Rimfire) cartridge, was introduced last year and is now in production. It is also offered in 22 Long Rifle and 22 Winchester Magnum Rimfire.

Wildey

The big Wildey gas-operated pistol is now available in a new chambering, the 44 Auto Mag. Well, the cartridge isn't exactly new, as it was the original magnum semiauto pistol cartridge–designed for the old Auto Mag pistol–and dates back prior to 1970. However, the round has not been commercially chambered in a factory production pistol since the demise of the Auto Mag in the early 1980s. There was a demand for a new pistol using this cartridge, and Wildey added it for 2003. It joins the original Wildey

HANDGUN NEWS

SIX-GUNS AND OTHERS

by John Taffin

WHEN I WAS a kid back in those dinosaur pre-television days, one of the most famous newscasters on radio was a man by the name of Gabriel Heater. He would always come on with the phrase: "Ah, there's good news tonight!" If he were alive he would be the perfect lead-in to announce what is going on in the world of six-guns. There really is good news—and lots

◀ Shooters can choose Peacekeepers from AWA with a hard chrome finish and a standard, or Thunderer, grip frame.

of it–for shooters. Dozens of new models are coming out, including those that are entirely original, and others that are simply upgrades-or slightly different versions-of existing six-guns.

Not only do we have new six-guns to talk about, but we also have both the smallest and largest revolver cartridges ever commercially produced being introduced in new six-guns this year. Those two cartridges are the 17 HMR (Hornady Magnum Rimfire) and the 500 S&W Magnum. The former is now being chambered in revolvers from Ruger, Smith & Wesson, and Taurus; the latter–at least for now–is found only in the new Model 500 X-Frame from Smith & Wesson.

Competition among the major manufacturers is exceptionally fierce to see who can get there *"fustest with the mostest."* This, of course, is great news for consumers as we reap the benefit of a wide range of both large and small six-guns for virtually any application. Not only is this going to be another great year for handgunners in general, and six-gunners in particular, I speculate that – in the words of the late Al Jolson, that great entertainer from the first half of the 20th century – "You ain't seen nothing yet." If we can continue to hold the anti-gunners at bay, the future will be both exciting and enjoyable. Let us take an alphabetical journey through many of the manufacturers viewing some of the models they are offering.

American Western Arms

American Western Arms (AWA) offers two replica Single-Action Armies known as the Longhorn and the Peacekeeper. The former is their standard-finished Single Action available in 45 Colt, 44-40, 44 Special, 38-40, and 357 Magnum. The Peacekeeper has the same chamberings; however, it is specially tuned, exquisitely finished, and also fitted with checkered rubber grips instead of the one-piece style found on the Longhorn. The Peacekeeper is as beautiful a Single-Action

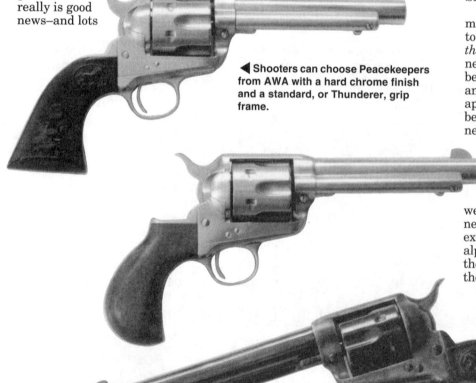

▶ AWA's top-of-the-line Peacekeeper, here shown in a 7 1/2-inch 44-40 and 4 3/4-inch 45 Colt, exhibits a deep blue finish, brilliant case colors, and eagle-style rubber grips.

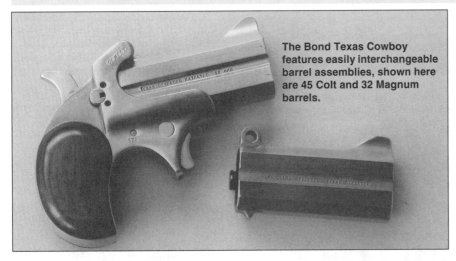

The Bond Texas Cowboy features easily interchangeable barrel assemblies, shown here are 45 Colt and 32 Magnum barrels.

Army replica as one is ever going to find anywhere. The top-of-the-line model Peacekeeper, in addition to a factory-tuned action, has an 11-degree forcing cone, 1st Generation-style cylinder flutes, and bone/charcoal case-hardened frame.

Both models feature a beveled ejector rod housing to keep the metal from digging into the leather on a tight holster, and both models can be had in nickel finish, while the Peacekeeper can also be ordered with the "blackpowder frame", distinctive because an angled screw in the front of the frame – rather than the spring-loaded cross-pin retainer – holds the cylinder pin in place. It is also available in a satin hard chrome finish that not only looks great, but also cleans up easily for those using blackpowder loads.

American Western Arms cylinders have virtually no end play or side-to-side movement; the one-piece walnut stocks on the Longhorn, and black rubber American Eagle grips on the Peacekeeper are individually fitted with no overlapping of grip or frame. AWA is now fitting their single actions with a coil mainspring. These are more reliable, and give a more even hammer pull and faster hammer fall than the old-style flat mainspring. The coil springs are available in three weights: 15#, 17#, and 19# and can be fitted to older six-guns by filing a small area behind the trigger guard part of the grip frame and using a coil-spring holding shelf that screws into the hole used for the original flat mainspring.

Bond Arms

Several years ago I tested the first Bond Derringer and discovered it was a good, strong two-shooter with two problems. The trigger pull

was very heavy, and the changing of barrel and shims took three hands, or more, to accomplish. That is all past. The Cowboy Derringer is exceptionally easy to use. Changing barrels *(each frame accepts all caliber barrels)* takes about one minute to accomplish, using an Allen wrench of the proper size. On the left side of the frame of the Cowboy Derringer is a spring-loaded camming lever that, when pushed down, unlatches the barrel assembly allowing it to move upwards to be unloaded and reloaded. Each barrel assembly has its own built-in

spring-loaded ejector. The Bond Cowboy Texas Defender Model is stainless steel and comes with grips of an impregnated laminated rosewood that are small, but they nestle comfortably in the hand. The hammer is of the rebounding type and a cross-bolt safety is found on the Bond and should–that is SHOULD–always be applied if the Bond is carried loaded. The Bond Cowboy/ Texas Defender Derringer comes in 32 Magnum, 357 Maximum, 9mm, 45ACP, 44 Special/44 Magnum, 40 S&W, 38 Special/357 Magnum, 45 Colt, and 45 Colt/.410.

The Bond Derringer is quality, and unlike some derringers on the market, is easy to operate one-handed. The trigger pull is not overly heavy and the hammer is easy to cock with the thumb of the shooting hand and, for all practical purposes for which such a little gun should be used, point of impact with both barrels is close enough.

Cimarron Firearms

Cimarron is now providing brand-new six-guns in what they call an original finish. This finish is actually what a six-gun would look like after much usage on a daily basis, after hundreds and

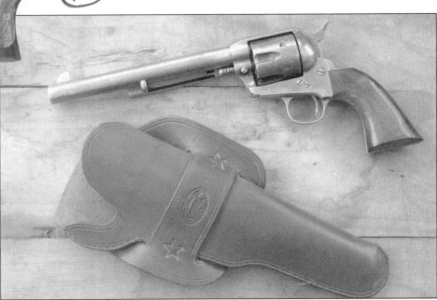

Available in either the standard finish *(shown)* or original finish, Cimarron's Wyatt Earp Buntline is an excellent shooter. Shield in the right grip commemorates the presentation of the Buntline Special to Earp.

It is a brand-new six-gun from Cimarron; however this 7 1/2-inch 44-40 looks 125 years old due to its 'original' finish. Period leather is by Will Ghormley.

Cimarron offers both the 45 New Thunderer *(top)*, and 38 Lightning Model. Custom grips are by Buffalo Brothers.

▼ Cimarron brings back a short but important time in history with their 1871-72 Open-Top, chambered in 44 Colt. Carved eagle grips are by Buffalo Brothers.

Colts chambered in 44-40 were called) with one-piece stocks and a 7 1/2-inch barrel has a finish earned with over 100 years of service. The new

hundreds of times being drawn and replaced in a leather holster. My original 1879-vintage Colt Frontier Six-Shooter, *(as the early*

'original' finish of the Cimarron Model P perfectly matches with what is left on my old Six-Shooter. The Cimarron's finish is not simply an in-the- white six-gun with no bluing. Instead it has age marks, blemishes—and even a small spot or two with a brownish patina. The one-piece stocks are also appropriately distressed. CFA also offers the Wyatt Earp Buntline Special 10-inch barrel 45 Colt in either blue/case color or original finish. Either way, it fairly reeks of history and, for most six-gunners, is also easy to shoot well due to the long barrel and great distance between sights.

Jamie Harvey of Cimarron Firearms shows off the new stainless steel Model P 45 Colt.

Cowboy Action Shooting has been responsible for the availability of replicas of most of the great single actions of the past, not only the well known Colt Single-Action Army and Remington Model 1875, but also the Richards Conversion, the Richards-Mason Conversion, and the 1871-72 Open-Top. Cimarron has offered all three of these, and currently offers the Richards-Mason and the Open-Top. While attending Range War in Fredericksburg, Texas I had the opportunity to visit the Cimarron Firearms facility—and came home with a pair of consecutively-numbered 1871-72 Open-Tops, chambered in 44 Colt.

The modern 44 Colt is simply a 44 Special cartridge case that has been slightly shortened, with the diameter of the rim turned down to allow six rounds to fit in the 1860 Army-sized cylinders of the Colt cartridge conversions. Open-Tops, with their connection to the past and mild recoil, are such a pleasure that it seemed reasonable to have them fitted with custom stocks. For grips I called upon Buffalo Brothers. They specialize in molded, antique-looking polymer grips for all the old six-guns, and their replicas. Using old-style patterns and modern coloring techniques, Buffalo Brothers offers ten different shades of historical antique coloring molded into the grip, as well as carvings such as those found on single actions in the middle of the 19th-century. For the Open-Tops I chose ivory grips with a carved Eagle symbol. They really set off these Open-Tops and make them extremely attractive.

Cimarron's newest offering is a Model P in stainless steel. These six-guns are made by Uberti and, as you read this, will be available in both 357 Magnum and 45 Colt in the three standard barrel lengths of 4 3/4, 5 1/2, and 7 1/2 inches. For the first time, those that pack a traditional single action in all kinds of weather will have the advantage of stainless steel's ability to withstand the elements. A bonus, for those shooting blackpowder, is that they are much easier to clean and maintain.

Colt's Manufacturing Company, Inc.

More good news from Colt this year. Two years ago the retail price of the Colt Single Action Army was $1,968. Last year this dropped by $438 to $1,530, and now Colt continues the trend with a new MSRP of $1,380. Some replicas are already

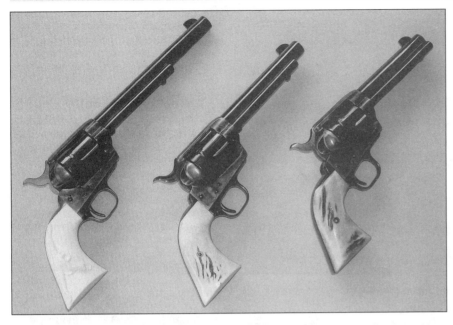

The Classic Colt Single Action Army has not only been lowered in price by nearly $600 over the past two years, it is now offered in all three standard barrel lengths. Custom stocks are extra.

running as high as $1,100 or more, so this may cause some six-gunners to take another look at the original Single Action Army. Colt has two advantages over the replicas: First, they are genuine Colts—no other single action can make that statement. Second, the Colt Single Action has more than a century and one-half of history behind it. Again, no other single action can make that claim.

A second piece of good news from Colt is that the Single Action Army is once again offered in the original 1873 Cavalry Model 7 1/2-inch barrel length. It has probably been a decade since shooters could have anything except 4 3/4- and 5 1/2-inch Single Actions from Colt. Now all three standard barrel lengths are available in 357 Magnum, 44-40, and 45 Colt. There is a downside, however, as the nickel-plate finish has been dropped from the catalog; now only the standard blued finish with a casehardened frame is offered. Grips are a checkered black composite with the rampant colt emblem at the top and the American Eagle at the bottom.

Colt also continues to offer their answer to Ruger's Vaquero—the Cowboy—in 45 Colt only and a choice of 4 3/4- and 5 1/2-inch barrel lengths. This six-gun is also offered only in the blued/casehardened finish. To round out their six-gun offerings, Colt continues to offer a stainless steel 44 Magnum Anaconda in barrel lengths of 4, 6, and 8 inches, as well as the 357 Python Elite in either of blue or stainless, and a barrel length choice of 4 or 6 inches. All double-action models feature adjustable sights with a red ramp front and white outline rear sight. Anacondas come equipped with finger-grooved rubber grips, while the Python Elite is the only Colt revolver currently offered with wooden stocks (finger-grooved combat-style walnut).

▶ New from EMF this year is the Great Western II, here shown in both the Californian and the satin nickel versions.

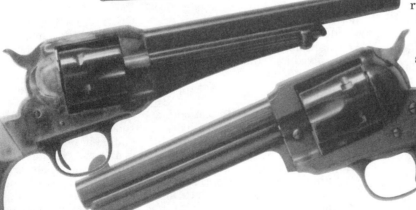

◀ ▶ EMF offers both the 1875 Remington and 1890 Remington in 45 Colt. Stocks are by Buffalo Brothers.

Forty-fours from Freedom Arms: Model 83 *(top)* chambered in 44 Magnum, and the new Model 97 set up for the 44 Special.

Freedom Arms' newest offering is the mid-framed Model 97, a five-shot 44 Special. This could well be the finest factory-manufactured 44 Special ever.

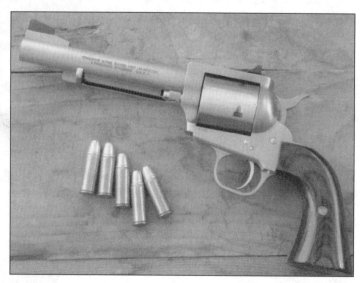

frame and hammer, while the 1890 is fully blued. The Model 1890 also has a round lanyard ring in the butt. Both six-guns proved to be well above average in the accuracy department for this type of revolver.

Freedom Arms

Freedom Arms full-sized five-shot revolver, the Model 83, continues to be produced in 454 Casull, 44 Magnum, 357 Magnum, 41 Magnum, 475 Linebaugh and 50AE. There is even a 22 LR version. These are simply the finest six-guns ever to come from a factory being, in fact, custom-built. Seven years ago, Freedom Arms introduced their mid-frame six-gun, the Model 97. The Model 97 is built exactly the same way as the larger Model 83, using the same materials and the same strict attention to tight tolerances and precision fitting. Although the Model 83 is available with both a Field Grade and Premier Grade finish, the Model 97 is thus far offered only in Premier Grade. Price-wise, the Model 97 costs about 12 percent less than a comparable Model 83 due to less material being used for the smaller gun, rather than any short-cuts or difference in manufacturing. The cylinders on the little gun are still line-bored as they are on the big gun.

Last year Freedom Arms introduced the Model 97 in 22 Long Rifle with an extra 22 Magnum cylinder. I have now had a chance to thoroughly test this grand little 22 and I can say the Model 97 22/22 Magnum really shoots! The performance of this Model 97 is superb with both cylinders using either 22 Long Rifle or 22 Magnum Rimfire ammunition resulting in groups of less than one-third of an inch for five shots at 25 yards. CCI's Mini-Mag Hollow Points, Remington's Yellow Jackets, and Winchester's High Velocity Hollow Points all came in well under one-third of an inch with the 22 Long Rifle cylinder in place, while CCI's Maxi-Mag Hollow Points delivered the same results with the 22 Magnum cylinder in use.

New for this year is the Model 97 chambered in 44 Special. Most dedicated and knowledgeable six-gunners agree the first 44 Special, the Smith & Wesson 1st Model Hand Ejector of 1907 is not only the finest double-action six-gun ever built, it is also the grandest of 44 Specials. Until now. The old Triple-Lock has met its match with the new Freedom Arms 44 Special.

I've been a connoisseur of 44 Specials since my first Smith & Wesson Model 1950 Target was acquired in 1959. I've had just about every 44

Early & Modern Firearms (EMF)

EMF imports a full line of quality revolvers and offers them under the Hartford label. In the past many of their replica six-guns have been manufactured by Armi San Marco, however they have now turned to Pietta to produce a new lineup of single-action six-guns that bear the Great Western name. Although labeled Great Western, these new six-guns are not replicas of the original replica, the Great Western, having the traditional Colt-style firing pin instead of the original frame-mounted firing pin of the original Great Western. Forty years after the demise of the Great Western Frontier Revolver, EMF is offering the Great Western II in nickel, satin nickel, full blue, or blue with a beautifully case-colored frame. Another version, known as The Cal-

ifornian, is offered with a standard finish. I have had the opportunity to test two 4 3/4-inch 45s; one a satin nickel Great Western II with one-piece polymer ivory stocks, the other a Californian with one-piece wood stocks. The less expensive Californian has the best-looking wooden stocks I have yet to find on any Italian replica. They are perfectly fitted and finished, and performed and shot well.

EMF also offers excellent copies of the Remington single actions. It has been my pleasure to test both a 7 1/2-inch Model 1875 and a 5 1/2-inch Model 1890, both chambered in 45 Colt. Cylinders lock up tightly, and I do mean tightly, and both are timed better than the average Italian replica. Actions are smooth, and mainsprings are also much lighter than found on Remington replicas from two decades ago. The Model 1875 is blued with a case-colored

Freedom Arms is now delivering the Model 97 22LR/22 WMR. This may well be most accurate 22 revolver ever offered to shooters.

Kelly Baker of Freedom Arms displays the new Model 97 44 Special.

Special ever manufactured: Smith & Wesson Triple-Lock, Model 1926, 1950 Military, 1950 Target, Model 24, and Model 624; Colt New Service, Single Action Army, and New Frontier; Great Western Frontier Model; Texas Longhorn Arms South Texas Army and Flat-Top Target; and many custom 44s built on Ruger 357 Magnum Blackhawk Flat-Tops and Three-Screws. None can surpass the Freedom Arms Model 97 for quality, accuracy, and portability. Many cannot understand the deep appreciation for the 44 Special, a cartridge that has been "surpassed" by so many big-bore magnums. For those that do understand, no explanation is necessary; for those that don't, no explanation is possible. It is a spiritual thing with many six-gunners.

Magnum Research

Magnum Research has long been known for the semi-automatic Desert Eagle. However, in recent years they have been offering the BFR *(Biggest Finest Revolver),* an all stainless-steel revolver offered in two frame sizes. The standard frame and cylinder *(they call it the Short Cylinder)* is chambered in 454 Casull, 22 Hornet, and 475 Linebaugh–which also handles the 480 Ruger. The Long Cylinder version handles the 45-70, 444 Marlin, 450 Marlin, or a 45 Colt version that also handles .410 shot shells.

This past year I have been shooting one of the Short Cylinder versions with a 6 1/2–inch barrel chambered in 480/475 Linebaugh. Instead of adjustable sights, it came from the factory fitted with a mounted scope and no iron sights whatsoever. The rubber grips supplied are not pretty but they certainly help in handling felt recoil. With a suggested retail price of $999, the BFR is the most affordable way to own a quality single-action revolver chambered in many large calibers.

The standard BFR rear sight is fully adjustable, and mated with an interchangeable front sight. Bar-

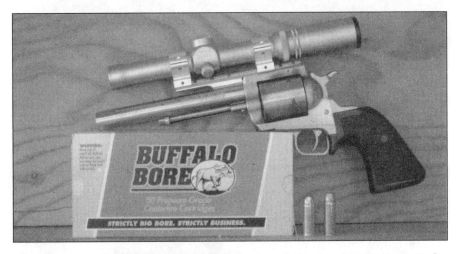

The BFR revolver from Magnum Research has proven to be an extremely accurate six-gun when using either 480 Ruger or 475 Linebaugh ammunition.

Navy Arms is now offering the Schofield Model chambered for 38 Special or 38 Long Colt. Grips are by Buffalo Brothers.

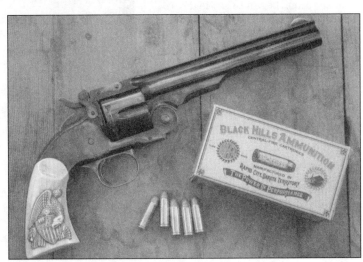

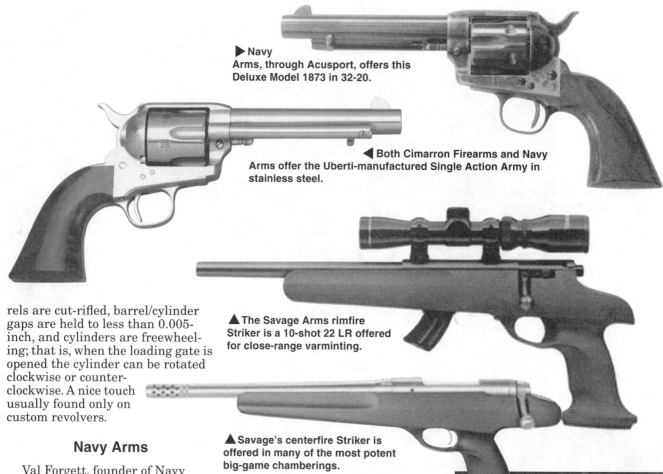

▶ Navy Arms, through Acusport, offers this Deluxe Model 1873 in 32-20.

◀ Both Cimarron Firearms and Navy Arms offer the Uberti-manufactured Single Action Army in stainless steel.

▲ The Savage Arms rimfire Striker is a 10-shot 22 LR offered for close-range varminting.

▲ Savage's centerfire Striker is offered in many of the most potent big-game chamberings.

rels are cut-rifled, barrel/cylinder gaps are held to less than 0.005-inch, and cylinders are freewheeling; that is, when the loading gate is opened the cylinder can be rotated clockwise or counter-clockwise. A nice touch usually found only on custom revolvers.

Navy Arms

Val Forgett, founder of Navy Arms and the Father of the Replica Firearms Industry passed away this past year at the age of 72. Navy Arms continues under the leadership of his son, Val Forgett III. We now have available a replica of virtually every single-action revolver from the 19th century, thanks to the efforts of several individuals. However, it all started back in the 1950s with Forgett introducing a copy of the 1851 Colt Navy. Forgett and Navy Arms were directly responsible for the introduction of Smith & Wesson single actions, beginning with the 1875 Schofield and followed by the Model #3 Russian.

New models from Navy Arms this year include two new Schofields. First is a Founders Model with a color-case-hardened receiver, polymer ivory grips, 7 1/2-inch barrel, and chambered in 45 Colt. The 38 Special Schofield joins the 45 Colt and 44-40 in both the 7 1/2-inch Cavalry and 5 1/2-inch Wells Fargo models.

Those who prefer Colt replicas have not been forgotten. Navy Arms' 1873 Single Actions are now offered as a Gunfighter Series with all standard springs replaced by custom Wolff springs, a nickel-plated backstrap and trigger guard, and black checkered grips. These are offered in

the three standard barrel lengths of 4 inches, 5 1/2 inches, and 7 1/2 inches in 357 Magnum, 44-40, and 45 Colt. For the first time, Navy Arms is also offering a stainless steel 1873 Single Action Army with the same black checkered grips and Wolff springs in all three barrel lengths, chambered in 357 Magnum or 45 Colt.

Finally from Navy Arms comes a Deluxe Model 1873 Single Action Army in 32-20. When the West was wild the most popular chamberings were 45 Colt, 44-40, and 38-40. However, as things began to settle down, around the turn-of-the-century, the 32-20 became very popular so is altogether fitting that Navy Arms would choose this chambering for their Deluxe Model. This version features a color-casehardened receiver and loading gate; charcoal- or fire-blue barrel, cylinder, and grip frame; hand-rubbed walnut stocks, and Wolff springs.

Savage

Savage not only produces some of the finest rifles available, they are also part of the handgunner's world with their Striker bolt-action pistol. All of these superbly accurate handguns have a left-handed bolt and a

Dale Donough of SIGARMS shows off the new Blaser 93 bolt-action pistol.

black ambidextrous synthetic stock, with a finger-groove pistol grip. Centerfire models are offered in both blue and stainless, a magazine capacity of two rounds and chambered in 243 Winchester, 7-08 and 308, while the 223 version is offered

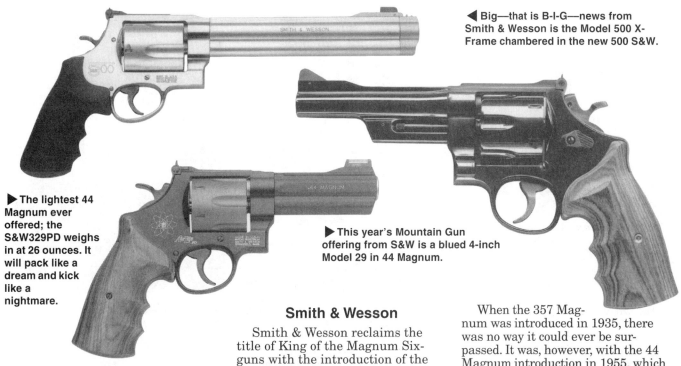

◀ Big—that is B-I-G—news from Smith & Wesson is the Model 500 X-Frame chambered in the new 500 S&W.

▶ The lightest 44 Magnum ever offered; the S&W329PD weighs in at 26 ounces. It will pack like a dream and kick like a nightmare.

▶ This year's Mountain Gun offering from S&W is a blued 4-inch Model 29 in 44 Magnum.

in blued steel only. For fanciers of the new short cartridges, a stainless-steel Striker is cataloged, chambered for the 270, 7mm, and 300 WSM. All centerfire Strikers have 14-inch barrels.

For those who prefer to hunt varmints with a rimfire, the Striker is available chambered in 22 WMR and 17 HMR with a 10-inch barrel and five-round magazine, while a 10-shot version can be had for everyone's favorite cartridge for plinking and relaxing, 22 Long Rifle. All Strikers come with scope bases already installed and button-rifled, free-floating barrels.

SIGARMS

No I'm not going to report on any semi-automatics from SIG. John Malloy handles that pleasant chore quite well. However, SIGARMS is offering a handgun that fits into my section. It is the Blaser R93 bolt-action hunting handgun. And a beauty it is! It is a straight-pull, bolt-action pistol built on the same action as the Blaser 93 Rifle, with free-floating interchangeable barrels. Barrels are hammer-forged, 14 inches in length; the stock is beautifully-figured walnut; and the forearm is furnished with a sling swivel for the attachment of a Harris bipod. Chambering options currently include the 223 Remington, 243 Winchester, 6mm BR, 270 Winchester, 308 Winchester, 30/06, 7-08, 7mm Remington Magnum, and the new 300WSM. With a price tag in the $2650 to $2800 range, only serious handgun hunters need apply.

Smith & Wesson

Smith & Wesson reclaims the title of King of the Magnum Six-guns with the introduction of the 500 S&W Magnum cartridge, and the X-frame Model 500 revolver to handle it. From the 1930s the 1960s it was all Smith & Wesson, as far as magnum chamberings were concerned, as they introduced (in succession) the 357 Magnum, the 44 Magnum, and the 41 Magnum. After that, the game plan changed as other companies and individuals introduced the 454 Casull, the 475 and 500 Linebaugh, the 357, 375, 445, 475, and 500 Maximums/SuperMags, and the 480 Ruger. Now Smith & Wesson is back on top of the mountain with the 500 Magnum.

When the 357 Magnum was introduced in 1935, there was no way it could ever be surpassed. It was, however, with the 44 Magnum introduction in 1955, which could never be challenged. Then came the 454 in the 1970s, and then

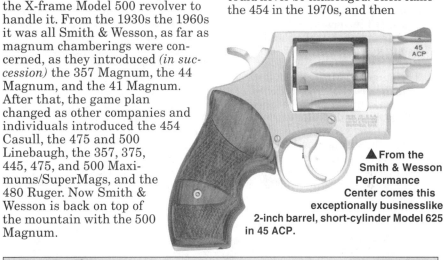

▲ From the Smith & Wesson Performance Center comes this exceptionally businesslike 2-inch barrel, short-cylinder Model 625 in 45 ACP.

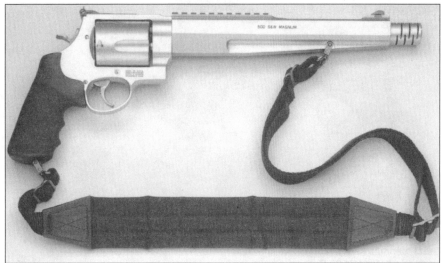

In addition to the standard Model 500, Smith & Wesson also offers this Performance Center model complete with built-in scope mount, sling swivels, and carrying strap.

Shooters now have a choice of six-guns chambered for the largest: 500 S&W, and smallest: 17HMR.

The four big-bore six-gun cartridges introduced by Smith & Wesson: 357 Magnum *(1935)*, 41 Magnum *(1964)*, 44 Magnum *(1955)*, and the 500 S&W *(2003)*.

Jim Rae of the Smith & Wesson Performance Center with a new S&W Model 500 Hunter Model.

the…. Well, you get the picture. With every new cartridge we felt we were at the top. We certainly have reached it now! I cannot see how we could come up with a more powerful cartridge for a handheld six-gun than the 500 that is, by the way, a slightly modified version of John Linebaugh's original 500 Maximum. The latter uses a 1.610-inch cartridge case with a 0.511-inch bullet, while Smith & Wesson's version has a 1.625-inch case and a true 0.500-inch bullet.

The standard Model 500 has an 8 3/8-inch ported barrel, stretched frame and cylinder to fit the longer cartridge, heavy underlug barrel, felt recoil-reducing rubber grips, stainless-steel finish, and a weight of 4 pounds that will be welcomed by most shooters. The Performance Center will be offering a 10-inch Model 500 with sling swivels and a scope mount base, and Smith & Wesson is at least contemplating an easy-packing 3-inch barrel version. Cor-Bon has three loads for the 500 S&W: a 275-grain Bar-

nes X-Bullet at 1665 fps with a muzzle energy of 1688 ft/lbs; a 400-grain SP at 1675 fps and 2500 ft/lbs; and a 440-grain Hard Cast, 1625 fps and 2580 ft/lbs! This is incredible power in a handheld revolver.

As stout as recoil of the Model 500 will be, it may be overshadowed by the second offering from Smith & Wesson—the 44 Magnum Model 329PD. We are used to titanium and scandium 357 Magnums, now it's time to get ready for light versions in 44 Magnum. The Model 329PD has a scandium frame, titanium cylinder, 4-inch barrel, black matte finish, Hi-Viz front sight, and weighs all of 26 ounces! When I asked Herb Belin of Smith & Wesson why it was equipped with wooden grips, he admitted after he fired it rubber

grips were more appropriate. So this Smith & Wesson comes with two pair of grips: Ahrends finger-groove wood and a Hogue rubber Monogrip. One will be able to tell what type of loads are being used by which grip is being employed. Recoil will be HEAVY.

Several other revolvers of note: Smith & Wesson is now chambering the 17 HMR in the medium-frame Model 647, with a companion Model 648 in 22 WMR. Both are 6-inch stainless steel six-guns with heavy underlug barrels. From the Performance Center we have the return of the blued Model 29 in a Mountain Gun version with a 4-inch tapered barrel. I have always felt the 357 Magnum Model 27 with a 3 1/2-inch

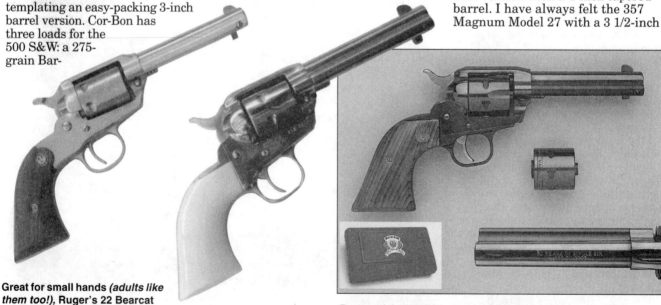

Great for small hands *(adults like them too!)*, Ruger's 22 Bearcat and 32 Single-Six with a short grip frame. One-piece style grips are by Get-A-Grip.

Ruger celebrates fifty years of fine single actions with this Anniversary Model 22 Single-Six 22LR/22WMR.

Ruger's standard model Old Army is now joined by a 5 1/2-inch version. Gunfighter grips are by Eagle grips, auxiliary 45 Colt cylinders are from Taylor's.

barrel was the most serious-looking double-action revolver around. Now the rather strange-looking Performance Center Model 625, with a two-inch barrel and a shortened cylinder to accommodate the 45 ACP, has surpassed it. Since much of the barrel is in the frame and extends to the front of the cylinder, only a small nub protrudes in front of the frame. Now that six-gun really looks serious!

Sturm, Ruger & Co.

In 1999, Ruger celebrated the 50th anniversary of the founding of their company by issuing an Anniversary Commemorative Model Red Eagle 22 semi-auto pistol. Now, four years later, it is time for the Ruger Single-Six 50th Anniversary Model. Bill Ruger correctly read the shooting public and resurrected the single-action revolver in 1953. He very wisely maintained the Colt grip shape, while scaling down the rest of the revolver to 22 rimfire size. The price in 1953 was a very afford-

able $63.25 and a whole box of 22s could be had for well under 50 cents. Single-Sixes have been favored by shooters ever since. The 50th Anniversary Model will feature a New Model Single-Six with a 4 5/8-inch barrel that will be marked "50 Years of Single-Six 1953 to 2003". Grips will be of coco bola and, for the first time ever, will have red eagle medallions. An extra cylinder chambered in 22 MRF will be included.

Last year Ruger reintroduced the 44 Magnum Super Blackhawk Hunter model, which I consider the greatest bargain available to the handgun hunter. With its 7 1/2-inch barrel, stainless-steel construction, and full-length barrel rib cut for the Ruger scope rings (included), a handgun hunter gets just about everything he needs. Now Ruger has made the Hunter Model even more attractive by providing a Bisley version. Most shooters find the Bisley grip frame handles felt recoil better than any other grip frame configuration. A great bargain just got better.

Ruger's Old Army, which is without doubt the finest cap and ball revolver ever produced, is now being offered in an easier-to-carry 5 1/2-inch version. It should find great favor with cowboy action shooters who prefer blackpowder. Cowboy action shooters will also appreciate that the 4 5/8-inch Bird's Head Vaquero is now offered in 357 Magnum. Last year Ruger introduced several rifles chambered in the new 17 HMR. They are followed with a 6 1/2-inch Single-Six chambered in this smallest of rimfires.

Two six-guns that were announced last year are now coming through regularly. Those two are the Bearcat in 22 rimfire and the Single-Six in 32 Magnum with a shorter grip frame—both in stainless steel. For these two small six-guns I used some of my grandkids as the field-testers and expert panel of judges to report upon their merits. Elyse *(17)*, Laura *(16)*, and Brian John *(10)*, joined me to test the newest Ruger single actions. The Bearcat has a very small grip frame that fits the smallest hands, and the newest 32 Magnum features a grip frame approximately 1/4-inch shorter *(top to bottom)* than the standard Blackhawk grip frame. The kids liked the way this grip frame fit their relatively small hands. They work pretty well for the rest of us, too.

Taylor's & Co.

Taylor's has producing a line of quality replicas for several years. However, the big news is that Taylor's is now distributing R&D conversion cylinders for both Remington replicas and Ruger Old Army percussion revolvers. I mentioned above the fact Ruger was now offering the Old Army in a 5 1/2-inch version. A pair of these was ordered in stainless steel, along with R&D 45 Colt conversion cylinders from Taylor's. The cylinders are not offered in stainless steel. However, one has a choice of blue or nickel finish, with the latter nicely matching the Ruger stainless-steel finish.

I was very impressed with the quality and workmanship of the cylinders and the fact that they work not only in these two Old Armies, but two older versions as well. To put these cylinders to use, the conversion ring is removed from the back, five cartridges are loaded in the six-shot cylinder, the conversion ring is replaced *(lining up the pin hole with the corresponding pin*

Taylor's & Co. now offers the R&D 45 Colt Conversion Cylinder for Ruger's Old Army, here shown in the new 5 1/2-inch stainless steel model fitted with Eagle's checkered buffalo horn Gunfighter grips.

TRENDS

▶ Taurus now offers the Raging Bull as a six-shot 41 Magnum.

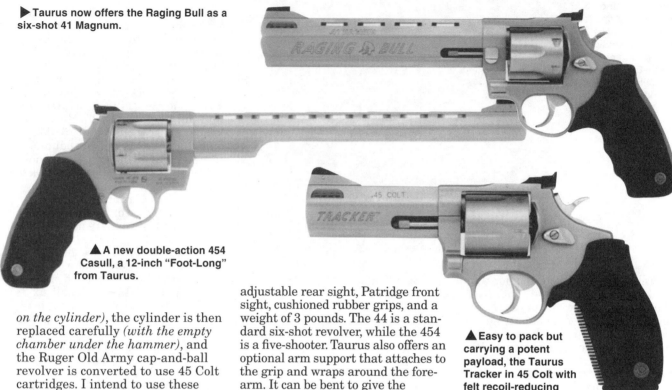

▲ A new double-action 454 Casull, a 12-inch "Foot-Long" from Taurus.

▲ Easy to pack but carrying a potent payload, the Taurus Tracker in 45 Colt with felt recoil-reducing Ribber grips.

on the cylinder), the cylinder is then replaced carefully *(with the empty chamber under the hammer)*, and the Ruger Old Army cap-and-ball revolver is converted to use 45 Colt cartridges. I intend to use these guns and cylinders to shoot both Frontier Cartridge and Plainsman in cowboy action shooting matches.

Taurus

This company just continues to amaze—they not let any grass grow under their feet. For the new 17 Hornady Magnum Rimfire they have not only chambered their pump-action rifle, they now are offering shooters 10 six-gun choices. Shooters have a choice of both blue and stainless eight-shooters, or the new Model 17SS12. The "12" of this model number denotes a foot-long barrel. I find myself captivated by these long barrels and I have been shooting both the 22 Long Rifle and 22 Winchester Rimfire Magnum versions since last year. To keep the weight down as much as possible, the long tubes are standard barrels rather than the heavy underlug style. This keeps the weight of the 17HMR version at just two ounces over three pounds. Taurus calls this the "Perfect Gun and Ammunition Match for Coyote, Rabbit, Squirrel, Crow and Other Small Game Hunting." They could well be right and to further ensure this they include a free scope mount base with each foot-long 17.

The 17HMR, 22LR, and 22WMR 12-inch six-guns are now joined by centerfire versions in both 357 Magnum and 218 Bee, as well as two big-game hunting models chambered in 44 Magnum and 454 Casull. All have a vent-ribbed standard barrel, fully

adjustable rear sight, Patridge front sight, cushioned rubber grips, and a weight of 3 pounds. The 44 is a standard six-shot revolver, while the 454 is a five-shooter. Taurus also offers an optional arm support that attaches to the grip and wraps around the forearm. It can be bent to give the required tension and has been given the *OK* by ATF.

Taurus' very popular Raging Bull has been offered in 44 Magnum, 454 Casull, and 480 Ruger. The connoisseur's other cartridge, the 41 Magnum has now been added to the line. Raging Bull's feature heavy underlug barrels, four ports on each side of the front sight, fully adjustable rear sight, Patridge front sight, and cushioned rubber grips. Scope mount bases are also offered. The Raging Bulls have now been joined by three other Raging Models, the Raging Hornet (22 Hornet), the Raging Bee (218 Bee), and the Raging Thirty (30 Carbine). These are all eight-shooters weighing two ounces over three pounds with their 10-inch barrels. Scope mounts are also available for these varmint pistols.

For those that are looking for an easy-to-pack but potent six-gun, Taurus offers four 4-inch, five-shot Trackers chambered in 357 Magnum, 41 Magnum, 45 ACP, and 45 Colt. All of these feature heavy underlug barrels and the felt recoil-reducing wraparound "Ribber" grips. All but the 41 are also offered in a 6 1/2-inch vent rib model. This latter version also comes in 17HMR and 218 Bee. Taurus of course continues to offer a full line of revolvers for concealed carry, including the 2-inch CIA and Protector, in 38 Special and 357 Magnum, including Total Titanium versions in 38. The CIA is a hammerless, DAO five-shooter, while the Protector has

just enough of the hammer spur showing to allow cocking for single-action fire. Both models feature finger-grooved rubber grips.

Thompson/Center

T/C's Contender opened up new vistas for the handgun hunter more than three decades ago. The standard Contender frame was replaced last year with the new G2 Contender featuring an easier-to-open action, more room for the hand between the back of the trigger guard and front of the grip, and a hammer-block safety that does not require the action be re-opened if the shooter decides to lower the hammer, and then re-cock. On the old models, once the hammer was lowered, the action had to be opened before it could be re-cocked. The G2 will accept all original Contender barrels; however, the grip frame is different and requires use of the new grip. As of this writing, G2s continue to be in short supply.

The G2 may be in short supply but the Encore is not. This stronger version of the Contender allows the use of high-pressure rifle cartridges above the level of the 44Magnum/30-30 Contender. The Encore is offered in both 12-inch and 15-inch easy opening models in such chamberings as 454 Casull, 480 Ruger, 22-250 Remington, 25-06, 7-08, 308, 30-06, 45-70,

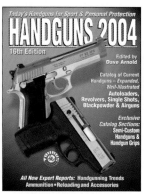
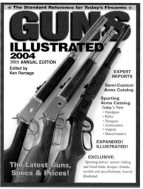
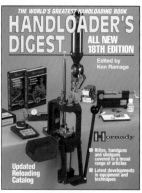

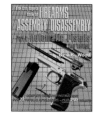

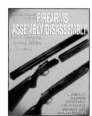

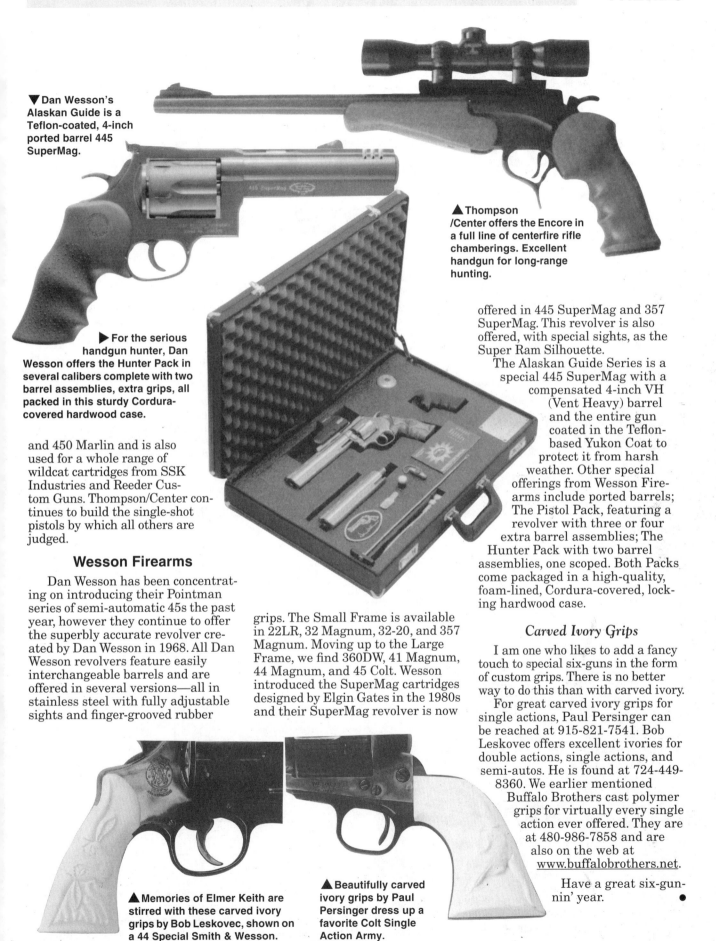

▼Dan Wesson's Alaskan Guide is a Teflon-coated, 4-inch ported barrel 445 SuperMag.

▲Thompson /Center offers the Encore in a full line of centerfire rifle chamberings. Excellent handgun for long-range hunting.

▶For the serious handgun hunter, Dan Wesson offers the Hunter Pack in several calibers complete with two barrel assemblies, extra grips, all packed in this sturdy Cordura-covered hardwood case.

and 450 Marlin and is also used for a whole range of wildcat cartridges from SSK Industries and Reeder Custom Guns. Thompson/Center continues to build the single-shot pistols by which all others are judged.

Wesson Firearms

Dan Wesson has been concentrating on introducing their Pointman series of semi-automatic 45s the past year, however they continue to offer the superbly accurate revolver created by Dan Wesson in 1968. All Dan Wesson revolvers feature easily interchangeable barrels and are offered in several versions—all in stainless steel with fully adjustable sights and finger-grooved rubber

grips. The Small Frame is available in 22LR, 32 Magnum, 32-20, and 357 Magnum. Moving up to the Large Frame, we find 360DW, 41 Magnum, 44 Magnum, and 45 Colt. Wesson introduced the SuperMag cartridges designed by Elgin Gates in the 1980s and their SuperMag revolver is now

offered in 445 SuperMag and 357 SuperMag. This revolver is also offered, with special sights, as the Super Ram Silhouette.

The Alaskan Guide Series is a special 445 SuperMag with a compensated 4-inch VH (Vent Heavy) barrel and the entire gun coated in the Teflon-based Yukon Coat to protect it from harsh weather. Other special offerings from Wesson Firearms include ported barrels; The Pistol Pack, featuring a revolver with three or four extra barrel assemblies; The Hunter Pack with two barrel assemblies, one scoped. Both Packs come packaged in a high-quality, foam-lined, Cordura-covered, locking hardwood case.

Carved Ivory Grips

I am one who likes to add a fancy touch to special six-guns in the form of custom grips. There is no better way to do this than with carved ivory.

For great carved ivory grips for single actions, Paul Persinger can be reached at 915-821-7541. Bob Leskovec offers excellent ivories for double actions, single actions, and semi-autos. He is found at 724-449-8360. We earlier mentioned Buffalo Brothers cast polymer grips for virtually every single action ever offered. They are at 480-986-7858 and are also on the web at www.buffalobrothers.net.

Have a great six-gunnin' year. ●

▲Memories of Elmer Keith are stirred with these carved ivory grips by Bob Leskovec, shown on a 44 Special Smith & Wesson.

▲Beautifully carved ivory grips by Paul Persinger dress up a favorite Colt Single Action Army.

Update: Ammunition, Ballistics And Components

by Holt Bodinson

SMITH & WESSON surprised us this year. The company who has given us the 357, 41, and 44 magnums upped the ante with the release of their 500 S&W Magnum, and a behemoth of a revolver to handle it.

Non-toxic projectiles are the rage. We see more signs of "green" bullets in the rifle and handgun ammunition lines each year.

Lots of great new reloading manuals are out in print, and most include data on the latest short magnums. Look for further information under Hodgdon, Hornady, Lee Precision, Lyman, Nosler, Sierra, and Swift.

Ballistic software is finally becoming more sophisticated and user-friendly. See the latest offerings under Lee Precision, Load from a Disk and Sierra.

It's been an intriguing year in ammunition, ballistics and components.

CCI-SPEER

CCI's extensive, sintered copper/tin, frangible bullet line just got bigger. New this year under the Blazer label is a 140-grain 45 ACP load clocking 1200 fps; a 90-grain 9mm load at 1350 fps; and a 105-grain 40 S&W loading at 1380 fps. Speer is introducing a 250-grain loading for that old stalwart, the 45 Colt, with a respectable velocity of 900 fps. In their component line, Speer has added a 210-grain 44 Magnum Gold Dot HP bullet and 185- and 200-grain Totally Metal Jacket bullets designed for 45 ACP velocities.

www.cci-ammunition.com
www.speer-bullets.com

Cor-Bon

When Smith &Wesson went looking for a new magnum handgun cartridge, Cor-Bon jumped at the chance to design the 500 S&W Magnum cartridge. The brass is being drawn right there in Sturgis, ND by Jamison International and the completed ammunition is being loaded by Cor-Bon. Initially, three

Smith&Wesson decided to capture the high ground with the release of their 500 S&W Magnum.

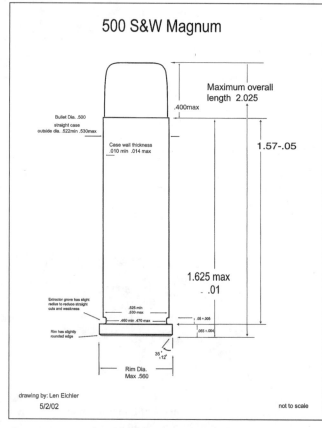

▲The 1.57-inch case length of S&W's new 500 illustrates how big this new cartridge really is.

Muzzleloaders will be pleased with Hodgdon's new 54-caliber Pyrodex pellet.

Hornady's two-volume reloading manual contains vital information on their new bullets and cartridge lines.

different 500 S&W loads are being offered: a 275-grain Barnes X bullet at 1665 fps; a 400-grain SP at 1675 fps; and a wrist-shocking 440-grain gas-checked LBT "wide flat nose" pill at 1625 fps. At the other end of the ballistic scale, Cor-Bon has teamed up with North American Arms (NAA) and created the 32NAA. The 32NAA is a bottlenecked 32-caliber cartridge based on a necked down 380 ACP case that fits in NAA's little pocket automatic, the Guardian. The resulting ballistics from the Guardian's 2.5-inch barrel are impressive. The 32NAA loaded with a 60-grain bullet achieves 1200 fps. Cor-Bon and NAA are now working on the 25NAA that will be a based on a 32ACP case. Stay tuned!
www.corbon.com

Environ Metal

Environ Metal is the manufacturer of Hevi-Shot products. New offerings include 40-caliber frangible bullets made from their proprietary, non-toxic alloy.
www.hevishot.com

GOEX

Clear Shot, Goex's popular, non-corrosive blackpowder replacement, is currently out of production. They hope to get it back on line in the future, but in the meantime, stock up on it. Several of their dis-

tributors still have it.
www.goexpowder.com

Hodgdon Powder

The traditional Pyrodex pellet line has been expanded to include 45-caliber/50-grain, 50-caliber/50-grain, 50-caliber/30-grain, and 54-caliber/60-grain loadings. There's a brand new Pyrodex brochure at your dealers that provides interesting loading data for metallic cartridges and shotshells, as well as muzzleloaders. There's a new "annual" reloading manual available that includes data for the latest short magnums plus 5000 other loads and some great articles from the past by Skeeter Skelton and Bob Milek.
www.hodgdon.com
www.pyrodex.com

Hornady

There's a lot of fresh loading data available in Hornady's new, two-volume reloading manual for many of the short magnums and other recent cartridge introductions. See Graf and Huntington listings for additional products.
www.hornady.com

Huntington

If you need brass, or bullets, or RCBS products, Huntington is the first stop. They are particularly strong in the rare and obsolete caliber department. They're the only source for 8mm Nambu bullets and carry the full Woodleigh line. How about 7mm-TCU or 500 Linebaugh brass? Huntington has them—plus they offer a unique service for cartridge collectors and handloaders. They will sell you a single case in every conceivable caliber for a very reasonable price. See their extensive catalog at www.huntington.com

Lee Precision

The father of the most affordable and unique reloading equipment line in the world, Richard Lee, has just released the 2nd edition of his book, Modern Reloading. This is the most personal and refreshingly

written reloading manual in the field. Within its 720 pages is a complete description of the history, theory and practice of reloading that includes original chapters on bullet casting, reduced loads, measuring powder by volume, pressure, and, of course, a full description of the design and function of Lee tools. There is loading data for cartridges not normally covered in other manuals and the case diagrams indicate the year of introduction and the capacity of the case in cc's. Released, too, this year is a brand new software program called "Lee Shooter." Contained in the program are detailed logs for storing and printing out your handloading data and firearm collection information; trajectory, energy, recoil, wind drift calculators; printable targets; the complete loading manuals of Accurate Arms, Alliant, Hodgdon, IMR and VihtaVuori—plus the Lee Precision catalog. Priced at only $19.98 plus postage, it's another great Lee bargain.
www.leeprecision.com

Liberty Shooting Supplies

Liberty's a great source for hard-to-find cast bullet designs. Recent introductions include bullets for the 32 Colt (heeled). There are old standbys–plus all standard calibers. Many bullets can be custom-sized to order. Liberty bullets are quality products.
www.libertyshootingsupplies.com

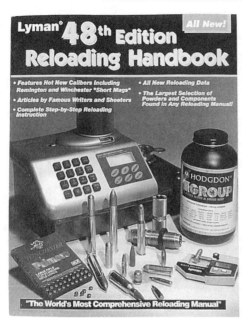

Lyman Reloading Handbook, 48th Edition.

Load From A Disk

An upgraded and expanded Version #4 of this popular program is now available.
www.loadammo.com/upgrade.htm

LYMAN

Lyman has just released the 48th Edition of its "Reloading Handbook." Advertised as the "world's most comprehensive reloading manual," it lives up to its reputation. Packed with lots of new data and powders and informative articles, the new manual has returned to the practice of indicating the potentially most accurate load. This is a "must have" reloading manual.

Magtech

"Guardian Gold" is the label for Magtech's latest line of jacketed hollowpoint ammunition for law enforcement and personal defense.

The new loading is available in 380, 38 Special, 357, 9mm, 40 S&W and 45 Auto. Also new is their "Clean Range" line—in 380, 38 Special, 9mm and 40 S&W—that features a fully encapsulated bullet and lead-free primer.
www.magtechammunition.com

Northern Precision

Imagine a bonded core, spitzer bullet for the 454 Casull that fits in a Freedom Arms cylinder. Northern Precision has them in weights from 300 to 375 grains. Call for their very unique catalog. (315) 493-1711

Nosler

Nosler has released a new 728-page reloading manual with lots of new data and new bullets. The graphic displays of loading density, as well as technical footnotes, make this manual a must.
www.nosler.com

Schroeder Bullets

Here's a small firm that specializes in old and odd size bullets and brass. Need some 7.92x33mm Kurz brass? Schroeder makes it. Interesting catalog. (619) 423-3523

Sellier & Bellot

NONTOX primers combined with TFMJ bullets are being offered in 9mm and 38 Special this year.
www.sb-usa.com

Sierra Bullets

Sierra's 5th Edition Rifle & Handgun Reloading Manual has been released and it's better than ever. Lots of new powders and cartridges. The exterior ballistics chapter has been condensed and rewritten so that the whole 1149-page manual now fits in one binder.

Released in concert with the new manual is Sierra's "INFINITY" Version 5.0 exterior ballistics software program. The program has been expanded to include the bullets of all major manufacturers and ammunition companies. A Windows format makes it user-friendly and flexible. No new bullets.
www.sierrabullets.com

Nosler's new 728-page reloading manual includes fresh data on the short magnums as well as on the latest Nosler and Combined Technology bullets.

Sierra's 5th Edition reloading manual includes the latest cartridges and powders and is bound in a single volume.

SSK Industries

After the appearance of the 500 S&W case, it didn't take JD long to create two new rounds for the Encore. Using the S&W basic case, he's necked it down to form the 475/500 and 458/500 JDJ Woodswalkers.
www.sskindustries.com

"Guardian Gold" is the label given Magtech's latest line of JHP ammunition for law enforcement and personal protection.

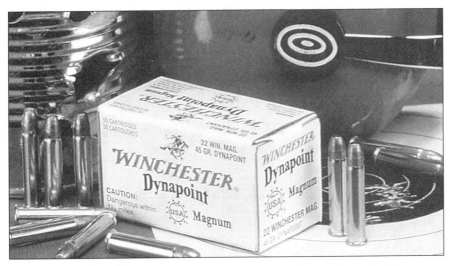

With the success of the Dyna Point design in the LR, Winchester is now loading a new Dyna Point in the 22 Rimfire Magnum.

The 500 S&W has been wildcatted already as evidenced by SSK's 458/500 and 475/500 Woodswalkers, pictured here with the parent 500.

The 22 WRF is being returned to the Winchester rimfire line.

Swift

Kudos to Swift for producing the highest quality handloading manual to date. Swift's hardbound Reloading Manual Number One is simply gorgeous. I laid my copy out on our coffee table. It offers extensive coverage of 49 rifle and pistol cartridges loaded with Swift's premium A-Frame and Scirocco bullets. The trajectory charts are adjacent to the loading data, and each cartridge is highlighted with an artist's rendering of game animal commonly associated with the caliber. It's a real collector's item. (785) 754-3959.

West Coast Bullets

How do you tell duty ammunition from frangible target ammo? West Coast produces non-toxic, sintered iron-tin-copper bullets for all popular handgun calibers–plus the 223 Winchester. To ensure none of their loaded frangible bullets are accidentally carried while an officer is on duty, they color their bullets purple, green; in fact, just about any color you want.

www.westcoastbullets.com

41 Magnum shooters will be delighted with Winchester's new 240-grain Platinum Tip loading in the handgun line.

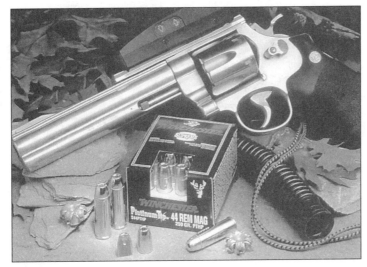

Winchester Ammunition

The old 22 WRF is back in the line, while the 22 Rimfire Magnum sports a new bullet, the 45-grain Dynapoint at 1550 fps. Will 41 Rem. Mag. fans be happy! Winchester is introducing a 240-grain Platinum Tip loading at 1250 fps.

www.winchester.com •

Starline

Some interesting new brass this year—480 Ruger, 41 Colt, 32 S&W and a special run of 475 Wildey–for Wildey. In the planning stages are the 45 Auto Rim and some hard-to-find metrics.

www.starlinebrass.com

Note: The actual ballistics obtained with your firearm can vary considerably from the advertised ballistics. Also, ballistics can vary from lot to lot with the same brand and type load.

Cartridge	Bullet Wt. Grs.	Velocity (fps) 22-1/2" Bbl.		Energy (ft. lbs.) 22-1/2" Bbl.		Mid-Range Traj. (in.)	Muzzle Velocity
		Muzzle	100 yds.	Muzzle	100 yds.	100 yds.	6" Bbl.
17 Aguila	20	1850	NA	NA	NA	NA	NA
17 HMR	17	2550	1902	245	136	NA	NA
22 Short Blank	—	—	—	—	—	—	—
22 Short CB	29	727	610	33	24	NA	706
22 Short Target	29	830	695	44	31	6.8	786
22 Short HP	27	1164	920	81	50	4.3	1077
22 Colibri	20	375	183	6	1	NA	NA
22 Super Colibri	20	500	441	11	9	NA	NA
22 Long CB	29	727	610	33	24	NA	706
22 Long HV	29	1180	946	90	57	4.1	1031
22 LR Ballistician	25	1100	760	65	30	NA	NA
22 LR Pistol Match	40	1070	890	100	70	4.6	940
22 LR Sub Sonic HP	38	1050	901	93	69	4.7	NA
22 LR Standard Velocity	40	1070	890	100	70	4.6	940
22 LR HV	40	1255	1016	140	92	3.6	1060
22 LR Silhoutte	42	1220	1003	139	94	3.6	1025
22 SSS	60	950	802	120	86	NA	NA
22 LR HV HP	40	1280	1001	146	89	3.5	1085
22 Velocitor GDHP	40	1435	0	0	0	NA	NA
22 LR Hyper HP	32/33/34	1500	1075	165	85	2.8	NA
22 LR Stinger HP	32	1640	1132	191	91	2.6	1395
22 LR Hyper Vel	30	1750	1191	204	93	NA	NA
22 LR Shot #12	31	950	NA	NA	NA	NA	NA
22 WRF LFN	45	1300	1015	169	103	3	NA
22 Win. Mag.	30	2200	1373	322	127	1.4	1610
22 Win. Mag. V-Max BT	33	2000	1495	293	164	0.60	NA
22 Win. Mag. JHP	34	2120	1435	338	155	1.4	NA
22 Win. Mag. JHP	40	1910	1326	324	156	1.7	1480
22 Win. Mag. FMJ	40	1910	1326	324	156	1.7	1480
22 Win. Mag. Dyna Point	45	1550	1147	240	131	2.60	NA
22 Win. Mag. JHP	50	1650	1280	300	180	1.3	NA
22 Win. Mag. Shot #11	52	1000	—	NA	—	—	NA

CENTERFIRE HANDGUN CARTRIDGES — BALLISTICS & PRICES

Notes: Blanks are available in 32 S&W, 38 S&W and 38 Special. "V" after barrel length indicates test barrel was vented to produce ballistics similar to a revolver with a normal barrel-to-cylinder gap. Ammo prices are per 50 rounds except when marked with an ** which signifies a 20 round box; *** signifies a 25-round box. Not all loads are available from all ammo manufacturers. Listed loads are those made by Remington, Winchester, Federal, and others. DISC. is a discontinued load. Prices are rounded to nearest whole dollar and will vary with brand and retail outlet. † = new bullet weight this year; "c" indicates a change in data.

Cartridge	Bullet Wgt. Grs.	VELOCITY (fps)			ENERGY (ft. lbs.)			Mid-Range Traj. (in.)		Bbl. Lgth. (in).	Est. Price/ box
		Muzzle	50 yds.	100 yds.	Muzzle	50 yds.	100 yds.	50 yds.	100 yds.		
221 Rem. Fireball	50	2650	2380	2130	780	630	505	0.2	0.8	10.5"	$15
25 Automatic	35	900	813	742	63	51	43	NA	NA	2"	$18
25 Automatic	45	815	730	655	65	55	40	1.8	7.7	2"	$21
25 Automatic	50	760	705	660	65	55	50	2.0	8.7	2"	$17
7.5mm Swiss	107	1010	NA	NA	240	NA	NA	NA	NA	NA	NEW
7.62mmTokarev	87	1390	NA	NA	365	NA	NA	0.6	NA	4.5"	NA
7.62 Nagant	97	1080	NA	NA	350	NA	NA	NA	NA	NA	NEW
7.63 Mauser	88	1440	NA	NA	405	NA	NA	NA	NA	NA	NEW
30 Luger	93†	1220	1110	1040	305	255	225	0.9	3.5	4.5"	$34
30 Carbine	110	1790	1600	1430	785	625	500	0.4	1.7	10"	$28
30-357 AeT	123	1992	NA	NA	1084	NA	NA	NA	NA	10"	NA
32 S&W	88	680	645	610	90	80	75	2.5	10.5	3"	$17
32 S&W Long	98	705	670	635	115	100	90	2.3	10.5	4"	$17
32 Short Colt	80	745	665	590	100	80	60	2.2	9.9	4"	$19
32 H&R Magnum	85	1100	1020	930	230	195	165	1.0	4.3	4.5"	$21
32 H&R Magnum	95	1030	940	900	225	190	170	1.1	4.7	4.5"	$19
32 Automatic	60	970	895	835	125	105	95	1.3	5.4	4"	$22
32 Automatic	60	1000	917	849	133	112	96			4"	NA
32 Automatic	65	950	890	830	130	115	100	1.3	5.6	NA	NA
32 Automatic	71	905	855	810	130	115	95	1.4	5.8	4"	$19
8mm Lebel Pistol	111	850	NA	NA	180	NA	NA	NA	NA	NA	NEW
8mm Steyr	112	1080	NA	NA	290	NA	NA	NA	NA	NA	NEW
8mm Gasser	126	850	NA	NA	200	NA	NA	NA	NA	NA	NEW
380 Automatic	60	1130	960	NA	170	120	NA	1.0	NA	NA	NA
380 Automatic	85/88	990	920	870	190	165	145	1.2	5.1	4"	$20
380 Automatic	90	1000	890	800	200	160	130	1.2	5.5	3.75"	$10
380 Automatic	95/100	955	865	785	190	160	130	1.4	5.9	4"	$20
38 Super Auto +P	115	1300	1145	1040	430	335	275	0.7	3.3	5"	$26
38 Super Auto +P	125/130	1215	1100	1015	425	350	300	0.8	3.6	5"	$26
38 Super Auto +P	147	1100	1050	1000	395	355	325	0.9	4.0	5"	NA
9x18mm Makarov	95	1000	NA	NA	NA	NA	NA	NA	NA	NA	NEW
9x18mm Ultra	100	1050	NA	NA	240	NA	NA	NA	NA	NA	NEW
9x23mm Largo	124	1190	1055	966	390	306	257	0.7	3.7	4"	NA
9x23mm Win.	125	1450	1249	1103	583	433	338	0.6	2.8	NA	NA
9mm Steyr	115	1180	NA	NA	350	NA	NA	NA	NA	NA	NEW
9mm Luger	88	1500	1190	1010	440	275	200	0.6	3.1	4"	$24
9mm Luger	90	1360	1112	978	370	247	191	NA	NA	4"	$26
9mm Luger	95	1300	1140	1010	350	275	215	0.8	3.4	4"	NA
9mm Luger	100	1180	1080	NA	305	255	NA	0.9	NA	4"	NA
9mm Luger	115	1155	1045	970	340	280	240	0.9	3.9	4"	$21
9mm Luger	123/125	1110	1030	970	340	290	260	1.0	4.0	4"	$23
9mm Luger	140	935	890	850	270	245	225	1.3	5.5	4"	$23
9mm Luger	147	990	940	900	320	290	265	1.1	4.9	4"	$26
9mm Luger +P	90	1475	NA	NA	437	NA	NA	NA	NA	NA	NA
9mm Luger +P	115	1250	1113	1019	399	316	265	0.8	3.5	4"	$27
9mm Federal	115	1280	1130	1040	420	330	280	0.7	3.3	4"V	$24
9mm Luger Vector	115	1155	1047	971	341	280	241	NA	NA	4"	NA
9mm Luger +P	124	1180	1089	1021	384	327	287	0.8	3.8	NA	NA
38 S&W	146	685	650	620	150	135	125	2.4	10.0	4"	$19
38 Short Colt	125	730	685	645	150	130	115	2.2	9.4	6"	$19
39 Special	100	950	900	NA	200	180	NA	1.3	NA	4"V	NA
38 Special	110	945	895	850	220	195	175	1.3	5.4	4"V	$23
38 Special	110	945	895	850	220	195	175	1.3	5.4	4"V	$23
38 Special	130	775	745	710	175	160	120	1.9	7.9	4"V	$22

CENTERFIRE HANDGUN CARTRIDGES — BALLISTICS & PRICES, continued

Notes: Blanks are available in 32 S&W, 38 S&W and 38 Special. "V" after barrel length indicates test barrel was vented to produce ballistics similar to a revolver with a normal barrel-to-cylinder gap. Ammo prices are per 50 rounds except when marked with an ** which signifies a 20 round box; *** signifies a 25-round box. Not all loads are available from all ammo manufacturers. Listed loads are those made by Remington, Winchester, Federal, and others. DISC. is a discontinued load. Prices are rounded to nearest whole dollar and will vary with brand and retail outlet. † = new bullet weight this year; "c" indicates a change in data.

Cartridge	Bullet Wgt. Grs.	VELOCITY (fps)			ENERGY (ft. lbs.)			Mid-Range Traj. (in.)		Bbl. Lgth. (in).	Est. Price/ box
		Muzzle	50 yds.	100 yds.	Muzzle	50 yds.	100 yds.	50 yds.	100 yds.		
38 Special Cowboy	140	800	767	735	199	183	168			7.5" V	NA
38 (Multi-Ball)	140	830	730	505	215	130	80	2.0	10.6	4"V	$10**
38 Special	148	710	635	565	165	130	105	2.4	10.6	4"V	$17
38 Special	158	755	725	690	200	185	170	2.0	8.3	4"V	$18
38 Special +P	95	1175	1045	960	290	230	195	0.9	3.9	4"V	$23
38 Special +P	110	995	925	870	240	210	185	1.2	5.1	4"V	$23
38 Special +P	125	975	929	885	264	238	218	1	5.2	4"	NA
38 Special +P	125	945	900	860	250	225	205	1.3	5.4	4"V	#23
38 Special +P	129	945	910	870	255	235	215	1.3	5.3	4"V	$11
38 Special +P	130	925	887	852	247	227	210	1.3	5.50	4"V	NA
38 Special +P	147/150(c)	884	NA	NA	264	NA	NA	NA	NA	4"V	$27
38 Special +P	158	890	855	825	280	255	240	1.4	6.0	4"V	$20
357 SIG	115	1520	NA	NA	593	NA	NA	NA	NA	NA	NA
357 SIG	124	1450	NA	NA	578	NA	NA	NA	NA	NA	NA
357 SIG	125	1350	1190	1080	510	395	325	0.7	3.1	4"	NA
357 SIG	150	1130	1030	970	420	355	310	0.9	4.0	NA	NA
356 TSW	115	1520	NA	NA	593	NA	NA	NA	NA	NA	NA
356 TSW	124	1450	NA	NA	578	NA	NA	NA	NA	NA	NA
356 TSW	135	1280	1120	1010	490	375	310	0.8	3.50	NA	NA
356 TSW	147	1220	1120	1040	485	410	355	0.8	3.5	5"	NA
357 Mag., Super Clean	105	1650									NA
357 Magnum	110	1295	1095	975	410	290	230	0.8	3.5	4"V	$25
357 (Med.Vel.)	125	1220	1075	985	415	315	270	0.8	3.7	4"V	$25
357 Magnum	125	1450	1240	1090	585	425	330	0.6	2.8	4"V	$25
357 (Multi-Ball)	140	1155	830	665	420	215	135	1.2	6.4	4"V	$11**
357 Magnum	140	1360	1195	1075	575	445	360	0.7	3.0	4"V	$25
357 Magnum	145	1290	1155	1060	535	430	360	0.8	3.5	4"V	$26
357 Magnum	150/158	1235	1105	1015	535	430	360	0.8	3.5	4"V	$25
357 Mag. Cowboy	158	800	761	725	225	203	185				NA
357 Magnum	165	1290	1189	1108	610	518	450	0.7	3.1	8-3/8"	NA
357 Magnum	180	1145	1055	985	525	445	390	0.9	3.9	4"V	$25
357 Magnum	180	1180	1088	1020	557	473	416	0.8	3.6	8"V	NA
357 Mag. CorBon F.A.	180	1650	1512	1386	1088	913	767	1.66	0.0		NA
357 Mag. CorBon	200	1200	1123	1061	640	560	500	3.19	0.0		NA
357 Rem. Maximum	158	1825	1590	1380	1170	885	670	0.4	1.7	10.5"	$14**
40 S&W	135	1140	1070	NA	390	345	NA	0.9	NA	4"	NA
40 S&W	155	1140	1026	958	447	362	309	0.9	4.1	4"	$14***
40 S&W	165	1150	NA	NA	485	NA	NA	NA	NA	4"	$18***
40 S&W	180	985	936	893	388	350	319	1.4	5.0	4"	$14***
40 S&W	180	1015	960	914	412	368	334	1.3	4.5	4"	NA
400 Cor-Bon	135	1450	NA	NA	630	NA	NA	NA	NA	5"	NA
10mm Automatic	155	1125	1046	986	436	377	335	0.9	3.9	5"	$26
10mm Automatic	170	1340	1165	1145	680	510	415	0.7	3.2	5"	$31
10mm Automatic	175	1290	1140	1035	650	505	420	0.7	3.3	5.5"	$11**
10mm Auto. (FBI)	180	950	905	865	361	327	299	1.5	5.4	4"	$16**
10mm Automatic	180	1030	970	920	425	375	340	1.1	4.7	5"	$16**
10mm Auto H.V.	180†	1240	1124	1037	618	504	430	0.8	3.4	5"	$27
10mm Automatic	200	1160	1070	1010	495	510	430	0.9	3.8	5"	$14**
10.4mm Italian	177	950	NA	NA	360	NA	NA	NA	NA	NA	NEW
41 Action Exp.	180	1000	947	903	400	359	326	0.5	4.2	5"	$13**
41 Rem. Magnum	170	1420	1165	1015	760	515	390	0.7	3.2	4"V	$33
41 Rem. Magnum	175	1250	1120	1030	605	490	410	0.8	3.4	4"V	$14**

Notes: Blanks are available in 32 S&W, 38 S&W and 38 Special. "V" after barrel length indicates test barrel was vented to produce ballistics similar to a revolver with a normal barrel-to-cylinder gap. Ammo prices are per 50 rounds except when marked with an ** which signifies a 20 round box; *** signifies a 25-round box. Not all loads are available from all ammo manufacturers. Listed loads are those made by Remington, Winchester, Federal, and others. DISC. is a discontinued load. Prices are rounded to nearest whole dollar and will vary with brand and retail outlet. † = new bullet weight this year; "c" indicates a change in data.

Cartridge	Bullet Wgt. Grs.	VELOCITY (fps)			ENERGY (ft. lbs.)			Mid-Range Traj. (in.)		Bbl. Lgth. (in).	Est. Price/ box
		Muzzle	50 yds.	100 yds.	Muzzle	50 yds.	100 yds.	50 yds.	100 yds.		
41 (Med. Vel.)	210	965	900	840	435	375	330	1.3	5.4	4"V	$30
41 Rem. Magnum	210	1300	1160	1060	790	630	535	0.7	3.2	4"V	$33
41 Rem. Magnum	240	1250	1151	1075	833	706	616	0.8	3.3	6.5V	NA
44 S&W Russian	247	780	NA	NA	335	NA	NA	NA	NA	NA	NA
44 S&W Special	180	980	NA	NA	383	NA	NA	NA	NA	6.5"	NA
44 S&W Special	180	1000	935	882	400	350	311	NA	NA	7.5"V	NA
44 S&W Special	200†	875	825	780	340	302	270	1.2	6.0	6"	$13**
44 S&W Special	200	1035	940	865	475	390	335	1.1	4.9	6.5"	$13**
44 S&W Special	240/246	755	725	695	310	285	265	2.0	8.3	6.5"	$26
44-40 Win. Cowboy	225	750	723	695	281	261	242				NA
44 Rem. Magnum	180	1610	1365	1175	1035	745	550	0.5	2.3	4"V	$18**
44 Rem. Magnum	200	1400	1192	1053	870	630	492	0.6	NA	6.5"	$20
44 Rem. Magnum	210	1495	1310	1165	1040	805	635	0.6	2.5	6.5"	$18**
44 (Med. Vel.)	240	1000	945	900	535	475	435	1.1	4.8	6.5"	$17
44 R.M. (Jacketed)	240	1180	1080	1010	740	625	545	0.9	3.7	4"V	$18**
44 R.M. (Lead)	240	1350	1185	1070	970	750	610	0.7	3.1	4"V	$29
44 Rem. Magnum	250	1180	1100	1040	775	670	600	0.8	3.6	6.5"V	$21
44 Rem. Magnum	250	1250	1148	1070	867	732	635	0.8	3.3	6.5"V	NA
44 Rem. Magnum	275	1235	1142	1070	931	797	699	0.8	3.3	6.5"	NA
44 Rem. Magnum	300	1200	1100	1026	959	806	702	NA	NA	7.5"	$17
44 Rem. Magnum	330	1385	1297	1220	1406	1234	1090	1.83	0.00	NA	NA
440 CorBon	260	1700	1544	1403	1669	1377	1136	1.58	NA	10"	NA
450 Short Colt/450 Revolver	226	830	NA	NA	350	NA	NA	NA	NA	NA	NEW
45 S&W Schofield	180	730	NA	NA	213	NA	NA	NA	NA	NA	NA
45 S&W Schofield	230	730	NA	NA	272	NA	NA	na			NA
45 Automatic	165	1030	930	NA	385	315	NA	1.2	NA	5"	NA
45 Automatic	185	1000	940	890	410	360	325	1.1	4.9	5"	$28
45 Auto. (Match)	185	770	705	650	245	204	175	2.0	8.7	5"	$28
45 Auto. (Match)	200	940	890	840	392	352	312	2.0	8.6	5"	$20
45 Automatic	200	975	917	860	421	372	328	1.4	5.0	5"	$18
45 Automatic	230	830	800	675	355	325	300	1.6	6.8	5"	$27
45 Automatic	230	880	846	816	396	366	340	1.5	6.1	5"	NA
45 Automatic +P	165	1250	NA	NA	573	NA	NA	NA	NA	NA	NA
45 Automatic +P	185	1140	1040	970	535	445	385	0.9	4.0	5"	$31
45 Automatic +P	200	1055	982	925	494	428	380	NA	NA	5"	NA
45 Super	185	1300	1190	1108	694	582	504	NA	NA	5"	NA
45 Win. Magnum	230	1400	1230	1105	1000	775	635	0.6	2.8	5"	$14**
45 Win. Magnum	260	1250	1137	1053	902	746	640	0.8	3.3	5"	$16**
45 Win. Mag. CorBon	320	1150	1080	1025	940	830	747	3.47			NA
455 Webley MKII	262	850	NA	NA	420	NA	NA	NA	NA	NA	NA
45 Colt	200	1000	938	889	444	391	351	1.3	4.8	5.5"	$21
45 Colt	225	960	890	830	460	395	345	1.3	5.5	5.5"	$22
45 Colt + P CorBon	265	1350	1225	1126	1073	884	746	2.65	0.0		NA
45 Colt + P CorBon	300	1300	1197	1114	1126	956	827	2.78	0.0		NA
45 Colt	250/255	860	820	780	410	375	340	1.6	6.6	5.5"	$27
454 Casull	250	1300	1151	1047	938	735	608	0.7	3.2	7.5"V	NA
454 Casull	260	1800	1577	1381	1871	1436	1101	0.4	1.8	7.5"V	NA
454 Casull	300	1625	1451	1308	1759	1413	1141	0.5	2.0	7.5"V	NA
454 Casull CorBon	360	1500	1387	1286	1800	1640	1323	2.01	0.0		NA
475 Linebaugh	400	1350	1217	1119	1618	1315	1112	NA	NA	NA	NA
480 Ruger	325	1350	1191	1076	1315	1023	835	2.6	0.0	7.5"	NA
50 Action Exp.	325	1400	1209	1075	1414	1055	835	0.2	2.3	6"	$24**
500 S&W	275	1665	1392	1183	1693	1184	854	1.5	NA	8.375	NA
500 S&W	400	1675	1472	1299	2493	1926	1499	1.3	NA	8.375	NA
500 S&W	440	1625	1367	1169	2581	1825	1337	1.6	NA	8.375	NA

40, 10mm
44
45, 50

WHAT U.S. COPS CARRY TODAY

by Massad Ayoob

◀ Having carried a number of service sidearms in nearly 30 years, the author currently wears a Ruger 45 auto to work at the department he serves.

BACKSPACE 20 YEARS from the cover date of this book. I was a sergeant on a municipal police department where I was authorized to carry a personally owned auto, usually a Colt 45, but the department issue gun was the Smith & Wesson Model 13 357 Magnum revolver. That was typical. Illinois had been alone among state police agencies to issue a semi-automatic service pistol, the Model 39 S&W

9mm they'd adopted in 1967, but now they had been joined by at least three other state law enforcement agencies. New Jersey troopers were now issued the HK P7M13, and both Connecticut and North Carolina had adopted the Beretta 92F for their state police. FBI was "revolvers only" for rank and file agents, but their

elite shock troops were issued autos. Their Hostage Rescue Team carried Browning Hi-Powers tuned by Wayne Novak, and local office FBI SWAT had the S&W Model 459. All were 9mm pistols, and the "wondernine" seemed to be the wave of the future in the collective police armory, even though the traditional six-shooter was still the predominant law enforcement sidearm.

A score of years makes a lot of difference. The service revolver as

The 40 Smith & Wesson, introduced in 1990, soon became America's favorite police handgun round, as ubiquitous as S&W's handcuffs shown. This is S&W's latest duty gun in that caliber, the cost-effective Value Series Model 410S in stainless.

The Glock is the best selling brand of pistol among police departments today. This is the G30 compact that holds 11 of these 45 ACP Taurus Hex rounds, the author's idea of a superb plainclothes/off duty police gun.

These are the four main service pistol duty calibers in use today. From top: 357 SIG, 9mm Luger, 45 ACP, and the most popular, 40 S&W.

The Safariland SS-III/070 security holster, containing a high-tech semi-automatic service pistol such as this Ruger P97 45 ACP.

Yesterday's duty holster paradigm: the Jordan holster with simple safety strap, here holding the S&W Model 10 38 Special that was once the nation's most popular service sidearm.

▲ **Today, the revolver reigns supreme only as a snub-nosed backup gun. From top, Ruger in 357 Mag, Taurus in 45 ACP, S&W Airlite in 38 Special.**

we knew it is all but extinct; no major law enforcement agency still mandates it for all personnel. Only a few thousand of NYPD's 40,000 cops still wear a Colt, Ruger, or S&W 38 in their duty holster. Among Chicago's 13,000 sworn officers, you can still find quite a few S&W or Colt 38s or 357s, all loaded with the trademark "Chicago round," the +P 38 Special cartridge with all-lead 158 grain semi-wadcutter hollowpoint. The occasional old head among nearly 10,000 LAPD officers still packs an adjustable sight S&W 38 Special. In one action news still from the infamous North Hollywood bank robbery shootout just a few years ago, a city cop can be seen carefully drawing a bead on the heavily armored, machinegun-wielding bandits with a six-inch heavy barrel K-38.

On many smaller departments, one still sees a veteran who stubbornly clings to the wheelgun. I hear there's a gray-haired uniform cop in San Diego who yet wears the old S&W 38 with which he has shot down multiple armed criminals; he feels no need for the 9mm autos almost all his colleagues wear to work. I know three hard-bitten veterans, a small town Indiana chief and a detective in the same state and a middle-aged street monster in Detroit, whose duty guns are Smith & Wesson 44 Magnums. All three are happy anachronisms in departments that now issue 40-caliber Glock semi-automatics.

Bert DuVernay, now a police chief, predicted when he was head of the Smith & Wesson Academy that soon the revolver's place would be as an off duty and backup gun. This has come to pass, particularly in the latter function. Modern compact, high performance autos have become the paradigm in off duty wear, and only as a backup gun do the snub-nose 38 and the "baby" 357 Magnum still keep the revolver dominant over the semi-automatic pistol among police.

Up From 9mm

Prior to 1990, cops on departments that only authorized one type of gun tended to split down the middle, with one faction favoring the proven potency of the 45 auto and the other seeking the high round count of the "wondernine." FBI attempted to split the difference in the late 1980s with the adoption of the S&W Model 1076 in 10mm Auto. John Hall, then head of the firearms training section of the Bureau, felt that with a reduced power load for more controllability, the 10mm would be a suitable compromise. The 10mm "FBI load" was powerful enough to satisfy the big-bore faction, and it was hoped that 10 or 11 rounds in the gun would be enough to make the high capacity crowd happy. Alas, the 10mm never caught on.

Meanwhile, at Smith & Wesson, gun-wise Tom Campbell had hooked up with Paul Liebenberg at the firm's Performance Center. Both were top-flight IPSC competitors, and Paul had developed a wildcat "10mm short" round that "made major" in that game, which he called the Centimeter. Tom realized that the Centimeter cartridge virtually duplicated the performance of the FBI's 180-grain subsonic round, and saw its law enforcement potential since this shorter cartridge would fit the handy envelope of a 9mm pistol. Campbell, Liebenberg, and Ed Hobbie did the research and brought in

▲ **Croatian-made Springfield Armory XD handles and shoots much like a Glock, and is being aggressively marketed to cops.**

Carrying nine rounds of fight-stopping 45 ACP like this proven Hydra-Shok, the S&W Model 4566 is a street-proven, heavy duty law enforcement sidearm.

Ruger SP101 357 Magnum small frame snubby is an ideal backup gun for many officers.

Winchester, and the result was the 1990 introduction of the 40 S&W cartridge, and their reinforced "9mm size" Model 4006 pistol to go with it. California Highway Patrol immediately became the first big department to adopt the 4006, and CHP uses that gun to this day with great reported satisfaction.

When the choice had been essentially between an eight-shot 45 and a 16-shot 9mm, a 12-shot 40 was a slice-it-down-the-middle Solomonic answer to the riddle. Soon, the 40 S&W was the most popular caliber for new handgun purchases by police departments. Glock immediately made the 40 option more attractive by producing their service size gun in that caliber, the G22, with 16 round capacity. By 2003, more state police agencies were issuing the 40 than any other, and FBI had been issuing that caliber to new agents for four years. Interest-

Working identically with only one round less of the same ammo, this lightweight compact S&W Model 457 makes an ideal off-duty counterpart. Most modern police autos come in similar "size families" for maximum skill transfer between uniform and plainclothes guns.

ingly, none of the "big three" municipal PDs went in that direction. 9mm remained the only auto pistol caliber NYPD authorized, and Chicago PD and LAPD by the 21st century had given armed personnel their choice of 9mm or 45 caliber.

Toward the middle of the 1990s, SIG and Federal Cartridge introduced the 357 SIG, essentially a cartridge case of 40 S&W external dimensions necked down to 9mm and spitting a 125-grain jacketed bullet at about 1350 feet per second. The intent was to duplicate the famous "lightning strike" one-shot stop potential that the 125-grain/1450 fps 357 Magnum revolver round had earned since its introduction in the 1970s, and for the most part the 357 SIG succeeded in achieving that goal. While never reaching the popularity of the 40 S&W, the 357 SIG made converts of numerous municipal and county police agencies, and state police including those of North Carolina (Beretta), New Mexico (Glock), and Delaware, Virginia, and Texas (SIG). The Secret Service, happy with their SIG P228s and 115 grain +P+ 9mm ammo, got more of the same when they upgraded to the SIG P229 and Winchester Ranger/SXT 357 SIG ammo. The Sky Marshals made exactly the same choice.

The 45 ACP was also increasing in popularity. Much of this had to do with the perception of too many stopping failures in actual shootings with the 9mm, particularly with the 147-grain subsonic JHP that FBI had popularized nationwide. The aforementioned LAPD and Chicago PD, as well as the Los Angeles County Sheriff's Department

(LASD) authorized privately owned 45 autos in response to their field personnel's complaints that the 9mm wasn't powerful enough. The San Bernardino, California, sheriff bought Glock 45s for his deputies for the same reason, upgrading from 9mm Glocks. Meanwhile, such Federal agencies as FBI, DEA, and the Marshal's Service had authorized 45s for years and still do. Among state police agencies, Tennessee is said to be switching from 40 to the Glock 45, and Idaho and New Hampshire have long been happy with the S&W 45.

The State Police agencies of the six New England states are a good bellwether. Not so long ago, all had medium-bore guns with Rhode Island carrying Ruger 357 revolvers, Maine and Connecticut 9mm Berettas, and New Hampshire 9mm S&Ws, while Vermont and Massachusetts had 9mm SIGs. Today, all have big-bore autos. Maine and New Hampshire have 45s (HK USP and S&W 4566, respectively) and the rest have 40s, with Rhode Island issuing the Beretta 96 and the others, SIG-Sauers.

In the Time of Polymer

Heckler and Koch actually offered the first plastic-frame police service pistol, the P9S, back in the '70s, but it was before its time. Only a handful of police entities adopted it, such as the conservation officers of Idaho and the SWAT team of South Carolina Law Enforcement Division. The concept faded until 1984, when the Glock burst on the scene in Europe. Adoptions by the police departments of St. Paul, Minnesota and Miami, Florida got the 18-shot 9mm Glock 17 on its way, and soon there was no stopping the family of Glock pistols. Light, reliable, exquisitely easy both to service mechanically and to learn to shoot fast and straight, the Glock was the single best selling brand of police duty handgun by the mid-1990s, with a market domination estimated as high as 65%. Their single best selling law enforcement service pistol in the United States is their full size, 16-shot 40, the Glock 22.

The Police Polymer Pistol Parade was on! HK introduced their excellent USP, which proved more affordable than the unique squeeze-cocking HK which had taken New Jersey and Utah state troopers by storm, but had proven too expensive to continue to be practical for governmental agencies that bought on bid. S&W wound up in court with Glock over their Sigma, which worked in a very similar fashion but with a front-loaded trigger pull. S&W still produces the Sigma, but it never caught on with police due to some highly publicized mechanical problems early on. Smith has a second police polymer option, however: their SW99, a joint production effort between their factory and Walther. Since S&W is now the sole U.S. agent for Walther, that brand's P99 makes three separate lines of polymer-framed service autos sold by Smith & Wesson.

Ruger improved both the ergonomics and the weight to power ratio of their ruggedly reliable service autos when they brought out the P95 9mm and P97 45 with plastic frames. SIG brought out their polymer-framed sig pro line in 1998, giving the primary features of the popular SIG-Sauer models now advertised as the "Classic" series, with better accuracy (at least in 40 caliber, it seemed) and at a much lower price. The Richmond, Virginia Police Department is one agency that reports complete satisfaction with their SIG Pro 357s in the field, and in 2001, a Richmond officer used his issue specimen to win the National Police Service Pistol championship.

Action Types

Thirty years ago, the rare cop with the "auto option" had but two choices. One was the cocked and locked single action (SA) auto typified by the Colt Government Model, and the other was a double action first-shot pistol that self-cocked itself for each subsequent shot. The latter has lately become known as a "traditional double action" (TDA). That identification was necessary because there are now no fewer than four distinct variations of semi-automatic pistol in use by American police.

One type has a long, heavy trigger pull for each shot. John Farnam aptly described this style as "self-decocking," and Wiley Clapp called it "double action only" (DAO). It was the latter term that stuck. The other is the niche that Glock carved for itself with what it calls "Safe Action" design: a uniform trigger pull for every shot, shorter in stroke length than most DAOs or the first shot on most TDAs, but not so short as with a cocked single action auto. Some departments have grouped the Safe Action in with the DAO as a single category.

▲Traditional service revolvers such as the S&W Model 13 357 (top, shown with Craig Spegel grips and many years of holster wear) have been replaced by higher firepower service pistols such as the SIG P226, below.

For instance, NYPD's written policy allows only DAO 9mm autos, with but three models specifically approved and left up to the individual officers' choice. These are, in order of popularity, the Glock 19, the S&W Model 5946, and the SIG P226 DAO. Chicago, on the other hand, expressly exempts the Glock from its list of approved autos, which must be double action only and encompass a number of models by Beretta, Ruger, SIG, and Smith & Wesson. (By contrast, LAPD authorizes only TDA pistols, limiting choice to the 9mm or 45 Beretta or S&W. The issue Beretta is of course the most popular 9mm, while S&W seems to rule the 45 roost for LA cops.)

Meanwhile, single action autos are enjoying a small comeback, almost entirely in the 1911 45 ACP format. Tacoma, Washington PD made news when it authorized the Kimber for all armed personnel. So did LAPD's SWAT team when, after

more than 30 years of issuing an assortment of refurbished 1911s taken from the confiscated weapons inventory, they issued each SWAT cop a pair of Kimber II pistols, one with and one without attached Sure-Fire flashlight. Meanwhile, FBI had long since gone to high-cap ParaOrdnance 45 autos for their Hostage Rescue Team, and single-stack Springfield Armory versions for each local office SWAT team. Denver is one large police department that still authorizes cocked and locked 45s for rank and file officers. So do many smaller county and municipal law enforcement agencies.

Ammunition

Hollowpoint ammunition is now the universal modern standard in policing. The last two holdouts for ball ammo among the big departments have gone with Gold Dots, with NYPD adopting the 124 grain +P+ for their 9mms with excellent results, and Detroit reportedly adopting the 180-grain 40 for their standard issue Glock 22s.

Most departments now use one or another "high tech" JHP that has been expressly developed to pass the extensive wound ballistics protocols developed by the FBI in the late 1980s. In addition to that CCI Gold Dot, popular police loads include the Federal Hydra-Shok, the Remington Golden Saber, and the Winchester SXT and Ranger designs that evolved from the ill-fated Black Talon bullet.

As light, powerful, and reliable as the Monadnock PR-24 baton that frames it here, HK USP pistols such as this 40 Compact have proven themselves in US police service.

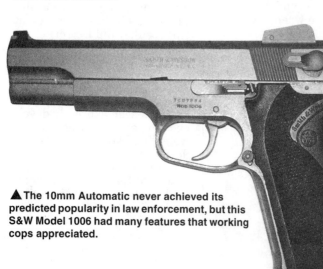

▲ Light rails allowing attachment of units like this Insights M3 flashlight, and potential for extended magazines like this 20-rounder, enhanced the auto pistol's tactical desirability for police. Pistol is latest generation SIG-Sauer P226 in 9mm.

Duty Rigs

There was a time, not so long ago, when it would have been laughable to even suggest that police utility belts and holsters would be made of anything other than leather, except perhaps for the combat web gear of a SWAT team. Things changed quickly, and style and cost had little to do with it.

More cops go out on disability from bad backs, by far, than from weapon-produced wounds. The heavy and rigid leather Sam Browne belt worn at the hips for long days has been identified as a major culprit. The loss-prevention specialists of the governments our law enforcement agencies serve slowly figured out that lightening the load would reduce the disability rate and net a significant cost saving to the taxpayers. Moreover, in the time of blood-borne pathogens, it was quickly learned that bodily fluids can be much more readily and cheaply removed from synthetics than from leather.

Cordura and other heavy duty, tightly woven fabrics were the first wave, and this "duty nylon" remains very popular. Traditionalists bemoaned its look, however, and soon we had ultra-light synthetics styled to resemble leather. Uncle Mike's Mirage and the latest style of Bianchi Accumold are leaders here, and the most high tech of all is the same substance rendered as the Levitation System designed for Safariland by competitive shooter and ex-FBI agent Bill Rogers. Soft plastic tubing runs along the edges of the Levitation's belt to soften pressure against the body and better distribute weight, and ingenious attachments hook holster, magazine pouches, handcuff case, nitrile glove carrier, etc. to the belt without leather loops that dig into underlying human tissue. The result is a new level of all-day comfort and fatigue reduction.

The switch from uniform holsters with a simple safety strap to true security rigs is all but complete, with the majority of our police wearing a snatch-resistant scabbard as part of their uniform. Safariland's concept of "security levels" has become as much a national standard as the FBI protocols for ammunition testing. A handgun in an open-top, pull-and-shoot holster would be deemed "Level Zero" in terms of snatch resistance. A thumb-break or snap-over safety strap is "Level One." A "Level Two" holster requires two movements before the draw can begin, usually the release of a safety strap plus rocking the gun in a certain direction to clear an internal securing niche. "Level Three" requires three actions before the draw can commence. The most popular holster today, with over a million units sold in the last twenty or so years, is the Rogers SS-III built by Safariland, also known as the Model 070. An updated version, the Raptor introduced in 2001, has modular options

that can bring it up to a hitherto unprecedented "Level Four" in terms of security.

Accessories

Extended capacity magazines are available for many models. Most new service pistols now have integral frame rails to attach white light units. At least 80% of currently issued police pistols have night sights. A small percentage of agencies have gone with recoil compensated pistols, such as Glock's "C" line, though upward-jetting muzzle flame from close combat shooting positions will probably keep that feature from ever becoming a universal standard.

Bottom Line

The working American police officer of today has the best guns ever, with the widest choice of brands, styles, and widely accepted calibers. He or she has the most tactically secure holsters, and the finest ammunition ever issued to law enforcement officers. This goes beyond the handgun. Modern police shotguns are far more versatile than the old riot guns, and state of the art semi-automatic rifles in the patrol function in more and more departments have augmented them. In terms of less lethal armament, modern pepper spray is vastly more effective than the old tear gas aerosols, and today's impact munitions are both more effective and more humane than the first generation "beanbag rounds." The old Taser had some shortcomings that seem to have been rectified with the current Advanced Taser. Training has likewise kept pace, and is the best that has ever been offered to law enforcement officers in terms of relevance to surviving armed encounters.

And, best of all, the evolution continues.

Approaching 30 years as a sworn police officer, Massad Ayoob is a captain in charge of training for a municipal police department in northern New England. From 1987 through this writing he has been in charge of the firearms committee of the American Society for Law Enforcement Training (ASLET). He has also taught for state, regional, national and international conferences of the International Association of Law Enforcement Firearms Instructors (IALEFI). The 1998 winner of the Outstanding American Handgunner Award, Massad has been law enforcement editor of "American Handgunner" magazine for more than 20 years. ●

▲ The 10mm Automatic never achieved its predicted popularity in law enforcement, but this S&W Model 1006 had many features that working cops appreciated.

GET A GRIP ON YOUR HANDGUN

And improve its performance

by David W. Arnold

▲ Ideally a grip should provide the shooter with a firm comfortable hold that permits the index finger to properly engage the trigger. The grip should also prevent movement in the hand during firing.

A HANDGUN'S GRIP or stock can greatly affect its shooting characteristics. Grips can affect accuracy, comfort, speed and appearance. Ideally a well-designed grip should provide a firm comfortable hold that points the gun naturally at the target so that the sights are aligned when the gun is brought to shoulder level for shooting. It must also enable the index finger to properly control the trigger and ensure that any recoil does not cause the grip to move in the hand causing the shooter's hold to be changed.

Grips can also greatly enhance a handgun's appearance. While not an essential attribute, it is certainly nice to have especially if the grip also enhances the handgun's performance.

For many years, factory handgun grips generally left much to be desired. Manufacturers were forced to provide a "one-size-fits-all" type of grip in an attempt to cater to different hand sizes.

In past years, auto pistols had factory grips that were generally superior to contemporary double-action revolvers. An exception was the Colt Single Action frontier revolver that was touted by many as having almost

perfect grips especially when compared to those of the modern double-action models. In fairness, factory handgun grips of today's handguns, including revolvers, are vastly improved. Nevertheless, there is often still some room for improvement. Fortunately there are a number of companies that offer a variety of after-market custom grips that should satisfy most shooters' needs.

So, if you have difficulty in controlling the trigger of your favorite handgun, consider investing in a set of custom grips.

Early model double-action revolvers like this Smith & Wesson Model 1917 45ACP (*top*) and Colt Official Police (*bottom*) left much to be desired as far as grips were concerned.

Early attempts by handgun companies was to fit revolvers like this Smith & Wesson Model 19 (*bottom*) and Colt Python (*top*) with larger target stocks based on the design of Walter Roper.

A common problem with early revolver grips was the annoying gap in the frame behind the trigger guard that allowed the gun to move in the hand when recoiling.

TRENDS

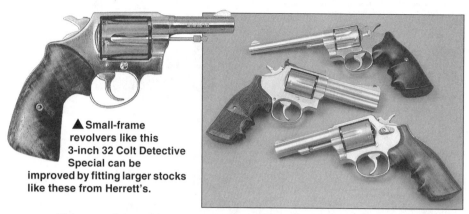

This excellent grip from Hogue leaves the revolver's backstrap exposed, improving the shooter's trigger engagement.

▲ Small-frame revolvers like this 3-inch 32 Colt Detective Special can be improved by fitting larger stocks like these from Herrett's.

There is a wide selection of well-designed custom grips available as illustrated by these three. The top two are from Eagle Grips; the bottom from Hogue Grips.

Trigger Control

Trigger control is the first essential of shooting a handgun effectively. The trigger is operated by the index finger. One should engage the face of the trigger with the first joint or pad of the trigger finger. Proper trigger engagement is especially important for controlling the long hard pull of double-action handguns.

Very often proper trigger engagement is compromised because a revolver's grip is too large or small. A grip that is too small is the easiest to correct. Installing larger stocks is the obvious solution and one that small-frame, short-barrel revolvers can often benefit from. Revolver grips that are too large are somewhat harder to correct. One solution is to install grips that are thinner and slimmer. Also replacing grips that encase the backstrap with one's that leave the same exposed can also work.

Autos that have grips that are too large are harder to rectify. Often

the only solution is to replace them with custom stocks that are thinner. With a 1911, using either an arched or straight mainspring housing can improve trigger engagement.

Recoil Control and Comfort

The recoil forces generated by firing a handgun can cause a number of problems. First and foremost is that ill fitting grips can be both painful and unpleasant. The other is the loss of a proper hold caused by the gun moving in the hand during recoil. Much of the problem is caused by the grip not fitting the hand properly. While some leeway is tolerable, an ill-fitting grip can make it hard to retain the same hold on the gun during firing.

As far as comfort is concerned, a grip that allows the gun to move in the hand can make shooting both painful and uncomfortable. Good fitting grips should be in contact with most of the hand. This helps in evenly distributing the recoil forces in the hand.

Early double-action revolver grips were especially bad in this respect because they left an annoying gap under the

frame behind the trigger guard that made it difficult to obtain a firm hold. An early solution was a grip adapter that effectively filled the gap. The problem was later solved when some manufacturers began offering large wood target-style grips that effectively eliminated the gap. The problem here was that such grips were often too large. The best solution is to fit a set of custom-made stocks that fit your hand. There are companies that offer a wide selection of sizes and styles. Some incorporate finger grooves that help in preventing movement in the hand during recoil.

One of the most effective grips for taking the bite out of recoil is a grip made of rubber. Some leave the backstrap exposed while others cover it. The latter is good for really heavy-recoiling guns, provided one's engagement of the trigger is not adversely affected.

Target Grips

The sport of target shooting probably places the most stringent demands on grips. The object is to provide grips that are comfortable, have a firm hold and enable the same hold to be taken every time the gun is picked up.

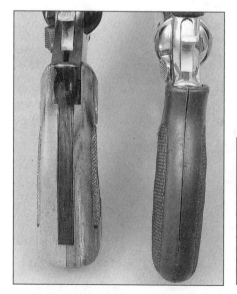

Another solution to large revolvers is to fit grips that are thinner than the originals.

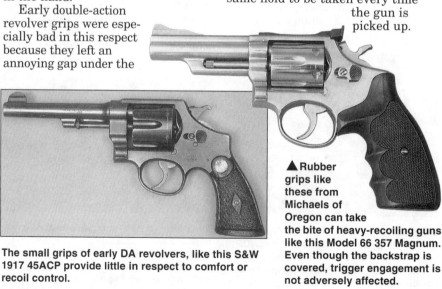

The small grips of early DA revolvers, like this S&W 1917 45ACP provide little in respect to comfort or recoil control.

▲ Rubber grips like these from Michaels of Oregon can take the bite of heavy-recoiling guns like this Model 66 357 Magnum. Even though the backstrap is covered, trigger engagement is not adversely affected.

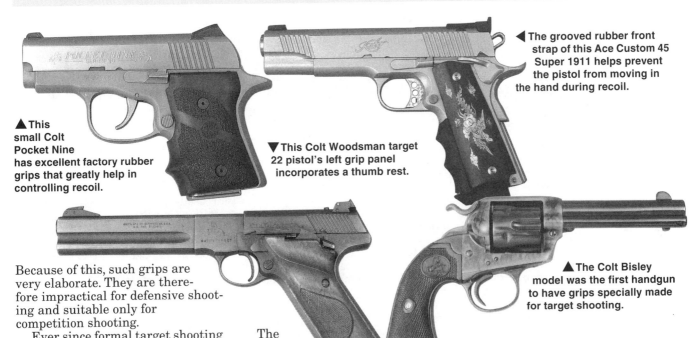

▲ This small Colt Pocket Nine has excellent factory rubber grips that greatly help in controlling recoil.

▼ This Colt Woodsman target 22 pistol's left grip panel incorporates a thumb rest.

◀ The grooved rubber front strap of this Ace Custom 45 Super 1911 helps prevent the pistol from moving in the hand during recoil.

▲ The Colt Bisley model was the first handgun to have grips specially made for target shooting.

Because of this, such grips are very elaborate. They are therefore impractical for defensive shooting and suitable only for competition shooting.

Ever since formal target shooting with handguns began, competitors have always tried to find ways of improving their equipment. Colt was the first manufacturer to appreciate the need for special handgun grips for target shooting. This is evident in the Bisley model that has a longer, more curved grip frame than the standard single actions.

In the early days, a number of competitors tried to improve the grips on their target pistol by adding clay or plastic wood to obtain a more form fitting hold. Another objective was to ensure that the same hold was taken on the gun every time it was fired.

It is a revelation how much a slight change in one's grip can alter where one's shots will group on the target. This is the main purpose of orthopedic grips, as these elaborately carved creations are generally called. The grips achieve this because they are carved to fit the shooter's hand as closely as possible. The carving of these grips is an art that is confined to a few grip makers in the world.

The first target handguns to have form-fitting grips were the early free pistols. These were often made by gunsmiths, much like the customized 1911s. These first such grips were hand-carved with supports for the thumb and the heel of the hand. Today's free pistol grips are almost glove-like, encasing the whole hand.

Modifications were made to other target arms, especially revolvers where shooters found the gap between the back of the trigger guard and the frontstrap uncomfortable. An early solution was the grip adaptor that filled the space with a detachable insert. A more permanent solution was the large stocks designed by Walter Roper, a well-known grip maker of the 1930s. He carved a grip that filled in the gap, while leaving the backstrap exposed. Later companies like Colt and Smith & Wesson began offering similar factory-made grips for their top-of-the-line target revolvers.

Grip design continued to progress after World War II. A common practice was to carve a platform for the thumb on the left side of the grip.

This was done to the factory grips of the Colt Woodsman 22 auto as well as to some of the High Standard target auto pistols. Some custom grip makers began offering revolver grips similar to those made by the factory, but incorporating a thumb rest.

There are, however, limits as to how elaborate grips can be made. In an attempt to create a level playing field for competitors, most of the target disciplines have rules that place restriction on which grips may be fitted to a handgun. The International Olympic Free Pistol rules are the most liberal of all as can be seen by the glove-fitting stocks fitted to the single-shot pistols used in this event. Even so, there still are some limitations such as that the grip must not provide any support to the shooter's wrist. The same rule also applies to most of the other International target events. In addition there are limitations on size, especially the width of the grip. To control this, handguns with grips installed have to be able to fit into a box of specified dimensions.

The target grip makers of today have still managed to do a lot within these limitations. International competition handguns invari-

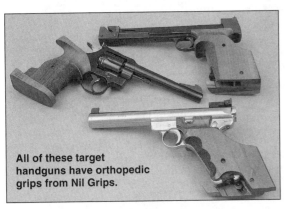

All of these target handguns have orthopedic grips from Nil Grips.

▶ Target grips are intended to give the hand maximum support. This set of orthopedic grips from Herrett's, are fitted to the author's Colt Python.

Ivory has always been sought after as an exotic material for cosmetic handgun grips.

Staghorn is another material used for decorative grips as have been fitted to this Colt New Frontier (*left*) and Ruger New Model Blackhawk (*right*).

ably have grips that incorporate a thumb rest as well as an adjustable heel platform. The grip is also custom made to fit all the contours of the shooter's hand to give maximum support while in the aim.

Virtually all the European target pistols come with factory-made orthopedic grips. Obviously these cannot fit everyone's hand perfectly. This is resolved by making the grips oversize so that the competitor can remove excess wood with a knife or file to get them to fit as required. In addition the area can be built up using epoxy putty or plastic wood. In fact it is rare to see a target arm that has not had some additional work done to it.

Custom-Made Target Grips

Without a doubt the best orthopedic grips are those made by an experienced grip maker.

I was fortunate in that we had a free pistol shooter called Frank Zangel who could carve a very good set of grips. He did a rough set for my custom-made Shooting Master that I finished off myself.

When I immigrated to the United States I purchased a very nice used Colt Officer's Model Match revolver that was, and still is, my premier target revolver. It had the standard factory stocks that I replaced with a nice set of Herrett orthopedic custom stocks made for my hand. Although Steve Herrett has passed on, his company is still active and continues to make custom target grips.

When I was active in target competition, the top grip maker who specialized in orthopedic grips was Hoffman of Germany. At a recent SHOT Show I came across a new grip maker called K.N. Nill from Germany. At first I thought I was looking at a selection of the famous Hoffman grips. The booth staff assured me that while Hoffman did not make the grips, they were as

good and even better. I immediately placed an order for a set for my Hammerli Raid Fire 22. After fitting them to the pistol I was pleased to find that they were a perfect fit for my hand. In the months that followed I ordered grips for my custom Ruger 22, Officer's Model Match and S&W Model 19 revolvers.

The first step in ordering a set of orthopedic grips is to make contact with the maker to determine if they can supply what you want for your particular handgun. Generally speaking you will not have to send your gun to them if it is a fairly popular model. To carve the grips to custom fit your hand you need to take a tracing of the outline of your strong hand. To do this simply place your hand with fingers slightly spread on a sheet of plain white paper and trace the outline with a soft pencil. Then mail the tracing to the maker with your order. All you have to do is wait. When the grips arrive, all that has to be done is to fit them to your gun.

Appearance

While this is probably the least importance attribute of custom grips, the fact is that many do enhance a handgun's appearance. A nice set of fine figured wood stocks that have been expertly checkered

Comestic grip can also be functional as well as appealing as displayed by these fitted to the author's engraved Colt King Cobra (*top*) and S&W Model 6509(*bottom*).

is a vast improvement over many of the austere plastic and synthetic factory grips.

One sport where appearance is an important consideration is the sport of Cowboy Action Shooting. Here competitors like to dress up in authentic Western garb and a fancy Colt Single Action revolver in one's holster would not be out of place. Single actions lend themselves to fancy grips made of exotic materials such as ivory, mother-of-pearl and stag horn.

In my opinion, shooting with a dressed-up quality revolver, especially a Colt Single Action, is a lot more gratifying than using some beat-up old replica with dinged wood or cracked hard rubber grips.●

SOURCES

Ahrends, Inc.
P.O. Box 203
Clarion, IA 50525
(515) 532-3449

Ajax custom Grips
9130 Viscount Row
Dallas, TX 75247
(214) 630-8893

Altamont Custom Grips
901 N Church St.
P.O.Box 309
Thomasville, IL 61878
(800) 626-5774

Butler Creek (Uncle Mike's)
290 Arden Dr.
Belgrade, MT 59714
(800) 423-8327

Eagle Grips
Eagle Business Center
460 Randy Rd.
Carol Stream, IL 60188
(800) 323-6144

Herrett's Stocks, Inc.
P.O.Box 741
Twin Falls, ID 83303
(208) 733-1498

Hogue Grips
P.O. Box 1138
Paso Robles, CA 93447
(800) 438-4747

Lett Custom Grips
672 Currier Rd.
Hopkinton, NH 03229-2652
(800) 421-5388

Nill Grips
P.O.Box 1916
Bandera, TX 78003
(830) 634-3131

Roy's Custom Grips
Rt 3, Box 174E
Lynchburg, VA 24504
(804) 993-3470

United State Fire-Arms Grips
55 Van Dyke Ave.
Hartford, CT 06106
(877) 227-6901

The Titanium and Scandium Revolution

Smith & Wesson started the compact lightweight exotic metal revolver trend with alloy frame and titanium cylinder Model 337 Airlite Ti 11-ounce 38 Chief Special (*left*) and scandium Model 360 12-ounce 357.

by Massad Ayoob

CIRCA 1950, MODERN handguns took a great leap forward. Vying for a fat contract for the USAF, Colt and Smith & Wesson alike experimented with aluminum revolvers that would arm military pilots with minimum-weight 38 Special revolvers. It became known as the Aircrewman Project. While neither gun became standard, these ultra-light revolvers proved two things. First, aluminum cylinders would not continually sustain high pressures. Second, aluminum frames *could* stand the gaff.

Colt was the first to take this technology to market. In the very early 1950s, they introduced the first two successful aluminum frame handguns. The Colt Commander evolved out of the U.S. military's study of lightweight 9mm autos to replace the venerable 1911A1 45. Initially produced in 9mm Luger, 38 Super, and 45 ACP, the Commander's slide and frame were three-quarters of an inch shorter than those of the commercial 1911A1, the Government Model. This plus the use of an aluminum alloy frame brought the weight of the 45-caliber model down from 39.5 ounces unloaded to 26.5 ounces.

The first commercial aluminum frame revolver was Colt's Cobra, introduced in the same period. It was simply the Detective Special rendered in a lightweight form. With 2-inch barrel in caliber 38 Special, the weight of this little six-

shooter came down from 21 ounces to about 15. Not many people were actually *carrying* 45 autos then – the snubnose 38 was the "in" gun for concealed carry, standard issue for plainclothes cops and almost as ubiquitous among armed citizens – and the Colt Cobra proved to be a great leap forward. It was an instant sales hit.

Smith & Wesson immediately gave chase. They called their aluminum frame revolvers Airweights, beginning with the Chief Special in 1952. These were followed within three years by an Airweight Military & Police, and the new shroud-hammered Bodyguard and "hammerless" Centennial, both J-frame five-shot 38 Specials. In fact, the latter two were *introduced* as Airweights, with all-steel versions created almost as afterthoughts. S&W also used the alumi-

num frame as the foundation for their classic Model 39 9mm auto, though for reasons I've never determined, the company never applied the Airweight sobriquet to its autos that were so constructed.

This great leap forward stopped in place. It would be nearly five decades before another metallurgical step of so great a distance was taken in the handgun world. As far back as the 1970s, gun companies studied titanium as handgun material. After all, what had made so-called "aircraft aluminum" strong enough for firearms frames was lacing it with a tiny bit of titanium, creating an alloy originally trademarked as "Duralumin," such as Alcoa #6 or equivalent. If a little titanium had been good, shouldn't more be better?

Smith & Wesson's Model 317 Airlite Ti was the first titanium revolver to actually hit the market. Chambered for the 22 LR, the revolver cylinder has an eight-round capacity, giving it a weight of only about 10 ounces.

▶The Taurus Model 941UL, a featherweight 8-shot 22 Magnum, is one of author's favorites. With negligible recoil, it put five CCI Maxi-Mag rounds into 2.05 inches at 25 yards despite its handy 2-inch barrel.

▶For best balance of portability with controllability in frequent rapid-fire training, author likes his centerfire snubbies in aluminum frame configuration, such as the Taurus Ultra-Lite.

It was not to be, at least not then. The engineers of the period said that titanium was a nightmare to work with. "It eats cutting tools for breakfast," said one. "Steel and aluminum *cut*, but titanium *tears*," said another. Sturm, Ruger Inc. aggressively pursued titanium gunmaking research in the mid-1980s, and whenever I saw Bill Ruger, Sr., I would ask him how he was coming with it. By the mid-1990s, he had pretty much given up on the concept. "Titanium is stronger than aluminum, but not as light, and it's hellishly expensive to buy and difficult to machine," he told me. In the end, Bill explained, he was just not convinced that the market wanted to pay a huge additional price for the degree of weight saving that titanium firearms construction would achieve.

Smith & Wesson, however, saw things differently. At the SHOT Show of February 1997, S&W stunned the handgun world with their introduction of the Model 317 Airlite Ti, an eight-shot snubnose revolver in 22 Long Rifle with aluminum alloy frame and barrel shroud, and titanium cylinder and barrel. The gun weighed only 10.9 ounces unloaded and 11.4 ounces loaded. It was the hit of the SHOT Show. Smith's creative advertising types demonstrated it hanging in midair, suspended from a helium balloon.

We in the field suspected that S&W's confidence in this titanium concept was a bit querulous. After all, they made the gun only in the piddling 22 Long Rifle chambering. Initial runs of the Model 317 were produced with a very strong mainspring and concomitantly extra-heavy trigger pull. The ostensible reason was to guarantee ignition with the broad range of rimfire cartridge head widths, but we thought that was BS; they had never needed extra-heavy springs in their all-steel or even Airweight 22 Kit Guns. Some of us speculated that they thought the titanium cylinder might be too soft and were allowing for down-the-road increase in headspace.

It turned out that we were wrong. S&W was merely exercising an abundance of caution. When the 317 came out, famous armorer Rick Devoid proved that he could install a standard J-frame mainspring and give you a helluva nice trigger pull with no loss of reliability. S&W soon followed with their Ladysmith version, with lighter spring and a much more manageable 8-pound double-action trigger pull, and soon all 317s were coming with decent triggers.

Then, in late 1998, S&W introduced Airlite Ti 38 Specials. They were rated for 38 Special +P and even +P+. There was, however, a caveat. In +P or hotter loads, you were limited to jacketed or semi-jacketed bullets. The reason was that +P recoil was so violent in these eleven-ounce guns, momentum would pull the bullets forward out of the cartridge cases. After two or three shots, an all-lead 158-grain slug would be protruding from the front of the cylinder, striking the forcing cone of the barrel as the cylinder turned. This stalled

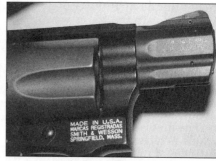

Small short-barrel revolvers are often unpleasant to shoot. The S&W Model 60 all-steel 357 (*top*) at 24 ounces, hurts to shoot with Magnums. The S&W Model 360 Sc Scandium 357 (*bottom*) at half the weight hurts at least twice as much to shoot with full-power 357 loads.

cylinder rotation and jammed the gun up solid. Jacketed bullets were more tightly crimped into the case mouth and didn't allow this. Realizing that recoil was going to be vicious with 38 Special hot loads, S&W offered these guns in the milder 32 H&R Magnum chambering, which also allowed a six-shot cylinder.

Soon S&W had upped the ante to 44 Special, introducing in 1999 the Model 296 Ti. Its five-shot titanium cylinder rotated within an L-size aluminum-alloy frame, and with its 2.5 inch barrel this gun weighed only 18.9 ounces, about the same as the old six-shot Model 12 K-frame 38 Special two-inch Airweight. The barrel was conspicuously marked "Max Bullet 200 Gr." It seemed, for a time, that titanium had finally reached its maximum cartridge potential.

Enter Taurus

Under the aggressive management of CEO Bob Morrison, Taurus International had become a handgun company that had thought into the future and outside of the box. Bob saw the titanium revolution coming and jumped into it with both feet. Soon, his company had trumped Smith & Wesson's ace with the Taurus Total Titanium series. Light and strong, these guns undersold the S&W by a significant margin at

The barrel of S&W Model 342 PD Airlite Ti. has a warning to use only jacketed ammunition. The recoil is so vicious in this super-light gun that it can pull lead bullets loose from cartridges in the chambers.

◀ This S&W 342 PD Titanium 38 is carried daily by a career cop for backup, loaded with 125-grain +P 38 Special hollowpoints.

◀ Author finds shroud-barrel S&W J-frames tend to shoot low. That's one reason he has these Crimson Trace LaserGrips on his titanium S&W Model 342 Airlite.

retail. There were other differences. These models were augmented in the Taurus line with the Ultra-Lite series, which used aircraft aluminum for the frame.

Taurus well understood the savage recoil that came with very light, very powerful guns, and took an approach different from Smith's. First, Taurus put compensated barrels on their Total Titanium guns in the serious calibers. While this would preclude firing from the hip or in the "protected gun position" because burning gases were vented upward and in these postures would endanger the shooter's face, it also made the guns far more controllable in conventional combat shooting stances. Perhaps more important for some users' needs, reduced jolting of the revolver upon recoil eliminated the need to load with specific cartridge variations. The shooter could use the most powerful lead bullet loads if he or she chose, without pulling them loose and locking up the gun. Second, Taurus made sure to put the softest "rubber" grips on these guns. Their Ribber grips, originally developed for their most powerful hunting handguns, proved to be exquisitely effective recoil absorbers on the most powerful of their Total Titanium carry revolvers.

The Taurus Total Titanium 357 Magnum was an instant hit. Such revolvers in calibers 44 Special and 45 Colt followed it. Then Taurus raised the bar by listing in its catalog a Total Titanium in a chambering previously unimagined in so light a revolver: the 41 Magnum.

Many felt that technologically Taurus had leapt ahead of Smith & Wesson. Naturally S&W had to up the ante.

The Step to Scandium

The metallurgists in the firearms industry had long been aware of scandium (Sc), but it had not been

available to them for practical purposes. Most of the world's supply of this rare element is found in what used to be called the Soviet Bloc, and the cold war had in effect blocked its availability to the free world. The material gave its owner a huge strategic advantage. Only recently has the American public been allowed to know what nervous Pentagon planners knew and kept top secret: Russian missiles with scandium nose-cones had allowed Soviet submarines to hide under Arctic ice packs. From these protected positions they could send the scandium-tipped ICBMs punching through the ice and on their way to NATO targets. In the time of the cold war, they were not about to make this material available to the Americans.

But now in the late 1990s, it was indeed available, albeit ridiculously expensive, and Smith & Wesson had set to work experimenting with it. They'd be damned if they'd be seen by the American shooter as copycatting Taurus, and they had learned that their buying public would pay a premium for something that gave them what they really wanted, so the market was there after all. Stronger than titanium, the Scandium option allowed Smith & Wesson to be comfortable with the hottest magnum cartridges.

Smith answered the Total Titanium 357 with the Model 386 Sc Mountain Lite, a seven-shot L-frame like the Taurus and weighing 18.5 ounces with 3 1/8-inch barrel, in 2001. They immediately followed with the PD (Personal Defense) version with 2.5-inch barrel weighing an ounce less.

But, simultaneously, they introduced the J-frame Sc guns in 357 Magnum. The "jacketed bullets only" rule was *definitely* in force here! With 1 7/8-inch barrels, these wee wheelguns weighed only 12 ounces unloaded, and the recoil was nothing less than savage. However, American shooters grabbed them up as fast as S&W could make them, the boycott of the "British owners sold us out" period and the very high price notwithstanding.

Early in 2003, the lighter weight/higher power race reached its zenith with S&W's introduction of the Model 329 Airlite PD. This six-shot, four-inch N-frame revolver weighed

only 26.85 ounces unloaded. Its construction comprised a metallurgical stew of no fewer than five different ingredients. The steel barrel was a stainless alloy, inside a barrel shroud crafted of the same 6061 "aircraft aluminum" alloy currently used in the long-proven Airweight models. The cylinder was titanium, the frame was scandium, and the internal lockwork was traditional carbon steel or "ordnance steel," 4140 or similar alloy.

The chambering was 44 Magnum.

Unbearable Lightness of Being

That movie title, "Unbearable Lightness of Being," takes on a new meaning when you shoot these guns. In 22 Long Rifle, the recoil of a Model 317 S&W or a Taurus Ultra-Lite is barely distinguishable from that of the all-steel equivalent. It's when you jack up the power level that you start paying the price.

When I wrote the current (fifth) edition of "THE COMPLETE BOOK OF

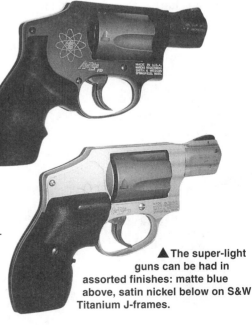

▲ The super-light guns can be had in assorted finishes: matte blue above, satin nickel below on S&W Titanium J-frames.

Futuristic trademark laser-engraved on Airlite Ti S&Ws supposedly depicts a molecule of titanium.

COMBAT HANDGUNNERY" for Krause Publications, I compared four S&W J-frames of identical size with different construction. Side by side on the firing line, I explained recoil and controllability of these 1 7/8-inch barrel fixed-sight revolvers ran in a distinct and predictable progression. The results condensed as follows:

"(Model 640 all-steel) It is very accurate, and head-shots at 25 yards are guaranteed if I do my part. Recoil with the +P is stiff, not fun, but not hard to handle either. Shooting a 50-round qualification course with it is no problem. It weights 19.5 ounces unloaded…(Model 442 Airweight) …the 50-round 'qual' course may not be fun with the now distinctly sharper recoil, but it is not my idea of torture, either. A perfect score on the qualification isn't that much harder to achieve…Weight is 15.8 ounces unloaded… (Model 342 Airlite Titanium) …The one qualification I shot with this was with jacketed CCI 158 grain +P. Recoil was so vicious I was glad I had a shooting glove in the car. When it was over, I was down two points. Rather than try again for a

perfect score, I took what I had. It was hurting to shoot the thing. This gun is not as accurate as the all-steel or Airweight, putting most 38 Special loads in 3-inch to 7-inch groups at 25 yards. Weight, unloaded, is 11.3 ounces. (Model 340 Sc Scandium) Chambered for 357 Magnum, this gun manages not to tear up the FBI load in the gun's chambers, but doesn't shoot it worth a damn for accuracy. Admittedly, this isn't the most accurate 38 Special cartridge made, but the load gives me about five inches at 25 yards with my Airweight, versus 15 inches of what I can only call spray out of this gun, with bullets showing signs of beginning to keyhole. Gun also shot way low. Recoil with Magnum loads was nothing less than savage…After five rounds, the hands were giving off that tingling sensation that says to the brain, 'WARNING! POTENTIAL NERVE DAMAGE.' When passed among people who shoot 44 Magnum and 480 Ruger revolvers for fun, the response was invariably, 'Those five shots were enough, thanks.' I didn't even try to shoot a 50-shot qualification with it. Unloaded weight is 12.0 ounces."

I haven't found the sleeve-barrel super-light S&Ws of Ti and Sc persuasion to be as accurate as the solid-barrel versions they descended from. I'm not sure that as produced at this time, they are as inherently accurate as the way Dan Wesson renders it. The Dan Wessons, all of which are all-steel, hold the barrel taut inside the shroud and deliver superb accuracy. In a hideout gun, of course, the accuracy of the S&Ws is probably adequate for the intended close-range purposes. Interestingly, I have found the Taurus Total Titaniums to have the same good accuracy as their all-steel counterpart models.

One S&W insider privately called the baby Magnum in scandium "a torture device" in terms of its recoil with full power 357 loads, and I found his assessment to be absolutely true. The bigger 386 Sc on the L-frame is unpleasant to shoot with magnums, but not nearly so objectionable as the same ammo in the J-frame.

Let's consider that 27-ounce 44 Magnum. As furnished, with Cocobolo grips that exposed the backstrap, the kick was merciless and created pain exceeded only by the

◀ **There are many style options in Ti/Sc revolvers. Top, S&W 337 has traditional DA/SA option for hiker who might want to take a precision shot at a small animal. Below, DA only Model 342 is better suited to pure self-defense needs.**

12-ounce J-frame with full 357 loads. Pachmayr grips that cushioned the backstrap made it more tolerable, and Pachmayr's softer Decelerator grips will be better yet. It's not a gun to shoot for fun. Most of the veteran shooters in the focus group at S&W stopped at six rounds, and some sooner than that. I shot it more, but wasn't up for a 50- or 60-shot qualification course with it, either. Yet, I could see it for the hiker or fisherman in big bear country (or lion country overseas) who needs this power level readily at hand but must absolutely minimize weight. Since it's not a hideout gun like the J-frames, putting on bigger stocks that more effectively cushion recoil is a much more practical option with the Model 329.

Finding the Balance

If you are looking at a super-light, super-powerful revolver, the advice of two great gun sages must be at least considered. Jeff Cooper said, classically, that such handguns were designed to be carried often and fired seldom. Bill Jordan, who inspired the 357 on a 38 frame that became the best-selling Combat Magnum, made it clear from the beginning that it was intended to be shot mostly with 38 Special, but carried with full power magnum rounds.

These two concepts would seem to make sense with the guns in question. A Taurus or Smith five-shot snub in the lightest weight isn't bad to shoot with feeble 38 wadcutters, and the mighty Model 329 will become "stimulating" with light 44 Special ammo and even fun to shoot with the yet milder 44 Russian "cowboy loads." But their *raison d'être* is, let's face it, personal defense. We learned long ago that practicing with mouse loads and carrying bear loads was not a recipe for competence in the way we would be firing when the chips were down.

For this writer, still a serving cop who has to qualify regularly with the backup gun and ammo he'll carry to work, the aluminum-framed Airweight S&W or Taurus Ultra-Lite seem to be the best balance between handy portability and constant full-power range work in rapid fire. However, for many people the only choice is a very light gun or none at all. As I said in that fifth edition of "COMPLETE BOOK OF COMBAT HANDGUNNERY," "For some, the super-light guns make carrying a gun *possible*. For that reason alone, I am grateful that these good guns exist." ●

IDPA matches are intended to duplicate a real life situation such as this car stage. More importantly, only practical guns and equipment may be used, like this Beretta 9x19mm LTT Custom.

Handguns of the International Defensive Pistol

The *Real* Practical Shooting Sport!

Article and photos by Walt Rauch

"**A**NY GUN WILL do...if you will" is the correct answer – almost – to the question of what handgun to get and use by someone who is interested in participating in International Defensive Pistol Association events. The same answer applies to someone looking for a handgun for personal self defense. And, in both instances, some handguns are better suited than others for the task at hand. This disparity leads to the next question of, "What is the 'right' or winning gun for the game?" Any shooting game favors one caliber or action type over another and, regardless of the questioner's avowed intent to simply better prepare himself for self defense, he will also want to do well in competition.

Now a curious thing takes place. The necessary artificiality of any defensive handgun sport will lead an entrant to choose and use a larger, heavier handgun than what he might pick for everyday carry. The truism of "no gun is too light or too small for carry and no gun is too big or too heavy in a gunfight" holds true here, as well. In IDPA shoots,

Police Chief Rob Haught wins his fair share of matches with a Beretta 92G Elite. Reloading behind cover, if available, is the rule in IDPA.

▶ This Heinie lightly-customized 1911 in 45 ACP with night sights and Heinie DOJ holster is a typical example of 1911s used in the Custom Pistol Division of IDPA.

Wilson Combat strong-side holster with Beretta 92 – good choices for both IDPA and self.

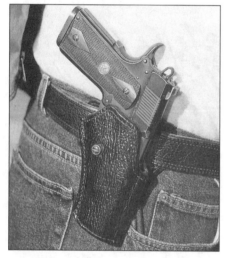

Bill Wilson, IDPA founder and president, is well represented with Wilson Combat-built 1911s and his own holster line.

as in real-world use, a full-sized fighting handgun is better for the task. In competition, though, corners are cut and advantages are sought that are not those that would be chosen in life-threatening problems, for as much as we all want to be best prepared to defend ourselves, we also like to do well when pitted against other like-minded folks in a sport. This having been said, the guns of IDPA do replicate or run close to those choices that are good for real-world survival.

To showcase the most frequently used guns of IDPA, the background and intent of the founders of IDPA is helpful. Philosophically, when the six of us – Bill Wilson, Ken Hackathorn, Larry Vickers, Dick Thomas, John Sayle and myself – got together (Larry by phone, as he was on assignment with the U.S. Army) in Marietta, Ohio in October 1996 to

create IDPA, we intended the sport to be, as our motto states, "The *Real Practical Shooting Sport.*" We wanted only practical, real-world handguns used in scenarios and exercises that simulated or replicated personal, life-threatening self-defense problems. We crafted the rules to eliminate, as much as possible, any perception that one type and caliber of handgun would be the "must-have-to-win" gun. We wanted to create a level playing field.

The IDPA rule book provides an overview of what is needed for the sport, with the underlying theme that, quoting from the book, "All equipment used in Defensive Pistol matches must meet the following simple guidelines: equipment must be practical for self-defense use, concealable, suitable for all-day continuous wear and must be worn in a manner that would be appropriate for all-day continuous wear. ...if you wouldn't carry it to defend yourself, you can't shoot or use it in Defensive Pistol competition."

We tried, to the best of our abilities, to be very clear on the subject of proper equipment. We all carry guns for self defense. Some of us have "seen the elephant" and have been founders and directors of other "practical" sports where the guns and equipment were permitted to evolve into extremely-specialized tools that often resulted in the spectacle of watching competitors carrying their scope-mounted, high-capacity, compensated, single-action 1911-type guns to the line in a gun bag, then carefully mounting them in orthopedic devices for the purpose of shooting copious quantities of custom-loaded specialty ammo at target arrays almost as large as those encountered by General George Armstrong Custer at the Battle of the Little Big Horn, where thousands of Indians annihilated his small U.S. Cavalry troop. Shooting a handgun in such a scenario is great fun, but certainly not *practical*!

IDPA courses of fire generally limit rounds fired on a stage to a maximum of 18. To keep the scenarios within the bounds of realism, the longest shot is strongly suggested to be no further than 15 yards and the number of no-shoot targets in the scenario should be in a ratio of one no-shoot to every three shoot targets.

Along with the strongly suggested guideline to limit the rounds fired on a stage,

the contestants are permitted to wear only two spare magazines or speed loaders on their belts. They can stuff more in their pockets and covering garments, but no one need look like a "Rambo" wannabe with magazines encompassing their girth. Our goal was to create and maintain a competition forum where the shooters use standard or slightly modified pistols in realistic scenarios – guns of the type that would normally be carried and used for self-defense. The idea is that the man, not the tool, rules the day. We almost *succeeded.*

With the idea of a level playing field paramount, we established four handgun divisions in which certain types of handguns and calibers are grouped togther. These include STOCK SERVICE PISTOL (SSP) Division for traditional double-action and safe-action guns such as the Beretta 92F, SIG, Ruger, Taurus, CZ and clones, Heckler & Koch and Glock 17. We also severely restricted any allowable modifications. The intent is to have SSP the "home" for out-of-the-box handguns of these action designs.

ENHANCED SERVICE PISTOL (ESP) Division is for various single-action guns and those that can be used in either double-action or single-action mode for the first shot such as the Walther and S&W P99, models based on the CZ-75 pistol and the Browning High-Power, as well as 1911 guns chambered for other than the 45 ACP cartridge, with loosened restrictions for modifications found to enhance the guns for self-defense use.

STOCK SERVICE REVOLVER (SSR) Division has the same limitations on modifications as are embodied in Stock Service Pistol, along with a 4-inch barrel-length limit. (Originally 5 inches, but later changed.)

We then put the 1911 single-column pistol chambered for the 45

▲The Smith & Wesson Model 625 45 ACP revolver with 4-inch barrel is the winning gun in IDPA's Stock Service Revolver Division. (Custom work by Jack Weigand.)

The Glock Practical/Tactical Models 34 (9x19mm) and 35 (40) predate IDPA's founding, but are ideal for the game.

extended thumb safeties, bevel mag wells and use a full-length guide rod, as long as it is not heavier than common steel. You can't muck it up with heavy barrels or compensators, change to some trick sight or appreciably alter the gun's overall original configuration. (One control put in place was the "IDPA box," which must fully contain the semi-auto handgun. We overlooked revolvers and they continue to be exempted from the "box" rule.)

Other rules that speak to our aims address ammunition, magazine capacity and holsters. We wanted to encourage the use of full-power ammo, although we set very reasonable minimum standards. The ammunition "power factor" is 125,000 for all calibers but the 45 ACP, which must have a power factor of 165,000. (Power Factor is gotten by multiplying the bullet weight by the velocity. For example, in 45 ACP a 200-grain bullet with a velocity of 825 fps equals 165,000.)

Magazine capacity restrictions were adopted for a couple of reasons. First, IDPA's courses of fire were to be and are realistic and as such the perceived need for high-capacity magazines doesn't exist. (We did not intend to encourage missing a lot, either.) Next, possession of high-capacity magazines by civilians is limited to those made prior to the enactment of the 1994 Federal Crime Law, after which any new high-capacity magazines are restricted to law enforcement and U.S. military personnel, with existing pre-ban magazines grandfathered into the law. The high-capacity magazines have therefore gotten expensive and we wanted the normal defensive handgun owner to be able to afford to shoot without taking out a second

Blade-Tech revolver holster and dual moon clip carriers are ideal for IDPA competition.

mortgage on his house.

In the Stock Service Pistol and Enhanced Service Pistol Divisions, you can load no more than ten rounds in the magazine, plus having one more chambered. While in Custom Defensive Pistol Division you can use either a seven- or eight-round magazine but you must continue to use the same-capacity magazine throughout the event. (It is possible to "game out" some scenarios by changing the number of rounds loaded to optimize the when and where of reloading.) Stock Service Revolvers may only have six rounds, regardless of cylinder capacity. Also, all guns must start in this fully-loaded condition except in a non-scenario stage (a standard marksmanship exercise).

All holsters and magazine carriers must be *practical* and as such are to be worn at or behind the strong-side hip. The rule book specifies the holsters that are permitted. If it's not listed in the book, it's not allowed. (However, because new rigs are appearing faster than dandelions in the Spring, holsters are continually being reviewed by the IDPA main office.) It's safe to figure that if it's a speed rig designed to give a perceived "edge," it's not allowed. If the holster is listed in the competition section of a catalog, save your money. (For safety, cross-draw, shoulder and other very practical concealment rigs, including fanny packs, are not allowed.)

If you already own a handgun for self-defense and want to try your hand at shooting IDPA events, you probably already own most of the necessary gear. IDPA asks for a standard or lightly customized handgun chambered for 9x19mm or above, a strong-side holster, three magazines or speed loaders and concealed carriers that affix to your

ACP in its own division – CUSTOM DEFENSIVE PISTOL (CDP), allowing those modifications thought to be beneficial for carry, *not competition*. (As a side note, any 45 ACP-chambered semi-auto can also compete in this division.)

Also, and only at the club level, there is a fifth Division – BACK-UP GUN (BUG) – where owners of the quintessential J-frame or Colt 2-inch revolver, as well as the myriad of mini semi-autos can compete in this subclass for awards. Stock Service Pistol/ revolver rules apply here, as well. (We thought that devising rules of equality for the BUG class was virtually impossible, so we limited its use to the local club level, where it is often shot as a stand-alone "fun" match or as a side event.) Finally, to try to hold any arms race at bay, IDPA doesn't award prizes or money, only trophies.

To favor the man not the tool, generally guns can be fiddled with in all Divisions, but only a little bit. You can change sights and grips, have internal action work done to improve function and accuracy and put on a custom finish. Depending on the division, you may add

Reloading a "moon clip" revolver can be as fast or more so than restuffing a semiauto pistol.

▲ Light modifications such as skate board tape for a more positive grip are allowed in IDPA's Stock Service Pistol Division.

The author using a 1986-manufactured Glock 17 in 9x19mm at an IDPA national championship match.

The CZ-75-pattern guns have a good following in IDPA.

belt. The IDPA way is that everyone can compete using a shoot-straight-out-of-the-box or lightly-customized blaster of his or her choice, drawing the gun from a concealable holster of the type that would be worn concealed under a coat. (For "first matches," my experience is that the local match director and fellow shooters will go out of their way to make you comfortable by lending gear and overlooking rules, except those that relate to safety. If you don't have enough gear, you can look to someone lending these to you or simply stuff the spare ammo in your pocket.)

Observing at your first match is always the best idea. This way you are not encumbered by the demands of the event. You can also question everyone (when they're not "next up to shoot," please). Quickly it will be obvious that any group of shooters are a competitive bunch and some guns, calibers and holsters are better suited for the game than others.

As IDPA is the newest and most-rapidly-growing handgun sport with almost 10,000 members currently and 242 affiliated clubs in the U.S., plus six foreign clubs. The "gun of choice" for each division has not yet solidified. Handgun manufacturers, taking note of the growth of IDPA as well as the matured nature of the other handgun sports, are creating new models and modifying existing ones to take advantage of this new IDPA market. (This also causes no end of consternation for IDPA administrators who are charged with maintaining the integrity and equality of the guns and gear.) Simply put, every handgun manufacturer wants their gun to be the "must-have-to-win" gun, while the administrators are hoping for no one gun to become dominant.

Looking at Stock Service Pistol Division, the 9x19mm has quickly become the most popular round, since using anything else gives no

competitive advantage but rather can hinder maximizing performance. (Nothing says you can't use full-powered ammunition giving off the largest fireball, though.) Also, 9x19mm ammo is the cheapest stuff to buy off the shelf.

The Glock 9x19mm pistol with its short-moving Safe-Action trigger is the choice of many competitors over other traditional double-action semi-autos. The perception is that the Glock action is easier to use when shooting multiple rounds on multiple targets. While this may be technically correct, winners use traditional double-action-first-shot/single-action-thereafter (DA/SA) handguns such as the Beretta 92 and SIG Arms Models 26 and 229 to win regional and national events. A good man with a DA/SA gun can win and often does.

Coming on strong is the Para-Ordnance LDA (Light Double Action) pistol built on a 1911 chassis that, like the Glock action, falls between the DA/SA action and the single action of the 1911. Another gun of this ilk is the Heckler & Koch USP with Law

Enforcement Modification (L.E.M.) action and the recently-introduced H&K Model HS 2000. These are what I term "cam action" guns, as those where the gun is cycled, the main-spring is fully compressed and retained in this state by an internal cam/sear. Moving the trigger against a light trigger return spring releases the cam and the stored energy of the mainspring driving the hammer or

Pocket revolvers are normally shot in the Back-Up Gun Division, but are often encountered as a "second" gun that is part of a course of fire at regional and national IDPA events. (Chris Edwards shooting.)

IDPA co-founder Ken Hackathorn uses his Wilson Combat 45 in a "house clearing" course of fire.

striker. This setup creates an appreciably better trigger pull.

These models were not created for IDPA competition but lend themselves well to the task, as do the SIG Arms all-steel rather than steel and aluminum pistols, with the increased weight definitely dampening recoil. Other manufacturers such as CZ and its clones, along with Taurus, have a smattering of representation but, so far, not in any significant numbers. They have great potential, though, because their selective DA/SA or SA-only actions can be used in both Stock Service Pistol (DA/SA) or Enhanced Service Pistol Division with their hammers raised and manual safety applied.

In Enhanced Service Pistol right now, the 38 Super 1911 is the most often seen gun for, I think, two reasons. First, those who shot in the other action sports already owned a single-column 1911 in this caliber, usually with a compensator, along with all the allied equipment and brass. By simply removing the compensator system, the owner retains a familiar handgun and now gains a legal IDPA gun setup for ESP.

The 9x19mm round in a 1911 is the new up and comer, fueled by the previously mentioned inexpensive factory 9x19mm ammunition. Springfield Armory is now making a 9x19mm 1911, as are some gunsmithing companies which have learned to make the gun and design work together. The combination suffered from a short-overall-length cartridge in a too long magazine. Springfield Armory redesigned the magazine and quickly learned the right combination of mainspring and recoil spring to insure 100% feeding with, at the least, factory-jacketed round-nose-shaped ammunition. The 40 S&W-chambered

1911 also has a dedicated following in this class, for with judicious hand loading, the combination is very soft shooting, brass for reloading is certainly plentiful and factory ammo is also reasonably priced.

The Browning High-Power has also had a resurgence of interest in 9x19mm, as well as the selective-action guns previously mentioned. ESP will, I believe, attract more shooters who find that, while they like the 1911, they are not comfortable firing the 45 ACP cartridge.

Stock Service Revolver permits any 4-inch or shorter barreled revolver chambered for 38 Special and loaded with no more than six rounds. I've seen Ruger Redhawks, Colt Pythons, the old reliable S&W Model 10, as well as S&W Model 66s with 2.5-inch barrels being shaken out over an IDPA course. The winning gun is the S&W Model 25 or Model 625 chambered for 45 ACP and shot using full-moon clips that hold all six rounds. The unit is simply inserted into the cylinder without the need to release the cartridges, as is the case when using a speedloader. This easy and relatively accident-free reload (no spilling of cartridges out of the speed loader while recharging the gun), coupled with the kicker that in this division, all revolver ammo, including the 45s, only have to meet the 125,000 power floor. This translates into being able to use really "wimp" loads if you choose to in large-frame guns. (One further note on revolver ammo power floors: The ammo must meet the minimum power factor fired from a 4-inch revolver, but you can shoot these loads from a shorter barreled gun without penalty.)

S&W's Model 625 is *the* revolver now used by the top guns, but the standard speed-loaded revolver is also viable and, since reloading "on

the clock is being de-emphasized, I foresee more interest in the old, reliable six-shot 38-caliber revolver as well. (IDPA scoring is a matter of the lowest score based on time winning, so reloading could be a major factor if not addressed by creating a downtime window for the task.

Custom Defensive Pistol Division is the home for the custom 1911 in 45 ACP. This is the lair of John Browning's 1911. Here is where all the factory and custom 1911s are shot, although any semi-auto chambered for the 45 ACP caliber can be used in this division. (For example, the Glock Models 21 and 30 in 45 ACP can be shot in Custom Defensive Pistol as well as Stock Service Pistol.) Winners use guns from what appears to be every 1911 manufacturer, either as complete guns or gunsmith-built. Although not broken out by caliber, the 2002 IDPA National Championship shooter survey shows the following 1911s used: Springfield (29), Wilson Combat (28), Kimber (23), Colt (17) and Caspian (11).

As I mentioned earlier, the guns are allowed to have frame checkering, high-visibility sights (often night sights), change of grips, trigger, grip safeties, thumb safeties and accuracy work – in short, light customizing.

In review, IDPA is the defensive-oriented Action Shooting sport where you can use your favorite self-defense handgun, be it any one of the popular Double-Action/Single-Actions pistols such as the Beretta, Taurus, Tanfoglio, Smith & Wesson semi-auto, SIG Arms or Glock. You can dust off your old S&W, Colt or Ruger revolver or, if you've gotten the 1911 bug and have a custom defensive 1911, use it. There's a place for all of these guns in IDPA!

For more information, contact the International Defensive Pistol Association, PO Box 639, Berryville, AR 72616-0639; telephone 870-545-3886; fax 870-545-3894; Website WWW.IDPA.COM; or E-mail IDPA.org@yournet.com. ●

Walt Rauch has recently authored *PRACTICALLY SPEAKING: AN ILLUSTRATED GUIDE to The Game, Guns and Gear of the International Defensive Pistol Association With Real-World Applications*, a comprehensive manual for anyone who is interested in the "how" and "why" of IDPA shooting events. To purchase a signed copy of Rauch's book for $24.95 plus $4.95 S/H, phone 610-825-4245.

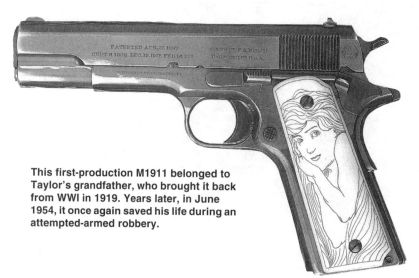

This first-production M1911 belonged to Taylor's grandfather, who brought it back from WWI in 1919. Years later, in June 1954, it once again saved his life during an attempted-armed robbery.

The Colt M1911 45

A Century Of Service

by Chuck Taylor

ALTHOUGH IT FIRST appeared shortly after the turn of the 20th century, the Colt Model 1911 45 ACP pistol continues to be the subject of intense discussion and no small amount of "improvement," some of which is legitimate, much of which is either superfluous or commercially motivated. Indeed, it's impossible to pick up a gun magazine and not see some form of M1911 pistol on the cover. Moreover, no handgun in history has been the subject of so many articles inside those magazines.

For 92 years, the Colt M1911 has dominated the handgun world. It has been used by dozens of nations and hundreds of police departments. It has seen combat in all four corners of the world, in two World Wars and countless "dirty little wars" and "police actions" in between.

It was the official service handgun of the U.S. Army from 1911 until the late 1980s and, though technically replaced by the Beretta M92 (M9), it actually continues in service, with

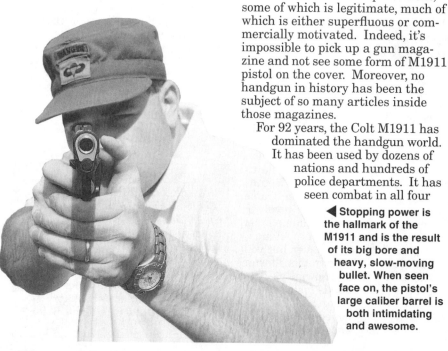

◄ Stopping power is the hallmark of the M1911 and is the result of its big bore and heavy, slow-moving bullet. When seen face on, the pistol's large caliber barrel is both intimidating and awesome.

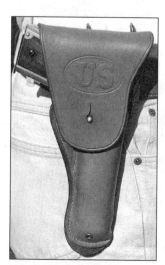

As the sidearm of the US military forces from 1911 until 1985, the 1911 was carried in this distinctive, leather flap holster.

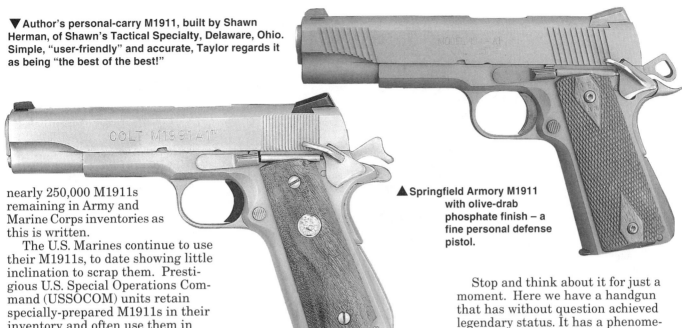

▼Author's personal-carry M1911, built by Shawn Herman, of Shawn's Tactical Specialty, Delaware, Ohio. Simple, "user-friendly" and accurate, Taylor regards it as being "the best of the best!"

▲Springfield Armory M1911 with olive-drab phosphate finish – a fine personal defense pistol.

nearly 250,000 M1911s remaining in Army and Marine Corps inventories as this is written.

The U.S. Marines continue to use their M1911s, to date showing little inclination to scrap them. Prestigious U.S. Special Operations Command (USSOCOM) units retain specially-prepared M1911s in their inventory and often use them in both counter-terrorist and military special-ops missions.

There is even a "SOCOM M1911," featuring high-visibility fixed sights, sharp edges removed, a crisp, light trigger and special weather/corrosion resistant finish. Though some erroneously believe that the special version of the Heckler & Koch USP (Mk-23) has become the standard SOCOM handgun, such is not true. SOCOM units maintain in their armories a vast array of weapons, including virtually all of the major handguns of the world. The Mk-23 is just one of these and is intended for special functions, not as a general-purpose sidearm.

For a number of years, I've trained various SOCOM units, including sensitive-mission Special Forces teams, and found that the M1911 was by far the most preferred handgun. Particularly after they had received state-of-the-art handgun training, the vast majority of SF personnel with whom I was

associated, came to fully appreciate the M1911's excellence.

Part of this occurred because they liked the superior stopping power of the 45 ACP over the 9mm. But most of it was caused by their recognizance of the M1911's superior human engineering. Its controls are located for easy, fast operation under high-speed stress. It is simple to fieldstrip and maintain and has a well-deserved reputation for mechanical reliability under adverse conditions.

Many non-professionals believe the M1911 must have extensive gunsmithing to reach its full potential, and some have even written articles on the subject, but such is untrue. It fact, it is this fixation on extensive gunsmithing that has caused the problem in the first place.

Stop and think about it for just a moment. Here we have a handgun that has without question achieved legendary status. It has a phenomenal reputation worldwide and is either *the* preferred handgun or at least one of the two or three most preferred handguns of every well-known handgun expert. How could all this have happened if it required extensive gunsmithing to be effective? The answer? It couldn't.

The real problem comes from a loss of *purpose* —a lack of clear perspective on the weapon's mission requirements. The M1911 45 doesn't need a full-length recoil spring guide, ambidextrous extended slide release levers, a match bushing, magazine well funnel, muzzle brake or (unless you're left-handed) an ambidextrous extended thumb safety to reach its full potential, especially as a combat weapon – quite the opposite. Doing all these things to it actually decreases its utility.

All it *really* needs are good low-profile high-visibility fixed sights, any sharp edges removed, a crisp

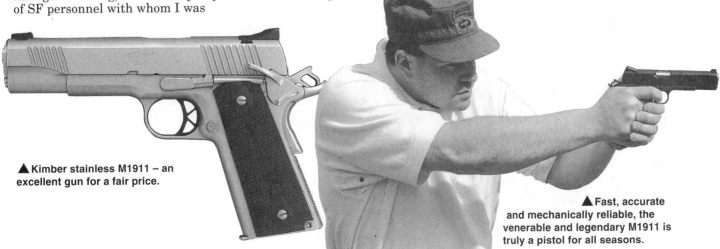

▲Kimber stainless M1911 – an excellent gun for a fair price.

▲Fast, accurate and mechanically reliable, the venerable and legendary M1911 is truly a pistol for all seasons.

▲ "Hell On The Border" Lightweight Commander fully customized by The Armory, Inc.

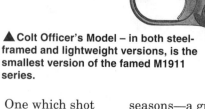
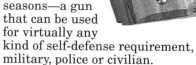

▲ Colt Officer's Model – in both steel-framed and lightweight versions, is the smallest version of the famed M1911 series.

trigger of decent poundage (say 3.5 to 5.0 pounds, depending upon the skill level of its user) and a finish appropriate to the natural environment in which its operator intends to carry it. You don't need to spend $2500 and wait two years for your M1911 to come back from the gunsmith. You don't want to add complex "bolt on" accessories to your M1911, Commander or Officer's Model, lest you run the very real risk of actually having it be less efficient than it was as it came out of the box.

Why has this happened? Because those who have fostered it, have forgotten the intended mission of the handgun. And in so doing, they forgot one of the cardinal rules of combat weaponcraft — simplicity. Putting it another way, the more complicated you make the weapon, the less mechanically reliable it will be. Removing tolerances critical to reliable functioning to "accurize" your M1911 isn't a good deal. I have yet to see a M1911 that was incapable of hitting a man in the chest at 50 meters, its officially stated maximum effective range.

In fact, I have yet to actually see a M1911 that wouldn't produce accuracy far superior to any shooter, especially under the high-stress, high-speed conditions inherent to any gunfight. Besides, which gun would you rather bet your life on:

One which shot into an inch at 50 meters, but wouldn't function reliably because it was too tight, or one that went "bang!" on demand, wet or dry, cold or hot, in the dust, mud or rain? I think the answer is obvious.

Loss of purpose? You bet it is. What has happened is that as the decades have passed, too many people have tried to make the M1911 into too many things, the solution to all problems, which it cannot be, then blame the gun for failure. If you want a target pistol to take to Camp Perry, fine; then perform those modifications to the pistol that are appropriate to that endeavor. If you want to shoot IPSC or IDPA competition, great; then have your gunsmith make appropriate modifications for that purpose. But if you intend to actually bet you life on your M1911 — or any other handgun, for that matter — then make only the four alterations mentioned previously. Other than these, the only real improvements in the M1911 have been its own mutations, the Lightweight and steel-framed Commander and Officer's Model. In these configurations, the M1911 series offers a gun for all

seasons—a gun that can be used for virtually any kind of self-defense requirement, military, police or civilian.

Another myth perpetrated about the M1911 is that in its aluminum-framed Lightweight Commander version, it lacks the ability to withstand a steady diet of service ammo. Nothing could be further from the truth. The Commander's frame is made from high tensile-strength aircraft-aluminum, not pot metal, and will last as long as any steel frame.

In fact, I have several LW Commanders that have digested over 30,000 rounds of full-powered service ammunition and are still going strong! As a matter of fact, because of their more pronounced harmonic vibration when the gun fires, I've had more cracked steel frames than aluminum ones.

So, carry and use your M1911 Government Model, Commander or Officer's Model 45 without reservation. Don't butcher them with inappropriate modifications. And when you do have them modified, have only those alterations made that will actually enhance its efficiency as a combat weapon.

The M1911 is truly a legendary handgun, and one which has by far surpassed all other handguns in its service life (over 92 years to date), reputation and capabilities. It has

Close-up view showing the M1911's well-located controls, making it one of the most "user friendly" pistols in history.

A favorite of many plainclothes narcotics officers for more than three decades, the M1911 is easily concealed because of its flatness.

Cocked and Locked – Condition One – is quite safe and the preferred mode when weapon is in "imminent use" mode.

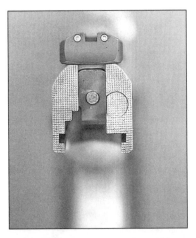

Older M1911s require better sights to bring them to full potential, while newer versions come "from the box" with them.

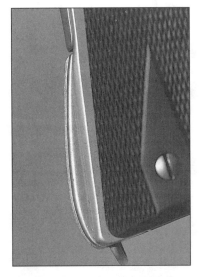

Both flat and arched mainspring housings can be found on the M1911. Flat housing was replaced with arched one in 1924 as part of the M1911A1 package.

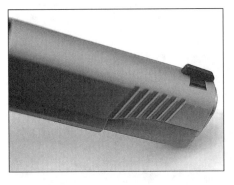

turers. As such, it is still *"The Great One,"* the standard against which all fighting handguns are measured, and anyone who says otherwise just hasn't been paying attention! Several of my Government Models and LW Commanders have saved my life a number of times. Set up correctly for best efficiency and used with a reasonable modicum of skill, the M1911 series pistol is still as good as it gets. I'll quite willingly bet my life on one anytime! ●

been produced in the millions and is, as this is written, being manufactured by no less than 15 manufac-

Short and long triggers can also be found on the M1911. Original version utilized a long trigger, which was replaced with a short one in 1924, also as part of the improved M1911A1 series.

Performance Specifications

MNFR	TYPE	WT (grs)	VEL (fps)	KE(ft lbs)
Cor-Bon	JHP	185	1133	528
Winchester-Western	JHP	185	876	315
Federal	JHP	185*	901	334
Remington-Peters	JHP	185*	914	343
Remington-Peters +P	JHP	185	1118	516
Super Vel	JHP	190*	1025	443
CCI-Speer	JHP	200*	1010	453
Cor-Bon	JHP	200	034	475
Cor-Bon	JHP	230	943	454
Federal H/Shok	JHP	230	840	360
Winchester Blk Tln	JHP	230*	924	436
Remington-Peters	FMJ	230	797	324
Winchester-Western	FMJ	230*	800	327
Federal	FMJ	230*	801	328
WCC-62 Mil BALL	FMJ	230*	799	326

TEST GUN = Commercial Colt Model 1911 Government Model with 5.0-inch barrel.

* = Ransom Rest 3-Shot group accuracy of 1.5 inches or better at 25 meters.

CHRONOGRAPH: Oehler Model 35P w/Printer
TEMPERATURE: 67 degrees F
HUMIDITY: 48%   **BAROMETER:** 29.89
ALTITUDE: 4896 FT. ASL

ACE CUSTOM 45 SUPER

Giving the 1911A Magnum Performance

by David W. Arnold

FEW HANDGUNS HAVE the reputation for hitting power and reliability as the Colt Government Model 45 Pistol of 1911. To be honest, its reputation has become somewhat exaggerated over the passage of time. Because of this, some valid questions have been raised about the true fight-stopping effectiveness of the pistol's cartridge the 45 ACP.

As has been the case with many cartridge developments, it was a handloader who came up with an improved cartridge for the 1911. Called the 45 Super, the cartridge has actually been in existence for some time. (It was developed over twenty years ago.)

▲ The 45 Super cartridge provides 1911-type pistols like this Kimber Custom Classic 45 ACP with a true Magnum performance.

Dean Grennell, a writer well known among handloaders of the post-World War II era, conceived the 45 Super. Grennel decided to explore the possibilities of improving the performance of the Colt 1911 and its cartridge by using new gunsmithing techniques and modern cartridge cases. He knew that the weakest part of the 45 ACP cartridge case was its case. When a round is chambered in a standard 1911, a significant portion of the case is unsupported over the feed ramp. This is not a problem with conventionally loaded ammunition, but it does limit attempts to increase ballistic performance.

Grennell examined the 451 Detonics magnum case that has

◀ The fact that the rear of a 45 ACP case is unsupported at the bottom rear of the chamber limits how much additional pressure it can safely handle.

thicker walls and a heavier web. This would provide the extra strength at the rear of the case where it was most needed. The case, however, is longer than that of the 45 ACP. It had to be trimmed to the correct length and the case mouth reamed to accept a 45 bullet. The finished product was a case capable of handling over 30,000 CUP of pressure compared to 19,000 CUP for a standard 45 ACP case. Grennell was able to work up loads that had a magnum performance using his new case.

Grennell used a standard Government Model that had a 22-pound Wolf recoil spring to enable it to withstand the increase in recoil. While the cartridge did provide enhanced performance, there were a number of functioning problems. One problem was that the thick walled Detonics cases had a tendency to bulge when heavier bullets were seated, causing chambering and feeding malfunctions. Another

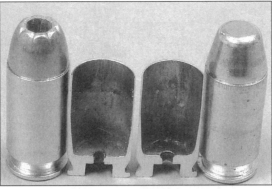

The 45 Super (*right*) is identical to the 45 ACP (*left*) in terms of external dimensions. The difference is that the Super cartridge case has been strengthened in the web area to enable it to handle the higher pressures.

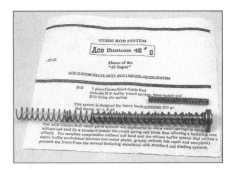

To handle the increased power of the 45 Super Ace Custom 45, the company that pioneered the cartridge makes this spring conversion kit.

problem was signs of excessive pressure when cartridges were loaded to higher velocities.

At this stage, Grennell did not have the time to resolve these problems. He turned the entire project over to the late Ace Hindman, a gunsmith experienced in the 1911 pistol. Ace was able to develop the 45 Super into a viable cartridge by working on both the pistol and the cartridge.

The case bulging problem was resolved by precision reaming the case mouth to the depth that the bullet was seated. The two other problems of failing to eject and pierced primers required some modifications to the pistol.

The failure to eject was due to the slide cycling too fast so that it trapped the case before it could be flung out of the ejection port. Ace resolved this by installing a stronger extractor and lowering the ejector port. The matter of pierced primers was due to the increased recoil caused the inertia firing pin to remain forward for too long after firing. This was resolved by installing a stronger firing pin spring and shortening the tip of the pin by .025-inch. The new firing pin still had sufficient energy to ignite the primer reliably.

To protect the gun from being battered, a heavy-duty dual-recoil spring system utilizing a full-length guide rod was installed. The latter incorporated a Delrin buffer to further cushion the effects of recoil.

These modifications made the 45 Super a reality and all that remained was to determine how far its performance in terms of power could be increased. The trouble was that the pistol gave no indication of excessive pressures with hotter loads.

Ace sought the help of Bruce Hodgdon of the Hodgdon Powder Company. Tests were run on various 45 Super loads. All showed that pressures were well within what was safe for both the pistol and the cartridge case.

The testing of 185-grain Nosler bullet velocities went as high as 1500 fps. While the pistol was not affected, the increase in recoil made it very difficult to control. Because of this loading was standardized at 1200 fps for the same bullet.

Ace then began to offer 45 Super customized pistols for shooters who wanted to take advantage of its magnum performance. An attractive feature of such pistols was that they could function perfectly well with standard velocity 45 ACP ammunition as well as with the 45 Supers.

Ace Hindman passed away in 1993 and his son Garry took over the reins of the company. Ace's shop continues to offer 45 Super custom work. Such pistols carry the banner "home of the 45 Super".

I first became acquainted with the 45 Super in 1995 when I was sent a pistol and a quantity of ammunition to evaluate for an article that I was assigned to do for *Handguns* magazine. At that time, a relatively new company called Triton was commercially manufacturing 45 Super ammunition.

Actually the commercial manufacture of 45 Super ammunition came at just the right time. Prior to that the only ammunition came from handloaders who had to use Detonic cases. Supplies of the latter were becoming increasingly difficult to obtain.

The pistol that accompanied the ammunition was a Springfield Armory 1911 A1 that the Ace custom shop had set up for shooting of 45 Super. The custom work was very well executed and compared favorably with customized pistols from other shops.

The author had this Kimber Custom Classic 45 ACP customized by Ace Custom for the 45 Super.

The author replaced his converted pistol grips with this nice set of pearl inlaid panels of unknown manufacturer. The rubber front strap was part of the Ace Custom conversion package.

The author specified Ace Custom to install a Bo-Mar adjustable rear sight and give his pistol the company's Ace Guard satin hard-chrome finish.

The pistol gave a very impressive performance on the range delivering above average accuracy with both Super and standard velocity 45 ACP. While recoil was certainly evident it was not excessive even when shooting with one hand. Reliability was also excellent with both types of ammunition.

In subsequent years I shot other 45 Super creations from the Ace Custom shop that included a Glock 20 and a Smith & Wesson 4506. Both pistols also delivered impressive performances.

As we entered the new century I decided to have one of my 1911s given the Ace 45 Super conversion treatment. The pistol that I selected was a Kimber Custom Combat 45 that I have had for some time. The pistol already had a number of custom features as it came out of the box. In addition it also delivered above average accuracy. However, I did request two features in addition to the 45 Super conversion. I asked for the Kimber fixed rear sight to be replaced with a Bo-Mar fully adjustable assembly and for the entire pistol to be given a satin-matte hard-chrome finish.

After a few weeks the completed project was returned. To say that I was pleased with the work is an understatement. The Bo-Mar sight installation was extremely well executed, as was the hard chrome plating. One feature that was included with the conversion package was a front strap attachment that incorporated finger grooves made of rubber.

At the time I had a very nice set of mother-of-pearl inlaid wood grips that I used to replace the factory rubber ones. When fitted to the pistol, the grips seemed as though they were made for it.

I was equally pleased with the pistol's performance. It was per-fectly reliable with both standard velocity 45 ACP and Super ammunition. Accuracy was good with the former and above average with the latter. As with the other 45 Supers I had shot, my Kimber was very pleasant to shoot even with the hot Super ammunition. Recoil, while definitely present, was neither excessive nor unpleasant.

I have done a fair amount of shooting with my Kimber, both with Super and regular 45 ammunition. The pistol has retained the same accuracy that it displayed after the conversion. In addition it has continued to be as reliable as ever.

On chrongraphing the ammunition, both Super cartridges consistently gave reading of 1294 fps, which is just under the manufacturers claim of 1300 fps. The temperature was just on 60 degrees Fahrenheit and the altitude was 3250 feet above sea level.

By way of comparison, some standard velocity Winchester Personal Protection 230-grain JHP fired on the same day produced average velocities of 785 fps. After firing, all the Super cases were recovered for examination. None displayed any indication of excessive pressure.

All things considered, the 45 Super is an impressive cartridge and I am surprised that it has not been more widely accepted. It delivers magnum performance safely and without beating up the pistol, in addition to excellent accuracy. Ace Custom has offered the concept to a number of handgun companies yet none have taken it up. The reason may be that companies are concerned about possible litigation suits that might arise even though the ammunition has proved to be perfectly safe in pistols that are modified in the manner that has been described.

Fortunately, ammunition is still being made by Buffalo Bore and Texas Ammunition, and Ace Custom 45 still does the conversion work. If you want to get more power out of your 1911 give serious consideration to the 45 super. I did and I'm happy with the result. •

BALLISTIC PERFORMANCE

AMMUNITION TYPE	AVERAGE VELOCITY FPS
Buffalo Bore 185-gr. 45 Super JHP	1254
Texas Ammunition 185-gr. 45 Super JHP XTP	1254
Winchester Personal Protection 230-gr. JHP	794
Cor-Bon 200-gr. JHP	794

NOTE: Velocities measured using Prochrono chronograph. Above figures are the averages of five individual shots fired with each ammunition type. Weather conditions were sunny and clear with mild crosswind. Altitude was 3250 feet above sea level. Temperature was 70 degrees F.

SOURCES

Ace Custom 45
1880 1/2 Upper Turtle Creek Road,
Kerville, TX 78028
(630) 257-4290
www.acecustom45.com

North American Arms New Potent 32 NAA Guardian

by Clair Rees

NEED A 32 pocket pistol? North American Arms now has both standard and high-test versions available. One puts 32 ACP power in a pint-sized package that tucks away out of sight almost anywhere, including the breast pocket of your shirt. The other chambers a new 32-caliber bottleneck cartridge and offers considerably more punch in a gun that's just a tad heavier and similarly easy to conceal.

When North American Arms introduced its 32 ACP Guardian pocket pistol in 1999, it caused quite a stir. While the new gun bore a striking resemblance to the prized, but perennially back-ordered Seecamp 32, the Guardian was designed for efficient mass production. Once manufacturing was in full swing, orders were quickly filled and you didn't have to pay a premium price to get your hands on one.

The Guardian offered another big advantage over the Seecamp. The Seecamp was designed to function with Winchester Silvertip 32 ACP loads only. It could be counted on to turn balky when fed any other fodder. In contrast, the Guardian was supposed to digest any and all 32 ACP factory loads. I tested one of the early Guardians, and it performed pretty much as advertised.

Later, North American Arms began offering a 380 ACP version of the Guardian. This upped the power ante in a gun just 1/2 inch longer and some five ounces heavier. The 380 Guardian quickly proved popular as a law enforcement backup weapon.

Then in 2002, the company kicked the Guardian up yet another notch. North American Arms surprised shooters everywhere by marrying the 32 ACP and 380 ACP cartridges to create the 32 NAA. The brainchild of Ed Sanow, editor of *Law &* *Order* magazine, this bottlenecked powerhouse was made by necking down a 380 ACP case to 32 caliber and loading it with a 60-grain jacketed hollowpoint bullet.

▲ The 32 NAA Guardian is North American Arm's newest pocket pistol that introduces a new bottleneck 32-caliber cartridge manufactured by Cor-bon.

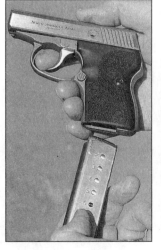

Bottlenecked 32 NAA cartridge (*left*) is produced by necking down 380 ACP brass to accept a 32-caliber bullet. The 32 ACP is at right.

The 32 NAA Guardian has a 6-shot magazine, giving a 6+1 round potential.

The new 32 NAA Guardian (*front*) is slightly larger and heavier than the original 32 ACP version (*rear*). The bottlenecked 32 NAA cartridge (*right*) packs more power.

Note shorter grip on 32 ACP Guardian, at right. This pistol is also 0.07 inch narrower than the new 32 NAA version.

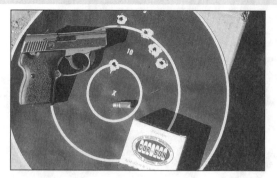

Fired offhand from seven yards, the 32 NAA Guardian consistently printed 3- to 3 1/4-inch 5-shot groups.

I've done a fair amount of shooting with the 32 NAA Guardian, and it's a real screamer as far as pocket pistols go. With 71-grain factory loads the original 32 ACP Guardian delivers some 780 feet per second (fps). Feed it lighter 60-grain ammo and you get around 900 fps. In contrast, chronographing 60-grain JHP 32 NAA CorBon loads 10 feet from the Guardian's muzzle resulted in an average velocity of 1249 fps. Some difference!

That translates into 208 footpounds (ft.-lbs.) of striking energy, which compares favorably with the 1200 fps and 200 ft.-lbs. churned up by 90-grain loads in the 380 Guardian.

The Guardian is a double-action-only auto pistol with an external hammer that—in its forward position—lies flush with the slide and frame. The only manual controls are the trigger, the slide release button at the rear right of the receiver, and the magazine release button conventionally located on the left side at the base of the trigger guard. There's no hammer spur or safety to deal with. You simply draw, point and shoot. The gun's fixed, low-profile sights are tiny, but serviceable. Takedown is accomplished by removing the magazine, then cycling the slide rearward and upward with one hand as you depress the slide release button with the other. The gun's small size and strong spring make disassembly a minor challenge, but this becomes easier with practice.

When I tested the 32 ACP Guardian, I encountered a few early hangups. Sometimes I had to manually ease the slide forward when chambering the first round from the magazine. After firing 50 rounds or so, feeding problems disappeared. I fed the little pistol a varied mixture of 60- and 71-grain 32 ACP factory loads, and it digested everything with only a couple of minor bobbles. In subsequent shooting, the gun has proven very reliable.

The abbreviated grip accommodated only my trigger finger, middle finger and thumb, so I curled the remaining digits under the butt. While the 13.5-ounce pocket pistol is pretty lively to shoot, the gun was relatively easy to manage. It also shot surprisingly well. In spite of a heavy 14-pound trigger and tiny sights, I was able to punch 2 3/4-inch 5-shot groups at seven yards with 71-grain Remington factory loads.

The newer 32 NAA Guardian is slightly larger and five ounces heavier. Its grip easily accommodates four fingers, leaving only one to curl underneath. Despite the gun's extra heft, it jumps back in your hand with noticeably more gusto than the 32 ACP version displays. Both guns come supplied with an extra magazine and a zippered nylon De Santis pouch, complete with belt clip.

Like the 32 ACP Guardian, the 32 NAA version choked a few times during initial break-in, but quickly settled down after 25 or 30 rounds. This gun has subsequently proven even more reliable than my 32 ACP model, possibly because the bottlenecked 32 NAA cartridge is less prone to feeding problems.

Again, accuracy was very good. Firing offhand, I was consistently able to punch 5-round groups measuring just over three inches across from seven yards.

Both North American Arms' pocket-sized powerhouses performed very well. Considering their diminutive size and heft, these guns were easy to shoot. At the same time, I wouldn't want to put 50 rapid-fire rounds through either of them during the same firing session. The 32 ACP and 32 NAA Guardians aren't intended for target work or casual plinking, but if you're looking for a light, easily concealed backup gun, either are ideally suited for the job. ●

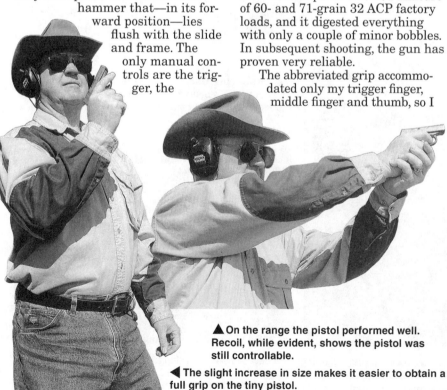

▲ On the range the pistol performed well. Recoil, while evident, shows the pistol was still controllable.

◀ The slight increase in size makes it easier to obtain a full grip on the tiny pistol.

Specifications

Model: NORTH AMERICAN 32NAA GUARDIAN
Maker: North American Arms, Inc., Dept. GAH, 2150 South 950 East, Provo, UT 84606-6285
Type: Double-action only auto pistol
Caliber: 32 NAA
Capacity: 6+1 rounds
Overall length: 4.75 in.
Height: 3.5 in.
Width: 0.92 inch
Barrel length: 2.5 in.
Overall length: 4.75 in.
Weight: 18.5 oz.
Sights: Fixed
Trigger: 13-pound pull
Grips: Stippled black synthetic
Finish: Matte stainless steel
Price: $449

GUN TESTS
SPRINGFIELD ARMORY'S XD PISTOL

by Chuck Taylor

BACK IN 2002, when Springfield Armory first unveiled their new "XD" pistol, I was skeptical. I was skeptical because XD stands for "Extreme Duty", and indeed, nearly every handgun manufacturer extols their weapons as being the best and thus suitable for the toughest of conditions.

To me, both "best" and "extreme duty" have unique connotations, because as a professional weapons and tactics consultant, writer and trainer, I must view them from the most serious perspective – life and death. Thus, when the terms are used, I tend to "take them with a grain of salt" until I'm satisfied that they actually possess the capabilities they're supposed to have.

Articles on the XD pistol have appeared a number of times in the various gun magazines, so I'll spare the reader a detailed history, except to say that: 1) It's the end-result of a decade-long refinement process conducted by several weapon-designers, and; 2) It's manufactured in Croatia.

These two points are significant because Croatia, a Baltic nation wracked for over a decade by civil war would hardly be thought to be a location wherein manufacturing facilities are sophisticated enough to produce such a highly innovative pistol. However, it obviously is!

Second, the XD's design shows that those who created it were not only cognizant of what makes a great handgun, but exceptionally cognizant! The XD simply oozes design superiority, not only from a mechanical standpoint, but also from the most overlooked and misunderstood, yet critical, standpoint of them all – human engineering — as well.

Available in three different configurations – service pistol, tactical

▲ Tough, accurate and exceptionally user-friendly, the XD pistol is irrefutably one of the best pistol designs ever produced and may well join the Colt M1911, Browning P-35 and Glock as a legendary handgun.

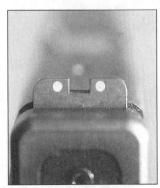

Fixed high-visibility front and rear sights with white horizontal 3-dot pattern for lowlight use provides maximum efficiency under a wide variety of light conditions and allow fast sight acquisition under stress.

Front grasping grooves on slide and light-mounting grooves on forward portion of frame are additional evidence of the XD's advanced design.

▶ **This is a close-up view of XD "Tactical" version. Slightly longer slide and barrel provide increased bullet velocity, while longer sight radius allows better sight acquisition at high speed.**

▼ **XD is exceptionally user-friendly, allowing novice shooters to achieve efficiency with it in a remarkably short time. Author's daughter Alexandra had no problem becoming quite adept with it after only a short orientation and training session with it.**

and subcompact – the XD demonstrates its designer's exceptional understanding of the fact that people must use the weapon. And as such, things like the way it feels, the way it points, how quickly it can be brought into action and the location of its operational controls are just as important as mechanical reliability. Another term for it is "user-friendliness" and it is in this particular category that the XD is especially superior.

Its grip is well-angled, yet small enough and thin enough to be comfortably held by nearly anyone, something not at all typical of most modern handguns. It also features an ambidextrous magazine release button assembly, allowing left-handed shooters to utilize the same magazine operational techniques for speed and tactical reloading and loading or unloading – as do their right-handed colleagues.

For easy chamber checking, especially in low light conditions, the XD also features a large loaded-chamber indicator directly on top of its slide, directly behind the ejection port. When a cartridge is indeed chambered, the indicator rises upward and is easily seen or, if light conditions are too dim, felt by

the operator, providing him with instantaneous knowledge whether the weapon is loaded or unloaded.

An easily seen or felt cocking indicator also protrudes from the rear of the slide for this same purpose.

As seen with the Glock, the XD has a trigger-blocking safety set into the front face of the trigger, but it also has a grip safety as well. As most readers are aware, there has been considerable criticism of the trigger-mounted safety over the last decade, even if it isn't legitimate. The weapon operator should never place his trigger finger inside the trigger guard until he's actually engaging a target and one would think that the fact would be obvious.

However, in today's world of civil liability hazards, there are continuous attempts to avoid placing the responsibility for negligent or accidental discharges where it belongs – on the operator – and instead focus it on the weapon. To preclude this, the XD's designers incorporated an additional grip-safety, thus effectively preventing both negligent (caused by deficient operator handling methods) and accidental

(inadvertent grabbing of an uncontrolled weapon and unintentionally placing one or two fingers on the trigger in the process) discharges.

The XD's superior human engineering doesn't stop there. It also features:

1. Integral grooves in the front portion of its polymer frame for flashlight attachment.

2. Grasping grooves both fore and aft to allow virtually any kind of slide manipulation technique.

3. A magazine well with a 60-degree bevel for quick and simple magazine insertion; both critically important factors in speed loading, tactical loading and even loading and unloading.

4. Twelve line-per-inch checkering on its front and back straps for fast, proper grip index in wet, cold or other stressful conditions.

▼ **Ambidextrous magazine release buttons are present on both left and right sides of frame and are easily operated by right or left-handed shooters.**

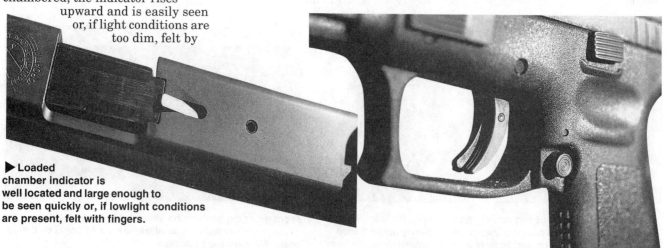

▶ **Loaded chamber indicator is well located and large enough to be seen quickly or, if lowlight conditions are present, felt with fingers.**

▲ Cocking indicator is also well located and large enough to feel with fingers in low light.

▶ Grip safety is unobtrusive, yet effective, adding another dimension to operator safety.

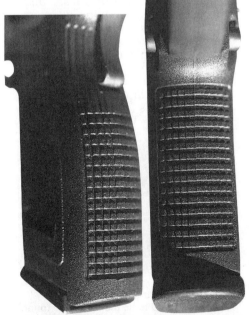

▶ Checkering on front and backstrap is sufficiently large to allow fast grip index even in wet conditions, but is without sharp edges that abrade skin and clothing.

5. High visibility low profile fixed sights with integral horizontal three-dot inserts for fast sight acquisition under the widest possible variety of light conditions.

6. A smooth, light double-action-only (DAO) trigger as it comes "from the box," thus eliminating the need for after-purchase gunsmithing to obtain tactically efficient, yet civil liability-resistant performance.

7. Two drop-free steel magazines in either 10-shot (civilian) or 15-shot (military/police) configurations for fast, easy speed loading or other functions requiring rapid magazine manipulation.

8. A dark gray matte finish on all metal parts to preclude light reflection.

9. Exceptional accuracy. With all three versions, I found that from a rest, I could place all my shots inside a six-inch circle at 100 meters.

10. Excellent functional (mechanical) reliability. Even though I used every kind of bullet type and configuration I could find – RNJ, RNL, JHP, JSP – all of my XDs have thus far functioned flawlessly, even in the cold, rain or dust. In fact, I have yet to experience a stoppage with them, even though I've fired some 4000 rounds through them.

11. Multiple caliber availability – 9mmP, 357 SIG & 40 S&W.

12. A lockable plastic hard case, making air-travel with the gun in a suitcase a less-stressful matter.

All of these characteristics combine to make a pistol that is so user-friendly that it is fast becoming acclaimed by both novice and expert alike. In the many military/police/civilian self-defense classes I teach around the world, I've found that my students find the XD to be extraordinarily easy to work with. Particularly for those with little experience with self-loaders, its simple operation and superior human engineering allow quick understanding and skill achievement.

But it doesn't stop there. Because the advantages of superior human engineering aren't limited to novices, the XD is also a good choice for those of higher skill levels. Time and time again, I've found that even master-class combat shooters find that they can transition to the XD from another type of weapon and regain their previous performance levels with astonishing quickness. In fact, to a man, every highly skilled shooter I have asked to evaluate the XD has commented that it's the easiest pistol to shoot well that they've ever seen.

This observation is further confirmed by my own performance with it. In July 2002, I shot the only perfect score produced thus far on the extremely difficult American Small Arms Academy Handgun Combat Master Qualification Course. By way of perspective, in the 22 years of its existence, there have only been 19 shooters who have successfully completed the ASAA HCM Qual Course.

During that time, I've successfully completed it nine times, using a Colt M1911 45 ACP, Colt LW Commander 45 ACP, Browning P35 9mmP, Browning P35 40 S&W, Glock 17 9mmP, Glock 22 40 S&W, Smith & Wesson M39 9mmP and a four-inch heavy-barreled Smith & Wesson M10 38 Spl. The ASAA HCM Course requires a minimum of 360 out of a possible 400 points – 90% — to pass and though I had previously shot a 396 with a Glock 17 9mmP, I'd never come any close to "cleaning the course" before.

So as you can see, the XD is a heck of a pistol and one well worth your consideration. It's tough, reliable, and phenomenally user-friendly and can be obtained in three configurations – standard, tactical or sub-compact – to fulfill nearly anyone's needs. And as if this isn't enough, it's available in all three versions at a more-than-fair price of less than $500.

In my book, that makes it a clear winner and though only time can tell if it will achieve the legendary status of the Colt M1911, Browning P35 and the Glock 17, it's my guess that it will. Regardless, I can honestly say that without hesitation, I'd bet my life on it nonetheless.

And what better endorsement can one give than that? •

► The Smith & Wesson SW1911 is a true 1911 pistol, even if it differs from those built for military use or by chief rival for decades, Colt Firearms.

Smith & Wesson's *New* 1911 Government Model 45 Pistol

by Frank W. James

COULD YOU IMAGINE the shock and surprise if General Motors decided they were going to build a "Cobra" sportscar? No, I don't mean a sportscar with the Cobra name, but a true Carroll Shelby deep blue/broad white stripes paint-scheme Cobra complete with a tube steel frame, uncomfortable seats and a 427 overhead valve engine that duplicated

the one made by Ford Motor Company in the late 1960s.

Naturally, this is impossible because Ford Motor Company has very carefully protected their trademarks against unauthorized use, but it would be possible to build a Cobra-

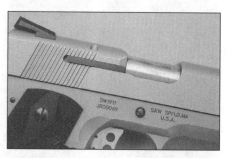

type sportscar because all of the patents pertaining to its particular design have expired. The same is true with the fabled 1911 pistol and an event as earth-shaking as the opening hypothesis "has" taken place because Smith & Wesson is manufacturing a 1911 pistol. That's right, they are making the 1911 pistol in 45 ACP and just as a reminder to those arriving late, 'ACP' in this instance stands for Automatic COLT Pistol. Smith & Wesson is making

The new 1911 (*bottom*) shown here with a Smith & Wesson Model 4506 (*top*) for a size comparison.

The SW1911 is fitted with a well proportioned beaver tail grip safety. It is large enough to protect the web of the shooter's hand. Yet, it is sufficiently discreet to maintain easy concealed carry.

The external extractor found on the SW1911 is said to be the same one found on the 4000 series of 40-caliber auto pistols from Smith & Wesson. The frame features the minimum in terms of explanations with its laser-engraved serial number and manufacturer's identity.

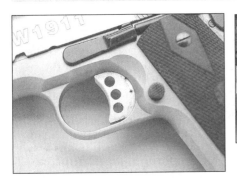

The author found the appearance of the trigger on the SW1911 to be less than what he expected from the prestigious firm in Springfield, Massachusetts. It was one of his few points of criticism.

The front of the grip features the same fine serrations seen on Smith & Wesson's Third Generation of auto pistols, but also note the well-rounded undercut at the junction where the triggerguard meets the grip frame.

The large loop hammer is a Chip McCormick unit and the corresponding sear appears identical to the same products offered by McCormick.

their own version of the pistol that Colt Firearms pioneered at the beginning of the 20th century.

It is not an exact copy, of course, because S & W engineers wanted to see where they could upgrade the pistol that was only a few decades ago made solely by their chief business competitor. Of course, the world is different now. Colt is a mere shadow of its former size. Additionally, it seems as if everyone in the gun business is making their own version of the 1911 pistol. Springfield Armory was the first to challenge Colt in the 1911 market, but in the last few years a wide number of manufacturers (starting with Kimber, then Dan Wesson and now followed by a host of others) have joined the rush to build 1911

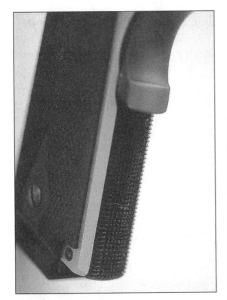

Like the original military issue 1911 pistol, the mainspring housing on the SW1911 remains flat in profile, but unlike the original this piece is made from aluminum and is checkered at 30 lines per inch.

pistols simply because it seems this market is virtually inexhaustible.

The Smith & Wesson Difference

As everyone knows, John Browning designed the original 1911 pistol and then Springfield Armory (the original government-owned arsenal, not a private firm) modified it in 1923 to become the 1911A1. The main differences between the 1911 pistol and the 1911A1 pistol were the latter pistol had a shorter trigger, a slightly extended comb (the rear portion) on the grip safety and the mainspring housing was changed from a flat piece to one that featured a pronounced arch and curve.

The new Smith & Wesson SW1911 shares much with both pistols, but there is little in terms of details they share in common. The first thing noticeable about the SW1911 is the fact that both the slide and frame are stainless steel, not carbon steel with a Parkerized finish. The finish on both the stainless steel frame and slide will be immediately recognized by anyone who has worked with a Smith & Wesson auto

pistol in the past decade because it features the same dull luster stainless finish Smith & Wesson has been using for several years now on most of their auto-pistol designs.

What is different for this 1911 pistol is the use of laser engraving for all the critical markings, including the serial number. Unlike the different models from other manufacturers, the manufacturer, model number and other essential bits of information are laser-engraved with dark gray lettering on the silver-colored stainless steel. I'm not being critical, it's just different than what you normally find on a 1911-type pistol.

The 1911 pistol has for decades been something of a paradox. Known foremost as a 'fighting' pistol, it was designed from the very beginning to utilize full metal jacketed bullets weighing 230 grains in 45 ACP. That is where things stood until the advent of the improved performance hollow-point bullets that have become the norm in law enforcement and self-defense circles for the past few decades. The 1911 pistol, being designed for full metal jacket ammunition, often had trou-

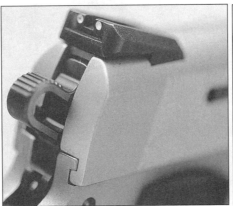 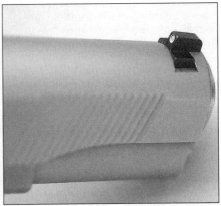

The rear sight on the SW1911 is the excellent, virtually snag-free Novak Lo Mount rear sight. It features two prominent white dots on either side of the square u-notch. The front sight is mounted to the front of the slide via a machine-cut dovetail and features a single white dot on the rear face of the blade sight.

The 45-caliber auto-pistol round is the best round available for self-defense in the minds of many and now Smith & Wesson is manufacturing the perfect 45-caliber auto-pistol, the 1911.

serves a dual role. The SW1911 has an internal firing pin safety, but unlike the one found on Series 80 Colt pistols which complicates the adjustment or lightening of the trigger pull, the SW1911 firing pin safety works off the grip safety and has nothing to do with the trigger mechanism. The result is the SW1911 firing pin safety does not inhibit the trigger pull in any way, shape or form. There is an increased resistenance felt in terms of engaging the grip safety, but once engaged, the pistol acts and feels like one made before the firing pin safety days. However, it should be emphasized the grip safety MUST be successfully engaged to deactivate the firing pin safety and thereby allow forward movement of the firing pin.

As to the actual trigger pull on the sample SW1911, an RCBS trigger pull scale measured the pull between 5.5 and 6.0 pounds on several different tests. Although this is still high, even for tuned street pistols, it is not unreasonable because the very first 1911 pistol I purchased brand new in the early 1970s was manufactured by Colt and had a trigger pull that scaled over nine pounds fresh out of the factory box.

The hammer is similar in appearance to those sold by Chip McCormick and features the often seen long oval opening in its center. The point here is competition applications have proven lighter is faster, so the less mass there is to the hammer is often considered a good thing. The sample SW1911 used for

ble adapting to other bullet designs and in recent years that has clouded its reputation greatly. A number of different 9mm pistol manufacturers have done a marvelous job of raising the bar, so to speak, in terms of functional reliability with hollow-point ammo and no one is more aware of this than Smith & Wesson, so they designed their 1911 pistol to work with hollow-point ammo from the very beginning, instead as an after-thought.

The new SW1911 features a barrel that comes throated and polished to accept the majority—if not all—of the hollow-point bullets currently available. (It ate everything I fed it during testing without a single hiccup and that included samples of Hornady, Federal Hi-Shok and Hydra-Shok, Speer Gold Dot and Cor-Bon ammunition.) Additionally, there is a small hole in the top of the barrel hood as a visual inspection point to check to see if the chamber is loaded. Like the original 1911 pistol and its follow-on, the SW1911 uses a bushing at the front of the barrel, only in this instance it is a match-grade bushing. Altogether, the barrel fit to the slide was very well done on the sample SW1911 as was the gun's ability to feed and function reliably with a mix of different hollow-point bullets.

The Individual Features

When you start examining the individual features you soon realize just how different this pistol is from those seen only 20 years ago. The Smith & Wesson SW1911 is a testament to the development of the 1911 pistol since the days of John Browning. The grip safety has always been

a contentious subject with both 1911 shooters and non-1911 aficionados. If it isn't extended far enough to cover the web of the hand, the hammer bites the shooter's hand. But, if it is too big then the pistol is hard to conceal for those who are interested in what many claim is the ultimate self-defense pistol. Smith & Wesson has solved the dilemma by installing a beavertail grip safety that features a pronounced outward hump at the bottom and a significant up-turn at the rear portion. This makes sure it protects the shooter's hand (regardless of size) as well as being sufficiently discreet for concealed carry.

However, the purpose of the upturned grip safety doesn't end there for the SW1911 pistol. It also

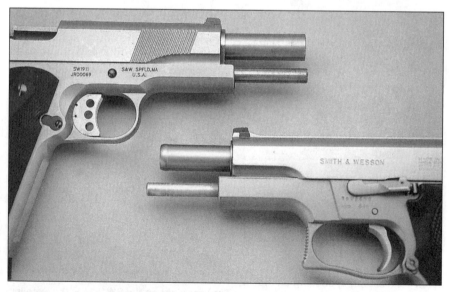

One of the shortcomings of the new SW1911, in the author's opinion, is the inclusion of the full-length guide-rod. This is a feature the SW1911 shares with the previous Model 4506 Smith & Wesson pistol.

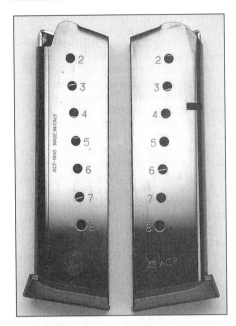

The SW1911 comes with two magazines, each capable of holding eight rounds. The magazines are made in Italy by ACT and are identical to those sold in the United States by Wayne Novak.

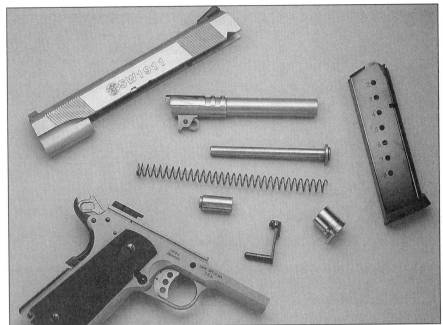

Fieldstripping the SW1911 pistol requires the same procedures found with any 1911 pistol featuring a full-length guide rod. Once stripped down to these basic components, cleaning and routine maintenance are easy to accomplish.

my evaluation was one of the first such pistols shipped from the factory and the only disappointment, in my view, in terms of its apparent quality was the appearance of the trigger used on the test pistol. The trigger was made from aluminum alloy and featured three holes and a serrated trigger face. Roll pins were used to fasten the trigger itself to the internal bow and the roll pins featured uneven edges as did the bottom part of the trigger. The whole ensemble had an overall 'shoddy' appearance, but in truth the trigger functioned flawlessly and could not be faulted on its function, only on its appearance.

Like all of the high-end Smith & Wesson auto-pistols of more than a decade, the SW1911 features the superb Novak Lo Mount sighting system. The rear Lo Mount sight features the now-standard two white dots on either side of the square u-notch and the front sight completes the sight picture with a short thick-bladed post featuring a single white dot on its rear face. Both the front and rear sight units are mounted to the top of the slide via a machine-cut dovetail in the slide. Windage adjustments are easily accomplished by drifting either the front or rear sights in their respective dovetail cuts. Elevation adjustments would require the replacement of the front sight blade with one either shorter or taller as the situation would demand, but

none were provided. The pistol—as delivered—seemed to be sighted in for 230-grain ammunition.

Major Differences

The big difference between the SW1911 and the guns produced by Colt over the years, as well as those made for military use, would be the use of an external extractor and the installation of a full-length guide-rod. The external extractor on 1911 pistols is a controversial subject among purists as some feel it adds little to the equation. Others feel an external extractor is more positive in terms of its purchase of the cartridge rim and is easier to maintain. The

counter-argument from the purists is the internal extractor is far easier to adjust and to clean in terms of daily maintenance. Reportedly, the external extractor used on the SW1911 is the same one manufactured by Smith & Wesson for the 40 S&W Model 4006 pistol.

The installation of the full-length guide rod is a feature found on many competition-only 1911 pistols. I am a critic of these devices and, yes, I do own 1911 pistols with full-length guide rods, but they were installed as part of the gunsmith's accurizing package. The biggest argument in favor of full-length guide rods is that some gunsmiths feel they keep the

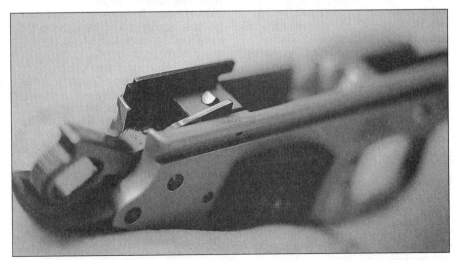

The firing pin stop is activated by action of the grip safety and not the trigger mechanism on the SW1911. As seen here the grip safety has been depressed, thereby raising the lever that activates the firing pin safety system located in the slide.

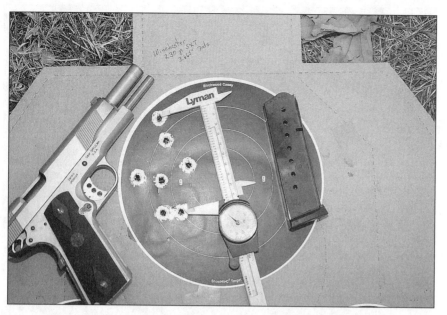

The author was a little disappointed in his target groups. Most often his best groups ran in the three inch-plus range for five rounds at 25 yards. The six-round group seen here, with one called flyer, measured just over 3.6 inches.

slide centered on the frame and thereby reduce side-to-side wear. There is little evidence to support or deny such claims. Others argue that full-length guide rods help keep the recoil spring contained and here Jeff Cooper had the best response: "Where the Hell is it going to go?" Full-length guide rods are often found on 1911 pistols from manufacturers other than Colt and one of the reasons not explained I think is the fact that some designs force the operator to start the take-down process with the slide locked open. That makes it virtually impossible to take the gun apart with a loaded chamber. That is not the case with the SW1911 as the take-down process actually starts with turning the muzzle bushing to release the spring plug and, yes, it can be done with the chamber loaded so be sure and check to make sure the magazine is removed and the chamber is empty before starting the take-down process.

Minor Differences

The minor differences between the SW1911 and the original military contract 45s include serrations on the front of the slide. It is no longer appropriate to use a thumb-in-the-triggerguard-front-finger-press-check to see if the chamber is loaded. Of course, in daylight situations a visual examination of the barrel hood will tell you if there is a shell casing present in the chamber, but in low-light environments the operator should retract the slide by grasping the front of the slide from under the pistol with the off-hand and retracting it to the point the trigger finger can be inserted into the chamber area. If the gun is loaded, the presence of the cartridge will be easily recognized and if it isn't then the chamber will be found empty.

What a lot of people don't realize is Springfield Armory in 1923 suggested the forward portion of the grip frame be knurled or checkered, and the suggestion was taken under advisement at the same time the other modifications resulted in the 1911A1 pistol. The idea, however, for checkering the front of the grip was rejected. Since then, of course, it has become a popular custom modification. The forward edge of the SW1911 grip frame is not checkered, but it is serrated and it's done in the same fashion as found on all the other S&W auto-pistols. Additionally, the junction where the trigger guard meets the grip frame is undercut, smoothed and contoured so the operator can get a 'higher' grip on the gun than that found with the original series military pistols.

The mainspring housing is flat, like the original 1911 pistol, but checkered in a 30 line-per-inch pattern. It is made from an aluminum alloy, so even though it is like the original, it is different in a couple of different ways what with the checkering and the alloy construction.

The magazine well opening has been beveled for easier insertion of the loaded magazine. Again, a feature developed from combat shooting competition over the last 30 to 40 years. The grip panels are soft rubber panels with large diamond centers surrounding each of the two grip screws used to secure the panel to the frame. The traditional Smith & Wesson trademark emblem is molded into each just below the top screw.

Two magazines came with the sample pistol and they are slightly different than those seen before. For one thing the single column tube body is highly polished and features a deep blue. The capacity is eight rounds, but they are slightly longer than a conventional seven round government model magazine. The bottom of the magazine is covered with a plastic floorplate and it does not seat flush with the bottom of the grip frame as it protrudes 5/16ths of an inch below the frame, but this extension also works well as a mag pad extension to insure the magazine is fully seated in the gun during a reload. These magazines are manufactured in Italy by ACT and they are identical to the ones offered by Wayne Novak.

As mentioned earlier during all of the range testing, the pistol functioned flawlessly throughout the different shooting sessions and it devoured a wide range of both factory and handloaded ammunition. The pressure required to depress the grip safety may have affected the resulting target groups to some extent because many of the groups were not as tight as one would prefer, but even at that none of them could be classified as 'bad'. The test SW1911 seemed to prefer Federal 230-grain Hydra-Shok above all others in terms of accuracy as it put four rounds into a group measuring 2.5 inches at 25 yards, but a fifth shot opened this up to 3.25 inches and here it was felt, as in most all the test groups, the pressure require to maintain the grip safety diminished some of the concentration necessary for really good shooting.

I doubt if General Motors will ever make a copy of the immortal Cobra. Why would they? They have the immortal Corvette, but Smith & Wesson has never really had a historic auto-pistol to compete with the 1911 pistol. Many have made Smith & Wesson the butt of jokes for this venture, but the fact is the SW1911 is a solid pistol, well built and, considering the cost of some of the models on the current market, it is offered at a competitive suggested retail price of around $935.

Would I be interested in purchasing one? I already have. ●

GUN TESTS

Ruger's 480 Super Redhawk

by Mark Hampton

◀ The new 480 revolver is the result of a collaborative effort of Sturm, Ruger and Hornady to create a powerful revolver and new cartridge for handgun hunters.

WHEN RUGER ANNOUNCED the first cartridge to bear the company's name, I got excited and wanted to learn more about this new development. The 480 Ruger was originally designed with the big game hunter in mind. Hornady joined forces with the Sturm, Ruger & Company to give the shooting fraternity the very first cartridge ever to bear the Ruger name. Both companies cooperatively worked to produce a big-bore revolver cartridge specifically designed with the big game hunter as their primary focus. Handgun hunters now have a new cartridge to pursue their favorite outdoor activity.

The Ruger 480 cartridge fills a niche between the ever-popular 44 Magnum and the powerful 454 Casull. Both of the older cartridges have served handgun hunters well in the past and now we have a new kid on the block. Hornady claims the new cartridge produces a muzzle velocity of 1350 fps with almost 50 % more muzzle energy than the 44 Magnum. When fired from a 7 1/2-inch barrel, even at 50 yards the cartridge is delivering over one thousand pounds of energy. These impressive numbers and awesome power come without the recoil of the 454 Casull. For all practical purposes the 480 Ruger delivers approximately 80 % of the power when compared to the 454 Casull, with much less recoil. All this is possible with Hornady's 325-grain XTP Magnum bullet. This is an ideal bullet for big game hunting. Hornady's premium jacketed hollowpoint bullet was specifically designed to withstand the higher velocities often produced by today's high performance handguns. I have always found Hornady's XTP bullets to work extremely well on big game such as wild boar and whitetail. This combination of gun/ammo from two industry giants will certainly fill the gap between two very popular hunting handgun cartridges, and just may very well be a "classic" in its infant stage.

Reloaders will find unfired brass available from Hornady. Unfortunately I did not have time before deadlines to work up any loads. For those hunters who do enjoy rolling their own handloads, the 480 Ruger will shine. Looking at the *Hodgdon*

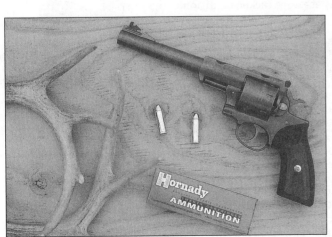

Open sighted revolvers like the new 480 Super Redhawk are ideally suited for close range hunting pursuits.

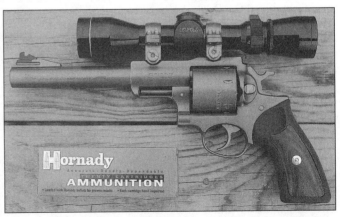

The author mounted this Leupold 2-8X scope on the big 480 Super Redhawk. It differs from the standard Redhawk by having a special non-reflective finish and a plain round cylinder.

The revolver delivered excellent accuracy, an essential requirement for handgun hunting.

Reloading Manual laying on my desk I find they have loads listed for two different bullet weights, both the 325- and 400-grain rounds listed are Hornady XTPs. Using H-110, the book lists over 1500 fps with the 325-grain XTP. When the big 400-grainer is ignited with the same powder it tops 1250 fps. These loads are all operating well under 48,000 psi. The company claims the 480 Ruger operates under normal handgun pressures so brass will not be under any undue stress and can be loaded many times. The 475 Linebaugh dies are used to load the 480 Ruger with several companies offering those dies including Hornady. This works under the same principal as loading 44 Special rounds with 44 Magnum dies.

When I received the Ruger Super Redhawk in 480 Ruger for testing and evaluation, a few days passed before I could get my hands on any factory Hornady ammo. I was like a kid at Christmas. Patience never was a strong point! Since there wasn't any ammo, I dry-fired the Ruger until my wife told me she was sick of hearing the hammer drop. To show a little progression of how we got to where we are today, Ruger first introduced the Redhawk back in 1979. At that time it was quite the advancement in design of heavy-frame, double-action revolvers. The demand for large caliber revolvers spurred by interest of handgun hunters encouraged the company to launch the Super Redhawk in 1986. Since Ruger had already produced the Super Redhawk to accommodate the mighty 454 Casull, it seemed a natural choice to use the same launching system for the new 480 Ruger. The gun just looks like a hunting revolver with the Target Grey all-weather finish that has no shiny appearance that might produce unwanted reflection, which may spook game. Ruger's patented cush-

ioned grips fit my fairly small hand well. These rubber grips with the wood insert in the middle added a pleasing look to the sixgun. My test revolver came with a 7 1/2-inch barrel although a 9 1/2-inch version is also available. As a personal choice if I were to hunt exclusively with a scoped revolver it would probably be the longer version. The gun tipped the scales at 53 ounces with the shorter barrel. This double-action revolver incorporates a one in 18" RH twist with six grooves in the stainless steel, hammer forged barrel. Other than being an ounce or so different than the 44 Magnum and 454 Casull, the Super Redhawk in 480 Ruger is dimensionally about the same. The swing-out unfluted cylinder, which holds six rounds, makes loading and unloading a simple task. This frequently overlooked feature is welcome especially if and when you find yourself in a hurry for whatever reason. It comes with an additional locking latch in the crane in front of the cylinder. This provides extra strength and safety. The cylinder opens by depressing the thumb button allowing for the release of the rear lock as well as the front latch. Sights on this gun came with an orange blade and the capability to interchange the front blade system to incorporate different colored front sights. The rear sights were adjustable with a white outline. The handgun comes with a high-impact case and gun lock with a suggested retail of $775. Even though it annoyed my wife, the gun handled nicely when dry-firing in the house. When the ammo arrived I immediately loaded the truck with all my shooting paraphernalia and headed to the range.

The weather was not cooperating with heavy fog looming over the range but that didn't deter the shooting session or my enthusiasm. I couldn't wait any longer as the targets were tacked to the backstop and placed 25 yards away. Barring the first shot that went off before I was ready, the group was more than acceptable, especially with open sights. The felt recoil was more than the 44 Magnum but still manageable. After getting bored punching paper I focused my attention to several rocks on the nearby pond bank. It didn't take a rocket sci-

entist to see the power behind the 480 Ruger as it blasted chunks of real estate up in the air. It was the end of February and hunting season was far away. Since I run a game ranch and knew where several big hogs were hanging out, heck, I had to see this gun in action! The rocks on the pond just weren't cutting it. Besides, my wife and I were out of pork steaks!

A few workdays passed before I had the opportunity to hunt. Before heading to the woods after a big mean hog I mounted a Leupold 2 1/2-8X scope on top of the gun. The frame topstrap is massive and provides for extra strength where scope rings attach plus in critical areas surrounding the barrel threads. Ruger's frame-integral scope mount dovetails and one-inch stainless rings came with the gun. It was relatively easy and simple to mount the scope. When getting the scope mounted you can see the huge portion of frame extension that swallows almost three inches of barrel. The barrel is also massive with a diameter of almost one inch. Anywhere you look on this gun it's easy to see heavy-duty, safety, strength, and reliability.

I sighted the gun in at 50 yards anticipating a shot similar to this when hunting for a pig. With the additional weight of Leupold's optics the gun now felt like a 44 Magnum during recoil. It wouldn't be a problem to spend an afternoon on the range shooting this gun with hunting-type ammo. With limited factory ammunition I had to conserve a few rounds for some pork chops and bacon. After getting the bullets to print dead-on from 50 yards, the gun was now shooting five-shot groups measuring a tad over two inches. This is certainly acceptable for hunting big game in typical revolver hunting conditions.

▶ **The revolver has a tad more recoil than the popular 44 Magnum but not enough to intimidate the author's wife.**

Practicing off-hand shooting is important if you plan to use the revolver for serious hunting in the field.

Under the proper circumstances I would not hesitate to fill a deer tag from 100 yards if the right shot presented itself. Now if I could just locate a big hog.

For many handgun hunters, chasing wild boar is a great off-season adventure. As this was being written it was the first part of March and all other big game seasons were closed. Wanting to see just how the 480 Ruger would perform under actual field conditions, there wasn't any other alternative. That's not necessarily a negative. Heck, stalking a big boar with a revolver is a challenge and great fun any time of the year. With the exception of whitetail deer, wild hogs are probably pursued as much as, often more than, other big game such as black bear, antelope, mule deer or elk. One thing for sure, if the 480 Ruger works on a big hog, it will certainly suffice for deer and black bear. After all, a really big hog will more than likely weigh as much as, or more than, most black bear taken every year.

I didn't have a holster that was made exactly for the scoped Ruger but found one that was made for a T/C that worked just as well. After 12 years of guiding hog hunters, many of which are handgun hunters, once in a while it's nice to go

out hunting by yourself. This particular day was overcast and cool, perfect for hunting hogs. We had a group of hunters who had just finished their hunt a few days before so I had a pretty good idea of where the pigs could be located. After having a little too much fun shooting the 480 Ruger at the range I found myself running low on ammo. With very few rounds to spare I was hoping one good shot in the right place would do the trick, if an opportunity did materialize. Working through the first patch of woods slowly yielded nothing. I checked a couple of wallows and a bedding area and still no sign of hogs. Working my way along a wooded ridge I soon came upon six good porkers with their noses down feeding. Luckily I spotted them before they laid eyes on me. They were rooting around digging up whatever they could find. I sat down with my back against a tree and watched. Slowly they eased toward my direction. The Ruger quietly slid out of the holster. I checked the variable power on the Leupold to make sure it was still resting on the 4X position. Finally, when the hogs got within 30 yards I noticed one was somewhat larger

than the other five. The wind was calm and not a factor. Unfortunately all the hogs were milling around and the one I wanted seemed to always be behind another. The Ruger was cocked very slowly not to make any noise as I took a rest off my knees. When the big hog was finally clear I lined the crosshairs up just behind the shoulders and slowly squeezed the trigger. The shot was almost perfect broadside from approximately 30 yards when the hammer dropped. I wasn't wearing any earplugs when the roar of the 480 Ruger broke the peace and tranquility of the late morning outing. I should have been wearing some ear protection! The big hog flinched and took off running with all the others. In a matter of seconds they all disappeared over the ridge, out of sight. I sat there a few minutes and lit a cigar, thinking and somewhat hoping the shot was good. A few moments later it was easy following a blood trail, which didn't go far. The big hog might have gone 40 yards before calling it quits. I wanted to recover the bullet but it made a clean pass through. That's a considerable amount of penetration when a 300-pound hog doesn't stop the bullet. The factory Hornady 475-caliber bullet did a superb job. However that didn't come as a big surprise.

Taking one animal with a particular gun/cartridge combination certainly doesn't make a person an expert by any means. It does give an insight on how effective this round will be on other similar sized big game. I believe the 480 Ruger will win the hearts of some handgun hunters looking for something different in a revolver. It has a bigger punch than the ever so popular 44 Magnum with less recoil of the 454 Casull. Plus, this combination will handle just about any game on the North American continent. And that will attract some serious handgun hunters! •

The author liked the handling qualities of the Ruger. Handgun Hunters who pursue boar, bear or big bucks will have a quality powerhouse of a revolver to pack in the field.

If the 480 Super Redhawk can tackle a big hog like this 300 pounder it will certainly handle a multitude of other hunting chores. The author used it to take this hog using Hornady's 325-grain JHP ammunition.

The Heckler & Koch P-7 Pistol

by Frank W. James

THE HECKLER & Koch P-7 will forever be known throughout the world of small arms as the "Squeeze-Cocker" pistol. It is a unique design that offered some natural advantages as well as more than a few major disadvantages, but at the time of its introduction it was innovative — a characteristic which can be said to apply to all Heckler & Koch firearms. The question is, however, was the HK P-7 Squeeze-Cocker a gun that came before its time or was it such a troubled design that for the P-7 there never was a right time?

The HK P-7 came into being as a result of a West German series of trials to standardize police pistols. The year was 1975 and West Germany realized their law enforcement agencies were behind the curve, so they put forth a set of requirements for a new pistol to arm all the major

▲ Even though it was a full-caliber pistol the P-7 (*bottom*) was surprisingly compact in term of length and width when compared with other pistols like this Colt Series 80 Government Model (*top*).

West German law enforcement agencies. The main thing was they wanted the 9x19mm round to be the common caliber, instead of any number of previously used calibers like 32 ACP or even 357 Magnum. They wanted a pistol that could be used instantly without the need to disengage a manual safety or, upon completion of firing, that did not require the reactivation of a manual safety in order to be rendered safe.

Three different firms submitted sample pistols for the ensuing trials and this contest was watched closely by many in the worldwide small arms community simply because the vast majority of the 9x19mm caliber pistols in popular use at that time were older designs like the Walther P-38, the Browning Hi-Power or some variation of a single action semi-auto John Browning design like those made in Spain.

Walther submitted the P5, while Sig-Sauer submitted the P6 and Heckler & Koch submitted the Polizei-Selbstlade-Pistole or PSP, that later become known as the P-7 when a couple of small changes were made. The HK P-7 is the smallest pistol of the three in terms of overall length, height and width. The overall length of the P-7 is slightly over 6.5 inches, but it is heavy thanks to its all steel construction at 31 ounces. The barrel length on the P-7 is 4.1 inches so it is not a large pistol. In fact, many would probably classify it, the P-7M8, as a large compact pistol if they were unfamiliar with the design and its origin.

▶ Heckler & Koch's P-7 squeeze-cocking pistol was a revolutionary design when it was first introduced in the late 1970s.

The Walther P5 was more compact than the World War II P-38, but it also shared many of the same components of that pistol and could arguably be said to have been a variation of the original pistol, if not a cleaned up duplicate. The SIG P6 was the same pistol American shooters came to know as the SIG P-225, which was a semi-auto pistol with the distinctive SIG double-action trigger mechanism and a decocking lever on the left side of the alloy frame. The P-225 employed a single-column magazine holding eight rounds of 9x19mm pistol that was the predecessor to the highly successful P-226 which used a double column magazine holding 15 rounds.

The Walther and SIG candidates for this trial used a double action trigger mechanism to meet the stated need of being capable of being readily engaged without a manual safety. Everyone thought the double-action trigger design was the only way you could answer this problem (after all wasn't that how they did it with revolvers?), but the engineers

The first P7s had eight-shot capacity magazines. This P7M8 was especially made with the American market in mind.

at Heckler & Koch looked at the problem and solved it in an entirely different manner. (Little did anyone suspect that Gaston Glock would solve this problem in yet another manner that would prove far more popular in American law enforcement than any of the three previously mentioned designs.)

What HK did was create a design that allowed the action, i.e. the striker assembly, to be cocked simply by grasping the grip portion of the pistol firmly. The HK P-7 had no conventional safety mechanisms of any kind. Grasping the pistol at the grip firmly cocked the action. On the front of the grip there was the 'squeeze-cocker', which was nothing more than a sheet metal shell which when compressed conformed to the shape on the front of the frame. Spring-loaded, this shell required a firm grasp with some force, but not an excessive amount, to compress it in order to cock the striker assembly in the slide. Once compressed, however, it was an easy task even for those with weak hands to maintain the firing grip. A unique feature of the squeeze-cocker was the fact it would also release the slide when the same was locked open after it had been depressed twice, so it could legitimately be said it was designed for speed.

One of the big advantages of the squeeze-cocker design was it allowed the HK engineers to equip the P-7 with a trigger in terms of felt-pull and smoothness that most experts could only dream about on a factory pistol. Many HK P-7 exhibited trigger pulls, once the squeeze-cocker had been depressed, that scaled

between three and four pounds in actual pull weights with 3 1/2 being a common trigger pull weight on many. This was both good and bad depending upon the shooter's level of expertise which will be explained in a moment in greater detail.

The action of the HK P-7 was a gas-retarded delayed-blowback action. The P-7 barrel, unlike all recoil operated designs, did not move. It was fixed solidly to the frame. In order to operate at a safe pressure level the gas pressure inside the barrel was bled off to a gas cylinder, located in the frame beneath the barrel, containing a piston which was directly connected to the front of the slide. This piston was used to hold the slide closed. The pressure which was bled into the gas cylinder worked against the piston and pushed forward on the slide until the pressure inside the barrel and behind the fired projectile had dropped to a point safe enough to open the chamber and cycle the slide.

Like the MP5 submachine gun the HK P-7 featured a fluted chamber which by way of explanation is a series of milled recesses surrounding the inside circumference of the chamber. These flutes allow gas pressure to 'float' the fired case off the wall of the chamber when extraction of the cartridge case takes place. In fact, many HK armorers feel the P-7 really didn't really need an extractor in the strictest sense because the flutes and the residual gas pressure in the barrel forced the fired case from the chamber and extracted it without need of a mechanical extractor.

The barrel on the PSP and subsequent P-7 was rifled in the then new polygonal rifling. Heckler & Koch builds many of the machines used to hammer forge barrels so it was easy for them to make a mandrel that hammer forged this rifling inside the barrel. Polygonal rifling is smooth lacking the traditional lands or grooves of conventional rifling, but appears to be a set of edgeless spirals inside the barrel. Many experts feel a tighter seal is achieved between the fired bullet and the barrel with polygonal rifling than that seen with traditional land and groove rifling.

The Many Different Squeeze-Cocker Pistols

Heckler & Koch originally introduced the squeeze-cocker pistol as the PSP. Many experts still feel that even today the HK PSP was probably the 'flattest' 9x19mm pistol ever made in terms of its slim width. It, however, used a heel clip magazine release and while HK wanted the West German contract they were already looking at sales in the United States as the possible pot of gold at the end of the rainbow. Unfortunately, the American market was not interested in any new semi-auto pistol design featuring a heel clip magazine release. So, the P-7 was born and here the difference was the introduction of a magazine release button at the junction where the trigger guard meets the pistol frame. Additionally, it was ambidextrous in that it was found on both sides of the pistol and it worked by pushing 'down' versus the traditional inward push of the mag release button.

This first P-7 model was correctly identified by the nomenclature P-7M8, where the suffix 'M8' indicated the capacity of the single column magazine. Although seldom seen in the United States and developed

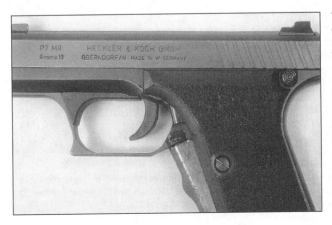

The pistol had a extremely simple manual of arms in terms of operation. Its only controls were an ambidextrous magazine catch, located on each side of the bottom of the trigger guard, a takedown button at the rear of the frame and, of course, the cocking lever that was incorporated as part of the frontstrap.

The cocking lever requires some 12 pounds of pressure to cock the striker but only a few pounds to keep it compressed.

After the last shot has been fired the slide is locked open. Releasing and compressing the slide releases it to close the action.

subsequent to the P-7M8 was a pistol that looked and operated almost identically to the P-7M8, but was called the P7PT8. The P7PT8 was never meant for use with live ammunition. Rather it was designed for use with plastic practice ammo. Not for tactical training exercises against human role players like Simunitions R modified pistols today, but for conventional style target practice in police station basements. (Live fire shooting ranges have always been scarce in West Germany and remain so to this day, even for law enforcement agencies.)

When the United States military told the world in the early 1980s the 1911 pistol would be replaced with a high capacity 9x19mm pistol, HK responded by developing the P7M13 that was submitted in the competition. The P7M13 used the same slide as the P7M8 but an entirely different frame and magazine. Due to the design parameters the high capacity 13 round magazine was somewhat funnel shaped. Unfortunately, it was probably the most expensive high-capacity 9x19mm pistol ever offered to the law enforcement or self-defense market during the 1980s and today are even more expensive when pre-ban P-7M13 magazines are offered for sale.

The P7K3 was actually a little smaller than the P7M8 because it was a different pistol, but it shared many of the same parts as its bigger brother. The P7K3 featured a barrel 3.8 inches in length and was available in three different calibers: 380 ACP, 32 ACP and 22 Long Rifle. Many who worked with the P7K3 felt it was the most accurate 380 ACP caliber pistol that was ever manufactured.

The last variant of the P7 design to be marketed by Heckler & Koch was the P7M10. This was their 40

S&W caliber version of this pistol and although the one I worked with many years ago functioned flawlessly and demonstrated great accuracy, I have to admit it was heavy, especially so when fully loaded with 10+1 180-gr 40 S&W rounds. I'm not sure what the fully loaded weight was, but empty the pistol weighed 39 ounces. So, the P7M10 suffered from excessive weight and what many felt was an exorbitant cost.

The Common Complaints

Because the P-7 utilized a gas-retarded action to delay the opening of the blowback action, it was essential to keep the gas cylinder clean. HK offered a gas cylinder cleaning brush as well as a gas cylinder reamer. Not only was carbon build-up a big problem with the P-7 gas cylinder but a poor choice in ammunition could absolutely render the pistol non-functional. Due to the gas port that bled gas into the cylinder it was impossible to shoot plain lead or cast lead bullets through a P-7. To do so was a quick way to plug up the gas cylinder with lead deposits and complicate the take-down because it sometimes froze the gas piston to the cylinder. Additionally, HK learned to their dismay that American shooters like to shoot reloaded ammunition that used plated bullets, and copper-plated bullets exhibited the same tendency to shave like cast lead bullets through the gas port into the gas cylinder. The P-7 design in

any form was a pistol that had to be kept spotlessly clean for complete reliability.

The biggest problem the P-7 faced in any of its variants, however, was the unintentional discharge of a loaded P-7 by its users. Especially troubling was the rate of negligent discharges among law enforcement officers equipped with an HK P-7. The problem became so severe in Germany that many departments formally banned the pistol from police use. In this country, departments like the New Jersey State Police simply got rid of them.

It's not that difficult to understand the problem when you realize that merely grasping the pistol cocks it. Add to this the fact it had an extremely light and smooth trigger and it is easy to see how a poorly trained or even a distracted officer could literally trigger an unintentional discharge. The idea behind the trigger was to eliminate the inconsistent trigger pull experience when the traditional double-action trigger

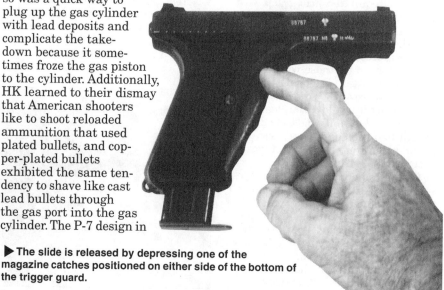

▶ The slide is released by depressing one of the magazine catches positioned on either side of the bottom of the trigger guard.

The field strip procedure is simple. Depressing the take down button releases the slide allowing it to be lifted up and off the rails.

The pistol takes down to four main components. Note the piston rod attached to the bottom of the slide. Gases are tapped from the chamber into a cylinder under the barrel to keep the action momentary closed on firing.

transitioned from the double action first shot to the subsequent single action second shot. In this respect, the trigger on the HK P-7 was extremely consistent and a literal joy on a formal target range, but where the problem arose was when the pistol was pulled quickly from the holster in an apparent life-threatening situation. It was not a pistol to be manipulated with course motor skills as it required fine motor skills for optimum operation and unfortunately these abilities are often lacking for most of us during periods of life-threatening stress.

That said the HK P-7 has always had a well earned reputation for accuracy. The fixed barrel and the gas retarded delayed blowback action together with the easy trigger pull created a combination of mechanical features that delivered extremely tight target groups for most any shooter. On the formal target with just a little instruction it was an easy

pistol for neophyte shooters to learn to shoot well because it was an easy gun to master in terms of shooter proficiency. It was the difficulty of controlling the pairing of the squeeze cocker shell with a light trigger that often proved to be the cause of the negligent discharge when drawn rapidly from the holster.

Conclusion

So, in answer to our original question, was the P-7 Squeeze-Cocker a pistol before its time or did time for the P-7 never exist in the first place? The general consensus of opinion would have to be that no matter how well made the Heckler & Koch P-7 was in any of its several variants, it was simply too 'different' for the market.

Yes, it answered all the requirements set forth by the German law enforcement requirements in the mid-1970s, and, yes, it was a great

piece of original engineering, but its execution failed to recognize the reality of lethal force confrontations. It failed, not because it was too difficult to use properly (unlike some of the products offered today), but because it was capable of firing when the operator wasn't aware he was actually pulling the trigger as he confronted a suspect.

Additionally, the P-7 was always a pistol that demanded a high degree of maintenance in the fact it had to be kept clean. It was never a pistol that you could ride hard, put up wet and then grab it in the morning and go again with complete confidence. Pure and simple, the gas cylinder was finicky in terms of carbon build-up as well as the ammunition fed through the gun. The net result of all this was it was soon realized it was not a pistol for military service whereas weapons in conflict may go days, if not weeks, without cleaning or service.

What will be remembered about the P-7 design is the fact it was an extremely accurate pistol. If one only shot on a formal target range where the conditions were far more controlled and the atmosphere somewhat relaxed in comparison to various duty activities, then the P-7 demonstrated qualities that many absolutely loved.

The thing that everyone will remember about the Heckler & Koch P-7 in any of its various variants is the fact it was the only pistol in the history of small arms to be known instantly as the "Squeeze-Cocker". •

The pistol has good high profile low-mount fixed sights. The extractor protrudes when the chamber is loaded.

Handloading for the

For large and dangerous animals the 44 Magnum is a good choice with the right loads. (*L-R*) a Sierra 180-grain JHP loaded with Hodgdon's H-110 is a fine choice for elk and other large animals, a Sierra 240-grain JHP in front of 23.0 grains of Hodgdon H-110 gives good penetration and expansion. A hardcast Keith SWC propelled by 20.5 grains of Alliant #2400 is the best all-around load, while a hardcast 280-grain flat-point in front of 18.0 grains of #2400 has great penetrative power.

Hunting Handgun

by Chuck Taylor

HAVING BEEN AN avid handgun hunter for over thirty years, I've watched with interest as the trend towards long-barreled, optically sighted handguns chambered for rifle cartridges continued to evolve. However, though such guns are irrefutably easier to bring home the bacon with, I've managed to resist the siren's song, preferring instead to utilize regular handguns and cartridges. To me, the limitations of the standard handgun make bagging a trophy game animal more difficult, is the whole point and the reason why I hunt with a handgun in the first place.

Why? Because I don't want it to be easier — I want it to be harder, more demanding, more challenging. I want it to demand superior stalking techniques and woodcraft, better marksmanship skills, more thoughtful load development. To me, though success is more elusive, it's considerably more satisfying when I overcome the limitations of conventional handguns, stalk closer, outsmart the animal at his own game and place the shot where it needs to be to put him down.

The result has been that I've spent the last three decades hunting all over the world with standard handguns. And as my skill increased, my preference for increased challenge caused me to utilize handguns of lesser and lesser power than before. As a result, I was forced to develop the loads needed to obtain my best efficiency with them. Indeed, developing a 9mm Parabellum or 38 Spl load that's capable of producing good results on game requires serious thought and extensive evaluation, both on the range and in the field.

When frangible bullets are utilized, maximum expansion is needed to produce the largest possible permanent wound channel. Yet, reliable expansion with JHPs has always been an elusive, if seductive, goal. Only careful bullet selection and load development can produce the velocities necessary to maximize the potential for expansion.

Of equal importance is that the loads are controllable and don't

A record book Fallow buck taken by the author at 100 meters with a single Sierra 180-grain JHP from a 6-inch S&W M29 44 Magnum.

(*Left*)6.0-grains of Alliant Unique behind a Hornady 90-grain XTP is a superb 9mm load for small and medium game, delivering 1300 fps from a 4 1/4-inch barrels. (*Right*) Best 45ACP load is 7.5 grains of Alliant Unique and a Hornady 165-grain XTP JHP performing extremely well out to 50-meters or so.

abuse the weapons in which they're used. Recoil is fully as much of an issue in the game field where quick follow-up shots might be needed. Penetration, too, is needed, because the bullet must reach vital organs to be effective and in order for that to happen, it must often smash through bones or substantial muscle bulk in the process.

So, over the past thirty or so years, I've spent a great deal of time, energy and, yes, money, pursuing the art and science of developing the best loads possible for each cartridge used in my hunting handguns – the 9mmP, 38 Spl. 357 magnum, 40 auto, 10mm auto, 44 Spl. 44 Magnum, 45 ACP, 45 Auto Rim and 45 Colt.

Now over a century old, the 9mm parabellum has gained considerable proliferation as a military service cartridge, but has not enjoyed much use as a hunting cartridge due to its minimal power. However, while the number of handguns chambered for it has increased fifty-fold, it continues to have a marginal reputation.

However, when Hornady introduced their XTP line of jacketed hollow points a few years ago, this all changed. The 90-grain XTP, loaded over 6.0 grains of Alliant UNIQUE (1300 fps from the 4 1/4-inch barrels typically found on 9mm service pistols), produces not only exceptional accuracy, but astonishing lethality and stopping power as well.

So much so, in fact, that those who witness its use on small and even medium game are astonished at its efficiency, noting that it mirrors the 357 Magnum, but without its heavy recoil or muzzle blast. Time and time again, I've been amazed how well it works—for the last five years downing a plethora of jackrabbits, cottontails, foxes and coyotes and bobcats with little difficulty.

But it doesn't stop there. It *also* works very well out to 75 meters or so on larger animals like whitetail, Sika, Fallow, Axis and mule deer, Catalina goats, Javelina and even mountain lion. Performance is text-

UNIQUE with a 110-grain XTP on small and medium game all the time, noting that it produces 1200 fps from my favorite 6-inch barreled S&W M14. It's also so accurate that I prefer it to a rifle out to 50 meters or so.

In the 357, this same 110-grain reaches over 1500 fps in a 6-inch barrel, expands completely and, surprisingly, considering its weight, stays together perfectly. Even in a 4-inch tube, it reaches over 1400 fps, which is plenty fast enough for expansion, but exhibits very little recoil. For some years now, I've been using it on small and medium game with excellent results.

For the larger medium game species such as mule deer and mountain lion, the 357 Magnum has much going for it, especially with the Remington 140-grain JHP, loaded with 16.0 grains of Alliant #2400. This excellent load produces 1420 fps from my 6-inch Colt Python, demonstrates excellent penetration and expansion and fine accuracy, all without too much recoil or muzzle blast. I even have a friend who's a hunting guide who swears it works beautifully on elk, too!

However, my preference for such critters is the hardcast

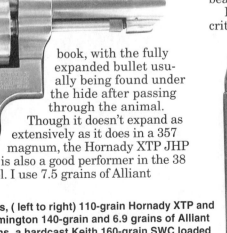

book, with the fully expanded bullet usually being found under the hide after passing through the animal. Though it doesn't expand as extensively as it does in a 357 magnum, the Hornady XTP JHP is also a good performer in the 38 Spl. I use 7.5 grains of Alliant

Author's preferred 38 Spl. Loads, (left to right) 110-grain Hornady XTP and 7.5 grains of Alliant Unique, Remington 140-grain and 6.9 grains of Alliant Unique and for heavy-framed guns, a hardcast Keith 160-grain SWC loaded with 12.0 grains of Alliant #2400.

Author's favorite 357 Magnum hunting loads are (left to right) Hornady 110-grain XTP JHP and 18.5-grains of Alliant #2400, Remington 140-grain JHP and 16.0-grains of #2400 and finally a hardcast 160-grain SWC and 14.0-grains of #2400.

Keith SWC (Lyman #358477) and 14.0 grains of #2400. From a 6-inch barrel, it reaches a bit over 1350 fps, penetrates marvelously and cuts a full-caliber permanent wound channel while it punches its way through bones and heavy muscle.

In my opinion, because of the limited velocities at which it can be driven, the 40 auto should be used with a 155-grain bullet, once again with the Hornady XTP being my choice. Loaded with 7.5 grains of UNIQUE, it reaches slightly over 1000 fps from a standard 4 1/4-inch service pistol barrel, nearly 1100 fps from a 5-inch Springfield Armory XD-40 Tactical and a full 1150 fps

from a 6-inch barreled Glock 24 longslide. Recoil is completely manageable and muzzle blast is minimal.

The hotter 10mm auto can be loaded somewhat hotter; of course, producing almost 1200 fps with the same bullet when loaded with 8.0 grains of UNIQUE and fired from either a Colt Delta or Glock 20. Recoil and muzzle blast are more pronounced, but remain tolerable. With 13.0 grains of #2400, the 180-grain XTP reaches a bit over 1100 fps, and provides just a bit more penetration for larger types of medium game like mule deer.

Long a favorite of mine, the 44 Spl. can be made to perform so well

as to perhaps be considered as being the best balanced of all the standard cartridges. From a 6 1/2-inch barrel, the Sierra 180-grain JHP and 19.0 grains of #2400 produces over 1300 fps, is highly accurate, expands quite well out to 75 meters or so and demonstrates only moderate recoil and muzzle blast. For all types of small, medium and even some larger animals like elk, it's therefore a fine choice.

If you're going after bigger, nastier critters like Russian boar or bear, a hardcast Keith 250-grain SWC and 15.5 grains of #2400 is hard to beat. From a 4-inch tube, 1076 fps is fairly typical, while from

Author's favorite 44 Special loads his preferred cartridge are (*left to right*) Sierra 180-grain JHP and 19.0-grains of Alliant #2400, Hornady XTP 240-grain JHP and 15-grains of Alliant #2400 and a Keith 250-hardcast SWC and 15.5-grains of Alliant-2400.

Author in the field shooting one of his favorite hunting handguns, a 6-inch Colt Python 357 Magnum.

a 6 1/2-inch barrel 1170 fps is easily achieved, providing good penetration and bone-breaking ability without too much recoil or muzzled blast. In fact, this particular load is my all-time favorite in the 44 Spl.

For those who prefer a heavy, frangible bullet, the Hornady XTP 240-grain JHP and 15.0 grains of #2400 is just what the doctor ordered. Accurate, tough and demonstrating good expansion out to a full 75 meters, it offers a nice balance of efficiency and weapon controllability.

In the mighty 44 Magnum, the Sierra 180-grain JHP produces only moderate recoil, superb accuracy, ultra-high velocities (which guarantee bullet expansion), good penetration and, for a 44 Maggie, low muzzle blast. Moreover, it's muzzle velocity of over 1500 fps gives it a nice, flat trajectory, allowing you to zero it at 75 or even 100 meters instead of the usual 50.

Sierra's 240-grain JHP and 23.0 grains of Hodgdon H-110 will give you almost 1300 fps from a 4-inch barreled S&W M29, while a 6 1/2-inch barrel boosts it to slightly over

The 45 Auto rim is another author favorite. (From left to right) Hornady 185-grain XTP JHP and 8.5-grains of Alliant Unique (for small to medium game),Speer 200-grain JHP and 8.0-grains of Unique (for small game) Sierra 240-grain JHP and 13.5- grains of #2400 (larger and thin-skinned game) and a hard cast Keith 250-grain SWC and 14.0-grains of #2400(for large and dangerous game).

1400 fps. Accuracy is good, though recoil is, shall we say, "noticeable." Penetration and bullet expansion is also excellent, so good, in fact, that many regard this particular load as being the best all-around 44 Magnum load available.

The Keith SWC (Lyman # 429421) with 20.5 grains of #2400 gives just under 1300 fps from a 4-inch S&W M29 and just over 1400 fps from a 6-incher. As with the 240-grain JHP load, recoil and muzzle blast is substantial, but penetration and bone-breaking ability is nothing less than superb, making it a fine choice for Russian boar, bear and other critters with potential anti-social tendencies!

If you really want to slam-dunk something, try the Buffalo Bullets 280-grain flat-point and 18.0

Recovered bullets from animals shot by author. (From left to right) 90-grain 9mm XTP JHP from a mule deer, 110-grain Hornady XTP JHP 357 Magnum from white tail buck, 140-grain Remington 357Magnum JHP, 180-grain JHP 44 Special from a mule deer and two hardcast Keith 250-grain SWCs from a black bear and a Russian boar respectively.

25-meter, 5-shot group shot over the author's jeep hood with a 5-inch S&W M625-2 using a 45 Auto Rim loaded with a 165-grain Hornady XTP JHP and 8.5-grains of Unique.

grains of #2400. Although not what I'd call fierce, recoil is, shall we say, substantial, and thus this particular load isn't for the faint of heart. But for big nasty beasties, it certainly gets the job done in direct proportion to how well you do yours as a marksman.

Long an underrated cartridge, the 45-Auto Rim can be made to perform quite admirably with the Hornady 185-grain XTP JHP and 8.5 grains of UNIQUE. From a 5-inch barreled S&W M625-2, 1150 fps is easily achieved and accuracy (one inch or better at 25 meters) is outstanding. I've shot several hundred jackrabbits with this particular load and found it to be devastating, literally turning them inside-out, but on whitetail or mule deer, it offers surprisingly good penetration as well as expansion.

For bigger animals like elk, boar and bear, the Sierra 240-grain JHP and 13.5 grains of #2400 gives right at 1000 fps from a 50-inch barrel and nearly 1050 fps from a 6-inch. Accuracy with this load, too, is excellent, though recoil is also substantial.

And, of course, if you want the best penetration and bone-breaking ability possible, the Keith 250-grain SWC (Lyman # 452424) and 14.0 grains of #2400 is as good as it gets. Also exceptionally accurate, it offers a full-caliber wound channel and fine penetration, making it a wonderful choice for elk, moose, bears and boars.

In a 7 1/2-inch Ruger Blackhawk, the venerable 45 Colt can also perform admirably on medium and large game. A Speer 200-grain JHP with 12.0 grains of UNIQUE and produces a little over 1400 fps, accuracy like a rifle and yet surprisingly moderate recoil and muzzle blast,

45 Colt can be loaded for higher performance. Taylor prefers (*left to right*) the Speer 200-grain JH with 12.0 grains of Unique for his Ruger, while for his S&W M25-2 he favors the Hornady 250-grain XTP JHP and 19.0-grains of #2400.

Texas whitetail buck dropped with a single hit at 55 meters with a Ruger Blacxkhawk 45 Colt and a Hornady 250-grain JHP.

making it a fine load for small and medium game.

At 1150 fps, 19.0 grains of #2400 and the Hornady XTP 250-grain JHP provide equally superb accuracy, but just a bit more recoil and muzzle blast, but not so much as to be considered oppressive. Bullet expansion is also quite good, often reaching the size of a five-cent piece of larger.

In fact, while on a Texas whitetail and Javelina hunt a few years ago, I encountered a nice boar at 60 meters. Obviously hoping to break visual contact with me, he quickly moved to a small clump of mesquite and stood very still, but his midsection was exposed, giving me a shot. Going kneeling, I quickly nailed him, noting a pronounced "Ooof!" when the bullet struck, knocking him down for good. Subsequent examination disclosed that the bullet had fully expanded, lodging on the off side under the hide—textbook performance.

Last, for big and/or hostile creatures, the Keith 250-grain SWC, also with 19.0 grains of #2400, is a fine choice. It gives excellent penetration, breaks bones spectacularly well and shoots into an inch at 25 meters in nearly any handgun in which it's used. I've used it on Russian boar, elk and mountain lion without a single failure and regard it as being the best general-purpose 45 Colt load available.

These, then, are my favorite handloads for handgun hunting. They've been developed, refined and proven by actual field use over the last 30 years and successfully bagged hundreds of animals, most with a single hit. They're all highly accurate, dependable and efficient and will give you good service if you "put 'em where they'll do the most good!"

Try them. I think you'll agree. Good luck and good hunting! ●

AUTHOR'S PREFERRED HUNTING HANDLOADS

CARTRIDGE	LOAD	POWDER	BULLET	WT.	B/LGTH	VEL
9mm Para	6.0	UNIQUE	Horn XTPJHP	90	4 1/4	1300
9mm Para	6.0	UNIQUE	Horn XTPJHP	90	5	1370
9mm Para	6.0	UNIQUE	Horn XTP JHP	90	6	1412
38 SPL	7.5	UNIQUE	Horn XTP JHP	110	4	1070
38 SPL	7.5	UNIQUE	Horn XTP JHP	110	6	1200
38 SPL	6.0	UNIQUE	REM JHP	140	6	1000
38 SPL	12.0	2400	Keith SWC	160	6	1050
357 MAG	18.5	2400	Horn XTP JHP	110	4	1488
357 MAG	18.5	2400	Horn XTP JHP	110	6 1/2	1570
357 MAG	16.0	2400	Rem JHP	140	6 1/2	1420
357 MAG	14.0	2400	Keith SWC	160	6 1/2	1360
40 AUTO	7.5	UNIQUE	Horn XTP JHP	155	4 1/4	1023
40 AUTO	7.5	UNIQUE	Horn XTP JHP	155	5	1080
40 AUTO	7.5	UNIQUE	Horn XTP JHP	155	6	1150
10mm	8.0	UNIQUE	Horn XTP JHP	155	5	1190
10mm	3.0	2400	Horn XTP JHP	180	5	1120
44 SPL	9.0	2400	Sierra JHP	180	6 1/2	1320
44 SPL	15.0	2400	Horn XTP JHP	240	4	1040
44 SPL	15.0	2400	Horn XTP JHP	240	6 1/2	1140
44 SPL	15.5	2400	Keith SWC	250	4	1076
44 SPL	5.5	2400	Keith SWC	250	6 1/2	1170
44 MAG	28.0	H-110	Sierra JHP	180	6 1/2	1542
44 MAG	23.0	H-110	Sierra JHP	240	4	1270
44 MAG	23.0	H-110	Sierra JHP	240	6 1/2	1434
44 MAG	20.5	2400	Keith SWC	250	4	1290
44 MAG	20.5	2400	Keith SWC	250	6 1/2	1412
44 MAG	18.0	2400	Flat Point	280	4	999
44 MAG	18.0	2400	Flat Point	280	6 1/2	1090
45 ACP	7.5	UNIQUE	Horn XTP JHP	185	5	1030
45 AR	8.5	UNIQUE	Horn XTP JHP	185	5	1150
45 AR	8.5	UNIQUE	Horn XTP JHP	185	6 1/2	1220
45 AR	8.0	UNIQUE	Speer JHP	200	5	1054
45 AR	8.0	UNIQUE	Speer JHP	200	6 1/2	1101
45 AR	3.5	2400	Sierra JHP	240	5	1001
45 AR	13.5	2400	Sierra JHP	240	6 1/2	1043
45 AR	14.0	2400	Keith SWC	250	5	1060
45 AR	14.0	2400	Keith SWC	250	6 1/2	1098
45 COLT	12.0	UNIQUE	Speer JHP	200	7 1/2	1410
45 COLT	19.0	2400	Horn XTP JHP	250	7 1/2	1150
45 COLT	19.0	2400	Keith SWC	250	7 1/2	1170

SELF-DEFENSE/CONCEALED CARRY

The Evolution of Defensive Handguns

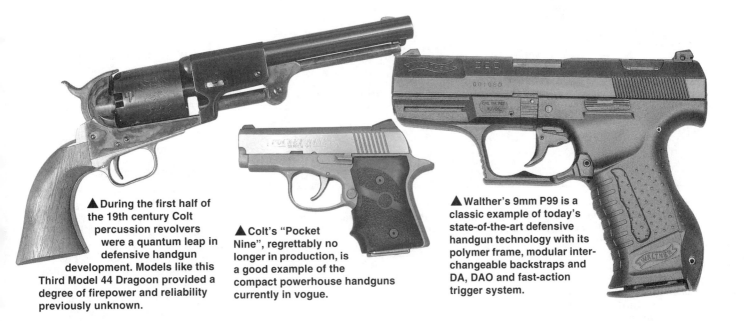

▲ During the first half of the 19th century Colt percussion revolvers were a quantum leap in defensive handgun development. Models like this Third Model 44 Dragoon provided a degree of firepower and reliability previously unknown.

▲ Colt's "Pocket Nine", regrettably no longer in production, is a good example of the compact powerhouse handguns currently in vogue.

▲ Walther's 9mm P99 is a classic example of today's state-of-the-art defensive handgun technology with its polymer frame, modular inter-changeable backstraps and DA, DAO and fast-action trigger system.

by David W. Arnold

THE HANDGUN HAS always been considered an important tool for self-defense since the first pistols appeared on the scene several centuries ago. This was especially so as pistols developed and became more portable and reliable. Early wheellock and flintlock pistols tended to be large, awkward and cumbersome. Such pistols were generally confined to carry in horse holsters attached to saddles. As pistols became more compact and reliable, they became more attractive for personal defense by gentleman to ward off attacks by footpads and other undesirables.

Further design advances such as the percussion cap and the revolver made handguns more desirable as personal defense arms. These improvements made handguns more attractive to the military and law enforcement. It is therefore not surprising that the civilian handgun market has been heavily influenced by what soldiers and police carry.

Handguns of the Frontier

The age of discovery, both in this country and elsewhere, increased the civilian demand for reliable firearms to put food on the table as well as to ward off attacks from predators—animal and human. Initially, settlers choose rifles and shotguns because they were better suited for hunting.

Over the years Colt percussion revolvers were refined by being made more compact. This 1852 Navy (*top*) and 1861 New Model Navy (*bottom*) were very popular with Civil War soldiers and frontiersmen alike.

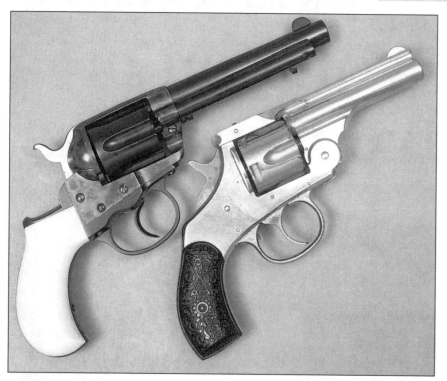

The introduction of double-action revolver saw the appearance of a variety of small inexpensive revolvers like this Harrington & Richardson break-top (*right*). Colt also introduced their more compact 38 Lightening revolver (*left*), the company's first double-action revolver.

Lawlessness in frontier towns created a need for firearms that were portable. The handgun was well suited for such use and the development of the first practical revolvers came just at the right time. As firearms were carried openly, civilians chose handguns used by the military—such as revolvers made by Colt, Remington and Smith & Wesson.

Although companies like Colt did good business making guns for civilian use, many probably acquired their revolvers from previous military service during the Civil and Indian wars. The Colt Single Action frontier revolver was equally popular with frontiersmen of all stripes, as well as the military and law officers.

There was some demand for more concealable handguns among gamblers, women of the night and others who frequented the saloons and bawdyhouses. They were well served with small revolvers of various manufacturers and a variety of single- and double-barrel derringers.

In the more settled eastern urban centers crime was the main concern of the average citizen then as it is today. While the same types of handguns were popular, guns were not carried openly as they were on the frontier. Smaller, more compact, handguns were more popular and by the end of the 19th century saw a proliferation of small inexpensive revolvers, usually of the break-top-design. These were often called "Suicide Specials", because they were cheap and purchased by individuals bent on self-destruction. Reputable manufacturers, like Colt and Smith & Wesson, also catered to this market by offering a line of smaller revolvers intended for home protection and concealed carry.

In the exploration of other remote lands such as Africa, Australia and India, civilians faced similar dangers. While many used American-made handguns, domestically made handguns were also adopted. The British-made Deane & Adams, Webley & Scott and Trantor revolvers saw considerable service in colonizing Britain's rapidly expanding overseas empire.

Double-Action Revolver Era

By the turn of the century, both here and elsewhere, frontiers had been largely settled. While the need for firearms to survive had largely diminished, there were now concerns of rising urban crime. The latest revolvers were the new double-action models and these were soon to be adopted by an increasing number of police forces. By now civilians were looking to see what the police were using when deciding what handgun to purchase. Consequently, handgun manufacturers found that what was popular with police sold equally well to the average citizen.

The swing-out cylinder double-action revolver that was generally found in most police holsters was considered the ultimate defense handgun. For a long period, both before and after World War II, the civilian and law enforcement handgun market was divided between Colt Fire-

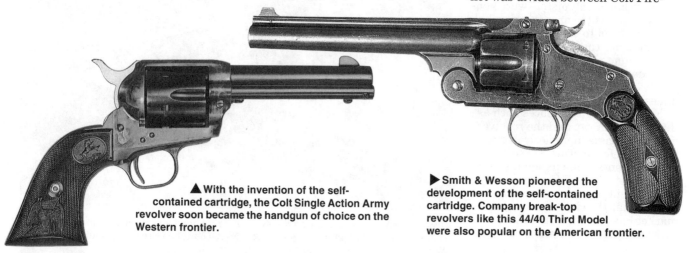

▲ With the invention of the self-contained cartridge, the Colt Single Action Army revolver soon became the handgun of choice on the Western frontier.

► Smith & Wesson pioneered the development of the self-contained cartridge. Company break-top revolvers like this 44/40 Third Model were also popular on the American frontier.

When police departments began to adopt Colt and Smith & Wesson revolvers models like this Colt Police Positive Special enjoyed good civilian sales.

Colt's short-barrel Detective Special introduced the concept of the compact revolver. Two inches was the common barrel length, although this 32 version has a three-inch barrel.

arms and Smith & Wesson. Two popular revolvers were the Colt Official Police and the Smith & Wesson Military & Police (later known as the Model 10) — or variations of both.

By 1950, police departments were issuing detectives, plainclothes personnel and off-duty officers short barrel small-frame 38 Special revolvers like the Colt Detective Special and Smith & Wesson's J-frame models. The lightweight aluminum-frame models like the Chief's Special Air weight, Colt Agent and Cobra were also popular. These revolvers also enjoyed considerable popularity among civilians because of their compactness and ease of concealment. And, in one form or another, they remained the main police and civilian defensive arms in this country right until the time departments began to make the changeover to the semi-automatic pistol in the 1980s.

During the 1960s Smith & Wesson had obtained a major share of the police revolver market, eventually becoming the dominant force by the mid-1970s. Colt retained a share of the civilian market, but Sturm, Ruger began to seriously challenge Smith & Wesson's domination of police sales with a line of reasonably priced, rugged and reliable double-action revolvers.

For many years the most used defensive revolvers tended to be of the fixed-sight type. Post-war revolvers began to display improved features such as better adjustable sights and large target grips. These were developed as the result of the demands of civilian target shooters and handgun hunters.

While the 38 Special round remained the cartridge of choice throughout the revolver era, more powerful calibers like the 357 Magnum were also introduced. These

cartridges had increased stopping power, but it came at a price. One problem was that the magnum revolvers tended to be big and cumbersome, and it presented problems for shooters with small hands. This was compounded by the difficulty of handling the violent recoil of the magnum ammunition.

The situation changed when mid-frame magnum revolvers were developed, like the Colt 357 and Python. They were user-friendlier for smaller hands. In the case of the Python, its heavy barrel with a full-length under lug helped in controlling recoil.

Smith & Wesson responded with their Model 19, a 357 Magnum using the popular medium-size K-frame. In terms of grip and general handling qualities, this is possibly

the most user-friendly service revolver of all time. As a result, the Model 19 and 66 (a stainless steel version) became one of the most popular law enforcement handguns of the period and was equally popular with civilians.

After some years in service, Smith & Wesson's K-frame 357 Magnums displayed evidence of accelerated wear from the continual use of magnum ammunition. This prompted the company to introduce the L-frame that is a compromise in size between the K-and L-frames. Towards the end of the 1960s Smith & Wesson introduced the first revolver to be made of stainless steel. Before long, the company was offering stainless versions of all its popular models.

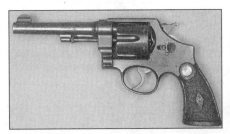

Smith & Wesson swing-out cylinder revolvers like this Model 1917 45 ACP enabled the company to become a major player in the defense handgun market.

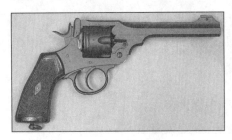

Large-caliber Webley & Scott break-top revolvers like this saw much use in the colonizing of the British Empire.

Revolvers like these enabled Smith & Wesson to obtain a dominant position in the defense handgun market for many years. (*From the top*) A model 65, a stainless steel 357 Magnum version of the famous Military & Police. A Model 66, the stainless steel version of the very popular Model 19 357 Magnum.

In Europe both police and civilians accepted auto pistols as defensive arms. The Walther PP series like this PPK/S are classic pistols that introduced the concept of the double-action auto pistol.

Although the semi-automatic pistol took some time to play a dominant role as a defensive handgun, there were exceptions: the Colt Government Model 45 of 1911 and the Colt Pocket pistol.

While revolvers continue to be used for civilian defense, many citizens have followed the police lead and switched to the semi-automatic pistol.

Auto Pistol as a Defensive Firearm

While the auto pistol was popular with both civilians and police in Europe, these arms took far longer to be accepted in America. This was in spite of the fact that the U.S. military adopted the Government Model 45 auto pistol in 1911. This pistol enjoyed some popularity with police officers, especially in the Southwest and in agencies where officers were allowed to choose their own personal arms. In addition, the chambering of the 1911 for the high velocity 38 Super during the 1930s made it a good choice for use against motorized robber gangs. The Government Model, therefore, saw some use by lawmen of the Roaring Twenties and Depression era.

The 1911 also enjoyed some popularity with civilians, possibly those who served in the Great War in Europe. Compact semi-automatics like the Colt Pocket pistol of 1908 were also popular with police and civilians.

A major strike against the auto pistol had been a poor reputation for reliability. Very often this was ammunition related. By the 1980s, however, improvements in both ammunition and auto pistol design had successfully made unreliability a problem of the past. Another perceived detraction was that the auto pistol was more complex than the revolver to operate and shoot. Having to cycle slides or disengage safeties slowed down getting such pistols into action.

The development of double-action auto pistols, like the Walther P38 provided a handgun with a trigger that is close to the revolver for the first shot and almost identical, in the case of double-action-only models.

In 1949, Smith & Wesson introduced America's first double-action 9mm auto pistol in the form of the Model 39, initially in the hope that it would be adopted by the military as a replacement for the Colt Government Model 45 pistol. When this did not occur, Smith & Wesson continued to manufacture the pistol for the civilian market and possible law enforcement market. The latter did not materialize until 1960 when the Illinois State Police made history by switching to the Model 39, becoming the first major American law enforcement agency to adopt a self-loading handgun.

The Illinois State Police decision did not result in a large number of other departments following suit.

After World War II, the Colt Python (*top*) started a trend of revolvers with full-lug, heavy barrels. Smith & Wesson responded with the Model 686 (*bottom*).

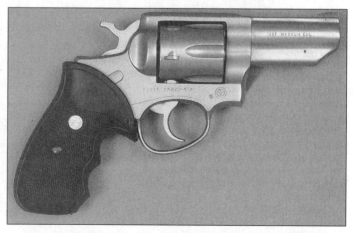

During the 1970s, Sturm Ruger challenged Smith & Wesson's dominance of the defensive revolver market with a line of rugged, reliable revolvers like this 357 Speed Six.

SELF-DEFENSE/CONCEALED CARRY

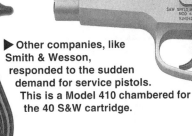

▶ Auto pistols were accepted and began to displace the revolver as the premier police and civilian defense handgun when the U.S. military chose the 9mm double-action Beretta Model 92 to replace the Colt 1911.

▶ Other companies, like Smith & Wesson, responded to the sudden demand for service pistols. This is a Model 410 chambered for the 40 S&W cartridge.

While a few smaller departments did switch to auto pistols, the majority of law enforcement departments elected to retain the revolver. The departments that did adopt or authorize auto pistols did not all choose the 9mm Smith & Wesson Model 39. A number adopted the Colt Government Model 45, perceiving it as having superior stopping power.

In addition, by the late 1970s handgun manufacturers were offering a new type of 9mm pistol with magazine capacities in excess of 11 rounds. In 1958, Smith & Wesson came out with their 14-shot version of the Model 39. Designated as the Model 59 it was adopted by a few agencies.

What really tipped the scales was the adoption of the 9mm Beretta 92, a double-action 15-shot by the U.S. military in 1985, as the country's new service pistol. This occurred at a time when there was a perception in the law enforcement community that drug dealers and street gangs were arming themselves with high-firepower firearms.

A number of departments began to replace their revolvers with 92s. Other handgun companies like Smith & Wesson, who lost out to Beretta in the military trials, found a ready market for their double-action pistols in law enforcement.

Initially the switch from revolver to auto pistol was limited to a few departments, but within a few years the trickle became a flood as more and more agencies began to adopt auto pistols. This demand created frenzy among handgun manufacturers as they rushed to grab a share of the police handgun market. In the early days major players were Beretta, Smith & Wesson and SIG-Sauer. This switch from the revolver to the auto pistol did not pass unnoticed by the public and civilian sales of double-action, high-capacity auto pistols showed a significant rise.

But the switch from revolver to double-action pistol had its problems. Departments found they had to invest in good training programs if the problems with safety manipulation, previously mentioned, were to be avoided. In addition, some officers experienced difficulty transitioning from the long, heavy double-action trigger pull for the first shot to the subsequent shorter, lighter trigger. Some other manufacturers provided an answer with double-action-only pistols that had the same long heavy pull for all shots. Since the hammer was never cocked on these pistols, they were simpler to operate. Having a trigger action so similar to the revolver also made training much easier.

One pistol that had a dramatic impact on American police agencies was the Austrian Glock pistol. Initially the pistol received bad press, reporting its plastic frame could not be detected by airport detection systems. When this was proved false, it was soon discovered that the pistol had many attributes that made it attractive to law enforcement. It has also proved to be a popular firearm with civilians. Today Glock has replaced Smith & Wesson as the major supplier of police handguns. Other handgun companies scrambled to come out with polymer pistols of their own design. As a result virtually all the major handgun companies have at least one plastic or polymer frame pistol in their inventory.

In terms of caliber, the 9mm was the choice of most agencies mainly because of the large number that could be accommodated in auto pistol magazines. It was not universally welcomed, however, as some questioned its stopping power effectiveness.

The Austrian Glock 17 grabbed a large share of the defensive handgun market and introduced the concept of a plastic frame. This pistol has had a laser aiming module added to it.

Most major handgun companies have followed Glock by introducing polymer-frame auto pistols of their own. Shown here is a S&W Sigma SW40 (*top*) and a Walther P99 (*bottom*).

This Para-Ordnance P14 is a good illustration of the current trend of developing large-caliber, high- capacity, very compact handguns intended for concealed carry.

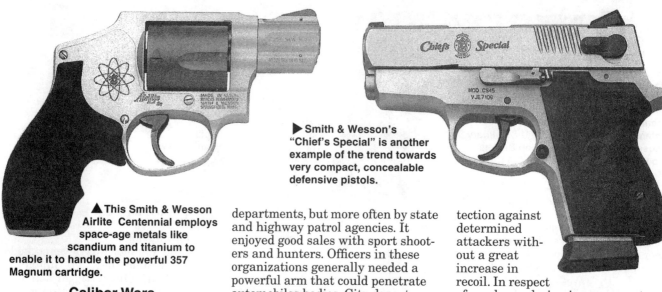

▶ Smith & Wesson's "Chief's Special" is another example of the trend towards very compact, concealable defensive pistols.

▲ This Smith & Wesson Airlite Centennial employs space-age metals like scandium and titanium to enable it to handle the powerful 357 Magnum cartridge.

Caliber Wars

During the revolver era law enforcement's cartridge of choice was the S&W 38 Special. The loading was invariably a 158-grain round nose lead bullet. Smith & Wesson introduced this cartridge in 1902. It was intended as a military cartridge to replace the unsatisfactory 38 Long Colt cartridge that had been found wanting in terms of stopping power during the Philippine insurrection of 1899 – 1913.

While the Special is quite similar to the 38 Long Colt in terms of performance, the former is a far more versatile cartridge. Because of its many virtues it remained the main American police and civilian defensive cartridge used right up until the semi-automatic pistol displaced the revolver.

The 38 Special was not immune from criticism and by the late 1950s and all through the '60s its effectiveness was questioned. During the 1930s there had been a number of attempts to improve the firepower of law enforcement, especially in the light of the motorized bank robbers of the time. The 38 Special had been found to be ineffective against motor vehicles and body armor. As a result, some police began to adopt larger calibers, like the 44 and 45. In addition, the firearms industry responded with more potent cartridges like the 38 Super and the S&W 357 Magnum. The latter cartridge was especially suited to the police revolvers because its bore dimensions were the same as the 38 Special. This meant that a 357 Magnum revolver could chamber and fire both cartridges.

During the 1930s the 357 Magnum was adopted by a few police departments, but more often by state and highway patrol agencies. It enjoyed good sales with sport shooters and hunters. Officers in these organizations generally needed a powerful arm that could penetrate automobiles bodies. City departments were hesitant to follow suit because of the possible danger to innocent bystanders from the high penetration ability of the magnum.

After the war a few departments did permit officers to carry the 357 Magnum, and even the more powerful 44 Magnum. Even though some departments adopted 357 Magnum revolvers, many restricted officers to carrying 38 Special ammunition. Generally civilians also preferred to feed their 357 Magnum revolvers with the milder, more pleasant-shooting 38 Special.

In an attempt to improve the police revolver's effectiveness, several handgun writers (notably Elmer Keith and Duke Roberts), called for a new cartridge of 40 caliber or larger. Smith & Wesson and Remington responded with a 41-caliber revolver and cartridge. In respect of the latter, both magnum and standard loads were offered.

Unfortunately, neither the revolver nor the cartridge was accepted in the numbers anticipated. One reason was probably its stiff recoil, while another was that 41 Magnum revolvers were big—often the same size as 44 Magnum revolvers. For this reason the 41 Magnum was not a hit with civilians, although it did garner a small and dedicated following among some handgun hunters.

The need for the 41 or other large calibers diminished by the 1970s as improvements in both 38 revolvers and ammunition largely overcame the stopping power problem. Ammunition companies began to offer improved high-velocity 38 Special ammunition with expanding bullets. Designated as +P and +P+ loads, this ammunition provided more protection against determined attackers without a great increase in recoil. In respect of revolvers, design improvements such as heavy barrels and better grip design helped make the increased recoil less intimidating. By the late 1970s and early 1980s law enforcement was facing a new perceived problem—firepower.

9mm Stopping Power Controversy

The adoption of the 9mm Luger cartridge as a replacement for the 45 ACP by the U.S. military drew considerable criticism from some quarters, mostly from adherents of the Colt 1911. These views seemed to be vindicated when two FBI agents were killed and four seriously wounded in a violent shooting confrontation with two heavily armed bank robbers in Florida during the fall of 1985. The bank robber's firearm was a 223 Ruger Mini 14 while the agents were armed with shotguns and their issue 38 Special and 9mm handguns.

Even though both robbers received several serious wounds, they continued to fight to the end. The most lethal bank robber, who was armed with the Mini-14, continued to fire even after he sustained one bullet wound that would prove to be eventually fatal. Ironically, an agent firing the 4-inch revolver loaded with 38 Specials neutralized him.

This incident caused the FBI to conduct an extensive study of the incident and bullet effectiveness. The study involved seeking the opinions of a number of firearm and ballistic authorities. The FBI drew up criteria for the ideal police cartridge based largely on laboratory data based on penetration, wound channel size and expansion obtained in ballistic gelatin. As a

▲ The use of titanium and scandium has been extended to large revolvers like this Smith & Wesson 44 Magnum "Mountain Lite."

result of this study, the FBI adopted a down-loaded version of a commercial 10mm cartridge that had been developed several years previously for an auto pistol called the Bren Ten. It was not a commercial success and only a few pistols were made for the cartridge, which was more powerful than the 45 ACP. Because it developed considerable recoil, the proposed FBI 10mm was reduced to be between the 45ACP and the 9mm in terms of power. Smith & Wesson agreed to develop a pistol for the cartridge.

Ironically Smith & Wesson, in collaboration with the Winchester ammunition company, had already developed a similar round in terms of ballistic performance. The cartridge called the 40 S&W had the same diameter as the 10mm but had a shorter case. This enabled the cartridge to be accommodated in a pistol of roughly the same size as the 9mm models being made by the company with very little modification. More important was the fact that the magazine capacity was not compromised to the same extent as the 10mm. In addition, the 10mm required a larger pistol to handle its greater power.

Even though there was very little difference in performance between the 40 and 10mm, the FBI declined to adopt 40 and stayed with the 10mm. Smith & Wesson's Model 1076 was adopted as the handgun for the new cartridge.

Unlike the FBI, other agencies were interested in the 40 S&W. The California Highway Patrol was the first major agency to adopt the new cartridge. When they announced interest in the 40, Glock quickly developed a pistol to compete against the Smith & Wesson pistol. The latter, however, was the pistol selected. Since then more and more

agencies have adopted the 40 S&W and most manufacturers now offer a pistol chambered for it.

During the 1990s, a cartridge that may prove as popular in the form of a bottleneck cartridge has joined the 40 S&W. Called the 357 SIG after the company that developed it, the new round has a performance similar to the famed revolver cartridge of the same caliber and it has been adopted by a number of agencies.

Cartridge development continued with ammunition companies producing ammunition with better performance in the areas of penetration and expansion. One of the downsides of the former is that rapid expansion can limit penetration into the vital areas of the body. In addition obstructions such as walls and glass can wreak havoc on expanding bullet's ability to penetrate.

Special ammunition is now being made that will penetrate human flesh and obstacles, including car windscreens, without losing effectiveness. There is also frangible ammunition that increases wounding by fragmenting. Such ammunition is also generally less likely to ricochet and injure innocent bystanders.

There is no doubt that over the last 50 years, improvements in ammunition have greatly increased handgun effectiveness far more than advances in the actual design of handguns. Serious civilian shooters pay close attention to police ammunition trends and generally use loads that are similar or close to what the cops use.

Bigger Yet Smaller

The last few years of the 20th century saw a number of important developments in handgun technology. The most significant is the use of space-age metals such as titanium, scandium and synthetic polymers in handgun construction.

These materials came at a time when there was an increased civilian demand for small, powerful and easily concealed handguns. The relaxing of concealed carry restriction by an increasing number of states prompted this.

Handgun makers have responded to this demand by developing an increasing number of small large-caliber, light revolvers and auto pis-

▶ This 40 S&W 40 tactical pistol has a rail in front of the trigger guard for mounting accessories such as flash-lights and laser aiming modules.

tols. This can be seen in an increase of very compact auto pistols chambered for large calibers such as 9mm, 40 S&W and 45 ACP.

Revolver advancement can be seen in the increase in short-barrel small revolvers chambered for powerhouse cartridges like the 357 Magnum. Cylinder capacities have also been increased. Today revolvers with 7- or 8-shot cylinders have become the rule instead of the exception.

Summary

A review of the history of defense handguns begs the question, just how good are the handguns of today compared to those of the past? The fact is that as far as handgun design is concerned, there has really been very little of significance since the 1930s in respect of either revolvers or auto pistols. What advances have occurred have really just fine-tuned existing designs. Even the Glock, that many consider to be a revolutionary design, employs several well-established concepts. Its greatest significance is really in the materials used in its construction, as well as its modular design.

The fact is that modern handguns are not any easier to shoot or more accurate. Great strides have, however, been made in materials and ammunition development. This has resulted in handguns being made that are smaller and lighter without sacrificing power or ammunition capacity. In this respect, today's handguns are superior.

Yet in spite of this, it is a moot question whether a citizen who is armed with a quality double-action revolver or semi-automatic pistol of 1930s vintage is less well protected than someone armed with the latest polymer-frame auto pistol. ●

COLONEL WALTER R. WALSH, USMC, RET.

1930s Gangster-era FBI Agent, U.S. Marine Corps Officer, Champion Marksman

Article and photos by Walt Rauch

COLONEL WALTER R. Walsh USMC, Ret., at the age of 95 (as of my interview with him on April 19 and 20, 2002) can now look back on a life of achievements that would take a legion of lesser men to accomplish. In an all-too-brief interview, I was able to get only the highlights of his exploits as a lawman, shooting champion and warrior. I beg the reader's forgiveness for unanswered questions, as I chose to cover as many topics as possible during the interview rather than getting the details of some at the expense of others.

Col. Walsh is now, arguably, the last of the 1930s FBI agents still alive. He came to the FBI after getting his Juris Doctor degree from the New Jersey School of Law (now part of Rutgers University). Along the way, he learned to shoot in the Civilian Marksmanship Training Corps and then as a member of the New Jersey National Guard.

If Col. Walsh's name sounds vaguely familiar, it should, as he is also the Marine, commissioned as a second lieutenant in the USMC

Reserve in 1938, who shot and killed a Japanese soldier with a 45 at 90 yards. He went on with his division to the occupation of North China. He also commanded one of two USMC scout-sniper schools during the Korean War and was Officer-In-Charge of the Weapons Training Battalion, Quantico Marine Base, Quantico, Virginia from 1962 until his retirement in 1969.

Col. Walsh was USMC Pistol Champion in 1946 and

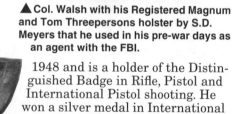

▲ Col. Walsh with his Registered Magnum and Tom Threepersons holster by S.D. Meyers that he used in his pre-war days as an agent with the FBI.

1948 and is a holder of the Distinguished Badge in Rifle, Pistol and International Pistol shooting. He won a silver medal in International Pistol at the 1952 Olympics and a team gold medal in Center-Fire Pistol. He captained and coached the U.S. team nationally and internationally, and is a long-time match official for the NRA Camp Perry National matches, Camp Perry, Ohio. As a FBI instructor, he co-designed the now-world-famous Police Pistol Course (PPC) used by law enforcement agencies around the world.

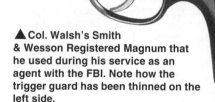

▲ Col. Walsh's Smith & Wesson Registered Magnum that he used during his service as an agent with the FBI. Note how the trigger guard has been thinned on the left side.

Self-Defense/Concealed Carry

◀ The right side of the Registered Magnum shows a revolver that has obviously seen a lot of use, but one that has been well cared for.

"Gang Busting" With the FBI

Col. Walsh joined the FBI in 1934 and was part of the first graduating class of agents authorized to be armed. As best he can recall, he was issued a 4-inch Colt Police Positive 38 Special, although he used a "45" (his term for the 1911A1 pistol), along with a pair of Smith & Wesson N-Frame Registered 357 Magnum revolvers. (More about these later.)

Special Agent Walsh came to the FBI in a turbulent time. J. Edgar Hoover was at the helm and to improve the tarnished image of the "Bureau of Investigation" renamed it the Federal Bureau of Investigation and set about developing a new breed of elite lawmen. New hires were to be accountants or lawyers only; Special Agent Walsh had the credentials.

Hoover had a major problem, though. The country was in the throes of a major crime wave being committed by organized gangs of ruthless and desperate men and the country wanted these men stopped...and stopped cold. The '30s were truly "hard times." The country was in the middle of the Great Depression, with millions out of work, banks closing, the stock market in shambles and most folks scratching hard to simply get by. Folks of this era were not soft by any means and the criminals were a product of the same environment! Hoover saw that the men he needed to stop the bandits were not the sorts that come from the ranks of accountants and lawyers. He needed gunmen – men with known abilities – who could shoot well, wouldn't flinch in the face of danger and who were not hesitant to "drop the hammer"...and Hoover hired them.

From what I've been able to learn, he found these men from within and without the fledgling organization. Col. Walsh, while a graduate lawyer, was already a national champion in both rifle and pistol. He was also a Marine. Some of the others, as Col. Walsh recalled their names, were Henry "Hank" Adams, Bill Nitchky (*phonetic spelling*), "Jelly" Brice, Bob Jones, Clarence Hurt and Charley Winstead. (*These last two were, according to Col. Walsh, responsible for getting John Dillinger.*) Some of these names are lost in the mists of time, while others have had their work documented, "Jelly" Brice being the most notable. It looks to me that Hoover created his own hunter/killer team and turned them loose.

I had the opportunity to interview Col. Walsh in April, 2002 at the Fairfax Rod and Gun Club in Mananas, Virginia, albeit for an all-too-brief period of time. We spent less than two hours together on two successive days, with Col. Walsh consenting to the taping of the interview. Rather than paraphrase his comments, I've chosen to provide portions of the transcript of the tape with italicized amplifications and explanations. This may well be the last time we are going to get the story from the man who was there, and his words much better convey the flavor of some of his exploits, such as with "Doc" Barker and the Brady Gang when he was an FBI agent, and his most well-known war time experience, that of shooting an enemy solder with a 1911 pistol at 90 yards.

Doc Barker

From the tape: "At the time, the bureau was small. Virtually everybody worked on major cases; leads were everywhere; a lot of them centered around Chicago. The Bakers were in the Chicago area. One day, one cold, rainy day, three or four of us were sent out to surveil Mildred Coolman (*phonetic*), Doc's (*Doc Barker's*) girlfriend. She wore a red fox fur coat. Now, a red fox fur coat stands out in Chicago. We had hardly parked when here comes a red fox fur coat (*worn by a woman*) out of an apartment building along with a guy who, in our wishful thinking, answered the description of Doc. (*Our*) Car hadn't even stopped and I was out... and across the street. As they walked, I tried to follow them as unobtrusively as possible. We got to a certain place and this individual who was with Mildred stopped and Mildred went on.

"I tried to contain myself and moped along and when I came up behind him I said, 'Stick 'em up, Doc. FBI!' I had this nice overcoat with big pockets and I had a 45 in my hand (*inside the pocket*). He looked around and was looking right down the muzzle of the 45. He started to run. I came up and down

The revolver has a Baughman ramp front sight, manufactured by King Sight Company and installed by Smith & Wesson.

Col. Walsh reshaped and thinned the Magna grip panels at the bottom as well as installing a Pachmayer grip adapter.

The bottom of the grip frame was rounded by Col. Walsh to better fit his hand.

The traditional humpback Registered Magnum hammer was shortened by Col. Walsh to eliminate snagging on his coat.

with it (the 45) (*more on this move later*) and he slipped in a muddy area (*fell*) and hit a car. Astride 'Doc' on the ground (*Walsh was on top of him*), I stuck my pistol in his ear and said, 'Don't move, you SOB!' I then realized I had no handcuffs, but one of the people in the car did. After Bob Jones, former chief of detectives in Dallas, got Doc on his feet and gave him a quick shake down, I asked, 'Where's your heater, Doc?' He said, 'I left it at the apartment. Ain't that a hell of a place for it.' I replied, 'No, you're lucky.' That's how we got Doc Barker."

Brady Gang

"The Brady Gang. They operated through the mid-west for the most part. They were at the head of the list – at the time the most sought-after. We didn't have much information. We got a rustle out of Baltimore, where the police chased a car; shots were exchanged, but no one was hurt. The Baltimore police came up with information that this might have been part of the Brady Gang. Then it just faded out.

"Then word got down a week or two later that some guy up in Bangor, Maine claimed to have seen these people. He ID them from an IO (*wanted poster*) in the Post Office. The Resident Agent investigated and got the mug shot book from Boston (*field office*). This guy in Bangor went through the mug shot book and ID them and did it a few times. They (*the FBI agents*) called down to Washington with the word and Inspector Gurney – he had been a former Sergeant with the San Francisco PD – got a couple people together. We went to Boston and picked up a couple agents and we got some guns there.

"We went up to Bangor on a Saturday and hit the joints, as we had an ID on the car. We didn't find anything, as we didn't go out far enough. They had been in town before this time, a week or two, and they had

THE BRADY GANG

The Brady Gang consisted of Alfred Brady, James Dalhover and Clarence Lee Schaffer, Jr. They had a brief but violent crime spree in the Midwest beginning in late 1935 until April 1936, committing about 150 armed holdups, at least, and possibly two murders – including an Indiana state trooper and an Indianapolis, IN police sergeant. The FBI gained jurisdiction under the newly-passed National Stolen Property Act when discarded jewelry boxes from a Kay jewelry store robbery in Lima, Ohio were found in Indiana

The gang was heavily armed. According to an article which appeared in the November, 1937 issue of *True Detective* magazine, the arms recovered after their final arrest or demise included "eight 45 caliber automatics pistols, seven 38 caliber revolvers, three 30 caliber machine guns with 350-round belts with 22 of these set for use from a car." (No further explanation of this was given.) Also, "five 32 caliber automatics, five 30 caliber rifles, one 30 caliber automatic rifle, two 12-gauge shotguns, one 45 caliber revolver, one 22 caliber revolver and two 22 caliber automatics." (No further details were listed.) In addition to this collection, the Brady Gang also had large quantities of ammunition, extra magazines and drums, as well as tear gas grenades.

been in a hardware or sporting goods store and bought a couple of Colt 32 semi-autos. They subtly asked the owner, 'You think you could get a 'Tommy gun'?' He told them, 'It could take a little while, but I think I can.' The plan was they would come back in a week or so.

(*The following*) "Monday, I was on my way from the apartment to the store and I spotted the car on the street. I got down to the store and called the apartment (*where the agents were staying*). Told them the car is at such and such a place. 'The police picked it up an hour ago on surveillance but they don't know where the occupants of the car are now.' It turned out there were two carloads of bad guys and while one stopped, the other was still looking for a parking place. From the stopped car, gang members Schaffer and Dalhover got out and Dalhover entered the store. There were two other agents who stopped the other car with Brady in it. They hit the car from both sides and ordered Brady out of the car. He (*Brady*) picked up a revolver on the way out and shot at the two agents (*who killed him*). This must have taken place almost simultaneously as Dalhover went into the (*hardware*)

Colonel Walsh showed the author his registered S&W Magnum during a meeting at the Colonel's club range in Virginia.

After explaining the modifications that he had made to his revolver Col. Walsh agreed to shoot a few rounds for the record.

store. I worked between the two counters. (*Walsh posed as a store employee.*) I drew on him and said, 'Stick 'em up.' (*Dalhover was held at gunpoint and relieved of a 45 1911 and a 32 ACP semi-auto, as well as two extra magazines for both.*)

"I started for the door and the glass shattered in my face. (*Schaffer, outside, fired at Walsh through the store window.*) We began to shoot back and forth. In the meantime, this agent (*name not recalled, but who was with Walsh in the store, hidden in the back*) came up with a 'Tommy gun' and he put all 20 bullets into Schaffer. He did it right; short bursts, right past my ear. I could feel the heat. This guy was lying in the middle of the street. In a few seconds, some woman said, 'Get this man to a hospital. He's still breathing.' Bill Nitchky said, '— that son of a bitch; get this man of ours to the hospital.' I got into the ambulance as a bullet had creased...had hit the grip of the gun in my right hand and my thumb opened up and my grip was slippery. (*He used two guns, one in either hand.*) One was a 45; the other was a 357 in the left.

Still have the 45 with the creased grip from the bullet."

The next day, when we resumed the interview, Col. Walsh apologized for not bringing the 45. He said he had left it with his daughter at her home and he didn't have time to get it, but he did bring his S&W Registered Magnum (see below). He was also chuckling as he said that I had missed a question. He pointed out I didn't ask him why he had a 45 and the Magnum. I told him that, since I used to carry both an S&W 4-inch Model 19 revolver and a 1911, the question never crossed my mind. He then explained that another agent didn't have a gun and Walsh offered him his choice, a 45 or the revolver. The agent chose the revolver. I then asked him why he brought three guns. He replied, grinning, "You can never have too many guns."

(Forgetting to bring a gun on the job is not uncommon, as strange as it seems. I recall another Secret Service agent and I were both dispatched to go to a last-minute posting on a protective assignment. When we arrived he turned to me and asked if I had brought a back-up gun that he could use. He said he left his revolver in his desk drawer. I lent him my second gun.)

The Jap Sniper Shot

Since the story about Col. Walsh shooting a Japanese sniper at 90 yards has been making the rounds since I was a boy, I thought I would get the story straight from the source.

Col. Walsh explained that while on Okinawa (*this was during and after the WWII battle for this island*), "I was Provost Marshal with the First Marine Division. I generally didn't carry a rifle; I carried a carbine. I was more familiar with a pistol...easier (*for him to shoot*). The soldier was spotted by Walsh. According to the Col., "He was a slow mover. He didn't keep with his crew, that's all. And I guess he wasn't ready to surrender. He was out there wandering around by himself. I shot him at 80 to 90 yards. He wasn't going to meet anybody."

I then asked Col. Walsh if he had used one hand or two to make the shot. He snapped back, "Gee, don't be stupid. I used two hands." I explained that this is the sort of detail readers want to know. He grunted and then said, "You know, with a 1911, up to about 100 yards you can hold on the silhouette target; you don't have to hold off the target. You get a hit." I moved on.

Guns

After being issued a Colt Police Positive 4-inch barrel 38 Special upon graduating from the first class of FBI special agents authorized to be armed, Special Agent Walsh found himself in Washington, DC. While there, he purchased a pair of Smith & Wesson "Registered" 357 Magnum revolvers that were ordered and received through Frank Baughman, who was also an FBI

In shooting his issue revolver Col. Walsh shot single action using a classic one-hand dueling target stance.

agent. (If this name sounds familiar, it should. Special Agent Baughman designed the now-world-known Baughman ramp front sight.)

Col. Walsh still owns serial number 48684. He said he sold the other gun while coming home to Arlington, Virginia from a vacation with his wife in San Diego, California. He had stopped to see another former special agent, last name Tanner, first name not recalled, who operated a hotel and casino in Las Vegas, Nevada. Col. Walsh said he regretted selling the gun and did attempt to buy it back, but Tanner wouldn't part with the gun. Walsh doesn't know the current whereabouts of the gun or Mr. Tanner. (My efforts to locate it have also been unsuccessful.)

The remaining Registered Magnum has a 4-inch barrel, blue, with Magna grips. Walsh pointed out he rounded the bottom edges of the Magna grips as well as the front and back of the bottom of the grip frame to fit his hand better. He also shortened the hammer spur because the hammer was tearing up his coats. He also thinned the trigger guard on the left side just forward of the trigger. (He's left-handed.) Col. Walsh brought the gun to the range in its holster, a Tom Threepersons rig made by S.D Myers. He said he liked the rig, but he had used a Burns-Martin rig for much of his work. The Burns-Martin holster is a metal-lined leather holster that is split down its front. The gun is drawn by pushing it through the tension of the steel bands that are "clamped" around it. Walsh said the leather had worn off all the metal and that he thought he just might get it repaired one of these days.

For those who might want to undertake the quest for the missing Walsh Registered Magnum, according to Roy Jinks, official S&W historian, S&W records reflect the following: Registered Numbers 1346 and 1347, with serial numbers 48684 and 48688, respectively, were ordered by Frank Baughman, Department of Justice, Rosalyn, Virginia and shipped from S&W on August 31, 1936. As written on the original order, "Both guns to have 4 inch barrels with front sight special quick draw like sketch. Sight at 25 yards with magnum ammunition, 6 o'clock hold, Magna grips. Same as sight on Certificate number 1345."

In examining the remaining Walsh revolver, the serrated ramp front sight is mounted in a King sight base. As I dry-fired the gun,

After his shooting demonstration, the author and the Colonel examine the target to confirm all shots are in the black. They were, with most grouped in the center rings.

the double action was very smooth and the single-action let-off was perfect. Col. Walsh mentioned that he had gunsmith A.E. Berdon work over the actions. (Berdon was a famous pistolsmith of the 1930s.)

Since we were at the Fairfax Rod and Gun Club and one of the pistol ranges is named in honor of the Colonel, I asked him if he would mind going to "his" range and firing a few rounds for posterity. Initially he demurred, explaining that two years ago when he last fired this gun at a bullseye he noted his "wobble area" had increased such that he was no longer satisfied with the quality of his handgun shooting, so he switched to shooting skeet because "I don't have to hold as long." (He uses a .410-bore gun.) He then said, "You shoot it."

When we got to the Walter R. Walsh range, a 25-yard bullseye target had been left up at 25 yards and had no holes in the black. I turned to the Colonel and said, "No one will give a rat's — about a photo of me shooting your gun. It has to be you." He paused, looked at me, nodded slightly and asked if I had any ammunition. I placed a box of Hornady 38 Special 125-grain XTP ammo on the shooting bench. Col. Walsh carefully examined the cartridges before deftly opening the cylinder and filling it with six rounds. With the gun still on the bench, he took a high, firm grip – high and firm enough that the flesh in the web of his hand rolled up against the top of the backstrap. He then pulled back slightly on the trigger with his forefinger enough to raise the hammer so he could thumb cock it with his off hand.

He took a classic bullseye shooting stance and raised the gun such that the muzzle was above the target and brought it back down to the bull; he broke the shot, calling it out

at 9 o'clock. He repeated this for every round, pausing on three repetitions to bring the gun back down to the bench before repeating the drill and when satisfied with his hold, he fired. He called the shots as he fired: "That one's at 4; I'm not sure of that one; that one's good." He said nothing out loud for the last two rounds. When he finished, he quickly and surely opened the cylinder, removed the empty cases and benched the revolver. As I started to ask him a question, he ignored me, turned and marched right down to the 25-yard line to see his hits. All his shots but one were centered in the black; one was in the lower outer portion of the black at 6 o'clock. He commented, "Didn't feel that one go."

Now if the reader will refer back to Col. Walsh's capture of "Doc" Barker, you will note that he said he "...came up and down with it" (the Registered magnum). I think, but didn't ask him, that he was going to fire and only Doc's fall saved his life!

End Notes

As far as how he helped design the PPC course, Col. Walsh recalled that in "'35-36, in that period, four or five of us were in Nitchky's apartment. We sat around the way we are BS-ing now. We would get on the floor, try this and that – discarded a lot. This group designed the PPC to start at 60 yards. Might have been too far."

I also asked him what his vision was now. He said it had gotten poorer and was now *only* 20-20.

I realize some topics cry out for more detail but, as in most matters, you take what you can, knowing that at least some history has been faithfully documented and preserved. •

HOLSTERS FOR CONCEALED CARRY

by Bob Campbell

I AM OFTEN asked what is the best holster for concealed carry? This is a question only the user can answer. With a hard look at his lifestyle, clothing choices and perhaps his occupation, the modern carrier has many choices. A concealed carry holster is not particularly complicated but is more complex than it first appears. A reinforced holster lip, double stitched tunnel loops, a tension screw and a sight track are often incorporated into the design.

A good concealed carry holster must have several of the attributes of a service or field holster, in addition to concealing the weapon from casual observation. Comfort, concealment, safety and retention are all important. A rapid presentation from the holster is also important. On the street the draw will be initiated by an attack. Assailants normally attack with the weapon in hand. Experienced peace officers have learned to meet danger with the gun in hand, but the average civilian will be drawing against a weapon that is already in the adver-

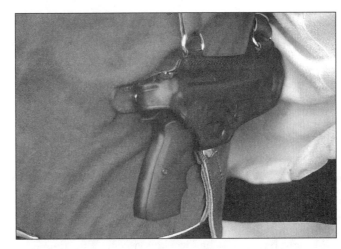

Shoulder holsters may not be as popular as other designs. This Don Hume rig is among the best on the market, with quality to rival or equal the best custom designs.

sary's hand. Surprise, discretion and concealment are important.

For most of us the strong side holster, worn on the belt, is the best choice. The holster should be tight against the body in normal wear, taking advantage of the natural depressions of the body for concealment. The gun should be presented in such a way that it is angled into

the draw. The cant of the holster should allow the user to draw the gun quickly. As an example, a tall person may need little angle in the grip; his hand may fall naturally on the gun butt. A shorter person with a high waist will need a more pronounced angle to move the gun butt forward to contact the hand quickly and efficiently. The drop from the

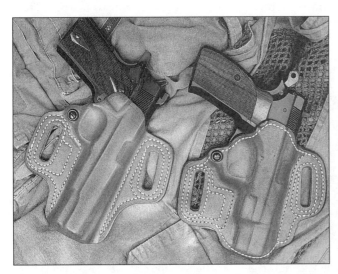

Here are a couple of variations on the pancake theme by High Noon holsters. The first carries the long heavy slide of the High Standard 45 quite well, the other is mated to a CZ 75 9mm pistol.

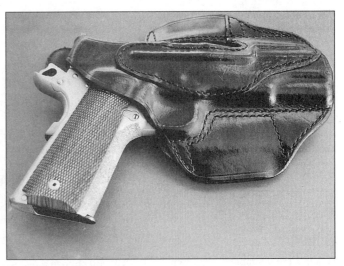

The author's Action Works custom 45 rides often in this Don Hume thumbreak. For the author's money this is one of the best mass-produced holsters.

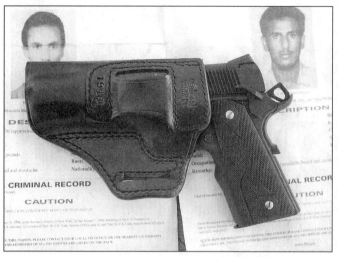
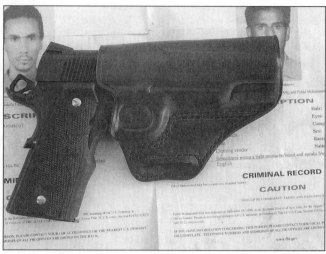

Alessi is a respected maker with a reputation second to none. The reverse or obverse of this Alessi holsters shows the preferred method of attachment, a long tunnel loop.

belt can be increased for those with more than a little middle aged spread. Otherwise, this bulge will push the handgun away from the body, compromising concealment. The Rapid Response from Wilson Combat is offered with just this type of drop. There are many considerations, but the custom holster maker can produce a well fitting holster perfectly suited to your needs. Take care in ordering, answer the questions correctly, check the right box, and satisfaction is assured.

There are nuances of design that are important. As an example, if you prefer the revolver, then a holster that places the cylinder of the revolver high on the belt, away from the hipbone, is preferred. The balance of the revolver is in the cylinder; the balance of an autoloader is in the handle. You cannot iron out the cylinder bulge of a revolver holster and make a good pistol holster. The better makers understand the difference, and revolver-and pistol-

specific holsters are readily available. The strong side high-ride belt holster is just about ideal for most types of carry. I suppose about 90 percent of my holsters are just that type. Among my favorites are the Kramer belt scabbard and Ken Null's Gibraltar. The best production holster for ready wear comes from Don Hume. Hume offers a production thumbbreak with a cut-down front and excellent double stitching. It has worked very well for me. Some users who chose the Browning High Power or Colt 1911, which require cocked and locked hammer, prefer a holster with a thumbbreak. There is nothing faster than this Don Hume design. If you opt for a holster from any maker with a thumbbreak, be certain the thumbbreak is reinforced. In other words, there will be hardened leather, plastic or metal support which keeps the thumbbreak from binding or flopping. Perhaps 80 percent of us will choose a strong side belt holster for

concealed carry, but there are a number of situations in which alternate styles work well.

I have been partial to the crossdraw holster for many reasons since I began carrying a handgun professionally. The rub is, only the very best designs offer any type of utility. A poor crossdraw is a nuisance, and there are quite a few poor crossdraws. The crossdraw should be worn just in front of the weak side hipbone, with an almost neutral angle. I have used the Liberty from Gordon Davis for over a decade with excellent results. Another good example comes from Kramer Leather, and a fine production type comes from Don Hume. The crossdraw is a good holster for those who are seated in a vehicle or seated behind a desk for much of the time. The gun hand can practically ride on the gun at all times when a good crossdraw is worn. The weak hand can draw the gun if necessary. When addressing a threat

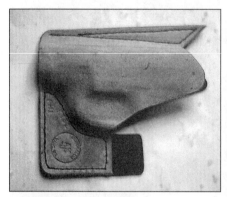

This is a fairly simple holster from AKJ Concealco for a small auto. It is well conceived and executed for the intended purpose.

If you choose a belt slide holster, this one from Aker Leather is among the best designs. It features good molding and a tension screw.

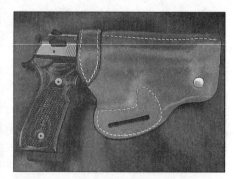

This is one of the author's favorite holsters, in the distinctive light tan that is the trademark of Blocker holsters. Note strong stitching and reinforced holster mouth.

◀ This well-used crossdraw from Kramer leather often carries the author's Springfield 45.

Alessi Talon and the Blocker ST 17. Inside-the-waist-band holsters are often made of slightly less rigid leather for comfort.

The inside-the-waistband holster that we judge all others by is the Summer Special from Milt Sparks. It was originally designed by California peace officer Bruce Nelson and licensed to the reputable Sparks company. This holster incorporated many features that made it a very successful holster. It has been copied, altered, and made cheaper but the current version from Sparks is faithful to the original, remaining a paradigm of concealed carry. It set the standard, and the standards are as follows:

The IWB holster must have a reinforced welt or holster mouth in order to allow reholstering the handgun after it is drawn. In other words, the holster must not collapse after the gun is drawn.

The IWB holster also must have some type of flap or cover to protect the gun from the corrosive salts of the body.

The IWB holster must have some type of sight track to prevent the common occurrence of the gun being drawn and the front sight appearing with a ball of lint, cotton or suede where the front sight should be. It is possible for a sharp ramp front sight to completely snag in a poor holster. Practice with your chosen holster will help you to avoid or discover these problems!

The IWB should be worn near the rear pants pocket, in the kidney position. Wearing an IWB over the spine can result in serious injury during a fall and this carry position is, therefore, not recommended. The IWB holster allows carrying a full-size handgun with relatively good concealment. Even a light windbreaker will conceal the handgun well with this type of holster, as the bottom of the holster does not fall below the beltline as the typical strong side holster will. The IWB can be worn under even a light sport shirt with good results. Some users report discomfort, but it is simply a matter of acclimation.

The draw from such a deep carry must be practiced often. There are two basic styles of draw with the inside the waistband holster. One requires the outer garments be pulled away by the weak hand while the gun is drawn with the strong hand. In the second style the strong hand, or drawing hand, brushes the garments away as the gun is drawn. I prefer the latter, as we will not always have the weak hand available. As a peace officer, I often carried the IWB on special assignments and off duty. In 23 years, my IWB holster was never a give away.

Quite a few cops and civilians alike seem to enjoy pocket carry. I do not care for pocket carry, but if you go this route be certain to obtain a good pocket-type holster. Don Hume makes one for the little Berettas that breaks up the outline of the backup gun—it looks like a wallet in the pocket. AKJ Concealco makes a decent little rig for the Kel Tec 32. Pocket holsters were among

from the weak side, draw and reaction is very good. The pistol is drawn toward the attacker and the weak hand meets the gun in front of the body. The holster should present the gun in the direction of the draw, and of course the crossdraw does not do so in the conventional sense. Tactics that maximize the crossdraw's advantages and minimize its weaknesses must be understood and utilized. Attackers are not always squared to us as the target is on the pistol range, and the crossdraw offers numerous advantages. The crossdraw is not for a novice; it demands skill and much practice.

A holster type I have used for many years is less comfortable than a standard belt design but offers excellent concealment. The inside-the-waistband or inside-the-trousers holster is worn between the trousers and shirt, and is attached to the belt by loops. There are a few good holsters that attach to the belt with a spring clip, but I strongly prefer a belt loop. The only spring clip models I can recommend have seen decades of use. These are the

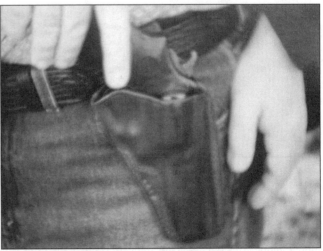

These two Kramer crossdraw holster illustrate a good draw angle and fit for an auto pistol and revolver.

This is a horsehide crossdraw from Rusty Sherrick—a very nice holster that works well in the field.

Both strong side and crossdraw holsters can ride close to the body and offer good concealment as this photo illustrates.

FBI tilt, a body-hugging design, and excellent stitching mark the quality of this Aker holster.

the first concealment holsters crafted, and some are decent, others are pretty lame attempts at holsters. Remember, there are different types for your clothing style. A holster designed for jeans will be termed a top loader, while trousers call for side-loading pocket holsters. There is a difference and care much be taken in ordering. When drawing from a pocket holster, you cannot jam your hand in the pocket and take a perfect grip on the gun. Your fist will not come out of the pocket with the gun. The gun must be drawn almost gingerly then the grip taken up. It is best to be armed, but the pocket holster is the least desirable of all carries. Recognizing the popularity of the carry, a number of makers have produced excellent holsters within the limitations of pocket carry. Pocket Concealment Systems makes other, more conventional holsters, and very good ones, but I learned most of what I know about pocket holsters in conversa-

tion and correspondence with this company. Their French Curve is perhaps the most suitable of all pocket holsters for the snubnose 38.

A racy—even sexy—type of holster is the shoulder holster. James Bond carried his PPK in a shoulder holster, and Dirty Harry managed to carry his far more serious armament of a 44 Magnum revolver in a Bianchi X 15 variant. Shoulder holsters come in two basic types, the ones that hold the gun horizontally and the ones that hold a handgun vertically. Either can be useful in a good example. DeSantis' New York Undercover is an example of a purpose-designed shoulder holster that works well. The shoulder holster demands a well-designed harness for proper fit, but just the same there are some that will feel the harness is choking them or constricting their blood flow. Women seem to adapt to shoulder holsters much more

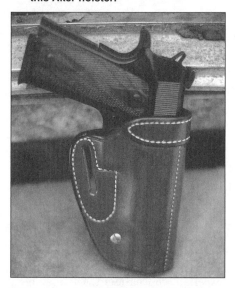

This is a modern version of the Gordon Davis Liberty crossdraw. Excellent stitching and fine design are guaranteed.

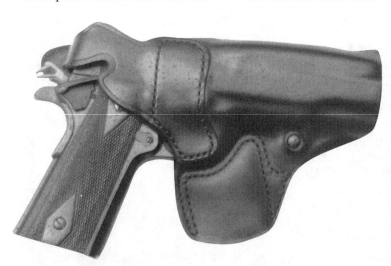

▲ This is the author's personal armament – a High Standard 45 with SFS trigger action. This holster is the standard issue of the FBI's Hostage Rescue Unit. It should be good enough for a retired cop!

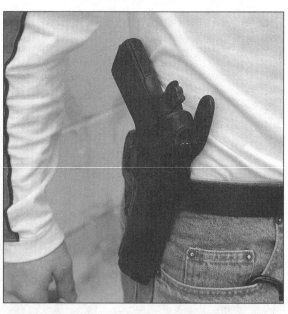

Sometimes, holsters have a better recommendation than the author can add to. This is the DeSantis HRT, standard issue of the FBI's Hostage Rescue Unit. A very good holster.

readily, perhaps because they are used to wearing a brassiere and are adroit at the nuances of adjustment.

A shoulder holster offers many of the advantages of a crossdraw holster. The shoulder holster is never as rigid as a belt holster. It moves and may flop forward when we lean forward. Still, for certain styles of clothing and especially when wearing a suitcoat, the shoulder holster does make a lot of sense. Be certain the outer jacket material is thick enough that the holster lines do not 'print' through the jacket. One of my more heavily muscled friends was a cause for hilarity when wearing a poorly designed shoulder harness beneath a windbreaker—it looked as if he was wearing a bra! A formidable officer of some reputation, he tended to go bargain basement in clothing and survival gear. He finally got the message and invested in a Blocker Lifeline shoulder holster. Take extra care in shoulder holster selection.

A serious fighting handgun can be concealed under even a light jacket with a good shoulder holster. Not long ago, I was wearing my New York Undercover when off duty, and was forced to collar four fellows who caused quite a stir on an otherwise quiet Sunday evening. I was not in uniform, but as I often do was wearing a jacket which has my agency's patches, my identification, and a badge emblem displayed. I asked the fellows to be kind enough to lean forward against their vehicle until my friends arrived to escort them to jail. One cut his eyes toward me—the proverbial targeting glance—then at his friends as he whispered, 'No pistoleo.' He made his move and I made mine. A solid uppercut properly delivered has stopped many a criminal before gunplay was necessary, but as he reeled I quickly drew my SIG P 220 and backed away from his compatriots. The attack was over. I am loath to draw my weapon for any reason other than real need, and the shoulder holster certainly concealed this 45 until the moment came.

There are a number of good shoulder holster designs for all around use. As an example, among the better choices on the market is offered by Don Hume. A mix of several materials including premium leather and modern elastic, this holster is among the most comfortable and easily adjusted I have used. I have carried my Accurate Plating Beretta 92 and two spare magazines quite often using the Don Hume holster. Concealment is there, but so is comfort. The weight of the firearm is well spread out due to the wonderfully designed shoulder harness. In short, a good shoulder holster is a fine load-bearing device. A poor one is a torture device.

There are a number of carry options that can be used well with practice. I abhor fanny packs and have never used one, but then I have been lucky. My personal situation has never called for anything more than a strong side belt holster or an IWB. Even if I were jogging in shorts, I could carry an IWB with an internal belt, an overlooked option. We usually carry rather small, light handguns when engaged in mundane pursuits and some ingenuity is required to conceal even them when lightly clad. But I have worn a simple fabric holster from Uncle Mikes attached to a velcro belt from the same firm while on special assignment. I wore no belt in my jeans. I could pull the shirt tail out, which I wore tucked, pretty quickly and draw my Star PD 45 with ease. At the time I fabricated this simple system, I was on loan from the sheriff's department to another agency. No one told me the chief of police of the town I was sent to was the owner of the illegal liquor and gambling den I was infiltrating! In any case, I was well-prepared for trouble and survived a number of 'bumps' by his prostitutes. They didn't bump the right place and probably figured I could not carry a gun without a belt. Today, I do not have to go to such lengths and often carry my stainless Taurus 38 in a simple strong side holster by Graham leather. A belt holster can fit under a pulled-out shirt or under a light jacket with discretion when carrying a light gun like the Taurus. I am not completely comfortable in one sense with such light armament, but perhaps the load of five Glaser Safety Slugs will suffice.

The subject of holster material is hotly debated, but in fact there are several good materials. Leather is by far the most popular. I am not speaking of thin suede-type holsters but quality leather holsters. Leather is readily tanned, lasts for years, retains its shape, and can be had in shades which are dull and do not draw attention. Horsehide is stronger per ounce of material and more resistant to water and solvent damage. It is worth the tariff, especially the shell horsehide type offered by Ken Null. Kydex is not resistant to wear, it is practically impervious! Oil, perspiration, solvent and other chemicals do not affect Kydex. Some Kydex is quite comfortable. My personal preference runs to quality leather and horsehide. I have had such good service from leather and horsehide I can hardly change at this date.

In closing, the holster should have a balance of comfort, concealability and speed. The holster should be properly mated to the belt. The holster should be angled into the draw, with an appropriate cant for the user's physique. Retention should lie in the fit of the holster, with a tight fit to the gun, perhaps a pinch in the triggerguard and, if you prefer, a strong, reliable thumbreak. Those are the facts. The rest is up to you—it's your hide. ●

HOLSTER MAKERS DIRECTORY

Alessi	2465 Niagra Falls Blvd., Amherst, NY 14228
Don Hume	PO 351 Miami, OK 74355
Aker Gunleather	2248 Main St. Ste. 6, Chula Vista, CA 91911
High Noon	PO 2138 Palm, Harbor, FL 34682
AKJ	PO 134, Rupert, ID 83350
Blocker	9396 SW Tigard, Tigard,OR 97223
Kramer	PO 112154, Tacoma, WA 98411
De Santis	PO 2039 149 Denton Ave., New Hyde Park, NY 11040
Sherrick	507 Mark Drive, Elizabethtown, PA 17022
Wild Bill	PO 1941, Garner, NC 27529
Gordon Davis	PO 1209, Chino Valley, AZ 86323
Null	161 School St. SW, Resaca, GA 30735
Wilson Combat	2234 CR 719-97, Berryville, AR 72616-4573
Taurisano	3695 Mohawk St., New Hartford, NY 13413

Care and Feeding of the Snub-Nose 38

by Dan C. Johnson

THERE IS NO shortage of opinions when it comes to defensive handguns. The debates rage from Internet forums to the local gun club, not to mention in the pages of the various gun magazines. Tactical Tupperware versus the 1911, 40S&W versus the 45 versus the 357 SIG and on and on. One caliber/ gun combination often overlooked in the stopping power debates just happens to be one of the most popular out in the real world. It is of course the 38 Special cartridge chambered in a small five-shot revolver with the short tube.

A snub-nose 38 is neither the most potent of self-defense handguns nor the easiest to hit with, but it is one of the handiest to carry in a caliber of sufficient power. Yes, the sufficient power part is debatable, but some of us weigh the slender odds we will actually need a gun against the certain inconveniences of carrying one. Unless one goes into abnormally dangerous areas or situations, many people are willing to sacrifice some power for day-to-day comfort. You can now get 357 Magnum power in the same small package but the recoil and muzzle blast are intimidating enough that many who own the mini magnums stoke the chambers with +P 38 loads. This equates to a lot of people who trust their lives to the venerable old 38 Special and short-barreled revolvers. Walk into any gun shop and look over the display cases and you may reach the same conclusion I did. The snub-nose 38 is here to stay.

Smith & Wesson introduced the 38 Special cartridge in 1902 in their Military & Police revolver. In spite of the Military designation of the gun, the 38 Special saw little use in the armed forces, but it was the standard police issue in most jurisdictions until well into the second half of the twentieth cen-

tury. Smith & Wesson first chambered the 38 Special cartridge in a small-frame 5-shot revolver in 1950, although it was preceded by the weaker 38

▶ The Smith & Wesson Chiefs Special was the first of the 5-shot two-inch 38 Special revolvers and remains popular today. (Knife is the Angelo Fluted Folder from Lone Wolf Knives)

Many people buy the snub-nose 38s for home defense, but the author feels a four-inch barrel revolver is better for this application.

S&W cartridge in the same configuration. The 38 S&W model was called the Terrier while the more potent model was named the Chiefs Special since it was aimed at the plain clothes police market. It was designed as a lighter, easier to carry alternative to the 38 service revolver and soon became enormously popular with police and civilians alike. Other companies have followed suit with a variety of similar designs. In fact, due to the widespread adoption of concealed carry laws, the civilian market in these guns is booming, with new models appearing regularly on dealer's shelves.

A good portion of these guns are sold to newcomers to handguns looking for a safe and simple-to-operate handgun for self-defense. The double-action revolver is an unbeatable choice for the novice but the downside is the short sight radius and tiny sights require a lot of practice for one to become proficient with the weapon. Snubbies are reliable, safe, and easy to carry but if a person is not willing to commit to the practice required to place their shots where they want them, quickly and under stress, there may be better choices. This is especially true if the handgun is to be kept at home rather than carried. A four-inch revolver is usually better suited for home-defense.

As with any firearm, the key to success is practice. Dave Ashmore checks out the results of some close-range point shooting.

I see the small 38 as more of an expert's gun, either as a highly reliable primary carry piece in low-risk situations or as a backup to a duty weapon. I might add that the snubbies are suited for more than protection from two-legged predators. They make an excellent trail or pack gun in areas where the larger four-legged beasts have been eliminated. I would not want to fend off a bear of any persuasion with one but wild dogs, coyotes (yes, coyote attacks are on the increase), or other assorted vermin, including mountain lions, could be repelled right handily with a few well-placed shots from a 38. They are also great for the legless critters when loaded with snake shot.

No matter what use you put these guns to, the handicap of the short barrel and tiny sights must be overcome. This is not to say these guns are not accurate. With practice they can be quite effective on even small targets out to twenty yards or so. Many times I have used my Chiefs Special loaded with wadcutters to take cottontails for the camp pot and have cleanly beheaded a number of rattlesnakes that invaded those camps. Accurate shots require adequate light, precise sight alignment, and a careful squeeze of the trigger in single-action mode. Most self-defense situations allow for none of these things.

That is why I also practice point shooting at close range on silhouettes with both a two-hand and one-hand hold. Most life-threatening encounters take place in low light and anyone who depends on being able to bring the small sights common on a snubnose into play is seriously deluding themselves in my opinion. Though nothing can replace extensive practice, there is another option that will allow anyone to connect better in low light. Crimson Trace Lasergrips project an aiming point on the target so that you can fire the gun accurately from any position in most any light.

Tune-ups

Due to their inherent ruggedness, some owners are prone to give little care to the revolver that rests on the nightstand or is occasionally dropped in a coat pocket. Many of these guns give years of reliable service with nothing more than an

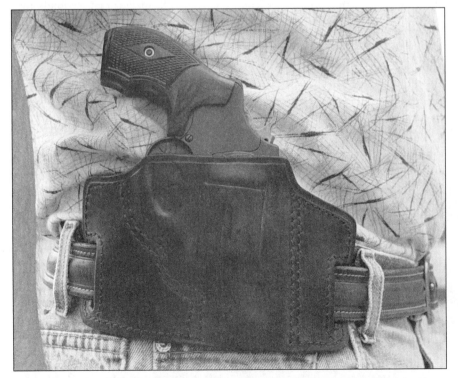

Many small 38s are carried in a coat pocket or purse but good leather can make the gun more accessible. Leather shown here is a C. Rusty Sherrick High-Ride.

There are so many excellent factory loads available that most owners of the snub-nose 38 do not reload for them but there are advantages to rolling your own.

Smoothing the action means polishing the mating surfaces of internal parts, the sides of the hammer, trigger, inside of the frame, etc. Very important—do not touch the sear engagements. Also remember, you only want to polish the surface of the metal, not remove it. Once the surfaces are polished, or even if you choose not to polish them, you may want to install an aftermarket spring kit. Most of today's double-action revolvers have very heavy springs to protect the manufacturer from liability. A kit like those available from Wolff can greatly lighten the trigger pull. Just don't go too light, especially on the hammer spring, as reliability may suffer.

Which Loads?

As popular as these guns are, there are varying opinions on the best load to carry in them for self-defense. Many people feel it is an either/or proposition. Either you can use lightweight hollowpoints and maybe get some expansion but limited penetration, or you can use a 158-grain lead semi-wadcutter bullet and insure penetration while sacrificing expansion. The consensus is the 38 Special does not have enough power to insure both expansion and penetration. Based on some recent tests I had run on a variety of 38 Special factory loads, I disagree.

occasional rubdown with an oily cloth but they certainly deserve better treatment. Just because they are not target guns does not mean regular bore cleaning and other routine maintenance should be skipped, particularly if you fire a lot of lead bullets. Likewise, contact points should be kept properly lubricated and clean. Personally, I'd tend to neglect a target or hunting firearm before one that I bet my life on.

Beyond routine maintenance, there are many things the average shooter can do to improve the ergonomics of these guns. The easiest and most common user project is to change the grips. Actually, aftermarket grips are not as critical as they once were since many of today's snubbies come from the factory with excellent hand-filling grips. It is still important, though,

to be sure the grip fits you well. Ideally the grip should afford a firm hold and naturally nestle in your hand for consistent accuracy in point shooting, yet should not diminish one of the major attributes of these guns: concealability.

CNC-machining and investment casting of parts has helped manufacturers maintain quality and keep prices in line to some degree but today's actions do not compare in smoothness to the hand-fitted models of bygone days. Most factory revolvers can use some tuning right out of the box. The goal is to smooth the action and lighten trigger pull without affecting reliability. Gun owners who possess the ability to completely disassemble the innards of their revolver and put it back together again can vastly improve most modern actions with a bit of effort.

I recently enlisted Jason Weaver of DVC Labs to gelatin-test some various 38 Special factory loads in the two-inch barrel. Mostly 125-grain hollowpoints and 158-grain SWC bullets were used, as they tend to be the most popular choices. All of the loads tested were +P rated except for one, the Hornady 125-grain factory load and surprisingly it outpaced several of the +P loads. I also included one handload, an old recipe that has been around for years and touted by some as the ultimate snubbie load. It consists of a swaged lead hollow-base wadcutter loaded backward so that the hollow base becomes a hollow point.

Each load was tested in bare gelatin as well as gelatin covered with three layers of cloth to simulate clothing. The latter test is very important when determining the effectiveness of a self-defense load since some hollowpoint bullets tend to clog up when passing through clothing and expand less or not at all. No gelatin test is foolproof, of course, and will not tell you exactly how a bullet will perform in a given situation on a live target. But ballistics experts have determined it is an

With marginal calibers like the 38 Special, premium bullets and loads are called for. Shown here is a recovered Winchester 130-grain SXT bullet that was fired into gelatin.

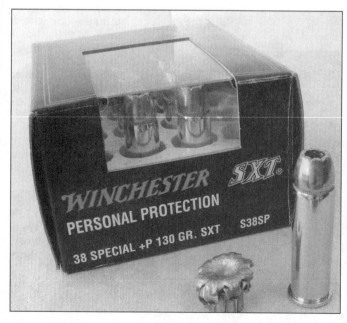

accurate enough test medium for making comparisons between bullets and will give you a good idea of how your bullet will penetrate and expand in flesh. Problem is, even these experts disagree somewhat on how to evaluate gelatin tests.

There are different factors to consider; it is easy when looking at gelatin tests to focus on one factor while overlooking another. With a low velocity/low energy load like the 38 Special, the main concern is likely penetration since no matter how much expansion occurs the bullet must reach the central nervous system to offer reliable stopping power. The consensus among most ballistics experts is that 12 to 15 inches of penetration in gelatin translates to optimum penetration on humans, so that is the first thing I look for when evaluating gelatin tests. Once I have identified the loads that give adequate penetration, I then consider expansion. I look not only for the bullet with the largest expanded diameter but also one that expands to roughly the same diameter in both bare and clothed gelatin.

When testing 38 Special factory loads, one of the first things you will notice is many of them display wide extremes in velocity. This is common with any low-pressure cartridge of relatively large case capacity. Powders of the proper burning rate leave a lot of empty space in the case and velocities vary depending on whether the powder is resting against the primer or forward against the bullet.

If you want to evaluate the consistency of your own favorite load, it is easy to do with a chronograph. Tilt the barrel down, then slowly raise it to level and fire through the sky screens. Then tilt the barrel up and lower it slowly to level before firing. Since the gun is usually brought up from the barrel-down position in self-defense applications, I consider the velocity achieved in this manner to be real world velocity for that load.

As to the loads evaluated by DVC labs, I'll just run through some general conclusions. Some of the high-dollar premium bullets pay dividends in the short-barreled 38. For example, Winchester's 130-grain SXT and Speer's Gold Dot 125-grain loads turned in stellar performances. Penetration was in the acceptable 12-to 15-inch range and expansion was excellent in both clothed and unclothed gelatin. Also notable was the Hornady 125-grain

Smooth grips as shown on this round butt S&W are a bit easier to conceal but a fuller grip handles recoil better. The grips on the gun and the rosewood boot grips are from Altamont. The rubber boot grip is from Uncle Mike.

XTP load, though it did not expand a lot, expansion was consistent and it gave excellent velocity for a standard-pressure load, beating out several of the +P entries, and offered a bit more penetration. The 158-grain lead SWCHP showed that it can offer some expansion, on bare gelatin at least, but really did not out-penetrate some of the 125-grain loads when it did expand. I was a little disappointed in the trick handload of a 148-grain backward wadcutter. It plugged up and failed to expand on clothed gelatin and under-penetrated a bit on bare.

Handloads

Many gun writers put forth the theory that handloads should not be used in self-defense due to legal concerns. The reasoning is a lawyer representing the thug you were forced to ventilate will claim you used some home-brewed concoction so deadly that it put his client's life in mortal danger. Foolish I know, but many foolish defenses have been won. I have written on this theory myself and even advanced it. Now, I am having second thoughts. It seems some thoughtful individuals have delved into recent legal cases and cannot find where this tactic was actually used in court. In other words, it is an interesting theory but has little real evidence to support it.

Legalities aside, there is much to recommend sticking to factory loads for self-defense. They are extremely reliable and offer a wide variety of excellent bullets for the purpose, plus they are nicely sealed against the elements. I doubt you could

really improve much on velocities in the 38 Special loadings either, at least not safely. The best reason I see to roll your own self-defense loads is the wide velocity extremes I mentioned earlier regarding some factory loads. There are some powders that fill the 38 case nicely and will give consistent velocities. For example, Hodgdon's Tite-Group is designed for just this purpose. Bulkier powders will leave more residue in the bore than the clean-burning faster powders but a dirty gun is not the main concern here.

Even if you stick with factory fodder for serious use, there is still good reason to reload the 38 snubnose. Practice is the key to accurate shot placement and reloading reduces the cost of that practice. It also allows you to tailor practice loads to match the point of impact of your self-defense loads. The short 38s tend to place different loads to different points on target and a bit of load experimentation is worth the effort. If you are going to learn accurate point shooting, it is critical the gun shoots where it is pointing.

Epilog

The short-barrel 38 will likely remain a favorite defense gun in the foreseeable future due to its many attributes. Some will still denigrate it for its lack of power, but even with increasingly more compact and potent alternatives on the market, the snub-nose will hold its own. It is a genuine American classic. •

NON-PEACEMAKER SINGLE ACTIONS

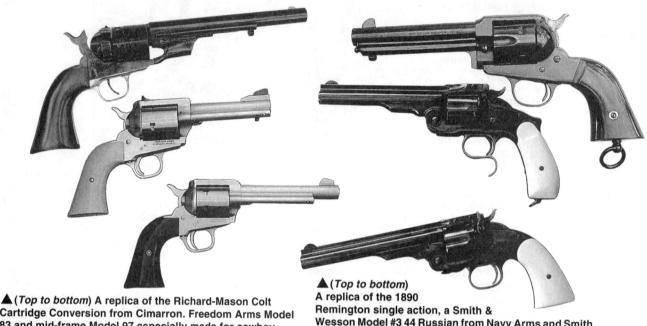

▲ (*Top to bottom*) A replica of the Richard-Mason Colt Cartridge Conversion from Cimarron. Freedom Arms Model 83 and mid-frame Model 97 especially made for cowboy action shooting.

▲ (*Top to bottom*) A replica of the 1890 Remington single action, a Smith & Wesson Model #3 44 Russian from Navy Arms and Smith & Wesson's resurrected 45 Schofield with Eagle Ultralvory grips.

FOR COWBOY-ACTION SHOOTING

by John Taffin

"THE SINGLE ACTION Is Dead." How many times has that song been sung over the past 100 plus years? It started with the appearance of the first modern double-action revolvers from Colt and Smith & Wesson in the last decade of the 19th century. It was sung again with the advent of the Colt 1911 Government Model. Why would anyone want an antiquated thumbcocker when they could choose a double action or semi-automatic? Somehow the Single Action Army held on although sales continued to decline until Colt would remove it from production in 1941. Colt announced it would never be made again. The Single Action really was dead.

Than a strange thing happened. Television began to spread across the country with much of the air

time being taken up by old "B" Western movies. A new generation discovered the Old West and the single-action sixgun. Two companies saw the desire and entered the marketplace. In 1953, Bill Ruger modernized the single action with all coil springs, reduced the frame size slightly, and chambered it in the affordable 22 Long Rifle. It has been a great seller for Ruger for half a century. One year after Ruger's 22 Single-Six arrived, another Bill at the other end of the country started producing a Colt replica. Great Westerns came out of a factory in Los Angeles owned by Bill Wilson. About the same time the sport of Fast Draw took off and even Colt decided

to resurrect the Single Action Army and the Second Generation of Model Ps arrived in 1956.

Great Western would disappear eight years after the return of the Colt Single Action Army, however,

Smith & Wesson replicas in both a five-inch Wells Fargo Model and 1st and 2nd Model Cavalry Schofields from Navy Arms and Cimarron Firearms. Antiqued grips are from Buffalo Brothers.

One of the great virtues of the Smith & Wesson design is the rapid operation for loading and unloading.

▶It's not a Colt Single Action, however the grip and hammer reach found on the Schofield Model fit most hands quite well.

Ruger would continue to produce Single-Sixes, Blackhawks, and Super Blackhawks. With the advent of the 1990s we saw the arrival of dozens of new semi-automatics in several new calibers. Now, not only was the single action dead, the double-action revolver was on the edge of extinction. Or so they said.

A new phenomenon arrived to once again pump new life into the single action. Cowboy action shooting started in California and began spreading across the country in the 1980s and was going full bore by the 1990s. Thousands upon thousands of competitors took up aliases, dressed Western, and created a tremendous demand for single actions. Replica revolvers had been around ever since the Great Westerns of the 1950s, however, we now saw a concerted effort to produce authentic copies of the Colt Single Action.

That was only the beginning. We soon had new versions of traditional shotguns and lever actions, all types of authentic western clothing and leather rigs, and who would have believed it, suddenly we could choose not only replicas of the Single Action Army but nearly every other single action produced in the last quarter of the 19th century as well. Many competitors in cowboy action shooting choose replicas of the original Colt Single Action Army of 1873, others go with the currently-produced 3rd Generation Single Action Army from Colt. However, shooters also have other choices and it is a feast for the eyes to attend a large cowboy action shooting match and enjoy looking at all of the different sixguns that are being used. Just as it was in the Old West, the New West offers great choices when it comes to selecting a single-action revolver.

Smith & Wesson: Before the Colt Single Action Army, there was the single-action Smith & Wesson. In fact, Smith & Wesson introduced the first successful cartridge-firing single-action revolver with the tip-up, seven-shot Model #1 in 1857. It was chambered in what has become the most popular cartridge of all times, the 22 rimfire. Smith & Wesson started working on a big-bore version and would have introduced it in the early 1860s had it not been for the coming of the Civil War. In 1869 the first top-break single action from Smith & Wesson was introduced as the S&W Model #3 American. When the latch on the barrel/cylinder assembly in front of the hammer was unlocked, the barrel and cylinder swung down 90 degrees automatically ejecting fired cases. The cylinder could be reloaded quickly, the barrel returned upwards, and the American #3 was back in action in a few seconds.

The Russians took a good look at the Smith & Wesson design and improved it two ways. The original 44 S&W American used a heel-type bullet such as still found in the 22 Long Rifle. The Russians modernized it by changing to a single diameter bullet that also had lube grooves inside the case. This was the 44

▲Unlike the solid-frame Colt Single Action, the Smith & Wesson unlatched in front of the hammer and the barrel then swung down for loading and unloading.

Russian cartridge that would be lengthened to become the 44 Special in 1907— which was then lengthened to the 44 Magnum in 1955. We can thank the Russians for coming up with the same type ammunition in use today. The Russians also changed the shape of the backstrap of the Smith & Wesson, adding a hump at the top to prevent the grip from sliding downwards in the hand as the gun was fired. This beautiful sixgun became known as the Model #3 Russian.

Not only did the Russians change the shape of the backstrap and grip frame, they also added a spur on the bottom of the trigger guard. This apparently served two purposes. Pictures exist showing Russian soldiers with their Model #3 shoved into a sash around their waist with the spur being used to prevent the sixgun from sliding downwards. I have also found that by placing the middle finger of my shooting hand on the spur a most secure and steady grip is afforded.

The Model #3 Russians were only produced in the 1870s; however, thanks to Navy Arms they are now available replicated in a beautifully finished and fitted new production model. These are available chambered only in the 44 Russian, with a 6-inch barrel. Until very recently, 44 Russian ammunition had not been available for over 50 years, however it is back from several ammunition manufacturers, while brass is available from Starline.

The Model #3 Russian is not as easy for me to shoot as a Colt Single Action. It is a little more awkward for me to reach the hammer when shooting one-handed; however, when using two hands and cocking with the off hand it can be handled quite

VINTAGE ARMS

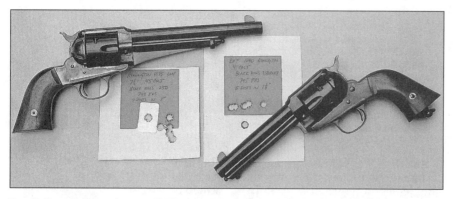

Remington replicas shoot well. These, a 7-inch Model 1875 and a 5-inch Model 1890 are chambered in 45 Colt and imported by EMF.

Remingtons, all replicas chambered in 45 Colt from Cimarron and EMF. Grips are by Buffalo Brothers.

speedily. Sights are very tiny, signifying pistoleros from the 1870s must have had very good eyes.

A second single-action Smith & Wesson available to shooters today is the 45 Schofield. Col. Schofield improved the Model #3 Smith & Wesson 44 by moving the locking latch from the barrel to the frame, which allowed it to be operated with one-hand instead of two. This could be tremendously important when operating on horseback. The caliber was also changed to 45 as the Army

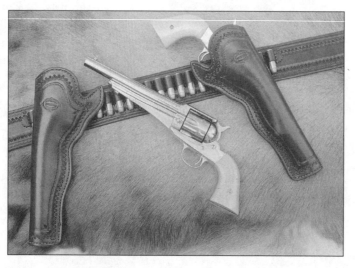

Pair of nickel-plated 1875 Remingtons from Navy Arms matched up with San Pedro Saddlery leather helps to turn the clock back 125 years.

had already purchased Colt Single Action Cavalry Models chambered in 45 Colt. However, the cylinder of the Smith & Wesson was too short to accept the 45 Colt so a new and shorter cartridge, the 45 S&W, was arrived at. The United States government purchased approximately 8,000 Schofield Models.

The 45 S&W could be used in six-guns chambered for the 45 Colt but not vice-versa. We are told that problems existed when outfits issued 45 Smith & Wessons wound

up with 45 Colt ammunition that would not chamber. Supposedly this was such a problem that the Army dropped the Schofield Model two years after it was adopted in 1875. Many of these guns had the barrel shortened and were sold to Wells Fargo. It is more likely that the Schofield was dropped simply because Smith & Wesson was so busy with a large contract for Russian Models for the Czar that they were no longer interested in manufacturing Schofields.

The Schofield Model, again thanks to Navy Arms, is available in replica form offered in the standard seven-inch Cavalry Model, a five-inch Wells Fargo version, and even in a three-inch "Sheriff's Model". Both blue and nickel finishes are offered as well as being chambered in both 45 Colt and 44-40. In 2000, Smith & Wesson resurrected the Schofield offering a special run chambered only in 45 S&W. Last year this became a standard offering through the Custom Shop but it has now been dropped. I would expect these Smith & Wesson-manufactured Schofields to increase in value over the next few years.

Remington: Eliphalet Remington goes back even farther than Sam Colt, Daniel Wesson, and Horace Smith when it comes to firearms. The history of Remington began in 1816 when Remington built his first rifle barrel. By 1839 it was "E. Remington & Son", which was then changed to "...Sons" in 1845. In 1856, Remington began manufacturing revolvers with the Fordyce Beals-designed 31 Pocket Revolver, followed closely by the Rider 31 Double Action Pocket Revolver.

Four years after Smith & Wesson's first big-bore cartridge firing revolver arrived with the American Model #3, Colt introduced the Colt Model P in 1873; and Remington followed two years later with the Model 1875 and a large contract for the Egyptian government. These "First Model" 1875s were chambered in 44 Remington. By 1878 the 45 Colt and 44-40 arrived in the Model 1875, and then in 1881, 7 1/2-inch Model 1875s were purchased for the Indian Police. The last batches of 1875s were made with 5 3/4-inch barrels and in 45 Colt chambering only. In 1886 E. Remington and Sons declared bankruptcy, however a new owner rescued the company as Remington Arms. The Model 1890 arrived only in 44-40 in both barrel lengths. Slightly over 2,000 Model 1890s

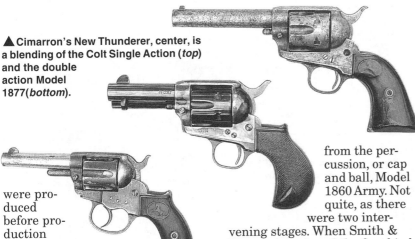

▲Cimarron's New Thunderer, center, is a blending of the Colt Single Action (*top*) and the double action Model 1877(*bottom*).

Cimarron's New Thunderer and Lightning are single actions, even though they resemble Colt's early double-action models.

were produced before production closed in 1894.

Today Italian-made replicas of both the 1875 and 1890 Model Remingtons are offered to shooters. They are easily distinguished from Colt Single Action replicas and each other due to the fact that the Model 1875 has a full web under the barrel and in front of the frame while it has been cut away on the 1890 sixgun. Both blue and nickel versions are offered, chambered in 45 Colt, 44-40 and 357 Magnum. Remington differs from the Colt in having a one-piece frame with the grip frame an integral part of the mainframe. For me, the hammer on a Remington is a little harder to reach than that on the Colt Single Action and there's also not quite as much room for my fingers between the back of the trigger guard and the front of the grip frame. Both EMF and Navy Arms offer replicas of the Remington. Good shootin' sixguns.

The First Colt Cartridge Revolvers: Many shooters have the mistaken idea that the Colt Single Action Army of 1873 came directly

from the percussion, or cap and ball, Model 1860 Army. Not quite, as there were two intervening stages. When Smith & Wesson introduced the first big-bore, cartridge-firing, single-action sixgun in 1869, Colt was caught totally flat-footed still clinging to the notion that shooters would always want to load their own by using powder, a round ball, and a percussion cap. When the Army, whose standard sidearm was the Colt 1860 Army, ordered 1,000 Smith & Wessons, Colt finally caught a picture of the future.

Smith & Wesson held the Rollin White patent for bored-through cylinders and it would be a few years before the patent would run out. Colt provided "modern" sixguns by converting both 1851 Navy and 1860 Army Models to cartridge-firing versions by retrofitting them with a new cylinder that would accept cartridges. They are appropriately known as Colt Cartridge Conversions. The first attempt was the Thuer Conversion that accepted a tapered cartridge that was inserted from the front of the cylinder. As expected, this version was not very practical and did not last very long. Next came the Richards, aad the,n the Richards-Mason Con-

version. They are easy to distinguish as the latter has a full-length ejector rod housing while the housing of the former stops about one inch in front of the cylinder. Remington cap and ball revolvers were also fitted with cartridge conversion cylinders in the early 1870s.

When the Army called for a series of tests to select a new sidearm, Colt's contribution was the 1871-72 Open-Top. This was not a cartridge conversion on the 1860 Army, but rather a totally new revolver. Had it not been for the Army insisting upon changes we may never have seen the advent of the Colt Single Action Army. The Open-Top followed the basic lines of the 1860 Army with, as the name suggests, the open-top frame as found on the 1860 rather than the solid frame found on the Remington percussion revolvers. It was also chambered in 44 caliber. The powers that be in the United States Army sent Colt back to the drawing board with two requests, solid top frame and 45 caliber. The result was the fabled Peacemaker.

Shooters can now relive the short but important part of history from 1869-1873 by shooting replicas of both the Colt Cartridge Conversions and the 1871-72 Open-Top. Cimarron Firearms offers Cartridge Conversions in an 1851 Model chambered in 38 Special/38 Long Colt and a 44 Colt 1860 Model as well as the 1871-72 Open-Top chambered in 44 Colt, 44 Russian, 45 S&W, and 38 Special/ 38 Long Colt. The modern 44 Colt cartridge is nothing more been a very slightly shortened 44 Special with a smaller diameter rim to be able to fit six rounds in the Model 1860-sized cylinder used in the Cartridge Conversions which is smaller in diameter than that found on the Colt Single Action Army. Ammunition is available from both

▲These three replica sixguns spanned the time period from the 1860 Army to the 1873 Peacemaker. From top left counterclockwise: a Richards Conversion, a Richards-Mason Conversion, and 1871-72 Open-Top.

For ease of cleaning it is difficult to beat the takedown feature of the Colt Cartridge Conversions.

Just as Colt did in the 1890s, Ruger now offers a Bisley Model (*top*) along with their standard single action, the Vaquero (*bottom*).

For those whose hands are too small for either the Bisley Model or Vaquero grip frames, Ruger now offers a 32 Single-Six (*bottom*) with a shortened grip frame.

Black Hills Ammunition and Ten-X, while Starline provides brass.

The Colts That Never Were: Four years after the introduction of the Single Action Army, Colt introduced their first double-action sixgun with the Model of 1877. Smaller than the Single Action Army it was known as the Lightning when chambered in 38 Long Colt and the Thunderer in 41 Long Colt. Although both of these models had the capability of being fired by simply pulling the trigger, they still loaded and unloaded the same as traditional single actions from Colt and Remington, that is, through a loading gate. The modern swing-out cylindered double-action revolver was still several years down the road.

Thanks to Cimarron Firearms, both the Lightning and Thunderer are back—not as double-action revolvers but rather single-action sixguns with the same backstrap profile as found on the Model 1877. This backstrap features a rounded butt with a hump at the top to keep the gun from shifting in the hand under recoil. The New Thunderer is nothing more than the standard Single Action Army with a new backstrap, while the Lightning is a smaller version of the same. The Thunderer version is offered in 45

Colt, 44-40, 44 Special, and 357 Magnum, while the smaller-framed Lightning accepts both 38 Special and 38 Long Colt cartridges.

Ruger's Variations on a Traditional Theme: In the early 1990s Ruger took a giant forward step backwards by giving their Blackhawk a traditional look. The Single-Six of 1953 and the Blackhawk of 1955 both featured a totally modern lockwork powered by coil springs rather than the flat springs of the Colt Single Action. The Blackhawk featured fully adjustable sights. With the growing popularity of cowboy action shooting, Ruger introduced the Vaquero version of the Blackhawk with Colt Single Action Army-type fixed sights. This made the Vaquero legal in the Traditional Class of cowboy action shooting. Since that time, Ruger has introduced three variations of the standard Vaquero. The Bisley Model Vaquero features a larger target-type grip frame with a lower riding, easier to cock, wide hammer; the Sheriff's Model Vaquero has a round-butted Bird's Head grip frame; and the third version is a 4 5/8-inch Vaquero-style stainless steel Single-Six chambered in 32 Magnum for

those shooters who cannot handle the recoil of the larger revolvers.

Unlike the 22 Single-Six, which has the standard Blackhawk grip frame the little 32 Single-Six is only offered with a Bird's Head or a shorter standard grip frame to accommodate those with small hands. The Bisley Model Vaquero is cataloged in 45 Colt, 44 Magnum and 357 Magnum calibers in blue/case-color and stainless finishes, with both 4 5/8-inch and 5 1/2-inch barrel lengths in the two big-bore chamberings and 5 1/2-inch only in 357 Magnum. The Sheriff's Model is offered in both blue/case color and stainless finishes in 357 Magnum with a 4 5/8-inch barrel and 45 Colt with a 3 1/2-inch barrel length.

Freedom Arms Model 97: Even Freedom Arms, best-known for its premium quality, factory custom-built, five-shot revolvers chambered in 454 Casull entered the cowboy action shooting arena with their first six-shot revolver in 1997. Chambered in 357 Magnum, with an extra cylinder in 38 Special available, the Model 97 is slightly smaller than a Colt Single Action and is offered to those cowboy action shooters who want the finest single-action revolver ever offered. The Model 97 is also chambered in 45 Colt, 41 Magnum, and 44 Special: all five-shooters—as well as a six-shot rimfire version in 22 Long Rifle with the option of a second cylinder chambered in 22 Rimfire Magnum.

In the 1870s, sixgunners had the choice of big-bore sixguns from several manufacturers with the top three being Colt, Remington, and Smith & Wesson. Now, thanks to replicas we have the same choices as well as thoroughly modern single actions such as the Ruger Vaquero and the Freedom Arms Model 97. Once in a while progress actually does us a favor. •

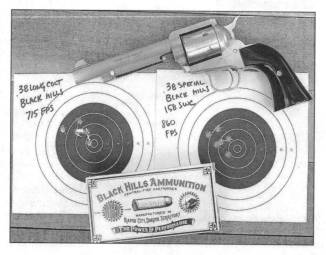

As expected, the Freedom Arms Model 97 shoots well with both 38 Long Colt and 38 Special ammunition from Black Hills.

Big-Bore Revolvers

▶ Short-barrel revolvers have a place in the handgun hunting battery. Two of these revolvers are from Smith & Wesson, while the one in the middle is a Freedom Arms five-shooter.

for Handgun Hunting

▲ Revolvers and boar hunting go hand in hand. This porker was taken with a Ruger Blackhawk in 357 Magnum.

by Mark Hampton

IT'S NO WONDER that handgun hunting continues to rise in popularity. More and more hunters are looking to add a bit of challenge into their outdoor experience and there seems to be an almost endless supply of high quality handguns available to make that endeavor more memorable and rewarding. The array of handguns, along with the added challenge of hunting with the short gun, really make the adventure appealing to many hunters, both men and women. For many of us, handgun hunting is more of an addiction. There are a lot of choices when it comes to hunting handguns. In an attempt to meet the needs and desires for many different preferences of shooters, we have at our disposal revolvers, autos, and single-shots. I guess that's why some of us prefer blondes while others succumb to brunettes or redheads; you know, the Dodge-Ford thing. For sixgun fans, the choice of revolvers has never been so good. There are some fine wheelguns available to make your handgun hunting pursuits more enjoyable, and successful. Plus they are just plain fun to shoot!

Why do hunters like packing a sixgun in the first place? Maybe it's because we have watched too many John Wayne movies or just an attraction to wheelguns perhaps? Everyone probably has a different reason or two but for me, it's the close range encounters that occur in the field that perk my interest in revolvers. Those encounters I am referring to include whitetail deer hunting in the woods, one of my favorite excursions. The most popular big game animal in America has many of us dreaming

This big pig was taken with a Mag-Na-Port Predator at range of around 20 yards. The Predator is basically a custom Ruger Super Blackhawk in 44 Magnum.

Pamela Atwood took this trophy dall sheep with a Freedom Arms 454 Casull.

Hunting revolvers are available in both single and double-action. Mounting revolvers with a scope depends on your preference or hunting methods.

about deer season long before it arrives. When shots are kept inside 100 yards, the revolver is a great choice for deer hunting. Many deer hunters, myself included, enjoy success by hunting from tree stands. The revolver can be easily carried and packed up a ladder stand in one of the many holsters today, safely and securely. Revolvers can adequately handle almost all woodswise whitetail encounters. But deer hunting is not the only place where the revolver is a top choice. Following a pack of hounds in pursuit of mountain lion, bear, or wild boar is another ideal situation for the sixgun. I have had my fair share of experiences trying to keep up with a bunch of dogs chasing enthusiastically after a cat, boar, or bear. Having a revolver strapped securely on your hip made running over hill and yonder much easier than packing a cumbersome rifle. And if whitetail deer—along with critters pursued by

hounds—is not enough to convince you to pack a revolver, you can always take the challenge of hunting elk, grizzly, or even African game with the wheelgun.

At a recent Safari Club International Convention I had the pleasure of getting to spend a few moments with Bob Baker, President of Freedom Arms. Bob is not only the head of this company but he is also an accomplished handgun hunter. Freedom Arms produces one the finest revolvers available today in their Model 83. This top-drawer

firearm was developed for the experienced hunter as a primary hunting rig for large or dangerous game. It can also be employed as a backup gun in certain circumstances. Several different barrel lengths are available including 4 3/4-, 6-, 7 1/2-, and 10-inch models. Both Premier and field-grade revolvers are manufactured with the same craftsmanship regarding materials and tolerances. I like both of these variations on this large-frame revolver. The Premier Grade appears with a brighter, brushed finish with much time and attention devoted to the cosmetic details. Grips on the Premier Grade are laminated hardwood with resin bonding and do not punish the hand during recoil. However,

This Freedom Arms 97 is chambered for 41 Magnum and is ideal for hunting whitetail deer.

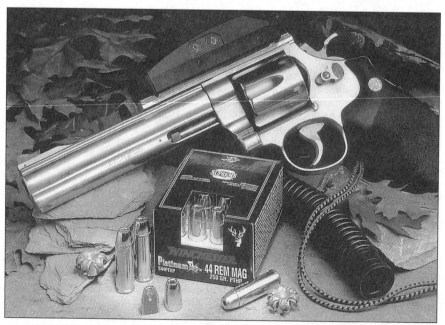

With today's quality handguns and ammunition, handgun hunters have never had it so good.

The Freedom Arms field-grade 454 Casull makes a powerful package for the hunter seeking big game.

This is the new Smith & Wesson Model 500 from the Performance Shop. For those who subscribe to "bigger is better", this offering should suffice.

many hunters prefer the Field Grade with a matte finish, which produces less glare under bright conditions. The Field Grade comes equipped with Pachmayr Presentation grips. The more economical Field Grade is available with a limited one-year warranty while the Premier Grade has a lifetime-limited warranty. These fine revolvers come in several calibers ideally suited for hunting purposes including 50 Action Express, 475 Linebaugh, 454 Casull, 44 Magnum, 41 Magnum, 357 Magnum, and the popular 22 Long Rifle for all of us small-game hunters. There is also a silhouette model available for competition shooting.

Another great offering from Freedom Arms is their Model 97. As a member of United Handgun Hunters Chapter of SCI, Bob had graciously donated a Model 97 chambered in 41 Magnum for a chapter fundraiser. I played with this model while talking to Bob in the Freedom Arms booth, hoping I would be lucky enough to win this firearm in the drawing. Unfortunately a friend of mine won this piece and I am sure he will use it. His name was Larry Kelly, one of the top handgun hunters of modern times. The Model 97 is a mid-frame revolver that fits my hand like a glove. The same craftsmanship and attention given to the large-frame revolvers is built into the Model 97. And boy, is this gun accurate! Five-shot versions are available in 45 Colt and 41 Magnum in 4 1/4-, 5 1/2-, and 7 1/2-inch barrel lengths. The six-shot version is chambered for 357 Magnum and 22 Long Rifle, with a 10-inch tube available for the rimfire.

I have been packing Freedom Arms revolvers around for many years. They have been on my side while hunting in Africa, Australia, and here in North America. These guns are truly some of the finest wheelguns available today. The people behind the guns are genuine, too. Bob Baker took his first whitetail deer while hunting with me

many years ago. It was a good 10-pointer that strolled too close past Bob's treestand. One well-placed shot from Bob's Model 97 in 357 Magnum yielded a fine 10-point Missouri buck and a winter's supply of venison. The folks behind Freedom Arms guns are hunters and understand our needs and wants.

Freedom Arms now offers Bear Track Cases, which are some of the most dependable and secure gun cases on the market. These cases have already established a reputation for being tough and capable of withstanding enraged baggage handlers. Several sizes, styles, and colors are available to fit many different types of handguns. Since I normally travel with two or even three large handguns, I like their Silhouette case that measures 27 x 15 x 6.5 inches and weighs 18 pounds. Traveling all over the world with handguns, it's nice to know they will arrive protected and secure from rough treatment. Bear Track Cases with their rugged construction allow me to travel in remote parts of the world with confidence that my guns will be ready for the hunt when we get there. I consider a high-quality gun case an investment worth every penny when it comes to protecting my guns.

Recently I have been shooting some big-bore revolvers from Magnum Research. If you are in the fraternity that believes bigger is better then you will find yourself longing for one of the company's BFR, which stands for Biggest Finest Revolver. At first glance the gun appears somewhat like a Super Blackhawk, but it isn't. The big gun does come with Pachmayr grips which helps cushion the hand during recoil. The cylinder can rotate freely when you

open the loading latch. As a matter of fact, the cylinder can rotate in the opposite direction if the need should arise. This facilitates both loading and unloading the gun with ease and could be considered "user friendly."

Two guns came for review: a 480 Ruger, along with the 45-70 and an extra cylinder in 450 Marlin. I really couldn't decide which one I liked best. First, the BFR is one of the only revolvers that come with a cylinder that accommodates both the 480 Ruger/475 Linebaugh. If you shove a 475 Linebaugh cartridge in cylinders not designed for it, the bullet will protrude beyond the cylinder, not allowing rotation. This gun came with a Leupold 2X scope mounted in an SSK base mount. The 45-70 was topped with a 2 1/2-8X Leupold. These were two very serious hunting handguns.

My good shooting buddy wanted to try the 480 Ruger first so we began our shooting at 50 yards. You could tell the cylinder lockup was very tight. When the hammer was

The top two scoped revolvers are from Magnum Research while the bottom one is a Taurus Raging Bull in 44 Magnum. All can handle most hunting situations.

The Taurus Raging Bull with an 8-inch barrel, compensator and cushioned grips is well balanced and pleasant to shoot.

cocked the action was smooth as silk. The ejector rod is fully shrouded. All barrels on these fine guns are hand-lapped and precision recessed-crowned. It doesn't take long to see this gun is built to handle heavy caliber rounds. The first, second, and third five-shot group fired measured right around two inches. Recoil was not the least bit intimidating. We were using factory ammo from Hornady utilizing their 325-grain XTP bullet. The XTP Magnum bullet is a jacketed hollow-point and makes for an ideal load for big game such as whitetail, wild boar, or a big black bear.

After taking the 480 Ruger through a few paces we then picked up the big 45-70. Both of us were a little apprehensive regarding the

anticipated recoil. Politely I allowed John first round with the gun. At the shot we were both pleasantly surprised. Recoil was amazingly mild. The load we were using happened to be some 400-grain Speers over a maximum load of powder for hunting purposes. With factory 45-70 ammo, this gun would be extremely mild mannered. The variable scope was setting in the 4X position where it remained during our shooting session. Accuracy was more than acceptable and we had no problems controlling the gun. The sheer weight of the massive revolver, nearly six pounds when loaded and scoped, along with proper balance contributes to its manageability. This big revolver chambered for the old and faithful

45-70 is no novelty, it's the real deal. John and I both were impressed!

Time did not allow us to run the 450 Marlin cylinder through the paces but it will happen. Currently the 450 Marlin BFR is the biggest bang you're going to find in a revolver. Don't be surprised to see some handgun hunters tackle really big game with this rig including bear, bison, Cape buffalo, or Asian buffalo.

Smith & Wesson has long been active in the handgun-hunting arena. One of my first real big-game hunting revolvers was a Model 29. The six-inch version accounted for the first whitetail deer I took with a handgun. Boy, was I a happy camper that day. Many handgun hunters today employ a variety of Smith & Wesson revolvers. For those that use a 357 Magnum, there are several models available. So many models that I am afraid to begin listing them for fear of omitting some. When I am guiding hog hunters, a Model 686 frequently can be found riding on my hip. The six-inch revolver rests in a radical cross-draw holster and provides comfort if a wounded hog happens to be in the forecast. Personally, I am not a huge fan of the 357 Magnum. When I do find myself packing one, it is stuffed full of 180-grain bullets.

For you 41 Magnum fans Smith & Wesson offers several models. While the 41 Magnum has never been, and will never be, as popular as the bigger 44 caliber, it still remains an efficient cartridge for medium-sized game like whitetail. The Model 57/657 line of revolvers fulfills many hunters desire to enjoy the not-so-popular 41 Magnum.

The Model 29 and 629, both chambered for the popular 44 Magnum, have seen much action in the field. Whitetail hunters can fill their tag and freezer with these double-action wheelguns, scoped or not. And there is a ton of factory ammunition available if you choose not to reload. This has been one of the most popular revolvers for hunting. After 12 years of guiding hunters on my ranch, many handgun hunters have packed some version of a Smith & Wesson 44 Magnum.

The big news from the company at this time is the introduction of the 50-caliber magnum cartridge. This massive cartridge will be launched from the new S & W Model 500 double-action revolver. The revolver will take shape on what the

The Magnum Research Biggest Finest Revolver chambered for the 45-70 cartridge. Thanks to its weight and balance recoil is not an issue.

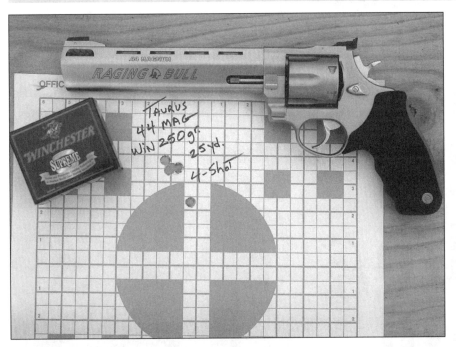

The raging bull is also capable of excellent accuracy, an essential for hunting game.

company dubs their X-frame. This new production model makes the Model 29/629 look small in comparison. The cartridge will initially be available in three factory bullet weights from Cor-Bon: a 275-grain hollow-point, 400-grain jacketed flat point, and a 440-grain cast offering. Cor-bon's factory listing of velocity using an 8 3/8-inch barrel with the 275-grain bullet is 1662 fps. The 400-grainer generates 1676 fps as the 440-grain cast bullet hits 1625 fps, with incredible whopping foot-pounds of energy approaching 2600! That's really impressive especially coming from a revolver.

The gun itself will be all stainless steel, double-action, wearing Hogue rubber grips. When I first laid eyes on one of these revolvers it struck me as big huge. And it is, weighing 72 ounces empty. By the time you fill the five chambers full of lead, mount a scope with base and rings, you will have a handful to say the least.

Right now plans are being made to take this newest offering from S&W to Africa this summer. I can't think of a better way to test the true capabilities of a hunting handgun. Maybe it will come up against a formidable opponent such as the nasty Cape buffalo or even something bigger! If the big 500 works on tough tenacious dangerous game, it will surely suffice on bear, elk, and moose. Who knows what might happen in Africa but it's going to be fun.

Single-action fans have the Ruger Super Blackhawk chambered in 44 Magnum to satisfy their cravings for a versatile, quality, time-proven performer. Available in several different barrel lengths, the Super Blackhawk has stood the test of time. In my younger days I have chased hounds all over hills and canyons chasing black bear, mountain lion, and wild hogs wearing a 10 1/2-inch barreled Ruger. It was simply a rugged, reliable handgun that you can count on in the time of need. The company's new Super Blackhawk Hunter model is made to accommodate optics right out of the box. This version has two cuts already machined on the 7 1/2-inch barrel's wide solid rib to accept factory-supplied stainless steel scope rings. Ruger has truly addressed the need for handgun hunters looking to mount a scope.

The new Hunter will handle all types of inclement weather with a buffed satin finish. The unfluted cylinder is designed to digest a consistent diet of factory magnum ammunition. The gun also comes with a rounded stainless steel grip frame and trigger guard. If you're in the market for a single-action hunting revolver that will last a lifetime, look no further.

For those hunters preferring double-action revolvers for whatever reason, the Super Redhawk is a natural. For years I have been shooting

and hunting with a custom 5 1/2-inch, Mag-na-ported Super Redhawk. It has always performed flawlessly time after time. Today we have a choice of Super Redhawks between the 44 Magnum, 480 Ruger, or 454 Casull. All serious big-game calibers designed with handgun hunters in mind. The Super Redhawk is a heavy-duty, well-constructed revolver capable of digesting heavy magnum loads consistently. The integral scope mounting system accepts a scope with simplicity. With three different barrel lengths, 5 1/2, 7 1/2, and 9 1/2 inches, handgun hunters have a choice depending on their likes and hunting applications.

Taurus International produces some fine revolvers with the hunter in mind including their 357 and 41 Magnum Tracker series. These quality firearms are well balanced and make a great choice for the hunter wishing to shoot either of the magnum calibers. The company's Model 425 is chambered in 41 Magnum and makes for an ideal packing gun. The Tracker holds five rounds of 41 Magnum ammo and comes with the exclusive Ribber Grip.

The Raging Bull Model 444 in 44 Magnum recently showed up on my doorstep. This is a first-class hunting revolver with a well-deserved reputation for rugged dependability. A double-lockup cylinder adds strength and safety. The factory porting feature works! I shot a bunch of factory 44 Magnum ammunition one afternoon on the range and couldn't believe how pleasant this gun reacted during recoil. The gun I was shooting wore an 8 3/8-inch heavy barrel and soft rubber grips, which helped cushion the gun while shooting magnum loads. It's no wonder more hunters and sportsmen are turning to Taurus for quality and dependable handguns.

WOW! What an incredible array of great revolvers capable of successfully engaging just about any hunting situation imaginable. If you are looking for a high-quality revolver for hunting purposes, the only dilemma I see is choosing which one. With so many fine handguns available today, it's difficult to decide which one will suit your needs and personal interest best. Oh well, what a delightful position to be in! ●

Hunting With the Self-Loading Pistol

by Chuck Taylor

This record book Corsican Ram was taken as he fled by author with a single raking shot from 40 meters with Colt M1911 45 ACP and a 200-grain Hensley & Gibbs SWC and 6.2 grains of Reliant Unique.

FOR THE LAST decade, the popularity of handgun hunting has increased tenfold, with more and more aficionados appearing all the time. Yet, most of the interest in the kind of weapons used has centered upon higher-powered handguns. Indeed, stories of 44 Magnums and even more powerful custom weapons have long dominated the hunting magazines, with less potent handguns being virtually ignored. Curiously, the self-loading – or "automatic" – pistol is in this category and has arbitrarily been regarded as being suitable only for military/police/civilian self-defense.

This is unfortunate, because the self-loader has much to offer, especially to what I call the "purist" handgun hunter, the fellow who takes his hunting seriously and thus pursues it in its most basic form. Hunters like this don't go for optical sights, powerful revolvers or rifle-caliber "carbines without a buttstock." Instead, they prefer to rely upon their woodcraft, stalking and marksmanship skills to get close to their quarry, then dispatch it with a well-placed shot to the appropriate vital area.

The handguns used for such hunting are service pistols, and are virtually identical to those used by the military/police/civilian sector as self-defense arms. Typically, they're chambered for the 9mm parabellum, 40 S&W, 10mm or 45 ACP and can be found in the usual array of designs – single action (SA), double-action (DA) and double-action only (DAO) – and in a number of variants of each central design type.

For example, let's take the Colt M1911. As we all know, "Olde Ugly" has been with us a long, long time and during its long tenure has evolved pretty much as far as its inherent characteristics permit. We know how to bring it to its full potential as far as accuracy, mechanical reliability and general "user friendliness" are concerned. Thus, adapting it for use as a hunting arm is relatively simple and largely a matter of individual preference and consideration.

The basic M1911 is currently manufactured by over a dozen companies, all of whom offer it in standard (Government Model), compact (Commander) and sub-compact (Officer's Model) configurations. The prospective hunter must then decide which type best suits his needs and then select which modifications, if any, best enhance its performance as a hunting arm.

Without a doubt, the two most popular SA autos are the M1911 and Browning P35. Both are among the earliest self-loaders to see service and are thus quite prolific and popular. Normally chambered for

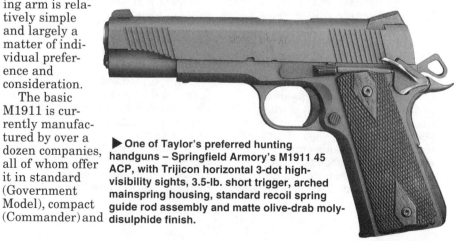

▶ One of Taylor's preferred hunting handguns – Springfield Armory's M1911 45 ACP, with Trijicon horizontal 3-dot high-visibility sights, 3.5-lb. short trigger, arched mainspring housing, standard recoil spring guide rod assembly and matte olive-drab moly-disulphide finish.

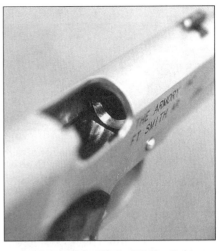

High-visibility sights, preferably with enhancement for use in low light conditions often typical of hunting situations, are a must. Author recommends the Trijicon horizontal 3-dot pattern for best results.

The use of exotic JHP or SWC bullet configurations for best results on game may require feedway polishing and/or reshaping to assure functional reliability under field conditions.

the 45 ACP cartridge, the M1911 continues to be the dominant handgun in many circles, as does the P35 in 9mmP. However, though they're nowhere as near popular, versions of both can also be found chambered for the 10mm auto and 40 S&W auto cartridges as well.

The classic DA is well represented by a plethora of guns from SIG, Smith & Wesson, Ruger and Beretta, to name but a few. And, as is experienced with the SA auto, they, too, are chambered for the entire range of service cartridges.

Unquestionably, the Glock is the most prolific DAO, though both Smith & Wesson and Beretta also offer a few. And, though only just beginning to appear in sizeable number on the U.S. market, Springfield Armory's excellent XD series is also becoming quite popular.

All of these guns share four common needs to reach their full potential as hunting arms. They all need sights quickly seen at high speed, particularly in the low light conditions typical of the hunting environment (dawn & dusk). They also need a crisp, clean light trigger pull, all sharp edges removed and an external finish appropriate to the natural

environment in which they're to be carried and used.

First, let's look at sights. High visibility doesn't necessarily mean that the rear sight must be adjustable, but given the wide variety of ammunition that might be used, adjustable sights are far more useful in the hunting environment than they are in a tactical one.

In addition, since the vast majority of encounters with game animals occur during twilight periods, tritium inserts are a good idea. They come in a number of configurations, but it's been my longtime experience that the horizontal 3-dot pattern is by far the most efficient. Sight alignment when game is engaged takes place quickly and the shot must be placed carefully. For such situations, no other alignment method is as fast as the 3-dot pattern.

A wide variety of bullet styles are also utilized for handgun hunting. What type you select is largely dependent upon what kind of game you're hunting, the terrain and vegetation in which you're hunting it and how well it feeds in the self-loader you've chosen to use. Personally, I've found Hor-

nady's XTP JHP to be by far the best performer on small and medium game, and even occasionally larger critters, as long as they're of the thin-skinned type.

In 9mmP, a handload consisting of the Hornady 90-grain XTP JHP and 6.0-grains of Reliant Unique produces right at 1300 fps from the 4 1/4-inch barrel of the typical service pistol, is exceptionally accurate, produces negligible recoil and demonstrates spectacular terminal ballistics totally disproportionate to its size. Time and time again, I've used this load successfully in the Glock 17, Browning P35, SIG P226, Beretta M92F and XD-9, successfully obtaining one-shot kills on even

Careful load and bullet selection is also required. Accuracy is important, of course, but so is feeding reliability and terminal ballistic performance. This being the case, author prefers a lead SWC in sub-sonic cartridges and the Hornady XTP JHP in those that are super-sonic.

Pre-hunt mastery of field shooting positions such as kneeling and prone greatly enhance the potential for success in the field.

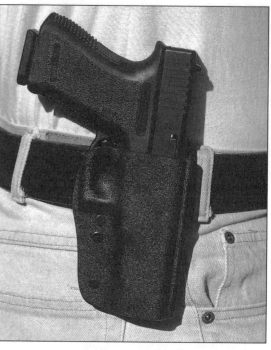

▲ Another of author's favorites – Glock 17 with 3.5-lb. trigger. Used with author's preferred handload of the Hornady 90-grain XTP JHP and 6.0 grains of Reliant Unique (1300 fps from typical 4-inch 9mm service pistol barrels), it performs magnificently even on larger thin-skinned animals such as elk.

A simple, yet rugged and secure holster is also needed. Taylor prefers the Kydex "Taylor Nighthawk," which he designed, produced by Cen-Dex Tactical, Inc.

mule deer at ranges out to a full 100-meters and occasionally beyond.

In fact, from the new XD-9 Tactical with 5-inch barrel, bullet velocities in the 1400 fps range are typical, as is also seen with the 6-inch barreled longslide Glock 17L. This is well within the range of performance expected of a healthy 357 Magnum, but without the blast and recoil.

In 40 S&W, the 155-grain XTP and 7.0-grains of Unique gives 1050 fps in the Glock 22 and 1150 fps in the longslide Glock 24, excellent accuracy and good terminal ballistics out to about 50 meters.

Though its popularity is on the wane, the 10mm auto is roughly the equivalent of a mid-range 41 magnum. And, while sharp recoil is typical of all full-house 10mm loads, a handload utilizing the 155-grain XTP JHP and 8.0-grains of Unique will give you about 1200 fps, good accuracy and excellent bullet expansion, making it a good all-around choice.

For those who prefer the 45 ACP, Hornady's 185-grain XTP JHP and 7.5 grains of Unique produces 1000 fps, while the 200-grain XTP and 7.0-grains slams out at about 950 fps. Both are exceptionally accurate, demonstrate good penetration and expansion, and are entirely suitable for the whole range of game animals out to 50-meters or so.

If dangerous animals like bear and wild boar are your quarry, I recommend you forego use of the 9mmP, and 40 S&W and instead use either the 10mm or 45 ACP. Since penetration is the paramount criteria for neutralizing such animals, I prefer to use hardcast SWC bullets to assure penetration through heavy muscle and bone, and the creation of the largest possible permanent wound channel.

With this in mind, 8.0 grains of Unique with a hard-cast 190-grain

SWC (1150 fps) brings the 10mm to its max, while the 200-grain Hensley & Gibbs #68 SWC and 7.5 grains of Unique (1000 fps) is about as good as it gets with the 45 ACP. Remember, however, that neither of these loads is the equivalent of a full-house 44 Magnum or heavy-loaded 45 Colt, so very careful shot-placement must be the order of the day.

As far as factory ammo goes, I find the 127-grain Winchester Ranger SXT JHP +P+ (1250 fps) and the Remington 115-grain JHP +P+ (1275 fps) to be the best 9mmP available. Although new and thus relatively untested on game, Federal's 357 SIG 125-grain JHP (1250 fps) is accurate and should also do well.

With the 40 S&W, the Ranger SXT 180-grain JHP (985 fps) is by far the best. If you're a 45 ACP buff, once again the Ranger SXT is the best choice, slamming its 230-grain JHP out of the 5-inch barrel of a typical Government Model M1911 at 870 fps.

Having said all this, regardless of your pistol's capability or the performance of its ammunition, successful results can only be obtained with careful shot placement. Service pistols just aren't as potent as the mag-

Near record-book bobcat, taken with a single shot to the chest from 45 meters by the author with Springfield Armory's new Xd-40.

nums, so care must be taken with shot angles and placement to ensure successful results. In many cases, particularly with dangerous game, shots directed against major bone mass are a poor choice because of penetration problems.

Thus, raking shots from the left or right rear and shots aimed directly into the animal's hindquarters don't usually produce good results because the bullet doesn't reach vital organs. This means that shots from the right or left side, placed behind the shoulder and, for dangerous game, even cranial shots are preferred.

Even if good judgment is exercised on shot angles, the only way you can guarantee good hit placement is to practice. Don't limit your practice to just fast weapon presentations and target engagement. Field conditions are often less than optimum in terms of vegetation and terrain, so spend a serious amount of your practice time and energy with field positions like kneeling and prone, too. In fact, I think once you perfect your skills with them, you'll be using them more often than not.

Last, think carefully about what kind of holster you want. Different kinds of hunting require different choices, so before you finalize your holster choice, think long and hard about your needs. I prefer a simple Kydex rig from Cen-Dex Tactical worn strong-side, with a spare magazine or two on my non-firing side, beside which I place my knife. It's compact, simple, rugged and secure, but very fast if a quick weapon presentation is needed.

These, then, are the things to consider if you want to hunt with the self-loading handgun. First, define your needs carefully. Second, keep your choice of weapon type, caliber and ammunition simple and focused on the kind of game you'll be hunting. Third, practice getting your weapon into action quickly and hitting targets in all kind of light conditions until it becomes second-nature.

Fourth, study the anatomy of the game you're hunting. Know the best shot angles and the maximum ranges at which you can expect good results. Remember that service pistols aren't as powerful as the magnums and as such, you'll have to get closer with them.

Having done all of this, don't forget your woodcraft. After all, if you can't stalk, then you can't get close enough and/or get the right angle to make the shot. This means paying attention to the wind, wearing cam-

Author with fine bull elk taken with a single frontal shot to the chest with Glock 24 40 S&W with 155-grain Hornady XTP JHP from 40 meters.

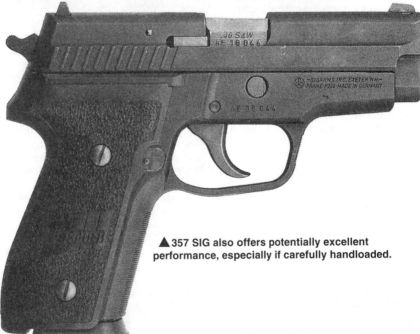

▲ 357 SIG also offers potentially excellent performance, especially if carefully handloaded.

ouflage clothes (that don't radiate ultra-violet light) and learning how to move slowly and smoothly across various types of terrain.

When you've done all this, you'll be ready – ready to enjoy the end-

less hours of pleasure afield, becoming very much one with the land around you. Handgun hunting is among the most pleasurable types of hunting and doing it with a self-loader, while clearly not for everyone, is among the most rewarding.

Try it! I think you'll agree. ●

Long Range Handgun Markmanship for the Field

by Mark Hampton

IT WASN'T TOO many years ago the thought of taking game beyond 200 yards with a handgun was nothing more than wishful thinking or maybe a hallucination. After all, handgun hunters were supposed to stalk game and get as close as absolutely possible before taking a shot. That's a big part of why so many hunters enjoy handgun hunting, the sheer challenge involved. We still are responsible for making a clean shot and harvesting game in a clean, quick, and humane fashion. But today's handguns allow us to take game out at 200 yards and well beyond, if we are properly prepared for this task. If you hunt long enough for a variety of different game, there will be times when getting within 100 yards, or less, to your quarry becomes virtually impossible. With shortened seasons and time restraints most of us have placed upon our lives, we really don't have twenty or thirty days to wait for the ideal opportunity to materialize. Perhaps the game we are hunting lives in an environment that makes close-range shooting unrealistic, such as antelope or mule deer in the wide-open spaces of the West. Maybe you're hunting

Sometime it is not possible to get close to one's prey in the field. In such instances the need for long range accuracy becomes essential. Shooting at extreme angles, either uphill or down, presents special challenges for the handgun hunter.

something like ibex or sheep that inhabit mountainous terrain and getting within 250 yards is tough. Regardless what circumstance you find yourself in, it's comforting to know that long shots are possible with today's handguns.

The first and foremost part of long-range shooting is choosing a handgun and cartridge combination that is capable of shooting minute-of-angle. This will focus our

attention to several of the single-shot handguns that are currently available. Thompson-Center Arms provides hunters and shooters with the versatile Contender, which will be replaced with the new G2 model. The folks in New Hampshire also manufacture the heavier and more beefed-up Encore, which is capable of handling higher-pressure cartridges than the Contender. Both guns have found favor

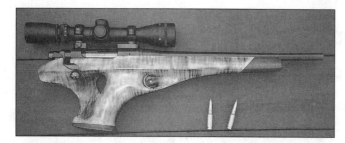

The out-of-production Remington XP-100 can still be found. And makes for an ideal long range tool. This particular 7BR is topped with a Burris 3-12X scope and wears a Fajen thumbhole stock.

The Savage Striker is an accurate bolt-action handgun. This one is chambered for the 22-250 cartridge.

Finding a good rest is important when shooting long distance. These shooting sticks, combined with bracing the back against a tree, help provide a very steady shooting platform.

in the hearts of handgun hunters. These guns are very accurate, reliable, and dependable. The interchangeable barrel option is appealing to many hunters and shooters. You can have one frame with the capability of adding a variety of barrels in different calibers and configurations to your personal handgun battery.

H-S Precision produces an extremely accurate bolt-action handgun they dub their Pro-Series 2000. This particular model comes in two different versions, a silhouette and varmint model, in 11 different calibers. I have one of their Varmint models in 308 Winchester wearing a 2-6X Bushnell scope and it is certainly a long-range handgun by every definition. The 2-inch wide forend rests nicely on top of a backpack.

The out-of-production Remington XP-100 is another excellent example of an accurate single-shot handgun. These fine bolt-action handguns can still be found floating around. They are extremely accurate when set-up properly and make great long range hunting guns. I have three XPs, two of which I use frequently in 7BR and a customized 284 Winchester. The other XP is resting peacefully, standing by as a spare. In terms of accuracy, these guns will outshoot the

vast majority of rifles. Quality gunsmiths can perform countless embellishments on these handguns making them unbelievably accurate.

Another bolt gun that is seeing a lot of action today is the Savage Striker. Unlike the XP, Savage incorporates the bolt on the left side of the action. In other words, right-handed shooters can hold the grip and work the bolt with their left hand. Some shooters appreciate this concept. Savage chambers the Striker in several calibers ideally suited for long-range shooting. Having shot one of these accurate bolt guns recently, I feel they benefit greatly by having a trigger job or an aftermarket replacement. The Striker is a lot of gun for the money and would make an ideal long-range handgun.

There are other handguns capable of MOA accuracy including the XL, MOA, and a new offering from Sigarms. I haven't had the pleasure of trying the new bolt-action handgun from Sig but it is built on the same action as the Blaser R93 rifle. This straight-pull, bolt-action hunting handgun is initially available in 10 popular calibers including the 7mm-08 and 308, two of my favorite whitetail

deer cartridges. Barrel length is 14 inches and even with a scope mounted the gun will tip the scales at less than five pounds. I can't wait to get my hands on this model. This should prove to be another welcome addition to the world of handgun hunting. Regardless which handgun you prefer, the main component that should be considered for long-range shooting is the accuracy potential.

I like handguns that are fairly heavy when shooting game from long distance. Most of my long-range guns weigh over five pounds when scoped. Some of them over six pounds. This is a lot of weight to carry while hunting, especially if you're walking a lot or climbing mountains. These large, single-shot handguns are not exactly easy to pack. They are bulky, cumbersome, awkward to carry whether you're walking, riding a horse, or packing up a mountain. However, when that once-in-a-lifetime shot materializes and you finally get that hard-earned trophy in the scope, that extra weight helps steady the crosshairs when the moment of truth arrives. It's amazing how quickly you forget about any inconvenience it may have caused. When resting on a backpack or shooting sticks, the additional weight of the handgun is obviously worth the trouble of packing, at least to me, especially when it helps place the bullet where it belongs.

Speaking of backpacks and shooting sticks makes me think of finding a good rest when attempting a long-range shot. We cannot take a shooting bench to the field but we can always look for a good solid rest. A lot depends on what type of terrain you find yourself hunting. In the mountains I always place my

This H-S Precision Pro-Series 2000 is chambered for 308 Winchester. The single-shot bolt action will outshoot a multitude of rifles.

In wide-open country out west, handgun hunters often find themselves shooting at long range. This Montana antelope was taken at long distance using a Thompson/center Arms Contender in 309 JDJ.

backpack on top of a boulder, which provides a fairly steady rest. Hunting areas where tall grass, weeds, or brush may obstruct your vision, I then turn to something like shooting sticks. It seems I am always on the lookout for something solid to help steady the crosshairs—like a fence post, stump, rock, or whatever happens to be handy at the time. Long-range precision shooting is simply not possible without a good steady rest, at least for most of us.

Shooting a handgun at long range can be a challenging task even if all conditions are right. Trying to place your bullet precisely with a hard-to-pull trigger becomes a bigger obstacle. In today's world it's difficult finding a factory trigger that is acceptable, at least for my preference. Really this is not the fault of the manufacturers, just our litigation-happy culture! It will behoove the shooter to have a trigger job performed by a competent gunsmith to eliminate any gritty spots or creep, and to adjust the break less than three pounds. If I only hunted in warm weather all of my triggers would be considerably less than two pounds. Hunting in cold weather keeps me from adjusting the trigger much lighter than 32 ounces as you don't want the gun to go off accidentally or unexpectedly. To increase the effectiveness of long range shooting, a good trigger is paramount.

Quality scopes are also high on the list of important equipment for long-range marksmanship. You cannot hit what you cannot see. The better you can see your target, the better chance you have of placing the bullet where you desire. Most of my long-range handguns

are topped with Burris Ballistic Plex 3-12X optics. If you are not familiar with the Ballistic Plex reticle, it maximizes the potential of long-range cartridges by positioning small lines below the vertical crosshair that coincide with bullet drop from 100 to 450 yards for many of the cartridges used by serious handgun shooters. This is a trajectory-compensating aid and once you get accustom to using it, with a little practice and a rangefinder, you have the ingredients to eliminate the guesswork out of long-range challenges. I like the variable because it gives me the option of turning the scope setting down to 3X if I am expecting something fairly close. For load development, varmint shooting, or big game hunting where the shot is way out there, I have the time to crank the power setting to a desired position. Other high-quality scopes are ideal for hunters including the Leupold 2 1/2-8X, Simmons 2-7X, and the Bushnell Elite 2-6X. I have used all of these models frequently and always have found them to be a handgun hunter's friend.

Choosing a cartridge and bullet combination is another very important aspect of long-range shooting. Everyone has his or her favorite round. Depending on what game you are chasing may dictate which caliber you choose. Varmint shooting often lends itself to long range opportunities that really present quite a challenge for the handgunner. The popular 223 Remington is a great round for varmint shooting. The cartridge is accurate and recoil almost non-existent, very user-friendly. It is not only my favorite

Prairie dog pursuits require precision shooting at long range. These outings offer the hunter a lot of shooting and excellent practice. Shown here is a T/C in 223 using Black Hills ammunition.

choice for varmints but according to sales of guns and reloading dies, many other shooters enjoy this 22-caliber round. When big game like pronghorn, mule deer, whitetail, and other such critters associated with long-range shooting are involved, rifle cartridges like the 260 Remington, 7-30 Waters, 7mm-08, and 308 Winchester are a few rounds that come to mind. There are many other cartridges out there that qualify, including a variety of wildcats that are capable of superb long-range performance.

Choosing a bullet to perform at distant ranges also becomes an important part of our long-range equation. Bullets with high ballistic coefficient (BC) will resist wind drag better than bullets with a lower number BC. Look in the pages of several reloading manuals such as Nosler, Hornady, Sierra, and Speer, to get a better understanding of how a particular bullet performs in this regard. Basically, long slender pointed bullets will sail through the air and deflect wind resistance better than large, flat-nosed bullets. Keep in mind, however, some bullets with the highest BC rating are specifically designed for target shooting and should not be used for hunting purposes.

It is most beneficial for us to know the trajectory of a particular cartridge and how it performs in the handgun we employ. As a hunter, I want and need to know where the bullet will strike at any given distance that I may be shooting. If I should entertain the

Mountain hunting often lends itself to long ranges opportunities. This ibex was taken in Mongolia from over 200-yards using an Encore in 308 Winchester.

thought of taking a big trophy mule deer out at 250 yards, then I better know for sure the trajectory of the bullet I'm sending down-range. We owe it to ourselves, and more importantly, to the game we pursue, to make a good clean shot and not wound any animal. It's our responsibility! Knowing the trajectory of your gun/load is of great importance when long-range shooting is undertaken. But knowing your trajectory is meaningless unless you know for certain the exact, or at least approximate, range you're shooting. That's why a rangefinder is a valuable tool. I always carry a Bushnell Pro Scout in my shirt pocket. It's always handy and can be used very quickly. When you have the time, and you don't always, it's nice to take a reading on your target to know exactly how far you're shooting. This eliminates a lot of guesswork. If you know the trajectory of your bullet, then are blessed with the knowledge of exactly how far the bullet will travel to your intended target, you will automatically stack the odds in your favor.

While we're on the subject, there are factors that affect the flight of the bullet. The first nemesis that comes to mind is wind. Have you ever shot at three hundred yards in a crosswind? If so, you know how much a bullet can be deflected off course. A prairie dog town is another good place to see what can happen if the wind picks up. Depending on many variables such as how much wind, what direction it's gusting, weight of the bullet, and distance involved, bullets can stray off their intended course by a surprising margin. Obviously smaller weight bullets are more easily affected by wind than larger caliber, heavier bullets. There are formulas that can equate this to an exact science but I'm not smart enough to memorize them. Being able to "dope the wind" comes from a lot of practice by actually shooting in windy conditions. On a recent mountain goat hunt in Alaska I found myself shooting from 316 yards in a crosswind. I knew there was a crosswind because the rain was coming down in a horizontal fashion! Unfortunately in all the excitement I forgot to allow for the windy conditions. To make a long story short, the end result was far from ideal. The "moral of the story" is first, recognize the wind factor and secondly, make the appropriate adjustments.

This new offering from Sigarms should be a welcome addition to handgun hunters looking for a long-range pistol. This model shown here by the author is topped with a quality scope and chambered for 223.

Don't let the wind intimidate you, just learn to deal with it.

There are other atmospheric conditions that affect bullet performance including altitude, barometric pressure, relative humidity, and let's not forget temperature. Yes, change in temperature will affect the muzzle velocity of the bullet. Generally speaking, the higher the temperature—the higher the velocity. Let's say you live in south Texas for example and you've been working up loads all summer long at sea level in 90 degree or above temperatures. You have finally settled on the perfect load knowing exactly where it shoots at various ranges and you're ready to go hunting. When you arrive in China for that blue sheep hunt you discover hunting will be conducted at 14,000 feet elevation with temperatures in the low teens. Will your bullet change impact from when you last shot it in Texas? You bet your boots it will! Drastic differences in environmental conditions will change the bullet's point of impact. For those of you who made straight "As" in math, there is a formula that can figure how the load will perform. I'm not mentioning any of this to alarm or confuse anyone; just want you to be aware of the many variables that can influence accuracy in long-range shooting.

Another stumbling block that often plagues long range shooting is the extreme uphill or downhill shot. Once again, there are mathematical formulas that will give you specific, more advanced information regarding this phenomenon. Since I cannot remember any of these numbers I must go another direction. Practically speaking, the bullet is affected by gravity in the horizontal distance involved. In other words, if I used the rangefinder and found it was

300 yards uphill or downhill to the target, but due to the extreme angle of the shot, the horizontal distance affecting the bullet was only 100 yards, you must shoot as if the quarry was only 100 yards away. You can understand why some of us tend to overshoot animals in this scenario. You may have the perception you're shooting 300 yards so there is a tendency to hold high.

Long-range marksmanship in the field is neither impossible nor is it only for the "experts." With the right equipment and a lot of practice, anyone is capable of making those 200-yard shots and beyond. I consider myself fortunate to have a shooting range on my farm where I have nine-inch steel plates placed out at 100, 150, 200, 250, and 300 yards. By shooting from various positions that I will encounter in the field such as off a backpack, shooting sticks, stump, or any other form of rest, it gives me the confidence needed when hunting situations occur. Shooting is a physical skill. As a former coach, I made my players practice a particular skill, the correct way, over and over again. So, in the heat of the battle this skill becomes second nature. They do not have to think twice, it just becomes routine. As shooters, we also need to practice the correct way, over and over again so we can perform when that big buck steps into a clearing. We owe it to the game we pursue to harvest each and every animal in a most humane and effective manner. Placing the bullet precisely where it belongs lessens the chance of wounding game. There is no substitute for practice. Besides, we don't want to miss out on any opportunity to enjoy shooting our favorite firearms! ●

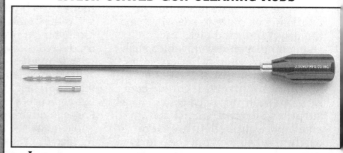

SHOOTER'S MARKETPLACE

ULTIMATE 500

MTM Case-Gard introduces 13 new products to make your shooting experience more organized and productive. Riflemen, shotgun, muzzleloaders and reloaders will find hundreds of items in their line of shooting products they can use.

Send $2.00 for a full-size catalog or look them up on their web site.

MTM MOLDED PRODUCTS COMPANY
P.O. Box 14117, Dayton, OH. 45414
Web: www.mtmcase-gard.com

COMBINATION RIFLE AND OPTICS REST

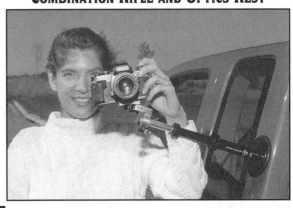

The Magna-Pod weighs less than two pounds, yet firmly supports more than most expensive tripods. It will hold 50 pounds at its low 9-inch height and over 10 pounds extended to 17 inches. It sets up in seconds where there is neither time nor space for a tripod and keeps your expensive equipment safe from knock-overs by kids, pets, pedestrians, or even high winds. It makes a great mono-pod for camcorders, etc., and its carrying box is less than 13" x 13" x 3 1/4" high for easy storage and access.

Attached to its triangle base it becomes an extremely stable table pod or rifle bench rest. The rifle yoke pictured in photo is included.

It's 5 pods in 1: Magna-Pod, Mono-Pod, Table-Pod, Shoulder-Pod and Rifle Rest. Send for free catalog.

SHEPHERD ENTERPRISES, INC.
Box 189, Waterloo, NE 68069
Phone: 402-779-2424 • Fax: 402-779-4010
E-mail: shepherd@shepherdscopes.com • Web: www.shepherdscopes.com

PREMIER HUNTING

John X Safaris offers premier hunting on a wide range of terrain that spans over 3,000,000 acres in South Africa. The leader in Plains Game hunting for over 20 years their clients have taken "eight" of the new or pending SCI top ten Kudu including #1 & 3, the # 1 and #6 Steenbuck, #8 Red Lechwe, #10 Eland as well as dozens more top twenty record book species. Their accommodations are rated four star and our chefs award winning. Their hunting areas are Malaria "FREE" and politically stable. Their package hunts currently run $3,450 for a seven day 5 animal package or $4,200 for a ten day six animal package. For more information visit their web site www.johnxsafaris.com or phone 901-409-1218 and speak to Dave Harwood.

LASERMAX
YOUR NEW SECURITY SYSTEM

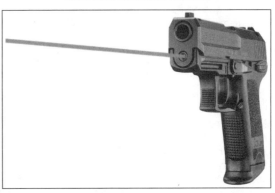

Rugged. Reliable. Consistent. Totally internal. Always stays aligned. User installed, with no gunsmithing. Use with any tactical lights. Fits all holsters. Ambidextrous switch at the take-down lever. Point-of-aim/impact is center of mass from 0 to 20 yds. Features pulsating beam more noticeable to the eye. Sights for all Glocks and most Sigs, including the P239 and P245. Available now: the HK USP Compact 40. Other models include M1911s, Berettas, Taurus and S&W. **LaserMax** offers law enforcement discounts and training programs.

LASERMAX, INC.
3495 Winton Place, Bldg. B, Rochester, NY 14623-2807
Toll-free Phone: (800) LASER-03 • Fax: (585) 272-5427
E-mail: customerservice@lasermax-inc.com
Web: www.lasermax-inc.com

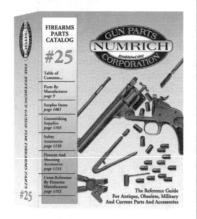

SHOOTER'S MARKETPLACE

PRECISION RIFLE REST

Bald Eagle Precision Machine Co. offers a rifle rest perfect for the serious benchrester or dedicated varminter.

"The Slingshot" or Next Generation has 60° front legs. The rest is constructed of aircraft-quality aluminum or fine grain cast iron and weighs 12 to 20 lbs. The finish is 3 coats of Imron clear. Primary height adjustments are made with a rack and pinion gear. Secondary adjustment uses a mariner wheel with thrust bearings for smooth operation. A hidden fourth leg allows for lateral movement on the bench.

Bald Eagle offers approximately 150 rest combinations to choose from, including windage adjustable, right or left hand, cast aluminum or cast iron.

Prices: $175.00 to $345.00

BALD EAGLE PRECISION MACHINE CO.
101-K Allison Street, Lock Haven, PA 17745
Phone: 570-748-6772 — Fax: 570-748-4443
Web: www.baldeaglemachine.com

FOLDING BIPODS

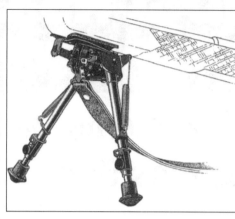

Harris Bipods clamp securely to most stud-equipped bolt-action rifles and are quick-detachable. With adapters, they will fit some other guns. On all models except the Model LM, folding legs have completely adjustable spring-return extensions. The sling swivel attaches to the clamp. This time-proven design is manufactured with heat-treated steel and hard alloys and has a black anodized finish.

Series S Bipods rotate 35° for instant leveling on uneven ground. Hinged base has tension adjustment and buffer springs to eliminate tremor or looseness in crotch area of bipod. They are otherwise similar to non-rotating Series 1A2.

Thirteen models are available from Harris Engineering; literature is free.

HARRIS ENGINEERING INC.
Dept: GD54, Barlow, KY 42024
Phone: 270-334-3633 • Fax: 270-334-3000

6x18x40 VARMINT/TARGET SCOPE

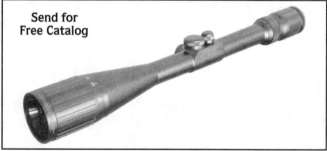

Send for
Free Catalog

The Shepherd 6x18x40 Varmint/Target Scope makes long-range varmint and target shooting child's play. Just pick the ranging circle that best fits your target (be it prairie dogs, coyotes or paper varmints) and Shepherd's exclusive, patented Dual Reticle Down Range System does the rest. You won't believe how far you can accurately shoot, even with rimfire rifles.

Shepherd's superior lens coating mean superior light transmission and tack-sharp resolution.

This new shockproof, waterproof scope features 1/4 minute-of-angle clicks on the ranging circles and friction adjustments on the crosshairs that allows fine-tuning to 0.001 MOA. A 40mm adjustable objective provides a 5.5-foot field of view at 100 yards (16x setting). 16.5 FOV @ 6X.

SHEPHERD ENTERPRISES, INC.
Box 189, Waterloo, NE 68069
Phone: 402-779-2424 • Fax: 402-779-4010
Email: shepherd@shepherdscopes.com • Web: www.shepherdscopes.com

CUSTOM RESTORATION/CASE COLORING

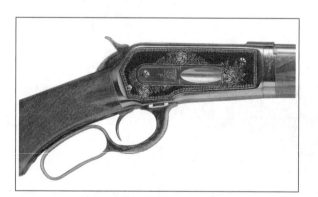

Doug Turnbull Restoration continues to offer bone charcoal case hardening work, matching the original case colors produced by Winchester, Colt, Marlin, Parker, L.C. Smith, Fox and other manufacturers. Also available is charcoal blue, known as Carbona or machine blue, a prewar finish used by most makers. "Specializing in the accurate recreation of historical metal finishes on period firearms, from polishing to final finishing. Including Bone Charcoal Color Case Hardening, Charcoal Bluing, Rust Blue, and Nitre Blue".

DOUG TURNBULL RESTORATION
P.O. Box 471, 6680 Rt 5&20, Dept SM2003
Bloomfield, New York 14469 • Phone/Fax: 585-657-6338
E-mail: turnbullrest@mindspring.com
Web: www.turnbullrestoration.com

SHOOTER'S MARKETPLACE

ULTIMATE 500

Gary Reeder Custom Guns, builder of full custom guns for over 25 years, and with over 50 different series of custom hunting handguns, cowboy guns, custom Encores and large caliber hunting rifles, has a free brochure for you. Or visit their website. One of the most popular is their Ultimate 500, chambered in the 500 S&W Magnum. This beefy 5-shot revolver is for the serious handgun hunter and is one of several series of large caliber handguns, such as 475 Linebaugh and 475 Maximum, 500 Linebaugh and 500 Maximum. For more information, contact:

GARY REEDER CUSTOM GUNS
2601 E. 7th Avenue, Flagstaff, AZ 86004
Phone: 928-527-4100 or 928-526-3313
Website: www.reedercustomguns.com

BLACK HILLS GOLD AMMUNITION

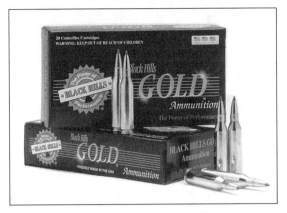

Black Hills Ammunition has introduced a new line of premium performance rifle ammunition. Calibers available in the Black Hills Gold Line are .243, .270, .308, .30-06, and .300 Win Mag. This line is designed for top performance in a wide range of hunting situations. Bullets used in this ammunition are the Barnes X-Bullet with XLC coating and the highly accurate Nosler Ballistic-Tip™.

Black Hills Ammunition is sold dealer direct. The Gold line is packaged in 20 rounds per box, 10 boxes per case. Black Hills pays all freight to dealers in the continental United States. Minimum dealer order is only one case.

BLACK HILLS AMMUNITION
P.O. Box 3090, Rapid City, SD 57709
Phone: 1-605-348-5150 • Fax: 1-605-348-9827
Web: www.black-hills.com

BEAR TRACK CASES

Designed by an Alaskan bush pilot! Polyurethane coated, zinc plated corners and feet, zinc plated—spring loaded steel handles, stainless steel hinges, high density urethane foam inside with a neoprene seal. Aluminum walls are standard at .070 with riveted ends. Committed to quality that will protect your valuables regardless of the transportation method you use. Exterior coating also protects other items from acquiring "aluminum black."

Many styles, colors and sizes available. Wheels come on large cases and special orders can be accommodated. Call for a brochure or visit online.

Bear Track Cases when top quality protection is a must.

BEAR TRACK CASES
314 Highway 239, Freedom, WY 83120
Phone: 307-883-2468 • Fax: 307-883-2005
Web: www.beartrackcases.com

DETACHABLE RINGS & BASES

A.R.M.S.® #22 Throw Lever Rings

All steel 30mm ring, secured with A.R.M.S.® dovetail system to an extruded aluminum platform. Built in no-mar patented buffer pads. Available in Low, Medium, and High height. Low height measures .925". Medium height measures 1.150". High height measures 1.450". Height is measured from the center of the optic to the bottom of the base.

Sugg. Retail $99.00
U.S. Patent No. 5,276,988 & 4,845,871
Item #37 to convert 30mm to 1",
   Suggested Retail $29.00

Call for dealer or distributor in your area.

A.R.M.S., INC.
230 W. Center St., West Bridgewater, MA 02379
Phone: (508) 584-7816 • Fax: (508) 588-8045
E-mail: sales@armsmounts • Web: www.armsmounts.com

SHOOTER'S MARKETPLACE

GUNSMITHING SUPPLIES

440 pages! Filled with more than 20,000, top, brand-name accessories to make your rifles, shotguns and handguns look and work better. Plus, 136 of those pages are filled with 9,000, genuine factory parts from 16 factories so you can repair guns to original equipment specs. A huge selection of specialized gunsmithing tools help you install those parts and accessories correctly. Books and videos teach you how to do general gun work and specific repairs, shoot better, identify collectables, reload your own ammo, and buy and sell guns. Full-time tech staff answers your questions. Selection. Service. Satisfaction - 100% guaranteed. Business discounts available.

Call 1-800-741-0015 or order on-line at:
www.brownells.com
Mention Department #AH7
Price of catalog refunded with order. $5.00

FOR THE SERIOUS RELOADER...

Rooster Labs' line of top-quality, innovative products...for individual and commercial reloaders...now includes:
- **ZAMBINI** 220° Pistol Bullet Lubricant (1x4 & 2x6)
- **HVR** 220° High Velocity Rifle Bullet Lube (1x4)
- **ROOSTER JACKET** Waterproof Liquid Bullet Film Lube
- **ROOSTER BRIGHT** Brass Case Polish Media Additive ...Brilliant!
- **CFL-56** Radical Case Forming Lube...for the Wildcatter
- **PDQ-21** Spray Case Sizing Lube...quick, no contamination
- **BP-7 BLACK POWDER** 210°Bullet Lube (1x4 solid)

Rooster LABORATORIES®
P.O. Box 414605, Kansas City, MO 64141
Phone: 816-474-1622 • Fax: 816-474-7622
E-mail: roosterlabs@aol.com
Web: www.roosterlabs.com

CLENZOIL FIELD & RANGE®

This is what museums, collectors, and competitive shooters are switching to in serious numbers.

Clenzoil Field & Range® is a remarkable one-step bore cleaner, lubricant, and long-term protectant that contains absolutely no teflon or silicone, so it never gets gummy or sticky.

A regional favorite for many years, Clenzoil is finally available nationwide. Clenzoil is signing up dealers daily, but your local shop may not carry it yet. If that's the case, you may order 24 hours a day by calling 1-800-OIL-IT-UP. Dealers may join the growing Clenzoil dealer network by calling 440-899-0482.

Clenzoil is a proud supplier to ArmaLite, Inc. and Ithaca Classic Doubles.

THE CLENZOIL CORPORATION
WORLDWIDE

25670 First Street, Westlake, OH 44145
Phone: 440-899-0482 • Fax: 440-899-0483

RUGER 10-22® COMPETITION MATCHED HAMMER AND SEAR KIT

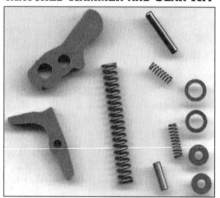

Precision EDM/CNC machined custom hammer and sear for your Ruger 10-22®. Both parts are machined from a solid billet of steel. Case hardened to RC-58-60. These are the highest quality drop in parts available on the market. They will produce a crisp 2-1/2 lbs. trigger pull. They are precision ground with Vapor hand honed engagement surfaces. Includes an Extra Power hammer spring, Extra Power disconnector spring, replacement trigger return spring, 2 hammer shims, and 2 trigger shims.

Price $55.95 plus $3.85 Priority Mail

POWER CUSTOM, INC.
29739 Hwy. J, Dept. KP, Gravois Mills, MO 65037
Phone: 1-573-372-5684 • Fax: 1-573-372-5799
Web: www.powercustom.com • E-mail: rwpowers@laurie.net

COMPLETE COMPACT CATALOG

HANDGUNS 2004

GUNDEX

GUNDEX

GUNDEX

GUNDEX

Browning Luxus Grade B2

Browning Luxus Renaissance Argent

Browning Luxus Renaissance OR

Ed Brown Classic Class A

Ed Brown Kobra Carry

Kimber Ultra CDP

Kimber Ultra Royal II

BRILEY 1911-STYLE AUTO PISTOLS

Caliber: 9mm Para., 38 Super, 40 S&W, 10-shot magazine; 45 ACP, 8-shot magazine. **Barrel:** 3.6" or 5". **Weight:** NA. **Length:** NA. **Grips:** Rosewood or rubber. **Sights:** Bo-Mar adjustable rear, Briley dovetail blade front. **Features:** Modular or Caspian alloy, carbon steel or stainless steel frame; match barrel and trigger group; lowered and flared ejection port; front and rear serrations on slide; beavertail grip safety; hot blue, hard chrome or stainless steel finish. Introduced 2000. Made in U.S. From Briley Manufacturing Inc.

Price: Fantom (3.6" bbl., fixed low-mount rear sight, armor coated lower receiver) . . . . from **$1,900.00**
Price: Fantom with two-port compensator . . . . from **$2,245.00**
Price: Advantage (5" bbl., adj. low-mount rear sight, checkered mainspring housing) . . . . from **$1,650.00**
Price: Versatility Plus (5" bbl., adj. low-mount rear sight, modular or Caspian frame) . . . . from **$1,850.00**
Price: Signature Series (5" bbl., adj. low-mount rear sight, 40 S&W only) . . . . from **$2,250.00**
Price: Plate Master (5" bbl. with compensator, lightened slide, Briley scope mount) . . . . from **$1,895.00**
Price: El Presidente (5" bbl. with Briley quad compensator, Briley scope mount) . . . . from **$2,550.00**

BROWNING HI-POWER LUXUS

The legendary Browning Hi-Power pistol still produced in Belgium is available in four grades in the Luxus series: Grade II, Renaissance Argent, Grade B2 and the gold-finished Renaissance OR. Other specifications NA.
Price: . . . . **NA**

ED BROWN CLASSIC CUSTOM AND CLASS A LIMITED 1911-STYLE AUTO PISTOLS

Caliber: 45 ACP; 7-shot magazine; 40 S&W, 400 Cor-Bon, 38 Super, 9x23, 9mm Para. **Barrel:** 4.25", 5", 6". **Weight:** NA. **Length:** NA. **Grips:** Hogue exotic checkered wood. **Sights:** Bo-Mar or Novak rear, blade front. **Features:** Blued or stainless steel frame; ambidextrous safety; beavertail grip safety; checkered forestrap and mainspring housing; match-grade barrel; slotted hammer; long lightweight or Videki short steel trigger. Many options offered. Made in U.S. by Ed Brown Products.

Price: Classic Custom (45 ACP, 5" barrel) . . . . from **$2,895.00**
Price: Class A Limited (all calibers; several bbl. lengths in competition and carry forms) . . . . from **$2,250.00**
Price: Commander Bobtail (most calibers, 4.25" bbl., has "bobtail" modification to reduce overall length) . . . . from **$2,300.00**

Price: Kobra (45 ACP only, 5" bbl., completely hand-fitted with heavy dehorning) . . . . from **$1,795.00**
Price: Kobra Carry (45 ACP only, 4.25" bbl., has exclusive snakeskin pattern on frame, top portion of mainspring housing and slide) . . . . from **$1,995.00**

KIMBER CUSTOM II 1911-STYLE AUTO PISTOLS

Caliber: 9mm Para., 38 Super, 9-shot magazines; 40 S&W, 8-shot magazine; 45 ACP, 7-shot magazine. **Barrel:** 5". **Weight:** 38 oz. **Length:** 8.7" overall. **Grips:** Black synthetic, smooth or double-diamond checkered rosewood, or double-diamond checkered walnut. **Sights:** McCormick low profile or Kimber adjustable rear, blade front. **Features:** Machined steel slide, frame and barrel; front and rear beveled slide serrations; cut and button-rifled, match-grade barrel; adjustable aluminum trigger; full-length guide rod; Commander-style hammer; high-ride beavertail safety; beveled magazine well. Other models available. Made in U.S. by Kimber Mfg. Inc.

Price: Custom II (black matte finish). **$730.00**
Price: Custom Royal II (polished blue finish, checkered rosewood grips) **$886.00**
Price: Custom Stainless II (satin-finished stainless steel frame and slide) **$832.00**
Price: Custom Target II (matte black or stainless finish, Kimber adj. sight) **$945.00**
Price: Custom Compact CDP II (4" bbl., alum. frame, tritium three-dot sights, 28 oz.) **$1,141.00**
Price: Custom Pro CDP II (4" bbl., alum. frame, tritium sights, full-length grip, 28 oz.) **$1,141.00**
Price: Ultra CDP II (3" bbl., aluminum frame, tritium sights, 25 oz.) **$1,141.00**
Price: Gold Match II (polished blue finish, hand-fitted barrel, ambid. safety) . . . . from **$1,168.00**
Price: Stainless Gold Match II (stainless steel frame and slide, hand-fitted bbl., amb. safety) . . . . **$1,315.00 to $1,345.00**

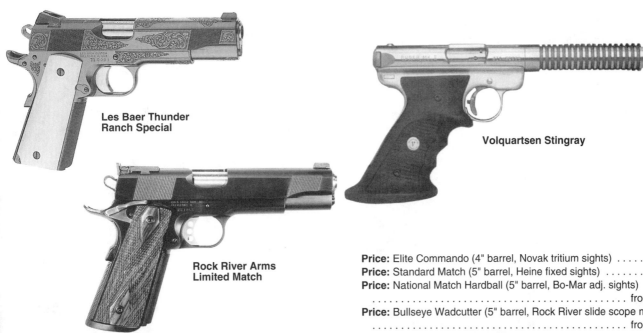

Les Baer Thunder
Ranch Special

Volquartsen Stingray

Rock River Arms
Limited Match

LES BAER CUSTOM 1911-STYLE AUTO PISTOLS

Caliber: 9mm Para., 38 Super, 40 S&W, 45 ACP, 400 Cor-Bon; 7- or 8-shot magazine. **Barrel:** 4-1/4", 5", 6". **Weight:** 28 to 40 oz. **Length:** NA. **Grips:** Checkered cocobolo. **Sights:** Low-mount combat fixed, combat fixed with tritium inserts or low-mount adjustable rear, dovetail front. **Features:** Forged steel or aluminum frame; slide serrated front and rear; lowered and flared ejection port; beveled magazine well; speed trigger with 4-pound pull; beavertail grip safety; ambidextrous safety. Other models available. Made in U.S. by Les Baer Custom.

Price: Baer 1911 Premier II 5" Model (5" bbl., optional stainless steel frame and slide) . . . . from **$1,498.00**
Price: Premier II 6" Model (6" barrel) . . . . from **$1,675.00**
Price: Premier II LW1 (forged aluminum frame, steel slide and barrel) . . . . from **$1,835.00**
Price: Custom Carry (4" or 5" barrel, steel frame) . . . . from **$1,728.00**
Price: Custom Carry (4" barrel, aluminum frame) . . . . from **$2,039.00**
Price: Swift Response Pistol (fixed tritium sights, Bear Coat finish) . . . . from **$2,339.00**
Price: Monolith (5" barrel and slide with extra-long dust cover) . . . . from **$1,660.00**
Price: Stinger (4-1/4" barrel, steel or aluminum frame) . . . from **$1,552.00**
Price: Thunder Ranch Special (tritium fixed combat sight, Thunder Ranch logo) . . . . from **$1,685.00**
Price: National Match Hardball (low-mount adj. sight; meets DCM rules) . . . . from **$1,425.00**
Price: Bullseye Wadcutter Pistol (Bo-Mar rib w/ adj. sight, guar. 2-1/2" groups) . . . . from **$1,560.00**
Price: Ultimate Master Combat (5" or 6" bbl., adj. sights, checkered front strap) . . . . from **$2,530.00**
Price: Ultimate Master Combat Compensated (four-port compensator, adj. sights) . . . . from **$2,558.00**

ROCK RIVER ARMS 1911-STYLE AUTO PISTOLS

Caliber: 9mm Para., 38 Super, 40 S&W, 45 ACP. **Barrel:** 4" or 5". **Weight:** NA. **Length:** NA. **Grips:** Double-diamond, checkered cocobolo or black synthetic. **Sights:** Bo-Mar low-mount adjustable, Novak fixed with tritium inserts, Heine fixed or Rock River scope mount; dovetail front blade. **Features:** Chrome-moly, machined steel frame and slide; slide serrated front and rear; aluminum speed trigger with 3.5-4 lb. pull; national match KART barrel; lowered and flared ejection port; tuned and polished extractor; beavertail grip safety; beveled mag. well. Other frames offered. Made in U.S. by Rock River Arms Inc.

Price: Elite Commando (4" barrel, Novak tritium sights) **$1,395.00**
Price: Standard Match (5" barrel, Heine fixed sights) **$1,150.00**
Price: National Match Hardball (5" barrel, Bo-Mar adj. sights) . . . . from **$1,275.00**
Price: Bullseye Wadcutter (5" barrel, Rock River slide scope mount) . . . . from **$1,380.00**
Price: Basic Limited Match (5" barrel, Bo-Mar adj. sights) from **$1,395.00**
Price: Limited Match (5" barrel, guaranteed 1-1/2" groups at 50 yards) . . . . from **$1,795.00**
Price: Hi-Cap Basic Limited (5" barrel, four frame choices) from **$1,895.00**
Price: Ultimate Match Achiever (5" bbl. with compensator, mount and Aimpoint) . . . . from **$2,255.00**
Price: Match Master Steel (5" bbl. with compensator, mount and Aimpoint) **$5,000.00**

STI COMPACT AUTO PISTOLS

Caliber: 9mm Para., 40 S&W. **Barrel:** 3.4". **Weight:** 28 oz. **Length:** 7" overall. **Grips:** Checkered double-diamond rosewood. **Sights:** Heine Low Mount fixed rear, slide integral front. **Features:** Similar to STI 2011 models except has compact frame, 7-shot magazine in 9mm (6-shot in 40 cal.), single-sided thumb safety, linkless barrel lockup system, matte blue finish. From STI International.
Price: (9mm Para. or 40 S&W) . . . . from **$746.50**

VOLQUARTSEN CUSTOM 22 CALIBER AUTO PISTOLS

Caliber: 22 LR; 10-shot magazine. **Barrel:** 3.5" to 10"; stainless steel air gauge. **Weight:** 2-1/2 to 3 lbs. 10 oz. **Length:** NA. **Grips:** Finger-grooved plastic or walnut. **Sights:** Adjustable rear and blade front or Weaver-style scope mount. **Features:** Conversions of Ruger Mk. II Auto pistol. Variety of configurations featuring compensators, underlug barrels, etc. Stainless steel finish; black Teflon finish available for additional $85; target hammer, trigger. Made in U.S. by Volquartsen Custom.
Price: 3.5 Compact (3.5" barrel, T/L adjustable rear sight, scope base optional) **$640.00**
Price: Deluxe (barrel to 10", T/L adjustable rear sight) **$675.00**
Price: Deluxe with compensator **$745.00**
Price: Masters (6.5" barrel, finned underlug, T/L adjustable rear sight, compensator) **$950.00**
Price: Olympic (7" barrel, recoil-reducing gas chamber, T/L adjustable rear sight) **$870.00**
Price: Stingray (7.5" ribbed, ported barrel; red-dot sight) **$995.00**
Price: Terminator (7.5" ported barrel, grooved receiver, scope rings) **$730.00**
Price: Ultra-Light Match (6" tensioned barrel, Weaver mount, weighs 2-1/2 lbs.) **$885.00**
Price: V-6 (6", triangular, ventilated barrel with underlug, T/L adj. sight) **$1,030.00**
Price: V-2000 (6" barrel with finned underlug, T/L adj. sight) . . **$1,095.00**
Price: V-Magic II (7.5" barrel, red-dot sight) **$1,055.00**

**Gary Reeder
Doc Holiday Classic**

**Gary Reeder
Ultimate 41**

**Gary Reeder
Black Widow**

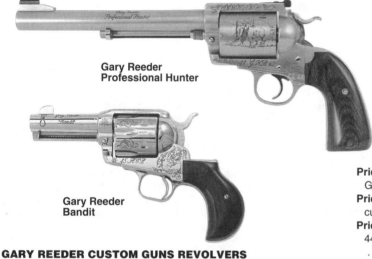

**Gary Reeder
Professional Hunter**

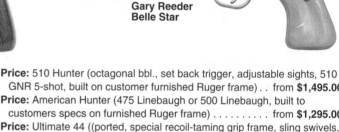

**Gary Reeder
Belle Star**

**Gary Reeder
Bandit**

GARY REEDER CUSTOM GUNS REVOLVERS

Caliber: 22 WMR, 22 Hornet, 218 Bee, 356 GMR, 41 GNR, 410 GNR, 510 GNR, 357 Magnum, 45 Colt, 44-40, 41 Magnum, 44 Magnum, 454 Casull, 475 Linebaugh, 500 Linebaugh. **Barrel:** 2-1/2" to 12". **Weight:** Varies by model. **Length:** Varies by model. **Grips:** Black Cape buffalo horn, laminated walnut, simulated pearl, black and ivory micarta, others. **Sights:** Notch fixed or adjustable rear, blade or ramp front. **Features:** Custom conversions of Ruger Vaquero, Blackhawk Bisley and Super Blackhawk frames. Jeweled hammer and trigger, tuned action, model name engraved on barrel, additional engraving on frame and cylinder, integral muzzle brake, finish available in high-polish or satin stainless steel or black Chromex finish. Also available on customer's gun at reduced cost. Other models available. Made in U.S. by Gary Reeder Custom Guns.

Price: Gamblers Classic (2-1/2" bbl., engraved cards and dice, no ejector rod housing) . . . . from **$995.00**

Price: Tombstone Classic (3-1/2" bbl. with gold bands, notch sight, birdshead grips) . . . . from **$995.00**

Price: Doc Holliday Classic (3-1/2" bbl., engraved cards and dice, white pearl grips) . . . . from **$995.00**

Price: Ultimate Vaquero (engraved barrel, frame and cylinder, made to customer specs) . . . . from **$995.00**

Price: Black Widow (4-5/8" bbl., black Chromex finish, black widow spider engraving). . . . . from **$1,095.00**

Price: Cowboy Classic (stainless finish, cattle brand engraved, limited to 100 guns) . . . . from **$995.00**

Price: African Hunter (6" bbl., with or without muzzle brake, 475 or 500 Linebaugh) (on your gun from) **$1,295.00**

Price: Alaskan Survivalist (3" bbl., Redhawk frame, engraved bear, 45 Colt or 44 Magnum) . . . . from **$1,095.00**

Price: Ultimate Back-Up (3-1/2" bbl., fixed sights, choice of animal engraving, 475 Linebaugh, 500 Linebaugh) (on your gun from)
. . . . **$1,295.00**

Price: Double Deuce (8" heavy bbl., adjustable sights, laminated grips, 22 WMR 8-shot) . . . . from **$1,195.00**

Price: Ultimate 41 (410 GNR 5-shot, built on customer furnished Ruger frame) . . . . from **$1,295.00**

Price: 510 Hunter (octagonal bbl., set back trigger, adjustable sights, 510 GNR 5-shot, built on customer furnished Ruger frame) . . from **$1,495.00**

Price: American Hunter (475 Linebaugh or 500 Linebaugh, built to customers specs on furnished Ruger frame) . . . . from **$1,295.00**

Price: Ultimate 44 ((ported, special recoil-taming grip frame, sling swivels, 44 Mag. 5-shot, built on customer furnished Ruger Hunter)
. . . . from **$1,295.00**

Price: Professional Hunter (stretch frame stainless 5-shot available in calibers including 475 Maximum and 500 Maximum). . . . from **$2,395.00**

Price: Classic 45 (shoots 45 Colt, 45 ACP or 45 Schofield without moon clips, built to customer specs on customer furnished Ruger frame)
. . . . from **$1,295.00**

Price: Belle Starr Classic (engraved with gunfighter grip, 32 H&R)
. . . . from **$1,095.00**

Price: Bandit (3-1/2" bbl., special Lightning style grip frame built on a Ruger Vaquero frame, engraved, set back trigger, Colt-style hammer)
. . . . from **$1,095.00**

Price: Southern Comfort (5 shot cylinder, heavy duty base pin, tear drop hammer, special set back trigger, interchangeable blade system, special gripframe, satin Vapor Honed finish) . . . . from **$1,095.00**

Price: Ultimate 480 (choice of barrel lengths in any caliber, full vapor honed stainless steel, satin finish Black Chromex or two-toned finish, 5 shot cylinder, heavy barrel, Gunfighter grip, full action job, custom laminated grips, freewheeling cylinder, Belt Mountain base pin) . . . . from **$995.00**

Price: Coyote Classic (chambered in 22 Hornet, 22 K-Hornet, 218 Bee, 218 Mashburn Bee, 17 Ackley Bee, 17 Ackley Hornet, 256 Winchester, 25-20, 6-shot unfluted cylinder, heavy 8" barrel, Super Blackhawk gripframe, finish of satin stainless, satin Black Chromex or high polished, comes with laminated cherry grips and Gunfighter grip) . . . . from **$995.00**

Price: Ultimate 50 (choice of barrel lengths in any centerfire caliber, 5 shot stainless steel 50 Action Express, freewheeling cylinder) from **$1,195.00**

Price: Ultimate Black Widow (475 Linebaugh or 500 Linebaugh, heavy duty 5 shot cylinder, heavy high grade barrel, Gunfighter Grip with black Micarta grips, Belt Mountain base pin) . . . . from **$1,295.00**

Price: 45 Backpacker (weighs 28 oz., comes in 45 Long Colt, all stainless except for lightweight aircraft aluminum gripframe, black Micarta grips, not recommended for Plus P ammo) . . . . from **$995.00**

Price: Rio Grande Classic (built on any caliber Vaquero in barrel length of choice, Gunfighter grip, engraving is old southwest type with a few western features, specially designed base pin, long tapered hammer . . . . from **$995.00**

SEMI-CUSTOM HANDGUNS — REVOLVERS

44 Linebaugh Long

500 Linebaugh Long

500 Linebaugh

LINEBAUGH CUSTOM SIXGUNS REVOLVERS

Caliber: 45 Colt, 44 Linebaugh Long, 458 Linebaugh, 475 Linebaugh, 500 Linebaugh, 500 Linebaugh Long, 445 Super Mag. **Barrel:** 4-3/4", 5-1/2", 6", 7-1/2"; other lengths available. **Weight:** NA. **Length:** NA. **Grips:** Dustin Linebaugh Custom made to customer's specs. **Sights:** Bowen steel rear or factory Ruger; blade front. **Features:**

Conversions using customer's Ruger Blackhawk Bisley and Vaquero Bisley frames. Made in U.S. by Linebaugh Custom Sixguns.
Price: Small 45 Colt conversion (rechambered cyl., new barrel) . . . . from **$1,200.00**
Price: Large 45 Colt conversion (oversized cyl., new barrel, 5- or 6-shot) . . . . from **$1,800.00**
Price: 475 Linebaugh, 500 Linebaugh conversions from **$1,800.00**
Price: Linebaugh and 445 Super Mag calibers on 357 Maximum frame . . . . from **$3,000.00**

SEMI-CUSTOM HANDGUNS — SINGLE SHOT

Gary Reeder Ultimate Encore

Gary Reeder Kodiak Hunter Dall Sheep

GARY REEDER CUSTOM GUNS CONTENDER AND ENCORE PISTOLS

Caliber: 22 Cheetah, 218 Bee, 22 K-Hornet, 22 Hornet, 218 Mashburn Bee, 22-250 Improved, 6mm/284, 7mm STW, 7mm GNR, 30 GNR, 338 GNR, 300 Win. Magnum, 338 Win. Magnum, 350 Rem. Magnum, 358 STA, 375 H&H, 378 GNR, 416 Remington, 416 GNR, 450 GNR, 475 Linebaugh, 500 Linebaugh, 50 Alaskan, 50 AE, 454 Casull; others available. **Barrel:** 8" to 15" (others available). **Weight:** NA. **Length:** Varies with barrel length. **Grips:** Walnut fingergroove. **Sights:** Express-style adjustable rear and barrel band front (Kodiak Hunter); none furnished most models. **Features:** Offers complete guns and barrels in the T/C Contender and Encore. Integral muzzle brake, engraved animals and model name, tuned action, high-polish or satin stainless steel or black Chromex finish. Made in U.S. by Gary Reeder Custom Guns.
Price: Kodiak Hunter (50 AE, 475 Linebaugh, 500 Linebaugh, 510 GNR, or 454 Casull, Kodiak bear and Dall sheep engravings) from **$1,195.00**
Price: Ultimate Encore (15" bbl. with muzzle brake, custom engraving) . . . . from **$1,095.00**

SSK INDUSTRIES CONTENDER AND ENCORE PISTOLS

Caliber: More than 200, including most standard pistol and rifle calibers, as well as 226 JDJ, 6mm JDJ, 257 JDJ, 6.5mm JDJ, 7mm JDJ, 6.5mm Mini-Dreadnaught, 30-06 JDJ, 280 JDJ, 375 JDJ, 6mm Whisper, 300 Whisper and 338 Whisper. **Barrel:** 10" to 26"; blued or stainless; variety of configurations. **Weight:** Varies with barrel length and features. **Length:** Varies with barrel length. **Grips:** Pachmayr, wood models available. **Features:** Offers frames, barrels and complete guns in the T/C Contender

SSK Industries Contender

and Encore. Fluted, diamond, octagon and round barrels; flatside Contender frames; chrome-plating; muzzle brakes; trigger jobs; variety of stocks and forends; sights and optics. Made in U.S. by SSK Industries.
Price: Blued Contender frame . . . . from **$390.00**
Price: Stainless Contender frame. from **$390.00**
Price: Blued Encore frame . . . . from **$290.00**
Price: Stainless Encore frame . . . . from **$318.00**
Price: Contender barrels . . . . from **$315.00**
Price: Encore barrels . . . . from **$340.00**

Includes models suitable for several forms of competition and other sporting purposes.

Accu-Tek HC-380

Accu-Tek XL-9

Auto-Ordnance 1911A1 Standard

Baer Custom Carry

Baer Premium II

Auto-Ordnance Deluxe

ACCU-TEK MODEL HC-380 AUTO PISTOL

Caliber: 380 ACP, 10-shot magazine. **Barrel:** 2.75". **Weight:** 26 oz. **Length:** 6" overall. **Grips:** Checkered black composition. **Sights:** Blade front, rear adjustable for windage. **Features:** External hammer; manual thumb safety with firing pin and trigger disconnect; bottom magazine release. Stainless steel construction. Introduced 1993. Price includes cleaning kit and gun lock. Made in U.S.A. by Accu-Tek.
Price: Satin stainless $249.00

ACCU-TEK XL-9 AUTO PISTOL

Caliber: 9mm Para., 5-shot magazine. **Barrel:** 3". **Weight:** 24 oz. **Length:** 5.6" overall. **Grips:** Black pebble composition. **Sights:** Three-dot system; rear adjustable for windage. **Features:** Stainless steel construction; double-action-only mechanism. Introduced 1999. Price includes cleaning kit and gun lock, two magazines. Made in U.S.A. by Accu-Tek.
Price: $267.00

AMERICAN DERRINGER LM-5 AUTOMATIC PISTOL

Caliber: 25 ACP, 5-shot magazine. **Barrel:** 2-1/4". **Weight:** 15 oz. **Length:** NA. **Grips:** Wood. **Sights:** Fixed. **Features:** Compact, stainless, semi-auto, single-action hammerless design. Hand assembled and fitted.
Price: $425.00

AUTO-ORDNANCE 1911A1 AUTOMATIC PISTOL

Caliber: 45 ACP, 7-shot magazine. **Barrel:** 5". **Weight:** 39 oz. **Length:** 8-1/2" overall. **Grips:** Checkered plastic with medallion. **Sights:** Blade front, rear adjustable for windage. **Features:** Same specs as 1911A1 military guns—parts interchangeable. Frame and slide blued; each radius has non-glare finish. Made in U.S.A. by Auto-Ordnance Corp.
Price: 45 ACP, blue. $511.00
Price: 45 ACP, Parkerized. $515.00
Price: 45 ACP Deluxe (three-dot sights, textured rubber
wraparound grips) $525.00

AUTAUGA 32 AUTO PISTOL

Caliber: 32 ACP, 6-shot magazine. **Barrel:** 2". **Weight:** 11.3 oz. **Length:** 4.3" overall. **Grips:** Black polymer. **Sights:** Fixed. **Features:** Double-action-only mechanism. Stainless steel construction. Uses Winchester Silver Tip ammunition.
Price: . . . . NA

BAER 1911 CUSTOM CARRY AUTO PISTOL

Caliber: 45 ACP, 7- or 10-shot magazine. **Barrel:** 5". **Weight:** 37 oz. **Length:** 8.5" overall. **Grips:** Checkered walnut. **Sights:** Baer improved ramp-style dovetailed front, Novak low-mount rear. **Features:** Baer forged NM frame, slide and barrel with stainless bushing; fitted slide to frame; double serrated slide (full-size only); Baer speed trigger with 4-lb. pull; Baer deluxe hammer and sear, tactical-style extended ambidextrous safety, beveled magazine well; polished feed ramp and throated barrel; tuned extractor; Baer extended ejector, checkered slide stop; lowered and flared ejection port, full-length recoil guide rod; recoil buff. Partial listing shown. Made in U.S.A. by Les Baer Custom, Inc.
Price: Standard size, blued. $1,640.00
Price: Standard size, stainless $1,690.00
Price: Comanche size, blued $1,640.00
Price: Comanche size, stainless. $1,690.00
Price: Comanche size, aluminum frame, blued slide $1,923.00
Price: Comanche size, aluminum frame, stainless slide. $1,995.00

BAER 1911 PREMIER II AUTO PISTOL

Caliber: 9x23, 38 Super, 400 Cor-Bon, 45 ACP, 7- or 10-shot magazine. **Barrel:** 5". **Weight:** 37 oz. **Length:** 8.5" overall. **Grips:** Checkered rosewood, double diamond pattern. **Sights:** Baer dovetailed front, low-mount Bo-Mar rear with hidden leaf. **Features:** Baer NM forged steel frame and barrel with stainless bushing; slide fitted to frame; double serrated slide; lowered, flared ejection port; tuned, polished extractor; Baer extended ejector, checkered slide stop, aluminum speed trigger with 4-lb. pull, deluxe Commander hammer and sear, beavertail grip safety with pad, beveled magazine well, extended ambidextrous safety; flat mainspring housing; polished feed ramp and throated barrel; 30 lpi checkered front strap. Made in U.S.A. by Les Baer Custom, Inc.
Price: Blued $1,428.00
Price: Stainless. $1,558.00
Price: 6" model, blued, from $1,595.00

BAER 1911 S.R.P. PISTOL

Caliber: 45 ACP. **Barrel:** 5". **Weight:** 37 oz. **Length:** 8.5" overall. **Grips:** Checkered walnut. **Sights:** Trijicon night sights. **Features:** Similar to the F.B.I. contract gun except uses Baer forged steel frame. Has Baer match barrel with supported chamber, Wolff springs, complete tactical action job. All parts Mag-na-fluxed; deburred for tactical carry. Has Baer Ultra Coat finish. Tuned for reliability. Contact Baer for complete details. Introduced 1996. Made in U.S.A. by Les Baer Custom, Inc.
Price: Government or Comanche length $2,240.00

HANDGUNS — AUTOLOADERS, SERVICE & SPORT

Beretta 92 Billennium

Beretta 96

Beretta M8000/8040 Cougar

Price: Model 87 Cheetah, wood, 22 LR, 7-shot **$599.00**
Price: Model 87 Target, plastic grips **$682.00**

BERETTA MODEL 92 BILLENNIUM LIMITED EDITION
Caliber: 9mm. **Grips:** Carbon fiber. **Sights:** 3 dot. **Features:** Single action. Semiauto. Steel frame, frame mounted safety. Only 2000 made worldwide.
Price: **$1,429.00**

BERETTA MODEL 92FS PISTOL
Caliber: 9mm Para., 10-shot magazine. **Barrel:** 4.9". **Weight:** 34 oz. **Length:** 8.5" overall. **Grips:** Checkered black plastic. **Sights:** Blade front, rear adjustable for windage. Tritium night sights available. **Features:** Double action. Extractor acts as chamber loaded indicator, squared trigger guard, grooved front and backstraps, inertia firing pin. Matte or blued finish. Introduced 1977. Made in U.S.A. and imported from Italy by Beretta U.S.A.
Price: With plastic grips **$691.00**
Price: Vertec with access rail **$726.00**
Price: Vertec Inox **$776.00**

Beretta Model 92FS/96 Brigadier Pistols
Similar to the Model 92FS/96 except with a heavier slide to reduce felt recoil and allow mounting removable front sight. Wrap-around rubber grips. Three-dot sights dovetailed to the slide, adjustable for windage. Weighs 35.3 oz. Introduced 1999.
Price: 9mm or 40 S&W, 10-shot **$748.00**
Price: Inox models (stainless steel) **$798.00**

Beretta Model 92FS Compact and Compact Type M Pistol
Similar to the Model 92FS except more compact and lighter: overall length 7.8"; 4.3" barrel; weighs 30.9 oz. Has Bruniton finish, chrome-lined bore, combat trigger guard, ambidextrous safety/decock lever. Single column 8-shot magazine (Type M), or double column 10-shot (Compact), 9mm only. Introduced 1998. Imported from Italy by Beretta U.S.A.
Price: Compact (10-shot) **$691.00**
Price: Compact Type M (8-shot) **$691.00**
Price: Compact Inox (stainless) **$748.00**
Price: Compact Type M Inox (stainless) **$748.00**

BERETTA MODEL 96 PISTOL
Same as the Model 92FS except chambered for 40 S&W. Ambidextrous safety mechanism with passive firing pin catch, slide safety/decocking lever, trigger bar disconnect. Has 10-shot magazine. Available with three-dot sights. Introduced 1992.
Price: Model 96, plastic grips **$691.00**
Price: Stainless, rubber grips **$798.00**
Price: Vertec with access rail **$726.00**
Price: Vertec Inox **$776.00**

BERETTA MODEL 80 CHEETAH SERIES DA PISTOLS
Caliber: 380 ACP, 10-shot magazine (M84); 8-shot (M85); 22 LR, 7-shot (M87). **Barrel:** 3.82". **Weight:** About 23 oz. (M84/85); 20.8 oz. (M87). **Length:** 6.8" overall. **Grips:** Glossy black plastic (wood optional at extra cost). **Sights:** Fixed front, drift-adjustable rear. **Features:** Double action, quick takedown, convenient magazine release. Introduced 1977. Imported from Italy by Beretta U.S.A.
Price: Model 84 Cheetah, plastic grips **$599.00**
Price: Model 85 Cheetah, plastic grips, 8-shot **$563.00**

Beretta Model 86 Cheetah
Similar to the 380-caliber Model 85 except has tip-up barrel for first-round loading. Barrel length is 4.4", overall length of 7.33". Has 8-shot magazine, walnut grips. Introduced 1989.
Price: **$599.00**

Beretta Model 21 Bobcat Pistol
Similar to the Model 950 BS. Chambered for 22 LR or 25 ACP. Both double action. Has 2.4" barrel, 4.9" overall length; 7-round magazine on 22 cal.; 8 rounds in 25 ACP, 9.9 oz., available in nickel, matte, engraved or blue finish. Plastic grips. Introduced in 1985.
Price: Bobcat, 22 or 25, blue **$292.00**
Price: Bobcat, 22, stainless **$315.00**
Price: Bobcat, 22 or 25, matte **$259.00**

BERETTA MODEL 3032 TOMCAT PISTOL
Caliber: 32 ACP, 7-shot magazine. **Barrel:** 2.45". **Weight:** 14.5 oz. **Length:** 5" overall. **Grips:** Checkered black plastic. **Sights:** Blade front, drift-adjustable rear. **Features:** Double action with exposed hammer; tip-up barrel for direct loading/unloading; thumb safety; polished or matte blue finish. Imported from Italy by Beretta U.S.A. Introduced 1996.
Price: Blue **$379.00**
Price: Matte **$349.00**
Price: Stainless **$428.00**
Price: Titanium **$589.00**
Price: With Tritium sights **$420.00**

BERETTA MODEL 8000/8040/8045 COUGAR PISTOL
Caliber: 9mm Para., 10-shot, 40 S&W, 10-shot magazine; 45 ACP, 8-shot. **Barrel:** 3.6". **Weight:** 33.5 oz. **Length:** 7" overall. **Grips:** Checkered plastic. **Sights:** Blade front, rear drift adjustable for windage. **Features:** Slide-mounted safety; rotating barrel; exposed hammer. Matte black Bruniton finish. Announced 1994. Imported from Italy by Beretta U.S.A.
Price: **$709.00**
Price: D model, 9mm, 40 S&W **$709.00**
Price: D model, 45 ACP **$764.00**

BERETTA MODEL 9000S COMPACT PISTOL
Caliber: 9mm Para., 40 S&W; 10-shot magazine. **Barrel:** 3.4". **Weight:** 26.8 oz. **Length:** 6.6". **Grips:** Soft polymer. **Sights:** Windage-adjustable white-dot rear, white-dot blade front. **Features:** Glass-reinforced polymer frame; patented tilt-barrel, open-slide locking system; chrome-lined barrel; external serrated hammer; automatic firing pin and manual safeties. Introduced 2000. Imported from Italy by Beretta USA.
Price: 9000S Type F (single and double action, external hammer) **$558.00**
Price: 9000S Type D (double-action only, no external hammer or safety) **$558.00**

Beretta Model 8000/8040/8045 Mini Cougar
Similar to the Model 8000/8040 Cougar except has shorter grip frame and weighs 27.6 oz. Introduced 1998. Imported from Italy by Beretta U.S.A.
Price: 9mm or 40 S&W **$709.00**
Price: 9mm or 40 S&W, DAO **$709.00**
Price: 45 ACP DAO **$764.00**

Beretta U22 Neos

Bersa Thunder 380

Browning Micro Buck Mark Standard

Browning Buck Mark Challenge

BERETTA MODEL U22 NEOS
Caliber: 22 LR, 10-shot magazine. **Barrel:** 4.2"; 6". **Weight:** 32 oz.; 36 oz. **Length:** 8.8"; 10.3". **Sights:** Target. **Features:** Integral rail for standard scope mounts, light, perfectly weighted, 100% American made by Beretta.
Price: **$265.00**
Price: Inox. **$315.00**
Price: DLX **$336.00**
Price: Inox. **$386.00**

BERSA THUNDER 380 AUTO PISTOLS
Caliber: 380 ACP, 7-shot (Thunder 380 Lite), 9-shot magazine (Thunder 380 DLX). **Barrel:** 3.5". **Weight:** 23 oz. **Length:** 6.6" overall. **Grips:** Black polymer. **Sights:** Blade front, notch rear adjustable for windage; three-dot system. **Features:** Double action; firing pin and magazine safeties. Available in blue, nickel, or duo tone. Introduced 1995. Distributed by Eagle Imports, Inc.
Price: Thunder 380, 7-shot, deep blue finish **$266.95**
Price: Thunder 380 Deluxe, 9-shot, satin nickel **$299.95**
Price: Thunder 380 Gold, 7-shot **$299.95**

NEW!

BERSA THUNDER 45 ULTRA COMPACT PISTOL
Similar to the Bersa Thunder 380 except in 45 ACP. Available in three finishes. Introduced 2003. Imported from Argentina by Eagle Imports, Inc.
Price: Thunder 45, matte blue **$400.95**
Price: Thunder 45, Duotone **$424.95**
Price: Thunder 45, Satin nickel **$441.95**

BLUE THUNDER/COMMODORE 1911-STYLE AUTO PISTOLS
Caliber: 45 ACP, 7-shot magazine. **Barrel:** 4-1/4", 5". **Weight:** NA. **Length:** NA. **Grips:** Checkered hardwood. **Sights:** Blade front, drift-adjustable rear. **Features:** Extended slide release and safety, spring guide rod, skeletonized hammer and trigger, magazine bumper, beavertail grip safety. Imported from the Philippines by Century International Arms Inc.
Price: .... **$464.80 to $484.80**

BROWNING HI-POWER 9mm AUTOMATIC PISTOL
Caliber: 9mm Para.,10-shot magazine. **Barrel:** 4-21/32". **Weight:** 32 oz. **Length:** 7-3/4" overall. **Grips:** Walnut, hand checkered, or black Polyamide. **Sights:** 1/8" blade front; rear screw-adjustable for windage and elevation. Also available with fixed rear (drift-adjustable for windage). **Features:** External hammer with half-cock and thumb safeties. A blow on the hammer cannot discharge a cartridge; cannot be fired with magazine removed. Fixed rear sight model available. Includes gun lock. Imported from Belgium by Browning.
Price: Fixed sight model, walnut grips **$680.00**
Price: Fully adjustable rear sight, walnut grips **$730.00**
Price: Mark III, standard matte black finish, fixed sight, moulded grips, ambidextrous safety **$662.00**

Browning Hi-Power Practical Pistol
Similar to the standard Hi-Power except has silver-chromed frame with blued slide, wrap-around Pachmayr rubber grips, round-style serrated hammer and removable front sight, fixed rear (drift-adjustable for windage). Available in 9mm Para. Includes gun lock. Introduced 1991.
Price: **$717.00**

BROWNING BUCK MARK STANDARD 22 PISTOL
Caliber: 22 LR, 10-shot magazine. **Barrel:** 5-1/2". **Weight:** 32 oz. **Length:** 9-1/2" overall. **Grips:** Black moulded composite with checkering. **Sights:** Ramp front, Browning Pro Target rear adjustable for windage and elevation. **Features:** All steel, matte blue finish or nickel, gold-colored trigger. Buck Mark Plus has laminated wood grips. Includes gun lock. Made in U.S.A. Introduced 1985. From Browning.
Price: Buck Mark Standard, blue **$286.00**
Price: Buck Mark Nickel, nickel finish with contoured rubber grips **$338.00**
Price: Buck Mark Plus, matte blue with laminated wood grips ... **$350.00**
Price: Buck Mark Plus Nickel, nickel finish, laminated wood grips **$383.00**

Browning Buck Mark Camper
Similar to the Buck Mark except 5-1/2" bull barrel. Weight is 34 oz. Matte blue finish, molded composite grips. Introduced 1999. From Browning.
Price: **$258.00**
Price: Camper Nickel, nickel finish, molded composite grips **$287.00**

Browning Buck Mark Challenge
Similar to the Buck Mark except has a lightweight barrel and smaller grip diameter. Barrel length is 5-1/2", weight is 25 oz. Introduced 1999. From Browning.
Price: **$320.00**

Browning Buck Mark Micro
Same as the Buck Mark Standard and Buck Mark Plus except has 4" barrel. Available in blue or nickel. Has 16-click Pro Target rear sight. Introduced 1992.
Price: Micro Standard, matte blue finish **$286.00**
Price: Micro Nickel, nickel finish **$338.00**
Price: Buck Mark Micro Plus, matte blue, lam. wood grips **$350.00**
Price: Buck Mark Micro Plus Nickel **$383.00**

Charles Daly M-1911-A1P

Cobra FS380

Cobra Patriot

Cobra CA32

Colt 1991 Model O

Colt 1991 Model O Commander

Colt XSE Model O Commander

Browning Buck Mark Bullseye

Same as the Buck Mark Standard except has 7-1/4" fluted barrel, matte blue finish. Weighs 36 oz.
Price: Bullseye Standard, molded composite grips **$420.00**
Price: Bullseye Target, contoured rosewood grips **$541.00**

Browning Buck Mark 5.5

Same as the Buck Mark Standard except has a 5-1/2" bull barrel with integral scope mount, matte blue finish.
Price: 5.5 Field, Pro-Target adj. rear sight,
contoured walnut grips **$459.00**
Price: 5.5 Target, hooded adj. target sights, contoured walnut grips
. . . . **$459.00**

Buck Mark Commemorative

Same as the Buck Mark Standard except has a 6-3/4" Challenger-style barrel, matte blue finish and scrimshaw-style, bonded ivory grips. Includes pistol rug. Limited to 1,000 guns.
Price: Commemorative **$437.00**

CHARLES DALY M-1911-A1P AUTOLOADING PISTOL

Caliber: 45 ACP, 7- or 10-shot magazine. **Barrel:** 5". **Weight:** 38 oz. **Length:** 8-3/4" overall. **Grips:** Checkered. **Sights:** Blade front, rear drift adjustable for windage; three-dot system. **Features:** Skeletonized combat hammer and trigger; beavertail grip safety; extended slide release; oversize thumb safety; Parkerized finish. Introduced 1996. Imported from the Philippines by K.B.I., Inc.
Price: **$469.95**

COBRA ENTERPRISES FS380 AUTO PISTOL

Caliber: 380 ACP, 7-shot magazine. **Barrel:** 3.5". **Weight:** 2.1 lbs. **Length:** 6-3/8" overall. **Grips:** Black composition. **Sights:** Fixed. **Features:** Choice of bright chrome, satin nickel or black finish. Introduced 2002. Made in U.S.A. by Cobra Enterprises.
Price: **$98.00**

Cobra Enterprises FS32 AUTO PISTOL

Caliber: 32 ACP, 8-shot magazine. **Barrel:** 3.5". **Weight:** 2.1 lbs. **Length:** 6-3/8" overall. **Grips:** Black composition. **Sights:** Fixed. **Features:** Choice of black, satin nickel or bright chrome finish. Introduced 2002. Made in U.S.A. by Cobra Enterprises.
Price: **$107.00**

Cobra Industries Patriot Pistol

Caliber: .380ACP, 9mm Luger,6-shot magazine. **Barrel:** 3.3". **Weight:** 20 oz. **Length:** 6" overall. **Grips:** Checkered polymer. **Sights:** Fixed. **Features:** Stainless steel slide with load indicator; double-action-only trigger system. Introduced 2002. Made in U.S.A. by Cobra Enterprises, Inc.
Price: . . . . About **$325.00**

Cobra Industries CA32, CA380

Caliber: 32ACP, 380 ACP. **Barrel:** 2.8" **Weight:** 22 oz. **Length:** 5.4". **Grips:** Laminated wood (CA32); Black molded synthetic (CA380). **Sights:** Fixed. **Features:** True pocket pistol size and styling without bulk. Made in U.S.A. by Cobra Enterprises.
Price: . . . . **NA**

COLT MODEL 1991 MODEL O AUTO PISTOL

Caliber: 45 ACP, 7-shot magazine. **Barrel:** 5". **Weight:** 38 oz. **Length:** 8.5" overall. **Grips:** Checkered black composition. **Sights:** Ramped blade front, fixed square notch rear, high profile. **Features:** Matte finish. Continuation of serial number range used on original G.I. 1911 A1 guns. Comes with one magazine and moulded carrying case. Introduced 1991.
Price: **$645.00**
Price: Stainless **$800.00**

Colt Model 1991 Model O Commander Auto Pistol

Similar to the Model 1991 A1 except has 4-1/4" barrel. Overall length is 7-3/4". Comes with one 7-shot magazine, molded case.
Price: Blue **$645.00**
Price: Stainless steel **$800.00**

COLT XSE SERIES MODEL O AUTO PISTOLS

Caliber: 45 ACP, 8-shot magazine. **Barrel:** 4.25", 5". **Grips:** Checkered, double diamond rosewood. **Sights:** Drift-adjustable three-dot combat. **Features:** Brushed stainless finish; adjustable, two-cut aluminum trigger; extended ambidextrous thumb safety; upswept beavertail with palm swell; elongated slot hammer; beveled magazine well. Introduced 1999. From Colt's Manufacturing Co., Inc.
Price: XSE Government (5" barrel) **$950.00**
Price: XSE Commander (4.25" barrel) **$950.00**

Colt XSE Lightweight Commander

Colt Defender

Colt Series 70

Colt 38 Super

Colt Gunsite

CZ 75B 9mm

CZ 75B Decocker

COLT XSE LIGHTWEIGHT COMMANDER AUTO PISTOL

Caliber: 45 ACP, 8-shot. **Barrel:** 4-1/4". **Weight:** 26 oz. **Length:** 7-3/4" overall. **Grips:** Double diamond checkered rosewood. **Sights:** Fixed, glare-proofed blade front, square notch rear; three-dot system. **Features:** Brushed stainless slide, nickeled aluminum frame; McCormick elongated-slot enhanced hammer, McCormick two-cut adjustable aluminum hammer. Made in U.S.A. by Colt's Mfg. Co., Inc.

Price: 45, stainless **$950.00**

COLT DEFENDER

Caliber: 40 S&W, 45 ACP, 7-shot magazine. **Barrel:** 3". **Weight:** 22-1/2 oz. **Length:** 6-3/4" overall. **Grips:** Pebble-finish rubber wraparound with finger grooves. **Sights:** White dot front, snag-free Colt competition rear. **Features:** Stainless finish; aluminum frame; combat-style hammer; Hi Ride grip safety, extended manual safety, disconnect safety. Introduced 1998. Made in U.S.A. by Colt's Mfg. Co.

Price: **$773.00**
Price: 41 Magnum Model, from. **$825.00**

COLT SERIES 70

NEW! **Caliber:** 45 ACP. **Barrel:** 5". **Weight:** NA **Length:** NA **Grips:** Rosewood with double diamond checkering pattern. **Sights:** Fixed. **Features:** A custom replica of the Original Series 70 pistol with a Series 70 firing system, original rollmarks. Introduced 2002. Made in U.S.A. by Colt's Manufacturing.

Price: . . . . **NA**

COLT 38 SUPER

NEW! **Caliber:** 38 Super **Barrel:** 5" **Weight:** NA. **Length:** 8-1/2" **Grips:** Checkered rubber (Stainless and blue models); Wood with double diamond checkering pattern (Bright stainless model). **Sights:** 3-dot. **Features:** Beveled magazine well, standard thumb safety and service-style grip safety. Introduced 2003. Made in U.S.A. by Colt's Mfg. Co.

Price: . . . . (Blue) **$864.00** (Stainless steel) **$943.00**
Price: . . . . (Bright stainless steel) **$1,152.00**

COLT GUNSITE PISTOL

NEW! **Caliber:** 45 ACP **Barrel:** 5". **Weight:** NA. **Length:** NA. **Grips:** Rosewood. **Sights:** Heinie, front; Novak, rear. **Features:** Contains most all of the Gunsite school recommended features such as Series 70 firing system, Smith & Alexander metal grip safety w/palm swell, serrated flat mainspring housing, dehorned all around. Available in blue or stainless steel. Introduced 2003. Made in U.S.A. by Colt's Mfg. Co.

Price: . . . . **NA**

CZ 75B AUTO PISTOL

Caliber: 9mm Para., 40 S&W, 10-shot magazine. **Barrel:** 4.7". **Weight:** 34.3 oz. **Length:** 8.1" overall. **Grips:** High impact checkered plastic. **Sights:** Square post front, rear adjustable for windage; three-dot system. **Features:** Single action/double action design; firing pin block safety; choice of black polymer, matte or high-polish blue finishes. All-steel frame. Imported from the Czech Republic by CZ-USA.

Price: Black polymer. **$472.00**
Price: Glossy blue. **$486.00**
Price: Dual tone or satin nickel **$486.00**
Price: 22 LR conversion unit. **$279.00**

CZ 75B Decocker

Similar to the CZ 75B except has a decocking lever in place of the safety lever. All other specifications are the same. Introduced 1999. Imported from the Czech Republic by CZ-USA.

Price: 9mm, black polymer **$467.00**
Price: 40 S&W **$481.00**

CZ 75B Compact Auto Pistol

Similar to the CZ 75 except has 10-shot magazine, 3.9" barrel and weighs 32 oz. Has removable front sight, non-glare ribbed slide top. Trigger guard is squared and serrated; combat hammer. Introduced 1993. Imported from the Czech Republic by CZ-USA.

Price: 9mm, black polymer **$499.00**
Price: Dual tone or satin nickel **$513.00**
Price: D Compact, black polymer **$526.00**

HANDGUNS

CZ 85

CZ 97B

CZ 75/85 Kadet

CZ 100

Dan Wesson Firearms
Pointman Major

CZ 75M IPSC Auto Pistol

Similar to the CZ 75B except has a longer frame and slide, slightly larger grip to accommodate new heavy-duty magazine. Ambidextrous thumb safety, safety notch on hammer; two-port in-frame compensator; slide racker; frame-mounted Firepoint red dot sight. Introduced 2001. Imported from the Czech Republic by CZ USA.

Price: 40 S&W, 10-shot mag. **$1,551.00**
Price: CZ 75 Standard IPSC (40 S&W, adj. sights) **$1,038.00**

CZ 85B Auto Pistol

Same gun as the CZ 75 except has ambidextrous slide release and safety-levers; non-glare, ribbed slide top; squared, serrated trigger guard; trigger stop to prevent overtravel. Introduced 1986. Imported from the Czech Republic by CZ-USA.

Price: Black polymer **$483.00**
Price: Combat, black polymer **$540.00**
Price: Combat, dual tone **$487.00**
Price: Combat, glossy blue **$499.00**

CZ 85 Combat

Similar to the CZ 85B (9mm only) except has an adjustable rear sight, adjustable trigger for overtravel, free-fall magazine, extended magazine catch. Does not have the firing pin block safety. Introduced 1999. Imported from the Czech Republic by CZ-USA.

Price: 9mm, black polymer **$540.00**
Price: 9mm, glossy blue **$566.00**
Price: 9mm, dual tone or satin nickel **$586.00**

CZ 83B DOUBLE-ACTION PISTOL

Caliber: 9mm Makarov, 32 ACP, 380 ACP, 10-shot magazine. **Barrel:** 3.8". **Weight:** 26.2 oz. **Length:** 6.8" overall. **Grips:** High impact checkered plastic. **Sights:** Removable square post front, rear adjustable for windage; three-dot system. **Features:** Single action/double action; ambidextrous magazine release and safety. Blue finish; non-glare ribbed slide top. Imported from the Czech Republic by CZ-USA.

Price: Blue **$378.00**
Price: Nickel **$397.00**

CZ 97B AUTO PISTOL

Caliber: 45 ACP, 10-shot magazine. **Barrel:** 4.85". **Weight:** 40 oz. **Length:** 8.34" overall. **Grips:** Checkered walnut. **Sights:** Fixed. **Features:** Single action/double action; full-length slide rails; screw-in barrel bushing; linkless barrel; all-steel construction; chamber loaded indicator; dual transfer bars. Introduced 1999. Imported from the Czech Republic by CZ-USA.

Price: Black polymer **$625.00**
Price: Glossy blue **$641.00**

CZ 75/85 KADET AUTO PISTOL

Caliber: 22 LR, 10-shot magazine. **Barrel:** 4.88". **Weight:** 36 oz. **Grips:** High impact checkered plastic. **Sights:** Blade front, fully adjustable rear. **Features:** Single action/double action mechanism; all-steel construction. Duplicates weight, balance and function of the CZ 75 pistol. Introduced 1999. Imported from the Czech Republic by CZ-USA.

Price: Black polymer **$486.00**

CZ 100 AUTO PISTOL

Caliber: 9mm Para., 40 S&W, 10-shot magazine. **Barrel:** 3.7". **Weight:** 24 oz. **Length:** 6.9" overall. **Grips:** Grooved polymer. **Sights:** Blade front with dot, white outline rear drift adjustable for windage. **Features:** Double action only with firing pin block; polymer frame, steel slide; has laser sight mount. Introduced 1996. Imported from the Czech Republic by CZ-USA.

Price: 9mm Para **$405.00**
Price: 40 S&W **$424.00**

DAN WESSON FIREARMS POINTMAN MAJOR AUTO PISTOL

Caliber: 45 ACP. **Barrel:** 5". **Grips:** Rosewood checkered. **Sights: Features:** Blued or stainless steel frame and serrated slide; Chip McCormick match-grade trigger group, sear and disconnect; match-grade barrel; high-ride beavertail safety; checkered slide release; high rib; interchangeable sight system; laser engraved. Introduced 2000. Made in U.S.A. by Dan Wesson Firearms.

Price: Model PM1-B (blued) **$799.00**
Price: Model PM1-S (stainless) **$799.00**

Dan Wesson Firearms Pointman Seven Auto Pistols

Similar to Pointman Major, dovetail adjustable target rear sight and dovetail target front sight. Available in blued or stainless finish. Introduced 2000. Made in U.S.A. by Dan Wesson Firearms.

Price: PM7 (blued frame and slide) **$999.00**
Price: PM7S (stainless finish) **$1,099.00**

Dan Wesson Firearms Pointman Guardian Auto Pistols

Similar to Pointman Major, more compact frame with 4.25" barrel. Avaiable in blued or stainless finish with fixed or adjustable sights. Introduced 2000. Made in U.S.A. by Dan Wesson Firearms.

Price: PMG-FS, all new frame (fixed sights) **$769.00**
Price: PMG-AS (blued frame and slide, adjustable sights) **$799.00**
Price: PMGD-FS Guardian Duce, all new frame (stainless frame and blued slide, fixed sights) **$829.00**
Price: PMGD-AS Guardian Duce (stainless frame and blued slide, adj. sights) **$799.00**

Dan Wesson Firearms
Major Aussie

Dan Wesson Firearms
Patriot Marksman

Desert Baby Eagle

Desert Eagle Mark XIX

Dan Wesson Firearms Major Tri-Ops Packs

Similar to Pointman Major. Complete frame assembly fitted to 3 match grade complete slide assemblied (9mm, 10mm, 40 S&W). Includes recoil springs and magazines that come in hard cases fashioned after high-grade European rifle case. Constructed of navy blue cordura stretched over hardwood with black leather trim and comfortable black leather wrapped handle. Brass corner protectors, dual combination locks, engraved presentation plate on the lid. Inside, the Tri-Ops Pack components are nested in precision die-cut closed cell foam and held sercurely in place by convoluted foam in the inside of the lid. Introduced 2002. Made in U.S.A. by Dan Wesson Firearms.
Price: TOP1B (blued), TOP1-S (stainless) **$2.459.00**

Dan Wesson Firearms Major Aussie

Similar to Pointman Major. Available in 45 ACP. Features Bomar-style adjustable rear target sight, unique slide top configuration exclusive to this model (features radius from the flat side surfaces of the slide to a narrow flat on top and then a small redius and reveal ending in a flat, low (1/16" high) sight rib 3/8" wide with lengthwise serrations). Clearly identified by the Southern Cross flag emblem laser engraved on the sides of the slide (available in 45 ACP only). Introduced 2002. Made in U.S.A. by Dan Wesson Firearms.
Price: PMA-B (blued) **$999.00**
Price: PMA-S (stainless) **$1,099.00**

Dan Wesson Firearms Pointman Minor Auto Pistol

Similar to Pointman Major. Full size (5") entry level IDPA or action pistol model with blued carbon alloy frame and round top slide, bead blast matte finish on frame and slide top and radius, satin-brushed polished finish on sides of slide, chromed barrel, dovetail mount fixed rear target sight and tactical/target ramp front sight, match trigger, skeletonized target hammer, high ride beavertail, fitted extractor, serrations on thumb safety, slide release and mag release, lowered and relieved ejection port, beveled mag well, exotic hardwood grips, serrated mainspring housing, laser engraved. Introduced 2000. Made in U.S.A. by Dan Wesson Firearms.
Price: Model PM2-P **$599.00**

Dan Wesson Firearms Pointman Hi-Cap Auto Pistol

Similar to Pointman Minor, full-size high-capacity (10-shot) magazine with 5" chromed barrel, blued finish and dovetail fixed rear sight. Match adjustable trigger, ambidextrous extended thumb safety, beavertail safety. Introduced 2001. From Dan Wesson Firearms.
Price: PMHC (Pointman High-Cap) **$689.00**

Dan Wesson Firearms Pointman Dave Pruitt Signature Series

Similar to other full-sized Pointman models, customized by Master Pistolsmith and IDPA Grand Master Dave Pruitt. Alloy carbon-steel with black oxide bluing and bead-blast matte finish. Front and rear chevron cocking serrations, dovetail mount fixed rear target sight and tactical/target ramp front sight, ramped match barrel with fitted match bushing and link, Chip McCormick (or equivalent) match grade trigger group, serrated ambidextrous tactical/carry thumb safety, high ride beavertail, serrated slide release and checkered mag release, match grade sear and hammer, fitted extractor, lowered and relieved ejection port, beveled mag well, full length 2-piece recoil spring guide rod, cocobolo double diamond checkered grips, serrated steel mainspring housing, special laser engraving. Introduced 2001. From Dan Wesson Firearms.
Price: PMDP (Pointman Dave Pruitt) **$899.00**

DAN WESSON FIREARMS PATRIOT 1911 PISTOL

Caliber: 45 ACP. **Grips:** Exotic exhibition grade cocobolo, double diamond hand cut checkering. **Sights:** New innovative combat/carry rear sight that completely encloses the dovetail. **Features:** The new Patriot Expert and Patriot Marksman are full size match grade series 70 1911s machined from steel forgings. Available in blued chome moly steel or stainless steel. Beveled mag well, lowered and flared ejection port, high sweep beavertail safety. Delivery begins in June 2002.
Price: Model PTM-B (blued) **$797.00**
Price: Model PTM-S (stainless) **$898.00**
Price: Model PTE-B (blued) **$864.00**
Price: Model PTE-S (stainless). **$971.00**

DESERT EAGLE MARK XIX PISTOL

Caliber: 357 Mag., 9-shot; 44 Mag., 8-shot; 50 Magnum, 7-shot. **Barrel:** 6", 10", interchangeable. **Weight:** 357 Mag.—62 oz.; 44 Mag.—69 oz.; 50 Mag.— 72 oz. **Length:** 10-1/4" overall (6" bbl.). **Grips:** Polymer; rubber available. **Sights:** Blade on ramp front, combat-style rear. Adjustable available. **Features:** Interchangeable barrels; rotating three-lug bolt; ambidextrous safety; adjustable trigger. Military epoxy finish. Satin, bright nickel, hard chrome, polished and blued finishes available. 10" barrel extra. Imported from Israel by Magnum Research, Inc.
Price: 357, 6" bbl., standard pistol **$1,199.00**
Price: 44 Mag., 6", standard pistol **$1,199.00**
Price: 50 Magnum, 6" bbl., standard pistol **$1,199.00**

DESERT BABY EAGLE PISTOLS

Caliber: 9mm Para., 40 S&W, 45 ACP, 10-round magazine. **Barrel:** 3.5", 3.7", 4.72". **Weight:** NA. **Length:** 7.25" to 8.25" overall. **Grips:** Polymer. **Sights:** Drift-adjustable rear, blade front. **Features:** Steel frame and slide; polygonal rifling to reduce barrel wear; slide safety; decocker. Reintroduced in 1999. Imported from Israel by Magnum Research Inc.
Price: Standard (9mm or 40 cal.; 4.72" barrel, 8.25" overall) **$499.00**
Price: Semi-Compact (9mm, 40 or 45 cal.; 3.7" barrel,
7.75" overall) **$499.00**
Price: Compact (9mm or 40 cal.; 3.5" barrel, 7.25" overall) **$499.00**
Price: Polymer (9mm or 40 cal; polymer frame; 3.25" barrel,
7.25" overall) **$499.00**

HANDGUNS

HANDGUNS — AUTOLOADERS, SERVICE & SPORT

EAA Witness

Ed Brown
Commander Bobtail

Ed Brown Kobra Carry

Entréprise Elite P500

Entréprise Boxer P500

Entréprise
Tactical 500

EAA WITNESS DA AUTO PISTOL
Caliber: 9mm Para., 10-shot magazine; 38 Super, 40 S&W, 10-shot magazine; 45 ACP, 10-shot magazine. **Barrel:** 4.50". **Weight:** 35.33 oz. **Length:** 8.10" overall. **Grips:** Checkered rubber. **Sights:** Undercut blade front, open rear adjustable for windage. **Features:** Double-action trigger system; round trigger guard; frame-mounted safety. Introduced 1991. Imported from Italy by European American Armory.

Price: 9mm, blue	**$449.00**
Price: 9mm, Wonder finish	**$459.00**
Price: 9mm Compact, blue, 10-shot	**$449.00**
Price: As above, Wonder finish	**$459.60**
Price: 40 S&W, blue	**$449.60**
Price: As above, Wonder finish	**$459.60**
Price: 40 S&W Compact, 9-shot, blue	**$449.60**
Price: As above, Wonder finish	**$459.60**
Price: 45 ACP, blue	**$449.00**
Price: As above, Wonder finish	**$459.60**
Price: 45 ACP Compact, 8-shot, blue	**$449.00**
Price: As above, Wonder finish	**$459.60**

EAA EUROPEAN MODEL AUTO PISTOLS
Caliber: 32 ACP or 380 ACP, 7-shot magazine. **Barrel:** 3.88". **Weight:** 26 oz. **Length:** 7-3/8" overall. **Grips:** European hardwood. **Sights:** Fixed blade front, rear drift-adjustable for windage. **Features:** Chrome or blue finish; magazine, thumb and firing pin safeties; external hammer; safety-lever takedown. Imported from Italy by European American Armory.
Price: Blue **$132.60**
Price: Wonder finish **$163.80**

EAA/BUL 1911 AUTO PISTOL
Caliber: 45 ACP. **Barrel:** 3", 4", 5". **Weight:** 24-30 oz. **Length:** 7-10". **Grips:** Full checkered. **Sights:** Tactical rear, dove tail front. **Features:** Lightweight polymer frame, extended beavertail, skeletonized trigger and hammer, beveled mag well.
Price: Blue **$559.00**
Price: Chrome **$599.00**

ED BROWN COMMANDER BOBTAIL
Caliber: 45 ACP, 400 Cor-Bon, 40 S&W, 357 SIG, 38 Super, 9mm Luger, 7-shot magazine. **Barrel:** 4.25". **Weight:** 34 oz. **Grips:** Hogue exotic wood. **Sights:** Customer preference front; fixed Novak low-mount, rear. Optional night inserts available. **Features:** Checkered forestrap and bobtailed mainspring housing. Other options available.
Price: **$2,300.00**

ED BROWN KOBRA, KOBRA CARRY
Caliber: 45 ACP, 7-shot magazine. **Barrel:** 5" (Kobra); 4.25" (Kobra Carry). **Weight:** 39 oz. (Kobra); 34 oz. (Kobra Carry). **Grips:** Hogue exotic wood. **Sights:** Ramp, front; fixed Novak low-mount night sights, rear. **Features:** Has snakeskin pattern serrations on forestrap and mainspring housing, denorned edges, beavertail grip safety.
Price: . . . . **$1,795.00** (Kobra); **$1,995.00** (Kobra Carry)

ENTRÉPRISE ELITE P500 AUTO PISTOL
Caliber: 45 ACP, 10-shot magazine. **Barrel:** 5". **Weight:** 40 oz. **Length:** 8.5" overall. **Grips:** Black ultra-slim, double diamond, checkered synthetic. **Sights:** Dovetailed blade front, rear adjustable for windage; three-dot system. **Features:** Reinforced dust cover; lowered and flared ejection port; squared trigger guard; adjustable match trigger; bolstered front strap; high grip cut; high ride beavertail grip safety; steel flat mainspring housing; extended thumb lock; skeletonized hammer, match grade sear, disconnector; Wolff springs. Introduced 1998. Made in U.S.A. by Entréprise Arms.
Price: **$739.90**

Entréprise Boxer P500 Auto Pistol
Similar to the Medalist model except has adjustable Competizione "melded" rear sight with dovetailed Patridge front; high mass chiseled slide with sweep cut; machined slide parallel rails; polished breech face and barrel channel. Introduced 1998. Made in U.S.A. by Entréprise Arms.
Price: **$1,399.00**

Entréprise Medalist P500 Auto Pistol
Similar to the Elite model except has adjustable Competizione "melded" rear sight with dovetailed Patridge front; machined slide parallel rails with polished breech face and barrel channel; front and rear slide serrations; lowered and flared ejection port; full-length one-piece guide rod with plug; National Match barrel and bushing; stainless firing pin; tuned match extractor; oversize firing pin stop; throated barrel and polished ramp; slide lapped to frame. Introduced 1998. Made in U.S.A. by Entréprise Arms.
Price: 45 ACP **$979.00**
Price: 40 S&W **$1,099.00**

Entréprise Tactical P500 Auto Pistol
Similar to the Elite model except has Tactical2 Ghost Ring sight or Novak lo-mount sight; ambidextrous thumb safety; front and rear slide serrations; full-length guide rod; throated barrel, polished ramp; tuned match extractor; fitted barrel and bushing; stainless firing pin; slide lapped to frame; dehorned. Introduced 1998. Made in U.S.A. by Entréprise Arms.
Price: **$979.90**
Price: Tactical Plus (full-size frame, Officer's slide) **$1,049.00**

FEG PJK-9HP

Felk MTF 450

Firestorm Mini

Firestorm 45 Gov't

Glock 17C

Glock 22

ERMA KGP68 AUTO PISTOL

Caliber: 32 ACP, 6-shot, 380 ACP, 5-shot. **Barrel:** 4". **Weight:** 22-1/2 oz. **Length:** 7-3/8" overall. **Grips:** Checkered plastic. **Sights:** Fixed. **Features:** Toggle action similar to original "Luger" pistol. Action stays open after last shot. Has magazine and sear disconnect safety systems.
Price: **$499.95**

FEG PJK-9HP AUTO PISTOL

Caliber: 9mm Para., 10-shot magazine. **Barrel:** 4.75". **Weight:** 32 oz. **Length:** 8" overall. **Grips:** Hand-checkered walnut. **Sights:** Blade front, rear adjustable for windage; three dot system. **Features:** Single action; polished blue or hard chrome finish; rounded combat-style serrated hammer. Comes with two magazines and cleaning rod. Imported from Hungary by K.B.I., Inc.
Price: Blue **$259.95**
Price: Hard chrome. **$259.95**

FEG SMC-380 AUTO PISTOL

Caliber: 380 ACP, 6-shot magazine. **Barrel:** 3.5". **Weight:** 18.5 oz. **Length:** 6.1" overall. **Grips:** Checkered composition with thumbrest. **Sights:** Blade front, rear adjustable for windage. **Features:** Patterned after the PPK pistol. Alloy frame, steel slide; double action. Blue finish. Comes with two magazines, cleaning rod. Imported from Hungary by K.B.I., Inc.
Price: **$224.95**

FELK MTF 450 AUTO PISTOL

Caliber: 9mm Para. (10-shot); 40 S&W (8-shot); 45 ACP (9-shot magazine). **Barrel:** 3.5". **Weight:** 19.9 oz. **Length:** 6.4" overall. **Grips:** Checkered. **Sights:** Blade front; adjustable rear. **Features:** Double-action-only trigger, striker fired; polymer frame; trigger safety, firing pin safety, trigger bar safety; adjustable trigger weight; fully interchangeable slide/barrel to change calibers. Introduced 1998. Imported by Felk Inc.
Price: **$395.00**
Price: 45 ACP pistol with 9mm and 40 S&W slide/barrel assemblies **$999.00**

FIRESTORM AUTO PISTOL

Features: 7 or 10 rd. double action pistols with matte, duotone or nickel finish. Distributed by SGS Importers International.
Price: 22 LR 10 rd, 380 7 rd. matte. **$264.95**
Price: Duotone **$274.95**
Price: Mini 9mm, 40 S&W, 10 rd. matte **$383.95**
Price: Duotone **$391.95**
Price: Nickel **$408.95**
Price: Mini 45, 7 rd. matte **$383.95**

Price: Duotone 45 . . . . **$399.95**
Price: Nickel 45 . . . . **$416.95**
Price: 45 Government, Compact, 7 rd. matte **$324.95**
Price: Duotone **$333.95**
Price: Extra magazines **$29.95-49.95**

GLOCK 17 AUTO PISTOL

Caliber: 9mm Para., 10-shot magazine. **Barrel:** 4.49". **Weight:** 22.04 oz. (without magazine). **Length:** 7.32" overall. **Grips:** Black polymer. **Sights:** Dot on front blade, white outline rear adjustable for windage. **Features:** Polymer frame, steel slide; double-action trigger with "Safe Action" system; mechanical firing pin safety, drop safety; simple takedown without tools; locked breech, recoil operated action. Adopted by Austrian armed forces 1983. NATO approved 1984. Imported from Austria by Glock, Inc.
Price: Fixed sight, with extra magazine, magazine loader, cleaning kit **$641.00**
Price: Adjustable sight **$671.00**
Price: Model 17L (6" barrel) **$800.00**
Price: Model 17C, ported barrel (compensated) **$646.00**

Glock 19 Auto Pistol

Similar to the Glock 17 except has a 4" barrel, giving an overall length of 6.85" and weight of 20.99 oz. Magazine capacity is 10 rounds. Fixed or adjustable rear sight. Introduced 1988.
Price: Fixed sight **$641.00**
Price: Adjustable sight **$671.00**
Price: Model 19C, ported barrel **$646.00**

Glock 20 10mm Auto Pistol

Similar to the Glock Model 17 except chambered for 10mm Automatic cartridge. Barrel length is 4.60", overall length is 7.59", and weight is 26.3 oz. (without magazine). Magazine capacity is 10 rounds. Fixed or adjustable rear sight. Comes with an extra magazine, magazine loader, cleaning rod and brush. Introduced 1990. Imported from Austria by Glock, Inc.
Price: Fixed sight **$700.00**
Price: Adjustable sight **$730.00**

Glock 21 Auto Pistol

Similar to the Glock 17 except chambered for 45 ACP, 10-shot magazine. Overall length is 7.59", weight is 25.2 oz. (without magazine). Fixed or adjustable rear sight. Introduced 1991.
Price: Fixed sight **$700.00**
Price: Adjustable sight **$730.00**

HANDGUNS

HANDGUNS — AUTOLOADERS, SERVICE & SPORT

Glock 26

Glock 30

Glock 31

Glock 35

Hammerli Trailside

Glock 22 Auto Pistol

Similar to the Glock 17 except chambered for 40 S&W, 10-shot magazine. Overall length is 7.28", weight is 22.3 oz. (without magazine). Fixed or adjustable rear sight. Introduced 1990.

Price: Fixed sight **$641.00**
Price: Adjustable sight **$671.00**
Price: Model 22C, ported barrel **$646.00**

Glock 23 Auto Pistol

Similar to the Glock 19 except chambered for 40 S&W, 10-shot magazine. Overall length is 6.85", weight is 20.6 oz. (without magazine). Fixed or adjustable rear sight. Introduced 1990.

Price: Fixed sight **$641.00**
Price: Model 23C, ported barrel **$646.00**
Price: Adjustable sight **$671.00**

GLOCK 26, 27 AUTO PISTOLS

Caliber: 9mm Para. (M26), 10-shot magazine; 40 S&W (M27), 9-shot magazine. **Barrel:** 3.46". **Weight:** 21.75 oz. **Length:** 6.29". **Grips:** Integral. Stippled polymer. **Sights:** Dot on front blade, fixed or fully adjustable white outline rear. **Features:** Subcompact size. Polymer frame, steel slide; double-action trigger with "Safe Action" system, three safeties. Matte black Tenifer finish. Hammer-forged barrel. Imported from Austria by Glock, Inc. Introduced 1996.

Price: Fixed sight **$641.00**
Price: Adjustable sight **$671.00**

GLOCK 29, 30 AUTO PISTOLS

Caliber: 10mm (M29), 45 ACP (M30), 10-shot magazine. **Barrel:** 3.78". **Weight:** 24 oz. **Length:** 6.7" overall. **Grips:** Integral. Stippled polymer. **Sights:** Dot on front, fixed or fully adjustable white outline rear. **Features:** Compact size. Polymer frame steel slide; double-recoil spring reduces recoil; Safe Action system with three safeties. Two magazines supplied. Introduced 1997. Imported from Austria by Glock, Inc.

Price: Fixed sight **$700.00**
Price: Adjustable sight **$730.00**

Glock 31/31C Auto Pistols

Similar to the Glock 17 except chambered for 357 Auto cartridge; 10-shot magazine. Overall length is 7.32", weight is 23.28 oz. (without magazine). Fixed or adjustable sight. Imported from Austria by Glock, Inc.

Price: Fixed sight **$641.00**
Price: Adjustable sight **$671.00**
Price: Model 31C, ported barrel **$646.00**

Glock 32/32C Auto Pistols

Similar to the Glock 19 except chambered for the 357 Auto cartridge; 10-shot magazine. Overall length is 6.85", weight is 21.52 oz. (without magazine). Fixed or adjustable sight. Imported from Austria by Glock, Inc.

Price: Fixed sight **$616.00**
Price: Adjustable sight **$644.00**
Price: Model 32C, ported barrel **$646.00**

Glock 33 Auto Pistol

Similar to the Glock 26 except chambered for the 357 Auto cartridge; 9-shot magazine. Overall length is 6.29", weight is 19.75 oz. (without magazine). Fixed or adjustable sight. Imported from Austria by Glock, Inc.

Price: Fixed sight **$641.00**
Price: Adjustable sight **$671.00**

GLOCK 34, 35 AUTO PISTOLS

Caliber: 9mm Para. (M34), 40 S&W (M35), 10-shot magazine. **Barrel:** 5.32". **Weight:** 22.9 oz. **Length:** 8.15" overall. **Grips:** Integral. Stippled polymer. **Sights:** Dot on front, fully adjustable white outline rear. **Features:** Polymer frame, steel slide; double-action trigger with "Safe Action" system; three safeties; Tenifer finish. Imported from Austria by Glock, Inc.

Price: Model 34, 9mm. **$770.00**
Price: Model 35, 40 S&W **$770.00**

GLOCK 36 AUTO PISTOL

Caliber: 45 ACP, 6-shot magazine. **Barrel:** 3.78". **Weight:** 20.11 oz. **Length:** 6.77" overall. **Grips:** Integral. Stippled polymer. **Sights:** Dot on front, fully adjustable white outline rear. **Features:** Polymer frame, steel slide; double-action trigger with "Safe Action" system; three safeties; Tenifer finish. Imported from Austria by Glock, Inc.

Price: Fixed sight **$700.00**
Price: Adj. sight **$730.00**

HAMMERLI "TRAILSIDE" TARGET PISTOL

Caliber: 22 LR. **Barrel:** 4.5", 6". **Weight:** 28 oz. **Grips:** Synthetic. **Sights:** Fixed. **Features:** 10-shot magazine. Imported from Switzerland by Sigarms. Distributed by Hammerli U.S.A.

Price: **$579.00**

HECKLER & KOCH USP AUTO PISTOL

Caliber: 9mm Para., 10-shot magazine, 40 S&W, 10-shot magazine. **Barrel:** 4.25". **Weight:** 28 oz. (USP40). **Length:** 6.9" overall. **Grips:** Non-slip stippled black polymer. **Sights:** Blade front, rear adjustable for windage. **Features:** New HK design with polymer frame, modified Browning action with recoil reduction system, single control lever. Special "hostile environment" finish on all metal parts. Available in SA/DA, DAO, left- and right-hand versions. Introduced 1993. Imported from Germany by Heckler & Koch, Inc.

Price: Right-hand **$827.00**
Price: Left-hand **$852.00**
Price: Stainless steel, right-hand **$888.00**
Price: Stainless steel, left-hand **$913.00**

HANDGUNS

Heckler & Koch
USP Compact

Heckler & Koch USP45

Heckler & Koch
USP45 Compact

Heckler & Koch
USP45 Tactical

Heckler & Koch
Elite

Heckler & Koch
Mark 23 Special Operations

Heckler & Koch P7M8

HECKLER & KOCH USP COMPACT AUTO PISTOL

Similar to the USP except has 3.58" barrel, measures 6.81" overall, and weighs 1.60 lbs. (9mm). Available in 9mm Para. 357 SIG or 40 S&W with 10-shot magazine. Introduced 1996. Imported from Germany by Heckler & Koch, Inc.

Price: Blue **$786.00**
Price: Blue with control lever on right **$821.00**
Price: Same as USP Compact DAO, enhanced trigger
performance **$821.00**

Heckler & Koch USP45 Auto Pistol

Similar to the 9mm and 40 S&W USP except chambered for 45 ACP, 10-shot magazine. Has 4.13" barrel, overall length of 7.87" and weighs 30.4 oz. Has adjustable three-dot sight system. Available in SA/DA, DAO, left- and right-hand versions. Introduced 1995. Imported from Germany by Heckler & Koch, Inc.

Price: Right-hand **$827.00**
Price: Left-hand **$862.00**
Price: Stainless steel right-hand **$888.00**
Price: Stainless steel left-hand **$923.00**

Heckler & Koch USP45 Compact

Similar to the USP45 except has stainless slide; 8-shot magazine; modified and contoured slide and frame; extended slide release; 3.80" barrel, 7.09" overall length, weighs 1.75 lbs.; adjustable three-dot sights. Introduced 1998. Imported from Germany by Heckler & Koch, Inc.

Price: With control lever on left, stainless **$909.00**
Price: As above, blue **$857.00**
Price: With control lever on right, stainless **$944.00**
Price: As above, blue **$892.00**

HECKLER & KOCH USP45 TACTICAL PISTOL

Caliber: 45 ACP, 10-shot magazine. **Barrel:** 4.92". **Weight:** 2.24 lbs. **Length:** 8.64" overall. **Grips:** Non-slip stippled polymer. **Sights:** Blade front, fully adjustable target rear. **Features:** Has extended threaded barrel with rubber O-ring; adjustable trigger; extended magazine floorplate; adjustable trigger stop; polymer frame. Introduced 1998. Imported from Germany by Heckler & Koch, Inc.

Price: **$1,124.00**

HECKLER & KOCH MARK 23 SPECIAL OPERATIONS PISTOL

Caliber: 45 ACP, 10-shot magazine. **Barrel:** 5.87". **Weight:** 43 oz. **Length:** 9.65" overall. **Grips:** Integral with frame; black polymer. **Sights:** Blade front, rear drift adjustable for windage; three-dot. **Features:** Polymer frame; double action; exposed hammer; short recoil, modified Browning action. Civilian version of the SOCOM pistol. Introduced 1996. Imported from Germany by Heckler & Koch, Inc.

Price: **$2,444.00**

HECKLER & KOCH USP EXPERT PISTOL

Combines features of the USP Tactical and HK Mark 23 pistols with a new slide design. Chambered for 45 ACP, .40 S&W & 9mm; 10-shot magazine. Has adjustable target sights, 5.20" barrel, 8.74" overall length, weighs 1.87 lbs. Match-grade single- and double-action trigger pull with adjustable stop; ambidextrous control levers; elongated target slide; barrel O-ring that seals and centers barrel. Suited to IPSC competition. Introduced 1999. Imported from Germany by Heckler & Koch, Inc.

Price: **$1,533.00**

HECKLER & KOCH ELITE

A long slide version of the USP combining features found on standard-sized and specialized models of the USP. Most noteworthy is the 6.2-inch barrel, making it the most accurate of the USP series. In 9mm and .45 ACP. Imported from Germany by Heckler & Koch, Inc. Introduced 2003.

Price: **$1,533.00**

HECKLER & KOCH P7M8 AUTO PISTOL

Caliber: 9mm Para., 8-shot magazine. **Barrel:** 4.13". **Weight:** 29 oz. **Length:** 6.73" overall. **Grips:** Stippled black plastic. **Sights:** Blade front, adjustable rear; three dot system. **Features:** Unique "squeeze cocker" in frontstrap cocks the action. Gas-retarded action. Squared combat-type trigger guard. Blue finish. Compact size. Imported from Germany by Heckler & Koch, Inc.

Price: P7M8, blued **$1,472.00**

HANDGUNS

Hi-Point 9MM Comp

Kahr K9

Kahr MK40

Kel-Tec P-11

HECKLER & KOCH P2000 GPM PISTOL
Caliber: 9mmx19; 10-shot magazine. 13- or 16-round law enforcment/military magazines. **Barrel:** 3.62". **Weight:** 21.87 ozs. **Length:** 7". **Grips:** Interchangeable panels. **Sights:** Fixed partridge style, drift adjustable for windage, standard 3-dot. **Features:** German Pistol Model incorporating features of the HK USP Compact such as the pre-cocked hammer system which combines the advantages of a cocked striker with the double action hammer system. Introduced 2003. Imported from Germany by Heckler & Koch, Inc.
Price: . . . . **NA**

HI-POINT FIREARMS 9MM COMP PISTOL
Caliber: 9mm, Para., 10-shot magazine. **Barrel:** 4". **Weight:** 39 oz. **Length:** 7.72" overall. **Grips:** Textured acetal plastic. **Sights:** Adjustable; low profile. **Features:** Single-action design. Scratch-resistant, non-glare blue finish, alloy frame. Muzzle brake/compensator. Compensator is slotted for laser or flashlight mounting. Introduced 1998. From MKS Supply, Inc.
Price: Matte black. **$159.00**

HI-POINT FIREARMS MODEL 9MM COMPACT PISTOL
Caliber: 9mm Para., 8-shot magazine. **Barrel:** 3.5". **Weight:** 29 oz. **Length:** 6.7" overall. **Grips:** Textured acetal plastic. **Sights:** Combat-style adjustable three-dot system; low profile. **Features:** Single-action design; frame-mounted magazine release; polymer or alloy frame. Scratch-resistant matte finish. Introduced 1993. Made in U.S.A. by MKS Supply, Inc.
Price: Black, alloy frame **$137.00**
Price: With polymer frame (29 oz.), non-slip grips **$137.00**
Price: Aluminum with polymer frame **$137.00**

Hi-Point Firearms Model 380 Polymer Pistol
Similar to the 9mm Compact model except chambered for 380 ACP, 8-shot magazine, adjustable three-dot sights. Weighs 29 oz. Polymer frame. Introduced 1998. Made in U.S.A. by MKS Supply.
Price: **$109.00**

Hi-Point Firearms 380 Comp Pistol
Similar to the 380 Polymer Pistol except has a 4" barrel with muzzle compensator; action locks open after last shot. Includes a 10-shot and an 8-shot magazine; trigger lock. Introduced 2001. Made in U.S.A. by MKS Supply Inc.
Price: **$125.00**
Price: With laser sight. **$190.00**

Hi-Point Firearms 45 Polymer Frame
Caliber: .45 ACP, 9-shot. **Barrel:** 4.5". **Weight:** 35 oz. **Sights:** Adjustable 3-dot. **Features:** Last round lock-open, grip mounted magazine release, magazine disconnect safety, integrated accessory rail. Introduced 2002. Made in U.S.A. by MKS Supply Inc.
Price: **$169.00**

IAI M-2000 PISTOL
Caliber: 45 ACP, 8-shot. **Barrel:** 5", (Compact 4.25"). **Weight:** 36 oz. **Length:** 8.5", (6" Compact). **Grips:** Plastic or wood. **Sights:** Fixed. **Features:** 1911 Government U.S. Army-style. Steel frame and slide parkerized. GI grip safety. Beveled feed ramp barrel. By IAI, Inc.
Price: **$465.00**

KAHR K9, K40 DA AUTO PISTOLS
Caliber: 9mm Para., 7-shot, 40 S&W, 6-shot magazine. **Barrel:** 3.5". **Weight:** 25 oz. **Length:** 6" overall. **Grips:** Wrap-around textured soft polymer. **Sights:** Blade front, rear drift adjustable for windage; bar-dot combat style. **Features:** Trigger-cocking double-action mechanism with passive firing pin block. Made of 4140 ordnance steel with matte black finish. Contact maker for complete price list. Introduced 1994. Made in U.S.A. by Kahr Arms.
Price: E9, black matte finish **$425.00**
Price: Matte black, night sights 9mm **$668.00**
Price: Matte stainless steel, 9mm. **$638.00**
Price: 40 S&W, matte black **$580.00**
Price: 40 S&W, matte black, night sights **$668.00**
Price: 40 S&W, matte stainless **$638.00**
Price: K9 Elite 98 (high-polish stainless slide flats, Kahr combat trigger), from **$694.00**
Price: As above, MK9 Elite 98, from **$694.00**
Price: As above, K40 Elite 98, from **$694.00**
Price: Covert, black, stainless slide, short grip **$599.00**
Price: Covert, black, tritium nite sights **$689.00**

Kahr K9 9mm Compact Polymer Pistol
Similar to K9 steel frame pistol except has polymer frame, matte stainless steel slide. Barrel length 3.5"; overall length 6"; weighs 17.9 oz. Includes two 7-shot magazines, hard polymer case, trigger lock. Introduced 2000. Made in U.S.A. by Kahr Arms.
Price: **$599.00**

Kahr MK9/MK40 Micro Pistol
Similar to the K9/K40 except is 5.5" overall, 4" high, has a 3" barrel. Weighs 22 oz. Has snag-free bar-dot sights, polished feed ramp, dual recoil spring system, DA-only trigger. Comes with 6- and 7-shot magazines. Introduced 1998. Made in U.S.A. by Kahr Arms.
Price: Matte stainless **$638.00**
Price: Elite 98, polished stainless, tritium night sights **$791.00**

KAHR PM9 PISTOL
Caliber: 9x19. **Barrel:** 3", 1:10 twist. **Weight:** 15.9 oz. **Length:** 5.3" overall. **Features:** Lightweight black polymer frame, polygonal rifling, stainless steel slide, DAO with passive striker block, trigger lock, hard case, 6 and 7 rd. mags.
Price: Matte stainless slide. **$622.00**
Price: Tritium night sights **$719.00**

KEL-TEC P-11 AUTO PISTOL
Caliber: 9mm Para., 10-shot magazine. **Barrel:** 3.1". **Weight:** 14 oz. **Length:** 5.6" overall. **Grips:** Checkered black polymer. **Sights:** Blade front, rear adjustable for windage. **Features:** Ordnance steel slide, aluminum frame. Double-action-only trigger mechanism. Introduced 1995. Made in U.S.A. by Kel-Tec CNC Industries, Inc.
Price: Blue **$314.00**
Price: Hard chrome. **$368.00**
Price: Parkerized **$355.00**

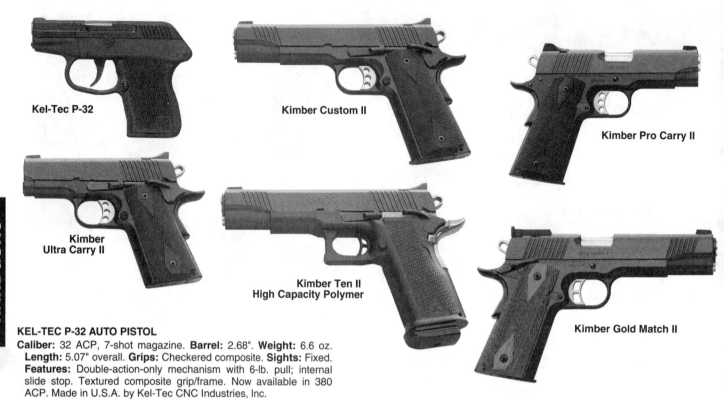

Kel-Tec P-32

Kimber Custom II

Kimber Pro Carry II

Kimber Ultra Carry II

Kimber Ten II High Capacity Polymer

Kimber Gold Match II

KEL-TEC P-32 AUTO PISTOL

Caliber: 32 ACP, 7-shot magazine. **Barrel:** 2.68". **Weight:** 6.6 oz. **Length:** 5.07" overall. **Grips:** Checkered composite. **Sights:** Fixed. **Features:** Double-action-only mechanism with 6-lb. pull; internal slide stop. Textured composite grip/frame. Now available in 380 ACP. Made in U.S.A. by Kel-Tec CNC Industries, Inc.

Price: Blue **$300.00**
Price: Hard chrome. **$340.00**
Price: Parkerized **$355.00**

KIMBER CUSTOM II AUTO PISTOL

Caliber: 45 ACP, 40 S&W, .38 Super. **Barrel:** 5", match grade, .40 S&W, .38 Super barrels ramped. **Weight:** 38 oz. **Length:** 8.7" overall. **Grips:** Checkered black rubber, walnut, rosewood. **Sights:** Dovetail front and rear, Kimber adjustable or fixed three dot (green) Meptrolight night sights. **Features:** Slide, frame and barrel machined from steel or stainless steel forgings. Match grade barrel, chamber and trigger group. Extended thumb safety, beveled magazine well, beveled front and rear slide serrations, high ride beavertail grip safety, checkered flat mainspring housing, kidney cut under trigger guard, high cut grip, match grade stainless steel berrel bushing, polished breech face, Commander-style hammer, lowered and flared ejection port, Wolff springs, bead blasted black oxide finish. Introduced in 1996. Made in U.S.A. by Kimber Mfg., Inc.

Price: Custom **$730.00**
Price: Custom Walnut (double-diamond walnut grips) **$752.00**
Price: Custom Stainless **$832.00**
Price: Custom Stainless 40 S&W **$870.00**
Price: Custom Stainless Target 45 ACP (stainless, adj. sight) . . . **$945.00**
Price: Custom Stainless Target 38 Super **$974.00**

Kimber Custom II Auto Pistol

Similar to Compact II, 4" bull barrel fitted directly to the stainless steel slide without a bushing, grip is .400" shorter than standard, no front serrations. Weighs 34 oz. 45 ACP only. Introduced in 1998. Made in U.S.A. by Kimber Mfg., Inc.

Price: **$870.00**

Kimber Pro Carry II Auto Pistol

Similar to Custom II, has aluminum frame, 4" bull barrel fitted directly to the slide without bushing. HD with stainless steel frame. Introduced 1998. Made in U.S.A. by Kimber Mfg., Inc.

Price: 45 ACP **$773.00**
Price: HD II **$879.00**
Price: Pro Carry HD II Stainless 45 ACP **$845.00**
Price: Pro Carry HD II Stainless 38 Spec. **$917.00**

Kimber Ultra Carry II Auto Pistol

Similar to Compact Stainless II, lightweight aluminum frame, 3" match grade bull barrel fitted to slide without bushing. Grips .400" shorter. Special slide stop. Low effort recoil. Weighs 25 oz. Introduced in 1999. Made in U.S.A. by Kimber Mfg., Inc.

Price: **$767.00**
Price: Stainless **$841.00**
Price: Stainless 40 S&W **$884.00**

Kimber Ten II High Capacity Polymer Pistol

Similar to Custom II, Pro Carry II and Ultra Carry II depending on barrel length. Ten-round magazine capacity (double stack and flush fitting). Polymer grip frame molded over stainless steel or aluminum (Ultra Ten II only) frame insert. Checkered front strap and belly of trigger guard. All models have fixed sights except Gold Match Ten II, which has adjustable sight. Frame grip dimensions approximate that of the standard 1911 for natural aiming and better recoil control. Ultra Ten II weight is 24 oz. Others 32-34 oz. Additional 14-round magazines available where legal. Much-improved version of the Kimber Polymer series. Made in U.S.A. by Kimber Mfg., Inc.

Price: Ultra Ten II **$850.00**
Price: Pro Carry Ten II **$828.00**
Price: Stainless Ten II **$812.00**

Kimber Gold Match II Auto Pistol

Similar to Custom II models. Includes stainless steel barrel with match grade chamber and barrel bushing, ambidextrous thumb safety, adjustable sight, premium aluminum trigger, hand-checkered double diamond rosewood grips. Barrel hand-fitted to bushing and slide for target accuracy. Made in U.S.A. by Kimber Mfg., Inc.

Price: Gold Match II **$1,169.00**
Price: Gold Match Stainless II 45 ACP **$1,315.00**
Price: Gold Match Stainless II 40 S&W **$1,345.00**

Kimber Gold Match Ten II Polymer Auto Pistol

Similar to Stainless Gold Match II. High capacity polymer frame with ten-round magazine. No ambi thumb safety. Polished flats add elegant look. Introduced 1999. Made in U.S.A. by Kimber Mfg., Inc.

Price: **$1,118.00**

HANDGUNS — AUTOLOADERS, SERVICE & SPORT

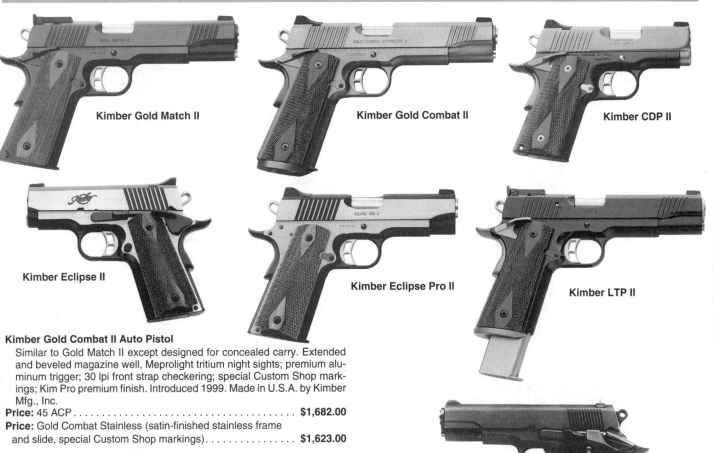

Kimber Gold Match II   Kimber Gold Combat II   Kimber CDP II

Kimber Eclipse II   Kimber Eclipse Pro II   Kimber LTP II

Kimber Gold Combat II Auto Pistol

Similar to Gold Match II except designed for concealed carry. Extended and beveled magazine well, Meprolight tritium night sights; premium aluminum trigger; 30 lpi front strap checkering; special Custom Shop markings; Kim Pro premium finish. Introduced 1999. Made in U.S.A. by Kimber Mfg., Inc.

Price: 45 ACP **$1,682.00**
Price: Gold Combat Stainless (satin-finished stainless frame
and slide, special Custom Shop markings) **$1,623.00**

Kimber CDP II Series Auto Pistol

Similar to Custom II, but designed for concealed carry. Aluminum frame. Standard features include stainless steel slide, Meprolight tritium three dot (green) dovetail-mounted night sights, match grade barrel and chamber, 30 LPI front strap checkering, two tone finish, ambidextrous thumb safety, hand-checkered double diamond rosewood grips. Introduced in 2000. Made in U.S.A. by Kimber Mfg., Inc.

Price: Ultra CDP II 40 S&W **$1,120.00**
Price: Ultra CDP II (3 barrel, short grip) **$1,084.00**
Price: Compact CDP II (4 barrel, short grip) **$1,084.00**
Price: Pro CDP II (4 barrel, full length grip) **$1,084.00**
Price: Custom CDP II (5 barrel, full length grip) **$1,084.00**

Kimber Eclipse II Series Auto Pistol

Similar to Custom II and other stainless Kimber pistol.s Stainless slide and frame, black anodized, two tone finish. Gray/black laminated grips. 30 LPI front strap checkering. All have night sights, with Target versions having Meprolight adjustable Bar/Dot version. Made in U.S.A. by Kimber Mfg., Inc.

Price: Eclipse Ultra II (3 barrel, short grip) **$1,052.00**
Price: Eclipse Pro II (4 barrel, full length grip) **$1,052.00**
Price: Eclipse Pro Target II (4 barrel, full length grip,
adjustable sight) **$1,153.00**
Price: Eclipse Custom II (5 barrel, full length grip) **$1,071.00**
Price: Eclipse Target II (5 barrel, full length grip,
adjustable sight) **$1,153.00**

Kimber LTP II Polymer Auto Pistol

Similar to Gold Match II. Built for Limited Ten competition. First Kimber pistol with new, innovative Kimber external extractor. KimPro premium finish. Stainless steel match grade barrel. Extended and beveled magazine well. Checkered front strap and trigger guard belly. Tungsten full length guide rod. Premium aluminum trigger. Ten-round single stack magazine. Wide ambidextrous thumb safety. Made in U.S.A. by Kimber Mfg., Inc.

Price: **$2,036.00**

Llama Micromax 380

Kimber Super Match II Auto Pistol

Similar to Gold Match II. Built for target and action shotting competition. Tested for accuracy. Target included. Stainless steel barrel and chamber. KimPro finish on stainless steel slide. Stainless steel frame. 30 LPI checkered front strap, premium aluminum trigger, Kimber adjustable sight. Introduced in 1999.

Price: **$1,926.00**

KORTH PISTOL

Caliber: .40 S&W, .357 SIG (9-shot); 9mm Para, 9x21 (10-shot). **Barrel:** 4" (standard), 5" (optional). Trigger **Weight:** 3.3 lbs. (single Action), 11 lbs. (double action). **Sights:** Fully adjustable. **Features:** All parts of surface-hardened steel; recoil-operated action, mechanically-locked via large pivoting bolot block maintaining parallel positioning of barrel during the complete cycle. Accessories include sound suppressor for qualified buyers. A masterpiece of German precision. Imported by Korth USA.

Price: **$5,413.00**

LLAMA MICROMAX 380 AUTO PISTOL

Caliber: 32 ACP, 8-shot, 380 ACP, 7-shot magazine. **Barrel:** 3-11/16". **Weight:** 23 oz. **Length:** 6-1/2" overall. **Grips:** Checkered high impact polymer. **Sights:** 3-dot combat. **Features:** Single-action design. Mini custom extended slide release; mini custom extended beavertail grip safety; combat-style hammer. Introduced 1997. Distributed by Import Sports, Inc.

Price: Matte blue **$281.95**
Price: Satin chrome (380 only) **$298.95**

HANDGUNS

Llama Minimax

Llama Max-1 Government Deluxe

North American Arms Guardian

Para-Ordnance P12.45

Para-Ordnance LDA

LLAMA MINIMAX SERIES

Caliber: 40 S&W, 7-shot; 45 ACP, 6-shot magazine. **Barrel:** 3-1/2". **Weight:** 35 oz. **Length:** 7-1/3" overall. **Grips:** Checkered rubber. **Sights:** Three-dot combat. **Features:** Single action, skeletonized combat-style hammer, extended slide release, cone-style barrel, flared ejection port. Introduced 1996. Distributed by Import Sports, Inc.

Price: Blue **$333.95**
Price: Duo-Tone finish (45 only) **$342.95**
Price: Satin chrome **$349.95**

Llama Minimax Sub-Compact Auto Pistol

Similar to the Minimax except has 3.14" barrel, weighs 31 oz.; 6.8" overall length; has 10-shot magazine with finger extension; beavertail grip safety. Introduced 1999. Distributed by Import Sports, Inc.

Price: 45 ACP, matte blue **$349.95**
Price: As above, satin chrome **$367.95**
Price: Duo-Tone finish (45 only) **$358.95**

LLAMA MAX-I AUTO PISTOLS

Caliber: 45 ACP, 7-shot. **Barrel:** 5-1/8". **Weight:** 36 oz. **Length:** 8-1/2" overall. **Grips:** Polymer. **Sights:** Blade front; three-dot system. **Features:** Single-action trigger; skeletonized combat-style hammer; steel frame; extended manual and grip safeties, matte finish. Introduced 1995. Distributed by Import Sports, Inc.

Price: 45 ACP, 7-shot, Government model **$324.95**

NORTH AMERICAN ARMS GUARDIAN PISTOL

Caliber: 32 ACP, 380 ACP, 32NAA, 6-shot magazine. **Barrel:** 2.1". **Weight:** 13.5 oz. **Length:** 4.36" overall. **Grips:** Black polymer. **Sights:** Fixed. **Features:** Double-action-only mechanism. All stainless steel construction; snag-free. Introduced 1998. Made in U.S.A. by North American Arms.

Price: . . . . **$408.00 to $449.00**

OLYMPIC ARMS OA-96 AR PISTOL

Caliber: 223. **Barrel:** 6", 8", 4140 chrome-moly steel. **Weight:** 5 lbs. **Length:** 15-3/4" overall. **Grips:** A2 stowaway pistol grip; no buttstock or receiver tube. **Sights:** Flat-top upper receiver, cut-down front sight base. **Features:** AR-15-type receivers with special bolt carrier; short aluminum hand guard; Vortex flash hider. Introduced 1996. Made in U.S.A. by Olympic Arms, Inc.

Price: **$858.00**

Olympic Arms OA-98 AR Pistol

Similar to the OA-93 except has removable 7-shot magazine, weighs 3 lbs. Introduced 1999. Made in U.S.A. by Olympic Arms, Inc.

Price: **$990.00**

PARA-ORDNANCE P-SERIES AUTO PISTOLS

Caliber: 9mm Para., 40 S&W, 45 ACP, 10-shot magazine. **Barrel:** 3", 3-1/2", 4-1/4", 5". **Weight:** From 24 oz. (alloy frame). **Length:** 8.5" overall. **Grips:** Textured composition. **Sights:** Blade front, rear adjustable for windage. High visibility three-dot system. **Features:** Available with alloy, steel or stainless steel frame with black finish (silver or stainless gun). Steel and stainless steel frame guns weigh 40 oz. (P14.45), 36 oz. (P13.45), 34 oz. (P12.45). Grooved match trigger, rounded combat-style hammer. Beveled magazine well. Manual thumb, grip and firing pin lock safeties. Solid barrel bushing. Contact maker for full details. Introduced 1990. Made in Canada by Para-Ordnance.

Price: Steel frame **$795.00**
Price: Alloy frame **$765.00**
Price: Stainless steel **$865.00**

Para-Ordnance Limited Pistols

Similar to the P-Series pistols except with full-length recoil guide system; fully adjustable rear sight; tuned trigger with overtravel stop; beavertail grip safety; competition hammer; front and rear slide serrations; ambidextrous safety; lowered ejection port; ramped match-grade barrel; dovetailed front sight. Introduced 1998. Made in Canada by Para-Ordnance.

Price: 9mm, 40 S&W, 45 ACP . . . . **$945.00 to $999.00**

Para-Ordnance LDA Auto Pistols

Similar to P-series except has double-action trigger mechanism. Steel frame with matte black finish, checkered composition grips. Available in 9mm Para., 40 S&W, 45 ACP. Introduced 1999. Made in Canada by Para-Ordnance.

Price: **$775.00**

Para-Ordnance LDA Limited Pistols

Similar to LDA, has ambidextrous safety, adjustable rear sight, front slide serrations and full-length recoil guide system. Made in Canada by Para-Ordnance.

Price: Black finish **$975.00**
Price: Stainless **$1,049.00**

PARA-ORDNANCE C5 45 LDA PARA CARRY

Caliber: 45 ACP. **Barrel:** 3", 6+1 shot. **Weight:** 30 oz. **Length:** 6.5". **Grips:** Double diamond checkered Cocobolo. **Features:** Stainless finish and receiver, "world's smallest DAO 45 auto." Para LDA trigger system and safeties.

Price: **$899.00**

HANDGUNS

Para-Ordnance C5
45 LDA Para Carry

Para-Ordnance C7
45 LDA Para Companion

Peters Stahl High Capacity

Peters Stahl Trophy Master

Peters Stahl Millenium

Phoenix
Arms HP22

Rock River Standard Match

Ruger P89

Ruger P90

PARA-ORDNANCE C7 45 LDA PARA COMPANION

Caliber: 45 ACP. **Barrel:** 3.5", 7+1 shot. **Weight:** 32 oz. **Length:** 7". **Grips:** Double diamond checkered Cocobolo. **Features:** Para LDA trigger system with Para LDA 3 safeties (slide lock, firing pin block and grip safety). Lightning speed, full size capacity.
Price: **$899.00**

PETERS STAHL AUTOLOADING PISTOLS

Caliber: 9mm Para., 45 ACP. **Barrel:** 5" or 6". **Grips:** Walnut or walnut with rubber wrap. **Sights:** Fully adjustable rear, blade front. **Features:** Stainless steel extended slide stop, safety and extended magazine release button; speed trigger with stop and approx. 3-lb. pull; polished ramp. Introduced 2000. Imported from Germany by Phillips & Rogers.
Price: High Capacity (accepts 15-shot magazines in 45 cal.; includes 10-shot magazine) **$1,695.00**
Price: Trophy Master (blued or stainless, 7-shot in 45,
8-shot in 9mm) **$1,995.00**
Price: Millenium Model (titanium coating on receiver and slide) **$2,195.00**

PHOENIX ARMS HP22, HP25 AUTO PISTOLS

Caliber: 22 LR, 10-shot (HP22), 25 ACP, 10-shot (HP25). **Barrel:** 3". **Weight:** 20 oz. **Length:** 5-1/2" overall. **Grips:** Checkered composition. **Sights:** Blade front, adjustable rear. **Features:** Single action, exposed hammer; manual hold-open; button magazine release. Available in satin nickel, polished blue finish. Introduced 1993. Made in U.S.A. by Phoenix Arms.
Price: With gun lock and cable lanyard. **$130.00**
Price: HP Rangemaster kit with 5" bbl., locking case
and assessories **$171.00**
Price: HP Deluxe Rangemaster kit with 3" and 5" bbls.,
2 mags., case **$210.00**

ROCK RIVER ARMS STANDARD MATCH AUTO PISTOL

Caliber: 45 ACP. **Barrel:** NA. **Weight:** NA. **Length:** NA. **Grips:** Cocobolo, checkered. **Sights:** Heine fixed rear, blade front. **Features:** Chrome-moly steel frame and slide; beavertail grip safety with raised pad; checkered slide stop; ambidextrous safety; polished feed ramp and extractor; aluminum speed trigger with 3.5 lb. pull. Made in U.S.A. From Rock River Arms.
Price: **$1,025.00**

ROCKY MOUNTAIN ARMS PATRIOT PISTOL

Caliber: 223, 10-shot magazine. **Barrel:** 7", with muzzle brake. **Weight:** 5 lbs. **Length:** 20.5" overall. **Grips:** Black composition. **Sights:** None furnished. **Features:** Milled upper receiver with enhanced Weaver base; milled lower receiver from billet plate; machined aluminum National Match handguard. Finished in DuPont Teflon-S matte black or NATO green. Comes with black nylon case, one magazine. Introduced 1993. From Rocky Mountain Arms, Inc.
Price: With A-2 handle top .... **$2,500.00 to $2,800.00**
Price: Flat top model. .... **$3,000.00 to $3,500.00**

RUGER P89 AUTOLOADING PISTOL

Caliber: 9mm Para., 10-shot magazine. **Barrel:** 4.50". **Weight:** 32 oz. **Length:** 7.84" overall. **Grips:** Grooved black synthetic composition. **Sights:** Square post front, square notch rear adjustable for windage, both with white dot inserts. **Features:** Double action, ambidextrous slide-mounted safety-levers. Slide 4140 chrome-moly steel or 400-series stainless steel, frame lightweight aluminum alloy. Ambidextrous magazine release. Blue, stainless steel. Introduced 1986; stainless 1990.
Price: P89, blue, extra mag and mag loader, plastic case locks . **$475.00**
Price: KP89, stainless, extra mag and mag loader,
plastic case locks **$525.00**

Ruger P93D

Ruger KP94D

Ruger KP95DAO

Ruger KMK 4

Ruger P89D Decocker Autoloading Pistol

Similar to standard P89 except has ambidextrous decocking levers in place of regular slide-mounted safety. Decocking levers move firing pin inside slide where hammer can not reach, while simultaneously blocking firing pin from forward movement—allows shooter to decock cocked pistol without manipulating trigger. Conventional thumb decocking procedures are therefore unnecessary. Blue, stainless steel. Introduced 1990.

Price: P89D, blue, extra mag and mag loader, plastic case locks **$475.00**

Price: KP89D, stainless, extra mag and mag loader,
plastic case locks **$525.00**

Ruger P89 Double-Action-Only Autoloading Pistol

Same as KP89 except operates only in double-action mode. Has spurless hammer, gripping grooves on each side of rear slide; no external safety or decocking lever. Internal safety prevents forward movement of firing pin unless trigger is pulled. Available 9mm Para., stainless steel only. Introduced 1991.

Price: Lockable case, extra mag and mag loader **$525.00**

RUGER P90 MANUAL SAFETY MODEL AUTOLOADING PISTOL

Caliber: 45 ACP, 8-shot magazine. **Barrel:** 4.50". **Weight:** 33.5 oz. **Length:** 7.75" overall. **Grips:** Grooved black synthetic composition. **Sights:** Square post front, square notch rear adjustable for windage, both with white dot. **Features:** Double action ambidextrous slide-mounted safety-levers move firing pin inside slide where hammer can not reach, simultaneously blocking firing pin from forward movement. Stainless steel only. Introduced 1991.

Price: KP90 with extra mag, loader, case and gunlock. **$565.00**
Price: P90 (blue). **$525.00**

Ruger KP90 Decocker Autoloading Pistol

Similar to the P90 except has a manual decocking system. The ambidextrous decocking levers move the firing pin inside the slide where the hammer can not reach it, while simultaneously blocking the firing pin from forward movement—allows shooter to decock a cocked pistol without manipulating the trigger. Available only in stainless steel. Overall length 7.75", weighs 33.5 oz. Introduced 1991.

Price: KP90D with case, extra mag and mag loading tool **$565.00**

RUGER P93 COMPACT AUTOLOADING PISTOL

Caliber: 9mm Para., 10-shot magazine. **Barrel:** 3.9". **Weight:** 31 oz. **Length:** 7.25" overall. **Grips:** Grooved black synthetic composition. **Sights:** Square post front, square notch rear adjustable for windage. **Features:** Front of slide crowned with convex curve; slide has seven finger grooves; trigger guard bow higher for better grip; 400-series stainless slide, lightweight alloy frame; also blue. Decocker-only or DAO-only. Includes hard case and lock. Introduced 1993. Made in U.S.A. by Sturm, Ruger & Co.

Price: KP93DAO, double-action-only **$575.00**
Price: KP93D ambidextrous decocker, stainless **$575.00**
Price: P93D, ambidextrous decocker, blue **$495.00**

Ruger KP94 Autoloading Pistol

Sized midway between full-size P-Series and compact P93. 4.25" barrel, 7.5" overall length, weighs about 33 oz. KP94 manual safety model; KP94DAO double-action-only (both 9mm Para., 10-shot magazine); KP94D is decocker-only in 40-caliber with 10-shot magazine. Slide gripping grooves roll over top of slide. KP94 has ambidextrous safety-levers; KP94DAO has no external safety, full-cock hammer position or decocking

lever; KP94D has ambidextrous decocking levers. Matte finish stainless slide, barrel, alloy frame. Also blue. Includes hard case and lock. Introduced 1994. Made in U.S.A. by Sturm, Ruger & Co.

Price: P94, P944, blue (manual safety) **$495.00**
Price: KP94 (9mm), KP944 (40-caliber) (manual
safety-stainless) **$575.00**
Price: KP94DAO (9mm), KP944DAO (40-caliber) **$575.00**
Price: KP94D (9mm), KP944D (40-caliber)-decock only **$575.00**

RUGER P95 AUTOLOADING PISTOL

Caliber: 9mm Para., 10-shot magazine. **Barrel:** 3.9". **Weight:** 27 oz. **Length:** 7.25" overall. **Grips:** Grooved; integral with frame. **Sights:** Blade front, rear drift adjustable for windage; three-dot system. **Features:** Moulded polymer grip frame, stainless steel or chrome-moly slide. Suitable for +P+ ammunition. Safety model, decocker or DAO. Introduced 1996. Made in U.S.A. by Sturm, Ruger & Co. Comes with lockable plastic case, spare magazine, loader and lock.

Price: P95 DAO double-action-only **$425.00**
Price: P95D decocker only **$425.00**
Price: KP95D stainless steel decocker only **$475.00**
Price: KP95DAO double-action only, stainless **$475.00**
Price: KP95 safety model, stainless steel **$475.00**
Price: P95 safety model, blued finish **$425.00**

RUGER P97 AUTOLOADING PISTOL

Caliber: 45ACP 8-shot magazine. **Barrel:** 4-1/8". **Weight:** 30-1/2 oz. **Length:** 7-1/4" overall. Grooved: Integral with frame. **Sights:** Blade front, rear drift adjustable for windage; three dot system. **Features:** Moulded polymer grip frame, stainless steel slide. Decocker or DAO. Introduced 1997. Made in U.S.A. by Sturm, Ruger & Co. Comes with lockable plastic case, spare magaline, loading tool.

Price: KP97D decocker only **$495.00**
Price: KP97DAO double-action only **$495.00**
Price: P97D decocker only, blued **$460.00**

RUGER MARK II STANDARD AUTOLOADING PISTOL

Caliber: 22 LR, 10-shot magazine. **Barrel:** 4-3/4" or 6". **Weight:** 35 oz. (4-3/4" bbl.). **Length:** 8-5/16" (4-3/4" bbl.). **Grips:** Checkered composition grip panels. **Sights:** Fixed, wide blade front, fixed rear. **Features:** Updated design of original Standard Auto. New bolt hold-open latch. 10-shot magazine, magazine catch, safety, trigger and new receiver contours. Introduced 1982.

Price: Blued (MK 4, MK 6) **$289.00**
Price: In stainless steel (KMK 4, KMK 6) **$379.00**

Ruger 22/45-P4

Ruger KP512

SIG Sauer P220

Ruger 22/45 Mark II Pistol

Similar to other 22 Mark II autos except has grip frame of Zytel that matches angle and magazine latch of Model 1911 45 ACP pistol. Available in 4" bull, 4-3/4" standard and 5-1/2" bull barrels. Comes with extra magazine, plastic case, lock. Introduced 1992.

Price: P4, 4" bull barrel, adjustable sights $275.00
Price: KP 4 (4-3/4" barrel), stainless steel, fixed sights $305.00
Price: KP512 (5-1/2" bull barrel), stainless steel, adj. sights $359.00
Price: P512 (5-1/2" bull barrel, all blue), adj. sights $275.00

SAFARI ARMS ENFORCER PISTOL

Caliber: 45 ACP, 6-shot magazine. **Barrel:** 3.8", stainless. **Weight:** 36 oz. **Length:** 7.3" overall. **Grips:** Smooth walnut with etched black widow spider logo. **Sights:** Ramped blade front, LPA adjustable rear. **Features:** Extended safety, extended slide release; Commander-style hammer; beavertail grip safety; throated, polished, tuned. Parkerized matte black or satin stainless steel finishes. Made in U.S.A. by Safari Arms.
Price: $630.00

SAFARI ARMS GI SAFARI PISTOL

Caliber: 45 ACP, 7-shot magazine. **Barrel:** 5", 416 stainless. **Weight:** 39.9 oz. **Length:** 8.5" overall. **Grips:** Checkered walnut. **Sights:** G.I.-style blade front, drift-adjustable rear. **Features:** Beavertail grip safety; extended thumb safety and slide release; Commander-style hammer. Parkerized finish. Reintroduced 1996.
Price: $439.00

SAFARI ARMS CARRIER PISTOL

Caliber: 45 ACP, 7-shot magazine. **Barrel:** 6", 416 stainless steel. **Weight:** 30 oz. **Length:** 9.5" overall. **Grips:** Wood. **Sights:** Ramped blade front, LPA adjustable rear. **Features:** Beavertail grip safety; extended controls; full-length recoil spring guide; Commander-style hammer. Throated, polished and tuned. Satin stainless steel finish. Introduced 1999. Made in U.S.A. by Safari Arms, Inc.
Price: $714.00

SAFARI ARMS COHORT PISTOL

Caliber: 45 ACP, 7-shot magazine. **Barrel:** 3.8", 416 stainless. **Weight:** 37 oz. **Length:** 8.5" overall. **Grips:** Smooth walnut with laser-etched black widow logo. **Sights:** Ramped blade front, LPA adjustable rear. **Features:** Combines the Enforcer model, slide and MatchMaster frame. Beavertail grip safety; extended thumb safety and slide release; Commander-style hammer. Throated, polished and tuned. Satin stainless finish. Introduced 1996. Made in U.S.A. by Safari Arms, Inc.
Price: $654.00

SAFARI ARMS MATCHMASTER PISTOL

Caliber: 45 ACP, 7-shot. **Barrel:** 5" or 6", 416 stainless steel. **Weight:** 38 oz. (5" barrel). **Length:** 8.5" overall. **Grips:** Smooth walnut. **Sights:** Ramped blade, LPA adjustable rear. **Features:** Beavertail grip safety; extended controls; Commander-style hammer; throated, polished, tuned.

Parkerized matte-black or satin stainless steel. Made in U.S.A. by Olympic Arms, Inc.
Price: 5" barrel $594.00
Price: 6" barrel $654.00

Safari Arms Carry Comp Pistol

Similar to the Matchmaster except has Wil Schueman-designed hybrid compensator system. Made in U.S.A. by Olympic Arms, Inc.
Price: $1,067.00

SEECAMP LWS 32 STAINLESS DA AUTO

Caliber: 32 ACP Win. Silvertip, 6-shot magazine. **Barrel:** 2", integral with frame. **Weight:** 10.5 oz. **Length:** 4-1/8" overall. **Grips:** Glass-filled nylon. **Sights:** Smooth, no-snag, contoured slide and barrel top. **Features:** Aircraft quality 17-4 PH stainless steel. Inertia-operated firing pin. Hammer fired double-action-only. Hammer automatically follows slide down to safety rest position after each shot—no manual safety needed. Magazine safety disconnector. Polished stainless. Introduced 1985. From L.W. Seecamp.
Price: $425.00

SEMMERLING LM-4 SLIDE-ACTION PISTOL

Caliber: 45 ACP, 4-shot magazine. **Barrel:** 2". **Weight:** 24 oz. **Length:** NA. **Grips:** NA. **Sights:** NA. **Features:** While outwardly appearing to be a semi-automatic, the Semmerling LM-4 is a unique and super compact pistol employing a thumb activated slide mechanism (the slide is manually retracted between shots). Hand-built and super reliable, it is intended for professionals in law enforcement and for concealed carry by licensed and firearms knowledgeable private citizens. From American Derringer Corp.
Price: $2,635.00

SIG SAUER P220 SERVICE AUTO PISTOL

Caliber: 45 ACP, (7- or 8-shot magazine). **Barrel:** 4-3/8". **Weight:** 27.8 oz. **Length:** 7.8" overall. **Grips:** Checkered black plastic. **Sights:** Blade front, drift adjustable rear for windage. Optional Siglite nightsights. **Features:** Double action. Decocking lever permits lowering hammer onto locked firing pin. Squared combat-type trigger guard. Slide stays open after last shot. Imported from Germany by SIGARMS, Inc.
Price: Blue SA/DA or DAO $790.00
Price: Blue, Siglite night sights $880.00
Price: K-Kote or nickel slide $830.00
Price: K-Kote or nickel slide with Siglite night sights. $930.00

SIG Sauer P220 Sport Auto Pistol

Similar to the P220 except has 4.9" barrel, ported compensator, all-stainless steel frame and slide, factory-tuned trigger, adjustable sights, extended competition controls. Overall length is 9.9", weighs 43.5 oz. Introduced 1999. From SIGARMS, Inc.
Price: $1,320.00

SIG Sauer P245 Compact

SIG Sauer Pro 2009

SIG Sauer P229 Sport

SIG Sauer P232

Smith & Wesson 457 TDA

SIG Sauer P245 Compact Auto Pistol

Similar to the P220 except has 3.9" barrel, shorter grip, 6-shot magazine, 7.28" overall length, and weighs 27.5 oz. Introduced 1999. From SIG-ARMS, Inc.

Price: Blue **$780.00**
Price: Blue, with Siglite sights. **$850.00**
Price: Two-tone **$830.00**
Price: Two-tone with Siglite sights. **$930.00**
Price: With K-Kote finish **$830.00**
Price: K-Kote with Siglite sights **$930.00**

SIG Sauer P229 DA Auto Pistol

Similar to the P228 except chambered for 9mm Para., 40 S&W, 357 SIG. Has 3.86" barrel, 7.08" overall length and 3.35" height. Weight is 30.5 oz. Introduced 1991. Frame made in Germany, stainless steel slide assembly made in U.S.; pistol assembled in U.S. From SIGARMS, Inc.

Price: **$795.00**
Price: With nickel slide **$890.00**
Price: Nickel slide Siglite night sights **$935.00**

SIG PRO AUTO PISTOL

Caliber: 9mm Para., 40 S&W, 10-shot magazine. **Barrel:** 3.86". **Weight:** 27.2 oz. **Length:** 7.36" overall. **Grips:** Composite and rubberized one-piece. **Sights:** Blade front, rear adjustable for windage. Optional Siglite night sights. **Features:** Polymer frame, stainless steel slide; integral frame accessory rail; replaceable steel frame rails; left- or right-handed magazine release. Introduced 1999. From SIGARMS, Inc.

Price: SP2340 (40 S&W) **$596.00**
Price: SP2009 (9mm Para.) **$596.00**
Price: As above with Siglite night sights **$655.00**

SIG Sauer P226 Service Pistol

Similar to the P220 pistol except has 4.4" barrel, and weighs 28.3 oz. 357 SIG or 40 S&W. Imported from Germany by SIGARMS, Inc.

Price: Blue SA/DA or DAO **$830.00**
Price: With Siglite night sights **$930.00**
Price: Blue, SA/DA or DAO 357 SIG. **$830.00**
Price: With Siglite night sights **$930.00**
Price: K-Kote finish, 40 S&W only or nickel slide **$830.00**
Price: K-Kote or nickel slide Siglite night sights **$930.00**
Price: Nickel slide 357 SIG **$875.00**
Price: Nickel slide, Siglite night sights **$930.00**

SIG Sauer P229 Sport Auto Pistol

Similar to the P229 except available in 357 SIG only; 4.8" heavy barrel; 8.6" overall length; weighs 40.6 oz.; vented compensator; adjustable target sights; rubber grips; extended slide latch and magazine release. Made of stainless steel. Introduced 1998. From SIGARMS, Inc.

Price: **$1,320.00**

SIG SAUER P232 PERSONAL SIZE PISTOL

Caliber: 380 ACP, 7-shot. **Barrel:** 3-3/4". **Weight:** 16 oz. **Length:** 6-1/2" overall. **Grips:** Checkered black composite. **Sights:** Blade front, rear adjustable for windage. **Features:** Double action/single action or DAO. Blowback operation, stationary barrel. Introduced 1997. Imported from Germany by SIGARMS, Inc.

Price: Blue SA/DA or DAO **$505.00**
Price: In stainless steel. **$545.00**
Price: With stainless steel slide, blue frame **$525.00**
Price: Stainless steel, Siglite night sights, Hogue grips **$585.00**

SIG SAUER P239 PISTOL

Caliber: 9mm Para., 8-shot, 357 SIG 40 S&W, 7-shot magazine. **Barrel:** 3.6". **Weight:** 25.2 oz. **Length:** 6.6" overall. **Grips:** Checkered black composite. **Sights:** Blade front, rear adjustable for windage. Optional Siglite night sights. **Features:** SA/DA or DAO; blackened stainless steel slide, aluminum alloy frame. Introduced 1996. Made in U.S.A. by SIGARMS, Inc.

Price: SA/DA or DAO **$620.00**
Price: SA/DA or DAO with Siglite night sights. **$720.00**
Price: Two-tone finish **$665.00**
Price: Two-tone finish, Siglite sights **$765.00**

SMITH & WESSON MODEL 22A SPORT PISTOL

Caliber: 22 LR, 10-shot magazine. **Barrel:** 4", 5-1/2", 7". **Weight:** 29 oz. **Length:** 8" overall. **Grips:** Two-piece polymer. **Sights:** Patridge front, fully adjustable rear. **Features:** Comes with a sight bridge with Weaver-style integral optics mount; alloy frame; .312" serrated trigger; stainless steel slide and barrel with matte blue finish. Introduced 1997. Made in U.S.A. by Smith & Wesson.

Price: 4" **$264.00**
Price: 5-1/2" **$292.00**
Price: 7" **$331.00**

SMITH & WESSON MODEL 457 TDA AUTO PISTOL

Caliber: 45 ACP, 7-shot magazine. **Barrel:** 3-3/4". **Weight:** 29 oz. **Length:** 7-1/4" overall. **Grips:** One-piece Xenoy, wrap-around with straight backstrap. **Sights:** Post front, fixed rear, three-dot system. **Features:** Aluminum alloy frame, matte blue carbon steel slide; bobbed hammer; smooth trigger. Introduced 1996. Made in U.S.A. by Smith & Wesson.

Price: **$591.00**

HANDGUNS

HANDGUNS — AUTOLOADERS, SERVICE & SPORT

Smith & Wesson 908

Smith & Wesson 4013 TSW

Smith & Wesson 410 DA

Smith & Wesson 910 DA

Smith & Wesson 3913 LadySmith

Smith & Wesson 4006

SMITH & WESSON MODEL 908 AUTO PISTOL

Caliber: 9mm Para., 8-shot magazine. **Barrel:** 3-1/2". **Weight:** 26 oz. **Length:** 6-13/16". **Grips:** One-piece Xenoy, wrap-around with straight backstrap. **Sights:** Post front, fixed rear, three-dot system. **Features:** Aluminum alloy frame, matte blue carbon steel slide; bobbed hammer; smooth trigger. Introduced 1996. Made in U.S.A. by Smith & Wesson.
Price: $535.00

SMITH & WESSON MODEL 4013, 4053 TSW AUTOS

Caliber: 40 S&W, 9-shot magazine. **Barrel:** 3-1/2". **Weight:** 26.4 oz. **Length:** 6-7/8" overall. **Grips:** Xenoy one-piece wrap-around. **Sights:** Novak three-dot system. **Features:** Traditional double-action system; stainless slide, alloy frame; fixed barrel bushing; ambidextrous decocker; reversible magazine catch, equipment rail. Introduced 1997. Made in U.S.A. by Smith & Wesson.
Price: Model 4013 TSW $886.00
Price: Model 4053 TSW, double-action-only. $886.00

Smith & Wesson Model 22S Sport Pistols

Similar to the Model 22A Sport except with stainless steel frame. Available only with 5-1/2" or 7" barrel. Introduced 1997. Made in U.S.A. by Smith & Wesson.
Price: 5-1/2" standard barrel. $358.00
Price: 5-1/2" bull barrel, wood target stocks with thumbrest $434.00
Price: 7" standard barrel. $395.00
Price: 5-1/2" bull barrel, two-piece target stocks with thumbrest . $353.00

SMITH & WESSON MODEL 410 DA AUTO PISTOL

Caliber: 40 S&W, 10-shot magazine. **Barrel:** 4". **Weight:** 28.5 oz. **Length:** 7.5 oz. **Grips:** One-piece Xenoy, wrap-around with straight backstrap. **Sights:** Post front, fixed rear; three-dot system. **Features:** Aluminum alloy frame; blued carbon steel slide; traditional double action with left-side slide-mounted decocking lever. Introduced 1996. Made in U.S.A. by Smith & Wesson.
Price: Model 410 . . . . $591.00
Price: Model 410, HiViz front sight $612.00

SMITH & WESSON MODEL 910 DA AUTO PISTOL

Caliber: 9mm Para., 10-shot magazine. **Barrel:** 4". **Weight:** 28 oz. **Length:** 7-3/8" overall. **Grips:** One-piece Xenoy, wrap-around with straight backstrap. **Sights:** Post front with white dot, fixed two-dot rear. **Features:** Alloy frame, blue carbon steel slide. Slide-mounted decocking lever. Introduced 1995.
Price: Model 910. . . . . $535.00
Price: Model 410, HiViz front sight $535.00

SMITH & WESSON MODEL 3913 TRADITIONAL DOUBLE ACTION

Caliber: 9mm Para., 8-shot magazine. **Barrel:** 3-1/2". **Weight:** 26 oz. **Length:** 6-13/16" overall. **Grips:** One-piece Delrin wrap-around, textured surface. **Sights:** Post front with white dot, Novak LoMount Carry with two dots. **Features:** Aluminum alloy frame, stainless slide (M3913) or blue steel slide (M3914). Bobbed hammer with no half-cock notch; smooth .304" trigger with rounded edges. Straight backstrap. Equipment rail. Extra magazine included. Introduced 1989.
Price: $760.00

Smith & Wesson Model 3913-LS LadySmith Auto

Similar to the standard Model 3913 except has frame that is upswept at the front, rounded trigger guard. Comes in frosted stainless steel with matching gray grips. Grips are ergonomically correct for a woman's hand. Novak LoMount Carry rear sight adjustable for windage, smooth edges for snag resistance. Extra magazine included. Introduced 1990.
Price: $782.00

Smith & Wesson Model 3953 DAO Pistol

Same as the Model 3913 except double-action-only. Model 3953 has stainless slide with alloy frame. Overall length 7"; weighs 25.5 oz. Extra magazine included. Equipment rail. Introduced 1990.
Price: $760.00

Smith & Wesson Model 3913TSW/3953TSW Auto Pistols

Similar to the Model 3913 and 3953 except TSW guns have tighter tolerances, ambidextrous manual safety/decocking lever, flush-fit magazine, delayed-unlock firing system; magazine disconnector. Compact alloy frame, stainless steel slide. Straight backstrap. Introduced 1998. Made in U.S.A. by Smith & Wesson.
Price: Single action/double action $760.00
Price: Double action only $760.00

SMITH & WESSON MODEL 4006 TDA AUTO

Caliber: 40 S&W, 10-shot magazine. **Barrel:** 4". **Weight:** 38.5 oz. **Length:** 7-7/8" overall. **Grips:** Xenoy wrap-around with checkered panels. **Sights:** Replaceable post front with white dot, Novak LoMount Carry fixed rear with two white dots, or micro. click adjustable rear with two white dots. **Features:** Stainless steel construction with non-reflective finish. Straight backstrap, quipment rail. Extra magazine included. Introduced 1990.
Price: With adjustable sights. $944.00
Price: With fixed sight $907.00
Price: With fixed night sights. $1,040.00
Price: With Saf-T-Trigger, fixed sights $927.00

HANDGUNS

HANDGUNS — AUTOLOADERS, SERVICE & SPORT

**Smith & Wesson
4566 TSW**

**Smith & Wesson
Sigma SW40V**

Smith & Wesson 99

SMITH & WESSON MODEL 4006 TSW

Caliber: 40, 10-shot. **Barrel:** 4". **Grips:** Straight back strap grip. **Sights:** Fixed Novak LoMount Carry. **Features:** Traditional double action, ambidextrous safety, Saf-T-Trigger, equipment rail, satin stainless.
Price: **$927.00**

Smith & Wesson Model 4043, 4046 DA Pistols

Similar to the Model 4006 except is double-action-only. Has a semi-bobbed hammer, smooth trigger, 4" barrel; Novak LoMount Carry rear sight, post front with white dot. Overall length is 7-1/2", weighs 28 oz. Model 4043 has alloy frame, equipment rail. Extra magazine included. Introduced 1991.
Price: Model 4043 (alloy frame) **$886.00**
Price: Model 4046 (stainless frame)..................... **$907.00**
Price: Model 4046 with fixed night sights **$1,040.00**

SMITH & WESSON MODEL 4500 SERIES AUTOS

Caliber: 45 ACP, 8-shot magazine. **Barrel:** 5" (M4506). **Weight:** 41 oz. (4506). **Length:** 8-1/2" overall. **Grips:** Xenoy one-piece wrap-around, arched or straight backstrap. **Sights:** Post front with white dot, adjustable or fixed Novak LoMount Carry on M4506. **Features:** M4506 has serrated hammer spur, equipment rail. All have two magazines. Contact Smith & Wesson for complete data. Introduced 1989.
Price: Model 4566 (stainless, 4-1/4", traditional DA, ambidextrous
safety, fixed sight) **$942.00**
Price: Model 4586 (stainless, 4-1/4", DA only) **$942.00**
Price: Model 4566 (stainless, 4-1/4" with Saf-T-Trigger,
fixed sight) **$961.00**

SMITH & WESSON MODEL 4513TSW/4553TSW PISTOLS

Caliber: 45 ACP, 7-shot magazine. **Barrel:** 3-3/4". **Weight:** 28 oz. (M4513TSW). **Length:** 6-7/8 overall. **Grips:** Checkered Xenoy; straight backstrap. **Sights:** White dot front, Novak LoMount Carry 2-Dot rear. **Features:** Model 4513TSW is traditional double action, Model 4553TSW is double action only. TSW series has tighter tolerances, ambidextrous manual safety/decocking lever, flush-fit magazine, delayed-unlock firing system; magazine disconnector. Compact alloy frame, stainless steel slide, equipment rail. Introduced 1998. Made in U.S.A. by Smith & Wesson.
Price: Model 4513TSW................................. **$924.00**
Price: Model 4553TSW................................. **$924.00**

SMITH & WESSON MODEL 4566 TSW

Caliber: 45 ACP. **Barrel:** 4-1/4", 8-shot . **Grips:** Straight back strap grip. **Sights:** Fixed Novak LoMount Carry. **Features:** Ambidextrous safety, equipment rail, Saf-T-Trigger, satin stainless finish. Traditional double action.
Price: **$961.00**

SMITH & WESSON MODEL 5900 SERIES AUTO PISTOLS

Caliber: 9mm Para., 10-shot magazine. **Barrel:** 4". **Weight:** 28-1/2 to 37-1/2 oz. (fixed sight); 38 oz. (adjustable sight). **Length:** 7-1/2" overall. **Grips:** Xenoy wrap-around with curved backstrap. **Sights:** Post front with white dot, fixed or fully adjustable with two white dots. **Features:** All stainless, stainless and alloy or carbon steel and alloy construction. Smooth .304" trigger, .260" serrated hammer. Equipment rail. Introduced 1989.
Price: Model 5906 (stainless, traditional DA, adjustable sight,
ambidextrous safety)................................... **$904.00**
Price: As above, fixed sight.............................. **$841.00**

Price: With fixed night sights............................. **$995.00**
Price: With Saf-T-Trigger................................ **$882.00**
Price: Model 5946 DAO (as above, stainless frame and slide)... **$863.00**

SMITH & WESSON ENHANCED SIGMA SERIES DAO PISTOLS

Caliber: 9mm Para., 40 S&W, 10-shot magazine. **Barrel:** 4". **Weight:** 26 oz. **Length:** 7.4" overall. **Grips:** Integral. **Sights:** White dot front, fixed rear; three-dot system. Tritium night sights available. **Features:** Ergonomic polymer frame; low barrel centerline; internal striker firing system; corrosion-resistant slide; Teflon-filled, electroless-nickel coated magazine, equipment rail. Introduced 1994. Made in U.S.A. by Smith & Wesson.
Price: SW9E, 9mm, 4" barrel, black finish, fixed sights **$447.00**
Price: SW9V, 9mm, 4" barrel, satin stainless, fixed night sights.. **$447.00**
Price: SW9VE, 4" barrel, satin stainless, Saf-T-Trigger,
fixed sights **$466.00**
Price: SW40E, 40 S&W, 4" barrel, black finish, fixed sights **$657.00**
Price: SW40V, 40 S&W, 4" barrel, black polymer, fixed sights ... **$447.00**
Price: SW40VE, 4" barrel, satin stainless, Saf-T-Trigger,
fixed sights **$466.00**

SMITH & WESSON MODEL CS9 CHIEF'S SPECIAL AUTO

Caliber: 9mm Para., 7-shot magazine. **Barrel:** 3". **Weight:** 20.8 oz. **Length:** 6-1/4" overall. **Grips:** Hogue wrap-around rubber. **Sights:** White dot front, fixed two-dot rear. **Features:** Traditional double-action trigger mechanism. Alloy frame, stainless or blued slide. Ambidextrous safety. Introduced 1999. Made in U.S.A. by Smith & Wesson.
Price: Blue or stainless................................. **$680.00**

Smith & Wesson Model CS40 Chief's Special Auto

Similar to CS9, chambered for 40 S&W (7-shot magazine), 3-1/4" barrel, weighs 24.2 oz., measures 6-1/2" overall. Introduced 1999. Made in U.S.A. by Smith & Wesson.
Price: Blue or stainless................................. **$717.00**

Smith & Wesson Model CS45 Chief's Special Auto

Similar to CS40, chambered for 45 ACP, 6-shot magazine, weighs 23.9 oz. Introduced 1999. Made in U.S.A. by Smith & Wesson.
Price: Blue or stainless................................. **$717.00**

SMITH & WESSON MODEL 99

Caliber: 9mm Para. 4" barrel; 40 S&W 4-1/8" barrel; 10-shot, adj. sights. **Features:** Traditional double action satin stainless, black polymer frame, equipment rail, Saf-T-Trigger.
Price: 4" barrel **$648.00**
Price: 4-1/8" barrel **$648.00**

SPRINGFIELD, INC. FULL-SIZE 1911A1 AUTO PISTOL

Caliber: 9mm Para., 9-shot; 38 Super, 9-shot; 40 S&W, 9-shot; 45 ACP, 7-shot. **Barrel:** 5". **Weight:** 35.6 oz. **Length:** 8-5/8" overall. **Grips:** Cocobolo. **Sights:** Fixed three-dot system. **Features:** Beveled magazine well; lowered and flared ejection port. All forged parts, including frame, barrel, slide. All new production. Introduced 1990. From Springfield, Inc.
Price: Mil-Spec 45 ACP, Parkerized **$559.00**
Price: Standard, 45 ACP, blued, Novak sights **$824.00**
Price: Standard, 45 ACP, stainless, Novak sights **$828.00**
Price: Lightweight 45 ACP (28.6 oz., matte finish, night sights).. **$877.00**
Price: 40 S&W, stainless **$860.00**
Price: 9mm, stainless **$837.00**

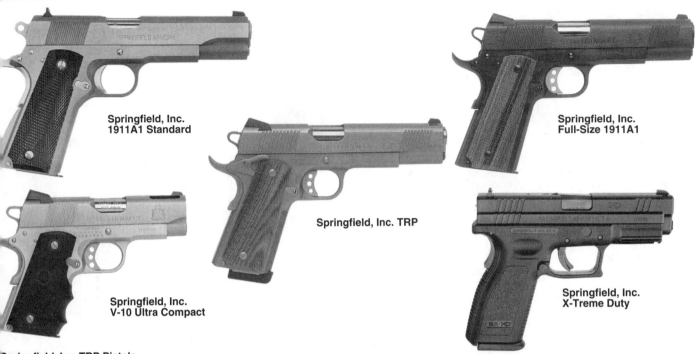

Springfield, Inc.
1911A1 Standard

Springfield, Inc. TRP

Springfield, Inc.
Full-Size 1911A1

Springfield, Inc.
V-10 Ultra Compact

Springfield, Inc.
X-Treme Duty

Springfield, Inc. TRP Pistols

Similar to 1911A1 except 45 ACP only, checkered front strap and main-spring housing, Novak Night Sight combat rear sight and matching dove-tailed front sight, tuned, polished extractor, oversize barrel link; lightweight speed trigger and combat action job, match barrel and bushing, extended ambidextrous thumb safety and fitted beavertail grip safety. Carry bevel on entire pistol; checkered cocobolo wood grips, comes with two Wilson 7-shot magazines. Frame is engraved "Tactical," both sides of frame with "TRP." Introduced 1998. From Springfield, Inc.

Price: Standard with Armory Kote finish **$1,395.00**
Price: Standard, stainless steel **$1,370.00**
Price: Standard with Operator Light Rail Armory Kote **$1,473.00**

Springfield, Inc. 1911A1 High Capacity Pistol

Similar to Standard 1911A1, available in 45 ACP with 10-shot magazine. Commander-style hammer, walnut grips, beveled magazine well, plastic carrying case. Can accept higher-capacity Para Ordnance magazines. Introduced 1993. From Springfield, Inc.

Price: Mil-Spec 45 ACP **$756.00**
Price: 45 ACP Ultra Compact (3-1/2" bbl.) **$909.00**

Springfield, Inc. 1911A1 V-Series Ported Pistols

Similar to standard 1911A1, scalloped slides with 10, 12 or 16 matching barrel ports to redirect powder gasses and reduce recoil and muzzle flip. Adjustable rear sight, ambi thumb safety, Videki speed trigger, and beveled magazine well. Checkered walnut grips standard. Available in 45 ACP, stainless or bi-tone. Introduced 1992.

Price: V-16 Long Slide, stainless **$1,121.00**
Price: Target V-12, stainless **$878.00**
Price: V-10 (Ultra-Compact, bi-tone) **$853.00**
Price: V-10 stainless **$863.00**

Springfield, Inc. 1911A1 Champion Pistol

Similar to standard 1911A1, slide is 4". Novak Night Sights. Delta hammer and cocobolo grips. Available in 45 ACP only; Parkerized or stainless. Introduced 1989.

Price: Stainless **$849.00**

Springfield Inc. Ultra Compact Pistol

Similar to 1911A1 Compact, shorter slide, 3.5" barrel, beavertail grip safety, beveled magazine well, Novak Low Mount or Novak Night Sights, Videki speed trigger, flared ejection port, stainless steel frame, blued slide, match grade barrel, rubber grips. Introduced 1996. From Springfield, Inc.

Price: Parkerized 45 ACP, Night Sights **$589.00**
Price: Stainless 45 ACP, Night Sights **$849.00**
Price: Lightweight, 9mm, stainless **$837.00**

Springfield Inc. Compact Lightweight

Mates a Springfield Inc. Champion length slide with the shorter Ultra-Compact forged alloy frame for concealability. In 45 ACP.

Price: **$733.00**

Springfield Inc. Long Slide 1911 A1 Pistol

Similar to Full Size model, 6" barrel and slide for increased sight radius and higher velocity, fully adjustable sights, muzzle-forward weight distribution for reduced recoil and quicker shot-to-shot recovery. From Springfield Inc.

Price: Target, 45 ACP, stainless with Night Sights **$1,049.00**
Price: Trophy Match, stainless with adj. sights **$1,452.00**
Price: V-16 stainless steel **$1,121.00**

SPRINGFIELD, INC. MICRO-COMPACT 1911A1 PISTOL

Caliber: 45 ACP, 40 S&W 6+1 capacity. **Barrel:** 3" 1:16 LH. **Weight:** 24 oz. **Length:** 5.7". **Sights:** Novak LoMount tritium. Dovetail front. **Features:** Forged frame and slide, ambi thumb safety, extreme carry bevel treatment, lockable plastic case, 2 magazines.

Price: . . . . **$993.00 to $1,021.00**

SPRINGFIELD, INC. X-TREME DUTY

Caliber: 9mm, 40 S&W, 357 Sig. **Barrel:** 4.08". **Weight:** 22.88 oz. **Length:** 7.2". **Sights:** Dovetail front and rear. **Features:** Lightweight, ultra high-impact polymer frame. Trigger, firing pin and grip safety. Two 10-rod steel easy glide magazines. Imported from Croatia.

Price: . . . . **$489.00 to $1,099.00**

STEYR M & S SERIES AUTO PISTOLS

Caliber: 9mm Para., 40 S&W, 357 SIG; 10-shot magazine. **Barrel:** 4" (3.58" for Model S). **Weight:** 28 oz. (22.5 oz. for Model S). **Length:** 7.05" overall (6.53" for Model S). **Grips:** Ultra-rigid polymer. **Sights:** Drift-adjustable, white-outline rear; white-triangle blade front. **Features:** Polymer frame; trigger-drop firing pin, manual and key-lock safeties; loaded chamber indicator; 5.5-lb. trigger pull; 111-degree grip angle enhances natural pointing. Introduced 2000. Imported from Austria by GSI Inc.

Price: Model M (full-sized frame with 4" barrel) **$609.95**
Price: Model S (compact frame with 3.58" barrel) **$609.95**
Price: Extra 10-shot magazines (Model M or S) **$39.00**

Taurus PT 22

Taurus PT-911

Taurus PT-938

Taurus PT-940

TAURUS MODEL PT 22/PT 25 AUTO PISTOLS

Caliber: 22 LR, 8-shot (PT 22); 25 ACP, 9-shot (PT 25). **Barrel:** 2.75". **Weight:** 12.3 oz. **Length:** 5.25" overall. **Grips:** Smooth rosewood or mother-of-pearl. **Sights:** Fixed. **Features:** Double action. Tip-up barrel for loading, cleaning. Blue, nickel, duotone or blue with gold accents. Introduced 1992. Made in U.S.A. by Taurus International.

Price: 22 LR, 25 ACP, blue, nickel or with duo-tone finish
with rosewood grips **$219.00**
Price: 22 LR, 25 ACP, blue with gold trim, rosewood grips...... **$234.00**
Price: 22 LR, 25 ACP, blue, nickel or duotone finish with checkered
wood grips... **$219.00**
Price: 22 LR, 25 ACP, blue with gold trim, mother of pearl grips . **$250.00**

TAURUS MODEL PT24/7

Caliber: 9mm, 10+1 shot; .40 Cal., 10+1 shot. **Barrel:** 4". **Weight:** 27.2 oz. **Length:** 7-18". **Grips:** RIBBER rubber-finned overlay on polymer. **Sights:** Adjustable. **Features:** Accessory rail, four safeties, blue or stainless finish, consistent trigger pull weight and travel. Introduced 2003. Imported from Brazil by Taurus Int'l. Manufacturing.

Price: 9mm **$578.00**
Price: .40 Cal. **$594.00**

TAURUS MODEL PT92 AUTO PISTOL

Caliber: 9mm Para., 10-shot mag. **Barrel:** 5". **Weight:** 34 oz. **Length:** 8.5" overall. **Grips:** Checkered rubber, rosewood, mother-of-pearl. **Sights:** Fixed notch rear. Three-dot sight system. Also offered with micrometer-click adjustable night sights. **Features:** Double action, ambidextrous 3-way hammer drop safety, allows cocked & locked carry. Blue, stainless steel, blue with gold highlights, stainless steel with gold highlights, forged aluminum frame, integral key-lock. .22 LR conversion kit available. Imported from Brazil by Taurus International Manufacturing.

Price: Blue .... **$578.00 to $672.00**

Taurus Model PT99 Auto Pistol

Similar to PT92, fully adjustable rear sight.
Price: Blue .... **$575.00 to $670.00**
Price: 22 Conversion kit for PT 92 and PT99 (includes barrel and slide)
.... **$266.00**

TAURUS MODEL PT-100/101 AUTO PISTOL

Caliber: 40 S&W, 10-shot mag. **Barrel:** 5". **Weight:** 34 oz. **Length:** 8-1/2". **Grips:** Checkered rubber, rosewood, mother-of-pearl. **Sights:** 3-dot fixed or adjustable; night sights available. **Features:** Single/double action with three-position safety/decocker. Re-introduced in 2001. Imported by Taurus International.

Price: PT100.............................. **$578.00 to $672.00**
Price: PT101.............................. **$594.00 to $617.00**

TAURUS MODEL PT-111 MILLENNIUM PRO AUTO PISTOL

Caliber: 9mm Para., 10-shot mag. **Barrel:** 3.25". **Weight:** 18.7 oz. **Length:** 6-1/8" overall. **Grips:** Polymer. **Sights:** 3-dot fixed; night sights available. Low profile, three-dot combat. **Features:** Double action only, polymer frame, matte stainless or blue steel slide, manual safety, integral key-lock. Deluxe models with wood grip inserts. Now issued in a third generation series with many cosmetic and internal improvements.

Price: .... **$445.00 to $539.00**

Taurus Model PT-111 Millennium Titanium Pistol

Similar to PT-111, titanium slide, night sights.
Price: **$586.00**

TAURUS PT-132 MILLENIUM PRO AUTO PISTOL

Caliber: 32 ACP, 10-shot mag. **Barrel:** 3.25". **Weight:** 18.7 oz. **Grips:** Polymer. **Sights:** 3-dot fixed; night sights available. **Features:** Double action only, polymer frame, matte stainless or blue steel slide, manual safety, integral key-lock action. Introduced 2001.

Price: .... **$445.00 to $461.00**

TAURUS PT-138 MILLENIUM PRO SERIES

Caliber: 380 ACP, 10-shot mag. **Barrel:** 3.25". **Weight:** 18.7 oz. **Grips:** Polymer. **Sights:** Fixed 3-dot fixed. **Features:** Double action only, polymer frame, matte stainless or blue steel slide, manual safety, integral key-lock.

Price: .... **$445.00 to $461.00**

TAURUS PT-140 MILLENIUM PRO AUTO PISTOL

Caliber: 40 S&W, 10-shot mag. **Barrel:** 3.25". **Weight:** 18.7 oz. **Grips:** Checkered polymer. **Sights:** 3-dot fixed; night sights available. **Features:** Double-action only; matte stainless or blue steel slide, black polymer frame, manual safety, integral key-lock action. From Taurus International.

Price: .... **$484.00 to $578.00**

TAURUS PT-145 MILLENIUM AUTO PISTOL

Caliber: 45 ACP, 10-shot mag. **Barrel:** 3.27". **Weight:** 23 oz. **Stock:** Checkered polymer. **Sights:** 3-dot fixed; night sights available. **Features:** Double-action only, matte stainless or blue steel slide, black polymer frame, manual safety, integral key-lock. From Taurus International.

Price: .... **$484.00 to $578.00**

TAURUS MODEL PT-911 AUTO PISTOL

Caliber: 9mm Para., 10-shot mag. **Barrel:** 4". **Weight:** 28.2 oz. **Length:** 7" overall. **Grips:** Checkered rubber, rosewood, mother-of-pearl. **Sights:** Fixed, three-dot blue or stainless; night sights optional. **Features:** Double action, semi-auto ambidextrous 3-way hammer drop safety, allows cocked and locked carry. Blue, stainless steel, blue with gold highlights, or stainless steel with gold highlights, forged aluminum frame, integral key-lock.

Price: .... **$523.00 to $617.00**

TAURUS MODEL PT-938 AUTO PISTOL

Caliber: 380 ACP, 10-shot mag. **Barrel:** 3.72". **Weight:** 27 oz. **Length:** 6.5" overall. **Grips:** Checkered rubber. **Sights:** Fixed, three-dot. **Features:** Double action, ambidextrous 3-way hammer drop allows cocked & locked carry. Forged aluminum frame. Integral key-lock. Imported by Taurus International.

Price: Blue **$516.00**
Price: Stainless....................................... **$531.00**

Taurus PT-945

Taurus PT-957

Walther PPK/S

Walther PPK

Walther P99

Walther P22

Wilkinson Sherry

TAURUS MODEL PT-940 AUTO PISTOL
Caliber: 40 S&W, 10-shot mag. **Barrel:** 3-5/8". **Weight:** 28.2 oz. **Length:** 7" overall. **Grips:** Checkered rubber, rosewood or mother-of-pearl. **Sights:** Fixed, three-dot blue or stainless; night sights optional. **Features:** Double action, semi-auto ambidextrous 3-way hammer drop safety, allows cocked & locked carry. Blue, stainless steel, blue with gold highlights, or stainless steel with gold hightlights, forged aluminum frame, integral key-lock.
Price: . . . . $523.00 to $617.00

TAURUS MODEL PT-945 SERIES
Caliber: 45 ACP, 8-shot mag. **Barrel:** 4.25". **Weight:** 28.2/29.5 oz. **Length:** 7.48" overall. **Grips:** Checkered rubber, rosewood or mother-of-pearl. **Sights:** Fixed, three-dot; night sights optional. **Features:** Double-action with ambidextrous 3-way hammer drop safety allows cocked & locked carry. Forged aluminum frame, PT-945C has poarted barrel/slide. Blue, stainless, blue with gold highlights, stainless with gold highlights, integral key-lock. Introduced 1995. Imported by Taurus International.
Price: . . . . $563.00 to $641.00

TAURUS MODEL PT-957 AUTO PISTOL
Caliber: 357 SIG, 10-shot mag. **Barrel:** 4". **Weight:** 28 oz. **Length:** 7" overall. **Grips:** Checkered rubber, rosewood or mother-of-pearl. **Sights:** Fixed, three-dot blue or stainless; night sights optional. **Features:** Double-action, blue, stainless steel, blue with gold accents or stainless with gold accents, ported barrel/slide, three-position safety with decocking lever and ambidextrous safety. Forged aluminum frame, integral key-lock. Introduced 1999. Imported by Taurus International.
Price: . . . . $525.00 to $620.00
Price: Non-ported . . . . $525.00 to $535.00

TAURUS MODEL 922 SPORT PISTOL
Caliber: .22 LR, 10-shot magazine. **Barrel:** 6". **Weight:** 24.8 oz. **Length:** 9-1/8". **Grips:** Polymer. **Sights:** Adjustable. **Features:** Matte blue steel finish, machined target crown, polymer frame, single and double action, easy disassembly for cleaning.
Price: . . . . (blue) $310.00
Price: . . . . (stainless) $328.00

WALTHER PPK/S AMERICAN AUTO PISTOL
Caliber: 380 ACP, 7-shot magazine. **Barrel:** 3.27". **Weight:** 23-1/2 oz. **Length:** 6.1" overall. **Stocks:** Checkered plastic. **Sights:** Fixed, white markings. **Features:** Double action; manual safety blocks firing pin and drops hammer; chamber loaded indicator on 32 and 380; extra finger rest magazine provided. Made entirely in the United States. Introduced 1980.
Price: 380 ACP only, blue $540.00
Price: As above, 32 ACP or 380 ACP, stainless $540.00

Walther PPK American Auto Pistol
Similar to Walther PPK/S except weighs 21 oz., has 6-shot capacity. Made in the U.S. Introduced 1986.
Price: Stainless, 32 ACP or 380 ACP $540.00
Price: Blue, 380 ACP only $540.00

WALTHER P99 AUTO PISTOL
Caliber: 9mm Para., 9x21, 40 S&W,10-shot magazine. **Barrel:** 4". **Weight:** 25 oz. **Length:** 7" overall. **Grips:** Textured polymer. **Sights:** Blade front (comes with three interchangeable blades for elevation adjustment), micrometer rear adjustable for windage. **Features:** Double-action mechanism with trigger safety, decock safety, internal striker safety; chamber loaded indicator; ambidextrous magazine release levers; polymer frame with interchangeable backstrap inserts. Comes with two magazines. Introduced 1997. Imported from Germany by Carl Walther USA.
Price: $799.00

Walther P990 Auto Pistol
Similar to the P99 except is double action only. Available in blue or silver tenifer finish. Introduced 1999. Imported from Germany by Carl Walther USA.
Price: $749.00

WALTHER P22 PISTOL
Caliber: 22 LR. **Barrel:** 3.4", 5". **Weight:** 19.6 oz. (3.4"), 20.3 oz. (5"). **Length:** 6.26", 7.83". **Grips:** NA. **Sights:** Interchangeable white dot, front, 2-dot adjustable, rear. **Features:** A rimfire version of the Walther P99 pistol, available in nickel slide with black frame, or green frame with black slide versions. Made in Germany and distributed in the U.S. by Smith & Wesson.
Price: . . . . NA

WILKINSON SHERRY AUTO PISTOL
Caliber: 22 LR, 8-shot magazine. **Barrel:** 2-1/8". **Weight:** 9-1/4 oz. **Length:** 4-3/8" overall. **Grips:** Checkered black plastic. **Sights:** Fixed, groove. **Features:** Cross-bolt safety locks the sear into the hammer. Available in all blue finish or blue slide and trigger with gold frame. Introduced 1985.
Price: $280.00

WILKINSON LINDA AUTO PISTOL
Caliber: 9mm Para. **Barrel:** 8-5/16". **Weight:** 4 lbs., 13 oz. **Length:** 12-1/4" overall. **Grips:** Checkered black plastic pistol grip, walnut forend. **Sights:** Protected blade front, aperture rear. **Features:** Fires from closed bolt. Semi-auto only. Straight blowback action. Cross-bolt safety. Removable barrel. From Wilkinson Arms.
Price: $675.00

Includes models suitable for several forms of competition and other sporting purposes.

Baer 1911 Ultimate Master

Baer 1911 Bullseye Wadcutter

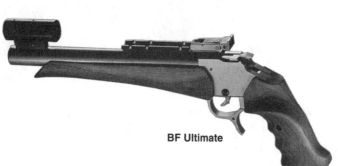

BF Ultimate

Browning Buck Mark Target 5.5

BAER 1911 ULTIMATE MASTER COMBAT PISTOL

Caliber: 9x23, 38 Super, 400 Cor-Bon 45 ACP (others available), 10-shot magazine. **Barrel:** 5", 6"; Baer NM. **Weight:** 37 oz. **Length:** 8.5" overall. **Grips:** Checkered rosewood. **Sights:** Baer dovetail front, low-mount Bo-Mar rear with hidden leaf. **Features:** Full-house competition gun. Baer forged NM blued steel frame and double serrated slide; Baer triple port, tapered cone compensator; fitted slide to frame; lowered, flared ejection port; Baer reverse recoil plug; full-length guide rod; recoil buff; beveled magazine well; Baer Commander hammer, sear; Baer extended ambidextrous safety, extended ejector, checkered slide stop, beavertail grip safety with pad, extended magazine release button; Baer speed trigger. Made in U.S.A. by Les Baer Custom, Inc.
Price: Compensated, open sights. **$2,476.00**
Price: 6" Model 400 Cor-Bon **$2,541.00**

BAER 1911 NATIONAL MATCH HARDBALL PISTOL

Caliber: 45 ACP, 7-shot magazine. **Barrel:** 5". **Weight:** 37 oz. **Length:** 8.5" overall. **Grips:** Checkered walnut. **Sights:** Baer dovetail front with undercut post, low-mount Bo-Mar rear with hidden leaf. **Features:** Baer NM forged steel frame, double serrated slide and barrel with stainless bushing; slide fitted to frame; Baer match trigger with 4-lb. pull; polished feed ramp, throated barrel; checkered front strap, arched mainspring housing; Baer beveled magazine well; lowered, flared ejection port; tuned extractor; Baer extended ejector, checkered slide stop; recoil buff. Made in U.S.A. by Les Baer Custom, Inc.
Price: **$1,335.00**

Baer 1911 Bullseye Wadcutter Pistol

Similar to National Match Hardball except designed for wadcutter loads only. Polished feed ramp and barrel throat; Bo-Mar rib on slide; full-length recoil rod; Baer speed trigger with 3-1/2-lb. pull; Baer deluxe hammer and sear; Baer beavertail grip safety with pad; flat mainspring housing checkered 20 lpi. Blue finish; checkered walnut grips. Made in U.S.A. by Les Baer Custom, Inc.
Price: From **$1,495.00**
Price: With 6" barrel, from **$1,690.00**

BF ULTIMATE SILHOUETTE HB SINGLE SHOT PISTOL

Caliber: 7mm U.S., 22 LR Match and 100 other chamberings. **Barrel:** 10.75" Heavy Match Grade with 11-degree target crown. **Weight:** 3 lbs.,

15 oz. **Length:** 16" overall. **Grips:** Thumbrest target style. **Sights:** Bo-Mar/Bond ScopeRib I Combo with hooded post front adjustable for height and width, rear notch available in .032", .062", .080" and .100" widths; 1/2-MOA clicks. **Features:** Designed to meet maximum rules for IHMSA Production Gun. Falling block action gives rigid barrel-receiver mating. Hand fitted and headspaced. Etched receiver; gold-colored trigger. Introduced 1988. Made in U.S.A. by E. Arthur Brown Co. Inc.
Price: **$669.00**

BF Classic Hunting Pistol

Similar to BF Ultimate Silhouette HB Single Shot Pistol, except no sights; drilled and tapped for scope mount. Barrels from 8" to 15". Variety of options offered. Made in U.S.A. by E. Arthur Brown Co. Inc.
Price: **$599.00**

BROWNING BUCK MARK SILHOUETTE

Caliber: 22 LR, 10-shot magazine. **Barrel:** 9-7/8". **Weight:** 53 oz. **Length:** 14" overall. **Grips:** Smooth walnut stocks and forend, or finger-groove walnut. **Sights:** Post-type hooded front adjustable for blade width and height; Pro Target rear fully adjustable for windage and elevation. **Features:** Heavy barrel with .900" diameter; 12-1/2" sight radius. Special sighting plane forms scope base. Introduced 1987. Made in U.S.A. From Browning.
Price: **$448.00**

Browning Buck Mark Target 5.5

Same as Buck Mark Silhouette, 5-1/2" barrel with .900" diameter. Hooded sights mounted on scope base that accepts optical or reflex sight. Rear sight is Browning fully adjustable Pro Target, front sight is adjustable post that customizes to different widths, can be adjusted for height. Contoured walnut grips with thumbrest, or finger-groove walnut. Matte blue finish. Overall length is 9-5/8", weighs 35-1/2 oz. Has 10-shot magazine. Introduced 1990. From Browning.
Price: **$425.00**
Price: Target 5.5 Gold (as above with gold anodized frame and
top rib) **$477.00**
Price: Target 5.5 Nickel (as above with nickel frame
and top rib) **$477.00**

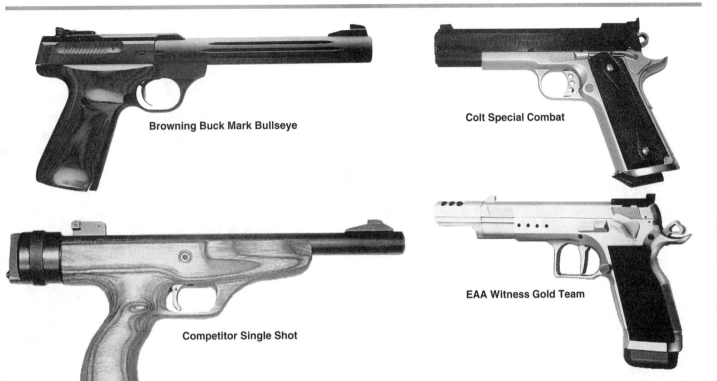

Browning Buck Mark Bullseye

Colt Special Combat

Competitor Single Shot

EAA Witness Gold Team

Browning Buck Mark Field 5.5

Same as Target 5.5, hoodless ramp-style front sight and low profile rear sight. Matte blue finish, contoured or finger-groove walnut stocks. Introduced 1991.
Price: **$425.00**

Browning Buck Mark Bullseye

Similar to Buck Mark Silhouette, 7-1/4" heavy barrel with three flutes per side; trigger adjusts from 2-1/2 to 5 lbs.; specially designed rosewood target or three-finger-groove stocks with competition-style heel rest, or with contoured rubber grip. Overall length 11-5/16", weighs 36 oz. Introduced 1996. Made in U.S.A. From Browning.
Price: With ambidextrous moulded composite stocks. **$389.00**
Price: With rosewood stocks, or wrap-around finger groove. **$500.00**

COLT GOLD CUP MODEL O PISTOL

Caliber: 45 ACP, 8-shot magazine. **Barrel:** 5", with new design bushing. **Weight:** 39 oz. **Length:** 8-1/2". **Grips:** Checkered rubber composite with silver-plated medallion. **Sights:** Patridge-style front, Bomar-style rear adjustable for windage and elevation, sight radius 6-3/4". **Features:** Arched or flat housing; wide, grooved trigger with adjustable stop; ribbed-top slide, hand fitted, with improved ejection port.
Price: Blue **$1,050.00**
Price: Stainless.................................... **$1,116.00**

COLT SPECIAL COMBAT GOVERNMENT

Caliber: 45 ACP. **Barrel:** 5" **Weight:** NA. **Length:** 8-1/2" **Grips:** Rosewood w/double diamond checkering pattern. **Sights:** Clark dovetail, front; Bomar adjustable, rear. **Features:** A competition ready pistol with enhancements such as skeletonized trigger, upswept grip safety, custom tuned action, polished feed ramp. Blue or satin nickel finish. Introduced 2003. Made in U.S.A. by Colt's Mfg. Co.
Price: **$1,640.00**

COMPETITOR SINGLE SHOT PISTOL

Caliber: 22 LR through 50 Action Express, including belted magnums. **Barrel:** 14" standard; 10.5" silhouette; 16" optional. **Weight:** About 59 oz. (14" bbl.). **Length:** 15.12" overall. **Grips:** Ambidextrous; synthetic (standard) or laminated or natural wood. **Sights:** Ramp front, adjustable rear. **Features:** Rotary canon-type action cocks on opening; cammed ejector; interchangeable barrels, ejectors. Adjustable single stage trigger, sliding

thumb safety and trigger safety. Matte blue finish. Introduced 1988. From Competitor Corp., Inc.
Price: 14", standard calibers, synthetic grip **$414.95**
Price: Extra barrels, from **$159.95**

CZ 75 CHAMPION COMPETITION PISTOL

Caliber: 9mm Para., 9x21, 40 S&W, 10-shot mag. **Barrel:** 4.49". **Weight:** 35 oz. **Length:** 9.44" overall. **Grips:** Black rubber. **Sights:** Blade front, fully adjustable rear. **Features:** Single-action trigger mechanism; three-port compensator (40 S&W, 9mm have two port) full-length guide rod; extended magazine release; ambidextrous safety; flared magazine well; fully adjustable match trigger. Introduced 1999. Imported from the Czech Republic by CZ USA.
Price: 9mm Para., 9x21, 40 S&W, dual-tone finish.......... **$1,551.00**

CZ 75 ST IPSC AUTO PISTOL

Caliber: 40 S&W, 10-shot magazine. **Barrel:** 5.12". **Weight:** 2.9 lbs. **Length:** 8.86" overall. **Grips:** Checkered walnut. **Sights:** Fully adjustable rear. **Features:** Single-action mechanism; extended slide release and ambidextrous safety; full-length slide rail; double slide serrations. Introduced 1999. Imported from the Czech Republic by CZ-USA.
Price: Dual-tone finish **$1,038.00**

EAA/BAIKAL IZH35 AUTO PISTOL

Caliber: 22 LR, 5-shot mag. **Barrel:** 6". **Grips:** Walnut; fully adjustable right-hand target-style. **Sights:** Fully adjustable rear, blade front; detachable scope mount. **Features:** Hammer-forged target barrel; machined steel receiver; adjustable trigger; manual slide hold back, grip and manual trigger-bar disconnect safeties; cocking indicator. Introduced 2000. Imported from Russia by European American Armory.
Price: Blued finish.................................. **$539.00**

EAA WITNESS GOLD TEAM AUTO

Caliber: 9mm Para., 9x21, 38 Super, 40 S&W, 45 ACP. **Barrel:** 5.1". **Weight:** 41.6 oz. **Length:** 9.6" overall. **Grips:** Checkered walnut, competition style. **Sights:** Square post front, fully adjustable rear. **Features:** Triple-chamber cone compensator; competition SA trigger; extended safety and magazine release; competition hammer; beveled magazine well; beavertail grip. Hand-fitted major components. Hard chrome finish. Match-grade barrel. From E.A.A. Custom Shop. Introduced 1992. From European American Armory.
Price: **$2,150.00**

Freedom Arms 83 22 Silhouette Class

Hammerli SP 20

High Standard Trophy

EAA Witness Silver Team Auto

Similar to Witness Gold Team, double-chamber compensator, oval magazine release, black rubber grips, double-dip blue finish. Super Sight and drilled and tapped for scope mount. Built for the intermediate competition shooter. Introduced 1992. From European American Armory Custom Shop.
Price: 9mm Para., 9x21, 38 Super, 40 S&W, 45 ACP. **$968.00**

ED BROWN CLASSIC CUSTOM PISTOL

Caliber: 45 ACP. **Barrel:** 5". **Weight:** 39 oz. **Grips:** Hogue exotic wood. **Sights:** Modified ramp or post, front; fully-adjustable Bo-Mar, rear. **Features:** Highly-polished slide, two-piece guide rod, oversize mag release, ambidextrous safety.
Price: **$2,895.00**

ED BROWN CLASS A LIMITED

Caliber: 45 ACP, 400 Cor-Bon, 10mm, 40 S&W, 357 SIG, 38 Super, 9x23, 9mm Luger, 7-shot magazine. **Barrel:** 4.25", 5". **Weight:** 34 to 39 oz. **Grips:** Hogue exotic wood. **Sights:** Customer preference, front; fixed Novak low-mount or fully-adjustable Bo-Mar, rear. **Features:** Checkered forestrap and mainspring housing, matte finished top sighting surface. Many options available.
Price: **$2,250.00**

ENTRÉPRISE TOURNAMENT SHOOTER MODEL I

Caliber: 45 ACP, 10-shot mag. **Barrel:** 6". **Weight:** 40 oz. **Length:** 8.5" overall. **Grips:** Black ultra-slim double diamond checkered synthetic. **Sights:** Dovetailed Patridge front, adjustable Competizione "melded" rear. **Features:** Oversized magazine release button; flared magazine well; fully machined parallel slide rails; front and rear slide serrations; serrated top of slide; stainless ramped bull barrel with fully supported chamber; full-length guide rod with plug; match extractor; stainless firing pin; match extractor; polished ramp; tuned match extractor; black oxide. Introduced 1998. Made in U.S.A. by Entréprise Arms.
Price: **$2,300.00**
Price: TSMIII (Satin chrome finish, two-piece guide rod) **$2,700.00**

EXCEL INDUSTRIES CP-45, XP-45 AUTO PISTOL

Caliber: 45 ACP, 6-shot & 10-shot mags. **Barrel:** 3-1/4". **Weight:** 31 oz. & 25 oz. **Length:** 6-3/8" overall. **Grips:** Checkered black nylon. **Sights:** Fully adjustable rear. **Features:** Stainless steel frame and slide; single action with external hammer and firing pin block, manual thumb safety; last-shot hold open. Includes gun lock and cleaning kit. Introduced 2001. Made in U.S.A. by Excel Industries Inc.
Price: CP-45 . . . . **$425.00**
Price: XP-45 . . . . **$465.00**

FEINWERKEBAU AW93 TARGET PISTOL

Caliber: 22. **Barrel:** 6". **Grips:** Fully adjustable orthopaedic. **Sights:** Fully adjustable micrometer. **Features:** Advanced Russian design with German craftmanship. Imported from Germany by Nygord Precision Products.
Price: **$1,495.00**

FREEDOM ARMS MODEL 83 22 FIELD GRADE SILHOUETTE CLASS

Caliber: 22 LR, 5-shot cylinder. **Barrel:** 10". **Weight:** 63 oz. **Length:** 15.5" overall. **Grips:** Black Micarta. **Sights:** Removable patridge front blade; Iron Sight Gun Works silhouette rear, click adjustable for windage and elevation (optional adj. front sight and hood). **Features:** Stainless steel, matte finish, manual sliding-bar safety system; dual firing pins, lightened hammer for fast lock time, pre-set trigger stop. Introduced 1991. Made in U.S.A. by Freedom Arms.

Price: Silhouette Class **$1,901.75**
Price: Extra fitted 22 WMR cylinder **$264.00**

FREEDOM ARMS MODEL 83 CENTERFIRE SILHOUETTE MODELS

Caliber: 357 Mag., 41 Mag., 44 Mag.; 5-shot cylinder. **Barrel:** 10", 9" (357 Mag. only). **Weight:** 63 oz. (41 Mag.). **Length:** 15.5", 14-1/2" (357 only). **Grips:** Pachmayr Presentation. **Sights:** Iron Sight Gun Works silhouette rear sight, replaceable adjustable front sight blade with hood. **Features:** Stainless steel, matte finish, manual sliding-bar safety system. Made in U.S.A. by Freedom Arms.
Price: Silhouette Models. **$1,634.85**

GAUCHER GP SILHOUETTE PISTOL

Caliber: 22 LR, single shot. **Barrel:** 10". **Weight:** 42.3 oz. **Length:** 15.5" overall. **Grips:** Stained hardwood. **Sights:** Hooded post on ramp front, open rear adjustable for windage and elevation. **Features:** Matte chrome barrel, blued bolt and sights. Other barrel lengths available on special order. Introduced 1991. Imported by Mandall Shooting Supplies.
Price: **$425.00**

HAMMERLI SP 20 TARGET PISTOL

Caliber: 22 LR, 32 S&W. **Barrel:** 4.6". **Weight:** 34.6-41.8 oz. **Length:** 11.8" overall. **Grips:** Anatomically shaped synthetic Hi-Grip available in five sizes. **Sights:** Integral front in three widths, adjustable rear with changeable notch widths. **Features:** Extremely low-level sight line; anatomically shaped trigger; adjustable JPS buffer system for different recoil characteristics. Receiver available in red, blue, gold, violet or black. Introduced 1998. Imported from Switzerland by SIGARMS, Inc and Hammerli Pistols USA.
Price: Hammerli 22 LR **$1,668.00**
Price: Hammerli 32 S&W **$1,743.00**

HAMMERLI X-ESSE SPORT PISTOL

An all-steel .22 LR target pistol with a Hi-Grip in a new anatomical shape and an adjustable hand rest. Made in Switzerland. Introduced 2003.
Price: **$710.00**

HARRIS GUNWORKS SIGNATURE JR. LONG RANGE PISTOL

Caliber: Any suitable caliber. **Barrel:** To customer specs. **Weight:** 5 lbs. **Stock:** Gunworks fiberglass. **Sights:** None furnished; comes with scope rings. **Features:** Right- or left-hand benchrest action of titanium or stainless steel; single shot or repeater. Comes with bipod. Introduced 1992. Made in U.S.A. by Harris Gunworks, Inc.
Price: **$2,700.00**

HANDGUNS — COMPETITION HANDGUNS

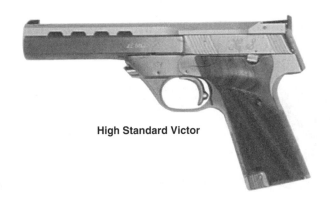

High Standard Victor

Ruger Mark II Target

HIGH STANDARD TROPHY TARGET PISTOL

Caliber: 22 LR, 10-shot mag. **Barrel:** 5-1/2" bull or 7-1/4" fluted. **Weight:** 44 oz. **Length:** 9.5" overall. **Stock:** Checkered hardwood with thumbrest. **Sights:** Undercut ramp front, frame-mounted micro-click rear adjustable for windage and elevation; drilled and tapped for scope mounting. **Features:** Gold-plated trigger, slide lock, safety-lever and magazine release; stippled front grip and backstrap; adjustable trigger and sear. Barrel weights optional. From High Standard Manufacturing Co., Inc.
Price: 5-1/2", scope base **$540.00**
Price: 7.25" **$689.00**
Price: 7.25", scope base **$625.00**

HIGH STANDARD VICTOR TARGET PISTOL

Caliber: 22 LR, 10-shot magazine. **Barrel:** 4-1/2" or 5-1/2"; push-button takedown. **Weight:** 46 oz. **Length:** 9.5" overall. **Stock:** Checkered hardwood with thumbrest. **Sights:** Undercut ramp front, micro-click rear adjustable for windage and elevation. Also available with scope mount, rings, no sights. **Features:** Stainless steel construction. Full-length vent rib. Gold-plated trigger, slide lock, safety-lever and magazine release; stippled front grip and backstrap; polished slide; adjustable trigger and sear. Comes with barrel weight. From High Standard Manufacturing Co., Inc.
Price: 4-1/2" scope base. **$564.00**
Price: 5-1/2", sights. **$625.00**
Price: 5-1/2" scope base. **$564.00**

KIMBER SUPER MATCH AUTO PISTOL

Caliber: 45 ACP, 7-shot magazine. **Barrel:** 5". **Weight:** 38 oz. **Length:** 18.7" overall. **Sights:** Blade front, Kimber fully adjustable rear. **Features:** Guaranteed to have shot 3" group at 50 yards. Stainless steel frame, black KimPro slide; two-piece magazine well; premium aluminum match-grade trigger; 30 lpi front strap checkering; stainless match-grade barrel; ambidextrous safety; special Custom Shop markings. Introduced 1999. Made in U.S.A. by Kimber Mfg., Inc.
Price: **$1,927.00**

KORTH MATCH REVOLVER

Caliber: .357 Mag., .38 Special, .32 S&W Long, 9mm Para., .22 WMR, .22 LR. **Barrel:** 5 π", 6". **Grips:** Adjustable match of oiled walnut with matte finish. **Sights:** Fully adjustable with rear sight leaves (wide th of sight notch: 3.4 mm, 3.5 mm, 3.6 mm), rear; undercut partridge, front. **Trigger:** Equipped with completely machined trigger shoe. Interchangeable caliber cylinders available as well as a variety of finishes. Made in Germany.
Price: . . . . From **$5,442.00**

MORINI MODEL 84E FREE PISTOL

Caliber: 22 LR, single shot. **Barrel:** 11.4". **Weight:** 43.7 oz. **Length:** 19.4" overall. **Grips:** Adjustable match type with stippled surfaces. **Sights:** Interchangeable blade front, match-type fully adjustable rear. **Features:** Fully adjustable electronic trigger. Introduced 1995. Imported from Switzerland by Nygord Precision Products.
Price: **$1,450.00**

PARDINI MODEL SP, HP TARGET PISTOLS

Caliber: 22 LR, 32 S&W, 5-shot magazine. **Barrel:** 4.7". **Weight:** 38.9 oz. **Length:** 11.6" overall. **Grips:** Adjustable; stippled walnut; match type. **Sights:** Interchangeable blade front, interchangeable, fully adjustable

rear. **Features:** Fully adjustable match trigger. Introduced 1995. Imported from Italy by Nygord Precision Products.
Price: Model SP (22 LR). **$995.00**
Price: Model HP (32 S&W) **$1,095.00**

PARDINI GP RAPID FIRE MATCH PISTOL

Caliber: 22 Short, 5-shot magazine. **Barrel:** 4.6". **Weight:** 43.3 oz. **Length:** 11.6" overall. **Grips:** Wrap-around stippled walnut. **Sights:** Interchangeable post front, fully adjustable match rear. Introduced 1995. Imported from Italy by Nygord Precision Products.
Price: Model GP **$1,095.00**
Price: Model GP-E Electronic, has special parts **$1,595.00**

PARDINI K22 FREE PISTOL

Caliber: 22 LR, single shot. **Barrel:** 9.8". **Weight:** 34.6 oz. **Length:** 18.7" overall. **Grips:** Wrap-around walnut; adjustable match type. **Sights:** Interchangeable post front, fully adjustable match open rear. **Features:** Removable, adjustable match trigger. Toggle bolt pushes cartridge into chamber. Barrel weights mount above the barrel. New upgraded model introduced in 2002. Imported from Italy by Nygord Precision Products.
Price: **$1,295.00**

PARDINI GT45 TARGET PISTOL

Caliber: 45, 9mm, 40 S&W. **Barrel:** 5", 6". **Grips:** Checkered fore strap. **Sights:** Interchangeable post front, fully adjustable match open rear. **Features:** Ambi-safeties, trigger pull adjustable. Fits Helweg Glock holsters for defense shooters. Imported from Italy by Nygord Precision Products.
Price: 5" **$1,050.00**
Price: 6" **$1,125.00**
Price: Frame mount available . . . . **$75.00 extra**
Price: Slide mount available . . . . **$35.00 extra**

PARDINI/NYGORD "MASTER" TARGET PISTOL

Caliber: 22 cal. **Barrel:** 5-1/2". **Grips:** Semi-wrap-around. **Sights:** Micrometer rear and red dot. **Features:** Elegant NRA "Bullseye" pistol. Superior balance of Pardini pistols. Revolutionary recirpcating internal weight barrel shroud. Imported from Italy by Nygord Precision Products.
Price: **$1,145.00**

RUGER MARK II TARGET MODEL AUTOLOADING PISTOL

Caliber: 22 LR, 10-shot magazine. **Barrel:** 6-7/8". **Weight:** 42 oz. **Length:** 11-1/8" overall. **Grips:** Checkered composition grip panels. **Sights:** .125" blade front, micro-click rear, adjustable for windage and elevation. Sight radius 9-3/8". Plastic case with lock included.
Features: Introduced 1982.
Price: Blued (MK-678) **$349.00**
Price: Stainless (KMK-678) **$439.00**

Ruger Mark II Government Target Model

Same gun as Mark II Target Model except has 6-7/8" barrel, higher sights and is roll marked "Government Target Model" on right side of receiver below rear sight. Identical in all aspects to military model used for training U.S. Armed Forces except for markings. Comes with factory test target, also lockable plastic case. Introduced 1987.
Price: Blued (MK-678G) **$425.00**
Price: Stainless (KMK-678G) **$509.00**

Ruger Mark II Government Target

Ruger Mark II Bull Barrel - MK10

Safari Arms Big Deuce

Smith & Wesson Model 41

Springfield, Inc. 1911A1 Bullseye Wadcutter

Ruger Stainless Competition Model Pistol
Similar to Mark II Government Target Model stainless pistol, 6-7/8" slab-sided barrel; receiver top is fitted with Ruger scope base of blued, chrome moly steel; has Ruger 1" stainless scope rings for mounting variety of optical sights; checkered laminated grip panels with right-hand thumbrest. Blued open sights with 9-1/4" radius. Overall length 11-1/8", weight 45 oz. Case and lock included. Introduced 1991.
Price: KMK-678GC $529.00

Ruger Mark II Bull Barrel
Same gun as Target Model except has 5-1/2" or 10" heavy barrel (10" meets all IHMSA regulations). Weight with 5-1/2" barrel is 42 oz., with 10" barrel, 51 oz. Case with lock included.
Price: Blued (MK-512) $349.00
Price: Blued (MK-10) $357.00
Price: Stainless (KMK-10) $445.00
Price: Stainless (KMK-512) $439.00

SAFARI ARMS BIG DEUCE PISTOL
Caliber: 45 ACP, 7-shot magazine. **Barrel:** 6", 416 stainless steel. **Weight:** 40.3 oz. **Length:** 9.5" overall. **Grips:** Smooth walnut. **Sights:** Ramped blade front, LPA adjustable rear. **Features:** Beavertail grip safety; extended thumb safety and slide release; Commander-style hammer. Throated, polished and tuned. Parkerized matte black slide with satin stainless steel frame. Introduced 1995. Made in U.S.A. by Safari Arms, Inc.
Price: $714.00

SMITH & WESSON MODEL 41 TARGET
Caliber: 22 LR, 10-shot clip. **Barrel:** 5-1/2", 7". **Weight:** 44 oz. (5-1/2" barrel). **Length:** 9" overall (5-1/2" barrel). **Grips:** Checkered walnut with modified thumbrest, usable with either hand. **Sights:** 1/8" Patridge on ramp base; micro-click rear adjustable for windage and elevation. **Features:** 3/8" wide, grooved trigger; adjustable trigger stop drilled and tapped.
Price: S&W Bright Blue, either barrel $958.00

SMITH & WESSON MODEL 22A TARGET PISTOL
Caliber: 22 LR, 10-shot magazine. **Barrel:** 5-1/2" bull. **Weight:** 38.5 oz. **Length:** 9-1/2" overall. **Grips:** Dymondwood with ambidextrous thumbrests and flared bottom or rubber soft touch with thumbrest. **Sights:** Patridge front, fully adjustable rear. **Features:** Sight bridge with Weaver-style integral optics mount; alloy frame, stainless barrel and slide; blue finish. Introduced 1997. Made in U.S.A. by Smith & Wesson.
Price: $367.00
Price: HiViz front sight $387.00

Smith & Wesson Model 22S Target Pistol
Similar to the Model 22A except has stainless steel frame. Introduced 1997. Made in U.S.A. by Smith & Wesson.
Price: $434.00
Price: HiViz front sight $453.00

SPRINGFIELD, INC. 1911A1 BULLSEYE WADCUTTER PISTOL
Caliber: 38 Super, 45 ACP. **Barrel:** 5". **Weight:** 45 oz. **Length:** 8.59" overall (5" barrel). **Grips:** Checkered walnut. **Sights:** Bo-Mar rib with undercut blade front, fully adjustable rear. **Features:** Built for wadcutter loads only. Has full-length recoil spring guide rod, fitted Videki speed trigger with 3.5-lb. pull; match Commander hammer and sear; beavertail grip safety; lowered and flared ejection port; tuned extractor; fitted slide to frame; recoil buffer system; beveled and polished magazine well; checkered front strap and steel mainspring housing (flat housing standard); polished and throated National Match barrel and bushing. Comes with two magazines with slam pads, plastic carrying case, test target. Introduced 1992. From Springfield, Inc.
Price: $1,499.00

Springfield, Inc. Expert

Springfield, Inc. N.M. Hardball

Springfield, Inc. Distinguished

Springfield, Inc. 1911A1 Trophy Match

Springfield, Inc. Basic Competition Pistol

Has low-mounted Bo-Mar adjustable rear sight, undercut blade front; match throated barrel and bushing; polished feed ramp; lowered and flared ejection port; fitted Videki speed trigger with tuned 3.5-lb. pull; fitted slide to frame; recoil buffer system; checkered walnut grips; serrated, arched mainspring housing. Comes with two magazines with slam pads, plastic carrying case. Introduced 1992. From Springfield, Inc.
Price: 45 ACP, blue, 5" only **$1,295.00**

Springfield, Inc. Expert Pistol

Similar to the Competition Pistol except has triple-chamber tapered cone compensator on match barrel with dovetailed front sight; lowered and flared ejection port; fully tuned for reliability; fitted slide to frame; extended ambidextrous thumb safety, extended magazine release button; beavertail grip safety; Pachmayr wrap-around grips. Comes with two magazines, plastic carrying case. Introduced 1992. From Springfield, Inc.
Price: 45 ACP, Duotone finish. **$1,724.00**
Price: Expert Ltd. (non-compensated) **$1,624.00**

Springfield, Inc. Distinguished Pistol

Has all the features of the 1911A1 Expert except is full-house pistol with deluxe Bo-Mar low-mounted adjustable rear sight; full-length recoil spring guide rod and recoil spring retainer; checkered frontstrap; S&A magazine well; walnut grips. Hard chrome finish. Comes with two magazines with slam pads, plastic carrying case. From Springfield, Inc.
Price: 45 ACP **$2,445.00**
Price: Distinguished Limited (non-compensated) **$2,345.00**

Springfield, Inc. 1911A1 N.M. Hardball Pistol

Has Bo-Mar adjustable rear sight with undercut front blade; fitted match Videki trigger with 4-lb. pull; fitted slide to frame; throated National Match barrel and bushing, polished feed ramp; recoil buffer system; tuned extractor; Herrett walnut grips. Comes with two magazines, plastic carrying case, test target. Introduced 1992. From Springfield, Inc.
Price: 45 ACP, blue **$1,336.00**

Springfield, Inc. Leatham Legend TGO Series Pistols

Three models of 5" barrel, .45 ACP 1911 pistols built for serious competition. TGO 1 has deluxe low mount BoMar rear sight, Dawson fiber optics front sight, 3.5 lb. trigger pull. TGO 2 has BoMar low mount adjustable rear sight, Dawson fiber optic front sight, 4.5 to 5 lb. trigger pull. TGO 3 has Springfield Armory fully adjustable rear sight with low mount BoMar cut Dawson fiber optic front sight, 4.5 to 5 lb. trigger.
Price: TGO 1 . . . . **$2,999.00**
Price: TGO 2 . . . . **$1,899.00**
Price: TGO 3 . . . . **$1,295.00**

Springfield, Inc. Trophy Match Pistol

Similar to Springfield, Inc.'s Full Size model, but designed for bullseye and action shooting competition. Available with a Service Model 5" frame with matching slide and barrel in 5" and 6" lengths. Fully adjustable sights, checkered frame front strap, match barrel and bushing. In 45 ACP only. From Springfield Inc.
Price: **$1,248.00**

STI EAGLE 5.0, 6.0 PISTOL

Caliber: 9mm, 9x21, 38 & 40 Super, 40 S&W, 10mm, 45 ACP, 10-shot magazine. **Barrel:** 5", 6" bull. **Weight:** 34.5 oz. **Length:** 8.62" overall. **Grips:** Checkered polymer. **Sights:** STI front, Novak or Heine rear. **Features:** Standard frames plus 7 others; adjustable match trigger; skeletonized hammer; extended grip safety with locator pad; match-grade fit of all parts. Many options available. Introduced 1994. Made in U.S.A. by STI International.
Price: . . . . (5.0 Eagle) **$1,794.00**, (6.0 Eagle) **$1,894.00**

STI EXECUTIVE PISTOL

Caliber: 40 S&W. **Barrel:** 5" bull. **Weight:** 39 oz. **Length:** 8-5/8". **Grips:** Gray polymer. **Sights:** Dawson fiber optic, front; STI adjustable rear. **Features:** Stainless mag. well, front and rear serrations on slide. Made in U.S.A. by STI.
Price: **$2,389.00**

STI TROJAN

Caliber: 9mm, 38 Super, 40S&W, 45 ACP. **Barrel:** 5", 6". **Weight:** 36 oz. **Length:** 8.5". **Grips:** Rosewood. **Sights:** STI front with STI adjustable rear. **Features:** Stippled front strap, flat top slide, one-piece steel guide rod.
Price: (Trojan 5") **$1,024.00**
Price: (Trojan 6", not available in 38 Super) **$1,232.50**

WALTHER GSP MATCH PISTOL

Caliber: 22 LR, 32 S&W Long (GSP-C), 5-shot magazine. **Barrel:** 4.22". **Weight:** 44.8 oz. (22 LR), 49.4 oz. (32). **Length:** 11.8" overall. **Grips:** Walnut. **Sights:** Post front, match rear adjustable for windage and elevation. **Features:** Available with either 2.2-lb. (1000 gm) or 3-lb. (1360 gm) trigger. Spare magazine, barrel weight, tools supplied. Imported from Germany by Nygord Precision Products.
Price: GSP, with case **$1,495.00**
Price: GSP-C, with case **$1,595.00**

HANDGUNS

*Includes models suitable for hunting and
competitive courses of fire, both police and international.*

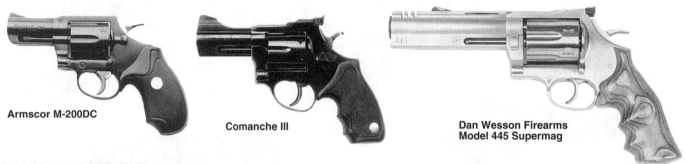

Armscor M-200DC

Comanche III

**Dan Wesson Firearms
Model 445 Supermag**

ARMSCOR M-200DC REVOLVER
Caliber: 38 Spec., 6-shot cylinder. **Barrel:** 2-1/2", 4". **Weight:** 22 oz. (2-1/2" barrel). **Length:** 7-3/8" overall (2-1/2" barrel). **Grips:** Checkered rubber. **Sights:** Blade front, fixed notch rear. **Features:** All-steel construction; floating firing pin, transfer bar ignition; shrouded ejector rod; blue finish. Reintroduced 1996. Imported from the Philippines by K.B.I., Inc.
Price: 2-1/2" **$199.99**
Price: 4" **$205.00**

ARMSPORT MODEL 4540 REVOLVER
Caliber: 38 Special. **Barrel:** 4". **Weight:** 32 oz **Length:** 9" overall. **Sights:** Fixed rear, blade front. **Features:** Ventilated rib; blued finish. Imported from Argentina by Armsport Inc.
Price: **$140.00**

COMANCHE I, II, III DA REVOLVERS
Features: Adjustable sights. Blue or stainless finish. Distributed by SGS Importers.
Price: I 22 LR, 6" bbl, 9-shot, blue **$236.95**
Price: I 22LR, 6" bbl, 9-shot, stainless **$258.95**
Price: II 38 Special, 3", 4" bbl, 6-shot, blue **$219.95**
Price: II 38 Special, 4" bbl, 6-shot, stainless **$236.95**
Price: III 357 Mag, 3", 4", 6" bbl, 6-shot, blue **$253.95**
Price: III 357 Mag, 3", 4", 6" bbl, 6-shot, stainless **$274.95**
Price: II 38 Special, 3" bbl, 6-shot, stainless steel **$236.95**

DAN WESSON FIREARMS MODEL 722 SILHOUETTE REVOLVER
Caliber: 22 LR, 6-shot. **Barrel:** 10", vent heavy. **Weight:** 53 oz. **Grips:** Combat style. **Sights:** Patridge-style front, .080" narrow notch rear. **Features:** Single action only. Satin brushed stainless finish. Reintroduced 1997. Made in U.S.A. by Dan Wesson Firearms.
Price: 722 VH10 (vent heavy 10" bbl.) **$888.00**
Price: 722 VH10 SRS1 (Super Ram Silhouette, Bo-Mar sights, front hood, trigger job). **$1,164.00**

DAN WESSON FIREARMS MODEL 3220/73220 TARGET REVOLVER
Caliber: 32-20, 6-shot. **Barrel:** 2.5", 4", 6", 8", 10" standard vent, vent heavy. **Weight:** 47 oz. (6" VH). **Length:** 11.25" overall. **Grips:** Hogue Gripper rubber (walnut, exotic hardwoods optional). **Sights:** Red ramp interchangeable front, fully adjustable rear. **Features:** Bright blue (3220) or stainless (73220). Reintroduced 1997. Made in U.S.A. by Dan Wesson Firearms.
Price: 3220 VH2.5 (blued, 2.5" vent heavy bbl.) **$643.00**
Price: 73220 VH10 (stainless 10" vent heavy bbl.)........... **$873.00**

DAN WESSON FIREARMS MODEL 40/740 REVOLVERS
Caliber: 357 Maximum, 6-shot. **Barrel:** 4", 6", 8", 10". **Weight:** 72 oz. (8" bbl.). **Length:** 14.3" overall (8" bbl.). **Grips:** Hogue Gripper rubber (walnut or exotic hardwood optional). **Sights:** 1/8" serrated front, fully adjustable rear. **Features:** Blue or stainless steel. Made in U.S.A. by Dan Wesson Firearms.
Price: Blue, 4". **$702.00**
Price: Blue, 6". **$749.00**

Price: Blue, 8". **$795.00**
Price: Blue, 10". **$858.00**
Price: Stainless, 4" **$834.00**
Price: Stainless, 6" **$892.00**
Price: Stainless, 8" slotted **$1,024.00**
Price: Stainless, 10" **$998.00**
Price: 4", 6", 8" Compensated, blue .... **$749.00 to $885.00**
Price: As above, stainless. .... **$893.00 to $1,061.00**

Dan Wesson Firearms Model 414/7414 and 445/7445 SuperMag Revolvers
Similar size and weight as Model 40 revolvers. Chambered for 414 SuperMag or 445 SuperMag cartridge. Barrel lengths of 4", 6", 8", 10". Contact maker for complete price list. Reintroduced 1997. Made in the U.S. by Dan Wesson Firearms.
Price: 4", vent heavy, blue or stainless **$904.00**
Price: 8", vent heavy, blue or stainless **$1,026.00**
Price: 10", vent heavy, blue or stainless **$1,103.00**
Price: Compensated models .... **$965.00 to $1,149.00**

DAN WESSON FIREARMS MODEL 22/722 REVOLVERS
Caliber: 22 LR, 22 WMR, 6-shot. **Barrel:** 2-1/2", 4", 6", 8" or 10"; interchangeable. **Weight:** 36 oz. (2-1/2"), 44 oz. (6"). **Length:** 9-1/4" overall (4" barrel). **Grips:** Hogue Gripper rubber (walnut, exotic woods optional). **Sights:** 1/8" serrated, interchangeable front, white outline rear adjustable for windage and elevation. **Features:** Built on the same frame as the Wesson 357; smooth, wide trigger with over-travel adjustment, wide spur hammer, with short double-action travel. Available in blue or stainless steel. Reintroduced 1997. Contact Dan Wesson Firearms for complete price list.
Price: 22 VH2.5/722 VH2.5 (blued or stainless 2-1/2" bbl.) **$551.00**
Price: 22VH10/722 VH10 (blued or stainless 10" bbl.) **$750.00**

Dan Wesson 722M Small Frame Revolver
Similar to Model 22/722 except chambered for 22 WMR. Blued or stainless finish, 2-1/2", 4", 6", 8" or 10" barrels.
Price: Blued or stainless finish .... **$643.00 to $873.00**

DAN WESSON FIREARMS MODEL 15/715 and 32/732 REVOLVERS
Caliber: 32-20, 32 H&R Mag. (Model 32), 357 Mag. (Model 15). **Barrel:** 2-1/2", 4", 6", 8" (M32), 2-1/2", 4", 6", 8", 10" (M15); vent heavy. **Weight:** 36 oz. (2-1/2" barrel). **Length:** 9-1/4" overall (4" barrel). **Grips:** Checkered, interchangeable. **Sights:** 1/8" serrated front, fully adjustable rear. **Features:** New Generation Series. Interchangeable barrels; wide, smooth trigger, wide hammer spur; short double-action travel. Available in blue or stainless. Reintroduced 1997. Made in U.S.A. by Dan Wesson Firearms. Contact maker for full list of models.
Price: Model 15/715, 2-1/2" (blue or stainless)............... **$551.00**
Price: Model 15/715, 8" (blue or stainless).................. **$612.00**
Price: Model 15/715, compensated .... **$704.00 to $827.00**
Price: Model 32/732, 4" (blue or stainless).................. **$674.00**
Price: Model 32/732, 8" (blue or stainless).................. **$766.00**

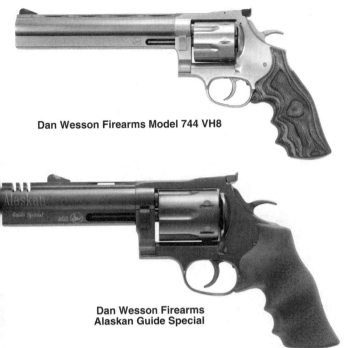

Dan Wesson Firearms Model 744 VH8

Dan Wesson Firearms
Alaskan Guide Special

Dan Wesson Firearms
Super Ram Silhouette

DAN WESSON FIREARMS MODEL 41/741, 44/744 and 45/745 REVOLVERS

Caliber: 41 Mag., 44 Mag., 45 Colt, 6-shot. **Barrel:** 4", 6", 8", 10"; interchangeable; 4", 6", 8" Compensated. **Weight:** 48 oz. (4"). **Length:** 12" overall (6" bbl.) **Grips:** Smooth. **Sights:** 1/8" serrated front, white outline rear adjustable for windage and elevation. **Features:** Available in blue or stainless steel. Smooth, wide trigger with adjustable over-travel, wide hammer spur. Available in Pistol Pac set also. Reintroduced 1997. Contact Dan Wesson Firearms for complete price list.
Price: 41 Mag., 4", vent heavy (blue or stainless) **$643.00**
Price: 44 Mag., 6", vent heavy (blue or stainless) **$689.00**
Price: 45 Colt, 8", vent heavy (blue or stainless) **$766.00**
Price: Compensated models (all calibers) . . . . **$812.00 to $934.00**

DAN WESSON FIREARMS LARGE FRAME SERIES REVOLVERS

Caliber: 41, 741/41 Magnum; 44, 744/44 Magnum; 45, 745/45 Long Colt; 360, 7360/357; 460, 7460/45. **Barrel:** 2"-10". **Weight:** 49 oz.-69 oz. **Grips:** Standard, Hogue rubber Gripper Grips. **Sights:** Standard front, serrated ramp with color insert. Standard rear, adustable wide notch. Other sight options available. **Features:** Available in blue or stainless steel. Smooth, wide trigger with overtravel, wide hammer spur. Double and single action.
Price: . . . . **$769.00 to $889.00**

DAN WESSON FIREARMS MODEL 360/7360 REVOLVERS

Caliber: 357 Mag. **Barrel:** 4", 6", 8", 10"; vent heavy. **Weight:** 64 oz. (8" barrel). **Grips:** Hogue rubber finger groove. **Sights:** Interchangeable ramp or Patridge front, fully adjustable rear. **Features:** New Generation Large Frame Series. Interchangeable barrels and grips; smooth trigger, wide hammer spur. Blue (360) or stainless (7360). Introduced 1999. Made in U.S.A. by Dan Wesson Firearms.
Price: 4" bbl., blue or stainless **$735.00**
Price: 10" bbl., blue or stainless **$873.00**
Price: Compensated models . . . . **$858.00 to $980.00**

DAN WESSON FIREARMS MODEL 460/7460 REVOLVERS

Caliber: 45 ACP, 45 Auto Rim, 45 Super, 45 Winchester Magnum and 460 Rowland. **Barrel:** 4", 6", 8", 10"; vent heavy. **Weight:** 49 oz. (4" barrel). **Grips:** Hogue rubber finger groove; interchangeable. **Sights:** Interchangeable ramp or Patridge front, fully adjustable rear. **Features:** New Generation Large Frame Series. Shoots five cartridges (45 ACP, 45 Auto Rim, 45 Super, 45 Winchester Magnum and 460 Rowland; six half-moon

clips for auto cartridges included). Interchangeable barrels and grips. Available with non-fluted cylinder and Slotted Lightweight barrel shroud. Introduced 1999. Made in U.S.A. by Dan Wesson Firearms.
Price: 4" bbl., blue or stainless **$735.00**
Price: 10" bbl., blue or stainless **$888.00**
Price: Compensated models . . . . **$919.00 to $1,042.00**

DAN WESSON FIREARMS STANDARD SILHOUETTE REVOLVERS

Caliber: 357 SuperMag/Maxi, 41 Mag., 414 SuperMag, 445 SuperMag. **Barrel:** 8", 10". **Weight:** 64 oz. (8" barrel). **Length:** 14.3" overall (8" barrel). **Grips:** Hogue rubber finger groove; interchangeable. **Sights:** Patridge front, fully adjustable rear. **Features:** Interchangeable barrels and grips, fluted or non-fluted cylinder, satin brushed stainless finish. Introduced 1999. Made in U.S.A. by Dan Wesson Firearms.
Price: 357 SuperMag/Maxi, 8" **$1,057.00**
Price: 41 Mag., 10" **$888.00**
Price: 414 SuperMag., 8" **$1,057.00**
Price: 445 SuperMag., 8" **$1,057.00**

Dan Wesson Firearms Super Ram Silhouette Revolver

Similar to Standard Silhouette except has 10 land and groove Laser Coat barrel, Bo-Mar target sights with hooded front, special laser engraving. Fluted or non-fluted cylinder. Introduced 1999. Made in U.S.A. by Dan Wesson Firearms.
Price: 357 SuperMag/Maxi, 414 SuperMag., 445 SuperMag., 8", blue or stainless **$1,364.00**
Price: 41 Magnum, 44 Magnum, 8", blue or stainless **$1,241.00**
Price: 41 Magnum, 44 Magnum, 10", blue or stainless **$1,333.00**

DAN WESSON FIREARMS ALASKAN GUIDE SPECIAL

Caliber: 445 SuperMag, 44 Magnum. **Barrel:** Compensated 4" vent heavy barrel assembly. **Features:** Stainless steel with baked on, non-glare, matte black coating, special laser engraving.
Price: Model 7445 VH4C AGS **$995.00**
Price: Model 744 VH4C AGS **$855.00**

EAA STANDARD GRADE REVOLVERS

Caliber: 38 Spec., 6-shot; 357 magnum, 6-shot. **Barrel:** 2", 4". **Weight:** 38 oz. (22 rimfire, 4"). **Length:** 8.8" overall (4" bbl.). **Grips:** Rubber with finger grooves. **Sights:** Blade front, fixed or adjustable on rimfires; fixed only on 32, 38. **Features:** Swing-out cylinder; hammer block safety; blue finish. Introduced 1991. Imported from Germany by European American Armory.
Price: 38 Special 2" **$249.00**
Price: 38 Special, 4" **$259.00**
Price: 357 Magnum, 2" **$259.00**
Price: 357 Magnum, 4" **$279.00**

KORTH COMBAT REVOLVER

Caliber: .357 Mag., .32 S&W Long, 9mm Para., .22 WMR, .22 LR. **Barrel:** 3", 4", 5-1/4", 6", 8". **Sights:** Fully-adjustable, rear; Baughman ramp, front. **Grips:** Walnut (checkered or smooth). Also available as a Target model in .22 LR, .38 Spl., .32 S&W Long, .357 Mag. with undercut partridge front sight; fully-adjustable rear. Made in Germany. Imported by Korth USA.
Price: . . . . From **$5,442.00**

Medusa Model 47   Ruger GP-161   Ruger KGP-141

Ruger KSP-331X

KORTH TROJA REVOLVER

Caliber: .357 Mag. **Barrel:** 6". **Finish:** Matte blue. **Grips:** Smooth, oversized finger contoured walnut. **Features:** Maintaining all of the precision German craftsmanship that has made this line famous, the final surface finish is not as finely polished as the firm's other products – thus the lower price. Introduced 2003. Imported from Germany by Korth USA.
Price: . . . . From **$3,995.00**

MEDUSA MODEL 47 REVOLVER

Caliber: Most 9mm, 38 and 357 caliber cartridges; 6-shot cylinder. **Barrel:** 2-1/2", 3", 4", 5", 6"; fluted. **Weight:** 39 oz. **Length:** 10" overall (4" barrel). **Grips:** Gripper-style rubber. **Sights:** Changeable front blades, fully adjustable rear. **Features:** Patented extractor allows gun to chamber, fire and extract over 25 different cartridges in the .355 to .357 range, without half-moon clips. Steel frame and cylinder; match quality barrel. Matte blue finish. Introduced 1996. Made in U.S.A. by Phillips & Rogers, Inc.
Price: **$899.00**

ROSSI MODEL 351/352 REVOLVERS

Caliber: 38 Special +P, 5-shot. **Barrel:** 2". **Weight:** 24 oz. **Length:** 6-1/2" overall. **Grips:** Rubber. **Sights:** Blade front, fixed rear. **Features:** Patented key-lock Taurus Security System; forged steel frame handles +P ammunition. Introduced 2001. Imported by BrazTech/Taurus.
Price: Model 351 (blued finish) **$298.00**
Price: Model 352 (stainless finish) **$345.00**

ROSSI MODEL 461/462 REVOLVERS

Caliber: 357 Magnum +P, 6-shot. **Barrel:** 2". **Weight:** 26 oz. **Length:** 6-1/2" overall. **Grips:** Rubber. **Sights:** Fixed. **Features:** Single/double action. Patented key-lock Taurus Security System; forged steel frame handles +P ammunition. Introduced 2001. Imported by BrazTech/Taurus.
Price: Model 461 (blued finish) **$298.00**
Price: Model 462 (stainless finish) **$345.00**

ROSSI MODEL 971/972 REVOLVERS

Caliber: 357 Magnum +P, 6-shot. **Barrel:** 4", 6". **Weight:** 40-44 oz. **Length:** 8-1/2" or 10-1/2" overall. **Grips:** Rubber. **Sights:** Fully adjustable. **Features:** Single/double action. Patented key-lock Taurus Security System; forged steel frame handles +P ammunition. Introduced 2001. Imported by BrazTech/Taurus.
Price: Model 971 (blued finish, 4" barrel) **$345.00**
Price: Model 972 (stainless steel finish, 6" barrel) **$391.00**

Rossi Model 851

Similar to Model 971/972, chambered for 38 Special +P. Blued finish, 4" barrel. Introduced 2001. From BrazTech/Taurus.
Price: **$298.00**

RUGER GP-100 REVOLVERS

Caliber: 38 Spec., 357 Mag., 6-shot. **Barrel:** 3", 3" full shroud, 4", 4" full shroud, 6", 6" full shroud. **Weight:** 3" barrel—35 oz., 3" full shroud—36 oz., 4" barrel—37 oz., 4" full shroud—38 oz. **Sights:** Fixed; adjustable on 4" full shroud, all 6" barrels. **Grips:** Ruger Santoprene Cushioned Grip with Goncalo Alves inserts. **Features:** Uses action, frame incorporating improvements and features of both the Security-Six and Redhawk revolvers. Full length, short ejector shroud. Satin blue and stainless steel.
Price: GP-141 (357, 4" full shroud, adj. sights, blue) **$499.00**
Price: GP-160 (357, 6", adj. sights, blue) **$499.00**
Price: GP-161 (357, 6" full shroud, adj. sights, blue), 46 oz. **$499.00**
Price: GPF-331 (357, 3" full shroud) **$495.00**

Price: GPF-340 (357, 4") **$495.00**
Price: GPF-341 (357, 4" full shroud). **$495.00**
Price: KGP-141 (357, 4" full shroud, adj. sights, stainless) **$555.00**
Price: KGP-160 (357, 6", adj. sights, stainless), 43 oz. **$555.00**
Price: KGP-161 (357, 6" full shroud, adj. sights, stainless) 46 oz. **$555.00**
Price: KGPF-330 (357, 3", stainless) **$555.00**
Price: KGPF-331 (357, 3" full shroud, stainless) **$555.00**
Price: KGPF-340 (357, 4", stainless), KGPF-840 (38 Special). . . **$555.00**
Price: KGPF-341 (357, 4" full shroud, stainless) **$555.00**
Price: KGPF-840 (38 Special, 4", stainless). **$555.00**

Ruger SP101 Double-Action-Only Revolver

Similar to standard SP101 except double-action-only with no single-action sear notch. Spurless hammer for snag-free handling, floating firing pin and Ruger's patented transfer bar safety system. Available with 2-1/4" barrel in 357 Magnum. Weighs 25 oz., overall length 7.06". Natural brushed satin, high-polish stainless steel. Introduced 1993.
Price: KSP321XL (357 Mag.) **$495.00**

RUGER SP101 REVOLVERS

Caliber: 22 LR, 32 H&R Mag., 6-shot; 38 Spec. +P, 357 Mag., 5-shot. **Barrel:** 2-1/4", 3-1/16", 4". **Weight:** (38 & 357 mag models) 2-1/4"—25 oz.; 3-1/16"—27 oz. **Sights:** Adjustable on 22, 32, fixed on others. **Grips:** Ruger Cushioned Grip with inserts. **Features:** Incorporates improvements and features found in the GP-100 revolvers into a compact, small frame, double-action revolver. Full-length ejector shroud. Stainless steel only. Introduced 1988.
Price: KSP-821X (2-1/4", 38 Spec.) **$495.00**
Price: KSP-831X (3-1/16", 38 Spec.) **$495.00**
Price: KSP-241X (4" heavy bbl., 22 LR), 34 oz. **$495.00**
Price: KSP-3231X (3-1/16", 32 H&R), 30 oz. **$495.00**
Price: KSP-321X (2-1/4", 357 Mag.). **$495.00**
Price: KSP-331X (3-1/16", 357 Mag.). **$495.00**
Price: KSP-3241X (32 Mag., 4" bbl) **$495.00**

HANDGUNS — DOUBLE ACTION REVOLVERS, SERVICE & SPORT

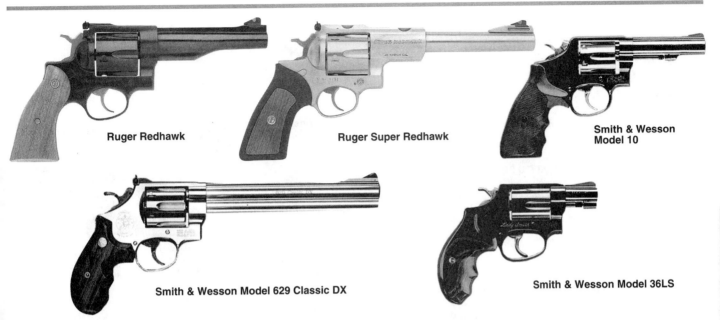

Ruger Redhawk

Ruger Super Redhawk

Smith & Wesson Model 10

Smith & Wesson Model 629 Classic DX

Smith & Wesson Model 36LS

RUGER REDHAWK
Caliber: 44 Rem. Mag., 45 Colt, 6-shot. **Barrel:** 5-1/2", 7-1/2". **Weight:** About 54 oz. (7-1/2" bbl.). **Length:** 13" overall (7-1/2" barrel). **Grips:** Square butt cushioned grip panels. **Sights:** Interchangeable Patridge-type front, rear adjustable for windage and elevation. **Features:** Stainless steel, brushed satin finish, blued ordnance steel. 9-1/2" sight radius. Introduced 1979.
Price: Blued, 44 Mag., 5-1/2" RH-445, 7-1/2" RH-44 . . . . **$585.00**
Price: Blued, 44 Mag., 7-1/2" RH44R, with scope mount, rings . . **$625.00**
Price: Stainless, 44 Mag., KRH445, 5-1/2", 7-1/2" KRH-44 . . . . . **$645.00**
Price: Stainless, 44 Mag., 7-1/2", with scope mount, rings KRH-44R. **$685.00**
Price: Stainless, 45 Colt, KRH455, 5-1/2", 7-1/2" KRH-45 . . . . . **$645.00**
Price: Stainless, 45 Colt, 7-1/2", with scope mount and rings KRH-45R. **$685.00**

Ruger Super Redhawk Revolver
Similar to standard Redhawk except has heavy extended frame with Ruger Integral Scope Mounting System on wide topstrap. Also available 454 Casull and 480 Ruger. Wide hammer spur lowered for better scope clearance. Incorporates mechanical design features and improvements of GP-100. Choice of 7-1/2" or 9-1/2" barrel, both ramp front sight base with Redhawk-style Interchangeable Insert sight blades, adjustable rear sight. Comes with Ruger "Cushioned Grip" panels with wood panels. Target gray stainless steel. Introduced 1987.
Price: KSRH-7 (7-1/2"), KSRH-9 (9-1/2"), 44 Mag. **$685.00**
Price: KSRH-7454 (7-1/2") 454 Casull, 9-1/2 KSRH-9454 . . . . . . **$775.00**
Price: KSRH-7480 (7-1/2") 480 Ruger **$775.00**
Price: KSRH-9480 (9-1/2") 480 Ruger **$775.00**

SMITH & WESSON MODEL 10 M&P HB REVOLVER
Caliber: 38 Spec., 6-shot. **Barrel:** 4". **Weight:** 33.5 oz. **Length:** 9-5/16" overall. **Grips:** Uncle Mike's Combat soft rubber; square butt. **Sights:** Fixed; ramp front, square notch rear.
Price: Blue **$496.00**

SMITH & WESSON COMMEMORATIVE MODEL 29
Features: Reflects original Model 29: 6-1/2" barrel, four-screw side plate, over-sized target grips, red vamp front and black blade rear sights, 150th Anniversary logo, engraved, gold-plated, blue, in wood presentation case. Limited.
Price: . . . . **NA**

SMITH & WESSON MODEL 629 REVOLVERS
Caliber: 44 Magnum, 44 S&W Special, 6-shot. **Barrel:** 5", 6", 8-3/8". **Weight:** 47 oz. (6" bbl.). **Length:** 11-3/8" overall (6" bbl.). **Grips:** Soft rubber; wood optional. **Sights:** 1/8" red ramp front, white outline rear, internal lock, adjustable for windage and elevation.
Price: Model 629, 4" **$717.00**
Price: Model 629, 6" **$739.00**
Price: Model 629, 8-3/8" barrel. **$756.00**

Smith & Wesson Model 629 Classic Revolver
Similar to standard Model 629, full-lug 5", 6-1/2" or 8-3/8" barrel, chamfered front of cylinder, interchangeable red ramp front sight with adjustable white outline rear, Hogue grips with S&W monogram, frame is drilled and tapped for scope mounting. Factory accurizing and endurance packages. Overall length with 5" barrel is 10-1/2"; weighs 51 oz. Introduced 1990.
Price: Model 629 Classic (stainless), 5", 6-1/2" **$768.00**
Price: As above, 8-3/8" **$793.00**
Price: Model 629 with HiViz front sight **$814.00**

Smith & Wesson Model 629 Classic DX Revolver
Similar to Model 629 Classic, offered only with 6-1/2" or 8-3/8" full-lug barrel, five front sights: red ramp, black Patridge, black Patridge with gold bead, black ramp, black Patridge with white dot, white outline rear sight, adjustable sight, internal lock. Hogue combat-style and wood round butt grip. Introduced 1991.
Price: Model 629 Classic DX, 6-1/2". **$986.00**
Price: As above, 8-3/8" **$1,018.00**

SMITH & WESSON MODEL 37 CHIEF'S SPECIAL & AIRWEIGHT
Caliber: 38 Spec. +P, 5-shot. **Barrel:** 1-7/8". **Weight:** 19-1/2 oz. (2" bbl.); 13-1/2 oz. (Airweight). **Length:** 6-1/2" (round butt). **Grips:** Round butt soft rubber. **Sights:** Fixed, serrated ramp front, square notch rear. Glass beaded finish.
Price: Model 37. . . . . **$523.00**

Smith & Wesson Model 637 Airweight Revolver
Similar to the Model 37 Airweight except has alloy frame, stainless steel barrel, cylinder and yoke; rated for 38 Spec. +P; Uncle Mike's Boot Grip. Weighs 15 oz. Introduced 1996. Made in U.S.A. by Smith & Wesson.
Price: **$548.00**

SMITH & WESSON MODEL 36LS, 60LS LADYSMITH
Caliber: .38 S&W Special +P, 5-shot. **Barrel:** 1-7/8". **Weight:** 20 oz. **Length:** 6-5/16 overall (1-7/8" barrel). **Grips:** Combat Dymondwood® grips with S&W monogram. **Sights:** Serrated ramp front, fixed notch rear. **Features:** Speedloader cutout. Comes in a fitted carry/storage case. Introduced 1989.
Price: Model 36LS **$518.00**
Price: Model 60LS, 2-1/8" barrel stainless, 357 Magnum. **$566.00**

HANDGUNS

16th EDITION • 179

Smith & Wesson Model 65LS

Smith & Wesson
Model 317 AirLite

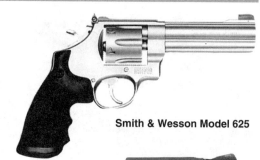

Smith & Wesson Model 625

Smith & Wesson
Model 340 PD Airlite Sc

SMITH & WESSON MODEL 60 CHIEF'S SPECIAL
Caliber: 357 Magnum, 5-shot. **Barrel:** 2-1/8" or 3". **Weight:** 24 oz. **Length:** 7-1/2 overall (3" barrel). **Grips:** Rounded butt synthetic grips. **Sights:** Fixed, serrated ramp front, square notch rear. **Features:** Stainless steel construction. 3" full lug barrel, adjustable sights, internal lock. Made in U.S.A. by Smith & Wesson.
Price: 2-1/8" barrel $541.00
Price: 3" barrel $574.00

SMITH & WESSON MODEL 65
Caliber: 357 Mag. and 38 Spec., 6-shot. **Barrel:** 4". **Weight:** 34 oz. **Length:** 9-5/16" overall (4" bbl.). **Grips:** Uncle Mike's Combat. **Sights:** 1/8" serrated ramp front, fixed square notch rear. **Features:** Heavy barrel. Stainless steel construction. Internal lock.
Price: $531.00

SMITH & WESSON MODEL 317 AIRLITE, 317 LADYSMITH REVOLVERS
Caliber: 22 LR, 8-shot. **Barrel:** 1-7/8" 3". **Weight:** 9.9 oz. **Length:** 6-3/16" overall. **Grips:** Dymondwood Boot or Uncle Mike's Boot. **Sights:** Serrated ramp front, fixed notch rear. **Features:** Aluminum alloy, carbon and stainless steels, and titanium construction. Short spur hammer, smooth combat trigger. Clear Cote finish. Introduced 1997. Made in U.S.A. by Smith & Wesson.
Price: With Uncle Mike's Boot grip $550.00
Price: With DymondWood Boot grip, 3" barrel, HiViz front sight, internal lock $600.00
Price: Model 317 LadySmith (DymondWood only, comes with display case) $596.00

SMITH & WESSON MODEL 64 STAINLESS M&P
Caliber: 38 Spec. +P, 6-shot. **Barrel:** 2", 3", 4". **Weight:** 34 oz. **Length:** 9-5/16" overall. **Grips:** Soft rubber. **Sights:** Fixed, 1/8" serrated ramp front, square notch rear. **Features:** Satin finished stainless steel, square butt.
Price: 2" $522.00
Price: 3", 4" $532.00

SMITH & WESSON MODEL 65LS LADYSMITH
Caliber: 357 Magnum, 38 Spec. +P, 6-shot. **Barrel:** 3". **Weight:** 31 oz. **Length:** 7.94" overall. **Grips:** Rosewood, round butt. **Sights:** Serrated ramp front, fixed notch rear. **Features:** Stainless steel with frosted finish. Smooth combat trigger, service hammer, shrouded ejector rod. Comes with case. Introduced 1992.
Price: $584.00

SMITH & WESSON MODEL 66 STAINLESS COMBAT MAGNUM
Caliber: 357 Mag. and 38 Spec. +P, 6-shot. **Barrel:** 2-1/2", 4", 6". **Weight:** 36 oz. (4" barrel). **Length:** 9-9/16" overall. **Grips:** Soft rubber. **Sights:** Red ramp front, micro-click rear adjustable for windage and elevation. **Features:** Satin finish stainless steel. Internal lock.
Price: 2-1/2" $590.00
Price: 4" $579.00
Price: 6" $608.00

SMITH & WESSON MODEL 67 COMBAT MASTERPIECE
Caliber: 38 Special, 6-shot. **Barrel:** 4". **Weight:** 32 oz. **Length:** 9-5/16" overall. **Grips:** Soft rubber. **Sights:** Red ramp front, micro-click rear adjustable for windage and elevation. **Features:** Stainless steel with satin finish. Smooth combat trigger, semi-target hammer. Introduced 1994.
Price: $585.00

Smith & Wesson Model 686 Magnum PLUS Revolver
Similar to the Model 686 except has 7-shot cylinder, 2-1/2", 4" or 6" barrel. Weighs 34-1/2 oz., overall length 7-1/2" (2-1/2" barrel). Hogue rubber grips. Internal lock. Introduced 1996. Made in U.S.A. by Smith & Wesson.
Price: 2-1/2" barrel $631.00
Price: 4" barrel $653.00
Price: 6" barrel $663.00

SMITH & WESSON MODEL 625 REVOLVER
Caliber: 45 ACP, 6-shot. **Barrel:** 5". **Weight:** 46 oz. **Length:** 11.375" overall. **Grips:** Soft rubber; wood optional. **Sights:** Patridge front on ramp, S&W micrometer click rear adjustable for windage and elevation. **Features:** Stainless steel construction with .400" semi-target hammer, .312" smooth combat trigger; full lug barrel. Glass beaded finish. Introduced 1989.
Price: 5" $745.00
Price: 4" with internal lock. $745.00

SMITH & WESSON MODEL 640 CENTENNIAL DA ONLY
Caliber: 357 Mag., 38 Spec. +P, 5-shot. **Barrel:** 2-1/8". **Weight:** 25 oz. **Length:** 6-3/4" overall. **Grips:** Uncle Mike's Boot Grip. **Sights:** Serrated ramp front, fixed notch rear. **Features:** Stainless steel. Fully concealed hammer, snag-proof smooth edges. Internal lock. Introduced 1995 in 357 Magnum.
Price: $599.00

SMITH & WESSON MODEL 617 K-22 MASTERPIECE
Caliber: 22 LR, 6- or 10-shot. **Barrel:** 4", 6", 8-3/8". **Weight:** 42 oz. (4" barrel). **Length:** NA. **Grips:** Soft rubber. **Sights:** Patridge front, adjustable rear. Drilled and tapped for scope mount. **Features:** Stainless steel with satin finish; 4" has .312" smooth trigger, .375" semi-target hammer; 6" has either .312" combat or .400" serrated trigger, .375" semi-target or .500" target hammer; 8-3/8" with .400" serrated trigger, .500" target hammer. Introduced 1990.
Price: 4" $644.00
Price: 6", target hammer, target trigger $625.00
Price: 6", 10-shot $669.00
Price: 8-3/8", 10 shot $679.00

SMITH & WESSON MODEL 610 CLASSIC HUNTER REVOLVER
Caliber: 10mm, 40 S&W, 6-shot cylinder. **Barrel:** 6-1/2" full lug. **Weight:** 52 oz. **Length:** 12" overall. **Grips:** Hogue rubber combat. **Sights:** Interchangeable blade front, micro-click rear adjustable for windage and elevation. **Features:** Stainless steel construction; target hammer, target trigger; unfluted cylinder; drilled and tapped for scope mounting. Introduced 1998.
Price: $785.00

SMITH & WESSON MODEL 340 PD AIRLITE Sc CENTENNIAL
Caliber: 357 Magnum, 38 Spec. +P, 5-shot. **Barrel:** 1-7/8". **Grips:** Rounded butt grip. **Sights:** HiViz front. **Features:** Synthetic grip, internal lock. Blue.
Price: $799.00

HANDGUNS — DOUBLE ACTION REVOLVERS, SERVICE & SPORT

Smith & Wesson Model 360 PD Airlite SC Chief's Special

Smith & Wesson Model 386 PD Airlite SC

Smith & Wesson Model 442

Smith & Wesson Model 696

Smith & Wesson Model 500

SMITH & WESSON MODEL 360 PD AIRLITE Sc CHIEF'S SPECIAL
Caliber: 357 Magnum, 38 Spec. +P, 5-shot. **Barrel:** 1-7/8". **Grips:** Rounded butt grip. **Sights:** Fixed. **Features:** Synthetic grip, internal lock. Stainless.
Price: Red ramp front **$767.00**
Price: HiViz front. **$781.00**

SMITH & WESSON MODEL 386 PD AIRLITE Sc
Caliber: 357 Magnum, 38 Spec. +P, 7-shot. **Barrel:** 2-1/2". **Grips:** Rounded butt grip. **Sights:** Adjustable, HiViz front. **Features:** Synthetic grip, internal lock.
Price: Blue **$815.00**

SMITH & WESSON MODEL 331, 332 AIRLITE Ti REVOLVERS
Caliber: 32 H&R Mag., 6-shot. **Barrel:** 1-7/8". **Weight:** 11.2 oz. (with wood grip). **Length:** 6-15/16" overall. **Grips:** Uncle Mike's Boot or Dymondwood Boot. **Sights:** Black serrated ramp front, fixed notch rear. **Features:** Aluminum alloy frame, barrel shroud and yoke; titanium cylinder; stainless steel barrel liner. Matte finish. Introduced 1999. Made in U.S.A. by Smith & Wesson.
Price: Model 331 Chiefs **$716.00**
Price: Model 332, internal lock **$734.00**

SMITH & WESSON MODEL 337 CHIEF'S SPECIAL AIRLITE Ti
Caliber: 38 Spec. +P, 5-shot. **Barrel:** 1-7/8". **Weight:** 11.2 oz. (Dymondwood grips). **Length:** 6-5/16" overall. **Grips:** Uncle Mike's Boot or Dymondwood Boot. **Sights:** Black serrated front, fixed notch rear. **Features:** Aluminum alloy frame, barrel shroud and yoke; titanium cylinder; stainless steel barrel liner. Matte finish. Introduced 1999. Made in U.S.A. by Smith & Wesson.
Price: **$716.00**

SMITH & WESSON MODEL 342 CENTENNIAL AIRLITE Ti
Caliber: 38 Spec. +P, 5-shot. **Barrel:** 1-7/8". **Weight:** 11.3 oz. (Dymondwood stocks). **Length:** 6-15/16" overall. **Grips:** Uncle Mike's Boot or Dymondwood Boot. **Sights:** Black serrated ramp front, fixed notch rear. **Features:** Aluminum alloy frame, barrel shroud and yoke; titanium cylinder; stainless steel barrel liner. Shrouded hammer. Matte finish. Internal lock. Introduced 1999. Made in U.S.A. by Smith & Wesson.
Price: **$734.00**

Smith & Wesson Model 442 Centennial Airweight
Similar to Model 640 Centennial, alloy frame giving weighs 15.8 oz. Chambered for 38 Special +P, 1-7/8" carbon steel barrel; carbon steel cylinder; concealed hammer; Uncle Mike's Boot grip. Fixed square notch rear sight, serrated ramp front. DA only, glass beaded finish. Introduced 1993.
Price: Blue **$547.00**

SMITH & WESSON MODEL 638 AIRWEIGHT BODYGUARD
Caliber: 38 Spec. +P, 5-shot. **Barrel:** 1-7/8". **Weight:** 15 oz. **Length:** 6-15/16" overall. **Grips:** Uncle Mike's Boot grip. **Sights:** Serrated ramp front, fixed notch rear. **Features:** Alloy frame, stainless cylinder and barrel; shrouded hammer. Glass beaded finish. Introduced 1997. Made in U.S.A. by Smith & Wesson.
Price: With Uncle Mike's Boot grip **$564.00**

Smith & Wesson Model 642 Airweight Revolver
Similar to Model 442 Centennial Airweight, stainless steel barrel, cylinder and yoke with matte finish; Uncle Mike's Boot Grip; DA only; weighs 15.8 oz. Introduced 1996. Made in U.S.A. by Smith & Wesson.
Price: **$571.00**

Smith & Wesson Model 642LS LadySmith Revolver
Same as Model 642 except has smooth combat wood grips, comes with deluxe soft case; Dymondwood grip; aluminum alloy frame, stainless cylinder, barrel and yoke; frosted matte finish. Weighs 15.8 oz. Introduced 1996. Made in U.S.A. by Smith & Wesson.
Price: 1-7/8" **$597.00**

SMITH & WESSON MODEL 649 BODYGUARD REVOLVER
Caliber: 357 Mag., 38 Spec. +P, 5-shot. **Barrel:** 2-1/8". **Weight:** 20 oz. **Length:** 6-5/16" overall. **Grips:** Uncle Mike's Combat. **Sights:** Black pinned ramp front, fixed notch rear. **Features:** Stainless steel construction; shrouded hammer; smooth combat trigger. Internal lock. Made in U.S.A. by Smith & Wesson.
Price: **$594.00**

SMITH & WESSON MODEL 657 REVOLVER
Caliber: 41 Mag., 6-shot. **Barrel:** 7-1/2" full lug. **Weight:** 48 oz. **Grips:** Soft rubber. **Sights:** Pinned 1/8" red ramp front, micro-click rear adjustable for windage and elevation. Target hammer, drilled and tapped, unfluted cylinder. **Features:** Stainless steel construction.
Price: **$706.00**

SMITH & WESSON MODEL 696 REVOLVER
Caliber: 44 Spec., 5-shot. **Barrel:** 3". **Weight:** 35.5 oz. **Length:** 8-1/4" overall. **Grips:** Uncle Mike's Combat. **Sights:** Red ramp front, click adjustable white outline rear. **Features:** Stainless steel construction; round butt frame; satin finish. Introduced 1997. Made in U.S.A. by Smith & Wesson.
Price: **$620.00**

SMITH & WESSON MODEL 500
Caliber: .50. **Barrel:** 8-3/8". **Weight:** 72.5 oz. **Length:** NA. **Grips:** Rubber. **Sights:** Interchangeable blade, front, adjustable rear. **Features:** Built on the massive, new X-Frame, recoil compensator, ball detent cylinder latch. Made in U.S.A. by Smith & Wesson.
Price: . . . . **NA**

HANDGUNS

16th EDITION • **181**

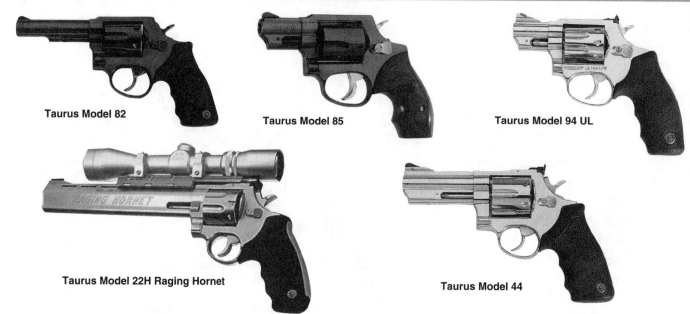

Taurus Model 82   Taurus Model 85   Taurus Model 94 UL

Taurus Model 22H Raging Hornet   Taurus Model 44

TAURUS SILHOUETTE REVOLVERS

Available in calibers from .22 LR through 454 Casull, the common trait is a 12" vent rib barrel. An optional arm support that wraps around the forearm is available.

Price: .... **$414.00 to $859.00**

TAURUS MODEL 17 "TRACKER"

Caliber: 17 HMR, 7-shot. **Barrel:** 6-1/2". **Weight:** 45.8 oz. **Grips:** Rubber. **Sights:** Adjustable. **Features:** Double action, matte stainless, integral key-lock.

Price: .... **$430.00 to $438.00**

TAURUS MODEL 17-12 TARGET "SILHOUETTE"

Caliber: 17 HMR, 7-shot. **Barrel:** 12". **Weight:** 57.8 oz. **Grips:** Rubber. **Sights:** Adjustable. **Features:** Vent rib, double action, adjustable main spring and trigger stop. Matte stainless, integral key-lock.

Price: **$430.00**

Taurus Model 17-C Series

Similar to the Models 17 Tracker and Silhouette series but 8-shot cylinder, 2", 4" or 5" barrel, blue or stainless finish and regular (24 oz.) or UltraLite (18.5 oz.) versions available. All models have target crown for enhanced accuracy.

Price: .... **$359.00 to $391.00**

TAURUS MODEL 63

Caliber: 22 LR, 10 + 1 shot. **Barrel:** 23". **Weight:** 97.9 oz. **Grips:** Premium hardwood. **Sights:** Adjustable. **Features:** Auto loading action, round barrel, manual firing pin block, integral security system lock, trigger guard mounted safety, blue or stainless finish.

Price: .... **$295.00 to $310.00**

TAURUS MODEL 65 REVOLVER

Caliber: 357 Mag., 6-shot. **Barrel:** 4". **Weight:** 38 oz. **Length:** 10-1/2" overall. **Grips:** Soft rubber. **Sights:** Fixed. **Features:** Double action, integral key-lock. Imported by Taurus International.

Price: Blue or matte stainless .... **$375.00 to $422.00**

Taurus Model 66 Revolver

Similar to Model 65, 4" or 6" barrel, 7-shot cylinder, adjustable rear sight. Integral key-lock action. Imported by Taurus International.

Price: Blue or matte stainless .... **$422.00 to $469.00**

Taurus Model 66 Silhouette Revolver

Similar to Model 6, 12" barrel, 7-shot cylinder, adjustable sight. Integral key-lock action, blue or matte stainless steel finish, rubber grips. Introduced 2001. Imported by Taurus International.

Price: .... **$414.00 to $461.00**

TAURUS MODEL 82 HEAVY BARREL REVOLVER

Caliber: 38 Spec., 6-shot. **Barrel:** 4", heavy. **Weight:** 36.5 oz. **Length:** 9-1/4" overall (4" bbl.). **Grips:** Soft black rubber. **Sights:** Serrated ramp front, square notch rear. **Features:** Double action, solid rib, integral key-lock. Imported by Taurus International.

Price: Blue or matte stainless .... **$352.00 to $398.00**

TAURUS MODEL 85 REVOLVER

Caliber: 38 Spec., 5-shot. **Barrel:** 2". **Weight:** 17-24.5 oz., titanium 13.5-15.4 oz. **Grips:** Rubber, rosewood or mother-of-pearl. **Sights:** Ramp front, square notch rear. **Features:** Blue, matte stainless, blue with gold accents, stainless with gold accents; rated for +P ammo. Integral key-lock. Introduced 1980. Imported by Taurus International.

Price: .... **$375.00 to $547.00**
Price: Total Titanium **$531.00**

TAURUS MODEL 94 REVOLVER

Caliber: 22 LR, 9-shot cylinder. **Barrel:** 2", 4", 5". **Weight:** 18.5-27.5 oz. **Grips:** Soft black rubber. **Sights:** Serrated ramp front, click-adjustable rear. **Features:** Double action, integral key-lock. Introduced 1989. Imported by Taurus International.

Price: Blue **$325.00**
Price: Matte stainless **$375.00**
Price: Model 94 UL, forged aluminum alloy, 18-18.5 oz. **$365.00**
Price: As above, stainless. **$410.00**

TAURUS MODEL 22H RAGING HORNET REVOLVER

Caliber: 22 Hornet, 8-shot. **Barrel:** 10". **Weight:** 50 oz. **Length:** 6.5" overall. **Grips:** Soft black rubber. **Sights:** Fully adjustable, scope mount base included. **Features:** Ventilated rib, stainless steel construction with matte finish. Double action, integral key-lock. Introduced 1999. Imported by Taurus International.

Price: **$898.00**

TAURUS MODEL 30C RAGING THIRTY

Caliber: 30 carbine, 8-shot. **Barrel:** 10". **Weight:** 72.3 oz. **Grips:** Soft black rubber. **Sights:** Adjustable. **Features:** Double action, ventilated rib, matte stainless, comes with five "Stellar" full-moon clips, integral key-lock.

Price: **$898.00**

TAURUS MODEL 44 REVOLVER

Caliber: 44 Mag., 6-shot. **Barrel:** 4", 6-1/2", 8-3/8". **Weight:** 44-3/4 oz. **Grips:** Rubber. **Sights:** Adjustable. **Features:** Double action. Integral key-lock. Introduced 1994. New Model 44S12 has 12" vent rib barrel. Imported from Brazil by Taurus International Manufacturing, Inc.

Price: Blue or stainless steel .... **$445.00 to $602.00**

Taurus Model 415

Taurus Model 608

Taurus Model 450

Taurus Model 454 Raging Bull

TAURUS MODEL 217 TARGET "SILHOUETTE"
Caliber: 218 Bee, 8-shot. **Barrel:** 12". **Weight:** 52.3 oz. **Grips:** Rubber. **Sights:** Adjustable. **Features:** Double action, ventilated rib, adjustable mainspring and trigger stop, matte stainless, integral key-lock.
Price: **$461.00**

TAURUS MODEL 218 RAGING BEE
Caliber: 218 Bee, 7-shot. **Barrel:** 10". **Weight:** 74.9 oz. **Grips:** Rubber. **Sights:** Adjustable rear. **Features:** Ventilated rib, adjustable action, matte stainless, integral key-lock. Also Available as Model 218SS6 Tracker with 6-1/2" vent rib barrel.
Price: . . . . (Raging Bee) **$898.00**
Price: . . . . (Tracker) **$406.00**

TAURUS MODEL 415 REVOLVER
Caliber: 41 Mag., 5-shot. **Barrel:** 2-1/2". **Weight:** 30 oz. **Length:** 7-1/8" overall. **Grips:** Rubber. **Sights:** Fixed. **Features:** Stainless steel construction; matte finish; ported barrel. Double action. Integral key-lock. Introduced 1999. Imported by Taurus International.
Price: **$508.00**
Price: Total Titanium **$602.00**

TAURUS MODEL 425/627 TRACKER REVOLVERS
Caliber: 357 Mag., 7-shot; 41 Mag., 5-shot. **Barrel:** 4" and 6". **Weight:** 28.8-40 oz. (titanium) 24.3-28. (6"). **Grips:** Rubber. **Sights:** Fixed front, adjustable rear. **Features:** Double action stainless steel, Shadow Gray or Total Titanium; vent rib (steel models only); integral key-lock action. Imported by Taurus International.
Price: . . . . **$508.00 to $516.00**
Price: Total Titanium **$688.00**

TAURUS MODEL 445
Caliber: 44 Special, 5-shot. **Barrel:** 2". **Weight:** 20.3-28.25 oz. **Length:** 6-3/4" overall. **Grips:** Rubber. **Sights:** Ramp front, notch rear. **Features:** Blue or stainless steel. Standard or DAO concealed hammer, optional porting. Introduced 1997. Imported by Taurus International.
Price: . . . . **$345.00 to $500.00**
Price: Total Titanium 19.8 oz. **$600.00**

TAURUS MODEL 455 "STELLAR TRACKER"
Caliber: 45 ACP, 5-shot. **Barrel:** 2", 4", 6". **Weight:** 28/33/38.4 oz. **Grips:** Rubber. **Sights:** Adjustable. **Features:** Double action, matte stainless, includes five "Stellar" full-moon clips, integral key-lock.
Price: **$523.00**

TAURUS MODEL 460 "TRACKER"
Caliber: 45 Colt, 5-shot. **Barrel:** 4" or 6". **Weight:** 33/38.4 oz. **Grips:** Rubber. **Sights:** Adjustable. **Features:** Double action, ventilated rib, matte stainless steel, comes with five "Stellar" full-moon clips.
Price: **$516.00**
Price: . . . . (Shadow gray, Total Titanium) **$688.00**

TAURUS MODEL 605 REVOLVER
Caliber: 357 Mag., 5-shot. **Barrel:** 2". **Weight:** 24 oz. **Grips:** Rubber. **Sights:** Fixed. **Features:** Double action, blue or stainless, concealed hammer models DAO, porting optional, integral key-lock. Introduced 1995. Imported by Taurus International.
Price: . . . . **$375.00 to $438.00**

Taurus Model 731 Revolver
Similar to the Taurus Model 605, except in .32 Magnum.
Price: . . . . **$438.00 to $531.00**

TAURUS MODEL 608 REVOLVER
Caliber: 357 Mag. 38 Spec., 8-shot. **Barrel:** 4", 6-1/2", 8-3/8". **Weight:** 44-57 oz. **Length:** 9-3/8" overall. **Grips:** Soft black rubber. **Sights:** Adjustable. **Features:** Double action, integral key-lock action. Available in blue or stainless. Introduced 1995. Imported by Taurus International.
Price: . . . . **$469.00 to $547.00**

Taurus Model 44 Series Revolver
Similar to Taurus Model 60 series, but in .44 Rem. Mag. With six-shot cylinder, blue and matte stainless finishes.
Price: . . . . **$500.00 to $578.00**

TAURUS MODEL 650CIA REVOLVER
Caliber: 357 Magnum, 5-shot. **Barrel:** 2". **Weight:** 24.5 oz. **Grips:** Rubber. **Sights:** Ramp front, square notch rear. **Features:** Double-action only, blue or matte stainless steel, integral key-lock, internal hammer. Introduced 2001. From Taurus International.
Price: . . . . **$406.00 to $453.00**

TAURUS MODEL 651 CIA REVOLVER
Caliber: 357 Magnum, 5-shot. **Barrel:** 2". **Weight:** 17-24.5 oz. **Grips:** Rubber. **Sights:** Fixed. **Features:** Concealed single action/double action design. Shrouded cockable hammer, blue, matte stainless, Shadow Gray, Total Titanium, integral key-lock. Made in Brazil. Imported by Taurus International Manufacturing, Inc.
Price: . . . . **$406.00 to $578.00**

TAURUS MODEL 450 REVOLVER
Caliber: 45 Colt, 5-shot. **Barrel:** 2". **Weight:** 21.2-22.3 oz. **Length:** 6-5/8" overall. **Grips:** Rubber. **Sights:** Ramp front, notch rear. **Features:** Double action, blue or stainless, ported, integral key-lock. Introduced 1999. Imported from Brazil by Taurus International.
Price: **$492.00**
Price: Ultra-Lite (alloy frame) **$523.00**
Price: Total Titanium, 19.2 oz. **$600.00**

TAURUS MODEL 444/454/480 RAGING BULL REVOLVERS
Caliber: 44 Mag., 45 LC, 454 Casull, 480 Ruger, 5-shot. **Barrel:** 5", 6-1/2", 8-3/8". **Weight:** 53-63 oz. **Length:** 12" overall (6-1/2" barrel). **Grips:** Soft black rubber. **Sights:** Patridge front, adjustable rear. **Features:** Double action, ventilated rib, ported, integral key-lock. Introduced 1997. Imported by Taurus International.
Price: Blue . . . . **$578.00 to $797.00**
Price: Matte stainless . . . . **$641.00 to $859.00**

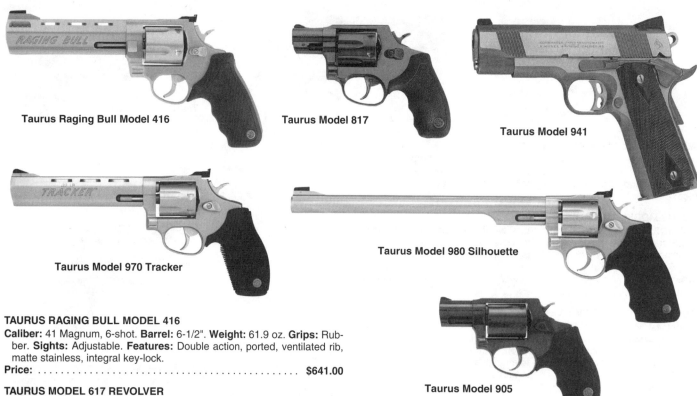

Taurus Raging Bull Model 416

Taurus Model 817

Taurus Model 941

Taurus Model 970 Tracker

Taurus Model 980 Silhouette

Taurus Model 905

TAURUS RAGING BULL MODEL 416
Caliber: 41 Magnum, 6-shot. **Barrel:** 6-1/2". **Weight:** 61.9 oz. **Grips:** Rubber. **Sights:** Adjustable. **Features:** Double action, ported, ventilated rib, matte stainless, integral key-lock.
Price: **$641.00**

TAURUS MODEL 617 REVOLVER
Caliber: 357 Magnum, 7-shot. **Barrel:** 2". **Weight:** 28.3 oz. **Length:** 6-3/4" overall. **Grips:** Soft black rubber. **Sights:** Fixed. **Features:** Double action, blue, shadow gray, bright spectrum blue or matte stainless steel, integral key-lock. Available with porting, concealed hammer. Introduced 1998. Imported by Taurus International.
Price: .... **$391.00 to $453.00**
Price: Total Titanium, 19.9 oz. **$602.00**

Taurus Model 445 Series Revolver
Similar to Taurus Model 617 series except in .44 Spl. with 5-shot cylinder.
Price: .... **$389.00 to $422.00**

Taurus Model 617ULT Revolver
Similar to Model 617 except aluminum alloy and titanium components, matte stainless finish, integral key-lock action. Weighs 18.5 oz. Available ported or non-ported. Introduced 2001. Imported by Taurus International.
Price: (5-shot cylinder) .... **$530.00 to $545.00**

TAURUS MODEL 817 ULTRA-LITE REVOLVER
Caliber: 38 Spec., 7-shot. **Barrel:** 2". **Weight:** 21 oz. **Length:** 6-1/2" overall. **Grips:** Soft rubber. **Sights:** Fixed. **Features:** Double action, integral key-lock. Rated for +P ammo. Introduced 1999. Imported from Brazil by Taurus International.
Price: Blue **$375.00**
Price: Blue, ported **$395.00**
Price: Matte, stainless. **$420.00**
Price: Matte, stainless, ported **$440.00**

TAURUS MODEL 850CIA REVOLVER
Caliber: 38 Special, 5-shot. **Barrel:** 2". **Weight:** 17-24.5 oz. **Grips:** Rubber. **Sights:** Ramp front, square notch rear. **Features:** Double action only, blue or matte stainless steel, rated for +P ammo, integral key-lock, internal hammer. Introduced 2001. From Taurus International.
Price: .... **$406.00 to $453.00**
Price: Total Titanium **$578.00**

TAURUS MODEL 851CIA REVOLVER
Caliber: 38 Spec., 5-shot. **Barrel:** 2". **Weight:** 17-24.5 oz. **Grips:** Rubber. **Sights:** Fixed-UL/ULT adjustable. **Features:** Concealed single action/double action design. Shrouded cockable hammer, blue, matte stainless, Total Titanium, blue or stainless UL and ULT, integral key-lock. Rated for +P ammo.
Price: .... **$406.00 to $578.00**

TAURUS MODEL 94, 941 REVOLVER
Caliber: 22 LR (Mod. 94), 22 WMR (Mod. 941), 8-shot. **Barrel:** 2", 4", 5". **Weight:** 27.5 oz. (4" barrel). **Grips:** Soft black rubber. **Sights:** Serrated ramp front, rear adjustable. **Features:** Double action, integral key-lock. Introduced 1992. Imported by Taurus International.
Price: Blue .... **$328.00 to $344.00**
Price: Stainless (matte) .... **$375.00 to $391.00**
Price: Model 941 Ultra Lite,
forged aluminum alloy, 2" .... **$359.00 to $375.00**
Price: As above, stainless. .... **$406.00 to $422.00**

TAURUS MODEL 970/971 TRACKER REVOLVERS
Caliber: 22 LR (Model 970), 22 Magnum (Model 971); 7-shot. **Barrel:** 6". **Weight:** 53.6 oz. **Grips:** Rubber. **Sights:** Adjustable. **Features:** Double barrel, heavy barrel with ventilated rib; matte stainless finish, integral key-lock. Introduced 2001. From Taurus International.
Price: .... **$391.00 to $406.00**

TAURUS MODEL 980/981 SILHOUETTE REVOLVERS
Caliber: 22 LR (Model 980), 22 Magnum (Model 981); 7-shot. **Barrel:** 12". **Weight:** 68 oz. **Grips:** Rubber. **Sights:** Adjustable. **Features:** Double action, heavy barrel with ventilated rib and scope mount, matte stainless finish, integral key-lock. Introduced 2001. From Taurus International.
Price: (Model 980) **$398.00**
Price: (Model 981) **$414.00**

TAURUS MODEL 905, 405, 455 PISTOL CALIBER REVOLVERS
Caliber: 9mm, .40, .45 ACP, 5-shot. **Barrel:** 2", 4", 6-1/2". **Weight:** 21 oz. to 40.8 oz. **Grips:** Rubber. **Sights:** Fixed, adjustable on Model 455SS6 in .45 ACP. **Features:** Produced as a backup gun for law enforcement officers who desire to carry the same caliber ammunition in their back-up revolver as they do in their service sidearm. Introduced 2003. Imported from Brazil by Taurus International Manufacturing, Inc.
Price: .... **$383.00 to $523.00**

Both classic six-shooters and modern adaptations for hunting and sport.

Century Model 100

Cimarron Lightning

Cimarron Model P

Cimarron Model P New Sheriff

Cimarron Bisley

Cimarron Roughrider

CABELA'S MILLENNIUM REVOLVER
Caliber: 45 Colt. **Barrel:** 4-3/4". **Weight:** NA. **Length:** 10" overall. **Grips:** Hardwood. **Sights:** Blade front, hammer notch rear. **Features:** Matte black finish; unpolished brass accents. Introduced 2001. From Cabela's.
Price: **$229.99**

CENTURY GUN DIST. MODEL 100 SINGLE-ACTION
Caliber: 30-30, 375 Win., 444 Marlin, 45-70, 50-70. **Barrel:** 6-1/2" (standard), 8", 10". **Weight:** 6 lbs. (loaded). **Length:** 15" overall (8" bbl.). **Grips:** Smooth walnut. **Sights:** Ramp front, Millett adjustable square notch rear. **Features:** Highly polished high tensile strength manganese bronze frame, blue cylinder and barrel; coil spring trigger mechanism. Contact maker for full price information. Introduced 1975. Made in U.S.A. From Century Gun Dist., Inc.
Price: 6-1/2" barrel, 45-70. . . . . **$2,000.00**

CIMARRON LIGHTNING SA
Caliber: 38 Colt, 38 Special. **Barrel:** 3-1/2", 4-3/4", 5-1/2". **Grips:** Smooth or checkered walnut. **Sights:** Blade front. **Features:** Replica of the Colt 1877 Lightning DA. Similar to Cimarron Thunderer™, except smaller grip frame to fit smaller hands. Standard blue, charcoal blue or nickel finish with forged, old model, or color case hardened frame. Introduced 2001. From Cimarron F.A. Co.
Price: . . . . **$489.00 to $554.00**

CIMARRON MODEL P
Caliber: 32 WCF, 38 WCF, 357 Mag., 44 WCF, 44 Spec., 45 Colt. **Barrel:** 4-3/4", 5-1/2", 7-1/2". **Weight:** 39 oz. **Length:** 10" overall (4" barrel). **Grips:** Walnut. **Sights:** Blade front, fixed or adjustable rear. **Features:** Uses "old model" blackpowder frame with "Bullseye" ejector or New Model frame. Imported by Cimarron F.A. Co.
Price: . . . . **$499.00 to $549.00**
Price: New Sheriff . . . . **$499.00 to $564.00**

Cimarron Bisley Model Single-Action Revolvers
Similar to 1873 Model P, special grip frame and trigger guard, knurled wide-spur hammer, curved trigger. Available in 357 Mag., 44 WCF, 44 Spl., 45 Colt. Introduced 1999. Imported by Cimarron F.A. Co.
Price: **$519.00**

Cimarron Flat Top Single-Action Revolvers
Similar to 1873 Model P, flat top strap with windage-adjustable rear sight, elevation-adjustable front sight. Available in 44 WCF, 45 Colt; 7-1/2" barrel. Introduced 1999. Imported by Cimarron F.A. Co.
Price: **$519.00**

CIMARRON MODEL "P" JR.
Caliber: 38 Special. **Barrel:** 3-1/2", 4-3/4", 5-1/2". **Grips:** Checkered walnut. **Sights:** Blade front. **Features:** Styled after 1873 Colt Peacemaker, except 20 percent smaller. Blue finish with color-case hardened frame; Cowboy Comp® action. Introduced 2001. From Cimarron F.A. Co.
Price: . . . . **$419.00 to $479.00**

CIMARRON ROUGHRIDER ARTILLERY MODEL SINGLE-ACTION
Caliber: 45 Colt. **Barrel:** 5-1/2". **Weight:** 39 oz. **Length:** 11-1/2" overall. **Grips:** Walnut. **Sights:** Fixed. **Features:** U.S. markings and cartouche, case-hardened frame and hammer; 45 Colt only. Imported by Cimarron F.A. Co.
Price: . . . . **$549.00 to $599.00**

Cimarron Thunderer

Colt Cowboy

Colt Single-Action Army

EAA Bounty Hunter

EMF Hartford

EMF 1894 Bisley

CIMARRON 1872 OPEN TOP REVOLVER
Caliber: 38, 44 Special, 45 S&W Schofield. **Barrel:** 5-1/2" and 7-1/2". **Grips:** Walnut. **Sights:** Blade front, fixed rear. **Features:** Replica of first cartridge-firing revolver. Blue, charcoal blue, nickel or Original® finish; Navy-style brass or steel Army-style frame. Introduced 2001 by Cimarron F.A. Co.
Price: .... **$529.00 to $599.00**

CIMARRON THUNDERER REVOLVER
Caliber: 357 Mag., 44 WCF, 44 Spl, 45 Colt, 6-shot. **Barrel:** 3-1/2", 4-3/4", 5-1/2", 7-1/2", with ejector. **Weight:** 38 oz. (3-1/2" barrel). **Grips:** Smooth walnut. **Sights:** Blade front, notch rear. **Features:** Thunderer grip; color case-hardened frame with balance blued. Introduced 1993. Imported by Cimarron F.A. Co.
Price: 3-1/2", 4-3/4", smooth grips .... **$519.00 to $549.00**
Price: As above, checkered grips .... **$564.00 to $584.00**
Price: 5-1/2", 7-1/2", smooth grips .... **$519.00 to $549.00**
Price: As above, checkered grips .... **$564.00 to $584.00**

COLT COWBOY SINGLE-ACTION REVOLVER
Caliber: 45 Colt, 6-shot. **Barrel:** 5-1/2". **Weight:** 42 oz. **Grips:** Black composition, first generation style. **Sights:** Blade front, notch rear. **Features:** Dimensional replica of Colt's original Peacemaker with medium-size color case-hardened frame; transfer bar safety system; half-cock loading. Introduced 1998. From Colt's Mfg. Co.
Price: About **$670.00**

COLT SINGLE-ACTION ARMY REVOLVER
Caliber: 44-40, 45 Colt, 6-shot. **Barrel:** 4-3/4", 5-1/2", 7-1/2". **Weight:** 40 oz. (4-3/4" barrel). **Length:** 10-1/4" overall (4-3/4" barrel). **Grips:** Black Eagle composite. **Sights:** Blade front, notch rear. **Features:** Available in full nickel finish with nickel grip medallions, or Royal Blue with color case-hardened frame, gold grip medallions. Reintroduced 1992.
Price: **$1,380.00**

EAA BOUNTY HUNTER SA REVOLVERS
Caliber: 22 LR/22 WMR, 357 Mag., 44 Mag., 45 Colt, 6-shot. **Barrel:** 4-1/2", 7-1/2". **Weight:** 2.5 lbs. **Length:** 11" overall (4-5/8" barrel). **Grips:** Smooth walnut. **Sights:** Blade front, grooved topstrap rear. **Features:** Transfer bar safety; three position hammer; hammer forged barrel. Introduced 1992. Imported by European American Armory.

Price: Blue or case-hardened............................ **$369.00**
Price: Nickel **$399.00**
Price: 22LR/22WMR, blue **$269.00**
Price: As above, nickel **$299.00**

EMF HARTFORD SINGLE-ACTION REVOLVERS
Caliber: 357 Mag., 32-20, 38-40, 44-40, 44 Spec., 45 Colt. **Barrel:** 4-3/4", 5-1/2", 7-1/2". **Weight:** 45 oz. **Length:** 13" overall (7-1/2" barrel). **Grips:** Smooth walnut. **Sights:** Blade front, fixed rear. **Features:** Identical to the original Colts with inspector cartouche on left grip, original patent dates and U.S. markings. All major parts serial numbered using original Colt-style lettering, numbering. Bullseye ejector head and color case-hardening on frame and hammer. Introduced 1990. From E.M.F.
Price: **$500.00**
Price: Cavalry or Artillery **$390.00**
Price: Nickel plated, add............................... **$125.00**
Price: Casehardened New Model frame................. **$365.00**

EMF 1894 Bisley Revolver
Similar to the Hartford single-action revolver except has special grip frame and trigger guard, wide spur hammer; available in 38-40 or 45 Colt, 4-3/4", 5-1/2" or 7-1/2" barrel. Introduced 1995. Imported by E.M.F.
Price: Casehardened/blue **$400.00**
Price: Nickel **$525.00**

EMF Hartford Pinkerton Single-Action Revolver
Same as the regular Hartford except has 4" barrel with ejector tube and birds head grip. Calibers: 357 Mag., 45 Colt. Introduced 1997. Imported by E.M.F.
Price: **$375.00**

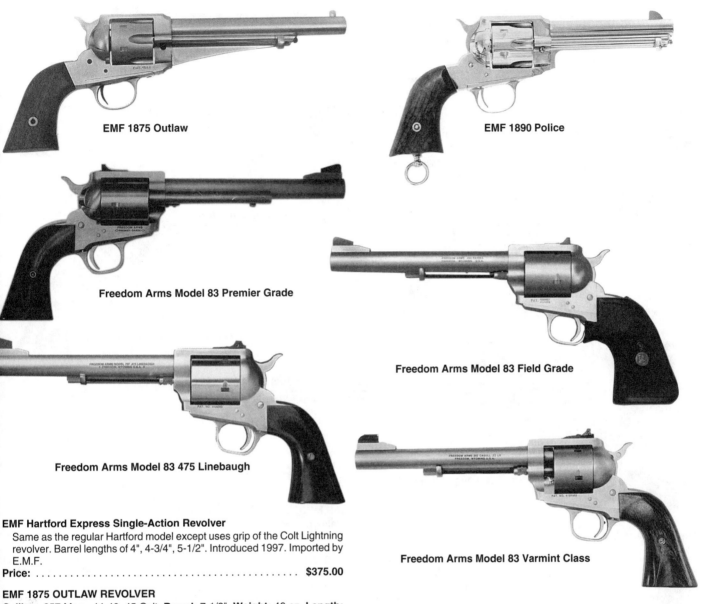

EMF 1875 Outlaw

EMF 1890 Police

Freedom Arms Model 83 Premier Grade

Freedom Arms Model 83 Field Grade

Freedom Arms Model 83 475 Linebaugh

Freedom Arms Model 83 Varmint Class

EMF Hartford Express Single-Action Revolver
 Same as the regular Hartford model except uses grip of the Colt Lightning revolver. Barrel lengths of 4", 4-3/4", 5-1/2". Introduced 1997. Imported by E.M.F.
Price: **$375.00**

EMF 1875 OUTLAW REVOLVER
Caliber: 357 Mag., 44-40, 45 Colt. **Barrel:** 7-1/2". **Weight:** 46 oz. **Length:** 13-1/2" overall. **Grips:** Smooth walnut. **Sights:** Blade front, fixed groove rear. **Features:** Authentic copy of 1875 Remington with firing pin in hammer; color case-hardened frame, blue cylinder, barrel, steel backstrap and brass trigger guard. Also available in nickel, factory engraved. Imported by E.M.F.
Price: All calibers **$575.00**
Price: Nickel **$735.00**

EMF 1890 Police Revolver
 Similar to the 1875 Outlaw except has 5-1/2" barrel, weighs 40 oz., with 12-1/2" overall length. Has lanyard ring in butt. No web under barrel. Calibers 357, 44-40, 45 Colt. Imported by E.M.F.
Price: All calibers **$590.00**
Price: Nickel **$750.00**

FREEDOM ARMS MODEL 83 PREMIER GRADE REVOLVER
Caliber: 357 Mag., 41 Mag., 44 Mag., 454 Casull, 475 Linebaugh, 50 AE, 5-shot. **Barrel:** 4-3/4", 6", 7-1/2", 9" (357 Mag. only), 10". **Weight:** 52.8 oz. **Length:** 13" (7-1/2" bbl.). **Grips:** Impregnated hardwood. **Sights:** Blade front, notch or adjustable rear. **Features:** All stainless steel construction; sliding bar safety system. Lifetime warranty. Made in U.S.A. by Freedom Arms, Inc.

Price: 454 Casull, 475 Linebaugh, 50 AE. **$2,058.00**
Price: 454 Casull, fixed sight **$1,979.00**
Price: 357 Mag., 41 Mag., 44 Mag. **$1,976.00**
Price: 44 Mag., fixed sight **$1,911.00**

Freedom Arms Model 83 Field Grade Revolver
 Model 83 frame. Weighs 52-56 oz. Adjustable rear sight, replaceable front blade, matte finish, Pachmayr grips. All stainless steel. Introduced 1988. Made in U.S.A. by Freedom Arms Inc.
Price: 454 Casull, 475 Linebaugh, 50 AE, adj. sights. **$1,591.00**
Price: 454 Casull, fixed sights. **$1,553.00**
Price: 357 Mag., 41 Mag., 44 Mag. **$1,527.00**

FREEDOM ARMS MODEL 83 VARMINT CLASS REVOLVERS
Caliber: 22 LR, 5-shot. **Barrel:** 5-1/8, 7-1/2". **Weight:** 58 oz. (7-1/2" bbl.). **Length:** 11-1/2" (7-1/2" bbl.). **Grips:** Impregnated hardwood. **Sights:** Steel base adjustable "V" notch rear sight and replaceable brass bead front sight. **Features:** Stainless steel, matte finish, manual sliding-bar system, dual firing pins, pre-set trigger stop. One year limited wararanty to original owner. Made in U.S.A. by Freedom Arms, Inc.
Price: Varmint Class **$1,828.00**
Price: Extra fitted 22 WMR cylinder **$264.00**

HANDGUNS — SINGLE ACTION REVOLVERS

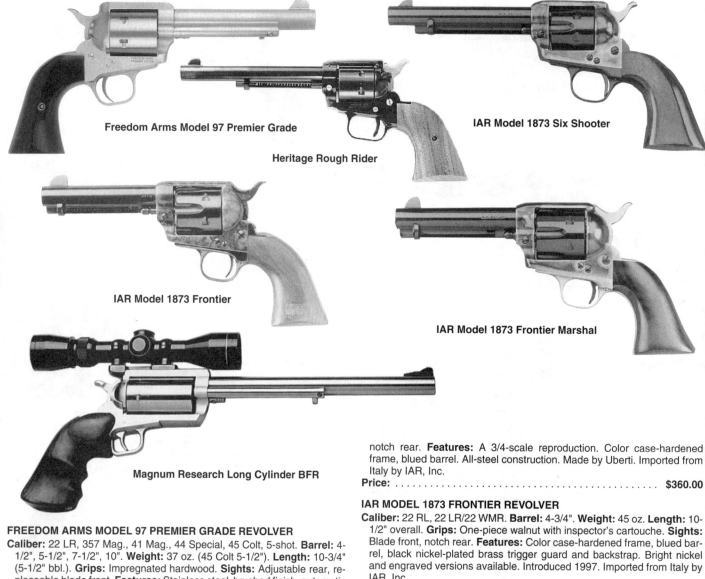

Freedom Arms Model 97 Premier Grade

Heritage Rough Rider

IAR Model 1873 Six Shooter

IAR Model 1873 Frontier

IAR Model 1873 Frontier Marshal

Magnum Research Long Cylinder BFR

FREEDOM ARMS MODEL 97 PREMIER GRADE REVOLVER
Caliber: 22 LR, 357 Mag., 41 Mag., 44 Special, 45 Colt, 5-shot. **Barrel:** 4-1/2", 5-1/2", 7-1/2", 10". **Weight:** 37 oz. (45 Colt 5-1/2"). **Length:** 10-3/4" (5-1/2" bbl.). **Grips:** Impregnated hardwood. **Sights:** Adjustable rear, replaceable blade front. **Features:** Stainless steel, brushed finish, automatic transfer bar safety system. Introduced in 1997. Made in U.S.A. by Freedom Arms.
Price: 357 Mag., 41 Mag., 45 Colt **$1,668.00**
Price: 357 Mag., 45 Colt, fixed sight **$1,576.00**
Price: Extra fitted cylinders 38 Special, 45 ACP **$264.00**
Price: 22 LR with sporting chambers **$1,732.00**
Price: Extra fitted 22 WMR cylinder **$264.00**
Price: Extra fitted 22 LR match grade cylinder **$476.00**
Price: 22 match grade chamber instead of 22 LR sport chamber
. . . . **$214.00**

HERITAGE ROUGH RIDER REVOLVER
Caliber: 22 LR, 22 LR/22 WMR combo, 6-shot. **Barrel:** 2-3/4", 3-1/2", 4-3/4", 6-1/2", 9". **Weight:** 31 to 38 oz. **Length:** NA. **Grips:** Exotic hardwood, laminated wood or mother of pearl; bird's head models offered. **Sights:** Blade front, fixed rear. Adjustable sight on 6-1/2" only. **Features:** Hammer block safety. High polish blue or nickel finish. Introduced 1993. Made in U.S.A. by Heritage Mfg., Inc.
Price: . . . . **$184.95 to $239.95**

IAR MODEL 1873 SIX SHOOTER
Caliber: 22 LR/22 WMR combo. **Barrel:** 5-1/2". **Weight:** 36-1/2" oz. **Length:** 11-3/8" overall. **Grips:** One-piece walnut. **Sights:** Blade front,

notch rear. **Features:** A 3/4-scale reproduction. Color case-hardened frame, blued barrel. All-steel construction. Made by Uberti. Imported from Italy by IAR, Inc.
Price: **$360.00**

IAR MODEL 1873 FRONTIER REVOLVER
Caliber: 22 RL, 22 LR/22 WMR. **Barrel:** 4-3/4". **Weight:** 45 oz. **Length:** 10-1/2" overall. **Grips:** One-piece walnut with inspector's cartouche. **Sights:** Blade front, notch rear. **Features:** Color case-hardened frame, blued barrel, black nickel-plated brass trigger guard and backstrap. Bright nickel and engraved versions available. Introduced 1997. Imported from Italy by IAR, Inc.
Price: **$380.00**
Price: Nickel-plated **$425.00**
Price: 22 LR/22WMR combo **$420.00**

IAR MODEL 1873 FRONTIER MARSHAL
Caliber: 357 Mag., 45 Colt. **Barrel:** 4-3/4", 5-1/2, 7-1/2". **Weight:** 39 oz. **Length:** 10-1/2" overall. **Grips:** One-piece walnut. **Sights:** Blade front, notch rear. **Features:** Bright brass trigger guard and backstrap, color case-hardened frame, blued barrel and cylinder. Introduced 1998. Imported from Italy by IAR, Inc.
Price: **$395.00**

MAGNUM RESEARCH BFR SINGLE-ACTION REVOLVER
(Long cylinder) Caliber: 45/70 Government, 444 Marlin, 45 LC/410, 450 Marlin, .500 S&W. **Barrel:** 7.5", 10". **Weight:** 4 lbs., 4.36 lbs. **Length:** 15", 17.5".
(Short cylinder) Caliber: 454 Casull, 22 Hornet, BFR 480/475. **Barrel:** 6.5", 7.5", 10". **Weight:** 3.2 lbs, 3.5 lbs., 4.36 lbs. (10"). **Length:** 12.75 (6"), 13.75", 16.25"
Sights: All have fully adjustable rear, black blade ramp front. **Features:** Stainless steel construction, rubber grips, all 5-shot capacity. Barrels are stress-relieved and cut rifled. Made in U.S.A. From Magnum Research, Inc.
Price: **$999.00**

HANDGUNS

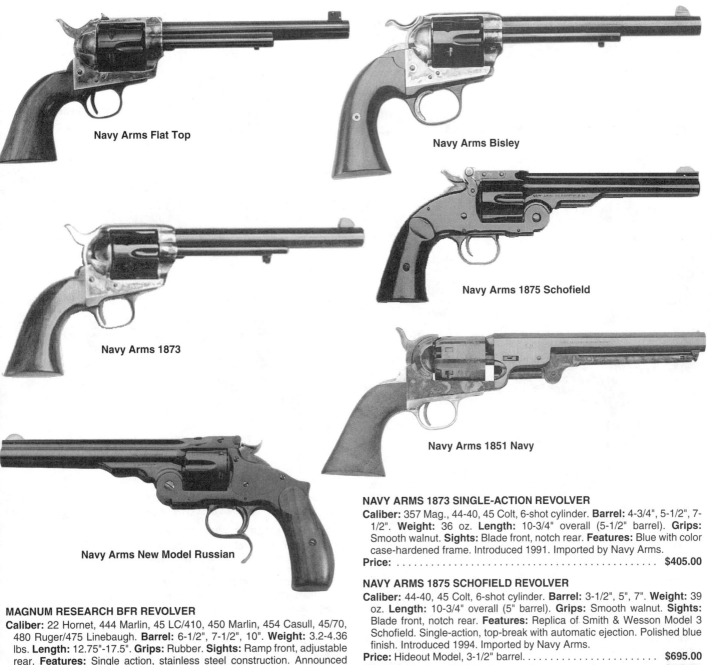

Navy Arms Flat Top

Navy Arms Bisley

Navy Arms 1873

Navy Arms 1875 Schofield

Navy Arms 1851 Navy

Navy Arms New Model Russian

MAGNUM RESEARCH BFR REVOLVER

Caliber: 22 Hornet, 444 Marlin, 45 LC/410, 450 Marlin, 454 Casull, 45/70, 480 Ruger/475 Linebaugh. **Barrel:** 6-1/2", 7-1/2", 10". **Weight:** 3.2-4.36 lbs. **Length:** 12.75"-17.5". **Grips:** Rubber. **Sights:** Ramp front, adjustable rear. **Features:** Single action, stainless steel construction. Announced 1998. Made in U.S.A. from Magnum Research.
Price: **$999.00**

NAVY ARMS FLAT TOP TARGET MODEL REVOLVER

Caliber: 45 Colt, 6-shot cylinder. **Barrel:** 7-1/2". **Weight:** 40 oz. **Length:** 13-1/4" overall. **Grips:** Smooth walnut. **Sights:** Spring-loaded German silver front, rear adjustable for windage. **Features:** Replica of Colt's Flat Top Frontier target revolver made from 1888 to 1896. Blue with color case-hardened frame. Introduced 1997. Imported by Navy Arms.
Price: **$450.00**

NAVY ARMS BISLEY MODEL SINGLE-ACTION REVOLVER

Caliber: 44-40 or 45 Colt, 6-shot cylinder. **Barrel:** 4-3/4", 5-1/2", 7-1/2". **Weight:** 40 oz. **Length:** 12-1/2" overall (7-1/2" barrel). **Grips:** Smooth walnut. **Sights:** Blade front, notch rear. **Features:** Replica of Colt's Bisley Model. Polished blue finish, color case-hardened frame. Introduced 1997. Imported by Navy Arms.
Price: . . . . **$425.00 to $460.00**

NAVY ARMS 1873 SINGLE-ACTION REVOLVER

Caliber: 357 Mag., 44-40, 45 Colt, 6-shot cylinder. **Barrel:** 4-3/4", 5-1/2", 7-1/2". **Weight:** 36 oz. **Length:** 10-3/4" overall (5-1/2" barrel). **Grips:** Smooth walnut. **Sights:** Blade front, notch rear. **Features:** Blue with color case-hardened frame. Introduced 1991. Imported by Navy Arms.
Price: **$405.00**

NAVY ARMS 1875 SCHOFIELD REVOLVER

Caliber: 44-40, 45 Colt, 6-shot cylinder. **Barrel:** 3-1/2", 5", 7". **Weight:** 39 oz. **Length:** 10-3/4" overall (5" barrel). **Grips:** Smooth walnut. **Sights:** Blade front, notch rear. **Features:** Replica of Smith & Wesson Model 3 Schofield. Single-action, top-break with automatic ejection. Polished blue finish. Introduced 1994. Imported by Navy Arms.
Price: Hideout Model, 3-1/2" barrel. **$695.00**
Price: Wells Fargo, 5" barrel **$695.00**
Price: U.S. Cavalry model, 7" barrel, military markings **$695.00**

NAVY ARMS NEW MODEL RUSSIAN REVOLVER

Caliber: 44 Russian, 6-shot cylinder. **Barrel:** 6-1/2". **Weight:** 40 oz. **Length:** 12" overall. **Grips:** Smooth walnut. **Sights:** Blade front, notch rear. **Features:** Replica of the S&W Model 3 Russian Third Model revolver. Spur trigger guard, polished blue finish. Introduced 1999. Imported by Navy Arms.
Price: **$769.00**

NAVY ARMS 1851 NAVY CONVERSION REVOLVER

Caliber: 38 Spec., 38 Long Colt. **Barrel:** 5-1/2", 7-1/2". **Weight:** 44 oz. **Length:** 14" overall (7-1/2" barrel). **Grips:** Smooth walnut. **Sights:** Bead front, notch rear. **Features:** Replica of Colt's cartridge conversion revolver. Polished blue finish with color case-hardened frame, silver plated trigger guard and backstrap. Introduced 1999. Imported by Navy Arms.
Price: **$165.00**

HANDGUNS — SINGLE ACTION REVOLVERS

Navy Arms 1860 Army

North American Mini

North American Mini-Master

North American Black Widow

Ruger "Bird's Head" Single Six

Ruger Blackhawk

Ruger SSMBH-4F

Ruger Bisley Single-Action

HANDGUNS

NAVY ARMS 1860 ARMY CONVERSION REVOLVER
Caliber: 38 Spec., 38 Long Colt. **Barrel:** 5-1/2", 7-1/2". **Weight:** 44 oz. **Length:** 13-1/2" overall (7-1/2" barrel). **Grips:** Smooth walnut. **Sights:** Blade front, notch rear. **Features:** Replica of Colt's conversion revolver. Polished blue finish with color case-hardened frame, full-size 1860 Army grip with blued steel backstrap. Introduced 1999. Imported by Navy Arms.
Price: **$190.00**

NORTH AMERICAN MINI REVOLVERS
Caliber: 22 Short, 22 LR, 22 WMR, 5-shot. **Barrel:** 1-1/8", 1-5/8". **Weight:** 4 to 6.6 oz. **Length:** 3-5/8" to 6-1/8" overall. **Grips:** Laminated wood. **Sights:** Blade front, notch fixed rear. **Features:** All stainless steel construction. Polished satin and matte finish. Engraved models available. From North American Arms.
Price: 22 Short, 22 LR . . . . **$186.00 to $221.00**
Price: 22 WMR, 1-1/8" or 1-5/8" bbl. **$205.00**
Price: 22 WMR, 1-1/8" or 1-5/8" bbl. with extra 22 LR cylinder. . . **$245.00**

NORTH AMERICAN MINI-MASTER
Caliber: 22 LR, 22 WMR, 17 HMR, 5-shot cylinder. **Barrel:** 4". **Weight:** 10.7 oz. **Length:** 7.75" overall. **Grips:** Checkered hard black rubber. **Sights:** Blade front, white outline rear adjustable for elevation, or fixed. **Features:** Heavy vent barrel; full-size grips. Non-fluted cylinder. Introduced 1989.
Price: Adjustable sight, 22 WMR, 17 HMR or 22 LR **$304.00**
Price: As above with extra WMR/LR cylinder **$343.00**
Price: Fixed sight, 22 WMR, 17 HMR or 22 LR **$286.00**
Price: As above with extra WMR/LR cylinder **$324.00**

North American Black Widow Revolver
Similar to Mini-Master, 2" heavy vent barrel. Built on 22 WMR frame. Non-fluted cylinder, black rubber grips. Available with Millett Low Profile fixed sights or Millett sight adjustable for elevation only. Overall length 5-7/8", weighs 8.8 oz. From North American Arms.
Price: Adjustable sight, 22 LR, 17 HMR or 22 WMR **$274.00**

Price: As above with extra WMR/LR cylinder **$312.00**
Price: Fixed sight, 22 LR, 17 HMR or 22 WMR **$256.00**
Price: As above with extra WMR/LR cylinder **$294.00**

RUGER NEW MODEL SINGLE SIX REVOLVER
Caliber: 32 H&R. **Barrel:** 4-5/8", 6-shot. **Grips:** Black Micarta "birds head", rosewood with color case. **Sights:** Fixed. **Features:** Instruction manual, high impact case, gun lock standard.
Price: Stainless, KSSMBH-4F, birds head **$576.00**
Price: Color case, SSMBH-4F, birds head **$576.00**
Price: Color case, SSM-4F-S, rosewood **$576.00**

RUGER NEW MODEL BLACKHAWK AND BLACKHAWK CONVERTIBLE
Caliber: 30 Carbine, 357 Mag./38 Spec., 41 Mag., 45 Colt, 6-shot. **Barrel:** 4-5/8" or 5-1/2", either caliber; 7-1/2" (30 Carbine and 45 Colt). **Weight:** 42 oz. (6-1/2" bbl.). **Length:** 12-1/4" overall (5-1/2" bbl.). **Grips:** American walnut. **Sights:** 1/8" ramp front, micro-click rear adjustable for windage and elevation. **Features:** Ruger transfer bar safety system, independent firing pin, hardened chrome-moly steel frame, music wire springs throughout. Case and lock included.
Price: Blue 30 Carbine, 7-1/2" (BN31) **$435.00**
Price: Blue, 357 Mag., 4-5/8", 6-1/2" (BN34, BN36) **$435.00**
Price: As above, stainless (KBN34, KBN36) **$530.00**
Price: Blue, 357 Mag./9mm Convertible, 4-5/8", 6-1/2" (BN34X, BN36X) includes extra cylinder **$489.00**
Price: Blue, 41 Mag., 4-5/8", 6-1/2" (BN41, BN42) **$435.00**
Price: Blue, 45 Colt, 4-5/8", 5-1/2", 7-1/2" (BN44, BN455, BN45) **$435.00**
Price: Stainless, 45 Colt, 4-5/8", 7-1/2" (KBN44, KBN45) **$530.00**
Price: Blue, 45 Colt/45 ACP Convertible, 4-5/8", 5-1/2" (BN44X, BN455X) includes extra cylinder **$489.00**

HANDGUNS — SINGLE ACTION REVOLVERS

Ruger Super Blackhawk Hunter

Ruger Vaquero

Ruger New Bearcat

Ruger Single-Six

Ruger Bisley-Vaquero

Ruger Bisley Single-Action Revolver

Similar to standard Blackhawk, hammer is lower with smoothly curved, deeply checkered wide spur. The trigger is strongly curved with wide smooth surface. Longer grip frame has hand-filling shape. Adjustable rear sight, ramp-style front. Unfluted cylinder and roll engraving, adjustable sights. Chambered for 357, 44 Mags. and 45 Colt; 7-1/2" barrel; overall length of 13"; weighs 48 oz. Plastic lockable case. Introduced 1985.
Price: RB-35W, 357Mag, RBD-44W, 44Mag, RB-45W, 45 Colt . . **$535.00**

RUGER NEW MODEL SUPER BLACKHAWK

Caliber: 44 Mag., 6-shot. Also fires 44 Spec. **Barrel:** 4-5/8", 5-1/2", 7-1/2", 10-1/2" bull. **Weight:** 48 oz. (7-1/2" bbl.), 51 oz. (10-1/2" bbl.). **Length:** 13-3/8" overall (7-1/2" bbl.). **Grips:** American walnut. **Sights:** 1/8" ramp front, micro-click rear adjustable for windage and elevation. **Features:** Ruger transfer bar safety system, fluted or un-fluted cylinder, steel grip and cylinder frame, round or square back trigger guard, wide serrated trigger, wide spur hammer. With case and lock.
Price: Blue, 4-5/8", 5-1/2", 7-1/2" (S458N, S45N, S47N) **$519.00**
Price: Blue, 10-1/2" bull barrel (S411N) **$529.00**
Price: Stainless, 4-5/8", 5-1/2", 7-1/2" (KS458N, KS45N, KS47N) **$535.00**
Price: Stainless, 10-1/2" bull barrel (KS411N) **$545.00**

RUGER NEW MODEL SUPER BLACKHAWK HUNTER

Caliber: 44 Mag., 6-shot. **Barrel:** 7-1/2", full-length solid rib, unfluted cylinder. **Weight:** 52 oz. **Length:** 13-5/8". **Grips:** Black laminated wood. **Sights:** Adjustable rear, replaceable front blade. **Features:** Reintroduced Ultimate SA revolver. Includes instruction manual, high-impact case, set 1" medium scope rings, gun lock, ejector rod as standard.
Price: $639.00

RUGER VAQUERO SINGLE-ACTION REVOLVER

Caliber: 357 Mag., 44-40, 44 Mag., 45 LC, 6-shot. **Barrel:** 4-5/8", 5-1/2", 7-1/2". **Weight:** 38-41 oz. **Length:** 13-1/8" overall (7-1/2" barrel). **Grips:** Smooth rosewood with Ruger medallion. **Sights:** Blade front, fixed notch rear. **Features:** Uses Ruger's patented transfer bar safety system and loading gate interlock with classic styling. Blued model color case-hardened finish on frame, rest polished and blued. Stainless has high-gloss. Introduced 1993. From Sturm, Ruger & Co.

Price: 357 Mag. BNV34, KBNV34 (4-5/8"), BNV35, KBNV35 (5-1/2") **$535.00**
Price: 44-40 BNV40, KBNV40 (4-5/8"). BNV405, KBNV405 (5-1/2"). BNV407, KBNV407 (7-1/2") **$535.00**
Price: 44 Mag., BNV474, KBNV474 (4-5/8"). BNV475, KBNV475 (5-1/2"). BNV477, KBNV477 (7-1/2") **$535.00**
Price: 45 LC, BN444, KBNV44 (4-5/8"). BNV455, KBNV455 (5-1/2"). BNV45, KBNV45 (7-1/2") **$535.00**
Price: 45 LC, BNVBH453, KBNVBH453 3-3/4" with "birds head" grip **$576.00**
Price: 357 Mag., RBNV35 (5-1/2") **$535.00**; KRBNV35 (5-1/2") . **$555.00**
Price: 45 LC, RBNV44 (4-5/8"), RBNV455 (5-1/2") **$535.00**
Price: 45 LC, KRBNV44 (4-5/8"), KRBNV455 (5-1/2") **$555.00**

Ruger Bisley-Vaquero Single-Action Revolver

Similar to Vaquero, Bisley-style hammer, grip and trigger, available in 357 Magnum, 44 Magnum and 45 LC only, 4-5/8" or 5-1/2" barrel. Smooth rosewood grips with Ruger medallion. Roll-engraved, unfluted cylinder. Introduced 1997. From Sturm, Ruger & Co.
Price: Color case-hardened frame, blue grip frame, barrel and cylinder, RBNV-475, RBNV-474, 44 Mag. **$535.00**
Price: High-gloss stainless steel, KRBNV-475, KRBNV-474 . . . . **$555.00**
Price: For simulated ivory grips add . . . . **$41.00 to $44.00**

RUGER NEW BEARCAT SINGLE-ACTION

Caliber: 22 LR, 6-shot. **Barrel:** 4". **Weight:** 24 oz. **Length:** 8-7/8" overall. **Grips:** Smooth rosewood with Ruger medallion. **Sights:** Blade front, fixed notch rear. **Features:** Reintroduction of the Ruger Bearcat with slightly lengthened frame, Ruger patented transfer bar safety system. Available in blue only. Introduced 1993. With case and lock. From Sturm, Ruger & Co.
Price: SBC4, blue **$379.00**
Price: KSBC-4, ss **$429.00**

RUGER MODEL SINGLE-SIX REVOLVER

Caliber: 32 H&R Magnum. **Barrel:** 4-5/8", 6-shot. **Weight:** 33 oz. **Length:** 10-1/8". **Grips:** Blue, rosewood, stainless, simulated ivory. **Sights:** Blade front, notch rear fixed. **Features:** Transfer bar and loading gate interlock safety, instruction manual, high impact case and gun lock.
Price: **$576.00**
Price: Blue, SSM4FS **$576.00**
Price: SS, KSSM4FSI **$576.00**

HANDGUNS

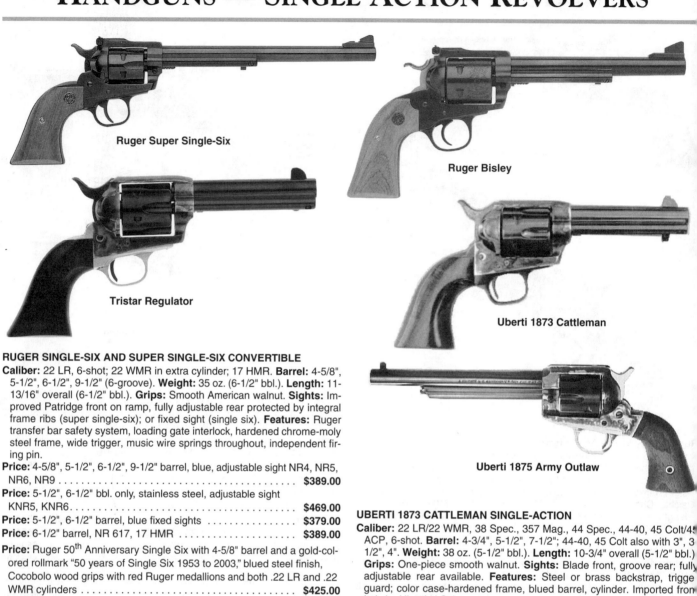

Ruger Super Single-Six

Tristar Regulator

Ruger Bisley

Uberti 1873 Cattleman

Uberti 1875 Army Outlaw

RUGER SINGLE-SIX AND SUPER SINGLE-SIX CONVERTIBLE
Caliber: 22 LR, 6-shot; 22 WMR in extra cylinder; 17 HMR. **Barrel:** 4-5/8", 5-1/2", 6-1/2", 9-1/2" (6-groove). **Weight:** 35 oz. (6-1/2" bbl.). **Length:** 11-13/16" overall (6-1/2" bbl.). **Grips:** Smooth American walnut. **Sights:** Improved Patridge front on ramp, fully adjustable rear protected by integral frame ribs (super single-six); or fixed sight (single six). **Features:** Ruger transfer bar safety system, loading gate interlock, hardened chrome-moly steel frame, wide trigger, music wire springs throughout, independent firing pin.
Price: 4-5/8", 5-1/2", 6-1/2", 9-1/2" barrel, blue, adjustable sight NR4, NR5, NR6, NR9 . . . . **$389.00**
Price: 5-1/2", 6-1/2" bbl. only, stainless steel, adjustable sight KNR5, KNR6. . . . . **$469.00**
Price: 5-1/2", 6-1/2" barrel, blue fixed sights **$379.00**
Price: 6-1/2" barrel, NR 617, 17 HMR **$389.00**
Price: Ruger 50th Anniversary Single Six with 4-5/8" barrel and a gold-colored rollmark "50 years of Single Six 1953 to 2003," blued steel finish, Cocobolo wood grips with red Ruger medallions and both .22 LR and .22 WMR cylinders **$425.00**

Ruger Bisley Small Frame Revolver
Similar to Single-Six, frame is styled after classic Bisley "flat-top." Most mechanical parts are unchanged. Hammer is lower and smoothly curved with deeply checkered spur. Trigger is strongly curved with wide smooth surface. Longer grip frame designed with hand-filling shape, and trigger guard is a large oval. Adjustable dovetail rear sight; front sight base accepts interchangeable square blades of various heights and styles. Unfluted cylinder and roll engraving. Weighs 41 oz. Chambered for 22 LR, 6-1/2" barrel only. Plastic lockable case. Introduced 1985.
Price: RB-22AW **$422.00**

SMITH & WESSON COMMEMORATIVE MODEL 2000
Caliber: 45 S&W Schofield. **Barrel:** 7". **Features:** 150th Anniversary logo, engraved, gold-plated, walnut grips, blue, original style hammer, trigger, and barrel latch. Wood presentation case. Limited.
Price: . . . . **NA**

TRISTAR/UBERTI REGULATOR REVOLVER
Caliber: 45 Colt. **Barrel:** 4-3/4", 5-1/2". **Weight:** 32-38 oz. **Length:** 8-1/4" overall (4-3/4" bbl.) **Grips:** One-piece walnut. **Sights:** Blade front, notch rear. **Features:** Uberti replica of 1873 Colt Model "P" revolver. Color-case hardened steel frame, brass backstrap and trigger guard, hammer-block safety. Imported from Italy by Tristar Sporting Arms.
Price: Regulator **$335.00**
Price: Regulator Deluxe (blued backstrap, trigger guard) **$367.00**

UBERTI 1873 CATTLEMAN SINGLE-ACTION
Caliber: 22 LR/22 WMR, 38 Spec., 357 Mag., 44 Spec., 44-40, 45 Colt/45 ACP, 6-shot. **Barrel:** 4-3/4", 5-1/2", 7-1/2"; 44-40, 45 Colt also with 3", 3 1/2", 4". **Weight:** 38 oz. (5-1/2" bbl.). **Length:** 10-3/4" overall (5-1/2" bbl.). **Grips:** One-piece smooth walnut. **Sights:** Blade front, groove rear; fully adjustable rear available. **Features:** Steel or brass backstrap, trigger guard; color case-hardened frame, blued barrel, cylinder. Imported from Italy by Uberti U.S.A.
Price: Steel backstrap, trigger guard, fixed sights **$410.00**
Price: Brass backstrap, trigger guard, fixed sights **$359.00**
Price: Bisley model. **$435.00**

Uberti 1873 Buckhorn Single-Action
A slightly larger version of the Cattleman revolver. Available in 44 Magnum or 44 Magnum/44-40 convertible, otherwise has same specs.
Price: Steel backstrap, trigger guard, fixed sights **$410.00**

UBERTI 1875 SA ARMY OUTLAW REVOLVER
Caliber: 357 Mag., 44-40, 45 Colt, 45 Colt/45 ACP convertible, 6-shot. **Barrel:** 5-1/2", 7-1/2". **Weight:** 44 oz. **Length:** 13-3/4" overall. **Grips:** Smooth walnut. **Sights:** Blade front, notch rear. **Features:** Replica of the 1875 Remington S.A. Army revolver. Brass trigger guard, color case-hardened frame, rest blued. Imported by Uberti U.S.A.
Price: **$483.00**
Price: 45 Colt/45 ACP convertible **$525.00**

UBERTI 1890 ARMY OUTLAW REVOLVER
Caliber: 357 Mag., 44-40, 45 Colt, 45 Colt/45 ACP convertible, 6-shot. **Barrel:** 5-1/2", 7-1/2". **Weight:** 37 oz. **Length:** 12-1/2" overall. **Grips:** American walnut. **Sights:** Blade front, groove rear. **Features:** Replica of the 1890 Remington single-action. Brass trigger guard, rest is blued. Imported by Uberti U.S.A.
Price: **$483.00**

HANDGUNS — SINGLE ACTION REVOLVERS

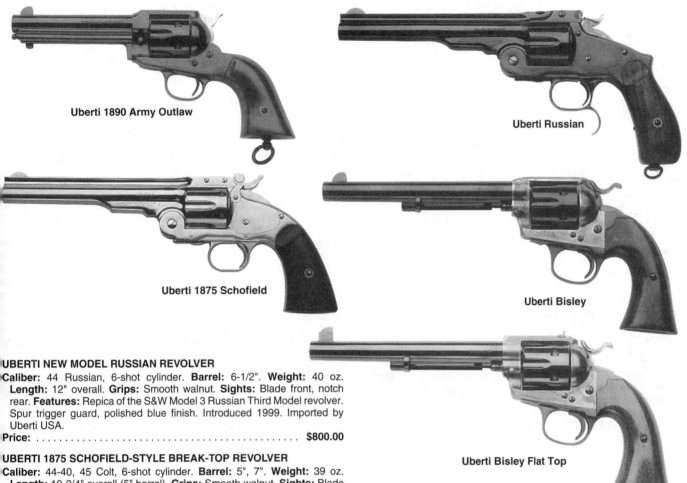

Uberti 1890 Army Outlaw

Uberti Russian

Uberti 1875 Schofield

Uberti Bisley

Uberti Bisley Flat Top

UBERTI NEW MODEL RUSSIAN REVOLVER
Caliber: 44 Russian, 6-shot cylinder. **Barrel:** 6-1/2". **Weight:** 40 oz. **Length:** 12" overall. **Grips:** Smooth walnut. **Sights:** Blade front, notch rear. **Features:** Repica of the S&W Model 3 Russian Third Model revolver. Spur trigger guard, polished blue finish. Introduced 1999. Imported by Uberti USA.
Price: **$800.00**

UBERTI 1875 SCHOFIELD-STYLE BREAK-TOP REVOLVER
Caliber: 44-40, 45 Colt, 6-shot cylinder. **Barrel:** 5", 7". **Weight:** 39 oz. **Length:** 10-3/4" overall (5" barrel). **Grips:** Smooth walnut. **Sights:** Blade front, notch rear. **Features:** Replica of Smith & Wesson Model 3 Schofield. Single-action, top-break with automatic ejection. Polished blue finish. Introduced 1994. Imported by Uberti USA.
Price: **$750.00**

UBERTI BISLEY MODEL SINGLE-ACTION REVOLVER
Caliber: 38-40, 357 Mag., 44 Spec., 44-40 or 45 Colt, 6-shot cylinder. **Barrel:** 4-3/4", 5-1/2", 7-1/2". **Weight:** 40 oz. **Length:** 12-1/2" overall (7-1/2" barrel). **Grips:** Smooth walnut. **Sights:** Blade front, notch rear. **Features:** Replica of Colt's Bisley Model. Polished blue finish, color case-hardened frame. Introduced 1997. Imported by Uberti USA.
Price: **$435.00**

Uberti Bisley Model Flat Top Target Revolver
Similar to standard Bisley model, flat top strap, 7-1/2" barrel only, spring-loaded German silver front sight blade, standing leaf rear sight adjustable for windage. Polished blue finish, color case-hardened frame. Introduced 1998. Imported by Uberti USA.
Price: **$435.00**

CONSULT

SHOOTER'S MARKETPLACE

Page 128, This Issue

U.S. FIRE-ARMS SINGLE ACTION ARMY REVOLVER
Caliber: 45 Colt (standard); .32 WCF, .38 WCF, .38 S&W, .41 Colt, .44WCF, .44 S&W (optional, additional charge), 6-shot cylinder. **Barrel:** 4-3/4", 5-1/2", 7-1/2". **Weight:** 37 oz. **Length:** NA. **Grips:** Hard rubber. **Sights:** Blade front, notch rear. **Features:** Recreation of original guns; 3" and 4" have no ejector. Available with all-blue, blue with color case-hardening, or full nickel-plate finish. Made in U.S.A. by United States Fire-Arms Mfg. Co.
Price: Blue/cased-colors............................... **$1,250.00**
Price: Carbonal blue/case-colors **$1,400.00**
Price: Nickel **$1,450.00**

U.S. Fire-Arms "China Camp" Cowboy Action Revolver
Similar to Single Action Army revolver, available in Silver Steel finish only. Offered in 4-3/4", 5-1/2", 7-1/2" barrels. Made in U.S.A. by United States Fire-Arms Mfg. Co.
Price: **$1,200.00**

U.S. FIRE-ARMS RODEO COWBOY ACTION REVOLVER
Caliber: 45 Colt. **Barrel:** 4-3/4", 5-1/2". **Grips:** Rubber. **Features:** Historically correct armory bone case hammer, blue satin finish, transfer bar safety system, correct solid firing pin. Entry level basic cowboy SASS gun for beginner or expert.
Price: **$550.00**

U.S. FIRE-ARMS UNITED STATES PRE-WAR
Caliber: .45 Colt, other caliber available. **Barrel:** 4-3/4", 5-1/2", 7-1/2". **Grips:** Hard rubber. **Features:** Armory bone case/Armory blue finish standard, cross-pin or black powder frame. Introduced 2002. Made in U.S.A. by United States Firearms Manufacturing Co.
Price: **$1,525.00**

HANDGUNS

Specially adapted single-shot and multi-barrel arms.

American Derringer Model 1

American Derringer Model 4

American Derringer Model 6

American Derringer Model 7

American Derringer Lady Derringer

American Derringer DA 38

AMERICAN DERRINGER MODEL 1

Caliber: 22 LR, 22 WMR, 30 Carbine, 30 Luger, 30-30 Win., 32 H&R Mag., 32-20, 380 ACP, 38 Super, 38 Spec., 38 Spec. shotshell, 38 Spec. +P, 9mm Para., 357 Mag., 357 Mag./45/410, 357 Maximum, 10mm, 40 S&W, 41 Mag., 38-40, 44-40 Win., 44 Spec., 44 Mag., 45 Colt, 45 Win. Mag., 45 ACP, 45 Colt/410, 45-70 single shot. **Barrel:** 3". **Weight:** 15-1/2 oz. (38 Spec.). **Length:** 4.82" overall. **Grips:** Rosewood, Zebra wood. **Sights:** Blade front. **Features:** Made of stainless steel with high-polish or satin finish. Two-shot capacity. Manual hammer block safety. Introduced 1980. Available in almost any pistol caliber. Contact the factory for complete list of available calibers and prices. From American Derringer Corp.

Price: 22 LR	$320.00
Price: 38 Spec.	$320.00
Price: 357 Maximum	$345.00
Price: 357 Mag.	$335.00
Price: 9mm, 380	$320.00
Price: 40 S&W	$335.00
Price: 44 Spec.	$398.00
Price: 44-40 Win.	$398.00
Price: 45 Colt	$385.00
Price: 30-30, 45 Win. Mag.	$460.00
Price: 41, 44 Mags.	$470.00
Price: 45-70, single shot	$387.00
Price: 45 Colt, 410, 2-1/2"	$385.00
Price: 45 ACP, 10mm Auto	$340.00

American Derringer Model 4

Similar to the Model 1 except has 4.1" barrel, overall length of 6", and weighs 16-1/2 oz.; chambered for 357 Mag., 357 Maximum, 45-70, 3" 410-bore shotshells or 45 Colt or 44 Mag. Made of stainless steel. Manual hammer block safety. Introduced 1980.

Price: 3" 410/45 Colt	$425.00
Price: 45-70	$560.00
Price: 44 Mag. with oversize grips	$515.00
Price: Alaskan Survival model (45-70 upper barrel, 410 or 45 Colt lower)	$475.00

American Derringer Model 6

Similar to the Model 1 except has 6" barrel chambered for 3" 410 shotshells or 22 WMR, 357 Mag., 45 ACP, 45 Colt; rosewood stocks; 8.2" o.a.l. and weighs 21 oz. Shoots either round for each barrel. Manual hammer block safety. Introduced 1980.

Price: 22 WMR	$440.00
Price: 357 Mag.	$440.00
Price: 45 Colt/410	$450.00
Price: 45 ACP	$440.00

American Derringer Model 7 Ultra Lightweight

Similar to Model 1 except made of high strength aircraft aluminum. Weighs 7-1/2 oz., 4.82" o.a.l., rosewood stocks. Available in 22 LR, 22 WMR, 32 H&R Mag., 380 ACP, 38 Spec., 44 Spec. Introduced 1980.

Price: 22 LR, WMR	$325.00
Price: 38 Spec.	$325.00
Price: 380 ACP	$325.00
Price: 32 H&R Mag/32 S&W Long	$325.00
Price: 44 Spec.	$565.00

American Derringer Model 10 Ultra Lightweight

Similar to the Model 1 except frame is of aluminum, giving weight of 10 oz. Stainless barrels. Available in 38 Spec., 45 Colt or 45 ACP only. Matte gray finish. Introduced 1980.

Price: 45 Colt	$385.00
Price: 45 ACP	$330.00
Price: 38 Spec.	$305.00

American Derringer Lady Derringer

Same as the Model 1 except has tuned action, is fitted with scrimshawed synthetic ivory grips; chambered for 32 H&R Mag. and 38 Spec.; 357 Mag., 45 Colt, 45/410. Deluxe Grade is highly polished; Deluxe Engraved is engraved in a pattern similar to that used on 1880s derringers. All come in a French fitted jewelry box. Introduced 1989.

Price: 32 H&R Mag.	$375.00
Price: 357 Mag.	$405.00
Price: 38 Spec.	$360.00
Price: 45 Colt, 45/410	$435.00

American Derringer Texas Commemorative

A Model 1 Derringer with solid brass frame, stainless steel barrel and rosewood grips. Available in 38 Spec., 44-40 Win., or 45 Colt. Introduced 1980.

Price: 38 Spec.	$365.00
Price: 44-40	$420.00
Price: Brass frame, 45 Colt	$450.00

AMERICAN DERRINGER DA 38 MODEL

Caliber: 22 LR, 9mm Para., 38 Spec., 357 Mag., 40 S&W. **Barrel:** 3". **Weight:** 14.5 oz. **Length:** 4.8" overall. **Grips:** Rosewood, walnut or other hardwoods. **Sights:** Fixed. **Features:** Double-action only; two-shots. Manual safety. Made of satin-finished stainless steel and aluminum. Introduced 1989. From American Derringer Corp.

Price: 22 LR	$435.00
Price: 38 Spec.	$460.00
Price: 9mm Para.	$445.00
Price: 357 Mag.	$450.00
Price: 40 S&W	$475.00

ANSCHUTZ MODEL 64P SPORT/TARGET PISTOL

Caliber: 22 LR, 22 WMR, 5-shot magazine. **Barrel:** 10". **Weight:** 3 lbs., 8 oz. **Length:** 18-1/2" overall. **Stock:** Choate Rynite. **Sights:** None furnished; grooved for scope mounting. **Features:** Right-hand bolt; polished blue finish. Introduced 1998. Imported from Germany by AcuSport.

Price: 22 LR	$455.95
Price: 22 WMR	$479.95

HANDGUNS — MISCELLANEOUS

Bond Arms Texas Defender

Bond Arms Century 2000 Defender

Cobra Big Bore

Cobra D-Series

Comanche Super Single Shot

Downsizer WSP Single Shot

IAR Model 1872 Derringer

Gaucher GN1 Silhouette

HANDGUNS

BOND ARMS DEFENDER DERRINGER

Caliber: 410 Buckshot or slug, 45 Colt/45 Schofield (2.5" chamber), 45 Colt (only), 450 Bond Super/45 ACP/45 Super, 44 Mag./44 Special/44 Russian, 10mm, 40 S&W, 357 SIG, 357 Maximum/357 Mag./38 Special, 357 Mag/38 Special & 38 Long Colt, 38 Short Colt, 9mm Luger (9x19), 32 H&R Mag./38 S&W Long/32 Colt New Police, 22 Mag., 22 LR., 38-40, 44-40. **Barrel:** 3", 3-1/2". **Weight:** 20-21 oz. **Length:** 5"-5-1/2". **Grips:** Exotic woods or animal horn. **Sights:** Blade front, fixed rear. **Features:** Interchangeable barrels, retracting and rebounding firing pins, cross-bolt safety, automatic extractor for rimmed calibers. Stainless steel construction. Right or left hand.
Price: Texas (with TG) 3" bbl. **$359.00**
Price: Super (with TG) 3" bbl., 450 Bond Super and 45 ACP . . . **$359.00**
Price: Cowboy (no TG) **$359.00**
Price: Century 2000 (with TG), Cowboy Century 2000 (no TG), 3-1/2" bbls., 410/45 Colt **$379.00**
Price: additional calibers available separately

BROWN CLASSIC SINGLE SHOT PISTOL

Caliber: 17 Ackley Hornet through 45-70 Govt. **Barrel:** 15" airgauged match grade. **Weight:** About 3 lbs., 7 oz. **Grips:** Walnut; thumbrest target style. **Sights:** None furnished; drilled and tapped for scope mounting. **Features:** Falling block action gives rigid barrel-receiver mating; hand-fitted and headspaced. Introduced 1998. Made in U.S.A. by E.A. Brown Mfg.
Price: **$499.00**

COBRA BIG BORE DERRINGERS

Caliber: 22 WMR, 38 Spec., 9mm Para. **Barrel:** 2.75". **Weight:** 11.5 oz. **Length:** 4.65" overall. **Grips:** Textured black synthetic. **Sights:** Blade front, fixed notch rear. **Features:** Alloy frame, steel-lined barrels, steel breech block. Plunger-type safety with integral hammer block. Chrome or black Teflon finish. Introduced 2002. Made in U.S.A. by Cobra Enterprises.
Price: **$98.00**
Price: 9mm Para **$104.00**

COBRA LONG-BORE DERRINGERS

Caliber: 22 WMR, 38 Spec., 9mm Para. **Barrel:** 3.5". **Weight:** 13 oz. **Length:** 5.65" overall. **Grips:** Textured black synthetic. **Sights:** Fixed. **Features:** Chrome or black Teflon finish. Larger than Davis D-Series models. Introduced 2002. Made in U.S.A. by Cobra Enterprises.
Price: **$104.00**
Price: 9mm Para. **$110.00**
Price: Big-Bore models (same calibers, 3/4" shorter barrels) **$98.00**

COBRA D-SERIES DERRINGERS

Caliber: 22 LR, 22 WMR, 25 ACP, 32 ACP. **Barrel:** 2.4". **Weight:** 9.5 oz. **Length:** 4" overall. **Grips:** Laminated wood or pearl. **Sights:** Blade front, fixed notch rear. **Features:** Choice of black Teflon or chrome finish; spur trigger. Introduced 2002. Made in U.S.A. by Cobra Enterprises.
Price: **$99.50**

COMANCHE SUPER SINGLE SHOT PISTOL

Caliber: 45 LC, 410 ga. **Barrel:** 10". **Sights:** Adjustable. **Features:** Blue finish, not available for sale in CA, MA. Distributed by SGS Importers International, Inc.
Price: **$174.95**
Price: Satin nickel **$191.95**
Price: Duo tone **$185.95**

DOWNSIZER WSP SINGLE SHOT PISTOL

Caliber: 357 Magnum, 45 ACP. **Barrel:** 2.10". **Weight:** 11 oz. **Length:** 3.25" overall. **Grips:** Black polymer. **Sights:** None. **Features:** Single shot, tip-up barrel. Double action only. Stainless steel construction. Measures .900" thick. Introduced 1997. From Downsizer Corp.
Price: **$499.00**

GAUCHER GN1 SILHOUETTE PISTOL

Caliber: 22 LR, single shot. **Barrel:** 10". **Weight:** 2.4 lbs. **Length:** 15.5" overall. **Grips:** European hardwood. **Sights:** Blade front, open adjustable rear. **Features:** Bolt action, adjustable trigger. Introduced 1990. Imported from France by Mandall Shooting Supplies.
Price: About **$525.00**
Price: Model GP Silhouette **$425.00**

IAR MODEL 1872 DERRINGER

Caliber: 22 Short. **Barrel:** 2-3/8". **Weight:** 7 oz. **Length:** 5-1/8" overall. **Grips:** Smooth walnut. **Sights:** Blade front, notch rear. **Features:** Gold or nickel frame with blue barrel. Reintroduced 1996 using original Colt designs and tooling for the Colt Model 4 Derringer. Made in U.S.A. by IAR, Inc.
Price: **$109.00**
Price: Single cased gun **$125.00**
Price: Double cased set **$215.00**

IAR MODEL 1866 DOUBLE DERRINGER

Caliber: 38 Special. **Barrel:** 2-3/4". **Weight:** 16 oz. **Grips:** Smooth walnut. **Sights:** Blade front, notch rear. **Features:** All steel construction. Blue barrel, color case-hardened frame. Uses original designs and tooling for the Uberti New Maverick Derringer. Introduced 1999. Made in U.S.A. by IAR, Inc.
Price: **$395.00**

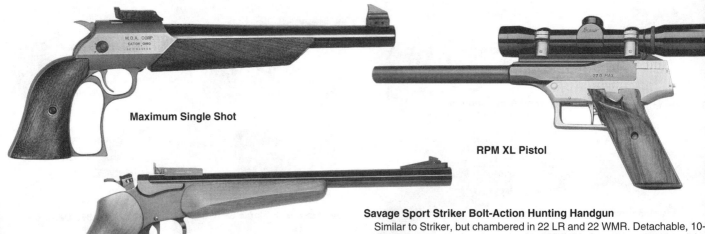

Maximum Single Shot

RPM XL Pistol

Thompson/Center C2 Contender

MAXIMUM SINGLE SHOT PISTOL
Caliber: 22 LR, 22 Hornet, 22 BR, 22 PPC, 223 Rem., 22-250, 6mm BR, 6mm PPC, 243, 250 Savage, 6.5mm-35M, 270 MAX, 270 Win., 7mm TCU, 7mm BR, 7mm-35, 7mm INT-R, 7mm-08, 7mm Rocket, 7mm Super-Mag., 30 Herrett, 30 Carbine, 30-30, 308 Win., 30x39, 32-20, 350 Rem. Mag., 357 Mag., 357 Maximum, 358 Win., 375 H&H, 44 Mag., 454 Casull. **Barrel:** 8-3/4", 10-1/2", 14". **Weight:** 61 oz. (10-1/2" bbl.); 78 oz. (14" bbl.). **Length:** 15", 18-1/2" overall (with 10-1/2" and 14" bbl., respectively). **Grips:** Smooth walnut stocks and forend. Also available with 17" finger groove grip. **Sights:** Ramp front, fully adjustable open rear. **Features:** Falling block action; drilled and tapped for M.O.A. scope mounts; integral grip frame/receiver; adjustable trigger; Douglas barrel (interchangeable). Introduced 1983. Made in U.S.A. by M.O.A. Corp.

Price: Stainless receiver, blue barrel **$799.00**
Price: Stainless receiver, stainless barrel **$883.00**
Price: Extra blued barrel **$254.00**
Price: Extra stainless barrel **$317.00**
Price: Scope mount **$60.00**

RPM XL SINGLE SHOT PISTOL
Caliber: 22 LR through 45-70. **Barrel:** 8", 10-3/4", 12", 14". **Weight:** About 60 oz. **Grips:** Smooth Goncalo Alves with thumb and heel rests. **Sights:** Hooded front with interchangeable post, or Patridge; ISGW rear adjustable for windage and elevation. **Features:** Barrel drilled and tapped for scope mount. Visible cocking indicator. Spring-loaded barrel lock, positive hammer-block safety. Trigger adjustable for weight of pull and over-travel. Contact maker for complete price list. Made in U.S.A. by RPM.

Price: XL Hunter model (action only) **$1,045.00**
Price: Extra barrel, 8" through 10-3/4" **$407.50**
Price: Extra barrel, 12" through 14" **$547.50**
Price: Muzzle brake **$160.00**
Price: Left hand action, add **$50.00**

SAVAGE STRIKER BOLT-ACTION HUNTING HANDGUN
Caliber: 223, 243, 7mm-08, 308, 300 WSM 2-shot mag. **Barrel:** 14". **Weight:** About 5 lbs. **Length:** 22-1/2" overall. **Stock:** Black composite ambidextrous mid-grip; grooved forend; "Dual Pillar" bedding. **Sights:** None furnished; drilled and tapped for scope mounting. **Features:** Short left-hand bolt with right-hand ejection; free-floated barrel; uses Savage Model 110 rifle scope rings/bases. Introduced 1998. Made in U.S.A. by Savage Arms, Inc.

Price: Model 510F (blued barrel and action). **$425.00**
Price: Model 516FSS (stainless barrel and action) **$462.00**
Price: Model 516FSAK (stainless, adjustable muzzle brake) . . . **$512.00**
Price: Model 516FSAK black stock (ss, aMB, 300WSM) **$588.00**

Savage Sport Striker Bolt-Action Hunting Handgun
Similar to Striker, but chambered in 22 LR and 22 WMR. Detachable, 10-shot magazine (5-shot magazine for 22 WMR). Overall length 19", weighs 4 lbs. Ambidextrous fiberglass/graphite composite rear grip. Drilled and tapped, scope mount installed. Introduced 2000. Made in U.S.A. by Savage Arms Inc.

Price: Model 501F (blue finish, 22LR) **$216.00**
Price: Model 501FXP with soft case, 1.25-4x28 scope **$258.00**
Price: Model 502F (blue finish, 22 WMR) **$238.00**

SPRINGFIELD M6 SCOUT PISTOL
Caliber: 22 LR/45 LC/.410, 22 Hornet, 45 LC/.410, **Barrel:** 10". **Weight:** NA. **Length:** NA. **Grip:** NA. **Sights:** NA. **Features:** Adapted from the U.S. Air Force M6 Survival Rifle, it is also available as a carbine with 16" barrel.
Price: . . . . **$169.00 to $197.00**
Price: Pistol/Carbine . . . . **$183.00 to $209.00**

THOMPSON/CENTER ENCORE PISTOL
Caliber: 22-250, 223, 260 Rem., 7mm-08, 243, 308, 270, 30-06, 44 Mag., 454 Casull, 480 Ruger, 444 Marlin single shot, 450 Marlin with muzzle tamer, no sights. **Barrel:** 12", 15", tapered round. **Weight:** NA. **Length:** 21" overall with 12" barrel. **Grips:** American walnut with finger grooves, walnut forend. **Sights:** Blade on ramp front, adjustable rear, or none. **Features:** Interchangeable barrels; action opens by squeezing the trigger guard; drilled and tapped for scope mounting; blue finish. Announced 1996. Made in U.S.A. by Thompson/Center Arms.

Price: . . . . **$582.00 to $588.00**
Price: Extra 12" barrels. **$258.00**
Price: Extra 15" barrels. **$263.00**
Price: 45 Colt/410 barrel, 12" **$282.00**
Price: 45 Colt/410 barrel, 15" **$297.00**

Thompson/Center Stainless Encore Pistol
Similar to blued Encore, made of stainless steel, available with 15" barrel in 223, 22-250, 243 Win., 7mm-08, 308, 30/06 Sprgfld., 45/70 Gov't., 45/410 VR. With black rubber grip and forend. Made in U.S.A. by Thompson/Center Arms.

Price: . . . . **$622.00 to $644.00**

Thompson/Center G2 Contender Pistol
A second generation Contender pistol maintaining the same barrel interchangeability with older Contender barrels and their corresponding forends (except Herrett forend). The G2 frame will not accept old-style grips due to the change in grip angle. Incorporates an automatic hammer block safety with built-in interlock. Features include trigger adjustable for overtravel, adjustable rear sight; ramp front sight blade, blued steel finish.
Price: **$566.75**

UBERTI ROLLING BLOCK TARGET PISTOL
Caliber: 22 LR, 22 WMR, 22 Hornet, 357 Mag., 45 Colt, single shot. **Barrel:** 9-7/8", half-round, half-octagon. **Weight:** 44 oz. **Length:** 14" overall. **Stock:** Walnut grip and forend. **Sights:** Blade front, fully adjustable rear. **Features:** Replica of the 1871 rolling block target pistol. Brass trigger guard, color case-hardened frame, blue barrel. Imported by Uberti U.S.A.
Price: **$410.00**

HANDGUNS

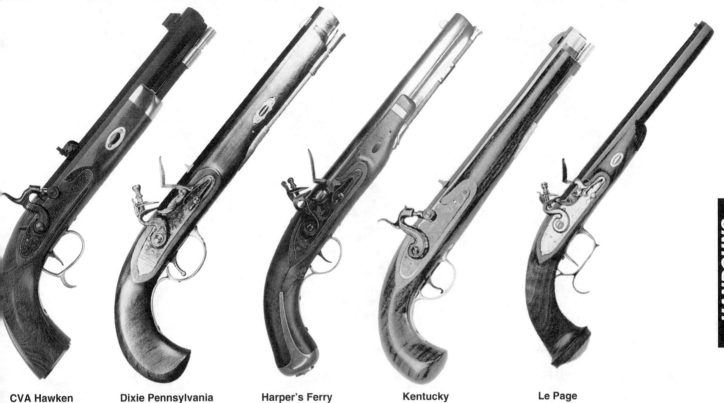

| CVA Hawken | Dixie Pennsylvania | Harper's Ferry | Kentucky | Le Page |

CVA HAWKEN PISTOL

Caliber: 50. **Barrel:** 9-3/4"; 15/16" flats. **Weight:** 50 oz. **Length:** 16-1/2" overall. **Stocks:** Select hardwood. **Sights:** Beaded blade front, fully adjustable open rear. **Features:** Color case-hardened lock, polished brass wedge plate, instep, ramrod thimble, trigger guard, grip cap. Imported by CVA.

Price: **$167.95**
Price: Kit **$127.95**

DIXIE PENNSYLVANIA PISTOL

Caliber: 44 (.430" round ball). **Barrel:** 10", (7/8" octagon). **Weight:** 2-1/2 labs. **Stocks:** Walnut-stained hardwood. **Sights:** Blade front, open rear drift-adjustable for windage; brass. **Features:** Available in flint only. Brass trigger guard, thimbles, instep, wedge plates; high-luster blue barrel. Imported from Italy by Dixie Gun Works.

Price: Finished **$215.00**
Price: Kit **$195.00**

FRENCH-STYLE DUELING PISTOL

Caliber: 44. **Barrel:** 10". **Weight:** 35 oz. **Length:** 15-3/4" overall. **Stocks:** Carved walnut. **Sights:** Fixed. **Features:** Comes with velvet-lined case and accessories. Imported by Mandall Shooting Supplies.

Price: **$295.00**

HARPER'S FERRY 1806 PISTOL

Caliber: 58 (.570" round ball). **Barrel:** 10". **Weight:** 40 oz. **Length:** 16" overall. **Stocks:** Walnut. **Sights:** Fixed. **Features:** Case-hardened lock, brass-mounted browned barrel. Replica of the first U.S. Gov't.-made flintlock pistol. Imported by Navy Arms, Dixie Gun Works.

Price: .... **$275.00 to $405.00**
Price: Kit (Dixie) **$249.00**

KENTUCKY FLINTLOCK PISTOL

Caliber: 44, 45. **Barrel:** 10-1/8". **Weight:** 32 oz. **Length:** 15-1/2" overall. **Stocks:** Walnut. **Sights:** Fixed. **Features:** Specifications, including caliber, weight and length may vary with importer. Case-hardened lock, blued barrel; available also as brass barrel flint Model 1821. Imported by Navy Arms, The Armoury, Dixie Gun Works.

Price: **$300.00**

Price: In kit form, from .... **$90.00 to $112.00**
Price: Single cased set (Navy Arms) **$360.00**
Price: Double cased set (Navy Arms) **$590.00**

Kentucky Percussion Pistol

Similar to flint version but percussion lock. Imported by The Armoury, Navy Arms, CVA (50-cal.).

Price: .... **$129.95 to $225.00**
Price: Blued steel barrel (CVA) **$167.95**
Price: Kit form (CVA) **$119.95**
Price: Steel barrel (Armoury) **$179.00**
Price: Single cased set (Navy Arms) **$355.00**
Price: Double cased set (Navy Arms) **$600.00**

LE PAGE PERCUSSION DUELING PISTOL

Caliber: 44. **Barrel:** 10", rifled. **Weight:** 40 oz. **Length:** 16" overall. **Stocks:** Walnut, fluted butt. **Sights:** Blade front, notch rear. **Features:** Double-set triggers. Blued barrel; trigger guard and buttcap are polished silver. Imported by Dixie Gun Works.

Price: **$450.00**

LYMAN PLAINS PISTOL

Caliber: 50 or 54. **Barrel:** 8"; 1:30" twist, both calibers. **Weight:** 50 oz. **Length:** 15" overall. **Stocks:** Walnut half-stock. **Sights:** Blade front, square notch rear adjustable for windage. **Features:** Polished brass trigger guard and ramrod tip, color case-hardened coil spring lock, spring-loaded trigger, stainless steel nipple, blackened iron furniture. Hooked patent breech, detachable belt hook. Introduced 1981. From Lyman Products.

Price: Finished **$244.95**
Price: Kit **$189.95**

PEDERSOLI MANG TARGET PISTOL

Caliber: 38. **Barrel:** 10.5", octagonal; 1:15" twist, **Weight:** 2.5 lbs. **Length:** 17.25" overall. **Stocks:** Walnut with fluted grip. **Sights:** Blade front, open rear adjustable for windage. **Features:** Browned barrel, polished breech plug, rest color case-hardened. Imported from Italy by Dixie Gun Works.

Price: **$895.00**

Lyman Plains Pistol   Pedersoli Mang   Queen Anne   Thompson/Center Encore   Traditions Pioneer   Traditions William Parker

QUEEN ANNE FLINTLOCK PISTOL

Caliber: 50 (.490" round ball). **Barrel:** 7-1/2", smoothbore. **Stocks:** Walnut. **Sights:** None. **Features:** Browned steel barrel, fluted brass trigger guard, brass mask on butt. Lockplate left in the white. Made by Pedersoli in Italy. Introduced 1983. Imported by Dixie Gun Works.

Price: **$245.00**
Price: Kit **$195.00**

THOMPSON/CENTER ENCORE 209x50 MAGNUM PISTOL

Caliber: 50. **Barrel:** 15"; 1:20" twist. **Weight:** About 4 lbs. Grips: American walnut grip and forend. **Sights:** Click-adjustable, steel rear, ramp front. **Features:** Uses 209 shotgun primer for closed-breech ignition; accepts charges up to 110 grains of FFg black powder or two, 50-grain Pyrodex pellets. Introduced 2000.

Price: **$611.00**
Price: (barrel only) **$325.00**

TRADITIONS BUCKHUNTER PRO IN-LINE PISTOL

Caliber: 50. **Barrel:** 9-1/2", round. **Weight:** 48 oz. **Length:** 14" overall. **Stocks:** Smooth walnut or black epoxy-coated hardwood grip and forend. **Sights:** Beaded blade front, folding adjustable rear. **Features:** Thumb safety; removable stainless steel breech plug; adjustable trigger, barrel drilled and tapped for scope mounting. From Traditions.

Price: With walnut grip **$229.00**
Price: Nickel with black grip **$239.00**
Price: With walnut grip and 12-1/2" barrel **$239.00**
Price: Nickel with black grip, muzzle brake and 14-3/4" fluted barrel. **$289.00**
Price: 45 cal. nickel w/bl. grip, muzzlebrake and 14-3/4" fluted bbl. **$289.00**

TRADITIONS KENTUCKY PISTOL

Caliber: 50. **Barrel:** 10"; octagon with 7/8" flats; 1:20" twist. **Weight:** 40 oz. **Length:** 15" overall. **Stocks:** Stained beech. **Sights:** Blade front, fixed rear. **Features:** Birds-head grip; brass thimbles; color case-hardened lock. Percussion only. Introduced 1995. From Traditions.

Price: Finished **$139.00**
Price: Kit. **$109.00**

TRADITIONS PIONEER PISTOL

Caliber: 45. **Barrel:** 9-5/8"; 13/16" flats, 1:16" twist. **Weight:** 31 oz. **Length:** 15" overall. **Stocks:** Beech. **Sights:** Blade front, fixed rear. **Features:**

Traditions Buckhunter Pro

V-type mainspring. Single trigger. German silver furniture, blackened hardware. From Traditions.

Price: **$139.00**
Price: Kit. **$119.00**

TRADITIONS TRAPPER PISTOL

Caliber: 50. **Barrel:** 9-3/4"; 7/8" flats; 1:20" twist. **Weight:** 2-3/4 lbs. **Length:** 16" overall. **Stocks:** Beech. **Sights:** Blade front, adjustable rear. **Features:** Double-set triggers; brass buttcap, trigger guard, wedge plate, forend tip, thimble. From Traditions.

Price: Percussion **$189.00**
Price: Flintlock **$209.00**
Price: Kit. **$149.00**

TRADITIONS VEST-POCKET DERRINGER

Caliber: 31. **Barrel:** 2-1/4"; brass. **Weight:** 8 oz. **Length:** 4-3/4" overall. **Stocks:** Simulated ivory. **Sights:** Beed front. **Features:** Replica of riverboat gamblers' derringer; authentic spur trigger. From Traditions.

Price: **$109.00**

TRADITIONS WILLIAM PARKER PISTOL

Caliber: 50. **Barrel:** 10-3/8"; 15/16" flats; polished steel. **Weight:** 37 oz. **Length:** 17-1/2" overall. **Stocks:** Walnut with checkered grip. **Sights:** Brass blade front, fixed rear. **Features:** Replica dueling pistol with 1:20" twist, hooked breech. Brass wedge plate, trigger guard, cap guard; separate ramrod. Double-set triggers. Polished steel barrel, lock. Imported by Traditions.

Price: **$269.00**

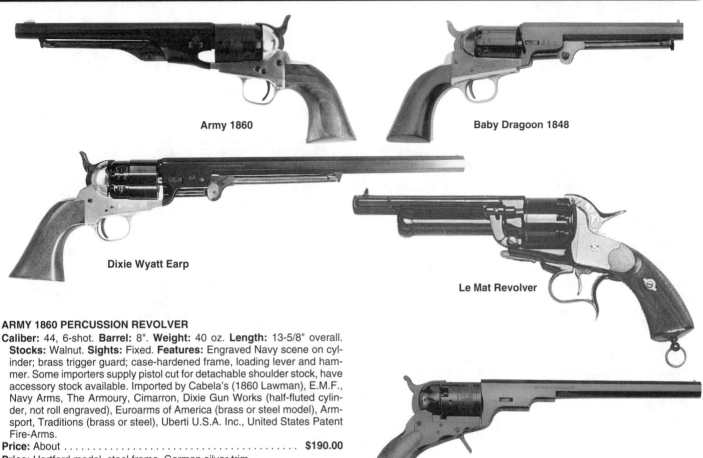

Army 1860

Baby Dragoon 1848

Dixie Wyatt Earp

Le Mat Revolver

Navy Arms 1836 Paterson

ARMY 1860 PERCUSSION REVOLVER

Caliber: 44, 6-shot. **Barrel:** 8". **Weight:** 40 oz. **Length:** 13-5/8" overall. **Stocks:** Walnut. **Sights:** Fixed. **Features:** Engraved Navy scene on cylinder; brass trigger guard; case-hardened frame, loading lever and hammer. Some importers supply pistol cut for detachable shoulder stock, have accessory stock available. Imported by Cabela's (1860 Lawman), E.M.F., Navy Arms, The Armoury, Cimarron, Dixie Gun Works (half-fluted cylinder, not roll engraved), Euroarms of America (brass or steel model), Armsport, Traditions (brass or steel), Uberti U.S.A. Inc., United States Patent Fire-Arms.

Price: About $190.00
Price: Hartford model, steel frame, German silver trim,
  cartouches (E.M.F.) $215.00
Price: Single cased set (Navy Arms) $300.00
Price: Double cased set (Navy Arms). $490.00
Price: 1861 Navy: Same as Army except 36-cal., 7-1/2" bbl., weighs 41 oz., cut for shoulder stock; round cylinder (fluted available), from Cabela's, CVA (brass frame, 44-cal.), United States Patent Fire-Arms
  . . . . **$99.95 to $385.00**
Price: Steel frame kit (E.M.F., Euroarms) . . . . $125.00 to $216.25
Price: Colt Army Police, fluted cyl., 5-1/2", 36-cal. (Cabela's) . . . $124.95
Price: With nickeled frame, barrel and backstrap, gold-tone fluted cylinder, trigger and hammer, simulated ivory grips (Traditions) $199.00

BABY DRAGOON 1848, 1849 POCKET, WELLS FARGO

Caliber: 31. **Barrel:** 3", 4", 5", 6"; seven-groove; RH twist. **Weight:** About 21 oz. **Stocks:** Varnished walnut. **Sights:** Brass pin front, hammer notch rear. **Features:** No loading lever on Baby Dragoon or Wells Fargo models. Unfluted cylinder with stagecoach holdup scene; cupped cylinder pin; no grease grooves; one safety pin on cylinder and slot in hammer face; straight (flat) mainspring. From Armsport, Cimarron F.A. Co., Dixie Gun Works, Uberti U.S.A. Inc.

Price: 6" barrel, with loading lever (Dixie Gun Works) $275.00
Price: 4" (Uberti USA Inc.) $335.00

CABELA'S 1860 ARMY SNUBNOSE REVOLVER

Caliber: .44. **Barrel:** 3". **Weight:** 2 lbs., 3 oz. **Length:** 9" overall. **Grips:** Hardwood. **Sights:** Blade front, hammer notch near. **Features:** Shortened barrels sans loading lever. Separate brass loading tool included.
Price: . . . . $149.99 (revolver only); $189.99 (with starter kit).

CABELA'S 1862 POLICE SNUBNOSE REVOLVER

Caliber: .36. **Barrel:** 3". **Weight:** 2 lbs., 3 oz. **Length:** 8.5" overall. **Grips:** Hardwood. **Sights:** Blade front, hammer notch rear. **Features:** Shortened barrel, removed loading lever. Separate brass loading tool included.
Price: . . . . $169.99 (revolver only); $209.99 (with starter kit).

DIXIE WYATT EARP REVOLVER

Caliber: 44. **Barrel:** 12", octagon. **Weight:** 46 oz. **Length:** 18" overall. **Stocks:** Two-piece walnut. **Sights:** Fixed. **Features:** Highly polished brass frame, backstrap and trigger guard; blued barrel and cylinder; case-hardened hammer, trigger and loading lever. Navy-size shoulder stock ($45) will fit with minor fitting. From Dixie Gun Works.
Price: $160.00

LE MAT REVOLVER

Caliber: 44/65. **Barrel:** 6-3/4" (revolver); 4-7/8" (single shot). **Weight:** 3 lbs., 7 oz. **Stocks:** Hand-checkered walnut. **Sights:** Post front, hammer notch rear. **Features:** Exact reproduction with all-steel construction; 44-cal. 9-shot cylinder, 65-cal. single barrel; color case-hardened hammer with selector; spur trigger guard; ring at butt; lever-type barrel release. From Navy Arms.
Price: Cavalry model (lanyard ring, spur trigger guard) $595.00
Price: Army model (round trigger guard, pin-type barrel release) . $595.00
Price: Naval-style (thumb selector on hammer) $595.00

NAVY ARMS NEW MODEL POCKET REVOLVER

Caliber: 31, 5-shot. **Barrel:** 3-1/2", octagon. **Weight:** 15 oz. **Length:** 7-3/4". **Stocks:** Two-piece walnut. **Sights:** Fixed. **Features:** Replica of the Remington New Model Pocket. Available with polisehd brass frame or nickel plated finish. Introduced 2000. Imported by Navy Arms.
Price: $300.00

NAVY ARMS 1836 PATERSON REVOLVER

Features: Hidden trigger, 36 cal., blued barrel, replica of 5-shooter, roll-engraved with stagecoach hold-up.
Price: . . . . $340.00 to $499.00

BLACKPOWDER REVOLVERS

North American Companion

**Navy Arms
1858 Army Percussion**

Pocket Police 1862

Rogers & Spencer

Ruger Old Army

NAVY MODEL 1851 PERCUSSION REVOLVER
Caliber: 36, 44, 6-shot. **Barrel:** 7-1/2". **Weight:** 44 oz. **Length:** 13" overall. **Stocks:** Walnut finish. **Sights:** Post front, hammer notch rear. **Features:** Brass backstrap and trigger guard; some have 1st Model squareback trigger guard, engraved cylinder with navy battle scene; case-hardened frame, hammer, loading lever. Imported by The Armoury, Cabela's, Cimarron F.A. Co., Navy Arms, E.M.F., Dixie Gun Works, Euroarms of America, Armsport, CVA (44-cal. only), Traditions (44 only), Uberti U.S.A. Inc., United States Patent Fire-Arms.

Price: Brass frame	**$99.95 to $385.00**
Price: Steel frame	**$130.00 to $285.00**
Price: Kit form	**$110.00 to $123.95**
Price: Engraved model (Dixie Gun Works)	**$182.50**
Price: Single cased set, steel frame (Navy Arms)	**$280.00**
Price: Double cased set, steel frame (Navy Arms)	**$455.00**
Price: Confederate Navy (Cabela's)	**$89.99**
Price: Hartford model, steel frame, German silver trim, cartouche (E.M.F.)	**$190.00**

NEW MODEL 1858 ARMY PERCUSSION REVOLVER
Caliber: 36 or 44, 6-shot. **Barrel:** 6-1/2" or 8". **Weight:** 38 oz. **Length:** 13-1/2" overall. **Stocks:** Walnut. **Sights:** Blade front, groove-in-frame rear. **Features:** Replica of Remington Model 1858. Also available from some importers as Army Model Belt Revolver in 36-cal., a shortened and lightened version of the 44. Target Model (Uberti U.S.A. Inc., Navy Arms) has fully adjustable target rear sight, target front, 36 or 44. Imported by Cabela's, Cimarron F.A. Co., CVA (as 1858 Army, brass frame, 44 only), Dixie Gun Works, Navy Arms, The Armoury, E.M.F., Euroarms of America (engraved, stainless and plain), Armsport, Traditions (44 only), Uberti U.S.A. Inc.

Price: Steel frame, about	**$99.95 to $280.00**
Price: Steel frame kit (Euroarms, Navy Arms)	**$115.95 to $150.00**
Price: Single cased set (Navy Arms)	**$290.00**
Price: Double cased set (Navy Arms)	**$480.00**
Price: Stainless steel Model 1858 (Euroarms, Uberti U.S.A. Inc., Cabela's, Navy Arms, Armsport, Traditions)	**$169.95 to $380.00**
Price: Target Model, adjustable rear sight (Cabela's, Euroarms, Uberti U.S.A. Inc., Stone Mountain Arms)	**$95.95 to $399.00**
Price: Brass frame (CVA, Cabela's, Traditions, Navy Arms)	**$79.95 to $159.95**
Price: As above, kit (Dixie Gun Works, Navy Arms)	**$145.00 to $188.95**
Price: Buffalo model, 44-cal. (Cabela's)	**$119.99**
Price: Hartford model, steel frame, German silver trim, cartouche (E.M.F.)	**$215.00**

NORTH AMERICAN COMPANION PERCUSSION REVOLVER
Caliber: 22. **Barrel:** 1-1/8". **Weight:** 5.1 oz. **Length:** 4-5/10" overall. **Stocks:** Laminated wood. **Sights:** Blade front, notch fixed rear. **Features:**

All stainless steel construction. Uses standard #11 percussion caps. Comes with bullets, powder measure, bullet seater, leather clip holster, gun rug. Long Rifle or Magnum frame size. Introduced 1996. Made in U.S. by North American Arms.

Price: Long Rifle frame	**$156.00**

North American Magnum Companion Percussion Revolver
Similar to the Companion except has larger frame. Weighs 7.2 oz., has 1-5/8" barrel, measures 5-7/16" overall. Comes with bullets, powder measure, bullet seater, leather clip holster, gun rag. Introduced 1996. Made in U.S. by North American Arms.

Price:	**$174.00**

POCKET POLICE 1862 PERCUSSION REVOLVER
Caliber: 36, 5-shot. **Barrel:** 4-1/2", 5-1/2", 6-1/2", 7-1/2". **Weight:** 26 oz. **Length:** 12" overall (6-1/2" bbl.). **Stocks:** Walnut. **Sights:** Fixed. **Features:** Round tapered barrel; half-fluted and rebated cylinder; case-hardened frame, loading lever and hammer; silver or brass trigger guard and backstrap. Imported by Dixie Gun Works, Navy Arms (5-1/2" only), Uberti U.S.A. Inc. (5-1/2", 6-1/2" only), United States Patent Fire-Arms and Cimarron F.A. Co.

Price: About	**$139.95 to $335.00**
Price: Single cased set with accessories (Navy Arms)	**$365.00**
Price: Hartford model, steel frame, German silver trim, cartouche (E.M.F.)	**$215.00**

ROGERS & SPENCER PERCUSSION REVOLVER
Caliber: 44. **Barrel:** 7-1/2". **Weight:** 47 oz. **Length:** 13-3/4" overall. **Stocks:** Walnut. **Sights:** Cone front, integral groove in frame for rear. **Features:** Accurate reproduction of a Civil War design. Solid frame; extra large nipple cut-out on rear of cylinder; loading lever and cylinder easily removed for cleaning. From Dixie Gun Works, Euroarms of America (standard blue, engraved, burnished, target models), Navy Arms.

Price:	**$160.00 to $299.95**
Price: Nickel-plated	**$215.00**
Price: Engraved (Euroarms)	**$287.00**
Price: Kit version	**$245.00 to $252.00**
Price: Target version (Euroarms)	**$239.00 to $270.00**
Price: Burnished London Gray (Euroarms)	**$245.00 to $270.00**

BLACKPOWDER REVOLVERS

Spiller & Burr

Texas Paterson

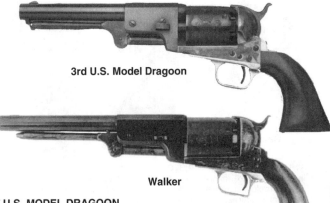

3rd U.S. Model Dragoon

Walker

RUGER OLD ARMY PERCUSSION REVOLVER
Caliber: 45, 6-shot. Uses .457" dia. lead bullets or 454 conical. **Barrel:** 7-1/2" (6-groove; 1:16" twist). **Weight:** 2-7/8 lbs. **Length:** 13-1/2" overall. **Stocks:** Rosewood. **Sights:** Ramp front, rear adjustable for windage and elevation; or fixed (groove). **Features:** Stainless steel; standard size nipples, chrome-moly steel cylinder and frame, same lockwork as original Super Blackhawk. Also stainless steel. Includes hard case and lock. Made in USA. From Sturm, Ruger & Co.
Price: Blued steel, fixed sight (Model BP-5F) $499.00
Price: Stainless steel, fixed sight (Model KBP-5F-I) $576.00
Price: Stainless steel (Model KBP-7) $535.00
Price: Blued steel (Model BP-7) $499.00
Price: Blued steel, fixed sight (BP-7F) $499.00
Price: Stainless steel, fixed sight (KBP-7F) $535.00

SHERIFF MODEL 1851 PERCUSSION REVOLVER
Caliber: 36, 44, 6-shot. **Barrel:** 5". **Weight:** 40 oz. **Length:** 10-1/2" overall. **Stocks:** Walnut. **Sights:** Fixed. **Features:** Brass backstrap and trigger guard; engraved navy scene; case-hardened frame, hammer, loading lever. Imported by E.M.F.
Price: Steel frame $169.95
Price: Brass frame $140.00

SPILLER & BURR REVOLVER
Caliber: 36 (.375" round ball). **Barrel:** 7", octagon. **Weight:** 2-1/2 lbs. **Length:** 12-1/2" overall. **Stocks:** Two-piece walnut. **Sights:** Fixed. **Features:** Reproduction of the C.S.A. revolver. Brass frame and trigger guard. Also available as a kit. From Dixie Gun Works, Navy Arms.
Price: $150.00
Price: Kit form (Dixie) $125.00
Price: Single cased set (Navy Arms) $270.00
Price: Double cased set (Navy Arms) $430.00

TEXAS PATERSON 1836 REVOLVER
Caliber: 36 (.375" round ball). **Barrel:** 7-1/2". **Weight:** 42 oz. **Stocks:** One-piece walnut. **Sights:** Fixed. **Features:** Copy of Sam Colt's first commercially-made revolving pistol. Has no loading lever but comes with loading tool. From Cimarron F.A. Co., Dixie Gun Works, Navy Arms, Uberti U.S.A. Inc.
Price: About $495.00
Price: With loading lever (Uberti U.S.A. Inc.) $450.00
Price: Engraved (Navy Arms) $485.00

UBERTI 1861 NAVY PERCUSSION REVOLVER
Caliber: 36. **Barrel:** 7-1/2", round. **Weight:** 40-1/2 oz. **Stocks:** One-piece oiled American walnut. **Sights:** Brass pin front, hammer notch rear. **Features:** Rounded trigger guard, German silver blade front sight, "creeping" loading lever. Available with fluted or round cylinder. Imported by Uberti U.S.A. Inc.
Price: Steel backstrap, trigger guard, cut for stock $265.00

1ST U.S. MODEL DRAGOON
Caliber: 44. **Barrel:** 7-1/2", part round, part octagon. **Weight:** 64 oz. **Stocks:** One-piece walnut. **Sights:** German silver blade front, hammer notch rear. **Features:** First model has oval bolt cuts in cylinder, square- back flared trigger guard, V-type mainspring, short trigger. Ranger and Indian scene roll-engraved on cylinder. Color case-hardened frame, loading lever, plunger and hammer; blue barrel, cylinder, trigger and wedge. Available with old-time charcoal blue or standard blue-black finish. Polished brass backstrap and trigger guard. From Cimarron F.A. Co., Dixie Gun Works, Uberti U.S.A. Inc., Navy Arms.
Price: . . . . $295.00 to $435.00

2nd U.S. Model Dragoon Revolver
Similar to the 1st Model except distinguished by rectangular bolt cuts in the cylinder. From Cimarron F.A. Co., Uberti U.S.A. Inc., United States Patent Fire-Arms, Navy Arms, Dixie Gunworks.
Price: . . . . $295.00 to $435.00

3rd U.S. Model Dragoon Revolver
Similar to the 2nd Model except for oval trigger guard, long trigger, modifications to the loading lever and latch. Imported by Cimarron F.A. Co., Uberti U.S.A. Inc., United States Patent Fire-Arms, Dixie Gunworks.
Price: Military model (frame cut for shoulder stock, steel backstrap) . . . . $295.00 to $435.00
Price: Civilian (brass backstrap, trigger guard) . . . . . $295.00 to $325.00

1862 POCKET NAVY PERCUSSION REVOLVER
Caliber: 36, 5-shot. **Barrel:** 5-1/2", 6-1/2", octagonal, 7-groove, LH twist. **Weight:** 27 oz. (5-1/2" barrel). **Length:** 10-1/2" overall (5-1/2" bbl.). **Stocks:** One-piece varnished walnut. **Sights:** Brass pin front, hammer notch rear. **Features:** Rebated cylinder, hinged loading lever, brass or silver-plated backstrap and trigger guard, color-cased frame, hammer, loading lever, plunger and latch, rest blued. Has original-type markings. From Cimarron F.A. Co., Uberti U.S.A. Inc., Dixie Gunworks.
Price: With brass backstrap, trigger guard . . . . $260.00 to $310.00

1861 Navy Percussion Revolver
Similar to Colt 1851 Navy except has round 7-1/2" barrel, rounded trigger guard, German silver blade front sight, "creeping" loading lever. Fluted or round cylinder. Imported by Cimarron F.A. Co., Uberti U.S.A. Inc., Dixie Gunworks.
Price: Steel backstrap, trigger guard, cut for stock . . . $255.00 to $300.00

WALKER 1847 PERCUSSION REVOLVER
Caliber: 44, 6-shot. **Barrel:** 9". **Weight:** 84 oz. **Length:** 15-1/2" overall. **Stocks:** Walnut. **Sights:** Fixed. **Features:** Case-hardened frame, loading lever and hammer; iron backstrap; brass trigger guard; engraved cylinder. Imported by Cabela's, Cimarron F.A. Co., Navy Arms, Dixie Gun Works, Uberti U.S.A. Inc., E.M.F., Cimarron, Traditions, United States Patent Fire-Arms.
Price: About . . . . $225.00 to $445.00
Price: Single cased set (Navy Arms) $405.00
Price: Deluxe Walker with French fitted case (Navy Arms) $540.00
Price: Hartford model, steel frame, German silver trim, cartouche (E.M.F.) $295.00

Gamo PT-80

Daisy 662X

EAA MP651K

ARS HUNTING MASTER AR6 PISTOL
Caliber: 22 (177 +20 special order). **Barrel:** 12" rifled. **Weight:** 3 lbs. **Length:** 18.25 overall. **Stock:** Indonesian walnut with checkered grip. **Sights:** Adjustable rear, blade front. **Features:** 6 shot repeater with rotary magazine, single or double action, receiver grooved for scope, hammer block and trigger block safeties.
Price: . . . . **NA**

BEEMAN P1 MAGNUM AIR PISTOL
Caliber: 177, 5mm, single shot. **Barrel:** 8.4". **Weight:** 2.5 lbs. **Length:** 11" overall. **Power:** Top lever cocking; spring-piston. **Stocks:** Checkered walnut. **Sights:** Blade front, square notch rear with click micrometer adjustments for windage and elevation. Grooved for scope mounting. **Features:** Dual power for 177 and 20-cal.: low setting gives 350-400 fps; high setting 500-600 fps. Rearward expanding mainspring simulates firearm recoil. All Colt 45 auto grips fit gun. Dry-firing feature for practice. Optional wooden shoulder stock. Imported by Beeman.
Price: 177, 5mm **$440.00**

BEEMAN P3 AIR PISTOL
Caliber: 177 pellet, single shot. **Barrel:** N/A. **Weight:** 1.7 lbs. **Length:** 9.6" overall. **Power:** Single-stroke pneumatic; overlever barrel cocking. **Grips:** Reinforced polymer. **Sights:** Adjustable rear, blade front. **Features:** Velocity 410 fps. Polymer frame; automatic safety; two-stage trigger; built-in muzzle brake.
Price: **$180.00**
Price: Combo **$285.00**

BEEMAN/FEINWERKBAU 103 PISTOL
Caliber: 177, single shot. **Barrel:** 10.1", 12-groove rifling. **Weight:** 2.5 lbs. **Length:** 16.5" overall. **Power:** Single-stroke pneumatic, underlever cocking. **Stocks:** Stippled walnut with adjustable palm shelf. **Sights:** Blade front, open rear adjustable for windage and elevation. Notch size adjustable for width. Interchangeable front blades. **Features:** Velocity 510 fps. Fully adjustable trigger. Cocking effort of 2 lbs. Imported by Beeman.
Price: Right-hand **$1,236.00**
Price: Left-hand **$1,275.00**

BEEMAN/FWB P34 MATCH AIR PISTOL
Caliber: 177, single shot. **Barrel:** 10-5/16", with muzzlebrake. **Weight:** 2.4 lbs. **Length:** 16.5" overall. **Power:** Pre-charged pneumatic. **Stocks:** Stippled walnut; adjustable match type. **Sights:** Undercut blade front, fully adjustable match rear. **Features:** Velocity to 525 fps; up to 200 shots per CO2 cartridge. Fully adjustable trigger; built-in muzzlebrake. Imported from Germany by Beeman.
Price: Right-hand **$1,395.00**
Price: Left-hand **$1,440.00**

BEEMAN HW70A AIR PISTOL
Caliber: 177, single shot. **Barrel:** 6-1/4", rifled. **Weight:** 38 oz. **Length:** 12-3/4" overall. **Power:** Spring, barrel cocking. **Stocks:** Plastic, with thumbrest. **Sights:** Hooded post front, square notch rear adjustable for windage and elevation. Comes with scope base. **Features:** Adjustable trigger, 31-lb. cocking effort, 440 fps MV; automatic barrel safety. Imported by Beeman.
Price: **$190.00**

BEEMAN/WEBLEY TEMPEST AIR PISTOL
Caliber: 177, 22, single shot. **Barrel:** 6-7/8". **Weight:** 32 oz. **Length:** 8.9" overall. **Power:** Spring-piston, break barrel. **Stocks:** Checkered black plastic with thumbrest. **Sights:** Blade front, adjustable rear. **Features:** Velocity to 500 fps (177), 400 fps (22). Aluminum frame; black epoxy finish; manual safety. Imported from England by Beeman.
Price: **$205.00**

Beeman/Webley Hurricane Air Pistol
Similar to the Tempest except has extended frame in the rear for a click-adjustable rear sight; hooded front sight; comes with scope mount. Imported from England by Beeman.
Price: **$255.00**

BENJAMIN SHERIDAN CO2 PELLET PISTOLS
Caliber: 177, 20, 22, single shot. **Barrel:** 6-3/8", rifled brass. **Weight:** 29 oz. **Length:** 9.8" overall. **Power:** 12-gram CO2 cylinder. **Stocks:** Walnut. **Sights:** High ramp front, fully adjustable notch rear. **Features:** Velocity to 500 fps. Turn-bolt action with

cross-bolt safety. Gives about 40 shots per CO2 cylinder. Black or nickel finish. Made in U.S. by Benjamin Sheridan Co.
Price: Black finish, EB17 (177), EB20 (20), ... **$190.00**

BENJAMIN SHERIDAN PNEUMATIC PELLET PISTOLS
Caliber: 177, 20, 22, single shot. **Barrel:** 9-3/8", rifled brass. **Weight:** 38 oz. **Length:**13-1/8" overall. **Power:** Underlever pnuematic, hand pumped. **Stocks:** Walnut stocks and pump handle. **Sights:** High ramp front, fully adjustable notch rear. **Features:** Velocity to 525 fps (variable). Bolt action with cross-bolt safety. Choice of black or nickel finish. Made in U.S. by Benjamin Sheridan Co.
Price: Black finish, HB17 (177), HB20 (20) **$190.00**
Price: HB22 (22) **$199.00**

BRNO TAU-7 CO2 MATCH PISTOL
Caliber: 177. **Barrel:** 10.24". **Weight:** 37 oz. **Length:** 15.75" overall. **Power:** 12.5-gram CO2 cartridge. **Stocks:** Stippled hardwood with adjustable palm rest. **Sights:** Blade front, open fully adjustable rear. **Features:** Comes with extra seals and counterweight. Blue finish. Imported by Great Lakes Airguns.
Price: **$299.50**

CROSMAN BLACK VENOM PISTOL
Caliber: 177 pellets, BB, 17-shot magazine; darts, single shot. **Barrel:** 4.75" smoothbore. **Weight:** 16 oz. **Length:** 10.8" overall. **Power:** Spring. **Sights:** Blade front, adjustable rear. **Features:** Velocity to 270 fps (BBs), 250 fps (pellets). Spring-fed magazine; cross-bolt safety. Made in U.S.A. by Crosman Corp.
Price: **$60.00**

CROSMAN MODEL 1377 AIR PISTOLS
Caliber: 177 (M1377), single shot. **Barrel:** 8", rifled steel. **Weight:** 39 oz. **Length:** 13-5/8". **Power:** Hand pumped. **Sights:** Blade front, rear adjustable for windage and elevation. **Features:** Bolt action moulded plastic grip, hand size pump forearm. Cross-bolt safety. From Crosman.
Price: **$60.00**

CROSMAN AUTO AIR II PISTOL
Caliber: BB, 17-shot magazine, 177 pellet, single shot. **Barrel:** 8-5/8" steel, smoothbore. **Weight:** 13 oz. **Length:** 10-3/4" overall. **Power:** CO2 Powerlet. **Stocks:** Grooved plastic. **Sights:** Blade front, adjustable rear; highlighted system. **Features:** Velocity to 480 fps (BBs), 430 fps (pellets). Semi-automatic action with BBs, single shot with pellets. Black. From Crosman.
Price: AAIIB **$38.00**
Price: AAIIBRD . . . . **NA**

CROSMAN MODEL 1008 REPEAT AIR
Caliber: 177, 8-shot pellet clip. **Barrel:** 4.25", rifled steel. **Weight:** 17 oz. **Length:** 8.625" overall. **Power:** CO2 Powerlet. **Stocks:** Checkered black plastic. **Sights:** Post front, adjustable rear. **Features:** Velocity about 430 fps. Break-open barrel for easy loading; single or double semi-automatic action; two 8-shot clips included. Optional carrying case available. From Crosman.
Price: **$60.00**
Price: Model 1008SB (silver and black finish), about **$60.00**

CROSMAN SEMI AUTO AIR PISTOL
Caliber: 177, pellets. **Barrel:** Rifled steel. **Weight:** 40 oz. **Length:** 8.63". **Power:** CO2. **Sights:** Blade front, rear adjustable. **Features:** Velocity up to 430 fps. Synthetic grips, zinc alloy frame. From Crosman.
Price: C40 . . . . **NA**

CROSMAN MAGNUM AIR PISTOLS
Caliber: 177, pellets. **Barrel:** Rifled steel. **Weight:** 27 oz. **Length:** 9.38". **Power:** CO2. **Sights:** Blade front, rear adjustable. **Features:** Single/double action accepts sights and scopes with standard 3/8" dovetail mount. Model 3576W features 6" barrel for increased accuracy. From Crosman.
Price: 3574W . . . . **NA**
Price: 3576W . . . . **NA**

DAISY/POWERLINE MODEL 15XT AIR PISTOL
Caliber: 177 BB, 15-shot built-in magazine. **Barrel:** NA. **Weight:** NA. **Length:** 7.21". **Power:** CO2. **Stocks:** NA. **Sights:** NA. **Features:** Velocity 425 fps. Made in the U.S.A. by Daisy Mfg. Co.
Price: **$36.95**
New! Price: 15XK Shooting Kit **$59.95**

HANDGUNS

DAISY/POWERLINE 717 PELLET PISTOL
Caliber: 177, single shot. **Barrel:** 9.61". **Weight:** 2.25 lbs. **Length:** 13-1/2" overall. **Stocks:** Moulded wood-grain plastic, with thumbrest. **Sights:** Blade and ramp front, micro-adjustable notch rear. **Features:** Single pump pneumatic pistol. Rifled steel barrel. Cross-bolt trigger block. Muzzle velocity 385 fps. From Daisy Mfg. Co.
Price: **$71.95**

DAISY/POWERLINE 1270 CO2 AIR PISTOL
Caliber: BB, 60-shot magazine. **Barrel:** Smoothbore steel. **Weight:** 17 oz. **Length:** 11.1" overall. **Power:** CO2 pump action. **Stocks:** Moulded black polymer. **Sights:** Blade on ramp front, adjustable rear. **Features:** Velocity to 420 fps. Crossbolt trigger block safety; plated finish. Made in U.S. by Daisy Mfg. Co.
Price: **$39.95**

DAISY/POWERLINE 93 AIR PISTOL
Caliber: BB, 15-shot magazine. **Barrel:** Smoothbore steel. **Weight:** 1.1 lbs. **Length:** 7.9" overall. **Power:** CO2 powered semi-auto. **Stocks:** Moulded brown checkered. **Sights:** Blade on ramp front, fixed open rear. **Features:** Velocity to 400 fps. Manual trigger block. Made in U.S.A. by Daisy Mfg. Co.
Price: **$48.95**

Daisy/Powerline 693 Air Pistol
Similar to Model 93 except has velocity to 235 fps.
Price: **$52.95**

DAISY/POWERLINE 622X PELLET PISTOL
Caliber: 22 (5.5mm), 6-shot. **Barrel:** Rifled steel. **Weight:** 1.3 lbs. **Length:** 8.5". **Power:** CO2. **Grips:** Molded black checkered. **Sights:** Fiber optic front, fixed open rear. **Features:** Velocity 225 fps. Rotary hammer block. Made by Daisy Mfg. Co.
Price: **$69.95**

DAISY/POWERLINE 45 AIR PISTOL
Caliber: BB, 13-shot magazine. **Barrel:** Rifled steel. **Weight:** 1.25 lbs. **Length:** 8.5" overall. **Power:** CO2 powered semi-auto. **Stocks:** Moulded black checkered. **Sights:** TRUGLO® fiber optic front, fixed open rear. **Features:** Velocity to 224 fps. Manual trigger block. Made in U.S.A. by Daisy Mfg. Co.
Price: **$54.95**

Daisy/Powerline 645 Air Pistol
Similar to Model 93 except has distinctive black and nickel-finish.
Price: **$59.95**

EAA/BAIKAL IZH-M46 TARGET AIR PISTOL
Caliber: 177, single shot. **Barrel:** 10". **Weight:** 2.4 lbs. **Length:** 16.8" overall. **Power:** Underlever single-stroke pneumatic. **Grips:** Adjustable wooden target. **Sights:** Micrometer fully adjustable rear, blade front. **Features:** Velocity about 420 fps. Hammer-forged, rifled barrel. Imported from Russia by European American Armory.
Price **$319.00**

EAA/BAIKAL MP-651K AIR PISTOL/RIFLE
Caliber: 177 pellet (8-shot magazine); 177 BB (23-shot). **Barrel:** 5.9" (17.25" with rifle attachment). **Weight:** 1.54 lbs. (3.3 lbs. with rifle attachment). **Length:** 9.4" (31.3" with rifle attachment) **Power:** CO2 cartridge, semi-automatic. **Stock:** Plastic. **Sights:** Notch rear/blade front (pistol); periscopic sighting system (rifle). **Features:** Velocity 328 fps. Unique pistol/rifle combination allows the pistol to be inserted into the rifle shell. Imported from Russia by European American Armory.
Price: **$99.00**

GAMO AUTO 45
Caliber: .177 (12-shot). **Barrel:** 4.25". **Weight:** 1.10 lbs. **Length:** 7.50". **Power:** CO2 cartridge, semi-automatic, 410 fps. **Stock:** Plastic. **Sights:** Rear sights adjusts for windage. **Features:** Looking very much like a Glock cartridge pistol, it fires in the double-action mode and has a manual safety. Imported from Spain by Gamo.
Price: **$99.95**

GAMO COMPACT TARGET PISTOL
Caliber: .177, single shot. **Barrel:** 8.26". **Weight:** 1.95 lbs. **Length:** 12.60. **Power:** Spring-piston, 400 fps. **Stock:** Walnut. **Sights:** Micro-adjustable. **Features:** Rifle steel barrel, adjustable match trigger, recoil and vibration-free. Imported from Spain by Gamo.
Price: **$229.95**

GAMO P-23, P-23 LASER PISTOL
Caliber: .177 (12-shot). **Barrel:** 4.25". **Weight:** 1 lb. **Length:** 7.5". **Power:** CO2 cartridge, semi-automatic, 410 fps. **Stock:** Plastic. **Sights:** NA. **Features:** Style somewhat like a Walther PPK cartridge pistol, an optional laser allows fast sight acquisition. Imported from Spain by Gamo.
Price: .... **$89.95**, (with laser) **$129.95**

GAMO PT-80, PT-80 LASER PISTOL
Caliber: .177 (8-shot). **Barrel:** 4.25". **Weight:** 1.2 lbs. **Length:** 7.2". **Power:** CO2 cartridge, semi-automatic, 410 fps. **Stock:** Plastic. **Sights:** 3-dot. **Features:** Available with optional laser sight and wit optional walnut grips. Imported from Spain by Gamo.
Price: .... **$108.95,** (with laser) **$129.95,** (with walnut grip) **$119.95**

"GAT" AIR PISTOL
Caliber: 177, single shot. **Barrel:** 7-1/2" cocked, 9-1/2" extended. **Weight:** 22 oz. **Power:** Spring-piston. **Stocks:** Cast checkered metal. **Sights:** Fixed. **Features:** Shoots pellets, corks or darts. Matte black finish. Imported from England by Stone Enterprises, Inc.
Price: **$24.95**

HAMMERLI AP40 AIR PISTOL
Caliber: 177. **Barrel:** 10". **Stocks:** Adjustable orthopaedic. **Sights:** Fully adjustable micrometer. **Features:** Sleek, light, well balanced and accurate. Imported from Switzerland by Nygord Precision Products.
Price: **$1,195.00**

MARKSMAN 2000 REPEATER PISTOL
Caliber: 177, 18-shot BB repeater. **Barrel:** 2-1/2", smoothbore. **Weight:** 24 oz. **Length:** 8-1/4" overall. **Power:** Spring. **Features:** Velocity to 200 fps. Thumb safety. Uses BBs, darts, bolts or pellets. Repeats with BBs only. From Marksman Products.
Price: **$27.00**

MARKSMAN 2005 LASERHAWK SPECIAL EDITION AIR PISTOL
Caliber: 177, 24-shot magazine. **Barrel:** 3.8", smoothbore. **Weight:** 22 oz. **Length:** 10.3" overall. **Power:** Spring-air. **Stocks:** Checkered. **Sights:** Fixed fiber optic front sight. **Features:** Velocity to 300 fps with Hyper-Velocity pellets. Square trigger guard with skeletonized trigger; extended barrel for greater velocity and accuracy. Shoots BBs, pellets, darts or bolts. Made in the U.S. From Marksman Products.
Price: **$32.00**

MORINI 162E MATCH AIR PISTOL
Caliber: 177, single shot. **Barrel:** 9.4". **Weight:** 32 oz. **Length:** 16.1" overall. **Power:** Scuba air. **Stocks:** Adjustable match type. **Sights:** Interchangeable blade front, fully adjustable match-type rear. **Features:** Power mechanism shuts down when pressure drops to a pre-set level. Adjustable electronic trigger. Imported from Switzerland by Nygord Precision Products.
Price: **$825.00**
Price: 162 EI **$1,075.00**

MORINI SAM K-11 AIR PISTOL
Caliber: 177. **Barrel:** 10". **Weight:** 38 oz. **Stocks:** Fully adjustable. **Sights:** Fully adjustable. **Features:** Improved trigger, more angle adjustment on grip. Sophisticated counter balance system. Deluxe aluminum case, two cylinders and manometer. Imported from Switzerland by Nygord Precision Products.
Price: **$975.00**

PARDINI K58 MATCH AIR PISTOL
Caliber: 177, single shot. **Barrel:** 9". **Weight:** 37.7 oz. **Length:** 15.5" overall. **Power:** Pre-charged compressed air; single-stroke cocking. **Stocks:** Adjustable match type; stippled walnut. **Sights:** Interchangeable post front, fully adjustable match rear. **Features:** Fully adjustable trigger. Short version K-2 available. Imported from Italy by Nygord Precision Products.
Price: **$795.00**
Price: K2S model, precharged air pistol, introduced in 1998 .... **$945.00**

RWS 9B/9N AIR PISTOLS
Caliber: 177, single shot. **Grips:** Plastic with thumbrest. **Sights:** Adjustable. **Features:** Spring-piston powered; 550 fps. Black or nickel finish. Imported from Spain by Dynamit Nobel-RWS.
Price: 9B **$169.00**
Price: 9N **$185.00**

STEYR LP 5CP MATCH AIR PISTOL
Caliber: 177, 5-shot magazine. **Weight:** 40.7 oz. **Length:** 15.2" overall. **Power:** Pre-charged air cylinder. **Stocks:** Adjustable match type. **Sights:** Interchangeable blade front, fully adjustable match rear. **Features:** Adjustable sight radius; fully adjustable trigger. Barrel compensator. One-shot magazine available. Imported from Austria by Nygord Precision Products.
Price: **$1,100.00**

STEYR LP10P MATCH PISTOL
Caliber: 177, single shot. **Barrel:** 9". **Weight:** 38.7 oz. **Length:** 15.3" overall. **Power:** Scuba air. **Stocks:** Fully adjustable Morini match, palm shelf, stippled walnut. **Sights:** Interchangeable blade in 4mm, 4.5mm or 5mm widths, fully adjustable open rear, interchangeable 3.5mm or 4mm leaves. **Features:** Velocity about 500 fps. Adjustable trigger, adjustable sight radius from 12.4" to 13.2". With compensator. New "aborber" eliminates recoil. Imported from Austria by Nygord Precision Products.
Price: **$1,175.00**

TECH FORCE SS2 OLYMPIC COMPETITION AIR PISTOL
Caliber: 177 pellet, single shot. **Barrel:** 7.4". **Weight:** 2.8 lbs. **Length:** 16.5" overall. **Power:** Spring piston, sidelever. **Grips:** Hardwood. **Sights:** Extended adjustable rear, blade front accepts inserts. **Features:** Velocity 520 fps. Recoilless design; adjustments allow duplication of a firearm's feel. Match-grade, adjustable trigger; includes carrying case. Imported from China by Compasseco Inc.
Price: **$295.00**

TECH FORCE 35 AIR PISTOL
Caliber: 177 pellet, single shot. **Weight:** 2.86 lbs. **Length:** 14.9" overall. **Power:** Spring piston, underlever. **Grips:** Hardwood. **Sights:** Micrometer adjustable rear, blade front. **Features:** Velocity 400 fps. Grooved for scope mount; trigger safety. Imported from China by Compasseco Inc.
Price: **$39.95**

Tech Force 8 Air Pistol
Similar to Tech Force 35, but with break-barrel action, ambidextrous polymer grips.
Price: **$59.95**

Tech Force S2-1 Air Pistol
Similar to Tech Force 8, more basic grips and sights for plinking.
Price: **$29.95**

AJAX

Grip materials include genuine stag, genuine buffalo horn, ivory polymer, white and black pearlite, exotic woods, buffalo polymer, pewter, genuine ivory and staglite (imitation stag horn). Available for most single- and double-action revolvers and semi-automatic pistols. Custom fittings are available.

Prices: Genuine stag . . . .$199.95 to $249.95
Prices: Genuine buffalo horn . . . .$60.00 to $80.00
Prices: Ivory polymer . . . .$35.00 to $90.00
Prices: Pearlite . . . .$35.00 to $90.00
Prices: Exotic woods (super walnut, cherrywood, black silverwood) . . . .$14.95 to $50.00
Prices: Buffalo polymer. . . . .$35.00 to $45.00
Prices: Pewter. . . . .$50.00 to $60.00
Prices: Genuine ivory . . . .$325.00 to $350.00
Prices: Staglite . . . .$49.95 to $59.95

GRIPS

ALUMNA GRIPS

Aluminum handgun grips available in several configurations including checkered, UltraLight, ThinLine, olive gray finish, laser engraved and Custom Deluxe with up to 3 engraved initials.
Prices:. . . . . **N/A**

ACCESSORIES

GRIPS

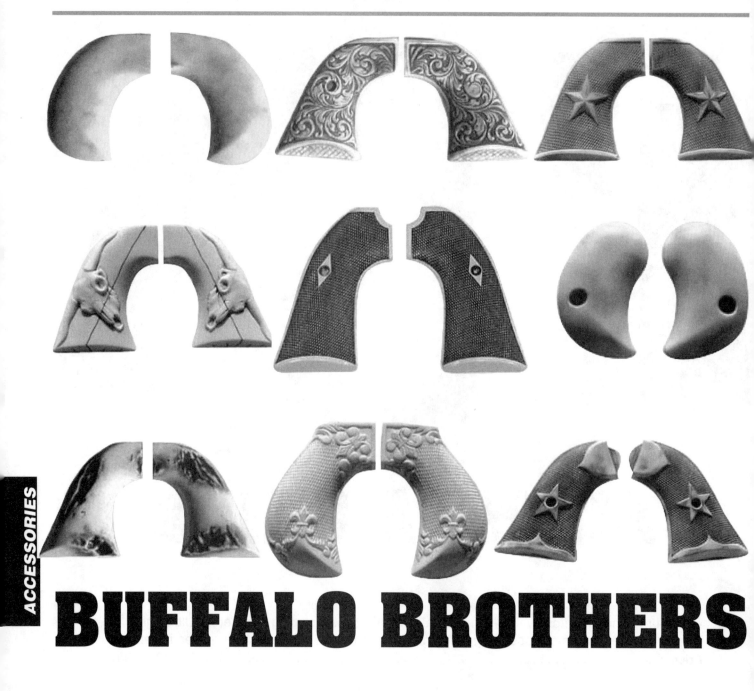

BUFFALO BROTHERS

Grips for single-action revolvers, derringers and others, made of polyurethane treated to yield an antique look. Wide variety of patterns, styles and colors available including some with simulated cracks, Americana motifs and checkering.

Prices:. . . . . $35.00 to $65.00

BUTLER CREEK (UNCLE MIKE'S)

Designed by handgun stock designer and craftsman Craig Spegel, revolver and pistol grips made of polymer are available for a wide range of handgun models. Revolver grips are made to be hand-filling, but not oversize. Finger grooves are provided on double-action revolver grips for good control. Revolver boot grips are designed not to "print" when used on concealed-carry revolvers, yet allow a controlled rapid draw. Pistol grips are specifically designed to maintain the original stock dimensions. Slip-on grips are offered in three sizes. Medium and large versions have finger grooves.

Prices: Revolver and handgun grips $20.95
Prices: Slip-on pistol grips $10.95

COAST IVORY

Offers handguns grips of genuine elephant ivory, genuine stag, California buckeye burl and other exotic woods, as well as polyester pearl.

Prices: Custom-fitted elephant ivory for 1911-style pistols $450.00
Prices: Custom-fitted ivory grips for Colt single-action revolvers . . . . $500.00 and up
Prices: Custom-fitted derringer pistol ivory grips . . . . $200.00 and up
Prices: Custom-fitted genuine stag grips for Colt single-action revolvers $190.00
Prices: Polyester pearl grips . . . . $60.00 to $85.00

ACCESSORIES

EAGLE GRIPS

Available grip materials include rosewood, buffalo horn, ebony, mother of pearl, American elk, polymer and ultra ivory (an imitation of elephant ivory). Can produce grips for virtually any handgun. Custom-fittings available.

Prices: Rosewood or ebony handgun grips . . . . **$39.95 to $59.95**
Prices: Compact revolver Secret Service grips. . . . . **$59.95 to $125.00**
Prices: Rosewood handgun thumb-rest grips (smooth finish) **$59.95**
Prices: Single-action revolver grips. . . . . **$59.95 to $99.95**

ACCESSORIES

FALCON INDUSTRIES, INC.

Producer of the Ergo Grip XT for 1911-type Government and Colt Commander-size frames. Made of textured nylon-based rigid polymer with pebble grain grip surface.

Price:.................................$22.00

ACCESSORIES

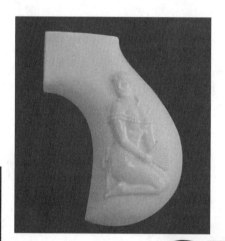
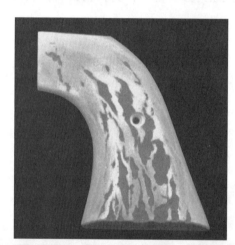
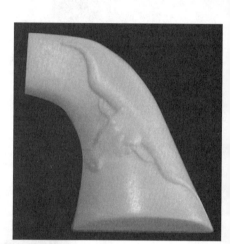

GRIPMAKER

Specializing in the production of original and authentic single-action revolver grip designs from the 1850s to 1890s. Made of white urethane which ages (yellows) like real ivory; also available in stag. Models available to fit Colt Single Action Army and similar models, blackpowder revolvers (1851 and 1861 Navy, 1860 Army), Ruger single actions, Smith & Wesson Schofield, #1 & #3 American and Model #3 Russian, and derringers.

Prices: Revolvers (urethane) . . . . $40.00 to $50.00; stag $60.00 to $70.00
Prices: Derringers (urethane) . . . .$20.00; stag $30.00

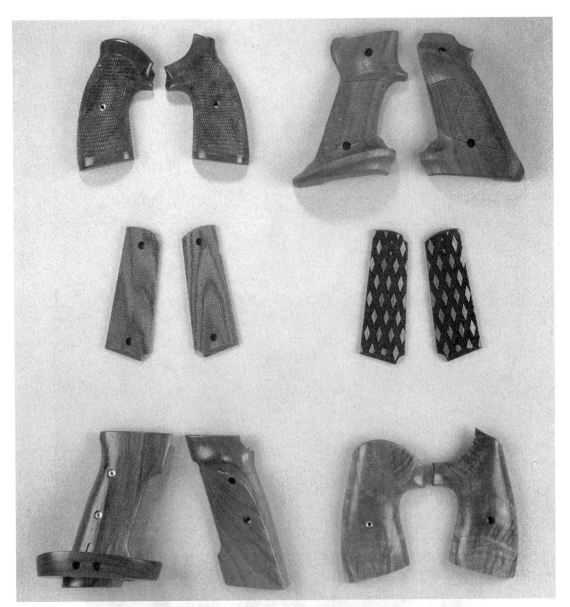

HERRETT'S STOCKS, INC.

Standard and custom hand-fitted grips made of American walnut. Exotic woods such as coco-bolo and bubinga are available on request. Grips are available in configurations including target, Camp Perry, combat, field, Jordan trooper, detective, and others. Offered in a variety of checkering patterns, or smooth finish.

Prices:. . . . . **$19.95 to $329.95**

GRIPS

HOGUE, INC.

Producer of a wide range of grips including the Monogrip, a one-piece design that slides on revolver frames from the bottom. HAND-ALL grip sleeves fit over the original grips of over 50 different handgun models. Grip materials include soft rubber, nylon, laminated hardwoods and fancy hardwoods such as cocobolo, goncalo alves, pau ferro, and kingwood. Single-action revolver grips are available in materials such as white and black micarta, white and black pearlized polymer, ebony, fancy walnut, ivory polymer and exotic hardwoods.

Prices: Revolver & pistol grips of rubber or nylon . . . . **$13.95 to $21.95**
Prices: Revolver & pistol grips of goncalo alves or pau ferro . . . . **$24.95 to $59.95**
Prices: Revolver & pistol grips of laminated or fancy woods. . . . . **$24.95 to $69.95**
Prices: Single-action revolver grips. . . . . **$39.95 to $79.95**

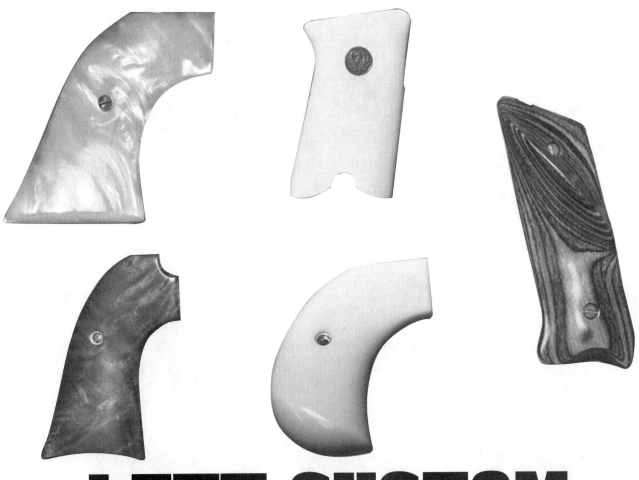

LETT CUSTOM GRIPS

Established in 1940, W.F. Lett Mfg., Inc. has been the principal OEM grip manufacturer for Sturm, Ruger & Co., Inc. since 1955. Grip materials include fancy hardwoods, such as Bolivian rosewood, zebrawood, bocote, goncalo alves and cocobola. Laminated grips are made of hardwood veneers impregnated with plastic resins. Other materials include black or ivory micarta, buffalo horn, simulated ivory, and pearl-LETT, a synthetic material offering the fiery beauty of genuine mother of pearl. Hand-checkering is available on many models.

Prices: Available for most Ruger handguns and Colt 1911 A-1 style pistols . . . . **$19.95 to $98.50**

GRIPS

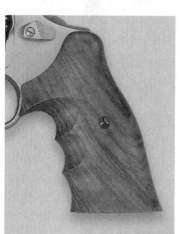
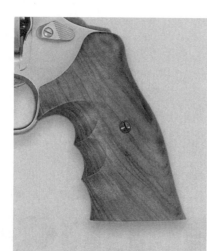

NILL GRIPS

Double-action revolver grips are available with closed or open backstrap area in walnut with smooth, stippled, checkered or Rhomlas finishes, with or without finger grooves in a variety of styles. Anatomical match grips with or without adjustable palm rest are available for standard cartridge handguns and air pistols, as are match grips for Olympic rapid-fire and free pistols.

Prices: Closed back revolver combat-style grips . . . . $67.90 to $116.00
Prices: Open back revolver combat-style grips. . . . .$62.90 to $88.90
Prices: Combat-style grips for pistols . . . .$54.90 to $137.50
Prices: Palm rest grips for revolvers . . . .$109.90 to $164.50
Prices: Anatomical match grips with adjustable palm rest . . . .$137.50 to $155.00

ACCESSORIES

GRIPS

PACHMAYR

Models available in rubber, combination wood and rubber (American Legend Series), and slip-on variations. Some have steel inserts to improve function and finger grooves and/or a palm swell is available on some models. Decelerator rubber grips are designed to dampen recoil on heavy-kicking handguns. Signature grips are available in full wrap-around or without coverage of the pistol backstrap for use on handguns such as the 1911-style pistols with grip safety mechanisms. Slip-on grips come in five sizes to fit virtually any handgun. Compac grips are for small, concealed carry handguns.

Prices:. . . . . $9.98 to $45.98

PEARCE GRIP

Producer of rubber grips for handgun models including those produced by Glock, Beretta, Colt, Makarov, Kahr Arms, Taurus and Para Ordnance. Highly contoured grips with palm swells, finger grooves and ultra-thin grip panels are available, depending on model.

Prices:. . . . .**$9.95 to $24.95**

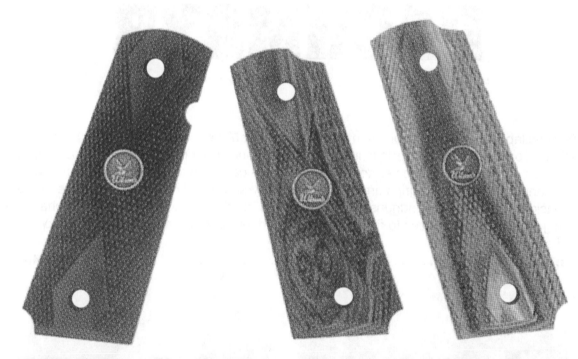

WILSON COMBAT

Grips for 1911-A1 style pistols in a variety of woods. Fully-checkered models available in cocobolo and diamondwood. Slim Line grips are laminated from cocobolo or diamondwood and are 1/3 the thickness of standard 1911-style grips. Exotic wood 1911 grips are offered in cocobolo, kingwood and diamondwood and have a double-diamond checkering pattern.

Price:. . . . .**$49.95 to $59.95**

CH4D Heavyduty Champion

Frame: Cast iron
Frame Type: O-frame
Die Thread: 7/8-14 or 1-14
Avg. Rounds Per Hour: NA
Ram Stroke: 3-1/4"
Weight: 26 lbs.
Features: 1.185" diameter ram with 16 square inches of bearing surface; ram drilled to allow passage of spent primers; solid steel handle; toggle that slightly breaks over the top dead center. Includes universal primer arm with large and small punches. From CH Tool & Die/4D Custom Die.
Price: $220.00

CH4D No. 444 4-Station "H" Press

Frame: Aluminum alloy
Frame Type: H-frame
Die Thread: 7/8-14
Avg. Rounds Per Hour: 200
Ram Stroke: 3-3/4"
Weight: 12 lbs.
Features: Two 7/8" solid steel shaft "H" supports; platen rides on permanently lubed bronze bushings; loads smallest pistol to largest magnum rifle cases and has strength to full-length resize. Includes four rams, large and small primer arm and primer catcher. From CH Tool & Die/4D Custom Die, Co.
Price: $195.00

CH4D No. 444-X Pistol Champ

Frame: Aluminum alloy
Frame Type: H-frame
Die Thread: 7/8-14
Avg. Rounds Per Hour: 200
Ram Stroke: 3-3/4"
Weight: 12 lbs.
Features: Tungsten carbide sizing die; Speed Seater seating die with tapered entrance to automatically align bullet on case mouth; automatic primer feed for large or small primers; push-button powder measure with easily changed bushings for 215 powder/load combinations; taper crimp die. Conversion kit for caliber changeover available. From CH Tool & Die/4D Custom Die, Co.
Price: .... $292.00-$316.50

New CORBIN CSP-2 MEGA MITE

Frame: N/A
Frame Type: N/A
Die Thread: 1-1/2 x 12
Avg. Rounds Per Hour: N/A
Ram Stroke: 6"
Weight: 70 lbs.
Features: Roller bearing linkage, hardened tool steel pivots, precision bush bushings glide on polished steel guide rods. Made for use with –H type (hydraulic) swage dies, it is capable of swaging rifle calibers up to .600 Nitro, lead shotgun slugs up to 12 gauge and the reloading of .50 BMG ammo. From Corbin Manufacturing.
Price: $750.00

FORSTER Co-Ax Press B-2

Frame: Cast iron
Frame Type: Modified O-frame
Die Thread: 7/8-14
Avg. Rounds Per Hour: 120
Ram Stroke: 4"
Weight: 18 lbs.
Features: Snap in/snap out die change; spent primer catcher with drop tube threaded into carrier below shellholder; automatic, handle-activated, cammed shellholder with opposing spring-loaded jaws to contact extractor groove; floating guide rods for alignment and reduced friction; no torque on the head due to design of linkage and pivots; shellholder jaws that float with die permitting case to center in the die; right- or left-hand operation; priming device for seating to factory specifications. "S" shellholder jaws included. From Forster Products.
Price: $298.00
Price: Extra shellholder jaws. $26.00

HOLLYWOOD Senior Press

Frame: Ductile iron
Frame Type: O-frame
Die Thread: 7/8-14
Avg. Rounds Per Hour: 50-100
Ram Stroke: 6-1/2"
Weight: 50 lbs.
Features: Leverage and bearing surfaces ample for reloading cartridges or swaging bullets. Precision ground one-piece 2-1/2" pillar with base; operating handle of 3/4" steel and 15" long; 5/8" steel tie-down rod fro added strength when swaging; heavy steel toggle and camming arms held by 1/2" steel pins in reamed holes. The 1-1/2" steel die bushing takes standard threaded dies; removed, it allows use of Hollywood shotshell dies. From Hollywood Engineering.
Price: $500.00

HOLLYWOOD Senior Turret Press

Frame: Ductile iron
Frame Type: H-frame
Die Thread: 7/8-14
Avg. Rounds Per Hour: 50-100
Ram Stroke: 6-1/2"
Weight: 50 lbs.
Features: Same features as Senior press except has three-position turret head; holes in turret may be tapped 1-1/2" or 7/8" or four of each. Height, 15". Comes complete with one turret indexing handle; one 1-1/2" to 7/8" die hole bushing; one 5/8" tie down bar for swaging. From Hollywood Engineering.
Price: $600.00

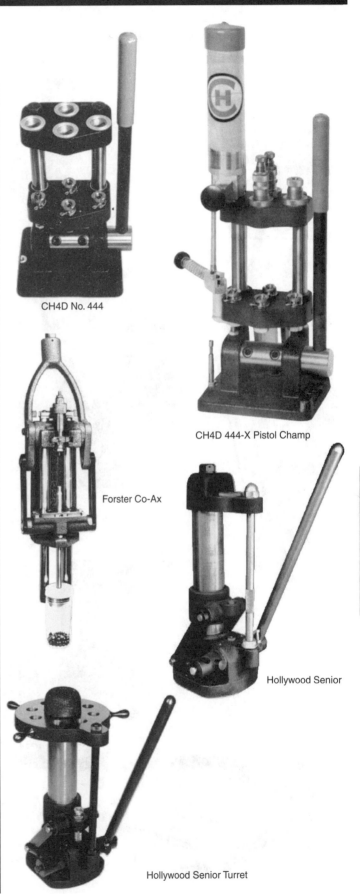

CH4D No. 444

CH4D 444-X Pistol Champ

Forster Co-Ax

Hollywood Senior

Hollywood Senior Turret

ACCESSORIES

METALLIC CARTRIDGE PRESSES

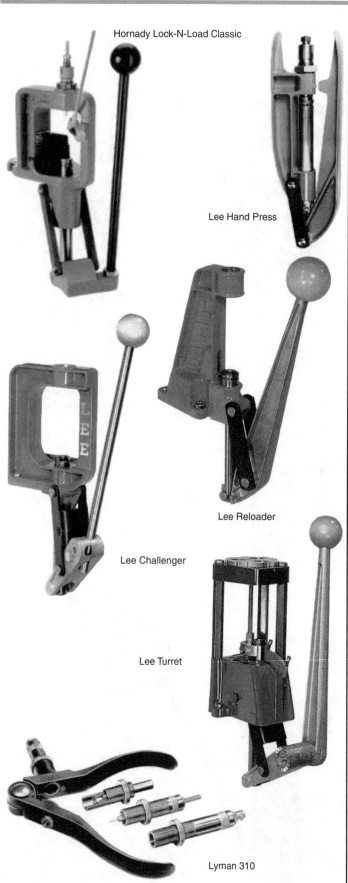

Hornady Lock-N-Load Classic

Lee Hand Press

Lee Reloader

Lee Challenger

Lee Turret

Lyman 310

HORNADY Lock-N-Load Classic

Frame: Die cast heat-treated aluminum alloy
Frame Type: O-frame
Die Thread: 7/8-14
Avg. Rounds Per Hour: NA
Ram Stroke: 3-5/8"
Weight: 14 lbs.

Features: Features Lock-N-Load bushing system that allows instant die changeovers. Solid steel linkage arms that rotate on steel pins; 30° angled frame design for improved visibility and accessibility; primer arm automatically moves in and out of ram for primer pickup and solid seating; two primer arms for large and small primers; long offset handle for increased leverage and unobstructed reloading; lifetime warranty. Comes as a package with primer catcher, PPS automatic primer feed and three Lock-N-Load die bushings. Dies and shellholder available separately or as a kit with primer catcher, positive priming system, automatic primer feed, three die bushings and reloading accessories. From Hornady Mfg. Co.
Price: Press and Three Die Bushings $99.95
Price: Classic Reloading Kit................................$259.95

LEE Hand Press

Frame: ASTM 380 aluminum
Frame Type: NA
Die Thread: 7/8-14
Avg. Rounds Per Hour: 100
Ram Stroke: 3-1/4"
Weight: 1 lb., 8 oz.

Features: Small and lightweight for portability; compound linkage for handling up to 375 H&H and case forming. Dies and shellholder not included. From Lee Precision, Inc.
Price: $26.98

LEE Challenger Press

Frame: ASTM 380 aluminum
Frame Type: O-frame
Die Thread: 7/8-14
Avg. Rounds Per Hour: 100
Ram Stroke: 3-1/2"
Weight: 4 lbs., 1 oz.

Features: Larger than average opening with 30° offset for maximum hand clearance; steel connecting pins; spent primer catcher; handle adjustable for start and stop positions; handle repositions for left- or right-hand use; shortened handle travel to prevent springing the frame from alignment. Dies and shellholders not included. From Lee Precision, Inc.
Price: $45.00

LEE Loader

Kit consists of reloading dies to be used with mallet or soft hammer. Neck sizes only. Comes with powder charge cup. From Lee Precision, Inc.
Price: $19.98

LEE Reloader Press

Frame: ASTM 380 aluminum
Frame Type: C-frame
Die Thread: 7/8-14
Avg. Rounds Per Hour: 100
Ram Stroke: 3"
Weight: 1 lb., 12 oz.

Features: Balanced lever to prevent pinching fingers; unlimited hand clearance; left- or right-hand use. Dies and shellholders not included. From Lee Precision, Inc.
Price: $26.98

LEE Turret Press

Frame: ASTM 380 aluminum
Frame Type: O-frame
Die Thread: 7/8-14
Avg. Rounds Per Hour: 300
Ram Stroke: 3"
Weight: 7 lbs., 2 oz.

Features: Replaceable turret lifts out by rotating 30°; T-primer arm reverses for large or small primers; built-in primer catcher; adjustable handle for right- or left-hand use or changing angle of down stroke; accessory mounting hole for Lee Auto-Disk powder measure. Optional Auto-Index rotates die turret to next station for semi-progressive use. Safety override prevents overstressing should turret not turn. From Lee Precision, Inc.
Price: $69.98
Price: With Auto-Index $83.98
Price: Four-Hole Turret with Auto-Index $85.98

LYMAN 310 Tool

Frame: Stainless steel
Frame Type: NA
Die Thread: 7/8-14
Avg. Rounds Per Hour: NA
Ram Stroke: NA
Weight: 10 oz.

Features: Compact, portable reloading tool for pistol or rifle cartridges. Adapter allows loading rimmed or rimless cases. Die set includes neck resizing/decapping die, primer seating chamber; neck expanding die; bullet seating die; and case head adapter. From Lyman Products Corp.
Price: Dies $45.00
Price: Handles $47.50
Price: Carrying pouch...$9.95

ACCESSORIES

METALLIC CARTRIDGE PRESSES

LYMAN AccuPress

Frame: Die cast
Frame Type: C-frame
Die Thread: 7/8-14
Avg. Rounds Per Hour: 75
Ram Stroke: 3.4"
Weight: 4 lbs.
Features: Reversible, contoured handle for bench mount or hand-held use; for rifle or pistol; compound leverage; Delta frame design. Accepts all standard powder measures. From Lyman Products Corp.
Price: $34.95

LYMAN Crusher II

Frame: Cast iron
Frame Type: O-frame
Die Thread: 7/8-14
Avg. Rounds Per Hour: 75
Ram Stroke: 3-7/8"
Weight: 19 lbs.
Features: Reloads both pistol and rifle cartridges; 1" diameter ram; 4-1/2" press opening for loading magnum cartridges; direct torque design; right- or left-hand use. New base design with 14 square inches of flat mounting surface with three bolt holes. Comes with priming arm and primer catcher. Dies and shellholders not included. From Lyman Products Corp.
Price: $116.50

LYMAN T-Mag II

Frame: Cast iron with silver metalflake powder finish
Frame Type: Turret
Die Thread: 7/8-14
Avg. Rounds Per Hour: 125
Ram Stroke: 3-13/16"
Weight: 18 lbs.
Features: Reengineered and upgraded with new turret system for ease of indexing and tool-free turret removal for caliber changeover; new flat machined base for bench mounting; new nickel-plated non-rust handle and links; and new silver hammertone powder coat finish for durability. Right- or left-hand operation; handles all rifle or pistol dies. Comes with priming arm and primer catcher. Dies and shellholders not included. From Lyman Products Corp.
Price: $164.95
Price: Extra turret $37.50

New MEACHAM ANYWHERE PORTABLE RELOADING PRESS

Frame: Anodized 6061 T6 aircraft aluminum
Frame Type: Cylindrical
Die Thread: 7/8-14
Avg. Rounds Per Hour: N/A
Ram Stroke: 2.7"
Weight: 2 lbs. (hand held); 5 lbs. (with docking kit)
Features: A light weight, portable press that can be used hand-held (or with a docking kit) can be clamped to a table top up to 9.75" thick. Docking kit includes a threaded powder measure mount and holder for the other die. Designed for neck sizing abd bullet seating of short action cartridges, it can be used for long action cartridges with the addition of an Easy Seater straight line seating die. Dies not included.
Price: $99.95
Price: (with docking kit) $144.95
Price: Easy Seater $114.95
Price: Re-De-Capper .... N/A

PONSNESS/WARREN Metal-Matic P-200

Frame: Die cast aluminum
Frame Type: Unconventional
Die Thread: 7/8-14
Avg. Rounds Per Hour: 200+
Weight: 18 lbs.
Features: Designed for straight-wall cartridges; die head with 10 tapped holes for holding dies and accessories for two calibers at one time; removable spent primer box; pivoting arm moves case from station to station. Comes with large and small primer tool. Optional accessories include primer feed, extra die head, primer speed feeder, powder measure extension and dust cover. Dies, powder measure and shellholder not included. From Ponsness/Warren.
Price: $215.00
Price: Extra die head $44.95
Price: Powder measure extension $29.95
Price: Primer feed $44.95
Price: Primer speed feed $14.50
Price: Dust cover $21.95

Turret handle disconnector

Lyman T-Mag II

Lyman Crusher II

Meacham Re-De-Capper

RCBS AmmoMaster Single

Ponsness/Warren Metal-Matic P-200

METALLIC CARTRIDGE PRESSES

RCBS Partner

RCBS Reloader Special-5

RCBS Rock Chucker

Redding Turret Press

Redding Boss

RCBS Partner

Frame: Aluminum
Frame Type: O-frame
Die Thread: 7/8-14
Avg. Rounds Per Hour: 50-60
Ram Stroke: 3-5/8"
Weight: 5 lbs.
Features: Designed for the beginning reloader. Comes with primer arm equipped with interchangeable primer plugs and sleeves for seating large and small primers. Shellholder and dies not included. Available in kit form (see Metallic Presses—Accessories). From RCBS.
Price:..$66.95

RCBS AmmoMaster Single

Frame: Aluminum base; cast iron top plate connected by three steel posts.
Frame Type: NA
Die Thread: 1-1/4"-12 bushing;
7/8-14 threads
Avg. Rounds Per Hour: 50-60
Ram Stroke: 5-1/4"
Weight: 19 lbs.
Features: Single-stage press convertible to progressive. Will form cases or swage bullets. Case detection system to disengage powder measure when no case is present in powder charging station; five-station shellplate; Uniflow Powder measure with clear powder measure adaptor to make bridged powders visible and correctable. 50-cal. conversion kit allows reloading 50 BMG. Kit includes top plate to accommodate either 1-3/8" x 12 or 1-1/2" x 12 reloading dies. Piggyback die plate for quick caliber change-overs available. Reloading dies not included. From RCBS.
Price:..$219.95
Price: 50 conversion kit............................$96.95
Price: Piggyback/AmmoMaster die plate.........$25.95
Price: Piggyback/AmmoMaster shellplate........$25.95
Price: Press cover................................$10.95

RCBS Reloader Special-5

Frame: Aluminum
Frame Type: 30° offset O-frame
Die Thread: 1-1/4"-12 bushing;
7/8-14 threads
Avg. Rounds Per Hour: 50-60
Ram Stroke: 3-1/16"
Weight: 7.5 lbs.
Features: Single-stage press convertible to progressive with RCBS Piggyback II. Primes cases during resizing operation. Will accept RCBS shotshell dies. From RCBS.
Price:..$119.95

RCBS Rock Chucker Supreme

Frame: Cast iron
Frame Type: O-frame
Die Thread: 1-1/4"-12 bushing;
7/8-14 threads
Avg. Rounds Per Hour: 50-60
Ram Stroke: 3-1/16"
Weight: 17 lbs.
Features: Redesigned to allow loading of longer cartridge cases. Made for heavy-duty reloading, case forming and bullet swaging. Provides 4" of ram bearing surface to support 1" ram and ensure alignment; ductile iron toggle blocks; hardened steel pins. Comes standard with Universal Primer Arm and primer catcher. Can be converted from single-stage to progressive with Piggyback II conversion unit. From RCBS.
Price:..$150.95

REDDING Turret Press

Frame: Cast iron
Frame Type: Turret
Die Thread: 7/8-14
Avg. Rounds Per Hour: NA
Ram Stroke: 3.4"
Weight: 23 lbs., 2 oz.
Features: Strength to reload pistol and magnum rifle, case form and bullet swage; linkage pins heat-treated, precision ground and in double shear; hollow ram to collect spent primers; removable turret head for caliber changes; progressive linkage for increased power as ram nears die; slight frame tilt for comfortable operation; rear turret support for stability and precise alignment; six-station turret head; priming arm for both large and small primers. Also available in kit form with shellholder, primer catcher and one die set. From Redding Reloading Equipment.
Price:..$298.50
Price: Kit......................................$336.00

REDDING Boss

Frame: Cast iron
Frame Type: O-frame
Die Thread: 7/8-14
Avg. Rounds Per Hour: NA
Ram Stroke: 3.4"
Weight: 11 lbs., 8 oz.
Features: 36° frame offset for visibility and accessibility; primer arm positioned at bottom ram travel; positive ram travel stop machined to hit exactly top-dead-center. Also available in kit form with shellholder and set of Redding A dies. From Redding Reloading Equipment.
Price:..$135.00
Price: Kit......................................$172.00

METALLIC CARTRIDGE PRESSES

REDDING Ultramag

Frame: Cast iron
Frame Type: Non-conventional
Die Thread: 7/8-14

Avg. Rounds Per Hour: NA
Ram Stroke: 4-1/8"
Weight: 23 lbs., 6 oz.

Features: Unique compound leverage system connected to top of press for tons of ram pressure; large 4-3/4" frame opening for loading outsized cartridges; hollow ram for spent primers. Kit available with shellholder and one set Redding A dies. From Redding Reloading Equipment.
Price: $298.50
Price: Kit $336.00

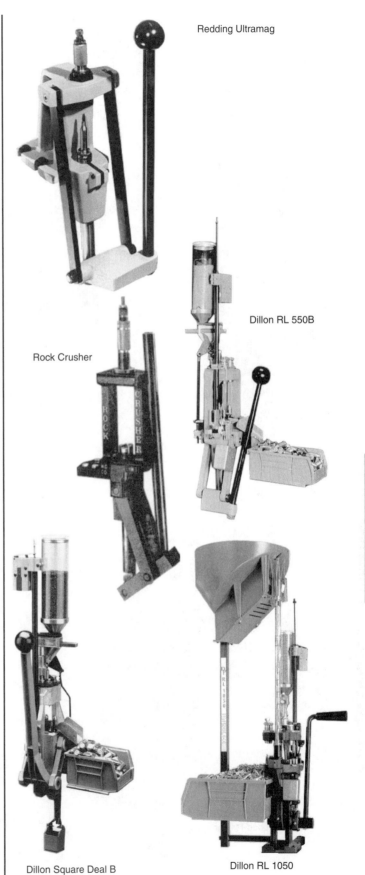

Redding Ultramag

ROCK CRUSHER Press

Frame: Cast iron
Frame Type: O-frame
Die Thread: 2-3/4"-12 with bushing reduced to 1-1/2"-12

Avg. Rounds Per Hour: 50
Ram Stroke: 6"
Weight: 67 lbs.

Features: Designed to load and form ammunition from 50 BMG up to 23x115 Soviet. Frame opening of 8-1/2"x3-1/2"; 1-1/2"x12"; bushing can be removed and bushings of any size substituted; ram pressure can exceed 10,000 lbs. with normal body weight; 40mm diameter ram. Angle block for bench mounting and reduction bushing for RCBS dies available. Accessories for Rock Crusher include powder measure, dies, shellholder, bullet puller, priming tool, case gauge and other accessories found elsewhere in this catalog. From The Old Western Scrounger.
Price: $795.00
Price: Angle block $57.95
Price: Reduction bushing $21.00
Price: Shellholder $47.25
Price: Priming tool, 50 BMG, 20 Lahti $65.10

Dillon RL 550B

Rock Crusher

PROGRESSIVE PRESSES

CORBIN BENCHREST S-PRESS

Frame: All steel
Frame Type: O-Frame
Die Thread: 7/8-14 and T-slot adapter

Avg. Rounds Per Hour: NA
Ram Stroke: 4"
Weight: 22 lbs.

Features: Roller bearing linkage, removeable head, right- or left-hand mount.
Price: $298.00

DILLON AT 500

Frame: Aluminum alloy
Frame Type: NA
Die Thread: 7/8-14

Avg. Rounds Per Hour: 200-300
Ram Stroke: 3-7/8"
Weight: NA

Features: Four stations; removable tool head to hold dies in alignment and allow caliber changes without die adjustment; manual indexing; capacity to be upgraded to progressive RL 550B. Comes with universal shellplate to accept 223, 22-250, 243, 30-06, 9mm, 38/357, 40 S&W, 45 ACP. Dies not included. From Dillon Precision Products.
Price: $193.95

DILLON RL 550B

Frame: Aluminum alloy
Frame Type: NA
Die Thread: 7/8-14

Avg. Rounds Per Hour: 500-600
Ram Stroke: 3-7/8"
Weight: 25 lbs.

Features: Four stations; removable tool head to hold dies in alignment and allow caliber changes without die adjustment; auto priming system that emits audible warning when primer tube is low; a 100-primer capacity magazine contained in DOM steel tube for protection; new auto powder measure system with simple mechanical connection between measure and loading platform for positive powder bar return; a separate station for crimping with star-indexing system; 220 ejected-round capacity bin; 3/4-lb. capacity powder measure. Height above bench, 35"; requires 3/4" bench overhang. Will reload 120 different rifle and pistol calibers. Comes with one caliber conversion kit. Dies not included. From Dillon Precision Products, Inc.
Price: $325.95

Dillon Square Deal B

Dillon RL 1050

METALLIC CARTRIDGE PRESSES

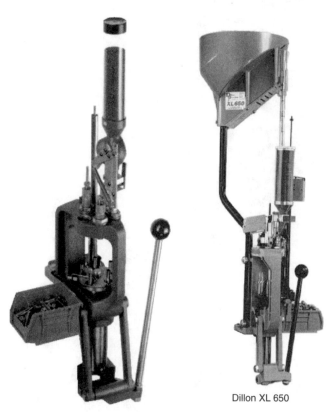

Hornady Lock-N-Load AP

Lee Load-Master

DILLON RL 1050

Frame: Ductile iron
Frame Type: Platform type
Die Thread: 7/8-14
Avg. Rounds Per Hour: 1000-1200
Ram Stroke: 2-5/16"
Weight: 62 lbs.
Features: Eight stations; auto case feed; primer pocket swager for military cartridge cases; auto indexing; removable tool head; auto prime system with 100-primer capacity; low primer supply alarm; positive powder bar return; auto powder measure; 515 ejected round bin capacity; 500-600 case feed capacity; 3/4-lb. capacity powder measure. Loads all pistol rounds as well as 30 M1 Carbine, 223, and 7.62x39 rifle rounds. Height above the bench, 43". Dies not included. From Dillon Precision Products, Inc.
Price: $1,199.95

DILLON Super 1050

Similar to RL1050, but has lengthened frame and short-stroke crank to accommodate long calibers.
Price: $1,299.95

DILLON Square Deal B

Frame: Zinc alloy
Frame Type: NA
Die Thread: None
(unique Dillon design)
Avg. Rounds Per Hour: 400-500
Ram Stroke: 2-5/16"
Weight: 17 lbs.
Features: Four stations; auto indexing; removable tool head; auto prime system with 100-primer capacity; low primer supply alarm; auto powder measure; positive powder bar return; 170 ejected round capacity bin; 3/4-lb. capacity powder measure. Height above the bench, 34". Comes complete with factory adjusted carbide die set. From Dillon Precision Products, Inc.
Price: $252.95

DILLON XL 650

Frame: Aluminum alloy
Frame Type: NA
Die Thread: 7/8-14
Avg. Rounds Per Hour: 800-1000
Ram Stroke: 4-9/16"
Weight: 46 lbs.
Features: Five stations; auto case feed; removable tool head; auto prime system with 100-primer capacity; low primer supply alarm; auto powder measure; positive powder bar return; 220 ejected round capacity bin; 3/4-lb. capacity powder measure. 500-600 case feed capacity with optional auto case feed. Loads all pistol/rifle calibers less than 3-1/2" in length. Height above the bench, 44"; 3/4" bench overhang required. From Dillon Precision Products, Inc.
Price: Less dies.. $443.95

HORNADY Lock-N-Load AP

Frame: Die cast heat-treated aluminum alloy
Frame Type: O-frame
Die Thread: 7/8-14
Avg. Rounds Per Hour: NA
Ram Stroke: 3-3/4"
Weight: 26 lbs.
Features: Features Lock-N-Load bushing system that allows instant die changeovers; five-station die platform with option of seating and crimping separately or adding taper-crimp die; auto prime with large and small primer tubes with 100-primer capacity and protective housing; brass kicker to eject loaded rounds into 80-round capacity cartridge catcher; offset operating handle for leverage and unobstructed operation; 2" diameter ram driven by heavy-duty cast linkage arms rotating on steel pins. Comes with five Lock-N-Load die bushings, shellplate, deluxe powder measure, auto powder drop, and auto primer feed and shut-off, brass kicker and primer catcher. Lifetime warranty. From Hornady Mfg. Co.
Price: $367.65

LEE Load-Master

Frame: ASTM 380 aluminum
Frame Type: O-frame
Die Thread: 7/8-14
Avg. Rounds Per Hour: 600
Ram Stroke: 3-1/4"
Weight: 8 lbs., 4 oz.
Features: Available in kit form only. A 1-3/4" diameter hard chrome ram for handling largest magnum cases; loads rifle or pistol rounds; five station press to factory crimp and post size; auto indexing with wedge lock mechanism to hold one ton; auto priming; removable turrets; four- tube case feeder with optional case collator and bullet feeder (late 1995); loaded round ejector with chute to optional loaded round catcher; quick change shellplate; primer catcher. Dies and shellholder for one caliber included. From Lee Precision, Inc.
Price: Rifle $320.00
Price: Pistol $330.00
Price: Extra turret $14.98
Price: Adjustable charge bar $9.98

Dillon XL 650

METALLIC CARTRIDGE PRESSES

LEE Pro 1000

Frame: ASTM 380 aluminum and steel
Frame Type: O-frame
Die Thread: 7/8-14
Avg. Rounds Per Hour: 600
Ram Stroke: 3-1/4"
Weight: 8 lbs., 7 oz.
Features: Optional transparent large/small or rifle case feeder; deluxe auto-disk case-activated powder measure; case sensor for primer feed. Comes complete with carbide die set (steel dies for rifle) for one caliber. Optional accessories include: case feeder for large/small pistol cases or rifle cases; shell plate carrier with auto prime, case ejector, auto-index and spare parts; case collator for case feeder. From Lee Precision, Inc.
Price: $199.98

PONSNESS/WARREN Metallic II

Frame: Die cast aluminum
Frame Type: H-frame
Die Thread: 7/8-14
Avg. Rounds Per Hour: 150+
Ram Stroke: NA
Weight: 32 lbs.
Features: Die head with five tapped 7/8-14 holes for dies, powder measure or other accessories; pivoting die arm moves case from station to station; depriming tube for removal of spent primers; auto primer feed; interchangeable die head. Optional accessories include additional die heads, powder measure extension tube to accommodate any standard powder measure, primer speed feeder to feed press primer tube without disassembly. Comes with small and large primer seating tools. Dies, powder measure and shellholder not included. From Ponsness/ Warren.
Price: $375.00
Price: Extra die head $56.95
Price: Primer speed feeder $14.50
Price: Powder measure extension $29.95
Price: Dust cover $27.95

RCBS Pro 2000™

Frame: Cast iron
Frame Type: H-Frame
Die Thread: 7/8 x 14
Avg. Rounds Per Hour: NA
Ram Stroke: NA
Weight: NA
Features: Five-station manual indexing; full-length sizing; removable die plate; fast caliber conversion. Uses APS Priming System. From RCBS.
Price: $516.95

RCBS Turret Press

Frame: Cast iron
Frame Type: NA
Die Thread: 7/8x14
Avg. Rounds Per Hour: 50 to 200
Ram Stroke: NA
Weight: NA
Features: Six-station turret head; positive alignment; on-press priming.
Price: $207.95

STAR Universal Pistol Press

Frame: Cast iron with aluminum base
Frame Type: Unconventional
Die Thread: 11/16-24 or 7/8-14
Avg. Rounds Per Hour: 300
Ram Stroke: NA
Weight: 27 lbs.
Features: Four or five-station press depending on need to taper crimp; handles all popular handgun calibers from 32 Long to 45 Colt. Comes completely assembled and adjusted with carbide dies (except 30 Carbine) and shellholder to load one caliber. Prices slightly higher for 9mm and 30 Carbine. From Star Machine Works.
Price: With taper crimp $1,055.00
Price: Without taper crimp $1,025.00
Price: Extra tool head, taper crimp $425.00
Price: Extra tool head, w/o taper crimp...................... $395.00

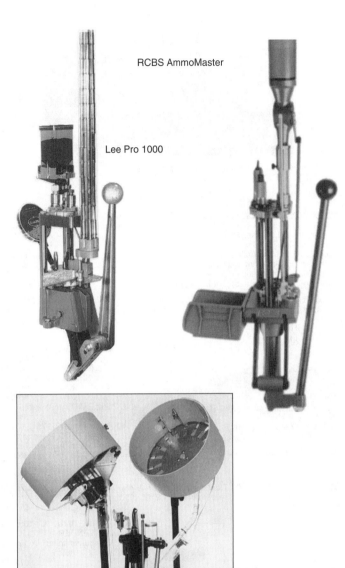

RCBS AmmoMaster

Lee Pro 1000

Fully-automated Star Universal

ACCESSORIES

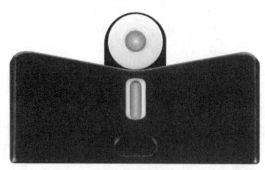

AO Express

Handgun Sights

AO EXPRESS SIGHTS Low-profile, snag-free express-type sights. Shallow V rear with white vertical line, white dot front. All-steel, matte black finish. Rear is available in different heights. Made for most pistols, many with double set-screws. From AO Sight Systems, Inc.
Price: Standard Set, front and rear. **$60.00**
Price: Big Dot Set, front and rear. **$60.00**
Price: Tritium Set, Standard or Big Dot. **$90.00**
Price: 24/7 Pro Express, Std. or Big Dot Tritium **$120.00**

BO-MAR DELUXE BMCS Gives 3/8" windage and elevation adjustment at 50 yards on Colt Gov't 45; sight radius under 7". For GM and Commander models only. Uses existing dovetail slot. Has shield-type rear blade.

Price: **$65.95**
Price: BMCS-2 (for GM and 9mm). **$68.95**
Price: Flat bottom . . . **$65.95**
Price: BMGC (for Colt Gold Cup), angled serrated blade, rear. . . **$68.95**
Price: BMGC front sight. **$12.95**
Price: BMCZ-75 (for CZ-75,TZ-75, P-9 and most clones). Works with factory front. **$68.95**

Bomar BMGS

BO-MAR FRONT SIGHTS Dovetail style for S&W 4506, 4516, 1076; undercut style (.250", .280", 5/16" high); Fast Draw style (.210", .250", .230" high).
Price: **$12.95**

BO-MAR BMU XP-100/T/C CONTENDER No gunsmithing required; has .080" notch.
Price: **$77.00**

BO-MAR BMML For muzzleloaders; has .062" notch, flat bottom.
Price: **$65.95**
Price: With 3/8" dovetail. **$65.95**

Bomar BMGC

Bomar BMU XP-100

Bomar BMML

Bomar BMR

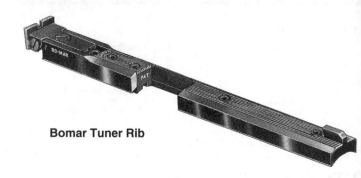

Bomar Tuner Rib

BO-MAR RUGER "P" ADJUSTABLE SIGHT Replaces factory front and rear sights.
Price: Rear sight. **$65.95**
Price: Front sight. **$12.00**

BO-MAR BMR Fully adjustable rear sight for Ruger MKI, MKII Bull barrel autos.
Price: Rear. **$65.95**
Price: Undercut front sight. **$12.00**

BO-MAR GLOCK Fully adjustable, all-steel replacement sights. Sight fits factory dovetail. Longer sight radius. Uses Novak Glock .275" high, .135" wide front, or similar.
Price: Rear sight. **$68.95**
Price: Front sight. **$20.95**

BO-MAR LOW PROFILE RIB & ACCURACY TUNER Streamlined rib with front and rear sights; 7 1/8" sight radius. Brings sight line closer to the bore than standard or extended sight and ramp. Weight 5 oz. Made for Colt Gov't 45, Super 38, and Gold Cup 45 and 38.
Price: **$140.00**

Bomar Combat Rib

BO-MAR COMBAT RIB For S&W Model 19 revolver with 4" barrel. Sight radius 5 3/4", weight 5 1/2 oz.
Price: **$127.00**

Bomar Winged Rib

BO-MAR WINGED RIB For S&W 4" and 6" length barrels—K-38, M10, HB 14 and 19. Weight for the 6" model is about 7 1/4 oz.
Price: **$140.00**

Bomar Cover-Up Rib

BO-MAR COVER-UP RIB Adjustable rear sight, winged front guards. Fits right over revolver's original front sight. For S&W 4" M-10HB, M-13, M-58, M-64 & 65, Ruger 4" models SDA-34, SDA-84, SS-34, SS-84, GF-34, GF-84.
Price: **$130.00**

ACCESSORIES

METALLIC SIGHTS

Chip McCormick "Drop In"

CHIP MCCORMICK "DROP-IN" A low mount sight that fits any 1911-style slide with a standard military-type dovetail sight cut (60x.290"). Dovetail front sights also available. From Chip McCormick Corp.
Price: **$47.95**

CHIP MCCORMICK FIXED SIGHTS Same sight picture (.110" rear - .110" front) that's become the standard for pro combat shooters. Low mount design with rounded edges. For 1911-style pistols. May require slide machining for installation. From Chip McCormick Corp.
Price: **$24.95**

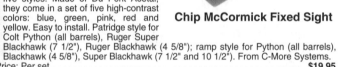

Chip McCormick Fixed Sight

C-MORE SIGHTS Replacement front sight blades offered in two types and five styles. Made of Du Pont Acetal, they come in a set of five high-contrast colors: blue, green, pink, red and yellow. Easy to install. Patridge style for Colt Python (all barrels), Ruger Super Blackhawk (7 1/2"), Ruger Blackhawk (4 5/8"); ramp style for Python (all barrels), Blackhawk (4 5/8"), Super Blackhawk (7 1/2" and 10 1/2"). From C-More Systems.
Price: Per set. **$19.95**

G.G. & G. GHOST RINGS Replaces the factory rear sight without gunsmithing. Black phosphate finish. Available for Colt M1911 and Commander, Beretta M92F, Glock, S&W, SIG Sauer.
Price: **$65.00**

Heinie Slant Pro

HEINIE SLANT PRO Made with a slight forward slant, the unique design of these rear sights is snag free for unimpeded draw from concealment. The combination of the slant and the rear serrations virtually eliminates glare. Made for most popular handguns. From Heinie Specialty Products.
Price: . . . . **$50.35 to $122.80**

HEINIE STRAIGHT EIGHT SIGHTS Consists of one tritium dot in the front sight and a slightly smaller Tritium dot in the rear sight. When aligned correctly, an elongated 'eight' is created. The Tritium dots are green in color. Designed with the belief that the human eye can correct vertical alignment faster than horizontal. Available for most popular handguns. From Heinie Specialty Products.
Price: . . . . **$104.95 to $122.80**

HEINIE CROSS DOVETAIL FRONT SIGHTS Made in a variety of heights, the standard dovetail is 60 degrees x .305" x .062" with a .002 taper. From Heinie Specialty Products.
Price: . . . . **$20.95 to $47.20**

JP GHOST RING Replacement bead front, ghost ring rear for Glock and M1911 pistols. From JP Enterprises.
Price: **$79.95**
Price: Bo-Mar replacement leaf with JP dovetail front bead. **$99.95**

LES BAER CUSTOM ADJUSTABLE LOW MOUNT REAR SIGHT Considered one of the top adjustable sights in the world for target shooting with 1911-style pistols. Available with Tritium inserts. From Les Baer Custom.
Price: . . . . **$49.00** (standard); **$99.00** (tritium)

LES BAER DELUXE FIXED COMBAT SIGHT A tactical-style sight with a very low profile. Incorporates a no-snag design and has serrations on sides. For 1911-style pistols. Available with Tritium inserts for night shooting. From Les Baer Custom.
Price: . . . . **$26.00** (standard); **$67.00** (with Tritium)

LES BAER DOVETAIL FRONT SIGHT Blank dovetail sight machined from bar stock. Can be contoured to many different configurations to meet user's needs. Available with Tritium insert. From Les Baer Custom.
Price: . . . . **$17.00** (standard); **$47.00** (with Tritium insert)

LES BAER FIBER OPTIC FRONT SIGHT Dovetail .330x65 degrees, .125" wide post, .185" high, .060" diameter. Red and green fiber optic. From Les Baer Custom.
Price: **$24.00**

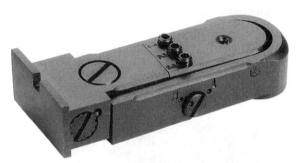

Les Baer PPC-Style Adjustable Rear Sight

LES BAER PPC-STYLE ADJUSTABLE REAR SIGHT Made for use with custom built 1911-style pistols, allows the user to preset three elevation adjustments for PPC-style shooting. Milling required for installation. Made from 4140 steel. From Les Baer Custom.
Price: **$120.00**

LES BAER DOVETAIL FRONT SIGHT WITH TRITIUM INSERT This fully contoured and finished front sight comes ready for gunsmith installation. From Les Baer Custom.
Price: **$47.00**

Les Baer Dovetail

MMC TACTICAL ADJUSTABLE SIGHTS Low-profile, snag free design. Twenty-two click positions for elevation, drift adjustable for windage. Machined from 4140 steel and heat treated to 40 RC. Tritium and non-tritium. Ten different configurations and colors. Three different finishes. For 1911s, all Glock, HK USP, S&W, Browning Hi-Power.
Price: Sight set, tritium. **$144.92**
Price: Sight set, white outline or white dot. **$99.90**
Price: Sight set, black. **$93.90**

MEPROLIGHT TRITIUM NIGHT SIGHTS Replacement sight assemblies for use in low-light conditions. Available for rifles, shotguns, handguns and bows. TRU-DOT models carry a 12-year warranty on the useable illumination, while non-TRU-DOT have a 5-year warranty. Contact Hesco, Inc. for complete list of available models.

Meprolight Glock

Meprolight Beretta

METALLIC SIGHTS

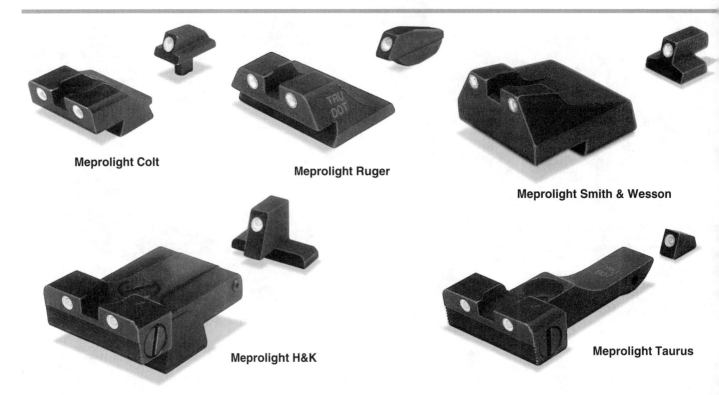

Meprolight Colt

Meprolight Ruger

Meprolight Smith & Wesson

Meprolight H&K

Meprolight Taurus

Price: Kahr K9, K40, fixed, TRU-DOT. $100.00
Price: Ruger P85, P89, P94, adjustable, TRU-DOT. $156.00
Price: Ruger Mini-14R sights. $140.00
Price: SIG Sauer P220, P225, P226, P228, adjustable, TRU-DOT. $156.00
Price: Smith&Wesson autos, fixed or adjustable, TRU-DOT. $100.00
Price: Taurus PT92, PT100, adjustable, TRU-DOT. $156.00
Price: Walther P-99, fixed, TRU-DOT. $100.00
Price: Shotgun bead. $32.00
Price: Beretta M92, Cougar, Brigadier, fixed, TRU-DOT. $100.00
Price: Browning Hi-Power, adjustable, TRU-DOT. $156.00
Price: Colt M1911 Govt., adjustable, TRU-DOT. $156.00

MILLETT SERIES 100 REAR SIGHTS All-steel highly visible, click adjustable. Blades in white outline, target black, silhouette, 3-dot. Fit most popular revolvers and autos.
Price: . . . . **$51.77 to $84.00**

rear sight available for most popular auto pistols and revolvers including Browning Hi-Power, Colt 1911 Government and Ruger P85.
Price: Front, from. **$16.80**
Price: Adjustable rear. **$55.60**

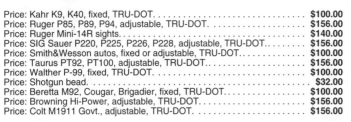

Millett Tritium Night Sight

Millett Colt

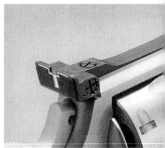

Millett Ruger

MILLETT BAR-DOT-BAR TRITIUM NIGHT SIGHTS Replacement front and rear combos fit most automatics. Horizontal tritium bars on rear, dot front sight.
Price: **$152.25**

MILLETT BAR/DOT Made with orange or white bar or dot for increased visibility. Available for Beretta 84, 85, 92S, 92SB, Browning, Colt Python & Trooper, Ruger GP 100, P85, Redhawk, Security Six.
Price: . . . . **$14.99 to $24.99**

MILLETT 3-DOT SYSTEM SIGHTS The 3-Dot System sights use a single white dot on the front blade and two dots flanking the rear notch. Fronts available in Dual-Crimp and Wide Stake-On styles, as well as special applications. Adjustable

MILLETT REVOLVER FRONT SIGHTS All-steel replacement front sights with either white or orange bar. Easy to install. For Ruger GP-100, Redhawk, Security-Six, Police-Six, Speed-Six, Colt Trooper, Diamondback, King Cobra, Peacemaker, Python, Dan Wesson 22 and 15-2.
Price: . . . . **$13.60 to $16.00**

MILLETT DUAL-CRIMP FRONT SIGHT Replacement front sight for automatic pistols. Dual-Crimp uses an all-steel two-point hollow rivet system. Available in eight heights and four styles. Has a skirted base that covers the front sight pad. Easily installed with the Millett Installation Tool Set. Available in Blaze Orange Bar, White Bar, Serrated Ramp, Plain Post. Available in heights of .185", .200", .225", .275", .312", .340" and .410".
Price: **$16.80**

MILLETT STAKE-ON FRONT SIGHT Replacement front sight for automatic pistols. Stake-On sights have skirted base that covers the front sight pad. Easily installed with the Millet Installation Tool Set. Available in seven heights and four styles—Blaze Orange Bar, White Bar, Serrated Ramp, Plain Post. Available for Glock 17L and 24 others.
Price: **$16.80**

ACCESSORIES

METALLIC SIGHTS

MILLETT ADJUSTABLE TARGET Positive light-deflection serration and slant to eliminate glare and sharp edge sight notch. Audible "click" adjustments. For AMT Hardballer, Beretta 84, 85, 92S, 92SB, Browning Hi-Power, Colt 1911 Government and Gold Cup, Colt revolvers, Dan Wesson 15, 41, 44, Ruger revolvers, Glock 17, 17L, 19, 20, 21, 22, 23.
Price: **$44.99**

MILLETT ADJUSTABLE WHITE OUTLINE Similar to the Target sight, except has a white outline on the blade to increase visibility. Available for the same handguns as the Target model, plus BRNO CZ-75/TZ-75/TA-90 without pin on front sight, and Ruger P85.
Price: . . . . **$44.99 to $49.99**

OMEGA OUTLINE SIGHT BLADES Replacement rear sight blades for Colt and Ruger single action guns and the Interarms Virginian Dragoon. Standard Outline available in gold or white notch outline on blue metal. From Omega Sales, Inc.
Price: **$10.00**

OMEGA MAVERICK SIGHT BLADES Replacement "peep-sight" blades for Colt, Ruger SAs, Virginian Dragoon. Three models available—No. 1, Plain; No. 2, Single Bar; No. 3, Double Bar Rangefinder. From Omega Sales, Inc.
Price: Each.. . . . . **$10.00**

ONE RAGGED HOLE Replacement rear sight ghost ring sight for Ruger handguns. Fits Blackhawks, Redhawks, Super Blackhawks, GP series and Mk. II target pistols with adjustable sights. From One Ragged Hole, Tallahassee, Florida.
Price: . . . . **NA**

Pachmayr Accu-Set

PACHMAYR ACCU-SET Low-profile, fully adjustable rear sight to be used with existing front sight. Available with target, white outline or 3-dot blade. Blue finish. Uses factory dovetail and locking screw. For Browning, Colt, Glock, SIG Sauer, S&W and Ruger autos. From Pachmayr.
Price: **$59.98**

P-T TRITIUM NIGHT SIGHTS Self-luminous tritium sights for most popular handguns, Colt AR-15, H&K rifles and shotguns. Replacement handgun sight sets available in 3- Dot style (green/green, green/yellow, green/orange) with bold outlines around inserts; Bar-Dot available in green/green with or without white outline rear sight. Functional life exceeds 15 years. From Innovative Weaponry, Inc.
Price: Handgun sight sets. **$99.95**
Price: Rifle sight sets. **$99.95**
Price: Rifle, front only.. . . . . **$49.95**
Price: Shotgun, front only.. . . . . **$49.95**

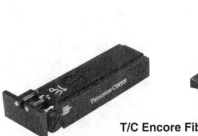

T/C Encore Fiber Optic Sight Set

T/C ENCORE FIBER OPTIC SIGHT SETS Click adjustable, steel rear sight and ramp-style front sight, both fitted with Tru-Glo™ fiber optics. Specifically-designed for the T/C Encore pistol series. From Thompson/Center arms.
Price **$49.35**

T/C ENCORE TARGET REAR SIGHT Precision, steel construction with click adjustments (via knurled knobs) for windage and elevation. Models available with low, medium and high blades. From Thompson/Center Arms.
Price:' **$54.00**

T/C Encore Target Rear Sight

Trijicon Night Sight   **Wichita Series 70/80 Sight**

TRIJICON NIGHT SIGHTS Three-dot night sight system uses tritium lamps in the front and rear sights. Tritium "lamps" are mounted in silicone rubber inside a metal cylinder. A polished crystal sapphire provides protection and clarity. Inlaid white outlines provide 3-dot aiming in daylight also. Available for most popular handguns including Glock 17, 19, 20, 21, 23, 24, 25, 26, 29, 30, H&K USP, Ruger P94, SIG P220, P225, 226, Colt 1911. Front and rear sets available. From Trijicon, Inc.
Price: . . . .**$80.00 to $299.00**

TRIJICON 3-DOT Self-luminous front iron night sight for the Ruger SP101.
Price: **$39.99**

WICHITA SERIES 70/80 SIGHT Provides click windage and elevation adjustments with precise repeatability of settings. Sight blade is grooved and angled back at the top to reduce glare. Available in Low Mount Combat or Low Mount Target styles for Colt 45s and their copies, S&W 645, Hi-Power, CZ 75 and others.
Price: Rear sight, target or combat. **$75.00**
Price: Front sight, Patridge or ramp. **$18.00**

WICHITA GRAND MASTER DELUXE RIBS Ventilated rib has wings machined into it for better sight acquisition and is relieved for Mag-Na-Porting. Milled to accept Weaver see-thru-style rings. Made of stainless; front and rear sights blued. Has Wichita Multi-Range rear sight system, adjustable front sight. Made for revolvers with 6" barrel.
Price: Model 301S, 301B (adj. sight K frames with custom bbl. of 1" to 1.032" dia. L and N frame with 1.062" to 1.100" dia. bbl.). **$225.00**
Price: Model 303S, 303B (adj. sight K, L, N frames with factory barrel). **$225.00**

WICHITA MULTI-RANGE QUICK CHANGE SIGHTING SYSTEM Multi-range rear sight can be pre-set to four positive repeatable range settings. Adjustable front sight allows compensation for changing lighting and weather conditions with just one front sight adjustment. Front sight comes with Lyman 17A Globe and set of apertures.
Price: Rear sight **$125.00**
Price: Front, sight **$95.00**

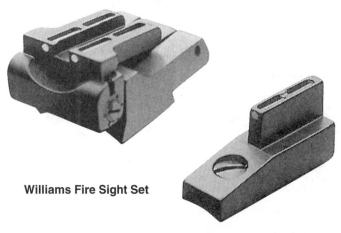

Williams Fire Sight Set

WILLIAMS FIRE SIGHT SETS Red fiber optic metallic sight replaces the original. Rear sight has two green fiber optic elements. Made of CNC-machined aluminum. Fits all Glocks, Ruger P-Series (except P-85), S&W 910, Colt Gov't. Model Series 80, Ruger GP 100 and Redhawk, and SIG Sauer (front only).
Price: Front and rear set **$39.95**
Price: SIG Sauer front. **$19.95**

WILSON ADJUSTABLE REAR SIGHTS Machined from steel, the click adjustment design requires simple cuts and no dovetails for installation. Available in several configurations: matte black standard blade with .128" notch; with .110" notch; with Tritium dots and .128" square or "U" shaped notch; and Combat Pyramid. From Wilson Combat.
Price: . . . . **$24.95 to $69.95**

METALLIC SIGHTS

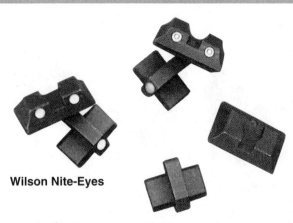

Wilson Nite-Eyes

Sight Attachments

MERIT OPTICAL ATTACHMENT For iron sight shooting with handgun or rifle. Instantly attached by rubber suction cup to prescription or shooting glasses. Swings aside. Aperture adjustable from .020" to .156".
Price: **$65.00**

WILSON NITE-EYES SIGHTS Low-profile, snag free design with green and yellow Tritium inserts. For 1911-style pistols. From Wilson Combat.
Price: **$119.95**

WILSON TACTICAL COMBAT SIGHTS Low-profile and snag-free in design, the sight employs the Combat Pyramid shape. For many 1911-style pistols and some Glock models. From Wilson Combat.
Price: **$139.95**

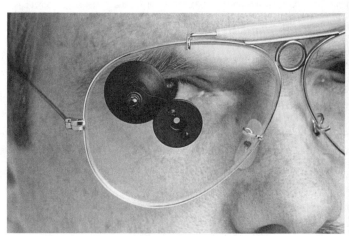

Merit Optical Attachment

MUZZLE BRAKES

JP Muzzle Brake

JP Muzzle Brake

Designed for single shot handguns, AR-15, Ruger Mini-14, Ruger Mini Thirty and other sporting rifles, the JP Muzzle Brake redirects high pressure gases against a large frontal surface which applies forward thrust to the gun. All gases are directed up, rearward and to the sides. Priced at **$79.95** (AR-15 or sporting rifles), **$89.95** (bull barrel and SKS, AK models), **$89.95** (Ruger Minis), Dual Chamber model **$79.95**. From JP Enterprises, Inc.

Laseraim

Simple, no-gunsmithing compensator reduces felt recoil and muzzle flip by up to 30 percent. Machined from single piece of Stainless Steel (Beretta/Taurus model made of aircraft aluminum). In black and polished finish. For Colt Government/Commander and Beretta/Taurus full-size pistols. Weighs 1 ounce. **$49.00**. From Laseraim Arms Inc.

Mag-Na-Port

Electrical Discharge Machining works on any firearm except those having non-conductive shrouded barrels. EDM is a metal erosion technique using carbon electrodes that control the area to be processed. The Mag-Na-Port venting process utilizes small trapezoidal openings to direct powder gases upward and outward to reduce recoil. No effect is had on bluing or nickeling outside the Mag-Na-Port area so no refinishing is needed. Rifle-style porting on single shot or large caliber handguns with barrels 7 1/2" or longer is **$115.00**; Dual Trapezoidal porting on most handguns with minimum barrel length of 3", **$115.00**; standard revolver porting, **$88.50**; porting through the slide and barrel for semi-autos, **$129.50**; traditional rifle porting, **$135.00**. Prices do not include shipping, handling and insurance. From Mag-Na-Port International.

Mag-Na-Brake

A screw-on brake under 2" long with progressive integrated exhaust chambers to neutralize expanding gases. Gases dissipate with an opposite twist to prevent the brake from unscrewing, and with a 5-degree forward angle to minimize sound pressure level. Available in blue, satin blue, bright or satin stainless. Standard and Light Contour installation cost **$195.00** for bolt-action rifles, many single action and single shot handguns. A knurled thread protector supplied at extra cost. Also available in Varmint style with exhaust chambers covering 220 degrees for prone-position shooters. From Mag-Na-Port International.

SSK Arrestor Brake

This is a true muzzle brake with an expansion chamber. It takes up about 1" of barrel and reduces velocity accordingly. Some Arrestors are added to a barrel, increasing its length. Said to reduce the felt recoil of a 458 to that approaching a 30-06. Can be set up to give zero muzzle rise in any caliber, and can be added to most guns. For handgun or rifle. Prices start at **$95.00**. Contact SSK Industries for full data.

ACCESSORIES

Maker and Model	Magn.	Field at 100 Yds. (feet)	Eye Relief (in.)	Length (in.)	Tube Dia. (in.)	W & E Adjustments	Weight (ozs.)	Price	Other Data
ADCO									
Magnum 50 mm[5]	0			4.1	45 mm	Int.	6.8	$269.00	[1]Multi-Color Dot system changes from red to green. [2]For airguns, paint ball, rimfires. Uses common lithium water battery. [3]Comes with standard dovetail mount. [4].75" dovetail mount; poly body; adj. intensity diode. [5]10 MOA dot; black or nickel. [6]Square format; with mount battery. From ADCO Sales.
MIRAGE Ranger 1"	0			5.2	1	Int.	3.9	159.00	
MIRAGE Ranger 30mm	0			5.5	30mm	Int.	5	159.00	
MIRAGE Competitor	0			5.5	30mm	Int.	5.5	229.00	
IMP Sight[2]	0			4.5		Int.	1.3	17.95	
Square Shooter 2[3]	0			5		Int.	5	99.00	
MIRAGE Eclipse[1]	0			5.5	30mm	Int.	5.5	229.00	
Champ Red Dot	0			4.5		Int.	2	33.95	
Vantage 1"	0			3.9	1	Int.	3.9	129.00	
Vantage 30mm	0			4.2	30mm	Int.	4.9	159.00	
Vision 2000[6]	0	60		4.7		Int.	6.2	79.00	
e-dot ESB[1]	0			4.12	1	Int.	3.7	139.00	
e-dot E1B	0			4.12	1	Int.	3.7	99.00	
e-dot ECB	0			3.8	30mm	Int.	6.4	99.00	
e-dot E30B	0			4.3	30mm	Int.	4.6	99.00	
AIMPOINT									
Comp	0			4.6	30mm	Int.	4.3	331.00	Illuminates red dot in field of view. Noparallax (dot does not need to be centered). Unlimited field of view and eye relief. On/off, adj. intensity. Dot covers 3" @100 yds. [1]Comes with 30mm rings, battery, lense cloth. [2]Requires 1" rings. Black fin ish. AP Comp avail. in black, blue, SS, camo. [3]Black finish (AP 5000-B); avail. with regular 3-min. or 10-min. Mag Dot as B2 or S2. [4]Band pass reflection coating for compatibility with night vision equipment; U.S. Army contract model; with anti-reflex coated lenses (Comp ML), **$359.00**. From Aimpoint U.S.A.
Comp M[4]	0			5	30mm	Int.	6.1	409.00	
Series 5000[3]	0			6	30mm	Int.	6	297.00	
Series 3000 Universal[2]	0			6.25	1	Int.	6	232.00	
Series 5000/2x[1]	2			7	30mm	Int.	9	388.00	
ARMSON O.E.G.									
Standard	0			5.125	1	Int.	4.3	202.00	Shown red dot aiming point. No batteries needed. Standard model fits 1" ring mounts (not incl.). Other O.E.G. models for shotguns and rifles can be special ordered. [1]Daylight Only Sight with .375" dovetail mount for 22s. Does not contain tritium. From Trijicon, Inc.
22 DOS[1]	0			3.75		Int.	3	127.00	
22 Day/Night	0			3.75		Int.	3	169.00	
M16/AR-15	0			5.125		Int.	5.5	226.00	
BEEMAN									
Pistol Scopes									
5021	2	19	10-24	9.1	1	Int.	7.4	85.50	All scopes have 5 point reticle, all glass fully coated lenses.
5020	1.5	14	11-16	8.3	.75	Int.	3.6	NA	
BSA									
Red Dot									
RD30[1]	0			3.8	30mm	Int.	5	59.95	[1]Red dot sights also available in 42mm and 50mm versions. From BSA.
PB30[1]	0			3.8	30mm	Int.	4.5	79.95	
BURRIS									
Speeddot 135[7]									
Red Dot	1			4.85	35mm	Int.	5	291.00	**Black Diamond & Fullfield:** All scopes avail. with Plex reticle. Steel-on-steel click adjustments. [1]Dot reticle on some models. [2]Matte satin finish. [3]Available with parallax adjustment (standard on 10x, 12x, 4-12x, 6-12x, 6-18x, 6x HBR and 3-12x Signature). [4]Silver matte finish extra. [5]Target knobs extra, standard on silhouette models. LER and XER with P.A., 6x HBR. [6]Available with Posi-Lock. **Signature Series:** LER=Long Eye Relief. **Speeddot 135:** [7]Waterproof, fogproof, coated lenses, 11 brightness settings; 3-MOA or 11-MOA dot size; includes Weaver-style rings and battery. **Partial listing shown.** Contact Burris for complete details.
Handgun									
1.50-4x LER[1,5,10]	1.6-3.	16-11	11-25	10.25	1	Int.	11	411.00	
2-7x LER[3,4,5,10]	2-6.5	21-7	7-27	9.5	1	Int.	12.6	458.00	
3-9x LER[4,5,10]	3.4-8.4	12-5	22-14	11	1	Int.	14	453.00	
2x LER[4,5,6]	1.7	21	10-24	8.75	1	Int.	6.8	286.00	
4x LER[1,4,5,6,10]	3.7	11	10-22	9.625	1	Int.	9	338.00	
10x LER[1,4,6]	9.5	4	8-12	13.5	1	Int.	14	460.00	

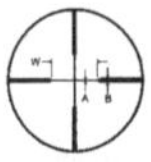

BUSHNELL (Bausch & Lomb Elite rifle scopes now sold under Bushnell brand)

Elite 3200 Handgun RainGuard

Maker and Model	Magn.	Field at 100 Yds. (feet)	Eye Relief (in.)	Length (in.)	Tube Dia. (in.)	W & E Adjustments	Weight (ozs.)	Price	Other Data
32-2632M[7]	2-6	10-4	20	9	1	Int.	10	444.95	[1]Also in silver finish. **Partial listings shown. Contact Bushnell Performance Optics for details.**
32-2632G	2-6	10-4	20	9	1	Int.	10	444.95	

Plex

Crosshair

Maker and Model	Magn.	Field at 100 Yds. (feet)	Eye Relief (in.)	Length (in.)	Tube Dia. (in.)	W & E Adjustments	Weight (ozs.)	Price	Other Data
LEUPOLD									
M8-2X EER[1]	1.7	21.2	12-24	7.9	1	Int.	6	312.50	Constantly centered reticles, choice of Duplex, tapered CPC, Leupold Dot, Crosshair and Dot. CPC and Dot reticles extra. [1]2x and 4x scopes have from 12"-24" of eye relief and are suitable for handguns, top ejection arms and muzzleloaders. Partial listing shown. **Contact Leupold for complete details.**
M8-2X EER Silver[1]	1.7	21.2	12-24	7.9	1	Int.	6	337.50	
M8-4X EER[1]	3.7	9	12-24	8.4	1	Int.	7	425.00	
M8-4X EER Silver[1]	3.7	9	12-24	8.4	1	Int.	7	425.00	

Duplex CPC Post & Duplex Leupold Dot Dot

Maker and Model	Magn.	Field at 100 Yds. (feet)	Eye Relief (in.)	Length (in.)	Tube Dia. (in.)	W & E Adjustments	Weight (ozs.)	Price	Other Data
SIGHTRON									
Pistol									
SII 1x28P[1]	1	30	9-24	9.49	1	Int.	8.46	212.95	[1]Satin black; also stainless. Rifle, pistol, shotgun scopes have aluminum tubes, Exac Trak adjustments. Lifetime warranty. From Sightron, Inc.
SII 2x28P[1]	2	16-10	9-24	9.49	1	Int.	8.28	212.95	
SIMMONS									
Prohunter Handgun									
7732[2]	2	22	9-17	8.75	1	Int.	7	109.99	[1]Black matte finish; also available in silver. [2]With 3V lithium battery, extension tube, polarizing filter, Weaver rings. **Only selected models shown.** Contact Simmons Outdoor Corp. for complete details.
7738[2]	4	15	11.8- 17.6	8.5	1	Int.	8	129.99	
82200[1]	2-6							159.99	

Truplex™ Smart ProDiamond® Crossbow

Maker and Model	Magn.	Field at 100 Yds. (feet)	Eye Relief (in.)	Length (in.)	Tube Dia. (in.)	W & E Adjustments	Weight (ozs.)	Price	Other Data
SWIFT									
Pistol									
679M 1.25-4x28	1.25-4	23-9	23-15	9.3	1	Int.	8.2	250.00	[1]Available in regular matte black or silver finish. Partial listing shown. From Swift Instruments.
Pistol Scopes									
661 4x32	4	90	10-22	9.2	1	Int.	9.5	130.00	
663 2x20[1]	2	18.3	9-21	7.2	1	Int.	8.4	130.00	
THOMPSON/CENTER RECOIL PROOF SERIES									
Pistol Scopes									
8315[1]	2.5-7	15-5	8-21, 8-11	9.25	1	Int.	9.2	349.00	[1]Black finish; silver optional. [2]Black; lighted reticle. From Thompson/Center Arms.
8326[2]	2.5-7	15-5	8-21, 8-11	9.25	1	Int.	10.5	416.00	
ULTRA DOT									
Ultra-Dot Sights[1]									
Ultra-Dot 25[2]	1			5.1	1	Int.	3.9	159.00	[1]Ultra Dot sights include rings, battery, polarized filter, and 5-year warranty. All models available in black or satin finish. [2]Illuminated red dot has eleven brightness settings. Shock-proof aluminum tube. From Ultra Dot Distribution.
Ultra-Dot 30[2]	1			5.1	30mm	Int.	4	179.00	
WEAVER									
Handgun									
H2[1-3]	2	21	4-29	8.5	1	Int.	6.7	161.43	[1]Gloss black. [2]Matte black. [3]Silver. All scopes are shock-proof, waterproof, and fogproof. Dual-X reticle available. From Weaver Products.
H4[1-3]	4	18	11.5-18	8.5	1	Int.	6.7	175.00	
VH4[1-3]	1.5-4	13.6-5.8	11-17	8.6	1	Int.	8.1	215.71	
VH8[1-2-3]	2.5-8	8.5-3.7	12.16	9.3	1	Int.	8.3	228.57	

Hunting scopes in general are furnished with a choice of reticlecrosshairs, post with crosshairs, tapered or blunt post, or dot crosshairs, etc. The great majority of target and varmint scopes have medium or fine crosshairs but post or dot reticles may be ordered. W=windage E=Elevation MOA=Minute of Angle or 1" (approx.) at 100 yards.

ACCESSORIES

LASER SIGHTS

Alpec Mini Shot

Laseraim LA5X

Laseraim LAX

Maker and Model	Wave length (nm)	Beam Color	Lens	Operating Temp. (degrees F.)	Weight (ozs.)	Price	Other Data
ALPEC							[1]Range 1000 yards. [2]Range 300 yards. Mini Shot II range 500 yards, output 650mm, **$129.95**. [3]Range 300 yards; Laser Shot II 500 yards; Super Laser Shot 1000 yards. Black or stainless finish aluminum; removable pressure or push-button switch. Mounts for most handguns, many rifles and shotguns. From Alpec Team, Inc.
Power Shot[1]	635	Red	Glass	NA	2.5	$199.95	
Mini Shot[2]	670	Red	Glass	NA	2.5	99.95	
Laser Shot[3]	670	Red	Glass	NA	3.0	99.95	
BEAMSHOT							[1]Black or silver finish; adj. for windage and elevation; 300-yd. range; also M1000/S (500- yd. range), M1000/u (800-yd.). [2]Black finish; 300-, 500-, 800-yd. models. All come with removable touch pad switch, 5" cable. Mounts to fit virtually any firearm. From Quarton USA Co.
1000[1]	670	Red	Glass		3.8	NA	
3000[2]	635/670	Red	Glass		2	NA	
1001/u	635	Red	Glass		3.8	NA	
780	780	Red	Glass		3.8	NA	
BSA							[1]Comes with mounts for 22/air rifle and Weaver-style bases.
LS650[1]	N/A	Red	N/A	N/A	N/A	49.95	
LASERAIM							[1]Red dot/laser combo; 300-yd. range: LA3xHD Hotdot has 500-yd. range **$249.00**; 4 MOA dot size, laser gives 2" dot size at 100 yds. [2]30mm obj. lens: 4 MOA dot at 100 yds: fits Weaver base. [3]300-yd range; 2" dot at 100 yds.; rechargeable Nicad battery [4]1.5-mile range; 1" dot at 100 yds.; 20+ hrs. batt. life. [5]1.5-mile range; 1" dot at 100 yds; rechargeable Nicad battery (comes with in-field charger); [6]Black or satin finish. With mount, **$169.00**. [7]Laser projects 2" dot at 100 yds.: with rotary switch; with Hotdot **$237.00**; with Hotdot touch switch **$357.00**. [8]For Glock 17-27; G1 Hotdot **$299.00**; price installed. [10]Fits std. Weaver base, no rings required; 6-MOA dot; seven brightness settings. All have w&e adj.; black or satin silver finish. From Laser aim Technologies, Inc.
LA10 Hotdot[4]					NA	199.00	
Lasers							
MA-35RB Mini Aimer[7]					1.0	129.00	
G1 Laser[8]					2.0	229.00	
LASER DEVICES							[1]For S&W P99 semi-auto pistols; also BA-2, 5 oz., **$339.00**. [2]For revolvers. [3]For HK, Walther P99. [4]For semi-autos. [5]For SIG-Pro pistol. [6]Universal, semi-autos. All avail. with Magnum Power Point (650nM) or daytime-visible Super Power Point (632nM) diode. Infrared diodes avail. for law enforcement. From Laser Devices, Inc.
BA-3[2]	632	Red	Glass		3.3	332.50	
BA-5[3]	632	Red	Glass		3.2	372.00	
Duty-Grade[4]	632	Red	Glass		3.5	372.00	
Las/Tac[1]	632	Red	Glass		5.5	298.00 to 477.00	

ACCESSORIES

LASER SIGHTS

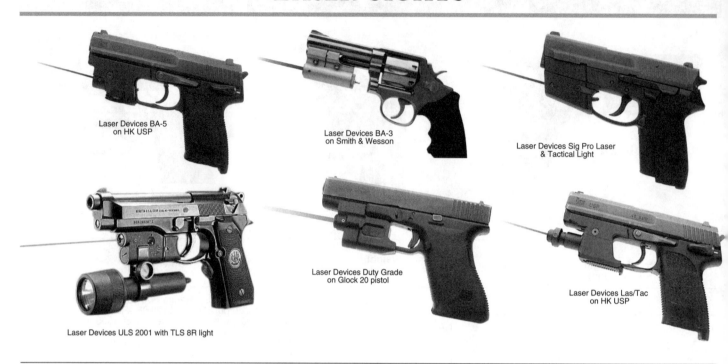

Laser Devices BA-5
on HK USP

Laser Devices BA-3
on Smith & Wesson

Laser Devices Sig Pro Laser
& Tactical Light

Laser Devices Duty Grade
on Glock 20 pistol

Laser Devices Las/Tac
on HK USP

Laser Devices ULS 2001 with TLS 8R light

Maker and Model	Wave length (nm)	Beam Color	Lens	Operating Temp. (degrees F.)	Weight (ozs.)	Price	Other Data
LASER DEVICES *(cont.)*							
ULS-2001[6]	632	Red	Glass		4.5	**210.95**	
Universal AR-2A	632	Red	Glass		4.5	**445.00**	
LASERGRIPS							Replaces existing grips with built-in laser high in the right grip panel. Integrated pressure sensi tive pad in grip activates the laser. Also has master on/off switch. [1]For Colt 1911/Commander. [2]For all Glock models. Option on/off switch. Requires factory installation. [3]For S&W K, L, N frames, round or square butt (LG-207); [4]For Taurus small-frame revolvers. [5]For Ruger SP-101. [6]For SIG Sauer P226. From Crimson Trace Corp. [7]For Beretta 92/96. [8]For Ruger MK II. [9]For S&W J-frame. [10]For Sig Sauer P228/229. [11]For Colt 1911 full size, wraparound. [12]For Beretta 92/96, wraparound. [13]For Colt 1911 compact, wraparound. [14]For S&W J-frame, rubber.
LG-201[1]	633	Red-Orange	Glass	NA		**299.00**	
LG-206[3]	633	Red-Orange	Glass	NA		**229.00**	
LG-085[4]	633	Red-Orange	Glass	NA		**229.00**	
LG-101[5]	633	Red-Orange	Glass	NA		**229.00**	
LG-226[6]	633	Red-Orange	Glass	NA		**229.00**	
GLS-630[2]	633	Red-Orange	Glass	NA		**595.00**	
LG202[7]	633	Red-Orange	Glass	NA		**299.00**	
LG203[8]	633	Red-Orange	Glass	NA		**299.00**	
LG205[9]	633	Red-Orange	Glass	NA		**299.00**	
LG229[10]	633	Red-Orange	Glass	NA		**299.00**	

LASER SIGHTS

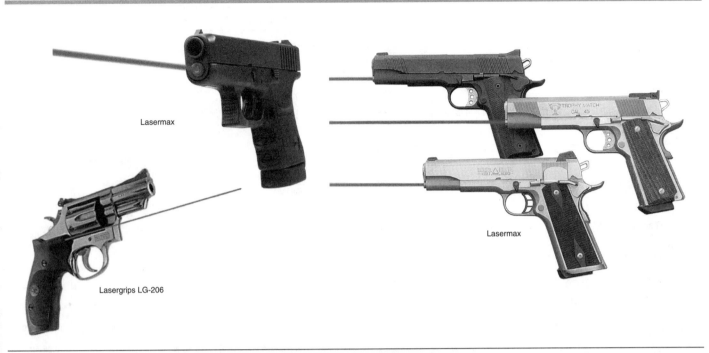

Lasermax

Lasergrips LG-206

Lasermax

Maker and Model	Wave length (nm)	Beam Color	Lens	Operating Temp. (degrees F.)	Weight (ozs.)	Price	Other Data
LASERGRIPS *(cont.)*							
LG301[11]	633	Red-Orange	Glass	NA		**329.00**	
LG302[12]	633	Red-Orange	Glass	NA		**329.00**	
LG304[13]	633	Red-Orange	Glass	NA		**329.00**	
LG305[14]	633	Red-Orange	Glass	NA		**299.00**	
LASERLYTE							[1]Dot/circle or dot/crosshair projection; black or stainless. [2]Also 635/645mm model. From Tac Star Laserlyte. in grip activates the laser. Also has master on/off switch.
LLX-0006-140/090[1]	635/645	Red			1.4	**159.95**	
WPL-0004-140/090[2]	670	Red			1.2	**109.95**	
TPL-0004-140/090[2]	670	Red			1.2	**109.95**	
T7S-0004-140[2]	670	Red			0.8	**109.95**	
LASERMAX							Replaces the recoil spring guide rod; includes a customized takedown lever that serves as the laser's instant on/off switch. Also has master on/off switch. For Glock, Smith & Wesson, Sigarms, Beretta, Colt, Kimber, Springfield Gov't. Model 1911, Heckler & Koch and select Taurus models. Installs in most pistols without gunsmithing. Battery life 1/2 hour to 2 hours in continuous use. From Laser Max.
LMS-1000 Internal Guide Rod	635	Red-Orange	Glass	40-120	.25	**389.00**	
NIGHT STALKER							Waterproof; LCD panel displays power remaining; programmable blink rate; constant or memory on. From Wilcox Industries.
S0 Smart	635	Red	NA	NA	2.46	**515.00**	

SCOPE RINGS & BASES

Maker, Model, Type	Adjust.	Scopes	Price
ADCO			
Std. Black or nickel		1"	$13.95
Std. Black or nickel		30mm	13.95
Rings Black or nickel		30mm w/ 3/8" grv.	13.95
Rings Black or nickel		1" raised 3/8" grv.	13.95
AIMTECH			
AMT Auto Mag II .22 Mag.	No	Weaver rail	$56.99
Astra .44 Mag Revolver	No	Weaver rail	63.25
Beretta/Taurus 92/99	No	Weaver rail	63.25
Browning Buckmark/Challenger II	No	Weaver rail	56.99
Browning Hi-Power	No	Weaver rail	63.25
Glock 17, 17L, 19, 23, 24 etc. no rail	No	Weaver rail	63.25
Glock 20, 21 no rail	No	Weaver rail	63.25
Glock 9mm and .40 with access. rail	No	Weaver rail	74.95
Govt. 45 Auto/.38 Super	No	Weaver rail	63.25
Hi-Standard (Mitchell version) 107	No	Weaver rail	63.25
H&K USP 9mm/40 rail mount	No	Weaver rail	74.95
Rossi 85/851/951 Revolvers	No	Weaver rail	63.25
Ruger Mk I, Mk II	No	Weaver rail	49.95
Ruger P85/P89	No	Weaver rail	63.25
S&W K, L, N frames	No	Weaver rail	63.25
S&W K, L, N with tapped top strap*	No	Weaver rail	69.95
S&W Model 41 Target 22	No	Weaver rail	63.25
S&W Model 52 Target 38	No	Weaver rail	63.25
S&W Model 99 Walther frame rail mount	No	Weaver rail	74.95
S&W 2nd Gen. 59/459/659 etc.	No	Weaver rail	56.99
S&W 3rd Gen. full size 5906 etc.	No	Weaver rail	69.95
S&W 422, 622, 2206	No	Weaver rail	56.99
S&W 645/745	No	Weaver rail	56.99
S&W Sigma	No	Weaver rail	64.95
Taurus PT908	No	Weaver rail	63.25
Taurus 44 6.5" bbl.	No	Weaver rail	69.95
Walther 99	No	Weaver rail	74.95

All mounts no-gunsmithing, iron sight usable. All mounts accommodate standard Weaver-style rings of all makers. From Aimtech division, L&S Technologies, Inc. *3-blade sight mount combination.

Maker, Model, Type	Adjust.	Scopes	Price
B-SQUARE			
Pistols (centerfire)			
Beretta 92, 96/Taurus 99	No	Weaver rail	69.95
Colt M1911	E only	Weaver rail	69.95
Desert Eagle	No	Weaver rail	69.95
Glock	No	Weaver rail	69.95
H&K USP, 9mm and 40 S&W	No	Weaver rail	69.95
Ruger P85/89	E only	Weaver rail	69.95
SIG Sauer P226	E only	Weaver rail	69.95
Pistols (rimfire)			
Browning Buck Mark	No	Weaver rail	32.95
Colt 22	No	Weaver rail	49.95
Ruger Mk I/II, bull or taper	No	Weaver rail	32.95-49.95
Smith & Wesson 41, 2206	No	Weaver rail	36.95-49.95
Revolvers			
Colt Anaconda/Python	No	Weaver rail	35.95-74.95
Ruger Single-Six	No	Weaver rail	64.95
Ruger GP-100	No	Weaver rail	64.95
Ruger Blackhawk, Super	No	Weaver rail	64.95
Ruger Redhawk, Super	No	Weaver rail	64.95
Smith & Wesson K, L, N	No	Weaver rail	36.95-74.95
Taurus 66, 669, 607, 608	No	Weaver rail	64.95

Prices shown for anodized black finish; add $10 for stainless finish. Partial listing of mounts shown here. Contact B-Square for complete listing and details.

Maker, Model, Type	Adjust.	Scopes	Price
BURRIS			
L.E.R. (LU) Mount Bases[1]	W only	1" split rings	24.00-52.00
L.E.R. No Drill-No Tap Bases[1,2,3]	W only	1" split rings	48.00-52.00

[1]Universal dovetail; accepts Burris, Universal, Redfield, Leupold rings. For Dan Wesson, S&W, Virginian, Ruger Blackhawk, Win. 94. [2]Selected rings and bases available with matte Safari or silver finish. [3]For S&W K, L, N frames, Colt Python, Dan Wesson with 6" or longer barrels.

Maker, Model, Type	Adjust.	Scopes	Price
CONETROL			
Pistol Bases, 2-or 3-ring[1]	W only		$149.88
Metric Rings[2]	W only	26mm, 26.5mm, 30mm	99.96-149.88

[1]For XP-100, T/C Contender, Colt SAA, Ruger Blackhawk, S&W and others. [2]26mm, 26.5mm, and 30mm rings made in projectionless style, in three heights. Three-ring mount for T/C Contender and other pistols in Conetrol's three grades. Any Conetrol mount available in stainless or Teflon for double regular cost of grade.

SCOPE RINGS & BASES

Maker, Model, Type	Adjust.	Scopes	Price
KRIS MOUNTS			
One Piece (T)[1]	No	1", 26mm split rings	12.98
[1]Blackhawk revolver. Mounts have oval hole to permit use of iron sights.			
LASER AIM	No	Laser Aim	19.99-69.00
Mounts Laser Aim above or below barrel. Avail. for most popular handguns. From Laser Aim Technologies, Inc.			
LEUPOLD			
STD Bases[1]	W only	One- or two-piece bases	24.60
[1]Base and two rings; Casull, Ruger, S&W, T/C; add $5.00 for silver finish.			
MILLETT			
One-Piece Bases[2]	Yes	1"	26.41
Handgun Bases, Rings[1]		1"	36.07-80.38
[1]Two- and three-ring sets for Colt Python, Trooper, Diamondback, Peacekeeper, Dan Wesson, Ruger Redhawk, Super Redhawk. [2]Turn-in bases and Weaver-style for most popular rifles and T/C Contender, XP-100 pistols. From Millett Sights.			
THOMPSON/CENTER			
Duo-Ring Mount[1]	No	1"	73.80
Weaver-Style Bases	No		13.00-42.50
Weaver-Style Rings[2]	No	1"	36.00
[1]Attaches directly to T/C Contender bbl., no drilling/tapping; also for T/C M/L rifles, needs base adapter; blue or stainless. [2]Medium and high; blue or silver finish. From Thompson/Center.			
WARNE			
Premier Series (all steel)			
T.P.A. (Permanently Attached)	No	1", 4 heights 30mm, 2 heights	87.75 98.55
Premier Series Rings fit Premier Series Bases			
Premier Series (all-steel Q.D. rings)			
Premier Series (all steel) Quick detachable lever	No	1", 4 heights 26mm, 2 heights 30mm, 3 heights	131.25 129.95 142.00
All-Steel One-Piece Base, ea.			38.50
All-Steel Two-Piece Base, ea.			14.00

Maker, Model, Type	Adjust.	Scopes	Price
Maxima Series (fits all Weaver-style bases)			
Permanently Attached[1]	No	1", 3 heights 30mm, 3 heights	25.50 36.00
Adjustable Double Lever[2]	No	1", 3 heights 30mm, 3 heights	72.60 80.75
Thumb Knob	No	1", 3 heights 30mm, 3 heights	59.95 68.25
Stainless-Steel Two-Piece Base, ea.			15.25
Vertically split rings with dovetail clamp, precise return to zero. Fit most popular rifles, handguns. Regular blue, matte blue, silver finish. 1All-Steel, non-Q.D. rings. 2All-steel, Q.D. rings. From Warne Mfg. Co.			
WEAVER			
Complete Mount Systems			
Pistol	No	1"	75.00-105.00
No Drill & Tap Pistol systems in gloss or silver for: Colt Python, Trooper, 357, Officer's Model; Ruger Single-Six, Security- Six (gloss finish only), Blackhawk, Super Blackhawk, Blackhawk SRM 357, Redhawk, Mini-14 Series (not Ranch), Ruger 22 Auto Pistols, Mark II; Smith & Wesson I- and current K-frames with adj. rear sights.			
WEIGAND			
Browning Buck Mark[1]	No		29.95
Integra Mounts[2]	No		39.95-69.00
S&W Revolver[3]	No		29.95
Ruger 10/22[4]	No		14.95-39.95
Ruger Revolver[5]	No		29.95
Taurus Revolver[4]	No		29.95-65.00
Lightweight Rings	No	1", 30mm	29.95-39.95
1911			
SM36	No	Weaver rail	99.95
APCMNT[7]	No		69.95
[1]No gunsmithing. [2]S&W K, L, N frames; Taurus vent rib models; Colt Anaconda/ Python; Ruger Redhawk; Ruger 10/22. [3]K, L, N frames. [4]Three models. [5]Redhawk, Blackhawk, GP-100. [6]3rd Gen.; drill and tap; without slots **$59.95**. [7]For Aimpoint Comp. Red Dot scope, silver only. From Weigand Combat Handguns, Inc.			
WIDEVIEW			
Desert Eagle Pistol Mount	No	1", 30mm	34.95-44.95
From Wideview Scope Mount Corp.			

NOTES

(S) — Side Mount; (T) — Top Mount; 22mm = .866", 25.4mm = 1.024"; 26.5mm = 1.045"; 30mm = 1.81".

ACCESSORIES

SPOTTING SCOPES

Bushnell Sentry

BAUSCH & LOMB DISCOVERER 15x to 60x zoom, 60mm objective. Constant focus throughout range. Field at 1000 yds. 38 ft (60x), 150 ft. (15x). Comes with lens caps. Length 17 1/2"; weight 48.5 oz.
Price:..$391.95

BAUSCH & LOMB ELITE 15x to 45x zoom, 60mm objective. Field at 1000 yds., 125-65 ft. Length is 12.2"; weight, 26.5 oz. Waterproof, armored. Tripod mount. Comes with black case.
Price:..$766.95

BAUSCH & LOMB ELITE ZOOM 20x-60x, 70mm objective. Roof prism. Field at 1000 yds. 90-50 ft. Length is 16"; weight 40 oz. Waterproof, armored. Tripod mount. Comes with black case.
Price: $921.95

BAUSCH & LOMB 80MM ELITE 20x-60x zoom, 80mm objective. Field of view at 1000 yds. 98-50 ft. (zoom). Weight 51 oz. (20x, 30x), 54 oz. (zoom); length 17". Interchangeable bayonet-style eyepieces. Built-in peep sight.
Price: With EDPrime Glass $1,276.95

BUSHNELL TROPHY 63mm objective, 20x-60x zoom. Field at 1000 yds. 90ft. (20x), 45 ft. (60x). Length 12.7"; weight 20 oz. Black rubber armored, waterproof. Case included.
Price: $421.95

BUSHNELL COMPACT TROPHY 50mm objective, 20x-50x zoom. Field at 1000 yds. 92 ft. (20x), 52 ft. (50x). Length 12.2"; weight 17 oz. Black rubber armored, waterproof. Case included.
Price:..$337.95

BUSHNELL SENTRY 16-32 zoom, 50mm objective. Field at 1000 yds. 140-65 ft. Length 8.7", weight 21.5 oz. Black rubber armored. Built-in peep sight. Comes with tripod and hardcase.
Price:..$205.95

BUSHNELL SPACEMASTER 20x-45x zoom. Long eye relief. Rubber armored, prismatic. 60mm objective. Field at 1000 yds. 90-58 ft. Minimum focus 20 ft. Length 12.7"; weight 43 oz.
Price: With tripod, carrying case and 20x-45x LER eyepiece............$560.95

BUSHNELL SPORTVIEW 12x-36x zoom, 50mm objective. Field at 100 yds. 160 ft. (12x), 90 ft. (36x). Length 14.6"; weight 25 oz.
Price: With tripod and carrying case $159.95

BUSHNELL XTRA-WIDE® 15-45x zoom, 60mm objective. Field at 1000 yds. 160-87 ft. Length 13"; weight 35 oz.
Price: $640.95

HERMES 1 70mm objective, 16x, 25x, 40x. Field at 1000 meters 160 ft. (16x), 75ft. (40x). Length 12.2"; weight 33 oz. From CZ-USA.
Price: Body $359.00
Price: 25x eyepiece $86.00
Price: 40x eyepiece $128.00

KOWA TS-500 SERIES Offset 45° or straight body. Comes with 20-40x zoom eyepiece or 20x fixed eyepiece. 50mm obj. Field of view at 1000 yds.: 171 ft. (20x fixed), 132-74 ft. (20-40x zoom). Length 8.9-10.4", weight 13.4-14.8 oz.
Price: TS-501 (offset 45° body w/20x fixed eyepiece) $258.00
Price: TS-502 (straight body w/20x fixed eyepiece) $231.00
Price: TS-501Z (offset 45° body w/20-40x zoom eyepiece) $321.00
Price: TS-502Z (straight body w/20-40x zoom eyepiece).........$290.00

KOWA TS-610 SERIES Offset 45° or straight body. Available with fluorite lens. Sunshade. 60mm obj. Field of view at 1000 yds.: 177 ft. (20xW), 154 ft. (22xW), 102 ft. (25x), 92 ft. (25xLER), 62 ft. (40x), 102-56 ft. (20-60x zoom). Length 11.2"; weight 27 oz. Note: Eyepieces for TSN 7mm series, TSN-660 series, and TS-610 series are interchangeable.
Price: TS-611 body (45° offset) $530.00
Price: TS-612 body (straight)............................$489.00

Price: TS-614 body (straight, fluorite lens)...........................$1,010.00
Price: TSE-Z2M (20-60x zoom eyepiece)..............................$231.00
Price: TSE-17HB (25x long eye relief eyepiece) $240.00
Price: TSE-15WM (27x wide angle eyepiece)............................$182.00
Price: TSE-21WB (20x wide angle high-grade eyepiece).................$230.00
Price: TSE-10PM (40x eyepiece)......................................$108.00
Price: TSE-16PM (25x eyepiece)......................................$108.00
Price: TSN-DA1 (digital photo adapter) $105.00
Price: Adapter rings for DA1..$43.00
Price: TSN-PA2 (800mm photo adapter)................................$269.00
Price: TSN-PA4 (1200mm photo adapter)...............................$330.00
Price: Camera mounts (for use with photo adapter) $30.00

KOWA TSN-660 SERIES Offset 45° or straight body. Fully waterproof. Available with fluorite lens. Sunshade and rotating tripod mount. 66mm obj., field of view at 1000 yds: 177 ft. (20x@), 154 ft. (27xW), 131 ft. (30xW), 102 ft. (25x), 92 ft. (25xLER), 62 ft. (40x), 108-79 ft. (20-40x Multi-Coated Zoom), 102-56 ft. (20-60x Zoom), 98-62 ft. (20-60x High Grade Zoom). Length 12.3"; weight 34.9-36.7 oz. Note: Eyepieces for TSN 77mm Series, TSN-660 Series, and TSN610 Series are interchangeable.
Price: TSN-661 body (45° offset) $660.00
Price: TSN-662 body (straight).......................................$610.00
Price: TSN-663 body (45° offset, fluorite lens).......................$1,070.00
Price: TSN-664 body (straight, fluorite lens).........................$1,010.00
Price: TSE-Z2M (20-60x zoom eyepiece)..............................$231.00
Price: TSE-Z4 (20-60x high-grade zoom eyepiece) $378.00
Price: TSE-Z6 (20-40x multi-coated zoom eyepiece)...................$250.00
Price: TSE-17HB (25x long eye relief eyepiece) $240.00
Price: TSE-14W (30x wide angle eyepiece)...........................$288.00
Price: TSE-21WB (20x wide angle eyepiece)..........................$230.00
Price: TSE-15PM (27x wide angle eyepiece)..........................$182.00
Price: TSE-10PM (40x eyepiece)......................................$108.00
Price: TSE-16PM (25x eyepiece)......................................$108.00
Price: TSNE5B (77x eyepiece)..$235.00
Price: TSNE7B (60x eyepiece)..$230.00
Price: TSN-DA1 (digital photo adapter) $105.00
Price: Adapter rings for DA1..$43.00
Price: TSN-PA2 (800mm photo adapter)................................$269.00
Price: TSN-PA4 (1200mm photo adapter)...............................$330.00
Price: Camera mounts (for use with photo adapter) $30.00

KOWA TSN-820 SERIES Offset 45° or straight body. Fully waterproof. Available with fluorite lens. Sunshade and rotating tripod mount. 82mm obj., field of view at 1000 yds: 75 ft (27xLER, 50xW), 126 ft. (32xW), 115-58 ft. (20-60xZoom). Length 15"; weight 49.4-52.2 oz.
Price: TSN-821M body (45° offset) $850.00
Price: TSN-822M body (straight)....................................$770.00
Price: TSN-823M body (45° offset, fluorite lens).....................$1,850.00
Price: TSN-824M body (straight, fluorite lens).......................$1,730.00
Price: TSE-Z7 (20-60x zoom eyepiece)...............................$433.00
Price: TSE-9W (50x wide angle eyepiece)............................$345.00
Price: TSE-14WB (32x wide angle eyepiece)..........................$366.00
Price: TSE-17HC (27x long eye relief eyepiece) $248.00
Price: TSN-Da1 (digital photo adapter) $105.00
Price: Adapter rings for DA1..$43.00
Price: TSN-PA2C (850mm photo adapter)..............................$300.00
Price: Camera mounts (for use with photo adapter) $30.00

LEUPOLD 12-40x60 VARIABLE 60mm objective, 12-40x. Field at 100 yds. 17.5-5.3 ft.; eye relief 1.2" (20x). Overall length 11.5", weight 32 oz. Rubber armored.
Price: $1,217.90

LEUPOLD 25x50 COMPACT 50mm objective, 25x. Field at 100 yds. 8.3 ft.; eye relief 1"; length overall 9.4"; weight 20.5 oz.
Price: Armored model...$848.20
Price: Packer Tripod $96.40

MIRADOR TTB SERIES Draw tube armored spotting scopes. Available with 75mm or 80mm objective. Zoom model (28x-62x, 80mm) is 11 7/8" (closed), weighs 50 oz. Field at 1000 yds. 70-42 ft. Comes with lens covers.
Price: 28-62x80mm...$1,133.95
Price: 32x80mm..$971.95
Price: 26-58x75mm...$989.95
Price: 30x75mm..$827.95

MIRADOR SSD SPOTTING SCOPES 60mm objective, 15x, 20x, 22x, 25x, 40x, 60x, 20-60x; field at 1000 yds. 37 ft.; length 10 1/4"; weight 33 oz.
Price: 25x $575.95
Price: 22x Wide Angle $593.95
Price: 20-60x Zoom..$746.95
Price: As above, with tripod, case $944.95

MIRADOR SIA SPOTTING SCOPES Similar to the SSD scopes except with 45° eyepiece. Length 12 1/4"; weight 39 oz.
Price: 25x $809.95
Price: 22x Wide Angle $827.95
Price: 20-60x Zoom..$980.95

MIRADOR SSR SPOTTING SCOPES 50mm or 60mm objective. Similar to SSD except rubber armored in black or camouflage. Length 11 1/8"; weight 31 oz.
Price: Black, 20x...$521.95
Price: Black, 18x Wide Angle $539.95
Price: Black, 16-48x Zoom..$692.95
Price: Black, 20x, 60mm, EER.......................................$692.95
Price: Black, 22x Wide Angle, 60mm $701.95
Price: Black, 20-60x Zoom..$854.95

SPOTTING SCOPES

MIRADOR SSF FIELD SCOPES Fixed or variable power, choice of 50mm, 60mm, 75mm objective lens. Length 9 3/4"; weight 20 oz. (15-32x50).
Price: 20x50mm **$359.95**
Price: 25x60mm **$440.95**
Price: 30x75mm **$584.95**
Price: 15-32x50mm Zoom **$548.95**
Price: 18-40x60mm Zoom **$629.95**
Price: 22-47x75mm Zoom **$773.95**

MIRADOR SRA MULTI ANGLE SCOPES Similar to SSF Series except eyepiece head rotates for viewing from any angle.
Price: 20x50mm **$503.95**
Price: 25x60mm **$647.95**
Price: 30x75mm **$764.95**
Price: 15-32x50mm Zoom **$692.95**
Price: 18-40x60mm Zoom **$836.95**
Price: 22-47x75mm Zoom **$953.95**

MIRADOR SIB FIELD SCOPES Short-tube, 45° scopes with porro prism design. 50mm and 60mm objective. Length 10 1/4"; weight 18.5 oz. (15-32x50mm); field at 1000 yds. 129-81 ft.
Price: 20x50mm **$386.95**
Price: 25x60mm **$449.95**
Price: 15-32x50mm Zoom **$575.95**
Price: 18-40x60mm Zoom **$638.95**

NIKON FIELDSCOPES 60mm and 78mm lens. Field at 1000 yds. 105 ft. (60mm, 20x), 126 ft. (78mm, 25x). Length 12.8" (straight 60mm), 12.6" (straight 78mm); weight 34.5- 47.5 oz. Eyepieces available separately.
Price: 60mm straight body **$499.99**
Price: 60mm angled body **$519.99**
Price: 60mm straight ED body **$779.99**
Price: 60mm angled ED body **$849.99**
Price: 78mm straight ED body **$899.99**
Price: 78mm angled ED body **$999.99**
Price: Eyepieces (15x to 60x) . . . . . **$146.95** to **$324.95**
Price: 20-45x eyepiece (25-56x for 78mm) **$320.55**

NIKON SPOTTING SCOPE 60mm objective, 20x fixed power or 15-45x zoom. Field at 1000 yds. 145 ft. (20x). Gray rubber armored. Straight or angled eyepiece. Weighs 44.2 oz., length 12.1" (20x).
Price: 20x60 fixed (with eyepiece) **$290.95**
Price: 15-45x zoom (with case, tripod, eyepiece) **$578.95**

PENTAX PF-80ED spotting scope 80mm objective lens available in 18x, 24x, 36x, 48x, 72x and 20-60x. Length 15.6", weight 11.9 to 19.2 oz.
Price: **$1,320.00**

SIGHTRON SII 2050X63 63mm objective lens, 20x-50x zoom. Field at 1000 yds 91.9 ft. (20x), 52.5 ft. (50x). Length 14"; weight 30.8 oz. Black rubber finish. Also available with 80mm objective lens.
Price: 63mm or 80mm **$339.95**

SIMMONS 1280 50mm objective, 15-45x zoom. Black matte finish. Ocular focus. Peep finder sight. Waterproof. FOV 95-51 ft. @ 1000 yards. Wgt. 33.5 oz., length 12".
Price: With tripod **$189.99**

SIMMONS 1281 60mm objective, 20-60x zoom. Black matte finish. Ocular focus. Peep finder sight. Waterproof. FOV 78-43 ft. @ 1000 yards. Wgt. 34.5 oz. Length 12".
Price: With tripod **$209.99**

SIMMONS 77206 PROHUNTER 50mm objectives, 25x fixed power. Field at 1000 yds. 113 ft.; length 10.25"; weighs 33.25 oz. Black rubber armored.
Price: With tripod case **$160.60**

SIMMONS 41200 REDLINE 50mm objective, 15x-45x zoom. Field at 1000 yds. 104-41 ft.; length 16.75"; weighs 32.75 oz.
Price: With hard case and tripod **$74.99**
Price: 20-60x, 60mm objective **$99.99**

SWAROVSKI CT EXTENDIBLE SCOPES 75mm or 85mm objective, 20-60x zoom, or fixed 15x, 22x, 30x, 32x eyepieces. Field at 1000 yds. 135 ft. (15x), 99 ft. (32x); 99 ft. (20x), 5.2 ft. (60x) for zoom. Length 12.4" (closed), 17.2" (open) for the CT75; 9.7"/17.2" for CT85. Weight 40.6 oz. (CT75), 49.4 oz. (CT85). Green rubber armored.
Price: CT75 body **$765.56**
Price: CT85 body **$1,094.44**
Price: 20-60x eyepiece **$343.33**
Price: 15x, 22x eyepiece **$232.22**
Price: 30x eyepiece **$265.55**

SWAROVSKI AT-80/ST-80 SPOTTING SCOPES 80mm objective, 20-60x zoom, or fixed 15x, 22x, 30x, 32x eyepieces. Field at 1000 yds. 135 ft. (15x), 99 ft. (32x); 99 ft. (20x), 52.5 ft. (60x) for zoom. Length 16" (AT-80), 15.6" (ST-80); weight 51.8 oz. Available with HD (high density) glass.
Price: AT-80 (angled) body **$1,094.44**
Price: ST-80 (straight) body **$1,094.44**
Price: With HD glass **$1,555.00**
Price: 20-60x eyepiece **$343.33**
Price: 15x, 22x eyepiece **$232.22**
Price: 30x eyepiece **$265.55**

SWIFT LYNX M836 15x-45x zoom, 60mm objective. Weight 7 lbs., length 14". Has 45° eyepiece, sunshade.
Price: **$315.00**

SWIFT NIGHTHAWK M849U 80mm objective, 20x-60x zoom, or fixed 19, 25x, 31x, 50x, 75x eyepieces. Has rubber armored body, 1.8x optical finder, retractable lens hood, 45° eyepiece. Field at 1000 yds. 60 ft. (28x), 41 ft. (75x). Length 13.4 oz.; weight 39 oz.
Price: Body only **$870.00**
Price: 20-68x eyepiece **$370.00**
Price: Fixed eyepieces . . . . . **$130.00** to **$240.00**
Price: Model 849 (straight) body **$795.00**

SWIFT NIGHTHAWK M850U 65mm objective, 16x-48x zoom, or fixed 19x, 20x, 25x, 40x, 60x eyepieces. Rubber armored with a 1.8x optical finder, retractable lens hood. Field at 1000 yds. 83 ft. (22x), 52 ft. (60x). Length 12.3"; weight 30 oz. Has 45° eyepiece.
Price: Body only **$650.00**
Price: 16x-48x eyepiece **$370.00**
Price: Fixed eyepieces . . . . . **$130.00** to **$240.00**
Price: Model 850 (straight) body **$575.00**

SWIFT LEOPARD M837 50mm objective, 25x. Length 9 11/16" to 10 1/2". Weight with tripod 28 oz. Rubber armored. Comes with tripod.
Price: **$160.00**

SWIFT TELEMASTER M841 60mm objective. 15x to 60x variable power. Field at 1000 yds. 160 feet (15x) to 40 feet (60x). Weight 3.25 lbs.; length 18" overall.
Price: **$399.50**

SWIFT PANTHER M844 15x-45x zoom or 22x WA, 15x, 20x, 40x. 60mm objective. Field at 1000 yds. 141 ft. (15x), 68 ft. (40x), 95-58 ft. (20x-45x).
Price: Body only **$380.00**
Price: 15x-45x zoom eyepiece **$120.00**
Price: 20x-45x zoom (long eye relief) eyepiece **$140.00**
Price: 15x, 20x, 40x eyepiece **$65.00**
Price: 22x WA eyepiece **$80.00**

SWIFT M700T 12x-36x, 50mm objective. Field of view at 100 yds. 16 ft. (12x), 9 ft. (36x). Length 14"; weight with tripod 3.22 lbs.
Price: **$225.00**

SWIFT SEARCHER M839 60mm objective, 20x, 40x. Field at 1000 yds. 118 ft. (30x), 59 ft. (40x). Length 12.6"; weight 3 lbs. Rotating eyepiece head for straight or 45° viewing.
Price: **$580.00**
Price: 30x, 50x eyepieces, each **$67.00**

TASCO 29TZBWP WATERPROOF SPOTTER 60mm objective lens, 20x-60x zoom. Field at 100 yds. 7 ft., 4 in. to 3 ft., 8 in. Black rubber armored. Comes with tripod, hard case.
Price: **$356.50**

TASCO WC28TZ WORLD CLASS SPOTTING SCOPE 50mm objective, 12-36x zoom. Field at 100 yds. World Class. 13-3.8 ft. Comes with tripod and case.
Price: **$220.00**

TASCO CW5001 COMPACT ZOOM 50mm objective, 12x-36x zoom. Field at 100 yds. 16 ft., 9 in. Includes photo adapter tube, tripod with panhead lever, case.
Price: **$280.00**

TASCO 3700WP WATERPROOF SPOTTER 50mm objective, 18x-36x zoom. Field at 100 yds. 12ft., 6 in. to 7 ft., 9 in. Black rubber armored. Comes with tripod, hard case.
Price: **$288.60**

TASCO 3700, 3701 SPOTTING SCOPE 50mm objective. 18x-36x zoom. Field at 100 yds. 12 ft., 6 in. to 7 ft., 9 in. Black rubber armored.
Price: Model 3700 (black, with tripod, case) **$237.00**
Price: Model 3701 (as above, brown camo) **$237.00**

TASCO 21EB ZOOM 50mm objective lens, 15x-45x zoom. Field at 100 yds. 11 ft. (15x). Weight 22 oz.; length 18.3" overall. Comes with panhead lever tripod.
Price: **$119.00**

TASCO 22EB ZOOM 60mm objective lens, 20x-60x zoom. Field at 100 yds. 7 ft., 2 in. (20x). Weight 28 oz.; length 21.5" overall. Comes with micro-adjustable tripod.
Price: **$183.00**

UNERTL "FORTY-FIVE" 54mm objective. 20x (single fixed power). Field at 100 yds. 10',10"; eye relief 1"; focusing range infinity to 33 ft. Weight about 32 oz.; overall length 15 3/4". With lens covers.
Price: With mono-layer magnesium coating **$810.00**

UNERTL STRAIGHT PRISMATIC 63.5mm objective, 24x. Field at 100 yds., 7 ft. Relative brightness, 6.96. Eye relief 1/2". Weight 40 oz.; length closed 19". Push-pull and screw-focus eyepiece. 16x and 32x eyepieces **$125.00** each.
Price: **$786.00**

UNERTL 20x STRAIGHT PRISMATIC 54mm objective, 20x. Field at 100 yds. 8.5 ft. Relative brightness 6.1. Eye relief 1/2". Weight 36 oz.; length closed 13 1/2". Complete with lens covers.
Price: **$695.00**

UNERTL TEAM SCOPE 100mm objective. 15x, 24x, 32x eyepieces. Field at 100 yds. 13 to 7.5 ft. Relative brightness, 39.06 to 9.79. Eye relief 2" to 1 1/2". Weight 13 lbs.; length 29 7/8" overall. Metal tripod, yoke and wood carrying case furnished (total weight 80 lbs.).
Price: **$3,624.50**

WEAVER 20x50 50mm objective. Field of view 124 ft. at 100 yds. Eye relief .85"; weighs 21 oz.; overall length 10". Waterproof, armored.
Price: **$249.99**

WEAVER 15-40x60 ZOOM 60mm objective. 15x-40x zoom. Field at 100 yds. 119 ft. (15x), 66 ft. (60x). Overall length 12.5", weighs 26 oz. Waterproof, armored.
Price: **$399.99**

ACCESSORIES

COMPENDIUM OF STATE LAWS GOVERNING FIREARMS

The following chart lists the main provisions of state firearms laws as of the date of publication. In addition to the state provisions, the purchase, sale, and, in certain circumstances, the possession and interstate transportation of firearms are regulated by the Federal Gun Control Act of 1968 as amended by the Firearms Owners' Protection Act of 1986. Also, cities and localities may have their own gun ordinances in addition to federal and state restrictions. Details may be obtained by contacting local law enforcement authorities or by consulting your state's firearms law digest compiled by the NRA Institute for Legislative Action.

STATE	GUN BAN	EXEMPTIONS TO NICS[2]	STATE WAITING PERIOD - NUMBER OF DAYS		LICENSE OR PERMIT TO PURCHASE		REGISTRATION		RECORD OF SALE REPORTED TO STATE OR LOCAL GOVT.
			HANDGUNS	LONG GUNS	HANDGUNS	LONG GUNS	HANDGUNS	LONG GUNS	
Alabama	—	—	—	—	—	—	—	—	X
Alaska	—	RTC	—	—	—	—	—	—	—
Arizona	—	RTC	—	—	—	—	—	—	—
Arkansas	—	RTC	—	—	—	—	—	—	—
California	X_{20}	—	10	10	—	—	X	—	X
Colorado	—	—	—	—	—	—	—	—	—
Connecticut	X_{20}	GRTC	$14_{14, 15}$	$14_{14, 15}$	X_{16}	—	—	—	X
Delaware	—	GRTC	—	—	—	—	—	—	—
Florida	—	GRTC	$3_{14, 15}$	—	—	—	—	—	—
Georgia	—	RTC	—	—	—	—	—	—	—
Hawaii	X_{20}	L, RTC	—	—	X_{16}	X_{16}	X_{12}	X_{12}	X
Idaho	—	RTC	—	—	—	—	—	—	—
Illinois	20	L	3	1	X_{16}	X_{16}	$—_4$	$—_4$	X
Indiana	—	RTC, O[3]	—	—	—	—	—	—	X
Iowa	—	L, RTC	—	—	X_{16}	—	—	—	X
Kansas	—	—	1	—	1	—	$—_1$	—	1
Kentucky	—	RTC	—	—	—	—	—	—	—
Louisiana	—	GRTC	—	—	—	—	—	—	—
Maine	—	—	—	—	—	—	—	—	—
Maryland	X_{20}	GRTC	7	7_9	8	—	—	—	X
Massachusetts	X_{20}	L, RTC	7	—	X_{16}	X_{16}	—	—	X
Michigan	—	L	—	—	X_{16}	—	X	—	X
Minnesota	—	L, GRTC	7_{16}	16	X_{16}	X_{16}	—	—	X
Mississippi	—	RTC[3]	—	—	—	—	—	—	—
Missouri	—	—	7	—	X_{16}	—	—	—	X
Montana	—	RTC	—	—	—	—	—	—	—
Nebraska	—	L	—	—	X	—	—	—	—
Nevada	—	RTC	1	—	—	—	1	—	—
New Hampshire	—	—	—	—	—	—	—	—	X
New Jersey	X_{20}	—	—	—	X_{16}	X_{16}	—	—	X
New Mexico	—	—	—	—	—	—	—	—	—
New York	X_{20}	L, RTC	—	—	X_{16}	16	X	7	X
North Carolina	—	L, RTC	—	—	X_{16}	—	—	—	X
North Dakota	—	RTC	—	—	—	—	—	—	X
Ohio	X_{20}	—	1	—	16	—	1	—	1
Oklahoma	—	RTC	—	—	—	—	—	—	—
Oregon	—	—	—	—	—	—	—	—	X
Pennsylvania	—	—	—	—	—	—	—	—	X
Rhode Island	—	—	7	7	—	—	—	—	X
South Carolina	—	RTC	8	—	8	—	—	—	X
South Dakota	—	GRTC	2	—	—	—	—	—	X
Tennessee	—	RTC	—	—	—	—	—	—	X
Texas	—	RTC[3]	—	—	—	—	—	—	—
Utah	—	RTC	—	—	—	—	—	—	—
Vermont	—	—	—	—	—	—	—	—	—
Virginia	X_{20}	—	1, 8	—	1,8	—	—	—	1
Washington	—	RTC	5_{10}	—	—	—	—	—	X
West Virginia	—	—	—	—	—	—	—	—	—
Wisconsin	—	—	2	—	—	—	—	—	X
Wyoming	—	RTC	—	—	—	—	—	—	—
District of Columbia	X_{20}	L	—	—	X_{16}	X_{16}	X_{16}	X	X

COMPENDIUM OF STATE LAWS GOVERNING FIREARMS

Since state laws are subject to frequent change, this chart is not to be considered legal advice or a restatement of the law. All fifty states have sportsmen's protections laws to halt harrassment.

Compiled by
NRA INSTITUTE FOR LEGISLATIVE ACTION
11250 WAPLES MILL ROAD
FAIRFAX, VIRGINIA 22030
www.nraila.org

STATE	STATE PROVISION FOR RIGHT-TO-CARRY CONCEALED[15]	CARRYING OPENLY PROHIBITED	OWNER ID CARDS OR LICENSING	FIREARM RIGHTS CONSTITUTIONAL PROVISION	STATE FIREARMS PREEMPTION LAWS	RANGE PROTECTION LAW
Alabama	R	X[11]	—	X	X	—
Alaska	R	—	—	X	—	X
Arizona	R	—	—	X	X	—
Arkansas	R	X[5]	—	X	X	X
California	L	X[6]	—	—	X	X
Colorado	L	1	—	X	—	X
Connecticut	R	X	—	X	X[17]	X
Delaware	L	—	—	X	X	X
Florida	R	X	—	X	X	X
Georgia	R	X	—	X	X	X
Hawaii	L	X	X	X	—	—
Idaho	R	—	—	X	X	X
Illinois	D	X	X	X	—	X
Indiana	R	X	—	X	X[18]	X
Iowa	L	X	—	—	X	X
Kansas	D	1	—	X	—	—
Kentucky	R	—	—	X	X	X
Louisiana	R	—	—	X	X	X
Maine	R	—	—	X	X	X
Maryland	L	X	—	—	X	X
Massachusetts	L	X	X	X	X[17]	X
Michigan	L	X[11]	—	X	X	X
Minnesota	L	X	—	—	X	—
Mississippi	R	—	—	X	X	—
Missouri	D	—	—	X	X	X
Montana	R	—	—	X	X	X
Nebraska	D	—	—	X	—	—
Nevada	R	—	—	X	X	X
New Hampshire	R	—	—	X	—	X
New Jersey	L	X	X	—	X[17]	X
New Mexico	D	—	—	X	X	—
New York	L	X	X	—	X[22]	X
North Carolina	R	—	—	X	X	X
North Dakota	R	X[6]	—	X	X	X
Ohio	D	1	16	X	—	X
Oklahoma	R	X[6]	—	X	X	X
Oregon	R	—	—	X	X	X
Pennsylvania	R	X[11]	—	X	X	X
Rhode Island	L	X	—	X	X	X
South Carolina	R	X	—	X	X	—
South Dakota	R	—	—	X	X	X
Tennessee	R	X[5]	—	X	X	X
Texas	R	X	—	X	X	—
Utah	R	X[6]	—	X	X	X
Vermont	R[19]	X[5]	—	X	X	X
Virginia	R	—	—	X	X	X
Washington	R	X[21]	—	X	X	—
West Virginia	R	—	—	X	X	X
Wisconsin	D	—	—	X	X	X
Wyoming	R	—	—	X	X	X
District of Columbia	L	X	X	NA	—	X

With over 20,000 "gun control" laws on the books in America, there are two challenges facing every gun owner. First, you owe it to yourself to become familiar with the federal laws on gun ownership. Only by knowing the laws can you avoid innocently breaking one.

Second, while federal legislation receives much more media attention, state legislatures and city councils make many more decisions regarding your right to own and carry firearms. NRA members and all gun owners must take extra care to be aware of anti-gun laws and ordinances at the state and local levels.

Notes:
1. In certain cities or counties.

2. **National Instant Check System (NICS) exemption codes:**
   RTC-Carry Permit Holders Exempt From NICS
   GRTC-Holders of RTC Permits issued before November 30, 1998 exempt from NICS. Holders of more recent permits are not exempt.
   L-Holders of state licenses to possess or purchase or firearms ID cards exempt from NICS.
   O-Other, See Note 3.

3. **NICS exemptions notes: Indiana:** Personal protection and hunting and target permits; **Mississippi:** Permit issued to security guards does **not** qualify.; **Texas:** Texas Peace Officer license, TCLEOSE Card, is grandfathered only.

4. Chicago only. No handgun not already registered may be possessed.

5. **Arkansas** prohibits carrying a firearm "with a purpose to employ it as a weapon against a person." **Tennessee** prohibits carrying "with the intent to go armed." **Vermont** prohibits carrying a firearm "with the intent or purpose of injuring another."

6. Loaded.

7. New York City only.

8. A permit is required to acquire another handgun before 30 days have elapsed following the acquisition of a handgun.

9. **Maryland** subjects purchases of "assault weapons" to a 7-day waiting period.

10. May be extended by police to 30 days in some circumstances. An individual not holding a driver's license must wait 90 days.

11. Carrying a handgun openly in a motor vehicle requires a license.

12. Every person arriving in **Hawaii** is required to register any firearm(s) brought into the State within 3 days of arrival of the person or firearm(s), whichever occurs later. Handguns purchased from licensed dealers must be registered within 5 days.

13. Concealed carry laws vary significantly between the states. Ratings reflect the real effect a state's particular laws have on the ability of citizens to carry firearms for self-defense.

14. Purchases from licensed dealers only.

15. The state waiting period does not apply to a person holding a valid permit or license to carry a firearm. In **Connecticut,** a hunting license also exempts the holder, for long gun purchases. In **Indiana,** only persons with unlimited carry permits are exempt.

16. **Connecticut:** A permit to purchase or a carry permit is required to obtain a handgun and a carry permit is required to transport a handgun outside your home. **District of Columbia:** No handgun may be possessed unless it was registered prior to Sept. 23, 1976 and re-registered by Feb. 5, 1977. A permit to purchase is required for a rifle or shotgun. **Hawaii:** Purchase permits, required for all firearms, may not be issued until 14 days after application. A handgun purchase permit is valid for 10 days, for one handgun; a long gun permit is valid for one year, for multiple long guns. **Illinois:** A Firearm Owner's Identification Card (FOI) is required to possess or purchase a firearm, must be issued to qualified applicants within 30 days, and is valid for 5 years. **Iowa:** A purchase permit is required for handguns, and is valid for one year, beginning three days

after issuance. **Massachusetts:** Firearms and feeding devices for firearms are divided into classes. Depending on the class, a firearm identification card (FID) or class A license or class B license is required to possess, purchase, or carry a firearm, ammunition therefore, or firearm feeding device, or "large capacity feeding device." **Michigan:** A handgun purchaser must obtain a license to purchase from local law enforcement, and within 10 days present the license and handgun to obtain a certificate of inspection. **Minnesota:** A handgun transfer or carrying permit, or a 7-day waiting period and handgun transfer report, is required to purchase handguns or "assault weapons" from a dealer. A permit or transfer report must be issued to qualified applicants within 7 days. A permit is valid for one year, a transfer report for 30 days. **Missouri:** A purchase permit is required for a handgun, must be issued to qualified applicants within 7 days, and is valid for 30 days. **New Jersey:** Firearm owners must possess an FID, which must be issued to qualified applicants within 30 days. To purchase a handgun, an FID and a purchase permit, which must be issued within 30 days to qualified applicants, is valid for 90 days, are required. An FID is required to purchase long guns. **New York:** Purchase, possession and/or carrying of a handgun require a single license, which includes any restrictions made upon the bearer. New York City also requires a license for long guns. **North Carolina:** To purchase a handgun, a license or permit is required, which must be issued to qualified applicants within 30 days. **Ohio:** Some cities require a permit-to-purchase or firearm owner ID card.

17. Preemption through judicial ruling. Local regulation may be instituted in **Massachusetts** if ratified by the legislature.

18. Except Gary and East Chicago and local laws enacted before January, 1994.

19. **Vermont** law respects your right to carry without a permit.

20. **California prohibits** "assault weapons" and commencing January 1, 2001, any "unsafe handgun." **Connecticut, New Jersey, New York City,** and other local jurisdictions in **New York,** and some local jurisdictions in **Ohio** prohibit "assault weapons." **Hawaii** prohibits "assault pistols." **Illinois:** Chicago, Evanston, Oak Park, Morton Grove, Winnetka, Wilmette, and Highland Park prohibit handguns; some cities prohibit other kinds of firearms. **Maryland** prohibits several small, low-caliber, inexpensive handguns and "assault pistols." **Massachusetts:** It is unlawful to sell, transfer or possess "any assuait weapon or large capacity feeding device" [more than 10 rounds] that was not legally possessed on September 13, 1994. **Ohio:** some cities prohibit handguns of certain magazine capacities." **Virginia** prohibits "Street Sweeper" shotguns. The **District of Columbia** prohibits new acquisition of handguns and any semi-automatic firearm capable of using a detachable ammunition magazine of more than 12 rounds capacity. (With respect to some of these laws and ordinances, individuals may retain prohibited firearms owned previously, with certain restrictions.)

21. Local jurisdictions may opt out of prohibition.

22. Preemption only applies to handguns.

Concealed carry codes:

R: Right-to-Carry: "shall issue" or less restrictive discretionary permit system (Ala., Conn.) (See also note #21.)
L: Right-to-Carry Limited by local authority's discretion over permit issuance.
D: Right-to-Carry Denied, no permit system exists; concealed carry is prohibited.

NL 00930

Rev.3/2001 5m

NRA · RIGHT-TO-CARRY RECIPROCITY GUIDE

- **The right to self-defense neither begins nor ends at a state border.**

- **A law-abiding citizen does not suffer a character change by crossing a state line.**

- **An "unalienable right" is not determined by geographical boundaries.**

- **A patchwork of state laws regarding the carrying of firearms can make criminals out of honest folks, especially those who frequently must travel the states to earn a living.**

- **Using data for all 3,054 U.S. counties from 1977 to 1994, University of Chicago Prof. John Lott finds that for each additional year a concealed handgun law is in effect the murder rate declines by 3%, robberies by over 2%, and the rape rate by 2%.**

In spite of the truth of these statements and the fact that nearly half of all Americans live in states that allow a law-abiding citizen to carry a firearm concealed for personal protection, it has not been commonplace that these same citizens could carry their firearm across states lines. NRA-ILA is working to pass right-to-carry reciprocity laws granting permit holders the ability to carry their firearms legally while visiting or traveling beyond their home state.

In order to assist NRA Members in determining which states recognize their permits, NRA-ILA has created this guide. **This guide is not to be considered as legal advice or a restatement of the law. It is important to remember that state carry laws vary considerably. Be sure to check with state and local authorities outside your home state for a complete listing of restrictions on carrying concealed in that state.** Many states restrict carrying in bars, restaurants (where alcohol is served), establishments where packaged alcohol is sold, schools, colleges, universities, churches, parks, sporting events, correctional facilities, courthouses, federal and state government offices/buildings, banks, airport terminals, police stations, polling places, any posted private property restricting the carrying of concealed firearms, etc. In addition to state restrictions, federal law prohibits carrying on military bases, in national parks and the sterile area of airports. National Forests usually follow laws of the state wherein the forest is located.

NOTE: Vermont does not issue permits, but allows carrying of concealed firearms if there is no intent to commit a crime. Vermont residents traveling to other states must first obtain a non-resident permit from that state—if available—prior to carrying concealed. Utah will honor any permit issued by another state or county for 60 consecutive days.

NOTE TO READERS: Right To Carry reciprocity and recognition between the various states is subject to frequent change through legislative action and regulatory interpretation. This information is the best available at the time of publication. This summary is not intended as legal advice or restatement of law.

•• **Last Revised 6/2002** ••

NRA - RIGHT-TO-CARRY RECIPROCITY GUIDE

Alabama

Right-to-Carry Law Type
Shall Issue

Issuing Authority:
County Sheriff
These states also recognize your permit:
Alaska, Florida, Georgia, Idaho, Indiana, Kentucky, Michigan, Mississippi, Montana, North Dakota, Utah, Vermont, Wyoming
Contact agency for non-resident permits if granted:
Permits not granted.
http://www.dps.state.al.us

Alaska

Right-to-Carry Law Type
Shall Issue

Issuing Authority:
State Trooper
These states also recognize your permit:
Alabama, Arizona, Florida, idaho, Indiana, Kentucky, Michigan, Montana, North Dakota, Oklahoma, Texas, Vermont, Wyoming
Contact agency for non-resident permits if granted:
Permits not granted.
http://www.dps.state.ak.us/ast/achp/

Arizona

Right-to-Carry Law Type
Shall Issue

Issuing Authority:
Arizona Department of Public Safety
These states also recognize your permit:
Alaska, Arkansas, Idaho, Indiana, Kentucky, Michigan, Montana, Texas, Utah, Vermont
Contact agency for non-resident permits if granted:
Arizona Department of Public Safety
http://www.dps.state.az.us/ccw/welcome.htm

Arkansas

Right-to-Carry Law Type
Shall Issue

Issuing Authority:
State Police
These states also recognize your permit:
Alaska, Arizona, Florida, Idaho, Indiana, Kentucky, Michigan, Montana, Oklahoma, South Carolina, Tennessee, Texas, Utah, Vermont, Wyoming
Contact agency for non-resident permits if granted:
Permits not granted.
http://www.state.ar.us/asp/handgun.html

California

Right-to-Carry Law Type
Discretionary Issue

Issuing Authority:
County Sheriff
These states also recognize your permit:
Idaho, Indiana, Kentucky, Michigan, Montana, Utah, Vermont
Contact agency for non-resident permits if granted:
Permits not granted.
http://caag.state.ca.us/

Colorado

Right-to-Carry Law Type
Discretionary Issue

Issuing Authority:
City Chief of Police/County Sheriff
These states also recognize your permit:
Idaho, Indiana, Kentucky, Michigan, Utah, Vermont
Contact agency for non-resident permits if granted:
Permits not granted.
http://www.state.co.us/gov_dir/cdps/csp.htm

Connecticut

Right-to-Carry Law Type
Shall Issue

Issuing Authority:
Department of Public Safety, Special Licenses & Firearms Unit
These states also recognize your permit:
Idaho, Indiana, Kentucky, Michigan, Montana, Utah, Vermont
Contact agency for non-resident permits if granted:
Dept. of Public Safety, Special Licenses Unit; (860) 685-8000
http://www.state.ct.us/dps/CSP.htm

Delaware

Right-to-Carry Law Type
Discretionary Issue

Issuing Authority:
Prothonotary of Superior Court
These states also recognize your permit:
Idaho, Indiana, Kentucky, Michigan, Montana, Utah, Vermont
Contact agency for non-resident permits if granted:
Permits not granted.
http://www.state.de.us/dsp/

Florida

Right-to-Carry Law Type
Shall Issue

Issuing Authority:
Department of State, Division of Licensing
These states also recognize your permit:
Alabama, Alaska, Arkansas, Georgia, Idaho, Indiana, Kentucky, Louisiana, Michigan, Mississippi, Montana, New Hampshire, North Dakota, Pennsylvania, Tennessee, Texas, Utah, Vermont, Wyoming
Contact agency for non-resident permits if granted:
Dept. of State, Division of Licensing; (850) 488-5381
http://licgweb.dos.state.fl.us/

Georgia

Right-to-Carry Law Type
Shall Issue

Issuing Authority:
County Probate Judge
These states also recognize your permit:
Alabama, Florida, Idaho, Indiana, Kentucky, Michigan, Montana, New Hampshire, Tennessee, Utah, Vermont
Contact agency for non-resident permits if granted:
Permits not granted.
http://www.ganet.org/ago/

NRA - RIGHT-TO-CARRY RECIPROCITY GUIDE

Hawaii
Right-to-Carry Law Type
Discretionary Issue

Issuing Authority:
Chief of Police
These states also recognize your permit:
Idaho, Indiana, Kentucky, Michigan, Montana, Utah, Vermont
Contact agency for non-resident permits if granted:
Permits not granted.
http://www.hawaii.gov/ag/index.html

Idaho
Right-to-Carry Law Type
Shall Issue

Issuing Authority:
County Sheriff
These states also recognize your permit:
Alabama, Alaska, Florida, Georgia, Indiana, Kentucky, Michigan, Montana, North Dakota, Utah, Vermont, Wyoming
Contact agency for non-resident permits if granted:
Any Sheriffs' Department
http://www./state.id.us/dle/dle.htm

Illinois
Right-to-Carry Law Type
Non-Issue

Issuing Authority:
Permits not available.
These states also recognize your permit:
None.
Contact agency for non-resident permits if granted:
Permits not granted.
http://www.state.il.us/isp/isphpage.htm

Indiana
Right-to-Carry Law Type
Shall Issue

Issuing Authority:
Chief Law Enforcement Officer of Municipality
These states also recognize your permit:
Alabama, Alaska, Florida, Georgia, Idaho, Kentucky, Michigan, Montana, Utah, Vermont, Wyoming
Contact agency for non-resident permits if granted:
Permits not granted.
http://www.state.in.us/isp/

Iowa
Right-to-Carry Law Type
Discretionary Issue

Issuing Authority:
(resident) Sheriff (non-resident) Commissioner of Public Safety
These states also recognize your permit:
Idaho, Indiana, Kentucky, Michigan, Montana, Utah, Vermont
Contact agency for non-resident permits if granted:
Commissioner of Public Safety; (515) 281-3211
http://www.state.ia.us/government/dps/index.html

Kansas
Right-to-Carry Law Type
Non-Issue

Issuing Authority:
Permits not available.
These states also recognize your permit:
None
Contact agency for non-resident permits if granted:
Permits not granted.
http://www.ink.org/public/ksag/

Kentucky
Right-to-Carry Law Type
Shall Issue

Issuing Authority:
State Police
These states also recognize your permit:
Alabama, Alaska, Arizona, Arkansas, Florida, Georgia, Idaho, Indiana, Louisiana, Michigan, Mississippi, Montana, N. Dakota, Pennsylvania, Tennessee, Texas, Utah, W. Virginia, Vermont, Wyoming
Contact agency for non-resident permits if granted:
Permits not granted.
http://www.state.ky.us/agencies/ksp/ksphome.htm#menu

Louisiana
Right-to-Carry Law Type
Shall Issue

Issuing Authority:
Department of Public Safety & Corrections
These states also recognize your permit:
Alaska, Florida, Idaho, Indiana, Kentucky, Michigan, Montana, Tennessee, Texas, Utah, Vermont, Virginia
Contact agency for non-resident permits if granted:
Permits not granted.
http://www.dps.state.la.us/stpolice.html

Maine
Right-to-Carry Law Type
Shall Issue

Issuing Authority:
Dept. of Public Safety, Maine State Police, Licensing Division
These states also recognize your permit:
Idaho, Indiana, Kentucky, Michigan, Montana, Utah, Vermont
Contact agency for non-resident permits if granted:
Chief of State Police; (207) 624-8775

Maryland
Right-to-Carry Law Type
Discretionary Issue

Issuing Authority:
Superintendent of State Police
These states also recognize your permit:
Alaska, Idaho, Indiana, Kentucky, Michigan, Montana, Utah, Vermont
Contact agency for non-resident permits if granted:
Superintendent of State Police
http://www.inform.umd.edu/UMS+State/MD_Resources/MDSP/handgun.html

REFERENCE

NRA - RIGHT-TO-CARRY RECIPROCITY GUIDE

Massachusetts

Right-to-Carry Law Type
Discretionary Issue

Issuing Authority:
Department of State Police, Firearms Record Bureau
These states also recognize your permit:
Alaska, Idaho, Indiana, Kentucky, Michigan, Montana, Utah, Vermont
Contact agency for non-resident permits if granted:
Permits are technically available for non-residents, but are rarely granted
http://www.state.ma.us/msp/firearms/index.htm

Montana

Right-to-Carry Law Type
Shall Issue

Issuing Authority:
County Sheriff
These states also recognize your permit:
Alaska, Florida, Idaho, Indiana, Kentucky, Michigan, North Dakota, Utah, Vermont, Wyoming
Contact agency for non-resident permits if granted:
Permits not granted.
http://www.doj.state.mt.us/ls/weaponslist.htm

Michigan

Right-to-Carry Law Type
Shall Issue

Issuing Authority:
County Gun Board/Sheriff
These states also recognize your permit:
Alabama, Alaska, Florida, Georgia, Idaho, Indiana, Kentucky, Montana, New Hampshire, North Dakota, Utah, Vermont, Wyoming
Contact agency for non-resident permits if granted:
Permits not granted.
http://www.msp.state.mi.us

Nebraska

Right-to-Carry Law Type
Non-Issue

Issuing Authority:
Permits not available.
These states also recognize your permit:
None.
Contact agency for non-resident permits if granted:
Permits not granted.
http://www.nebraska-state-patrol.org/

Minnesota

Right-to-Carry Law Type
Discretionary Issue

Issuing Authority:
Chief of Police/County Sheriff
These states also recognize your permit:
Idaho, Indiana, Kentucky, Michigan, Montana, Utah, Vermont
Contact agency for non-resident permits if granted:
Permits not granted.
http://www.dps.state.mn.us/

Nevada

Right-to-Carry Law Type
Shall Issue

Issuing Authority:
County Sheriff
These states also recognize your permit:
Alaska, Idaho, Indiana, Kentucky, Michigan, Montana, Utah, Vermont
Contact agency for non-resident permits if granted:
In person with any County Sheriff
http://www.state.nv.us/ag

Mississippi

Right-to-Carry Law Type
Shall Issue

Issuing Authority:
Department of Public Safety
These states also recognize your permit:
Alabama, Florida, Idaho, Indiana, Kentucky, Michigan, Montana, Tennessee, Utah, Vermont, Wyoming
Contact agency for non-resident permits if granted:
Permits not granted.
http://www.dps.state.ms.us/

New Hampshire

Right-to-Carry Law Type
Shall Issue

Issuing Authority:
Selectman/Mayor or Chief of Police
These states also recognize your permit:
Alabama, Alaska, Florida, Georgia, Idaho, Indiana, Kentucky, Michigan, North Dakota, Utah, Vermont, Wyoming
Contact agency for non-resident permits if granted:
Director of State Police; (603) 271-3575
http://www.state.nh.us.nhsp.index.html

Missouri

Right-to-Carry Law Type
Non-Issue

Issuing Authority:
Permits not available.
These states also recognize your permit:
None.
Contact agency for non-resident permits if granted:
Permits not granted.
http://www.dps.state.mo.us/home/dpshome.htm

New Jersey

Right-to-Carry Law Type
Discretionary Issue

Issuing Authority:
Chief of Police/Superintendent of State Police
These states also recognize your permit:
Idaho, Indiana, Kentucky, Michigan, Montana, Utah, Vermont
Contact agency for non-resident permits if granted:
Superintendent of State Police; (609) 882-2000 ext. 2664 (technically available but rarely granted)
http://www.njsp.org/front.html

REFERENCE

NRA - RIGHT-TO-CARRY RECIPROCITY GUIDE

New Mexico

Right-to-Carry Law Type
Non-Issue

Issuing Authority:
Permits not available.
These states also recognize your permit:
None
Contact agency for non-resident permits if granted:
Permits not granted.
http://www.dps.nm.org/

New York

Right-to-Carry Law Type
Discretionary Issue

Issuing Authority:
Varies by county
These states also recognize your permit:
Idaho, Indiana, Michigan, Montana, Utah, Vermont
Contact agency for non-resident permits if granted:
Permits not granted.
http://www.troopers.state.ny.us/

North Carolina

Right-to-Carry Law Type
Shall Issue

Issuing Authority:
County Sheriff
These states also recognize your permit:
Alaska, Idaho, Indiana, Kentucky, Michigan, Montana, Utah, Vermont, Virginia
Contact agency for non-resident permits if granted:
Permits not granted.
http://www.jus.state.nc.us

North Dakota

Right-to-Carry Law Type
Shall Issue

Issuing Authority:
Chief of the Bureau of Criminal Investigation
These states also recognize your permit:
Alabama, Alaska, Florida, Kentucky, Michigan, Montana, New Hampshire, Wyoming
Contact agency for non-resident permits if granted:
Chief of the Bureau of Criminal Investigation
http://www.ag.state.nd.us/BCI/BCI.html

Ohio

Right-to-Carry Law Type
Non-Issue

Issuing Authority:
Permits not available.
These states also recognize your permit:
None.
Contact agency for non-resident permits if granted:
Permits not granted.
http://www.ag.state.oh.us/

Oklahoma

Right-to-Carry Law Type
Shall Issue

Issuing Authority:
State Bureau of Investigation
These states also recognize your permit:
Alaska, Arkansas, Idaho, Indiana, Kentucky, Michigan, Montana, Texas, Utah, Virginia, Vermont, Wyoming
Contact agency for non-resident permits if granted:
Permits not granted.
http://www.osbi.state.ok.us/

Oregon

Right-to-Carry Law Type
Shall Issue

Issuing Authority:
County Sheriff
These states also recognize your permit:
Alaska, Idaho, Indiana, Kentucky, Michigan, Montana, Utah, Vermont
Contact agency for non-resident permits if granted:
Discretionary to residents of contiguous states only
http://www.osp.state.or.us/html/index_high.html

Pennsylvania

Right-to-Carry Law Type
Shall Issue

Issuing Authority:
County Sheriff or Chief of Police
These states also recognize your permit:
Florida, Idaho, Indiana, Kentucky, Michigan, Montana, Utah, Vermont
Contact agency for non-resident permits if granted:
Any Sheriff's Department
http://www.state.pa.us/PA_Exec/State_Police/

Rhode Island

Right-to-Carry Law Type
Discretionary Issue

Issuing Authority:
Attorney General
These states also recognize your permit:
Idaho, Indiana, Kentucky, Michigan, Montana, Utah, Vermont
Contact agency for non-resident permits if granted:
Attorney General by mail only (no phone calls) send self-addressed stamped envelope to: Dept. of Attorney General 150 South Main Street Providence, RI 02903 Attn: Bureau of Criminal Identification
http://www.riag.state.ri.us

South Carolina

Right-to-Carry Law Type
Shall Issue

Issuing Authority:
S.C. Law Enforcement Division
These states also recognize your permit:
Alaska, Arkansas, Idaho, Indiana, Kentucky, Michigan, Montana, Tennessee, Utah, Vermont, Virginia, Wyoming
Contact agency for non-resident permits if granted:
Permits not granted.

REFERENCE

NRA - RIGHT-TO-CARRY RECIPROCITY GUIDE

South Dakota
Right-to-Carry Law Type
Shall Issue

Issuing Authority:
Chief of Police/County Sheriff
These states also recognize your permit:
Idaho, Indiana, Kentucky, Michigan, Utah, Vermont
Contact agency for non-resident permits if granted:
Permits not granted.
http://www.state.sd.us/state/executive/dcr/hp/page1sdh.htm

Tennessee
Right-to-Carry Law Type
Shall Issue

Issuing Authority:
Department of Public Safety
These states also recognize your permit:
Alaska, Arkansas, Florida, Georgia, Idaho, Indiana, Kentucky,
Louisiana, Michigan, Mississippi, Montana, South Carolina, Texas,
Utah, Virginia, Vermont
Contact agency for non-resident permits if granted:
Permits not granted.
http://www.state.tn.us/safety/

Texas
Right-to-Carry Law Type
Shall Issue

Issuing Authority:
Department of Public Safety
These states also recognize your permit:
Arizona, Arkansas, Florida, Idaho, Indiana, Kentucky, Louisiana,
Michigan, Montana, Oklahoma, Tennessee, Utah, Virginia, Vermont
Contact agency for non-resident permits if granted:
Department of Public Safety. Call (800) 224-5744 or (512) 424-7293.
http://www.txdps.state.tx.us./administration/crime_records/chl/
reciprocity.htm

Utah
Right-to-Carry Law Type
Shall Issue

Issuing Authority:
Department of Public Safety
These states also recognize your permit:
Alabama, Alaska, Arizona, Florida, Idaho, Indiana, Kentucky,
Michigan, Montana, Oklahoma, South Carolina, Vermont, Wyoming
Contact agency for non-resident permits if granted:
Department of Public Safety; (801) 965-4484
http://www.bci.state.ut.us/

Vermont
Right-to-Carry Law Type
Shall Issue

Issuing Authority:
Permits not required.
These states also recognize your permit:
None
Contact agency for non-resident permits if granted:
Permits not required
http://www.state.vt.us/atg/

Virginia
Right-to-Carry Law Type
Shall Issue

Issuing Authority:
State Circuit Court of residence
These states also recognize your permit:
Idaho, Indiana, Kentucky, Michigan, Montana, Tennessee, Utah, West
Virginia, Vermont
Contact agency for non-resident permits if granted:
Permits not granted.
http://www.vsp.state.va.us/vsp.html

Washington
Right-to-Carry Law Type
Shall Issue

Issuing Authority:
Chief of Police/Sheriff
These states also recognize your permit:
Idaho, Indiana, Kentucky, Michigan, Montana, Utah, Vermont,
Virginia
Contact agency for non-resident permits if granted:
Permits not granted.
http://www.wa.gov/wsp/wsphome.htm

West Virginia
Right-to-Carry Law Type
Shall Issue

Issuing Authority:
County Sheriff
These states also recognize your permit:
Alaska, Idaho, Indiana, Kentucky, Michigan, Montana, Utah,
Virginia, Vermont
Contact agency for non-resident permits if granted:
Permits not granted.
http://www.wvstatepolice.com/legal/legal.shtml

Wisconsin
Right-to-Carry Law Type
Non-Issue

Issuing Authority:
Permits not available.
These states also recognize your permit:
None.
Contact agency for non-resident permits if granted:
Permits not granted.
http://www.doj.state.wi.us/

Wyoming
Right-to-Carry Law Type
Shall Issue

Issuing Authority:
Attorney General
These states also recognize your permit:
Alabama, Alaska, Florida, Georgia, Idaho, Indiana, Kentucky,
Michigan, Mississippi, Montana, North Dakota, Oklahoma, South
Carolina, Utah, Vermont
Contact agency for non-resident permits if granted:
Permits not granted.
http://www.state.wy.us/~ag/index.html

REFERENCE

UNITED STATES

ALABAMA

labama Gun Collectors Assn.
ecretary, P.O. Box 70965,
uscaloosa, AL 35407

ALASKA

laska Gun Collectors Assn., Inc.
.W. Floyd, Pres., 5240 Little Tree,
nchorage, AK 99507

ARIZONA

rizona Arms Assn.
on DeBusk, President, 4837
ryce Ave., Glendale, AZ 85301

CALIFORNIA

alifornia Cartridge Collectors ssn.
ick Montgomery, 1729 Christina,
tockton, CA
5204/209-463-7216 evs.
alifornia Waterfowl Assn.
630 Northgate Blvd., #150,
acramento, CA 95834
reater Calif. Arms & Collectors ssn.
onald L. Bullock, 8291 Carburton
t., Long Beach, CA 90808-3302
os Angeles Gun Ctg. Collectors ssn.
H. Ruffra, 20810 Amie Ave., Apt.
9, Torrance, CA 90503
tock Gun Players Assn.
038 Appian Way, Long Beach,
A, 90803

COLORADO

olorado Gun Collectors Assn.
.E.(Bud) Greenwald, 2553 S.
uitman St., Denver, CO
0219/303-935-3850
ocky Mountain Cartridge ollectors Assn.
ohn Roth, P.O. Box 757, Conifer,
O 80433

CONNECTICUT

e Connecticut Gun Guild, Inc.
ick Fraser, P.O. Box 425,
Vindsor, CT 06095

FLORIDA

nified Sportsmen of Florida
.O. Box 6565, Tallahassee, FL
2314

GEORGIA

eorgia Arms Collectors Assn., nc.
ichael Kindberg, President, P.O.
ox 277, Alpharetta, GA
0239-0277

ILLINOIS

linois State Rifle Assn.
.O. Box 637, Chatsworth, IL
0921
ississippi Valley Gun & artridge Coll. Assn.
ob Filbert, P.O. Box 61, Port
yron, IL 61275/309-523-2593
auk Trail Gun Collectors
ordell M. Matson, P.O. Box 1113,
ilan, IL 61264
Wabash Valley Gun Collectors ssn., Inc.
oger L. Dorsett, 2601 Willow Rd.,
rbana, IL 61801/217-384-7302

INDIANA

ndiana State Rifle & Pistol Assn.
hos. Glancy, P.O. Box 552,
hesterton, IN 46304
outhern Indiana Gun Collectors ssn., Inc.
heila McClary, 309 W. Monroe
t., Boonville, IN
7601/812-897-3742

IOWA

Beaver Creek Plainsmen Inc.
Steve Murphy, Secy., P.O. Box 298,
Bondurant, IA 50035
Central States Gun Collectors Assn.
Dennis Greischar, Box 841, Mason
City, IA 50402-0841

KANSAS

Kansas Cartridge Collectors Assn.
Bob Linder, Box 84, Plainville, KS
67663

KENTUCKY

Kentuckiana Arms Collectors Assn.
Charles Billips, President, Box
1776, Louisville, KY 40201
Kentucky Gun Collectors Assn., Inc.
Ruth Johnson, Box 64,
Owensboro, KY
42302/502-729-4197

LOUISIANA

Washitaw River Renegades
Sandra Rushing, P.O. Box 256,
Main St., Grayson, LA 71435

MARYLAND

Baltimore Antique Arms Assn.
Mr. Cillo, 1034 Main St.,
Darlington, MD 21304

MASSACHUSETTS

Bay Colony Weapons Collectors, Inc.
John Brandt, Box 111, Hingham,
MA 02043
Massachusetts Arms Collectors
Bruce E. Skinner, P.O. Box 31, No.
Carver, MA 02355/508-866-5259

MICHIGAN

Association for the Study and Research of .22 Caliber Rimfire Cartridges
George Kass, 4512 Nakoma Dr.,
Okemos, MI 48864

MINNESOTA

Sioux Empire Cartridge Collectors Assn.
Bob Cameron, 14597 Glendale
Ave. SE, Prior Lake, MN 55372

MISSISSIPPI

Mississippi Gun Collectors Assn.
Jack E. Swinney, P.O. Box 16323,
Hattiesburg, MS 39402

MISSOURI

Greater St. Louis Cartridge Collectors Assn.
Don MacChesney, 634 Scottsdale
Rd., Kirkwood, MO 63122-1109
Mineral Belt Gun Collectors Assn.
D.F. Saunders, 1110 Cleveland
Ave., Monett, MO 65708
Missouri Valley Arms Collectors Assn., Inc.
L.P Brammer II, Membership
Secy., P.O. Box 33033, Kansas
City, MO 64114

MONTANA

Montana Arms Collectors Assn.
Dean E. Yearout, Sr., Exec. Secy.,
1516 21st Ave. S., Great Falls, MT
59405
Weapons Collectors Society of Montana
R.G. Schipf, Ex. Secy., 3100
Bancroft St., Missoula, MT
59801/406-728-2995

NEBRASKA

Nebraska Cartridge Collectors Club
Gary Muckel, P.O. Box 84442,
Lincoln, NE 68501

NEW HAMPSHIRE

New Hampshire Arms Collectors, Inc.
James Stamatelos, Secy., P.O. Box
5, Cambridge, MA 02139

NEW JERSEY

Englishtown Benchrest Shooters Assn.
Michael Toth, 64 Cooke Ave.,
Carteret, NJ 07008
Jersey Shore Antique Arms Collectors
Joe Sisia, P.O. Box 100, Bayville,
NJ 08721-0100
New Jersey Arms Collectors Club, Inc.
Angus Laidlaw, Vice President,
230 Valley Rd., Montclair, NJ
07042/201-746-0939; e-mail:
acclaidlaw@juno.com

NEW YORK

Iroquois Arms Collectors Assn.
Bonnie Robinson, Show Secy.,
P.O. Box 142, Ransomville, NY
14131/716-791-4096
Mid-State Arms Coll. & Shooters Club
Jack Ackerman, 24 S. Mountain
Terr., Binghamton, NY 13903

NORTH CAROLINA

North Carolina Gun Collectors Assn.
Jerry Ledford, 3231-7th St. Dr. NE,
Hickory, NC 28601

OHIO

Ohio Gun Collectors Assn.
P.O. Box 9007, Maumee, OH
43537-9007/419-897-0861;
Fax:419-897-0860
Shotshell Historical and Collectors Society
Madeline Bruemmer, 3886 Dawley
Rd., Ravenna, OH 44266
The Stark Gun Collectors, Inc.
William I. Gann, 5666 Waynesburg
Dr., Waynesburg, OH 44688

OREGON

Oregon Arms Collectors Assn., Inc.
Phil Bailey, P.O. Box 13000-A,
Portland, OR
97213-0017/503-281-6864;
off.:503-281-0918
Oregon Cartridge Collectors Assn.
Boyd Northrup, P.O. Box 285,
Rhododendron, OR 97049

PENNSYLVANIA

Presque Isle Gun Collectors Assn.
James Welch, 156 E. 37 St., Erie,
PA 16504

SOUTH CAROLINA

Belton Gun Club, Inc.
Attn. Secretary, P.O. Box 126,
Belton, SC 29627/864-369-6767
Gun Owners of South Carolina
Membership Div.: William Strozier,
Secretary, P.O. Box 70, Johns
Island, SC
29457-0070/803-762-3240;
Fax:803-795-0711;
e-mail:76053.222@compuserve.
com

SOUTH DAKOTA

Dakota Territory Gun Coll. Assn., Inc.
Curt Carter, Castlewood, SD 57223

TENNESSEE

Smoky Mountain Gun Coll. Assn., Inc.
Hugh W. Yabro, President, P.O.
Box 23225, Knoxville, TN 37933

Tennessee Gun Collectors Assn., Inc.
M.H. Parks, 3556 Pleasant Valley
Rd., Nashville, TN 37204-3419

TEXAS

Houston Gun Collectors Assn., Inc.
P.O. Box 741429, Houston, TX
77274-1429
Texas Gun Collectors Assn.
Bob Eder, Pres., P.O. Box 12067, El
Paso, TX 79913/915-584-8183
Texas State Rifle Assn.
1131 Rockingham Dr., Suite 101,
Richardson, TX 75080-4326

VIRGINIA

Virginia Gun Collectors Assn., Inc.
Addison Hurst, Secy., 38802
Charlestown Height, Waterford, VA
20197/540-882-3543

WASHINGTON

Association of Cartridge Collectors on the Pacific Northwest
Robert Jardin, 14214 Meadowlark
Drive KPN, Gig Harbor, WA 98329
Washington Arms Collectors, Inc.
Joyce Boss, P.O. Box 389, Renton,
WA, 98057-0389/206-255-8410

WISCONSIN

Great Lakes Arms Collectors Assn., Inc.
Edward C. Warnke, 2913
Woodridge Lane, Waukesha, WI
53188
Wisconsin Gun Collectors Assn., Inc.
Lulita Zellmer, P.O. Box 181,
Sussex, WI 53089

WYOMING

Wyoming Weapons Collectors
P.O. Box 284, Laramie, WY
82073/307-745-4652 or 745-9530

NATIONAL ORGANIZATIONS

Amateur Trapshooting Assn.
David D. Bopp, Exec. Director, 601
W. National Rd., Vandalia, OH
45377/937-898-4638;
Fax:937-898-5472
American Airgun Field Target Assn.
5911 Cherokee Ave., Tampa, FL
33604
American Coon Hunters Assn.
Opal Johnston, P.O. Cadet, Route
1, Box 492, Old Mines, MO 63630
American Custom Gunmakers Guild
Jan Billeb, Exec. Director, 22 Vista
View Drive, Cody, WY 82414-9606
(307) 587-4297 (phone/fax).
Email: acgg@acgg.org Website:
www.acgg.org
American Defense Preparedness Assn.
Two Colonial Place, 2101 Wilson
Blvd., Suite 400, Arlington, VA
22201-3061
American Paintball League
P.O. Box 3561, Johnson City, TN
37602/800-541-9169
American Pistolsmiths Guild
Alex B. Hamilton, Pres., 1449 Blue
Crest Lane, San Antonio, TX
78232/210-494-3063
American Police Pistol & Rifle Assn.
3801 Biscayne Blvd., Miami, FL
33137

American Single Shot Rifle Assn.
Charles Kriegel, Secy., 1346C
Whispering Woods Drive, West
Carrollton OH
45449/937-866-9064. Website:
www.assra.com
American Society of Arms Collectors
George E. Weatherly, P.O. Box
2567, Waxahachie, TX 75165
American Tactical Shooting Assn.(A.T.S.A.)
c/o Skip Gochenour, 2600 N. Third
St., Harrisburg, PA
17110/717-233-0402;
Fax:717-233-5340
Association of Firearm and Tool Mark Examiners
Lannie G. Emanuel, Secy.,
Southwest Institute of Forensic
Sciences, P.O. Box 35728, Dallas,
TX 75235/214-920-5979;
Fax:214-920-5928; Membership
Secy., Ann D. Jones, VA Div. of
Forensic Science, P.O. Box 999,
Richmond, VA
23208/804-786-4706;
Fax:804-371-8328
Boone & Crockett Club
250 Station Dr., Missoula, MT
59801-2753
Browning Collectors Assn.
Secretary:Scherrie L. Brennac,
2749 Keith Dr., Villa Ridge, MO
63089/314-742-0571
The Cast Bullet Assn., Inc.
Ralland J. Fortier, Editor, 4103
Foxcraft Dr., Traverse City, MI
49684
Citizens Committee for the Right to Keep and Bear Arms
Natl. Hq., Liberty Park, 12500 NE
Tenth Pl., Bellevue, WA 98005
Colt Collectors Assn.
25000 Highland Way, Los Gatos,
CA 95030/408-353-2658
Ducks Unlimited, Inc.
Natl. Headquarters, One Waterfowl
Way, Memphis, TN
38120/901-758-3937
Fifty Caliber Shooters Assn.
PO Box 111, Monroe UT
84754-0111/435-527-9245;
Fax: 435-527-0948
Firearms Coalition/Neal Knox Associates
Box 6537, Silver Spring, MD
20906/301-871-3006
Firearms Engravers Guild of America
Rex C. Pedersen, Secy., 511 N.
Rath Ave., Lundington, MI
49431/616-845-7695(Phone and
Fax)
Foundation for North American Wild Sheep
720 Allen Ave., Cody, WY
82414-3402/web site:
http://iigi.com/os/non/fnaws/fnaw
s.htm; e-mail:
fnaws@wyoming.com
Freedom Arms Collectors Assn.
P.O. Box 160302, Miami, FL
33116-0302
Garand Collectors Assn.
P.O. Box 181, Richmond, KY
40475
German Gun Collectors Assn. U.S.A.
PO Box 385, Meriden, NH
03770/603-469-3438
Fax: 603-469-3800 Website:
www.germanguns.com; email:
jaeger@valley.net
Glock Collectors Assn.
PO Box 1063, Maryland Heights,
MO 63043/314-878-2061 Website:
www.glockcollectors.com

ARMS ASSOCIATIONS

Glock Shooting Sports Foundation
PO Box 309, Smyrna, GA 30081
770-432-1202 Website:
www.gssfonline.com
Golden Eagle Collectors Assn. (G.E.C.A.)
Chris Showler, 11144 Slate Creek Rd., Grass Valley, CA 95945
Gun Owners of America
8001 Forbes Place, Suite 102, Springfield, VA 22151/703-321-8585
Handgun Hunters International
J.D. Jones, Director, P.O. Box 357 MAG, Bloomingdale, OH 43910
Harrington & Richardson Gun Coll. Assn.
George L. Cardet, 330 S.W. 27th Ave., Suite 603, Miami, FL 33135
High Standard Collectors' Assn.
John J. Stimson, Jr., Pres., 540 W. 92nd St., Indianapolis, IN 46260 Website: www.highstandard.org
Hopkins & Allen Arms & Memorabilia Society (HAAMS)
P.O. Box 187, 1309 Pamela Circle, Delphos, OH 45833
International Ammunition Association, Inc.
C.R. Punnett, Secy., 8 Hillock Lane, Chadds Ford, PA 19317/610-358-1285;Fax:610-3 58-1560
International Benchrest Shooters
Joan Borden, RR1, Box 250BB, Springville, PA 18844/717-965-2366
International Blackpowder Hunting Assn.
P.O. Box 1180, Glenrock, WY 82637/307-436-9817
IHMSA (Intl. Handgun Metallic Silhouette Assn.)
PO Box 368, Burlington, IA 52601 Website: www.ihmsa.org
International Society of Mauser Arms Collectors
Michael Kindberg, Pres., P.O. Box 277, Alpharetta, GA 30239-0277
Jews for the Preservation of Firearms Ownership (JPFO) 501(c)(3)
2872 S. Wentworth Ave., Milwaukee, WI 53207/414-769-0760; Fax:414-483-8435
The Mannlicher Collectors Assn.
Membership Office: P.O. Box 1249, The Dalles, Oregon 97058
Marlin Firearms Collectors Assn., Ltd.
Dick Paterson, Secy., 407 Lincoln Bldg., 44 Main St., Champaign, IL 61820
Merwin Hulbert Association,
2503 Kentwood Ct., High Point, NC 27265
Miniature Arms Collectors/Makers Society, Ltd.
Ralph Koebbeman, Pres., 4910 Kilburn Ave., Rockford, IL 61101/815-964-2569
M1 Carbine Collectors Assn. (M1-CCA)
623 Apaloosa Ln., Gardnerville, NV 89410-7840
National Association of Buckskinners (NAB)
Territorial Dispatch—1800s Historical Publication, 4701 Marion St., Suite 324, Livestock Exchange Bldg., Denver, CO 80216/303-297-9671
The National Association of Derringer Collectors
P.O. Box 20572, San Jose, CA 95160

National Assn. of Federally Licensed Firearms Dealers
Andrew Molchan, 2455 E. Sunrise, Ft. Lauderdale, FL 33304
National Association to Keep and Bear Arms
P.O. Box 78336, Seattle, WA 98178
National Automatic Pistol Collectors Assn.
Tom Knox, P.O. Box 15738, Tower Grove Station, St. Louis, MO 63163
National Bench Rest Shooters Assn., Inc.
Pat Ferrell, 2835 Guilford Lane, Oklahoma City, OK 73120-4404/405-842-9585; Fax: 405-842-9575
National Muzzle Loading Rifle Assn.
Box 67, Friendship, IN 47021 / 812-667-5131. Website: www.nmlra@nmlra.org
National Professional Paintball League (NPPL)
540 Main St., Mount Kisco, NY 10549/914-241-7400
National Reloading Manufacturers Assn.
One Centerpointe Dr., Suite 300, Lake Oswego, OR 97035
National Rifle Assn. of America
11250 Waples Mill Rd., Fairfax, VA 22030 / 703-267-1000. Website: www.nra.org
National Shooting Sports Foundation, Inc.
Robert T. Delfay, President, Flintlock Ridge Office Center, 11 Mile Hill Rd., Newtown, CT 06470-2359/203-426-1320; FAX: 203-426-1087
National Skeet Shooting Assn.
Dan Snyuder, Director, 5931 Roft Road, San Antonio, TX 78253-9261/800-877-5338. Website: nssa-nsca.com
National Sporting Clays Association
Ann Myers, Director, 5931 Roft Road, San Antonio, TX 78253-9261/800-877-5338. Website: nssa-nsca.com
National Wild Turkey Federation, Inc.
P.O. Box 530, 770 Augusta Rd., Edgefield, SC 29824
North American Hunting Club
P.O. Box 3401, Minnetonka, MN 55343/612-936-9333; Fax: 612-936-9755
North American Paintball Referees Association (NAPRA)
584 Cestaric Dr., Milpitas, CA 95035
North-South Skirmish Assn., Inc.
Stevan F. Meserve, Exec. Secretary, 507 N. Brighton Court, Sterling, VA 20164-3919
Old West Shooter's Association
712 James Street, Hazel TX 76020 817-444-2049
Remington Society of America
Gordon Fosburg, Secretary, 11900 North Brinton Road, Lake, MI 48623
Rocky Mountain Elk Foundation
P.O. Box 8249, Missoula, MT 59807-8249/406-523-4500;Fax: 406-523-4581 Website: www.rmef.org
Ruger Collector's Assn., Inc.
P.O. Box 240, Greens Farms, CT 06436
Safari Club International
4800 W. Gates Pass Rd., Tucson, AZ 85745/520-620-1220

Sako Collectors Assn., Inc.
Jim Lutes, 202 N. Locust, Whitewater, KS 67154
Second Amendment Foundation
James Madison Building, 12500 NE 10th Pl., Bellevue, WA 98005
Single Action Shooting Society (SASS)
23255-A La Palma Avenue, Yorba Linda, CA 92887/714-694-1800; FAX: 714-694-1815/email: sasseot@aol.com Website: www.sassnet.com
Smith & Wesson Collectors Assn.
Cally Pletl, Admin. Asst.,PO Box 444, Afton, NY 13730
The Society of American Bayonet Collectors
P.O. Box 234, East Islip, NY 11730-0234
Southern California Schuetzen Society
Dean Lillard, 34657 Ave. E., Yucaipa, CA 92399
Sporting Arms and Ammunition Manufacturers' Institute (SAAMI)
Flintlock Ridge Office Center, 11 Mile Hill Rd., Newtown, CT 06470-2359/203-426-4358; FAX: 203-426-1087
Sporting Clays of America (SCA)
Ron L. Blosser, Pres., 9257 Buckeye Rd., Sugar Grove, OH 43155-9632/614-746-8334; Fax: 614-746-8605
Steel Challenge
23234 Via Barra, Valencia CA 91355 Website: www.steelchallenge.com
The Thompson/Center Assn.
Joe Wright, President, Box 792, Northboro, MA 01532/508-845-6960
U.S. Practical Shooting Assn./IPSC
Dave Thomas, P.O. Box 811, Sedro Woolley, WA 98284/360-855-2245 Website: www.uspsa.org
U.S. Revolver Assn.
Brian J. Barer, 40 Larchmont Ave., Taunton, MA 02780/508-824-4836
U.S. A. Shooting
U.S. Olympic Shooting Center, One Olympic Plaza, Colorado Springs, CO 80909/719-578-4670. Website: wwwusashooting.org
The Varmint Hunters Assn., Inc.
Box 759, Pierre, SD 57501/Member Services 800-528-4868
Weatherby Collectors Assn., Inc.
P.O. Box 478, Pacific, MO 63069 Website: www.weatherbycollectors.com Email: WCAsecretary@aol.com
The Wildcatters
P.O. Box 170, Greenville, WI 54942
Winchester Arms Collectors Assn.
P.O. Box 230, Brownsboro, TX 75756/903-852-4027
The Women's Shooting Sports Foundation (WSSF)
4620 Edison Avenue, Ste. C, Colorado Springs, CO 80915/719-638-1299; FAX: 719-638-1271/email: wssf@worldnet.att.net

ARGENTINA
Asociacion Argentina de Coleccionistas de Armes y Municiones
Castilla de Correos No. 28, Succursal I B, 1401 Buenos Aires, Republica Argentina

AUSTRALIA
Antique & Historical Arms Collectors of Australia
P.O. Box 5654, GCMC Queensland 9726, Australia
The Arms Collector's Guild of Queensland Inc.
Ian Skennerton, P.O. Box 433, Ashmore City 4214, Queensland, Australia
Australian Cartridge Collectors Assn., Inc.
Bob Bennett, 126 Landscape Dr., E. Doncaster 3109, Victoria, Australia
Sporting Shooters Assn. of Australia, Inc.
P.O. Box 2066, Kent Town, SA 5071, Australia

CANADA
ALBERTA
Canadian Historical Arms Society
P.O. Box 901, Edmonton, Alb., Canada T5J 2L8
National Firearms Assn.
Natl. Hq: P.O. Box 1779, Edmonton, Alb., Canada T5J 2P1
BRITISH COLUMBIA
The Historical Arms Collectors of B.C. (Canada)
Harry Moon, Pres., P.O. Box 50117, South Slope RPO, Burnaby, BC V5J 5G3, Canada/604-438-0950; Fax:604-277-3646
ONTARIO
Association of Canadian Cartridge Collectors
Monica Wright, RR 1, Millgrove, ON, LOR IVO, Canada
Tri-County Antique Arms Fair
P.O. Box 122, RR #1, North Lancaster, Ont., Canada K0C 1Z0

EUROPE
BELGIUM
European Cartridge Research Assn.
Graham Irving, 21 Rue Schaltin, 4900 Spa, Belgium/32.87.77.43.40; Fax:32.87.77.27.51
CZECHOSLOVAKIA
Spolecnost Pro Studium Naboju (Czech Cartridge Research Assn.)
JUDr. Jaroslav Bubak, Pod Homolko 1439, 26601 Beroun 2, Czech Republic
DENMARK
Aquila Dansk Jagtpatron Historic Forening (Danish Historical Cartridge Collectors Club)
Steen Elgaard Møller, Ulriksdalsvej 7, 4840 Nr. Alslev, Denmark 10045-53846218;Fax:00455384 6209
ENGLAND
Arms and Armour Society
Hon. Secretary A. Dove, P.O. Box 10232, London, 5W19 2ZD, England
Dutch Paintball Federation
Aceville Publ., Castle House 97 High Street, Colchester, Essex C01 1TH, England/011-44-206-564840
European Paintball Sports Foundation
c/o Aceville Publ., Castle House 97 High St., Colchester, Essex, C01 1TH, England
Historical Breechloading Smallarms Assn.
D.J. Penn M.A., Secy., P.O. Box

12778, London SE1 6BX, Englan Journal and newsletter are $23 a yr., including airmail.
National Rifle Assn.
(Great Britain) Bisley Camp, Brookwood, Woking Surrey GU2 OPB, England/01483.797777; Fax 014730686275
United Kingdom Cartridge Club
Ian Southgate, 20 Millfield, Elmle Castle, Nr. Pershore, Worcestershire, WR10 3HR, England

FRANCE
STAC-Western Co.
3 Ave. Paul Doumer (N.311); 78360 Montesson, France/01.30.53-43-65; Fax: 01.30.53.19.10

GERMANY
Bund Deutscher Sportschützen e.v. (BDS)
Borsigallee 10, 53125 Bonn 1, Germany
Deutscher Schützenbund
Lahnstrasse 120, 65195 Wiesbaden, Germany

SPAIN
Asociacion Espanola de Coleccionistas de Cartuchos (A.E.C.C.)
Secretary: Apdo. Correos No. 1086, 2880-Alcala de Henares (Madrid), Spain. President: Apdo. Correos No. 682, 50080 Zaragoza Spain

SWEDEN
Scandinavian Ammunition Research Assn.
c/o Morten Stoen, Annerudstubben 3, N-1383 Asker Norway

NEW ZEALAND
New Zealand Cartridge Collectors Club
Terry Castle, 70 Tiraumea Dr., Pakuranga, Auckland, New Zealand
New Zealand Deerstalkers Assn.
P.O. Box 6514 TE ARO, Wellington, New Zealand

SOUTH AFRICA
Historical Firearms Soc. of South Africa
P.O. Box 145, 7725 Newlands, Republic of South Africa
Republic of South Africa Cartridge Collectors Assn.
Arno Klee, 20 Eugene St., Malanshof Randburg, Gauteng 2194, Republic of South Africa
S.A.A.C.A.
(Southern Africa Arms and Ammunition Assn.)
Gauteng office: P.O. Box 7597, Weltevreden Park, 1715, Republic of South Africa/011-679-1151; Fax: 011-679-1131; e-mail: saaaca@iafrica.com. Kwa-Zulu Natal office: P.O. Box 4065, Northway, Kwazulu-Natal 4065, Republic of South Africa
SAGA
(S.A. Gunowners' Assn.)
P.O. Box 35203, Northway, Kwazulu-Natal 4065, Republic of South Africa

PERIODICAL PUBLICATIONS

AFTA News (M)
5911 Cherokee Ave., Tampa, FL 33604. Official newsletter of the American Airgun Field Target Assn.

ction Pursuit Games Magazine (M)
CFW Enterprises, Inc., 4201 W. Vanowen Pl., Burbank, CA 91505 818-845-2656. $4.99 single copy U.S., $5.50 Canada. Editor: Dan Reeves. World's leading magazine of paintball sports.

ir Gunner Magazine
4 The Courtyard, Denmark St., Wokingham, Berkshire RG11 2AZ, England/011-44-734-771677. $U.S. $44 for 1 yr. Leading monthly airgun magazine in U.K.

irgun Ads
Box 33, Hamilton, MT 59840/406-363-3805; Fax: 406-363-4117. $35 1 yr. (for first mailing; $20 for second mailing; $35 for Canada and foreign orders.) Monthly tabloid with extensive For Sale and Wanted airgun listings.

he Airgun Letter
Gapp, Inc., 4614 Woodland Rd., Ellicott City, MD 21042-6329/410-730-5496; Fax: 410-730-9544; e-mail: staff@airgnltr.net; http://www.airgunletter.com. $21 U.S., $24 Canada, $27 Mexico and $33 other foreign orders, 1 yr. Monthly newsletter for airgun users and collectors.

irgun World
4 The Courtyard, Denmark St., Wokingham, Berkshire RG40 2AZ, England/011-44-734-771677. Call for subscription rates. Oldest monthly airgun magazine in the U.K., now a sister publication to Air Gunner.

laska Magazine
Morris Communications, 735 Broad Street, Augusta, GA 30901/706-722-6060. Hunting, Fishing and Life on the Last Frontier articles of Alaska and western Canada.

merican Firearms Industry
Nat'l. Assn. of Federally Licensed Firearms Dealers, 2455 E. Sunrise Blvd., Suite 916, Ft. Lauderdale, FL 33304. $35.00 yr. For firearms retailers, distributors and manufacturers.

merican Guardian
NRA, 11250 Waples Mill Rd., Fairfax, VA 22030. Publications division. $15.00 1 yr. Magazine features personal protection; home-self-defense; family recreation shooting; women's issues; etc.

merican Gunsmith
Belvoir Publications, Inc., 75 Holly Hill Lane, Greenwich, CT 06836-2626/203-661-6111. $49.00 (12 issues). Technical journal of firearms repair and maintenance.

merican Handgunner*
Publisher's Development Corp., 591 Camino de la Reina, Suite 200, San Diego, CA 92108/800-537-3006 $16.95 yr. Articles for handgun enthusiasts, competitors, police and hunters.

merican Hunter (M)
National Rifle Assn., 11250 Waples Mill Rd., Fairfax, VA 22030 (Same address for both.) Publications Div. $35.00 yr. Wide scope of hunting articles.

merican Rifleman (M)
National Rifle Assn., 11250 Waples Mill Rd., Fairfax, VA 22030 (Same address for both). Publications Div. $35.00 yr. Firearms articles of all kinds.

merican Survival Guide
McMullen Angus Publishing, Inc., 774 S. Placentia Ave., Placentia, CA 92670-6846. 12 issues $19.95/714-572-2255; FAX: 714-572-1864.

rmes & Tir*
c/o FABECO, 38, rue de Trévise 75009 Paris, France. Articles for hunters, collectors, and shooters. French text.

rms Collecting (Q)
Museum Restoration Service, P.O. Box 70, Alexandria Bay, NY 13607-0070. $22.00 yr.; $62.00 3 yrs.; $112.00 5 yrs.

ustralian Shooter (formerly Australian Shooters Journal)
Sporting Shooters' Assn. of Australia, Inc., P.O. Box 2066, Kent Town SA 5071, Australia. $60.00 yr. locally; $65.00 yr. overseas surface mail. Hunting and shooting articles.

he Backwoodsman Magazine
P.O. Box 627, Westcliffe, CO 81252. $16.00 for 6 issues per yr.; $30.00 for 2 yrs.; sample copy $2.75. Subjects include muzzle-loading, woodslore, primitive survival, trapping, homesteading, blackpowder cartridge guns, 19th century how-to.

lack Powder Cartridge News (Q)
SPG, Inc., P.O. Box 761, Livingston, MT 59047/Phone/Fax: 406-222-8416. $17 yr. (4 issues) ($6 extra 1st class mailing). For the blackpowder cartridge enthusiast.

lackpowder Hunting (M)
Intl. Blackpowder Hunting Assn., P.O. Box 1180Z, Glenrock, WY 82637/307-436-9817. $20.00 1 yr., $36.00 2 yrs. How-to and where-to features by experts on hunting; shooting; ballistics; traditional and modern blackpowder rifles, shotguns, pistols and cartridges.

lack Powder Times
P.O. Box 234, Lake Stevens, WA 98258. $20.00 yr.; add $5 per year for Canada, $10 per year other foreign. Tabloid newspaper for blackpowder activities; test reports.

lade Magazine
Krause Publications, 700 East State St., Iola, WI 54990-0001. $25.98 for 12 issues. Foreign price (including Canada-Mexico) $50.00. A magazine for all enthusiasts of handmade, factory and antique knives.

Caliber
GFI-Verlag, Theodor-Heuss Ring 62, 50668 K"ln, Germany. For hunters, target shooters and reloaders.

The Caller (Q) (M)
National Wild Turkey Federation, P.O. Box 530, Edgefield, SC 29824. Tabloid newspaper for members; 4 issues per yr. (membership fee $25.00)

Cartridge Journal (M)
Robert Mellichamp, 907 Shirkmere, Houston, TX 77008/713-869-0558. Dues $12 for U.S. and Canadian members (includes the newsletter); 6 issues.

The Cast Bullet*(M)
Official journal of The Cast Bullet Assn. Director of Membership, 203 E. 2nd St., Muscatine, IA 52761. Annual membership dues $14, includes 6 issues.

COLTELLI, che Passione (Q)
Casella postale N.519, 20101 Milano, Italy/Fax:02-48402857. $15 1 yr., $27 2 yrs. Covers all types of knives—collecting, combat, historical. Italian text.

Combat Handguns*
Harris Publications, Inc., 1115 Broadway, New York, NY 10010.

Deer & Deer Hunting Magazine
Krause Publications, 700 E. State St., Iola, WI 54990-0001. $19.95 yr. (9 issues). For the serious deer hunter. Website: www.krause.com

The Derringer Peanut (M)
The National Association of Derringer Collectors, P.O. Box 20572, San Jose, CA 95160. A newsletter dedicated to developing the best derringer information. Write for details.

Deutsches Waffen Journal
Journal-Verlag Schwend GmbH, Postfach 100340, D-74503 Schwäbisch Hall, Germany/0791-404-500; FAX:0791-404-505 and 404-424. DM102 p. yr. (interior); DM125.30 (abroad), postage included. Antique and modern arms and equipment. German text.

Double Gun Journal
P.O. Box 550, East Jordan, MI 49727/800-447-1658. $35 for 4 issues.

Ducks Unlimited, Inc. (M)
1 Waterfowl Way, Memphis, TN 38120

The Engraver (M) (Q)
P.O. Box 4365, Estes Park, CO 80517/970-586-2388; Fax: 970-586-0394. Mike Dubber, editor. The journal of firearms engraving.

The Field
King's Reach Tower, Stamford St., London SE1 9LS England. £36.40 U.K. 1 yr.; 49.90 (overseas, surface mail) yr.; £82.00 (overseas, air mail) yr. Hunting and shooting articles, and all country sports.

Field & Stream
Time4 Media, Two Park Ave., New York, NY 10016/212-779-5000. Monthly shooting column. Articles on hunting and fishing.

Field Tests
Belvoir Publications, Inc., 75 Holly Hill Lane; P.O. Box 2626, Greenwich, CT 06836-2626/203-661-6111; 800-829-3361 (subscription line). U.S. & Canada $29 1 yr., $58 2 yrs.; all other countries $45 1 yr., $90 2 yrs. (air).

Fur-Fish-Game
A.R. Harding Pub. Co., 2878 E. Main St., Columbus, OH 43209. $15.95 yr. Practical guidance regarding trapping, fishing and hunting.

The Gottlieb-Tartaro Report
Second Amendment Foundation, James Madison Bldg., 12500 NE 10th Pl., Bellevue, WA 98005/206-454-7012;Fax:206-451-3959. $30 for 12 issues. An insiders guide for gun owners.

Gray's Sporting Journal
Gray's Sporting Journal, P.O. Box 1207, Augusta, GA 30903. $36.95 per yr. for 6 issues. Hunting and fishing journals. Expeditions and Guides Book (Annual Travel Guide).

Gun List†
700 E. State St., Iola, WI 54990. $36.98 yr. (26 issues); $65.98 2 yrs. (52 issues). Indexed market publication for firearms collectors and active shooters; guns, supplies and services. Website: www.krause.com

Gun News Digest (Q)
Second Amendment Fdn., P.O. Box 488, Station C, Buffalo, NY 14209/716-885-6408;Fax:716-884-4471. $10 U.S.; $20 foreign.

The Gun Report
World Wide Gun Report, Inc., Box 38, Aledo, IL 61231-0038. $33.00 yr. For the antique and collectable gun dealer and collector.

Gunmaker (M) (Q)
ACGG, P.O. Box 812, Burlington, IA 52601-0812. The journal of custom gunmaking.

The Gunrunner
Div. of Kexco Publ. Co. Ltd., Box 565G, Lethbridge, Alb., Canada T1J 3Z4. $23.00 yr., sample $2.00. Monthly newspaper, listing everything from antiques to artillery.

Gun Show Calendar (Q)
700 E. State St., Iola, WI 54990. $14.95 yr. (4 issues). Gun shows listed; chronologically and by state. Website: www.krause.com

Gun Tests
11 Commerce Blvd., Palm Coast, FL 32142. The consumer resource for the serious shooter. Write for information.

Gun Trade News
Bruce Publishing Ltd., P.O. Box 82, Wantage, Ozon OX12 7A8, England/44-1-235-771770; Fax: 44-1-235-771848. Britain's only "trade only" magazine exclusive to the gun trade.

Gun Week†
Second Amendment Foundation, P.O. Box 488, Station C, Buffalo, NY 14209. $35.00 yr. U.S. and possessions; $45.00 yr. other countries. Tabloid paper on guns, hunting, shooting and collecting (36 issues).

Gun World
Y-Visionary Publishing, LP 265 South Anita Drive, Ste. 120, Orange, CA 92868. $21.97 yr.; $34.97 2 yrs. For the hunting, reloading and shooting enthusiast.

Guns & Ammo
Primedia, 6420 Wilshire Blvd., Los Angeles, CA 90048/213-782-2780. $23.94 yr. Guns, shooting, and technical articles.

Guns
Publishers Development Corporation, P.O. Box 85201, San Diego, CA 92138/800-537-3006. $19.95 yr. In-depth articles on a wide range of guns, shooting equipment and related accessories for gun collectors, hunters and shooters.

Guns Review
Ravenhill Publishing Co. Ltd., Box 35, Standard House, Bonhill St., London EC 2A 4DA, England. £20.00 sterling (approx. U.S. $38 USA & Canada) yr. For collectors and shooters.

H.A.C.S. Newsletter (M)
Harry Moon, Pres., P.O. Box 50117, South Slope RPO, Burnaby BC, V5J 5G3, Canada/604-438-0950; Fax:604-277-3646. $25 p. yr. U.S. and Canada. Official newsletter of The Historical Arms Collectors of B.C. (Canada).

Handgunner*
Richard A.J. Munday, Seychelles house, Brightlingsen, Essex CO7 ONN, England/012063-305201. £18.00 (sterling).

Handguns
Primedia, 6420 Wilshire Blvd., Los Angeles, CA 90048/323-782-2868. $23/94 yr. For the handgunning and shooting enthusiast.

Handloader*
Wolfe Publishing Co., 2626 Stearman Road, Ste. A, Prescott, AZ 86301/520-445-7810;Fax:520-778-5124. $22.00 yr. The journal of ammunition reloading.

INSIGHTS*
NRA, 11250 Waples Mill Rd., Fairfax, VA 22030. Editor, John E. Robbins. $15.00 yr., which includes NRA junior membership; $10.00 for adult subscriptions (12 issues). Plenty of details for the young hunter and target shooter; emphasizes gun safety, marksmanship training, hunting skills.

International Arms & Militaria Collector (Q)
Arms & Militaria Press, P.O. Box 80, Labrador, Qld. 4215, Australia. A$39.50 yr. (U.S. & Canada), 2 yrs. A$77.50; A$37.50 (others), 1 yr., 2 yrs. $73.50 all air express mail; surface mail is less. Editor: Ian D. Skennerton.

International Shooting Sport*/UIT Journal
International Shooting Union (UIT), Bavariaring 21, D-80336 Munich, Germany. Europe: (Deutsche Mark) DM44.00 yr., 2 yrs. DM83.00; outside Europe: DM50.00 yr., 2 yrs. DM95.00 (air mail postage included.) For international sport shooting.

Internationales Waffen-Magazin
Habegger-Verlag Zürich, Postfach 9230, CH-8036 Zürich, Switzerland. SF 105.00 (approx. U.S. $73.00) surface mail for 10 issues. Modern and antique arms, self-defense. German text; English summary of contents.

The Journal of the Arms & Armour Society (M)
A. Dove, P.O. Box 10232, London, SW19 2ZD England. £15.00 surface mail; £20.00 airmail sterling only yr. Articles for the historian and collector.

Journal of the Historical Breechloading Smallarms Assn.
Published annually. P.O. Box 12778, London, SE1 6XB, England. $21.00 yr. Articles for the collector plus mailings of short articles on specific arms, reprints, newsletters, etc.

Knife World
Knife World Publications, P.O. Box 3395, Knoxville, TN 37927. $15.00 yr.; $25.00 2 yrs. Published monthly for knife enthusiasts and collectors. Articles on custom and factory knives; other knife-related interests, monthly column on knife identification, military knives.

Man At Arms*
P.O. Box 460, Lincoln, RI 02865. $27.00 yr., $52.00 2 yrs. plus $8.00 for foreign subscribers. The N.R.A. magazine of arms collecting-investing, with excellent articles for the collector of antique arms and militaria.

The Mannlicher Collector (Q)(M)
Mannlicher Collectors Assn., Inc., P.O. Box 7144, Salem Oregon 97303. $20/ yr. subscription included in membership.

*Published bi-monthly
† Published weekly
‡Published three times per month. All others are published monthly.

M=Membership requirements; write for details.
Q=Published Quarterly.

REFERENCE

PERIODICAL PUBLICATIONS

MAN/MAGNUM
S.A. Man (Pty) Ltd., P.O. Box 35204, Northway, Durban 4065, Republic of South Africa. SA Rand 200.00 for 12 issues. Africa's only publication on hunting, shooting, firearms, bushcraft, knives, etc.

The Marlin Collector (M)
R.W. Paterson, 407 Lincoln Bldg., 44 Main St., Champaign, IL 61820.

Muzzle Blasts (M)
National Muzzle Loading Rifle Assn., P.O. Box 67, Friendship, IN 47021/812-667-5131. $35.00 yr. annual membership. For the blackpowder shooter.

Muzzleloader Magazine*
Scurlock Publishing Co., Inc., Dept. Gun, Route 5, Box 347-M, Texarkana, TX 75501. $18.00 U.S.; $22.50 U.S./yr. for foreign subscribers. The publication for blackpowder shooters.

National Defense (M)*
American Defense Preparedness Assn., Two Colonial Place, Suite 400, 2101 Wilson Blvd., Arlington, VA 22201-3061/703-522-1820; FAX: 703-522-1885. $35.00 yr. Articles on both military and civil defense field, including weapons, materials technology, management.

National Knife Magazine (M)
Natl. Knife Coll. Assn., 7201 Shallowford Rd., P.O. Box 21070, Chattanooga, TN 37424-0070. Membership $35 yr.; $65.00 International yr.

National Rifle Assn. Journal (British) (Q)
Natl. Rifle Assn. (BR.), Bisley Camp, Brookwood, Woking, Surrey, England. GU24, OPB. £24.00 Sterling including postage.

National Wildlife*
Natl. Wildlife Fed., 1400 16th St. NW, Washington, DC 20036, $16.00 yr. (6 issues); International Wildlife, 6 issues, $16.00 yr. Both, $22.00 yr., includes all membership benefits. Write attn.: Membership Services Dept., for more information.

New Zealand GUNS*
Waitekauri Publishing, P.O. 45, Waikino 3060, New Zealand. $NZ90.00 (6 issues) yr. Covers the hunting and firearms scene in New Zealand.

New Zealand Wildlife (Q)
New Zealand Deerstalkers Assoc., Inc., P.O. Box 6514, Wellington, N.Z. $30.00 (N.Z.). Hunting, shooting and firearms/game research articles.

North American Hunter* (M)
P.O. Box 3401, Minnetonka, MN 55343/612-936-9333; e-mail: huntingclub@pclink.com. $18.00 yr. (7 issues). Articles on all types of North American hunting.

Outdoor Life
Time4 Media, Two Park Ave., New York, NY 10016. $16.95/yr. Extensive coverage of hunting and shooting. Shooting column by Jim Carmichel.

La Passion des Courteaux (Q)
Phenix Editions, 25 rue Mademoiselle, 75015 Paris, France. French text.

Paintball Games International Magazine
Aceville Publications, Castle House, 97 High St., Colchester, Essex, England CO1 1TH/011-44-206-564840. Write for subscription rates. Leading magazine in the U.K. covering competitive paintball activities.

Paintball News
PBN Publishing, P.O. Box 1608, 24 Henniker St., Hillsboro, NH 03244/603-464-6080. $35 U.S. 1 yr. Bi-weekly. Newspaper covering the sport of paintball, new product reviews and industry features.

Paintball Sports (Q)
Paintball Publications, Inc., 540 Main St., Mount Kisco, NY 10549/941-241-7400. $24.75 U.S. 1 yr., $32.75 foreign. Covering the competitive paintball scene.

Performance Shooter
Belvoir Publications, Inc., 75 Holly Hill Lane, Greenwich, CT 06836-2626/203-661-6111. $45.00 yr. (12 issues). Techniques and technology for improved rifle and pistol accuracy.

Petersen's HUNTING Magazine
Primedia, 6420 Wilshire Blvd., Los Angeles, CA 90048. $19.94 yr.; Canada $29.34 yr.; foreign countries $29.94 yr. Hunting articles for all game; test reports.

P.I. Magazine
America's Private Investigation Journal, 755 Bronx Dr., Toledo, OH 43609. Chuck Klein, firearms editor with column about handguns.

Pirsch
BLV Verlagsgesellschaft mbH, Postfach 400320, 80703 Munich, Germany/089-12704-0;Fax:089-12705-354. German text.

Point Blank
Citizens Committee for the Right to Keep and Bear Arms (sent to contributors), Liberty Park, 12500 NE 10th Pl., Bellevue, WA 98005

POINTBLANK (M)
Natl. Firearms Assn., Box 4384 Stn. C, Calgary, AB T2T 5N2, Canada. Official publication of the NFA.

The Police Marksman*
6000 E. Shirley Lane, Montgomery, AL 36117. $17.95 yr. For law enforcement personnel.

Police Times (M)
3801 Biscayne Blvd., Miami, FL 33137/305-573-0070.

Popular Mechanics
Hearst Corp., 224 W. 57th St., New York, NY 10019. Firearms, camping, outdoor oriented articles.

Precision Shooting
Precision Shooting, Inc., 222 McKee St., Manchester, CT 06040. $37.00 yr. U.S. Journal of the International Benchrest Shooters, and target shooting in general. Also considerable coverage of varmint shooting, as well as big bore, small bore, schuetzen, lead bullet, wildcats and precision reloading.

Rifle*
Wolfe Publishing Co., 2626 Stearman Road, Ste. A, Prescott, AZ 86301/520-445-7810; Fax: 520-778-5124. $19.00 yr. The sporting firearms journal.

Rifle's Hunting Annual
Wolfe Publishing Co., 2626 Stearman Road, Ste. A, Prescott, AZ 86301/520-445-7810; Fax: 520-778-5124. $4.99 Annual. Dedicated to the finest pursuit of the hunt.

Rod & Rifle Magazine
Lithographic Serv. Ltd., P.O. Box 38-138, Wellington, New Zealand. $50.00 yr. (6 issues). Hunting, shooting and fishing articles.

Safari* (M)
Safari Magazine, 4800 W. Gates Pass Rd., Tucson, AZ 85745/602-620-1220. $55.00 (6 times). The journal of big game hunting, published by Safari Club International. Also publish Safari Times, a monthly newspaper, included in price of $55.00 national membership.

Second Amendment Reporter
Second Amendment Foundation, James Madison Bldg., 12500 NE 10th Pl., Bellevue, WA 98005. $15.00 yr. (non-contributors).

Shoot! Magazine*
Shoot! Magazine Corp., 1770 West State Stret PMB 340, Boise ID 83702/208-368-9920; Fax: 208-338-8428. Website: www.shootmagazine.com $32.95 (6 times/yr.). Articles of interest to the cowboy action shooter, or others interested the Western-era firearms and ammunition.

Shooter's News
23146 Lorain Rd., Box 349, North Olmsted, OH 44070/216-979-5258;Fax:216-979-5259. $29 U.S. 1 yr., $54 2 yrs.; $52 foreign surface. A journal dedicated to precision riflery.

Shooting Industry
Publisher's Dev. Corp., 591 Camino de la Reina, Suite 200, San Diego, CA 92108. $50.00 yr. To the trade. $25.00.

Shooting Sports USA
National Rifle Assn. of America, 11250 Waples Mill Road, Fairfax, VA 22030. Annual subscriptions for NRA members are $5 for classified shooters and $10 for non-classified shooters. Non-NRA member subscriptions are $15. Covering events, techniques and personalities in competitive shooting.

Shooting Sportsman*
P.O. Box 11282, Des Moines, IA 50340/800-666-4955 (for subscriptions). Editorial: P.O. Box 1357, Camden, ME 04843. $19.95 for six issues. The magazine of wingshooting and fine guns.

The Shooting Times & Country Magazine (England)†
IPC Magazines Ltd., King's Reach Tower, Stamford St, 1 London SE1 9LS, England/0171-261-6180;Fax:0171-261-7179. £65 (approx. $98.00) yr.; £79 yr. overseas (52 issues). Game shooting, wild fowling, hunting, game fishing and firearms articles. Britain's best selling field sports magazine.

Shooting Times
Primedia, 2 News Plaza, P.O. Box 1790, Peoria, IL 61656/309-682-6626. $16.97 yr. Guns, shooting, reloading; articles on every gun activity.

The Shotgun News‡
Primedia, 2 News Plaza, P.O. Box 1790, Peoria, IL 61656/800-495-8362. $28.95 yr.; foreign subscription call for rates. Sample copy $4.00. Gun ads of all kinds.

SHOT Business
National Shooting Sports Foundation, Flintlock Ridge Office Center, 11 Mile Hill Rd., Newtown, CT 06470-2359/203-426-1320; FAX: 203-426-1087. For the shooting, hunting and outdoor trade retailer.

Shotgun Sports
P.O. Box 6810, Auburn, CA 95604/916-889-2220; FAX:916-889-9106. $31.00 yr. Trapshooting how-to's, shotshell reloading, shotgun patterning, shotgun tests and evaluations, Sporting Clays action, waterfowl/upland hunting. Call 1-800-676-8920 for a free sample copy.

The Single Shot Exchange Magazine
PO Box 1055, York SC 29745/803-628-5326 phone/fax. $31.50/yr., monthly. Articles of interest to the blackpowder cartridge shooter and antique arms collector.

Single Shot Rifle Journal* (M)
Editor John Campbell, PO Box 595, Bloomfield Hills, MI 48303/248-458-8415. Email: jcampbell@chemistri.com Annual dues $35 for 6 issues. Journal of the American Single Shot Rifle Assn.

The Sixgunner (M)
Handgun Hunters International, P.O. Box 357, MAG, Bloomingdale, OH 43910

The Skeet Shooting Review
National Skeet Shooting Assn., 5931 Roft Rd., San Antonio, TX 78253. $20.00 yr. (Assn. membership includes mag.) Competition results, personality profiles of top Skeet shooters, how-to articles, technical, reloading information.

Soldier of Fortune
Subscription Dept., P.O. Box 348, Mt. Morris, IL 61054. $29.9 yr.; $39.95 Canada; $50.95 foreign.

Sporting Clays Magazine
Patch Communications, 5211 South Washington Ave., Titusville, FL 32780/407-268-5010; FAX: 407-267-7216. $29.95 yr. (12 issues). Official publication of the National Sporting Clays Association.

Sporting Goods Business
Miller Freeman, Inc., One Penn Plaza, 10th Fl., New York, N 10119-0004. Trade journal.

Sporting Goods Dealer
Two Park Ave., New York, NY 10016. $100.00 yr. Sporting goods trade journal.

Sporting Gun
Bretton Court, Bretton, Peterborough PE3 8DZ, England. £27.00 (approx. U.S. $36.00), airmail £35.50 yr. For the gam and clay enthusiasts.

The Squirrel Hunter
P.O. Box 368, Chireno, TX 75937. $14.00 yr. Articles about squirrel hunting.

Stott's Creek Calendar
Stott's Creek Printers, 2526 S 475 W, Morgantown, IN 46160/317-878-5489. 1 yr (3 issues) $11.50; 2 yrs. (6 issues) $20.00. Lists all gun shows everywhere in convenient calenda form; call for information.

Super Outdoors
2695 Aiken Road, Shelbyville, KY 40065/502-722-9463; 800-404-6064; Fax: 502-722-8093. Mark Edwards, publisher. Contact for details.

TACARMI
Via E. De Amicis, 25; 20123 Milano, Italy. $100.00 yr. approx. Antique and modern guns. (Italian text.)

Territorial Dispatch—1800s Historical Publication (M)
National Assn. of Buckskinners, 4701 Marion St., Suite 324, Livestock Exchange Bldg., Denver, CO 80216. Michael A. Nester & Barbara Wyckoff, editors. 303-297-9671.

Trap & Field
1000 Waterway Blvd., Indianapolis, IN 46202. $25.00 yr. Official publ. Amateur Trapshooting Assn. Scores, averages, trapshooting articles.

Turkey Call* (M)
Natl. Wild Turkey Federation, Inc., P.O. Box 530, Edgefield, SC 29824. $25.00 with membership (6 issues per yr.)

Turkey & Turkey Hunting*
Krause Publications, 700 E. State St., Iola, WI 54990-0001. $13.95 (6 issue p. yr.). Magazine with leading-edge articles on all aspects of wild turkey behavior, biology and the successful ways to hunt better with that info. Learn the proper techniques to calling, the right equipment, and more.

The Accurate Rifle
Precisions Shooting, Inc., 222 Mckee Street, Manchester CT 06040. $37 yr. Dedicated to the rifle accuracy enthusiast.

The U.S. Handgunner* (M)
U.S. Revolver Assn., 40 Larchmont Ave., Taunton, MA 02780. $10.00 yr. General handgun and competition articles. Bi-monthly sent to members.

U.S. Airgun Magazine
P.O. Box 2021, Benton, AR 72018/800-247-4867; Fax: 501-316-8549. 10 issues a yr. Cover the sport from hunting, 10-meter, field target and collecting. Write for details.

The Varmint Hunter Magazine (Q)
The Varmint Hunters Assn., Box 759, Pierre, SD 57501/800-528-4868. $24.00 yr.

Waffenmarkt-Intern
GFI-Verlag, Theodor-Heuss Ring 62, 50668 K"ln, Germany. Only for gunsmiths, licensed firearms dealers and their suppliers in Germany, Austria and Switzerland.

Wild Sheep (M) (Q)
Foundation for North American Wild Sheep, 720 Allen Ave., Cody, WY 82414. Website: http://iigi.com/os/non/fnaws/fnaws.htm; e-mail: fnaws@wyoming.com. Official journal of the foundation.

Wisconsin Outdoor Journal
Krause Publications, 700 E. State St., Iola, WI 54990-0001. $17.97 yr. (8 issues). For Wisconsin's avid hunters and fishermen, with features from all over that state with regional reports, legislative updates, etc. Website: www.krause.com

Women & Guns
P.O. Box 488, Sta. C, Buffalo, NY 14209. $24.00 yr. U.S.; $72.00 foreign (12 issues). Only magazine edited by and for women gun owners.

World War II*
Cowles History Group, 741 Miller Dr. SE, Suite D-2, Leesburg, VA 20175-8920. Annual subscriptions $19.95 U.S.; $25.95 Canada; 43.95 foreign. The title says it—WWII; good articles, ads, etc.

*Published bi-monthly
† Published weekly
‡Published three times per month. All others are published monthly.

M=Membership requirements; write for details.
Q=Published Quarterly.

REFERENCE

THE HANDGUNNER'S LIBRARY

FOR COLLECTOR ◆ HUNTER ◆ SHOOTER ◆ OUTDOORSMAN

IMPORTANT NOTICE TO BOOK BUYERS

Books listed here may be bought from Ray Riling Arms Books Co., 6844 Gorsten St., P.O. Box 18925, Philadelphia, PA 19119, Phone 215/438-2456; FAX: 215-438-5395. E-Mail: sales@rayrilingarms-books.com. Larry Riling is the researcher and compiler of "The Arms Library" and a seller of gun books for over 32 years. The Riling stock includes books classic and modern, many hard-to-find items, and many not obtainable elsewhere. These pages list a portion of the current stock. They offer prompt, complete service, with delayed shipments occurring only on out-of-print or out-of-stock books.

Visit our web site at **www.rayrilingarmsbooks.com** and order all of your favorite titles on line from our secure site.

NOTICE FOR ALL CUSTOMERS: Remittance in U.S. funds must accompany all orders. For your convenience we now accept VISA, Master-Card & American Express. For shipments in the U.S. add $7.00 for the 1st book and $2.00 for each additional book for postage and insurance. Mini-mum order $10.00. International Orders add $13.00 for the 1st book and $5.00 for each additional book. All International orders are shipped at the buyer's risk unless an additional $5 for insurance is included. USPS does not offer insurance to all countries unless shipped Air-Mail please e-mail or call for pricing.

Payments in excess of order or for "Backorders" are credited or fully re-funded at request. Books "As-Ordered" are not returnable except by permis-sion and a handling charge on these of 10% or $2.00 per book which ever is greater is deducted from refund or credit. Only Pennsylvania customers must include current sales tax.

A full variety of arms books also available from Rutgers Book Center, 127 Raritan Ave., Highland Park, NJ 08904/908-545-4344; FAX: 908-545-6686 or I.D.S.A. Books, 1324 Stratford Drive, Piqua, OH 45356/937-773-4203; FAX: 937-778-1922.

BALLISTICS AND HANDLOADING

ABC's of Reloading, 6th Edition, by C. Rodney James and the editors of Handloader's Digest, DBI Books, a division of Krause Publications, Iola, WI, 1997. 288 pp., illus. Paper covers. $21.95

The definitive guide to every facet of cartridge and shotshell reloading.

Accurate Arms Loading Guide Number 2, by Accurate Arms. McEwen, TN: Accurate Arms Company, Inc., 2000. Paper Covers. $18.95

Includes new data on smokeless powders XMR4064 and XMP5744 as well as a special section on Cowboy Action Shooting. The new manual includes 50 new pages of data. An appendix includes nominal rotor charge weights, bullet diameters.

American Cartridge, The, by Charles Suydam, Borden Publishing Co. Alhambra, CA, 1986. 184 pp., illus. Softcover $24.95

An illustrated study of the rimfire cartridge in the United States.

Ammo and Ballistics, by Robert W. Forker, Safari Press, Inc., Huntington Beach, CA., 1999. 252 pp., illustrated. Paper covers. $18.95

Ballistic data on 125 calibers and 1,400 loads out to 500 yards.

Ammunition: Grenades and Projectile Munitions, by Ian V. Hogg, Stackpole Books, Mechanicsburg, PA, 1998. 144 pp., illus. $22.95

Concise guide to modern ammunition. International coverage with detailed specifications and illustrations.

Barnes Reloading Manual #2, Barnes Bullets, American Fork, UT, 1999. 668 pp., illus. $24.95

Features data and trajectories on the new weight X, XBT and Solids in calibers from .22 to .50 BMG.

Black Powder Guide, 2nd Edition, by George C. Nonte, Jr., Stoeger Publishing Co., So. Hackensack, NJ, 1991. 288 pp., illus. Paper covers. $14.95

How-to instructions for selection, repair and maintenance of muzzleloaders, making your own bullets, restoring and refinishing, shooting techniques.

Blackpowder Loading Manual, 3rd Edition, by Sam Fadala, DBI Books, a division of Krause Publications, Iola, WI, 1995. 368 pp., illus. Paper covers. $20.95

Revised and expanded edition of this landmark blackpowder loading book. Covers hundreds of loads for most of the popular blackpowder rifles, handguns and shotguns.

Cartridges of the World, 9th Edition, by Frank Barnes, Krause Publications, Iola, WI, 2000. 512 pp., illus. Paper covers. $27.95

Completely revised edition of the general purpose reference work for which collectors, police, scientists and laymen reach first for answers to cartridge identification questions.

Cartridge Reloading Tools of the Past, by R.H. Chamberlain and Tom Quigley, Tom Quigley, Castle Rock, WA, 1998. 167 pp., illustrated. Paper covers. $25.00

A detailed treatment of the extensive Winchester and Ideal line of handloading tools and bullet molds, plus Remington, Marlin, Ballard, Browning, Maynard, and many others.

Cast Bullets for the Black Powder Rifle, by Paul A. Matthews, Wolfe Publishing Co., Prescott, AZ, 1996. 133 pp., illus. Paper covers. $22.50

The tools and techniques used to make your cast bullet shooting a success.

Complete Blackpowder Handbook, 4th Edition, by Sam Fadala, DBI Books, a division of Krause Publications, Iola, WI, 2001. 400 pp., illus. Paper covers. $22.95

Expanded and completely rewritten edition of the definitive book on the subject of blackpowder.

Complete Reloading Manual, One Book / One Caliber. California: Load Books USA, 2000. $7.95 each

Containing unabridged information from U. S. Bullet and Powder Makers. With thousands of proven and tested loads, plus dozens of various bullet designs and different powders. Spiral bound. Available in all Calibers.

Designing and Forming Custom Cartridges for Rifles and Handguns, by Ken Howell. Precision Shooting, Manchester, CT. 2002. 600 pages, illus. $59.95

The classic work in its field, out of print for the last few years, and virtually unobtainable on the used book market, now returns in an exact reprint of the original. Some 600 pages, full size (8 1/2" x 11"), hard covers. Dozens of cartridge drawings never published anywhere before-dozens you've never heard of (guaranteed!). Precisely drawn to the dimensions specified by men who designed them, the factories that made them, and the authorities that set the standards. All drawn to the same format and scale (1.5x)-for most, how to form them from brass. Some 450 pages of them, two to a page. Plus other practical information.

Early Loading Tools & Bullet Molds, Pioneer Press, 1988. 88 pages, illustrated. Softcover. $7.50

Handbook for Shooters and Reloaders, by P.O. Ackley, Salt Lake City, UT, 1998, (Vol. I), 567 pp., illus. Includes a separate exterior ballistics chart. $21.95 (Vol. II), a new printing with specific new material. 495 pp., illus. $20.95

Handgun Stopping Power; The Definitive Study, by Marshall & Sandow. Boulder, CO: Paladin Press, 1992. 240 pages. $45.00

Offers accurate predictions of the stopping power of specific loads in calibers from .380 Auto to .45 ACP, as well as such specialty rounds as the Glaser Safety Slug, Federal Hydra-Shok, MagSafe, etc. This is the definitive methodology for predicting the stopping power of handgun loads, the first to take into account what really happens when a bullet meets a man.

Handloader's Manual of Cartridge Conversions, 2nd Revised Edition by John J. Donnelly, Stoeger Publishing Co., So. Hackensack, NJ, 2002. Unpaginated. $39.95

From 14 Jones to 70-150 Winchester in English and American cartridges, and from 4.85 U.K. to 15.2x28R Gevelot in metric cartridges. Over 900 cartridges described in detail.

Hatcher's Notebook, by S. Julian Hatcher, Stackpole Books, Harrisburg, PA, 1992. 488 pp., illus. $39.95

A reference work for shooters, gunsmiths, ballisticians, historians, hunters and collectors.

History and Development of Small Arms Ammunition; Volume 2 Centerfire: Primitive, and Martial Long Arms. by George A. Hoyem. Oceanside, CA: Armory Publications, 1991. 303 pages, illustrated. $60.00

Covers the blackpowder military centerfire rifle, carbine, machine gun and volley gun ammunition used in 28 nations and dominions, together with the firearms that chambered them.

REFERENCE

THE HANDGUNNER'S LIBRARY

History and Development of Small Arms Ammunition; Volume 4, American Military Rifle Cartridges. Oceanside, CA: Armory Publications, 1998. 244pp., illus. $60.00

Carries on what Vol. 2 began with American military rifle cartridges. Now the sporting rifle cartridges are at last organized by their originators-235 individual case types designed by eight makers of single shot rifles and four of magazine rifles from .50-140 Winchester Express to .22-15-60 Stevens. plus experimentals from .70-150 to .32-80. American Civil War enthusiasts and European collectors will find over 150 primitives in Appendix A to add to those in Volumes One and Two. There are 16 pages in full color of 54 box labels for Sharps, Remington and Ballard cartridges. There are large photographs with descriptions of 15 Maynard, Sharps, Winchester, Browning, Freund, Remington-Hepburn, Farrow and other single shot rifles, some of them rare one of a kind specimens.

Hodgdon Powder Data Manual #27, Hodgdon Powder Co., Shawnee Mission, KS, 1999. 800 pp. $27.95

Reloading data for rifle and pistol loads.

Hodgdon Shotshell Data Manual, Hodgdon Powder Co., Shawnee Mission, KS, 1999. 208 pp. $19.95

Contains hundreds of loads for lead shot, buck shot, slugs, bismuth shot and steel shot plus articles on ballistics, patterning, special reloads and much more.

Home Guide to Cartridge Conversions, by Maj. George C. Nonte Jr., The Gun Room Press, Highland Park, NJ, 1976. 404 pp., illus. $24.95

Revised and updated version of Nonte's definitive work on the alteration of cartridge cases for use in guns for which they were not intended.

Hornady Handbook of Cartridge Reloading, 5th Edition, Vol. I and II, Edited by Larry Steadman, Hornady Mfg. Co., Grand Island, NE, 2000., illus. $49.95

2 Volumes; Volume 1, 773 pp.; Volume 2, 717 pp. New edition of this famous reloading handbook covers rifle and handgun reloading data and ballistic tables.
Latest loads, ballistic information, etc.

How-To's for the Black Powder Cartridge Rifle Shooter, by Paul A. Matthews, Wolfe Publishing Co., Prescott, AZ, 1995. 45 pp. Paper covers. $22.50

Covers lube recipes, good bore cleaners and over-powder wads. Tips include compressing powder charges, combating wind resistance, improving ignition and much more.

Illustrated Reference of Cartridge Dimensions, The, edited by Dave Scovill, Wolfe Publishing Co., Prescott, AZ, 1994. 343 pp., illus. Paper covers. $19.00

A comprehensive volume with over 300 cartridges. Standard and metric dimensions have been taken from SAAMI drawings and/or fired cartridges.

Lee Modern Reloading, by Richard Lee, 350 pp. of charts and data and 85 illustrations. 512 pp. $24.95

Bullet casting, lubricating and author's formula for calculating proper charges for cast bullets. Includes virtually all current load data published by the powder suppliers. Exclusive source of volume measured loads.

Loading the Black Powder Rifle Cartridge, by Paul A Matthews, Wolfe Publishing Co., Prescott, AZ, 1993. 121 pp., illus. Paper covers. $22.50

Author Matthews brings the blackpowder cartridge shooter valuable information on the basics, including cartridge care, lubes and moulds, powder charges and developing and testing loads in his usual authoritative style.

Loading the Peacemaker—Colt's Model P, by Dave Scovill, Wolfe Publishing Co., Prescott, AZ, 1996. 227 pp., illus. $24.95

A comprehensive work about the history, maintenance and repair of the most famous revolver ever made, including the most extensive load data ever published.

Lyman Cast Bullet Handbook, 3rd Edition, edited by C. Kenneth Ramage, Lyman Publications, Middlefield, CT, 1980. 416 pp., illus. Paper covers. $19.95

Information on more than 5000 tested cast bullet loads and 19 pages of trajectory and wind drift tables for cast bullets.

Lyman Black Powder Handbook, 2nd Edition, edited by C. Kenneth Ramage, Lyman Products for Shooters, Middlefield, CT, 2000. 239 pp., illus. Paper covers. $19.95

Comprehensive load information for the modern blackpowder shooter.

Lyman Pistol & Revolver Handbook, 2nd Edition, edited by Thomas J. Griffin, Lyman Products Co., Middlefield, CT, 1996. 287 pp., illus. Paper covers. $18.95

The most up-to-date loading data available including the hottest new calibers, like 40 S&W, 9x21, 9mm Makarov, 9x25 Dillon and 454 Casull.

Lyman Reloading Handbook No. 48, edited by Edward A. Matunas, Lyman Publications, Middlefield, CT, 2003. 480 pp., illus. Paper covers. $24.95

A comprehensive reloading manual complete with "How to Reload" information. Expanded data section with all the newest rifle and pistol calibers.

Lyman Shotshell Handbook, 4th Edition, edited by Edward A. Matunas, Lyman Products Co., Middlefield, CT, 1996. 330 pp., illus. Paper covers. $24.95

Has 9000 loads, including slugs and buckshot, plus feature articles and a full color I.D. section.

Lyman's Guide to Big Game Cartridges & Rifles, by Edward Matunas, Lyman Publishing Corporation, Middlefield, CT, 1994. 287 pp., illus. Paper covers. $17.95

A selection guide to cartridges and rifles for big game—antelope to elephant.

Military Rifle and Machine Gun Cartridges, by Jean Huon, Alexandria, VA: Ironside International, 1995. 1st edition. 378 pages, over 1,000 photos. $34.95

Superb reference text.

Modern Combat Ammunition, by Duncan Long, Paladin Press, Boulder, CO, 1997, soft cover, photos, illus., 216 pp. $34.00

Now, Paladin's leading weapons author presents his exhaustive evaluation of the stopping power of modern rifle, pistol, shotgun and machine gun rounds based on actual case studies of shooting incidents. He looks at the hot new cartridges that promise to dominate well into the next century .40 S&W, 10mm auto, sub-sonic 9mm's - as well as the trusted standbys. Find out how to make your own exotic tracers, fléchette and sabot rounds, caseless ammo and fragmenting bullets.

Modern Exterior Ballistics, by Robert L. McCoy, Schiffer Publishing Co., Atglen, PA, 1999. 128 pp. $95.00

Advanced students of exterior ballistics and flight dynamics will find this comprehensive textbook on the subject a useful addition to their libraries.

Modern Reloading, by Richard Lee, Inland Press, 1996. 510 pp., illus. $24.98

The how-to's of rifle, pistol and shotgun reloading plus load data for rifle and pistol calibers.

Modern Reloading 2nd Edition, by Richard Lee, Inland Press, 2003. 623 pp., illus. $29.95

The how-to's of rifle, pistol and shotgun reloading plus load data for rifle and pistol calibers.

Modern Sporting Rifle Cartridges, by Wayne van Zwoll, Stoeger Publishing Co., Wayne, NJ, 1998. 310 pp., illustrated. Paper covers. $21.95

Illustrated with hundreds of photos and backed up by dozens of tables and schematic drawings, this four-part book tells the story of how rifle bullets and cartridges were developed and, in some cases, discarded.

Mr. Single Shot's Cartridge Handbook, by Frank de Haas, Mark de Haas, Orange City, IA, 1996. 116 pp., illus. Paper covers. $21.50

This book covers most of the cartridges, both commercial and wildcat, that the author has known and used.

Nosler Reloading Manual #5, edited by Gail Root, Nosler Bullets, Inc., Bend, OR, 2002. 516 pp., illus. $29.99

Combines information on their Ballistic Tip, Partition and Handgun bullets with traditional powders and new powders never before used, plus trajectory information from 100 to 500 yards.

Paper Jacket, The, by Paul Matthews, Wolfe Publishing Co., Prescott, AZ, 1991. Paper covers. $14.50

Up-to-date and accurate information about paper-patched bullets.

Reloading Tools, Sights and Telescopes for S/S Rifles, by Gerald O. Kelver, Brighton, CO, 1982. 163 pp., illus. Softcover. $15.00

A listing of most of the famous makers of reloading tools, sights and telescopes with a brief description of the products they manufactured.

Reloading for Shotgunners, 4th Edition, by Kurt D. Fackler and M.L. McPherson, DBI Books, a division of Krause Publications, Iola, WI, 1997. 320 pp., illus. Paper covers. $19.95

Expanded reloading tables with over 11,000 loads. Bushing charts for every major press and component maker. All new presentation on all aspects of shotshell reloading by two of the top experts in the field.

Rimfire Cartridge in the United States and Canada, The, Illustrated history of rimfire cartridges, manufacturers, and the products made from 1857-1984. by John L. Barber, Thomas Publications, Gettysburg, PA 2000. 1st edition. Profusely illustrated. 221 pages. $50.00

The author has written an encyclopedia of rimfire cartridges from the .22 to the massive 1.00 in. Gatling. Fourteen chapters, six appendices and an excellent bibliography make up a reference volume that all cartridge collectors should aquire.

Shotshells & Ballistics. Long Beach, CA: Safari Press, 2002. 275pp, photos. Softcover. $19.95

There is a bewildering array of commercially loaded shotgun shells for sale, from the .410 to the 10-gauge. In fact, there are more types of shells and shot sizes on the market now than ever before. With this overwhelming selection of shells available, here, finally, is a practical, reasonably priced book that makes sense of it all. It lists commercially available shotshell loads from the .410-bore to the 10-gauge, in all shot sizes available, different shot types (lead, steel, bismuth, tungsten, and others) so that the shooter or hunter can quickly find what will be best for the gun he has and the game or targets he wants to shoot. Each shotgun shell with each loading has its own table--over 1,600 tables!!--showing shot size; weight of shot; recoil; average number of pellets in the shell; manufacturer's order number; shell length and type of hull; type of wad; and whether the shot is buffered or not. In addition, each table contains data that details velocity (in 10-yard intervals from 0 to 70 yards); average pellet energy; and time of flight in seconds. This book includes complete listings and tables of every load made from the following manufacturers: Aguilla, Armscorp, ARMUSA, Baschieri & Pellagri, Bismuth Cartridge Company, Clever, Dionisi, Dynamit Nobel, Eley Hawk, Federal, Fiocchi, Hevi-Shot (now loaded exclusively by Remington), Kent, Lightfield, Nobel

Sport, PMC, RIO, Remington, Rotweil, Sellier & Bellot, RST, RWS, and Winchester. In addition, this informative reference contains authoritative articles on the history and development of shotshells, the components and technical data that govern production of shotshells, what load and shot size to use for what type of game or target, and much more. Never before has so much information on shotshells and ballistics been placed in a single book. Accentuated with photos from the field and the range, this is a reference book unlike any other.

Sierra Reloading Manual, 5th Edition: Rifle and Handgun Manual of Reloading Data. Sedalia, MO: Sierra Bullets, 2003. 5th edition. Hardcover. $39.95

This 1152 page manual retains the popular three-ring binder format and has been modernized with new cartridge information, histories and reloading recommendations. New bullets, new cartridges and new powders make this manual a necessity in every reloader's library.

Sixgun Cartridges and Loads, by Elmer Keith, The Gun Room Press, Highland Park, NJ, 1986. 151 pp., illus. $24.95

A manual covering the selection, uses and loading of the most suitable and popular revolver cartridges. Originally published in 1936. Reprint.

Speer Reloading Manual No. 13, edited by members of the Speer research staff, Omark Industries, Lewiston, ID, 1999. 621 pp., illustrated. $24.95

With thirteen new sections containing the latest technical information and reloading trends for both novice and expert in this latest edition. More than 9,300 loads are listed, including new propellant powders from Accurate Arms, Alliant, Hodgdon and Vihtavuori.

Stopping Power: A Practical Analysis of the Latest Handgun Ammunition, by Marshall & Sanow. Boulder, CO: Paladin Press, 2002. 1st edition. 600+ photos, 360 pp. Softcover. $49.95

If you want to know how handgun ammunition will work against human targets in the future, you must look at how similar ammo has worked against human targets in the past. Stopping Power bases its conclusions on real-world facts from real-world gunfights. It provides the latest street results of actual police and civilian shootings in all of the major handgun calibers, from .22 LR to .45 ACP, plus more than 30 chapters of vital interest to all gun owners. The only thing worse than being involved in a gunfight is losing one. The info. in this book will help you choose the right bullets for your gun so you don't lose.

Street Stoppers, The Latest Handgun Stopping Power Street Results, by Marshall & Lanow. Boulder, CO, Paladin Press, 1996. 374 pages, illus. Softcover. $42.95

Street Stoppers is the long-awaited sequel to Handgun Stopping Power. It provides the latest results of real-life shootings in all of the major handgun calibers, plus more than 25 thought-provoking chapters that are vital to anyone interested in firearms, would ballistics, and combat shooting. This book also covers the street results of the hottest new caliber to hit the shooting world in years, the .40 Smith & Wesson. Updated street results of the latest exotic ammunition including Remington Golden Saber and CCI-Speer Gold Dot, plus the venerable offerings from MagSafe, Glaser, Cor-Bon and others. A fascinating look at the development of Hydra-Shok ammunition is included.

Understanding Ballistics, Revised 2nd Edition by Robert A. Rinker, Mulberry House Publishing Co., Corydon, IN, 2000. 430 pp., illus Paper covers. New, Revised and Expanded. 2nd Edition. $24.95

Explains basic to advanced firearm ballistics in understandable terms.

Why Not Load Your Own?, by Col. T. Whelen, Gun Room Press, Highland Park, NJ 1996, 4th ed., rev. 237 pp., illus. $20.00

A basic reference on handloading, describing each step, materials and equipment. Includes loads for popular cartridges.

Wildcat Cartridges Volumes 1 & 2 Combination, by the editors of Handloaders magazine, Wolfe Publishing Co., Prescott, AZ, 1997. 350 pp., illus. Paper covers. $39.95

A profile of the most popular information on wildcat cartridges that appeared in the Handloader magazine.

COLLECTORS

18th Century Weapons of the Royal Welsh Fuziliers from Flixton Hall, by Goldstein, Erik. Thomas Publications, Gettysburg, PA: 2002. 1st edition. 126 pages, illustrated with B & W photos. Softcover. $19.95

Ackermann Military Prints: Uniforms of the British and Indian Armies 1840-1855, The, by Carman, William Y. with Robert W. Kenny Jr. Schiffer Publications, Atglen, PA: 2002. 1st edition. 176 pages, with over 160 color images. $69.95

Accoutrements of the United States Infantry, Riflemen, and Dragoons 1834-1839. by R.T. Huntington, Historical Arms Series No. 20. Canada: Museum Restoration. 58 pp. illus. Softcover. $8.95

Although the 1841 edition of the U.S. Ordnance Manual provides ample information on the equipment that was in use during the 1840s, it is evident that the patterns of equipment that it describes were not introduced until 1838 or 1839. This guide is intended to fill this gap in our knowledge by providing an overview of what we now know about the accoutrements that were issued to the regular infantryman, rifleman, and dragoon, in the 1830's with excursions into earlier and later years.

Age of the Gunfighter; Men and Weapons on the Frontier 1840-1900, by Joseph G. Rosa, University of Oklahoma Press, Norman, OK, 1999. 192 pp., illustrated. Paper covers. $21.95

Stories of gunfighters and their encounters and detailed descriptions of virtually every firearm used in the old West.

Air Guns, by Eldon G. Wolff, Duckett's Publishing Co., Tempe, AZ, 1997. 204 pp., illus Paper covers. $35.00

Historical reference covering many makers, European and American guns, canes and more.

Allied and Enemy Aircraft: May 1918; Not to be Taken from the Front Lines, Historical Arms Series No. 27. Canada: Museum Restoration. Softcover. $8.95

The basis for this title is a very rare identification manual published by the French government in 1918 that illustrated 60 aircraft with three or more views: French, English American, German, Italian, and Belgian, which might have been seen over the trenches ofFrance. Each is describe in a text translated from the original French. This is probably the most complete collection of illustrations of WW1 aircraft which has survived.

American Military and Naval Belts, 1812-1902, by Dorsey, R. Stephen. Eugene, OR: Collectors Library, 2002. 1st edition. Hardcover. $80.00

With introduction by Norm Flayderman, this massive work is the NEW key reference on Sword Belts, Waist Belts, Sabre Belts, Shoulder Belts and Cartridge Belts (looped and non-looped). At over 460 pages, this 8.5x 11 inch book offers over 840 photos (primarily in colour) and original period drawings. In addition, this work offers the first, comprehensive research on the Anson Mills Woven Cartridge Belts: the man, the company and its personalities, the belt-related patents and the government contracts from 1880 through 1902. This book is a "must" for all accoutrements collectors, military historians and museums.

American Military Belt Plates, by O'Donnell, Michael J. and J. Duncan Campbell. Alexandria, VA: O'Donnell Publishing, 2000. 2nd edition. 614 pages, illus. Hardcover $49.00

At last available and well worth the wait! This massive study encompasses all the known plates from the Revolutionary War through the Spanish-American conflict. A sweeping, handsomely presented study that covers 1776 through 1910. Over 1,025 specimens are illustrated front and back along with many images of soldiers wearing various plates.

American Military Saddle, 1776-1945, The, by R. Stephen Dorsey & Kenneth L. McPheeters, Collector's Library, Eugene, OR, 1999. 400 pp., illustrated. $59.95

The most complete coverage of the subject ever writeen on the American Military Saddle. Nearly 1000 actual photos and official drawings, from the major public and private collections in the U.S. and Great Britain.

American Police Collectibles; Dark Lanterns and Other Curious Devices, by Matthew G. Forte, Turn of the Century Publishers, Upper Montclair, NJ, 1999. 248 pp., illustrated. $24.95

For collectors of police memorabilia (handcuffs, police dark lanterns, mechanical and chain nippers, rattles, billy clubs and nightsticks) and police historians.

Ammunition; Small Arms, Grenades, and Projected Munitions, by Greenhill Publishing. 144 pp., Illustrated. $22.95

The best concise guide to modern ammunition available today. Covers ammo for small arms, grenades, and projected munitions. 144 pp., Illustrated. As New – Hardcover.

Antique Guns, the Collector's Guide, 2nd Edition, edited by John Traister, Stoeger Publishing Co., So. Hackensack, NJ, 1994. 320 pp., illus. Paper covers. $19.95

Covers a vast spectrum of pre-1900 firearms: those manufactured by U.S. gunmakers as well as Canadian, French, German, Belgian, Spanish and other foreign firms.

Arming the Glorious Cause; Weapons of the Second War for Independence, by James B. Whisker, Daniel D. Hartzler and Larry W. Tantz, Old Bedford Village Press, Bedford, PA., 1998. 175 pp., illustrated. $45.00

A photographic study of Confederate weapons.

Arms & Accoutrements of the Mounted Police 1873-1973, by Roger F. Phillips and Donald J. Klancher, Museum Restoration Service, Ont., Canada, 1982. 224 pp., illus. $49.95

A definitive history of the revolvers, rifles, machine guns, cannons, ammunition, swords, etc. used by the NWMP, the RNWMP and the RCMP during the first 100 years of the Force.

Arms and Armor in the Art Institute of Chicago. By Waltler J. Karcheski, Bulfinch, New York 1999. 128 pp., 103 color photos, 12 black & white illustrations. $50.00

The George F. Harding Collection of arms and armor is the most visited installation at the Art Institute of Chicago - a testament to the enduring appeal of swords, muskets and the other paraphernalia of medieval and early modern war. Organized both chronologically and by type of weapon, this book captures the best of this astonishing collection in 115 striking photographs - most in color - accompanied by illuminating text. Here are intricately filigreed breastplates and ivory-handled crossbows, samurai katana and Toledo-steel scimitars, elaborately decorated maces and beautifully carved flintlocks - a treat for anyone who has ever been beguiled by arms, armor and the age of chivalry.

Arms and Armor in Colonial America 1526-1783, by Harold Peterson, Dover Publishing, New York, 2000. 350 pages with over 300 illustrations, index, bibliography & appendix. Softcover. $34.95

Over 200 years of firearms, ammunition, equipment & edged weapons.

Arms and Armor: The Cleveland Museum of Art. By Stephen N. Fliegel, Abrams, New York, 1998. 172 color photos, 17 halftones. 181 pages. $49.50

Intense look at the culture of the warrior and hunter, with an intriguing discussion of the decorative arts found on weapons and armor, set against the background of political and social history. Also provides information on the evolution of armor, together with manufacture and decoration, and weapons as technology and art.

Arms Makers of Maryland, by Daniel D. Hartzler, George Shumway, York, PA, 1975. 200 pp., illus. $50.00

A thorough study of the gunsmiths of Maryland who worked during the late 18th and early 19th centuries.

Arms Makers of Pennsylvania, by James B. Whisker, Selinsgrove, PA, Susquehanna Univ. Press, 1990. 1st edition. 218 pages, illustrated in black and white and color. $50.00

Concentrates primarily on the cottage industry gunsmiths & gun makers who worked in the Keystone State from it's early years through 1900.

Arms Makers of Western Pennsylvania, by James B. Whisker, Old Bedford Village Press. 1st edition. This deluxe hard bound edition has 176 pages, $50.00

Printed on fine coated paper, with many large photographs, and detailed text describing the period, lives, tools, and artistry of the Arms Makers of Western Pennsylvania.

Arsenal Of Freedom: The Springfield Armory 1890-1948, by Lt. Col. William Brophy, Andrew Mowbray, Inc., Lincoln, RI,1997. 20 pgs. of photos. 400 pages. As new — Softcover. $29.95

A year by year account drawn from offical records. Packed with reports, charts, tables, line drawings, and 20 page photo section.

Artistic Ingredients of the Longrifle, by George Shumway Publisher, 1989 102 pp., with 94 illus. $20.00

After a brief review of Pennsylvania-German folk art and architecture, to establish the artistic enviroment in which the longrifle was made, the author demonstrates that the sophisticated rococo decoration on the many of the finer longrifles is comparable to the best rococo work of Philadelphia cabinet makers and silversmiths.

Art of Miniature Firearms: Centuries of Craftsmanship, The, by Miniature Arms Society. Plainfield, IL: MAS Publications, 1999. 1st edition. Hardcover. $100.00

This volume of miniature arms includes some of the finest collector's items in existence, from antique replicas to contemporary pieces made by premium craftsmen working today, many of whom are members of the Miniature Arms Society. Beautiful color photographs highlight details of miniature firearms, including handguns, shoulder guns, and machine guns; cannon weaponry; weapons systems such as suits of armor, crossbows, and Gatling guns; and hand weapons, which include bows and arrows, daggers, knives, swords, maces, and spears. Also featured are exquisite replicas of accessories, from gun cases to cavalry saddles. 335 pages, full color photos.

Art of Gun Engraving, The, by Claude Gaier and Pietro Sabatti, Knickerbocker Press, N.Y., 1999. 160 pp., illustrated. $34.95

The richness and detail lavished on early firearms represents a craftmanship nearly vanished. Beginning with crossbows in the 100's, hunting scenes, portraits, or mythological themes are intricately depicted within a few square inches of etched metal. The full-color photos contained herein recaptures this lost art with exquisite detail.

Artillery Fuses of the Civil War, by Jones, Charles H., O'Donnell Publishing, Alexandria, VA: 2001. 1st edition. Hardcover. $34.00

Chuck Jones has been recognized as the leading authority on Civil War fuses for decades. Over the course of "Artillery Fuses" 167 pages Mr. Jones imparts the reader with the culmination of his life-long study of the subject with well-researched text and hundreds of photographs of every type of Civil War fuse known. The book is hardbound, color format, printed on lustrous glossy paper. A valuable reference for every serious Civil War collector.

Astra Automatic Pistols, by Leonardo M. Antaris, FIRAC Publishing Co., Sterling, CO, 1989. 248 pp., illus. $55.00

Charts, tables, serial ranges, etc. The definitive work on Astra pistols.

Ballard: The Great American Single Shot Rifle, by John T. Dutcher. Denver, CO: Privately Printed, 2002. 1st edition. 380 pages, illustrated with black & white photos, with 8-page color insert. Hardcover. New in New Dust Jacket. $79.95

Basic Documents on U.S. Martial Arms, commentary by Col. B. R. Lewis, reissue by Ray Riling, Phila., PA, 1956 and 1960. *Rifle Musket Model 1855.*

The first issue rifle of musket caliber, a muzzle loader equipped with the Maynard Primer, 32 pp. *Rifle Musket Model 1863.* The typical Union muzzle-loader of the Civil War, 26 pp. *Breech-Loading Rifle Musket Model 1866.* The first of our 50-caliber breechloading rifles, 12 pp. *Remington Navy Rifle Model 1870.* A commercial type breech-loader made at Springfield, 16 pp. *Lee Straight Pull Navy Rifle Model 1895.* A magazine cartridge arm of 6mm caliber. 23 pp. *Breech-Loading Arms* (five models) 27 pp. *Ward-Burton Rifle Musket 1871*-16 pp. Each $10.00

Battle Weapons of the American Revolution, by George C. Neuman Scurlock Publishing Co., Texarkana, TX, 2001. 400 pp. Illus. Softcovers $34.95

The most extensive photographic collection of Revolutionary War weapons ever in one volume. More than 1,600 photos of over 500 muskets, rifles, swords, bayonets, knives and other arms used by both sides in America's War for Independence.

Bedford County Rifle and Its Makers, The, by George Shumway. 40pp illustrated, Softcover. $10.00

The authors study of the graceful and distinctive muzzle-loading rifles made in Bedford County, Pennsylvania. Stands as a milestone on the long path to the understanding of America's longrifles.

Belgian Rattlesnake; The Lewis Automatic Machine Gun, The, by William M. Easterly, Collector Grade Publications, Cobourg, Ontario, Canada, 1998. 584 pp., illustrated. $79.95

The most complete account ever published on the life and times of Colonel Isaac Newton Lewis and his crowning invention, the Lewis Automatic machine gun.

Beretta Automatic Pistols, by J.B. Wood, Stackpole Books, Harrisburg, PA, 1985. 192 pp., illus. $24.95

Only English-language book devoted to the Beretta line. Includes all important models.

Best of Holland & Holland, England's Premier Gunmaker, The, by McIntosh, Michael & Roosenburg, Jan G. Safari Press, Inc., Long Beach, CA: 2002. 1st edition. 298 pages. Profuse color illustrations. $69.95

Holland & Holland has had a long history of not only building London's "best" guns but also providing superior guns--the ultimate gun in finish, engraving, and embellishment. From the days of old in which a maharaja would order 100 fancifully engraved H&H shotguns for his guests to use at his duck shoot to the recent elaborately decorated sets depicting the Apollo 11 moon landing or the history of the British Empire, all of these guns represent the zenith in the art and craft of gunmaking and engraving. These and other H&H guns in the series named "Products of Excellence" are a cut above the ordinary H&H gun and hark back to a time when the British Empire ruled over one-third of the globe--a time when rulers, royalty, and the rich worldwide came to H&H for a gun that would elevate them above the crowd. In this book master gunwriter and acknowledged English gun expert Michael McIntosh and former H&H director Jan Roosenburg show us in words and pictures the finest products ever produced by H&H and, many would argue, by any gun company on earth. From a dainty and elegant .410 shotgun with gold relief engraving of scenes from Greek and Roman antiquity to the massive .700 Nitro Express double rifle, some of the most expensive and opulent guns ever produced on earth parade through these pages. An overview of the Products of Excellence series is given as well as a description and history of these special H&H guns. Never before have so many superlative guns from H&H--or any other maker for that manner--been displayed in one book. Many photos shown are firearms from private collections, which cannot be seen publicly anywhere except in this book. In addition, many interesting details and a general history of H&H are provided.

Big Guns, Civil War Siege, Seacoast, and Naval Cannon, The, by Edwin Olmstead, Wayne E. Stark, and Spencer C. Tucker, Museum Restoration Service, Bloomfield, Ontario, Canada, 1997. 360 pp., illustrated. $80.00

This book is designed to identify and record the heavy guns available to both sides by the end of the Civil War.

Blue Book of Air Guns, 2nd Edition, edited by S.P. Fjestad, Blue Book Publications, Inc. Minneapolis, MN 2002. $14.95

This new 2nd edition simply contains more airgun values and information than any other single publication.

Blue Book of Gun Values, 23rd Edition, edited by S.P. Fjestad, Blue Book Publications, Inc. Minneapolis, MN 2003. $39.95

This new 23rd edition simply contains more firearms values and information than any other single publication. Expanded to over 1,600 pages featuring over 100,000 firearms prices, the new Blue Book of Gun Values also contains over Ω million words of text – no other book is even close! Most of the information contained in this publication is simply not available anywhere else, for any price!

Blue Book of Modern Black Powder Values, 2nd Edtion by Dennis Adler, Blue Book Publications, Inc. Minneapolis, MN 2002. 200 pp., illustrated. 41 color photos. Softcover. $17.95

This new title contains more up-to-date black powder values and related information than any other single publication. With 163 pages, this new book will keep you up to date on modern black powder models and prices, including most makes & models introduced this year!

Blunderbuss 1500-1900, The, by James D. Forman, Historical Arms Series No. 32. Canada: Museum Restoration, 1994. An excellent and authoritative booklet giving tons of information on the Blunderbuss, a very neglected subject. 40 pages, illustrated. Softcover. $8.95

REFERENCE

Boarders Away I: With Steel-Edged Weapons & Polearms, by William Gilkerson, Andrew Mowbray, Inc. Publishers, Lincoln, RI, 1993. 331 pages. $48.00

Contains the essential 24 page chapter 'War at Sea' which sets the historical and practical context for the arms discussed. Includeds chapters on, Early Naval Weapons, Boarding Axes, Cutlasses, Officers Fighting Swords and Dirks, and weapons at hand of Random Mayhem.

Boarders Away, Volume II: Firearms of the Age of Fighting Sail, by William Gilkerson, Andrew Mowbray, Inc. Publishers, Lincoln, RI, 1993. 331 pp., illus. $65.00

Covers the pistols, muskets, combustibles and small cannon used aboard American and European fighting ships, 1626-1826.

Boston's Gun Bible, by Boston T. Party, Ignacio, CO: Javelin Press, August 2000. Expanded Edition. Softcover. $28.00

This mammoth guide for gun owners everywhere is a completely updated and expanded edition (more than 500 new pages!) of Boston T. Party's classic Boston on Guns and Courage. Pulling no punches, Boston gives new advice on which shoulder weapons and handguns to buy and why before exploring such topics as why you should consider not getting a concealed carry permit, what guns and gear will likely be outlawed next, how to spend within your budget, why you should go to a quality defensive shooting academy now, which guns and gadgets are inferior and why, how to stay off illegal government gun registration lists, how to spot an undercover agent trying to entrap law-abiding gun owners and much more.

Breech-Loading Carbines of the United States Civil War Period, by Brig. Gen. John Pitman, Armory Publications, Tacoma, WA, 1987. 94 pp., illus. $29.95

The first in a series of previously unpublished manuscripts originated by the late Brigadier General John Putnam. Exploded drawings showing parts actual size follow each sectioned illustration.

Breech-Loading Single-Shot Rifle, The, by Major Ned H. Roberts and Kenneth L. Waters, Wolfe Publishing Co., Prescott, AZ, 1995. 333 pp., illus. $28.50

A comprehensive and complete history of the evolution of the Schutzen and single-shot rifle.

Bren Gun Saga, The, by Thomas B. Dugelby, Collector Grade Publications, Cobourg, Ontario, Canada, 1999, revised and expanded edition. 406 pp., illustrated. $65.95

A modern, definitive book on the Bren in this revised expanded edition, which in terms of numbers of pages and illustrations is nearly twice the size of the original.

British Board of Ordnance Small Arms Contractors 1689-1840, by De Witt Bailey, Rhyl, England: W. S. Curtis, 2000. 150 pp. $18.00

Thirty years of research in the Archives of the Ordnance Board in London has identified more than 600 of these suppliers. The names of many can be found marking the regulation firearms of the period. In the study, the contractors are identified both alphabetically and under a combination of their date period together with their specialist trade.

British Enfield Rifles, The, Volume 1, The SMLE Mk I and Mk III Rifles, by Charles R. Stratton, North Cape Pub. Tustin, CA, 1997. 150 pp., illus. Paper covers. $16.95

A systematic and thorough examination on a part-by-part basis of the famous British battle rifle that endured for nearly 70 years as the British Army's number one battle rifle.

British Enfield Rifles, Volume 2, No.4 and No.5 Rifles, by Charles R. Stratton, North Cape Publications, Tustin, CA, 1999. 150 pp., illustrated. Paper covers. $16.95

The historical background for the development of both rifles describing each variation and an explanation of all the "marks", "numbers" and codes found on most parts.

British Enfield Rifles, Volume 4, The Pattern 1914 and U. S. Model 1917 Rifles, by Charles R. Stratton, North Cape Publications, Tustin, CA, 2000. Paper covers. $16.95

One of the lease know American and British collectible military rifles is analyzed on a part by part basis. All markings and codes, refurbishment procedures and WW 2 upgrade are included as are the varios sniper rifle versions.

British Falling Block Breechloading Rifle from 1865, The, by Jonathan Kirton, Tom Rowe Books, Maynardsville, TN, 2nd edition, 1997. 380 pp., illus. $70.00

Expanded 2nd edition of a comprehensive work on the British falling block rifle.

British Gun Engraving, by Douglas Tate, Safari Press, Inc., Huntington Beach, CA, 1999. 240 pp., illustrated. Limited, signed and numbered edition, in a slipcase. $80.00

A historic and photographic record of the last two centuries.

British Military Flintlock Rifles 1740-1840. 264 pages with over 320 photographs. Hardcover. $47.95

With a remarkable weath of data about the Rifleman and Regiments that carried these weapons, by Bailey, De Witt. Andrew Mowbray, Inc. Lincoln, RI:, 2002. 1st edition. Pattern 1776 Rifles, The Ferguson Breechloader, The Famous Baker Rifle, Rifles of the Hessians and other German Mercenaries,

American Loylist Rifles, Rifles given to indians, Cavalry Rifles and Rifled Carbines, Bayonets, Accoutrements, Ammunition and more.

British Service Rifles and Carbines 1888-1900, by Alan M. Petrillo, Excaliber Publications, Latham, NY, 1994. 72 pp., illus, Paper covers. $11.95

A complete review of the Lee-Metford and Lee-Enfield rifles and carbines.

British Single Shot Rifles, Volume 1, Alexander Henry, by Wal Winfer, Tom Rowe, Maynardsville, TN, 1998, 200 pp., illus. $50.00

Detailed Study of the single shot rifles made by Henry. Illustrated with hundreds of photographs and drawings.

British Single Shot Rifles Volume 2, George Gibbs, by Wal Winfer, Tom Rowe, Maynardsville, TN, 1998. 177 pp., illus. $50.00

Detailed study of the rifles made by Gibbs. Hundreds of photos.

British Single Shot Rifles, Volume 3, Jeffery, by Wal Winfer, Rowe Publications, Rochester, N.Y., 1999. 260 pp., illustrated. $60.00

The Farquharsen as made by Jeffery and his competitors, Holland & Holland, Bland, Westley, Manton, etc. Large section on the development of nitro cartridges including the .600.

British Single Shot Rifles, Vol. 4; Westley Richards, by Wal Winfer, Rowe Publications, Rochester, N.Y., 2000. 265 pages, illustrated, photos. $60.00

In his 4th volume Winfer covers a detailed study of the Westley Richards single shot rifles, including Monkey Tails, Improved Martini, 1872,1873, 1878,1881, 1897 Falling Blocks. He also covers Westley Richards Cartridges, History and Reloading information.

British Small Arms Ammunition, 1864-1938 (Other than .303 inch), by Peter Labbett, Armory Publications, Seattle, WA. 1993, 358 pages, illus. Four-color dust jacket. $79.00

A study of British military rifle, handgun, machine gun, and aiming tube ammunition through 1 inch from 1864 to 1938. Photo-illustrated including the firearms that chambered the cartridges.

British Soldier's Firearms from Smoothbore to Rifled Arms, The, 1850-1864, by Dr. C.H. Roads, R&R Books, Livonia, NY, 1994. 332 pp., illus. $49.00

A reprint of the classic text covering the development of British military hand and shoulder firearms in the crucial years between 1850 and 1864.

British Sporting Guns & Rifles, compiled by George Hoyem, Armory Publications, Coeur d'Alene, ID, 1997. 1024 pp., illus. In two volumes. $250.00

Eighteen old sporting firearms trade catalogs and a rare book reproduced with their color covers in a limited, signed and numbered edition.

Browning Dates of Manufacture, compiled by George Madis, Art and Reference House, Brownsboro, TX, 1989. 48 pp. $10.00

Gives the date codes and product codes for all models from 1824 to the present.

Buffalo Bill's Wild West: An American Legend, by R.L. Wilson and Greg Martine, Random House, N.Y., 1999. 3,167 pp., illustrated. $60.00

Over 225 color plates and 160 black-and-white illustrations, with in-depth text and captions, the colorful arms, posters, photos, costumes, saddles, accoutrement are brought to life.

Bullard Firearms, by Jamieson, G. Scott, Schiffer Publications, Atglen, PA 2002. 1st edition. 400 pages, with over 1100 color and b/w photographs, charts, diagrams. Hardcover. $100.00

Bullard Firearms is the story of a mechanical genius whose rifles and cartridges were the equal of any made in America in the 1880s, yet little of substance had been written about James H. Bullard or his arms prior to 1988 when the first edition called Bullard Arms was published. This greatly expanded volume with over 1,000 black and white and 150 color plates, most not previously published answers many of the questions posed in the first edition. The book is divided into eleven chapters each covering a different aspect of the Bullard story. For example, chapter two discusses Bullard's pioneering automotive work for the Overman Automobile Company (he was probably first to use a metal body on a production automobile (1899). Chapters four through eight outline in detail the large-frame repeaters, the small-frame repeaters, the solid-frame single-shot rifles, the detachable-interchangeable barrel model single-shots and lastly the very rare military and experimental models. Each model is covered in depth with many detailed photographs of the interior parts and workings of the repeaters. Chapter nine covers the fascinating and equally unknown world of Bullard cartridges and reloading tools. The final chapter outlines in chart form almost 500 Bullard rifles by serial number, caliber and type. Quick and easy to use, this book is a real benefit for collectors and dealers alike.

Burning Powder, compiled by Major D.B. Wesson, Wolfe Publishing Company, Prescott, AZ, 1992. 110 pp. Soft cover. $10.95

A rare booklet from 1932 for Smith & Wesson collectors.

Burnside Breech Loading Carbines, The, by Edward A. Hull, Andrew Mowbray, Inc., Lincoln, RI, 1986. 95 pp., illus. $16.00

No. 1 in the "Man at Arms Monograph Series." A model-by-model historical/technical examination of one of the most widely used cavalry weapons of the American Civil War based upon important and previously unpublished research.

REFERENCE

Camouflage Uniforms of European and NATO Armies; 1945 to the Present, by J. F. Borsarello, Atglen, PA: Schiffer Publications. Over 290 color and b/w photographs, 120 pages. Softcover. $29.95

This full-color book covers nearly all of the NATO, and other European armies' camouflaged uniforms, and not only shows and explains the many patterns, but also their efficacy of design. Described and illustrated are the variety of materials tested in over forty different armies, and includes the history of obsolete trial tests from 1945 to the present time. More than two hundred patterns have been manufactured since World War II using various landscapes and seasonal colors for their look. The Vietnam and Gulf Wars, African or South American events, as well as recent Yugoslavian independence wars have been used as experimental terrains to test a variety of patterns. This book provides a superb reference for the historian, reenactor, designer, and modeler.

Camouflage Uniforms of the Waffen-SS A Photographic Reference, by Michael Beaver, Schiffer Publishing, Atglen, PA. Over 1,000 color and b/w photographs and illustrations, 296 pages. $69.95

Finally a book that unveils the shroud of mystery surrounding Waffen-SS camouflage clothing. Illustrated here, both in full color and in contemporary black and white photographs, this unparalleled look at Waffen-SS combat troops and their camouflage clothing will benefit both the historian and collector.

Canadian Gunsmiths from 1608: A Checklist of Tradesmen, by John Belton, Historical Arms Series No. 29. Canada: Museum Restoration, 1992. 40 pp., 17 illustrations. Softcover. $8.95

This Checklist is a greatly expanded version of HAS No. 14, listing the names, occupation, location, and dates of more than 1,500 men and women who worked as gunmakers, gunsmiths, armorers, gun merchants, gun patent holders, and a few other gun related trades. A collection of contemporary gunsmiths' letterhead have been provided to add color and depth to the study.

Cap Guns, by James Dundas, Schiffer Publishing, Atglen, PA, 1996. 160 pp., illus. Paper covers. $29.95

Over 600 full-color photos of cap guns and gun accessories with a current value guide.

Carbines of the Civil War, by John D. McAulay, Pioneer Press, Union City, TN, 1981. 123 pp., illus. Paper covers. $12.95

A guide for the student and collector of the colorful arms used by the Federal cavalry.

Carbines of the U.S. Cavalry 1861-1905, by John D. McAulay, Andrew Mowbray Publishers, Lincoln, RI, 1996. $35.00

Covers the crucial use of carbines from the beginning of the Civil War to the end of the cavalry carbine era in 1905.

Cartridge Carbines of the British Army, by Alan M. Petrillo, Excalibur Publications, Latham, NY, 1998. 72 pp., illustrated. Paper covers. $11.95

Begins with the Snider-Enfield which was the first regulation cartridge carbine introduced in 1866 and ends with the .303 caliber No.5, Mark 1 Enfield.

Cartridge Catalogues, compiled by George Hoyem, Armory Publications, Coeur d'Alene, ID., 1997. 504 pp., illus. $125.00

Fourteen old ammunition makers' and designers' catalogs reproduced with their color covers in a limited, signed and numbered edition. Completely revised edition of the general purpose reference work for which collectors, police, scientists and laymen reach first for answers to cartridge identification questions.

Cartridge Reloading Tools of the Past, by R.H. Chamberlain and Tom Quigley, Tom Quigley, Castle Rock, WA, 1998. 167 pp., illustrated. Paper covers. $25.00

A detailed treatment of the extensive Winchester and Ideal lines of handloading tools and bulletmolds plus Remington, Marlin, Ballard, Browning and many others.

Cartridges for Collectors, by Fred Datig, Pioneer Press, Union City, TN, 1999. In three volumes of 176 pp. each. Vol.1 (Centerfire); Vol.2 (Rimfire and Misc.) types; Vol.3 (Additional Rimfire, Centerfire, and Plastic.). All illustrations are shown in full-scale drawings. Volume 1, softcover only, $19.95. Volumes 2 & 3, Hardcover $19.95

Civil War Arms Makers and Their Contracts, edited by Stuart C. Mowbray and Jennifer Heroux, Andrew Mowbray Publishing, Lincoln, RI, 1998. 595 pp. $39.50

A facsimile reprint of the Report by the Commissioner of Ordnance and Ordnance Stores, 1862.

Civil War Arms Purchases and Deliveries, edited by Stuart C. Mowbray, Andrew Mowbray Publishing, Lincoln, RI, 1998. 300pp., illus. $39.50

A facsimile reprint of the master list of Civil War weapons purchases and deliveries including Small Arms, Cannon, Ordnance and Projectiles.

Civil War Breech Loading Rifles, by John D. McAulay, Andrew Mowbray, Inc., Lincoln, RI, 1991. 144 pp., illus. Paper covers. $15.00

All the major breech-loading rifles of the Civil War and most, if not all, of the obscure types are detailed, illustrated and set in their historical context.

Civil War Cartridge Boxes of the Union Infantryman, by Paul Johnson, Andrew Mowbray, Inc., Lincoln, RI, 1998. 352 pp., illustrated. $45.00

There were four patterns of infantry cartridge boxes used by Union forces during the Civil War. The author describes the development and subsequent pattern changes to these cartridge boxes.

Civil War Collector's Price Guide; Expanded Millennium Edition, by North South Trader. Orange, VA: Publisher's Press, 2000. 9th edition. 260 pps., illus. Softcover. $29.95

All updated prices, scores of new listings, and hundreds of new pictures! It's the one reference work no collector should be without. An absolute must.

Civil War Commanders, by Dean Thomas, Thomas Publications, Gettysburg, PA. 1998. 72 pages, illustrated, photos. Paper Covers. $9.95

138 photographs and capsule biographies of Union and Confederate officers. A convenient personalities reference guide.

Civil War Guns, by William B. Edwards, Thomas Publications, Gettysburg, PA, 1997. 444 pp., illus. $40.00

The complete story of Federal and Confederate small arms; design, manufacture, identifications, procurement issue, employment, effectiveness, and postwar disposal by the recognized expert.

Civil War Infantryman: In Camp, On the March, And in Battle, by Dean Thomas, Thomas Publications, Gettysburg, PA. 1998. 72 pages, illustrated, Softcovers. $12.95

Uses first-hand accounts to shed some light on the "common soldier" of the Civil War from enlistment to muster-out, including camp, marching, rations, equipment, fighting, and more.

Civil War Pistols, by John D. McAulay, Andrew Mowbray Inc., Lincoln, RI, 1992. 166 pp., illus. $38.50

A survey of the handguns used during the American Civil War.

Civil War Projectiles II; Small Arms & Field Artillery, With Supplement, by McKee, W. Reid, and M. E. Mason, Jr. Orange, VA: Publisher's Press, 2001. 202 pages, illus. Hardcover. $40.00

The standard reference work is now available. Essential for every Civil War bullet collector.

Civil War Sharps Carbines and Rifles, by Earl J. Coates and John D. McAulay, Thomas Publications, Gettysburg, PA, 1996. 108 pp., illus. Paper covers. $12.95

Traces the history and development of the firearms including short histories of specific serial numbers and the soldiers who received them.

Civil War Small Arms of the U.S. Navy and Marine Corps, by John D. McAulay, Mowbray Publishing, Lincoln, RI, 1999. 186 pp., illustrated. $39.00

The first reliable and comprehensive guide to the firearms and edged weapons of the Civil War Navy and Marine Corps.

Cody Buffalo Bill Collector's Guide with Values, The W.F., by James W. Wojtowicz, Collector Books, Paducah, KY, 1998. 271 pp., illustrated. $24.95

A profusion of colorful collectibles including lithographs, programs, photographs, books, medals, sheet music, guns, etc. and today's values.

Col. Burton's Spiller & Burr Revolver, by Matthew W. Norman, Mercer University Press, Macon, GA, 1997. 152 pp., illus. $22.95

A remarkable archival research project on the arm together with a comprehensive story of the establishment and running of the factory.

Collector's Guide to United States Combat Shotguns, A, by Bruce N. Canfield, Andrew Mowbray Inc., Lincoln, RI, 1992. 184 pp., illus. Paper covers. $24.00

This book provides full coverage of combat shotguns, from the earliest examples right up to the Gulf War and beyond.

Collector's Guide to Winchester in the Service, A, by Bruce N. Canfield, Andrew Mowbray, Inc., Lincoln, RI, 1991. 192 pp., illus. Paper covers. $22.00

The firearms produced by Winchester for the national defense. From Hotchkiss to the M14, each firearm is examined and illustrated.

Collector's Guide to the '03 Springfield, A, by Bruce N. Canfield, Andrew Mowbray Inc., Lincoln, RI, 1989. 160 pp., illus. Paper covers. $22.00

A comprehensive guide follows the '03 through its unparalleled tenure of service. Covers all of the interesting variations, modifications and accessories of this highly collectible military rifle.

Collector's Illustrated Encyclopedia of the American Revolution, by George C. Neumann and Frank J. Kravic, Rebel Publishing Co., Inc., Texarkana, TX, 1989. 286 pp., illus. $36.95

A showcase of more than 2,300 artifacts made, worn, and used by those who fought in the War for Independence.

Colonial Frontier Guns, by T.M. Hamilton, Pioneer Press, Union City, TN, 1988. 176 pp., illus. Paper covers. $17.50

A complete study of early flint muskets of this country.

Colt: An American Legend, by R.L. Wilson, Artabras, New York, 1997. 406 pages, fully illustrated, most in color. $35.00

A reprint of the commemorative album celebrates 150 years of the guns of Samuel Colt and the manufacturing empire he built, with expert discussion of every model ever produced, the innovations of each model and variants, updated model and serial number charts and magnificent photographic showcases of the weapons.

Colt Engraving Book, The, Volumes I & II, by R. L. Wilson. Privately printed, 2001. Each volume is approximately 500 pages, with 650 illustrations, most in color. $390.00

This third edition from the original texts of 1974 and 1982 has been fine-tuned and dramatically expanded, and is by far the most illuminating and complete. With over 1,200 illustrations, more than 2/3 of which are in color, this book joins the author's The Book of Colt Firearms, and Fine Colts as companion volumes. Approximately 1,000 pages in two volumes, each signed by the author, serial numbered, and strictly limited to 3000 copies. Volume I covers from the Paterson and pre-Paterson period through c.1921 (end of the Helfricht period). Volume II commences with Kornbrath, and Glahn, and covers Colt embellished arms from c.1919 through 2000.

Colt Model 1905 Automatic Pistol, The, by John Potocki, Andrew Mowbray Publishing, Lincoln, RI, 1998. 191 pp., illus. $28.00
> Covers all aspects of the Colt Model 1905 Automatic Pistol, from its invention by the legendary John Browning to its numerous production variations.

Colt Peacemaker British Model, by Keith Cochran, Cochran Publishing Co., Rapid City, SD, 1989. 160 pp., illus. $35.00
> Covers those revolvers Colt squeezed in while completing a large order of revolvers for the U.S. Cavalry in early 1874, to those magnificent cased target revolvers used in the pistol competitions at Bisley Commons in the 1890s.

Colt Peacemaker Encyclopedia, by Keith Cochran, Keith Cochran, Rapid City, SD, 1986. 434 pp., illus. $60.00
> A must book for the Peacemaker collector.

Colt Peacemaker Encyclopedia, Volume 2, by Keith Cochran, Cochran Publishing Co., SD, 1992. 416 pp., illus. $60.00
> Included in this volume are extensive notes on engraved, inscribed, historical and noted revolvers, as well as those revolvers used by outlaws, lawmen, movie and television stars.

Colt Presentations: From The Factory Ledgers 1856-1869, by Herbert G. Houze. Lincoln, RI: Andrew Mowbray, Inc., 2003. 112 pages, 45 b&w photos. Softcover. $21.95
> Samuel Colt was a generous man. He also used gifts to influence government decision makers. But after Congress investigated him in 1854, Colt needed to hide the gifts from prying eyes, which makes it very difficult for today's collectors to document the many revolvers presented by Colt and the factory. Using the original account journals of the Colt's Patent Fire Arms Manufacturing Co., renowned arms authority Herbert G. Houze finally gives us the full details behind hundreds of the most exciting Colts ever made.

Colt Revolvers and the Tower of London, by Joseph G. Rosa, Royal Armouries of the Tower of London, London, England, 1988. 72 pp., illus. Soft covers. $15.00
> Details the story of Colt in London through the early cartridge period.

Colt's SAA Post War Models, by George Garton, The Gun Room Press, Highland Park, NJ, 1995. 166 pp., illus. $39.95
> Complete facts on the post-war Single Action Army revolvers. Information on calibers, production numbers and variations taken from factory records.

Colt Single Action Army Revolvers: The Legend, the Romance and the Rivals, by "Doc" O'Meara, Krause Publications, Iola, WI, 2000. 160 pp., illustrated with 250 photos in b&w and a 16 page color section. $34.95
> Production figures, serial numbers by year, and rarities.

Colt Single Action Army Revolvers and Alterations, by C. Kenneth Moore, Mowbray Publishers, Lincoln, RI, 1999. 112 pp., illustrated. $35.00
> A comprehensive history of the revolvers that collectors call "Artillery Models." These are the most historical of all S.A.A. Colts, and this new book covers all the details.

Colt Single Action Army Revolvers and the London Agency, by C. Kenneth Moore, Andrew Mowbray Publishers, Lincoln, RI, 1990. 144 pp., illus. $35.00
> Drawing on vast documentary sources, this work chronicles the relationship between the London Agency and the Hartford home office.

Colt U.S. General Officers' Pistols, The, by Horace Greeley IV, Andrew Mowbray Inc., Lincoln, RI, 1990. 199 pp., illus. $38.00
> These unique weapons, issued as a badge of rank to General Officers in the U.S. Army from WWII onward, remain highly personal artifacts of the military leaders who carried them. Includes serial numbers and dates of issue.

Colts from the William M. Locke Collection, by Frank Sellers, Andrew Mowbray Publishers, Lincoln, RI, 1996. 192 pp., illus. $55.00
> This important book illustrates all of the famous Locke Colts, with captions by arms authority Frank Sellers.

Colt's Dates of Manufacture 1837-1978, by R.L. Wilson, published by Maurie Albert, Coburg, Australia; N.A. distributor Madis Books, TX, 1997. 61 pp. $7.50
> An invaluable pocket guide to the dates of manufacture of Colt firearms up to 1978.

Colt's Pocket '49: Its Evolution Including the Baby Dragoon and Wells Fargo, by Robert Jordan and Darrow Watt, privately printed, Loma Mar, CA 2000. 304 pages, with 984 color photos, illus. Beautifully bound in a deep blue leather like case. $125.00
> Detailed information on all models and covers engaving, cases, accoutrements, holsters, fakes, and much more. Included is a summary booklet containing information such as serial numbers, production ranges & identifing photos. This book is a masterpiece on its subject.

Complete Guide to all United States Military Medals 1939 to Present, by Colonel Frank C. Foster, Medals of America Press, Fountain Inn, SC, 2000. 121 pp,.illustrated, photos. $29.95
> Complete criteria for every Army, Navy, Marines, Air Force, Coast Guard, and Merchant Marine awards since 1939. All decorations, service medals, and

ribbons shown in full-color and accompanied by dates and campaigns as well as detailed descriptions on proper wear and display.

Complete Guide to the M1 Garand and the M1 Carbine, by Bruce N. Canfield, 2nd printing, Andrew Mowbray Inc., Lincoln, RI, 1999. 296 pp., illus. $39.50
> Expanded and updated coverage of both the M1 Garand and the M1 Carbine, with more than twice as much information as the author's previous book on this topic.

Complete Guide to U.S. Infantry Weapons of the First War, The, by Bruce Canfield, Andrew Mowbray, Publisher, Lincoln, RI, 2000. 304 pp., illus. $39.95
> The definitive study of the U.S. Infantry weapons used in WWI.

Complete Guide to U.S. Infantry Weapons of World War Two, The, by Bruce Canfield, Andrew Mowbray, Publisher, Lincoln, RI, 1995. 303 pp., illus. $39.95
> A definitive work on the weapons used by the United States Armed Forces in WWII.

Confederate Belt Buckles & Plates, by Mullinax, Steve E. O'Donnell Publishing, Alexandria, VA: 1999. Expanded edition. Hardbound, 247 pages, illus. Hardcover. $34.00
> Hundreds of crisp photographs augment this classic study of Confederate accoutrement plates.

Confederate Carbines & Musketoons Cavalry Small Arms manufactured in and for the Southern Confederacy 1861-1865, by Murphy, John M. Santa Ana, CA: Privately Printed, 2002. Reprint. 320 pages, illustrated with B & W drawings and photos. Color Frontis by Don Troiani. Hardcover. $79.95
> This is Dr. Murphy's first work on Confederate arms. See also "Confederate Rifles & Muskets". Exceptional photography compliments the text. John Murphy has one of the finest collections of Confederate arms known.

Confederate Rifles & Muskets Infantry Small Arms Manufactured in the Southern Confederacy 1861-1865, by Murphy, John M. Santa Ana, CA: Privately Printed, 1996. Reprint. 768pp, 8pp color plates, profusely illustrated. Hardcover. $119.95
> The first in-depth and academic analysis and discussion of the "long" longarms produced in the South and for the Confederacy during the American Civil War. The collection of Dr. Murphy is doubtless the largest and finest grouping of Confederate longarms in private hands today.

Confederate Saddles & Horse Equipment, by Knopp, Ken R. Orange, VA: Publisher's Press, 2002. 194 pps., illus. Hardcover. $39.95
> Confederate Saddles & Horse Equipment is a pioneer work on the subject. After ten years of research Ken Knopp has compiled a thorough and fascinating study of the little-known field of Confederate saddlery and equipment. His analysis of ordnance operations coupled with his visual presentation of surviving examples offers an indispensable source for collectors and historians.

Concise Guide to the Artillery at Gettysburg, A, by Gregory Coco, Thomas Publications, Gettysburg, PA, 1998. 96 pp., illus. Paper Covers. $10.00
> Coco's tenth book on Gettysburg is a beginner's guide to artillery and its use at the battle. It covers the artillery batteries describing the types of cannons, shells, fuses, etc.using interesting narrative and human interest stories.

Cooey Firearms, Made in Canada 1919-1979, by John A. Belton, Museum Restoration, Canada, 1998. 36pp., with 46 illus. Paper Covers. $8.95
> More than 6 million rifles and at least 67 models, were made by this small Canadian riflemaker. They have been identified from the first 'Cooey Canuck' through the last variations made by the 'Winchester-Cooey'. Each is descibed and most are illustrated in this first book on The Cooey.

Cowboy Collectibles and Western Memorabilia, by Bob Bell and Edward Vebell, Schiffer Publishing, Atglen, PA, 1992. 160 pp., illus. Paper covers. $29.95
> The exciting era of the cowboy and the wild west collectibles including rifles, pistols, gun rigs, etc.

Cowboy Culture: The Last Frontier of American Antiques, by Michael Friedman, Schiffer Publishing, Ltd., West Chester, PA, 1992. 300 pp., illustrated.
> Covers the artful aspects of the old west, the antiques and collectibles. Illustrated with clear color plates of over 1,000 items such as spurs, boots, guns, saddles etc.

Cowboy and Gunfighter Collectible, by Bill Mackin, Mountain Press Publishing Co., Missoula, MT, 1995. 178 pp., illus. Paper covers. $25.00
> A photographic encyclopedia with price guide and makers' index.

Cowboys and the Trappings of the Old West, by William Manns and Elizabeth Clair Flood, Zon International Publishing Co., Santa Fe, NM, 1997, 1st edition. 224 pp., illustrated. $45.00
> A pictorial celebration of the cowboys dress and trappings.

Cowboy Hero Cap Pistols, by Rudy D'Angelo, Antique Trader Books, Dubuque, IA, 1998. 196 pp., illus. Paper covers. $34.95
> Aimed at collectors of cap pistols created and named for famous film and television cowboy heros, this in-depth guide hits all the marks. Current values are given.

THE HANDGUNNER'S LIBRARY

Custom Firearms Engraving, by Tom Turpin, Krause Publications, Iola, WI, 1999. 208 pp., illustrated. $49.95

Over 200 four-color photos with more than 75 master engravers profiled. Engravers Directory with addresses in the U.S. and abroad.

Daisy Air Rifles & BB Guns: The First 100 Years, by Punchard, Neal. St. Paul, MN: Motorbooks, 2002. 1st edition. Hardcover, 10 x 10, 156 pp, 300 color. Hardcover. $29.95

Flash back to the days of your youth and recall fond memories of your Daisy. Daisy Air Rifles and BB Guns looks back fondly on the first 100 years of Daisy BB rifles and pistols, toy and cork guns, accessories, packaging, period advertising and literature. Wacky ads and catalogs conjure grins of pure nostalgia as chapters reveal how Daisy used a combination of savvy business sense and quality products to dominate the market.

Decorations, Medals, Ribbons, Badges and Insignia of the United States Army; World War 2 to Present, The, by Col. Frank C. Foster, Medals of America Press, Fountain Inn, SC. 2001. 145 pages, illustrated. $29.95

The most complete guide to United States Army medals, ribbons, rank, insignia nad patches from WWII to the present day. Each medal and insignia shown in full color. Includes listing of respective criteria and campaigns.

Decorations, Medals, Ribbons, Badges and Insignia of the United States Navy; World War 2 to Present, The, by James G. Thompson, Medals of America Press, Fountain Inn, SC. 2000. 123 pages, illustrated. $29.95

The most complete guide to United States Army medals, ribbons, rank, insignia nad patches from WWII to the present day. Each medal and insignia shown in full color. Includes listing of respective criteria and campaigns.

Derringer in America, The, Volume 1, The Percussion Period, by R.L. Wilson and L.D. Eberhart, Andrew Mowbray Inc., Lincoln, RI, 1985. 271 pp., illus. $48.00

A long awaited book on the American percussion deringer.

Derringer in America, The, Volume 2, The Cartridge Period, by L.D. Eberhart and R.L. Wilson, Andrew Mowbray Inc., Publishers, Lincoln, RI, 1993. 284 pp., illus. $65.00

Comprehensive coverage of cartridge deringers organized alphabetically by maker. Includes all types of deringers known by the authors to have been offered to the American market.

Devil's Paintbrush: Sir Hiram Maxim's Gun, The, by Dolf Goldsmith, 3rd Edition, expanded and revised, Collector Grade Publications, Toronto, Canada, 2002. 384 pp., illus. $79.95

The classic work on the world's first true automatic machine gun.

Dr. Josephus Requa Civil War Dentist and the Billinghurst-Requa Volley Gun, by John M. Hyson, Jr., & Margaret Requa DeFrancisco, Museum Restoration Service, Bloomfield, Ont., Canada, 1999. 36 pp., illus. Paper covers. $8.95

The story of the inventor of the first practical rapid-fire gun to be used during the American Civil War.

Dutch Luger (Parabellum) A Complete History, The, by Bas J. Martens and Guus de Vries, Ironside International Publishers, Inc., Alexandria, VA, 1995. 268 pp., illus. $49.95

The history of the Luger in the Netherlands. An extensive description of the Dutch pistol and trials and the different models of the Luger in the Dutch service.

Eagle on U.S. Firearms, The, by John W. Jordan, Pioneer Press, Union City, TN, 1992. 140 pp., illus. Paper covers. $17.50

Stylized eagles have been stamped on government owned or manufactured firearms in the U.S. since the beginning of our country. This book lists and illustrates these various eagles in an informative and refreshing manner.

Encyclopedia of Rifles & Handguns; A Comprehensive Guide to Firearms, edited by Sean Connolly, Chartwell Books, Inc., Edison, NJ., 1996. 160 pp., illustrated. $26.00

A lavishly illustrated book providing a comprehensive history of military and civilian personal firepower.

Eprouvettes: A Comprehensive Study of Early Devices for the Testing of Gunpowder, by R.T.W. Kempers, Royal Armouries Museum, Leeds, England, 1999. 352 pp., illustrated with 240 black & white and 28 color plates. $125.00

The first comprehensive study of eprouvettes ever attempted in a single volume.

European Firearms in Swedish Castles, by Kaa Wennberg, Bohuslaningens Boktryckeri AB, Uddevalla, Sweden, 1986. 156 pp., illus. $50.00

The famous collection of Count Keller, the Ettersburg Castle collection, and others. English text.

Fifteen Years in the Hawken Lode, by John D. Baird, The Gun Room Press, Highland Park, NJ, 1976. 120 pp., illus. $24.95

A collection of thoughts and observations gained from many years of intensive study of the guns from the shop of the Hawken brothers.

'51 Colt Navies, by Nathan L. Swayze, The Gun Room Press, Highland Park, NJ, 1993. 243 pp., illus. $59.95

The Model 1851 Colt Navy, its variations and markings.

Fighting Iron, by Art Gogan, Andrew Mowbray, Inc., Lincoln, R.I., 2002. 176 pp., illustrated. $28.00

It doesn't matter whether you collect guns, swords, bayonets or accountrement— sooner or later you realize that it all comes down to the metal. If you don't understand the metal you don't understand your collection.

Fine Colts, The Dr. Joseph A. Murphy Collection, by R.L. Wilson, Sheffield Marketing Associates, Inc., Doylestown, PA, 1999. 258 pp., illustrated. Limited edition signed and numbered. $99.00

This lavish new work covers exquisite, deluxe and rare Colt arms from Paterson and other percussion revolvers to the cartridge period and up through modern times.

Firearms, by Derek Avery, Desert Publications, El Dorado, AR, 1999. 95 pp., illustrated. $9.95

The firearms included in this book are by necessity only a selection, but nevertheless one that represents the best and most famous weapons seen since the Second World War.

Firearms and Tackle Memorabilia, by John Delph, Schiffer Publishing, Ltd., West Chester, PA, 1991. 124 pp., illus. $39.95

A collector's guide to signs and posters, calendars, trade cards, boxes, envelopes, and other highly sought after memorabilia. With a value guide.

Firearms of the American West 1803-1865, Volume 1, by Louis A. Garavaglia and Charles Worman, University of Colorado Press, Niwot, CO, 1998. 402 pp., illustrated. $59.95

Traces the development and uses of firearms on the frontier during this period.

Firearms of the American West 1866-1894, by Louis A. Garavaglia and Charles G. Worman, University of Colorado Press, Niwot, CO, 1998. 416 pp., illus. $59.95

A monumental work that offers both technical information on all of the important firearms used in the West during this period and a highly entertaining history of how they were used, who used them, and why.

Firearms from Europe, 2nd Edition, by David Noe, Larry W. Yantz, Dr. James B. Whisker, Rowe Publications, Rochester, N.Y., 2002. 192 pp., illustrated. $45.00

A history and description of firearms imported during the American Civil War by the United States of America and the Confederate States of America.

Firepower from Abroad, by Wiley Sword, Andrew Mowbray Publishing, Lincoln, R.I., 2000. 120 pp., illustrated. $23.00

The Confederate Enfield and the LeMat revolver and how they reached the Confederate market.

Flayderman's Guide to Antique American Firearms and Their Values, 8th Edition, edited by Norm Flayderman, Krause Publications, Iola, WI, 2001. 692 pp., illus. Paper covers. $34.95

A completely updated and new edition with more than 3,600 models and variants extensively described with all marks and specifications necessary for quick identification.

FN-FAL Rifle, et al, The, by Duncan Long, Paladin Press, Boulder, CO, 1999. 144 pp., illustrated. Paper covers. $18.95

Detailed descriptions of the basic models produced by Fabrique Nationale and the myriad variants that evolved as a result of the firearms universal acceptance.

.45-70 Springfield; Book 1, The, by Frasca, Albert and Robert Hill. Frasca, Albert and Robert Hill. Frasca Publishing, 2000. Memorial edition. Hardback with gold embossed cover and spine. $95.00

The Memorial Edition reprint of The .45-70 Springfield was done to honor Robert H. Hill who was an outstanding Springfield collector, historian, researcher, and gunsmith. Only 1000 of these highly regarded books were printed using the same binding and cover material as the original 1980 edition. The book is considered The Bible for .45-70 Springfield Trapdoor collectors.

.45-70 Springfield Book II 1865-1893, The, by Frasca, Albert. Frasca Publishing, Springfield, Ohio 1997 Hardback with gold embossed cover and spine. The book has 400+ pages and 400+ photographs which cover ALL the trapdoor Springfield models. A MUST for the trapdoor collector! Hardback with gold embossed cover and spine. $85.00

.45-70 Springfield, The, by Joe Poyer and Craig Riesch, North Cape Publications, Tustin, CA, 1996. 150 pp., illus. Paper covers. $16.95

A revised and expanded second edition of a best-selling reference work organized by serial number and date of production to aid the collector in identifying popular "Trapdoor" rifles and carbines.

The French 1935 Pistols, by Eugene Medlin and Colin Doane, Eugene Medlin, El Paso, TX, 1995. 172 pp., illus. Paper covers. $25.95

The development and identification of successive models, fakes and variants, holsters and accessories, and serial numbers by dates of production.

Freund & Bro. Pioneer Gunmakers to the West, by F.J. Pablo Balentine, Graphic Publishers, Newport Beach, CA, 1997. 380 pp., illustrated $69.95

The story of Frank W. and George Freund, skilled German gunsmiths who plied their trade on the Western American frontier during the final three decades of the nineteenth century.

REFERENCE

The Handgunner's Library

Fusil de Tulole in New France, 1691-1741, The, by Russel Bouchard, Museum Restorations Service, Bloomfield, Ontario, Canada, 1997. 36 pp., illus. Paper covers. $8.95

The development of the company and the identification of their arms.

Game Guns & Rifles: Percussion to Hammerless Ejector in Britain, by Richard Akehurst, Trafalgar Square, N. Pomfret, VT, 1993. 192 pp., illus. $39.95

Long considered a classic this important reprint covers the period of British gunmaking between 1830-1900.

Gas Trap Garand, The, by Billy Pyle, Collector Grade Publications, Cobourg, Ontario, Canada, 1999 316 pp., illustrated. $59.95

The in-depth story of the rarest Garands of them all, the initial 80 Model Shop rifles made under the personal supervision of John Garand himself in 1934 and 1935, and the first 50,000 plus production "gas trap" M1's manufactured at Springfield Armory between August, 1937 and August, 1940.

George Schreyer, Sr. and Jr., Gunmakers of Hanover, Pennsylvania, by George Shumway, George Shumway Publishers, York, PA, 1990. 160pp., illus. $50.00

This monograph is a detailed photographic study of almost all known surviving long rifles and smoothbore guns made by highly regarded gunsmiths George Schreyer, Sr. and Jr.

German Assault Rifle 1935-1945, The, by Peter R. Senich, Paladin Press, Boulder, CO, 1987. 328 pp., illus. $60.00

A complete review of machine carbines, machine pistols and assault rifles employed by Hitler's Wehrmacht during WWII.

German K98k Rifle, 1934-1945, The: The Backbone of the Wehrmacht, by Richard D. Law, Collector Grade Publications, Toronto, Canada, 1993. 336 pp., illus. $69.95

The most comprehensive study ever published on the 14,000,000 bolt-action K98k rifles produced in Germany between 1934 and 1945.

German Machine Guns, by Daniel D. Musgrave, revised edition, Ironside International Publishers, Inc. Alexandria, VA, 1992. 586 pp., 650 illus. $49.95

The most definitive book ever written on German machineguns. Covers the introduction and development of machineguns in Germany from 1899 to the rearmament period after WWII.

German Military Rifles and Machine Pistols, 1871-1945, by Hans Dieter Gotz, Schiffer Publishing Co., West Chester, PA, 1990. 245 pp., illus. $35.00

This book portrays in words and pictures the development of the modern German weapons and their ammunition including the scarcely known experimental types.

Glossary of the Construction, Decoration and Use of Arms and Armor in All Countries and in All Times, A, by George Cameron Stone., Dover Publishing, New York 1999. Softcover. $39.95

An exhaustive study of arms and armor in all countries through recorded history - from the stone age up to the second world war. With over 4500 Black & White Illustrations. This Dover edition is an unabridged republication of the work originally published in 1934 by the Southworth Press, Portland MA. A new Introduction has been specially prepared for this edition.

Government Models, The, by William H.D. Goddard, Andrew Mowbray Publishing, Lincoln, RI, 1998. 296 pp., illustrated. $58.50

The most authoritative source on the development of the Colt model of 1911.

Grasshoppers and Butterflies, by Adrian B. Caruana, Museum Restoration Service, Alexandria, Bay, N.Y., 1999. 32 pp., illustrated. Paper covers. $8.95

No.39 in the Historical Arms Series. The light 3 pounders of Pattison and Townsend.

Greener Story, The, by Graham Greener, Quiller Press, London, England, 2000. 256 pp., illustrated with 32 pages of color photos. $64.50

W.W. Greener, his family history, inventions, guns, patents, and more.

Greenhill Dictionary of Guns And Gunmakers: From Colt's First Patent to the Present Day, 1836-2001, The, by John Walter, Greenhill Publishing, 2001, 1st edition, 576 pages, illustrated with 200 photos, 190 trademarks and 40 line drawings, Hardcover: $59.95

Covers military small arms, sporting guns and rifles, air and gas guns, designers, inventors, patentees, trademarks, brand names and monograms.

Guide to American Trade Catalogs 1744-1900, A, by Lawrence B. Romaine, Dover Publications, New York, NY. 422 pp., illus. Paper covers. $12.95

Guide to Ballard Breechloaders, A, by George J. Layman, Pioneer Press, Union City, TN, 1997. 261 pp., illus. Paper covers. $19.95

Documents the saga of this fine rifle from the first models made by Ball & Williams of Worcester, to its production by the Marlin Firearms Co, to the cessation of 19th century manufacture in 1891, and finally to the modern reproductions made in the 1990's.

Guide to Civil War Artillery Projectiles, A, by Jack W. Melton, and Lawrence E. Pawl . Kennesaw, GA: Kennesaw Mounton Press, 1996

The concise pictorial study belongs on the shelf of every enthusiast. Hundreds of crisp photographs and a wealth of rich, well-researched information. 96 pps., illus. Softcover. $9.95

Guide to the Maynard Breechloader, A, by George J. Layman, George J. Layman, Ayer, MA, 1993. 125 pp., illus. Paper covers. $11.95

The first book dedicated entirely to the Maynard family of breech-loading firearms. Coverage of the arms is given from the 1850s through the 1880s.

Guide to U. S. Army Dress Helmets 1872-1904, A, by Kasal and Moore, North Cape Publications, 2000. 88 pp., illus. Paper covers. $15.95

This thorough study provides a complete description of the Model 1872 & 1881 dress helmets worn by the U.S. Army. Including all componets from bodies to plates to plumes & shoulder cords and tells how to differentiate the originals from reproductions. Extensively illustrated with photographs, '8 pages in full color' of complete helmets and their components.

The Gun and Its Development, by W.W. Greener, New York: Lyons Press, 2002. 9th edition. Rewritten, and with many additional illustrations. 804 pages plus advertising section. Contains over 700 illustrations plus many tables. Softcover. $19.95

A famed book of great value, truly encyclopedic in scope and sought after by firearms collectors.

Gun Collecting, by Geoffrey Boothroyd, Sportsman's Press, London, 1989. 208 pp., illus. $29.95

The most comprehensive list of 19th century British gunmakers and gunsmiths ever published.

Gunmakers of London 1350-1850 with Supplement, by Howard L. Blackmore, Museum Restoration Service, Alexandria Bay, NY, 1999. 222 pp., illus. $135.00

A listing of all the known workmen of gun making in the first 500 years, plus a history of the guilds, cutlers, armourers, founders, blacksmiths, etc. 260 gunmarks are illustrated. Supplement is 156 pages, and Begins with an introductory chapter on "foreighn" gunmakers followed by records of all the new information found about previously unidentified armourers, gunmakers and gunsmiths. 2 Volumes Slipcased

Guns that Won the West: Firearms of the American Frontier, 1865-1898, The, by John Walter, Stackpole Books, Inc., Mechanicsburg, PA.,1999. 256 pp., illustrated. $34.95

Here is the story of the wide range of firearms from pistols to rifles used by plainsmen and settlers, gamblers, native Americans and the U.S. Army.

Gunsmiths of Illinois, by Curtis L. Johnson, George Shumway Publishers, York, PA, 1995. 160 pp., illus. $50.00

Genealogical information is provided for nearly one thousand gunsmiths. Contains hundreds of illustrations of rifles and other guns, of handmade origin, from Illinois.

Gunsmiths of Manhattan, 1625-1900: A Checklist of Tradesmen, The, by Michael H. Lewis, Museum Restoration Service, Bloomfield, Ont., Canada, 1991. 40 pp., illus. Paper covers. $8.95

This listing of more than 700 men in the arms trade in New York City prior to about the end of the 19th century will provide a guide for identification and further research.

Guns of Dagenham: Lanchester, Patchett, Sterling, The, by Peter Laidler and David Howroyd, Collector Grade Publications, Inc., Cobourg, Ont., Canada, 1995. 310 pp., illus. $39.95

An in-depth history of the small arms made by the Sterling Company of Dagenham, Essex, England, from 1940 until Sterling was purchased by British Aerospace in 1989 and closed.

Guns of the Western Indian War, by R. Stephen Dorsey, Collector's Library, Eugene, OR, 1997. 220 pp., illus. Paper covers. $30.00

The full story of the guns and ammunition that made western history in the turbulent period of 1865-1890.

Gun Powder Cans & Kegs, by Ted & David Bacyk and Tom Rowe, Rowe Publications, Rochester, NY, 1999. 150 pp., illus. $65.00

The first book devoted to powder tins and kegs. All cans and kegs in full color. With a price guide and rarity scale.

Gun Tools, Their History and Identification by James B. Shaffer, Lee A. Rutledge and R. Stephen Dorsey, Collector's Library, Eugene, OR, 1992. 375 pp., illus. $30.00

Written history of foreign and domestic gun tools from the flintlock period to WWII.

Gun Tools, Their History and Identifications, Volume 2, by Stephen Dorsey and James B. Shaffer, Collectors' Library, Eugene, OR, 1997. 396 pp., illus. Paper covers. $30.00

Gun tools from the Royal Armouries Museum in England, Pattern Room, Royal Ordnance Reference Collection in Nottingham and from major private collections.

Gunsmiths of Maryland, by Daniel D. Hartzler and James B. Whisker, Old Bedford Village Press, Bedford, PA, 1998. 208 pp., illustrated. $40.00

Covers firelock Colonial period through the breech-loading patent models. Featuring longrifles.

Gunsmiths of Virginia, by Daniel D. Hartzler and James B. Whisker, Old Bedford Village Press, Bedford, PA, 1992. 206 pp., illustrated. $40.00

A photographic study of American longrifles.

Gunsmiths of West Virginia, by Daniel D. Hartzler and James B. Whisker, Old Bedford Village Press, Bedford, PA, 1998. 176 pp., illustrated. $40.00

A photographic study of American longrifles.

REFERENCE

Hall's Military Breechloaders, by Peter A. Schmidt, Andrew Mowbray Publishers, Lincoln, RI, 1996. 232 pp., illus. $55.00

The whole story behind these bold and innovative firearms.

Handgun, The, by Geoffrey Boothroyd, David and Charles, North Pomfret, VT, 1989. 566 pp., illus. $50.00

Every chapter deals with an important period in handgun history from the 14th century to the present.

Handguns & Rifles: The Finest Weapons from Around the World, by Ian Hogg, Random House Value Publishing, Inc., N.Y., 1999. 128 pp., illustrated. $18.98

The serious gun collector will welcome this fully illustrated examination of international handguns and rifles. Each entry covers the history of the weapon, what purpose it serves, and its advantages and disadvantages.

Hawken Rifle: Its Place in History, The, by Charles E. Hanson, Jr., The Fur Press, Chadron, NE, 1979. 104 pp., illus. Paper covers. $15.00

A definitive work on this famous rifle.

Hawken Rifles, The Mountain Man's Choice, by John D. Baird, The Gun Room Press, Highland Park, NJ, 1976. 95 pp., illus. $29.95

Covers the rifles developed for the Western fur trade. Numerous specimens are described and shown in photographs.

High Standard: A Collector's Guide to the Hamden & Hartford Target Pistols, by Tom Dance, Andrew Mowbray, Inc., Lincoln, RI, 1991. 192 pp., illus. Paper covers. $24.00

From Citation to Supermatic, all of the production models and specials made from 1951 to 1984 are covered according to model number or series.

Historical Hartford Hardware, by William W. Dalrymple, Colt Collector Press, Rapid City, SD, 1976. 42 pp., illus. Paper covers. $10.00

Historically associated Colt revolvers.

History and Development of Small Arms Ammunition, The, Volume 2, by George A. Hoyem, Armory Publications, Oceanside, CA, 1991. 303 pp., illus. $65.00

Covers the blackpowder military centerfire rifle, carbine, machine gun and volley gun ammunition used in 28 nations and dominions, together with the firearms that chambered them.

History and Development of Small Arms Ammunition, The, Volume 4, by George A. Hoyem, Armory Publications, Seattle, WA, 1998. 200 pp., illustrated $65.00

A comprehensive book on American black powder and early smokeless rifle cartridges.

History of Colt Firearms, The, by Dean Boorman, Lyons Press, New York, NY, 2001. 144 pp., illus. $29.95

Discover the fascinating story of the world's most famous revolver, complete with more than 150 stunning full-color photographs.

History of the German Steel Helmet: 1916-1945, by Ludwig Baer. Bender Publishing, San Jose, CA, 2001. 448 pages, nearly 1,000 photos & illustrations. $54.95

This publication is the most complete and detailed German steel helmet book ever produced, with in-depth documentated text and nearly 1,000 photographs and illustrations encompassing all German steel helmets from 1916 through 1945. The regulations, modifications and use of camouflage are carefully clarified for the Imperial Army, Reichswehr and the numerous 3rd Reich organizations.

History of Modern U.S. Military Small Arms Ammunition. Volume 1, 1880-1939, revised by F.W. Hackley, W.H. Woodin and E.L. Scranton, Thomas Publications, Gettysburg, PA, 1998. 328 pp., illus. $49.95

This revised edition incorporates all publicly available information concerning military small arms ammunition for the period 1880 through 1939 in a single volume.

History of Modern U.S. Military Small Arms Ammunition. Volume 2, 1940-1945 by F.W. Hackley, W.H. Woodin and E.L. Scranton. Gun Room Press, Highland Park, NJ, 300 + pages, illustrated. $39.95

Based on decades of original research conducted at the National Archives, numerous military, public and private museums and libraries, as well as individual collections, this edition incorporates all publicly available information concerning military small arms ammunition for the period 1940 through 1945.

The History of Smith & Wesson Firearms, by Dean Boorman, Lyons Press, New York, NY, 2002. 144 pp., illustrated in full color. Hardcover. New dust jacket. $29.95

The definitive guide to one of the world's best-known firearms makers. Takes the story through the years of the Military & Police .38 & of the Magnum cartridge, to today's wide range of products for law-enforcement customers.

The History of Winchester Rifles, by Dean Boorman, Lyons Press, New York, NY, 2001. 144 pp., illus. $29.95

A captivating and wonderfully photographed history of one of the most legendary names in gun lore. 150 full-color photos.

History of Winchester Firearms 1866-1992, The, sixth edition, updated, expanded, and revised by Thomas Henshaw, New Win Publishing, Clinton, NJ, 1993. 280 pp., illus. $27.95

This classic is the standard reference for all collectors and others seeking the facts about any Winchester firearm, old or new.

Honour Bound: The Chauchat Machine Rifle, by Gerard Demaison and Yves Buffetaut, Collector Grade Publications, Inc., Cobourg, Ont., Canada, 1995. $39.95.

The story of the CSRG (Chauchat) machine rifle, the most manufactured automatic weapon of World War One.

Hunting Weapons From the Middle Ages to the Twentieth Century, by Howard L. Blackmore, Dover Publications, Meneola, NY, 2000. 480 pp. illustrated. Paper covers. $16.95

Dealing mainly with the different classes of weapons used in sport—swords, spears, crossbows, guns, and rifles—from the Middle Ages until the present day.

Identification Manual on the .303 British Service Cartridge, No. 1-Ball Ammunition, by B.A. Temple, I.D.S.A. Books, Piqua, OH, 1986. 84 pp., 5? illus. $12.50

Identification Manual on the .303 British Service Cartridge, No. 2-Blank Ammunition, by B.A. Temple, I.D.S.A. Books, Piqua, OH, 1986. 95 pp., 5? illus. $12.50

Identification Manual on the .303 British Service Cartridge, No. 3-Special Purpose Ammunition, by B.A. Temple, I.D.S.A. Books, Piqua, OH, 1987. 8? pp., 49 illus. $12.50

Identification Manual on the .303 British Service Cartridge, No. 4-Dummy Cartridges Henry 1869-c.1900, by B.A. Temple, I.D.S.A. Books, Piqua, OH, 1988. 84 pp., 70 illus. $12.50

Identification Manual on the .303 British Service Cartridge, No. 5-Dummy Cartridges (2), by B.A. Temple, I.D.S.A. Books, Piqua, OH, 1994. 78 pp. $12.50

Illustrated Book of Guns, The, by David Miller, Salamander Books, N.Y., N.Y., 2000. 304 pp., illustrated in color. $34.95

An illustrated directory of over 1,000 military and sporting firearms.

Illustrated Encyclopedia of Civil War Collectibles, The, by Chuck Lawliss, Henry Holt and Co., New York, NY, 1997. 316 pp., illus. Paper covers. $22.9?

A comprehensive guide to Union and Confederate arms, equipment, uniforms, and other memorabilia.

Illustrations of United States Military Arms 1776-1903 and Their Inspector's Marks, compiled by Turner Kirkland, Pioneer Press, Union City, TN, 1988. 37 pp., illus. Paper covers. $7.00

Reprinted from the 1949 Bannerman catalog. Valuable information for both the advanced and beginning collector.

Indian War Cartridge Pouches, Boxes and Carbine Boots, by R. Stephen Dorsey, Collector's Library, Eugene, OR, 1993. 156 pp., illus. Paper Covers. $20.00

The key reference work to the cartridge pouches, boxes, carbine sockets and boots of the Indian War period 1865-1890.

International Armament, with History, Data, Technical Information and Photographs of Over 800 Weapons, by George Johnson. Alexandria, VA, Ironside International, 2002. 2nd edition, new printing. Over 947 pages illustrated with over 800 photos. Hardcover. $59.95

The development and progression of modern military small arms. All significant weapons have been included and examined in depth. Over 800 photographs and illustrations with both historical and technical data. Two volumes are now bound into one book.

Introduction to the Civil War Small Arms, An, by Earl J. Coates and Dean S. Thomas, Thomas Publishing Co., Gettysburg, PA, 1990. 96 pp., illus. Paper covers. $10.00

The small arms carried by the individual soldier during the Civil War.

Japanese Rifles of World War Two, by Duncan O. McCollum, Excalibur Publications, Latham, NY, 1996. 64 pp., illus. Paper covers. $18.95

A sweeping view of the rifles and carbines that made up Japan's arsenal during the conflict.

Kalashnikov "Machine Pistols, Assault Rifles, and Machine Guns, 1945 to the Present", by John Walter, Paladin Press, Boulder, CO, 1999, hardcover photos, illus., 146 pp. $22.95

This exhaustive work published by Greenhill Military Manuals features a gun-by-gun directory of Kalashnikov variants. Technical specifications and illustrations are provided throughout, along with details of sights, bayonets, markings and ammunition. A must for the serious collector and historian.

Kentucky Pistol, The, by Roy Chandler and James Whisker, Old Bedford Village Press, Bedford, PA, 1997. 225 pp., illus. $60.00

A photographic study of Kentucky pistols from famous collections.

Kentucky Rifle, The, by Captain John G.W. Dillin, George Shumway Publisher, York, PA, 1993. 221 pp., illus. $50.00

This well-known book was the first attempt to tell the story of the American longrifle. This edition retains the original text and illustrations with supplemental footnotes provided by Dr. George Shumway.

Know Your Broomhandle Mausers, by R.J. Berger, Blacksmith Corp. Southport, CT, 1996. 96 pp., illus. Paper covers. $14.95

An interesting story on the big Mauser pistol and its variations.

THE HANDGUNNER'S LIBRARY

Law Enforcement Memorabilia Price and Identification Guide, by Monty McCord, DBI Books a division of Krause Publications, Inc. Iola, WI, 1999. 208 pp., illustrated. Paper covers. $19.95

An invaluable reference to the growing wave of law enforcement collectors. Hundreds of items are covered from miniature vehicles to clothes, patches, and restraints.

Legendary Sporting Guns, by Eric Joly, Abbeville Press, New York, N.Y., 1999. 228 pp., illustrated. $65.00

A survey of hunting through the ages and relates how many different types of firearms were created and refined for use afield.

Legends and Reality of the AK, by Val Shilin and Charlie Cutshaw, Paladen Press, Boulder, CO, 2000. 192 pp., illustrated. Paper covers. $35.00

A behind-the-scenes look at history, design and impact of the Kalashnikov family of weapons.

LeMat, the Man, the Gun, by Valmore J. Forgett and Alain F. and Marie-Antoinette Serpette, Navy Arms Co., Ridgefield, NJ, 1996. 218 pp., illus. $49.95

The first definitive study of the Confederate revolvers invention, development and delivery by Francois Alexandre LeMat.

Light 6-Pounder Battalion Gun of 1776, The, by Adrian Caruana, Museum Restoration Service, Bloomfield, Ontario, Canada, 2001. 76 pp., illus. Paper covers. $8.95

London Gun Trade, 1850-1920, The, by Joyce E. Gooding, Museum Restoration Service, Bloomfield, Ontario, Canada, 2001. 48 pp., illus. Paper covers. $8.95

Names, dates and locations of London gunmakers working between 1850 and 1920 are listed. Compiled from the original Kelly's Post Office Directories of the City of London.

London Gunmakers and the English Duelling Pistol, 1770-1830, The, by Keith R. Dill, Museum Restoration Service, Bloomfield, Ontario, Canada, 1997. 36 pp., illus. Paper covers. $8.95

Ten gunmakers made London one of the major gunmaking centers of the world. This book examines how the design and construction of their pistols contributed to that reputation and how these characteristics may be used to date flintlock arms.

Longrifles of Pennsylvania, Volume 1, Jefferson, Clarion & Elk Counties, by Russel H. Harringer, George Shumway Publisher, York, PA, 1984. 200 pp., illus. $50.00

First in series that will treat in great detail the longrifles and gunsmiths of Pennsylvania.

Luger Handbook, The, by Aarron Davis, Krause Publications, Iola, WI, 1997. 112 pp., illus. Paper covers. $9.95

Quick reference to classify Luger models and variations with complete details including proofmarks.

Lugers at Random, by Charles Kenyon, Jr., Handgun Press, Glenview, IL, 1990. 420 pp., illus. $59.95

A new printing of this classic, comprehensive reference for all Luger collectors.

Luger Story, The, by John Walter, Stackpole Books, Mechanicsburg, PA, 2001. 256 pp., illus. Paper Covers $19.95

The standard history of the world's most famous handgun.

M1 Carbine, by Larry Ruth, Gun room Press, Highland Park, NJ, 1987. 291 pp., illus. Paper $19.95

The origin, development, manufacture and use of this famous carbine of World War II.

M-1 Carbine—A Revolution in Gun-Stocking, The, by Grafton H. Cook II and Barbara W. Cook. Lincoln, RI: Andrew Mowbray, Inc., 2002. 1st edition. 208 pages, heavily illustrated with 157 rare photographs of the guns and the men and women who made them. Softcover. $29.95

Shows you, step by step, how M1 Carbine stocks were made, right through to assembly with the hardware. Learn about M1 Carbine development, and how the contracting and production process actually worked. Also contains lots of detailed information about other military weapons, like the M1A1, the M1 Garand, the M14 and much, much more. Includes more than 200 short biographies of the people who made M1 Carbines. The depth of this information will amaze you. Shows and explains the machinery used to make military rifle stocks during World War II, with photos of these remarkable machines and data about when they were invented and shipped. Explains why walnut gunstocks are so very difficult to make, and why even large gun manufacturers are usually unable to do this specialized work.

M1 Carbine: Owner's Guide, The by Scott A. Duff, Scott A. Duff, Export, PA, 1997. 126 pp., illus. Paper covers. $21.95

This book answers the questions M1 owners most often ask concerning maintenance activities not encounted by military users.

M1 Garand: Owner's Guide, The by Scott A. Duff, Scott A. Duff, Export, PA, 1998. 132 pp., illus. Paper covers. $21.95

This book answers the questions M1 owners most often ask concerning maintenance activities not encounted by military users.

M1 Garand Serial Numbers and Data Sheets, The by Scott A. Duff, Export, PA, 1995. 101 pp., illus. Paper covers. $11.95

Provides the reader with serial numbers related to dates of manufacture and a large sampling of data sheets to aid in identification or restoration.

M1 Garand 1936 to 1957, The by Joe Poyer and Craig Riesch, North Cape Publications, Tustin, CA, 1996. 216 pp., illus. Paper covers. $19.95

Describes the entire range of M1 Garand production in text and quick-scan charts.

M1 Garand: Post World War, The by Scott A. Duff, Scott A. Duff, Export, PA, 1990. 139 pp., illus. Soft covers. $21.95

A detailed account of the activities at Springfield Armory through this period. International Harvester, H&R, Korean War production and quantities delivered. Serial numbers.

M1 Garand: World War 2, The by Scott A. Duff, Scott A. Duff, Export, PA, 2001. 210 pp., illus. Paper covers. $34.95

The most comprehensive study available to the collector and historian on the M1 Garand of World War II.

Machine Guns, by Ian V. Hogg. Iola, WI: Krause Publications, 2002. 1st edition. 336 pages, illustrated with b & w photos with a 16 page color section. Softcover. $29.95

A detailed history of the rapid-fire gun, 14th century to present. Covers the development, history and specifications.

Maine Made Guns and Their Makers, by Dwight B. Demeritt Jr., Maine State Museum, Augusta, ME, 1998. 209 pp., illustrated. $55.00

An authoritative, biographical study of Maine gunsmiths.

Marlin Firearms: A History of the Guns and the Company That Made Them, by Lt. Col. William S. Brophy, USAR, Ret., Stackpole Books, Harrisburg, PA, 1989. 672 pp., illus. $80.00

The definitive book on the Marlin Firearms Co. and their products.

Martini-Henry .450 Rifles & Carbines, by Dennis Lewis, Excalibur Publications, Latham, NY, 1996. 72 pp., illus. Paper covers. $11.95

The stories of the rifles and carbines that were the mainstay of the British soldier through the Victorian wars.

Mauser Bolt Rifles, by Ludwig Olson, F. Brownell & Son, Inc., Montezuma, IA, 1999. 364 pp., illus. $59.95

The most complete, detailed, authoritative and comprehensive work ever done on Mauser bolt rifles. Completely revised deluxe 3rd edition.

Mauser Military Rifles of the World, 2nd Edition, by Robert Ball, Krause Publications, Iola, WI, 2000. 304 pp., illustrated with 1,000 b&w photos and a 48 page color section. $44.95

This 2nd edition brings more than 100 new photos of these historic rifles and the wars in which they were carried.

Mauser Military Rifle Markings, by Terence W. Lapin, Arlington, VA: Hyrax Publishers, LLC, 2001. 167 pages, illustrated. 2nd edition. Revised and expanded. Softcover. $22.95

A general guide to reading and understanding the often mystifying markings found on military Mauser Rifles. Includes German Regimental markings as well as German police markings and W.W. 2 German Mauser subcontractor codes. A handy reference to take to gun shows.

Mauser Smallbores Sporting, Target and Training Rifles, by Jon Speed, Collector Grade Publications, Cobourg, Ontario, Canada 1998. 349 pp., illustrated. $67.50

A history of all the smallbore sporting, target and training rifles produced by the legendary Mauser-Werke of Obendorf Am Neckar.

Military Holsters of World War 2, by Eugene J. Bender, Rowe Publications, Rochester, NY, 1998. 200 pp., illustrated. $45.00

A revised edition with a new price guide of the most definitive book on this subject.

Military Pistols of Japan, by Fred L. Honeycutt, Jr., Julin Books, Palm Beach Gardens, FL, 1997. 168 pp., illus. $42.00

Covers every aspect of military pistol production in Japan through WWII.

Military Remington Rolling Block Rifle, The, by George Layman, Pioneer Press, TN, 1998. 146 pp., illus. Paper covers. $24.95

A standard reference for those with an interest in the Remington rolling block family of firearms.

Military Rifles of Japan, 5th Edition, by F.L. Honeycutt, Julin Books, Lake Park, FL, 1999. 208 pp., illus. $42.00

A new revised and updated edition. Includes the early Murata-period markings, etc.

Military Small Arms Data Book, by Ian V. Hogg, Stackpole Books, Mechanicsburg, PA, 1999. $44.95. 336 pp., illustrated.

Data on more than 1,500 weapons. Covers a vast range of weapons from pistols to anti-tank rifles. Essential data, 1870-2000, in one volume.

MP38, 40, 40/1 & 41 Submachine Gun, The, by de Vries & Martens. Propaganda Photo Series, Volume II. Alexandria, VA: Ironside International, 2001. 1st edition. 150 pages, illustrated with 200 high quality black & white photos. Hardcover. $34.95

Covers all essential information on history and development, ammunition and accessories, codes and markings, and contains photos of nearly every model and accessory. Includes a unique selection of original German WWII propoganda photos, most never published before.

REFERENCE

16th EDITION • **261**

THE HANDGUNNER'S LIBRARY

Modern Beretta Firearms, by Gene Gangarosa, Jr., Stoeger Publishing Co., So. Hackensack, NJ, 1994. 288 pp., illus. Paper covers. $16.95

Traces all models of modern Beretta pistols, rifles, machine guns and combat shotguns.

Modern Gun Values, The Gun Digest Book of, 11th Edition, by the Editors of Gun Digest. Krause Publications, Iola, WI., 2002. 560 pp. illus. Paper covers. $21.95

Greatly updated and expanded edition describing and valuing over 7,000 firearms manufactured from 1900 to 1996. The standard for valuing modern firearms.

Modern Gun Identification & Value Guide, 13th Edition, by Russell and Steve Quertermous, Collector Books, Paducah, KY, 1998. 504 pp., illus. Paper covers. $14.95

Features current values for over 2,500 models of rifles, shotguns and handguns, with over 1,800 illustrations.

More Single Shot Rifles, by James C. Grant, The Gun Room Press, Highland Park, NJ, 1976. 324 pp., illus. $35.00

Details the guns made by Frank Wesson, Milt Farrow, Holden, Borchardt, Stevens, Remington, Winchester, Ballard and Peabody-Martini.

Mortimer, the Gunmakers, 1753-1923, by H. Lee Munson, Andrew Mowbray Inc., Lincoln, RI, 1992. 320 pp., illus. $65.00

Seen through a single, dominant, English gunmaking dynasty this fascinating study provides a window into the classical era of firearms artistry.

Mosin-Nagant Rifle, The, by Terence W. Lapin, North Cape Publications, Tustin, CA, 1998. 30 pp., illustrated. Paper covers. $19.95

The first ever complete book on the Mosin-Nagant rifle written in English. Covers every variation.

Navy Luger, The, by Joachim Gortz and John Walter, Handgun Press, Glenview, IL, 1988. 128 pp., illus. $24.95

The 9mm Pistole 1904 and the Imperial German Navy. A concise illustrated history.

New World of Russian Small Arms and Ammunition, The, by Charlie Cutshaw, Paladin Press, Boulder, CO, 1998. 160 pp., illustrated. $42.95

Detailed descriptions, specifications and first-class illustrations of the AN-94, PSS silent pistol, Bizon SMG, Saifa-12 tactical shotgun, the GP-25 grenade launcher and more cutting edge Russian weapons.

Number 5 Jungle Carbine, The, by Alan M. Petrillo, Excalibur Publications, Latham, NY, 1994. 32 pp., illus. Paper covers. $7.95

A comprehensive treatment of the rifle that collectors have come to call the "Jungle Carbine"—the Lee-Enfield Number 5, Mark 1.

Observations on Colt's Second Contract, November 2, 1847, by G. Maxwell Longfield and David T. Basnett, Museum Restoration Service, Bloomfield, Ontario, Canada, 1997. 36 pp., illus. Paper covers. $6.95

This study traces the history and the construction of the Second Model Colt Dragoon supplied in 1848 to the U.S. Cavalry.

Official Price Guide to Gun Collecting, by R.L. Wilson, Ballantine/House of Collectibles, New York, NY, 1998. 450 pp., illus. Paper covers. $21.50

Covers more than 30,000 prices from Colt revolvers to Winchester rifles and shotguns to German Lugers and British sporting rifles and game guns.

Official Price Guide to Military Collectibles, 6th edition, by Richard J. Austin, Random House, Inc., New York, NY, 1998. 200 pp., illus. Paper cover. $20.00

Covers weapons and other collectibles from wars of the distant and recent past. More than 4,000 prices are listed. Illustrated with 400 black & white photos plus a full-color insert.

Official Soviet SVD Manual, The, by Major James F. Gebhardt (Ret.) Paladin Press, Boulder, CO, 1999. 112 pp., illustrated. Paper covers. $15.00

Operating instructions for the 7.62mm Dragunov, the first Russian rifle developed from scratch specifically for sniping.

Old Gunsights: A Collector's Guide, 1850 to 2000, by Nicholas Stroebel, Krause Publications, Iola, WI, 1998. 320 pp., illus. Paper covers. $29.95

An in-depth and comprehensive examination of old gunsights and the rifles on which they were used to get accurate feel for prices in this expanding market.

Old Rifle Scopes, by Nicholas Stroebel, Krause Publications, Iola, WI, 2000. 400 pp., illustrated. Paper covers. $31.95

This comprehensive collector's guide takes aim at more than 120 scope makers and 60 mount makers and features photos and current market values for 300 scopes and mounts manufactured from 1950-1985.

Ordnance Tools, Accessories & Appendages of the M1 Rifle, by Billy Pyle. Houston, TX: Privately Printed, 2002. 2nd edition. 206 pages, illustrated with b & w photos. Softcover $40.00

This is the new updated second edition with over 350 pictures and drawings - 30 of which are new. Part I contains accessories, appendages, and equipment including such items as bayonets, blank firing attachments, cheek pads, cleaning equipment, clips, flash hiders, grenade launchers, scabbards, slings, telescopes and mounts, winter triggers, and much more. Part II covers ammunition, grenades, and pyrotechnics. Part III shows the inspection gages. Part IV presents the ordnance tools, fixtures, and assemblies. Part V contains miscellaneous items related to the M1 Rifle such as arms racks, rifle racks, clip loading machine, and other devices.

Orders, Decorations and Badges of the Socialist Republic of Vietnam and the National Front for the Liberation of South Vietnam, by Edward J. Emering. Schiffer Publications, Atglen, PA. 2000. 96 pages, 190 color and b/w photographs, line drawings. $24.95

The Orders and Decorations of the "enemy" during the Vietnam War have remained shrouded in mystery for many years. References to them are scarce and interrogations of captives during the war often led to the proliferation of misinformation concerning them. Includes value guide.

Packing Iron, by Richard C. Rattenbury, Zon International Publishing, Millwood, NY, 1993. 216 pp., illus. $45.00

The best book yet produced on pistol holsters and rifle scabbards. Over 300 variations of holster and scabbards are illustrated in large, clear plates.

Painted Steel, Steel Pots Volume 2, by Chris Armold. Bender Publishing, San Jose, CA, 2001. 384 pages - 1,053 photos (hundreds in color) $57.95

From the author of "Steel Pots: The History of America's Steel Combat Helmets" comes "Painted Steel: Steel Pots, Vol. II." This companion volume features detailed chapters on painted and unit marked helments of WWI and WWII, plus a variety of divisional, regimental and subordinate markings. Special full-color plates detail subordinate unit markings such as the tactical markings used by the U.S. 2nd Division in WWI. In addition, insignia and specialty markings such as USN beach battalion, Army engineers, medics, MP and airborne division tactical markings are examined. For those interested in American armored forces, a complete chapter is devoted to the history of the U.S. tank and combat vehicle crewman's helmet from WWI to present. Other chapters provide tips on reproductions and fake representations of U.S. helmets and accessories. With over 1,000 photos and images (many in color), "Painted Steel" will be a prized addition to any collector's reference bookshelf.

Parabellum: A Technical History of Swiss Lugers, by Vittorio Bobba, Priuli & Verlucca, Editori, Torino, Italy, 1996. Italian and English text. Illustrated. $100.00

Patents for Inventions, Class 119 (Small Arms), 1855-1930. British Patent Office, Armory Publications, Oceanside, CA, 1993. 7 volume set. $375.00

Contains 7980 abridged patent descriptions and their sectioned line drawings, plus a 37-page alphabetical index of the patentees.

Pattern Dates for British Ordnance Small Arms, 1718-1783, by DeWitt Bailey, Thomas Publications, Gettysburg, PA, 1997. 116 pp., illus. Paper covers. $20.00

The weapons discussed in this work are those carried by troops sent to North America between 1737 and 1783, or shipped to them as replacement arms while in America.

Peters & King, by Thomas D. Schiffer. Krause Publications, Iola, WI 2002. 1st edition. 256 pages, 200+ black & white photos with a 32 page color section. Hardcover. $44.95

Discover the history behind Peters Cartridge and King Powder and see how they shaped the arms industry into what it is today and why their products fetch hundreds and even thousands of dollars at auctions. Current values are provided for their highly collectible product packaging and promotional advertising premiums such as powder kegs, tins, cartridge boxes, and calendars.

Pitman Notes on U.S. Martial Small Arms and Ammunition, 1776-1933, Volume 2, Revolvers and Automatic Pistols, The, by Brig. Gen. John Pitman, Thomas Publications, Gettysburg, PA, 1990. 192 pp., illus. $29.95

A most important primary source of information on United States military small arms and ammunition.

Plates and Buckles of the American Military 1795-1874, by Sydney C. Kerksis, Orange, VA: Publisher's Press, 1998. 5th edition. 568 pages, illustrated with 100's of black and white photos. Hardcover. $39.00

The single most comprehensive reference for U.S. and Confederate plates.

Plains Rifle, The, by Charles Hanson, Gun Room Press, Highland Park, NJ, 1989. 169 pp., illus. $35.00

All rifles that were made with the plainsman in mind, including pistols.

Powder and Ball Small Arms, by Martin Pegler, Windrow & Green, London, 1998. 128 pp., illus. $39.95

Part of the new "Live Firing Classic Weapons" series featuring full color photos of experienced shooters dressed in authentic costumes handling, loading and firing historic weapons.

Powder Flask Book, The, by Ray Riling, R&R Books, Livonia, NY, 1993. 514 pp., illus. $69.95

The complete book on flasks of the 19th century. Exactly scaled pictures of 1,600 flasks are illustrated.

Proud Promise: French Autoloading Rifles, 1898-1979, by Jean Huon, Collector Grade Publications, Inc., Cobourg, Ont., Canada, 1995. 216 pp., illus. $39.95

The author has finally set the record straight about the importance of French contributions to modern arms design.

E. C. Prudhomme's Gun Engraving Review, by E. C. Prudhomme, R&R Books, Livonia, NY, 1994. 164 pp., illus. $60.00

As a source for engravers and collectors, this book is an indispensable guide to styles and techniques of the world's foremost engravers.

REFERENCE

THE HANDGUNNER'S LIBRARY

Purdey Gun and Rifle Makers: The Definitive History, by Donald Dallas, Quiller Press, London, 2000. 245 pp., illus. Color throughout. $100.00

A limited edition of 3,000 copies. Signed and numbered. With a PURDEY book plate.

Queen Anne Pistol, 1660-1780: A History of the Turn-Off Pistol, The, by John W. Burgoyne, Bloomfield, Ont. CANADA: Museum Restoration Service, 2002. 1st edition — Historical Arms New Series No. 1. ISBN: 0-88855-0154. 120 pages. Pictorial Hardcover. $35.00

A detailed, fast moving, thoroughly researched text and almost 200 cross-referenced illustrations. This distinctive breech-loading arm was developed in the middle years of the 17th century but found popularity during the reign of the monarch (1702-1714), by whose name it is known.

Red Shines the Sun: A Pictorial History of the Fallschirm-Infantrie, by Eric Queen. San Jose, CA: R. James Bender Publishing, 2003. 1st edition. Hardcover. $69.95

A culmination of 12 years of research, this reference work traces the history of the Army paratroopers of the Fallschirm-Infanterie from their origins in 1937, to the expansion to battalion strength in 1938, then on through operations at Wola Gulowska (Poland), and Moerdijk (Holland). This 240 page comprehensive look at their history is supported by 600 images, many of which are in full color, and nearly 90% are previously unpublished. This work also features original examples of nearly all documents awarded to the Army paratroopers, as well as the most comprehensive study to date of the Army paratrooper badge or Fallschirmschützenabzeichen (Heer). Original examples of all known variations (silver, aluminum, cloth, feinzink) are pictured in full color. If you are interested in owning one of these badges, this book can literally save you from making a $2,000.00 mistake.

Reloading Tools, Sights and Telescopes for Single Shot Rifles, by Gerald O. Kelver, Brighton, CO, 1982. 163 pp., illus. Paper covers. $13.95

A listing of most of the famous makers of reloading tools, sights and telescopes with a brief description of the products they manufactured.

The Remington-Lee Rifle, by Eugene F. Myszkowski, Excalibur Publications, Latham, NY, 1995. 100 pp., illus. Paper covers. $22.50

Features detailed descriptions, including serial number ranges, of each model from the first Lee Magazine Rifle produced for the U.S. Navy to the last Remington-Lee Small Bores shipped to the Cuban Rural Guard.

Remington 'America's Oldest Gunmaker' The Official Authorized History Of The Remington Arms Company, by Roy Marcot. Madison, NC: Remington Arms Company, 1999. 1st edition. 312 pages, with 167 black & white illustrations, plus 291 color plates. $79.95

This is without a doubt the finest history of that firm ever to have been compiled. Based on firsthand research in the Remington companies archives, it is extremely well written.

Remington's Vest Pocket Pistols, by Hatfield, Robert E. Lincoln, RI: Andrew Mowbray, Inc., 2002. 117 pages. Hardcover. $29.95

While Remington Vest Pocket Pistols have always been popular with collectors, very little solid information has been available about them. Such simple questions such as "When were they made?"..."How many were produced?"...and "What calibers were they available in?" have all remained unanswered. This new book, based upon years of study and a major survey of surviving examples, attempts to answer these critical questions. Specifications, markings, mechanical design and patents are also presented here. Inside you will find 100+ photographs, serial number data, exploded views of all four Remington Vest Pocket Pistol sizes, component parts lists and a guide to disassembly and reassembly. Also includes a discussion of Vest Pocket Wire-Stocked Buggy/Bicycle rifles, plus the documented serial number story.

Revolvers of the British Services 1854-1954, by W.H.J. Chamberlain and A.W.F. Taylerson, Museum Restoration Service, Ottawa, Canada, 1989. 80 pp., illus. $27.50

Covers the types issued among many of the United Kingdom's naval, land or air services.

Rifles of the World, by Oliver Achard, Chartwell Books, Inc., Edison, NJ, 141 pp., illus. $24.95

A unique insight into the world of long guns, not just rifles, but also shotguns, carbines and all the usual multi-barreled guns that once were so popular with European hunters, especially in Germany and Austria.

Round Ball to Rimfire, Vol. 1, by Dean Thomas, Thomas Publications, Gettysburg, PA, 1997. 144 pp., illus. $49.95

The first of a two-volume set of the most complete history and guide for all small arms ammunition used in the Civil War. The information includes data from research and development to the arsenals that created it.

Round Ball to Rimfire: A History of Civil War Small Arms Ammunition, Vol. 2. by Dean Thomas, Thomas Publications, Gettysburg, PA 2002. 528 pages. Hardcover. $49.95

Completely discusses the ammunition for Federal Breechloading Carbines and Rifles. The seven chapters with eighteen appendices detailing the story of the twenty-seven or so different kinds of breechloaders actually purchased or ordered by the Ordnance Department during the Civil War. The book is conveniently divided by the type of priming — external or internal — and then alphabetically by maker or supplier. A wealth of new information and research has proven that these weapons either functioned properly or were inadequate relative to the design and ingenuity of the proprietary cartridges.

Russell M. Catron and His Pistols, by Warren H. Buxton, Ucross Books, Los Alamos, NM, 1998. 224 pp., illustrated. Paper covers. $49.50

An unknown American firearms inventor and manufacturer of the mid twentieth century. Military, commerical, ammunition.

SAFN-49 and The FAL, The, by Joe Poyer and Dr. Richard Feirman, North Cape Publications, Tustin, CA, 1998. 160 pp., illus. Paper covers. $14.95

The first complete overview of the SAFN-49 battle rifle, from its pre-World War 2 beginnings to its military service in countries as diverse as the Belgian Congo and Argentina. The FAL was "light" version of the SAFN-49 and it became the Free World's most adopted battle rifle.

Sauer & Sohn, Sauer "Dein Waffenkamerad" Volume 2, J. P., by Cate & Krause, Walsworth Publishing, Chattanooga, TN, 2000. 440 pp., illus. $69.95

A historical study of Sauer automatic pistols. This new volume includes a great deal of new knowledge that has surfaced about the firm J.P. Sauer. You will find new photos, documentation, serial number ranges and historial facts which will expand the knowledge and interest in the oldest and best of the German firearms companies.

Scottish Firearms, by Claude Blair and Robert Woosnam-Savage, Museum Restoration Service, Bloomfield, Ont., Canada, 1995. 52 pp., illus. Paper covers. $8.95

This revision of the first book devoted entirely to Scottish firearms is supplemented by a register of surviving Scottish long guns.

Scottish Pistol, The, by Martin Kelvin. Fairleigh Dickinson University Press, Dist. By Associated University Presses, Cranbury, NJ, 1997. 256 pp., illus. $49.50

The Scottish pistol, its history, manufacture and design.

Sharps Firearms, by Frank Seller, Frank M. Seller, Denver, CO, 1998. 358 pp., illus. $59.95

Traces the development of Sharps firearms with full range of guns made including all martial variations.

Simeon North: First Official Pistol Maker of the United States, by S. North and R. North, The Gun Room Press, Highland Park, NJ, 1972. 207 pp., illus. $15.95

Reprint of the rare first edition.

SKS Carbine, The, by Steve Kehaya and Joe Poyer, North Cape Publications, Tustin, CA, 1997. 150 pp., illus. Paper covers. $16.95

The first comprehensive examination of a major historical firearm used through the Vietnam conflict to the diamond fields of Angola.

SKS Type 45 Carbines, The, by Duncan Long, Desert Publications, El Dorado, AZ, 1992. 110 pp., illus. Paper covers. $19.95

Covers the history and practical aspects of operating, maintaining and modifying this abundantly available rifle.

Smith & Wesson 1857-1945, by Robert J. Neal and Roy G. Jinks, R&R Books, Livonia, NY, 1996. 434 pp., illus. $50.00

The bible for all existing and aspiring Smith & Wesson collectors.

Sniper Variations of the German K98k Rifle, by Richard D. Law, Collector Grade Publications, Ontario, Canada, 1997. 240 pp., illus. $47.50

Volume 2 of "Backbone of the Wehrmacht" the author's in-depth study of the German K98k rifle. This volume concentrates on the telescopic-sighted rifle of choice for most German snipers during World War 2.

Southern Derringers of the Mississippi Valley, by Turner Kirkland, Pioneer Press, Tenn., 1971. 80 pp., illus., paper covers. $4.00

A guide for the collector, and a much-needed study.

Soviet Russian Postwar Military Pistols and Cartridges, by Fred A. Datig, Handgun Press, Glenview, IL, 1988. 152 pp., illus. $29.95

Thoroughly researched, this definitive sourcebook covers the development and adoption of the Makarov, Stechkin and the new PSM pistols. Also included in this source book is coverage on Russian clandestine weapons and pistol cartridges.

Soviet Russian Tokarev "TT" Pistols and Cartridges 1929-1953, by Fred Datig, Graphic Publishers, Santa Ana, CA, 1993. 168 pp., illus. $39.95

Details of rare arms and their accessories are shown in hundreds of photos. It also contains a complete bibliography and index.

Spencer Repeating Firearms, by Roy M. Marcot. New York: Rowe Publications, 2002. 316 pages; numerous B&W photos & illustrations. Hardcover. $65.00

Sporting Collectibles, by Jim and Vivian Karsnitz, Schiffer Publishing Ltd., West Chester, PA, 1992. 160 pp., illus. Paper covers. $29.95.

The fascinating world of hunting related collectibles presented in an informative text.

Springfield 1903 Rifles, The, by Lt. Col. William S. Brophy, USAR, Ret., Stackpole Books Inc., Harrisburg, PA, 1985. 608 pp., illus. $75.00

The illustrated, documented story of the design, development, and production of all the models, appendages, and accessories.

Springfield Armory Shoulder Weapons 1795-1968, by Robert W.D. Ball, Antique Trader Books, Dubuque, IA, 1998. 264 pp., illus. $34.95

This book documents the 255 basic models of rifles, including test and trial rifles, produced by the Springfield Armory. It features the entire history of rifles and carbines manufactured at the Armory, the development of each weapon with specific operating characteristics and procedures.

Springfield Model 1903 Service Rifle Production and Alteration, 1905-1910, by C.S. Ferris and John Beard, Arvada, CO, 1995. 66 pp., illus. Paper covers. $12.50

A highly recommended work for any serious student of the Springfield Model 1903 rifle.

Springfield Shoulder Arms 1795-1865, by Claud E. Fuller, S. & S. Firearms, Glendale, NY, 1996. 76 pp., illus. Paper covers. $14.95

Exact reprint of the scarce 1930 edition of one of the most definitive works on Springfield flintlock and percussion muskets ever published.

SS Headgear, by Kit Wilson. Johnson Reference Books, Fredericksburg, VA. 72 pages, 15 full-color plates and over 70 black and white photos. $16.50

An excellent source of information concerning all types of SS headgear, to include Allgemeine-SS, Waffen-SS, visor caps, helmets, overseas caps, M-43's and miscellaneous headgear. Also included is a guide on the availability and current values of SS headgear. This guide was compiled from auction catalogs, dealer price lists, and input from advanced collectors in the field.

SS Helmets: A Collector's Guide, Vol 1, by Kelly Hicks. Johnson Reference Books, Fredericksburg, VA. 96 pages, illustrated. $17.50

Deals only with SS helmets and features some very nice color close-up shots of the different SS decals used. Also, has some nice color shots of entire helmets. Over 85 photographs, 27 in color. The author has documented most of the known types of SS helmets, and describes in detail all of the vital things to look for in determining the originality, style type, and finish. Complete descriptions of each helmet are provided along with detailed close-ups of interior and exterior views of the markings and insignia. Also featured are several period photos of helmets in wear.

SS Helmets: A Collector's Guide, Vol 2, by Kelly Hicks. Johnson Reference Books, Fredericksburg, VA. 2000. 128 pages. 107 full-color photos, 14 period photos. $25.00

Volume II contains dozen of highly detailed, full-color photos of rare and original SS and Field Police helmets, featuring both sides as well as interior view. The very best graphics techniques ensure that these helmets are presented in such a way that the reader can 'almost feel' the different paint textures of the camo and factory finishes. The outstanding decal section offers detailed close-ups of original SS and Police decals, and in conjunction with Volume I, completes the documentation of virtually all types of original decal variations used between 1934 and 1945.

SS Uniforms, Insignia and Accoutrements, by A. Hayes. Schiffer Publications, Atglen, PA. 1996. 248 pages, with over 800 color and b/w photographs. $69.95

This new work explores in detailed color the complex subject of Allgemeine and Waffen-SS uniforms, insignia, and accoutrements. Hundreds of authentic items are extensively photographed in close-up to enable the reader to examine and study.

Steel Pots: The History of America's Steel Combat Helmets, by Chris Armold. Bender Publishing, San Jose, CA, 2000. $47.95

Packed with hundreds of color photographs, detailed specification diagrams and supported with meticulously researched data, this book takes the reader on a fascinating visual journey covering 80 years of American helmet design and development. From the classic Model 1917 "Doughboy" helmet to the distinctive ballistic "Kelvar" helmet, Steel Pots will introduce you to over 50 American helmet variations. Also, rare WWI experimental helmets to specialized WWII aircrew anti-flak helmets, plus liners, suspensions, chinstraps, camouflage covers, nets and even helmet radios!

Standard Catalog of Firearms, 13th Edition, by Ned Schwing, Krause Publications, Iola, WI, 2003.1382 Pages, illustrated. 6,000+ b&w photos plus a 16-page color section. Paper covers. $34.95

This is the largest, most comprehensive and best-selling firearm book of all time! And this year's edition is a blockbuster for both shooters and firearm collectors. More than 14,000 firearms are listed and priced in up to six grades of condition. That's almost 100,000 prices! Gun enthusiasts will love the new full-color section of photos highlighting the finest firearms sold at auction this past year.

Steel Canvas: The Art of American Arms, by R.L. Wilson, Random House, NY, 1995, 384 pp., illus. $65.00

Presented here for the first time is the breathtaking panorama of America's extraordinary engravers and embellishers of arms, from the 1700s to modern times.

Stevens Pistols & Pocket Rifles, by K.L. Cope, Museum Restoration Service, Alexandria Bay, NY, 1992. 114 pp., illus. $24.50

This is the story of the guns and the man who designed them and the company which he founded to make them.

Sumptuous Flaske, The, by Herbert G. Houze, Andrew Mowbray, Inc., Lincoln, RI, 1989. 158 pp., illus. Soft covers. $35.00

Catalog of a recent show at the Buffalo Bill Historical Center bringing together some of the finest European and American powder flasks of the 16th to 19th centuries.

Swedish Mauser Rifles, The, by Steve Kehaya and Joe Poyer, North Cape Publications, Tustin, CA, 1999. 267 pp., illustrated. Paper covers. $19.95

Every known variation of the Swedish Mauser carbine and rifle is described including all match and target rifles and all sniper fersions. Includes serial number and production data.

System Lefaucheaux, by Chris C. Curtis, with a Foreword by Norm Flayderman. Armslore Press, 2002. 312 pages, heavily illustrated with b & w photos. Hardcover. $44.95

The study of pinfire cartridge arms including their role in the American Civil War.

Televisions Cowboys, Gunfighters & Cap Pistols, by Rudy A. D'Angelo, Antique Trader Books, Norfolk, VA, 1999. 287 pp., illustrated in color and black and white. Paper covers. $31.95

Over 850 beautifully photographed color and black and white images of cap guns, actors, and the characters they portrayed in the "Golden Age of TV Westerns. With accurate descriptions and current values.

Thompson: The American Legend, by Tracie L. Hill, Collector Grade Publications, Ontario, Canada, 1996. 584 pp., illus. $85.00

The story of the first American submachine gun. All models are featured and discussed.

Thoughts on the Kentucky Rifle in its Golden Age by Kindig, Joe K. III. York, PA: George Shumway Publisher, 2002. Annotated Second Edition. 561pp; Illustrated. Hardcover. $85.00

The definitive book on the Kentucky Rifle, illustrating 266 of these guns in 856 detailed photographs. This scarce title, long out of print, is once again available.

Toys that Shoot and other Neat Stuff, by James Dundas, Schiffer Books, Atglen, PA, 1999. 112 pp., illustrated. Paper covers. $24.95

Shooting toys from the twentieth century, especially 1920's to 1960's, in over 420 color photographs of BB guns, cap shooters, marble shooters, squirt guns and more. Complete with a price guide.

Trapdoor Springfield, The, by M.D. Waite and B.D. Ernst, The Gun Room Press, Highland Park, NJ, 1983. 250 pp., illus. $39.95

The first comprehensive book on the famous standard military rifle of the 1873-92 period.

Treasures of the Moscow Kremlin: Arsenal of the Russian Tsars, A Royal Armories and the Moscow Kremlin exhibition. HM Tower of London 13, June 1998 to 11 September, 1998. BAS Printers, Over Wallop, Hampshire, England. XXII plus 192 pp. over 180 color illustrations. Text in English and Russian. $65.00

For this exchibition catalog each of the 94 objects on display are photographed and described in detail to provide a most informative record of this important exhibition.

U.S. Army Headgear 1812-1872, by Langellier, John P. and C. Paul Loane. Atglen, PA: Schiffer Publications, 2002. 167 pages, with over 350 color and b/w photos. $69.95

This profusely illustrated volume represents more than three decades of research in public and private collections by military historian John P. Langellier and Civil War authority C. Paul Loane. Hardcover.

U.S. Army Rangers & Special Forces of World War II Their War in Photographs, by Robert Todd Ross. Atglen, PA: Schiffer Publications, 2002. 216 pages, over 250 b/w & color photographs. Hardcover. $59.95

Never before has such an expansive view of World War II elite forces been offered in one volume. An extensive search of public and private archives unearthed an astonishing number of rare and never before seen images, including color. Most notable are the nearly twenty exemplary photographs of Lieutenant Colonel William O. Darby's Ranger Force in Italy, taken by Robert Capa, considered by many to be the greatest combat photographer of all time. Complementing the period photographs are numerous color plates detailing the rare and often unique items of insignia, weapons, and equipment that marked the soldiers whose heavy task it was to Lead the Way. Includes rare, previously unpublished photographs by legendary combat photographer Robert Capa.

U.S. Breech-Loading Rifles and Carbines, Cal. 45, by Gen. John Pitman, Thomas Publications, Gettysburg, PA, 1992. 192 pp., illus. $29.95

The third volume in the Pitman Notes on U.S. Martial Small Arms and Ammunition, 1776-1933. This book centers on the "Trapdoor Springfield" models.

U.S. Handguns of World War 2: The Secondary Pistols and Revolvers, by Charles W. Pate, Andrew Mowbray, Inc., Lincoln, RI, 1998. 515 pp., illus. $39.00

This indispensable new book covers all of the American military handguns of World War 2 except for the M1911A1 Colt automatic.

United States Martial Flintlocks, by Robert M. Reilly, Mowbray Publishing Co., Lincoln, RI, 1997. 264 pp., illus. $40.00

A comprehensive history of American flintlock longarms and handguns (mostly military) c. 1775 to c. 1840.

U.S. Martial Single Shot Pistols, by Daniel D. Hartzler and James B. Whisker, Old Bedford Village Pess, Bedford, PA, 1998. 128 pp., illus. $45.00

A photographic chronicle of military and semi-martial pistols supplied to the U.S. Government and the several States.

U.S. Military Arms Dates of Manufacture from 1795, by George Madis, David Madis, Dallas, TX, 1995. 64 pp. Soft covers. $9.95

Lists all U.S. military arms of collector interest alphabetically, covering about 250 models.

REFERENCE

U.S. Military Small Arms 1816-1865, by Robert M. Reilly, The Gun Room Press, Highland Park, NJ, 1983. 270 pp., illus. $39.95
Covers every known type of primary and secondary martial firearms used by Federal forces.

U.S. M1 Carbines: Wartime Production, by Craig Riesch, North Cape Publications, Tustin, CA, 1994. 72 pp., illus. Paper covers. $16.95
Presents only verifiable and accurate information. Each part of the M1 Carbine is discussed fully in its own section; including markings and finishes.

U.S. Naval Handguns, 1808-1911, by Fredrick R. Winter, Andrew Mowbray Publishers, Lincoln, RI, 1990. 128 pp., illus. $26.00
The story of U.S. Naval handguns spans an entire century—included are sections on each of the important naval handguns within the period.

Uniform and Dress Army and Navy of the Confederate States of America. (Official Regulations), by Confederate States of America. Ray Riling Arms Books, Philadelphia, PA. 1960. $20.00
A portfolio containing a complete set of nine color plates especially prepared for framing Reproduced in exactly 200 sets from the very rare Richmond, VA., 1861 regulations.

Uniform Buttons of the United States 1776-1865, by Warren K. Tice. Thomas Publications, Gettysburg, PA. 1997. 520 pages over 3000 illustrations. $60.00
A timely work on US uniform buttons for a growing area of collecting. This work interrelates diverse topics such as manufacturing processes, history of manufacturing companies, known & recently discovered button patterns and the unist that wore them.

Uniforms & Equipment of the Imperial German Army 1900-1918: A Study in Period Photographs, by Charles Woolley. Schiffer Publications, Atglen, PA. 2000. 375 pages, over 500 b/w photographs and 50 color drawings. $69.95
Features formal studio portraits of pre-war dress and wartime uniforms of all arms. Also contains photo postal cards taken in the field of Infantry, Pionier, Telegraph-Signal, Landsturm, and Mountain Troops, vehicles, artillery, musicians, the Bavarian Leib Regiment, specialized uniforms and insignia, small arms close-ups, unmotorized transport, group shots and Balloon troops and includes a 60 page full-color uniform section reproduced from rare 1914 plates. Fully illustrated.

Uniforms & Equipment of the Imperial German Army 1900-1918: A Study in Period Photographs, Volume 2. by Charles Woolley. Schiffer Publications, Atglen, PA. 2000. 320 pages, over 500 b/w photographs and 50 color drawings. $69.95
Contains over 500 never before published photographic images of Imperial German military subjects. This initial volume, of a continuing study, features formal studio portraits of pre-war dress and wartime uniforms of all arms. It also contains photo postal cards taken in the field of Infantry, Pionier, Telegraph-Signal, Landsturm and Mountain Troops, Vehicles, Artillery, Musicians, the Bavarian Leib Regiment, specialized uniforms and insignia, small arms close-ups, unmotorized transport, group shots and Balloon troops.

Uniforms of the Third Reich: A Study in Photographs, by Maguire Hayes. Schiffer Publications, Atglen, PA. 1997. 200 pages, with over 400 color photographs. $69.95
This new book takes a close look at a variety of authentic World War II era German uniforms including examples from the Army, Luftwaffe, Kriegsmarine, Waffen-SS, Allgemeine-SS, Hitler Youth and Political Leaders. The pieces are shown in large full frame front and rear shots, and in painstaking detail to show tailors tags, buttons, insignia detail etc. and allow the reader to see what the genuine article looks like. Various accoutrements worn with the uniforms are also included to aid the collector.

Uniforms of The United States Army, 1774-1889, by Henry Alexander Ogden. Dover Publishing, Mineola, NY. 1998. 48 pages of text plus 44 color plates. Softcover. $9.95
A republication of the work published by the quarter-master general, United States army in 1890. A striking collection of lithographs and a marvelous archive of military, social, and costume history portraying the gamut of U.S. Army uniforms from fatigues to full dress, between 1774 and 1889.

Uniforms, Organization, and History of the NSKK/NSFK, by John R. Angolia & David Littlejohn. Bender Publishing, San Jose, CA, 2000. $44.95
This work is part of the on-going study of political organizations that formed the structure of the Hitler hierarchy, and is authored by two of the most prominent authorities on the subject of uniforms and insignia of the Third Reich. This comprehensive book covers details on the NSKK and NSFK such as history, organization, uniforms, insignia, special insignia, flags and standards, gorgets, daggers, awards, "day badges," and much more!

Uniforms of the Waffen-SS; Black Service Uniform —LAH Guard Uniform— SS Earth-Grey Service Uniform—Model 1936 Field Service Uniform— 1939-1940 —1941 Volume 1, by Michael D. Beaver. Schiffer Publications, Atglen, PA. 2002. 272 pages, with 500 color, and black and white photos. $79.95
This spectacular work is a heavily documented record of all major clothing articles of the Waffen-SS. Hundreds of unpublished photographs were used in production. Original and extremely rare SS uniforms of various types are carefully photographed and presented here. Among the subjects covered in this multi volume series are field-service uniforms, sports, drill, dress, armored personnel, tropical, and much more. A large updated chapter on SS camouflage clothing is also provided. Special chapters on the SD and

concentration camp personnel assist the reader in differentiating these elements from combat units of the Waffen-SS. Difficult areas such as mountain and ski troops, plus ultra-rare pre-war uniforms are covered. Included are many striking and exquisite uniforms worn by such men as Himmler, Dietrich, Ribbentrop (father and son), Wolff, Demelhuber, and many others. From the enlisted man to the top of the SS empire, this book covers it all. This book is indispensable and an absolute must-have for any serious historian of World War II German uniforms.

Uniforms of the Waffen-SS; 1942-1943 — 1944-1945 — Ski Uniforms — Overcoats — White Service Uniforms — Tropical Clothing, Volume 2, by Michael D. Beaver. Schiffer Publications, Atglen, PA. 2002. 272 pages, with 500 color, and black and white photos. $79.95

Uniforms of the Waffen-SS; Sports and Drill Uniforms — Black Panzer Uniform — Camouflage — Concentration Camp Personnel-SD-SS Female Auxiliaries, Volume 3, by Michael D. Beaver. Schiffer Publications, Atglen, PA. 2002. 272 pages, with 500 color, and black and white photos. $79.95

U.S. Silent Service - Dolphins & Combat Insignia 1924-1945, by David Jones. Bender Publishing, San Jose, CA, 2001. 224 pages, 532 photos. (most in full color) $39.95
After eight years of extensive research, the publication of this book is a submarine buff and collectord̃s dream come true. This beautiful full-color book chronicles, with period letters and sketches, the developmental history of US submarine insignia prior to 1945. It also contains many rare and never before published photographs, plus interviews with WWII submarine veterans, from enlisted men to famous skippers. Each insignia is photographed (obverse and reverse) and magnified in color. All known contractors are covered plus embroidered versions, mess dress variations, the Roll of Honor, submarine combat insignia, battleflags, launch memorabilia and related submarine collectibles (postal covers, match book covers, jewelry, posters, advertising art, postcards, etc.)

Variations of Colt's New Model Police and Pocket Breech Loading Pistols, by Breslin, John D., Pirie, William Q., & Price, David E.: Lincoln, RI: Andrew Mowbray Publishers, 2002. 1st edition. 158 pages, heavily illustrated with over 160 photographs and superb technical detailed drawings and diagrams. Pictorial Hardcover. $37.95
A type-by-type guide to what collectors call small frame conversions.

Walther: A German Legend, by Manfred Kersten, Safari Press, Inc., Huntington Beach, CA, 2000. 400 pp., illustrated. $85.00
This comprehensive book covers, in rich detail, all aspects of the company and its guns, including an illustrious and rich history, the WW2 years, all the pistols (models 1 through 9), the P-38, P-88, the long guns, .22 rifles, centerfires, Wehrmacht guns, and even a gun that could shoot around a corner.

Walther Pistols: Models 1 Through P99, Factory Variations and Copies, by Dieter H. Marschall, Ucross Books, Los Alamos, NM. 2000. 140 pages, with 140 b & w illustrations, index. Paper Covers. $19.95
This is the English translation, revised and updated, of the highly successful and widely acclaimed German language edition. This book provides the collector with a reference guide and overview of the entire line of the Walther military, police, and self-defense pistols from the very first to the very latest. Models 1-9, PP, PPK, MP, AP, HP, P.38, P1, P4, P38K, P5, P88, P99 and the Manurhin models. Variations, where issued, serial ranges, calibers, marks, proofs, logos, and design aspects in an astonishing quantity and variety are crammed into this very well researched and highly regarded work.

Walther Handgun Story: A Collector's and Shooter's Guide, The, by Gene Gangarosa, Steiger Publications, 1999. 300., illustrated. Paper covers. $21.95
Covers the entire history of the Walther empire. Illustrated with over 250 photos.

Walther P-38 Pistol, by Maj. George Nonte, Desert Publications, Cornville, AZ, 1982. 100 pp., illus. Paper covers. $12.95
Complete volume on one of the most famous handguns to come out of WWII. All models covered.

Walther Models PP & PPK, 1929-1945 – Volume 1, by James L. Rankin, Coral Gables, FL, 1974. 142 pp., illus. $40.00
Complete coverage on the subject as to finish, proofmarks and Nazi Party inscriptions.

Walther Volume II, Engraved, Presentation and Standard Models, by James L. Rankin, J.L. Rankin, Coral Gables, FL, 1977. 112 pp., illus. $40.00
The new Walther book on embellished versions and standard models. Has 88 photographs, including many color plates.

Walther, Volume III, 1908-1980, by James L. Rankin, Coral Gables, FL, 1981. 226 pp., illus. $40.00
Covers all models of Walther handguns from 1908 to date, includes holsters, grips and magazines.

Winchester Bolt Action Military & Sporting Rifles 1877 to 1937, by Herbert G. Houze, Andrew Mowbray Publishing, Lincoln, RI, 1998. 295 pp., illus. $45.00
Winchester was the first American arms maker to commercially manufacture a bolt action repeating rifle, and this book tells the exciting story of these Winchester bolt actions.

REFERENCE

THE HANDGUNNER'S LIBRARY

Winchester Book, The, by George Madis, David Madis Gun Book Distributor, Dallas, TX, 2000. 650 pp., illus. $54.50

A new, revised 25th anniversary edition of this classic book on Winchester firearms. Complete serial ranges have been added.

Winchester Dates of Manufacture 1849-1984, by George Madis, Art & Reference House, Brownsboro, TX, 1984. 59 pp. $7.50

A most useful work, compiled from records of the Winchester factory.

Winchester Model 1876 "Centennial" Rifle, The, by Houze, Herbert G. Lincoln, RI: Andrew Mowbray, Inc., 2001. Illustrated with over 180 black and white photographs. 192 Pages. Hardcover. $45.00

The first authoritative study of the Winchester Model 1876 written using the company's own records. This book dispels the myth that the Model 1876 was merely a larger version of the Winchester company's famous Model 1873 and instead traces its true origins to designs developed immediately after the American Civil War. The specifics of the model-such as the numbers made in its standard calibers, barrel lengths, finishes and special order features-are fully listed here for the first time. In addition, the actual processes and production costs involved in its manufacture are also completely documented. For Winchester collectors, and those interested in the mechanics of the 19th-century arms industry, this book provides a wealth of previously unpublished information.

Winchester Engraving, by R.L. Wilson, Beinfeld Books, Springs, CA, 1989. 500 pp., illus. $135.00

A classic reference work of value to all arms collectors.

Winchester Handbook, The, by George Madis, Art & Reference House, Lancaster, TX, 1982. 287 pp., illus. $26.95

The complete line of Winchester guns, with dates of manufacture, serial numbers, etc.

Winchester-Lee Rifle, The, by Eugene Myszkowski, Excalibur Publications, Tucson, AZ 2000. 96 pp., illustrated. Paper Covers. $22.95

The development of the Lee Straight Pull, the cartridge and the approval for military use. Covers details of the inventor and memorabilia of Winchester-Lee related material.

Winchester Lever Action Repeating Firearms, Vol. 1, The Models of 1866, 1873 and 1876, by Arthur Pirkle, North Cape Publications, Tustin, CA, 1995. 112 pp., illus. Paper covers. $19.95

Complete, part-by-part description, including dimensions, finishes, markings and variations throughout the production run of these fine, collectible guns.

Winchester Lever Action Repeating Rifles, Vol. 2, The Models of 1886 and 1892, by Arthur Pirkle, North Cape Publications, Tustin, CA, 1996. 150 pp., illus. Paper covers. $19.95

Describes each model on a part-by-part basis by serial number range complete with finishes, markings and changes.

Winchester Lever Action Repeating Rifles, Volume 3, The Model of 1894, by Arthur Pirkle, North Cape Publications, Tustin, CA, 1998. 150 pp., illus. Paper covers. $19.95

The first book ever to provide a detailed description of the Model 1894 rifle and carbine.

Winchester Lever Legacy, The, by Clyde "Snooky" Williamson, Buffalo Press, Zachary, LA, 1988. 664 pp., illustrated. $75.00

A book on reloading for the different calibers of the Winchester lever action rifle.

Winchester Model 94: The First 100 Years, The, by Robert C. Renneberg, Krause Publications, Iola, WI, 1991. 208 pp., illus. $34.95

Covers the design and evolution from the early years up to the many different editions that exist today.

Winchester Rarities, by Webster, Krause Publications, Iola, WI, 2000. 208 pp., with over 800 color photos, illus. $49.95

This book details the rarest of the rare; the one-of-a-kind items and the advertising pieces from years gone by. With nearly 800 full color photos and detailed pricing provided by experts in the field, this book gives collectors and enthusiasts everything they need.

Winchester Shotguns and Shotshells, by Ronald W. Stadt, Krause Publications, Iola, WI, 1995. 256 pp., illus. $34.95

The definitive book on collectible Winchester shotguns and shotshells manufactured through 1961.

Winchester Single-Shot—Volume 1; A History and Analysis, The, by John Campbell, Andrew Mowbray, Inc., Lincoln RI, 1995. 272 pp., illus. $55.00

Covers every important aspect of this highly-collectible firearm.

Winchester Single-Shot—Volume 2; Old Secrets and New Discoveries, The, by John Campbell, Andrew Mowbray, Inc., Lincoln RI, 2000. 280 pp., illus. $55.00

An exciting follow-up to the classic first volume.

Winchester Slide-Action Rifles, Volume 1: Model 1890 & 1906, by Ned Schwing, Krause Publications, Iola, WI, 1992. 352 pp., illus. $39.95

First book length treatment of models 1890 & 1906 with over 50 charts and tables showing significant new information about caliber style and rarity.

Worldwide Webley and the Harrington and Richardson Connection, by Stephen Cuthbertson, Ballista Publishing and Distributing Ltd., Gabriola Island, Canada, 1999. 259 pp., illus. $50.00

A masterpiece of scholarship. Over 350 photographs plus 75 original documents, patent drawings, and advertisements accompany the text.

GENERAL

Action Shooting: Cowboy Style, by John Taffin, Krause Publications, Iola, WI, 1999. 320 pp., illustrated. $39.95

Details on the guns and ammunition. Explanations of the rules used for many events. The essential cowboy wardrobe.

Advanced Muzzleloader's Guide, by Toby Bridges, Stoeger Publishing Co., So. Hackensack, NJ, 1985. 256 pp., illus. Paper covers. $14.95

The complete guide to muzzle-loading rifles, pistols and shotguns—flintlock and percussion.

Aids to Musketry for Officers & NCOs, by Capt. B.J. Friend, Excalibur Publications, Latham, NY, 1996. 40 pp., illus. Paper covers. $7.95

A facsimile edition of a pre-WWI British manual filled with useful information for training the common soldier.

Air Gun Digest, 3rd Edition, by J.I. Galan, DBI Books, a division of Krause Publications, Iola, WI, 1995. 258 pp., illus. Paper covers. $19.95

Everything from A to Z on air gun history, trends and technology.

American Air Rifles, by House, James E. Krause Publications, Iola, WI. 2002. 1st edition. 208 pages, with 198 b&w photos. Softcover. $22.95

Air rifle ballistics, sights, pellets, games, and hunting caliber recommendations are thoroughly explained to help shooters get the most out of their American air rifles. Evaluation of more than a dozen American-made and American-imported air rifle models.

American B.B. Gun: A Collector's Guide, The, by Dunathan, Arni T. A.S. Barnes And Co., Inc., South Brunswick. 2001. 154 pages, illustrated with nearly 200 photographs, drawings and detailed diagrams. Hardcover. $35.00

American and Imported Arms, Ammunition and Shooting Accessories, Catalog No. 18 of the Shooter's Bible, Stoeger, Inc., reprinted by Fayette Arsenal, Fayetteville, NC, 1988. 142 pp., illus. Paper covers. $10.95

A facsimile reprint of the 1932 Stoeger's Shooter's Bible.

America's Great Gunmakers, by Wayne van Zwoll, Stoeger Publishing Co., So. Hackensack, NJ, 1992. 288 pp., illus. Paper covers. $16.95

This book traces in great detail the evolution of guns and ammunition in America and the men who formed the companies that produced them.

Armed and Female, by Paxton Quigley, E.P. Dutton, New York, NY, 1989. 237 pp., illus. $16.95

The first complete book on one of the hottest subjects in the media today, the arming of the American woman.

Arming the Glorious Cause: Weapons of the Second War for Independence, by James B. Whisker, Daniel D. Hartzler and Larry W. Yantz, R & R Books, Livonia, NY, 1998. 175 pp., illustrated. $45.00.

A photographic study of Confederate weapons.

Arms and Armour in Antiquity and the Middle Ages, by Charles Boutell, Stackpole Books, Mechanicsburg, PA, 1996. 352 pp., illus. $22.95

Detailed descriptions of arms and armor, the development of tactics and the outcome of specific battles.

Arms & Armor in the Art Institute of Chicago, by Walter J. Karcheski, Jr., Bulfinch Press, Boston, MA, 1995. 128 pp., illus. $35.00

Now, for the first time, the Art Institute of Chicago's arms and armor collection is presented in the visual delight of 103 color illustrations.

Arms for the Nation: Springfield Longarms, edited by David C. Clark, Scott A. Duff, Export, PA, 1994. 73 pp., illus. Paper covers. $9.95

A brief history of the Springfield Armory and the arms made there.

Arsenal of Freedom, The Springfield Armory, 1890-1948: A Year-by-Year Account Drawn from Official Records, compiled and edited by Lt. Col. William S. Brophy, USAR Ret., Andrew Mowbray, Inc., Lincoln, RI, 1991. 400 pp., illus. Soft covers. $29.95

A "must buy" for all students of American military weapons, equipment and accoutrements.

Assault Pistols, Rifles and Submachine Guns, by Duncan Long, Paladin Press, Boulder, CO, 1997, 8 1/2 x 11, soft cover, photos, illus. 152 pp. $21.95

This book offers up-to-date, practical information on how to operate and field-strip modern military, police and civilian combat weapons. Covers new developments and trends such as the use of fiber optics, liquid-recoil systems and lessening of barrel length are covered. Troubleshooting procedures, ballistic tables and a list of manufacturers and distributors are also included.

Assault Weapons, 5th Edition, The Gun Digest Book of, edited by Jack Lewis and David E. Steele, DBI Books, a division of Krause Publications, Iola, WI, 2000. 256 pp., illustrated. Paper covers. $21.95

This is the latest word on true assault weaponry in use today by international military and law enforcement organizations.

Benchrest Shooting Primer, The, by Brennan, Dave (Editor). Precision Shooting, Inc., Manchester, CT 2000. 2nd edition. 420 pages, illustrated with black and white photographs, drawings and detailed diagrams. Pictorial softcover. $24.95

> The very best articles on shooting and reloading for the most challenging of all the rifle accuracy disciplines...benchrest shooting.

Black Powder, Pig Lead and Steel Silhouettes, by Matthews, Paul A. Wolfe Publishing, Prescott, AZ, 2002. 132 pages, illustrated with black and white photographs and detailed drawings and diagrams. Softcover. $16.95

Book of the Crossbow The, by Sir Ralph Payne-Gallwey, Dover Publications, Mineola, NY, 1996. 416 pp., illus. Paper covers. $14.95

> Unabridged republication of the scarce 1907 London edition of the book on one of the most devastating hand weapons of the Middle Ages.

British Small Arms of World War 2, by Ian D. Skennerton, I.D.S.A. Books, Piqua, OH, 1988. 110 pp., 37 illus. $25.00

Carbine And Shotgun Speed Shooting: How To Hit Hard And Fast In Combat, by Moses, Steve. Paladin Press, Boulder, CO. 2002. 96 pages, illus. Softcover $18.00

> In this groundbreaking book, he breaks down the mechanics of speed shooting these weapons, from stance and grip to sighting, trigger control and more, presenting them in a concise and easily understood manner. Whether you wish to further your defensive, competitive or recreational shooting skills, you will find this book a welcome resource for learning to shoot carbines and shotguns with the speed and accuracy that are so critical at short distances.

Combat Handgunnery, 5th Edition, The Gun Digest Book of, by Chuck Taylor, DBI Books, a division of Krause Publications, Iola, WI, 2002. 256 pp., illus. Paper covers. $21.95

> This edition looks at real world combat handgunnery from three different perspectives—military, police and civilian.

Complete Blackpowder Handbook, 4th Edition, The, by Sam Fadala, DBI Books, a division of Krause Publications, Iola, WI, 2002. 400 pp., illus. Paper covers. $21.95

> Expanded and completely rewritten edition of the definitive book on the subject of blackpowder.

Complete .50-caliber Sniper Course, The, by Dean Michaelis, Paladin Press, Boulder, CO, 2000. 576 pp, illustrated, $60.00

> The history from German Mauser T-Gewehr of World War 1 to the Soviet PTRD and beyond. Includes the author's Program of Instruction for Special Operations Hard-Target Interdiction Course.

cowboy Action Shooting, by Charly Gullett, Wolfe Publishing Co., Prescott, AZ, 1995. 400 pp., illus. Paper covers. $24.50

> The fast growing of the shooting sports is comprehensively covered in this text— the guns, loads, tactics the fun and flavor of this Old West era competition.

Custom Firearms Engraving, by Tom Turpin, Krause Publications, Iola, WI, 1999. 208 pp., illustrated. $49.95

> Provides a broad and comprehensive look at the world of firearms engraving. The exquisite styles of more than 75 master engravers are shown on beautiful examples of handguns, rifles, shotguns, and other firearms, as well as knives.

Dead On, by Tony Noblitt and Warren Gabrilska, Paladin Press, Boulder, CO, 1998. 176 pp., illustrated. Paper covers. $22.00

> The long-range marksman's guide to extreme accuracy.

Elmer Keith: The Other Side of A Western Legend, by Gene Brown., Precision Shooting, Inc., Manchester, CT 2002. 1st edition. 168 pages, illustrated with black and white photographs. Softcover. $19.95

> An updated and expanded edition of his original work, incorporating new tales and information that has come to light in the past six years. Additional photos have been added, and the expanded work has been professionally edited and formatted. Gene Brown was a long time friend of Keith, and today is unquestionably the leading authority on Keith's books. The chapter on the topic is worth the price of admission by itself.

Encyclopedia of Native American Bows, Arrows and Quivers, by Steve Allely and Jim Hamm, The Lyons Press, N.Y., 1999. 160 pp., illustrated. $29.95

> A landmark book for anyone interested in archery history, or Native Americans.

Exercise of Armes, The, by Jacob de Gheyn, edited and with an introduction by Bas Kist, Dover Publications, Inc., Mineola, NY, 1999. 144 pp., illustrated. Paper covers. $14.95

> Republications of all 117 engravings from the 1607 classic military manual. A meticulously accurate portrait of uniforms and weapons of the 17th century Netherlands.

Federal Civil War Shelter Tent, The, by Gaede, Frederick C., Alexandria, VA: O'Donnell Publishing, 2001. 1st edition. 134 pages, and illustrated. Softcover $20.00

> This is a great monograph for all Civil War collectors. The text covers everything from government patents, records, and contract data to colorful soldier's descriptions. In addition, it is extensively illustrated with drawings and photos of over 30 known examples with close-ups of stitching, fastening buttons, and some that were decorated with soldier's art. This book is a well-presented study by a leading researcher, collector, and historian.

Fighting Iron; A Metals Handbook for Arms Collectors, by Art Gogan, Mowbray Publishers, Inc., Lincoln, RI, 2002. 176 pp., illustrated. $28.00

> A guide that is easy to use, explains things in simple English and covers all of the different historical periods that we are interested in.

Fighting Submachine Gun, Machine Pistol, and Shotgun, a Hands-On Evaluation, The, by Timothy J. Mullin, Paladin Press, Boulder, CO, 1999. 224 pp., illustrated. Paper covers. $35.00

> An invaluable reference for military, police and civilian shooters who may someday need to know how a specific weapon actually performs when the targets are shooting back and the margin of errors is measured in lives lost.

Fireworks: A Gunsight Anthology, by Jeff Cooper, Paladin Press, Boulder, CO, 1998. 192 pp., illus. Paper cover. $27.00

> A collection of wild, hilarious, shocking and always meaningful tales from the remarkable life of an American firearms legend.

Frank Pachmayr: The Story of America's Master Gunsmith and his Guns, by John Lachuk, Safari Press, Huntington Beach, CA, 1996. 254 pp., illus. First edition, limited, signed and slipcased. $85.00; Second printing trade edition. $50.00

> The colorful and historically significant biography of Frank A. Pachmayr, America's own gunsmith emeritus.

From a Stranger's Doorstep to the Kremlin Gate, by Mikhail Kalashnikov, Ironside International Publishers, Inc., Alexandria, VA, 1999. 460 pp., illustrated. $34.95

> A biography of the most influential rifle designer of the 20th century. His AK-47 assault rifle has become the most widely used (and copied) assault rifle of this century.

Frontier Rifleman, The, by H.B. LaCrosse Jr., Pioneer Press, Union City, TN, 1989. 183 pp., illus. Soft covers. $17.50

> The Frontier rifleman's clothing and equipment during the era of the American Revolution, 1760-1800.

Gatling Gun: 19th Century Machine Gun to 21st Century Vulcan, The, by Joseph Berk, Paladin Press, Boulder, CO, 1991. 136 pp., illus. $34.95

> Here is the fascinating on-going story of a truly timeless weapon, from its beginnings during the Civil War to its current role as a state-of-the-art modern combat system.

German Artillery of World War Two, by Ian V. Hogg, Stackpole Books, Mechanicsburg, PA, 1997. 304 pp., illus. $44.95

> Complete details of German artillery use in WWII.

Gone Diggin: Memoirs of A Civil War Relic Hunter, by Toby Law. Orange, VA: Publisher's Press, 2002. 1st edition signed. ISBN: 0942365138. 151 pages, illustrated with black & white photos. $24.95

> The true story of one relic hunter's life - the author kept exacting records of every relic hunt and every relic hunter he was with working with.

Grand Old Lady of No Man's Land: The Vickers Machine Gun, by Dolf L. Goldsmith, Collector Grade Publications, Cobourg, Canada, 1994. 600 pp., illus. $79.95

> Goldsmith brings his years of experience as a U.S. Army armourer, machine gun collector and shooter to bear on the Vickers, in a book sure to become a classic in its field.

Grenade Recognition Manual, Volume 1, U.S. Grenades & Accessories, The, by Darryl W. Lynn, Service Publications, Ottawa, Canada, 1998. 112 pp., illus. Paper covers. $29.95

> This new book examines the hand grenades of the United States beginning with the hand grenades of the U.S. Civil War and continues through to the present.

Grenade Recognition Manual, Vol. 2, British and Commonwealth Grenades and Accessories, The, by Darryl W. Lynn, Printed by the Author, Ottawa, Canada, 2001. 201 pp., illustrated with over 200 photos and drawings. Paper covers. $40.00

> Covers British, Australian, and Canadian Grenades. It has the complete British Numbered series, most of the L series as well as the Australian and Canadian grenades in use. Also covers Launchers, fuzes and lighters, launching cartridges, fillings, and markings.

Gun Digest 2003, 57th Edition, edited by Ken Ramage, DBI Books a division of Krause Publications, Iola, WI, 2002. 544 pp., illustrated. Paper covers. $27.95

> This all new 56th edition continues the editorial excellence, quality, content and comprehensive cataloguing that firearms enthusiasts have come to know and expect. The most read gun book in the world for the last half century.

Gun Engraving, by C. Austyn, Safari Press Publication, Huntington Beach, CA, 1998. 128 pp., plus 24 pages of color photos. $50.00

> A well-illustrated book on fine English and European gun engravers. Includes a fantastic pictorial section that lists types of engravings and prices.

Gun Notes, Volume 1, by Elmer Keith, Safari Press, Huntington Beach, CA, 2002. 219 pp., illustrated Softcover. $24.95

> A collection of Elmer Keith's most interesting columns and feature stories that appeared in "Guns & Ammo" magazine from 1961 to the late 1970's.

Gun Notes, Volume 2, by Elmer Keith, Safari Press, Huntington Beach, CA, 2002. 292 pp., illustrated. Softcover. $24.95

THE HANDGUNNER'S LIBRARY

Covers articles from Keith's monthly column in "Guns & Ammo" magazine during the period from 1971 through Keith's passing in 1982.

Gun Talk, edited by Dave Moreton, Winchester Press, Piscataway, NJ, 1973. 256 pp., illus. $9.95
> A treasury of original writing by the top gun writers and editors in America. Practical advice about every aspect of the shooting sports.

Gun That Made the Twenties Roar, The, by Wm. J. Helmer, rev. and enlarged by George C. Nonte, Jr., The Gun Room Press, Highland Park, NJ, 1977. Over 300 pp., illus. $24.95
> Historical account of John T. Thompson and his invention, the infamous "Tommy Gun."

Gun Trader's Guide, 24th Edition, published by Stoeger Publishing Co., Wayne, NJ, 2002. 592 pp., illus. Paper covers. $23.95
> Complete specifications and current prices for used guns. Prices of over 5,000 handguns, rifles and shotguns both foreign and domestic.

Gunfighter, Man or Myth?, The, by Joseph G. Rosa, Oklahoma Press, Norman, OK, 1969. 229 pp., illus. (including weapons). Paper covers. $14.95
> A well-documented work on gunfights and gunfighters of the West and elsewhere. Great treat for all gunfighter buffs.

Guns Illustrated 2003, 23rd Edition, edited by Ken Ramage, DBI Books a division of Krause Publications, Iola, WI, 2003. 352 pp., illustrated. Softcovers. $22.95
> Highly informative, technical articles on a wide range of shooting topics by some of the top writers in the industry. A catalog section lists more than 3,000 firearms currently manufactured in or imported to the U.S.

Guns Of The Old West, by Dean K. Boorman, New York: Lyons Press, 2002. Color & b&w illus, 144 pgs. Hardcover. $29.95
> An illustrated history of the firearms used by pioneers, hunters, soldiers, lawmen, & the lawless.

Guns & Shooting: A Selected Bibliography, by Ray Riling, Ray Riling Arms Books Co., Phila., PA, 1982. 434 pp., illus. Limited, numbered edition. $75.00
> A limited edition of this superb bibliographical work, the only modern listing of books devoted to guns and shooting.

Guns, Bullets, and Gunfighters, by Jim Cirillo, Paladin Press, Boulder, CO, 1996. 119 pp., illus. Paper covers. $16.00
> Lessons and tales from a modern-day gunfighter.

Hidden in Plain Sight, "A Practical Guide to Concealed Handgun Carry" (Revised 2nd Edition), by Trey Bloodworth and Mike Raley, Paladin Press, Boulder, CO, 1997, 5 1/2 x 8 1/2, softcover, photos, 176 pp. $20.00
> Concerned with how to comfortably, discreetly and safely exercise the privileges granted by a CCW permit? This invaluable guide offers the latest advice on what to look for when choosing a CCW, how to dress for comfortable, effective concealed carry, traditional and more unconventional carry modes, accessory holsters, customized clothing and accessories, accessibility data based on draw-time comparisons and new holsters on the market. Includes 40 new manufacturer listings.

HK Assault Rifle Systems, by Duncan Long, Paladin Press, Boulder, CO, 1995. 110 pp., illus. Paper covers. $27.95
> The little known history behind this fascinating family of weapons tracing its beginnings from the ashes of World War Two to the present time.

Hunting Time: Adventures In Pursuit Of North American Big Game: A Forty Year Chronicle, The, by John E. Howard, Deforest, WI: Saint Huberts Press, 2002. 1st edition. ISBN: 0963309447. 537 pages, illustrated with drawings. Hardcover. $29.95
> From a novice's first hunt for whitetailed deer in his native Wisconsin, to a seasoned hunter's pursuit of a Boone and Crockett Club record book caribou in the northwest territories, the author carries the reader along on his forty year journey through the big game fields of North America.

I Remember Skeeter, compiled by Sally Jim Skelton, Wolfe Publishing Co., Prescott, AZ, 1998. 401 pp., illus. Paper covers. $19.95
> A collection of some of the beloved storyteller's famous works interspersed with anecdotes and tales from the people who knew best.

Indian Tomahawks and Frontiersmen Belt Axes, by Daniel Hartzler & James Knowles. New Windsor, MD: Privately Printed, 2002. 4th revised edition. 279 pages, illustrated with photos and drawings. Hardcover. $65.00
> This fourth revised edition has over 160 new tomahawks and trade axes added since the first edition, also a list of 205 makers names. There are 15 chapters from the earliest known tomahawks to the present day. Some of the finest tomahawks in the country are shown in this book with 31 color plates. This comprehensive study is invaluable to any collector.

Jack O'Connor Catalogue of Letters, by Enzler-Herring, E. Cataloguer. Agoura CA: Trophy Room Books, 2002. 262 pages, 18 illustrations. Hardcover. $55.00
> During a sixteen year period beginning in 1960, O'Connor exchanged many letters with his pal, John Jobson. Material from nearly three hundred of these has been assembled and edited by Ellen Enzler Herring and published in chronological order. A number of the letters have been reproduced in full or part. They offer considerable insight into the beloved gun editor and "Dean of Outdoor Writers"over and beyond what we know about him from his books.

Jack O'Connor — The Legendary Life of America's Greatest Gunwriter, by R. Anderson. Long Beach, CA: Safari Press, 2002. 1st edition. 240pp, profuse photos. Hardcover. $29.95
> This is the book all hunters in North America have been waiting for—the long-awaited biography on Jack O'Connor! Jack O'Connor was the preeminent North American big-game hunter and gunwriter of the twentieth century, and Robert Anderson's masterfully written new work is a blockbuster filled with fascinating facts and stories about this controversial character. With the full cooperation of the O'Connor children, Anderson spent three years interviewing O'Connor's family and friends as well as delving into JOC's papers, photos, and letters, including the extensive correspondence between O'Connor and Bob Householder, and the O'Connor papers from Washington State University. O'Connor's lifelong friend Buck Buckner has contributed two chapters on his experiences with the master of North American hunting.

Kill or Get Killed, by Col. Rex Applegate, Paladin Press, Boulder, CO, 1996. 400 pp., illus. $49.95
> The best and longest-selling book on close combat in history.

Long-Range War: Sniping in Vietnam, The, by Peter R. Senich, Paladin Press, Boulder, CO, 1999. 280 pp., illus. Softcover $59.95
> The most complete report on Vietnam-era sniping ever documented.

Manual for H&R Reising Submachine Gun and Semi-Auto Rifle, edited by George P. Dillman, Desert Publications, El Dorado, AZ, 1994. 81 pp., illus. Paper covers. $12.95
> A reprint of the Harrington & Richardson 1943 factory manual and the rare military manual on the H&R submachine gun and semi-auto rifle.

Manufacture of Gunflints, The, by Sydney B.J. Skertchly, facsimile reprint with new introduction by Seymour de Lotbiniere, Museum Restoration Service, Ontario, Canada, 1984. 90 pp., illus. $24.50
> Limited edition reprinting of the very scarce London edition of 1879.

Master Tips, by J. Winokur, Potshot Press, Pacific Palisades, CA, 1985. 96 pp., illus. Paper covers. $11.95
> Basics of practical shooting.

Military and Police Sniper, The, by Mike R. Lau, Precision Shooting, Inc., Manchester, CT, 1998. 352 pp., illustrated. Paper covers. $44.95
> Advanced precision shooting for combat and law enforcement.

Military Rifle & Machine Gun Cartridges, by Jean Huon, Paladin Press, Boulder, CO, 1990. 392 pp., illus. $34.95
> Describes the primary types of military cartridges and their principal loadings, as well as their characteristics, origin and use.

Military Small Arms of the 20th Century, 7th Edition, by Ian V. Hogg and John Weeks, DBI Books, a division of Krause Publications, Iola, WI, 2000. 416 pp., illustrated. Paper covers. $24.95
> Cover small arms of 46 countries. Over 800 photographs and illustrations.

Modern Custom Guns, Walnut, Steel, and Uncommon Artistry, by Tom Turpin, Krause Publications, Iola, WI, 1997. 206 pp., illus. $49.95
> From exquisite engraving to breathtaking exotic woods, the mystique of today's custom guns is expertly detailed in word and awe-inspiring color photos of rifles, shotguns and handguns.

Modern Law Enforcement Weapons & Tactics, 2nd Edition, by Tom Ferguson, DBI Books, a division of Krause Publications, Iola, WI, 1991. 256 pp., illus. Paper covers. $18.95
> An in-depth look at the weapons and equipment used by law enforcement agencies of today.

Modern Machine Guns, by John Walter, Stackpole Books, Inc. Mechanicsburg, PA, 2000. 144 pp., with 146 illustrations. $22.95
> A compact and authoritative guide to post-war machine-guns. A gun-by-gun directory identifying individual variants and types including detailed evaluations and technical data.

Modern Sporting Guns, by Christopher Austyn, Safari Press, Huntington Beach, CA, 1994. 128 pp., illus. $40.00
> A discussion of the "best" English guns; round action, over-and-under, boxlocks, hammer guns, bolt action and double rifles as well as accessories.

More Complete Cannoneer, The, by M.C. Switlik, Museum & Collectors Specialties Co., Monroe, MI, 1990. 199 pp., illus. $19.95
> Compiled agreeably to the regulations for the U.S. War Department, 1861, and containing current observations on the use of antique cannons.

MP-40 Machine Gun, The, Desert Publications, El Dorado, AZ, 1995. 32 pp., illus. Paper covers. $11.95
> A reprint of the hard-to-find operating and maintenance manual for one of the most famous machine guns of World War II.

Naval Percussion Locks and Primers, by Lt. J. A. Dahlgren, Museum Restoration Service, Bloomfield, Canada, 1996. 140 pp., illus. $35.00
> First published as an Ordnance Memoranda in 1853, this is the finest existing study of percussion locks and primers origin and development.

Official Soviet AKM Manual, The, translated by Maj. James F. Gebhardt (Ret.), Paladin Press, Boulder, CO, 1999. 120 pp., illustrated. Paper covers. $18.00
> This official military manual, available in English for the first time, was originally published by the Soviet Ministry of Defence. Covers the history, function, maintenance, assembly and disassembly, etc. of the 7.62mm AKM assault rifle.

THE HANDGUNNER'S LIBRARY

One-Round War: U.S.M.C. Scout-Snipers in Vietnam, The, by Peter Senich, Paladin Press, Boulder, CO, 1996. 384 pp., illus. Paper covers $59.95
Sniping in Vietnam focusing specifically on the Marine Corps program.

Parker Brothers: Knight of the Trigger, by Ed Muderlak. A Fact-Based Historical Novel Describing the Life and Times of Captain Arthur William du Bray, 1848-1928. Davis, IL: Old Reliable Publishing, 2002. 223 pages. $25.00
Knight of the Trigger tells the story of the Old West when Parker's most famous gun salesman traveled the country by rail, competing in the pigeon ring, hunting with the rich and famous, and selling the "Old Reliable" Parker shotgun. The life and times of Captain Arthur William du Bray, Parker Brothers' on-the-road sales agent from 1884 to 1926, is described in a novelized version of his interesting life.

Powder Horns and Their Architecture and Decoration as Used by the Soldier, Indian, Sailor and Traders of the Era, by Madison Grant. York, PA: Privately Printed, 1987. 165 pages, profusely illustrated. Hardcover. $45.00
Covers homemade pieces from the late eighteenth and early nineteenth centuries.

Practically Speaking: An Illustrated Guide — The Game, Guns and Gear of the International Defensive Pistol Association, by Walt Rauch. Lafayette Hills, PA: Privately Printed, 2002. 1st edition. Softcover. $24.95
The game, guns and gear of the International Defensive Pistol Association with real-world applications. 79 pages, illustated with drawings and color photos.

Present Sabers: A Popular History of the U.S. Horse Cavalry, by Allan T. Heninger, Tucson, AZ: Excalibur Publications, 2002. 1st edition. 160 pages, with 148 photographs, 45 illustrations and 4 charts. Softcover. $24.95
An illustrated history of America's involvement with the horse cavalry, from its earliest beginnings during the Revolutionary War through it's demise in World War 2. The book also contains several appendices, as well as depictions of the regular insignia of all the U.S. Cavalry units.

Principles of Personal Defense, by Jeff Cooper, Paladin Press, Boulder, CO, 1999. 56 pp., illustrated. Paper covers $14.00
This revised edition of Jeff Cooper's classic on personal defense offers great new illustrations and a new preface while retaining the timeliness theory of individual defense behavior presented in the original book.

Quotable Hunter, The, edited by Jay Cassell and Peter Fiduccia, The Lyons Press, N.Y., 1999. 224 pp., illustrated. $20.00
This collection of more than three hundred memorable quotes from hunters through the ages captures the essence of the sport, with all its joys idiosyncrasies, and challenges.

Rifleman Went to War, A, by H. W. McBride, Lancer Militaria, Mt. Ida, AR, 1987. 398 pp., illus. $29.95
The classic account of practical marksmanship on the battlefields of World War I.

Sharpshooting for Sport and War, by W.W. Greener, Wolfe Publishing Co., Prescott, AZ, 1995. 192 pp., illus. $30.00
This classic reprint explores the *first* expanding bullet; service rifles; shooting positions; trajectories; recoil; external ballistics; and other valuable information.

Shooter's Bible 2003, The, No. 94, edited by William S. Jarrett, Stoeger Publishing Co., Wayne, NJ, 2002. 576 pp., illustrated. Paper covers. $23.95
Over 3,000 firearms currently offered by major American and foreign gunmakers. Represented are handguns, rifles, shotguns and black powder arms with complete specifications and retail prices.

Shooting to Live, by Capt. W. E. Fairbairn & Capt. E. A. Sykes, Paladin Press, Boulder, CO, 1997, 4 1/2 x 7, soft cover, illus., 112 pp. $14.00
Shooting to Live is the product of Fairbairn's and Sykes' practical experience with the handgun. Hundreds of incidents provided the basis for the first true book on life-or-death shootouts with the pistol. Shooting to Live teaches all concepts, considerations and applications of combat pistol craft.

Shooting Buffalo Rifles of the Old West, by Mike Venturino, MLV Enterprises, Livingston, MT, 2002. 278 pages, illustrated with black and white photos. Softcover. $30.00
This tome will take you through the history, the usage, the many models, and the actual shooting (and how to's) of the many guns that saw service on the Frontier and are lovingly called "Buffalo Rifles" today. If you love to shoot your Sharps, Ballards, Remingtons, or Springfield "Trapdoors" for hunting or competition, or simply love Old West history, your library WILL NOT be complete without this latest book from Mike Venturino!

Shooting Colt Single Actions, by Mike Venturino, MLV Enterprises, Livingston, MT 1997. 205 pp., illus. Black and white photos throughout. Softcover. $25.00
A complete examination of the Colt Single Action including styles, calibers and generations.

Shooting Lever Guns Of The Old West, by Mike Venturino, MLV Enterprises, Livingston, MT, 1999. 300 pp., illustrated. Softcover. $27.95
Shooting the lever action type repeating rifles of our American West.

Shooting Sixguns of the Old West, by Mike Venturino, MLV Enterprises, Livingston, MT, 1997. 221 pp., illus. Paper covers. $26.50
A comprehensive look at the guns of the early West: Colts, Smith & Wesson and Remingtons, plus blackpowder and reloading specs.

Sniper Training, FM 23-10, Reprint of the U.S. Army field manual of August, 1994, Paladin Press, Boulder, CO, 1995. 352pp., illus. Paper covers. $30.00
The most up-to-date U.S. military sniping information and doctrine.

Sniping in France, by Major H. Hesketh-Prichard, Lancer Militaria, Mt. Ida, AR, 1993. 224 pp., illus. $24.95
The author was a well-known British adventurer and big game hunter. He was called upon in the early days of "The Great War" to develop a program to offset an initial German advantage in sniping. How the British forces came to overcome this advantage.

Special Warfare: Special Weapons, by Kevin Dockery, Emperor's Press, Chicago, IL, 1997. 192 pp., illus. $29.95
The arms and equipment of the UDT and SEALS from 1943 to the present.

Sporting Collectibles, by Dr. Stephen R. Irwin, Stoeger Publishing Co., Wayne, NJ, 1997. 256 pp., illus. Paper covers. $19.95
A must book for serious collectors and admirers of sporting collectibles.

Sporting Craftsmen: A Complete Guide to Contemporary Makers of Custom-Built Sporting Equipment, The, by Art Carter, Countrysport Press, Traverse City, MI, 1994. 240 pp., illus. $35.00
Profiles leading makers of centerfire rifles; muzzleloading rifles; bamboo fly rods; fly reels; flies; waterfowl calls; decoys; handmade knives; and traditional longbows and recurves.

Street Smart Gun Book, The, by John Farnam, Police Bookshelf, Concord, NH, 1986. 45 pp., illus. Paper covers. $11.95
Weapon selection, defensive shooting techniques, and gunfight-winning tactics from one of the world's leading authorities.

Stress Fire, Vol. 1: Stress Fighting for Police, by Massad Ayoob, Police Bookshelf, Concord, NH, 1984. 149 pp., illus. Paper covers. $11.95
Gunfighting for police, advanced tactics and techniques.

Survival Guns, by Mel Tappan, Desert Publications, El Dorado, AZ, 1993. 456 pp., illus. Paper covers. $25.00
Discusses in a frank and forthright manner which handguns, rifles and shotguns to buy for personal defense and securing food, and the ones to avoid.

Tactical Advantage, The, by Gabriel Suarez, Paladin Press, Boulder, CO, 1998. 216 pp., illustrated. Paper covers. $22.00
Learn combat tactics that have been tested in the world's toughest schools.

Tactical Marksman, by Dave M. Lauch, Paladin Press, Boulder, CO, 1996. 165 pp., illus. Paper covers. $35.00
A complete training manual for police and practical shooters.

Thompson Guns 1921-1945, Anubis Press, Houston, TX, 1980. 215 pp., illus. Paper covers. $15.95
Facsimile reprinting of five complete manuals on the Thompson submachine gun.

To Ride, Shoot Straight, and Speak the Truth, by Jeff Cooper, Paladin Press, Boulder, CO, 1997, 5 1/2 x 8 1/2, soft-cover, illus., 384 pp. $32.00
Combat mind-set, proper sighting, tactical residential architecture, nuclear war - these are some of the many subjects explored by Jeff Cooper in this illustrated anthology. The author discusses various arms, fighting skills and the importance of knowing how to defend oneself, and one's honor, in our rapidly changing world.

Trailriders Guide to Cowboy Action Shooting, by James W. Barnard, Pioneer Press, Union City, TN, 1998. 134 pp., plus 91 photos, drawings and charts. Paper covers. $24.95
Covers the complete spectrum of this shooting discipline, from how to dress to authentic leather goods, which guns are legal, calibers, loads and ballistics.

Ultimate Sniper, The, by Major John L. Plaster, Paladin Press, Boulder, CO, 1994. 464 pp., illus. Paper covers. $49.95
An advanced training manual for military and police snipers.

Uniforms and Equipment of the Imperial Japanese Army in World War 2, by Mike Hewitt. Atglen, PA: Schiffer Publications, 2002. 176 pages, with over 520 color and b/w photos. Hardcover. $59.95

Unrepentant Sinner, by Col. Charles Askins, Paladin Press, Boulder, CO, 2000. 322 pp., illustrated. $29.95
The autobiography of Colonel Charles Askins.

U.S. Marine Corp Rifle and Pistol Marksmanship, 1935, reprinting of a government publication, Lancer Militaria, Mt. Ida, AR, 1991. 99 pp., illus. Paper covers. $11.95
The old corps method of precision shooting.

U.S. Marine Corps Scout/Sniper Training Manual, Lancer Militaria, Mt. Ida, AR, 1989. Soft covers. $27.95
Reprint of the original sniper training manual used by the Marksmanship Training Unit of the Marine Corps Development and Education Command in Quantico, Virginia.

U.S. Marine Corps Scout-Sniper, World War II and Korea, by Peter R. Senich, Paladin Press, Boulder, CO, 1994. 236 pp., illus. $44.95
The most thorough and accurate account ever printed on the training, equipment and combat experiences of the U.S. Marine Corps Scout-Snipers.

U.S. Marine Corps Sniping, Lancer Militaria, Mt. Ida, AR, 1989. Irregular pagination. Soft covers. $18.95
A reprint of the official Marine Corps FMFM1-3B.

REFERENCE

THE HANDGUNNER'S LIBRARY

U.S. Marine Uniforms—1912-1940, by Jim Moran. Williamstown, NJ: Phillips Publications, 2001. 174 pages, illustrated with black and white photographs. Hardcover. $49.95

Weapons of the Waffen-SS, by Bruce Quarrie, Sterling Publishing Co., Inc., 1991. 168 pp., illus. $24.95.

An in-depth look at the weapons that made Hitler's Waffen-SS the fearsome fighting machine it was.

Winchester Era, The, by David Madis, Art & Reference House, Brownsville, TX, 1984. 100 pp., illus. $19.95

Story of the Winchester company, management, employees, etc.

With British Snipers to the Reich, by Capt. C. Shore, Lander Militaria, Mt. Ida, AR, 1988. 420 pp., illus. $29.95

One of the greatest books ever written on the art of combat sniping.

World's Machine Pistols and Submachine Guns - Vol. 2a 1964 to 1980, The, by Nelson & Musgrave, Ironside International, Alexandria, VA, 2000. 673 pages, illustrated. $59.95

Containing data, history and photographs of over 200 weapons. With a special section covering shoulder stocked automatic pistols, 100 additional photos.

World's Sniping Rifles, The, by Ian V. Hogg, Paladin Press, Boulder, CO, 1998. 144 pp., illustrated. $22.95

A detailed manual with descriptions and illustrations of more than 50 high-precision rifles from 14 countries and a complete analysis of sights and systems.

GUNSMITHING

Accurizing the Factory Rifle, by M.L. McPhereson, Precision Shooting, Inc., Manchester, CT, 1999. 335 pp., illustrated. Paper covers. $44.95

A long-awaiting book, which bridges the gap between the rudimentary (mounting sling swivels, scope blocks and that general level of accomplishment) and the advanced (precision chambering, barrel fluting, and that general level of accomplishment) books that are currently available today.

Art of Engraving, The, by James B. Meek, F. Brownell & Son, Montezuma, IA, 1973. 196 pp., illus. $38.95

A complete, authoritative, imaginative and detailed study in training for gun engraving. The first book of its kind—and a great one.

Artistry in Arms, The R. W. Norton Gallery, Shreveport, LA, 1970. 42 pp., illus. Paper covers. $9.95.

The art of gunsmithing and engraving.

Checkering and Carving of Gun Stocks, by Monte Kennedy, Stackpole Books, Harrisburg, PA, 1962. 175 pp., illus. $39.95

Revised, enlarged cloth-bound edition of a much sought-after, dependable work.

Firearms Assembly/Disassembly, Part I: Automatic Pistols, 2nd Revised Edition, The Gun Digest Book of, by J.B. Wood, DBI Books, a division of Krause Publications, Iola, WI, 1999. 480 pp., illus. Paper covers. $24.95

Covers 58 popular autoloading pistols plus nearly 200 variants of those models integrated into the text and completely cross-referenced in the index.

Firearms Assembly/Disassembly Part II: Revolvers, Revised Edition, The Gun Digest Book of, by J.B. Wood, DBI Books, a division of Krause Publications, Iola, WI, 1990. 480 pp., illus. Paper covers. $19.95

Covers 49 popular revolvers plus 130 variants. The most comprehensive and professional presentation available to either hobbyist or gunsmith.

Firearms Assembly/Disassembly Part III: Rimfire Rifles, Revised Edition, The Gun Digest Book of, by J. B. Wood, DBI Books, a division of Krause Publications, Iola, WI., 1994. 480 pp., illus. Paper covers. $19.95

Greatly expanded edition covering 65 popular rimfire rifles plus over 100 variants all completely cross-referenced in the index.

Firearms Assembly/Disassembly Part IV: Centerfire Rifles, Revised Edition, The Gun Digest Book of, by J.B. Wood, DBI Books, a division of Krause Publications, Iola, WI, 1991. 480 pp., illus. Paper covers. $19.95

Covers 54 popular centerfire rifles plus 300 variants. The most comprehensive and professional presentation available to either hobbyist or gunsmith.

Firearms Assembly/Disassembly, Part V: Shotguns, Revised Edition, The Gun Digest Book of, by J.B. Wood, DBI Books, a division of Krause Publications, Iola, WI, 1992. 480 pp., illus. Paper covers. $19.95

Covers 46 popular shotguns plus over 250 variants with step-by-step instructions on how to dismantle and reassemble each. The most comprehensive and professional presentation available to either hobbyist or gunsmith.

Firearms Assembly/Disassembly Part VI: Law Enforcement Weapons, The Gun Digest Book of, by J.B. Wood, DBI Books, a division of Krause Publications, Iola, WI, 1981. 288 pp., illus. Paper covers. $16.95

Step-by-step instructions on how to completely dismantle and reassemble the most commonly used firearms found in law enforcement arsenals.

Firearms Assembly 3: The NRA Guide to Rifle and Shotguns, NRA Books, Wash., DC, 1980. 264 pp., illus. Paper covers. $13.95

Text and illustrations explaining the takedown of 125 rifles and shotguns, domestic and foreign.

Firearms Assembly 4: The NRA Guide to Pistols and Revolvers, NRA Books, Wash., DC, 1980. 253 pp., illus. Paper covers. $13.95

Text and illustrations explaining the takedown of 124 pistol and revolver models, domestic and foreign.

Firearms Bluing and Browning, By R.H. Angier, Stackpole Books, Harrisburg, PA. 151 pp., illus. $19.95

A world master gunsmith reveals his secrets of building, repairing and renewing a gun, quite literally, lock, stock and barrel. A useful, concise text on chemical coloring methods for the gunsmith and mechanic.

Firearms Disassembly—With Exploded Views, by John A. Karns & John E. Traister, Stoeger Publishing Co., S. Hackensack, NJ, 1995. 320 pp., illus. Paper covers. $19.95

Provides the do's and don'ts of firearms disassembly. Enables owners and gunsmiths to disassemble firearms in a professional manner.

Guns and Gunmaking Tools of Southern Appalachia, by John Rice Irwin, Schiffer Publishing Ltd., 1983. 118 pp., illus. Paper covers. $9.95

The story of the Kentucky rifle.

Gunsmith Of Grenville County: Building The American Longrifle, The, by Peter Alexander, Texarkana, TX: Scurlock Publishing Co., 2002. Stiff paper covers. $45.00

The most extensive how to book on building longrifles ever published. Takes you through every step of building your own longrifle, from shop set up and tools to engraving, carving and finishing. 400 pages, with hundreds of illustrations, and six color photos of original rifles. Wire O Bind spine will lay flat on the workbench.

Gunsmithing: Pistols & Revolvers, by Patrick Sweeney, DBI Books, a division of Krause Publications, Iola, WI, 1998. 352 pp., illus. Paper covers. $24.95

Do-it-Yourself projects, diagnosis and repair for pistols and revolvers.

Gunsmithing: Rifles, by Patrick Sweeney, Krause Publications, Iola, WI, 1999. 352 pp., illustrated. Paper covers. $24.95

Tips for lever-action rifles. Building a custom Ruger 10/22. Building a better hunting rifle.

Gunsmith Kinks, by F.R. (Bob) Brownell, F. Brownell & Son, Montezuma, IA, 1st ed., 1969. 496 pp., well illus. $22.98

A widely useful accumulation of shop kinks, short cuts, techniques and pertinent comments by practicing gunsmiths from all over the world.

Gunsmith Kinks 2, by Bob Brownell, F. Brownell & Son, Publishers, Montezuma, IA, 1983. 496 pp., illus. $22.95

A collection of gunsmithing knowledge, shop kinks, new and old techniques, shortcuts and general know-how straight from those who do them best—the gunsmiths.

Gunsmith Kinks 3, edited by Frank Brownell, Brownells Inc., Montezuma, IA, 1993. 504 pp., illus. $24.95

Tricks, knacks and "kinks" by professional gunsmiths and gun tinkerers. Hundreds of valuable ideas are given in this volume.

Gunsmith Kinks 4, edited by Frank Brownell, Brownells Inc., Montezuma, IA, 2001. 564 pp., illus. $27.75

332 detailed illustrations. 560+ pages with 706 separate subject headings and over 5000 cross-indexed entries. An incredible gold mine of information.

Gunsmithing, by Roy F. Dunlap, Stackpole Books, Harrisburg, PA, 1990. 742 pp., illus. $34.95

A manual of firearm design, construction, alteration and remodeling. For amateur and professional gunsmiths and users of modern firearms.

Gunsmithing at Home: Lock, Stock and Barrel, by John Traister, Stoeger Publishing Co., Wayne, NJ, 1997. 320 pp., illus. Paper covers. $19.95

A complete step-by-step fully illustrated guide to the art of gunsmithing.

Gunsmith's Manual, The, by J.P. Stelle and Wm. B. Harrison, The Gun Room Press, Highland Park, NJ, 1982. 376 pp., illus. $19.95

For the gunsmith in all branches of the trade.

Home Gunsmithing the Colt Single Action Revolvers, by Loren W. Smith, Ray Riling Arms Books, Co., Phila., PA, 2001. 119 pp., illus. $29.95

Affords the Colt Single Action owner detailed, pertinent information on the operating and servicing of this famous and historic handgun.

Mauser M98 & M96, by R.A. Walsh, Wolfe Publishing Co., Prescott, AR, 1998. 123 pp., illustrated. Paper covers. $32.50

How to build your own favorite custom Mauser rifle from two of the best bolt action rifle designs ever produced—the military Mauser Model 1898 and Model 1896 bolt rifles.

Mr. Single Shot's Gunsmithing-Idea-Book, by Frank de Haas, Mark de Haas, Orange City, IA, 1996. 168 pp., illus. Paper covers. $21.50

Offers easy to follow, step-by-step instructions for a wide variety of gunsmithing procedures all reinforced by plenty of photos.

Pistolsmithing, by George C. Nonte, Jr., Stackpole Books, Harrisburg, PA, 1974. 560 pp., illus. $34.95

A single source reference to handgun maintenance, repair, and modification at home, unequaled in value.

REFERENCE

THE HANDGUNNER'S LIBRARY

Practical Gunsmithing, by the editors of American Gunsmith, DBI Books, a division of Krause Publications, Iola, WI, 1996. 256 pp., illus. Paper covers. $19.95

A book intended primarily for home gunsmithing, but one that will be extremely helpful to professionals as well.

Professional Stockmaking, by D. Wesbrook, Wolfe Publishing Co., Prescott AZ, 1995. 308 pp., illus. $54.00

A step-by-step how-to with complete photographic support for every detail of the art of working wood into riflestocks.

Recreating the American Longrifle, by William Buchele, et al, George Shumway Publisher, York, Pa, 5th edition, 1999. 175 pp., illustrated. $40.00

Includes full size plans for building a Kentucky rifle.

Story of Pope's Barrels, The, by Ray M. Smith, R&R Books, Livonia, NY, 1993. 203 pp., illus. $39.00

A reissue of a 1960 book whose author knew Pope personally. It will be of special interest to Schuetzen rifle fans, since Pope's greatest days were at the height of the Schuetzen-era before WWI.

Survival Gunsmithing, by J.B. Wood, Desert Publications, Cornville, AZ, 1986. 92 pp., illus. Paper covers. $11.95

A guide to repair and maintenance of the most popular rifles, shotguns and handguns.

Tactical 1911, The, by Dave Lauck, Paladin Press, Boulder, CO, 1998. 137 pp., illus. Paper covers. $20.00

Here is the only book you will ever need to teach you how to select, modify, employ and maintain your Colt.

HANDGUNS

Advanced Master Handgunning, by Charles Stephens, Paladin Press, Boulder, CO., 1994. 72 pp., illus. Paper covers. $14.00

Secrets and surefire techniques for winning handgun competitions.

Advanced Tactical Marksman More High Performance Techniques for Police, Military, and Practical Shooters, by Lauck, Dave M. Paladin Press, Boulder, CO 2002. 1st edition. 232 pages, photos, illus. Softcover. $35.00

Lauck, one of the most respected names in high-performance shooting and gunsmithing, refines and updates his 1st book . Dispensing with overcomplicated mil-dot formulas and minute-of-angle calculations, Lauck shows you how to achieve superior accuracy and figure out angle shots, streamline the zero process, hit targets at 2,000 yards, deal with dawn and dusk shoots, train for real-world scenarios, choose optics and accessories and create a mobile shooting platform. He also demonstrates the advantages of his custom reticle design and describes important advancements in the MR-30PG shooting system.

American Beauty: The Prewar Colt National Match Government Model Pistol, by Timothy Mullin, Collector Grade Publications, Canada, 1999. 72 pp., 69 illus. $34.95

69 illustrations, 20 in full color photos of factory engraved guns and other authenticated upgrades, including rare 'double-carved' ivory grips.

Ayoob Files: The Book, The, by Massad Ayoob, Police Bookshelf, Concord, NH, 1995. 223 pp., illus. Paper covers. $14.95

The best of Massad Ayoob's acclaimed series in American Handgunner magazine.

Belgian Browning Pistols 1889-1949, The, by Vanderlinden, Anthony. Wet Dog Publications, Geensboro, NC 2001. Limited edition of 2000 copies, signed by the author. 243 pages, plus index. Illustrated with black and white photos. Hardcover. $65.00

Includes the 1899 compact, 1899 Large, 1900,01903, Grand Browning, 1910, 1922 Grand Rendement and high power pistols. Also includes a chapter on holsters.

Big Bore Handguns, by Taffin, John, Krause Publishing, Iola, WI: 2002. 1st edition. 352 Pages, 320 b&w photos with a 16-page color section. Hardcover. $39.95

Gives honest reviews and an inside look at shooting, hunting, and competing with the biggest handguns around. Covers handguns from major gunmakers, as well as handgun customizing, accessories, reloading, and cowboy activities. Significant coverage is also given to handgun customizing, accessories, reloading, and popular shooting hobbies including hunting and cowboy activities. Accessories consist of stocks, handgun holster rigs, and much more. Firearms include single-shot pistols, revolvers, and semi-automatics.

Big Bore Sixguns, by John Taffin, Krause Publications, Iola, WI, 1997. 336 pp., illus. $39.95

The author takes aim on the entire range of big bores from .357 Magnums to .500 Maximums, single actions and cap-and-ball sixguns to custom touches for big bores.

Browning High Power Automatic Pistol (Expanded Edition), The, by Blake R. Stevens, Collector Grade Publications, Canada, 1996. 310 pages, with 313 illus. $49.95

An in-depth chronicle of seventy years of High Power history, from John M Browning's original 16-shot prototypes to the present. Profusely illustrated with rare original photos and drawings from the FN Archive to describe virtually every sporting and military version of the High Power. The numerous modifications made to the basic design over the years are, for the first time, accurately arranged in chronological order, thus permitting the dating of any High Power to within a few years of its production. Full details on the WWII Canadian-made Inglis Browning High Power pistol. The Expanded Edition contains 30 new pages on the interesting Argentine full-auto High Power, the latest FN 'MK3' and BDA9 pistols, plus FN's revolutionary P90 5.7x28mm Personal Defence Weapon, and more!

Browning Hi-Power Pistols, Desert Publications, Cornville, AZ, 1982. 20 pp., illus. Paper covers. $11.95

Covers all facets of the various military and civilian models of the Browning Hi-Power pistol.

Canadian Military Handguns 1855-1985, by Clive M. Law, Museum Restoration Service, Bloomfield, Ont. Canada, 1994. 130pp., illus. $40.00

A long-awaited and important history for arms historians and pistol collectors.

Collecting U.S. Pistols & Revolvers, 1909-1945, by J. C. Harrison. The Arms Chest, Okla. City, OK. 1999. 2nd edition (revised). 185 pages, illus. with pictures and drawings. Spiral bound. $35.00

Valuable and detailed reference book for the collector of U.S. Pistols & Revolvers. Identifies standard issue original military models of the M1911, M1911A1 and M1917Cal .45 Pistols and Revolvers as produced by all manufacturers from 1911 through 1945. Plus .22 ACE Models, National Match Models, and similar foreign military models produced by Colt or manufactured under Colt license. Plus Arsenal repair, refinish and Lend-Lease Models.

Colt .45 Auto Pistol, The, compiled from U.S. War Dept. Technical Manuals, and reprinted by Desert Publications, Cornville, AZ, 1978. 80 pp., illus. Paper covers. $11.95

Covers every facet of this famous pistol from mechanical training, manual of arms, disassembly, repair and replacement of parts.

Colt Automatic Pistols, by Donald B. Bady, Pioneer Press, Union City, TN, 1999. 368 pp., illustrated. Softcover. $19.95

A revised and enlarged edition of a key work on a fascinating subject. Complete information on every Colt automatic pistol.

Combat Handgunnery, 5th Edition, by Chuck Taylor, Krause Publications, Iola, WI, 2002. 256 pp., illus. Paper covers. $21.95

This all-new edition looks at real world combat handgunnery from three different perspectives—military, police and civilian.

Combat Revolvers, by Duncan Long, Paladin Press, Boulder, CO, 1999, 8 1/2 x 11, soft cover, 115 photos, 152 pp. $21.95

This is an uncompromising look at modern combat revolvers. All the major foreign and domestic guns are covered: the Colt Python, S&W Model 29, Ruger GP 100 and hundreds more. Know the gun that you may one day stake your life on.

Complete Guide to Compact Handguns, by Gene Gangarosa, Jr., Stoeger Publishing Co., Wayne, NJ, 1997. 228 pp., illus. Paper covers. $22.95

Includes hundreds of compact firearms, along with text results conducted by the author.

Complete Guide to Service Handguns, by Gene Gangarosa, Jr., Stoeger Publishing Co., Wayne, NJ, 1998. 320 pp., illus. Paper covers. $22.95

The author explores the revolvers and pistols that are used around the globe by military, law enforcement and civilians.

Concealable Pocket Pistols: How to Choose and Use Small-Caliber Handguns, McLeod, Terence. Paladin Press, 2001. 1st edition. 80 pages. Softcover. $14.00

Small-caliber handguns are often maligned as too puny for serious self-defense, but millions of Americans own and carry these guns and have used them successfully to stop violent assaults. This is the first book ever devoted to eliminating the many misconceptions about the usefulness of these popular guns. "Pocket pistols" are small, easily concealed, inexpensive semiautomatic handguns in .22, .25, .32 and .380 calibers. Their small size and hammerless design enable them to be easily concealed and carried so they are immediately accessible in an emergency. Their purpose is not to knock an assailant off his feet with fire-breathing power (which no handgun is capable of doing) but simply to deter or stop his assault by putting firepower in your hands when you need it most. Concealable Pocket Pistols addresses every aspect of owning, carrying and shooting small-caliber handguns in a realistic manner. It cuts right to the chase and recommends a handful of the best pistols on the market today as well as the best ammunition for them. It then gets into the real-world issues of how to carry a concealed pocket pistol, how to shoot it under stress and how to deal with malfunctions quickly and efficiently. In an emergency, a small-caliber pistol in the pocket is better than the .357 Magnum left at home. Find out what millions of Americans already know about these practical self-defense tools.

Custom Government Model Pistol, The, by Layne Simpson, Wolfe Publishing Co., Prescott, AZ, 1994. 639 pp., illus. Paper covers. $26.95

The book about one of the world's greatest firearms and the things pistolsmiths do to make it even greater.

CZ-75 Family: The Ultimate Combat Handgun, The, by J.M. Ramos, Paladin Press, Boulder, CO, 1990. 100 pp., illus. Soft covers. $25.00

An in-depth discussion of the early-and-late model CZ-75s, as well as the many newest additions to the Czech pistol family.

REFERENCE

THE HANDGUNNER'S LIBRARY

Encyclopedia of Pistols & Revolvers, by A.E. Hartnik, Knickerbocker Press, New York, NY, 1997. 272 pp., illus. $19.95
A comprehensive encyclopedia specially written for collectors and owners of pistols and revolvers.

Engraved Handguns of .22 Calibre, by John S. Laidacker, Atglen, PA: Schiffer Publications, 2003. 1st edition. 192 pages, with over 400 color and b/w photos. $69.95

Experiments of a Handgunner, by Walter Roper, Wolfe Publishing Co., Prescott, AZ, 1989. 202 pp., illus. $37.00
A limited edition reprint. A listing of experiments with functioning parts of handguns, with targets, stocks, rests, handloading, etc.

Farnam Method of Defensive Handgunning, The, by John S. Farnam, Police Bookshelf, 1999. 191 pp., illus. Paper covers. $24.00
A book intended to not only educate the new shooter, but also to serve as a guide and textbook for his and his instructor's training courses.

Fast and Fancy Revolver Shooting, by Ed. McGivern, Anniversary Edition, Winchester Press, Piscataway, NJ, 1984. 484 pp., illus. $19.95
A fascinating volume, packed with handgun lore and solid information by the acknowledged dean of revolver shooters.

German Handguns: The Complete Book of the Pistols and Revolvers of Germany, 1869 To The Present, by Ian Hogg. Greenhill Publishing, 2001. 320 pages, 270 illustrations. Hardcover. $49.95
Ian Hogg examines the full range of handguns produced in Germany from such classics as the Luger M1908, Mauser HsC and Walther PPK, to more unusual types such as the Reichsrevolver M1879 and the Dreyse 9mm. He presents the key data (length, weight, muzzle velocity, and range) for each weapon discussed and also gives its date of introduction and service record, evaluates and discusses peculiarities, and examines in detail particular strengths and weaknesses.

Glock: The New Wave in Combat Handguns, by Peter Alan Kasler, Paladin Press, Boulder, CO, 1993. 304 pp., illus. $27.00
Kasler debunks the myths that surround what is the most innovative handgun to be introduced in some time.

Glock's Handguns, by Duncan Long, Desert Publications, El Dorado, AR, 1996. 180 pp., illus. Paper covers. $19.95
An outstanding volume on one of the world's newest and most successful firearms of the century.

Gun Digest Book of the 1911, The, by Patrick Sweeney. Krause Publications, Iola, WI, 2002. 336 pages, with 700 b&w photos. Softcover. $27.95
Compete guide of all models and variations of the Model 1911. The author also includes repair tips and information on buying a used 1911.

Hand Cannons: The World's Most Powerful Handguns, by Duncan Long, Paladin Press, Boulder, CO, 1995. 208 pp., illus. Paper covers. $22.00
Long describes and evaluates each powerful gun according to their features.

Handgun, The, by Geoffrey Boothroyd, Safari Press, Inc., Huntington Beach, CA, 1999. 566 pp., illustrated. $50.00
A very detailed history of the handgun. Now revised and a completely new chapter written to take account of developments since the 1970 edition.

Handguns 2003, 14th Edition, edited by Ken Ramage, DBI Books a division of Krause Publications, Iola, WI, 2002. 352 pp., illustrated. Paper covers. $22.95
Top writers in the handgun industry give you a complete report on new handgun developments, testfire reports on the newest introductions and previews on what's ahead.

Handgun Stopping Power "The Definitive Study", by Evan P. Marshall & Edwin J. Sanow, Paladin Press, Boulder, CO, 1997, soft cover, photos, 240 pp. $45.00
Dramatic first-hand accounts of the results of handgun rounds fired into criminals by cops, storeowners, cabbies and others are the heart and soul of this long-awaited book. This is the definitive methodology for predicting the stopping power of handgun loads, the first to take into account what really happens when a bullet meets a man.

Heckler & Koch's Handguns, by Duncan Long, Desert Publications, El Dorado, AR, 1996. 142 pp., illus. Paper covers. $19.95.
Traces the history and the evolution of H&K's pistols from the company's beginning at the end of WWII to the present.

Hidden in Plain Sight, by Trey Bloodworth & Mike Raley, Professional Press, Chapel Hill, NC, 1995. Paper covers. $19.95.
A practical guide to concealed handgun carry.

High Standard: A Collectors Guide to the Hamden & Hartford Target Pistols, Dance, Tom. Andrew Mowbray, Inc., Lincoln, RI: 1999. 192 pp., Heavily illustrated with black & white photographs and technical drawings. $24.00
From Citation to Supermatic, all of the production models and specials made from 1951 to 1984 are covered according to model number or series, making it easy to understand the evolution to this favorite of shooters and collectors.

High Standard Automatic Pistols 1932-1950, by Charles E. Petty, The Gunroom Press, Highland Park, NJ, 1989. 124 pp., illus. $14.95
A definitive source of information for the collector of High Standard arms.

Hi-Standard Pistols and Revolvers, 1951-1984, by James Spacek, James Spacek, Chesire, CT, 1998. 128 pp., illustrated. Paper covers. $12.50
Technical details, marketing features and instruction/parts manual of every model High Standard pistol and revolver made between 1951 and 1984. Most accurate serial number information available.

Hi-Standard Pistol Guide, The, by Burr Leyson, Duckett's Sporting Books, Tempe AZ, 1995. 128 pp., illus. Paper covers. $26.00
Complete information on selection, care and repair, ammunition, parts, and accessories.

How to Become a Master Handgunner: The Mechanics of X-Count Shooting, by Charles Stephens, Paladin Press, Boulder, CO, 1993. 64 pp., illus. Paper covers. $14.00
Offers a simple formula for success to the handgunner who strives to master the technique of shooting accurately.

Illustrated Encyclopedia of Handguns, by A.B. Zhuk, Stackpole Books, Mechanicsburg, PA, 2002. 256 pp., illus. Softcover, $24.95
Identifies more than 2,000 military and commercial pistols and revolvers with details of more than 100 popular handgun cartridges.

Inglis Diamond: The Canadian High Power Pistol, The, by Clive M. Law, Collector Grade Publications, Canada, 2001. 312 pp., illustrated. $49.95
This definitive work on Canada's first and indeed only mass produced handgun, in production for a very brief span of time and consequently made in relatively few numbers, the venerable Inglis-made Browning High Power covers the pistol's initial history, the story of Chinese and British adoption, use post-war by Holland, Australia, Greece, Belgium, New Zealand, Peru, Brasil and other countries. All new information on the famous light-weights and the Inglis Diamond variations. Completely researched through official archives in a dozen countries. Many of the bewildering variety of markings have never been satisfactorily explained until now. Also included are many photos of holsters and accessories.

Instinct Combat Shooting, by Chuck Klein, The Goose Creek, IN, 1989. 49 pp., illus. Paper covers. $12.00
Defensive handgunning for police.

Know Your 45 Auto Pistols—Models 1911 & A1, by E.J. Hoffschmidt, Blacksmith Corp., Southport, CT, 1974. 58 pp., illus. Paper covers. $14.95
A concise history of the gun with a wide variety of types and copies.

Know Your Ruger Single Actions: The Second Decade 1963-1973, by John C. Dougan. Blacksmith Corp., North Hampton, OH, 1994. 143 pp., illus. Paper covers. $19.95

Know Your Ruger S/A Revolvers 1953-1963 (Revised Edition), by John C. Dougan. Blacksmith Corp., North Hampton, OH, 2002. 191 pp., illus. Paper covers. $19.95

Know Your Walther P38 Pistols, by E.J. Hoffschmidt, Blacksmith Corp., Southport, CT, 1974. 77 pp., illus. Paper covers. $14.95
Covers the Walther models Armee, M.P., H.P., P.38—history and variations.

Know Your Walther PP & PPK Pistols, by E.J. Hoffschmidt, Blacksmith Corp., Southport, CT, 1975. 87 pp., illus. Paper covers. $14.95
A concise history of the guns with a guide to the variety and types.

La Connaissance du Luger, Tome 1, by Gerard Henrotin, H & L Publishing, Belguim, 1996. 144 pages, illustrated. $45.00
(The Knowledge of Luger, Volume 1, translated.) Black & white and color photos. French text.

Living with Glocks: The Complete Guide to the New Standard in Combat Handguns, by Robert H Boatman, Boulder, CO: Paladin Press, 2002. 1st edition. ISBN: 1581603401. 184 pages, illustrated. Hardcover. $29.95
In this book he explains why in no uncertain terms. In addition to demystifying the enigmatic Glock trigger, Boatman describes and critiques each Glock model in production. Separate chapters on the G36, the enhanced G20 and the full-auto G18 emphasize the job-specific talents of these standout models for those seeking insight on which Glock pistol might best meet their needs. And for those interested in optimizing their Glock's capabilities, this book addresses all the peripherals – holsters, ammo, accessories, silencers, modifications and conversions, training programs and more. Whether your focus is on concealed carry, home protection, hunting, competition, training or law enforcement.

Luger Handbook, The, by Aarron Davis, Krause Publications, Iola, WI, 1997. 112 pp., illus. Paper covers. $9.95
Now you can identify any of the legendary Luger variations using a simple decision tree. Each model and variation includes pricing information, proof marks and detailed attributes in a handy, user-friendly format. Plus, it's fully indexed. Instantly identify that Luger!

Lugers of Ralph Shattuck, by Ralph Shattuck, Peoria, AZ, 2000. 49 pages, illus. Hardcover. $29.95
49 pages, illustrated with maps and full color photos of here to now never before shown photos of some of the rarest lugers ever. Written by one of the world's renowned collectors. A MUST have book for any Luger collector.

Lugers at Random (Revised Format Edition), by Charles Kenyon, Jr., Handgun Press, Glenview, IL, 2000. 420 pp., illus. $59.95
A new printing of this classic, comprehensive reference for all Luger collectors.

Luger Story, The, by John Walter, Stackpole Books, Mechanicsburg, PA, 2001. 256 pp., illus. Paper Covers. $19.95
The standard history of the world's most famous handgun.

REFERENCE

THE HANDGUNNER'S LIBRARY

Mauser Self-Loading Pistol, The, by Belford & Dunlap, Borden Publ. Co., Alhambra, CA. Over 200 pp., 300 illus., large format. $29.95

The long-awaited book on the "Broom Handles," covering their inception in 1894 to the end of production. Complete and in detail: pocket pistols, Chinese and Spanish copies, etc.

Mental Mechanics of Shooting: How to Stay Calm at the Center, by Vishnu Karmakar and Thomas Whitney. Littleton, CO: Center Vision, Inc., 2001. 144 pages. Softcover. $19.95

Not only will this book help you stay free of trigger jerk, it will help you in all areas of your shooting.

9mm Parabellum; The History & Development of the World's 9mm Pistols & Ammunition, by Klaus-Peter Konig and Martin Hugo, Schiffer Publishing Ltd., Atglen, PA, 1993. 304 pp., illus. $39.95

Detailed history of 9mm weapons from Belgium, Italy, Germany, Israel, France, USA, Czechoslovakia, Hungary, Poland, Brazil, Finland and Spain.

Official 9mm Markarov Pistol Manual, The, translated into English by Major James Gebhardt, U.S. Army (Ret.), Desert Publications, El Dorado, AR, 1996. 84 pp., illus. Paper covers. $12.95

The information found in this book will be of enormous benefit and interest to the owner or a prospective owner of one of these pistols.

Official Soviet 7.62mm Handgun Manual, The, by Translation by Maj. James F. Gebhardt Ret.), Paladin Press, Boulder, CO, 1997, soft cover, illus., 104 pp. $20.00

This Soviet military manual, now available in English for the first time, covers instructions for use and maintenance of two side arms, the Nagant 7.62mm revolver, used by the Russian tsarist armed forces and later the Soviet armed forces, and the Tokarev7.62mm semi-auto pistol, which replaced the Nagant.

P-08 Parabellum Luger Automatic Pistol, The, edited by J. David McFarland, Desert Publications, Cornville, AZ, 1982. 20 pp., illus. Paper covers. $13.95

Covers every facet of the Luger, plus a listing of all known Luger models.

P08 Luger Pistol, The, by de Vries & Martens. Alexandria, VA: Ironside International, 2002. 152 pages, illustrated with 200 high quality black & white photos. Hardcover. $34.95

Covers all essential information on history and development, ammunition and accessories, codes and markings, and contains photos of nearly every model and accessory. Includes a unique selection of original German WWII propaganda photos, most never published before.

P-38 Automatic Pistol, by Gene Gangarosa, Jr., Stoeger Publishing Co., S. Hackensack, NJ, 1993. 272 pp., illus. Paper covers. $16.95

This book traces the origins and development of the P-38, including the momentous political forces of the World War II era that caused its near demise and, later, its rebirth.

P-38 Pistol: The Walther Pistols, 1930-1945. Volume 1, The, by Warren Buxton, Ucross Books, Los Alamos, MN 1999. $68.50

A limited run reprint of this scarce and sought-after work on the P-38 Pistol. 328 pp. with 160 illustrations.

P-38 Pistol: The Contract Pistols, 1940-1945. Volume 2, The, by Warren Buxton, Ucross Books, Los Alamos, MN 1999. 256 pp. with 237 illustrations. $68.50

P-38 Pistol: Postwar Distributions, 1945-1990. Volume 3, The, by Warren Buxton, Ucross Books, Los Alamos, MN 1999. $68.50

Plus an addendum to Volumes 1 & 2. 272 pp. with 342 illustrations.

Parabellum - A Technical History of Swiss Lugers, by V. Bobba, Italy.1998. 224pp, profuse color photos, large format. $100.00

The is the most beautifully illustrated and well-documented book on the Swiss Lugers yet produced. This splendidly produced book features magnificent images while giving an incredible amount of detail on the Swiss Luger. In-depth coverage of key issues include: the production process, pistol accessories, charts with serial numbers, production figures, variations, markings, patent drawings, etc. Covers the Swiss Luger story from 1894 when the first Bergmann-Schmeisser models were tested till the commercial model 1965. Shows every imaginable production variation in amazing detail and full color! A must for all Luger collectors. This work has been produced in an extremely attractive package using quality materials throughout and housed in a protective slipcase.

Report of Board on Tests of Revolvers and Automatic Pistols, From the Annual Report of the Chief of Ordnance, 1907. Reprinted by J.C. Tillinghast, Marlow, NH, 1969. 34 pp., 7 plates, paper covers. $9.95

A comparison of handguns, including Luger, Savage, Colt, Webley-Fosbery and other makes.

Ruger "P" Family of Handguns, The, by Duncan Long, Desert Publications, El Dorado, AZ, 1993. 128 pp., illus. Paper covers. $14.95

A full-fledged documentary on a remarkable series of Sturm Ruger handguns.

Ruger .22 Automatic Pistol, Standard/Mark I/Mark II Series, The, by Duncan Long, Paladin Press, Boulder, CO, 1989. 168 pp., illus. Paper covers. $16.00

The definitive book about the pistol that has served more than 1 million owners so well.

Semiautomatic Pistols in Police Service and Self Defense, The, by Massad Ayoob, Police Bookshelf, Concord, NH, 1990. 25 pp., illus. Soft covers. $11.95.

First quantitative, documented look at actual police experience with 9mm and 45 police service automatics.

Shooting Colt Single Actions, by Mike Venturino, Livingston, MT, 1997. 205 pp., illus. Paper covers. $25.00

A definitive work on the famous Colt SAA and the ammunition it shoots.

Sig Handguns, by Duncan Long, Desert Publications, El Dorado, AZ, 1995. 150 pp., illus. Paper covers. $19.95

The history of Sig/Sauer handguns, including Sig, Sig-Hammerli and Sig/Sauer variants.

Sixgun Cartridges and Loads, by Elmer Keith, reprint edition by The Gun Room Press, Highland Park, NJ, 1984. 151 pp., illus. $24.95

A manual covering the selection, use and loading of the most suitable and popular revolver cartridges.

Sixguns, by Elmer Keith, Wolfe Publishing Company, Prescott, AZ, 1992. 336 pp. Paper covers. $29.95. Hardcover $35.00

The history, selection, repair, care, loading, and use of this historic frontiersman's friend—the one-hand firearm.

Smith & Wesson's Automatics, by Larry Combs, Desert Publications, El Dorado, AZ, 1994. 143 pp., illus. Paper covers. $19.95

A must for every S&W auto owner or prospective owner.

Spanish Handguns: The History of Spanish Pistols and Revolvers, by Gene Gangarosa, Jr., Stoeger Publishing Co., Accokeek, MD, 2001. 320 pp., illustrated. B & W photos. Paper covers. $21.95

Standard Catalog of Smith & Wesson; 2nd Edition, by Jim Supica and Richard Nahas.Krause Publications, Iola, WI: 2001. 2nd edition. 272 Pages, 350 b&w photos, with a 16 page color section. Pictorial Hardcover. $34.95

Clearly details 775 Smith & Wesson models, knives, holsters, ammunition and police items with complete pricing information, illustrated glossary and index.

Star Firearms, by Leonardo M. Antaris, Davenport, IA: Firac Publications Co., 2002. 640 pages, with over 1,100 b/w photos, 47 pages in full color. Hardcover. $119.95

The definitive work on Star's many models with a historical context, with a review of their mechanical features, & details their development throughout production plus tables of proof marks & codes, serial numbers, annual summaries, procurements by Spanish Guardia Civil & Spanish Police, exports to Bulgaria, Germany, & Switzerland during WW2; text also covers Star's .22 rifles & submachine guns & includes a comprehensive list of Spanish trade names matched to manufacturer for arms made prior to the Spanish Civil War (1936-1939).

Street Stoppers: The Latest Handgun Stopping Power Street Results, by Evan P. Marshall & Edwin J. Sandow, Paladin Press, Boulder, CO, 1997. 392 pp., illus. Paper covers. $42.95

Compilation of the results of real-life shooting incidents involving every major handgun caliber.

Tactical 1911, The, by Dave Lauck, Paladin Press, Boulder, CO, 1999. 152 pp., illustrated. Paper covers. $22.00

The cop's and SWAT operator's guide to employment and maintenance.

Tactical Pistol, The, by Gabriel Suarez with a foreword by Jeff Cooper, Paladin Press, Boulder, CO, 1996. 216 pp., illus. Paper covers. $25.00

Advanced gunfighting concepts and techniques.

Thompson/Center Contender Pistol, The, by Charles Tephens, Paladin Press, Boulder, CO, 1997. 58 pp., illus. Paper covers. $14.00

How to tune and time, load and shoot accurately with the Contender pistol.

.380 Enfield No. 2 Revolver, The, by Mark Stamps and Ian Skennerton, I.D.S.A. Books, Piqua, OH, 1993. 124 pp., 80 illus. Paper covers. $19.95

Truth About Handguns, The, by Duane Thomas, Paladin Press, Boulder, CO, 1997. 136 pp., illus. Paper covers. $18.00

Exploding the myths, hype, and misinformation about handguns.

Walther Pistols: Models 1 Through P99, Factory Variations and Copies, by Dieter H. Marschall, Ucross Books, Los Alamos, NM. 2000. 140 pages, with 140 b & w illustrations, index. Paper Covers. $19.95

This is the English translation, revised and updated, of the highly successful and widely acclaimed German language edition. This book provides the collector with a reference guide and overview of the entire line of the Walther military, police, and self-defense pistols from the very first to the very latest. Models 1-9, PP, PPK, MP, AP, HP, P.38, P1, P4, P38K, P5, P88, P99 and the Manurhin models. Variations, where issued, serial ranges, calibers, marks, proofs, logos, and design aspects in an astonishing quantity and variety are crammed into this very well researched and highly regarded work.

U.S. Handguns of World War 2, The Secondary Pistols and Revolvers, by Charles W. Pate, Mowbray Publishers, Lincoln, RI, 1997. 368 pp., illus. $39.00

This indispensable new book covers all of the American military handguns of W.W.2 except for the M1911A1

REFERENCE

DIRECTORY OF THE HANDGUNNING TRADE

HANDGUNS 2004

REFERENCE

AMMUNITION COMPONENTS, SHOTSHELL

A.W. Peterson Gun Shop, Inc.
Ballistic Product, Inc.
Blount, Inc., Sporting Equipment Div.
CCI Ammunition ATK
Cheddite, France S.A.
Claybuster Wads & Harvester Bullets
Garcia National Gun Traders, Inc.
Peterson Gun Shop, Inc., A.W.
Precision Reloading, Inc.
Ravell Ltd.
Tar-Hunt Custom Rifles, Inc.
Vitt/Boos

AMMUNITION COMPONENTS-- BULLETS, POWDER, PRIMERS, CASES

A.W. Peterson Gun Shop, Inc.
Acadian Ballistic Specialties
Accuracy Unlimited
Accurate Arms Co., Inc.
Action Bullets & Alloy Inc.
ADCO Sales, Inc.
Alaska Bullet Works, Inc.
Alliant Techsystems Smokeless Powder Group
Allred Bullet Co.
Alpha LaFranck Enterprises
American Products, Inc.
Arizona Ammunition, Inc.
Armfield Custom Bullets
A-Square Co.
Atlantic Rose, Inc.
Baer's Hollows
Ballard Rifle & Cartridge Co., LLC
Barnes
Barnes Bullets, Inc.
Beartooth Bullets
Bell Reloading, Inc.
Berger Bullets Ltd.
Berry's Mfg., Inc.
Big Bore Bullets of Alaska
Big Bore Express
Bitterroot Bullet Co.
Black Belt Bullets (See Big Bore Express)
Black Hills Shooters Supply
Black Powder Products
Blount, Inc., Sporting Equipment Div.
Blue Mountain Bullets
Brenneke GmbH
Briese Bullet Co., Inc.
Brown Co., E. Arthur
Brown Dog Ent.
BRP, Inc. High Performance Cast Bullets
Buck Stix-SOS Products Co.
Buckeye Custom Bullets
Buckskin Bullet Co.
Buffalo Arms Co.
Buffalo Bullet Co., Inc.
Buffalo Rock Shooters Supply
Bullseye Bullets
Bull-X, Inc.
Butler Enterprises
Cambos Outdoorsman
Canyon Cartridge Corp.
Cascade Bullet Co., Inc.
Cast Performance Bullet Company
Casull Arms Corp.
CCI Ammunition ATK
Champion's Choice, Inc.
Cheddite, France S.A.
CheVron Bullets
Chuck's Gun Shop
Clean Shot Technologies
Competitor Corp., Inc.

Cook Engineering Service
Corbin Mfg. & Supply, Inc.
Cummings Bullets
Curtis Cast Bullets
Curtis Gun Shop (See Curtis Cast Bullets)
Custom Bullets by Hoffman
Dakota Arms, Inc.
Davide Pedersoli and Co.
DKT, Inc.
Dohring Bullets
Eichelberger Bullets, Wm.
Federal Cartridge Co.
Fiocchi of America, Inc.
Forkin, Ben (See Belt MTN Arms)
Forkin Arms
Fowler Bullets
Fowler, Bob (See Black Powder Products)
Foy Custom Bullets
Freedom Arms, Inc.
Garcia National Gun Traders, Inc.
Gehmann, Walter (See Huntington Die Specialties)
GOEX, Inc.
Golden Bear Bullets
Gotz Bullets
Grayback Wildcats
Green Mountain Rifle Barrel Co., Inc.
Grier's Hard Cast Bullets
GTB
Gun City
Harris Enterprises
Harrison Bullets
Hart & Son, Inc.
Hawk Laboratories, Inc. (See Hawk, Inc.)
Hawk, Inc.
Haydon Shooters Supply, Russ
Heidenstrom Bullets
Hercules, Inc. (See Alliant Techsystems, Smokeless)
Hi-Performance Ammunition Company
Hirtenberger AG
Hobson Precision Mfg. Co.
Hodgdon Powder Co.
Hornady Mfg. Co.
HT Bullets
Hunters Supply, Inc.
Huntington Die Specialties
Impact Case & Container, Inc.
Imperial Magnum Corp.
IMR Powder Co.
Intercontinental Distributors, Ltd.
J&D Components
J&L Superior Bullets (See Huntington Die Special)
J.R. Williams Bullet Co.
James Calhoon Mfg.
James Calhoon Varmint Bullets
Jamison International
Jensen Bullets
Jensen's Firearms Academy
Jericho Tool & Die Co., Inc.
Jester Bullets
JLK Bullets
JRP Custom Bullets
Ka Pu Kapili
Kaswer Custom, Inc.
Keith's Bullets
Keng's Firearms Specialty, Inc./US Tactical Systems
Ken's Kustom Kartridges
Kent Cartridge Mfg. Co. Ltd.
KLA Enterprises
Knight Rifles
Knight Rifles (See Modern Muzzle Loading, Inc.)
Lapua Ltd.
Lawrence Brand Shot (See Precision Reloading)
Legend Products Corp.
Liberty Shooting Supplies
Lightning Performance Innovations, Inc.

Lindsley Arms Cartridge Co.
Littleton, J. F.
Lomont Precision Bullets
Lyman Products Corp.
Magnus Bullets
Maine Custom Bullets
Maionchi-L.M.I.
Marchmon Bullets
Markesbery Muzzle Loaders, Inc.
MarMik, Inc.
Marshall Fish Mfg. Gunsmith Sptg. Co.
MAST Technology, Inc.
McMurdo, Lynn (See Specialty Gunsmithing)
Meister Bullets (See Gander Mountain)
Men-Metallwerk Elisenhuette GmbH
Merkuria Ltd.
Michael's Antiques
Midway Arms, Inc.
Mitchell Bullets, R.F.
MI-TE Bullets
Montana Precision Swaging
Mountain State Muzzleloading Supplies, Inc.
Mulhern, Rick
Murmur Corp.
Nagel's Custom Bullets
National Bullet Co.
Naval Ordnance Works
North American Shooting Systems
North Devon Firearms Services
Northern Precision Custom Swaged Bullets
Nosler, Inc.
OK Weber, Inc.
Oklahoma Ammunition Co.
Old Wagon Bullets
Oregon Trail Bullet Company
Pacific Cartridge, Inc.
Pacific Rifle Co.
Page Custom Bullets
Pease Accuracy
Penn Bullets
Peterson Gun Shop, Inc., A.W.
Petro-Explo Inc.
Phillippi Custom Bullets, Justin
Pinetree Bullets
PMC/Eldorado Cartridge Corp.
Polywad, Inc.
Pony Express Reloaders
Power Plus Enterprises, Inc.
Precision Delta Corp.
Prescott Projectile Co.
Price Bullets, Patrick W.
PRL Bullets, c/o Blackburn Enterprises
Professional Hunter Supplies (See Star Custom Bullets)
Proofmark Corp.
R.I.S. Co., Inc.
Rainier Ballistics Corp.
Ramon B. Gonzalez Guns
Ravell Ltd.
Redwood Bullet Works
Reloading Specialties, Inc.
Remington Arms Co., Inc.
Rhino
Robinson H.V. Bullets
Rubright Bullets
Russ Haydon's Shooters' Supply
SAECO (See Redding Reloading Equipment)
Scharch Mfg., Inc.-Top Brass
Schneider Bullets
Schroeder Bullets
Schumakers Gun Shop
Scot Powder
Seebeck Assoc., R.E.
Shappy Bullets
Sharps Arms Co., Inc., C.
Shilen, Inc.
Sierra Bullets
SOS Products Co. (See Buck Stix-SOS Products Co.)

Southern Ammunition Co., Inc.
Specialty Gunsmithing
Speer Bullets
Spencer's Rifle Barrels, Inc.
SSK Industries
Stanley Bullets
Star Ammunition, Inc.
Star Custom Bullets
Starke Bullet Company
Starline, Inc.
Stewart's Gunsmithing
Swift Bullet Co.
T.F.C. S.p.A.
Taracorp Industries, Inc.
Tar-Hunt Custom Rifles, Inc.
TCCI
TCSR
The A.W. Peterson Gun Shop, Inc.
The Gun Works
The Ordnance Works
Thompson Bullet Lube Co.
Thompson Precision
TMI Products (See Haselbauer Products, Jerry)
Traditions Performance Firearms
Trico Plastics
True Flight Bullet Co.
Tucson Mold, Inc.
Unmussig Bullets, D. L.
USAC
Vann Custom Bullets
Vihtavuori Oy/Kaltron-Pettibone
Vincent's Shop
Viper Bullet and Brass Works
Walters Wads
Warren Muzzleloading Co., Inc.
Watson Trophy Match Bullets
Weatherby, Inc.
Western Nevada West Coast Bullets
Widener's Reloading & Shooting Supply, Inc.
Winchester Div. Olin Corp.
Winkle Bullets
Woodleigh (See Huntington Die Specialties)
Worthy Products, Inc.
Wyant Bullets
Wyoming Custom Bullets
Zero Ammunition Co., Inc.

AMMUNITION, COMMERCIAL

3-Ten Corp.
A.W. Peterson Gun Shop, Inc.
Ace Custom 45's, Inc.
Ad Hominem
Air Arms
American Ammunition
Arizona Ammunition, Inc.
Arms Corporation of the Philippines
Arundel Arms & Ammunition, Inc., A.
A-Square Co.
Atlantic Rose, Inc.
Badger Shooters Supply, Inc.
Ballistic Product, Inc.
Ben William's Gun Shop
Benjamin/Sheridan Co., Crosman
Big Bear Arms & Sporting Goods, Inc.
Black Hills Ammunition, Inc.
Blammo Ammo
Blount, Inc., Sporting Equipment Div.
Brenneke GmbH
Buffalo Bullet Co., Inc.
Bull-X, Inc.
Cabela's
Cambos Outdoorsman
Casull Arms Corp.
CBC
Champion's Choice, Inc.
Cor-Bon Inc./Glaser LLC

Crosman Airguns
Cubic Shot Shell Co., Inc.
Daisy Outdoor Products
Dead Eye's Sport Center
Delta Arms Ltd.
Delta Frangible Ammunition LLC
Dynamit Nobel-RWS, Inc.
Effebi SNC-Dr. Franco Beretta
Eley Ltd.
Elite Ammunition
Estate Cartridge, Inc.
Federal Cartridge Co.
Fiocchi of America, Inc.
Garcia National Gun Traders, Inc.
Garrett Cartridges, Inc.
Garthwaite Pistolsmith, Inc., Jim
Gibbs Rifle Co., Inc.
Gil Hebard Guns Inc.
Glaser LLC
Glaser Safety Slug, Inc.
GOEX, Inc.
Goodwin's Gun Shop
Gun City
Hansen & Co.
Hart & Son, Inc.
Hi-Performance Ammunition Company
Hirtenberger AG
Hornady Mfg. Co.
Hunters Supply, Inc.
Intercontinental Distributors, Ltd.
Ion Industries, Inc.
Keng's Firearms Specialty, Inc./US Tactical Systems
Kent Cartridge America, Inc.
Kent Cartridge Mfg. Co. Ltd.
Knight Rifles
Lapua Ltd.
Lethal Force Institute (See Police Bookshelf)
Lock's Philadelphia Gun Exchange
Magnum Research, Inc.
MagSafe Ammo Co.
Magtech Ammunition Co. Inc.
Maionchi-L.M.I.
Mandall Shooting Supplies Inc.
Markell,Inc.
Marshall Fish Mfg. Gunsmith Sptg. Co.
McBros Rifle Co.
Men-Metallwerk Elisenhuette GmbH
Mullins Ammunition
New England Ammunition Co.
Oklahoma Ammunition Co.
Omark Industries, Div. of Blount, Inc.
Outdoor Sports Headquarters, Inc.
P.S.M.G. Gun Co.
Pacific Cartridge, Inc.
Paragon Sales & Services, Inc.
Parker & Sons Shooting Supply
Parker Gun Finishes
Peterson Gun Shop, Inc., A.W.
PMC/Eldorado Cartridge Corp.
Police Bookshelf
Polywad, Inc.
Pony Express Reloaders
Precision Delta Corp.
Pro Load Ammunition, Inc.
R.E.I.
Ravell Ltd.
Remington Arms Co., Inc.
Rucker Dist. Inc.
RWS (See US Importer-Dynamit Nobel-RWS, Inc.)
Sellier & Bellot, USA Inc.
Southern Ammunition Co., Inc.
Speer Bullets
TCCI
The A.W. Peterson Gun Shop, Inc.
The BulletMakers Workshop
The Gun Room Press
The Gun Works
Thompson Bullet Lube Co.
USAC
VAM Distribution Co. LLC

Victory USA
Vihtavuori Oy/Kaltron-Pettibone
Visible Impact Targets
Voere-KGH GmbH
Weatherby, Inc.
Westley Richards & Co.
Whitestone Lumber Corp.
Widener's Reloading & Shooting Supply, Inc.
William E. Phillips Firearms
Winchester Div. Olin Corp.
Zero Ammunition Co., Inc.

AMMUNITION, CUSTOM

3-Ten Corp.
A.W. Peterson Gun Shop, Inc.
Accuracy Unlimited
AFSCO Ammunition
Allred Bullet Co.
American Derringer Corp.
American Products, Inc.
Arizona Ammunition, Inc.
Arms Corporation of the Philippines
Atlantic Rose, Inc.
Ballard Rifle & Cartridge Co., LLC
Bear Arms
Belding's Custom Gun Shop
Berger Bullets Ltd.
Big Bore Bullets of Alaska
Black Hills Ammunition, Inc.
Blue Mountain Bullets
Brynin, Milton
Buckskin Bullet Co.
CBC
CFVentures
Champlin Firearms, Inc.
Cubic Shot Shell Co., Inc.
Custom Tackle and Ammo
Dakota Arms, Inc.
Dead Eye's Sport Center
Delta Frangible Ammunition LLC
DKT, Inc.
Elite Ammunition
Estate Cartridge, Inc.
GDL Enterprises
GOEX, Inc.
Grayback Wildcats
Hirtenberger AG
Hobson Precision Mfg. Co.
Horizons Unlimited
Hornady Mfg. Co.
Hunters Supply, Inc.
James Calhoon Mfg.
James Calhoon Varmint Bullets
Jensen Bullets
Jensen's Custom Ammunition
Jensen's Firearms Academy
Kaswer Custom, Inc.
Kent Cartridge Mfg. Co. Ltd.
L. E. Jurras & Assoc.
L.A.R. Mfg., Inc.
Lethal Force Institute (See Police Bookshelf)
Lindsley Arms Cartridge Co.
Linebaugh Custom Sixguns
Loch Leven Industries/Convert-A-Pell
MagSafe Ammo Co.
MAST Technology, Inc.
McBros Rifle Co.
McMurdo, Lynn (See Specialty Gunsmithing)
Men-Metallwerk Elisenhuette GmbH
Milstor Corp.
Mullins Ammunition
Oklahoma Ammunition Co.
P.S.M.G. Gun Co.
Peterson Gun Shop, Inc., A.W.
Phillippi Custom Bullets, Justin
Police Bookshelf
Power Plus Enterprises, Inc.
Precision Delta Corp.

Professional Hunter Supplies (See Star Custom Bullets)
R.E.I.
Ramon B. Gonzalez Guns
Sandia Die & Cartridge Co.
SOS Products Co. (See Buck Stix-SOS Products Co.)
Specialty Gunsmithing
Spencer's Rifle Barrels, Inc.
SSK Industries
Star Custom Bullets
Stewart's Gunsmithing
The A.W. Peterson Gun Shop, Inc.
The BulletMakers Workshop
The Country Armourer
Unmussig Bullets, D. L.
Vitt/Boos
Vulpes Ventures, Inc. Fox Cartridge Division
Warren Muzzleloading Co., Inc.
Watson Trophy Match Bullets
Worthy Products, Inc.
Zero Ammunition Co., Inc.

AMMUNITION, FOREIGN

A.W. Peterson Gun Shop, Inc.
Ad Hominem
AFSCO Ammunition
Armscorp USA, Inc.
Atlantic Rose, Inc.
B&P America
Beeman Precision Airguns
Cape Outfitters
CBC
Cheddite, France S.A.
Cubic Shot Shell Co., Inc.
Dead Eye's Sport Center
DKT, Inc.
Dynamit Nobel-RWS, Inc.
E. Arthur Brown Co.
Fiocchi of America, Inc.
First Inc., Jack
Gamebore Division, Polywad Inc.
Gibbs Rifle Co., Inc.
GOEX, Inc.
Goodwin's Gun Shop
Gunsmithing, Inc.
Hansen & Co.
Heidenstrom Bullets
Hirtenberger AG
Hornady Mfg. Co.
I.S.S.
Intrac Arms International
K.B.I. Inc.
MagSafe Ammo Co.
Maionchi-L.M.I.
Mandall Shooting Supplies Inc.
Marksman Products
MAST Technology, Inc.
Merkuria Ltd.
Mullins Ammunition
Navy Arms Company
Oklahoma Ammunition Co.
P.S.M.G. Gun Co.
Paragon Sales & Services, Inc.
Peterson Gun Shop, Inc., A.W.
Petro-Explo Inc.
Precision Delta Corp.
R.E.T. Enterprises
Ramon B. Gonzalez Guns
RWS (See US Importer-Dynamit Nobel-RWS, Inc.)
Samco Global Arms, Inc.
Sentinel Arms
Southern Ammunition Co., Inc.
Speer Bullets
Stratco, Inc.
T.F.C. S.p.A.
The A.W. Peterson Gun Shop, Inc.
The BulletMakers Workshop
The Paul Co.
Victory Ammunition
Vihtavuori Oy/Kaltron-Pettibone
Vulpes Ventures, Inc. Fox Cartridge Division

Wolf Performance Ammunition

ANTIQUE ARMS DEALER

Ackerman & Co.
Ad Hominem
Antique American Firearms
Antique Arms Co.
Aplan Antiques & Art, James O.
Armoury, Inc., The
Arundel Arms & Ammunition, Inc., A.
Ballard Rifle & Cartridge Co., LLC
Bear Mountain Gun & Tool
Bob's Tactical Indoor Shooting Range & Gun Shop
Buffalo Arms Co.
Cape Outfitters
Carlson, Douglas R, Antique American Firearms
CBC-BRAZIL
Chadick's Ltd.
Chambers Flintlocks Ltd., Jim
Champlin Firearms, Inc.
Chuck's Gun Shop
Clements' Custom Leathercraft, Chas
Cole's Gun Works
D&D Gunsmiths, Ltd.
David R. Chicoine
Dixie Gun Works
Dixon Muzzleloading Shop, Inc.
Duffy, Charles E (See Guns Antique & Modern DBA)
Ed's Gun House
Enguix Import-Export
Fagan & Co.Inc
Flayderman & Co., Inc.
Fulmer's Antique Firearms, Chet
George Madis Winchester Consultants
Getz Barrel Co.
Glass, Herb
Goergen's Gun Shop, Inc.
Golden Age Arms Co.
Goodwin's Gun Shop
Gun Hunter Books (See Gun Hunter Trading Co.)
Gun Hunter Trading Co.
Guns Antique & Modern DBA / Charles E. Duffy
Hallowell & Co.
Hammans, Charles E.
HandCrafts Unltd (See Clements' Custom Leather)
Handgun Press
Hansen & Co.
Hunkeler, A (See Buckskin Machine Works
Imperial Miniature Armory
James Wayne Firearms for Collectors and Investors
Kelley's
Knight's Mfg. Co.
Ledbetter Airguns, Riley
LeFever Arms Co., Inc.
Lever Arms Service Ltd.
Lock's Philadelphia Gun Exchange
Log Cabin Sport Shop
Logdewood Mfg.
Mandall Shooting Supplies Inc.
Marshall Fish Mfg. Gunsmith Sptg. Co.
Martin's Gun Shop
Michael's Antiques
Mid-America Recreation, Inc.
Montana Outfitters, Lewis E. Yearout
Muzzleloaders Etcetera, Inc.
Navy Arms Company
New England Arms Co.
Olathe Gun Shop
Peter Dyson & Son Ltd.
Pony Express Sport Shop
Powder Horn Ltd.
Ravell Ltd.

Reno, Wayne
Retting, Inc., Martin B
Robert Valade Engraving
Rutgers Book Center
Samco Global Arms, Inc.
Sarco, Inc.
Scott Fine Guns Inc., Thad
Shootin' Shack
Sportsmen's Exchange & Western Gun Traders, Inc.
Steves House of Guns
Stott's Creek Armory, Inc.
The Gun Room
The Gun Room Press
The Gun Works
Turnbull Restoration, Doug
Vic's Gun Refinishing
Vintage Arms, Inc.
Wallace, Terry
Westley Richards & Co.
Wild West Guns
William Fagan & Co.
Winchester Sutler, Inc., The
Wood, Frank (See Classic Guns, Inc.)
Yearout, Lewis E. (See Montana Outfitters)

APPRAISER - GUNS, ETC.

A.W. Peterson Gun Shop, Inc.
Ackerman & Co.
Antique Arms Co.
Armoury, Inc., The
Arundel Arms & Ammunition, Inc., A.
Barta's Gunsmithing
Beitzinger, George
Blue Book Publications, Inc.
Bob's Tactical Indoor Shooting Range & Gun Shop
Bullet N Press
Butterfield's
Cape Outfitters
Chadick's Ltd.
Champlin Firearms, Inc.
Christie's East
Chuilli, Stephen
Clark Firearms Engraving
Clements' Custom Leathercraft, Chas
Cole's Gun Works
Colonial Arms, Inc.
Colonial Repair
Corry, John
Custom Tackle and Ammo
D&D Gunsmiths, Ltd.
David R. Chicoine
DGR Custom Rifles
Dietz Gun Shop & Range, Inc.
Dixie Gun Works
Dixon Muzzleloading Shop, Inc.
Duane's Gun Repair (See DGR Custom Rifles)
Ed's Gun House
Eversull Co., Inc.
Fagan & Co.Inc
Ferris Firearms
Flayderman & Co., Inc.
Forty Five Ranch Enterprises
Francotte & Cie S.A. Auguste
Frontier Arms Co.,Inc.
Gene's Custom Guns
George E. Mathews & Son, Inc.
George Madis Winchester Consultants
Gerald Pettinger Books (See Pettinger Books)
Getz Barrel Co.
Gillmann, Edwin
Gilmore Sports Concepts
Goergen's Gun Shop, Inc.
Golden Age Arms Co.
Goodwin's Gun Shop
Griffin & Howe, Inc.

Griffin & Howe, Inc.
Griffin & Howe, Inc.
Groenewold, John
Gun City
Gun Hunter Books (See Gun Hunter Trading Co.)
Gun Hunter Trading Co.
Guncraft Books (See Guncraft Sports Inc.)
Guncraft Sports Inc.
Gunsmithing, Inc.
Hallowell & Co.
Hammans, Charles E.
HandCrafts Unltd (See Clements' Custom Leather)
Handgun Press
Hank's Gun Shop
Hansen & Co.
Irwin, Campbell H.
Island Pond Gun Shop
Ithaca Classic Doubles
Jackalope Gun Shop
James Wayne Firearms for Collectors and Investors
Jensen's Custom Ammunition
Kelley's
L.L. Bean, Inc.
Lampert, Ron
LaRocca Gun Works
Ledbetter Airguns, Riley
LeFever Arms Co., Inc.
Lock's Philadelphia Gun Exchange
Log Cabin Sport Shop
Logdewood Mfg.
Lomont Precision Bullets
Long, George F.
Mahony, Philip Bruce
Mandall Shooting Supplies Inc.
Marshall Fish Mfg. Gunsmith Sptg. Co.
Martin's Gun Shop
Mathews & Son, Inc., George E.
McCann Industries
McCann's Machine & Gun Shop
Mercer Custom Guns
Montana Outfitters, Lewis E. Yearout
Muzzleloaders Etcetera, Inc.
Navy Arms Company
New England Arms Co.
Nitex Gun Shop
Olathe Gun Shop
P&M Sales & Services, LLC
Pasadena Gun Center
Pentheny de Pentheny
Peterson Gun Shop, Inc., A.W.
Pettinger Books, Gerald
Pony Express Sport Shop
Powder Horn Ltd.
R.A. Wells Custom Gunsmith
R.E.T. Enterprises
Ramon B. Gonzalez Guns
Retting, Inc., Martin B
Robert Valade Engraving
Rutgers Book Center
Scott Fine Guns Inc., Thad
Shootin' Shack
Spencer Reblue Service
Sportsmen's Exchange & Western Gun Traders, Inc.
Steven Dodd Hughes
Stott's Creek Armory, Inc.
Stratco, Inc.
Ten-Ring Precision, Inc.
The A.W. Peterson Gun Shop, Inc.
The Gun Room Press
The Gun Shop
The Gun Works
The Orvis Co.
The Swampfire Shop (See Peterson Gun Shop, Inc.)
Thurston Sports, Inc.
Vic's Gun Refinishing
Walker Arms Co., Inc.
Wallace, Terry
Wasmundt, Jim

Weber & Markin Custom Gunsmiths
Werth, T. W.
Whildin & Sons Ltd, E.H.
Whitestone Lumber Corp.
Wichita Arms, Inc.
Wild West Guns
William Fagan & Co.
Williams Shootin' Iron Service, The Lynx-Line
Winchester Sutler, Inc., The
Wood, Frank (See Classic Guns, Inc.)
Yearout, Lewis E. (See Montana Outfitters)

AUCTIONEER - GUNS, ETC.

'Little John's" Antique Arms
Buck Stix-SOS Products Co.
Butterfield's
Christie's East
Fagan & Co.Inc
Sotheby's

BOOKS & MANUALS (PUBLISHERS & DEALERS)

"Su-Press-On", Inc.
Alpha 1 Drop Zone
American Handgunner Magazine
Armory Publications
Arms & Armour Press
Ballistic Product, Inc.
Ballistic Product, Inc.
Barnes Bullets, Inc.
Bauska Barrels
Beartooth Bullets
Beeman Precision Airguns
Blacksmith Corp.
Blacktail Mountain Books
Blue Book Publications, Inc.
Blue Ridge Machinery & Tools, Inc.
Boone's Custom Ivory Grips, Inc.
Brown Co., E. Arthur
Brownells, Inc.
Bullet N Press
C. Sharps Arms Co. Inc./Montana Armory
Cape Outfitters
Cheyenne Pioneer Products
Colonial Repair
Corbin Mfg. & Supply, Inc.
DBI Books Division of Krause Publications
deHaas Barrels
Dixon Muzzleloading Shop, Inc.
Excalibur Publications
Executive Protection Institute
Galati International
Gerald Pettinger Books (See Pettinger Books)
Golden Age Arms Co.
Gun City
Gun List (See Krause Publications)
Guncraft Books (See Guncraft Sports Inc.)
Guncraft Sports Inc.
Gunnerman Books
GUNS Magazine
Gunsmithing, Inc.
H&P Publishing
Handgun Press
Harris Publications
Hawk Laboratories, Inc. (See Hawk, Inc.)
Hawk, Inc.
Heritage/VSP Gun Books
Hodgdon Powder Co.
Home Shop Machinist, The Village Press Publications
Hornady Mfg. Co.
Huntington Die Specialties

I.D.S.A. Books
Info-Arm
Ironside International Publishers, Inc.
Jantz Supply
Kelley's
King & Co.
Koval Knives
Krause Publications, Inc.
L.B.T.
Lapua Ltd.
Lebeau-Courally
Lethal Force Institute (See Police Bookshelf)
Lyman Products Corp.
Madis Books
Magma Engineering Co.
Mandall Shooting Supplies Inc.
MarMik, Inc.
Montana Armory, Inc .(See C. Sharps Arms Co. Inc.)
Mountain South
Mountain State Muzzleloading Supplies, Inc.
Mulberry House Publishing
Navy Arms Company
Numrich Gun Parts Corporation
OK Weber, Inc.
Outdoor Sports Headquarters, Inc.
Paintball Games International Magazine Aceville
Pejsa Ballistics
Petersen Publishing Co.
Pettinger Books, Gerald
PFRB Co.
Police Bookshelf
Precision Shooting, Inc.
Professional Hunter Supplies (See Star Custom Bullets)
Ravell Ltd.
Ray Riling Arms Books Co.
Remington Double Shotguns
Russ Haydon's Shooters' Supply
Rutgers Book Center
S&S Firearms
Safari Press, Inc.
Saunders Gun & Machine Shop
Scharch Mfg., Inc.-Top Brass
Scharch Mfg., Inc.-Top Brass
Semmer, Charles (See Remington Double Shotguns)
Sharps Arms Co., Inc., C.
Shotgun Sports Magazine, dba Shootin' Accessories Ltd.
Sierra Bullets
Speer Bullets
SPG LLC
Stackpole Books
Star Custom Bullets
Stewart Game Calls, Inc., Johnny
Stoeger Industries
Stoeger Publishing Co. (See Stoeger Industries)
Swift Bullet Co.
The A.W. Peterson Gun Shop, Inc.
The Gun Room Press
The Gun Works
The NgraveR Co.
Thomas, Charles C.
Track of the Wolf, Inc.
Trafalgar Square
Trotman, Ken
Tru-Balance Knife Co.
Vega Tool Co.
Vintage Industries, Inc.
VSP Publishers (See Heritage/VSP Gun Books)
W.E. Brownell Checkering Tools
WAMCO-New Mexico
Wells Creek Knife & Gun Works
Wilderness Sound Products Ltd.
Williams Gun Sight Co.
Wolfe Publishing Co.
Wolf's Western Traders

BULLET CASTING, ACCESSORIES

Ballisti-Cast, Inc.
Buffalo Arms Co.
Bullet Metals
Cast Performance Bullet Company
CFVentures
Cooper-Woodward
Davide Pedersoli and Co.
Ferguson, Bill
Huntington Die Specialties
Lee Precision, Inc.
Lithi Bee Bullet Lube
Lyman Products Corp.
Magma Engineering Co.
Ox-Yoke Originals, Inc.
Rapine Bullet Mould Mfg. Co.
SPG LLC
The A.W. Peterson Gun Shop, Inc.
The Hanned Line
United States Products Co.

BULLET CASTING, FURNACES & POTS

Ballisti-Cast, Inc.
Buffalo Arms Co.
Bullet Metals
Ferguson, Bill
GAR
Lee Precision, Inc.
Lyman Products Corp.
Magma Engineering Co.
Rapine Bullet Mould Mfg. Co.
RCBS/ATK
The A.W. Peterson Gun Shop, Inc.
The Gun Works
Thompson Bullet Lube Co.

BULLET CASTING, LEAD

Action Bullets & Alloy Inc.
Ames Metal Products
Belltown Ltd.
Buckskin Bullet Co.
Buffalo Arms Co.
Bullet Metals
Bullseye Bullets
Hunters Supply, Inc.
Jericho Tool & Die Co., Inc.
Lee Precision, Inc.
Lithi Bee Bullet Lube
Magma Engineering Co.
Montana Precision Swaging
Ox-Yoke Originals, Inc.
Penn Bullets
Proofmark Corp.
SPG LLC
Splitfire Sporting Goods, L.L.C.
The A.W. Peterson Gun Shop, Inc.
The Gun Works
Walters Wads

BULLET PULLERS

Battenfeld Technologies
Davide Pedersoli and Co.
Hollywood Engineering
Huntington Die Specialties
Royal Arms Gunstocks
The A.W. Peterson Gun Shop, Inc.
The Gun Works

BULLET TOOLS

Brynin, Milton
Camdex, Inc.
Corbin Mfg. & Supply, Inc.
Cumberland Arms
Eagan, Donald V.
Holland's Gunsmithing
Hollywood Engineering
Lee Precision, Inc.

Niemi Engineering, W. B.
North Devon Firearms Services
Rorschach Precision Products
Sport Flite Manufacturing Co.
The A.W. Peterson Gun Shop, Inc.
The Hanned Line
WTA Manufacturing

BULLET, CASE & DIE LUBRICANTS

Beartooth Bullets
Bonanza (See Forster Products)
Brown Co., E. Arthur
Buckskin Bullet Co.
Buffalo Arms Co.
Camp-Cap Products
CFVentures
Cooper-Woodward
CVA
E-Z-Way Systems
Ferguson, Bill
Forster Products
GAR
Guardsman Products
Heidenstrom Bullets
Hollywood Engineering
Hornady Mfg. Co.
Imperial (See E-Z-Way Systems)
Knoell, Doug
L.B.T.
Le Clear Industries (See E-Z-Way Systems)
Lee Precision, Inc.
Lithi Bee Bullet Lube
MI-TE Bullets
Paco's (See Small Custom Mould & Bullet Co.)
RCBS Operations/ATK
Reardon Products
Rooster Laboratories
Shay's Gunsmithing
Small Custom Mould & Bullet Co.
Tamarack Products, Inc.
The Hanned Line
Uncle Mike's (See Michaels of Oregon Co.)
Warren Muzzleloading Co., Inc.
Widener's Reloading & Shooting Supply, Inc.
Young Country Arms

CARTRIDGES FOR COLLECTORS

Ackerman & Co.
Ad Hominem
Armory Publications
Cameron's
Campbell, Dick
Cartridge Transfer Group, Pete de Coux
Cherry Creek State Park Shooting Center
Cole's Gun Works
Colonial Repair
Cubic Shot Shell Co., Inc.
de Coux, Pete (See Cartridge Transfer Group)
Duane's Gun Repair (See DGR Custom Rifles)
Ed's Gun House
Ed's Gun House
Enguix Import-Export
Epps, Ellwood/Isabella
First Inc., Jack
Forty Five Ranch Enterprises
George Madis Winchester Consultants
Goergen's Gun Shop, Inc.
Goodwin's Gun Shop
Grayback Wildcats
Gun City
Gun Hunter Books (See Gun Hunter Trading Co.)

Gun Hunter Trading Co.
Jack First, Inc.
Kelley's
Liberty Shooting Supplies
Mandall Shooting Supplies Inc.
MAST Technology, Inc.
Michael's Antiques
Montana Outfitters, Lewis E. Yearout
Numrich Gun Parts Corporation
Pasadena Gun Center
Samco Global Arms, Inc.
SOS Products Co. (See Buck Stix-SOS Products Co.)
Stone Enterprises Ltd.
The Country Armourer
The Gun Room Press
Ward & Van Valkenburg
Yearout, Lewis E. (See Montana Outfitters)

CASE & AMMUNITION PROCESSORS, INSPECTORS, BOXERS

Ammo Load, Inc.
Ben's Machines
Hafner World Wide, Inc.
Scharch Mfg., Inc.-Top Brass
The A.W. Peterson Gun Shop, Inc.

CASE CLEANERS & POLISHING MEDIA

Battenfeld Technologies
Belltown Ltd.
Buffalo Arms Co.
G96 Products Co., Inc.
Huntington Die Specialties
Lee Precision, Inc.
Penn Bullets
The A.W. Peterson Gun Shop, Inc.
The Gun Works
Tru-Square Metal Products Inc.
VibraShine, Inc.

CASE PREPARATION TOOLS

Battenfeld Technologies
CONKKO
High Precision
Hoehn Sales, Inc.
Huntington Die Specialties
J. Dewey Mfg. Co., Inc.
K&M Services
Lee Precision, Inc.
Match Prep-Doyle Gracey
Plum City Ballistic Range
RCBS Operations/ATK
Russ Haydon's Shooters' Supply
Sinclair International, Inc.
Stoney Point Products, Inc.
The A.W. Peterson Gun Shop, Inc.

CASE TRIMMERS, TRIM DIES & ACCESSORIES

Buffalo Arms Co.
Creedmoor Sports, Inc.
Fremont Tool Works
Goodwin's Gun Shop
Hollywood Engineering
K&M Services
Lyman Products Corp.
Match Prep-Doyle Gracey
OK Weber, Inc.
Ozark Gun Works
RCBS/ATK
Redding Reloading Equipment
The A.W. Peterson Gun Shop, Inc.
Time Precision

REFERENCE

PRODUCT & SERVICE DIRECTORY

CASE TUMBLERS, VIBRATORS, MEDIA & ACCESSORIES

4-D Custom Die Co.
Battenfeld Technologies
Berry's Mfg., Inc.
Dillon Precision Products, Inc.
Goodwin's Gun Shop
Penn Bullets
Raytech Div. of Lyman Products Corp.
The A.W. Peterson Gun Shop, Inc.
Tru-Square Metal Products Inc.
VibraShine, Inc.

CASES, CABINETS, RACKS & SAFES - GUN

All Rite Products, Inc.
Allen Co., Bob
Allen Co., Inc.
Allen Sportswear, Bob (See Allen Co., Bob)
Alumna Sport by Dee Zee
American Display Co.
American Security Products Co.
Americase
Art Jewel Enterprises Ltd.
Ashby Turkey Calls
Bagmaster Mfg., Inc.
Barramundi Corp.
Berry's Mfg., Inc.
Big Spring Enterprises "Bore Stores"
Bill's Custom Cases
Bison Studios
Black Sheep Brand
Brauer Bros.
Brown, H. R. (See Silhouette Leathers)
Browning Arms Co.
Bushmaster Hunting & Fishing
Cannon Safe, Inc.
Chipmunk (See Oregon Arms, Inc.)
Cobalt Mfg., Inc.
CONKKO
Connecticut Shotgun Mfg. Co.
D&L Industries (See D.J. Marketing)
D.J. Marketing
Dara-Nes, Inc. (See Nesci Enterprises, Inc.)
Deepeeka Exports Pvt. Ltd.
Doskocil Mfg. Co., Inc.
DTM International, Inc.
EMF Co., Inc.
English, Inc., A.G.
Enhanced Presentations, Inc.
Eversull Co., Inc.
Fort Knox Security Products
Freedom Arms, Inc.
Frontier Safe Co.
Galati International
GALCO International Ltd.
Gun-Ho Sports Cases
Hall Plastics, Inc., John
Hastings
Homak
Hoppe's Div. Penguin Industries, Inc.
Hunter Co., Inc.
Hydrosorbent Products
Impact Case & Container, Inc.
Johanssons Vapentillbehor, Bert
Johnston Bros. (See C&T Corp. TA Johnson Brothers)
Kalispel Case Line
Kane Products, Inc.
KK Air International (See Impact Case & Container Co.)
Knock on Wood Antiques
Kolpin Mfg., Inc.
Lakewood Products LLC
Liberty Safe

Mandall Shooting Supplies Inc.
Marsh, Mike
McWelco Products
Morton Booth Co.
MPC
MTM Molded Products Co., Inc.
Nalpak
Necessary Concepts, Inc.
Nesci Enterprises Inc.
Oregon Arms, Inc. (See Rogue Rifle Co., Inc.)
Outa-Site Gun Carriers
Pflumm Mfg. Co.
Poburka, Philip (See Bison Studios)
Powell & Son (Gunmakers) Ltd., William
Protektor Model
Prototech Industries, Inc.
Rogue Rifle Co., Inc.
Schulz Industries
Southern Security
Sportsman's Communicators
Sun Welding Safe Co.
Sweet Home, Inc.
Talmage, William G.
The Outdoor Connection, Inc.
The Surecase Co.
Tinks & Ben Lee Hunting Products (See Wellington)
Trulock Tool
Universal Sports
W. Waller & Son, Inc.
Whitestone Lumber Corp.
Wilson Case, Inc.
Woodstream
Zanotti Armor, Inc.
Ziegel Engineering

CHOKE DEVICES, RECOIL ABSORBERS & RECOIL PADS

3-Ten Corp.
Action Products, Inc.
Allen Co., Bob
Allen Sportswear, Bob (See Allen Co., Bob)
Answer Products Co.
Arms Ingenuity Co.
Baer Custom Inc., Les
Bansner's Ultimate Rifles, LLC
Bartlett Engineering
Battenfeld Technologies
Briley Mfg. Inc.
Brooks Tactical Systems-Agrip
Brownells, Inc.
B-Square Company, Inc.
Buffer Technologies
Bull Mountain Rifle Co.
C&H Research
Cation
Chicasaw Gun Works
Clearview Products
Colonial Arms, Inc.
Connecticut Shotgun Mfg. Co.
CRR, Inc./Marble's Inc.
Danuser Machine Co.
Dina Arms Corporation
Gentry Custom Gunmaker, David
Goodwin's Gun Shop
Graybill's Gun Shop
Gruning Precision Inc.
Harry Lawson Co.
Hastings
Haydel's Game Calls, Inc.
Hogue Grips
Holland's Gunsmithing
I.N.C. Inc (See Kickeez I.N.C., Inc.)
J.P. Enterprises Inc.
Jackalope Gun Shop
Jenkins Recoil Pads, Inc.
KDF, Inc.
Kickeez I.N.C., Inc.
Lawson Co., Harry
London Guns Ltd.

Lyman Products Corp.
Mag-Na-Port International, Inc.
Mandall Shooting Supplies Inc.
Marble Arms (See CRR, Inc./Marble's Inc.)
Menck, Gunsmith Inc., T.W.
Middlebrooks Custom Shop
Morrow, Bud
Nelson/Weather-Rite, Inc.
One Of A Kind
Original Box, Inc.
P.S.M.G. Gun Co.
Palsa Outdoor Products
Parker & Sons Shooting Supply
Pro-Port Ltd.
Que Industries, Inc.
Shotguns Unlimited
Simmons Gun Repair, Inc.
Sound Technology
Stan Baker Sports
Stone Enterprises Ltd.
The A.W. Peterson Gun Shop, Inc.
Truglo, Inc.
Trulock Tool
Uncle Mike's (See Michaels of Oregon Co.)
Universal Sports
Virgin Valley Custom Guns
Vortek Products, Inc.
Williams Gun Sight Co.
Wilsom Combat
Wise Guns, Dale

CHRONOGRAPHS & PRESSURE TOOLS

Air Rifle Specialists
Brown Co., E. Arthur
C.W. Erickson's L.L.C.
Canons Delcour
Clearview Products
Competition Electronics, Inc.
Custom Chronograph, Inc.
D&H Precision Tooling
Hege Jagd-u. Sporthandels GmbH
Hutton Rifle Ranch
Kent Cartridge Mfg. Co. Ltd.
Mac-1 Airgun Distributors
Oehler Research,Inc.
P.A.C.T., Inc.
Romain's Custom Guns, Inc.
Savage Arms, Inc.
Stratco, Inc.
Tepeco

CLEANERS & DEGREASERS

Barnes Bullets, Inc.
Belltown Ltd.
Camp-Cap Products
G96 Products Co., Inc.
Goodwin's Gun Shop
Hafner World Wide, Inc.
Half Moon Rifle Shop
Kleen-Bore,Inc.
LEM Gun Specialties, Inc. The Lewis Lead Remover
Modern Muzzleloading, Inc.
Northern Precision Custom Swaged Bullets
Parker & Sons Shooting Supply
Parker Gun Finishes
Perazone-Gunsmith, Brian
PrOlixr Lubricants
R&S Industries Corp.
Ramon B. Gonzalez Guns
Rusteprufe Laboratories
Sheffield Knifemakers Supply, Inc.
Shooter's Choice Gun Care
Sierra Specialty Prod. Co.
Spencer's Rifle Barrels, Inc.
The A.W. Peterson Gun Shop, Inc.
The Gun Works
United States Products Co.

CLEANING & REFINISHING SUPPLIES

AC Dyna-tite Corp.
Alpha 1 Drop Zone
American Gas & Chemical Co., Ltd
Answer Products Co.
Armite Laboratories
Atlantic Mills, Inc.
Atsko/Sno-Seal, Inc.
Barnes Bullets, Inc.
Battenfeld Technologies
Beeman Precision Airguns
Belltown Ltd.
Bill's Gun Repair
Birchwood Casey
Blount, Inc., Sporting Equipment Div.
Blount/Outers ATK
Blue and Gray Products Inc. (See Ox-Yoke Originals)
Break-Free, Inc.
Bridgers Best
Brown Co., E. Arthur
Brownells, Inc.
C.S. Van Gorden & Son, Inc.
Cambos Outdoorsman
Cambos Outdoorsman
Camp-Cap Products
CONKKO
Connecticut Shotgun Mfg. Co.
Creedmoor Sports, Inc.
CRR, Inc./Marble's Inc.
Custom Products (See Jones Custom Products)
Cylinder & Slide, Inc., William R. Laughridge
Dara-Nes, Inc. (See Nesci Enterprises, Inc.)
Deepeeka Exports Pvt. Ltd.
Desert Mountain Mfg.
Du-Lite Corp.
Dykstra, Doug
E&L Mfg., Inc.
Eezox, Inc.
Ekol Leather Care
Faith Associates
Flitz International Ltd.
Fluoramics, Inc.
Frontier Products Co.
G96 Products Co., Inc.
Golden Age Arms Co.
Guardsman Products
Gunsmithing, Inc.
Hafner World Wide, Inc.
Half Moon Rifle Shop
Heatbath Corp.
Hoppe's Div. Penguin Industries, Inc.
Hornady Mfg. Co.
Hydrosorbent Products
Iosso Products
J. Dewey Mfg. Co., Inc.
Jantz Supply
Jantz Supply
Johnston Bros. (See C&T Corp. TA Johnson Brothers)
Jonad Corp.
K&M Industries, Inc.
Kellogg's Professional Products
Kent Cartridge Mfg. Co. Ltd.
Kesselring Gun Shop
Kleen-Bore,Inc.
Knight Rifles
Laurel Mountain Forge
Lee Supplies, Mark
LEM Gun Specialties, Inc. The Lewis Lead Remover
List Precision Engineering
LPS Laboratories, Inc.
Lyman Products Corp.
Mac-1 Airgun Distributors
Mandall Shooting Supplies Inc.
Marble Arms (See CRR, Inc./Marble's Inc.)
Mark Lee Supplies

Micro Sight Co.
Minute Man High Tech Industries
Mountain State Muzzleloading Supplies, Inc.
MTM Molded Products Co., Inc.
Muscle Products Corp.
Nesci Enterprises Inc.
Northern Precision Custom Swaged Bullets
Now Products, Inc.
October Country Muzzleloading
Old World Oil Products
Omark Industries, Div. of Blount, Inc.
Original Mink Oil, Inc.
Otis Technology, Inc.
Outers Laboratories Div. of ATK
Ox-Yoke Originals, Inc.
Parker & Sons Shooting Supply
Parker Gun Finishes
Pendleton Royal, c/o Swingler Buckland Ltd.
Perazone-Gunsmith, Brian
Pete Rickard, Inc.
Peter Dyson & Son Ltd.
Precision Airgun Sales, Inc.
PrOlixr Lubricants
Pro-Shot Products, Inc.
R&S Industries Corp.
Radiator Specialty Co.
Rooster Laboratories
Russ Haydon's Shooters' Supply
Rusteprufe Laboratories
Rusty Duck Premium Gun Care Products
Saunders Gun & Machine Shop
Schumakers Gun Shop
Sheffield Knifemakers Supply, Inc.
Shooter's Choice Gun Care
Shotgun Sports Magazine, dba Shootin' Accessories Ltd.
Silencio/Safety Direct
Sinclair International, Inc.
Sno-Seal, Inc. (See Atsko/Sno-Seal, Inc.)
Southern Bloomer Mfg. Co.
Splitfire Sporting Goods, L.L.C.
Starr Trading Co., Jedediah
Stoney Point Products, Inc.
Svon Corp.
T.F.C. S.p.A.
TDP Industries, Inc.
Tetra Gun Care
Texas Platers Supply Co.
The A.W. Peterson Gun Shop, Inc.
The Dutchman's Firearms, Inc.
The Lewis Lead Remover (See LEM Gun Specialties)
The Paul Co.
Track of the Wolf, Inc.
United States Products Co.
Van Gorden & Son Inc., C. S.
Venco Industries, Inc. (See Shooter's Choice Gun Care)
VibraShine, Inc.
Volquartsen Custom Ltd.
Warren Muzzleloading Co., Inc.
Watson Trophy Match Bullets
WD-40 Co.
Wick, David E.
Willow Bend
Wolf's Western Traders
Young Country Arms

COMPUTER SOFTWARE - BALLISTICS

Action Target, Inc.
AmBr Software Group Ltd.
Arms Software
Arms, Programming Solutions (See Arms Software)
Barnes Bullets, Inc.
Canons Delcour
Corbin Mfg. & Supply, Inc.
Data Tech Software Systems

PRODUCT & SERVICE DIRECTORY

Hodgdon Powder Co.
.I.T. Ltd.
ensen Bullets
Lent Cartridge Mfg. Co. Ltd.
Maionchi-L.M.I.
ehler Research,Inc.
utdoor Sports Headquarters, Inc.
.A.C.T., Inc.
ejsa Ballistics
owley Computer (See Hutton Rifle Ranch)
CBS Operations/ATK
ierra Bullets
he Ballistic Program Co., Inc.
he Country Armourer
he Gun Works
ioga Engineering Co., Inc.
V. Square Enterprises

CUSTOM GUNSMITH

&W Repair
A.A. Arms, Inc.
cadian Ballistic Specialties
ccuracy Unlimited
ce Custom 45's, Inc.
cra-Bond Laminates
dair Custom Shop, Bill
hlman Guns
l Lind Custom Guns
ldis Gunsmithing & Shooting Supply
lpha Precision, Inc.
lpine Indoor Shooting Range
mrine's Gun Shop
nswer Products Co.
ntique Arms Co.
rmament Gunsmithing Co., Inc.
rms Craft Gunsmithing
rms Ingenuity Co.
rmscorp USA, Inc.
rtistry in Wood
rt's Gun & Sport Shop, Inc.
rundel Arms & Ammunition, Inc., A.
utauga Arms, Inc.
Badger Creek Studio
Baelder, Harry
Baer Custom Inc., Les
Bain & Davis, Inc.
Bansner's Ultimate Rifles, LLC
Barnes Bullets, Inc.
Baron Technology
Barta's Gunsmithing
Bear Arms
Bear Mountain Gun & Tool
Beaver Lodge (See Fellowes, Ted)
Behlert Precision, Inc.
Beitzinger, George
Belding's Custom Gun Shop
Ben William's Gun Shop
Bengtson Arms Co., L.
Bill Adair Custom Shop
Billings Gunsmiths
BlackStar AccuMax Barrels
BlackStar Barrel Accurizing (See BlackStar AccuMax)
Bob Rogers Gunsmithing
Bond Custom Firearms
Borden Ridges Rimrock Stocks
Borovnik KG, Ludwig
Bowen Classic Arms Corp.
Brace, Larry D.
Briese Bullet Co., Inc.
Briganti, A.J.
Briley Mfg. Inc.
Broad Creek Rifle Works, Ltd.
Brockman's Custom Gunsmithing
Broken Gun Ranch
Brown Precision, Inc.
Brown Products, Inc., Ed
Buchsenmachermeister
Buckhorn Gun Works
Budin, Dave
Bull Mountain Rifle Co.
Bullberry Barrel Works, Ltd.

Burkhart Gunsmithing, Don
Cache La Poudre Rifleworks
Cambos Outdoorsman
Cambos Outdoorsman
Campbell, Dick
Carolina Precision Rifles
Carter's Gun Shop
Caywood, Shane J.
CBC-BRAZIL
Chambers Flintlocks Ltd., Jim
Champlin Firearms, Inc.
Chicasaw Gun Works
Chuck's Gun Shop
Chuilli, Stephen
Clark Custom Guns, Inc.
Clark Firearms Engraving
Classic Arms Company
Classic Arms Corp.
Clearview Products
Cleland's Outdoor World, Inc
Coffin, Charles H.
Cogar's Gunsmithing
Cole's Gun Works
Colonial Arms, Inc.
Colonial Repair
Colorado Gunsmithing Academy
Colorado School of Trades
Colt's Mfg. Co., Inc.
Conrad, C. A.
Corkys Gun Clinic
Cox, Ed. C.
Cullity Restoration
Custom Gun Stocks
Custom Single Shot Rifles
D&D Gunsmiths, Ltd.
Dangler, Homer L.
D'Arcy Echols & Co.
Darlington Gun Works, Inc.
Dave's Gun Shop
David Miller Co.
David R. Chicoine
David W. Schwartz Custom Guns
Davis, Don
Del-Sports, Inc.
Delorge, Ed
DGR Custom Rifles
DGS, Inc., Dale A. Storey
Dietz Gun Shop & Range, Inc.
Dilliott Gunsmithing, Inc.
Donnelly, C. P.
Duane A. Hobbie Gunsmithing
Duane's Gun Repair (See DGR Custom Rifles)
Duffy, Charles E (See Guns Antique & Modern DBA)
Duncan's Gun Works, Inc.
E. Arthur Brown Co.
Eckelman Gunsmithing
Ed Brown Products, Inc.
Eggleston, Jere D.
Entre`prise Arms, Inc.
Erhardt, Dennis
Eversull Co., Inc.
Evolution Gun Works Inc.
F.I., Inc. - High Standard Mfg. Co.
FERLIB
Ferris Firearms
Fisher, Jerry A.
Fisher Custom Firearms
Fleming Firearms
Flynn's Custom Guns
Forkin, Ben (See Belt MTN Arms)
Forkin Arms
Forster, Kathy (See Custom Checkering)
Forster, Larry L.
Forthofer's Gunsmithing & Knifemaking
Francesca, Inc.
Francotte & Cie S.A. Auguste
Fred F. Wells/Wells Sport Store
Frontier Arms Co.,Inc.
Fullmer, Geo. M.
G.G. & G.
Galaxy Imports Ltd., Inc.
Garthwaite Pistolsmith, Inc., Jim
Gary Reeder Custom Guns

Gator Guns & Repair
Genecco Gun Works
Gene's Custom Guns
Gentry Custom Gunmaker, David
George E. Mathews & Son, Inc.
George Hoenig, Inc.
Gillmann, Edwin
Gilman-Mayfield, Inc.
Gilmore Sports Concepts
Giron, Robert E.
Goens, Dale W.
Gonic Arms/North American Arm
Goodling's Gunsmithing
Goodwin's Gun Shop
Grace, Charles E.
Grayback Wildcats
Graybill's Gun Shop
Green, Roger M.
Greg Gunsmithing Repair
Gre-Tan Rifles
Griffin & Howe, Inc.
Griffin & Howe, Inc.
Griffin & Howe, Inc.
Gruning Precision Inc.
Guncraft Books (See Guncraft Sports Inc.)
Guncraft Sports Inc.
Guncraft Sports, Inc.
Guns Antique & Modern DBA / Charles E. Duffy
Gunsite Custom Shop
Gunsite Gunsmithy (See Gunsite Custom Shop)
Gunsite Training Center
Gunsmithing Ltd.
Hamilton, Alex B (See Ten-Ring Precision, Inc)
Hammans, Charles E.
Hammerli Service-Precision Mac
Hammond Custom Guns Ltd.
Hank's Gun Shop
Hanson's Gun Center, Dick
Harris Gunworks
Harry Lawson Co.
Hart & Son, Inc.
Hart Rifle Barrels,Inc.
Hartmann & Weiss GmbH
Harwood, Jack O.
Hawken Shop, The (See Dayton Traister)
Hecht, Hubert J, Waffen-Hecht
Heilmann, Stephen
Heinie Specialty Products
Hensley, Gunmaker, Darwin
High Bridge Arms, Inc
High Performance International
High Precision
Highline Machine Co.
Hill, Loring F.
Hiptmayer, Armurier
Hiptmayer, Klaus
Hoag, James W.
Hodgson, Richard
Hoehn Sales, Inc.
Hofer Jagdwaffen, P.
Holland's Gunsmithing
Huebner, Corey O.
Hunkeler, A (See Buckskin Machine Works
Imperial Magnum Corp.
Irwin, Campbell H.
Island Pond Gun Shop
Israel Arms International, Inc.
Ivanoff, Thomas G. (See Tom's Gun Repair)
J&S Heat Treat
J.J. Roberts / Engraver
Jack Dever Co.
Jackalope Gun Shop
James Calhoon Mfg.
James Calhoon Varmint Bullets
Jamison's Forge Works
Jarrett Rifles, Inc.
Jarvis, Inc.
Jay McCament Custom Gunmaker
Jeffredo Gunsight
Jensen's Custom Ammunition

Jim Norman Custom Gunstocks
Jim's Gun Shop (See Spradlin's)
Jim's Precision, Jim Ketchum
John Norrell Arms
John Rigby & Co.
Jones Custom Products, Neil A.
Juenke, Vern
K. Eversull Co., Inc.
KDF, Inc.
Keith's Custom Gunstocks
Ken Eyster Heritage Gunsmiths, Inc.
Ken Starnes Gunmaker
Ketchum, Jim (See Jim's Precision)
Kilham & Co.
King's Gun Works
KLA Enterprises
Klein Custom Guns, Don
Kleinendorst, K. W.
KOGOT
Korzinek Riflesmith, J.
L. E. Jurras & Assoc.
LaFrance Specialties
Lampert, Ron
LaRocca Gun Works
Larry Lyons Gunworks
Lathrop's, Inc.
Laughridge, William R (See Cylinder & Slide Inc)
Lawson Co., Harry
Lazzeroni Arms Co.
LeFever Arms Co., Inc.
Linebaugh Custom Sixguns
List Precision Engineering
Lock's Philadelphia Gun Exchange
Lone Star Rifle Company
Long, George F.
Mag-Na-Port International, Inc.
Mahony, Philip Bruce
Mahony, Philip Bruce
Mahovsky's Metalife
Makinson, Nicholas
Mandall Shooting Supplies Inc.
Marshall Fish Mfg. Gunsmith Sptg. Co.
Martin's Gun Shop
Martz, John V.
Mathews & Son, Inc., George E.
Mazur Restoration, Pete
McCann's Muzzle-Gun Works
McCluskey Precision Rifles
McGowen Rifle Barrels
McMillan Rifle Barrels
MCS, Inc.
Mercer Custom Guns
Michael's Antiques
Mid-America Recreation, Inc.
Middlebrooks Custom Shop
Miller Arms, Inc.
Miller Custom
Mills Jr., Hugh B.
Moeller, Steve
Monell Custom Guns
Montgomery Community College
Morrison Custom Rifles, J. W.
Morrow, Bud
Mo's Competitor Supplies (See MCS, Inc.)
Mowrey's Guns & Gunsmithing
Mullis Guncraft
Muzzleloaders Etcetera, Inc.
NCP Products, Inc.
Neil A. Jones Custom Products
Nelson's Custom Guns, Inc.
Nettestad Gun Works
New England Arms Co.
New England Custom Gun Service
Newman Gunshop
Nicholson Custom
Nickels, Paul R.
Nicklas, Ted
Nitex Gun Shop
North American Shooting Systems
Nu-Line Guns,Inc.
Old World Gunsmithing
Olson, Vic

Ottmar, Maurice
Ox-Yoke Originals, Inc.
Ozark Gun Works
P&M Sales & Services, LLC
P.S.M.G. Gun Co.
PAC-NOR Barreling
Pagel Gun Works, Inc.
Parker & Sons Shooting Supply
Parker Gun Finishes
Pasadena Gun Center
Paterson Gunsmithing
Paulsen Gunstocks
Peacemaker Specialists
PEM's Mfg. Co.
Pence Precision Barrels
Pennsylvania Gunsmith School
Penrod Precision
Pentheny de Pentheny
Performance Specialists
Pete Mazur Restoration
Peter Dyson & Son Ltd.
Peterson Gun Shop, Inc., A.W.
Piquette's Custom Engraving
Plum City Ballistic Range
Powell & Son (Gunmakers) Ltd., William
Power Custom, Inc.
Professional Hunter Supplies (See Star Custom Bullets)
Quality Custom Firearms
R&J Gun Shop
R.A. Wells Custom Gunsmith
Ramon B. Gonzalez Guns
Ray's Gunsmith Shop
Renfrew Guns & Supplies
Ridgetop Sporting Goods
Ries, Chuck
RMS Custom Gunsmithing
Robert Valade Engraving
Robinson, Don
Rocky Mountain Arms, Inc.
Romain's Custom Guns, Inc.
Ron Frank Custom Classic Arms
Ruger's Custom Guns
Rupert's Gun Shop
Savage Arms, Inc.
Schiffman, Mike
Schumakers Gun Shop
Score High Gunsmithing
Sharp Shooter Supply
Shaw, Inc., E. R. (See Small Arms Mfg. Co.)
Shay's Gunsmithing
Shockley, Harold H.
Shooters Supply
Shootin' Shack
Shooting Specialties (See Titus, Daniel)
Shotguns Unlimited
Silver Ridge Gun Shop (See Goodwin, Fred)
Simmons Gun Repair, Inc.
Singletary, Kent
Siskiyou Gun Works (See Donnelly, C. P.)
Skeoch, Brian R.
Sklany's Machine Shop
Slezak, Jerome F.
Small Arms Mfg. Co.
Small Arms Specialists
Smith, Art
Snapp's Gunshop
Sound Technology
Speiser, Fred D.
Spencer Reblue Service
Spencer's Rifle Barrels, Inc.
Splitfire Sporting Goods, L.L.C.
Sportsmen's Exchange & Western Gun Traders, Inc.
Springfield Armory
Springfield, Inc.
SSK Industries
Star Custom Bullets
Steelman's Gun Shop
Steffens, Ron
Steven Dodd Hughes
Stiles Custom Guns

Stott's Creek Armory, Inc.
Sturgeon Valley Sporters
Sullivan, David S .(See Westwind Rifles Inc.)
Swann, D. J.
Swenson's 45 Shop, A. D.
Swift River Gunworks
Szweda, Robert (See RMS Custom Gunsmithing)
Taconic Firearms Ltd., Perry Lane
Talmage, William G.
Tank's Rifle Shop
Tar-Hunt Custom Rifles, Inc.
Tarnhelm Supply Co., Inc.
Taylor & Robbins
Ten-Ring Precision, Inc.
Terry K. Kopp Professional Gunsmithing
The A.W. Peterson Gun Shop, Inc.
The Competitive Pistol Shop
The Custom Shop
The Gun Shop
The Gun Works
The Orvis Co.
The Robar Co.'s, Inc.
The Swampfire Shop (See Peterson Gun Shop, Inc.)
Theis, Terry
Thompson, Randall (See Highline Machine Co.)
Thurston Sports, Inc.
Time Precision
Tom's Gun Repair, Thomas G. Ivanoff
Tom's Gunshop
Trevallion Gunstocks
Trulock Tool
Tucker, James C.
Turnbull Restoration, Doug
Unmussig Bullets, D. L.
Upper Missouri Trading Co.
Van Horn, Gil
Van Patten, J. W.
Van's Gunsmith Service
Vest, John
Vic's Gun Refinishing
Vintage Arms, Inc.
Virgin Valley Custom Guns
Volquartsen Custom Ltd.
Walker Arms Co., Inc.
Wallace, Terry
Wasmundt, Jim
Wayne E. Schwartz Custom Guns
Weatherby, Inc.
Weber & Markin Custom Gunsmiths
Weems, Cecil
Werth, T. W.
Wessinger Custom Guns & Engraving
Western Design (See Alpha Gunsmith Division)
Westley Richards & Co.
Westwind Rifles, Inc., David S. Sullivan
White Barn Wor
White Rifles, Inc.
Wichita Arms, Inc.
Wiebe, Duane
Wild West Guns
William E. Phillips Firearms
Williams Gun Sight Co.
Williams Shootin' Iron Service, The Lynx-Line
Williamson Precision Gunsmithing
Wilsom Combat
Winter, Robert M.
Wise Guns, Dale
Wiseman and Co., Bill
Wood, Frank (See Classic Guns, Inc.)
Working Guns
Wright's Gunstock Blanks
Yankee Gunsmith "Just Glocks"
Zeeryp, Russ

CUSTOM METALSMITH

A&W Repair
Ackerman & Co.
Ahlman Guns
Alaskan Silversmith, The
Aldis Gunsmithing & Shooting Supply
Alpha Precision, Inc.
Amrine's Gun Shop
Answer Products Co.
Antique Arms Co.
Artistry in Wood
Baer Custom Inc., Les
Baron Technology
Bear Mountain Gun & Tool
Behlert Precision, Inc.
Beitzinger, George
Bengtson Arms Co., L.
Bill Adair Custom Shop
Billings Gunsmiths
Billingsley & Brownell
Bob Rogers Gunsmithing
Bowen Classic Arms Corp.
Brace, Larry D.
Briganti, A.J.
Broad Creek Rifle Works, Ltd.
Brown Precision, Inc.
Buckhorn Gun Works
Bull Mountain Rifle Co.
Bullberry Barrel Works, Ltd.
Carter's Gun Shop
Caywood, Shane J.
Checkmate Refinishing
Cleland's Outdoor World, Inc
Colonial Repair
Colorado Gunsmithing Academy
Craftguard
Crandall Tool & Machine Co.
Cullity Restoration
Custom Single Shot Rifles
D&D Gunsmiths, Ltd.
D&H Precision Tooling
D'Arcy Echols & Co.
Dave's Gun Shop
Delorge, Ed
DGS, Inc., Dale A. Storey
Dietz Gun Shop & Range, Inc.
Dilliott Gunsmithing, Inc.
Duane's Gun Repair (See DGR Custom Rifles)
Duncan's Gun Works, Inc.
Erhardt, Dennis
Eversull Co., Inc.
Ferris Firearms
Fisher, Jerry A.
Forster, Larry L.
Forthofer's Gunsmithing & Knifemaking
Francesca, Inc.
Fred F. Wells/Wells Sport Store
Fullmer, Geo. M.
Genecco Gun Works
Gentry Custom Gunmaker, David
Grace, Charles E.
Grayback Wildcats
Graybill's Gun Shop
Green, Roger M.
Gunsmithing Ltd.
Hamilton, Alex B (See Ten-Ring Precision, Inc)
Harry Lawson Co.
Hartmann & Weiss GmbH
Harwood, Jack O.
Hecht, Hubert J, Waffen-Hecht
Heilmann, Stephen
Highline Machine Co.
Hiptmayer, Armurier
Hiptmayer, Klaus
Hoag, James W.
Holland's Gunsmithing
Island Pond Gun Shop
Ivanoff, Thomas G. (See Tom's Gun Repair)
J J Roberts Firearm Engraver
J&S Heat Treat
J.J. Roberts / Engraver

Jamison's Forge Works
Jay McCament Custom Gunmaker
Jeffredo Gunsight
KDF, Inc.
Ken Eyster Heritage Gunsmiths, Inc.
Ken Starnes Gunmaker
Kilham & Co.
Klein Custom Guns, Don
Kleinendorst, K. W.
Lampert, Ron
LaRocca Gun Works
Larry Lyons Gunworks
Lawson Co., Harry
List Precision Engineering
Mahovsky's Metalife
Makinson, Nicholas
Mandall Shooting Supplies Inc.
Mazur Restoration, Pete
McCann Industries
McCann's Machine & Gun Shop
Mid-America Recreation, Inc.
Miller Arms, Inc.
Montgomery Community College
Morrison Custom Rifles, J. W.
Morrow, Bud
Mullis Guncraft
Nelson's Custom Guns, Inc.
Nettestad Gun Works
New England Custom Gun Service
Nicholson Custom
Nitex Gun Shop
Noreen, Peter H.
Nu-Line Guns,Inc.
Olson, Vic
Ozark Gun Works
P.S.M.G. Gun Co.
Pagel Gun Works, Inc.
Parker & Sons Shooting Supply
Parker Gun Finishes
Pasadena Gun Center
Penrod Precision
Pete Mazur Restoration
Precision Specialties
Quality Custom Firearms
R.A. Wells Custom Gunsmith
Rice, Keith (See White Rock Tool & Die)
Robert Valade Engraving
Rocky Mountain Arms, Inc.
Romain's Custom Guns, Inc.
Ron Frank Custom Classic Arms
Score High Gunsmithing
Simmons Gun Repair, Inc.
Singletary, Kent
Skeoch, Brian R.
Sklany's Machine Shop
Small Arms Specialists
Smith, Art
Smith, Sharmon
Snapp's Gunshop
Spencer Reblue Service
Spencer's Rifle Barrels, Inc.
Sportsmen's Exchange & Western Gun Traders, Inc.
SSK Industries
Steffens, Ron
Stiles Custom Guns
Taylor & Robbins
Ten-Ring Precision, Inc.
The A.W. Peterson Gun Shop, Inc.
The Custom Shop
The Gun Shop
The Robar Co.'s, Inc.
Thompson, Randall (See Highline Machine Co.)
Tom's Gun Repair, Thomas G. Ivanoff
Turnbull Restoration, Doug
Van Horn, Gil
Van Patten, J. W.
Waldron, Herman
Wallace, Terry
Weber & Markin Custom Gunsmiths
Werth, T. W.

Wessinger Custom Guns & Engraving
White Rock Tool & Die
Wiebe, Duane
Wild West Guns
Williams Shootin' Iron Service, The Lynx-Line
Williamson Precision Gunsmithing
Winter, Robert M.
Wise Guns, Dale
Wood, Frank (See Classic Guns, Inc.)
Wright's Gunstock Blanks
Zufall, Joseph F.

DECOYS

Ad Hominem
Baekgaard Ltd.
Belding's Custom Gun Shop
Bill Russ Trading Post
Boyds' Gunstock Industries, Inc.
Carry-Lite, Inc.
Farm Form Decoys, Inc.
Feather, Flex Decoys
Flambeau Products Corp.
G&H Decoys,Inc.
Grand Slam Hunting Products
Herter's Manufacturing Inc.
Hiti-Schuch, Atelier Wilma
Klingler Woodcarving
L.L. Bean, Inc.
Molin Industries, Tru-Nord Division
Murphy, R.R. Co., Inc.
Original Deer Formula Co., The.
Quack Decoy & Sporting Clays
Sports Innovations Inc.
Tanglefree Industries
The A.W. Peterson Gun Shop, Inc.
Woods Wise Products

DIE ACCESSORIES, METALLIC

High Precision
King & Co.
MarMik, Inc.
Rapine Bullet Mould Mfg. Co.
Redding Reloading Equipment
Royal Arms Gunstocks
Sport Flite Manufacturing Co.
The A.W. Peterson Gun Shop, Inc.
Wolf's Western Traders

DIES, METALLIC

4-D Custom Die Co.
Badger Creek Studio
Buffalo Arms Co.
Dakota Arms, Inc.
Dillon Precision Products, Inc.
Dixie Gun Works
Fremont Tool Works
Goodwin's Gun Shop
Gruning Precision Inc.
Jones Custom Products, Neil A.
King & Co.
Lee Precision, Inc.
Montana Precision Swaging
Neil A. Jones Custom Products
Ozark Gun Works
Rapine Bullet Mould Mfg. Co.
RCBS Operations/ATK
RCBS/ATK
Redding Reloading Equipment
Romain's Custom Guns, Inc.
Spencer's Rifle Barrels, Inc.
Sport Flite Manufacturing Co.
SSK Industries
The A.W. Peterson Gun Shop, Inc.
Vega Tool Co.
Wolf's Western Traders

DIES, SHOTSHELL

Goodwin's Gun Shop
Lee Precision, Inc.
MEC, Inc.
The A.W. Peterson Gun Shop, Inc.

DIES, SWAGE

4-D Custom Die Co.
Bullet Swaging Supply, Inc.
Goodwin's Gun Shop
Hollywood Engineering
Montana Precision Swaging
Sport Flite Manufacturing Co.
The A.W. Peterson Gun Shop, Inc.

ENGRAVER, ENGRAVING TOOLS

Ackerman & Co.
Adair Custom Shop, Bill
Ahlman Guns
Alaskan Silversmith, The
Alfano, Sam
Allard, Gary/Creek Side Metal & Woodcrafters
Allen Firearm Engraving
Altamont Co.
American Pioneer Video
Baron Technology
Barraclough, John K.
Bates Engraving, Billy
Bill Adair Custom Shop
Billy Bates Engraving
Boessler, Erich
Brooker, Dennis
Buchsenmachermeister
Churchill, Winston G.
Clark Firearms Engraving
Collings, Ronald
Creek Side Metal & Woodcrafters
Cullity Restoration
Cupp, Alana, Custom Engraver
Custom Single Shot Rifles
Dayton Traister
Delorge, Ed
Dolbare, Elizabeth
Drain, Mark
Dremel Mfg. Co.
Dubber, Michael W.
Engraving Artistry
Engraving Only
Evans Engraving, Robert
Eversull Co., Inc.
Firearms Engraver's Guild of America
Flannery Engraving Co., Jeff W
Forty Five Ranch Enterprises
Fountain Products
Francotte & Cie S.A. Auguste
Frank Knives
Fred F. Wells/Wells Sport Store
French, Artistic Engraving, J. R.
Gary Reeder Custom Guns
Gene's Custom Guns
George Madis Winchester Consultants
Glimm's Custom Gun Engraving
Golden Age Arms Co.
Gournet Artistic Engraving
Grant, Howard V.
GRS / Glendo Corp.
Gurney, F. R.
Half Moon Rifle Shop
Harris Gunworks
Harris Hand Engraving, Paul A.
Harwood, Jack O.
Hawken Shop, The (See Dayton Traister)
Hiptmayer, Armurier
Hiptmayer, Heidemarie
Hofer Jagdwaffen, P.
Ingle, Ralph W.

PRODUCT & SERVICE DIRECTORY

J Roberts Firearm Engraver
.J. Roberts / Engraver
antz Supply
eff W. Flannery Engraving Co.
im Blair Engraving
ohn J. Adams & Son Engravers
ane, Edward
ehr, Roger
elly, Lance
en Eyster Heritage Gunsmiths,
   Inc.
enneth W. Warren Engraver
lingler Woodcarving
arry Lyons Gunworks
eFever Arms Co., Inc.
eibowitz, Leonard
indsay Engraving & Tools
ittle Trees Ramble (See Scott
   Pilkington)
McCombs, Leo
McDonald, Dennis
McKenzie, Lynton
Mele, Frank
Mid-America Recreation, Inc.
Mittermeier, Inc., Frank
Montgomery Community College
Nelson, Gary K.
New Orleans Jewelers Supply Co.
edersen, C. R.
edersen, Rex C.
eter Hale/Engraver
ilgrim Pewter,Inc. (See Bell
   Originals Inc. Sid)
ilkington, Scott (See Little Trees
   Ramble)
iquette's Custom Engraving
otts, Wayne E.
uality Custom Firearms
abeno, Martin
alph Bone Engraving
eed, Dave
eno, Wayne
iggs, Jim
obert Evans Engraving
obert Valade Engraving
ohner, Hans
ohner, John
osser, Bob
undell's Gun Shop
unge, Robert P.
am Welch Gun Engraving
ampson, Roger
chiffman, Mike
heffield Knifemakers Supply, Inc.
herwood, George
ingletary, Kent
mith, Mark A.
mith, Ron
mokey Valley Rifles
SK Industries
teve Kamyk Engraver
wanson, Mark
he Gun Room
he NgraveR Co.
heis, Terry
hiewes, George W.
hirion Gun Engraving, Denise
iramontez Engraving
orhes, David
V.E. Brownell Checkering Tools
Vagoner, Vernon G.
Vallace, Terry
Varenski, Julie
Veber & Markin Custom
   Gunsmiths
Vells, Rachel
Vessinger Custom Guns &
   Engraving
iegel Engineering

GAME CALLS

Adventure Game Calls
African Import Co.
Ashby Turkey Calls
Bill Russ Trading Post

Bostick Wildlife Calls, Inc.
Cedar Hill Game Calls, Inc.
Crit'R Call (See Rocky Mountain
   Wildlife Products)
Custom Calls
D-Boone Ent., Inc.
Deepeeka Exports Pvt. Ltd.
Dr. O's Products Ltd.
Duck Call Specialists
Faulhaber Wildlocker
Faulk's Game Call Co., Inc.
Fibron Products, Inc.
Glynn Scobey Duck & Goose Calls
Goodwin's Gun Shop
Grand Slam Hunting Products
Green Head Game Call Co.
Hally Caller
Haydel's Game Calls, Inc.
Herter's Manufacturing Inc.
Hunter's Specialties Inc.
Keowee Game Calls
Kingyon, Paul L. (See Custom
   Calls)
Knight & Hale Game Calls
Lohman Mfg. Co., Inc.
Mallardtone Game Calls
Moss Double Tone, Inc.
Oakman Turkey Calls
Original Deer Formula Co., The.
Outdoor Sports Headquarters, Inc.
Pete Rickard, Inc.
Philip S. Olt Co.
Primos, Inc.
Protektor Model
Quaker Boy, Inc.
Rocky Mountain Wildlife Products
Sceery Game Calls
Sports Innovations Inc.
Stewart Game Calls, Inc., Johnny
Sure-Shot Game Calls, Inc.
Tanglefree Industries
The A.W. Peterson Gun Shop, Inc.
Tinks & Ben Lee Hunting Products
   (See Wellington)
Tink's Safariland Hunting Corp.
Wellington Outdoors
Wilderness Sound Products Ltd.
Woods Wise Products
Wyant's Outdoor Products, Inc.

GAUGES, CALIPERS & MICROMETERS

Blue Ridge Machinery & Tools, Inc.
Goodwin's Gun Shop
Gruning Precision Inc.
Huntington Die Specialties
K&M Services
King & Co.
Spencer's Rifle Barrels, Inc.
Starrett Co., L. S.
Stoney Point Products, Inc.

GUN PARTS, U.S. & FOREIGN

"Su-Press-On", Inc.
A.A. Arms, Inc.
Ahlman Guns
Amherst Arms
Antique Arms Co.
Armscorp USA, Inc.
Auto-Ordnance Corp.
B.A.C.
Badger Shooters Supply, Inc.
Ballard Rifle & Cartridge Co., LLC
Bar-Sto Precision Machine
Bear Mountain Gun & Tool
Billings Gunsmiths
Bill's Gun Repair
Bob's Gun Shop
Briese Bullet Co., Inc.
Brown Products, Inc., Ed
Brownells, Inc.
Bryan & Assoc.

Buffer Technologies
Cambos Outdoorsman
Cambos Outdoorsman
Cape Outfitters
Caspian Arms, Ltd.
CBC-BRAZIL
Chicasaw Gun Works
Ciener Inc., Jonathan Arthur
Cole's Gun Works
Colonial Arms, Inc.
Colonial Repair
Colt's Mfg. Co., Inc.
Custom Riflestocks, Inc., Michael
   M. Kokolus
Cylinder & Slide, Inc., William R.
   Laughridge
David R. Chicoine
Delta Arms Ltd.
DGR Custom Rifles
Dibble, Derek A.
Dixie Gun Works
Duane's Gun Repair (See DGR
   Custom Rifles)
Duffy, Charles E (See Guns Antique
   & Modern DBA)
E.A.A. Corp.
Elliott Inc., G. W.
EMF Co., Inc.
Enguix Import-Export
Entre`prise Arms, Inc.
European American Armory Corp
   (See E.A.A. Corp)
Evolution Gun Works Inc.
F.I., Inc. - High Standard Mfg. Co.
Faloon Industries, Inc.
Federal Arms Corp. of America
Fleming Firearms
Forrest Inc., Tom
Gentry Custom Gunmaker, David
Glimm's Custom Gun Engraving
Goodwin's Gun Shop
Granite Mountain Arms, Inc.
Greider Precision
Gre-Tan Rifles
Groenewold, John
Gun Hunter Books (See Gun Hunter
   Trading Co.)
Gun Hunter Trading Co.
Guns Antique & Modern DBA /
   Charles E. Duffy
Gunsmithing, Inc.
Hastings
Hawken Shop, The (See Dayton
   Traister)
High Performance International
I.S.S.
Irwin, Campbell H.
Jack First, Inc.
Jamison's Forge Works
Jonathan Arthur Ciener, Inc.
Kimber of America, Inc.
Knight's Mfg. Co.
Krico Deutschland GmbH
LaFrance Specialties
Lampert, Ron
LaPrade
Laughridge, William R (See
   Cylinder & Slide Inc)
Leapers, Inc.
List Precision Engineering
Lodewick, Walter H.
Logdewood Mfg.
Long, George F.
Mandall Shooting Supplies Inc.
Markell,Inc.
Martin's Gun Shop
McCormick Corp., Chip
MCS, Inc.
Merkuria Ltd.
Mid-America Recreation, Inc.
Morrow, Bud
Mo's Competitor Supplies (See
   MCS, Inc.)
North Star West
Northwest Arms
Nu-Line Guns,Inc.
Numrich Gun Parts Corporation

Nygord Precision Products, Inc.
Olathe Gun Shop
Olympic Arms Inc.
P.S.M.G. Gun Co.
Pacific Armament Corp
Pennsylvania Gun Parts Inc
Performance Specialists
Peter Dyson & Son Ltd.
Peterson Gun Shop, Inc., A.W.
Ranch Products
Randco UK
Ravell Ltd.
Retting, Inc., Martin B
Romain's Custom Guns, Inc.
Ruger (See Sturm, Ruger & Co.,
   Inc.)
Rutgers Book Center
S&S Firearms
Sabatti SPA
Samco Global Arms, Inc.
Sarco, Inc.
Shockley, Harold H.
Shootin' Shack
Silver Ridge Gun Shop (See
   Goodwin, Fred)
Simmons Gun Repair, Inc.
Smires, C. L.
Smith & Wesson
Southern Ammunition Co., Inc.
Sportsmen's Exchange & Western
   Gun Traders, Inc.
Springfield Sporters, Inc.
Springfield, Inc.
Steyr Mannlicher GmbH P Co KG
STI International
Strayer-Voigt, Inc.
Sturm Ruger & Co. Inc.
Sunny Hill Enterprises, Inc.
T&S Industries, Inc.
Tank's Rifle Shop
Tarnhelm Supply Co., Inc.
Terry K. Kopp Professional
   Gunsmithing
The A.W. Peterson Gun Shop, Inc.
The Gun Room Press
The Gun Shop
The Gun Works
The Southern Armory
The Swampfire Shop (See Peterson
   Gun Shop, Inc.)
VAM Distribution Co. LLC
Vektor USA
Vintage Arms, Inc.
W. Waller & Son, Inc.
W.C. Wolff Co.
Walker Arms Co., Inc.
Wescombe, Bill (See North Star
   West)
Whitestone Lumber Corp.
Wild West Guns
Williams Mfg. of Oregon
Winchester Sutler, Inc., The
Wise Guns, Dale
Wisners Inc/Twin Pine Armory

GUNS & GUN PARTS, REPLICA & ANTIQUE

Ackerman & Co.
Ahlman Guns
Armi San Paolo
Auto-Ordnance Corp.
Ballard Rifle & Cartridge Co., LLC
Bear Mountain Gun & Tool
Billings Gunsmiths
Bob's Gun Shop
Buffalo Arms Co.
Cache La Poudre Rifleworks
Campbell, Dick
Cash Mfg. Co., Inc.
CBC-BRAZIL
CCL Security Products
Chambers Flintlocks Ltd., Jim
Chicasaw Gun Works
Cimarron F.A. Co.
Cogar's Gunsmithing

Cole's Gun Works
Colonial Repair
Colt Blackpowder Arms Co.
Colt's Mfg. Co., Inc.
Custom Riflestocks, Inc., Michael
   M. Kokolus
Custom Single Shot Rifles
David R. Chicoine
Delhi Gun House
Delta Arms Ltd.
Dilliott Gunsmithing, Inc.
Dixie Gun Works
Dixon Muzzleloading Shop, Inc.
Ed's Gun House
Euroarms of America, Inc.
Flintlocks, Etc.
George E. Mathews & Son, Inc.
Getz Barrel Co.
Golden Age Arms Co.
Goodwin's Gun Shop
Groenewold, John
Gun Hunter Books (See Gun Hunter
   Trading Co.)
Gun Hunter Trading Co.
Hastings
Heidenstrom Bullets
Hunkeler, A (See Buckskin Machine
   Works
IAR Inc.
Imperial Miniature Armory
Ithaca Classic Doubles
Jack First, Inc.
Ken Starnes Gunmaker
Kokolus, Michael M. (See Custom
   Riflestocks In)
L&R Lock Co.
Leonard Day
List Precision Engineering
Lock's Philadelphia Gun Exchange
Logdewood Mfg.
Lone Star Rifle Company
Lucas, Edward E
Mandall Shooting Supplies Inc.
Martin's Gun Shop
Mathews & Son, Inc., George E.
Mid-America Recreation, Inc.
Mountain State Muzzleloading
   Supplies, Inc.
Mowrey Gun Works
Navy Arms Company
Neumann GmbH
North Star West
Numrich Gun Parts Corporation
Olathe Gun Shop
Parker & Sons Shooting Supply
Pasadena Gun Center
Pecatonica River Longrifle
PEM's Mfg. Co.
Peter Dyson & Son Ltd.
Pony Express Sport Shop
R.A. Wells Custom Gunsmith
Randco UK
Ravell Ltd.
Retting, Inc., Martin B
Rutgers Book Center
S&S Firearms
Samco Global Arms, Inc.
Sarco, Inc.
Shootin' Shack
Silver Ridge Gun Shop (See
   Goodwin, Fred)
Simmons Gun Repair, Inc.
Sklany's Machine Shop
Southern Ammunition Co., Inc.
Starr Trading Co., Jedediah
Stott's Creek Armory, Inc.
Taylor's & Co., Inc.
Tennessee Valley Mfg.
The A.W. Peterson Gun Shop, Inc.
The Gun Room Press
The Gun Works
Tiger-Hunt Gunstocks
Turnbull Restoration, Doug
Upper Missouri Trading Co.
Vintage Industries, Inc.
Vortek Products, Inc.
VTI Gun Parts

PRODUCT & SERVICE DIRECTORY

Weber & Markin Custom
  Gunsmiths
Wescombe, Bill (See North Star
  West)
Whitestone Lumber Corp.
Winchester Sutler, Inc., The

GUNS, AIR

Air Arms
Air Rifle Specialists
Air Venture Airguns
AirForce Airguns
Airrow
Allred Bullet Co.
Arms Corporation of the
  Philippines
BEC, Inc.
Beeman Precision Airguns
Benjamin/Sheridan Co., Crosman
Brass Eagle, Inc.
Brocock Ltd.
Bryan & Assoc.
BSA Guns Ltd.
Compasseco, Ltd.
Component Concepts, Inc.
Conetrol Scope Mounts
Crosman Airguns
Daisy Outdoor Products
Daystate Ltd.
Domino
Dynamit Nobel-RWS, Inc.
European American Armory Corp
  (See E.A.A. Corp)
Feinwerkbau Westinger &
  Altenburger
Gamo USA, Inc.
Gaucher Armes, S.A.
Great Lakes Airguns
Groenewold, John
Hammerli Service-Precision Mac
I.S.S.
IAR Inc.
J.G. Anschutz GmbH & Co. KG
Labanu, Inc.
Leapers, Inc.
List Precision Engineering
Mac-1 Airgun Distributors
Marksman Products
Maryland Paintball Supply
Merkuria Ltd.
Nationwide Airgun Repair
Nygord Precision Products, Inc.
Olympic Arms Inc.
Pardini Armi Srl
Precision Airgun Sales, Inc.
Precision Sales International, Inc.
Ripley Rifles
Robinson, Don
RWS (See US Importer-Dynamit
  Nobel-RWS, Inc.)
S.G.S. Sporting Guns Srl.
Safari Arms/Schuetzen Pistol
  Works
Savage Arms, Inc.
Smart Parts
Smith & Wesson
Steyr Mannlicher GmbH P Co KG
Stone Enterprises Ltd.
The A.W. Peterson Gun Shop, Inc.
The Gun Room Press
The Park Rifle Co., Ltd.
Tippman Pneumatics, Inc.
Tristar Sporting Arms, Ltd.
Trooper Walsh
UltraSport Arms, Inc.
Visible Impact Targets
Vortek Products, Inc.
Walther GmbH, Carl
Webley and Scott Ltd.
Weihrauch KG, Hermann
Whiscombe (See U.S. Importer-
  Pelaire Products)

GUNS, FOREIGN MANUFACTURER U.S. IMPORTER

Accuracy Internationl Precision
  Rifles (See U.S.)
Accuracy Int'l. North America, Inc.
Ad Hominem
Air Arms
Armas Garbi, S.A.
Armas Kemen S. A. (See U.S.
  Importers)
Armi Perazzi S.p.A.
Armi San Marco (See U.S.
  Importers-Taylor's & Co I
Armi Sport (See U.S. Importers-
  Cape Outfitters)
Arms Corporation of the
  Philippines
Armscorp USA, Inc.
Arrieta S.L.
Astra Sport, S.A.
Atamec-Bretton
AYA (See U.S. Importer-New
  England Custom Gun Serv
B.A.C.
B.C. Outdoors
BEC, Inc.
Benelli Armi S.p.A.
Benelli USA Corp
Beretta S.p.A., Pietro
Beretta U.S.A. Corp.
Bernardelli S.p.A., Vincenzo
Bersa S.A.
Bertuzzi (See U.S. Importer-New
  England Arms Co)
Bill Hanus Birdguns
Blaser Jagdwaffen GmbH
Borovnik KG, Ludwig
Bosis (See U.S. Importer-New
  England Arms Co.)
Brenneke GmbH
Browning Arms Co.
Bryan & Assoc.
BSA Guns Ltd.
Cabanas (See U.S. Importer-
  Mandall Shooting Supply
Cabela's
Cape Outfitters
CBC
Chapuis Armes
Churchill (See U.S. Importer-Ellett
  Bros.)
Conetrol Scope Mounts
Cosmi Americo & Figlio s.n.c.
Crucelegui, Hermanos (See U.S.
  Importer-Mandall)
Cubic Shot Shell Co., Inc.
Daewoo Precision Industries Ltd.
Dakota (See U.S. Importer-EMF
  Co., Inc.)
Dakota Arms, Inc.
Daly, Charles (See U.S. Importer)
Davide Pedersoli and Co.
Domino
Dumoulin, Ernest
Eagle Imports, Inc.
EAW (See U.S. Importer-New
  England Custom Gun Serv
Ed's Gun House
Effebi SNC-Dr. Franco Beretta
EMF Co., Inc.
Eversull Co., Inc.
F.A.I.R.
Fabarm S.p.A.
FEG
Feinwerkbau Westinger &
  Altenburger
Felk Pistols Inc.
FERLIB
Fiocchi Munizioni S.p.A. (See U.S.
  Importer-Fiocch
Firearms Co Ltd. / Alpine (See U.S.
  Importer-Mandall
Firearms International
Flintlocks, Etc.

Franchi S.p.A.
Galaxy Imports Ltd., Inc.
Gamba S.p.A. Societa Armi
  Bresciane Srl
Gamo (See U.S. Importers-Arms
  United Corp, Daisy M
Gaucher Armes, S.A.
Gibbs Rifle Co., Inc.
Glock GmbH
Goergen's Gun Shop, Inc.
Griffin & Howe, Inc.
Griffin & Howe, Inc.
Griffin & Howe, Inc.
Grulla Armes
Hammerli Ltd.
Hammerli USA
Hartford (See U.S. Importer-EMF
  Co. Inc.)
Hartmann & Weiss GmbH
Heckler & Koch, Inc.
Hege Jagd-u. Sporthandels GmbH
Helwan (See U.S. Importer-
  Interarms)
Holland & Holland Ltd.
Howa Machinery, Ltd.
I.A.B. (See U.S. Importer-Taylor's
  & Co. Inc.)
IAR Inc.
IGA (See U.S. Importer-Stoeger
  Industries)
Ignacio Ugartechea S.A.
Imperial Magnum Corp.
Imperial Miniature Armory
Import Sports Inc.
Inter Ordnance of America LP
Intrac Arms International
J.G. Anschutz GmbH & Co. KG
JSL Ltd (See U.S. Importer-
  Specialty Shooters)
K. Eversull Co., Inc.
Kimar (See U.S. Importer-IAR,Inc)
Korth Germany GmbH
Krico Deutschland GmbH
Krieghoff Gun Co., H.
Lakefield Arms Ltd. (See Savage
  Arms, Inc.)
Lapua Ltd.
Laurona Armas Eibar, S.A.L.
Lebeau-Courally
Lever Arms Service Ltd.
Llama Gabilondo Y Cia
London Guns Ltd.
M. Thys (See U.S. Importer-
  Champlin Firearms Inc)
Magtech Ammunition Co. Inc.
Mandall Shooting Supplies Inc.
Marocchi F.lli S.p.A.
Mauser Werke Oberndorf
  Waffensysteme GmbH
McCann Industries
MEC-Gar S.R.L.
Merkel
Miltex, Inc
Morini (See U.S. Importers-
  Mandall Shooting Supply)
New England Custom Gun Service
New SKB Arms Co.
Norica, Avnda Otaola
Norinco
Norma Precision AB (See U.S.
  Importers-Dynamit)
Northwest Arms
Nygord Precision Products, Inc.
OK Weber, Inc.
Para-Ordnance Mfg., Inc.
Pardini Armi Srl
Perugini Visini & Co. S.r.l.
Peters Stahl GmbH
Pietta (See U.S. Importers-Navy
  Arms Co, Taylor's
Piotti (See U.S. Importer-Moore &
  Co, Wm. Larkin)
PMC/Eldorado Cartridge Corp.
Powell & Son (Gunmakers) Ltd.,
  William
Prairie Gun Works
Ramon B. Gonzalez Guns

Rizzini F.lli (See U.S. Importers-
  Moore & C England)
Rizzini SNC
Robinson Armament Co.
Rossi Firearms
Rottweil Compe
Rutten (See U.S. Importer-Labanu
  Inc)
RWS (See US Importer-Dynamit
  Nobel-RWS, Inc.)
S.A.R.L. G. Granger
S.I.A.C.E. (See U.S. Importer-IAR
  Inc)
Sabatti SPA
Sako Ltd (See U.S. Importer-
  Stoeger Industries)
San Marco (See U.S. Importers-
  Cape Outfitters-EMF
Sarsilmaz Shotguns - Turkey (see
  B.C. Outdoors)
Sauer (See U.S. Importers-Paul
  Co., The, Sigarms I
Savage Arms (Canada), Inc.
SIG
Sigarms, Inc.
SIG-Sauer (See U.S. Importer-
  Sigarms Inc.)
SKB Shotguns
Small Arms Specialists
Societa Armi Bresciane Srl (See
  U.S. Importer-Cape
Sphinx Systems Ltd.
Springfield Armory
Springfield, Inc.
Starr Trading Co., Jedediah
Steyr Mannlicher GmbH P Co KG
T.F.C. S.p.A.
Tanfoglio Fratelli S.r.l.
Tanner (See U.S. Importer-Mandall
  Shooting Supply)
Tar-Hunt Custom Rifles, Inc.
Taurus International Firearms (See
  U.S. Importer)
Taurus S.A. Forjas
Taylor's & Co., Inc.
Techno Arms (See U.S. Importer-
  Auto-Ordnance Corp
The A.W. Peterson Gun Shop, Inc.
Tikka (See U.S. Importer-Stoeger
  Industries)
TOZ (See U.S. Importer-Nygord
  Precision Products)
Ugartechea S. A., Ignacio
Ultralux (See U.S. Importer-Keng's
  Firearms)
Unique/M.A.P.F.
Valtro USA, Inc
Verney-Carron
Voere-KGH GmbH
Walther GmbH, Carl
Weatherby, Inc.
Webley and Scott Ltd.
Weihrauch KG, Hermann
Westley Richards & Co.
Whiscombe (See U.S. Importer-
  Pelaire Products)
Wolf (See J.R. Distributing)
Yankee Gunsmith "Just Glocks"
Zabala Hermanos S.A.

GUNS, FOREIGN- IMPORTER

Accuracy International
AcuSport Corporation
Air Rifle Specialists
American Frontier Firearms Mfg.,
  Inc
Auto-Ordnance Corp.
B.A.C.
B.C. Outdoors
Bell's Legendary Country Wear
Benelli USA Corp
Big Bear Arms & Sporting Goods,
  Inc.
Bill Hanus Birdguns

Bridgeman Products
British Sporting Arms
Browning Arms Co.
Cape Outfitters
Century International Arms, Inc.
Champion Shooters' Supply
Champion's Choice, Inc.
Chapuis USA
Cimarron F.A. Co.
CVA
CZ USA
Dixie Gun Works
Dynamit Nobel-RWS, Inc.
E&L Mfg., Inc.
E.A.A. Corp.
Eagle Imports, Inc.
Ellett Bros.
EMF Co., Inc.
Euroarms of America, Inc.
Eversull Co., Inc.
Fiocchi of America, Inc.
Flintlocks, Etc.
Franzen International,Inc (See U.S.
  Importer for)
G.U. Inc (See U.S. Importer for
  New SKB Arms Co.)
Galaxy Imports Ltd., Inc.
Gamba, USA
Gamo USA, Inc.
Giacomo Sporting USA
Glock, Inc.
Gremmel Enterprises
GSI, Inc.
Guncraft Books (See Guncraft
  Sports Inc.)
Guncraft Sports Inc.
Gunsite Custom Shop
Gunsite Training Center
Hammerli USA
I.S.S.
IAR Inc.
Imperial Magnum Corp.
Imperial Miniature Armory
Import Sports Inc.
Intrac Arms International
K. Eversull Co., Inc.
K.B.I. Inc.
Kemen America
Keng's Firearms Specialty, Inc./US
  Tactical Systems
Krieghoff International,Inc.
Labanu, Inc.
Legacy Sports International
Lion Country Supply
London Guns Ltd.
Magnum Research, Inc.
Marx, Harry (See U.S. Importer for
  FERLIB)
MCS, Inc.
MEC-Gar U.S.A., Inc.
Navy Arms Company
New England Arms Co.
Nygord Precision Products, Inc.
OK Weber, Inc.
P.S.M.G. Gun Co.
Para-Ordnance, Inc.
Parker Reproductions
Pelaire Products
Perazzi U.S.A. Inc.
Powell Agency, William
Precision Sales International, Inc.
Rocky Mountain Armoury
S.D. Meacham
Safari Arms/Schuetzen Pistol
  Works
Samco Global Arms, Inc.
Savage Arms, Inc.
Scott Fine Guns Inc., Thad
Sigarms, Inc.
SKB Shotguns
Small Arms Specialists
Southern Ammunition Co., Inc.
Specialty Shooters Supply, Inc.
Springfield, Inc.
Stoeger Industries
Stone Enterprises Ltd.

Swarovski Optik North America Ltd.
Tar-Hunt Custom Rifles, Inc.
Taurus Firearms, Inc.
Taylor's & Co., Inc.
The A.W. Peterson Gun Shop, Inc.
The Gun Shop
The Orvis Co.
The Paul Co.
Track of the Wolf, Inc.
Traditions Performance Firearms
Tristar Sporting Arms, Ltd.
Trooper Walsh
U.S. Importer-Wm. Larkin Moore
VAM Distribution Co. LLC
Vektor USA
Vintage Arms, Inc.
VTI Gun Parts
Westley Richards Agency USA (See U.S. Importer for
Wingshooting Adventures

GUNS, SURPLUS, PARTS & AMMUNITION

Ahlman Guns
Alpha 1 Drop Zone
Armscorp USA, Inc.
Arundel Arms & Ammunition, Inc., A.
B.A.C.
Bondini Paolo
Cambos Outdoorsman
Century International Arms, Inc.
Cole's Gun Works
Conetrol Scope Mounts
Delta Arms Ltd.
Ed's Gun House
First Inc., Jack
Fleming Firearms
Forrest Inc., Tom
Garcia National Gun Traders, Inc.
Goodwin's Gun Shop
Gun City
Gun Hunter Books (See Gun Hunter Trading Co.)
Gun Hunter Trading Co.
Hank's Gun Shop
Hege Jagd-u. Sporthandels GmbH
Jackalope Gun Shop
Ken Starnes Gunmaker
LaRocca Gun Works
Lever Arms Service Ltd.
Log Cabin Sport Shop
Martin's Gun Shop
Navy Arms Company
Nevada Pistol Academy, Inc.
Northwest Arms
Numrich Gun Parts Corporation
Oil Rod and Gun Shop
Olathe Gun Shop
Paragon Sales & Services, Inc.
Pasadena Gun Center
Power Plus Enterprises, Inc.
Ravell Ltd.
Retting, Inc., Martin B
Rutgers Book Center
Samco Global Arms, Inc.
Sarco, Inc.
Shootin' Shack
Silver Ridge Gun Shop (See Goodwin, Fred)
Simmons Gun Repair, Inc.
Sportsmen's Exchange & Western Gun Traders, Inc.
Springfield Sporters, Inc.
T.F.C. S.p.A.
Tarnhelm Supply Co., Inc.
The A.W. Peterson Gun Shop, Inc.
The Gun Room Press
Thurston Sports, Inc.
Williams Shootin' Iron Service, The Lynx-Line

GUNS, U.S. MADE

3-Ten Corp.
A.A. Arms, Inc.
Accu-Tek
Ace Custom 45's, Inc.
Acra-Bond Laminates
Ad Hominem
Airrow
Allred Bullet Co.
American Derringer Corp.
American Frontier Firearms Mfg., Inc
AR-7 Industries, LLC
ArmaLite, Inc.
Armscorp USA, Inc.
A-Square Co.
Austin & Halleck, Inc.
Autauga Arms, Inc.
Auto-Ordnance Corp.
Baer Custom Inc., Les
Ballard Rifle & Cartridge Co., LLC
Barrett Firearms Manufacturer, Inc.
Bar-Sto Precision Machine
Benjamin/Sheridan Co., Crosman
Beretta S.p.A., Pietro
Beretta U.S.A. Corp.
Big Bear Arms & Sporting Goods, Inc.
Bill Russ Trading Post
Bond Arms, Inc.
Borden Ridges Rimrock Stocks
Borden Rifles Inc.
Brockman's Custom Gunsmithing
Brown Co., E. Arthur
Brown Products, Inc., Ed
Browning Arms Co.
Bryan & Assoc.
Bushmaster Firearms
C. Sharps Arms Co. Inc./Montana Armory
Cabela's
Calico Light Weapon Systems
Cambos Outdoorsman
Cape Outfitters
Casull Arms Corp.
CCL Security Products
Century Gun Dist. Inc.
Champlin Firearms, Inc.
Charter 2000
Cobra Enterprises, Inc.
Colt's Mfg. Co., Inc.
Competitor Corp., Inc.
Conetrol Scope Mounts
Connecticut Shotgun Mfg. Co.
Connecticut Valley Classics (See CVC, BPI)
Cooper Arms
Crosman Airguns
Cumberland Arms
Cumberland Mountain Arms
CVA
Daisy Outdoor Products
Dakota Arms, Inc.
Dan Wesson Firearms
Dayton Traister
Dixie Gun Works
Downsizer Corp.
DS Arms, Inc.
DunLyon R&D Inc.
E&L Mfg., Inc.
E. Arthur Brown Co.
Eagle Arms, Inc. (See ArmaLite, Inc.)
Ed Brown Products, Inc.
Emerging Technologies, Inc. (See Laseraim Technologies, Inc.)
Entre`prise Arms, Inc.
Essex Arms
Excel Industries Inc.
F.I., Inc. - High Standard Mfg. Co.
Fletcher-Bidwell, LLC.
FN Manufacturing
Fort Worth Firearms
Freedom Arms, Inc.
Fulton Armory
Galena Industries AMT

Garcia National Gun Traders, Inc.
Gary Reeder Custom Guns
Genecco Gun Works
Gentry Custom Gunmaker, David
George Hoenig, Inc.
George Madis Winchester Consultants
Gibbs Rifle Co., Inc.
Gil Hebard Guns Inc.
Gilbert Equipment Co., Inc.
Goergen's Gun Shop, Inc.
Goodwin's Gun Shop
Granite Mountain Arms, Inc.
Grayback Wildcats
Gunsite Custom Shop
Gunsite Gunsmithy (See Gunsite Custom Shop)
H&R 1871.LLC
Hammans, Charles E.
Hammerli USA
Harrington & Richardson (See H&R 1871, Inc.)
Harris Gunworks
Hart & Son, Inc.
Hatfield Gun
Hawken Shop, The (See Dayton Traister)
Heritage Firearms (See Heritage Mfg., Inc.)
Heritage Manufacturing, Inc.
Hesco-Meprolight
High Precision
Hi-Point Firearms/MKS Supply
HJS Arms, Inc.
H-S Precision, Inc.
Hutton Rifle Ranch
IAR Inc.
Imperial Miniature Armory
Israel Arms International, Inc.
Ithaca Classic Doubles
Ithaca Gun Company LLC
J.P. Enterprises Inc.
Jim Norman Custom Gunstocks
John Rigby & Co.
John's Custom Leather
K.B.I. Inc.
Kahr Arms
Kehr, Roger
Kelbly's
Kel-Tec CNC Industries, Inc.
Kimber of America, Inc.
Knight Rifles
Knight's Mfg. Co.
Kolar
L.A.R. Mfg., Inc.
L.W. Seecamp Co., Inc.
LaFrance Specialties
Lakefield Arms Ltd. (See Savage Arms, Inc.)
Laseraim Technologies, Inc.
Lever Arms Service Ltd.
Ljutic Industries, Inc.
Lock's Philadelphia Gun Exchange
Lomont Precision Bullets
Lone Star Rifle Company
Mag-Na-Port International, Inc.
Magnum Research, Inc.
Mandall Shooting Supplies Inc.
Marlin Firearms Co.
Maverick Arms, Inc.
McBros Rifle Co.
McCann Industries
Mid-America Recreation, Inc.
Miller Arms, Inc.
MKS Supply, Inc. (See Hi-Point Firearms)
MOA Corporation
Montana Armory, Inc .(See C. Sharps Arms Co. Inc.)
MPI Stocks
Navy Arms Company
NCP Products, Inc.
New Ultra Light Arms, LLC
Noreen, Peter H.
North American Arms, Inc.
North Star West
Northwest Arms

Nowlin Mfg. Co.
Olympic Arms Inc.
Oregon Arms, Inc. (See Rogue Rifle Co., Inc.)
P&M Sales & Services, LLC
Parker & Sons Shooting Supply
Parker Gun Finishes
Phillips & Rogers, Inc.
Phoenix Arms
Precision Small Arms Inc.
ProWare, Inc.
Ramon B. Gonzalez Guns
Rapine Bullet Mould Mfg. Co.
Remington Arms Co., Inc.
Robinson Armament Co.
Rock River Arms
Rocky Mountain Arms, Inc.
Rogue Rifle Co., Inc.
Rogue River Rifleworks
Rohrbaugh
Romain's Custom Guns, Inc.
RPM
Ruger (See Sturm, Ruger & Co., Inc.)
Safari Arms/Schuetzen Pistol Works
Savage Arms (Canada), Inc.
Searcy Enterprises
Sharps Arms Co., Inc., C.
Shiloh Rifle Mfg.
Sklany's Machine Shop
Small Arms Specialists
Smith & Wesson
Sound Technology
Spencer's Rifle Barrels, Inc.
Springfield Armory
Springfield, Inc.
SSK Industries
STI International
Stoeger Industries
Strayer-Voigt, Inc.
Sturm Ruger & Co. Inc.
Sunny Hill Enterprises, Inc.
T&S Industries, Inc.
Taconic Firearms Ltd., Perry Lane
Tank's Rifle Shop
Tar-Hunt Custom Rifles, Inc.
Taurus Firearms, Inc.
Texas Armory (See Bond Arms, Inc.)
The A.W. Peterson Gun Shop, Inc.
The Gun Room Press
The Gun Works
Thompson/Center Arms
Tristar Sporting Arms, Ltd.
U.S. Fire Arms Mfg. Co., Inc.
U.S. Repeating Arms Co., Inc.
Visible Impact Targets
Volquartsen Custom Ltd.
Wallace, Terry
Weatherby, Inc.
Wescombe, Bill (See North Star West)
Wessinger Custom Guns & Engraving
Whildin & Sons Ltd, E.H.
Whitestone Lumber Corp.
Wichita Arms, Inc.
Wichita Arms, Inc.
Wildey, Inc.
Wilsom Combat
Z-M Weapons

GUNSMITH SCHOOL

American Gunsmithing Institute
Bull Mountain Rifle Co.
Colorado Gunsmithing Academy
Colorado School of Trades
Cylinder & Slide, Inc., William R. Laughridge
Lassen Community College, Gunsmithing Dept.
Laughridge, William R (See Cylinder & Slide Inc)
Log Cabin Sport Shop

Modern Gun Repair School
Montgomery Community College
Murray State College
North American Correspondence Schools The Gun Pro
Nowlin Mfg. Co.
NRI Gunsmith School
Pennsylvania Gunsmith School
Piedmont Community College
Pine Technical College
Professional Gunsmiths of America
Smith & Wesson
Southeastern Community College
Spencer's Rifle Barrels, Inc.
Trinidad St. Jr. Col. Gunsmith Dept.
Wright's Gunstock Blanks
Yavapai College

GUNSMITH SUPPLIES, TOOLS & SERVICES

Ace Custom 45's, Inc.
Actions by "T" Teddy Jacobson
Alaskan Silversmith, The
Aldis Gunsmithing & Shooting Supply
Alley Supply Co.
Allred Bullet Co.
Alpec Team, Inc.
American Frontier Firearms Mfg., Inc
American Gunsmithing Institute
Baer Custom Inc., Les
Ballard Rifle & Cartridge Co., LLC
Bar-Sto Precision Machine
Bauska Barrels
Bear Mountain Gun & Tool
Bengtson Arms Co., L.
Bill's Gun Repair
Blue Ridge Machinery & Tools, Inc.
Boyds' Gunstock Industries, Inc.
Break-Free, Inc.
Briley Mfg. Inc.
Brockman's Custom Gunsmithing
Brown Products, Inc., Ed
Brownells, Inc.
Bryan & Assoc.
B-Square Company, Inc.
Buffer Technologies
Bull Mountain Rifle Co.
Bushmaster Firearms
C.S. Van Gorden & Son, Inc.
Carbide Checkering Tools (See J&R Engineering)
Carter's Gun Shop
Caywood, Shane J.
CBC-BRAZIL
Chapman Manufacturing Co.
Chicasaw Gun Works
Choate Machine & Tool Co., Inc.
Ciener Inc., Jonathan Arthur
Colonial Arms, Inc.
Colorado School of Trades
Colt's Mfg. Co., Inc.
Conetrol Scope Mounts
Corbin Mfg. & Supply, Inc.
CRR, Inc./Marble's Inc.
Cumberland Arms
Cumberland Mountain Arms
Custom Checkering Service, Kathy Forster
D'Arcy Echols & Co.
Dem-Bart Checkering Tools, Inc.
Dixie Gun Works
Dixie Gun Works
Dremel Mfg. Co.
Du-Lite Corp.
Efficient Machinery Co.
Entre`prise Arms, Inc.
Erhardt, Dennis
Evolution Gun Works Inc.
Faith Associates
Faloon Industries, Inc.
FERLIB
Fisher, Jerry A.
Forgreens Tool & Mfg., Inc.

Forkin, Ben (See Belt MTN Arms)
Forster, Kathy (See Custom Checkering)
Gentry Custom Gunmaker, David
Goodwin's Gun Shop
Grace Metal Products
Gre-Tan Rifles
Gruning Precision Inc.
Gunline Tools
Half Moon Rifle Shop
Hammond Custom Guns Ltd.
Hastings
Henriksen Tool Co., Inc.
High Performance International
High Precision
Holland's Gunsmithing
Ironsighter Co.
Israel Arms International, Inc.
Ivanoff, Thomas G. (See Tom's Gun Repair)
J&R Engineering
J&S Heat Treat
J. Dewey Mfg. Co., Inc.
Jantz Supply
Jenkins Recoil Pads, Inc.
JGS Precision Tool Mfg., LLC
Jonathan Arthur Ciener, Inc.
Jones Custom Products, Neil A.
Kailua Custom Guns Inc.
Kasenit Co., Inc.
Kleinendorst, K. W.
Korzinek Riflesmith, J.
LaBounty Precision Reboring, Inc
LaFrance Specialties
Laurel Mountain Forge
Lea Mfg. Co.
Lee Supplies, Mark
List Precision Engineering
Lock's Philadelphia Gun Exchange
London Guns Ltd.
Mahovsky's Metalife
Marble Arms (See CRR, Inc./Marble's Inc.)
Mark Lee Supplies
Marsh, Mike
Martin's Gun Shop
McFarland, Stan
Menck, Gunsmith Inc., T.W.
Metalife Industries (See Mahovsky's Metalife)
Michael's Antiques
Micro Sight Co.
Midway Arms, Inc.
MMC
Mo's Competitor Supplies (See MCS, Inc.)
Mowrey's Guns & Gunsmithing
Neil A. Jones Custom Products
New England Custom Gun Service
Ole Frontier Gunsmith Shop
Olympic Arms Inc.
Parker & Sons Shooting Supply
Parker Gun Finishes
Paulsen Gunstocks
PEM's Mfg. Co.
Perazone-Gunsmith, Brian
Peter Dyson & Son Ltd.
Power Custom, Inc.
Practical Tools, Inc.
Precision Specialties
R.A. Wells Custom Gunsmith
Ranch Products
Ransom International Corp.
Reardon Products
Rice, Keith (See White Rock Tool & Die)
Robert Valade Engraving
Rocky Mountain Arms, Inc.
Romain's Custom Guns, Inc.
Royal Arms Gunstocks
Rusteprufe Laboratories
Sharp Shooter Supply
Shooter's Choice Gun Care
Simmons Gun Repair, Inc.
Smith Abrasives, Inc.
Southern Bloomer Mfg. Co.
Spencer Reblue Service

Spencer's Rifle Barrels, Inc.
Spradlin's
Starr Trading Co., Jedediah
Starrett Co., L. S.
Stiles Custom Guns
Stoney Point Products, Inc.
Sullivan, David S .(See Westwind Rifles Inc.)
Sunny Hill Enterprises, Inc.
T&S Industries, Inc.
T.W. Menck Gunsmith Inc.
Tank's Rifle Shop
Texas Platers Supply Co.
The A.W. Peterson Gun Shop, Inc.
The Dutchman's Firearms, Inc.
The Gun Works
The NgraveR Co.
The Robar Co.'s, Inc.
Theis, Terry
Tom's Gun Repair, Thomas G. Ivanoff
Track of the Wolf, Inc.
Trinidad St. Jr. Col. Gunsmith Dept.
Trulock Tool
Turnbull Restoration, Doug
United States Products Co.
Van Gorden & Son Inc., C. S.
Venco Industries, Inc. (See Shooter's Choice Gun Care)
W.C. Wolff Co.
Warne Manufacturing Co.
Washita Mountain Whetstone Co.
Weigand Combat Handguns, Inc.
Wessinger Custom Guns & Engraving
White Rock Tool & Die
Wilcox All-Pro Tools & Supply
Wild West Guns
Will-Burt Co.
Williams Gun Sight Co.
Williams Shootin' Iron Service, The Lynx-Line
Willow Bend
Windish, Jim
Winter, Robert M.
Wise Guns, Dale
Wright's Gunstock Blanks
Yavapai College
Ziegel Engineering

HANDGUN ACCESSORIES

"Su-Press-On", Inc.
A.A. Arms, Inc.
Ace Custom 45's, Inc.
Action Direct, Inc.
ADCO Sales, Inc.
Aimtech Mount Systems
Ajax Custom Grips, Inc.
Alpha 1 Drop Zone
American Derringer Corp.
American Frontier Firearms Mfg., Inc
Arms Corporation of the Philippines
Astra Sport, S.A.
Autauga Arms, Inc.
Badger Creek Studio
Baer Custom Inc., Les
Bagmaster Mfg., Inc.
Bar-Sto Precision Machine
Behlert Precision, Inc.
Berry's Mfg., Inc.
Bill's Custom Cases
Blue and Gray Products Inc. (See Ox-Yoke Originals)
Bond Custom Firearms
Bowen Classic Arms Corp.
Bridgeman Products
Broken Gun Ranch
Brooks Tactical Systems-Agrip
Brown Products, Inc., Ed
Bushmaster Hunting & Fishing
Butler Creek Corp.
Cannon Safe, Inc.

Centaur Systems, Inc.
Central Specialties Ltd (See Trigger Lock Division
Charter 2000
Cheyenne Pioneer Products
Chicasaw Gun Works
Ciener Inc., Jonathan Arthur
Clark Custom Guns, Inc.
Classic Arms Company
Conetrol Scope Mounts
Crimson Trace Lasers
CRR, Inc./Marble's Inc.
Cylinder & Slide, Inc., William R. Laughridge
D&L Industries (See D.J. Marketing)
D.J. Marketing
Dade Screw Machine Products
Delhi Gun House
DeSantis Holster & Leather Goods, Inc.
Dixie Gun Works
Doskocil Mfg. Co., Inc.
E&L Mfg., Inc.
E. Arthur Brown Co.
E.A.A. Corp.
Ed Brown Products, Inc.
Essex Arms
European American Armory Corp (See E.A.A. Corp)
Evolution Gun Works Inc.
F.I., Inc. - High Standard Mfg. Co.
Faloon Industries, Inc.
Federal Arms Corp. of America
Feinwerkbau Westinger & Altenburger
Fisher Custom Firearms
Fleming Firearms
Freedom Arms, Inc.
G.G. & G.
Galati International
GALCO International Ltd.
Garcia National Gun Traders, Inc.
Garthwaite Pistolsmith, Inc., Jim
Gil Hebard Guns Inc.
Gilmore Sports Concepts
Glock, Inc.
Goodwin's Gun Shop
Gould & Goodrich
Gremmel Enterprises
Gun-Alert
Gun-Ho Sports Cases
H.K.S. Products
Hafner World Wide, Inc.
Hammerli USA
Heinie Specialty Products
Henigson & Associates, Steve
Hill Speed Leather, Ernie
Hi-Point Firearms/MKS Supply
Hobson Precision Mfg. Co.
Hoppe's Div. Penguin Industries, Inc.
H-S Precision, Inc.
Hunter Co., Inc.
Impact Case & Container, Inc.
J.P. Enterprises Inc.
Jarvis, Inc.
JB Custom
Jeffredo Gunsight
Jim Noble Co.
John's Custom Leather
Jonathan Arthur Ciener, Inc.
Kalispel Case Line
KeeCo Impressions, Inc.
King's Gun Works
KK Air International (See Impact Case & Container Co.)
L&S Technologies, Inc. (See Aimtech Mount Systems)
Lakewood Products LLC
LaserMax, Inc.
Loch Leven Industries/Convert-A-Pell
Lock's Philadelphia Gun Exchange
Lohman Mfg. Co., Inc.
Mag-Na-Port International, Inc.
Magnolia Sports,Inc.

Mag-Pack Corp.
Mahony, Philip Bruce
Mandall Shooting Supplies Inc.
Marble Arms (See CRR, Inc./Marble's Inc.)
Markell,Inc.
McCormick Corp., Chip
MEC-Gar S.R.L.
Menck, Gunsmith Inc., T.W.
Merkuria Ltd.
Middlebrooks Custom Shop
Millett Sights
Mogul Co./Life Jacket
MTM Molded Products Co., Inc.
No-Sho Mfg. Co.
Numrich Gun Parts Corporation
Omega Sales
Outdoor Sports Headquarters, Inc.
Ox-Yoke Originals, Inc.
Pachmayr Div. Lyman Products
Pager Pal
Palmer Security Products
Parker & Sons Shooting Supply
Pearce Grip, Inc.
Perazone-Gunsmith, Brian
Phoenix Arms
Practical Tools, Inc.
Precision Small Arms Inc.
Protektor Model
Ram-Line ATK
Ranch Products
Ransom International Corp.
Ringler Custom Leather Co.
RPM
Seecamp Co. Inc., L. W.
Simmons Gun Repair, Inc.
Sound Technology
Southern Bloomer Mfg. Co.
Springfield Armory
Springfield, Inc.
SSK Industries
Sturm Ruger & Co. Inc.
T.F.C. S.p.A.
Tactical Defense Institute
Tanfoglio Fratelli S.r.l.
The A.W. Peterson Gun Shop, Inc.
The Concealment Shop, Inc.
The Gun Works
The Keller Co.
The Protector Mfg. Co., Inc.
Thompson/Center Arms
Trigger Lock Division / Central Specialties Ltd.
Trijicon, Inc.
Triple-K Mfg. Co., Inc.
Truglo, Inc.
Tyler Manufacturing & Distributing
United States Products Co.
Universal Sports
Volquartsen Custom Ltd.
W. Waller & Son, Inc.
W.C. Wolff Co.
Warne Manufacturing Co.
Weigand Combat Handguns, Inc.
Wessinger Custom Guns & Engraving
Western Design (See Alpha Gunsmith Division)
Whitestone Lumber Corp.
Wild West Guns
Williams Gun Sight Co.
Wilsom Combat
Yankee Gunsmith "Just Glocks"
Ziegel Engineering

HANDGUN GRIPS

A.A. Arms, Inc.
African Import Co.
Ahrends, Kim (See Custom Firearms, Inc)
Ajax Custom Grips, Inc.
Altamont Co.
American Derringer Corp.
American Frontier Firearms Mfg., Inc

American Gripcraft
Arms Corporation of the Philippines
Art Jewel Enterprises Ltd.
Baelder, Harry
Baer Custom Inc., Les
Big Bear Arms & Sporting Goods, Inc.
Bob's Gun Shop
Boone Trading Co., Inc.
Boone's Custom Ivory Grips, Inc.
Boyds' Gunstock Industries, Inc.
Brooks Tactical Systems-Agrip
Brown Products, Inc., Ed
Clark Custom Guns, Inc.
Cole-Grip
Colonial Repair
Crimson Trace Lasers
Custom Firearms (See Ahrends, Kim)
Cylinder & Slide, Inc., William R. Laughridge
Dixie Gun Works
E.A.A. Corp.
EMF Co., Inc.
Essex Arms
European American Armory Corp (See E.A.A. Corp)
F.I., Inc. - High Standard Mfg. Co.
Faloon Industries, Inc.
Feinwerkbau Westinger & Altenburger
Fibron Products, Inc.
Fisher Custom Firearms
Forrest Inc., Tom
Garthwaite Pistolsmith, Inc., Jim
Goodwin's Gun Shop
Herrett's Stocks, Inc.
HIP-GRIP Barami Corp.
Hogue Grips
H-S Precision, Inc.
Huebner, Corey O.
I.S.S.
Israel Arms International, Inc.
John Masen Co. Inc.
KeeCo Impressions, Inc.
Kim Ahrends Custom Firearms, Inc.
Korth Germany GmbH
Lett Custom Grips
Linebaugh Custom Sixguns
Lyman Products Corp.
Mandall Shooting Supplies Inc.
Michaels Of Oregon, Co.
Millett Sights
N.C. Ordnance Co.
Newell, Robert H.
Northern Precision Custom Swaged Bullets
Pachmayr Div. Lyman Products
Pardini Armi Srl
Parker & Sons Shooting Supply
Perazone-Gunsmith, Brian
Pilgrim Pewter,Inc. (See Bell Originals Inc. Sid)
Precision Small Arms Inc.
Radical Concepts
Rosenberg & Son, Jack A
Roy's Custom Grips
Spegel, Craig
Stoeger Industries
Sturm Ruger & Co. Inc.
Sunny Hill Enterprises, Inc.
Tactical Defense Institute
Taurus Firearms, Inc.
The A.W. Peterson Gun Shop, Inc.
Tirelli
Triple-K Mfg. Co., Inc.
Tyler Manufacturing & Distributing
U.S. Fire Arms Mfg. Co., Inc.
Uncle Mike's (See Michaels of Oregon Co.)
Vintage Industries, Inc.
Volquartsen Custom Ltd.
Western Mfg. Co.
Whitestone Lumber Corp.
Wright's Gunstock Blanks

PRODUCT & SERVICE DIRECTORY

HEARING PROTECTORS

Aero Peltor
Ajax Custom Grips, Inc.
Brown Co., E. Arthur
Browning Arms Co.
Creedmoor Sports, Inc.
David Clark Co., Inc.
Dillon Precision Products, Inc.
Dixie Gun Works
E-A-R, Inc.
Electronic Shooters Protection,
    Inc.
Gentex Corp.
Goodwin's Gun Shop
Gunsmithing, Inc.
Hoppe's Div. Penguin Industries,
    Inc.
Kesselring Gun Shop
Mandall Shooting Supplies Inc.
North Specialty Products
Parker & Sons Shooting Supply
Paterson Gunsmithing
Peltor, Inc. (See Aero Peltor)
R.E.T. Enterprises
Ridgeline, Inc.
Rucker Dist. Inc.
Silencio/Safety Direct
Sound Technology
Tactical Defense Institute
The A.W. Peterson Gun Shop, Inc.
The Gun Room Press
Triple-K Mfg. Co., Inc.
Watson Trophy Match Bullets
Whitestone Lumber Corp.

HOLSTERS & LEATHER GOODS

A&B Industries,Inc (See Top-Line
    USA Inc)
A.A. Arms, Inc.
Action Direct, Inc.
Action Products, Inc.
Aker International, Inc.
AKJ Concealco
Alessi Holsters, Inc.
Arratoonian, Andy (See Horseshoe
    Leather Products)
Autauga Arms, Inc.
Bagmaster Mfg., Inc.
Baker's Leather Goods, Roy
Bandcor Industries, Div. of Man-
    Sew Corp.
Bang-Bang Boutique (See Holster
    Shop, The)
Beretta S.p.A., Pietro
Bianchi International, Inc.
Bond Arms, Inc.
Brocock Ltd.
Brooks Tactical Systems-Agrip
Brown, H. R. (See Silhouette
    Leathers)
Browning Arms Co.
Bull-X, Inc.
Cape Outfitters
Cathey Enterprises, Inc.
Chace Leather Products
Churchill Glove Co., James
Cimarron F.A. Co.
Classic Old West Styles
Clements' Custom Leathercraft,
    Chas
Cobra Sport S.r.l.
Colonial Repair
Counter Assault
Delhi Gun House
DeSantis Holster & Leather Goods,
    Inc.
Dillon Precision Products, Inc.
Dixie Gun Works
Ekol Leather Care
El Paso Saddlery Co.
EMF Co., Inc.
Faust Inc., T. G.
Freedom Arms, Inc.

Gage Manufacturing
GALCO International Ltd.
Garcia National Gun Traders, Inc.
Gil Hebard Guns Inc.
Gilmore Sports Concepts
GML Products, Inc.
Goodwin's Gun Shop
Gould & Goodrich
Gun Leather Limited
Gunfitters
Hafner World Wide, Inc.
HandCrafts Unltd (See Clements'
    Custom Leather)
Hank's Gun Shop
Heinie Specialty Products
Henigson & Associates, Steve
Hill Speed Leather, Ernie
HIP-GRIP Barami Corp.
Hobson Precision Mfg. Co.
Hogue Grips
Horseshoe Leather Products
Hume, Don
Hunter Co., Inc.
Jim Noble Co.
John's Custom Leather
K.L. Null Holsters Ltd.
Kane Products, Inc.
Kirkpatrick Leather Co.
Kolpin Mfg., Inc.
Korth Germany GmbH
Kramer Handgun Leather
L.A.R. Mfg., Inc.
Lawrence Leather Co.
Lock's Philadelphia Gun Exchange
Lone Star Gunleather
Magnolia Sports,Inc.
Mandall Shooting Supplies Inc.
Markell,Inc.
Marksman Products
Michaels Of Oregon, Co.
Minute Man High Tech Industries
Navy Arms Company
No-Sho Mfg. Co.
Null Holsters Ltd. K.L.
October Country Muzzleloading
Ojala Holsters, Arvo
Oklahoma Leather Products,Inc.
Old West Reproductions,Inc. R.M.
    Bachman
Pager Pal
Parker & Sons Shooting Supply
Pathfinder Sports Leather
Protektor Model
PWL Gunleather
Ramon B. Gonzalez Guns
Renegade
Ringler Custom Leather Co.
Rogue Rifle Co., Inc.
Safariland Ltd., Inc.
Safety Speed Holster, Inc.
Scharch Mfg., Inc.-Top Brass
Schulz Industries
Second Chance Body Armor
Silhouette Leathers
Smith Saddlery, Jesse W.
Sparks, Milt
Stalker, Inc.
Starr Trading Co., Jedediah
Strong Holster Co.
Stuart, V. Pat
Tabler Marketing
Tactical Defense Institute
Ted Blocker Holsters, Inc.
Tex Shoemaker & Sons, Inc.
Thad Rybka Custom Leather
    Equipment
The A.W. Peterson Gun Shop, Inc.
The Concealment Shop, Inc.
The Gun Works
The Keller Co.
The Outdoor Connection, Inc.
Torel, Inc.
Triple-K Mfg. Co., Inc.
Tristar Sporting Arms, Ltd.
Tyler Manufacturing & Distributing
Uncle Mike's (See Michaels of
    Oregon Co.)

Venus Industries
Walt's Custom Leather, Walt
    Whinnery
Watson Trophy Match Bullets
Westley Richards & Co.
Whinnery, Walt (See Walt's
    Custom Leather)
Wild Bill's Originals
Wilsom Combat

HUNTING & CAMP GEAR, CLOTHING, ETC.

Ace Sportswear, Inc.
Action Direct, Inc.
Action Products, Inc.
Adventure 16, Inc.
Adventure Game Calls
All Rite Products, Inc.
Allen Co., Bob
Allen Sportswear, Bob (See Allen
    Co., Bob)
Alpha 1 Drop Zone
Armor (See Buck Stop Lure Co.,
    Inc.)
Atlanta Cutlery Corp.
Atsko/Sno-Seal, Inc.
B.B. Walker Co.
Baekgaard Ltd.
Bagmaster Mfg., Inc.
Barbour, Inc.
Bauer, Eddie
Bear Archery
Beaver Park Product, Inc.
Beretta S.p.A., Pietro
Better Concepts Co.
Bill Russ Trading Post
Boonie Packer Products
Boss Manufacturing Co.
Browning Arms Co.
Buck Stop Lure Co., Inc.
Bushmaster Hunting & Fishing
Cambos Outdoorsman
Cambos Outdoorsman
Camp-Cap Products
Carhartt,Inc.
Churchill Glove Co., James
Clarkfield Enterprises, Inc.
Classic Old West Styles
Clements' Custom Leathercraft,
    Chas
Coghlan's Ltd.
Cold Steel Inc.
Coleman Co., Inc.
Coulston Products, Inc.
Counter Assault
Dakota Corp.
Danner Shoe Mfg. Co.
Deepeeka Exports Pvt. Ltd.
Dr. O's Products Ltd.
Duofold, Inc.
Dynalite Products, Inc.
E-A-R, Inc.
Ekol Leather Care
Forrest Tool Co.
Fox River Mills, Inc.
Frontier
G&H Decoys,Inc.
Gerber Legendary Blades
Glacier Glove
Grand Slam Hunting Products
HandCrafts Unltd (See Clements'
    Custom Leather)
High North Products, Inc.
Hinman Outfitters, Bob
Hodgman, Inc.
Houtz & Barwick
Hunter's Specialties Inc.
James Churchill Glove Co.
John's Custom Leather
K&M Industries, Inc.
Kamik Outdoor Footwear
Kolpin Mfg., Inc.
L.L. Bean, Inc.
LaCrosse Footwear, Inc.
Leapers, Inc.

MAG Instrument, Inc.
Mag-Na-Port International, Inc.
Marathon Rubber Prods. Co., Inc.
McCann Industries
McCann's Machine & Gun Shop
Molin Industries, Tru-Nord Division
Murphy, R.R. Co., Inc.
Nelson/Weather-Rite, Inc.
North Specialty Products
Northlake Outdoor Footwear
Original Deer Formula Co., The.
Original Mink Oil, Inc.
Palsa Outdoor Products
Partridge Sales Ltd., John
Pointing Dog Journal, Village Press
    Publications
Powell & Son (Gunmakers) Ltd.,
    William
Pro-Mark Div. of Wells Lamont
Ringler Custom Leather Co.
Robert Valade Engraving
Rocky Shoes & Boots
Scansport, Inc.
Sceery Game Calls
Schaefer Shooting Sports
Servus Footwear Co.
Simmons Outdoor Corp.
Sno-Seal, Inc. (See Atsko/Sno-
    Seal, Inc.)
Streamlight, Inc.
Swanndri New Zealand
T.H.U. Enterprises, Inc.
TEN-X Products Group
The A.W. Peterson Gun Shop, Inc.
The Orvis Co.
The Outdoor Connection, Inc.
Tink's Safariland Hunting Corp.
Torel, Inc.
Triple-K Mfg. Co., Inc.
United Cutlery Corp.
Venus Industries
Wakina by Pic
Walls Industries, Inc.
Wideview Scope Mount Corp.
Wilderness Sound Products Ltd.
Winchester Sutler, Inc., The
Wolverine Footwear Group
Woolrich, Inc.
Wyoming Knife Corp.
Yellowstone Wilderness Supply

KNIVES & KNIFEMAKER'S SUPPLIES

A.G. Russell Knives, Inc.
Action Direct, Inc.
Adventure 16, Inc.
African Import Co.
Aitor-Cuchilleria Del Norte S.A.
American Target Knives
Art Jewel Enterprises Ltd.
Atlanta Cutlery Corp.
B&D Trading Co., Inc.
Barteaux Machete
Belltown Ltd.
Benchmark Knives (See Gerber
    Legendary Blades)
Beretta S.p.A., Pietro
Beretta U.S.A. Corp.
Big Bear Arms & Sporting Goods,
    Inc.
Bill Russ Trading Post
Bill's Custom Cases
Boker USA, Inc.
Boone Trading Co., Inc.
Boone's Custom Ivory Grips, Inc.
Bowen Knife Co., Inc.
Brooks Tactical Systems-Agrip
Browning Arms Co.
Buck Knives, Inc.
Buster's Custom Knives
Camillus Cutlery Co.
Campbell, Dick
Case & Sons Cutlery Co., W R
Chicago Cutlery Co.

Clements' Custom Leathercraft,
    Chas
Cold Steel Inc.
Coleman Co., Inc.
Compass Industries, Inc.
Crosman Blades (See Coleman Co.,
    Inc.)
CRR, Inc./Marble's Inc.
Cutco Cutlery
damascususa@inteliport.com
Dan's Whetstone Co., Inc.
Deepeeka Exports Pvt. Ltd.
Degen Inc. (See Aristocrat Knives)
Delhi Gun House
DeSantis Holster & Leather Goods,
    Inc.
Diamond Machining Technology,
    Inc. (See DMT)
Dixie Gun Works
EdgeCraft Corp., S. Weiner
Empire Cutlery Corp.
Eze-Lap Diamond Prods.
Flitz International Ltd.
Forrest Tool Co.
Forthofer's Gunsmithing &
    Knifemaking
Fortune Products, Inc.
Frank Knives
Frost Cutlery Co.
Galati International
George Ibberson (Sheffield) Ltd.
Gerber Legendary Blades
Gibbs Rifle Co., Inc.
Glock, Inc.
Golden Age Arms Co.
H&B Forge Co.
Hafner World Wide, Inc.
Hammans, Charles E.
HandCrafts Unltd (See Clements'
    Custom Leather)
Harris Publications
High North Products, Inc.
Hoppe's Div. Penguin Industries,
    Inc.
Hunter Co., Inc.
Imperial Schrade Corp.
J.A. Blades, Inc. (See Christopher
    Firearms Co.)
J.A. Henckels Zwillingswerk Inc.
Jackalope Gun Shop
Jantz Supply
Jenco Sales, Inc.
Jim Blair Engraving
Johnson Wood Products
KA-BAR Knives
Kasenit Co., Inc.
Kershaw Knives
Knifeware, Inc.
Koval Knives
Lamson & Goodnow Mfg. Co.
Lansky Sharpeners
Leapers, Inc.
Leatherman Tool Group, Inc.
Lethal Force Institute (See Police
    Bookshelf)
Linder Solingen Knives
Mandall Shooting Supplies Inc.
Marble Arms (See CRR,
    Inc./Marble's Inc.)
Marshall Fish Mfg. Gunsmith Sptg.
    Co.
Matthews Cutlery
McCann Industries
McCann's Machine & Gun Shop
Molin Industries, Tru-Nord Division
Mountain State Muzzleloading
    Supplies, Inc.
Normark Corp.
October Country Muzzleloading
Outdoor Edge Cutlery Corp.
Pilgrim Pewter,Inc. (See Bell
    Originals, Inc. Sid)
Plaza Cutlery, Inc.
Police Bookshelf
Queen Cutlery Co.
R&C Knives & Such
R. Murphy Co., Inc.

Randall-Made Knives
Ringler Custom Leather Co.
Robert Valade Engraving
Rodgers & Sons Ltd., Joseph (See George Ibberson)
Scansport, Inc.
Schiffman, Mike
Sheffield Knifemakers Supply, Inc.
Smith Saddlery, Jesse W.
Springfield Armory
Spyderco, Inc.
T.F.C. S.p.A.
The A.W. Peterson Gun Shop, Inc.
The Creative Craftsman, Inc.
The Gun Room
The Gun Works
Theis, Terry
Traditions Performance Firearms
Traditions Performance Firearms
Tru-Balance Knife Co.
United Cutlery Corp.
Utica Cutlery Co.
Venus Industries
W.R. Case & Sons Cutlery Co.
Washita Mountain Whetstone Co.
Weber Jr., Rudolf
Wells Creek Knife & Gun Works
Wenger North America/Precise Int'l
Western Cutlery (See Camillus Cutlery Co.)
Whinnery, Walt (See Walt's Custom Leather)
Wideview Scope Mount Corp.
Wostenholm (See Ibberson [Sheffield] Ltd., George)
Wyoming Knife Corp.

LABELS, BOXES & CARTRIDGE HOLDERS

Ballistic Product, Inc.
Berry's Mfg., Inc.
Brocock Ltd.
Brown Co., E. Arthur
Cabinet Mtn. Outfitters Scents & Lures
Cheyenne Pioneer Products
Del Rey Products
DeSantis Holster & Leather Goods, Inc.
Flambeau Products Corp.
Goodwin's Gun Shop
Hafner World Wide, Inc.
J&J Products, Inc.
Kolpin Mfg., Inc.
Liberty Shooting Supplies
Midway Arms, Inc.
MTM Molded Products Co., Inc.
Pendleton Royal, c/o Swingler Buckland Ltd.
Protektor Model
Ziegel Engineering

LEAD WIRES & WIRE CUTTERS

Ames Metal Products
Big Bore Express
Bullet Swaging Supply, Inc.
Goodwin's Gun Shop
Liberty Metals
Lightning Performance Innovations, Inc.
Montana Precision Swaging
Northern Precision Custom Swaged Bullets
Sport Flite Manufacturing Co.
Star Ammunition, Inc.
Unmussig Bullets, D. L.

LOAD TESTING & PRODUCT TESTING

Ballistic Research

Bitterroot Bullet Co.
Bridgeman Products
Briese Bullet Co., Inc.
Buckskin Bullet Co.
Bull Mountain Rifle Co.
CFVentures
Claybuster Wads & Harvester Bullets
Clearview Products
D&H Precision Tooling
Dead Eye's Sport Center
Defense Training International, Inc.
Duane's Gun Repair (See DGR Custom Rifles)
Gruning Precision Inc.
Gun Hunter Books (See Gun Hunter Trading Co.)
Gun Hunter Trading Co.
H.P. White Laboratory, Inc.
Hank's Gun Shop
Henigson & Associates, Steve
Hutton Rifle Ranch
J&J Sales
Jackalope Gun Shop
Jensen Bullets
L. E. Jurras & Assoc.
Liberty Shooting Supplies
Linebaugh Custom Sixguns
Lomont Precision Bullets
Maionchi-L.M.I.
MAST Technology, Inc.
McMurdo, Lynn (See Specialty Gunsmithing)
Middlebrooks Custom Shop
Modern Gun Repair School
Multiplex International
Northwest Arms
Oil Rod and Gun Shop
Plum City Ballistic Range
R.A. Wells Custom Gunsmith
Ramon B. Gonzalez Guns
Rupert's Gun Shop
Small Custom Mould & Bullet Co.
SOS Products Co. (See Buck Stix-SOS Products Co.)
Spencer's Rifle Barrels, Inc.
Tar-Hunt Custom Rifles, Inc.
Trinidad St. Jr. Col. Gunsmith Dept.
Vulpes Ventures, Inc. Fox Cartridge Division
W. Square Enterprises
X-Spand Target Systems

LOADING BLOCKS, METALLIC & SHOTSHELL

Battenfeld Technologies
Buffalo Arms Co.
Huntington Die Specialties
Jericho Tool & Die Co., Inc.
Sinclair International, Inc.
The A.W. Peterson Gun Shop, Inc.

LUBRISIZERS, DIES & ACCESSORIES

Ballisti-Cast, Inc.
Ben's Machines
Buffalo Arms Co.
Cast Performance Bullet Company
Cooper-Woodward
Corbin Mfg. & Supply, Inc.
GAR
Hart & Son, Inc.
Javelina Lube Products
Lee Precision, Inc.
Lithi Bee Bullet Lube
Lyman Products Corp.
Magma Engineering Co.
RCBS Operations/ATK
Redding Reloading Equipment
SPG LLC
The A.W. Peterson Gun Shop, Inc.
Thompson Bullet Lube Co.

United States Products Co.
WTA Manufacturing

MOULDS & MOULD ACCESSORIES

Ad Hominem
American Products, Inc.
Ballisti-Cast, Inc.
Buffalo Arms Co.
Bullet Swaging Supply, Inc.
Cast Performance Bullet Company
Corbin Mfg. & Supply, Inc.
Davide Pedersoli and Co.
GAR
Huntington Die Specialties
Lee Precision, Inc.
Lyman Products Corp.
Magma Engineering Co.
NEI Handtools, Inc.
Old West Bullet Moulds
Penn Bullets
Rapine Bullet Mould Mfg. Co.
RCBS Operations/ATK
Redding Reloading Equipment
S&S Firearms
Small Custom Mould & Bullet Co.
The A.W. Peterson Gun Shop, Inc.
The Gun Works
Wolf's Western Traders

MUZZLE-LOADING GUNS, BARRELS & EQUIPMENT

Accuracy Unlimited
Ackerman & Co.
Adkins, Luther
Allen Mfg.
Armi San Paolo
Armoury, Inc., The
Austin & Halleck, Inc.
Bauska Barrels
Beaver Lodge (See Fellowes, Ted)
Bentley, John
Big Bore Express
Birdsong & Assoc., W. E.
Black Powder Products
Blount/Outers ATK
Blue and Gray Products Inc. (See Ox-Yoke Originals)
Bridgers Best
Buckskin Bullet Co.
Bullberry Barrel Works, Ltd.
Butler Creek Corp.
Cabela's
Cache La Poudre Rifleworks
California Sights (See Fautheree, Andy)
Cash Mfg. Co., Inc.
Caywood Gunmakers
CBC-BRAZIL
Chambers Flintlocks Ltd., Jim
Chicasaw Gun Works
Cimarron F.A. Co.
Claybuster Wads & Harvester Bullets
Cogar's Gunsmithing
Colonial Repair
Colt Blackpowder Arms Co.
Conetrol Scope Mounts
Cousin Bob's Mountain Products
Cumberland Arms
Cumberland Mountain Arms
Curly Maple Stock Blanks (See Tiger-Hunt)
CVA
Dangler, Homer L.
Davide Pedersoli and Co.
Dayton Traister
deHaas Barrels
Delhi Gun House
Dixie Gun Works
Dixie Gun Works
Dixon Muzzleloading Shop, Inc.

EMF Co., Inc.
Euroarms of America, Inc.
Feken, Dennis
Fellowes, Ted
Flintlocks, Etc.
Fort Hill Gunstocks
Fowler, Bob (See Black Powder Products)
Frontier
Getz Barrel Co.
Goergen's Gun Shop
Golden Age Arms Co.
Gonic Arms/North American Arm
Goodwin's Gun Shop
Green Mountain Rifle Barrel Co., Inc.
H&R 1871.LLC
Hastings
Hawken Shop, The (See Dayton Traister)
Hege Jagd-u. Sporthandels GmbH
Hodgdon Powder Co.
Hoppe's Div. Penguin Industries, Inc.
Hornady Mfg. Co.
House of Muskets, Inc., The
Hunkeler, A (See Buckskin Machine Works)
IAR Inc.
Impact Case & Container, Inc.
Ironsighter Co.
J. Dewey Mfg. Co., Inc.
Jamison's Forge Works
Jones Co., Dale
K&M Industries, Inc.
Kalispel Case Line
Kennedy Firearms
Knight Rifles
Knight Rifles (See Modern Muzzle Loading, Inc.)
Kolar
L&R Lock Co.
L&S Technologies Inc. (See Aimtech Mount Systems)
Lakewood Products LLC
Legend Products Corp.
Lodgewood Mfg.
Log Cabin Sport Shop
Lothar Walther Precision Tool Inc.
Lyman Products Corp.
Markesbery Muzzle Loaders, Inc.
Marlin Firearms Co.
McCann's Muzzle-Gun Works
Michaels Of Oregon, Co.
Millennium Designed Muzzleloaders
Modern Muzzleloading, Inc.
Mountain State Muzzleloading Supplies, Inc.
Mowrey Gun Works
Mt. Alto Outdoor Products
Navy Arms Company
Newman Gunshop
North Star West
October Country Muzzleloading
Oklahoma Leather Products,Inc.
Olson, Myron
Orion Rifle Barrel Co.
Ox-Yoke Originals, Inc.
Pacific Rifle Co.
Parker & Sons Shooting Supply
Parker Gun Finishes
Pecatonica River Longrifle
Peter Dyson & Son Ltd.
Pioneer Arms Co.
Prairie River Arms
Rusty Duck Premium Gun Care Products
S&S Firearms
Selsi Co., Inc.
Simmons Gun Repair, Inc.
Sklany's Machine Shop
Smokey Valley Rifles
South Bend Replicas, Inc.
Southern Bloomer Mfg. Co.
Splitfire Sporting Goods, L.L.C.
Starr Trading Co., Jedediah

Stone Mountain Arms
Sturm Ruger & Co. Inc.
Taylor's & Co., Inc.
Tennessee Valley Mfg.
The A.W. Peterson Gun Shop, Inc.
The Gun Works
The Hawken Shop
Thompson Bullet Lube Co.
Thompson/Center Arms
Tiger-Hunt Gunstocks
Track of the Wolf, Inc.
Traditions Performance Firearms
Truglo, Inc.
Uncle Mike's (See Michaels of Oregon Co.)
Universal Sports
Upper Missouri Trading Co.
Venco Industries, Inc. (See Shooter's Choice Gun Care)
Virgin Valley Custom Guns
Voere-KGH GmbH
W.E. Birdsong & Assoc.
Warne Manufacturing Co.
Warren Muzzleloading Co., Inc.
Wescombe, Bill (See North Star West)
White Rifles, Inc.
William E. Phillips Firearms
Woodworker's Supply
Wright's Gunstock Blanks
Young Country Arms
Ziegel Engineering

PISTOLSMITH

A.W. Peterson Gun Shop, Inc.
Acadian Ballistic Specialties
Accuracy Unlimited
Ace Custom 45's, Inc.
Actions by "T" Teddy Jacobson
Adair Custom Shop, Bill
Ahlman Guns
Ahrends, Kim (See Custom Firearms, Inc)
Aldis Gunsmithing & Shooting Supply
Alpha Precision, Inc.
Alpine Indoor Shooting Range
Armament Gunsmithing Co., Inc.
Arundel Arms & Ammunition, Inc., A.
Badger Creek Studio
Baer Custom Inc., Les
Bain & Davis, Inc.
Banks, Ed
Bar-Sto Precision Machine
Behlert Precision, Inc.
Ben William's Gun Shop
Bengtson Arms Co., L.
Bill Adair Custom Shop
Billings Gunsmiths
Bowen Classic Arms Corp.
Broken Gun Ranch
Caraville Manufacturing
Chicasaw Gun Works
Clark Custom Guns, Inc.
Cleland's Outdoor World, Inc
Colonial Repair
Colorado School of Trades
Colt's Mfg. Co., Inc.
Corkys Gun Clinic
Custom Firearms (See Ahrends, Kim)
Cylinder & Slide, Inc., William R. Laughridge
D&D Gunsmiths, Ltd.
D&L Sports
David R. Chicoine
Dayton Traister
Dilliott Gunsmithing, Inc.
Ellicott Arms, Inc. / Woods Pistolsmithing
Evolution Gun Works Inc.
F.I., Inc. - High Standard Mfg. Co.
Ferris Firearms
Fisher Custom Firearms

PRODUCT & SERVICE DIRECTORY

Forkin, Ben (See Belt MTN Arms)
Forkin Arms
Francesca, Inc.
G.G. & G.
Garthwaite Pistolsmith, Inc., Jim
Gary Reeder Custom Guns
Genecco Gun Works
Gentry Custom Gunmaker, David
George E. Mathews & Son, Inc.
Greider Precision
Guncraft Sports Inc.
Guncraft Sports, Inc.
Gunsite Custom Shop
Gunsite Gunsmithy (See Gunsite Custom Shop)
Gunsite Training Center
Hamilton, Alex B (See Ten-Ring Precision, Inc)
Hammerli Service-Precision Mac
Hammond Custom Guns Ltd.
Hank's Gun Shop
Hanson's Gun Center, Dick
Harris Gunworks
Harwood, Jack O.
Hawken Shop, The (See Dayton Traister)
Heinie Specialty Products
High Bridge Arms, Inc
Highline Machine Co.
Hoag, James W.
Irwin, Campbell H.
Island Pond Gun Shop
Ivanoff, Thomas G. (See Tom's Gun Repair)
J&S Heat Treat
Jarvis, Inc.
Jeffredo Gunsight
Jensen's Custom Ammunition
Jungkind, Reeves C.
Kaswer Custom, Inc.
Ken Starnes Gunmaker
Kilham & Co.
Kim Ahrends Custom Firearms, Inc.
King's Gun Works
La Clinique du .45
LaFrance Specialties
LaRocca Gun Works
Lathrop's, Inc.
Lawson, John G (See Sight Shop, The)
Leckie Professional Gunsmithing
Linebaugh Custom Sixguns
List Precision Engineering
Long, George F.
Mag-Na-Port International, Inc.
Mahony, Philip Bruce
Mahovsky's Metalife
Mandall Shooting Supplies Inc.
Marvel, Alan
Mathews & Son, Inc., George E.
McCann's Machine & Gun Shop
MCS, Inc.
Middlebrooks Custom Shop
Miller Custom
Mitchell's Accuracy Shop
MJK Gunsmithing, Inc.
Modern Gun Repair School
Montgomery Community College
Mo's Competitor Supplies (See MCS, Inc.)
Mowrey's Guns & Gunsmithing
Mullis Guncraft
NCP Products, Inc.
Novak's, Inc.
Nowlin Mfg. Co.
Olathe Gun Shop
Paris, Frank J.
Pasadena Gun Center
Peacemaker Specialists
PEM's Mfg. Co.
Performance Specialists
Peterson Gun Shop, Inc., A.W.
Pierce Pistols
Piquette's Custom Engraving
Power Custom, Inc.
Precision Specialties

Ramon B. Gonzalez Guns
Randco UK
Ries, Chuck
Rim Pac Sports, Inc.
Rocky Mountain Arms, Inc.
RPM
Ruger's Custom Guns
Score High Gunsmithing
Shooters Supply
Shootin' Shack
Singletary, Kent
Springfield, Inc.
SSK Industries
Swenson's 45 Shop, A. D.
Swift River Gunworks
Ten-Ring Precision, Inc.
Terry K. Kopp Professional Gunsmithing
The A.W. Peterson Gun Shop, Inc.
The Gun Works
The Robar Co.'s, Inc.
The Sight Shop
Thompson, Randall (See Highline Machine Co.)
Thurston Sports, Inc.
Tom's Gun Repair, Thomas G. Ivanoff
Turnbull Restoration, Doug
Vic's Gun Refinishing
Volquartsen Custom Ltd.
Walker Arms Co., Inc.
Walters Industries
Wardell Precision Handguns Ltd.
Wessinger Custom Guns & Engraving
White Barn Wor
Wichita Arms, Inc.
Wild West Guns
Williams Gun Sight Co.
Williamson Precision Gunsmithing
Wilsom Combat
Wright's Gunstock Blanks

POWDER MEASURES, SCALES, FUNNELS & ACCESSORIES

4-D Custom Die Co.
Battenfeld Technologies
Buffalo Arms Co.
Dillon Precision Products, Inc.
Fremont Tool Works
Frontier
GAR
High Precision
Hoehn Sales, Inc.
Jones Custom Products, Neil A.
Modern Muzzleloading, Inc.
Neil A. Jones Custom Products
Peter Dyson & Son Ltd.
Precision Reloading, Inc.
Ramon B. Gonzalez Guns
RCBS Operations/ATK
RCBS/ATK
Redding Reloading Equipment
Saunders Gun & Machine Shop
Spencer's Rifle Barrels, Inc.
The A.W. Peterson Gun Shop, Inc.
Vega Tool Co.
VibraShine, Inc.
VTI Gun Parts

PRESS ACCESSORIES, METALLIC

Buffalo Arms Co.
Corbin Mfg. & Supply, Inc.
Efficient Machinery Co.
Hollywood Engineering
Huntington Die Specialties
R.E.I.
Redding Reloading Equipment
The A.W. Peterson Gun Shop, Inc.
Thompson Tool Mount
Vega Tool Co.

PRESS ACCESSORIES, SHOTSHELL

Efficient Machinery Co.
Hollywood Engineering
Lee Precision, Inc.
MEC, Inc.
Precision Reloading, Inc.
R.E.I.
The A.W. Peterson Gun Shop, Inc.

PRESSES, ARBOR

Blue Ridge Machinery & Tools, Inc.
Goodwin's Gun Shop
K&M Services
RCBS Operations/ATK
Spencer's Rifle Barrels, Inc.
The A.W. Peterson Gun Shop, Inc.

PRESSES, METALLIC

4-D Custom Die Co.
Battenfeld Technologies
Dillon Precision Products, Inc.
Fremont Tool Works
Goodwin's Gun Shop
Hornady Mfg. Co.
Huntington Die Specialties
Lee Precision, Inc.
Midway Arms, Inc.
R.E.I.
Ramon B. Gonzalez Guns
RCBS Operations/ATK
RCBS/ATK
Redding Reloading Equipment
Spencer's Rifle Barrels, Inc.
The A.W. Peterson Gun Shop, Inc.

PRESSES, SHOTSHELL

Ballistic Product, Inc.
Dillon Precision Products, Inc.
Goodwin's Gun Shop
Hornady Mfg. Co.
MEC, Inc.
Precision Reloading, Inc.
Spolar Power Load Inc.
The A.W. Peterson Gun Shop, Inc.

PRESSES, SWAGE

Bullet Swaging Supply, Inc.
The A.W. Peterson Gun Shop, Inc.

PRIMING TOOLS & ACCESSORIES

Goodwin's Gun Shop
Hart & Son, Inc.
Huntington Die Specialties
K&M Services
RCBS Operations/ATK
Simmons, Jerry
Sinclair International, Inc.
The A.W. Peterson Gun Shop, Inc.

REBORING & RERIFLING

Ahlman Guns
Bauska Barrels
BlackStar AccuMax Barrels
BlackStar Barrel Accurizing (See BlackStar AccuMax)
Buffalo Arms Co.
Champlin Firearms, Inc.
Ed's Gun House
Fred F. Wells/Wells Sport Store
H&S Liner Service
Ivanoff, Thomas G. (See Tom's Gun Repair)
Jackalope Gun Shop
LaBounty Precision Reboring, Inc

NCP Products, Inc.
Pence Precision Barrels
Redman's Rifling & Reboring
Rice, Keith (See White Rock Tool & Die)
Ridgetop Sporting Goods
Savage Arms, Inc.
Shaw, Inc., E. R. (See Small Arms Mfg. Co.)
Siegrist Gun Shop
Simmons Gun Repair, Inc.
Stratco, Inc.
Terry K. Kopp Professional Gunsmithing
The Gun Works
Time Precision
Tom's Gun Repair, Thomas G. Ivanoff
Turnbull Restoration, Doug
Van Patten, J. W.
White Rock Tool & Die
Zufall, Joseph F.

RELOADING TOOLS AND ACCESSORIES

4-D Custom Die Co.
Advance Car Mover Co., Rowell Div.
American Products, Inc.
Ammo Load, Inc.
Armfield Custom Bullets
Armite Laboratories
Arms Corporation of the Philippines
Atlantic Rose, Inc.
Atsko/Sno-Seal, Inc.
Bald Eagle Precision Machine Co.
Ballistic Product, Inc.
Belltown Ltd.
Ben William's Gun Shop
Ben's Machines
Berger Bullets Ltd.
Berry's Mfg., Inc.
Blount, Inc., Sporting Equipment Div.
Blue Mountain Bullets
Blue Ridge Machinery & Tools, Inc.
Bonanza (See Forster Products)
Break-Free, Inc.
Brown Co., E. Arthur
BRP, Inc. High Performance Cast Bullets
Brynin, Milton
B-Square Company, Inc.
Buck Stix-SOS Products Co.
Buffalo Arms Co.
Bull Mountain Rifle Co.
Bullseye Bullets
C&D Special Products (See Claybuster Wads & Harvester Bullets)
Camdex, Inc.
Camp-Cap Products
Canyon Cartridge Corp.
Case Sorting System
CH Tool & Die Co. (See 4-D Custom Die Co.)
CheVron Bullets
Claybuster Wads & Harvester Bullets
CONKKO
Cook Engineering Service
Crouse's Country Cover
Cumberland Arms
Curtis Cast Bullets
Custom Products (See Jones Custom Products)
CVA
D.C.C. Enterprises
Davide Pedersoli and Co.
Davis, Don
Davis Products, Mike
Denver Instrument Co.
Dillon Precision Products, Inc.
Dropkick

E&L Mfg., Inc.
Eagan, Donald V.
Eezox, Inc.
Eichelberger Bullets, Wm.
Enguix Import-Export
Euroarms of America, Inc.
E-Z-Way Systems
Federated-Fry (See Fry Metals)
Feken, Dennis
Ferguson, Bill
First Inc., Jack
Fisher Custom Firearms
Flambeau Products Corp.
Flitz International Ltd.
Forster Products
Fremont Tool Works
Fry Metals
Gehmann, Walter (See Huntington Die Specialties)
Graf & Sons
Graphics Direct
Graves Co.
Green, Arthur S.
Greenwood Precision
GTB
Gun City
Hanned Precision (See The Hanned Line)
Harrell's Precision
Harris Enterprises
Harrison Bullets
Haydon Shooters Supply, Russ
Heidenstrom Bullets
High Precision
Hirtenberger AG
Hodgdon Powder Co.
Hoehn Sales, Inc.
Holland's Gunsmithing
Hondo Ind.
Hornady Mfg. Co.
Howell Machine
Hunters Supply, Inc.
Hutton Rifle Ranch
Image Ind. Inc.
Imperial Magnum Corp.
INTEC International, Inc.
Iosso Products
J&L Superior Bullets (See Huntington Die Special)
Javelina Lube Products
JGS Precision Tool Mfg., LLC
JLK Bullets
Jonad Corp.
Jones Custom Products, Neil A.
Jones Moulds, Paul
K&M Services
Kapro Mfg. Co. Inc. (See R.E.I.)
Knoell, Doug
Korzinek Riflesmith, J.
L.A.R. Mfg., Inc.
L.E. Wilson, Inc.
Lapua Ltd.
Le Clear Industries (See E-Z-Way Systems)
Lee Precision, Inc.
Legend Products Corp.
Liberty Metals
Liberty Shooting Supplies
Lightning Performance Innovations, Inc.
Lithi Bee Bullet Lube
Littleton, J. F.
Lock's Philadelphia Gun Exchange
Lortone Inc.
Lyman Instant Targets, Inc. (See Lyman Products)
Lyman Products Corp.
MA Systems
Magma Engineering Co.
MarMik, Inc.
Marquart Precision Co.
Match Prep-Doyle Gracey
Mayville Engineering Co. (See MEC, Inc.)
MCS, Inc.
MEC, Inc.
Midway Arms, Inc.

PRODUCT & SERVICE DIRECTORY

MI-TE Bullets
Montana Armory, Inc .(See C. Sharps Arms Co. Inc.)
Mo's Competitor Supplies (See MCS, Inc.)
Mountain South
Mountain State Muzzleloading Supplies, Inc.
MTM Molded Products Co., Inc.
Multi-Scale Charge Ltd.
MWG Co.
Navy Arms Company
Newman Gunshop
North Devon Firearms Services
Old West Bullet Moulds
Omark Industries, Div. of Blount, Inc.
Original Box, Inc.
Outdoor Sports Headquarters, Inc.
Paco's (See Small Custom Mould & Bullet Co.)
Paragon Sales & Services, Inc.
Pease Accuracy
Pinetree Bullets
Ponsness/Warren
Prairie River Arms
Prime Reloading
Professional Hunter Supplies (See Star Custom Bullets)
Pro-Shot Products, Inc.
R.A. Wells Custom Gunsmith
R.E.I.
R.I.S. Co., Inc.
Rapine Bullet Mould Mfg. Co.
Reloading Specialties, Inc.
Rice, Keith (See White Rock Tool & Die)
Rochester Lead Works
Rooster Laboratories
Rorschach Precision Products
SAECO (See Redding Reloading Equipment)
Sandia Die & Cartridge Co.
Saunders Gun & Machine Shop
Saville Iron Co. (See Greenwood Precision)
Seebeck Assoc., R.E.
Sharp Shooter Supply
Sharps Arms Co., Inc., C.
Shiloh Rifle Mfg.
Sierra Specialty Prod. Co.
Silver Eagle Machining
Skip's Machine
Small Custom Mould & Bullet Co.
Sno-Seal, Inc. (See Atsko/Sno-Seal, Inc.)
SOS Products Co. (See Buck Stix-SOS Products Co.)
Spencer's Rifle Barrels, Inc.
SPG LLC
SSK Industries
Stalwart Corporation
Star Custom Bullets
Starr Trading Co., Jedediah
Stillwell, Robert
Stoney Point Products, Inc.
Stratco, Inc.
Tamarack Products, Inc.
Taracorp Industries, Inc.
TCCI
TCSR
TDP Industries, Inc.
Tetra Gun Care
The Hanned Line
The Protector Mfg. Co., Inc.
Thompson/Center Arms
TMI Products (See Haselbauer Products, Jerry)
Vega Tool Co.
Venco Industries, Inc. (See Shooter's Choice Gun Care)
VibraShine, Inc.
Vibra-Tek Co.
Vihtavuori Oy/Kaltron-Pettibone
Vitt/Boos
W.B. Niemi Engineering
W.J. Riebe Co.

WD-40 Co.
Webster Scale Mfg. Co.
White Rock Tool & Die
Widener's Reloading & Shooting Supply, Inc.
Wise Custom Guns
Woodleigh (See Huntington Die Specialties)
Yesteryear Armory & Supply
Young Country Arms

RESTS BENCH, PORTABLE AND ACCESSORIES

Adventure 16, Inc.
Armor Metal Products
Bald Eagle Precision Machine Co.
Bartlett Engineering
Battenfeld Technologies
Blount/Outers ATK
Browning Arms Co.
B-Square Company, Inc.
Bull Mountain Rifle Co.
Canons Delcour
Clift Mfg., L. R.
Desert Mountain Mfg.
Efficient Machinery Co.
Greenwood Precision
Harris Engineering Inc.
Hidalgo, Tony
Hoehn Sales, Inc.
Hoppe's Div. Penguin Industries, Inc.
J&J Sales
Keng's Firearms Specialty, Inc./US Tactical Systems
Kolpin Mfg., Inc.
Kramer Designs
Midway Arms, Inc.
Millett Sights
Protektor Model
Ransom International Corp.
Russ Haydon's Shooters' Supply
Saville Iron Co. (See Greenwood Precision)
Sinclair International, Inc.
Stoney Point Products, Inc.
T.H.U. Enterprises, Inc.
The A.W. Peterson Gun Shop, Inc.
The Outdoor Connection, Inc.
Thompson Target Technology
Tonoloway Tack Drives
Varmint Masters, LLC
Wichita Arms, Inc.
Zanotti Armor, Inc.
Ziegel Engineering

RIFLE BARREL MAKER

Airrow
American Safe Arms, Inc.
Bauska Barrels
BlackStar AccuMax Barrels
BlackStar Barrel Accurizing (See BlackStar AccuMax)
Border Barrels Ltd.
Brown Co., E. Arthur
Buchsenmachermeister
Bullberry Barrel Works, Ltd.
Bushmaster Firearms
Canons Delcour
Carter's Gun Shop
Christensen Arms
Cincinnati Swaging
deHaas Barrels
Dilliott Gunsmithing, Inc.
DKT, Inc.
Donnelly, C. P.
Douglas Barrels, Inc.
Fred F. Wells/Wells Sport Store
Gaillard Barrels
Gary Schneider Rifle Barrels Inc.
Getz Barrel Co.
Granite Mountain Arms, Inc.

Green Mountain Rifle Barrel Co., Inc.
Gruning Precision Inc.
Half Moon Rifle Shop
Harris Gunworks
Hart Rifle Barrels,Inc.
Hastings
Hofer Jagdwaffen, P.
H-S Precision, Inc.
Jackalope Gun Shop
Krieger Barrels, Inc.
Lilja Precision Rifle Barrels
Lothar Walther Precision Tool Inc.
McGowen Rifle Barrels
McMillan Rifle Barrels
Mid-America Recreation, Inc.
Modern Gun Repair School
Morrison Precision
N.C. Ordnance Co.
Obermeyer Rifled Barrels
Olympic Arms Inc.
Orion Rifle Barrel Co.
PAC-NOR Barreling
Pence Precision Barrels
Rogue Rifle Co., Inc.
Sabatti SPA
Savage Arms, Inc.
Schneider Rifle Barrels, Inc., Gary
Shaw, Inc., E. R. (See Small Arms Mfg. Co.)
Shilen, Inc.
Siskiyou Gun Works (See Donnelly, C. P.)
Small Arms Mfg. Co.
Specialty Shooters Supply, Inc.
Spencer's Rifle Barrels, Inc.
Strutz Rifle Barrels, Inc., W. C.
Swift River Gunworks
Terry K. Kopp Professional Gunsmithing
The Gun Works
The Wilson Arms Co.
Turnbull Restoration, Doug
Unmussig Bullets, D. L.
Verney-Carron
Virgin Valley Custom Guns
Wiseman and Co., Bill

SCOPES, MOUNTS, ACCESSORIES, OPTICAL EQUIPMENT

A.R.M.S., Inc.
Accu-Tek
Ackerman, Bill (See Optical Services Co.)
Action Direct, Inc.
ADCO Sales, Inc.
Aimtech Mount Systems
Air Rifle Specialists
Air Venture Airguns
All Rite Products, Inc.
Alley Supply Co.
Alpec Team, Inc.
Apel GmbH, Ernst
ArmaLite, Inc.
Arundel Arms & Ammunition, Inc., A.
B.A.C.
Badger Creek Studio
Baer Custom Inc., Les
Bansner's Ultimate Rifles, LLC
Barrett Firearms Manufacturer, Inc.
Beaver Park Product, Inc.
BEC, Inc.
Beeman Precision Airguns
Ben William's Gun Shop
Benjamin/Sheridan Co., Crosman
Bill Russ Trading Post
BKL Technologies
Blount, Inc., Sporting Equipment Div.
Blount/Outers ATK
Borden Rifles Inc.
Brockman's Custom Gunsmithing
Brocock Ltd.

Brown Co., E. Arthur
Brownells, Inc.
Brunton U.S.A.
BSA Optics
B-Square Company, Inc.
Bull Mountain Rifle Co.
Burris Co., Inc.
Bushmaster Firearms
Bushnell Sports Optics Worldwide
Butler Creek Corp.
Cabela's
Carl Zeiss Inc.
Center Lock Scope Rings
Chuck's Gun Shop
Clark Custom Guns, Inc.
Clearview Mfg. Co., Inc.
Compass Industries, Inc.
Compasseco, Ltd.
Concept Development Corp.
Conetrol Scope Mounts
Creedmoor Sports, Inc.
Crimson Trace Lasers
Crosman Airguns
Custom Quality Products, Inc.
D.C.C. Enterprises
Daisy Outdoor Products
Del-Sports, Inc.
DHB Products
E. Arthur Brown Co.
Eclectic Technologies, Inc.
Edmund Scientific Co.
Ednar, Inc.
Eggleston, Jere D.
Emerging Technologies, Inc. (See Laseraim Technologies, Inc.)
Entre`prise Arms, Inc.
Euro-Imports
Evolution Gun Works Inc.
Excalibur Electro Optics Inc.
Excel Industries Inc.
Faloon Industries, Inc.
Farr Studio, Inc.
Federal Arms Corp. of America
Freedom Arms, Inc.
Fujinon, Inc.
G.G. & G.
Galati International
Gentry Custom Gunmaker, David
Gil Hebard Guns Inc.
Gilmore Sports Concepts
Goodwin's Gun Shop
GSI, Inc.
Gun South, Inc. (See GSI, Inc.)
Guns Div. of D.C. Engineering, Inc.
Gunsmithing, Inc.
Hakko Co. Ltd.
Hammerli USA
Harris Gunworks
Harvey, Frank
Highwood Special Products
Hiptmayer, Armurier
Hiptmayer, Klaus
HiTek International
Holland's Gunsmithing
Impact Case & Container, Inc.
Ironsighter Co.
Jeffredo Gunsight
Jena Eur
Jerry Phillips Optics
Jewell Triggers, Inc.
John Masen Co. Inc.
John's Custom Leather
Kahles A. Swarovski Company
Kalispel Case Line
KDF, Inc.
Keng's Firearms Specialty, Inc./US Tactical Systems
Kesselring Gun Shop
Kimber of America, Inc.
Knight's Mfg. Co.
Kowa Optimed, Inc.
KVH Industries, Inc.
Kwik-Site Co.
L&S Technologies Inc. (See Aimtech Mount Systems)
L.A.R. Mfg., Inc.
Laser Devices, Inc.

Laseraim Technologies, Inc.
LaserMax, Inc.
Leapers, Inc.
Leica USA, Inc.
Leupold & Stevens, Inc.
List Precision Engineering
Lohman Mfg. Co., Inc.
Lomont Precision Bullets
London Guns Ltd.
Mac-1 Airgun Distributors
Mag-Na-Port International, Inc.
Mandall Shooting Supplies Inc.
Marksman Products
Maxi-Mount Inc.
McBros Rifle Co.
McCann's Machine & Gun Shop
McMillan Optical Gunsight Co.
MCS, Inc.
MDS
Merit Corp.
Military Armament Corp.
Millett Sights
Mirador Optical Corp.
Mitchell Optics, Inc.
MMC
Mo's Competitor Supplies (See MCS, Inc.)
MWG Co.
Navy Arms Company
New England Custom Gun Service
Nikon, Inc.
Norincoptics (See BEC, Inc.)
Olympic Optical Co.
Optical Services Co.
Orchard Park Enterprise
Oregon Arms, Inc. (See Rogue Rifle Co., Inc.)
Ozark Gun Works
Parker & Sons Shooting Supply
Parsons Optical Mfg. Co.
PECAR Herbert Schwarz GmbH
PEM's Mfg. Co.
Pentax Corp.
PMC/Eldorado Cartridge Corp.
Precision Sport Optics
Premier Reticles
R.A. Wells Custom Gunsmith
Ram-Line ATK
Ramon B. Gonzalez Guns
Ranch Products
Randolph Engineering Inc.
Rice, Keith (See White Rock Tool & Die)
Robinson Armament Co.
Rogue Rifle Co., Inc.
Romain's Custom Guns, Inc.
S&K Scope Mounts
Saunders Gun & Machine Shop
Schmidt & Bender, Inc.
Schumakers Gun Shop
Scope Control, Inc.
Score High Gunsmithing
Seecamp Co. Inc., L. W.
Segway Industries
Selsi Co., Inc.
Sharp Shooter Supply
Shepherd Enterprises, Inc.
Sightron, Inc.
Simmons Outdoor Corp.
Six Enterprises
Southern Bloomer Mfg. Co.
Spencer's Rifle Barrels, Inc.
Splitfire Sporting Goods, L.L.C.
Sportsmatch U.K. Ltd.
Springfield Armory
Springfield, Inc.
SSK Industries
Stiles Custom Guns
Stoeger Industries
Stoney Point Products, Inc.
Sturm Ruger & Co. Inc.
Sunny Hill Enterprises, Inc.
Swarovski Optik North America Ltd.
Swift Instruments, Inc.
T.K. Lee Co.
Talley, Dave

PRODUCT & SERVICE DIRECTORY

Tasco Sales, Inc.
Tele-Optics
The A.W. Peterson Gun Shop, Inc.
The Outdoor Connection, Inc.
Thompson/Center Arms
Traditions Performance Firearms
Trijicon, Inc.
Truglo, Inc.
Ultra Dot Distribution
Uncle Mike's (See Michaels of
  Oregon Co.)
Unertl Optical Co., Inc.
United Binocular Co.
United States Optics Technologies,
  Inc.
Virgin Valley Custom Guns
Visible Impact Targets
Voere-KGH GmbH
Warne Manufacturing Co.
Warren Muzzleloading Co., Inc.
Watson Trophy Match Bullets
Weaver Products ATK
Weaver Scope Repair Service
Weigand Combat Handguns, Inc.
Wessinger Custom Guns &
  Engraving
Westley Richards & Co.
White Rifles, Inc.
White Rock Tool & Die
Whitestone Lumber Corp.
Wideview Scope Mount Corp.
Wilcox Industries Corp.
Wild West Guns
Williams Gun Sight Co.
York M-1 Conversions
Zanotti Armor, Inc.

SHELLHOLDERS

Corbin Mfg. & Supply, Inc.
Fremont Tool Works
Goodwin's Gun Shop
Hart & Son, Inc.
Hollywood Engineering
Huntington Die Specialties
K&M Services
King & Co.
RCBS Operations/ATK
Redding Reloading Equipment
The A.W. Peterson Gun Shop, Inc.
Vega Tool Co.

SHOOTING/TRAINING SCHOOL

Alpine Indoor Shooting Range
American Gunsmithing Institute
American Small Arms Academy
Auto Arms
Beretta U.S.A. Corp.
Bob's Tactical Indoor Shooting
  Range & Gun Shop
Bridgeman Products
Chapman Academy of Practical
  Shooting
Chelsea Gun Club of New York City
  Inc.
Cherry Creek State Park Shooting
  Center
CQB Training
Defense Training International, Inc.
Executive Protection Institute
Ferris Firearms
Front Sight Firearms Training
  Institute
G.H. Enterprises Ltd.
Gene's Custom Guns
Griffin & Howe, Inc.
Griffin & Howe, Inc.
Griffin & Howe, Inc.
Guncraft Books (See Guncraft
  Sports Inc.)
Guncraft Sports Inc.
Guncraft Sports, Inc.
Gunsite Training Center

Henigson & Associates, Steve
Jensen's Custom Ammunition
Jensen's Firearms Academy
Kemen America
L.L. Bean, Inc.
Lethal Force Institute (See Police
  Bookshelf)
Loch Leven Industries/Convert-A-
  Pell
Long, George F.
McMurdo, Lynn (See Specialty
  Gunsmithing)
Mendez, John A.
NCP Products, Inc.
Nevada Pistol Academy, Inc.
North American Shooting Systems
North Mountain Pine Training
  Center (See Executive
Nowlin Mfg. Co.
Paxton Quigley's Personal
  Protection Strategies
Pentheny de Pentheny
Performance Specialists
Police Bookshelf
SAFE
Shoot Where You Look
Shooter's World
Shooters, Inc.
Sigarms, Inc.
Smith & Wesson
Specialty Gunsmithing
Starlight Training Center, Inc.
Tactical Defense Institute
The Firearm Training Center
The Midwest Shooting School
The Shooting Gallery
Thunder Ranch
Western Missouri Shooters
  Alliance
Yankee Gunsmith "Just Glocks"
Yavapai Firearms Academy Ltd.

SHOTSHELL MISCELLANY

American Products, Inc.
Ballistic Product, Inc.
Bridgeman Products
Goodwin's Gun Shop
Lee Precision, Inc.
MEC, Inc.
Precision Reloading, Inc.
R.E.I.
RCBS Operations/ATK
T&S Industries, Inc.
The A.W. Peterson Gun Shop, Inc.
The Gun Works
Vitt/Boos
Ziegel Engineering

SIGHTS, METALLIC

100 Straight Products, Inc.
Accura-Site (See All's, The Jim
  Tembelis Co., Inc.)
Ad Hominem
Alley Supply Co.
All's, The Jim J. Tembelis Co., Inc.
Alpec Team, Inc.
Andela Tool & Machine, Inc.
AO Sight Systems
ArmaLite, Inc.
Ashley Outdoors, Inc.
Aspen Outfitting Co.
Axtell Rifle Co.
B.A.C.
Baer Custom Inc., Les
Ballard Rifle & Cartridge Co., LLC
BEC, Inc.
Bob's Gun Shop
Bo-Mar Tool & Mfg. Co.
Bond Custom Firearms
Bowen Classic Arms Corp.
Brockman's Custom Gunsmithing
Brooks Tactical Systems-Agrip

Brown Co., E. Arthur
Brown Dog Ent.
Brownells, Inc.
Buffalo Arms Co.
Bushmaster Firearms
C. Sharps Arms Co. Inc./Montana
  Armory
California Sights (See Fautheree,
  Andy)
Campbell, Dick
Cape Outfitters
Cape Outfitters
Cash Mfg. Co., Inc.
Center Lock Scope Rings
Champion's Choice, Inc.
C-More Systems
Colonial Repair
CRR, Inc./Marble's Inc.
Davide Pedersoli and Co.
DHB Products
Dixie Gun Works
DPMS (Defense Procurement
  Manufacturing Services, Inc.)
E. Arthur Brown Co.
Evolution Gun Works Inc.
Faloon Industries, Inc.
Farr Studio, Inc.
G.G. & G.
Garthwaite Pistolsmith, Inc., Jim
Goergen's Gun Shop, Inc.
Goodwin's Gun Shop
Guns Div. of D.C. Engineering, Inc.
Gunsmithing, Inc.
Hank's Gun Shop
Heidenstrom Bullets
Heinie Specialty Products
Hesco-Meprolight
Hiptmayer, Armurier
Hiptmayer, Klaus
I.S.S.
Innovative Weaponry Inc.
J.G. Anschutz GmbH & Co. KG
J.P. Enterprises Inc.
Keng's Firearms Specialty, Inc./US
  Tactical Systems
Knight Rifles
Knight's Mfg. Co.
L.P.A. Inc.
Leapers, Inc.
List Precision Engineering
London Guns Ltd.
Lyman Instant Targets, Inc. (See
  Lyman Products)
Mandall Shooting Supplies Inc.
Marble Arms (See CRR,
  Inc./Marble's Inc.)
MCS, Inc.
MEC-Gar S.R.L.
Meprolight (See Hesco-
  Meprolight)
Merit Corp.
Mid-America Recreation, Inc.
Middlebrooks Custom Shop
Millett Sights
MMC
Modern Muzzleloading, Inc.
Montana Armory, Inc .(See C.
  Sharps Arms Co. Inc.)
Montana Vintage Arms
Mo's Competitor Supplies (See
  MCS, Inc.)
Navy Arms Company
New England Custom Gun Service
Newman Gunshop
Novak's, Inc.
OK Weber, Inc.
One Ragged Hole
Parker & Sons Shooting Supply
PEM's Mfg. Co.
Perazone-Gunsmith, Brian
RPM
Sharps Arms Co., Inc., C.
Slug Site
STI International
T.F.C. S.p.A.
Talley, Dave
Tank's Rifle Shop

The A.W. Peterson Gun Shop, Inc.
The Gun Doctor
Trijicon, Inc.
Truglo, Inc.
United States Optics Technologies,
  Inc.
Warne Manufacturing Co.
Weigand Combat Handguns, Inc.
Wichita Arms, Inc.
Wild West Guns
Williams Gun Sight Co.
Wilsom Combat
Wilsom Combat

STOCK MAKER

Acra-Bond Laminates
Al Lind Custom Guns
Amrine's Gun Shop
Antique Arms Co.
Artistry in Wood
Aspen Outfitting Co.
Bain & Davis, Inc.
Bansner's Ultimate Rifles, LLC
Baron Technology
Belding's Custom Gun Shop
Billings Gunsmiths
Bob Rogers Gunsmithing
Boltin, John M.
Borden Ridges Rimrock Stocks
Bowerly, Kent
Boyds' Gunstock Industries, Inc.
Brace, Larry D.
Briganti, A.J.
Brown Precision, Inc.
Buchsenmachermeister
Bull Mountain Rifle Co.
Bullberry Barrel Works, Ltd.
Burkhart Gunsmithing, Don
Cambos Outdoorsman
Cambos Outdoorsman
Caywood, Shane J.
Chicasaw Gun Works
Chuck's Gun Shop
Claro Walnut Gunstock Co.
Coffin, Charles H.
Colorado Gunsmithing Academy
Custom Riflestocks, Inc., Michael
  M. Kokolus
Custom Single Shot Rifles
Custom Stocking
D&D Gunsmiths, Ltd.
Dangler, Homer L.
D'Arcy Echols & Co.
DGR Custom Rifles
DGR Custom Rifles
DGS, Inc., Dale A. Storey
Erhardt, Dennis
Eversull Co., Inc.
Fieldsport Ltd.
Fisher, Jerry A.
Forster, Larry L.
Fred F. Wells/Wells Sport Store
Gary Goudy Classic Stocks
Genecco Gun Works
Gene's Custom Guns
George E. Mathews & Son, Inc.
Gillmann, Edwin
Grace, Charles E.
Great American Gunstock Co.
Gruning Precision Inc.
Gunsmithing Ltd.
Hank's Gun Shop
Harper's Custom Stocks
Harry Lawson Co.
Heilmann, Stephen
Hensley, Gunmaker, Darwin
Heydenberk, Warren R.
High Tech Specialties, Inc.
Hofer Jagdwaffen, P.
Huebner, Corey O.
Island Pond Gun Shop
Jack Dever Co.
Jamison's Forge Works
Jay McCament Custom Gunmaker
Jim Norman Custom Gunstocks

John Rigby & Co.
K. Eversull Co., Inc.
Keith's Custom Gunstocks
Ken Eyster Heritage Gunsmiths,
  Inc.
Klein Custom Guns, Don
L. E. Jurras & Assoc.
Larry Lyons Gunworks
Marshall Fish Mfg. Gunsmith Sptg.
  Co.
Mathews & Son, Inc., George E.
McGowen Rifle Barrels
Mercer Custom Guns
Mid-America Recreation, Inc.
Mitchell, Jack
Modern Gun Repair School
Morrow, Bud
Nelson's Custom Guns, Inc.
Nettestad Gun Works
Nickels, Paul R.
Paul and Sharon Dressel
Paul D. Hillmer Custom Gunstocks
Paulsen Gunstocks
Pawling Mountain Club
Pecatonica River Longrifle
Pentheny de Pentheny
Quality Custom Firearms
R&J Gun Shop
R.A. Wells Custom Gunsmith
Ralph Bone Engraving
RMS Custom Gunsmithing
Ron Frank Custom Classic Arms
Royal Arms Gunstocks
Ruger's Custom Guns
Six Enterprises
Skeoch, Brian R.
Smith, Art
Smith, Sharmon
Speiser, Fred D.
Steven Dodd Hughes
Stott's Creek Armory, Inc.
Sturgeon Valley Sporters
Talmage, William G.
Taylor & Robbins
The Custom Shop
Tiger-Hunt Gunstocks
Trico Plastics
Tucker, James C.
Turnbull Restoration, Doug
Vest, John
Walker Arms Co., Inc.
Wayne E. Schwartz Custom Guns
Weber & Markin Custom
  Gunsmiths
Wenig Custom Gunstocks
Wiebe, Duane
Wild West Guns
Williamson Precision Gunsmithing
Winter, Robert M.
Working Guns

STOCKS (COMMERCIAL)

Accuracy Unlimited
Acra-Bond Laminates
Ahlman Guns
Al Lind Custom Guns
Arms Ingenuity Co.
Arundel Arms & Ammunition, Inc.,
  A.
Aspen Outfitting Co.
B.A.C.
Baelder, Harry
Balickie, Joe
Bansner's Ultimate Rifles, LLC
Barnes Bullets, Inc.
Battenfeld Technologies
Beitzinger, George
Belding's Custom Gun Shop
Bell & Carlson, Inc.
Blount, Inc., Sporting Equipment
  Div.
Blount/Outers ATK
Bob's Gun Shop
Borden Ridges Rimrock Stocks
Borden Rifles Inc.

REFERENCE

Wald

PRODUCT & SERVICE DIRECTORY

Bowerly, Kent
Boyds' Gunstock Industries, Inc.
Brockman's Custom Gunsmithing
Brown Co., E. Arthur
Buckhorn Gun Works
Bull Mountain Rifle Co.
Butler Creek Corp.
Cali'co Hardwoods, Inc.
Cape Outfitters
Caywood, Shane J.
Chambers Flintlocks Ltd., Jim
Chicasaw Gun Works
Chuilli, Stephen
Claro Walnut Gunstock Co.
Coffin, Charles H.
Coffin, Jim (See Working Guns)
Colonial Repair
Colorado Gunsmithing Academy
Colorado School of Trades
Conrad, C. A.
Curly Maple Stock Blanks (See Tiger-Hunt)
Custom Checkering Service, Kathy Forster
Custom Riflestocks, Inc., Michael M. Kokolus
D&D Gunsmiths, Ltd.
D&G Precision Duplicators (See Greene Precision)
David W. Schwartz Custom Guns
Davide Pedersoli and Co.
DGR Custom Rifles
Duane's Gun Repair (See DGR Custom Rifles)
Duncan's Gun Works, Inc.
Eggleston, Jere D.
Erhardt, Dennis
Eversull Co., Inc.
Faloon Industries, Inc.
Faloon Industries, Inc.
Fibron Products, Inc.
Fieldsport Ltd.
Fisher, Jerry A.
Folks, Donald E.
Forster, Kathy (See Custom Checkering)
Forthofer's Gunsmithing & Knifemaking
Francotte & Cie S.A. Auguste
Game Haven Gunstocks
George Hoenig, Inc.
Gervais, Mike
Gillmann, Edwin
Giron, Robert E.
Goens, Dale W.
Golden Age Arms Co.
Goodwin's Gun Shop
Great American Gunstock Co.
Green, Roger M.
Greenwood Precision
Guns Div. of D.C. Engineering, Inc.
Gunsmithing Ltd.
Hammerli USA
Hanson's Gun Center, Dick
Harper's Custom Stocks
Harris Gunworks
Harry Lawson Co.
Hart & Son, Inc.
Harwood, Jack O.
Hecht, Hubert J, Waffen-Hecht
Hensley, Gunmaker, Darwin
High Tech Specialties, Inc.
Hiptmayer, Armurier
Hiptmayer, Klaus
Hogue Grips
H-S Precision, Inc.
Huebner, Corey O.
Island Pond Gun Shop
Israel Arms International, Inc.
Ivanoff, Thomas G. (See Tom's Gun Repair)
Jackalope Gun Shop

Jarrett Rifles, Inc.
Jay McCament Custom Gunmaker
Jim Norman Custom Gunstocks
John Masen Co. Inc.
Johnson Wood Products
KDF, Inc.
Keith's Custom Gunstocks
Kelbly, Inc.
Kilham & Co.
Klingler Woodcarving
Kokolus, Michael M. (See Custom Riflestocks In)
Lawson Co., Harry
Mandall Shooting Supplies Inc.
McBros Rifle Co.
McDonald, Dennis
McMillan Fiberglass Stocks, Inc.
Michaels Of Oregon, Co.
Mid-America Recreation, Inc.
Miller Arms, Inc.
Mitchell, Jack
Morrison Custom Rifles, J. W.
MPI Stocks
MWG Co.
NCP Products, Inc.
Nelson's Custom Guns, Inc.
New England Arms Co.
New England Custom Gun Service
Newman Gunshop
Nickels, Paul R.
Oil Rod and Gun Shop
Old World Gunsmithing
One Of A Kind
Ottmar, Maurice
Pagel Gun Works, Inc.
Paragon Sales & Services, Inc.
Parker & Sons Shooting Supply
Paul and Sharon Dressel
Paul D. Hillmer Custom Gunstocks
Paulsen Gunstocks
Pawling Mountain Club
Pecatonica River Longrifle
PEM's Mfg. Co.
Pohl, Henry A. (See Great American Gun Co.)
Powell & Son (Gunmakers) Ltd., William
Precision Gun Works
R&J Gun Shop
R.A. Wells Custom Gunsmith
Ram-Line ATK
Ramon B. Gonzalez Guns
Rampart International
Reagent Chemical & Research, Inc.
Reiswig, Wallace E. (See Claro Walnut Gunstock)
Richards Micro-Fit Stocks
RMS Custom Gunsmithing
Robinson, Don
Robinson Armament Co.
Robinson Firearms Mfg. Ltd.
Romain's Custom Guns, Inc.
Ron Frank Custom Classic Arms
Royal Arms Gunstocks
Saville Iron Co. (See Greenwood Precision)
Schiffman, Curt
Schiffman, Mike
Score High Gunsmithing
Simmons Gun Repair, Inc.
Six Enterprises
Speiser, Fred D.
Stan De Treville & Co.
Stiles Custom Guns
Swann, D. J.
Swift River Gunworks
Szweda, Robert (See RMS Custom Gunsmithing)
T.F.C. S.p.A.
Talmage, William G.
Tecnolegno S.p.A.
The A.W. Peterson Gun Shop, Inc.

The Gun Shop
The Orvis Co.
Tiger-Hunt Gunstocks
Tirelli
Tom's Gun Repair, Thomas G. Ivanoff
Track of the Wolf, Inc.
Trevallion Gunstocks
Tuttle, Dale
Vic's Gun Refinishing
Vintage Industries, Inc.
Virgin Valley Custom Guns
Volquartsen Custom Ltd.
Walker Arms Co., Inc.
Weber & Markin Custom Gunsmiths
Weems, Cecil
Wenig Custom Gunstocks
Werth, T. W.
Western Mfg. Co.
Wild West Guns
Williams Gun Sight Co.
Windish, Jim
Winter, Robert M.
Working Guns
Wright's Gunstock Blanks
Zeeryp, Russ

STUCK CASE REMOVERS

Goodwin's Gun Shop
Huntington Die Specialties
MarMik, Inc.
The A.W. Peterson Gun Shop, Inc.
Tom's Gun Repair, Thomas G. Ivanoff

TARGETS, BULLET & CLAYBIRD TRAPS

Action Target, Inc.
Air Arms
American Target
Autauga Arms, Inc.
Beeman Precision Airguns
Benjamin/Sheridan Co., Crosman
Beomat of America, Inc.
Birchwood Casey
Blount, Inc., Sporting Equipment Div.
Blount/Outers ATK
Blue and Gray Products Inc. (See Ox-Yoke Originals)
Brown Precision, Inc.
Bull-X, Inc.
Champion Target Co.
Creedmoor Sports, Inc.
Crosman Airguns
D.C.C. Enterprises
Daisy Outdoor Products
Detroit-Armor Corp.
Diamond Mfg. Co.
Federal Champion Target Co.
G.H. Enterprises Ltd.
Hiti-Schuch, Atelier Wilma
H-S Precision, Inc.
Hunterjohn
J.G. Dapkus Co., Inc.
Kennebec Journal
Kleen-Bore,Inc.
Lakefield Arms Ltd. (See Savage Arms, Inc.)
Leapers, Inc.
Littler Sales Co.
Lyman Instant Targets, Inc. (See Lyman Products)
Marksman Products
Mendez, John A.
Mountain Plains Industries

MSR Targets
Muscle Products Corp.
N.B.B., Inc.
National Target Co.
North American Shooting Systems
Outers Laboratories Div. of ATK
Ox-Yoke Originals, Inc.
Palsa Outdoor Products
Passive Bullet Traps, Inc. (See Savage Range Systems, Inc.)
PlumFire Press, Inc.
Precision Airgun Sales, Inc.
Protektor Model
Quack Decoy & Sporting Clays
Remington Arms Co., Inc.
Rockwood Corp.
Rocky Mountain Target Co.
Savage Range Systems, Inc.
Schaefer Shooting Sports
Seligman Shooting Products
Shooters Supply
Shoot-N-C Targets (See Birchwood Casey)
Target Shooting, Inc.
The A.W. Peterson Gun Shop, Inc.
Thompson Target Technology
Trius Traps, Inc.
Universal Sports
Visible Impact Targets
Watson Trophy Match Bullets
Woods Wise Products
World of Targets (See Birchwood Casey)
X-Spand Target Systems

TAXIDERMY

African Import Co.
Bill Russ Trading Post
Kulis Freeze Dry Taxidermy
Montgomery Community College
World Trek, Inc.

TRAP & SKEET SHOOTER'S EQUIPMENT

Allen Co., Bob
Allen Sportswear, Bob (See Allen Co., Bob)
American Products, Inc.
Bagmaster Mfg., Inc.
Ballistic Product, Inc.
Beomat of America, Inc.
Beretta S.p.A., Pietro
Blount/Outers ATK
Bridgeman Products
C&H Research
Cape Outfitters
Claybuster Wads & Harvester Bullets
Fiocchi of America, Inc.
G.H. Enterprises Ltd.
Hoppe's Div. Penguin Industries, Inc.
Hunter Co., Inc.
Jamison's Forge Works
Jenkins Recoil Pads, Inc.
Jim Noble Co.
Kalispel Case Line
Kolar
Lakewood Products LLC
Ljutic Industries, Inc.
Mag-Na-Port International, Inc.
Maionchi-L.M.I.
MEC, Inc.
Moneymaker Guncraft Corp.
MTM Molded Products Co., Inc.
NCP Products, Inc.
Pachmayr Div. Lyman Products
Palsa Outdoor Products
Perazone-Gunsmith, Brian

Pro-Port Ltd.
Protektor Model
Quack Decoy & Sporting Clays
Randolph Engineering Inc.
Remington Arms Co., Inc.
Rhodeside, Inc.
Shooting Specialties (See Titus, Daniel)
Shotgun Sports Magazine, dba Shootin' Accessories Ltd.
Stan Baker Sports
T&S Industries, Inc.
TEN-X Products Group
The Gun Works
Trius Traps, Inc.
Truglo, Inc.
Universal Sports
Warne Manufacturing Co.
Weber & Markin Custom Gunsmiths
X-Spand Target Systems
Ziegel Engineering

TRIGGERS, RELATED EQUIPMENT

Actions by "T" Teddy Jacobson
B&D Trading Co., Inc.
Baer Custom Inc., Les
Behlert Precision, Inc.
Bond Custom Firearms
Boyds' Gunstock Industries, Inc.
Bull Mountain Rifle Co.
Chicasaw Gun Works
Dayton Traister
Electronic Trigger Systems, Inc.
Eversull Co., Inc.
Feinwerkbau Westinger & Altenburger
Gentry Custom Gunmaker, David
Goodwin's Gun Shop
Hart & Son, Inc.
Hawken Shop, The (See Dayton Traister)
Hoehn Sales, Inc.
Holland's Gunsmithing
Impact Case & Container, Inc.
J.P. Enterprises Inc.
Jewell Triggers, Inc.
John Masen Co. Inc.
Jones Custom Products, Neil A.
K. Eversull Co., Inc.
KK Air International (See Impact Case & Container Co.)
Knight's Mfg. Co.
L&R Lock Co.
List Precision Engineering
London Guns Ltd.
M.H. Canjar Co.
Mahony, Philip Bruce
Master Lock Co.
Miller Single Trigger Mfg. Co.
NCP Products, Inc.
Neil A. Jones Custom Products
Nowlin Mfg. Co.
PEM's Mfg. Co.
Penrod Precision
Ramon B. Gonzalez Guns
Robinson Armament Co.
Schumakers Gun Shop
Sharp Shooter Supply
Shilen, Inc.
Simmons Gun Repair, Inc.
Spencer's Rifle Barrels, Inc.
Tank's Rifle Shop
Target Shooting, Inc.
The A.W. Peterson Gun Shop, Inc.
The Gun Works
Watson Trophy Match Bullets

REFERENCE

MANUFACTURER'S DIRECTORY

A

A Zone Bullets, 2039 Walter Rd., Billings, MT 59105 / 800-252-3111; FAX: 406-248-1961

A&B Industries,Inc (See Top-Line USA Inc)

A&W Repair, 2930 Schneider Dr., Arnold, MO 63010 / 617-287-3725

A.A. Arms, Inc., 4811 Persimmont Ct., Monroe, NC 28110 / 704-289-5356; or 800-935-1119; FAX: 704-289-5859

A.B.S. III, 9238 St. Morritz Dr., Fern Creek, KY 40291

A.G. Russell Knives, Inc., 1920 North 26th Street, Springdale, AR 72764 / 479-751-7341; FAX: 479-751-4520 ag@agrussell.com agrussell.com

A.R.M.S., Inc., 230 W. Center St., West Bridgewater, MA 02379-1620 / 508-584-7816; FAX: 508-588-8045

A.W. Peterson Gun Shop, Inc., 4255 W. Old U.S. 441, Mt. Dora, FL 32757-3299 / 352-383-4258; FAX: 352-735-1001

AC Dyna-tite Corp., 155 Kelly St., P.O. Box 0984, Elk Grove Village, IL 60007 / 847-593-5566; FAX: 847-593-1304

Acadian Ballistic Specialties, P.O. Box 787, Folsom, LA 70437 / 504-796-0078 gunsmith@neasolft.com

Accuracy International, Foster, PO Box 111, Wilsall, MT 59086 / 406-587-7922; FAX: 406-585-9434

Accuracy Internationl Precision Rifles (See U.S.)

Accuracy Int'l. North America, Inc., PO Box 5267, Oak Ridge, TN 37831 / 423-482-0330; FAX: 423-482-0336

Accuracy Unlimited, 16036 N. 49 Ave., Glendale, AZ 85306 / 602-978-9089; FAX: 602-978-9089 fglenn@cox.net www.glenncustom.com

Accuracy Unlimited, 7479 S. DePew St., Littleton, CO 80123

Accura-Site (See All's, The Jim Tembelis Co., Inc.)

Accurate Arms Co., Inc., 5891 Hwy. 230 West, McEwen, TN 37101 / 931-729-4207; FAX: 931-729-4211 email@accuratecompanies.com www.accuratepowder.com

Accu-Tek, 4510 Carter Ct., Chino, CA 91710

Ace Custom 45's, Inc., 1880 1/2 Upper Turtle Creek Rd., Kerrville, TX 78028 / 830-257-4290; FAX: 830-257-5724 www.acecustom45.com

Ace Sportswear, Inc., 700 Quality Rd., Fayetteville, NC 28306 / 919-323-1223; FAX: 919-323-5392

Ackerman & Co., Box 133 US Highway Rt. 7, Pownal, VT 05261 / 802-823-9874 muskets@togsther.net

Ackerman, Bill (See Optical Services Co.)

Acra-Bond Laminates, 134 Zimmerman Rd., Kalispell, MT 59901 / 406-257-9003; FAX: 406-257-9003 merlins@digisys.net www.acrabondlaminates.com

Action Bullets & Alloy Inc., RR 1, P.O. Box 189, Quinter, KS 67752 / 785-754-3609; FAX: 785-754-3629 bullets@ruraltel.net

Action Direct, Inc., P.O. Box 770400, Miami, FL 33177 / 305-969-0056; FAX: 530-734-3760 www.action-direct.com

Action Products, Inc., 22 N. Mulberry St., Hagerstown, MD 21740 / 301-797-1414; FAX: 301-733-2073

Action Target, Inc., PO Box 636, Provo, UT 84603 / 801-377-8033; FAX: 801-377-8096

Actions by "T" Teddy Jacobson, 16315 Redwood Forest Ct., Sugar Land, TX 77478 / 281-277-4008; FAX: 281-277-9112 tjacobson@houston.rr.com www.actionsbyt.com

AcuSport Corporation, 1 Hunter Place, Bellefontaine, OH 43311-3001 / 513-593-7010; FAX: 513-592-5625

Ad Hominem, 3130 Gun Club Lane, RR #3, Orillia, ON L3V 6H3 CANADA / 705-689-5303; FAX: 705-689-5303

Adair Custom Shop, Bill, 2886 Westridge, Carrollton, TX 75006

ADCO Sales, Inc., 4 Draper St. #A, Woburn, MA 01801 / 781-935-1799; FAX: 781-935-1011

Adkins, Luther, 1292 E. McKay Rd., Shelbyville, IN 46176-8706 / 317-392-3795

Advance Car Mover Co., Rowell Div., P.O. Box 1, 240 N. Depot St., Juneau, WI 53039 / 414-386-4464; FAX: 414-386-4416

Adventure 16, Inc., 4620 Alvarado Canyon Rd., San Diego, CA 92120 / 619-283-6314

Adventure Game Calls, R.D. 1, Leonard Rd., Spencer, NY 14883 / 607-589-4611

Aero Peltor, 90 Mechanic St., Southbridge, MA 01550 / 508-764-5500; FAX: 508-764-0188

African Import Co., 22 Goodwin Rd, Plymouth, MA 02360 / 508-746-8552; FAX: 508-746-0404

AFSCO Ammunition, 731 W. Third St., P.O. Box L, Owen, WI 54460 / 715-229-2516

Ahlman Guns, 9525 W. 230th St., Morristown, MN 55052 / 507-685-4243; FAX: 507-685-4280 www.ahlmans.com

Ahrends, Kim (See Custom Firearms, Inc), Box 203, Clarion, IA 50525 / 515-532-3449; FAX: 515-532-3926

Aimtech Mount Systems, P.O. Box 223, Thomasville, GA 31799 / 229-226-4313; FAX: 229-227-0222 mail@aimtech-mounts.com www.aimtech-mounts.com

Air Arms, Hailsham Industrial Park, Diplocks Way, Hailsham, E. Sussex, BN27 3JF ENGLAND / 011-0323-845853

Air Rifle Specialists, P.O. Box 138, 130 Holden Rd., Pine City, NY 14871-0138 / 607-734-7340; FAX: 607-733-3261 ars@stny.rr.com www.air-rifles.com

Air Venture Airguns, 9752 E. Flower St., Bellflower, CA 90706 / 562-867-6355

AirForce Airguns, P.O. Box 2478, Fort Worth, TX 76113 / 817-451-8966; FAX: 817-451-1613 www.airforceairguns.com

Airrow, 11 Monitor Hill Rd., Newtown, CT 06470 / 203-270-6343

Aitor-Cuchilleria Del Norte S.A., Izelaieta, 17, 48260, Ermua, S SPAIN / 43-17-08-50 info@aitor.com www.ailor.com

Ajax Custom Grips, Inc., 9130 Viscount Row, Dallas, TX 75247 / 214-630-8893; FAX: 214-630-4942

Aker International, Inc., 2248 Main St., Suite 6, Chula Vista, CA 91911 / 619-423-5182; FAX: 619-423-1363 aker@akerleather.com www.akerleather.com

AKJ Concealco, P.O. Box 871596, Vancouver, WA 98687-1596 / 360-891-8222; FAX: 360-891-8221 Concealco@aol.com www.greatholsters.com

Al Lind Custom Guns, P.O. Box 97268, Tacoma, WA 98497 / 253-584-6361; FAX: 253-584-6361

Alana Cupp Custom Engraver, P.O. Box 207, Annabella, UT 84711 / 801-896-4834

Alaska Bullet Works, Inc., 9978 Crazy Horse Drive, Juneau, AK 99801 / 907-789-3834; FAX: 907-789-3433

Alaskan Silversmith, The, 2145 Wagner Hollow Rd., Fort Plain, NY 13339 / 518-993-3983 sidbell@capital.net www.sidbell.cizland.com

Aldis Gunsmithing & Shooting Supply, 502 S. Montezuma St., Prescott, AZ 86303 / 602-445-6723; FAX: 602-445-6763

Alessi Holsters, Inc., 2465 Niagara Falls Blvd., Amherst, NY 14228-3527 / 716-691-5615

Alex, Inc., 3420 Cameron Bridge Rd., Manhattan, MT 59741-8523 / 406-282-7396; FAX: 406-282-7396

Alfano, Sam, 36180 Henry Gaines Rd., Pearl River, LA 70452 / 504-863-3364; FAX: 504-863-7715

All American Lead Shot Corp., P.O. Box 224566, Dallas, TX 75062

All Rite Products, Inc., 9554 Wells Circle, Suite D, West Jordan, UT 84088-6226 / 800-771-8471; FAX: 801-280-8302 www.allriteproducts.com

Allard, Gary/Creek Side Metal & Woodcrafters, Fishers Hill, VA 22626 / 703-465-3903

Allen Co., Bob, 214 SW Jackson, P.O. Box 477, Des Moines, IA 50315 / 515-283-2191; or 800-685-7020; FAX: 515-283-0779

Allen Co., Inc., 525 Burbank St., Broomfield, CO 80020 / 303-469-1857; or 800-876-8600; FAX: 303-466-7437

Allen Firearm Engraving, P.O. Box 155, Camp Verde, AZ 86322 / 928-567-6711; FAX: 928-567-3901 rosebudmkco@aol.com

Allen Mfg., 6449 Hodgson Rd., Circle Pines, MN 55014 / 612-429-8231

Allen Sportswear, Bob (See Allen Co., Bob)

Alley Supply Co., PO Box 848, Gardnerville, NV 89410 / 775-782-3800; FAX: 775-782-3827 jetalley@aol.com www.alleysupplyco.com

Alliant Techsystems Smokeless Powder Group, P.O. Box 6, Rt. 114, Bldg. 229, Radford, VA 24141-0096 www.alliantpowder.com

Allred Bullet Co., 932 Evergreen Drive, Logan, UT 84321 / 435-752-6983; FAX: 435-752-6983

All's, The Jim J. Tembelis Co., Inc., 216 Loper Ct., Neenah, WI 54956 / 920-725-5251; FAX: 920-725-5251

Alpec Team, Inc., 201 Ricken Backer Cir., Livermore, CA 94550 / 510-606-8245; FAX: 510-606-4279

Alpha 1 Drop Zone, 2121 N. Tyler, Wichita, KS 67212 / 316-729-0800; FAX: 316-729-4262 www.alpha1dropzone.com

Alpha LaFranck Enterprises, P.O. Box 81072, Lincoln, NE 68501 / 402-466-3193

Alpha Precision, Inc., 3238 Della Slaton Rd., Comer, GA 30629-2212 / 706-783-2131 jim@alphaprecisioninc.com www.alphaprecisioninc.com

Alpine Indoor Shooting Range, 2401 Government Way, Coeur d'Alene, ID 83814 / 208-676-8824; FAX: 208-676-8824

Altamont Co., 901 N. Church St., P.O. Box 309, Thomasboro, IL 61878 / 217-643-3125; or 800-626-5774; FAX: 217-643-7973

Alumna Sport by Dee Zee, 1572 NE 58th Ave., P.O. Box 3090, Des Moines, IA 50316 / 800-798-9899

Amadeo Rossi S.A., Rua: Amadeo Rossi, 143, Sao Leopoldo, RS 93030-220 BRAZIL / 051-592-5566

AmBr Software Group Ltd., P.O. Box 301, Reistertown, MD 21136-0301 / 800-888-1917; FAX: 410-526-7212

American Ammunition, 3545 NW 71st St., Miami, FL 33147 / 305-835-7400; FAX: 305-694-0037

American Derringer Corp., 127 N. Lacy Dr., Waco, TX 76705 / 800-642-7817 or 254-799-9111; FAX: 254-799-7935

American Display Co., 55 Cromwell St., Providence, RI 02907 / 401-331-2464; FAX: 401-421-1264

American Frontier Firearms Mfg., Inc, PO Box 744, Aguanga, CA 92536 / 909-763-0014; FAX: 909-763-0014

American Gas & Chemical Co., Ltd, 220 Pegasus Ave, Northvale, NJ 07647 / 201-767-7300

American Gripcraft, 3230 S Dodge 2, Tucson, AZ 85713 / 602-790-1222

American Gunsmithing Institute, 1325 Imola Ave #504, Napa, CA 94559 / 707-253-0462; FAX: 707-253-7149

MANUFACTURER'S DIRECTORY

American Handgunner Magazine, 591 Camino de la Reina, Ste. 200, San Diego, CA 92108 / 619-297-5350; FAX: 619-297-5353

American Pioneer Video, PO Box 50049, Bowling Green, KY 42102-2649 / 800-743-4675

American Products, Inc., 14729 Spring Valley Road, Morrison, IL 61270 / 815-772-3336; FAX: 815-772-8046

American Safe Arms, Inc., 1240 Riverview Dr., Garland, UT 84312 / 801-257-7472; FAX: 801-785-8156

American Security Products Co., 11925 Pacific Ave., Fontana, CA 92337 / 909-685-9680; or 800-421-6142; FAX: 909-685-9685

American Small Arms Academy, P.O. Box 12111, Prescott, AZ 86304 / 602-778-5623

American Target, 1328 S. Jason St., Denver, CO 80223 / 303-733-0433; FAX: 303-777-0311

American Target Knives, 1030 Brownwood NW, Grand Rapids, MI 49504 / 616-453-1998

Americase, P.O. Box 271, 1610 E. Main, Waxahachie, TX 75165 / 800-880-3629; FAX: 214-937-8373

Ames Metal Products, 4323 S. Western Blvd., Chicago, IL 60609 / 773-523-3230 or 800-255-6937; FAX: 773-523-3854

Amherst Arms, P.O. Box 1457, Englewood, FL 34295 / 941-475-2020; FAX: 941-473-1212

Ammo Load, Inc., 1560 E. Edinger, Suite G, Santa Ana, CA 92705 / 714-558-8858; FAX: 714-569-0319

Amrine's Gun Shop, 937 La Luna, Ojai, CA 93023 / 805-646-2376

Amsec, 11925 Pacific Ave., Fontana, CA 92337

Analog Devices, Box 9106, Norwood, MA 02062

Andela Tool & Machine, Inc., RD3, Box 246, Richfield Springs, NY 13439

Anderson Manufacturing Co., Inc., 22602 53rd Ave. SE, Bothell, WA 98021 / 206-481-1858; FAX: 206-481-7839

Andres & Dworsky KG, Bergstrasse 18, A-3822 Karlstein, Thaya, AUSTRIA / 0 28 44-285; FAX: 02844 28619 andres.dnorsky@wvnet.as

Angelo & Little Custom Gun Stock Blanks, P.O. Box 240046, Dell, MT 59724-0046

Answer Products Co., 1519 Westbury Drive, Davison, MI 48423 / 810-653-2911

Antique American Firearms, P.O. Box 71035, Dept. GD, Des Moines, IA 50325 / 515-224-6552

Antique Arms Co., 1110 Cleveland Ave., Monett, MO 65708 / 417-235-6501

AO Sight Systems, 2401 Ludelle St., Fort Worth, TX 76105 / 888-744-4880 or 817-536-0136; FAX: 817-536-3517

Apel GmbH, Ernst, Am Kirschberg 3, D-97218, Gerbrunn, GERMANY / 0 (931) 707192 info@eaw.de www.eaw.de

Aplan Antiques & Art, James O., James O., HC 80, Box 793-25, Piedmont, SD 57769 / 605-347-5016

AR-7 Industries, LLC, 998 N. Colony Rd., Meriden, CT 06450 / 203-630-3536; FAX: 203-630-3637

Arizona Ammunition, Inc., 21421 No. 14th Ave., Suite E, Phoenix, AZ 85027 / 623-516-9004; FAX: 623-516-9012 www.azammo.com

ArmaLite, Inc., P.O. Box 299, Geneseo, IL 61254 / 800-336-0184 or 309-944-6939; FAX: 309-944-6949

Armament Gunsmithing Co., Inc., 525 Rt. 22, Hillside, NJ 07205 / 908-686-0960; FAX: 718-738-5019 armamentgunsmithing@worldnet.att.net

Armas Garbi, S.A., 12-14 20.600 Urki, 12, Eibar (Guipuzcoa), / 943203873; FAX: 943203873 armosgarbi@euskalnet.n

Armas Kemen S. A. (See U.S. Importers)

Armfield Custom Bullets, 10584 County Road 100, Carthage, MO 64836 / 417-359-8480; FAX: 417-359-8497

Armi Perazzi S.p.A., Via Fontanelle 1/3, 1-25080, Botticino Mattina, / 030-2692591; FAX: 030 2692594

Armi San Marco (See U.S. Importers-Taylor's & Co I

Armi San Paolo, 172-A, I-25062, via Europa, ITALY / 030-2751725

Armi Sport (See U.S. Importers-Cape Outfitters)

Armite Laboratories, 1560 Superior Ave., Costa Mesa, CA 92627 / 213-587-7768; FAX: 213-587-5075

Armoloy Co. of Ft. Worth, 204 E. Daggett St., Fort Worth, TX 76104 / 817-332-5604; FAX: 817-335-6517

Armor (See Buck Stop Lure Co., Inc.)

Armor Metal Products, P.O. Box 4609, Helena, MT 59604 / 406-442-5560; FAX: 406-442-5650

Armory Publications, 17171 Bothall Way NE, #276, Seattle, WA 98155 / 206-364-7653; FAX: 206-362-9413 armorypub@aol.com www.grocities.com/armorypub

Armoury, Inc., The, Rt. 202, Box 2340, New Preston, CT 06777 / 860-868-0001; FAX: 860-868-2919

Arms & Armour Press, Wellington House, 125 Strand, London, WC2R 0BB ENGLAND / 0171-420-5555; FAX: 0171-240-7265

Arms Corporation of the Philippines, Bo. Parang Marikina, Metro Manila, PHILIPPINES / 632-941-6243 or 632-941-6244; FAX: 632-942-0682

Arms Craft Gunsmithing, 1106 Linda Dr., Arroyo Grande, CA 93420 / 805-481-2830

Arms Ingenuity Co., P.O. Box 1, 51 Canal St., Weatogue, CT 06089 / 203-658-5624

Arms Software, 4851 SW Madrona St., Lake Oswego, OR 97035 / 800-366-5559 or 503-697-0533; FAX: 503-697-3337

Arms, Programming Solutions (See Arms Software)

Armscorp USA, Inc., 4424 John Ave., Baltimore, MD 21227 / 410-247-6200; FAX: 410-247-6205 info@armscorpusa.com www.armscorpusa.com

Arratoonian, Andy (See Horseshoe Leather Products)

Arrieta S.L., Morkaiko 5, 20870, Elgoibar, SPAIN / 34-43-743150; FAX: 34-43-743154

Art Jewel Enterprises Ltd., Eagle Business Ctr., 460 Randy Rd., Carol Stream, IL 60188 / 708-260-0400

Artistry in Wood, 134 Zimmerman Rd., Kalispell, MT 59901 / 406-257-9003; FAX: 406-257-9167 merlins@digisys.net www.acrabondlaminates.com

Art's Gun & Sport Shop, Inc., 6008 Hwy. Y, Hillsboro, MO 63050

Arundel Arms & Ammunition, Inc., A., 24A Defense St., Annapolis, MD 21401 / 410-224-8683

Arvo Ojala Holsters, P.O. Box 98, N. Hollywood, CA 91603 / 818-222-9700; FAX: 818-222-0401

Ashby, David. See: ASHBY TURKEY CALLS

Ashby Turkey Calls, David L. Ashby, P.O. Box 1653, Ozark, MO 65721-1653

Ashley Outdoors, Inc., 2401 Ludelle St., Fort Worth, TX 76105 / 888-744-4880; FAX: 800-734-7939

Aspen Outfitting Co., Jon Hollinger, 9 Dean St., Aspen, CO 81611 / 970-925-3406

A-Square Co., 205 Fairfield Ave., Jeffersonville, IN 47130 / 812-283-0577; FAX: 812-283-0375

Astra Sport, S.A., Apartado 3, 48300 Guernica, Espagne, SPAIN / 34-4-6250100; FAX: 34-4-6255186

Atamec-Bretton, 19 rue Victor Grignard, F-42026, St.-Etienne (Cedex 1, / 77-93-54-69; FAX: 33-77-93-57-98

Atlanta Cutlery Corp., 2143 Gees Mill Rd., Box 839 CIS, Conyers, GA 30207 / 800-883-0300; FAX: 404-388-0246

Atlantic Mills, Inc., 1295 Towbin Ave., Lakewood, NJ 08701-5934 / 800-242-7374

Atlantic Rose, Inc., P.O. Box 10717, Bradenton, FL 34282-0717

Atsko/Sno-Seal, Inc., 2664 Russell St., Orangeburg, SC 29115 / 803-531-1820; FAX: 803-531-2139 info@atsko.com www.atsko.com

Auguste Francotte & Cie S.A., rue du Trois Juin 109, 4400 Herstal-Liege, BELGIUM / 32-4-248-13-18; FAX: 32-4-948-11-79

Austin & Halleck, Inc., 2150 South 950 East, Provo, UT 84606-6285 / 877-543-3256; or 801-374-9990; FAX: 801-374-9998 www.austinhallek.com

Austin Sheridan USA, Inc., P.O. Box 577, 36 Haddam Quarter Rd., Durham, CT 06422 / 860-349-1772; FAX: 860-349-1771 swalzer@palm.net

Autauga Arms, Inc., Pratt Plaza Mall No. 13, Prattville, AL 36067 / 800-262-9563; FAX: 334-361-2961

Auto Arms, 738 Clearview, San Antonio, TX 78228 / 512-434-5450

Auto-Ordnance Corp., PO Box 220, Blauvelt, NY 10913 / 914-353-7770

Autumn Sales, Inc. (Blaser), 1320 Lake St., Fort Worth, TX 76102 / 817-335-1634; FAX: 817-338-0119

Avnda Otaola Norica, 16 Apartado 68, 20600, Eibar,

AWC Systems Technology, P.O. Box 41938, Phoenix, AZ 85080-1938 / 602-780-1050; FAX: 602-780-2967

Axtell Rifle Co., 353 Mill Creek Road, Sheridan, MT 59749 / 406-842-5814

AYA (See U.S. Importer-New England Custom Gun Serv

B

B&D Trading Co., Inc., 3935 Fair Hill Rd., Fair Oaks, CA 95628 / 800-334-3790 or 916-967-9366; FAX: 916-967-4873

B&P America, 12321 Brittany Cir., Dallas, TX 75230 / 972-726-9069

B.A.C., 17101 Los Modelos St., Fountain Valley, CA 92708 / 435-586-3286

B.B. Walker Co., PO Box 1167, 414 E Dixie Dr, Asheboro, NC 27204 / 910-625-1380; FAX: 910-625-8125

B.C. Outdoors, Larry McGhee, PO Box 61497, Boulder City, NV 89006 / 702-294-3056; FAX: 702-294-0413 jdalton@pmcammo.com www.pmcammo.com

B.M.F. Activator, Inc., 12145 Mill Creek Run, Plantersville, TX 77363 / 936-894-2397; FAX: 936-894-2397

Badger Creek Studio, 1629 Via Monserate, Fallbrook, CA 92028 / 760-723-9279; or 619-728-2663

Badger Shooters Supply, Inc., P.O. Box 397, Owen, WI 54460 / 800-424-9069; FAX: 715-229-2332

Baekgaard Ltd., 1855 Janke Dr., Northbrook, IL 60062 / 708-498-3040; FAX: 708-493-3106

Baelder, Harry, Alte Goennebeker Strasse 5, 24635, Rickling, GERMANY / 04328-722732; FAX: 04328-722733

Baer Custom Inc., Les, 29601 34th Ave., Hillsdale, IL 61257 / 309-658-2716; FAX: 309-658-2610

Baer's Hollows, P.O. Box 284, Eads, CO 81036 / 719-438-5718

Bagmaster Mfg., Inc., 2731 Sutton Ave., St. Louis, MO 63143 / 314-781-8002; FAX: 314-781-3363

Bain & Davis, Inc., 307 E. Valley Blvd., San Gabriel, CA 91776-3522 / 626-573-4241 baindavis@aol.com

Baker, Stan. See: STAN BAKER SPORTS

Baker's Leather Goods, Roy, PO Box 893, Magnolia, AR 71754 / 870-234-0344 pholsters@ipa.net

Bald Eagle Precision Machine Co., 101-A Allison St., Lock Haven, PA 17745 / 570-748-6772; FAX: 570-748-4443

Balickie, Joe, 408 Trelawney Lane, Apex, NC 27502 / 919-362-5185

Ballard, Donald. See: BALLARD INDUSTRIES

Ballard Industries, Donald Ballard Sr., PO Box 2035, Arnold, CA 95223 / 408-996-0957; FAX: 408-257-6828

Ballard Rifle & Cartridge Co., LLC, 113 W. Yellowstone Ave., Cody, WY 82414 / 307-587-4914; FAX: 307-527-6097 ballard@wyoming.com www.ballardrifles.com

Ballistic Product, Inc., 20015 75th Ave. North, Corcoran, MN 55340-9456 / 763-494-9237; FAX: 763-494-9236 info@ballisticproducts.com www.ballisticproducts.com

Ballistic Research, 1108 W. May Ave., McHenry, IL 60050 / 815-385-0037

Ballisti-Cast, Inc., P.O. Box 1057, Minot, ND 58702-1057 / 701-497-3333; FAX: 701-497-3335

Bandcor Industries, Div. of Man-Sew Corp., 6108 Sherwin Dr., Port Richey, FL 34668 / 813-848-0432

Bang-Bang Boutique (See Holster Shop, The)

Banks, Ed, 2011 Alabama Ave., Savannah, GA 31404-2721 / 912-987-4665

Bansner's Ultimate Rifles, LLC, P.O. Box 839, 261 E. Main St., Adamstown, PA 19501 / 717-484-2370; FAX: 717-484-0523 bansner@aol.com www.bansnersrifle.com

Barbour, Inc., 55 Meadowbrook Dr., Milford, NH 03055 / 603-673-1313; FAX: 603-673-6510

Barnes, 4347 Tweed Dr., Eau Claire, WI 54703-6302

Barnes Bullets, Inc., P.O. Box 215, American Fork, UT 84003 / 801-756-4222 or 800-574-9200; FAX: 801-756-2465 email@barnesbullets.com www.barnesbullets.com

Baron Technology, 62 Spring Hill Rd., Trumbull, CT 06611 / 203-452-0515; FAX: 203-452-0663 dbaron@baronengraving.com www.baronengraving.com

Barraclough, John K., 55 Merit Park Dr., Gardena, CA 90247 / 310-324-2574

Barramundi Corp., P.O. Drawer 4259, Homosassa Springs, FL 32687 / 904-628-0200

Barrett Firearms Manufacturer, Inc., P.O. Box 1077, Murfreesboro, TN 37133 / 615-896-2938; FAX: 615-896-7313

Bar-Sto Precision Machine, 73377 Sullivan Rd., PO Box 1838, Twentynine Palms, CA 92277 / 760-367-2747; FAX: 760-367-2407 barsto@eee.org www.barsto.com

Barta's Gunsmithing, 10231 US Hwy. 10, Cato, WI 54230 / 920-732-4472

Barteaux Machete, 1916 SE 50th Ave., Portland, OR 97215-3238 / 503-233-5880

Bartlett Engineering, 40 South 200 East, Smithfield, UT 84335-1645 / 801-563-5910

Bates Engraving, Billy, 2302 Winthrop Dr. SW, Decatur, AL 35603 / 256-355-3690 bbrn@aol.com

Battenfeld Technologies, 5875 W. Van Horn Tavern Rd., Columbia, MO 65203 / 573-445-9200; FAX: 573-447-4158 battenfeldtechnologies.com

Bauer, Eddie, 15010 NE 36th St., Redmond, WA 98052

Baumgartner Bullets, 3011 S. Alane St., W. Valley City, UT 84120

Bauska Barrels, 105 9th Ave. W., Kalispell, MT 59901 / 406-752-7706

Bear Archery, RR 4, 4600 Southwest 41st Blvd., Gainesville, FL 32601 / 904-376-2327

Bear Arms, 374-A Carson Road, St. Mathews, SC 29135

Bear Mountain Gun & Tool, 120 N. Plymouth, New Plymouth, ID 83655 / 208-278-5221; FAX: 208-278-5221

Beartooth Bullets, PO Box 491, Dept. HLD, Dover, ID 83825-0491 / 208-448-1865 bullets@beartoothbullets.com beartoothbullets.com

Beaver Lodge (See Fellowes, Ted)

Beaver Park Product, Inc., 840 J St., Penrose, CO 81240 / 719-372-6744

BEC, Inc., 1227 W. Valley Blvd., Suite 204, Alhambra, CA 91803 / 626-281-5751; FAX: 626-293-7073

Beeks, Mike. See: GRAYBACK WILDCATS

Beeman Precision Airguns, 5454 Argosy Dr., Huntington Beach, CA 92649 / 714-890-4800; FAX: 714-890-4808

Behlert Precision, Inc., P.O. Box 288, 7067 Easton Rd., Pipersville, PA 18947 / 215-766-8681 or 215-766-7301; FAX: 215-766-8681

Beitzinger, George, 116-20 Atlantic Ave., Richmond Hill, NY 11419 / 718-847-7661

Belding's Custom Gun Shop, 10691 Sayers Rd., Munith, MI 49259 / 517-596-2388

Bell & Carlson, Inc., Dodge City Industrial Park, 101 Allen Rd., Dodge City, KS 67801 / 800-634-8586 or 620-225-6688; FAX: 620-225-6688 email@bellandcarlson.com www.bellandcarlson.com

Bell Reloading, Inc., 1725 Harlin Lane Rd., Villa Rica, GA 30180

Bell's Gun & Sport Shop, 3309-19 Mannheim Rd, Franklin Park, IL 60131

Bell's Legendary Country Wear, 22 Circle Dr., Bellmore, NY 11710 / 516-679-1158

Belltown Ltd., 11 Camps Rd., Kent, CT 06757 / 860-354-5750; FAX: 860-354-6764

Ben William's Gun Shop, 1151 S. Cedar Ridge, Duncanville, TX 75137 / 214-780-1807

Benchmark Knives (See Gerber Legendary Blades)

Benelli Armi S.p.A., Via della Stazione, 61029, Urbino, ITALY / 39-722-307-1; FAX: 39-722-327427

Benelli USA Corp, 17603 Indian Head Hwy, Accokeek, MD 20607 / 301-283-6981; FAX: 301-283-6988 benelliusa.com

Bengtson Arms Co., L., 6345-B E. Akron St., Mesa, AZ 85205 / 602-981-6375

Benjamin/Sheridan Co., Crosman, Rts. 5 and 20, E. Bloomfield, NY 14443 / 716-657-6161; FAX: 716-657-5405 www.crosman.com

Ben's Machines, 1151 S. Cedar Ridge, Duncanville, TX 75137 / 214-780-1807; FAX: 214-780-0316

Bentley, John, 128-D Watson Dr., Turtle Creek, PA 15145

Beomat of America, Inc., 300 Railway Ave., Campbell, CA 95008 / 408-379-4829

Beretta S.p.A., Pietro, Via Beretta, 18, 25063, Gardone Vae Trompia, ITALY / 39-30-8341-1 info@benetta.com www.benetta.com

Beretta U.S.A. Corp., 17601 Beretta Drive, Accokeek, MD 20607 / 301-283-2191; FAX: 301-283-0435

Berger Bullets Ltd., 5443 W. Westwind Dr., Glendale, AZ 85310 / 602-842-4001; FAX: 602-934-9083

Bernardelli, Vincenzo, P.O. Box 460243, Houston, TX 77056-8243 www.bernardelli.com

Bernardelli S.p.A., Vincenzo, 125 Via Matteotti, PO Box 74, Brescia, ITALY / 39-30-8912851-2-3; FAX: 39-30-8910249

Berry's Mfg., Inc., 401 North 3050 East St., St. George, UT 84770 / 435-634-1682; FAX: 435-634-1683 sales@berrysmfg.com www.berrysmfg.com

Bersa S.A., Benso Bonadimani, Magallanes 775 B1704 FLC, Ramos Mejia, ARGENTINA / 011-4656-2377; FAX: 011-4656-2093+ info@bersa-sa.com.dr www.bersa-sa.com.ar

Bert Johanssons Vapentillbehor, S-430 20 Veddige, SWEDEN,

Bertuzzi (See U.S. Importer-New England Arms Co)

Better Concepts Co., 663 New Castle Rd., Butler, PA 16001 / 412-285-9000

Beverly, Mary, 3201 Horseshoe Trail, Tallahassee, FL 32312

Bianchi International, Inc., 100 Calle Cortez, Temecula, CA 92590 / 909-676-5621; FAX: 909-676-6777

Big Bear Arms & Sporting Goods, Inc., 1112 Milam Way, Carrollton, TX 75006 / 972-416-8051 or 800-400-BEAR; FAX: 972-416-0771

Big Bore Bullets of Alaska, PO Box 521455, Big Lake, AK 99652 / 907-373-2673; FAX: 907-373-2673 doug@mtaonline.net ww.awloo.com/bbb/index.

Big Bore Express, 16345 Midway Rd., Nampa, ID 83651 / 208-466-9975; FAX: 208-466-6927 bigbore.com

Big Spring Enterprises "Bore Stores", P.O. Box 1115, Big Spring Rd., Yellville, AR 72687 / 870-449-5297; FAX: 870-449-4446

Bilal, Mustafa. See: TURK'S HEAD PRODUCTIONS

Bilinski, Bryan. See: FIELDSPORT LTD.

Bill Adair Custom Shop, 2886 Westridge, Carrollton, TX 75006 / 972-418-0950

Bill Austin's Calls, Box 284, Kaycee, WY 82639 / 307-738-2552

Bill Hanus Birdguns, P.O. Box 533, Newport, OR 97365 / 541-265-7433; FAX: 541-265-7400 www.billhanusbirdguns.com

Bill Russ Trading Post, William A. Russ, 23 William St., Addison, NY 14801-1326 / 607-359-3896

Bill Wiseman and Co., P.O. Box 3427, Bryan, TX 77805 / 409-690-3456; FAX: 409-690-0156

Billeb, Stepehn. See: QUALITY CUSTOM FIREARMS

Billings Gunsmiths, 1841 Grand Ave., Billings, MT 59102 / 406-256-8390; FAX: 406-256-6530 blgsgunsmiths@msn.com www.billingsgunsmiths.net

Billingsley & Brownell, P.O. Box 25, Dayton, WY 82836 / 307-655-9344

Bill's Custom Cases, P.O. Box 2, Dunsmuir, CA 96025 / 530-235-0177; FAX: 530-235-4959 billscustomcases@mindspring.com

Bill's Gun Repair, 1007 Burlington St., Mendota, IL 61342 / 815-539-5786

Billy Bates Engraving, 2302 Winthrop Dr. SW, Decatur, AL 35603 / 256-355-3690 bbrn@aol.com

Birchwood Casey, 7900 Fuller Rd., Eden Prairie, MN 55344 / 800-328-6156 or 612-937-7933; FAX: 612-937-7979

Birdsong & Assoc., W. E., 1435 Monterey Rd., Florence, MS 39073-9748 / 601-366-8270

Bismuth Cartridge Co., 3500 Maple Ave., Suite 1650, Dallas, TX 75219 / 214-521-5880; FAX: 214-521-9035

Bison Studios, 1409 South Commerce St., Las Vegas, NV 89102 / 702-388-2891; FAX: 702-383-9967

Bitterroot Bullet Co., P.O. Box 412, 2001 Cedar Ave., Lewiston, ID 83501-0412 / 208-743-5635; FAX: 208-743-5635 brootbil@lewiston.com

BKL Technologies, PO Box 5237, Brownsville, TX 78523

Black Belt Bullets (See Big Bore Express)

REFERENCE

MANUFACTURER'S DIRECTORY

Black Hills Ammunition, Inc., P.O. Box 3090, Rapid City, SD 57709-3090 / 605-348-5150; FAX: 605-348-9827

Black Hills Shooters Supply, P.O. Box 4220, Rapid City, SD 57709 / 800-289-2506

Black Powder Products, 67 Township Rd. 1411, Chesapeake, OH 45619 / 614-867-8047

Black Sheep Brand, 3220 W. Gentry Parkway, Tyler, TX 75702 / 903-592-3853; FAX: 903-592-0527

Blacksmith Corp., P.O. Box 280, North Hampton, OH 45349 / 800-531-2665; FAX: 937-969-8399 sales@blacksmith.com www.blacksmithcorp.com

BlackStar AccuMax Barrels, 11501 Brittmoore Park Drive, Houston, TX 77041 / 281-721-6040; FAX: 281-721-6041

BlackStar Barrel Accurizing (See BlackStar AccuMax)

Blacktail Mountain Books, 42 First Ave. W., Kalispell, MT 59901 / 406-257-5573

Blammo Ammo, P.O. Box 1677, Seneca, SC 29679 / 803-882-1768

Blaser Jagdwaffen GmbH, D-88316, Isny Im Allgau, GERMANY

Blount, Inc., Sporting Equipment Div., 2299 Snake River Ave., P.O. Box 856, Lewiston, ID 83501 / 800-627-3640 or 208-746-2351; FAX: 208-799-3904

Blount/Outers ATK, P..O Box 39, Onalaska, WI 54650 / 608-781-5800; FAX: 608-781-0368

Blue and Gray Products Inc. (See Ox-Yoke Originals)

Blue Book Publications, Inc., 8009 34th Ave. S., Ste. 175, Minneapolis, MN 55425 / 800-877-4867 or 612-854-5229; FAX: 612-853-1486 bluebook@bluebookinc.com www.bluebookinc.com

Blue Mountain Bullets, 64146 Quail Ln., Box 231, John Day, OR 97845 / 541-820-4594; FAX: 541-820-4594

Blue Ridge Machinery & Tools, Inc., P.O. Box 536-GD, Hurricane, WV 25526 / 800-872-6500; FAX: 304-562-5311 blueridgemachine@worldnet.att.net www.blueridgemachinery.com

BMC Supply, Inc., 26051 - 179th Ave. S.E., Kent, WA 98042

Bob Allen Co.214 SW Jackson, P.O. Box 477, Des Moines, IA 50315 / 800-685-7020; FAX: 515-283-0779

Bob Rogers Gunsmithing, P.O. Box 305, 344 S. Walnut St., Franklin Grove, IL 61031 / 815-456-2685; FAX: 815-456-2777

Bob's Gun Shop, P.O. Box 200, Royal, AR 71968 / 501-767-1970; FAX: 501-767-1970 gunparts@hsnp.com www.gun-parts.com

Bob's Tactical Indoor Shooting Range & Gun Shop, 90 Lafayette Rd., Salisbury, MA 01952 / 508-465-5561

Boessler, Erich, Am Vogeltal 3, 97702, Munnerstadt, GERMANY

Boker USA, Inc., 1550 Balsam Street, Lakewood, CO 80215 / 303-462-0662; FAX: 303-462-0668 sales@bokerusa.com bokerusa.com

Boltin, John M., P.O. Box 644, Estill, SC 29918 / 803-625-2185

Bo-Mar Tool & Mfg. Co., 6136 State Hwy. 300, Longview, TX 75604 / 903-759-4784; FAX: 903-759-9141 marykor@earthlink.net bo-mar.com

Bonadimani, Benso. See: BERSA S.A.

Bonanza (See Forster Products), 310 E. Lanark Ave., Lanark, IL 61046 / 815-493-6360; FAX: 815-493-2371

Bond Arms, Inc., P.O. Box 1296, Granbury, TX 76048 / 817-573-4445; FAX: 817-573-5636

Bond Custom Firearms, 8954 N. Lewis Ln., Bloomington, IN 47408 / 812-332-4519

Bondini Paolo, Via Sorrento 345, San Carlo di Cesena, ITALY / 0547-663-240; FAX: 0547-663-780

Boone Trading Co., Inc., PO Box 669, Brinnon, WA 98320 / 800-423-1945; or 360-796-4330; FAX: 360-796-4511 sales@boonetrading.com boonetrading.com

Boone's Custom Ivory Grips, Inc., 562 Coyote Rd., Brinnon, WA 98320 / 206-796-4330

Boonie Packer Products, P.O. Box 12517, Salem, OR 97309-0517 / 800-477-3244; or 503-581-3244; FAX: 503-581-3191 booniepacker@aol.com www.booniepacker.com

Borden Ridges Rimrock Stocks, RR 1 Box 250 BC, Springville, PA 18844 / 570-965-2505; FAX: 570-965-2328

Borden Rifles Inc., RD 1, Box 250BC, Springville, PA 18844 / 717-965-2505; FAX: 717-965-2328

Border Barrels Ltd., Riccarton Farm, Newcastleton, SCOTLAND UK

Borovnik KG, Ludwig, 9170 Ferlach, Bahnhofstrasse 7, AUSTRIA / 042 27 24 42; FAX: 042 26 43 49

Bosis (See U.S. Importer-New England Arms Co.)

Boss Manufacturing Co., 221 W. First St., Kewanee, IL 61443 / 309-852-2131; or 800-447-4581; FAX: 309-852-0848

Bostick Wildlife Calls, Inc., P.O. Box 728, Estill, SC 29918 / 803-625-2210; or 803-625-4512

Bowen Classic Arms Corp., PO Box 67, Louisville, TN 37777 / 865-984-3583 www.bowenclassicarms.com

Bowen Knife Co., Inc., P.O. Box 590, Blackshear, GA 31516 / 912-449-4794

Bowerly, Kent, 710 Golden Pheasant Dr., Redmond, OR 97756 / 541-923-3501 jkbowerly@aol.com

Boyds' Gunstock Industries, Inc., 25376 403 Rd. Ave., Mitchell, SD 57301 / 605-996-5011; FAX: 605-996-9878

Brace, Larry D., 771 Blackfoot Ave., Eugene, OR 97404 / 541-688-1278; FAX: 541-607-5833

Brass Eagle, Inc., 7050A Bramalea Rd., Unit 19, Mississauga,, ON L4Z 1C7 CANADA / 416-848-4844

Brauer Bros., 1520 Washington Avenue., St. Louis, MO 63103 / 314-231-2864; FAX: 314-249-4952 www.brauerbros.com

Break-Free, Inc., 1035 S. Linwood Ave., Santa Ana, CA 92705 / 714-953-1900; FAX: 714-953-0402

Brenneke GmbH, P.O. Box 1646, 30837 Langenhagen, Langenhagen, GERMANY / +49-511-97262-0; FAX: +49-511-97262-62 info@brenneke.de brenneke.com

Bridgeman Products, Harry Jaffin, 153 B Cross Slope Court, Englishtown, NJ 07726 / 732-536-3604; FAX: 732-972-1004

Bridgers Best, P.O. Box 1410, Berthoud, CO 80513

Briese Bullet Co., Inc., RR1, Box 108, Tappen, ND 58487 / 701-327-4578; FAX: 701-327-4579

Brigade Quartermasters, 1025 Cobb International Blvd., Dept. VH, Kennesaw, GA 30144-4300 / 404-428-1248; or 800-241-3125; FAX: 404-426-7726

Briganti, A.J., 512 Rt. 32, Highland Mills, NY 10930 / 914-928-9573

Briley Mfg. Inc., 1230 Lumpkin, Houston, TX 77043 / 800-331-5718; or 713-932-6995; FAX: 713-932-1043

Brill, R. See: ROYAL ARMS INTERNATIONAL

British Sporting Arms, RR1, Box 130, Millbrook, NY 12545 / 914-677-8303

Broad Creek Rifle Works, Ltd., 120 Horsey Ave., Laurel, DE 19956 / 302-875-5446; FAX: 302-875-1448 bcrw4guns@aol.com

Brockman's Custom Gunsmithing, P.O. Box 357, Gooding, ID 83330 / 208-934-5050

Brocock Ltd., 43 River Street, Digbeth, Birmingham, B5 5SA ENGLAND / 011-021-773-1200; FAX: 011-021-773-1211 sales@brocock.co.un www.brocock.co.uk

Broken Gun Ranch, 10739 126 Rd., Spearville, KS 67876 / 316-385-2587; FAX: 316-385-2597

Brooker, Dennis, Rt. 1, Box 12A, Derby, IA 50068 / 515-533-2103

Brooks Tactical Systems-Agrip, 279-C Shorewood Ct., Fox Island, WA 98333 / 253-549-2866 FAX: 253-549-2703 brooks@brookstactical.com www.brookstactical.com

Brown, H. R. (See Silhouette Leathers)

Brown Co., E. Arthur, 3404 Pawnee Dr., Alexandria, MN 56308 / 320-762-8847

Brown Dog Ent., 2200 Calle Camelia, 1000 Oaks CA 91360 / 805-497-2318; FAX: 805-497-1618

Brown Precision, Inc., 7786 Molinos Ave., Los Molinos, CA 96055 / 530-384-2506; FAX: 916-384-1638 www.brownprecision.com

Brown Products, Inc., Ed, 43825 Muldrow Trail, Perry, MO 63462 / 573-565-3261; FAX: 573-565-2791 www.edbrown.com

Brownells, Inc., 200 S. Front St., Montezuma, IA 50171 / 641-623-5401; FAX: 641-623-3896 orderdesk@brownells.com www.brownells.com

Browning Arms Co., One Browning Place, Morgan, UT 84050 / 801-876-2711; FAX: 801-876-3331

Browning Arms Co. (Parts & Service), 3005 Arnold Tenbrook Rd., Arnold, MO 63010 / 617-287-6800; FAX: 617-287-9751

BRP, Inc. High Performance Cast Bullets, 1210 Alexander Rd., Colorado Springs, CO 80909 / 719-633-0658

Brunton U.S.A., 620 E. Monroe Ave., Riverton, WY 82501 / 307-856-6559; FAX: 307-856-1840

Bryan & Assoc., R D Sauls, PO Box 5772, Anderson, SC 29623-5772 / 864-261-6810 bryanandac@aol.com www.huntersweb.com/bryanandac

Brynin, Milton, P.O. Box 383, Yonkers, NY 10710 / 914-779-4333

BSA Guns Ltd., Armoury Rd. Small Heath, Birmingham B11 2PP, ENGLAND / 011-021-772-8543; FAX: 011-021-773-0845 sales@bsagun.com www.bsagun.com

BSA Optics, 3911 SW 47th Ave., Ste. 914, Ft. Lauderdale, FL 33314 / 954-581-2144; FAX: 954-581-3165 4info@basaoptics.com www.bsaoptics.com

B-Square Company, Inc., ;, P.O. Box 11281, 2708 St. Louis Ave., Ft. Worth, TX 76110 / 817-923-0964 or 800-433-2909; FAX: 817-926-7012

Buchsenmachermeister, Peter Hofer Jagdwaffen Buchsenmachermeister, Kirchgasse 24 A-9170, Ferlach, AUSTRIA / 43 4227 3683; FAX: 43 4227 368330 peterhofer@hoferwaffen.com www.hoferwaffen.com

Buck Knives, Inc., 1900 Weld Blvd., P.O. Box 1267, El Cajon, CA 92020 / 619-449-1100; or 800-326-2825; FAX: 619-562-5774 8

Buck Stix-SOS Products Co., Box 3, Neenah, WI 54956

Buck Stop Lure Co., Inc., 3600 Grow Rd. NW, P.O. Box 636, Stanton, MI 48888 / 517-762-5091; FAX: 517-762-5124

Buckeye Custom Bullets, 6490 Stewart Rd., Elida OH 45807 / 419-641-4463

Buckhorn Gun Works, 8109 Woodland Dr., Black Hawk, SD 57718 / 605-787-6472

Buckskin Bullet Co., P.O. Box 1893, Cedar City, UT 84721 / 435-586-3286

Budin, Dave, Main St., Margaretville, NY 12455 / 914-568-4103; FAX: 914-586-4105

MANUFACTURER'S DIRECTORY

Budin, Dave. See: DEL-SPORTS, INC.
Buenger Enterprises/Goldenrod Dehumidifier, 3600 S. Harbor Blvd., Oxnard, CA 93035 / 800-451-6797; or 805-985-5828; FAX: 805-985-1534
Buffalo Arms Co., 660 Vermeer Ct., Ponderay, ID 83852 / 208-263-6953; FAX: 208-265-2096 www.buffaloarms.com
Buffalo Bullet Co., Inc., 12637 Los Nietos Rd., Unit A, Santa Fe Springs, CA 90670 / 800-423-8069; FAX: 562-944-5054
Buffalo Gun Center, 3385 Harlem Rd., Buffalo, NY 14225 / 716-833-2581; FAX: 716-833-2265 www.buffaloguncenter.com
Buffalo Rock Shooters Supply, R.R. 1, Ottawa, IL 61350 / 815-433-2471
Buffer Technologies, P.O. Box 104930, Jefferson City, MO 65110 / 573-634-8529; FAX: 573-634-8522
Bull Mountain Rifle Co., 6327 Golden West Terrace, Billings, MT 59106 / 406-656-0778
Bullberry Barrel Works, Ltd., 2430 W. Bullberry Ln., Hurricane, UT 84737 / 435-635-9866; FAX: 435-635-0348 fred@bullberry.com www.bullberry.com
Bullet Metals, Bill Ferguson, P.O. Box 1238, Sierra Vista, AZ 85636 / 520-458-5321; FAX: 520-458-1421 info@theantimonyman.com www.bullet-metals.com
Bullet N Press, 1210 Jones St., Gastonia, NC 28052 / 704-853-0265 bnpress@quik.com www.nemaine.com/bnpress
Bullet Swaging Supply, Inc., P.O. Box 1056, 303 McMillan Rd., West Monroe, LA 71291 / 318-387-3266; FAX: 318-387-7779 leblackmon@colla.com
Bullseye Bullets, 1808 Turkey Creek Rd. #9, Plant City, FL 33567 / 800-741-6343 bbullets8100@aol.com
Bull-X, Inc., 411 E. Water St., Farmer City, IL 61842-1556 / 309-928-2574 or 800-248-3845; FAX: 309-928-2130
Burkhart Gunsmithing, Don, P.O. Box 852, Rawlins, WY 82301 / 307-324-6007
Burnham Bros., P.O. Box 1148, Menard, TX 78659 / 915-396-4572; FAX: 915-396-4574
Burris Co., Inc., PO Box 1747, 331 E. 8th St., Greeley, CO 80631 / 970-356-1670; FAX: 970-356-8702
Bushmaster Firearms, 999 Roosevelt Trail, Windham, ME 04062 / 800-998-7928; FAX: 207-892-8068 info@bushmaster.com www.bushmaster.com
Bushmaster Hunting & Fishing, 451 Alliance Ave., Toronto, ON M6N 2J1 CANADA / 416-763-4040; FAX: 416-763-0623
Bushnell Sports Optics Worldwide, 9200 Cody, Overland Park, KS 66214 / 913-752-3400 or 800-423-3537; FAX: 913-752-3550
Buster's Custom Knives, P.O. Box 214, Richfield, UT 84701 / 801-896-5319
Butler Creek Corp., 2100 S. Silverstone Way, Meridian, ID 83642-8151 / 800-423-8327 or 406-388-1356; FAX: 406-388-7204
Butler Enterprises, 834 Oberting Rd., Lawrenceburg, IN 47025 / 812-537-3584
Butterfield's, 220 San Bruno Ave., San Francisco, CA 94103 / 415-861-7500; FAX: 415-861-0183 arms@butterfields.com www.butterfields.com
Buzz Fletcher Custom Stockmaker, 117 Silver Road, P.O. Box 189, Taos, NM 87571 / 505-758-3486

C

C&D Special Products (See Claybuster Wads & Harvester Bullets)
C&H Research, 115 Sunnyside Dr., Box 351, Lewis, KS 67552 / 316-324-5445888-324-5445; FAX:

620-324-5984 info@mercuryrecoil.com www.mercuryrecoil.com
C. Palmer Manufacturing Co., Inc., P.O. Box 220, West Newton, PA 15089 / 412-872-8200; FAX: 412-872-8302
C. Sharps Arms Co. Inc./Montana Armory, 100 Centennial Dr., PO Box 885, Big Timber, MT 59011 / 406-932-4353; FAX: 406-932-4443
C.S. Van Gorden & Son, Inc., 1815 Main St., Bloomer, WI 54724 / 715-568-2612 vangorden@bloomer.net
C.W. Erickson's L.L.C., 530 Garrison Ave. NE, PO Box 522, Buffalo, MN 55313 / 763-682-3665; FAX: 763-682-4328 www.archerhunter.com
Cabanas (See U.S. Importer-Mandall Shooting Supply
Cabela's, One Cabela Drive, Sidney, NE 69160 / 308-254-5505; FAX: 308-254-8420
Cabinet Mtn. Outfitters Scents & Lures, P.O. Box 766, Plains, MT 59859 / 406-826-3970
Cache La Poudre Rifleworks, 140 N. College, Ft. Collins, CO 80524 / 920-482-6913
Cali'co Hardwoods, Inc., 3580 Westwind Blvd., Santa Rosa, CA 95403 / 707-546-4045; FAX: 707-546-4027 calicohardwoods@msn.com
Calico Light Weapon Systems, 1489 Greg St., Sparks, NV 89431
California Sights (See Fautheree, Andy)
Cambos Outdoorsman, 532 E. Idaho Ave., Ontario, OR 97914 / 541-889-3135; FAX: 541-889-2633
Cambos Outdoorsman, Fritz Hallberg, 532 E. Idaho Ave, Ontario, OR 97914 / 541-889-3135; FAX: 541-889-2633
Camdex, Inc., 2330 Alger, Troy, MI 48083 / 810-528-2300; FAX: 810-528-0989
Cameron's, 16690 W. 11th Ave., Golden, CO 80401 / 303-279-7365; FAX: 303-628-5413 ncnoremac@aol.com
Camillus Cutlery Co., 54 Main St., Camillus, NY 13031 / 315-672-8111; FAX: 315-672-8832
Campbell, Dick, 20000 Silver Ranch Rd., Conifer, CO 80433 / 303-697-0150; FAX: 303-697-0150 dicksknives@aol.com
Camp-Cap Products, P.O. Box 3805, Chesterfield, MO 63006 / 314-532-4340; FAX: 314-532-4340
Cannon Safe, Inc., 216 S. 2nd Ave. #BLD-932, San Bernardino, CA 92400 / 310-692-0636; or 800-242-1055; FAX: 310-692-7252
Canons Delcour, Rue J.B. Cools, B-4040, Herstal, BELGIUM / 32.(0)42.40.61.40; FAX: 32(0)42.40.22.88
Canyon Cartridge Corp., P.O. Box 152, Albertson, NY 11507 / 516-294-8946
Cape Outfitters, 599 County Rd. 206, Cape Girardeau, MO 63701 / 573-335-4103; FAX: 573-335-1555
Caraville Manufacturing, P.O. Box 4545, Thousand Oaks, CA 91359 / 805-499-1234
Carbide Checkering Tools (See J&R Engineering)
Carhartt,Inc., P.O. Box 600, 3 Parklane Blvd., Dearborn, MI 48121 / 800-358-3825; or 313-271-8460; FAX: 313-271-3455
Carl Walther GmbH, B.P. 4325, D-89033, Ulm, GERMANY
Carl Zeiss Inc., 13005 N. Kingston Ave., Chester, VA 23836 / 800-441-3005; FAX: 804-530-8481
Carlson, Douglas R, Antique American Firearms, P.O. Box 71035, Dept GD, Des Moines, IA 50325 / 515-224-6552
Carolina Precision Rifles, 1200 Old Jackson Hwy., Jackson, SC 29831 / 803-827-2069
Carrell, William. See: CARRELL'S PRECISION FIREARMS
Carrell's Precision Firearms, William Carrell, 1952 W.Silver Falls Ct., Meridian, ID 83642-3837
Carry-Lite, Inc., P.O. Box 1587, Fort Smith, AR 72902 / 479-782-8971; FAX: 479-783-0234

Carter's Gun Shop, 225 G St., Penrose, CO 81240 / 719-372-6240
Cartridge Transfer Group, Pete de Coux, HC 30 Box 932 G, Prescott, AZ 86305-7447 / 928-776-8285; FAX: 928-776-8276 pdbullets@commspeed.net
Cascade Bullet Co., Inc., 2355 South 6th St., Klamath Falls, OR 97601 / 503-884-9316
Cascade Shooters, 2155 N.W. 12th St., Redwood, OR 97756
Case & Sons Cutlery Co., W R, Owens Way, Bradford, PA 16701 / 814-368-4123; or 800-523-6350; FAX: 814-768-5369
Case Sorting System, 12695 Cobblestone Creek Rd., Poway, CA 92064 / 619-486-9340
Cash Mfg. Co., Inc., P.O. Box 130, 201 S. Klein Dr., Waunakee, WI 53597-0130 / 608-849-5664; FAX: 608-849-5664
Caspian Arms, Ltd., 14 North Main St., Hardwick, VT 05843 / 802-472-6454; FAX: 802-472-6709
Cast Performance Bullet Company, PO Box 153, Riverton, WY 82501 / 307-857-2940; FAX: 307-857-3132 castperform@wyoming.com castperformance.com
Casull Arms Corp., P.O. Box 1629, Afton, WY 83110 / 307-886-0200
Cathey Enterprises, Inc., P.O. Box 2202, Brownwood, TX 76804 / 915-643-2553; FAX: 915-643-3653
Cation, 2341 Alger St., Troy, MI 48083 / 810-689-0658; FAX: 810-689-7558
Caywood, Shane J., P.O. Box 321, Minocqua, WI 54548 / 715-277-3866
Caywood Gunmakers, 18 King's Hill Estates, Berryville, AR 72616 / 870-423-4741 www.caywoodguns.com
CBC, Avenida Humberto de Campos 3220, 09400-000, Ribeirao Pires, SP, BRAZIL / 55-11-742-7500; FAX: 55-11-459-7385
CBC-BRAZIL, 3 Cuckoo Lane, Honley, Yorkshire HD7 2BR, ENGLAND / 44-1484-661062; FAX: 44-1484-663709
CCG Enterprises, 5217 E. Belknap St., Halton City, TX 76117 / 800-819-7464
CCI Ammunition ATK, P.O. Box 856, Lewiston, ID 83501 / 208-746-2351 www.cci_ammunition.com
CCL Security Products, 199 Whiting St, New Britain, CT 06051 / 800-733-8588
Cedar Hill Game Calls, Inc., 238 Vic Allen Rd, Downsville, LA 71234 / 318-982-5632; FAX: 318-368-2245
Centaur Systems, Inc., 1602 Foothill Rd., Kalispell, MT 59901 / 406-755-8609; FAX: 406-755-8609
Center Lock Scope Rings, 9901 France Ct., Lakeville, MN 55044 / 612-461-2114
Central Specialties Ltd (See Trigger Lock Division
Century Gun Dist. Inc., 1467 Jason Rd., Greenfield, IN 46140 / 317-462-4524
Century International Arms, Inc., 1161 Holland Dr, Boca Raton, FL 33487
CFVentures, 509 Harvey Dr., Bloomington, IN 47403-1715 paladinwilltravel@yahoo.com
CH Tool & Die Co. (See 4-D Custom Die Co.), 711 N Sandusky St., P.O. Box 889, Mt. Vernon, OH 43050-0889 / 740-397-7214; FAX: 740-397-6600
Chace Leather Products, 507 Alden St., Fall River, MA 02722 / 508-678-7556; FAX: 508-675-9666
Chadick's Ltd., P.O. Box 100, Terrell, TX 75160 / 214-563-7577
Chambers Flintlocks Ltd., Jim, 116 Sams Branch Rd., Candler, NC 28715 / 828-667-8361; FAX: 828-665-0852 www.flintlocks.com
Champion Shooters' Supply, P.O. Box 303, New Albany, OH 43054 / 614-855-1603; FAX: 614-855-1209

16th EDITION • 295

Champion Target Co., 232 Industrial Parkway, Richmond, IN 47374 / 800-441-4971

Champion's Choice, Inc., 201 International Blvd., LaVergne, TN 37086 / 615-793-4066; FAX: 615-793-4070 champ.choice@earthlink.net www.champchoice.com

Champlin Firearms, Inc., P.O. Box 3191, Woodring Airport, Enid, OK 73701 / 580-237-7388; FAX: 580-242-6922 info@champlinarms.com www.champlinarms.com

Chapman Academy of Practical Shooting, 4350 Academy Rd., Hallsville, MO 65255 / 573-696-5544; FAX: 573-696-2266 ha@chapmanacademy.com

Chapman, J Ken. See: OLD WEST BULLET MOULDS

Chapman Manufacturing Co., 471 New Haven Rd., PO Box 250, Durham, CT 06422 / 860-349-9228; FAX: 860-349-0084 sales@chapmanmfg.com www.chapmanmfg.com

Chapuis Armes, 21 La Gravoux, BP15, 42380, St. Bonnet-le-Chatea, FRANCE / (33)77.50.06.96

Chapuis USA, 416 Business Park, Bedford, KY 40006

Charter 2000, 273 Canal St, Shelton, CT 06484 / 203-922-1652

Checkmate Refinishing, 370 Champion Dr., Brooksville, FL 34601 / 352-799-5774; FAX: 352-799-2986 checkmatecustom.com

Cheddite, France S.A., 99 Route de Lyon, F-26501, Bourg-les-Valence, FRANCE / 33-75-56-4545; FAX: 33-75-56-3587 export@cheddite.com

Chelsea Gun Club of New York City Inc., 237 Ovington Ave., Apt. D53, Brooklyn, NY 11209 / 718-836-9422; or 718-833-2704

Cherry Creek State Park Shooting Center, 12500 E. Belleview Ave., Englewood, CO 80111 / 303-693-1765

Chet Fulmer's Antique Firearms, P.O. Box 792, Rt. 2 Buffalo Lake, Detroit Lakes, MN 56501 / 218-847-7712

CheVron Bullets, RR1, Ottawa, IL 61350 / 815-433-2471

Cheyenne Pioneer Products, PO Box 28425, Kansas City, MO 64188 / 816-413-9196; FAX: 816-455-2859 cheyennepp@aol.com www.cartridgeboxes.com

Chicago Cutlery Co., 1536 Beech St., Terre Haute, IN 47804 / 800-457-2665

Chicasaw Gun Works, 4 Mi. Mkr., Pluto Rd., Box 868, Shady Spring, WV 25918-0868 / 304-763-2848; FAX: 304-763-3725

Chipmunk (See Oregon Arms, Inc.)

Choate Machine & Tool Co., Inc., P.O. Box 218, 116 Lovers Ln., Bald Knob, AR 72010 / 501-724-6193; or 800-972-6390; FAX: 501-724-5873

Christensen Arms, 192 East 100 North, Fayette, UT 84630 / 435-528-7999; FAX: 435-528-7494 www.christensenarms.com

Christie's East, 20 Rockefeller Plz., New York, NY 10020-1902 / 212-606-0406 christics.com

Chu Tani Ind., Inc., P.O. Box 2064, Cody, WY 82414-2064

Chuck's Gun Shop, P.O. Box 597, Waldo, FL 32694 / 904-468-2264

Chuilli, Stephen, 8895 N. Military Trl. Ste., Ste. 201E, Palm Beach Gardens, FL 33410

Churchill (See U.S. Importer-Ellett Bros.)

Churchill, Winston G., 2838 20 Mile Stream Rd., Proctorville, VT 05153 / 802-226-7772

Churchill Glove Co., James, PO Box 298, Centralia, WA 98531 / 360-736-2816; FAX: 360-330-0151

CIDCO, 21480 Pacific Blvd., Sterling, VA 22170 / 703-444-5353

Ciener Inc., Jonathan Arthur, 8700 Commerce St., Cape Canaveral, FL 32920 / 321-868-2200; FAX: 321-868-2201

Cimarron F.A. Co., P.O. Box 906, Fredericksburg, TX 78624-0906 / 830-997-9090; FAX: 830-997-0802 cimgraph@koc.com www.cimarron-firearms.com

Cincinnati Swaging, 2605 Marlington Ave., Cincinnati, OH 45208

Clark Custom Guns, Inc., 336 Shootout Lane, Princeton, LA 71067 / 318-949-9884; FAX: 318-949-9829

Clark Firearms Engraving, P.O. Box 80746, San Marino, CA 91118 / 818-287-1652

Clarkfield Enterprises, Inc., 1032 10th Ave., Clarkfield, MN 56223 / 612-669-7140

Claro Walnut Gunstock Co., 1235 Stanley Ave., Chico, CA 95928 / 530-342-5188; FAX: 530-342-5199 wally@clarowalnutgunstock.com www.clarowalnutgunstock.com

Classic Arms Company, Rt 1 Box 120F, Burnet, TX 78611 / 512-756-4001

Classic Arms Corp., P.O. Box 106, Dunsmuir, CA 96025-0106 / 530-235-2000

Classic Old West Styles, 1060 Doniphan Park Circle C, El Paso, TX 79936 / 915-587-0684

Claybuster Wads & Harvester Bullets, 309 Sequoya Dr., Hopkinsville, KY 42240 / 800-922-6287 or 800-284-1746; FAX: 502-885-8088 50

Clean Shot Technologies, 21218 St. Andrews Blvd. Ste 504, Boca Raton, FL 33433 / 888-866-2532

Clearview Mfg. Co., Inc., 413 S. Oakley St., Fordyce, AR 71742 / 501-352-8557; FAX: 501-352-7120

Clearview Products, 3021 N. Portland, Oklahoma City, OK 73107

Cleland's Outdoor World, Inc, 10306 Airport Hwy, Swanton, OH 43558 / 419-865-4713; FAX: 419-865-5865

Clements' Custom Leathercraft, Chas, 1741 Dallas St., Aurora, CO 80010-2018 / 303-364-0403; FAX: 303-739-9824 gryphons@home.com kuntaoslcat.com

Clenzoil Worldwide Corp, Jack Fitzgerald, 25670 1st St., Westlake, OH 44145-1430 / 440-899-0482; FAX: 440-899-0483

Clift Mfg., L. R., 3821 Hammonton Rd., Marysville, CA 95901 / 916-755-3390; FAX: 916-755-3393

Clymer Mfg. Co., 1645 W. Hamlin Rd., Rochester Hills, MI 48309-3312 / 248-853-5555; FAX: 248-853-1530

C-More Systems, P.O. Box 1750, 7553 Gary Rd., Manassas, VA 20108 / 703-361-2663; FAX: 703-361-5881

Cobalt Mfg., Inc., 4020 Mcewen Rd Ste 180, Dallas, TX 75244-5090 / 817-382-8986; FAX: 817-383-4281

Cobra Enterprises, Inc., 1960 S. Milestone Drive, Suite F, Salt Lake City, UT 84104 FAX: 801-908-8301 www.cobrapistols@networld.com

Cobra Sport S.r.l., Via Caduti Nei Lager No. 1, 56020 San Romano, Montopoli v/Arno (Pi, ITALY / 0039-571-450490; FAX: 0039-571-450492

Coffin, Charles H., 3719 Scarlet Ave., Odessa, TX 79762 / 915-366-4729; FAX: 915-366-4729

Coffin, Jim (See Working Guns)

Coffin, Jim. See: WORKING GUNS

Cogar's Gunsmithing, 206 Redwine Dr., Houghton Lake, MI 48629 / 517-422-4591

Coghlan's Ltd., 121 Irene St., Winnipeg, MB R3T 4C7 CANADA / 204-284-9550; FAX: 204-475-4127

Cold Steel Inc., 3036 Seaborg Ave. Ste. A, Ventura, CA 93003 / 800-255-4716; or 800-624-2363; FAX: 805-642-9727

Cole-Grip, 16135 Cohasset St., Van Nuys, CA 91406 / 818-782-4424

Coleman Co., Inc., 250 N. St. Francis, Wichita, KS 67201

Cole's Gun Works, Old Bank Building, Rt. 4 Box 250, Moyock, NC 27958 / 919-435-2345

Collings, Ronald, 1006 Cielta Linda, Vista, CA 92083

Colonial Arms, Inc., P.O. Box 636, Selma, AL 36702-0636 / 334-872-9455; FAX: 334-872-9540 colonialarms@mindspring.com www.colonialarms.com

Colonial Repair, 47 Navarre St., Roslindale, MA 02131-4725 / 617-469-4951

Colorado Gunsmithing Academy, RR 3 Box 79B, El Campo, TX 77437 / 719-336-4099 or 800-754-2046; FAX: 719-336-9642

Colorado School of Trades, 1575 Hoyt St., Lakewood, CO 80215 / 800-234-4594; FAX: 303-233-4723

Colt Blackpowder Arms Co., 110 8th Street, Brooklyn, NY 11215 / 718-499-4678; FAX: 718-768-8056

Colt's Mfg. Co., Inc., PO Box 1868, Hartford, CT 06144-1868 / 800-962-COLT; or 860-236-6311; FAX: 860-244-1449

Compass Industries, Inc., 104 East 25th St., New York, NY 10010 / 212-473-2614 or 800-221-9904; FAX: 212-353-0826

Compasseco, Ltd., 151 Atkinson Hill Ave., Bardtown, KY 40004 / 502-349-0910

Competition Electronics, Inc., 3469 Precision Dr., Rockford, IL 61109 / 815-874-8001; FAX: 815-874-8181

Competitor Corp., Inc., Appleton Business Center, 30 Tricnit Road Unit 16, New Ipswich, NH 03071 / 603-878-3891; FAX: 603-878-3950

Component Concepts, Inc., 530 S Springbrook Road, Newberg, OR 97132 / 503-554-8095; FAX: 503-554-9370 cci@cybcon.com www.phantomonline.com

Concept Development Corp., 16610 E. Laser Drive, Suite 5, Fountain Hills, AZ 85268-6644

Conetrol Scope Mounts, 10225 Hwy. 123 S., Seguin, TX 78155 / 830-379-3030 or 800-CONETROL; FAX: 830-379-3030 email@conetrol.com www.conetrol.com

CONKKO, P.O. Box 40, Broomall, PA 19008 / 215-356-0711

Connecticut Shotgun Mfg. Co., P.O. Box 1692, 35 Woodland St., New Britain, CT 06051 / 860-225-6581; FAX: 860-832-8707

Connecticut Valley Classics (See CVC, BPI)

Conrad, C. A., 3964 Ebert St., Winston-Salem, NC 27127 / 919-788-5469

Cook Engineering Service, 891 Highbury Rd., Vict, 3133 AUSTRALIA

Cooper Arms, P.O. Box 114, Stevensville, MT 59870 / 406-777-0373; FAX: 406-777-5228

Cooper-Woodward, 3800 Pelican Rd., Helena, MT 59602 / 406-458-3800 dolymama@msn.com

Corbin Mfg. & Supply, Inc., 600 Industrial Circle, P.O. Box 2659, White City, OR 97503 / 541-826-5211; FAX: 541-826-8669 sales@corbins.com www.corbins.com

Cor-Bon Inc./Glaser LLC, P.O. Box 173, 1311 Industry Rd., Sturgis, SD 57785 / 605-347-4544 or 800-221-3489; FAX: 605-347-5055 email@corbon.com www.corbon.com

Corkys Gun Clinic, 4401 Hot Springs Dr., Greeley, CO 80634-9226 / 970-330-0516

Corry, John, 861 Princeton Ct., Neshanic Station, NJ 08853 / 908-369-8019

Cosmi Americo & Figlio s.n.c., Via Flaminia 307, Ancona, ITALY / 071-888208; FAX: 39-071-887008

Coulston Products, Inc., P.O. Box 30, 201 Ferry St. Suite 212, Easton, PA 18044-0030 / 215-253-0167; or 800-445-9927; FAX: 215-252-1511

Counter Assault, 120 Industrial Court, Kalispell, MT 59901 / 406-257-4740; FAX: 406-257-6674

Cousin Bob's Mountain Products, 7119 Ohio River Blvd., Ben Avon, PA 15202 / 412-766-5114; FAX: 412-766-5114

Cox, Ed. C., RD 2, Box 192, Prosperity, PA 15329 / 412-228-4984

CP Bullets, 1310 Industrial Hwy #5-6, South Hampton, PA 18966 / 215-953-7264; FAX: 215-953-7275

CQB Training, P.O. Box 1739, Manchester, MO 63011

Craftguard, 3624 Logan Ave., Waterloo, IA 50703 / 319-232-2959; FAX: 319-234-0804

Crandall Tool & Machine Co., 19163 21 Mile Rd., Tustin, MI 49688 / 616-829-4430

Creedmoor Sports, Inc., P.O. Box 1040, Oceanside, CA 92051 / 767-757-5529; FAX: 760-757-5558 shoot@creedmoorsports.com www.creedmoorsports.com

Creek Side Metal & Woodcrafters, Fishers Hill, VA 22626 / 703-465-3903

Creighton Audette, 19 Highland Circle, Springfield, VT 05156 / 802-885-2331

Crimson Trace Lasers, 8090 SW Cirrus Dr., Beverton, OR 97008 / 800-442-2406; FAX: 503-627-0166 www.crimsontrace.com

Crit'R Call (See Rocky Mountain Wildlife Products)

Crosman Airguns, Rts. 5 and 20, E. Bloomfield, NY 14443 / 716-657-6161; FAX: 716-657-5405

Crosman Blades (See Coleman Co., Inc.)

Crouse's Country Cover, P.O. Box 160, Storrs, CT 06268 / 860-423-8736

CRR, Inc./Marble's Inc., 420 Industrial Park, P.O. Box 111, Gladstone, MI 49837 / 906-428-3710; FAX: 906-428-3711

Crucelegui, Hermanos (See U.S. Importer-Mandall)

Cubic Shot Shell Co., Inc., 98 Fatima Dr., Campbell, OH 44405 / 330-755-0349

Cullity Restoration, 209 Old Country Rd., East Sandwich, MA 02537 / 508-888-1147

Cumberland Arms, 514 Shafer Road, Manchester, TN 37355 / 800-797-8414

Cumberland Mountain Arms, P.O. Box 710, Winchester, TN 37398 / 615-967-8414; FAX: 615-967-9199

Cummings Bullets, 1417 Esperanza Way, Escondido, CA 92027

Cupp, Alana, Custom Engraver, PO Box 207, Annabella, UT 84711 / 801-896-4834

Curly Maple Stock Blanks (See Tiger-Hunt)

Curtis Cast Bullets, 527 W. Babcock St., Bozeman, MT 59715 / 406-587-8117; FAX: 406-587-8117

Curtis Gun Shop (See Curtis Cast Bullets)

Custom Bullets by Hoffman, 2604 Peconic Ave., Seaford, NY 11783

Custom Calls, 607 N. 5th St., Burlington, IA 52601 / 319-752-4465

Custom Checkering Service, Kathy Forster, 2124 S.E. Yamhill St., Portland, OR 97214 / 503-236-5874

Custom Chronograph, Inc., 5305 Reese Hill Rd., Sumas, WA 98295 / 360-988-7801

Custom Firearms (See Ahrends, Kim)

Custom Gun Stocks, 3062 Turners Bend Rd, McMinnville, TN 37110 / 615-668-3912

Custom Products (See Jones Custom Products)

Custom Quality Products, Inc., 345 W. Girard Ave., P.O. Box 71129, Madison Heights, MI 48071 / 810-585-1616; FAX: 810-585-0644

Custom Riflestocks, Inc., Michael M. Kokolus, 7005 Herber Rd., New Tripoli, PA 18066 / 610-298-3013; FAX: 610-298-2431 mkokolus@prodigy.net

Custom Single Shot Rifles, 9651 Meadows Lane, Guthrie, OK 73044 / 405-282-3634

Custom Stocking, Mike Yee, 29927 56 Pl. S., Auburn, WA 98001 / 253-839-3991

Custom Tackle and Ammo, P.O. Box 1886, Farmington, NM 87499 / 505-632-3539

Cutco Cutlery, P.O. Box 810, Olean, NY 14760 / 716-372-3111

CVA, 5988 Peachtree Corners East, Norcross, GA 30071 / 770-449-4687; FAX: 770-242-8546 info@cva.com www.cva.com

Cylinder & Slide, Inc., William R. Laughridge, 245 E. 4th St., Fremont, NE 68025 / 402-721-4277; FAX: 402-721-0263 bill@cylinder-slide.com www.clinder-slide.com

CZ USA, PO Box 171073, Kansas City, KS 66117 / 913-321-1811; FAX: 913-321-4901

D

D&D Gunsmiths, Ltd., 363 E. Elmwood, Troy, MI 48083 / 810-583-1512; FAX: 810-583-1524

D&G Precision Duplicators (See Greene Precision)

D&H Precision Tooling, 7522 Barnard Mill Rd., Ringwood, IL 60072 / 815-653-4011

D&L Industries (See D.J. Marketing)

D&L Sports, P.O. Box 651, Gillette, WY 82717 / 307-686-4008

D.C.C. Enterprises, 259 Wynburn Ave., Athens, GA 30601

D.J. Marketing, 10602 Horton Ave., Downey, CA 90241 / 310-806-0891; FAX: 310-806-6231

Dade Screw Machine Products, 2319 NW 7th Ave., Miami, FL 33127 / 305-573-5050

Daewoo Precision Industries Ltd., 34-3 Yeoeuido-Dong, Yeongdeungoo-GU 15th Fl., Seoul, KOREA

Daisy Outdoor Products, P.O. Box 220, Rogers, AR 72757 / 479-636-1200; FAX: 479-636-0573 www.daisy.com

Dakota (See U.S. Importer-EMF Co., Inc.)

Dakota Arms, Inc., 130 Industry Road, Sturgis, SD 57785 / 605-347-4686; FAX: 605-347-4459 info@dakotaarms.com www.dakotaarms.com

Dakota Corp., 77 Wales St., P.O. Box 543, Rutland, VT 05701 / 802-775-6062; or 800-451-4167; FAX: 802-773-3919

Daly, Charles (See U.S. Importer), P.O. Box 6625, Harrisburg, PA 17112 / 717-540-8518 www.charlesdaly.com

Da-Mar Gunsmith's Inc., 102 1st St., Solvay, NY 13209

damascususa@inteliport.com, 149 Deans Farm Rd., Tyner, NC 27980 / 252-221-2010; FAX: 252-221-2010 damascususa@inteliport.com

Dan Wesson Firearms, 119 Kemper Lane, Norwich, NY 13815 / 607-336-1174; FAX: 607-336-2730

Danforth, Mikael. See: VEKTOR USA

Dangler, Homer L., 2870 Lee Marie Dr., Adrian, MI 49220 / 517-266-1997

Danner Shoe Mfg. Co., 12722 NE Airport Way, Portland, OR 97230 / 503-251-1100; or 800-345-0430; FAX: 503-251-1119

Dan's Whetstone Co., Inc., 130 Timbs Place, Hot Springs, AR 71913 / 501-767-1616; FAX: 501-767-9598 questions@danswhetstone.com www.danswhetstone.com

Danuser Machine Co., 550 E. Third St., P.O. Box 368, Fulton, MO 65251 / 573-642-2246; FAX: 573-642-2240 sales@danuser.com www.danuser.com

Dara-Nes, Inc. (See Nesci Enterprises, Inc.)

D'Arcy Echols & Co., PO Box 421, Millville, UT 84326 / 435-755-6842

Darlington Gun Works, Inc., P.O. Box 698, 516 S. 52 Bypass, Darlington, SC 29532 / 803-393-3931

Dart Bell/Brass (See MAST Technology)

Darwin Hensley Gunmaker, PO Box 329, Brightwood, OR 97011 / 503-622-5411

Data Tech Software Systems, 19312 East Eldorado Drive, Aurora, CO 80013

Dave Norin Schrank's Smoke & Gun, 2010 Washington St., Waukegan, IL 60085 / 708-662-4034

Dave's Gun Shop, P.O. Box 2824, Casper, WY 82602-2824 / 307-754-9724

David Clark Co., Inc., PO Box 15054, Worcester, MA 01615-0054 / 508-756-6216; FAX: 508-753-5827 sales@davidclark.com www.davidclark.com

David Condon, Inc., 109 E. Washington St., Middleburg, VA 22117 / 703-687-5642

David Miller Co., 3131 E Greenlee Rd, Tucson, AZ 85716 / 520-326-3117

David R. Chicoine, 1210 Jones Street, Gastonia, NC 28052 / 704-853-0265 bnpress@quik.com

David W. Schwartz Custom Guns, 2505 Waller St., Eau Claire, WI 54703 / 715-832-1735

Davide Pedersoli and Co., Via Artigiani 57, Gardone VT, Brescia 25063, ITALY / 030-8912402; or 030-8915000; FAX: 030-8911019 info@davidepedersoli.com www.davide_pedersoli.com

Davis, Don, 1619 Heights, Katy, TX 77493 / 713-391-3090

Davis Industries (See Cobra Enterprises, Inc.)

Davis Products, Mike, 643 Loop Dr., Moses Lake, WA 98837 / 509-765-6178; or 509-766-7281

Daystate Ltd., Birch House Lanee, Cotes Heath Staffs, ST15.022, ENGLAND / 01782-791755; FAX: 01782-791617

Dayton Traister, 4778 N. Monkey Hill Rd., P.O. Box 593, Oak Harbor, WA 98277 / 360-679-4657; FAX: 360-675-1114

DBI Books Division of Krause Publications, 700 E. State St., Iola, WI 54990-0001 / 715-445-2214

D-Boone Ent., Inc., 5900 Colwyn Dr., Harrisburg, PA 17109

de Coux, Pete (See Cartridge Transfer Group)

Dead Eye's Sport Center, 76 Baer Rd., Shickshinny, PA 18655 / 570-256-7432 deadeyeprizz@aol.com

Deepeeka Exports Pvt. Ltd., D-78, Saket, Meerut-250-006, INDIA / 011-91-121-640363 or ; FAX: 011-91-121-640988 deepeeka@poboxes.com www.deepeeka.com

Defense Training International, Inc., 749 S. Lemay, Ste. A3-337, Ft. Collins, CO 80524 / 303-482-2520; FAX: 303-482-0548

Degen Inc. (See Aristocrat Knives)

deHaas Barrels, 20049 W. State Hwy. Z, Ridgeway, MO 64481 / 660-872-6308

Del Rey Products, P.O. Box 5134, Playa Del Rey, CA 90296-5134 / 213-823-0494

Delhi Gun House, 1374 Kashmere Gate, New Delhi 110 006, INDIA / 2940974; or 394-0974; FAX: 2917344 dgh@vsnl.com

Delorge, Ed, 6734 W. Main, Houma, LA 70360 / 985-223-0206

Del-Sports, Inc., Dave Budin, Box 685, 817 Main St., Margaretville, NY 12455 / 845-586-4103; FAX: 845-586-4105

Delta Arms Ltd., P.O. Box 1000, Delta, VT 84624-1000

Delta Enterprises, 284 Hagemann Drive, Livermore, CA 94550

Delta Frangible Ammunition LLC, P.O. Box 2350, Stafford, VA 22555-2350 / 540-720-5778 or 800-339-1933; FAX: 540-720-5667 dfa@dfanet.com www.dfanet.com

Dem-Bart Checkering Tools, Inc., 1825 Bickford Ave., Snohomish, WA 98290 / 360-568-7356 walt@dembartco.com www.dembartco.com

Denver Instrument Co., 6542 Fig St., Arvada, CO 80004 / 800-321-1135; or 303-431-7255; FAX: 303-423-4831

DeSantis Holster & Leather Goods, Inc., P.O. Box 2039, 149 Denton Ave., New Hyde Park, NY

MANUFACTURER'S DIRECTORY

11040-0701 / 516-354-8000; FAX: 516-354-7501

Desert Mountain Mfg., P.O. Box 130184, Coram, MT 59913 / 800-477-0762; or 406-387-5361; FAX: 406-387-5361

Detroit-Armor Corp., 720 Industrial Dr. No. 112, Cary, IL 60013 / 708-639-7666; FAX: 708-639-7694

DGR Custom Rifles, 4191 37th Ave. SE, Tappen, ND 58487 / 701-327-8135

DGS, Inc., Dale A. Storey, 1117 E. 12th, Casper, WY 82601 / 307-237-2414; FAX: 307-237-2414 dalest@trib.com www.dgsrifle.com

DHB Products, 336 River View Dr., Verona, VA 24482-2547 / 703-836-2648

Diamond Machining Technology, Inc. (See DMT)

Diamond Mfg. Co., P.O. Box 174, Wyoming, PA 18644 / 800-233-9601

Dibble, Derek A., 555 John Downey Dr., New Britain, CT 06051 / 203-224-2630

Dietz Gun Shop & Range, Inc., 421 Range Rd., New Braunfels, TX 78132 / 210-885-4662

Dilliott Gunsmithing, Inc., 657 Scarlett Rd., Dandridge, TN 37725 / 865-397-9204 gunsmithd@aol.com www.dilliottgunsmithing.com

Dillon Precision Products, Inc., 8009 East Dillon's Way, Scottsdale, AZ 85260 / 480-948-8009; or 800-762-3845; FAX: 480-998-2786 sales@dillonprecision.com www.dillonprecision.com

Dina Arms Corporation, P.O. Box 46, Royersford, PA 19468 / 610-287-0266; FAX: 610-287-0266

Dixie Gun Works, P.O. Box 130, Union City, TN 38281 / 731-885-0700; FAX: 731-885-0440 info@dixiegunworks.com www.dixiegunworks.com

Dixon Muzzleloading Shop, Inc., 9952 Kunkels Mill Rd., Kempton, PA 19529 / 610-756-6271 dixonmuzzleloading.com

DKT, Inc., 14623 Vera Drive, Union, MI 49130-9744 / 800-741-7083 orders; FAX: 616-641-2015

DLO Mfg., 10807 SE Foster Ave., Arcadia, FL 33821-7304

DMT--Diamond Machining Technology Inc., 85 Hayes Memorial Dr., Marlborough, MA 01752 FAX: 508-485-3924

Dohring Bullets, 100 W. 8 Mile Rd., Ferndale, MI 48220

Dolbare, Elizabeth, P.O. Box 502, Dubois, WY 82513-0502

Domino, PO Box 108, 20019 Settimo Milanese, Milano, ITALY / 1-39-2-33512040; FAX: 1-39-2-33511587

Donnelly, C. P., 405 Kubli Rd., Grants Pass, OR 97527 / 541-846-6604

Doskocil Mfg. Co., Inc., P.O. Box 1246, 4209 Barnett, Arlington, TX 76017 / 817-467-5116; FAX: 817-472-9810

Douglas Barrels, Inc., 5504 Big Tyler Rd., Charleston, WV 25313-1398 / 304-776-1341; FAX: 304-776-8560 www.benchrest.com/douglas

Downsizer Corp., P.O. Box 710316, Santee, CA 92072-0316 / 619-448-5510 www.downsizer.com

DPMS (Defense Procurement Manufacturing Services, Inc.), 13983 Industry Avenue, Becker, MN 55308 / 800-578-DPMS; or 763-261-5600 FAX: 763-261-5599

Dr. O's Products Ltd., P.O. Box 111, Niverville, NY 12130 / 518-784-3333; FAX: 518-784-2800

Drain, Mark, SE 3211 Kamilche Point Rd., Shelton, WA 98584 / 206-426-5452

Dremel Mfg. Co., 4915-21st St., Racine, WI 53406

Dri-Slide, Inc., 411 N. Darling, Fremont, MI 49412 / 616-924-3950

Dropkick, 1460 Washington Blvd., Williamsport, PA 17701 / 717-326-6561; FAX: 717-326-4950

DS Arms, Inc., P.O. Box 370, 27 West 990 Industrial Ave., Barrington, IL 60010 / 847-277-7258; FAX: 847-277-7259 www.dsarms.com

DTM International, Inc., 40 Joslyn Rd., P.O. Box 5, Lake Orion, MI 48362 / 313-693-6670

Duane A. Hobbie Gunsmithing, 2412 Pattie Ave, Wichita, KS 67216 / 316-264-8266

Duane's Gun Repair (See DGR Custom Rifles)

Dubber, Michael W., P.O. Box 312, Evansville, IN 47702 / 812-424-9000; FAX: 812-424-6551

Duck Call Specialists, P.O. Box 124, Jerseyville, IL 62052 / 618-498-9855

Duffy, Charles E (See Guns Antique & Modern DBA), Williams Lane, PO Box 2, West Hurley, NY 12491 / 914-679-2997

Du-Lite Corp., 171 River Rd., Middletown, CT 06457 / 203-347-2505; FAX: 203-347-9404

Dumoulin, Ernest, Rue Florent Boclinville 8-10, 13-4041, Votten, BELGIUM / 41 27 78 92

Duncan's Gun Works, Inc., 1619 Grand Ave., San Marcos, CA 92069 / 760-727-0515

DunLyon R&D Inc., 52151 E. US Hwy. 60, Miami, AZ 85539 / 928-473-9027

Duofold, Inc., RD 3 Rt. 309, Valley Square Mall, Tamaqua, PA 18252 / 717-386-2666; FAX: 717-386-3652

Dybala Gun Shop, P.O. Box 1024, FM 3156, Bay City, TX 77414 / 409-245-0866

Dykstra, Doug, 411 N. Darling, Fremont, MI 49412 / 616-924-3950

Dynalite Products, Inc., 215 S. Washington St., Greenfield, OH 45123 / 513-981-2124

Dynamit Nobel-RWS, Inc., 81 Ruckman Rd., Closter, NJ 07624 / 201-767-7971; FAX: 201-767-1589

E

E&L Mfg., Inc., 4177 Riddle By Pass Rd., Riddle, OR 97469 / 541-874-2137; FAX: 541-874-3107

E. Arthur Brown Co., 3404 Pawnee Dr., Alexandria, MN 56308 / 320-762-8847

E.A.A. Corp., P.O. Box 1299, Sharpes, FL 32959 / 407-639-4842; or 800-536-4442; FAX: 407-639-7006

Eagan, Donald V., P.O. Box 196, Benton, PA 17814 / 717-925-6134

Eagle Arms, Inc. (See ArmaLite, Inc.)

Eagle Grips, Eagle Business Center, 460 Randy Rd., Carol Stream, IL 60188 / 800-323-6144; or 708-260-0400; FAX: 708-260-0486

Eagle Imports, Inc., 1750 Brielle Ave., Unit B1, Wanamassa, NJ 07712 / 908-493-0333

E-A-R, Inc., Div. of Cabot Safety Corp., 5457 W. 79th St., Indianapolis, IN 46268 / 800-327-3431; FAX: 800-488-8007

EAW (See U.S. Importer-New England Custom Gun Serv

Eckelman Gunsmithing, 3125 133rd St. SW, Fort Ripley, MN 56449 / 218-829-3176

Eclectic Technologies, Inc., 45 Grandview Dr., Suite A, Farmington, CT 06034

Ed Brown Products, Inc., P.O. Box 492, Perry, MO 63462 / 573-565-3261; FAX: 573-565-2791 edbrown@edbrown.com www.edbrown.com

Edenpine, Inc. c/o Six Enterprises, Inc., 320 D Turtle Creek Ct., San Jose, CA 95125 / 408-999-0201; FAX: 408-999-0216

EdgeCraft Corp., S. Weiner, 825 Southwood Road, Avondale, PA 19311 / 610-268-0500; or 800-342-3255; FAX: 610-268-3545 www.edgecraft.com

Edmisten Co., P.O. Box 1293, Boone, NC 28607

Edmund Scientific Co., 101 E. Gloucester Pike, Barrington, NJ 08033 / 609-543-6250

Ednar, Inc., 2-4-8 Kayabacho, Nihonbashi Chuo-ku, Tokyo, JAPAN / 81(Japan)-3-3667-1651; FAX: 81-3-3661-8113

Ed's Gun House, Ed Kukowski, P.O. Box 62, Minnesota City, MN 55959 / 507-689-2925

Eezox, Inc., P.O. Box 772, Waterford, CT 06385-0772 / 800-462-3331; FAX: 860-447-3484

Effebi SNC-Dr. Franco Beretta, via Rossa, 4, 25062, ITALY / 030-2751955; FAX: 030-2180414

Efficient Machinery Co., 12878 N.E. 15th Pl., Bellevue, WA 98005 / 425-453-9318 or 800-375-8554; FAX: 425-453-9311 priemc@aol.com www.sturdybench.com

Eggleston, Jere D., 400 Saluda Ave., Columbia, SC 29205 / 803-799-3402

Eichelberger Bullets, Wm., 158 Crossfield Rd., King Of Prussia, PA 19406

Ekol Leather Care, P.O. Box 2652, West Lafayette, IN 47906 / 317-463-2250; FAX: 317-463-7004

El Paso Saddlery Co., P.O. Box 27194, El Paso, TX 79926 / 915-544-2233; FAX: 915-544-2535 epsaddlery.com www.epsaddlery.com

Electro Prismatic Collimators, Inc., 1441 Manatt St., Lincoln, NE 68521

Electronic Shooters Protection, Inc., 15290 Gadsden Ct., Brighton, CO 80603 / 800-797-7791; FAX: 303-659-8668

Electronic Trigger Systems, Inc., PO Box 13, 230 Main St. S., Hector, MN 55342 / 320-848-2760; FAX: 320-848-2760

Eley Ltd., P.O. Box 705, Witton, Birmingham, B6 7UT ENGLAND / 021-356-8899; FAX: 021-331-4173

Elite Ammunition, P.O. Box 3251, Oakbrook, IL 60522 / 708-366-9006

Ellett Bros., 267 Columbia Ave., P.O. Box 128, Chapin, SC 29036 / 803-345-3751; or 800-845-3711; FAX: 803-345-3820

Ellicott Arms, Inc. / Woods Pistolsmithing, 8390 Sunset Dr., Ellicott City, MD 21043 / 410-465-7979

Elliott Inc., G. W., 514 Burnside Ave, East Hartford, CT 06108 / 203-289-5741; FAX: 203-289-3137

EMAP USA, 6420 Wilshire Blvd., Los Angeles, CA 90048 / 213-782-2000; FAX: 213-782-2867

Emerging Technologies, Inc. (See Laseraim Technologies, Inc.)

EMF Co., Inc., 1900 E. Warner Ave., Suite 1-D, Santa Ana, CA 92705 / 949-261-6611; FAX: 949-756-0133

Empire Cutlery Corp., 12 Kruger Ct., Clifton, NJ 07013 / 201-472-5155; FAX: 201-779-0759

English, Inc., A.G., 708 S. 12th St., Broken Arrow, OK 74012 / 918-251-3399 agenglish@wedzone.net www.agenglish.com

Engraving Artistry, 36 Alto Rd., Burlington, CT 06013 / 203-673-6837 bobburt44@hotmail.com

Engraving Only, Box 55 Rabbit Gulch, Hill City, SD 57745 / 605-574-2239

Enguix Import-Export, Alpujarras 58, Alzira, Valencia, SPAIN / (96) 241 43 95; FAX: (96) 241 43 95

Enhanced Presentations, Inc., 5929 Market St., Wilmington, NC 28405 / 910-799-1622; FAX: 910-799-5004

Enlow, Charles, 895 Box, Beaver, OK 73932 / 405-625-4487

Entre`prise Arms, Inc., 15861 Business Center Dr., Irwindale, CA 91706

EPC, 1441 Manatt St., Lincoln, NE 68521 / 402-476-3946

Epps, Ellwood/Isabella, Box 341, Washago, ON L0K 2B0 CANADA / 705-689-5348

MANUFACTURER'S DIRECTORY

Erhardt, Dennis, 4508 N. Montana Ave., Helena, MT 59602 / 406-442-4533

Essex Arms, P.O. Box 363, Island Pond, VT 05846 / 802-723-6203; FAX: 802-723-6203

Estate Cartridge, Inc., 900 Bob Ehlen Dr., Anoka, MN 55303-7502 / 409-856-7277; FAX: 409-856-5486

Euber Bullets, No. Orwell Rd., Orwell, VT 05760 / 802-948-2621

Euroarms of America, Inc., P.O. Box 3277, Winchester, VA 22604 / 540-662-1863; FAX: 540-662-4464 www.euroarms.net

Euro-Imports, 905 W. Main St. E., El Cajon, CA 92020 / 619-442-7005; FAX: 619-442-7005

European American Armory Corp (See E.A.A. Corp)

Evans Engraving, Robert, 332 Vine St, Oregon City, OR 97045 / 503-656-5693 norbob-ore@msn.com

Eversull Co., Inc., 1 Tracemont, Boyce, LA 71409 / 318-793-8728; FAX: 318-793-5483 bestguns@aol.com

Evolution Gun Works Inc., 4050 B-8 Skyron Dr., Doylestown, PA 18901 / 215-348-9892; FAX: 215-348-1056 egw@pil.net www.egw-guns.com

Excalibur Electro Optics Inc., P.O. Box 400, Fogelsville, PA 18051-0400 / 610-391-9105; FAX: 610-391-9220

Excalibur Publications, P.O. Box 35369, Tucson, AZ 85740 / 520-575-9057 militarypubs@earthlink.net

Excel Industries Inc., 4510 Carter Ct., Chino, CA 91710 / 909-627-2404; FAX: 909-627-7817

Executive Protection Institute, P.O. Box 802, Berryville, VA 22611 / 540-554-2540 ruk.@creslink.net www.personalprotecion.com

Eze-Lap Diamond Prods., P.O. Box 2229, 15164 West State St., Westminster, CA 92683 / 714-847-1555; FAX: 714-897-0280

E-Z-Way Systems, PO Box 4310, Newark, OH 43058-4310 / 614-345-6645; or 800-848-2072; FAX: 614-345-6600

F

F.A.I.R., Via Gitti, 41, 25060 Marcheno (Bres, ITALY / 030/861162-8610344; FAX: 030/8610179 info@fair.it www.fair.it

F.I., Inc. - High Standard Mfg. Co., 5200 Mitchelldale St., Ste. E17, Houston, TX 77092-7222 / 713-462-4200; or 800-272-7816; FAX: 713-681-5665 info@highstandard.com www.highstandard.com

Fabarm S.p.A., Via Averolda 31, 25039 Travagliato, Brescia, ITALY / 030-6863629; FAX: 030-6863684 info@fabarm.com www.fabarm.com

Fagan & Co.Inc, 22952 15 Mile Rd, Clinton Township, MI 48035 / 810-465-4637; FAX: 810-792-6996

Faith Associates, PO Box 549, Flat Rock, NC 28731-0549 FAX: 828-697-6827

Faloon Industries, Inc., P.O. Box 1060, Tijeras, NM 87059 / 505-281-3783

Far North Outfitters, Box 1252, Bethel, AK 99559

Farm Form Decoys, Inc., 1602 Biovu, P.O. Box 748, Galveston, TX 77553 / 409-744-0762; or 409-765-6361; FAX: 409-765-8513

Farr Studio, Inc., 183 Hunters Rd., Washington, VA 22747-2001 / 615-638-8825

Farrar Tool Co., Inc., 11855 Cog Hill Dr., Whittier, CA 90601-1902 / 310-863-4367; FAX: 310-863-5123

Faulhaber Wildlocker, Dipl.-Ing. Norbert Wittasek, Seilergasse 2, A-1010 Wien, AUSTRIA / OM-43-1-5137001; FAX: 43-1-5137001 faulhaber1ut@net.at

Faulk's Game Call Co., Inc., 616 18th St., Lake Charles, LA 70601 / 318-436-9726; FAX: 318-494-7205

Faust Inc., T. G., 544 minor St, Reading, PA 19602 / 610-375-8549; FAX: 610-375-4488

Fautheree, Andy, P.O. Box 4607, Pagosa Springs, CO 81157 / 970-731-5003; FAX: 970-731-5009

Feather, Flex Decoys, 4500 Doniphan Dr., Neosho, MO 64850 / 318-746-8596; FAX: 318-742-4815

Federal Arms Corp. of America, 7928 University Ave., Fridley, MN 55432 / 612-780-8780; FAX: 612-780-8780

Federal Cartridge Co., 900 Ehlen Dr., Anoka, MN 55303 / 612-323-2300; FAX: 612-323-2506

Federal Champion Target Co., 232 Industrial Parkway, Richmond, IN 47374 / 800-441-4971; FAX: 317-966-7747

Federated-Fry (See Fry Metals)

FEG, Budapest, Soroksariut 158, H-1095, HUNGARY

Feinwerkbau Westinger & Altenburger, Neckarstrasse 43, 78727, Oberndorf a. N., GERMANY / 07423-814-0; FAX: 07423-814-200 info@feinwerkbau.de www.feinwerkbau.de

Feken, Dennis, Rt. 2, Box 124, Perry, OK 73077 / 405-336-5611

Felk Pistols Inc., 2121 Castlebridge Rd., Midlothian, VA 23113 / 804-794-3744; FAX: 208-988-4834

Fellowes, Ted, Beaver Lodge, 9245 16th Ave. SW, Seattle, WA 98106 / 206-763-1698

Ferguson, Bill, P.O. Box 1238, Sierra Vista, AZ 85636 / 520-458-5321; FAX: 520-458-9125

Ferguson, Bill. See: BULLET METALS

FERLIB, Via Parte 33 Marcheno/BS, Marcheno/BS, ITALY / 00390308610191; FAX: 00390308966882 info@ferlib.com www.ferlib.com

Ferris Firearms, 7110 F.M. 1863, Bulverde, TX 78163 / 210-980-4424

Fibron Products, Inc., P.O. Box 430, Buffalo, NY 14209-0430 / 716-886-2378; FAX: 716-886-2394

Fieldsport Ltd., Bryan Bilinski, 3313 W South Airport Rd., Traverse City, MI 49684 / 616-933-0767

Fiocchi Munizioni S.p.A. (See U.S. Importer-Fiocch

Fiocchi of America, Inc., 5030 Fremont Rd., Ozark, MO 65721 / 417-725-4118 or 800-721-2666; FAX: 417-725-1039

Firearms Co Ltd. / Alpine (See U.S. Importer-Mandall

Firearms Engraver's Guild of America, 332 Vine St., Oregon City, OR 97045 / 503-656-5693

Firearms International, 5709 Hartsdale, Houston, TX 77036 / 713-460-2447

First Inc., Jack, 1201 Turbine Dr., Rapid City, SD 57701 / 605-343-9544; FAX: 605-343-9420

Fisher, Jerry A., 631 Crane Mt. Rd., Big Fork, MT 59911 / 406-837-2722

Fisher Custom Firearms, 2199 S. Kittredge Way, Aurora, CO 80013 / 303-755-3710

Fitzgerald, Jack. See: CLENZOIL WORLDWIDE CORP

Flambeau Products Corp., 15981 Valplast Rd., Middlefield, OH 44062 / 216-632-1631; FAX: 216-632-1581

Flannery Engraving Co., Jeff W, 11034 Riddles Run Rd, Union, KY 41091 / 606-384-3127

Flayderman & Co., Inc., PO Box 2446, Ft Lauderdale, FL 33303 / 954-761-8855

Fleming Firearms, 7720 E 126th St. N, Collinsville, OK 74021-7016 / 918-665-3624

Fletcher-Bidwell, LLC., 305 E. Terhune St., Viroqua, WI 54665-1631 / 866-637-1860 fbguns@netscape.net

Flintlocks, Etc., 160 Rossiter Rd., P.O. Box 181, Richmond, MA 01254 / 413-698-3822; FAX: 413-698-3866 flintetc@berkshire.rr.com

Flitz International Ltd., 821 Mohr Ave., Waterford, WI 53185 / 414-534-5898; FAX: 414-534-2991

Fluoramics, Inc., 18 Industrial Ave., Mahwah, NJ 07430 / 800-922-0075; FAX: 201-825-7035

Flynn's Custom Guns, P.O. Box 7461, Alexandria, LA 71306 / 318-455-7130

FN Manufacturing, PO Box 24257, Columbia, SC 29224 / 803-736-0522

Folks, Donald E., 205 W. Lincoln St., Pontiac, IL 61764 / 815-844-7901

Foothills Video Productions, Inc., P.O. Box 651, Spartanburg, SC 29304 / 803-573-7023; or 800-782-5358

Foredom Electric Co., Rt. 6, 16 Stony Hill Rd., Bethel, CT 06801 / 203-792-8622

Forgett, Valmore. See: NAVY ARMS COMPANY

Forgreens Tool & Mfg., Inc., PO Box 955, Robert Lee, TX 76945 / 915-453-2800; FAX: 915-453-2460

Forkin, Ben (See Belt MTN Arms)

Forkin Arms, 205 10th Avenue S.W., White Sulphur Spring, MT 59645 / 406-547-2344

Forrest Inc., Tom, PO Box 326, Lakeside, CA 92040 / 619-561-5800; FAX: 619-561-0227

Forrest Tool Co., P.O. Box 768, 44380 Gordon Lane, Mendocino, CA 95460 / 707-937-2141; FAX: 717-937-1817

Forster, Kathy (See Custom Checkering)

Forster, Larry L., P.O. Box 212, 216 Highway 13 E., Gwinner, ND 58040-0212 / 701-678-2475

Forster Products, 310 E Lanark Ave, Lanark, IL 61046 / 815-493-6360; FAX: 815-493-2371

Fort Hill Gunstocks, 12807 Fort Hill Rd., Hillsboro, OH 45133 / 513-466-2763

Fort Knox Security Products, 1051 N. Industrial Park Rd., Orem, UT 84057 / 801-224-7233; or 800-821-5216; FAX: 801-226-5493

Fort Worth Firearms, 2006-B, Martin Luther King Fwy., Ft. Worth, TX 76104-6303 / 817-536-0718; FAX: 817-535-0290

Forthofer's Gunsmithing & Knifemaking, 5535 U.S. Hwy 93S, Whitefish, MT 59937-8411 / 406-862-2674

Fortune Products, Inc., 205 Hickory Creek Rd, Marble Falls, TX 78654 / 210-693-6111; FAX: 210-693-6394

Forty Five Ranch Enterprises, Box 1080, Miami, OK 74355-1080 / 918-542-5875

Foster, . See: ACCURACY INTERNATIONAL

Fountain Products, 492 Prospect Ave., West Springfield, MA 01089 / 413-781-4651; FAX: 413-733-8217

4-D Custom Die Co., 711 N. Sandusky St., PO Box 889, Mt. Vernon, OH 43050-0889 / 740-397-7214; FAX: 740-397-6600 info@ch4d.com ch4d.com

Fowler Bullets, 806 Dogwood Dr., Gastonia, NC 28054 / 704-867-3259

Fowler, Bob (See Black Powder Products)

Fox River Mills, Inc., P.O. Box 298, 227 Poplar St., Osage, IA 50461 / 515-732-3798; FAX: 515-732-5128

Foy Custom Bullets, 104 Wells Ave., Daleville, AL 36322

Francesca, Inc., 3115 Old Ranch Rd., San Antonio, TX 78217 / 512-826-2584; FAX: 512-826-8211

Franchi S.p.A., Via del Serpente 12, 25131, Brescia, ITALY / 030-3581833; FAX: 030-3581554

Francotte & Cie S.A. Auguste, rue de Trois Juin 109, 4400 Herstal-Liege, BELGIUM / 32-4-248-13-18; FAX: 32-4-948-11-79

Frank Knives, 13868 NW Keleka Pl., Seal Rock, OR 97376 / 541-563-3041; FAX: 541-563-3041

MANUFACTURER'S DIRECTORY

Frank Mittermeier, Inc., P.O. Box 2G, 3577 E. Tremont Ave., Bronx, NY 10465 / 718-828-3843

Franzen International,Inc (See U.S. Importer for)

Fred F. Wells/Wells Sport Store, 110 N Summit St., Prescott, AZ 86301 / 928-445-3655 www.wellssportstore@aol.com

Freedom Arms, Inc., P.O. Box 150, Freedom, WY 83120 / 307-883-2468; FAX: 307-883-2005

Fremont Tool Works, 1214 Prairie, Ford, KS 67842 / 316-369-2327

French, Artistic Engraving, J. R., 1712 Creek Ridge Ct, Irving, TX 75060 / 214-254-2654

Front Sight Firearms Training Institute, P.O. Box 2619, Aptos, CA 95001 / 800-987-7719; FAX: 408-684-2137

Frontier, 2910 San Bernardo, Laredo, TX 78040 / 956-723-5409; FAX: 956-723-1774

Frontier Arms Co.,Inc., 401 W. Rio Santa Cruz, Green Valley, AZ 85614-3932

Frontier Products Co., 2401 Walker Rd, Roswell, NM 88201-8950 / 614-262-9357

Frontier Safe Co., 3201 S. Clinton St., Fort Wayne, IN 46806 / 219-744-7233; FAX: 219-744-6678

Frost Cutlery Co., P.O. Box 22636, Chattanooga, TN 37422 / 615-894-6079; FAX: 615-894-9576

Fry Metals, 4100 6th Ave., Altoona, PA 16602 / 814-946-1611

Fujinon, Inc., 10 High Point Dr., Wayne, NJ 07470 / 201-633-5600; FAX: 201-633-5216

Fullmer, Geo. M., 2499 Mavis St., Oakland, CA 94601 / 510-533-4193

Fulmer's Antique Firearms, Chet, PO Box 792, Rt 2 Buffalo Lake, Detroit Lakes, MN 56501 / 218-847-7712

Fulton Armory, 8725 Bollman Place No. 1, Savage, MD 20763 / 301-490-9485; FAX: 301-490-9547

Furr Arms, 91 N. 970 W., Orem, UT 84057 / 801-226-3877; FAX: 801-226-3877

G

G C Bullet Co. Inc., 40 Mokelumne River Dr., Lodi, CA 95240

G&H Decoys,Inc., P.O. Box 1208, Hwy. 75 North, Henryetta, OK 74437 / 918-652-3314; FAX: 918-652-3400

G.G. & G., 3602 E. 42nd Stravenue, Tucson, AZ 85713 / 520-748-7167; FAX: 520-748-7583 ggg3@aol.com www.ggg3.com

G.H. Enterprises Ltd., Bag 10, Okotoks, AB T0L 1T0 CANADA / 403-938-6070

G.U. Inc (See U.S. Importer for New SKB Arms Co.)

G.W. Elliott, Inc., 514 Burnside Ave., East Hartford, CT 06108 / 203-289-5741; FAX: 203-289-3137

G96 Products Co., Inc., 85 5th Ave, Bldg. #6, Paterson, NJ 07544 / 973-684-4050; FAX: 973-684-3848 g96prod@aol

Gage Manufacturing, 663 W. 7th St., A, San Pedro, CA 90731 / 310-832-3546

Gaillard Barrels, P.O. Box 21, Pathlow, SK S0K 3B0 CANADA / 306-752-3769; FAX: 306-752-5969

Gain Twist Barrel Co. Rifle Works and Armory, 707 12th Street, Cody, WY 82414 / 307-587-4919; FAX: 307-527-6097

Galati International, P.O. Box 10, 616 Burley Ridge Rd., Wesco, MO 65586 / 636-584-0785; FAX: 573-775-4308 support@galatiinternational.com www.galatiinternational.com

Galaxy Imports Ltd., Inc., P.O. Box 3361, Victoria, TX 77903 / 361-573-4867; FAX: 361-576-9622 galaxy@cox_internet.com

GALCO International Ltd., 2019 W. Quail Ave., Phoenix, AZ 85027 / 602-258-8295; or 800-874-2526; FAX: 602-582-6854

Galena Industries AMT, 5463 Diaz St, Irwindale, CA 91706 / 626-856-8883; FAX: 626-856-8878

Gamba S.p.A. Societa Armi Bresciane Srl, Renato, Via Artigiani 93, ITALY / 30-8911640; FAX: 30-8911648

Gamba, USA, P.O. Box 60452, Colorado Springs, CO 80960 / 719-578-1145; FAX: 719-444-0731

Game Haven Gunstocks, 13750 Shire Rd., Wolverine, MI 49799 / 616-525-8257

Gamebore Division, Polywad Inc., P.O. Box 7916, Macon, GA 31209 / 478-477-0669 or 800-998-0669

Gamo (See U.S. Importers-Arms United Corp, Daisy M

Gamo USA, Inc., 3911 SW 47th Ave., Suite 914, Ft. Lauderdale, FL 33314 / 954-581-5822; FAX: 954-581-3165 gamousa@gate.net www.gamo.com

Gander Mountain, Inc., 12400 Fox River Rd., Wilmont, WI 53192 / 414-862-6848

GAR, 590 McBride Avenue, West Paterson, NJ 07424 / 973-754-1114; FAX: 973-754-1114 garreloading@aol.com

Garcia National Gun Traders, Inc., 225 SW 22nd Ave., Miami, FL 33135 / 305-642-2355

Garrett Cartridges, Inc., P.O. Box 178, Chehalis, WA 98532 / 360-736-0702 www.garrettcartridges.com

Garthwaite Pistolsmith, Inc., Jim, 12130 State Route 405, Watsontown, PA 17777 / 570-538-1566; FAX: 570-538-2965 www.garthwaite.com

Gary Goudy Classic Stocks, 1512 S. 5th St., Dayton, WA 99328 / 509-382-2726 goudy@innw.net

Gary Reeder Custom Guns, 2601 7th Avenue East, Flagstaff, AZ 86004 / 928-526-3313; FAX: 928-527-0840 gary@reedercustomguns.com www.reedercustomguns.com

Gary Schneider Rifle Barrels Inc., 12202 N. 62nd Pl., Scottsdale, AZ 85254 / 602-948-2525

Gator Guns & Repair, 7952 Kenai Spur Hwy., Kenai, AK 99611-8311

Gaucher Armes, S.A., 46 rue Desjoyaux, 42000, Saint-Etienne, FRANCE / 04-77-33-38-92; FAX: 04-77-61-95-72

GDL Enterprises, 409 Le Gardeur, Slidell, LA 70460 / 504-649-0693

Gehmann, Walter (See Huntington Die Specialties)

Genco, P.O. Box 5704, Asheville, NC 28803

Genecco Gun Works, 10512 Lower Sacramento Rd., Stockton, CA 95210 / 209-951-0706; FAX: 209-931-3872

Gene's Custom Guns, P.O. Box 10534, White Bear Lake, MN 55110 / 651-429-5105; FAX: 651-429-7365

Gentex Corp., 5 Tinkham Ave., Derry, NH 03038 / 603-434-0311; FAX: 603-434-3002 sales@derry.gentexcorp.com www.derry.gentexcorp.com

Gentner Bullets, 109 Woodlawn Ave., Upper Darby, PA 19082 / 610-352-9396

Gentry Custom Gunmaker, David, 314 N Hoffman, Belgrade, MT 59714 / 406-388-GUNS davidgent@mcn.net www.gentrycustom.com

George & Roy's, PO Box 2125, Sisters, OR 97759-2125 / 503-228-5424; or 800-553-3022; FAX: 503-225-9409

George E. Mathews & Son, Inc., 10224 S. Paramount Blvd., Downey, CA 90241 / 562-862-6719; FAX: 562-862-6719

George Hoenig, Inc., 6521 Morton Dr., Boise, ID 83704 / 208-375-1116; FAX: 208-375-1116

George Ibberson (Sheffield) Ltd., 25-31 Allen St., Sheffield, S3 7AW ENGLAND / 0114-2766123; FAX: 0114-2738465

sales@ebbintongroupco.uk www.eggintongroup.co.uk

George Madis Winchester Consultants, George Madis, P.O. Box 545, Brownsboro, TX 75756 / 903-852-6480; FAX: 903-852-3045 gmadis@earthlink.com www.georgemadis.com

Gerald Pettinger Books (See Pettinger Books), 47827 300th Ave., Russell, IA 50238 / 641-535-2239 gpettinger@lisco.com

Gerber Legendary Blades, 14200 SW 72nd Ave., Portland, OR 97223 / 503-639-6161; or 800-950-6161; FAX: 503-684-7008

Gervais, Mike, 3804 S. Cruise Dr., Salt Lake City, UT 84109 / 801-277-7729

Getz Barrel Co., P.O. Box 88, Beavertown, PA 17813 / 717-658-7263

Giacomo Sporting USA, 6234 Stokes Lee Center Rd., Lee Center, NY 13363

Gibbs Rifle Co., Inc., 211 Lawn St., Martinsburg, WV 25401 / 304-262-1651; FAX: 304-262-1658

Gil Hebard Guns Inc., 125 Public Square, Knoxville, IL 61448 / 309-289-2700; FAX: 309-289-2233

Gilbert Equipment Co., Inc., 960 Downtowner Rd., Mobile, AL 36609 / 205-344-3322

Gillmann, Edwin, 33 Valley View Dr., Hanover, PA 17331 / 717-632-1662 gillmaned@super-pa.net

Gilman-Mayfield, Inc., 3279 E. Shields, Fresno, CA 93703 / 209-221-9415; FAX: 209-221-9419

Gilmore Sports Concepts, 5949 S. Garnett, Tulsa, OK 74146 / 918-250-3810; FAX: 918-250-3845 gilmore@webzone.net www.gilmoresports.com

Giron, Robert E., 12671 Cousins Rd.., Peosta, IA 52068 / 412-731-6041

Glacier Glove, 4890 Aircenter Circle, Suite 210, Reno, NV 89502 / 702-825-8225; FAX: 702-825-6544

Glaser LLC, P.O. Box 173, Sturgis, SD 57785 / 605-347-4544 or 800-221-3489; FAX: 605-347-5055 email@corbon.com www.safetyslug.com

Glaser Safety Slug, Inc., PO Box 8223, Foster City, CA 94404 / 800-221-3489; FAX: 510-785-6685 safetyslug.com

Glass, Herb, PO Box 25, Bullville, NY 10915 / 914-361-3021

Glimm, Jerome. See: GLIMM'S CUSTOM GUN ENGRAVING

Glimm's Custom Gun Engraving, Jerome C. Glimm, 19 S. Maryland, Conrad, MT 59425 / 406-278-3574 jandlglimm@mcn.net

Glock GmbH, P.O. Box 50, A-2232, Deutsch Wagram, AUSTRIA

Glock, Inc., PO Box 369, Smyrna, GA 30081 / 770-432-1202; FAX: 770-433-8719

Glynn Scobey Duck & Goose Calls, Rt. 3, Box 37, Newbern, TN 38059 / 731-643-6128

GML Products, Inc., 394 Laredo Dr., Birmingham, AL 35226 / 205-979-4867

Gner's Hard Cast Bullets, 1107 11th St., LaGrande, OR 97850 / 503-963-8796

Goens, Dale W., P.O. Box 224, Cedar Crest, NM 87008 / 505-281-5419

Goergen's Gun Shop, Inc., 17985 538th Ave., Austin, MN 55912 / 507-433-9280; FAX: 507-433-9280

GOEX, Inc., P.O. Box 659, Doyline, LA 71023-0659 / 318-382-9300; FAX: 318-382-9303 mfahringer@goexpowder.com www.goexpowder.com

Golden Age Arms Co., 115 E. High St., Ashley, OH 43003 / 614-747-2488

Golden Bear Bullets, 3065 Fairfax Ave., San Jose, CA 95148 / 408-238-9515

Gonic Arms/North American Arm, 134 Flagg Rd., Gonic, NH 03839 / 603-332-8456 or 603-332-8457

Goodling's Gunsmithing, 1950 Stoverstown Road, Spring Grove, PA 17362 / 717-225-3350

Goodwin, Fred. See: GOODWIN'S GUN SHOP

Goodwin's Gun Shop, Fred Goodwin, Sherman Mills, ME 04776 / 207-365-4451

Gotz Bullets, 11426 Edgemere Ter., Roscoe, IL 61073-8232

Gould & Goodrich, 709 E. McNeil, Lillington, NC 27546 / 910-893-2071; FAX: 910-893-4742

Gournet Artistic Engraving, Geoffroy Gournet, 820 Paxinosa Ave., Easton, PA 18042 / 610-559-0710 www.geoffroygournet.com

Gournet, Geoffroy. See: GOURNET ARTISTIC ENGRAVING

Grace, Charles E., 1006 Western Ave., Trinidad, CO 81082 / 719-846-9435

Grace Metal Products, P.O. Box 67, Elk Rapids, MI 49629 / 616-264-8133

Graf & Sons, 4050 S Clark St., Mexico, MO 65265 / 573-581-2266; FAX: 573-581-2875

Grand Slam Hunting Products, Box 121, 25454 Military Rd., Cascade, MD 21719 / 301-241-4900; FAX: 301-241-4900 rlj6call@aol.com

Granite Mountain Arms, Inc., 3145 W Hidden Acres Trail, Prescott, AZ 86305 / 520-541-9758; FAX: 520-445-6826

Grant, Howard V., Hiawatha 15, Woodruff, WI 54568 / 715-356-7146

Graphics Direct, P.O. Box 372421, Reseda, CA 91337-2421 / 818-344-9002

Graves Co., 1800 Andrews Ave., Pompano Beach, FL 33069 / 800-327-9103; FAX: 305-960-0301

Grayback Wildcats, Mike Beeks, 5306 Bryant Ave., Klamath Falls, OR 97603 / 541-884-1072

Graybill's Gun Shop, 1035 Ironville Pike, Columbia, PA 17512 / 717-684-2739

Great American Gunstock Co., 3420 Industrial Drive, Yuba City, CA 95993 / 800-784-4867; FAX: 530-671-3906 gunstox@oro.net www.gunstocks.com

Great Lakes Airguns, 6175 S. Park Ave, Hamburg, NY 14075 / 716-648-6666; FAX: 716-648-6666 www.greatlakesairguns.com

Green, Arthur S., 485 S. Robertson Blvd., Beverly Hills, CA 90211 / 310-274-1283

Green, Roger M., P.O. Box 984, 435 E. Birch, Glencock, WY 82637 / 307-436-9804

Green Head Game Call Co., RR 1, Box 33, Lacon, IL 61540 / 309-246-2155

Green Mountain Rifle Barrel Co., Inc., P.O. Box 2670, 153 West Main St., Conway, NH 03818 / 603-447-1095; FAX: 603-447-1099

Greenwood Precision, P.O. Box 407, Rogersville, MO 65742 / 417-725-2330

Greg Gunsmithing Repair, 3732 26th Ave. North, Robbinsdale, MN 55422 / 612-529-8103

Greg's Superior Products, P.O. Box 46219, Seattle, WA 98146

Greider Precision, 431 Santa Marina Ct., Escondido, CA 92029 / 760-480-8892; FAX: 760-480-9800 greider@msn.com

Gremmel Enterprises, 2111 Carriage Drive, Eugene, OR 97408-7537 / 541-302-3000

Gre-Tan Rifles, 29742 W.C.R. 50, Kersey, CO 80644 / 970-353-6176; FAX: 970-356-5940 www.gtrtooling.com

Grier's Hard Cast Bullets, 1107 11th St., LaGrande, OR 97850 / 503-963-8796

Griffin & Howe, Inc., 36 W. 44th St., Suite 1011, New York, NY 10036 / 212-921-0980 info@griffinhowe.com www.griffinhowe.com

Griffin & Howe, Inc., 33 Claremont Rd., Bernardsville, NJ 07924 / 908-766-2287; FAX: 908-766-1068 info@griffinhowe.com www.griffinhowe.com

Griffin & Howe, Inc., 340 W Putnam Avenue, Greenwich, CT 06830 / 203-618-0270 info@griffinhowe.com www.griffinhowe.com

Grifon, Inc., 58 Guinam St., Waltham, MS 02154

Groenewold, John, P.O. Box 830, Mundelein, IL 60060 / 847-566-2365; FAX: 847-566-4065 jgairguns@direcway.com http://jwww.gairguns.aupal.com/augmpubl.

GRS / Glendo Corp., P.O. Box 1153, 900 Overlander St., Emporia, KS 66801 / 620-343-1084; or 800-836-3519; FAX: 620-343-9640 glendo@glendo.com www.glendo.com

Grulla Armes, Apartado 453, Avda Otaloa 12, Eiber, SPAIN

Gruning Precision Inc., 7101 Jurupa Ave., No. 12, Riverside, CA 92504 / 909-289-4371; FAX: 909-689-7791 gruningprecision@earthlink.net www.gruningprecision.com

GSI, Inc., 7661 Commerce Ln., Trussville, AL 35173 / 205-655-8299

GTB, 482 Comerwood Court, San Francisco, CA 94080 / 650-583-1550

Guarasi, Robert. See: WILCOX INDUSTRIES CORP.

Guardsman Products, 411 N. Darling, Fremont, MI 49412 / 616-924-3950

Gun City, 212 W. Main Ave., Bismarck, ND 58501 / 701-223-2304

Gun Hunter Books (See Gun Hunter Trading Co.), 5075 Heisig St., Beaumont, TX 77705 / 409-835-3006; FAX: 409-838-2266 gunhuntertrading@hotmail.com

Gun Hunter Trading Co., 5075 Heisig St., Beaumont, TX 77705 / 409-835-3006; FAX: 409-838-2266 gunhuntertrading@hotmail.com

Gun Leather Limited, 116 Lipscomb, Ft. Worth, TX 76104 / 817-334-0225; FAX: 800-247-0609

Gun List (See Krause Publications), 700 E State St., Iola, WI 54945 / 715-445-2214; FAX: 715-445-4087

Gun South, Inc. (See GSI, Inc.)

Gun Vault, 7339 E Acoma Dr., Ste. 7, Scottsdale, AZ 85260 / 602-951-6855

Gun-Alert, 1010 N. Maclay Ave., San Fernando, CA 91340 / 818-365-0864; FAX: 818-365-1308

Guncraft Books (See Guncraft Sports Inc.), 10737 Dutchtown Rd, Knoxville, TN 37932 / 865-966-4545; FAX: 865-966-4500 findit@guncraft.com www.usit.net/guncraft

Guncraft Sports Inc., 10737 Dutchtown Rd., Knoxville, TN 37932 / 865-966-4545; FAX: 865-966-4500 findit@guncraft.com www.usit.net/guncraft

Guncraft Sports, Inc., Marie C. Wiest, 10737 Dutchtown Rd., Knoxville, TN 37932 / 865-966-4545; FAX: 865-966-4500 www.guncraft.com

Gunfitters, P.O. Box 426, Cambridge, WI 53523-0426 / 608-764-8128 gunfitters@aol.com www.gunfitters.com

Gun-Ho Sports Cases, 110 E. 10th St., St. Paul, MN 55101 / 612-224-9491

Gunline Tools, 2950 Saturn St., "O", Brea, CA 92821 / 714-993-5100; FAX: 714-572-4128

Gunnerman Books, P.O. Box 81697, Rochester Hills, MI 48308 / 989-729-7018

Guns Antique & Modern DBA / Charles E. Duffy, Williams Lane, West Hurley, NY 12491 / 914-679-2997

Guns Div. of D.C. Engineering, Inc., 8633 Southfield Fwy., Detroit, MI 48228 / 313-271-7111 or 800-886-7623; FAX: 313-271-7112 guns@rifletech.com www.rifletech.com

GUNS Magazine, 591 Camino de la Reina, Suite 200, San Diego, CA 92108 / 619-297-5350; FAX: 619-297-5353

Gunsite Custom Shop, P.O. Box 451, Paulden, AZ 86334 / 520-636-4104; FAX: 520-636-1236

Gunsite Gunsmithy (See Gunsite Custom Shop)

Gunsite Training Center, P.O. Box 700, Paulden, AZ 86334 / 520-636-4565; FAX: 520-636-1236

Gunsmithing Ltd., 57 Unquowa Rd., Fairfield, CT 06430 / 203-254-0436; FAX: 203-254-1535

Gunsmithing, Inc., 30 West Buchanan St., Colorado Springs, CO 80907 / 719-632-3795; FAX: 719-632-3493

Gurney, F. R., Box 13, Sooke, BC V0S 1N0 CANADA / 604-642-5282; FAX: 604-642-7859

H

H&B Forge Co., Rt. 2, Geisinger Rd., Shiloh, OH 44878 / 419-895-1856

H&P Publishing, 7174 Hoffman Rd., San Angelo, TX 76905 / 915-655-5953

H&R 1871.LLC, 60 Industrial Rowe, Gardner, MA 01440 / 508-632-9393; FAX: 508-632-2300 hr1871@hr1871.com www.hr1871.com

H&S Liner Service, 515 E. 8th, Odessa, TX 79761 / 915-332-1021

H. Krieghoff Gun Co., Boschstrasse 22, D-89079, Ulm, GERMANY / 731-401820; FAX: 731-4018270

H.K.S. Products, 7841 Founion Dr., Florence, KY 41042 / 606-342-7841; or 800-354-9814; FAX: 606-342-5865

H.P. White Laboratory, Inc., 3114 Scarboro Rd., Street, MD 21154 / 410-838-6550; FAX: 410-838-2802

Hafner World Wide, Inc., PO Box 1987, Lake City, FL 32055 / 904-755-6481; FAX: 904-755-6595 hafner@isgroupe.net

Hakko Co. Ltd., 1-13-12, Narimasu, Itabashiku Tokyo, JAPAN / 03-5997-7870/2; FAX: 81-3-5997-7840

Half Moon Rifle Shop, 490 Halfmoon Rd., Columbia Falls, MT 59912 / 406-892-4409 halfmoonrs@centurytel.net

Hall Manufacturing, 142 CR 406, Clanton, AL 35045 / 205-755-4094

Hall Plastics, Inc., John, P.O. Box 1526, Alvin, TX 77512 / 713-489-8709

Hallberg, Fritz. See: CAMBOS OUTDOORSMAN

Hallowell & Co., P.O. Box 1445, Livingston, MT 59047 / 406-222-4770; FAX: 406-222-4792 morris@hallowellco.com www.hallowellco.com

Hally Caller, 443 Wells Rd., Doylestown, PA 18901 / 215-345-6354; FAX: 215-345-8892 info@hallycaller.com www.hallycaller.com

Hamilton, Alex B (See Ten-Ring Precision, Inc)

Hammans, Charles E., P.O. Box 788, 2022 McCracken, Stuttgart, AR 72160-0788 / 870-673-1388

Hammerli Ltd., Seonerstrasse 37, CH-5600, SWITZERLAND / 064-50 11 44; FAX: 064-51 38 27

Hammerli Service-Precision Mac, Rudolf Marent, 9711 Tiltree St., Houston, TX 77075 / 713-946-7028

Hammerli USA, 19296 Oak Grove Circle, Groveland, CA 95321 FAX: 209-962-5311

Hammond Custom Guns Ltd., 619 S. Pandora, Gilbert, AZ 85234 / 602-892-3437

HandCrafts Unltd (See Clements' Custom Leather), 1741 Dallas St, Aurora, CO 80010-2018 / 303-364-0403; FAX: 303-739-9824 gryphons@home.com kuntaoslcat.com

Handgun Press, P.O. Box 406, Glenview, IL 60025 / 847-657-6500; FAX: 847-724-8831 handgunpress@earth-link.net

Hank's Gun Shop, Box 370, 50 West 100 South, Monroe, UT 84754 / 801-527-4456

Hanned Precision (See The Hanned Line)

Hansen & Co., 244-246 Old Post Rd., Southport, CT 06490 / 203-259-6222; FAX: 203-254-3832

MANUFACTURER'S DIRECTORY

Hanson's Gun Center, Dick, 233 Everett Dr, Colorado Springs, CO 80911

Hanusin, John, 3306 Commercial, Northbrook, IL 60062 / 708-564-2706

Harford (See U.S. Importer-EMF Co. Inc.)

Harper's Custom Stocks, 928 Lombrano St., San Antonio, TX 78207 / 210-732-7174

Harrell's Precision, 5756 Hickory Dr., Salem, VA 24153 / 540-380-2683

Harrington & Richardson (See H&R 1871, Inc.)

Harris Engineering Inc., Dept GD54, Barlow, KY 42024 / 502-334-3633; FAX: 502-334-3000

Harris Enterprises, P.O. Box 105, Bly, OR 97622 / 503-353-2625

Harris Gunworks, 11240 N. Cave Creek Rd., Ste. 104, Phoenix, AZ 85020 / 602-582-9627; FAX: 602-582-5178

Harris Hand Engraving, Paul A., 113 Rusty Ln, Boerne, TX 78006-5746 / 512-391-5121

Harris Publications, 1115 Broadway, New York, NY 10010 / 212-807-7100; FAX: 212-627-4678

Harrison Bullets, 6437 E. Hobart St., Mesa, AZ 85205

Harry Lawson Co., 3328 N. Richey Blvd., Tucson, AZ 85716 / 520-326-1117

Hart & Son, Inc., Robert W., 401 Montgomery St., Nescopeck, PA 18635 / 717-752-3655; FAX: 717-752-1088

Hart Rifle Barrels,Inc., PO Box 182, 1690 Apulia Rd., Lafayette, NY 13084 / 315-677-9841; FAX: 315-677-9610 hartrb@aol.com hartbarrels.com

Hartford (See U.S. Importer-EMF Co. Inc.)

Hartmann & Weiss GmbH, Rahlstedter Bahnhofstr. 47, 22143, Hamburg, GERMANY / (40) 677 55 85; FAX: (40) 677 55 92 hartmannundweisst-online.de

Harvey, Frank, 218 Nightfall, Terrace, NV 89015 / 702-558-6998

Harwood, Jack O., 1191 S. Pendlebury Lane, Blackfoot, ID 83221 / 208-785-5368

Hastings, P.O. Box 224, Clay Center, KS 67432 / 785-632-3169; FAX: 785-632-6554

Hatfield Gun, 224 N. 4th St., St. Joseph, MO 64501

Hawk Laboratories, Inc. (See Hawk, Inc.), 849 Hawks Bridge Rd, Salem, NJ 08079 / 609-299-2700; FAX: 609-299-2800

Hawk, Inc., 849 Hawks Bridge Rd., Salem, NJ 08079 / 609-299-2700; FAX: 609-299-2800

Hawken Shop, The (See Dayton Traister)

Haydel's Game Calls, Inc., 5018 Hazel Jones Rd., Bossier City, LA 71111 / 318-746-3586; FAX: 318-746-3711

Haydon Shooters Supply, Russ, 15018 Goodrich Dr. NW, Gig Harbor, WA 98329-9738 / 253-857-7557; FAX: 253-857-7884

Heatbath Corp., P.O. Box 2978, Springfield, MA 01101 / 413-543-3381

Hecht, Hubert J, Waffen-Hecht, PO Box 2635, Fair Oaks, CA 95628 / 916-966-1020

Heckler & Koch GmbH, PO Box 1329, 78722 Oberndorf, Neckar, GERMANY / 49-7423179-0; FAX: 49-7423179-2406

Heckler & Koch, Inc., 21480 Pacific Blvd., Sterling, VA 20166-8900 / 703-450-1900; FAX: 703-450-8160 www.hecklerkoch-usa.com

Hege Jagd-u. Sporthandels GmbH, P.O. Box 101461, W-7770, Ueberlingen a. Boden, GERMANY

Heidenstrom Bullets, Dalghte 86-3660 Rjukan, 35091818, NORWAY, olau.joh@online.tuo

Heilmann, Stephen, P.O. Box 657, Grass Valley, CA 95945 / 530-272-8758; FAX: 530-274-0285 sheilmann@jps.net www.metalwood.com

Heinie Specialty Products, 301 Oak St., Quincy, IL 62301-2500 / 217-228-9500; FAX: 217-228-9502 rheinie@heinie.com www.heinie.com

Helwan (See U.S. Importer-Interarms)

Henigson & Associates, Steve, PO Box 2726, Culver City, CA 90231 / 310-305-8288; FAX: 310-305-1905

Henriksen Tool Co., Inc., 8515 Wagner Creek Rd., Talent, OR 97540 / 541-535-2309; FAX: 541-535-2309

Henry Repeating Arms Co., 110 8th St., Brooklyn, NY 11215 / 718-499-5600

Hensley, Gunmaker, Darwin, PO Box 329, Brightwood, OR 97011 / 503-622-5411

Heppler, Keith. See: KEITH'S CUSTOM GUNSTOCKS

Hercules, Inc. (See Alliant Techsystems, Smokeless)

Heritage Firearms (See Heritage Mfg., Inc.)

Heritage Manufacturing, Inc., 4600 NW 135th St., Opa Locka, FL 33054 or 305-685-5966; FAX: 305-687-6721 infohmi@heritagemfg.com www.heritagemfg.com

Heritage/VSP Gun Books, P.O. Box 887, McCall, ID 83638 / 208-634-4104; FAX: 208-634-3101

Herrett's Stocks, Inc., P.O. Box 741, Twin Falls, ID 83303 / 208-733-1498

Herter's Manufacturing Inc., 111 E. Burnett St., P.O. Box 518, Beaver Dam, WI 53916-1811 / 414-887-1765; FAX: 414-887-8444

Hesco-Meprolight, 2139 Greenville Rd., LaGrange, GA 30241 / 706-884-7967; FAX: 706-882-4683

Hesse Arms, Robert Hesse, 1126 70th Street E., Inver Grove Heights, MN 55077-2416 / 651-455-5760; FAX: 612-455-5760

Hesse, Robert. See: HESSE ARMS

Heydenberk, Warren R., 1059 W. Sawmill Rd., Quakertown, PA 18951 / 215-538-2682

Hickman, Jaclyn, Box 1900, Glenrock, WY 82637

Hidalgo, Tony, 12701 SW 9th Pl., Davie, FL 33325 / 954-476-7645

High Bridge Arms, Inc, 3185 Mission St., San Francisco, CA 94110 / 415-282-8358

High North Products, Inc., P.O. Box 2, Antigo, WI 54409 / 715-627-2331; FAX: 715-623-5451

High Performance International, 5734 W. Florist Ave., Milwaukee, WI 53218 / 414-466-9040

High Precision, Bud Welsh, 80 New Road, E. Amherst, NY 14051 / 716-688-6344; FAX: 716-688-0425 welsh5168@aol.com www.high-precision.com

High Tech Specialties, Inc., P.O. Box 839, 293 E Main St., Rear, Adamstown, PA 19501 / 717-484-0405; FAX: 717-484-0523 bansner@aol.com www.bansmersrifle.com/hightech

Highline Machine Co., Randall Thompson, 654 Lela Place, Grand Junction, CO 81504 / 970-434-4971

Highwood Special Products, 1531 E. Highwood, Pontiac, MI 48340

Hi-Grade Imports, 8655 Monterey Rd., Gilroy, CA 95021 / 408-842-9301; FAX: 408-842-2374

Hill, Loring F., 304 Cedar Rd., Elkins Park, PA 19027

Hill Speed Leather, Ernie, 4507 N 195th Ave, Litchfield Park, AZ 85340 / 602-853-9222; FAX: 602-853-9235

Hinman Outfitters, Bob, 107 N Sanderson Ave, Bartonville, IL 61607-1839 / 309-691-8132

Hi-Performance Ammunition Company, 484 State Route 366, Apollo, PA 15613 / 412-327-8100

HIP-GRIP Barami Corp., P.O. Box 252224, West Bloomfield, MI 48325-2224 / 248-738-0462; FAX: 248-738-2542 hipgripja@aol.com www.hipgrip.com

Hi-Point Firearms/MKS Supply, 8611-A North Dixie Dr., Dayton, OH 45414 / 877-425-4867; FAX: 937-454-0503 www.hi-pointfirearms.com

Hiptmayer, Armurier, RR 112 750, P.O. Box 136, Eastman, PQ J0E 1P0 CANADA / 514-297-2492

Hiptmayer, Heidemarie, RR 112 750, P.O. Box 136, Eastman, PQ J0E 1P0 CANADA / 514-297-2492

Hiptmayer, Klaus, RR 112 750, P.O. Box 136, Eastman, PQ J0E 1P0 CANADA / 514-297-2492

Hirtenberger AG, Leobersdorferstrasse 31, A-2552, Hirtenberg, / 43(0)2256 81184; FAX: 43(0)2256 81808 www.hirtenberger.ot

HiTek International, 484 El Camino Real, Redwood City, CA 94063 / 415-363-1404; or 800-54-NIGHT; FAX: 415-363-1408

Hiti-Schuch, Atelier Wilma, A-8863 Predlitz, Pirming, Y1 AUSTRIA / 0353418278

HJS Arms, Inc., P.O. Box 3711, Brownsville, TX 78523-3711 / 956-542-2767; FAX: 956-542-2767

Hoag, James W., 8523 Canoga Ave., Suite C, Canoga Park, CA 91304 / 818-998-1510

Hobson Precision Mfg. Co., 210 Big Oak Ln, Brent, AL 35034 / 205-926-4662; FAX: 205-926-3193 cahobbob@dbtech.net

Hodgdon Powder Co., 6231 Robinson, Shawnee Mission, KS 66202 / 913-362-9455; FAX: 913-362-1307

Hodgman, Inc., 1750 Orchard Rd., Montgomery, IL 60538 / 708-897-7555; FAX: 708-897-7558

Hodgson, Richard, 9081 Tahoe Lane, Boulder, CO 80301

Hoehn Sales, Inc., 2045 Kohn Road, Wright City, MO 63390 / 636-745-8144; FAX: 636-745-8144 hoehnsal@usmo.com

Hofer Jagdwaffen, P., Buchsenmachermeister, Kirchgasse 24, A-9170 Ferlach, AUSTRIA / 43 4227 3683; FAX: 43 4227 368330 peterhofer@hoferwaffen.com www.hoferwaffen.com

Hoffman New Ideas, 821 Northmoor Rd., Lake Forest, IL 60045 / 312-234-4075

Hogue Grips, P.O. Box 1138, Paso Robles, CA 93447 / 800-438-4747 or 805-239-1440; FAX: 805-239-2553

Holland & Holland Ltd., 33 Bruton St., London, ENGLAND / 44-171-499-4411; FAX: 44-171-408-7962

Holland's Gunsmithing, P.O. Box 69, Powers, OR 97466 / 541-439-5155; FAX: 541-439-5155

Hollinger, Jon. See: ASPEN OUTFITTING CO.

Hollywood Engineering, 10642 Arminta St., Sun Valley, CA 91352 / 818-842-8376; FAX: 818-504-4168

Homak, 5151 W. 73rd St., Chicago, IL 60638-6613 / 312-523-3100; FAX: 312-523-9455

Home Shop Machinist, The Village Press Publications, P.O. Box 1810, Traverse City, MI 49685 / 800-447-7367; FAX: 616-946-3289

Hondo Ind., 510 S. 52nd St., l04, Tempe, AZ 85281

Hoppe's Div. Penguin Industries, Inc., P.O. Box 1690, Oregon City, OR 97045-0690 / 610-384-6000

Horizons Unlimited, P.O. Box 426, Warm Springs, GA 31830 / 706-655-3603; FAX: 706-655-3603

Hornady Mfg. Co., P.O. Box 1848, Grand Island, NE 68802 / 800-338-3220 or 308-382-1390; FAX: 308-382-5761

Horseshoe Leather Products, Andy Arratoonian, The Cottage Sharow, Ripon U.K., ENGLAND U.K. / 44-1765-605858 andy@horseshoe.co.uk www.horseshoe.co.uk

House of Muskets, Inc., The, PO Box 4640, Pagosa Springs, CO 81157 / 970-731-2295

Houtz & Barwick, P.O. Box 435, W. Church St., Elizabeth City, NC 27909 / 800-775-0337; or 919-335-4191; FAX: 919-335-1152

Howa Machinery, Ltd., Sukaguchi, Shinkawa-cho Nishikasugai-gun, Aichi 452-8601, JAPAN / 81-52-408-1231; FAX: 81-52-409-4855 howa@howa.co.jp http://www.howa.cojpl

302 • HANDGUNS 2004

Howell Machine, 815 1/2 D St., Lewiston, ID 83501 / 208-743-7418

H-S Precision, Inc., 1301 Turbine Dr., Rapid City, SD 57701 / 605-341-3006; FAX: 605-342-8964

HT Bullets, 244 Belleville Rd., New Bedford, MA 02745 / 508-999-3338

Hubert J. Hecht Waffen-Hecht, P.O. Box 2635, Fair Oaks, CA 95628 / 916-966-1020

Huebner, Corey O., PO Box 564, Frenchtown, MT 59834 / 406-721-7168

Huey Gun Cases, 820 Indiana St., Lawrence, KS 66044-2645 / 816-444-1637; FAX: 816-444-1637 hueycases@aol.com www.hueycases.com

Hume, Don, P.O. Box 351, Miami, OK 74355 / 800-331-2686; FAX: 918-542-4340 info@donhume.com www.donhume.com

Hunkeler, A (See Buckskin Machine Works, 3235 S 358th St., Auburn, WA 98001 / 206-927-5412

Hunter Co., Inc., 3300 W. 71st Ave., Westminster, CO 80030 / 303-427-4626; FAX: 303-428-3980

Hunterjohn, PO Box 771457, St. Louis, MO 63177 / 314-531-7250

Hunter's Specialties Inc., 6000 Huntington Ct. NE, Cedar Rapids, IA 52402-1268 / 319-395-0321; FAX: 319-395-0326

Hunters Supply, Inc., P.O. Box 313, Tioga, TX 76271 / 940-437-2458; FAX: 940-437-2228 hunterssupply@hotmail.com www.hunterssupply.net

Huntington Die Specialties, 601 Oro Dam Blvd., Oroville, CA 95965 / 530-534-1210; FAX: 530-534-1212 buy@huntingtons.com www.huntingtons.com

Hutton Rifle Ranch, P.O. Box 170317, Boise, ID 83717 / 208-345-8781 www.martinbrevik@aol.com

Hydrosorbent Products, PO Box 437, Ashley Falls, MA 01222 / 800-448-7903; FAX: 413-229-8743 orders@dehumidify.com www.dehumidify.com

I

I.A.B. (See U.S. Importer-Taylor's & Co. Inc.)

I.D.S.A. Books, 1324 Stratford Drive, Piqua, OH 45356 / 937-773-4203; FAX: 937-778-1922

I.N.C. Inc (See Kickeez I.N.C., Inc.)

I.S.S., P.O. Box 185234, Ft. Worth, TX 76181 / 817-595-2090; FAX: 817-595-2090 iss@concentric.net

I.S.W., 106 E. Cairo Dr., Tempe, AZ 85282

IAR Inc., 33171 Camino Capistrano, San Juan Capistrano, CA 92675 / 949-443-3642; FAX: 949-443-3647 sales@iar-arms.com iar-arms.com

Ide, K. See: STURGEON VALLEY SPORTERS

IGA (See U.S. Importer-Stoeger Industries)

Ignacio Ugartechea S.A., Chonta 26, Eibar, 20600 SPAIN / 43-121257; FAX: 43-121669

Image Ind. Inc., 382 Balm Court, Wood Dale, IL 60191 / 630-766-2402; FAX: 630-766-7373

Impact Case & Container, Inc., P.O. Box 1129, Rathdrum, ID 83858 / 877-687-2452; FAX: 208-687-0632 bradk@icc-case.com www.icc-case.com

Imperial (See E-Z-Way Systems), PO Box 4310, Newark, OH 43058-4310 / 614-345-6645; FAX: 614-345-6600 ezway@infinet.com www.jcunald.com

Imperial Magnum Corp., P.O. Box 249, Oroville, WA 98844 / 604-495-3131; FAX: 604-495-2816

Imperial Miniature Armory, 10547 S. Post Oak Road, Houston, TX 77035-3305 / 713-729-8428; FAX: 713-729-2274 miniguns@aol.com www.1800miniature.com

Imperial Schrade Corp., 7 Schrade Ct., Box 7000, Ellenville, NY 12428 / 914-647-7601; FAX: 914-647-8701 csc@schradeknives.com www.schradeknives.com

Import Sports Inc., 1750 Brielle Ave., Unit B1, Wanamassa, NJ 07712 / 908-493-0302; FAX: 908-493-0301

IMR Powder Co., 1080 Military Turnpike, Suite 2, Plattsburgh, NY 12901 / 518-563-2253; FAX: 518-563-6916

Info-Arm, P.O. Box 1262, Champlain, NY 12919 / 514-955-0355; FAX: 514-955-0357

Ingle, Ralph W., Engraver, 112 Manchester Ct., Centerville, GA 31028 / 478-953-5824 riengraver@aol.com www.fega.com

Innovative Weaponry Inc., 2513 E. Loop 820 N., Fort Worth, TX 76118 / 817-284-0099 or 800-334-3573

INTEC International, Inc., P.O. Box 5708, Scottsdale, AZ 85261 / 602-483-1708

Inter Ordnance of America LP, 3305 Westwood Industrial Dr, Monroe, NC 28110-5204 / 704-821-8337; FAX: 704-821-8523

Intercontinental Distributors, Ltd., PO Box 815, Beulah, ND 58523

Intrac Arms International, 5005 Chapman Hwy., Knoxville, TN 37920

Ion Industries, Inc., 3508 E Allerton Ave., Cudahy, WI 53110 / 414-486-2007; FAX: 414-486-2017

Iosso Products, 1485 Lively Blvd., Elk Grove Village, IL 60007 / 847-437-8400; FAX: 847-437-8478

Iron Bench, 12619 Bailey Rd., Redding, CA 96003 / 916-241-4623

Ironside International Publishers, Inc., 3000 S. Eaos St., Arlington, VA 22202 / 703-684-6111; FAX: 703-683-5486

Ironsighter Co., P.O. Box 85070, Westland, MI 48185 / 734-326-8731; FAX: 734-326-3378 www.ironsighter.com

Irwin, Campbell H., 140 Hartland Blvd., East Hartland, CT 06027 / 203-653-3901

Island Pond Gun Shop, Cross St., Island Pond, VT 05846 / 802-723-4546

Israel Arms International, Inc., 1085 Gessner Rd., Ste. F, Houston, TX 77055 / 713-789-0745; FAX: 713-914-9515 iaipro@wt.net www.israelarms.com

Ithaca Classic Doubles, Stephen Lamboy, No. 5 Railroad St., Victor, NY 14564 / 716-924-2710; FAX: 716-924-2737 ithacadoubles.com

Ithaca Gun Company LLC, 901 Rt. 34 B, King Ferry, NY 13081 / 315-364-7171; FAX: 315-364-5134 info@ithacagun.com

Ivanoff, Thomas G. (See Tom's Gun Repair)

J

J J Roberts Firearm Engraver, 7808 Lake Dr, Manassas, VA 20111 / 703-330-0448; FAX: 703-264-8600 james..roberts@angelfire.com www.angelfire.com/va2/engraver

J&D Components, 75 East 350 North, Orem, UT 84057-4719 / 801-225-7007

J&J Products, Inc., 9240 Whitmore, El Monte, CA 91731 / 818-571-5228; FAX: 800-927-8361

J&J Sales, 1501 21st Ave. S., Great Falls, MT 59405 / 406-727-9789 www.j&jsales.us

J&L Superior Bullets (See Huntington Die Special)

J&R Engineering, P.O. Box 77, 200 Lyons Hill Rd., Athol, MA 01331 / 508-249-9241

J&R Enterprises, 4550 Scotts Valley Rd., Lakeport, CA 95453

J&S Heat Treat, 803 S. 16th St., Blue Springs, MO 64015 / 816-229-2149; FAX: 816-228-1135

J. Dewey Mfg. Co., Inc., P.O. Box 2014, Southbury, CT 06488 / 203-264-3064; FAX: 203-262-6907 deweyrods@worldnet.att.net www.deweyrods.com

J. Korzinek Riflesmith, RD 2, Box 73D, Canton, PA 17724 / 717-673-8512

J.A. Blades, Inc. (See Christopher Firearms Co.)

J.A. Henckels Zwillingswerk Inc., 9 Skyline Dr., Hawthorne, NY 10532 / 914-592-7370

J.G. Anschutz GmbH & Co. KG, Daimlerstr. 12, D-89079 Ulm, Ulm, GERMANY / 49 731 40120; FAX: 49 731 4012700 JGA-info@anschuetz-sport.com www.anschuetz-sport.com

J.G. Dapkus Co., Inc., Commerce Circle, P.O. Box 293, Durham, CT 06422 www.explodingtargets.com

J.I.T. Ltd., P.O. Box 230, Freedom, WY 83120 / 708-494-0937

J.J. Roberts / Engraver, 7808 Lake Dr., Manassas, VA 20111 / 703-330-0448 jjrengraver@aol.com www.angelfire.com/va2/engraver

J.P. Enterprises Inc., P.O. Box 378, Hugo, MN 55110 / 612-486-9064; FAX: 612-482-0970

J.R. Williams Bullet Co., 2008 Tucker Rd., Perry, GA 31069 / 912-987-0274

J.W. Morrison Custom Rifles, 4015 W. Sharon, Phoenix, AZ 85029 / 602-978-3754

J/B Adventures & Safaris Inc., 2275 E. Arapahoe Rd., Ste. 109, Littleton, CO 80122-1521 / 303-771-0977

Jack A. Rosenberg & Sons, 12229 Cox Ln., Dallas, TX 75234 / 214-241-6302

Jack Dever Co., 8520 NW 90th St., Oklahoma City, OK 73132 / 405-721-6393 jbdever1@home.com

Jack First, Inc., 1201 Turbine Dr., Rapid City, SD 57703 / 605-343-8481; FAX: 605-343-9420

Jack Jonas Appraisals & Taki, 13952 E. Marina Dr., #604, Aurora, CO 80014

Jackalope Gun Shop, 1048 S. 5th St., Douglas, WY 82633 / 307-358-3441

Jaffin, Harry. See: BRIDGEMAN PRODUCTS

Jagdwaffen, Peter. See: BUCHSENMACHERMEISTER

James Calhoon Mfg., Shambo Rte. 304, Havre, MT 59501 / 406-395-4079 www.jamescalhoon.com

James Calhoon Varmint Bullets, Shambo Rt., 304, Havre, MT 59501 / 406-395-4079 www.jamescalhoon.com

James Churchill Glove Co., PO Box 298, Centralia, WA 98531 / 360-736-2816; FAX: 360-330-0151 churchillglove@localaccess.com

James Wayne Firearms for Collectors and Investors, 2608 N. Laurent, Victoria, TX 77901 / 361-578-1258; FAX: 361-578-3559

Jamison International, Marc Jamison, 3551 Mayer Ave., Sturgis, SD 57785 / 605-347-5090; FAX: 605-347-4704 jbell2@masttechnology.com

Jamison, Marc. See: JAMISON INTERNATIONAL

Jamison's Forge Works, 4527 Rd. 6.5 NE, Moses Lake, WA 98837 / 509-762-2659

Jantz Supply, 309 West Main Dept HD, Davis, OK 73030-0584 / 580-369-2316; FAX: 580-369-3082 jantz@brightok.net www.knifemaking.com

Jarrett Rifles, Inc., 383 Brown Rd., Jackson, SC 29831 / 803-471-3616 www.jarrettrifles.com

Jarvis, Inc., 1123 Cherry Orchard Lane, Hamilton, MT 59840 / 406-961-4392

Javelina Lube Products, PO Box 337, San Bernardino, CA 92402 / 714-882-5847; FAX: 714-434-6937

Jay McCament Custom Gunmaker, Jay McCament, 1730-134th St. Ct. S., Tacoma, WA 98444 / 253-531-8832

JB Custom, P.O. Box 6912, Leawood, KS 66206 / 913-381-2329

Jeff W. Flannery Engraving Co., 11034 Riddles Run Rd., Union, KY 41091 / 606-384-3127 engraving@fuse.net http://home.fuse.net/engraving/

Jeffredo Gunsight, P.O. Box 669, San Marcos, CA 92079 / 760-728-2695

MANUFACTURER'S DIRECTORY

Jena Eur, PO Box 319, Dunmore, PA 18512
Jenco Sales, Inc., P.O. Box 1000, Manchaca, TX 78652 / 800-531-5301; FAX: 800-266-2373 jencosales@sbcglobal.net
Jenkins Recoil Pads, Inc., 5438 E. Frontage Ln., Olney, IL 62450 / 618-395-3416
Jensen Bullets, RR 1 Box 187, Arco, ID 83213 / 208-785-5590
Jensen's Custom Ammunition, 5146 E. Pima, Tucson, AZ 85712 / 602-325-3346; FAX: 602-322-5704
Jensen's Firearms Academy, 1280 W. Prince, Tucson, AZ 85705 / 602-293-8516
Jericho Tool & Die Co., Inc., 2917 St. Hwy. 7, Bainbridge, NY 13733 / 607-563-8222; FAX: 607-563-8560 jerichotool.com www.jerichotool.com
Jerry Phillips Optics, P.O. Box L632, Langhorne, PA 19047 / 215-757-5037; FAX: 215-757-7097
Jesse W. Smith Saddlery, 0499 County Road J, Pritchett, CO 81064 / 509-325-0622
Jester Bullets, Rt. 1 Box 27, Orienta, OK 73737
Jewell Triggers, Inc., 3620 Hwy. 123, San Marcos, TX 78666 / 512-353-2999; FAX: 512-392-0543
J-Gar Co., 183 Turnpike Rd., Dept. 3, Petersham, MA 01366-9604
JGS Precision Tool Mfg., LLC, 60819 Selander Rd., Coos Bay, OR 97420 / 541-267-4331; FAX: 541-267-5996 jgstools@harborside.com www.jgstools.com
Jim Blair Engraving, P.O. Box 64, Glenrock, WY 82637 / 307-436-8115 jblairengrav@msn.com
Jim Noble Co., 1305 Columbia St, Vancouver, WA 98660 / 360-695-1309; FAX: 360-695-6835 jnobleco@aol.com
Jim Norman Custom Gunstocks, 14281 Cane Rd., Valley Center, CA 92082 / 619-749-6252
Jim's Gun Shop (See Spradlin's)
Jim's Precision, Jim Ketchum, 1725 Moclips Dr., Petaluma, CA 94952 / 707-762-3014
JLK Bullets, 414 Turner Rd., Dover, AR 72837 / 501-331-4194
Johanssons Vapentillbehor, Bert, S-430 20, Veddige, SWEDEN
John Hall Plastics, Inc., P.O. Box 1526, Alvin, TX 77512 / 713-489-8709
John J. Adams & Son Engravers, 7040 VT Rt 113, Vershire, VT 05079 / 802-685-0019
John Masen Co. Inc., 1305 Jelmak, Grand Prairie, TX 75050 / 817-430-8732; FAX: 817-430-1715
John Norrell Arms, 2608 Grist Mill Rd, Little Rock, AR 72207 / 501-225-7864
John Partridge Sales Ltd., Trent Meadows Rugeley, Staffordshire, WS15 2HS ENGLAND
John Rigby & Co., 500 Linne Rd. Ste. D, Paso Robles, CA 93446 / 805-227-4236; FAX: 805-227-4723 jribgy@calinet www.johnrigbyandco.com
Johnny Stewart Game Calls, Inc., P.O. Box 7954, 5100 Fort Ave., Waco, TX 76714 / 817-772-3261; FAX: 817-772-3670
John's Custom Leather, 523 S. Liberty St., Blairsville, PA 15717 / 724-459-6802; FAX: 724-459-5996
Johnson Wood Products, 34897 Crystal Road, Strawberry Point, IA 52076 / 563-933-6504 johnsonwoodproducts@yahoo.com
Johnston Bros. (See C&T Corp. TA Johnson Brothers)
Jonad Corp., 2091 Lakeland Ave., Lakewood, OH 44107 / 216-226-3161
Jonathan Arthur Ciener, Inc., 8700 Commerce St., Cape Canaveral, FL 32920 / 321-868-2200; FAX: 321-868-2201
Jones Co., Dale, 680 Hoffman Draw, Kila, MT 59920 / 406-755-4684

Jones Custom Products, Neil A., 17217 Brookhouser Rd., Saegertown, PA 16433 / 814-763-2769; FAX: 814-763-4228
Jones, J. See: SSK INDUSTRIES
Jones Moulds, Paul, 4901 Telegraph Rd, Los Angeles, CA 90022 / 213-262-1510
JP Sales, Box 307, Anderson, TX 77830
JRP Custom Bullets, RR2 2233 Carlton Rd., Whitehall, NY 12887 / 518-282-0084 or 802-438-5548
JSL Ltd (See U.S. Importer-Specialty Shooters)
Juenke, Vern, 25 Bitterbush Rd., Reno, NV 89523 / 702-345-0225
Jungkind, Reeves C., 509 E. Granite St., Llano, TX 78643-3055 / 512-442-1094
Jurras, L. See: L. E. JURRAS & ASSOC.
Justin Phillippi Custom Bullets, P.O. Box 773, Ligonier, PA 15658 / 412-238-9671

K

K&M Industries, Inc., Box 66, 510 S. Main, Troy, ID 83871 / 208-835-2281; FAX: 208-835-5211
K&M Services, 5430 Salmon Run Rd., Dover, PA 17315 / 717-292-3175; FAX: 717-292-3175
K. Eversull Co., Inc., 1 Tracemont, Boyce, LA 71409 / 318-793-8728; FAX: 318-793-5483 bestguns@aol.com
K.B.I. Inc., P.O. Box 6625, Harrisburg, PA 17112 / 717-540-8518; FAX: 717-540-8567
K.L. Null Holsters Ltd., 161 School St. NW, Hill City Station, Resaca, GA 30735 / 706-625-5643; FAX: 706-625-9392 ken@klnullholsters.com www.klnullholsters.com
Ka Pu Kapili, P.O. Box 745, Honokaa, HI 96727 / 808-776-1644; FAX: 808-776-1731
KA-BAR Knives, 1125 E. State St., Olean, NY 14760 / 800-282-0130; FAX: 716-373-6245 info@ka-bar.com www.ka-bar.com
Kahles A. Swarovski Company, 2 Slater Rd., Cranston, RI 02920 / 401-946-2220; FAX: 401-946-2587
Kahr Arms, PO Box 220, 630 Route 303, Blauvelt, NY 10913 / 845-353-7770; FAX: 845-353-7833 www.kahr.com
Kailua Custom Guns Inc., 51 N. Dean Street, Coquille, OR 97423 / 541-396-5413 kailuacustom@aol.com www.kailuacustom.com
Kalispel Case Line, P.O. Box 267, Cusick, WA 99119 / 509-445-1121
Kamik Outdoor Footwear, 554 Montee de Liesse, Montreal, PQ H4T 1P1 CANADA / 514-341-3950; FAX: 514-341-1861
Kane, Edward, P.O. Box 385, Ukiah, CA 95482 / 707-462-2937
Kane Products, Inc., 5572 Brecksville Rd., Cleveland, OH 44131 / 216-524-9962
Kapro Mfg. Co. Inc. (See R.E.I.)
Kasenit Co., Inc., 13 Park Ave., Highland Mills, NY 10930 / 914-928-9595; FAX: 914-928-7292
Kaswer Custom, Inc., 13 Surrey Drive, Brookfield, CT 06804 / 203-775-0564; FAX: 203-775-6872
KDF, Inc., 2485 Hwy. 46 N., Seguin, TX 78155 / 830-379-8141; FAX: 830-379-5420
KeeCo Impressions, Inc., 346 Wood Ave., North Brunswick, NJ 08902 / 800-468-0546
Kehr, Roger, 2131 Agate Ct. SE, Lacy, WA 98503 / 360-491-0691
Keith's Bullets, 942 Twisted Oak, Algonquin, IL 60102 / 708-658-3520
Keith's Custom Gunstocks, Keith M. Heppler, 540 Banyan Circle, Walnut Creek, CA 94598 / 925-934-3509; FAX: 925-934-3143 kmheppler@hotmail.com
Kelbly, Inc., 7222 Dalton Fox Lake Rd., North Lawrence, OH 44666 / 216-683-4674; FAX: 216-683-7349

Kelley's, P.O. Box 125, Woburn, MA 01801-0125 / 800-879-7273; FAX: 781-272-7077 kels@star.net www.kelsmilitary.com
Kellogg's Professional Products, 325 Pearl St., Sandusky, OH 44870 / 419-625-6551; FAX: 419-625-6167 skwigton@aol.com
Kelly, Lance, 1723 Willow Oak Dr., Edgewater, FL 32132 / 904-423-4933
Kel-Tec CNC Industries, Inc., PO Box 236009, Cocoa, FL 32923 / 407-631-0068; FAX: 407-631-1169
Kemen America, 2550 Hwy. 23, Wrenshall, MN 55797 / 218-384-3670 patrickl@midwestshootingschool.com midwestshootingschool.com
Ken Eyster Heritage Gunsmiths, Inc., 6441 Bishop Rd., Centerburg, OH 43011 / 740-625-6131; FAX: 740-625-7811
Ken Starnes Gunmaker, 15940 SW Holly Hill Rd, Hillsboro, OR 97123-9033 / 503-628-0705; FAX: 503-443-2096 kstarnes@kdsa.com
Keng's Firearms Specialty, Inc./US Tactical Systems, 875 Wharton Dr., P.O. Box 44405, Atlanta, GA 30336-1405 / 404-691-7611; FAX: 404-505-8445
Kennebec Journal, 274 Western Ave., Augusta, ME 04330 / 207-622-6288
Kennedy Firearms, 10 N. Market St., Muncy, PA 17756 / 717-546-6695
Kenneth W. Warren Engraver, P.O. Box 2842, Wenatchee, WA 98807 / 509-663-6123; FAX: 509-665-6123
Ken's Kustom Kartridges, 331 Jacobs Rd., Hubbard, OH 44425 / 216-534-4595
Kent Cartridge America, Inc., PO Box 849, 1000 Zigor Rd., Kearneysville, WV 25430
Kent Cartridge Mfg. Co. Ltd., Unit 16 Branbridges Industrial Esta, Tonbridge, Kent, ENGLAND / 622-872255; FAX: 622-872645
Keowee Game Calls, 608 Hwy. 25 North, Travelers Rest, SC 29690 / 864-834-7204; FAX: 864-834-7831
Kershaw Knives, 25300 SW Parkway Ave., Wilsonville, OR 97070 / 503-682-1966; or 800-325-2891; FAX: 503-682-7168
Kesselring Gun Shop, 4024 Old Hwy. 99N, Burlington, WA 98233 / 360-724-3113; FAX: 360-724-7003 info@kesselrings.com www.kesselrings.com
Ketchum, Jim (See Jim's Precision)
Kickeez I.N.C., Inc., 301 Industrial Dr, Carl Junction, MO 64834-8806 / 419-649-2100; FAX: 417-649-2200 kickey@ipa.net
Kilham & Co., Main St., P.O. Box 37, Lyme, NH 03768 / 603-795-4112
Kim Ahrends Custom Firearms, Inc., Box 203, Clarion, IA 50525 / 515-532-3449; FAX: 515-532-3926
Kimar (See U.S. Importer-IAR,Inc)
Kimber of America, Inc., 1 Lawton St., Yonkers, NY 10705 / 800-880-2418; FAX: 914-964-9340
King & Co., P.O. Box 1242, Bloomington, IL 61702 / 309-473-3964; FAX: 309-473-2161
King's Gun Works, 1837 W. Glenoaks Blvd., Glendale, CA 91201 / 818-956-6010; FAX: 818-548-8606
Kingyon, Paul L. (See Custom Calls)
Kirkpatrick Leather Co., PO Box 677, Laredo, TX 78040 / 956-723-6631; FAX: 956-725-0672 mike@kirkpatrickleather.com www.kirkpatrickleather.com
KK Air International (See Impact Case & Container Co.)
KLA Enterprises, P.O. Box 2028, Eaton Park, FL 33840 / 941-682-2829; FAX: 941-682-2829
Kleen-Bore,Inc., 16 Industrial Pkwy., Easthampton, MA 01027 / 413-527-0300; FAX: 413-527-2522 info@kleen-bore.com www.kleen-bore.com

Klein Custom Guns, Don, 433 Murray Park Dr, Ripon, WI 54971 / 920-748-2931 daklein@charter.net

Kleinendorst, K. W., RR 1, Box 1500, Hop Bottom, PA 18824 / 717-289-4687

Klingler Woodcarving, P.O. Box 141, Thistle Hill, Cabot, VT 05647 / 802-426-3811

Knifeware, Inc., P.O. Box 3, Greenville, WV 24945 / 304-832-6878

Knight & Hale Game Calls, Box 468, Industrial Park, Cadiz, KY 42211 / 502-924-1755; FAX: 502-924-1763

Knight Rifles, 21852 Hwy. J46, P.O. Box 130, Centerville, IA 52544 / 515-856-2626; FAX: 515-856-2628

Knight Rifles (See Modern Muzzle Loading, Inc.)

Knight's Mfg. Co., 7750 Ninth St. SW, Vero Beach, FL 32968 / 561-562-5697; FAX: 561-569-2955 civiliansales@knightarmco.com

Knock on Wood Antiques, 355 Post Rd., Darien, CT 06820 / 203-655-9031

Knoell, Doug, 9737 McCardle Way, Santee, CA 92071 / 619-449-5189

Knopp, Gary. See: SUPER 6 LLC

KOGOT, 410 College, Trinidad, CO 81082 / 719-846-9406; FAX: 719-846-9406

Kokolus, Michael M. (See Custom Riflestocks In)

Kolar, 1925 Roosevelt Ave., Racine, WI 53406 / 414-554-0800; FAX: 414-554-9093

Kolpin Mfg., Inc., P.O. Box 107, 205 Depot St., Fox Lake, WI 53933 / 414-928-3118; FAX: 414-928-3687

Korth Germany GmbH, Robert Bosch Strasse, 11, D-23909, 23909 Ratzeburg, GERMANY / 4541-840363; FAX: 4541-84 05 35

Korth USA, 437R Chandler St., Tewksbury, MA 01876 / 978-851-8656; FAX: 978-851-9462 info@korthusa.com www.korthusa.com

Korzinek Riflesmith, J., RD 2 Box 73D, Canton, PA 17724 / 717-673-8512

Koval Knives, 5819 Zarley St., Suite A, New Albany, OH 43054 / 614-855-0777; FAX: 614-855-0945 koval@kovalknives.com www.kovalknives.com

Kowa Optimed, Inc., 20001 S. Vermont Ave., Torrance, CA 90502 / 310-327-1913; FAX: 310-327-4177

Kramer Designs, P.O. Box 129, Clancy, MT 59634 / 406-933-8658; FAX: 406-933-8658

Kramer Handgun Leather, P.O. Box 112154, Tacoma, WA 98411 / 800-510-2666; FAX: 253-564-1214 www.kramerleather.com

Krause Publications, Inc., 700 E. State St., Iola, WI 54990 / 715-445-2214; FAX: 715-445-4087

Krico Deutschland GmbH, Nurnbergerstrasse 6, D-90602, Pyrbaum, GERMANY / 09180-2780; FAX: 09180-2661

Krieger Barrels, Inc., 2024 Mayfield Rd, Richfield, WI 53076 / 262-628-8558; FAX: 262-628-8748

Krieghoff Gun Co., H., Boschstrasse 22, D-89079 Elm, GERMANY or 731-4018270

Krieghoff International,Inc., 7528 Easton Rd., Ottsville, PA 18942 / 610-847-5173; FAX: 610-847-8691

Kukowski, Ed. See: ED'S GUN HOUSE

Kulis Freeze Dry Taxidermy, 725 Broadway Ave., Bedford, OH 44146 / 216-232-8352; FAX: 216-232-7305 jkulis@kastaway.com kastaway.com

KVH Industries, Inc., 110 Enterprise Center, Middletown, RI 02842 / 401-847-3327; FAX: 401-849-0045

Kwik-Site Co., 5555 Treadwell St., Wayne, MI 48184 / 734-326-1500; FAX: 734-326-4120 kwiksiteco@aol.com

L

L&R Lock Co., 1137 Pocalla Rd., Sumter, SC 29150 / 803-775-6127; FAX: 803-775-5171

L&S Technologies Inc. (See Aimtech Mount Systems)

L. Bengtson Arms Co., 6345-B E. Akron St., Mesa, AZ 85205 / 602-981-6375

L. E. Jurras & Assoc., L. E. Jurras, P.O. Box 680, Washington, IN 47501 / 812-254-6170; FAX: 812-254-6170 jurasgun@rtcc.net

L.A.R. Mfg., Inc., 4133 W. Farm Rd., West Jordan, UT 84088 / 801-280-3505; FAX: 801-280-1972

L.B.T., Judy Smith, HCR 62, Box 145, Moyie Springs, ID 83845 / 208-267-3588

L.E. Wilson, Inc., Box 324, 404 Pioneer Ave., Cashmere, WA 98815 / 509-782-1328; FAX: 509-782-7200

L.L. Bean, Inc., Freeport, ME 04032 / 207-865-4761; FAX: 207-552-2802

L.P.A. Inc., Via Alfieri 26, Gardone V.T., Brescia, ITALY / 30-891-14-81; FAX: 30-891-09-51

L.R. Clift Mfg., 3821 Hammonton Rd., Marysville, CA 95901 / 916-755-3390; FAX: 916-755-3393

L.W. Seecamp Co., Inc., PO Box 255, New Haven, CT 06502 / 203-877-3429; FAX: 203-877-3429 seecamp@optonline.net

La Clinique du .45, 1432 Rougemont, Chambly,, PQ J3L 2L8 CANADA / 514-658-1144

Labanu, Inc., 2201-F Fifth Ave., Ronkonkoma, NY 11779 / 516-467-6197; FAX: 516-981-4112

LaBoone, Pat. See: THE MIDWEST SHOOTING SCHOOL

LaBounty Precision Reboring, Inc, 7968 Silver Lake Rd., PO Box 186, Maple Falls, WA 98266 / 360-599-2047; FAX: 360-599-3018

LaCrosse Footwear, Inc., 18550 NE Riverside Parkway, Portland, OR 97230 / 503-766-1010; or 800-323-2668; FAX: 503-766-1015

LaFrance Specialties, P.O. Box 87933, San Diego, CA 92138 / 619-293-3373; FAX: 619-293-7087 timlafrance@att.net

Lake Center Marina, PO Box 670, St. Charles, MO 63302 / 314-946-7500

Lakefield Arms Ltd. (See Savage Arms, Inc.)

Lakewood Products LLC, 275 June St., Berlin, WI 54923 / 800-872-8458; FAX: 920-361-7719 lakewood@dotnet.com www.lakewoodproducts.com

Lamboy, Stephen. See: ITHACA CLASSIC DOUBLES

Lampert, Ron, Rt. 1, 44857 Schoolcraft Trl., Guthrie, MN 56461 / 218-854-7345

Lamson & Goodnow Mfg. Co., 45 Conway St., Shelburne Falls, MA 03170 / 413-625-6564; or 800-872-6564; FAX: 413-625-9816 www.lamsonsharp.com

Lansky Levine, Arthur. See: LANSKY SHARPENERS

Lansky Sharpeners, Arthur Lansky Levine, PO Box 50830, Las Vegas, NV 89016 / 702-361-7511; FAX: 702-896-9511

LaPrade, PO Box 250, Ewing, VA 24248 / 423-733-2615

Lapua Ltd., P.O. Box 5, Lapua, FINLAND / 6-310111; FAX: 6-4388991

LaRocca Gun Works, 51 Union Place, Worcester, MA 01608 / 508-754-2887; FAX: 508-754-2887 www.laroccagunworks.com

Larry Lyons Gunworks, 110 Hamilton St., Dowagiac, MI 49047 / 616-782-9478

Laser Devices, Inc., 2 Harris Ct. A-4, Monterey, CA 93940 / 831-373-0701; FAX: 831-373-0903 sales@laserdevices.com www.laserdevices.com

Laseraim Technologies, Inc., P.O. Box 3548, Little Rock, AR 72203 / 501-375-2227

Laserlyte, 2201 Amapola Ct., Torrance, CA 90501

LaserMax, Inc., 3495 Winton Place, Bldg. B, Rochester, NY 14623-2807 / 800-527-3703; FAX: 716-272-5427 customerservice@lasermax-inc.com www.lasermax-inc.com

Lassen Community College, Gunsmithing Dept., P.O. Box 3000, Hwy. 139, Susanville, CA 96130 / 916-251-8800; FAX: 916-251-8838

Lathrop's, Inc., Inc., 5146 E. Pima, Tucson, AZ 85712 / 520-881-0266; or 800-875-4867; FAX: 520-322-5704

Laughridge, William R (See Cylinder & Slide Inc)

Laurel Mountain Forge, P.O. Box 52, Crown Point, IN 46308 / 219-548-2950; FAX: 219-548-2950

Laurona Armas Eibar, S.A.L., Avenida de Otaola 25, P.O. Box 260, Eibar 20600, SPAIN / 34-43-700600; FAX: 34-43-700616

Lawrence Brand Shot (See Precision Reloading)

Lawrence Leather Co., P.O. Box 1479, Lillington, NC 27546 / 910-893-2071; FAX: 910-893-4742

Lawson Co., Harry, 3328 N Richey Blvd., Tucson, AZ 85716 / 520-326-1117; FAX: 520-326-1117

Lawson, John. See: THE SIGHT SHOP

Lawson, John G (See Sight Shop, The)

Lazzeroni Arms Co., PO Box 26696, Tucson, AZ 85726 / 888-492-7247; FAX: 520-624-4250

Le Clear Industries (See E-Z-Way Systems), PO Box 4310, Newark, OH 43058-4310 / 614-345-6645; FAX: 614-345-6600

Lea Mfg. Co., 237 E. Aurora St., Waterbury, CT 06720 / 203-753-5116

Leapers, Inc., 7675 Five Mile Rd., Northville, MI 48167 / 248-486-1231; FAX: 248-486-1430

Leatherman Tool Group, Inc., 12106 NE Ainsworth Cir., P.O. Box 20595, Portland, OR 97294 / 503-253-7826; FAX: 503-253-7830

Lebeau-Courally, Rue St. Gilles, 386 4000, Liege, BELGIUM / 042-52-48-43; FAX: 32-4-252-2008 info@lebeau-courally.com www.lebeau-courally.com

Leckie Professional Gunsmithing, 546 Quarry Rd., Ottsville, PA 18942 / 215-847-8594

Ledbetter Airguns, Riley, 1804 E Sprague St, Winston Salem, NC 27107-3521 / 919-784-0676

Lee Precision, Inc., 4275 Hwy. U, Hartford, WI 53027 / 262-673-3075; FAX: 262-673-9273 info@leeprecision.com www.leeprecision.com

Lee Supplies, Mark, 9901 France Ct., Lakeville, MN 55044 / 612-461-2114

LeFever Arms Co., Inc., 6234 Stokes, Lee Center Rd., Lee Center, NY 13363 / 315-337-6722; FAX: 315-337-1543

Legacy Sports International, 206 S. Union St., Alexandria, VA 22314 / 703-548-4837 www.legacysports.com

Legend Products Corp., 21218 Saint Andrews Blvd., Boca Raton, FL 33433-2435

Leibowitz, Leonard, 1205 Murrayhill Ave., Pittsburgh, PA 15217 / 412-361-5455

Leica USA, Inc., 156 Ludlow Ave., Northvale, NJ 07647 / 201-767-7500; FAX: 201-767-8666

LEM Gun Specialties, Inc. The Lewis Lead Remover, P.O. Box 2855, Peachtree City, GA 30269-2024 / 770-487-0556

Leonard Day, 6 Linseed Rd Box 1, West Hatfield, MA 01088-7505 / 413-337-8369

Les Baer Custom,Inc., 29601 34th Ave., Hillsdale, IL 61257 / 309-658-2716; FAX: 309-658-2610

LesMerises, Felix. See: ROCKY MOUNTAIN ARMOURY

Lethal Force Institute (See Police Bookshelf), PO Box 122, Concord, NH 03301 / 603-224-6814; FAX: 603-226-3554

Lett Custom Grips, 672 Currier Rd., Hopkinton, NH 03229-2652 / 800-421-5388; FAX: 603-226-4580 info@lettgrips.com www.lettgrips.com

Leupold & Stevens, Inc., 14400 NW Greenbrier Pky., Beaverton, OR 97006 / 503-646-9171; FAX: 503-526-1455

Lever Arms Service Ltd., 2131 Burrard St., Vancouver, BC V6J 3H7 CANADA / 604-736-2711; FAX: 604-738-3503

MANUFACTURER'S DIRECTORY

Lew Horton Dist. Co., Inc., 15 Walkup Dr., Westboro, MA 01581 / 508-366-7400; FAX: 508-366-5332

Liberty Metals, 2233 East 16th St., Los Angeles, CA 90021 / 213-581-9171; FAX: 213-581-9351 libertymfgsolder@hotmail.com

Liberty Safe, 999 W. Utah Ave., Payson, UT 84651-1744 / 800-247-5625; FAX: 801-489-6409

Liberty Shooting Supplies, P.O. Box 357, Hillsboro, OR 97123 / 503-640-5518; FAX: 503-640-5518 info@libertyshootingsupplies.com www.libertyshootingsupplies.com

Lightning Performance Innovations, Inc., RD1 Box 555, Mohawk, NY 13407 / 315-866-8819; FAX: 315-867-5701

Lilja Precision Rifle Barrels, P.O. Box 372, Plains, MT 59859 / 406-826-3084; FAX: 406-826-3083 lilja@riflebarrels.com www.riflebarrels.com

Lincoln, Dean, Box 1886, Farmington, NM 87401

Linder Solingen Knives, 4401 Sentry Dr., Tucker, GA 30084 / 770-939-6915; FAX: 770-939-6738

Lindsay Engraving & Tools, Steve Lindsay, 3714 W. Cedar Hills, Kearney, NE 68845 / 308-236-7885 steve@lindsayengraving.com www.handgravers.com

Lindsay, Steve. See: LINDSAY ENGRAVING & TOOLS

Lindsley Arms Cartridge Co., P.O. Box 757, 20 College Hill Rd., Henniker, NH 03242 / 603-428-3127

Linebaugh Custom Sixguns, P.O. Box 455, Cody, WY 82414 / 307-645-3332 www.sitgunner.com

Lion Country Supply, P.O. Box 480, Port Matilda, PA 16870

List Precision Engineering, Unit 1 Ingley Works, 13 River Road, Barking, ENGLAND / 011-081-594-1686

Lithi Bee Bullet Lube, 1728 Carr Rd., Muskegon, MI 49442 / 616-788-4479

"Little John's" Antique Arms, 1740 W. Laveta, Orange, CA 92668

Little Trees Ramble (See Scott Pilkington)

Littler Sales Co., 20815 W. Chicago, Detroit, MI 48228 / 313-273-6888; FAX: 313-273-1099 littlerptg@aol.com

Littleton, J. F., 275 Pinedale Ave., Oroville, CA 95966 / 916-533-6084

Ljutic Industries, Inc., 732 N. 16th Ave., Suite 22, Yakima, WA 98902 / 509-248-0476; FAX: 509-576-8233 ljuticgun.net www.ljuticgun.com

Llama Gabilondo Y Cia, Apartado 290, E-01080, Victoria, spain, SPAIN

Loch Leven Industries/Convert-A-Pell, P.O. Box 2751, Santa Rosa, CA 95405 / 707-573-8735; FAX: 707-573-0369

Lock's Philadelphia Gun Exchange, 6700 Rowland Ave., Philadelphia, PA 19149 / 215-332-6225; FAX: 215-332-4800 locks.gunshop@verizon.net

Lodewick, Walter H., 2816 NE Halsey St., Portland, OR 97232 / 503-284-2554

Lodgewood Mfg., P.O. Box 611, Whitewater, WI 53190 / 262-473-5444; FAX: 262-473-6448 lodgewd@idcnet.com lodgewood.com

Log Cabin Sport Shop, 8010 Lafayette Rd., Lodi, OH 44254 / 330-948-1082; FAX: 330-948-4307 logcabin@logcabinshop.com www.logcabinshop.com

Logan, Harry M., Box 745, Honokaa, HI 96727 / 808-776-1644

Logdewood Mfg., P.O. Box 611, Whitewater, WI 53190 / 262-473-5444; FAX: 262-473-6448 lodgewd@idcnet.com www.lodgewood.com

Lohman Mfg. Co., Inc., 4500 Doniphan Dr., P.O. Box 220, Neosho, MO 64850 / 417-451-4438; FAX: 417-451-2576

Lomont Precision Bullets, 278 Sandy Creek Rd, Salmon, ID 83467 / 208-756-6819; FAX: 208-756-6824 www.klomont.com

London Guns Ltd., Box 3750, Santa Barbara, CA 93130 / 805-683-4141; FAX: 805-683-1712

Lone Star Gunleather, 1301 Brushy Bend Dr., Round Rock, TX 78681 / 512-255-1805

Lone Star Rifle Company, 11231 Rose Road, Conroe, TX 77303 / 936-856-3363 dave@lonestar.com

Long, George F., 1500 Rogue River Hwy., Ste. F, Grants Pass, OR 97527 / 541-476-7552

Lortone Inc., 2856 NW Market St., Seattle, WA 98107

Lothar Walther Precision Tool Inc., 3425 Hutchinson Rd., Cumming, GA 30040 / 770-889-9998; FAX: 770-889-4919 lotharwalther@mindspring.com www.lothar-walther.com

LPS Laboratories, Inc., 4647 Hugh Howell Rd., P.O. Box 3050, Tucker, GA 30084 / 404-934-7800

Lucas, Edward E, 32 Garfield Ave., East Brunswick, NJ 08816 / 201-251-5526

Lupton, Keith. See: PAWLING MOUNTAIN CLUB

Lyman Instant Targets, Inc. (See Lyman Products)

Lyman Products Corp., 475 Smith Street, Middletown, CT 06457-1541 / 800-423-9704; FAX: 860-632-1699 lymansales@cshore.com www.lymanproducts.com

M

M. Thys (See U.S. Importer-Champlin Firearms Inc)

M.H. Canjar Co., 6510 Raleigh St., Arvada, CO 80003 / 303-295-2638; FAX: 303-295-2638

MA Systems, P.O. Box 894, Pryor, OK 74362-0894 / 918-479-6378

Mac-1 Airgun Distributors, 13974 Van Ness Ave., Gardena, CA 90249-2900 / 310-327-3581; FAX: 310-327-0238 mac1@maclairgun.com www.mac1airgun.com

Madis Books, 2453 West Five Mile Pkwy., Dallas, TX 75233 / 214-330-7168

Madis, George. See: GEORGE MADIS WINCHESTER CONSULTANTS

MAG Instrument, Inc., 1635 S. Sacramento Ave., Ontario, CA 91761 / 909-947-1006; FAX: 909-947-3116

Magma Engineering Co., P.O. Box 161, 20955 E. Ocotillo Rd., Queen Creek, AZ 85242 / 602-987-9008; FAX: 602-987-0148

Mag-Na-Port International, Inc., 41302 Executive Dr., Harrison Twp., MI 48045-1306 / 586-469-6727; FAX: 586-469-0425 email@magnaport.com www.magnaport.com

Magnolia Sports,Inc., 211 W. Main, Magnolia, AR 71753 / 501-234-8410; or 800-530-7816; FAX: 501-234-8117

Magnum Power Products, Inc., P.O. Box 17768, Fountain Hills, AZ 85268

Magnum Research, Inc., 7110 University Ave. NE, Minneapolis, MN 55432 / 800-772-6168 or 763-574-1868; FAX: 763-574-0109 info@magnumresearch.com

Magnus Bullets, P.O. Box 239, Toney, AL 35773 / 256-420-8359; FAX: 256-420-8360

Mag-Pack Corp., P.O. Box 846, Chesterland, OH 44026 / 440-285-9480 magpack@hotmail.com

MagSafe Ammo Co., 4700 S US Highway 17/92, Casselberry, FL 32707-3814 / 407-834-9966; FAX: 407-834-8185 www.magsafeonline.com

Magtech Ammunition Co. Inc., 837 Boston Rd #12, Madison, CT 06443 / 203-245-8983; FAX: 203-245-2883 rfine@mactechammunition.com www.mactech.com.br

Mahony, Philip Bruce, 67 White Hollow Rd., Lime Rock, CT 06039-2418 / 203-435-9341 filbalony-redbeard@snet.net

Mahovsky's Metalife, R.D. 1, Box 149a Eureka Road, Grand Valley, PA 16420 / 814-436-7747

Maine Custom Bullets, RFD 1, Box 1755, Brooks, ME 04921

Maionchi-L.M.I., Via Di Coselli-Zona, Industriale Di Guamo 55060, Lucca, ITALY / 011 39-583 94291

Makinson, Nicholas, RR 3, Komoka, ON N0L 1R0 CANADA / 519-471-5462

Malcolm Enterprises, 1023 E. Prien Lake Rd., Lake Charles, LA 70601

Mallardtone Game Calls, 10406 96th St., Court West, Taylor Ridge, IL 61284 / 309-798-2481; FAX: 309-798-2501

Mandall Shooting Supplies Inc., 3616 N. Scottsdale Rd., Scottsdale, AZ 85251 / 480-945-2553; FAX: 480-949-0734

Marathon Rubber Prods. Co., Inc., 1009 3rd St, Wausau, WI 54403-4765 / 715-845-6255

Marble Arms (See CRR, Inc./Marble's Inc.)

Marchmon Bullets, 8191 Woodland Shore Dr., Brighton, MI 48116

Marent, Rudolf. See: HAMMERLI SERVICE-PRECISION MAC

Mark Lee Supplies, 9901 France Ct., Lakeville, MN 55044 / 952-461-2114; FAX: 952-461-2194 marklee55044@usfamily.net

Markell,Inc., 422 Larkfield Center 235, Santa Rosa, CA 95403 / 707-573-0792; FAX: 707-573-9867

Markesbery Muzzle Loaders, Inc., 7785 Foundation Dr., Ste. 6, Florence, KY 41042 / 606-342-5553 or 606-342-2380

Marksman Products, 5482 Argosy Dr., Huntington Beach, CA 92649 / 714-898-7535; or 800-822-8005; FAX: 714-891-0782

Marlin Firearms Co., 100 Kenna Dr., North Haven, CT 06473 / 203-239-5621; FAX: 203-234-7991

MarMik, Inc., 2116 S. Woodland Ave., Michigan City, IN 46360 / 219-872-7231; FAX: 219-872-7231

Marocchi F.lli S.p.A, Via Galileo Galilei 8, I-25068 Zanano, ITALY

Marquart Precision Co., P.O. Box 1740, Prescott, AZ 86302 / 520-445-5646

Marsh, Mike, Croft Cottage, Main St., Derbyshire, DE4 2BY ENGLAND / 01629 650 669

Marshall Enterprises, 792 Canyon Rd., Redwood City, CA 94062

Marshall Fish Mfg. Gunsmith Sptg. Co., Rd. Box 2439, Westport, NY 12993 / 518-962-4897; FAX: 518-962-4897

Martin B. Retting Inc., 11029 Washington, Culver City, CA 90232 / 213-837-2412

Martini & Hagn, 1264 Jimsmith Lake Rd, Cranbrook, BC V1C 6V6 CANADA / 250-417-2926; FAX: 250-417-2928

Martin's Gun Shop, 937 S. Sheridan Blvd., Lakewood, CO 80226 / 303-922-2184

Martz, John V., 8060 Lakeview Lane, Lincoln, CA 95648 FAX: 916-645-3815

Marvel, Alan, 3922 Madonna Rd., Jarretsville, MD 21084 / 301-557-6545

Marx, Harry (See U.S. Importer for FERLIB)

Maryland Paintball Supply, 8507 Harford Rd., Parkville, MD 21234 / 410-882-5607

MAST Technology, Inc., 14555 US Hwy. 95 S., P.O. Box 60969, Boulder City, NV 89006 / 702-293-6969; FAX: 702-293-7255 info@masttechnology.com www.bellammo.com

Master Lock Co., 2600 N. 32nd St., Milwaukee, WI 53245 / 414-444-2800

Match Prep-Doyle Gracey, P.O. Box 155, Tehachapi, CA 93581 / 661-822-5383; FAX: 661-823-8680

Manufacturer's Directory

Mathews & Son, Inc., George E., 10224 S Paramount Blvd, Downey, CA 90241 / 562-862-6719; FAX: 562-862-6719

Matthews Cutlery, 4401 Sentry Dr., Tucker, GA 30084 / 770-939-6915

Mauser Werke Oberndorf Waffensysteme GmbH, Postfach 1349, 78722, Oberndorf/N., GERMANY

Maverick Arms, Inc., 7 Grasso Ave., P.O. Box 497, North Haven, CT 06473 / 203-230-5300; FAX: 203-230-5420

Maxi-Mount Inc., P.O. Box 291, Willoughby Hills, OH 44096-0291 / 440-944-9456; FAX: 440-944-9456 maximount454@yahoo.com

Mayville Engineering Co. (See MEC, Inc.)

Mazur Restoration, Pete, 13083 Drummer Way, Grass Valley, CA 95949 / 530-268-2412

McBros Rifle Co., P.O. Box 86549, Phoenix, AZ 85080 / 602-582-3713; FAX: 602-581-3825

McCament, Jay. See: JAY MCCAMENT CUSTOM GUNMAKER

McCann Industries, P.O. Box 641, Spanaway, WA 98387 / 253-537-6919; FAX: 253-537-6919 mccann.machine@worldnet.att.net www.mccannindustries.com

McCann's Machine & Gun Shop, P.O. Box 641, Spanaway, WA 98387 / 253-537-6919; FAX: 253-537-6993 mccann.machine@worldnet.att.net www.mccannindustries.com

McCann's Muzzle-Gun Works, 14 Walton Dr., New Hope, PA 18938 / 215-862-2728

McCluskey Precision Rifles, 10502 14th Ave. NW, Seattle, WA 98177 / 206-781-2776

McCombs, Leo, 1862 White Cemetery Rd., Patriot, OH 45658 / 740-256-1714

McCormick Corp., Chip, 1715 W. FM 1626 Ste. 105, Manchaca, TX 78652 / 800-328-CHIP; FAX: 512-462-0009

McDonald, Dennis, 8359 Brady St., Peosta, IA 52068 / 319-556-7940

McFarland, Stan, 2221 Idella Ct., Grand Junction, CO 81505 / 970-243-4704

McGhee, Larry. See: B.C. OUTDOORS

McGowen Rifle Barrels, 5961 Spruce Lane, St. Anne, IL 60964 / 815-937-9816; FAX: 815-937-4024

Mchalik, Gary. See: ROSSI FIREARMS

McKenzie, Lynton, 6940 N. Alvernon Way, Tucson, AZ 85718 / 520-299-5090

McMillan Fiberglass Stocks, Inc., 1638 W. Knudsen Dr. #102, Phoenix, AZ 85027 / 602-582-9635; FAX: 602-581-3825

McMillan Optical Gunsight Co., 28638 N. 42nd St., Cave Creek, AZ 85331 / 602-585-7868; FAX: 602-585-7872

McMillan Rifle Barrels, P.O. Box 3427, Bryan, TX 77805 / 409-690-3456; FAX: 409-690-0156

McMurdo, Lynn (See Specialty Gunsmithing), PO Box 404, Afton, WY 83110 / 307-886-5535

MCS, Inc., 166 Pocono Rd., Brookfield, CT 06804-2023 / 203-775-1013; FAX: 203-775-9462

McWelco Products, 6730 Santa Fe Ave., Hesperia, CA 92345 / 619-244-8876; FAX: 619-244-9398 products@mcwelco.com www.mawelco.com

MDS, P.O. Box 1441, Brandon, FL 33509-1441 / 813-653-1180; FAX: 813-684-5953

Measurement Group Inc., Box 27777, Raleigh, NC 27611

Measures, Leon. See: SHOOT WHERE YOU LOOK

MEC, Inc., 715 South St., Mayville, WI 53050 / 414-387-4500; FAX: 414-387-5802 reloaders@mayul.com www.mayvl.com

MEC-Gar S.R.L., Via Madonnina 64, Gardone V.T. Brescia, ITALY / 39-30-8912687; FAX: 39-30-8910065

MEC-Gar U.S.A., Inc., Hurley Farms Industr. Park, 115, Hurley Road 6G, Oxofrd, CT 06478 / 203-262-1525; FAX: 203-262-1719 mecgar@aol.com www.mec-gar.com

Mech-Tech Systems, Inc., 1602 Foothill Rd., Kalispell, MT 59901 / 406-755-8055

Meister Bullets (See Gander Mountain)

Mele, Frank, 201 S. Wellow Ave., Cookeville, TN 38501 / 615-526-4860

Menck, Gunsmith Inc., T.W., 5703 S 77th St, Ralston, NE 68127

Mendez, John A., P.O. Box 620984, Orlando, FL 32862 / 407-344-2791

Men-Metallwerk Elisenhuette GmbH, P.O. Box 1263, Nassau/Lahn, D-56372 GERMANY / 2604-7819

Meprolight (See Hesco-Meprolight)

Mercer Custom Guns, 216 S Whitewater Ave, Jefferson, WI 53549 / 920-674-3839

Merit Corp., PO Box 9044, Schenectady, NY 12309 / 518-346-1420 sales@meritcorporation.com www.meritcorporation.com

Merkel, Schutzenstrasse 26, D-98527 Suhl, Suhl, GERMANY FAX: 011-49-3681-854-203 www.merkel-waffen.de

Merkuria Ltd., Argentinska 38, 17005, Praha 7 CZECH, REPUBLIC / 422-875117; FAX: 422-809152

Metal Merchants, PO Box 186, Walled Lake, MI 48390-0186

Metalife Industries (See Mahovsky's Metalife)

Michael's Antiques, Box 591, Waldoboro, ME 04572

Michaels Of Oregon, Co., P.O. Box 1690, Oregon City, OR 97045 www.michaels-oregon.com

Micro Sight Co., 242 Harbor Blvd., Belmont, CA 94002 / 415-591-0769; FAX: 415-591-7531

Microfusion Alfa S.A., Paseo San Andres N8, P.O. Box 271, Eibar, 20600 SPAIN / 34-43-11-89-16; FAX: 34-43-11-40-38

Mid-America Recreation, Inc., 1328 5th Ave., Moline, IL 61265 / 309-764-5089; FAX: 309-764-5089 fmilcusguns@aol.com www.midamericarecreation.com

Middlebrooks Custom Shop, 7366 Colonial Trail East, Surry, VA 23883 / 757-357-0881; FAX: 757-365-0442

Midway Arms, Inc., 5875 W. Van Horn Tavern Rd., Columbia, MO 65203 / 800-243-3220; or 573-445-6363; FAX: 573-446-1018

Midwest Gun Sport, 1108 Herbert Dr., Zebulon, NC 27597 / 919-269-5570

Midwest Sport Distributors, Box 129, Fayette, MO 65248

Mike Davis Products, 643 Loop Dr., Moses Lake, WA 98837 / 509-765-6178; or 509-766-7281

Military Armament Corp., P.O. Box 120, Mt. Zion Rd., Lingleville, TX 76461 / 817-965-3253

Millennium Designed Muzzleloaders, PO Box 536, Routes 11 & 25, Limington, ME 04049 / 207-637-2316

Miller Arms, Inc., P.O. Box 260 Purl St., St. Onge, SD 57779 / 605-642-5160; FAX: 605-642-5160

Miller Custom, 210 E. Julia, Clinton, IL 61727 / 217-935-9362

Miller Single Trigger Mfg. Co., 6680 Rt. 5-20, P.O. Box 471, Bloomfield, NY 14469 / 585-657-6338

Millett Sights, 7275 Murdy Circle, Adm. Office, Huntington Beach, CA 92647 / 714-842-5575 or 800-645-5388; FAX: 714-843-5707

Mills Jr., Hugh B., 3615 Canterbury Rd., New Bern, NC 28560 / 919-637-4631

Milstor Corp., 80-975 Indio Blvd., Indio, CA 92201 / 760-775-9998; FAX: 760-775-5229 milstor@webtv.net

Miltex, Inc, 700 S Lee St, Alexandria, VA 22314-4332 / 888-642-9123; FAX: 301-645-1430

Minute Man High Tech Industries, 10611 Canyon Rd. E., Suite 151, Puyallup, WA 98373 / 800-233-2734

Mirador Optical Corp., P.O. Box 11614, Marina Del Rey, CA 90295-7614 / 310-821-5587; FAX: 310-305-0386

Mitchell, Jack, c/o Geoff Gaebe, Addieville East Farm, 200 Pheasant Dr, Mapleville, RI 02839 / 401-568-3185

Mitchell Bullets, R.F., 430 Walnut St, Westernport, MD 21562

Mitchell Optics, Inc., 2072 CR 1100 N, Sidney, IL 61877 / 217-688-2219; or 217-621-3018; FAX: 217-688-2505 mitche1@attglobal.net

Mitchell's Accuracy Shop, 68 Greenridge Dr., Stafford, VA 22554 / 703-659-0165

MI-TE Bullets, 1396 Ave. K, Ellsworth, KS 67439 / 785-472-4575; FAX: 785-472-5579

Mittermeier, Inc., Frank, PO Box 2G, 3577 E Tremont Ave., Bronx, NY 10465 / 718-828-3843

Mixson Corp., 7635 W. 28th Ave., Hialeah, FL 33016 / 305-821-5190; or 800-327-0078; FAX: 305-558-9318

MJK Gunsmithing, Inc., 417 N. Huber Ct., E. Wenatchee, WA 98802 / 509-884-7683

MKS Supply, Inc. (See Hi-Point Firearms)

MMC, 5050 E. Belknap St., Haltom City, TX 76117 / 817-831-9557; FAX: 817-834-5508

MOA Corporation, 2451 Old Camden Pike, Eaton, OH 45320 / 937-456-3669 www.moaguns.com

Modern Gun Repair School, PO Box 846, Saint Albans, VT 05478 / 802-524-2223; FAX: 802-524-2053 jfwp@dlilearn.com www.mgsinfoadlifearn.com

Modern Muzzleloading, Inc., P.O. Box 130, Centerville, IA 52544 / 515-856-2626

Moeller, Steve, 1213 4th St., Fulton, IL 61252 / 815-589-2300

Mogul Co./Life Jacket, 500 N. Kimball Rd., Ste. 109, South Lake, TX 76092

Molin Industries, Tru-Nord Division, P.O. Box 365, 204 North 9th St., Brainerd, MN 56401 / 218-829-2870

Monell Custom Guns, 228 Red Mills Rd., Pine Bush, NY 12566 / 914-744-3021

Moneymaker Guncraft Corp., 1420 Military Ave., Omaha, NE 68131 / 402-556-0226

Montana Armory, Inc .(See C. Sharps Arms Co. Inc.), 100 Centennial Dr., P.O. Box 885, Big Timber, MT 59011 / 406-932-4353; FAX: 406-932-4443

Montana Outfitters, Lewis E. Yearout, 308 Riverview Dr. E., Great Falls, MT 59404 / 406-761-0859

Montana Precision Swaging, P.O. Box 4746, Butte, MT 59702 / 406-494-0600; FAX: 406-494-0600

Montana Rifleman, Inc., 2593A Hwy. 2 East, Kalispell, MT 59901 / 406-755-4867

Montana Vintage Arms, 2354 Bear Canyon Rd., Bozeman, MT 59715

Montgomery Community College, PO Box 787-GD, Troy, NC 27371 / 910-576-6222; or 800-839-6222; FAX: 910-576-2176 hammondp@mcc.montgomery.cc.nc.us www.montgomery.cc.nc.us

Morini (See U.S. Importers-Mandall Shooting Supply)

Morrison Custom Rifles, J. W., 4015 W Sharon, Phoenix, AZ 85029 / 602-978-3754

Morrison Precision, 6719 Calle Mango, Hereford, AZ 85615 / 520-378-6207 morprec@c2i2.com

Morrow, Bud, 11 Hillside Lane, Sheridan, WY 82801-9729 / 307-674-8360

Morton Booth Co., P.O. Box 123, Joplin, MO 64802 / 417-673-1962; FAX: 417-673-3642

Mo's Competitor Supplies (See MCS, Inc.)

Moss Double Tone, Inc., P.O. Box 1112, 2101 S. Kentucky, Sedalia, MO 65301 / 816-827-0827

REFERENCE

MANUFACTURER'S DIRECTORY

Mountain Plains Industries, 244 Glass Hollow Rd., Alton, VA 22920 / 800-687-3000; FAX: 540-456-8134

Mountain South, P.O. Box 381, Barnwell, SC 29812 / FAX: 803-259-3227

Mountain State Muzzleloading Supplies, Inc., Box 154-1, Rt. 2, Williamstown, WV 26187 / 304-375-7842; FAX: 304-375-3737

Mowrey Gun Works, P.O. Box 246, Waldron, IN 46182 / 317-525-6181; FAX: 317-525-9595

Mowrey's Guns & Gunsmithing, 119 Fredericks St., Canajoharie, NY 13317 / 518-673-3483

MPC, P.O. Box 450, McMinnville, TN 37110-0450 / 615-473-5513; FAX: 615-473-5516 thebox@blomand.net www.mpc-thebox.com

MPI Stocks, PO Box 83266, Portland, OR 97283 / 503-226-1215; FAX: 503-226-2661

MSR Targets, P.O. Box 1042, West Covina, CA 91793 / 818-331-7840

Mt. Alto Outdoor Products, Rt. 735, Howardsville, VA 24562

MTM Molded Products Co., Inc., 3370 Obco Ct., Dayton, OH 45414 / 937-890-7461; FAX: 937-890-1747

Mulberry House Publishing, P.O. Box 2180, Apache Junction, AZ 85217 / 888-738-1567; FAX: 480-671-1015

Mulhern, Rick, Rt. 5, Box 152, Rayville, LA 71269 / 318-728-2688

Mullins Ammunition, Rt. 2 Box 304N, Clintwood, VA 24228 / 540-926-6772; FAX: 540-926-6092 www.extremeshockusa

Mullis Guncraft, 3523 Lawyers Road E., Monroe, NC 28110 / 704-283-6683

Multiplex International, 26 S. Main St., Concord, NH 03301 FAX: 603-796-2223

Multipropulseurs, La Bertrandiere, 42580, FRANCE / 77 74 01 30; FAX: 77 93 19 34

Multi-Scale Charge Ltd., 3269 Niagara Falls Blvd., N. Tonawanda, NY 14120 / 905-566-1255; FAX: 905-276-6295

Mundy, Thomas A., 69 Robbins Road, Somerville, NJ 08876 / 201-722-2199

Murmur Corp., 2823 N. Westmoreland Ave., Dallas, TX 75222 / 214-630-5400

Murphy, R.R. Murphy Co., Inc. See: MURPHY, R.R. CO., INC.

Murphy, R.R. Co., Inc., R.R. Murphy Co., Inc. Murphy, P.O. Box 102, Ripley, TN 38063 / 901-635-4003; FAX: 901-635-2320

Murray State College, 1 Murray Campus St., Tishomingo, OK 73460 / 508-371-2371

Muscle Products Corp., 112 Fennell Dr., Butler, PA 16002 / 800-227-7049 or 724-283-0567; FAX: 724-283-8310 mpc@mpc_home.com www.mpc_home.com

Muzzleloaders Etcetera, Inc., 9901 Lyndale Ave. S., Bloomington, MN 55420 / 952-884-1161 www.muzzleloaders-etcetera.com

MWG Co., P.O. Box 971202, Miami, FL 33197 / 800-428-9394 or 305-253-8393; FAX: 305-232-1247

N

N.B.B., Inc., 24 Elliot Rd., Sterling, MA 01564 / 508-422-7538; or 800-942-9444

N.C. Ordnance Co., P.O. Box 3254, Wilson, NC 27895 / 919-237-2440; FAX: 919-243-9845

Nagel's Custom Bullets, 100 Scott St., Baytown, TX 77520-2849

Nalpak, 1937-C Friendship Drive, El Cajon, CA 92020 / 619-258-1200

Nastoff, Steve. See: NASTOFFS 45 SHOP, INC.

Nastoffs 45 Shop, Inc., Steve Nastoff, 1057 Laverne Dr., Youngstown, OH 44511

National Bullet Co., 1585 E. 361 St., Eastlake, OH 44095 / 216-951-1854; FAX: 216-951-7761

National Target Co., 4690 Wyaconda Rd., Rockville, MD 20852 / 800-827-7060 or 301-770-7060; FAX: 301-770-7892

Nationwide Airgun Repair, 2310 Windsor Forest Dr, Louisville, KY 40272 / 502-937-2614; FAX: 812-637-1463 airgunrepair@aol.com

Naval Ordnance Works, Rt. 2, Box 919, Sheperdstown, WV 25443 / 304-876-0998

Navy Arms Co., Inc., 219 Lawn St., Martinsburg, WV 25401 / 304-262-1651; FAX: 304-262-1658

Navy Arms Company, Valmore J. Forgett Jr., 815 22nd Street, Union City, NJ 07087 / 201-863-7100; FAX: 201-863-8770 info@navyarms.com www.navyarms.com

NCP Products, Inc., 3500 12th St. N.W., Canton, OH 44708 / 330-456-5130; FAX: 330-456-5234

Necessary Concepts, Inc., P.O. Box 571, Deer Park, NY 11729 / 516-667-8509; FAX: 516-667-8588

NEI Handtools, Inc., 51583 Columbia River Hwy., Scappoose, OR 97056 / 503-543-6776; FAX: 503-543-7865 nei@columbia-center.com www.neihandtools.com

Neil A. Jones Custom Products, 17217 Brookhouser Road, Saegertown, PA 16433 / 814-763-2769; FAX: 814-763-4228

Nelson, Gary K., 975 Terrace Dr., Oakdale, CA 95361 / 209-847-4590

Nelson, Stephen. See: NELSON'S CUSTOM GUNS, INC.

Nelson/Weather-Rite, Inc., 14760 Santa Fe Trail Dr., Lenexa, KS 66215 / 913-492-3200; FAX: 913-492-8749

Nelson's Custom Guns, Inc., Stephen Nelson, 7430 Valley View Dr. N.W., Corvallis, OR 97330 / 541-745-5232 nelsons-custom@attbi.com

Nesci Enterprises Inc., P.O. Box 119, Summit St., East Hampton, CT 06424 / 203-267-2588

Nesika Bay Precision, 22239 Big Valley Rd., Poulsbo, WA 98370 / 206-697-3830

Nettestad Gun Works, 38962 160th Avenue, Pelican Rapids, MN 56572 / 218-863-4301

Neumann GmbH, Am Galgenberg 6, 90575, GERMANY / 09101/8258; FAX: 09101/6356

Nevada Pistol Academy, Inc., 4610 Blue Diamond Rd., Las Vegas, NV 89139 / 702-897-1100

New England Ammunition Co., 1771 Post Rd. East, Suite 223, Westport, CT 06880 / 203-254-8048

New England Arms Co., Box 278, Lawrence Lane, Kittery Point, ME 03905 / 207-439-0593; FAX: 207-439-0525 info@newenglandarms.com www.newenglandarms.com

New England Custom Gun Service, 438 Willow Brook Rd., Plainfield, NH 03781 / 603-469-3450; FAX: 603-469-3471 bestguns@cyborportal.net www.newenglandcustom.com

New Orleans Jewelers Supply Co., 206 Charters St., New Orleans, LA 70130 / 504-523-3839; FAX: 504-523-3836

New SKB Arms Co., C.P.O. Box 1401, Tokyo, JAPAN / 81-3-3943-9550; FAX: 81-3-3943-0695

New Ultra Light Arms, LLC, 1024 Grafton Rd., Morgantown, WV 26508 / 304-292-0600; FAX: 304-292-9662 newultralightarm@cs.com www.NewUltraLightArm

Newark Electronics, 4801 N. Ravenswood Ave., Chicago, IL 60640

Newell, Robert H., 55 Coyote, Los Alamos, NM 87544 / 505-662-7135

Newman Gunshop, 2035 Chester Ave. #411, Ottumwa, IA 52501-3715 / 515-937-5775

Nicholson Custom, 17285 Thornlay Road, Hughesville, MO 65334 / 816-826-8746

Nickels, Paul R., 4328 Seville St., Las Vegas, NV 89121 / 702-435-5318

Nicklas, Ted, 5504 Hegel Rd., Goodrich, MI 48438 / 810-797-4493

Niemi Engineering, W. B., Box 126 Center Rd., Greensboro, VT 05841 / 802-533-7180; FAX: 802-533-7141

Nikon, Inc., 1300 Walt Whitman Rd., Melville, NY 11747 / 516-547-8623; FAX: 516-547-0309

Nitex Gun Shop, P.O. Box 1706, Uvalde, TX 78801 / 830-278-8843

Noreen, Peter H., 5075 Buena Vista Dr., Belgrade, MT 59714 / 406-586-7383

Norica, Avnda Otaola, 16 Apartado 68, Eibar, SPAIN

Norinco, 7A Yun Tan N, Beijing, CHINA

Norincoptics (See BEC, Inc.)

Norma Precision AB (See U.S. Importers-Dynamit)

Normark Corp., 10395 Yellow Circle Dr., Minnetonka, MN 55343-9101 / 612-933-7060; FAX: 612-933-0046

North American Arms, Inc., 2150 South 950 East, Provo, UT 84606-6285 / 800-821-5783; or 801-374-9990; FAX: 801-374-9998

North American Correspondence Schools The Gun Pro, Oak & Pawney St., Scranton, PA 18515 / 717-342-7701

North American Shooting Systems, P.O. Box 306, Osoyoos, BC V0H 1V0 CANADA / 604-495-3131; FAX: 604-495-2816

North Devon Firearms Services, 3 North St., Braunton, EX33 1AJ ENGLAND / 01271 813624; FAX: 01271 813624

North Mountain Pine Training Center (See Executive

North Specialty Products, 10091 Stageline St., Corona, CA 92883 / 714-524-1665

North Star West, P.O. Box 488, Glencoe, CA 95232 / 209-293-7010 northstarwest.com

Northern Precision Custom Swaged Bullets, 329 S. James St., Carthage, NY 13619 / 315-493-1711

Northlake Outdoor Footwear, P.O. Box 10, Franklin, TN 37065-0010 / 615-794-1556; FAX: 615-790-8005

Northside Gun Shop, 2725 NW 109th, Oklahoma City, OK 73120 / 405-840-2353

Northwest Arms, 26884 Pearl Rd., Parma, ID 83660 / 208-722-6771; FAX: 208-722-1062

No-Sho Mfg. Co., 10727 Glenfield Ct., Houston, TX 77096 / 713-723-5332

Nosler, Inc., P.O. Box 671, Bend, OR 97709 / 800-285-3701 or 541-382-3921; FAX: 541-388-4667

Novak's, Inc., 1206 1/2 30th St., P.O. Box 4045, Parkersburg, WV 26101 / 304-485-9295; FAX: 304-428-6722

Now Products, Inc., P.O. Box 27608, Tempe, AZ 85285 / 800-662-6063; FAX: 480-966-0890

Nowlin Mfg. Co., 20622 S 4092 Rd, Claremore, OK 74017 / 918-342-0689; FAX: 918-342-0624 nowlinguns@msn.com nowlinguns.com

NRI Gunsmith School, P.O. Box 182968, Columbus, OH 43218-2968

Nu-Line Guns,Inc., 1053 Caulks Hill Rd., Harvester, MO 63304 / 314-441-4500; or 314-447-4501; FAX: 314-447-5018

Null Holsters Ltd. K.L., 161 School St NW, Resaca, GA 30735 / 706-625-5643; FAX: 706-625-9392

Numrich Arms Corp., 203 Broadway, W. Hurley, NY 12491

Numrich Gun Parts Corporation, 226 Williams Lane, P.O. Box 299, West Hurley, NY 12491 / 866-686-7424; FAX: 877-GUNPART info@gunpartscorp.com www.@-gunparts.com

Nygord Precision Products, Inc., P.O. Box 12578, Prescott, AZ 86304 / 928-717-2315; FAX: 928-717-2198 nygords@northlink.com www.nygordprecision.com

MANUFACTURER'S DIRECTORY

O

O.F. Mossberg & Sons,Inc., 7 Grasso Ave., North Haven, CT 06473 / 203-230-5300; FAX: 203-230-5420

Oakman Turkey Calls, RD 1, Box 825, Harrisonville, PA 17228 / 717-485-4620

Obermeyer Rifled Barrels, 23122 60th St., Bristol, WI 53104 / 262-843-3537; FAX: 262-843-2129

October Country Muzzleloading, P.O. Box 969, Dept. GD, Hayden, ID 83835 / 208-772-2068; FAX: 208-772-9230 ocinfo@octobercountry.com www.octobercountry.com

Oehler Research,Inc., P.O. Box 9135, Austin, TX 78766 / 512-327-6900 or 800-531-5125; FAX: 512-327-6903 www.oehler-research.com

Oil Rod and Gun Shop, 69 Oak St., East Douglas, MA 01516 / 508-476-3687

Ojala Holsters, Arvo, PO Box 98, N Hollywood, CA 91603 / 503-669-1404

OK Weber, Inc., P.O. Box 7485, Eugene, OR 97401 / 541-747-0458; FAX: 541-747-5927 okweber@pacinfo www.okweber.com

Oker's Engraving, P.O. Box 126, Shawnee, CO 80475 / 303-838-6042

Oklahoma Ammunition Co., 3701A S. Harvard Ave., No. 367, Tulsa, OK 74135-2265 / 918-396-3187; FAX: 918-396-4270

Oklahoma Leather Products,Inc., 500 26th NW, Miami, OK 74354 / 918-542-6651; FAX: 918-542-6653

Olathe Gun Shop, 716-A South Rogers Road, Olathe, KS 66062 / 913-782-6900; FAX: 913-782-6902 info@olathegunshop.com www.olathegunshop.com

Old Wagon Bullets, 32 Old Wagon Rd., Wilton, CT 06897

Old West Bullet Moulds, J Ken Chapman, P.O. Box 519, Flora Vista, NM 87415 / 505-334-6970

Old West Reproductions,Inc. R.M. Bachman, 446 Florence S. Loop, Florence, MT 59833 / 406-273-2615; FAX: 406-273-2615 rick@oldwestreproductions.com www.oldwestreproduction.com

Old World Gunsmithing, 2901 SE 122nd St., Portland, OR 97236 / 503-760-7681

Old World Oil Products, 3827 Queen Ave. N., Minneapolis, MN 55412 / 612-522-5037

Ole Frontier Gunsmith Shop, 2617 Hwy. 29 S., Cantonment, FL 32533 / 904-477-8074

Olson, Myron, 989 W. Kemp, Watertown, SD 57201 / 605-886-9787

Olson, Vic, 5002 Countryside Dr., Imperial, MO 63052 / 314-296-8086

Olympic Arms Inc., 620-626 Old Pacific Hwy. SE, Olympia, WA 98513 / 360-456-3471; FAX: 360-491-3447 info@olyarms.com www.olyarms.com

Olympic Optical Co., P.O. Box 752377, Memphis, TN 38175-2377 / 901-794-3890; or 800-238-7120; FAX: 901-794-0676 80

Omark Industries, Div. of Blount, Inc., 2299 Snake River Ave., P.O. Box 856, Lewiston, ID 83501 / 800-627-3640 or 208-746-2351

Omega Sales, P.O. Box 1066, Mt. Clemens, MI 48043 / 810-469-7323; FAX: 810-469-0425

100 Straight Products, Inc., P.O. Box 6148, Omaha, NE 68106 / 402-556-1055; FAX: 402-556-1055

One Of A Kind, 15610 Purple Sage, San Antonio, TX 78255 / 512-695-3364

One Ragged Hole, P.O. Box 13624, Tallahassee, FL 32317-3624

Op-Tec, P.O. Box L632, Langhorn, PA 19047 / 215-757-5037

Optical Services Co., P.O. Box 1174, Santa Teresa, NM 88008-1174 / 505-589-3833

Orchard Park Enterprise, P.O. Box 563, Orchard Park, NY 14127 / 616-656-0356

Oregon Arms, Inc. (See Rogue Rifle Co., Inc.)

Oregon Trail Bullet Company, PO Box 529, Dept. P, Baker City, OR 97814 / 800-811-0548; FAX: 514-523-1803

Original Box, Inc., 700 Linden Ave., York, PA 17404 / 717-854-2897; FAX: 717-845-4276

Original Deer Formula Co., The., PO Box 1705, Dickson, TN 37056 / 800-874-6965; FAX: 615-446-0646 deerformula1@aol.com

Original Mink Oil, Inc., 10652 NE Holman, Portland, OR 97220 / 503-255-2814; or 800-547-5895; FAX: 503-255-2487

Orion Rifle Barrel Co., RR2, 137 Cobler Village, Kalispell, MT 59901 / 406-257-5649

Otis Technology, Inc., RR 1 Box 84, Boonville, NY 13309 / 315-942-3320

Ottmar, Maurice, Box 657, 113 E. Fir, Coulee City, WA 99115 / 509-632-5717

Outa-Site Gun Carriers, 219 Market St., Laredo, TX 78040 / 210-722-4678; or 800-880-9715; FAX: 210-726-4858

Outdoor Edge Cutlery Corp., 4699 Nautilus Ct. S. Ste. 503, Boulder, CO 80301-5310 / 303-652-8212; FAX: 303-652-8238

Outdoor Enthusiast, 3784 W. Woodland, Springfield, MO 65807 / 417-883-9841

Outdoor Sports Headquarters, Inc., 967 Watertower Ln., West Carrollton, OH 45449 / 513-865-5855; FAX: 513-865-5962

Outers Laboratories Div. of ATK, Route 2, P.O. Box 39, Onalaska, WI 54650 / 608-781-5800; FAX: 608-781-0368

Ox-Yoke Originals, Inc., 34 Main St., Milo, ME 04463 / 800-231-8313; or 207-943-7351; FAX: 207-943-2416

Ozark Gun Works, 11830 Cemetery Rd., Rogers, AR 72756 / 479-631-1024; FAX: 479-631-1024 ogw@hotmail.com www.eocities.com/ocarkgunworks

P

P&M Sales & Services, LLC, 4697 Tote Rd. Bldg. H-B, Comins, MI 48619 / 989-848-8364; FAX: 989-848-8364 mail@pmsales-online.com

P.A.C.T., Inc., P.O. Box 531525, Grand Prairie, TX 75053 / 214-641-0049

P.S.M.G. Gun Co., 10 Park Ave., Arlington, MA 02174 / 617-646-8845; FAX: 617-646-2133

Pachmayr Div. Lyman Products, 475 Smith St., Middletown, CT 06457 / 860-632-2020; or 800-225-9626; FAX: 860-632-1699 lymansales@cshore.com www.pachmayr.com

Pacific Armament Corp, 4813 Enterprise Way, Unit K, Modesto, CA 95356 / 209-545-2800 gunsparts@att.net

Pacific Cartridge, Inc., 2425 Salashan Loop Road, Ferndale, WA 98248 / 360-366-4444; FAX: 360-366-4445

Pacific Rifle Co., PO Box 1473, Lake Oswego, OR 97035 / 503-538-7437

PAC-NOR Barreling, 99299 Overlook Rd., P.O. Box 6188, Brookings, OR 97415 / 503-469-7330; FAX: 503-469-7331 info@pac-nor.com www.pac-nor.com

Paco's (See Small Custom Mould & Bullet Co.)

Page Custom Bullets, P.O. Box 25, Port Moresby, NEW GUINEA

Pagel Gun Works, Inc., 1407 4th St. NW, Grand Rapids, MN 55744 / 218-326-3003

Pager Pal, 200 W Pleasantview, Hurst, TX 76054 / 800-561-1603; FAX: 817-285-8769 www.pagerpal.com

Paintball Games International Magazine Aceville, Castle House 97 High St., Essex, ENGLAND / 011-44-206-564840

Palmer Security Products, 2930 N. Campbell Ave., Chicago, IL 60618 / 773-267-0200; FAX: 773-267-8080 info@palmersecurity.com www.palmersecurity.com

Palsa Outdoor Products, P.O. Box 81336, Lincoln, NE 68501 / 402-488-5288; FAX: 402-488-2321

Paragon Sales & Services, Inc., 2501 Theodore St, Crest Hill, IL 60435-1613 / 815-725-9212; FAX: 815-725-8974

Para-Ordnance Mfg., Inc., 980 Tapscott Rd., Scarborough, ON M1X 1E7 CANADA / 416-297-7855; FAX: 416-297-1289

Para-Ordnance, Inc., 1919 NE 45th St., Ste 215, Ft. Lauderdale, FL 33308 info@paraord.com www.paraord.com

Pardini Armi Srl, Via Italica 154, 55043, Lido Di Camaiore Lu, ITALY / 584-90121; FAX: 584-90122

Paris, Frank J., 17417 Pershing St., Livonia, MI 48152-3822

Parker & Sons Shooting Supply, 9337 Smoky Row Road, Strawberry Plains, TN 37871 / 865-933-3286; FAX: 865-932-8586

Parker Gun Finishes, 9337 Smokey Row Rd., Strawberry Plains, TN 37871 / 423-933-3286; FAX: 865-932-8586

Parker Reproductions, 114 Broad St., Flemington, NJ 11232 / 718-499-6220; FAX: 718-499-6143

Parsons Optical Mfg. Co., PO Box 192, Ross, OH 45061 / 513-867-0820; FAX: 513-867-8380 psscopes@concentric.net

Partridge Sales Ltd., John, Trent Meadows, Rugeley, ENGLAND

Pasadena Gun Center, 206 E. Shaw, Pasadena, TX 77506 / 713-472-0417; FAX: 713-472-1322

Passive Bullet Traps, Inc. (See Savage Range Systems, Inc.)

Paterson Gunsmithing, 438 Main St., Paterson, NJ 07502 / 201-345-4100

Pathfinder Sports Leather, 2920 E. Chambers St., Phoenix, AZ 85040 / 602-276-0016

Patrick W. Price Bullets, 16520 Worthley Drive, San Lorenzo, CA 94580 / 510-278-1547

Pattern Control, 114 N. Third St., P.O. Box 462105, Garland, TX 75046 / 214-494-3551; FAX: 214-272-8447

Paul A. Harris Hand Engraving, 113 Rusty Lane, Boerne, TX 78006-5746 / 512-391-5121

Paul and Sharon Dressel, 209 N. 92nd Ave., Yakima, WA 98908 / 509-966-9233; FAX: 509-966-3365 dressels@nwinfo.net www.dressels.com

Paul D. Hillmer Custom Gunstocks, 7251 Hudson Heights, Hudson, IA 50643 / 319-988-3941

Paul Jones Moulds, 4901 Telegraph Rd., Los Angeles, CA 90022 / 213-262-1510

Paulsen Gunstocks, Rt. 71, Box 11, Chinook, MT 59523 / 406-357-3403

Pawling Mountain Club, Keith Lupton, PO Box 573, Pawling, NY 12564 / 914-855-3825

Paxton Quigley's Personal Protection Strategies, 9903 Santa Monica Blvd., 300, Beverly Hills, CA 90212 / 310-281-1762 www.defend-net.com/paxton

Payne Photography, Robert, Robert, P.O. Box 141471, Austin, TX 78714 / 512-272-4554

Peacemaker Specialists, P.O. Box 157, Whitmore, CA 96096 / 530-472-3438 www.peacemakerspecialists.com

Pearce Grip, Inc., PO Box 40367, Fort Worth, TX 76140 / 206-485-5488; FAX: 206-488-9497

Pease Accuracy, Bob, P.O. Box 310787, New Braunfels, TX 78131 / 210-625-1342

PECAR Herbert Schwarz GmbH, Kreuzbergstrasse 6, 10965, Berlin, GERMANY / 004930-785-7383; FAX: 004930-785-1934 michael.schwart@pecar-berlin.de www.pecar-berlin.de

Pecatonica River Longrifle, 5205 Nottingham Dr., Rockford, IL 61111 / 815-968-1995; FAX: 815-968-1996

Pedersen, C. R., 2717 S. Pere Marquette Hwy., Ludington, MI 49431 / 231-843-2061; FAX: 231-845-7695 fega@fega.com

Pedersen, Rex C., 2717 S. Pere Marquette Hwy., Ludington, MI 49431 / 231-843-2061; FAX: 231-845-7695 fega@fega.com

Peifer Rifle Co., P.O. Box 192, Nokomis, IL 62075-0192 / 217-563-7050; FAX: 217-563-7060

Pejsa Ballistics, 1314 Marquette Ave., Apt 807, Minneapolis, MN 55403 / 612-374-3337; FAX: 612-374-5383

Pelaire Products, 5346 Bonky Ct., W. Palm Beach, FL 33415 / 561-439-0691; FAX: 561-967-0052

Peltor, Inc. (See Aero Peltor)

PEM's Mfg. Co., 5063 Waterloo Rd., Atwater, OH 44201 / 216-947-3721

Pence Precision Barrels, 7567 E. 900 S., S. Whitley, IN 46787 / 219-839-4745

Pendleton Royal, c/o Swingler Buckland Ltd., 4/7 Highgate St., Birmingham, ENGLAND / 44 121 440 3060; or 44 121 446 5898; FAX: 44 121 446 4165

Pendleton Woolen Mills, P.O. Box 3030, 220 N.W. Broadway, Portland, OR 97208 / 503-226-4801

Penn Bullets, P.O. Box 756, Indianola, PA 15051

Pennsylvania Gun Parts Inc, P.O. Box 665, 300 Third St, East Berlin, PA 17316-0665 / 717-259-8010; FAX: 717-259-0057

Pennsylvania Gunsmith School, 812 Ohio River Blvd., Avalon, Pittsburgh, PA 15202 / 412-766-1812; FAX: 412-766-0855 pgs@pagunsmith.com www.pagunsmith.com

Penrod Precision, 312 College Ave., PO Box 307, N. Manchester, IN 46962 / 260-982-8385; FAX: 260-982-1819

Pentax Corp., 35 Inverness Dr. E., Englewood, CO 80112 / 303-799-8000; FAX: 303-790-1131

Pentheny de Pentheny, 2352 Baggett Ct., Santa Rosa, CA 95401 / 707-573-1390; FAX: 707-573-1390

Perazone-Gunsmith, Brian, Cold Spring Rd., Roxbury, NY 12474 / 607-326-4088; FAX: 607-326-3140

Perazzi U.S.A. Inc., 1010 West Tenth, Azusa, CA 91702 / 626-334-1234; FAX: 626-334-0344 perazziusa@aol.com

Performance Specialists, 308 Eanes School Rd., Austin, TX 78746 / 512-327-0119

Perugini Visini & Co. S.r.l., Via Camprelle, 126, 25080 Nuvolera, ITALY / 30-6897535; FAX: 30-6897821 peruvisi@virgilia.it

Pete Mazur Restoration, 13083 Drummer Way, Grass Valley, CA 95949 / 530-268-2412; FAX: 530-268-2412

Pete Rickard, Inc., 115 Roy Walsh Rd, Cobleskill, NY 12043 / 518-234-2731: FAX: 518-234-2454 rickard@telenet.net www.peterickard.com

Peter Dyson & Son Ltd., 3 Cuckoo Lane, Honley Huddersfield, Yorkshire, HD7 2BR ENGLAND / 44-1484-661062; FAX: 44-1484-663709 info@peterdyson.co.uk www.peterdyson.com

Peter Hale/Engraver, 800 E. Canyon Rd., Spanish Fork, UT 84660 / 801-798-8215

Peters Stahl GmbH, Stettiner Strasse 42, D-33106, Paderborn, GERMANY / 05251-750025; FAX: 05251-75611

Petersen Publishing Co., 6420 Wilshire Blvd., Los Angeles, CA 90048 / 213-782-2000; FAX: 213-782-2867

Peterson Gun Shop, Inc., A.W., 4255 W. Old U.S. 441, Mt. Dora, FL 32757-3299 / 352-383-4258; FAX: 352-735-1001

Petro-Explo Inc., 7650 U.S. Hwy. 287, Suite 100, Arlington, TX 76017 / 817-478-8888

Pettinger Books, Gerald, 47827 300th Ave., Russell, IA 50238 / 641-535-2239 gpettinger@lisco.com

Pflumm Mfg. Co., 10662 Widmer Rd., Lenexa, KS 66215 / 800-888-4867; FAX: 913-451-7857

PFRB Co., P.O. Box 1242, Bloomington, IL 61702 / 309-473-3964 or 800-914-5464; FAX: 309-473-2161

Philip S. Olt Co., P.O. Box 550, 12662 Fifth St., Pekin, IL 61554 / 309-348-3633; FAX: 309-348-3300

Phillippi Custom Bullets, Justin, P.O. Box 773, Ligonier, PA 15658 / 724-238-2962; FAX: 724-238-9671 jrp@wpa.net http://www.wpa.net~jrphil

Phillips & Rogers, Inc., 100 Hilbig #C, Conroe, TX 77301 / 409-435-0011

Phoenix Arms, 1420 S. Archibald Ave., Ontario, CA 91761 / 909-947-4843; FAX: 909-947-6798

Photronic Systems Engineering Company, 6731 Via De La Reina, Bonsall, CA 92003 / 619-758-8000

Piedmont Community College, P.O. Box 1197, Roxboro, NC 27573 / 336-599-1181; FAX: 336-597-3817 www.piedmont.cc.nc.us

Pierce Pistols, 55 Sorrellwood Lane, Sharpsburg, GA 30277-9523 / 404-253-8192

Pietta (See U.S. Importers-Navy Arms Co, Taylor's

Pilgrim Pewter,Inc. (See Bell Originals Inc. Sid)

Pilkington, Scott (See Little Trees Ramble)

Pine Technical College, 1100 4th St., Pine City, MN 55063 / 800-521-7463; FAX: 612-629-6766

Pinetree Bullets, 133 Skeena St., Kitimat, BC V8C 1Z1 CANADA / 604-632-3768; FAX: 604-632-3768

Pioneer Arms Co., 355 Lawrence Rd., Broomall, PA 19008 / 215-356-5203

Piotti (See U.S. Importer-Moore & Co, Wm. Larkin)

Piquette, Paul. See: PIQUETTE'S CUSTOM ENGRAVING

Piquette's Custom Engraving, Paul R. Piquette, 80 Bradford Dr., Feeding Hills, MA 01030 / 413-789-4582; FAX: 413-786-8118 ppiquette@aol.com www.pistoldynamics.com

Plaza Cutlery, Inc., 3333 Bristol, 161 South Coast Plaza, Costa Mesa, CA 92626 / 714-549-3932

Plum City Ballistic Range, N2162 80th St., Plum City, WI 54761 / 715-647-2539

PlumFire Press, Inc., 30-A Grove Ave., Patchogue, NY 11772-4112 / 800-695-7246; FAX: 516-758-4071

PMC/Eldorado Cartridge Corp., P.O. Box 62508, 12801 U.S. Hwy. 95 S., Boulder City, NV 89005 / 702-294-0025; FAX: 702-294-0121 kbauer@pmcammo.com www.pmcammo.com

Poburka, Philip (See Bison Studios)

Pohl, Henry A. (See Great American Gun Co.)

Pointing Dog Journal, Village Press Publications, P.O. Box 968, Dept. PGD, Traverse City, MI 49685 / 800-272-3246; FAX: 616-946-3289

Police Bookshelf, PO Box 122, Concord, NH 03301 / 603-224-6814; FAX: 603-226-3554

Polywad, Inc., P.O. Box 7916, Macon, GA 31209 / 478-477-0669; or 800-998-0669 polywadmpb@aol.com www.polywad.com

Ponsness/Warren, 768 Ohio St., Rathdrum, ID 83858 / 800-732-0706; FAX: 208-687-2233

Pony Express Reloaders, 608 E. Co. Rd. D, Suite 3, St. Paul, MN 55117 / 612-483-9406; FAX: 612-483-9884

Pony Express Sport Shop, 23404 Lyons Ave., PMB 448, Newhall, CA 91321-2511 / 818-895-1231

Potts, Wayne E., 912 Poplar St., Denver, CO 80220 / 303-355-5462

Powder Horn Ltd., PO Box 565, Glenview, IL 60025 / 305-565-6060

Powell & Son (Gunmakers) Ltd., William, 35-37 Carrs Lane, Birmingham, B4 7SX ENGLAND / 121-643-0689; FAX: 121-631-3504

Powell Agency, William, 22 Circle Dr., Bellmore, NY 11710 / 516-679-1158

Power Custom, Inc., 29739 Hwy. J, Gravois Mills, MO 65037 / 573-372-5684; FAX: 573-372-5799 rwpowers@laurie.net www.powercustom.com

Power Plus Enterprises, Inc., PO Box 38, Warm Springs, GA 31830 / 706-655-2132

Powley Computer (See Hutton Rifle Ranch)

Practical Tools, Inc., 7067 Easton Rd., P.O. Box 133, Pipersville, PA 18947 / 215-766-7301; FAX: 215-766-8681

Prairie Gun Works, 1-761 Marion St., Winnipeq, MB R2J 0K6 CANADA / 204-231-2976; FAX: 204-231-8566

Prairie River Arms, 1220 N. Sixth St., Princeton, IL 61356 / 815-875-1616 or 800-445-1541; FAX: 815-875-1402

Pranger, Ed G., 1414 7th St., Anacortes, WA 98221 / 206-293-3488

Precision Airgun Sales, Inc., 5247 Warrensville Ctr Rd., Maple Hts., OH 44137 / 216-587-5005; FAX: 216-587-5005

Precision Cast Bullets, 101 Mud Creek Lane, Ronan, MT 59864 / 406-676-5135

Precision Delta Corp., PO Box 128, Ruleville, MS 38771 / 662-756-2810; FAX: 662-756-2590

Precision Firearm Finishing, 25 N.W. 44th Avenue, Des Moines, IA 50313 / 515-288-8680; FAX: 515-244-3925

Precision Gun Works, 104 Sierra Rd.Dept. GD, Kerrville, TX 78028 / 830-367-4587

Precision Reloading, Inc., PO Box 122, Stafford Springs, CT 06076 / 860-684-7979; FAX: 860-684-6788 info@precisionreloading.com www.precisionreloading.com

Precision Sales International, Inc., PO Box 1776, Westfield, MA 01086 / 413-562-5055; FAX: 413-562-5056 precision-sales.com

Precision Shooting, Inc., 222 McKee St., Manchester, CT 06040 / 860-645-8776; FAX: 860-643-8215 www.precisionshooting.com

Precision Small Arms Inc., 9272 Jeronimo Rd, Ste 121, Irvine, CA 92618 / 800-554-5515; or 949-768-3530; FAX: 949-768-4808 www.tcbebe.com

Precision Specialties, 131 Hendom Dr., Feeding Hills, MA 01030 / 413-786-3365; FAX: 413-786-3365

Precision Sport Optics, 15571 Producer Lane, Unit G, Huntington Beach, CA 92649 / 714-891-1309; FAX: 714-892-6920

Premier Reticles, 920 Breckinridge Lane, Winchester, VA 22601-6707 / 540-722-0601; FAX: 540-722-3522

Prescott Projectile Co., 1808 Meadowbrook Road, Prescott, AZ 86303

Preslik's Gunstocks, 4245 Keith Ln., Chico, CA 95926 / 916-891-8236

Price Bullets, Patrick W., 16520 Worthley Dr., San Lorenzo, CA 94580 / 510-278-1547

Prime Reloading, 30 Chiswick End, Meldreth, ROYSTON UK / 0763-260636

Primos, Inc., P.O. Box 12785, Jackson, MS 39236-2785 / 601-366-1288; FAX: 601-362-3274

PRL Bullets, c/o Blackburn Enterprises, 114 Stuart Rd., Ste. 110, Cleveland, TN 37312 / 423-559-0340

Pro Load Ammunition, Inc., 5180 E. Seltice Way, Post Falls, ID 83854 / 208-773-9444; FAX: 208-773-9441

Professional Gunsmiths of America, Rt 1 Box 224, Lexington, MO 64067 / 660-259-2636

Professional Hunter Supplies (See Star Custom Bullets), PO Box 608, 468 Main St., Ferndale, CA 95536 / 707-786-9140; FAX: 707-786-9117 wmebride@humboldt.com

PrOlixr Lubricants, P.O. Box 1348, Victorville, CA 92393 / 760-243-3129; FAX: 760-241-0148 prolix@accex.net www.prolixlubricant.com

Pro-Mark Div. of Wells Lamont, 6640 W. Touhy, Chicago, IL 60648 / 312-647-8200

Proofmark Corp., P.O. Box 610, Burgess, VA 22432 / 804-453-4337; FAX: 804-453-4337 proofmark@rivnet.net

Pro-Port Ltd., 41302 Executive Dr., Harrison Twp., MI 48045-1306 / 586-469-6727; FAX: 586-469-0425 e-mail@magnaport.com www.magnaport.com

Pro-Shot Products, Inc., P.O. Box 763, Taylorville, IL 62568 / 217-824-9133; FAX: 217-824-8861

Protektor Model, 1-11 Bridge St., Galeton, PA 16922 / 814-435-2442 mail@protektormodel.com www.protektormodel.com

Prototech Industries, Inc., 10532 E Road, Delia, KS 66418 / 785-771-3571; prototec@grapevine.net

ProWare, Inc., 15847 NE Hancock St., Portland, OR 97230 / 503-239-0159

PWL Gunleather, P.O. Box 450432, Atlanta, GA 31145 / 800-960-4072; FAX: 770-822-1704 covert@pwlusa.com www.pwlusa.com

Pyramyd Stone Inter. Corp., 2447 Suffolk Lane, Pepper Pike, OH 44124-4540

Q

Quack Decoy & Sporting Clays, 4 Ann & Hope Way, P.O. Box 98, Cumberland, RI 02864 / 401-723-8202; FAX: 401-722-5910

Quaker Boy, Inc., 5455 Webster Rd., Orchard Parks, NY 14127 / 716-662-3979; FAX: 716-662-9426

Quality Arms, Inc., Box 19477, Dept. GD, Houston, TX 77224 / 281-870-8377; FAX: 281-870-8524 arrieta2@excite.com www.gunshop.com

Quality Custom Firearms, Stepehn Billeb, 22 Vista View Drive, Cody, WY 82414 / 307-587-4278; FAX: 307-587-4297 stevebilleb@wyoming.com

Que Industries, Inc., PO Box 2471, Everett, WA 98203 / 425-303-9088; FAX: 206-514-3266 queinfo@queindustries.com

Queen Cutlery Co., PO Box 500, Franklinville, NY 14737 / 800-222-5233; FAX: 800-299-2618

R

R&C Knives & Such, 2136 CANDY CANE WALK, Manteca, CA 95336-9501 / 209-239-3722; FAX: 209-825-6947

R&D Gun Repair, Kenny Howell, RR1 Box 283, Beloit, WI 53511

R&J Gun Shop, 337 S. Humbolt St., Canyon City, OR 97820 / 541-575-2130 rjgunshop@highdestertnet.com

R&S Industries Corp., 8255 Brentwood Industrial Dr., St. Louis, MO 63144 / 314-781-5169 ron@miraclepolishingcloth.com www.miraclepolishingcloth.com

R. Murphy Co., Inc., 13 Groton-Harvard Rd., P.O. Box 376, Ayer, MA 01432 / 617-772-3481

R.A. Wells Custom Gunsmith, 3452 1st Ave., Racine, WI 53402 / 414-639-5223

R.E. Seebeck Assoc., P.O. Box 59752, Dallas, TX 75229

R.E.I., P.O. Box 88, Tallevast, FL 34270 / 813-755-0085

R.E.T. Enterprises, 2608 S. Chestnut, Broken Arrow, OK 74012 / 918-251-GUNS; FAX: 918-251-0587

R.F. Mitchell Bullets, 430 Walnut St., Westernport, MD 21562

R.I.S. Co., Inc., 718 Timberlake Circle, Richardson, TX 75080 / 214-235-0933

R.T. Eastman Products, P.O. Box 1531, Jackson, WY 83001 / 307-733-3217; or 800-624-4311

Rabeno, Martin, 92 Spook Hole Rd., Ellenville, NY 12428 / 845-647-2129; FAX: 845-647-2129 fancygun@aol.com

Radack Photography, Lauren, 21140 Jib Court L-12, Aventura, FL 33180 / 305-931-3110

Radiator Specialty Co., 1900 Wilkinson Blvd., P.O. Box 34689, Charlotte, NC 28234 / 800-438-6947; FAX: 800-421-9525

Radical Concepts, P.O. Box 1473, Lake Grove, OR 97035 / 503-538-7437

Rainier Ballistics Corp., 4500 15th St. East, Tacoma, WA 98424 / 800-638-8722 or 206-922-7589; FAX: 206-922-7854

Ralph Bone Engraving, 718 N. Atlanta St., Owasso, OK 74055 / 918-272-9745

Ram-Line ATK, P.O. Box 39, Onalaska, WI 54650

Ramon B. Gonzalez Guns, P.O. Box 370, Monticello, NY 12701 / 914-794-4515

Rampart International, 2781 W. MacArthur Blvd., B-283, Santa Ana, CA 92704 / 800-976-7240 or 714-557-6405

Ranch Products, P.O. Box 145, Malinta, OH 43535 / 313-277-3118; FAX: 313-565-8536

Randall-Made Knives, P.O. Box 1988, Orlando, FL 32802 / 407-855-8075

Randco UK, 286 Gipsy Rd., Welling, DA16 1JJ ENGLAND / 44 81 303 4118

Randolph Engineering Inc., 26 Thomas Patten Dr., Randolph, MA 02368 / 781-961-6070; FAX: 781-961-0337

Randy Duane Custom Stocks, 7822 Church St., Middletown, VA 22645-9521

Range Brass Products Company, P.O. Box 218, Rockport, TX 78381

Ranger Shooting Glasses, 26 Thomas Patten Dr., Randolph, MA 02368 / 800-541-1405; FAX: 617-986-0337

Ransom International Corp., 1027 Spire Dr, Prescott, AZ 86302 / 520-778-7899; FAX: 520-778-7993 ransom@primenet.com www.ransom-intl.com

Rapine Bullet Mould Mfg. Co., 9503 Landis Lane, East Greenville, PA 18041 / 215-679-5413; FAX: 215-679-9795

Ravell Ltd., 289 Diputacion St., 08009, Barcelona, SPAIN / 34(3) 4874486; FAX: 34(3) 4881394

Ray Riling Arms Books Co., 6844 Gorsten St., Philadelphia, PA 19119 / 215-438-2456; FAX: 215-438-5395 sales@rayrilingarmsbooks.com www.rayrilingarmsbooks.com

Ray's Gunsmith Shop, 3199 Elm Ave., Grand Junction, CO 81504 / 970-434-6162; FAX: 970-434-6162

Raytech Div. of Lyman Products Corp., 475 Smith Street, Middletown, CT 06457-1541 / 860-632-2020 or 800-225-9626; FAX: 860-632-1699 lymansales@cshore.com www.lymanproducts.com

RCBS Operations/ATK, 605 Oro Dam Blvd., Oroville, CA 95965 / 530-533-5191 or 800-533-5000; FAX: 530-533-1647 www.rcbs.com

RCBS/ATK, 605 Oro Dam Blvd., Oroville, CA 95965 / 800-533-5000; FAX: 916-533-1647

Reagent Chemical & Research, Inc., 114 Broad St., Flemington, NJ 11232 / 718-499-6220; FAX: 718-499-6143

Reardon Products, P.O. Box 126, Morrison, IL 61270 / 815-772-3155

Red Diamond Dist. Co., 1304 Snowdon Dr., Knoxville, TN 37912

Redding Reloading Equipment, 1089 Starr Rd., Cortland, NY 13045 / 607-753-3331; FAX: 607-756-8445 techline@redding-reloading.com www.redding-reloading.com

Redfield Media Resource Center, 4607 N.E. Cedar Creek Rd., Woodland, WA 98674 / 360-225-5000; FAX: 360-225-7616

Redman's Rifling & Reboring, 189 Nichols Rd., Omak, WA 98841 / 509-826-5512

Redwood Bullet Works, 3559 Bay Rd., Redwood City, CA 94063 / 415-367-6741

Reed, Dave, Rt. 1, Box 374, Minnesota City, MN 55959 / 507-689-2944

Reimer Johannsen, Inc., 438 Willow Brook Rd., Plainfield, NH 03781 / 603-469-3450; FAX: 603-469-3471

Reiswig, Wallace E. (See Claro Walnut Gunstock

Reloaders Equipment Co., 4680 High St., Ecorse, ML 48229

Reloading Specialties, Inc., Box 1130, Pine Island, MN 55463 / 507-356-8500; FAX: 507-356-8800

Remington Arms Co., Inc., 870 Remington Drive, P.O. Box 700, Madison, NC 27025-0700 / 800-243-9700; FAX: 910-548-8700

Remington Double Shotguns, 7885 Cyd Dr., Denver, CO 80221 / 303-429-6947

Renato Gamba S.p.A.-Societa Armi Bresciane Srl., Via Artigiani 93, 25063 Gardone, Val Trompia (BS), ITALY / 30-8911640; FAX: 30-8911648

Renegade, PO Box 31546, Phoenix, AZ 85046 / 602-482-6777; FAX: 602-482-1952

Renfrew Guns & Supplies, R.R. 4, Renfrew, ON K7V 3Z7 CANADA / 613-432-7080

Reno, Wayne, 2808 Stagestop Road, Jefferson, CO 80456

Republic Arms, Inc. (See Cobra Enterprises, Inc.)

Retting, Inc., Martin B, 11029 Washington, Culver City, CA 90232 / 213-837-2412

RG-G, Inc., PO Box 935, Trinidad, CO 81082 / 719-845-1436

RH Machine & Consulting Inc, PO Box 394, Pacific, MO 63069 / 314-271-8465

Rhino, P.O. Box 787, Locust, NC 28097 / 704-753-2198

Rhodeside, Inc., 1704 Commerce Dr., Piqua, OH 45356 / 513-773-5781

Rice, Keith (See White Rock Tool & Die)

Richards Micro-Fit Stocks, 8331 N. San Fernando Ave., Sun Valley, CA 91352 / 818-767-6097; FAX: 818-767-7121

Ridgeline, Inc., Bruce Sheldon, P.O. Box 930, Dewey, AZ 86327-0930 / 800-632-5900; FAX: 520-632-5900

Ridgetop Sporting Goods, P.O. Box 306, 42907 Hilligoss Ln. East, Eatonville, WA 98328 / 360-832-6422; FAX: 360-832-6422

Ries, Chuck, 415 Ridgecrest Dr., Grants Pass, OR 97527 / 503-476-5623

Riggs, Jim, 206 Azalea, Boerne, TX 78006 / 210-249-8567

Riley Ledbetter Airguns, 1804 E. Sprague St., Winston Salem, NC 27107-3521 / 919-784-0676

Rim Pac Sports, Inc., 1034 N. Soldano Ave., Azusa, CA 91702-2135

Ringler Custom Leather Co., 31 Shining Mtn. Rd., Powell, WY 82435 / 307-645-3255

Ripley Rifles, 42 Fletcher Street, Ripley, Derbyshire, DE5 3LP ENGLAND / 011-0773-748353

Rizzini F.lli (See U.S. Importers-Moore & C England)

Rizzini SNC, Via 2 Giugno, 7/7Bis-25060, Marcheno (Brescia), ITALY

RLCM Enterprises, 110 Hill Crest Drive, Burleson, TX 76028

RMS Custom Gunsmithing, 4120 N. Bitterwell, Prescott Valley, AZ 86314 / 520-772-7626

Robert Evans Engraving, 332 Vine St., Oregon City, OR 97045 / 503-656-5693

Robert Valade Engraving, 931 3rd Ave., Seaside, OR 97138 / 503-738-7672

Robinett, R. G., P.O. Box 72, Madrid, IA 50156 / 515-795-2906

Robinson, Don, Pennsylvania Hse, 36 Fairfax Crescent, W Yorkshire, ENGLAND / 0422-364458

REFERENCE

Robinson Armament Co., PO Box 16776, Salt Lake City, UT 84116 / 801-355-0401; FAX: 801-355-0402 zdf@robarm.com www.robarm.com

Robinson Firearms Mfg. Ltd., 1699 Blondeaux Crescent, Kelowna, BC V1Y 4J8 CANADA / 604-868-9596

Robinson H.V. Bullets, 3145 Church St., Zachary, LA 70791 / 504-654-4029

Rochester Lead Works, 76 Anderson Ave., Rochester, NY 14607 / 716-442-8500; FAX: 716-442-4712

Rock River Arms, 101 Noble St., Cleveland, IL 61241

Rockwood Corp., Speedwell Division, 136 Lincoln Blvd., Middlesex, NJ 08846 / 800-243-8274; FAX: 980-560-7475

Rocky Mountain Armoury, Mr. Felix LesMerises, 610 Main Street, P.O. Box 691, Frisco, CO 80443-0691 / 970-668-0136; FAX: 970-668-4484 felix@rockymountainarmoury.com

Rocky Mountain Arms, Inc., 1813 Sunset Pl, Unit D, Longmont, CO 80501 / 800-375-0846; FAX: 303-678-8766

Rocky Mountain Target Co., 3 Aloe Way, Leesburg, FL 34788 / 352-365-9598

Rocky Mountain Wildlife Products, P.O. Box 999, La Porte, CO 80535 / 970-484-2768; FAX: 970-484-0807 critrcall@earthlink.net www.critrcall.com

Rocky Shoes & Boots, 294 Harper St., Nelsonville, OH 45764 / 800-848-9452; or 614-753-1951; FAX: 614-753-4024

Rodgers & Sons Ltd., Joseph (See George Ibberson)

Rogue Rifle Co., Inc., P.O. Box 20, Prospect, OR 97536 / 541-560-4040; FAX: 541-560-4041

Rogue River Rifleworks, 500 Linne Road #D, Paso Robles, CA 93446 / 805-227-4706; FAX: 805-227-4723 rrrifles@calinet.com

Rohner, Hans, 1148 Twin Sisters Ranch Rd., Nederland, CO 80466-9600

Rohner, John, 186 Virginia Ave, Asheville, NC 28806 / 303-444-3841

Rohrbaugh, P.O. Box 785, Bayport, NY 11705 / 631-363-2843; FAX: 631-363-2681 API380@aol.com

Romain's Custom Guns, Inc., RD 1, Whetstone Rd., Brockport, PA 15823 / 814-265-1948 romwhetstone@penn.com

Ron Frank Custom Classic Arms, 7131 Richland Rd., Ft. Worth, TX 76118 / 817-284-9300; FAX: 817-284-9300 rfrank3974@aol.com

Rooster Laboratories, P.O. Box 414605, Kansas City, MO 64141 / 816-474-1622; FAX: 816-474-7622

Rorschach Precision Products, 417 Keats Cir., Irving, TX 75061 / 214-790-3487

Rosenberg & Son, Jack A, 12229 Cox Ln, Dallas, TX 75234 / 214-241-6302

Ross, Don, 12813 West 83 Terrace, Lenexa, KS 66215 / 913-492-6982

Rosser, Bob, 1824 29th Ave. So., Suite 214, Homewood, AL 35209 / 205-870-4422; FAX: 205-870-4421 www.hand-engravers.com

Rossi Firearms, Gary Mchalik, 16175 NW 49th Ave, Miami, FL 33014-6314 / 305-474-0401; FAX: 305-623-7506

Rottweil Compe, 1330 Glassell, Orange, CA 92667

Roy Baker's Leather Goods, PO Box 893, Magnolia, AR 71754 / 870-234-0344

Royal Arms Gunstocks, 919 8th Ave. NW, Great Falls, MT 59404 / 406-453-1149 royalarms@lmt.net www.lmt.net/~royalarms

Royal Arms International, R J Brill, P.O. Box 6083, Woodland Hills, CA 91365 / 818-704-5110; FAX: 818-887-2059 royalarms.com

Roy's Custom Grips, 793 Mt. Olivet Church Rd, Lynchburg, VA 24504 / 434-993-3470

RPM, 15481 N. Twin Lakes Dr., Tucson, AZ 85739 / 520-825-1233; FAX: 520-825-3333

Rubright Bullets, 1008 S. Quince Rd., Walnutport, PA 18088 / 215-767-1339

Rucker Dist. Inc., P.O. Box 479, Terrell, TX 75160 / 214-563-2094

Ruger (See Sturm, Ruger & Co., Inc.)

Ruger, Chris. See: RUGER'S CUSTOM GUNS

Ruger's Custom Guns, Chris Ruger, 1050 Morton Blvd., Kingston, NY 12401 / 845-336-7106; FAX: 845-336-7106 rugerscustom@outdrs.net rugergunsmith.com

Rundell's Gun Shop, 6198 Frances Rd., Clio, MI 48420 / 313-687-0559

Runge, Robert P., 1120 Helderberg Trl. #1, Berne, NY 12023-2909

Rupert's Gun Shop, 2202 Dick Rd., Suite B, Fenwick, MI 48834 / 517-248-3252 17rupert@pathwaynet.com

Russ Haydon's Shooters' Supply, 15018 Goodrich Dr. NW, Gig Harbor, WA 98329 / 253-857-7557; FAX: 253-857-7884 www.shooters-supply.com

Russ, William. See: BILL RUSS TRADING POST

Rusteprufe Laboratories, 1319 Jefferson Ave., Sparta, WI 54656 / 608-269-4144; FAX: 608-366-1972 rusteprufe@centurytel.net www.rusteprufe.com

Rusty Duck Premium Gun Care Products, 7785 Foundation Dr., Suite 6, Florence, KY 41042 / 606-342-5553; FAX: 606-342-5556

Rutgers Book Center, 127 Raritan Ave., Highland Park, NJ 08904 / 732-545-4344; FAX: 732-545-6686 gunbooks@rutgersgunbooks.com www.rutgersgunbooks.com

Rutten (See U.S. Importer-Labanu Inc)

RWS (See US Importer-Dynamit Nobel-RWS, Inc.), 81 Ruckman Rd., Closter, NJ 07624 / 201-767-7971; FAX: 201-767-1589

S

S&K Scope Mounts, RD 2 Box 72E, Sugar Grove, PA 16350 / 814-489-3091; or 800-578-9862; FAX: 814-489-5466 comments@scopemounts.com www.scopemounts.com

S&S Firearms, 74-11 Myrtle Ave., Glendale, NY 11385 / 718-497-1100; FAX: 718-497-1105

S.A.R.L. G. Granger, 66 cours Fauriel, 42100, Saint Etienne, FRANCE / 04 77 25 14 73; FAX: 04 77 38 66 99

S.C.R.C., PO Box 660, Katy, TX 77492-0660 FAX: 713-578-2124

S.D. Meacham, 1070 Angel Ridge, Peck, ID 83545

S.G.S. Sporting Guns Srl., Via Della Resistenza, 37 20090, Buccinasco, ITALY / 2-45702446; FAX: 2-45702464

S.I.A.C.E. (See U.S. Importer-IAR Inc)

Sabatti SPA, Via A Volta 90, 25063 Gandome V.T.(BS), Brescia, ITALY / 030-8912207-831312; FAX: 030-8912059 info@sabatti.it www.sabatti.com

SAECO (See Redding Reloading Equipment)

Safari Arms/Schuetzen Pistol Works, 620-626 Old Pacific Hwy. SE, Olympia, WA 98513 / 360-459-3471; FAX: 360-491-3447 info@yarms.com www.olyarms.com

Safari Press, Inc., 15621 Chemical Lane B, Huntington Beach, CA 92649 / 714-894-9080; FAX: 714-894-4949

Safariland Ltd., Inc., 3120 E. Mission Blvd., P.O. Box 51478, Ontario, CA 91761 / 909-923-7300; FAX: 909-923-7400

SAFE, PO Box 864, Post Falls, ID 83877 / 208-773-3624; FAX: 208-773-6819 staysafe@safe-llc.com www.safe-llc.com

Safety Speed Holster, Inc., 910 S. Vail Ave., Montebello, CA 90640 / 323-723-4140; FAX:

323-726-6973 e-mail@safetyspeedholster.com www.safetyspeedholster.com

Saf-T-Lok Corp., 18245 SE, Tesquesta, FL 33469 / 800-723-8565

Sako Ltd (See U.S. Importer-Stoeger Industries)

Sam Welch Gun Engraving, Sam Welch, HC 64 Box 2110, Moab, UT 84532 / 435-259-8131

Samco Global Arms, Inc., 6995 NW 43rd St., Miami, FL 33166 / 305-593-9782; FAX: 305-593-1014 samco@samcoglobal.com www.samcoglobal.com

Sampson, Roger, 2316 Mahogany St., Mora, MN 55051 / 612-679-4868

San Marco (See U.S. Importers-Cape Outfitters-EMF

Sandia Die & Cartridge Co., 37 Atancacio Rd. NE, Auquerque, NM 87123 / 505-298-5729

Sarco, Inc., 323 Union St., Stirling, NJ 07980 / 908-647-3800; FAX: 908-647-9413

Sarsilmaz Shotguns - Turkey (see B.C. Outdoors)

Sauer (See U.S. Importers-Paul Co., The, Sigarms I

Sauls, R. See: BRYAN & ASSOC.

Saunders Gun & Machine Shop, 145 Delhi Rd, Manchester, IA 52057 / 563-927-4026

Savage Arms (Canada), Inc., 248 Water St., P.O. Box 1240, Lakefield, ON K0L 2H0 CANADA / 705-652-8000; FAX: 705-652-8431

Savage Arms, Inc., 100 Springdale Rd., Westfield, MA 01085 / 413-568-7001; FAX: 413-562-7764

Savage Range Systems, Inc., 100 Springdale Rd., Westfield, MA 01085 / 413-568-7001; FAX: 413-562-1152

Saville Iron Co. (See Greenwood Precision)

Savino, Barbara J., P.O. Box 51, West Burke, VT 05871-0051

Scansport, Inc., P.O. Box 700, Enfield, NH 03748 / 603-632-7654

Sceery Game Calls, P.O. Box 6520, Sante Fe, NM 87502 / 505-471-9110; FAX: 505-471-3476

Schaefer Shooting Sports, P.O. Box 1515, Melville, NY 11747-0515 / 516-643-5466; FAX: 516-643-2426 robert@robertschaefer.com www.schaefershooting.com

Scharch Mfg., Inc.-Top Brass, 10325 Co. Rd. 120, Salida, CO 81201 / 719-539-7242; or 800-836-4683; FAX: 719-539-3021 scharch@chaffee.net www.topbraass.tv

Scherer, Liz. See: SCHERER SUPPLIES

Scherer Supplies, Liz Scherer, Box 250, Ewing, VA 24248 FAX: 423-733-2073

Schiffman, Curt, 3017 Kevin Cr., Idaho Falls, ID 83402 / 208-524-4684

Schiffman, Mike, 8233 S. Crystal Springs, McCammon, ID 83250 / 208-254-9114

Schmidt & Bender, Inc., P.O. Box 134, Meriden, NH 03770 / 603-469-3565; FAX: 603-469-3471 scopes@cyberportal.net www.schmidtbender.com

Schmidtke Group, 17050 W. Salentine Dr., New Berlin, WI 53151-7349

Schneider Bullets, 3655 West 214th St., Fairview Park, OH 44126

Schneider Rifle Barrels, Inc., Gary, 12202 N 62nd Pl., Scottsdale, AZ 85254 / 602-948-2525

Schroeder Bullets, 1421 Thermal Ave., San Diego, CA 92154 / 619-423-3523; FAX: 619-423-8124

Schulz Industries, 16247 Minnesota Ave., Paramount, CA 90723 / 213-439-5903

Schumakers Gun Shop, 512 Prouty Corner Lp. A, Colville, WA 99114 / 509-684-4848

Scope Control, Inc., 5775 Co. Rd. 23 SE, Alexandria, MN 56308 / 612-762-7295

Score High Gunsmithing, 9812-A, Cochiti SE, Albuquerque, NM 087123 / 800-326-5632 or 505-292-5532; FAX: 505-292-2592

Scot Powder, Rt.1 Box 167, McEwen, TN 37101 / 800-416-3006; FAX: 615-729-4211

Scott Fine Guns Inc., Thad, PO Box 412, Indianola, MS 38751 / 601-887-5929

Searcy Enterprises, PO Box 584, Boron, CA 93596 / 760-762-6771; FAX: 760-762-0191

Second Chance Body Armor, P.O. Box 578, Central Lake, MI 49622 / 616-544-5721; FAX: 616-544-9824

Seebeck Assoc., R.E., P. O. Box 59752, Dallas, TX 75229

Seecamp Co. Inc., L. W., PO Box 255, New Haven, CT 06502 / 203-877-3429; FAX: 203-877-3429

Segway Industries, P.O. Box 783, Suffern, NY 10901-0783 / 914-357-5510

Seligman Shooting Products, Box 133, Seligman, AZ 86337 / 602-422-3607 shootssp@yahoo.com

Sellier & Bellot, USA Inc., P.O. Box 27006, Shawnee Mission, KS 66225 / 913-685-0916; FAX: 913-685-0917

Selsi Co., Inc., P.O. Box 10, Midland Park, NJ 07432-0010 / 201-935-0388; FAX: 201-935-5851

Semmer, Charles (See Remington Double Shotguns), 7885 Cyd Dr, Denver, CO 80221 / 303-429-6947

Sentinel Arms, P.O. Box 57, Detroit, MI 48231 / 313-331-1951; FAX: 313-331-1456

Servus Footwear Co., 1136 2nd St., Rock Island, IL 61204 / 309-786-7741; FAX: 309-786-9808

Shappy Bullets, 76 Milldale Ave., Plantsville, CT 06479 / 203-621-3704

Sharp Shooter Supply, 4970 Lehman Road, Delphos, OH 45833 / 419-695-3179

Sharps Arms Co., Inc., C., 100 Centennial, Box 885, Big Timber, MT 59011 / 406-932-4353

Shaw, Inc., E. R. (See Small Arms Mfg. Co.)

Shay's Gunsmithing, 931 Marvin Ave., Lebanon, PA 17042

Sheffield Knifemakers Supply, Inc., PO Box 741610, Orange City, FL 32774-1107 / 386-775-6453; FAX: 386-774-5754

Sheldon, Bruce. See: RIDGELINE, INC.

Shepherd Enterprises, Inc., Box 189, Waterloo, NE 68069 / 402-779-2424; FAX: 402-779-4010 sshepherd@shepherdscopes.com www.shepherdscopes.com

Sherwood, George, 46 N. River Dr., Roseburg, OR 97470 / 541-672-3159

Shilen, Inc., 205 Metro Park Blvd., Ennis, TX 75119 / 972-875-5318; FAX: 972-875-5402

Shiloh Rifle Mfg., 201 Centennial Dr., Big Timber, MT 59011 / 406-932-4454; FAX: 406-932-5627 lucinda@shilohrifle.com www.shilohrifle.com

Shockley, Harold H., 204 E. Farmington Rd., Hanna City, IL 61536 / 309-565-4524

Shoot Where You Look, Leon Measures, Dept GD, 408 Fair, Livingston, TX 77351

Shooters Arms Manufacturing Inc., Rivergate Mall, Gen. Maxilom Ave., Cebu City 6000, PHILIPPINES / 6332-254-8478 www.shootersarms.com.ph

Shooter's Choice Gun Care, 15050 Berkshire Ind. Pky., Middlefield, OH 44062 / 440-834-8888; FAX: 440-834-3388 www.shooterschoice.com

Shooter's Edge Inc., 3313 Creekstone Dr., Fort Collins, CO 80525

Shooters Supply, 1120 Tieton Dr., Yakima, WA 98902 / 509-452-1181

Shooter's World, 3828 N. 28th Ave., Phoenix, AZ 85017 / 602-266-0170

Shooters, Inc., 5139 Stanart St., Norfolk, VA 23502 / 757-461-9152; FAX: 757-461-9155 gflocker@aol.com

Shootin' Shack, 357 Cypress Drive, No. 10, Tequesta, FL 33469 / 561-842-0990; FAX: 561-545-4861

Shooting Specialties (See Titus, Daniel)

Shooting Star, 1715 FM 1626 Ste 105, Manchaca, TX 78652 / 512-462-0009

Shoot-N-C Targets (See Birchwood Casey)

Shotgun Sports, P.O. Box 6810, Auburn, CA 95604 / 530-889-2220; FAX: 530-889-9106 custsrv@shotgunsportsmagazine.com shotgunsportsmagazine.com

Shotgun Sports Magazine, dba Shootin' Accessories Ltd., P.O. Box 6810, Auburn, CA 95604 / 916-889-2220 custsrv@shotgunsportsmagazine.com shotgunspotsmagazine.com

Shotguns Unlimited, 2307 Fon Du Lac Rd., Richmond, VA 23229 / 804-752-7115

Siegrist Gun Shop, 8752 Turtle Road, Whittemore, MI 48770 / 989-873-3929

Sierra Bullets, 1400 W. Henry St., Sedalia, MO 65301 / 816-827-6300; FAX: 816-827-6300

Sierra Specialty Prod. Co., 1344 Oakhurst Ave., Los Altos, CA 94024 FAX: 415-965-1536

SIG, CH-8212 Neuhausen, SWITZERLAND

Sigarms, Inc., Corporate Park, Exeter, NH 03833 / 603-772-2302; FAX: 603-772-9082 www.sigarms.com

Sightron, Inc., 1672B Hwy. 96, Franklinton, NC 27525 / 919-528-8783; FAX: 919-528-0995 info@sightron.com www.sightron.com

Signet Metal Corp., 551 Stewart Ave., Brooklyn, NY 11222 / 718-384-5400; FAX: 718-388-7488

SIG-Sauer (See U.S. Importer-Sigarms Inc.)

Silencio/Safety Direct, 56 Coney Island Dr., Sparks, NV 89431 / 800-648-1812 or 702-354-4451; FAX: 702-359-1074

Silent Hunter, 1100 Newton Ave., W. Collingswood, NJ 08107 / 609-854-3276

Silhouette Leathers, P.O. Box 1161, Gunnison, CO 81230 / 303-641-6639 oldshooter@yahoo.com

Silver Eagle Machining, 18007 N. 69th Ave., Glendale, AZ 85308

Silver Ridge Gun Shop (See Goodwin, Fred)

Simmons, Jerry, 715 Middlebury St., Goshen, IN 46528-2717 / 574-533-8546

Simmons Gun Repair, Inc., 700 S. Rogers Rd., Olathe, KS 66062 / 913-782-3131; FAX: 913-782-4189

Simmons Outdoor Corp., 6001 Oak Canyon, Irvine, CA 92618 / 949-451-1450; FAX: 949-451-1460 www.meade.com

Sinclair International, Inc., 2330 Wayne Haven St., Fort Wayne, IN 46803 / 260-493-1858; FAX: 260-493-2530 sales@sinclairintl.com www.sinclairintl.com

Singletary, Kent, 4538 W Carol Ave., Glendale, AZ 85302 / 602-526-6836 kent@kscustom www.kscustom.com

Siskiyou Gun Works (See Donnelly, C. P.)

Six Enterprises, 320-D Turtle Creek Ct., San Jose, CA 95125 / 408-999-0201; FAX: 408-999-0216

SKB Shotguns, 4325 S. 120th St., Omaha, NE 68137 / 800-752-2767; FAX: 402-330-8040 skb@skbshotguns.com www.skbshotguns.com

Skeoch, Brian R., PO Box 279, Glenrock, WY 82637 / 307-436-9655 brianskeoch@aol.com

Skip's Machine, 364 29 Road, Grand Junction, CO 81501 / 303-245-5417

Sklany's Machine Shop, 566 Birch Grove Dr., Kalispell, MT 59901 / 406-755-4257

Slezak, Jerome F., 1290 Marlowe, Lakewood (Cleveland), OH 44107 / 216-221-1668

Slug Site, Ozark Wilds, 21300 Hwy. 5, Versailles, MO 65084 / 573-378-6430 john@ebeling.com john.ebeling.com

Small Arms Mfg. Co., 5312 Thoms Run Rd., Bridgeville, PA 15017 / 412-221-4343; FAX: 412-221-4303

Small Arms Specialists, 443 Firchburg Rd, Mason, NH 03048 / 603-878-0427; FAX: 603-878-3905 miniguns@empire.net miniguns.com

Small Custom Mould & Bullet Co., Box 17211, Tucson, AZ 85731

Smart Parts, 1203 Spring St., Latrobe, PA 15650 / 412-539-2660; FAX: 412-539-2298

Smires, C. L., 5222 Windmill Lane, Columbia, MD 21044-1328

Smith & Wesson, 2100 Roosevelt Ave., Springfield, MA 01104 / 413-781-8300; FAX: 413-731-8980

Smith, Art, 230 Main St. S., Hector, MN 55342 / 320-848-2760; FAX: 320-848-2760

Smith, Mark A., P.O. Box 182, Sinclair, WY 82334 / 307-324-7929

Smith, Michael, 2612 Ashmore Ave., Red Bank, TN 37415 / 615-267-8341

Smith, Ron, 5869 Straley, Ft. Worth, TX 76114 / 817-732-6768

Smith, Sharmon, 4545 Speas Rd., Fruitland, ID 83619 / 208-452-6329 sharmon@fmtc.com

Smith Abrasives, Inc., 1700 Sleepy Valley Rd., P.O. Box 5095, Hot Springs, AR 71902-5095 / 501-321-2244; FAX: 501-321-9232

Smith, Judy. See: L.B.T.

Smith Saddlery, Jesse W., 0499 County Road J, Pritchett, CO 81064 / 509-325-0622

Smokey Valley Rifles, E1976 Smokey Valley Rd, Scandinavia, WI 54977 / 715-467-2674

Snapp's Gunshop, 6911 E. Washington Rd., Clare, MI 48617 / 989-386-9226

Sno-Seal, Inc. (See Atsko/Sno-Seal, Inc.)

Societa Armi Bresciane Srl (See U.S. Importer-Cape

SOS Products Co. (See Buck Stix-SOS Products Co.), Box 3, Neenah, WI 54956

Sotheby's, 1334 York Ave. at 72nd St., New York, NY 10021 / 212-606-7260

Sound Technology, Box 391, Pelham, AL 35124 / 205-664-5860; or 907-486-2825 rem700P@sprintmail.com www.soundtechsilencers.com

South Bend Replicas, Inc., 61650 Oak Rd.., South Bend, IN 46614 / 219-289-4500

Southeastern Community College, 1015 S. Gear Ave., West Burlington, IA 52655 / 319-752-2731

Southern Ammunition Co., Inc., 4232 Meadow St., Loris, SC 29569-3124 / 803-756-3262; FAX: 803-756-3583

Southern Bloomer Mfg. Co., P.O. Box 1621, Bristol, TN 37620 / 615-878-6660; FAX: 615-878-8761

Southern Security, 1700 Oak Hills Dr., Kingston, TN 37763 / 423-376-6297; FAX: 800-251-9992

Sparks, Milt, 605 E. 44th St. No. 2, Boise, ID 83714-4800

Spartan-Realtree Products, Inc., 1390 Box Circle, Columbus, GA 31907 / 706-569-9101; FAX: 706-569-0042

Specialty Gunsmithing, Lynn McMurdo, P.O. Box 404, Afton, WY 83110 / 307-886-5535

Specialty Shooters Supply, Inc., 3325 Griffin Rd., Suite 9mm, Fort Lauderdale, FL 33317

Speer Bullets, PO Box 856, Lewiston, ID 83501 / 208-746-2351; www.speer-bullets.com

Spegel, Craig, P.O. Box 387, Nehalem, OR 97131 / 503-368-5653

Speiser, Fred D., 2229 Dearborn, Missoula, MT 59801 / 406-549-8133

Spencer Reblue Service, 1820 Tupelo Trail, Holt, MI 48842 / 517-694-7474

Spencer's Rifle Barrels, Inc., 4107 Jacobs Creek Dr, Scottsville, VA 24590 / 804-293-6836; FAX: 804-293-6836 www.spencerriflebarrels.com

REFERENCE

MANUFACTURER'S DIRECTORY

SPG LLC, P.O. Box 1625, Cody, WY 82414 / 307-587-7621; FAX: 307-587-7695 spg@cody.wtp.net www.blackpowderspg.com

Sphinx Systems Ltd., Gesteigtstrasse 12, CH-3800, Matten, BRNE, SWITZERLAND

Splitfire Sporting Goods, L.L.C., P.O. Box 1044, Orem, UT 84059-1044 / 801-932-7950; FAX: 801-932-7959 www.splitfireguns.com

Spolar Power Load Inc., 17376 Filbert, Fontana, CA 92335 / 800-227-9667

Sport Flite Manufacturing Co., PO Box 1082, Bloomfield Hills, MI 48303 / 248-647-3747

Sporting Clays Of America, 9257 Bluckeye Rd, Sugar Grove, OH 43155-9632 / 740-746-8334; FAX: 740-746-8605

Sports Innovations Inc., P.O. Box 5181, 8505 Jacksboro Hwy., Wichita Falls, TX 76307 / 817-723-6015

Sportsman Safe Mfg. Co., 6309-6311 Paramount Blvd., Long Beach, CA 90805 / 800-266-7150; or 310-984-5445

Sportsman's Communicators, 588 Radcliffe Ave., Pacific Palisades, CA 90272 / 800-538-3752

Sportsmatch U.K. Ltd., 16 Summer St. Leighton,, Buzzard Beds, Bedfordshire, LU7 8HT ENGLAND / 01525-381638; FAX: 01525-851236 info@sportsmatch-uk.com www.sportsmatch-uk.com

Sportsmen's Exchange & Western Gun Traders, Inc., 560 S. C St., Oxnard, CA 93030 / 805-483-1917

Spradlin's, 457 Shannon Rd, Texas CreekCotopaxi, CO 81223 / 719-275-7105; FAX: 719-275-3852 spradlins@prodigy.net www.spradlins.net

Springfield Armory, 420 W. Main St, Geneseo, IL 61254 / 309-944-5631; FAX: 309-944-3676 sales@springfield-armory.com www.springfieldarmory.com

Springfield Sporters, Inc., RD 1, Penn Run, PA 15765 / 412-254-2626; FAX: 412-254-9173

Springfield, Inc., 420 W. Main St., Geneseo, IL 61254 / 309-944-5631; FAX: 309-944-3676

Spyderco, Inc., 20011 Golden Gate Canyon Rd., Golden, CO 80403 / 800-525-7770; or 800-525-7770; FAX: 303-278-2229 sales@spyderco.com www.spyderco.com

SSK Industries, J. D. Jones, 590 Woodvue Lane, Wintersville, OH 43953 / 740-264-0176; FAX: 740-264-2257 www.sskindustries.com

Stackpole Books, 5067 Ritter Rd., Mechanicsburg, PA 17055-6921 / 717-796-0411 or 800-732-3669; FAX: 717-796-0412 tmanney@stackpolebooks.com www.stackpolebooks.com

Stalker, Inc., P.O. Box 21, Fishermans Wharf Rd., Malakoff, TX 75148 / 903-489-1010

Stalwart Corporation, PO Box 46, Evanston, WY 82931 / 307-789-7687; FAX: 307-789-7688

Stan Baker Sports, Stan Baker, 10000 Lake City Way, Seattle, WA 98125 / 206-522-4575

Stan De Treville & Co., 4129 Normal St., San Diego, CA 92103 / 619-298-3393

Stanley Bullets, 2085 Heatheridge Ln., Reno, NV 89509

Star Ammunition, Inc., 5520 Rock Hampton Ct., Indianapolis, IN 46268 / 800-221-5927; FAX: 317-872-5847

Star Custom Bullets, PO Box 608, 468 Main St., Ferndale, CA 95536 / 707-786-9140; FAX: 707-786-9117 wmebridge@humboldt.com

Star Machine Works, PO Box 1872, Pioneer, CA 95666 / 209-295-5000

Starke Bullet Company, P.O. Box 400, 605 6th St. NW, Cooperstown, ND 58425 / 888-797-3431

Starkey Labs, 6700 Washington Ave. S., Eden Prairie, MN 55344

Starkey's Gun Shop, 9430 McCombs, El Paso, TX 79924 / 915-751-3030

Starlight Training Center, Inc., Rt. 1, P.O. Box 88, Bronaugh, MO 64728 / 417-843-3555

Starline, Inc., 1300 W. Henry St., Sedalia, MO 65301 / 660-827-6640; FAX: 660-827-6650 info@starlinebrass.com http://www.starlinebrass.com

Starr Trading Co., Jedediah, PO Box 2007, Farmington Hills, MI 48333 / 810-683-4343; FAX: 810-683-3282

Starrett Co., L. S., 121 Crescent St., Athol, MA 01331 / 978-249-3551; FAX: 978-249-8495

Steelman's Gun Shop, 10465 Beers Rd., Swartz Creek, MI 48473 / 810-735-4884

Steffens, Ron, 18396 Mariposa Creek Rd., Willits, CA 95490 / 707-485-0873

Stegall, James B., 26 Forest Rd., Wallkill, NY 12589

Steve Henigson & Associates, P.O. Box 2726, Culver City, CA 90231 / 310-305-8288; FAX: 310-305-1905

Steve Kamyk Engraver, 9 Grandview Dr., Westfield, MA 01085-1810 / 413-568-0457 stevek201@attbi

Steven Dodd Hughes, P.O. Box 545, Livingston, MT 59047 / 406-222-9377; FAX: 406-222-9377

Steves House of Guns, Rt. 1, Minnesota City, MN 55959 / 507-689-2573

Stewart Game Calls, Inc., Johnny, PO Box 7954, 5100 Fort Ave, Waco, TX 76714 / 817-772-3261; FAX: 817-772-3670

Stewart's Gunsmithing, P.O. Box 5854, Pietersburg North 0750, Transvaal, SOUTH AFRICA / 01521-89401

Steyr Mannlicher GmbH P Co KG, Mannlicherstrasse 1, 4400 Steyr, Steyr, AUSTRIA / 0043-7252-896-0; FAX: 0043-7252-78620 office@steyr-mannlicher.com www.steyr-mannlicher.com

STI International, 114 Halmar Cove, Georgetown, TX 78628 / 800-959-8201; FAX: 512-819-0465 www.stiguns.com

Stiles Custom Guns, 76 Cherry Run Rd., Box 1605, Homer City, PA 15748 / 712-479-9945

Stillwell, Robert, 421 Judith Ann Dr., Schertz, TX 78154

Stoeger Industries, 17603 Indian Head Hwy., Suite 200, Accokeek, MD 20607-2501 / 301-283-6300; FAX: 301-283-6986 www.stoegerindustries.com

Stoeger Publishing Co. (See Stoeger Industries)

Stone Enterprises Ltd., 426 Harveys Neck Rd., PO Box 335, Wicomico Church, VA 22579 / 804-580-5114; FAX: 804-580-8421

Stone Mountain Arms, 5988 Peachtree Corners E., Norcross, GA 30071 / 800-251-9412

Stoney Point Products, Inc., P.O. Box 234, 1822 N Minnesota St., New Ulm, MN 56073-0234 / 507-354-3360; FAX: 507-354-7236 stoney@newulmtel.net www.stoneypoint.com

Storm, Gary, P.O. Box 5211, Richardson, TX 75083 / 214-385-0862

Stott's Creek Armory, Inc., 2526 S. 475W, Morgantown, IN 46160 / 317-878-5489; FAX: 317-878-9489 sccalendar@aol.com www.sccalendar.com

Stratco, Inc., P.O. Box 2270, Kalispell, MT 59901 / 406-755-1221; FAX: 406-755-1226

Strayer, Sandy. See: STRAYER-VOIGT, INC.

Strayer-Voigt, Inc., Sandy Strayer, 3435 Ray Orr Blvd, Grand Prairie, TX 75050 / 972-513-0575

Streamlight, Inc., 1030 W. Germantown Pike, Norristown, PA 19403 / 215-631-0600; FAX: 610-631-0712

Strong Holster Co., 39 Grove St., Gloucester, MA 01930 / 508-281-3300; FAX: 508-281-6321

Strutz Rifle Barrels, Inc., W. C., P.O. Box 611, Eagle River, WI 54521 / 715-479-4766

Stuart, V. Pat, Rt.1, Box 447-S, Greenville, VA 24440 / 804-556-3845

Sturgeon Valley Sporters, K. Ide, P.O. Box 283, Vanderbilt, MI 49795 / 517-983-4338

Sturm Ruger & Co. Inc., 200 Ruger Rd., Prescott, AZ 86301 / 928-541-8820; FAX: 520-541-8850 www.ruger.com

Sullivan, David S .(See Westwind Rifles Inc.)

Summit Specialties, Inc., P.O. Box 786, Decatur, AL 35602 / 205-353-0634; FAX: 205-353-9818

Sun Welding Safe Co., 290 Easy St. No.3, Simi Valley, CA 93065 / 805-584-6678; or 800-729-SAFE; FAX: 805-584-6169 sunwelding.com

Sunny Hill Enterprises, Inc., W1790 Cty. HHH, Malone, WI 53049 / 920-795-4722; FAX: 920-795-4822

"Su-Press-On", Inc., P.O. Box 09161, Detroit, MI 48209 / 313-842-4222

Super 6 LLC, Gary Knopp, 3806 W. Lisbon Ave., Milwaukee, WI 53208 / 414-344-3343; FAX: 414-344-0304

Sure-Shot Game Calls, Inc., P.O. Box 816, 6835 Capitol, Groves, TX 77619 / 409-962-1636; FAX: 409-962-5465

Survival Arms, Inc., 273 Canal St., Shelton, CT 06484-3173 / 203-924-6533; FAX: 203-924-2581

Svon Corp., 2107 W. Blue Heron Blvd., Riviera Beach, FL 33404 / 508-881-8852

Swann, D. J., 5 Orsova Close, Eltham North Vic., 3095 AUSTRALIA / 03-431-0323

Swanndri New Zealand, 152 Elm Ave., Burlingame, CA 94010 / 415-347-6158

Swanson, Mark, 975 Heap Avenue, Prescott, AZ 86301 / 928-778-4423

Swarovski Optik North America Ltd., 2 Slater Rd., Cranston, RI 02920 / 401-946-2220; or 800-426-3089; FAX: 401-946-2587

Sweet Home, Inc., P.O. Box 900, Orrville, OH 44667-0900

Swenson's 45 Shop, A. D., 3839 Ladera Vista Rd, Fallbrook, CA 92028-9431

Swift Bullet Co., P.O. Box 27, 201 Main St., Quinter, KS 67752 / 913-754-3959; FAX: 913-754-2359

Swift Instruments, Inc., 952 Dorchester Ave., Boston, MA 02125 / 617-436-2960; FAX: 617-436-3232

Swift River Gunworks, 450 State St., Belchertown, MA 01007 / 413-323-4052

Szweda, Robert (See RMS Custom Gunsmithing)

T

T&S Industries, Inc., 1027 Skyview Dr., W. Carrollton, OH 45449 / 513-859-8414

T.F.C. S.p.A., Via G. Marconi 118, B, Villa Carcina 25069, ITALY / 030-881271; FAX: 030-881826

T.G. Faust, Inc., 544 Minor St., Reading, PA 19602 / 610-375-8549; FAX: 610-375-4488

T.H.U. Enterprises, Inc., P.O. Box 418, Lederach, PA 19450 / 215-256-1665; FAX: 215-256-9718

T.K. Lee Co., 1282 Branchwater Ln., Birmingham, AL 35216 / 205-913-5222 odonmich@aol.com www.scopedot.com

T.W. Menck Gunsmith Inc., 5703 S. 77th St., Ralston, NE 68127 guntools@cox.net http://llwww.members.cox.net/guntools

Tabler Marketing, 2554 Lincoln Blvd., Suite 555, Marina Del Rey, CA 90291 / 818-755-4565; FAX: 818-755-0972

Taconic Firearms Ltd., Perry Lane, PO Box 553, Cambridge, NY 12816 / 518-677-2704; FAX: 518-677-5974

Tactical Defense Institute, 2174 Bethany Ridges, West Union, OH 45693 / 937-544-7228; FAX: 937-544-2887

Talley, Dave, P.O. Box 821, Glenrock, WY 82637 / 307-436-8724; or 307-436-9315

Talmage, William G., 10208 N. County Rd. 425 W., Brazil, IN 47834 / 812-442-0804

MANUFACTURER'S DIRECTORY

Talon Industries Inc. (See Cobra Enterprises, Inc.)
Tamarack Products, Inc., PO Box 625, Wauconda, IL 60084 / 708-526-9333; FAX: 708-526-9353
Tanfoglio Fratelli S.r.l., via Valtrompia 39, 41, Brescia, ITALY / 30-8910361; FAX: 30-8910183
Tanglefree Industries, 1261 Heavenly Dr., Martinez, CA 94553 / 800-982-4868; FAX: 510-825-3874
Tank's Rifle Shop, P.O. Box 474, Fremont, NE 68026-0474 / 402-727-1317 jtank@tanksrifleshop.com www.tanksrifleshop.com
Tanner (See U.S. Importer-Mandall Shooting Supply)
Taracorp Industries, Inc., 1200 Sixteenth St., Granite City, IL 62040 / 618-451-4400
Target Shooting, Inc., PO Box 773, Watertown, SD 57201 / 605-882-6955; FAX: 605-882-8840
Tar-Hunt Custom Rifles, Inc., 101 Dogtown Rd., Bloomsburg, PA 17815 / 570-784-6368; FAX: 570-784-6368 www.tar-hunt.com
Tarnhelm Supply Co., Inc., 431 High St., Boscawen, NH 03303 / 603-796-2551; FAX: 603-796-2918 info@tarnhelm.com www.tarnhelm.com
Tasco Sales, Inc., 2889 Commerce Pky., Miramar, FL 33025
Taurus Firearms, Inc., 16175 NW 49th Ave., Miami, FL 33014 / 305-624-1115; FAX: 305-623-7506
Taurus International Firearms (See U.S. Importer)
Taurus S.A. Forjas, Avenida Do Forte 511, Porto Alegre, RS BRAZIL 91360 / 55-51-347-4050; FAX: 55-51-347-3065
Taylor & Robbins, P.O. Box 164, Rixford, PA 16745 / 814-966-3233
Taylor's & Co., Inc., 304 Lenoir Dr., Winchester, VA 22603 / 540-722-2017; FAX: 540-722-2018
TCCI, P.O. Box 302, Phoenix, AZ 85001 / 602-237-3823; FAX: 602-237-3858
TCSR, 3998 Hoffman Rd., White Bear Lake, MN 55110-4626 / 800-328-5323; FAX: 612-429-0526
TDP Industries, Inc., P.O. Box 249, Ottsville, PA 18942-0249 / 215-345-8687; FAX: 215-345-6057
Techno Arms (See U.S. Importer- Auto-Ordnance Corp
Tecnolegno S.p.A., Via A. Locatelli, 6 10, 24019 Zogno, I ITALY / 0345-55111; FAX: 0345-55155
Ted Blocker Holsters, Inc., 9396 S.W. Tigard St., Tigard, OR 97223 / 800-650-9742; FAX: 503-670-9692 www.tedblocker.com
Tele-Optics, 630 E. Rockland Rd., PO Box 6313, Libertyville, IL 60048 / 847-362-7757; FAX: 847-362-7757
Tennessee Valley Mfg., 14 County Road 521, Corinth, MS 38834 / 601-286-5014
Ten-Ring Precision, Inc., Alex B. Hamilton, 1449 Blue Crest Lane, San Antonio, TX 78232 / 210-494-3063; FAX: 210-494-3066
TEN-X Products Group, 1905 N Main St, Suite 133, Cleburne, TX 76031-1305 / 972-243-4016; or 800-433-2225; FAX: 972-243-4112
Tepeco, P.O. Box 342, Friendswood, TX 77546 / 713-482-2702
Terry K. Kopp Professional Gunsmithing, Rt 1 Box 224, Lexington, MO 64067 / 816-259-2636
Testing Systems, Inc., 220 Pegasus Ave., Northvale, NJ 07647
Tetra Gun Care, 8 Vreeland Rd., Florham Park, NJ 07932 / 973-443-0004; FAX: 973-443-0263
Tex Shoemaker & Sons, Inc., 714 W. Cienega Ave., San Dimas, CA 91773 / 909-592-2071; FAX: 909-592-2378

texshoemaker@texshoemaker.com www.texshoemaker.com
Texas Armory (See Bond Arms, Inc.)
Texas Platers Supply Co., 2453 W. Five Mile Parkway, Dallas, TX 75233 / 214-330-7168
Thad Rybka Custom Leather Equipment, 2050 Canoe Creek Rd., Springvale, AL 35146-6709
Thad Scott Fine Guns, Inc., P.O. Box 412, Indianola, MS 38751 / 601-887-5929
The A.W. Peterson Gun Shop, Inc., 4255 West Old U.S. 441, Mount Dora, FL 32757-3299 / 352-383-4258
The Accuracy Den, 25 Bitterbrush Rd., Reno, NV 89523 / 702-345-0225
The Ballistic Program Co., Inc., 2417 N. Patterson St., Thomasville, GA 31792 / 912-228-5739 or 800-368-0835
The BulletMakers Workshop, RFD 1 Box 1755, Brooks, ME 04921
The Competitive Pistol Shop, 5233 Palmer Dr., Ft. Worth, TX 76117-2433 / 817-834-8479
The Concealment Shop, Inc., 617 W. Kearney St., Ste. 205, Mesquite, TX 75149 / 972-289-8997; or 800-444-7090; FAX: 972-289-4410 concealmentshop@email.msn.com www.theconcealmentshop.com
The Country Armourer, P.O. Box 308, Ashby, MA 01431-0308 / 508-827-6797; FAX: 508-827-4845
The Creative Craftsman, Inc., 95 Highway 29 North, P.O. Box 331, Lawrenceville, GA 30246 / 404-963-2112; FAX: 404-513-9488
The Custom Shop, 890 Cochrane Crescent, Peterborough, ON K9H 5N3 CANADA / 705-742-6693
The Dutchman's Firearms, Inc., 4143 Taylor Blvd., Louisville, KY 40215 / 502-366-0555
The Ensign-Bickford Co., 660 Hopmeadow St., Simsbury, CT 06070
The Firearm Training Center, 9555 Blandville Rd., West Paducah, KY 42086 / 502-554-5886
The Fouling Shot, 6465 Parfet St., Arvada, CO 80004
The Gun Doctor, 435 East Maple, Roselle, IL 60172 / 708-894-0668
The Gun Room, 1121 Burlington, Muncie, IN 47302 / 765-282-9073; FAX: 765-282-5270 bshstleguns@aol.com
The Gun Room Press, 127 Raritan Ave., Highland Park, NJ 08904 / 732-545-4344; FAX: 732-545-6686 gunbooks@rutgersgunbooks.com www.rutgersgunbooks.com
The Gun Shop, 5550 S. 900 East, Salt Lake City, UT 84117 / 801-263-3633
The Gun Shop, 62778 Spring Creek Rd., Montrose, CO 81401
The Gun Works, 247 S. 2nd St., Springfield, OR 97477 / 541-741-4118; FAX: 541-988-1097 gunworks@worldnet.att.net www.thegunworks.com
The Gunsight, 1712 North Placentia Ave., Fullerton, CA 92631
The Gunsmith in Elk River, 14021 Victoria Lane, Elk River, MN 55330 / 612-441-7761
The Hanned Line, P.O. Box 2387, Cupertino, CA 95015-2387 smith@hanned.com www.hanned.com
The Hawken Shop, P.O. Box 593, Oak Harbor, WA 98277 / 206-679-4657; FAX: 206-675-1114
The Keller Co., P.O. Box 4057, Port Angeles, WA 98363-0997 / 214-770-8585
The Lewis Lead Remover (See LEM Gun Specialties)
The Midwest Shooting School, Pat LaBoone, 2550 Hwy. 23, Wrenshall, MN 55797 / 218-384-3670 shootingschool@starband.net
The NgraveR Co., 67 Wawecus Hill Rd., Bozrah, CT 06334 / 860-823-1533

The Ordnance Works, 2969 Pidgeon Point Road, Eureka, CA 95501 / 707-443-3252
The Orvis Co., Rt. 7, Manchester, VT 05254 / 802-362-3622; FAX: 802-362-3525
The Outdoor Connection, Inc., 7901 Panther Way, Waco, TX 76712-6556 / 800-533-6076 or 254-772-5575; FAX: 254-776-3553 floyd@outdoorconnection.com www.outdoorconnection.com
The Park Rifle Co., Ltd., Unit 6a Dartford Trade Park, Power Mill Lane, Dartford DA7 7NX, ENGLAND / 011-0322-222512
The Paul Co., 27385 Pressonville Rd., Wellsville, KS 66092 / 785-883-4444; FAX: 785-883-2525
The Protector Mfg. Co., Inc., 443 Ashwood Place, Boca Raton, FL 33431 / 407-394-6011
The Robar Co.'s, Inc., 21438 N. 7th Ave., Suite B, Phoenix, AZ 85027 / 623-581-2648 www.robarguns.com
The School of Gunsmithing, 6065 Roswell Rd., Atlanta, GA 30328 / 800-223-4542
The Shooting Gallery, 8070 Southern Blvd., Boardman, OH 44512 / 216-726-7788
The Sight Shop, John G. Lawson, 1802 E. Columbia Ave., Tacoma, WA 98404 / 253-474-5465 parahellum9@aol.com www.thesightshop.org
The Southern Armory, 25 Millstone Road, Woodlawn, VA 24381 / 703-238-1343; FAX: 703-238-1453
The Surecase Co., 233 Wilshire Blvd., Ste. 900, Santa Monica, CA 90401 / 800-92ARMLOC
The Swampfire Shop (See Peterson Gun Shop, Inc.)
The Wilson Arms Co., 63 Leetes Island Rd., Branford, CT 06405 / 203-488-7297; FAX: 203-488-0135
Theis, Terry, 21452 FM 2093, Harper, TX 78631 / 830-864-4438
Thiewes, George W., 14329 W. Parada Dr., Sun City West, AZ 85375
Things Unlimited, 235 N. Kimbau, Casper, WY 82601 / 307-234-5277
Thirion Gun Engraving, Denise, PO Box 408, Graton, CA 95444 / 707-829-1876
Thomas, Charles C., 2600 S. First St., Springfield, IL 62794 / 217-789-8980; FAX: 217-789-9130
Thompson Bullet Lube Co., P.O. Box 409, Wills Point, TX 75169 / 866-476-1500; FAX: 866-476-1500 thompsonbulletlube.com www.thompsonbulletlube.com
Thompson Precision, 110 Mary St., P.O. Box 251, Warren, IL 61087 / 815-745-3625
Thompson, Randall. See: HIGHLINE MACHINE CO.
Thompson Target Technology, 4804 Sherman Church Ave. S.W., Canton, OH 44710 / 330-484-6480; FAX: 330-491-1087 www.thompsontarget.com
Thompson Tool Mount, 1550 Solomon Rd., Santa Maria, CA 93455 / 805-934-1281 ttm@pronet.net www.thompsontoolmount.com
Thompson, Randall (See Highline Machine Co.)
Thompson/Center Arms, P.O. Box 5002, Rochester, NH 03866 / 603-332-2394; FAX: 603-332-5133 tech@tcarms.com www.tcarms.com
3-Ten Corp., P.O. Box 269, Feeding Hills, MA 01030 / 413-789-2086; FAX: 413-789-1549
Thunden Ranch, HCR 1, Box 53, Mt. Home, TX 78058 / 830-640-3138
Thurston Sports, Inc., RD 3 Donovan Rd., Auburn, NY 13021 / 315-253-0966
Tiger-Hunt Gunstocks, Box 379, Beaverdale, PA 15921 / 814-472-5161 tigerhunt4@aol.com www.gunstockwood.com
Tikka (See U.S. Importer-Stoeger Industries)
Time Precision, 4 Nicholas Sq., New Milford, CT 06776-3506 / 203-775-8343

REFERENCE

16th EDITION • 315

Tinks & Ben Lee Hunting Products (See Wellington)

Tink's Safariland Hunting Corp., P.O. Box 244, 1140 Monticello Rd., Madison, GA 30650 / 706-342-4915; FAX: 706-342-7568

Tioga Engineering Co., Inc., P.O. Box 913, 13 Cone St., Wellsboro, PA 16901 / 570-724-3533; FAX: 570-724-3895 tiogaeng@epix.net

Tippman Pneumatics, Inc., 3518 Adams Center Rd., Fort Wayne, IN 46806 / 219-749-6022; FAX: 219-749-6619

Tirelli, Snc Di Tirelli Primo E.C., Via Matteotti No. 359, Gardone V.T. Brescia, I ITALY / 030-8912819; FAX: 030-832240

TM Stockworks, 6355 Maplecrest Rd., Fort Wayne, IN 46835 / 219-485-5389

TMI Products (See Haselbauer Products, Jerry)

Tom Forrest, Inc., P.O. Box 326, Lakeside, CA 92040 / 619-561-5800; FAX: 619-561-0227

Tombstone Smoke`n' Deals, PO Box 31298, Phoenix, AZ 85046 / 602-905-7013; FAX: 602-443-1998

Tom's Gun Repair, Thomas G. Ivanoff, 76-6 Rt. Southfork Rd., Cody, WY 82414 / 307-587-6949

Tom's Gunshop, 3601 Central Ave., Hot Springs, AR 71913 / 501-624-3856

Tonoloway Tack Drives, HCR 81, Box 100, Needmore, PA 17238

Torel, Inc., 1708 N. South St., P.O. Box 592, Yoakum, TX 77995 / 512-293-2341; FAX: 512-293-3413

TOZ (See U.S. Importer-Nygord Precision Products)

Track of the Wolf, Inc., 18308 Joplin St. NW, Elk River, MN 55330-1773 / 763-633-2500; FAX: 763-633-2550

Traditions Performance Firearms, P.O. Box 776, 1375 Boston Post Rd., Old Saybrook, CT 06475 / 860-388-4656; FAX: 860-388-4657 info@traditionsfirearms.com www.traditionsfirearms.com

Trafalgar Square, P.O. Box 257, N. Pomfret, VT 05053 / 802-457-1911

Trail Visions, 5800 N. Ames Terrace, Glendale, WI 53209 / 414-228-1328

Trax America, Inc., PO Box 898, 1150 Eldridge, Forrest City, AR 72335 / 870-633-0410; or 800-232-2327; FAX: 870-633-4788 trax@ipa.net www.traxamerica.com

Treadlok Gun Safe, Inc., 1764 Granby St. NE, Roanoke, VA 24012 / 800-729-8732; or 703-982-6881; FAX: 703-982-1059

Treemaster, P.O. Box 247, Guntersville, AL 35976 / 205-878-3597

Trevallion Gunstocks, 9 Old Mountain Rd., Cape Neddick, ME 03902 / 207-361-1130

Trico Plastics, 28061 Diaz Rd., Temecula, CA 92590 / 909-676-7714; FAX: 909-676-0267 ustinfo@ustplastics.com www.tricoplastics.com

Trigger Lock Division / Central Specialties Ltd., 220-D Exchange Dr., Crystal Lake, IL 60014 / 847-639-3900; FAX: 847-639-3972

Trijicon, Inc., 49385 Shafer Ave., P.O. Box 930059, Wixom, MI 48393-0059 / 248-960-7700 or 800-338-0563

Trilby Sport Shop, 1623 Hagley Rd., Toledo, OH 43612-2024 / 419-472-6222

Trilux, Inc., P.O. Box 24608, Winston-Salem, NC 27114 / 910-659-9438; FAX: 910-768-7720

Trinidad St. Jr. Col. Gunsmith Dept., 600 Prospect St., Trinidad, CO 81082 / 719-846-5631; FAX: 719-846-5667

Triple-K Mfg. Co., Inc., 2222 Commercial St., San Diego, CA 92113 / 619-232-2066; FAX: 619-232-7675 sales@triplek.com www.triplek.com

Tristar Sporting Arms, Ltd., 1814 Linn St. #16, N. Kansas City, MO 64116-3627 / 816-421-1400;

FAX: 816-421-4182 tristar@blity-it.net www.tristarsportingarms

Trius Traps, Inc., P.O. Box 25, 221 S. Miami Ave., Cleves, OH 45002 / 513-941-5682; FAX: 513-941-7970 triustraps@fuse.net www.triustraps.com

Trooper Walsh, 2393 N Edgewood St, Arlington, VA 22207

Trotman, Ken, 135 Ditton Walk, Unit 11, Cambridge, CB5 8PY ENGLAND / 01223-211030; FAX: 01223-212317 www.kentrolman.com

Tru-Balance Knife Co., P.O. Box 140555, Grand Rapids, MI 49514 / 616-647-1215

True Flight Bullet Co., 5581 Roosevelt St., Whitehall, PA 18052 / 610-262-7630; FAX: 610-262-7806

Truglo, Inc., P.O. Box 1612, McKinna, TX 75070 / 972-774-0300; FAX: 972-774-0323 www.truglosights.com

Trulock Tool, PO Box 530, Whigham, GA 31797 / 229-762-4678; FAX: 229-762-4050 trulockchokes@hotmail.com trulockchokes.com

Tru-Square Metal Products Inc., 640 First St. SW, P.O. Box 585, Auburn, WA 98071 / 253-833-2310; or 800-225-1017; FAX: 253-833-2349 t-tumbler@qwest.net

Tucker, James C., P.O. Box 1212, Paso Robles, CA 93447-1212

Tucson Mold, Inc., 930 S. Plumer Ave., Tucson, AZ 85719 / 520-792-1075; FAX: 520-792-1075

Turk's Head Productions, Mustafa Bilal, 908 NW 50th St., Seattle, WA 98107-3634 / 206-782-4164; FAX: 206-783-5677 info@turkshead.com www.turkshead.com

Turnbull Restoration, Doug, 6680 Rt. 5 & 20, P.O. Box 471, Bloomfield, NY 14469 / 585-657-6338; FAX: 585-657-6338 turnbullrest@mindspring.com www.turnbullrestoration.com

Tuttle, Dale, 4046 Russell Rd., Muskegon, MI 49445 / 616-766-2250

Tyler Manufacturing & Distributing, 3804 S. Eastern, Oklahoma City, OK 73129 / 405-677-1487; or 800-654-8415

U

U.S. Fire Arms Mfg. Co., Inc., 55 Van Dyke Ave., Hartford, CT 06106 / 877-227-6901; FAX: 800-644-7265 usfirearms.com

U.S. Importer-Wm. Larkin Moore, 8430 E. Raintree Ste. B-7, Scottsdale, AZ 85260

U.S. Repeating Arms Co., Inc., 275 Winchester Ave., Morgan, UT 84050-9333 / 801-876-3440; FAX: 801-876-3737

U.S. Tactical Systems (See Keng's Firearms Specialty)

Ugartechea S. A., Ignacio, Chonta 26, Eibar, SPAIN / 43-121257; FAX: 43-121046

Ultra Dot Distribution, P.O. Box 362, 6304 Riverside Dr., Yankeetown, FL 34498 / 352-447-2255; FAX: 352-447-2266

Ultralux (See U.S. Importer-Keng's Firearms)

UltraSport Arms, Inc., 1955 Norwood Ct., Racine, WI 53403 / 414-554-3237; FAX: 414-554-9731

Uncle Bud's, HCR 81, Box 100, Needmore, PA 17238 / 717-294-6000; FAX: 717-294-6005

Uncle Mike's (See Michaels of Oregon Co.)

Unertl Optical Co., Inc., 103 Grand Avenue, P.O. Box 895, Mars, PA 16046-0895 / 724-625-3810; FAX: 724-625-3819 unertl@nauticom.net www.unertloptics.net

Unique/M.A.P.F., 10 Les Allees, 64700, Hendaye, FRANCE / 33-59 20 71 93

UniTec, 1250 Bedford SW, Canton, OH 44710 / 216-452-4017

United Binocular Co., 9043 S. Western Ave., Chicago, IL 60620

United Cutlery Corp., 1425 United Blvd., Sevierville, TN 37876 / 865-428-2532; or 800-548-0835; FAX: 865-428-2267

United States Optics Technologies, Inc., 5900 Dale St., Buena Park, CA 90621 / 714-994-4901; FAX: 714-994-4904 www.usoptics.com

United States Products Co., 518 Melwood Ave., Pittsburgh, PA 15213-1136 / 412-621-2130; FAX: 412-621-8740 sales@us-products.com www.us-products.com

Universal Sports, PO Box 532, Vincennes, IN 47591 / 812-882-8680; FAX: 812-882-8680

Unmussig Bullets, D. L., 7862 Brentford Dr., Richmond, VA 23225 / 804-320-1165

Upper Missouri Trading Co., P.O. Box 100, 304 Harold St., Crofton, NE 68730-0100 / 402-388-4844

USAC, 4500-15th St. East, Tacoma, WA 98424 / 206-922-7589

Utica Cutlery Co., 820 Noyes St., Utica, NY 13503 / 315-733-4663; FAX: 315-733-6602

V

V.H. Blackinton & Co., Inc., 221 John L. Dietsch, Attleboro Falls, MA 02763-0300 / 508-699-4436; FAX: 508-695-5349

Valdada Enterprises, P.O. Box 773122, 31733 County Road 35, Steamboat Springs, CO 80477 / 970-879-2983; FAX: 970-879-0851 www.valdada.com

Valtro USA, Inc, 1281 Andersen Dr., San Rafael, CA 94901 / 415-256-2575; FAX: 415-256-2576

VAM Distribution Co. LLC, 1141-B Mechanicsburg Rd., Wooster, OH 44691 www.rex10.com

Van Gorden & Son Inc., C. S., 1815 Main St., Bloomer, WI 54724 / 715-568-2612

Van Horn, Gil, P.O. Box 207, Llano, CA 93544

Van Patten, J. W., P.O. Box 145, Foster Hill, Milford, PA 18337 / 717-296-7069

Vann Custom Bullets, 330 Grandview Ave., Novato, CA 94947

Van's Gunsmith Service, 224 Route 69-A, Parish, NY 13131 / 315-625-7251

Varmint Masters, LLC, Rick Vecqueray, PO Box 6724, Bend, OR 97708 / 541-318-7306; FAX: 541-318-7306 varmintmasters@bendcable.com www.varmintmasters.net

Vecqueray, Rick. See: VARMINT MASTERS, LLC

Vega Tool Co., c/o T.R. Ross, 4865 Tanglewood Ct., Boulder, CO 80301 / 303-530-0174 clanlaird@aol.com www.vegatool.com

Vektor USA, Mikael Danforth, 5139 Stanart St, Norfolk, VA 23502 / 888-740-0837; or 757-455-8895; FAX: 757-461-9155

Venco Industries, Inc. (See Shooter's Choice Gun Care)

Venus Industries, P.O. Box 246, Sialkot-1, PAKISTAN FAX: 92 432 85579

Verney-Carron, BP 72-54 Boulevard Thiers, 42002 St Etienne Cedex 1, St Etienne Cedex 1, FRANCE / 33-477791500; FAX: 33-477790702 email@verney-carron.com www.verney-carron.com

Vest, John, 1923 NE 7th St., Redmond, OR 97756 / 541-923-8898

VibraShine, Inc., PO Box 577, Taylorsville, MS 39168 / 601-785-9854; FAX: 601-785-9874

Vibra-Tek Co., 1844 Arroya Rd., Colorado Springs, CO 80906 / 719-634-8611; FAX: 719-634-6886

Vic's Gun Refinishing, 6 Pineview Dr., Dover, NH 03820-6422 / 603-742-0013

Victory Ammunition, PO Box 1022, Milford, PA 18337 / 717-296-5768; FAX: 717-296-9298

Victory USA, P.O. Box 1021, Pine Bush, NY 12566 / 914-744-2060; FAX: 914-744-5181

Vihtavuori Oy, FIN-41330 Vihtavuori, FINLAND, / 358-41-3779211; FAX: 358-41-3771643

Vihtavuori Oy/Kaltron-Pettibone, 1241 Ellis St., Bensenville, IL 60106 / 708-350-1116; FAX: 708-350-1606

Viking Video Productions, P.O. Box 251, Roseburg, OR 97470

Vincent's Shop, 210 Antoinette, Fairbanks, AK 99701

Vincenzo Bernardelli S.p.A., 125 Via Matteotti, P.O. Box 74, Gardone V.T., Bresci, 25063 ITALY / 39-30-8912851-2-3; FAX: 39-30-8910249

Vintage Arms, Inc., 6003 Saddle Horse, Fairfax, VA 22030 / 703-968-0779; FAX: 703-968-0780

Vintage Industries, Inc., 781 Big Tree Dr., Longwood, FL 32750 / 407-831-8949; FAX: 407-831-5346

Viper Bullet and Brass Works, 11 Brock St., Box 582, Norwich, ON N0J 1P0 CANADA

Viramontez Engraving, Ray Viramontez, 601 Springfield Dr., Albany, GA 31721 / 229-432-9683 sgtvira@aol.com

Viramontez, Ray. See: VIRAMONTEZ ENGRAVING

Virgin Valley Custom Guns, 450 E 800 N #20, Hurricane, UT 84737 / 435-635-8941; FAX: 435-635-8943 vvcguns@infowest.com www.virginvalleyguns.com

Visible Impact Targets, Rts. 5 & 20, E. Bloomfield, NY 14443 / 716-657-6161; FAX: 716-657-5405

Vitt/Boos, 1195 Buck Hill Rd., Townshend, VT 05353 / 802-365-9232

Voere-KGH GmbH, Untere Sparchen 56, A-6330 Kufstein, Tirol, AUSTRIA / 0043-5372-62547; FAX: 0043-5372-65752 voere@aon.com www.voere.com

Volquartsen Custom Ltd., 24276 240th Street, PO Box 397, Carroll, IA 51401 / 712-792-4238; FAX: 712-792-2542 vcl@netins.net www.volquartsen.com

Vorhes, David, 3042 Beecham St., Napa, CA 94558 / 707-226-9116; FAX: 707-253-7334

Vortek Products, Inc., P.O. Box 871181, Canton, MI 48187-6181 / 313-397-5656; FAX: 313-397-5656

VSP Publishers (See Heritage/VSP Gun Books), PO Box 887, McCall, ID 83638 / 208-634-4104; FAX: 208-634-3101

VTI Gun Parts, P.O. Box 509, Lakeville, CT 06039 / 860-435-8068; FAX: 860-435-8146 mail@vtigunparts.com www.vtigunparts.com

Vulpes Ventures, Inc. Fox Cartridge Division, P.O. Box 1363, Bolingbrook, IL 60440-7363 / 630-759-1229

W

W. Square Enterprises, 9826 Sagedale Dr., Houston, TX 77089 / 281-484-0935; FAX: 281-464-9940 lfdw@pdq.net www.loadammo.com

W. Waller & Son, Inc., 2221 Stoney Brook Rd., Grantham, NH 03753-7706 / 603-863-4177 www.wallerandson.com

W.B. Niemi Engineering, Box 126 Center Road, Greensboro, VT 05841 / 802-533-7180 or 802-533-7141

W.C. Wolff Co., PO Box 458, Newtown Square, PA 19073 / 610-359-9600; or 800-545-0077; mail@gunsprings.com www.gunsprings.com

W.E. Birdsong & Assoc., 1435 Monterey Rd., Florence, MS 39073-9748 / 601-366-8270

W.E. Brownell Checkering Tools, 9390 Twin Mountain Cir., San Diego, CA 92126 / 858-695-2479; FAX: 858-695-2479

W.J. Riebe Co., 3434 Tucker Rd., Boise, ID 83703

W.R. Case & Sons Cutlery Co., Owens Way, Bradford, PA 16701 / 814-368-4123; or 800-523-6350; FAX: 814-368-1736 jsullivan@wrcase.com www.wrcase.com

Wagoner, Vernon G., 2325 E. Encanto St., Mesa, AZ 85213-5917 / 480-835-1307

Wakina by Pic, 24813 Alderbrook Dr., Santa Clarita, CA 91321 / 800-295-8194

Waldron, Herman, Box 475, 80 N. 17th St., Pomeroy, WA 99347 / 509-843-1404

Walker Arms Co., Inc., 499 County Rd. 820, Selma, AL 36701 / 334-872-6231; FAX: 334-872-6262

Wallace, Terry, 385 San Marino, Vallejo, CA 94589 / 707-642-7041

Walls Industries, Inc., P.O. Box 98, 1905 N. Main, Cleburne, TX 76033 / 817-645-4366; FAX: 817-645-7946 www.wallsoutdoors.com

Walters Industries, 6226 Park Lane, Dallas, TX 75225 / 214-691-6973

Walters, John. See: WALTERS WADS

Walters Wads, John Walters, 500 N. Avery Dr., Moore, OK 73160 / 405-799-0376; FAX: 405-799-7727 www.tinwadman@cs.com

Walther America, PO Box 22, Springfield, MA 01102 / 413-747-3443 www.walther-usa.com

Walther GmbH, Carl, B.P. 4325, D-89033 Ulm, GERMANY

Walt's Custom Leather, Walt Whinnery, 1947 Meadow Creek Dr., Louisville, KY 40218 / 502-458-4361

WAMCO-New Mexico, P.O. Box 205, Peralta, NM 87042-0205 / 505-869-0826

Ward & Van Valkenburg, 114 32nd Ave. N., Fargo, ND 58102 / 701-232-2351

Ward Machine, 5620 Lexington Rd., Corpus Christi, TX 78412 / 512-992-1221

Wardell Precision Handguns Ltd., 48851 N. Fig Springs Rd., New River, AZ 85027-8513 / 602-465-7995

Warenski, Julie, 590 E. 500 N., Richfield, UT 84701 / 801-896-5319; FAX: 801-896-5319

Warne Manufacturing Co., 9057 SE Jannsen Rd., Clackamas, OR 97015 / 503-657-5590 or 800-683-5590; FAX: 503-657-5695 info@warnescopemounts.com www.warnescopemounts.com

Warren Muzzleloading Co., Inc., Hwy. 21 North, P.O. Box 100, Ozone, AR 72854 / 501-292-3268

Washita Mountain Whetstone Co., P.O. Box 378, Lake Hamilton, AR 71951 / 501-525-3914

Wasmundt, Jim, P.O. Box 511, Fossil, OR 97830

Watson Bros., 39 Redcross Way, SE1 1H6, London, ENGLAND FAX: 44-171-403-336

Watson Trophy Match Bullets, 467 Pine Loop, Frostproof, FL 33843 / 863-635-7948 or 864-244-7948 cbestbullet@aol.com

Wayne E. Schwartz Custom Guns, 970 E. Britton Rd., Morrice, MI 48857 / 517-625-4079

Wayne Firearms For Collectors & Investors

Wayne Specialty Services, 260 Waterford Drive, Florissant, MO 63033 / 413-831-7083

WD-40 Co., 1061 Cudahy Pl., San Diego, CA 92110 / 619-275-1400; FAX: 619-275-5823

Weatherby, Inc., 3100 El Camino Real, Atascadero, CA 93422 / 805-466-1767; FAX: 805-466-2527 www.weatherby.com

Weaver Products ATK, P.O. Box 39, Onalaska, WI 54650 / 800-648-9624 or 608-781-5800; FAX: 608-781-0368

Weaver Scope Repair Service, 1121 Larry Mahan Dr., Suite B, El Paso, TX 79925 / 915-593-1005

Webb, Bill, 6504 North Bellefontaine, Kansas City, MO 64119 / 816-453-7431

Weber & Markin Custom Gunsmiths, 4-1691 Powick Rd., Kelowna, BC V1X 4L1 CANADA / 250-762-7575; FAX: 250-861-3655 www.weberandmarkinguns.com

Weber Jr., Rudolf, P.O. Box 160106, D-5650, GERMANY / 0212-592136

Webley and Scott Ltd., Frankley Industrial Park, Tay Rd., Birmingham, B45 0PA ENGLAND / 011-021-453-1864; FAX: 0121-457-7846 guns@webley.co.uk www.webley.co.uk

Webster Scale Mfg. Co., P.O. Box 188, Sebring, FL 33870 / 813-385-6362

Weems, Cecil, 510 W Hubbard St., Mineral Wells, TX 76067-4847 / 817-325-1462

Weigand Combat Handguns, Inc., 1057 South Main Rd., Mountain Top, PA 18707 / 570-868-8358; FAX: 570-868-5218 sales@jackweigand.com www.scopemount.com

Weihrauch KG, Hermann, Industriestrasse 11, 8744 Mellrichstadt, Mellrichstadt, GERMANY

Welch, Sam. See: SAM WELCH GUN ENGRAVING

Wellington Outdoors, P.O. Box 244, 1140 Monticello Rd., Madison, GA 30650 / 706-342-4915; FAX: 706-342-7568

Wells, Rachel, 110 N. Summit St., Prescott, AZ 86301 / 928-445-3655 wellssportstore@aol.com

Wells Creek Knife & Gun Works, 32956 State Hwy. 38, Scottsburg, OR 97473 / 541-587-4202; FAX: 541-587-4223

Welsh, Bud. See: HIGH PRECISION

Wenger North America/Precise Int'l, 15 Corporate Dr., Orangeburg, NY 10962 / 800-431-2996; FAX: 914-425-4700

Wenig Custom Gunstocks, 103 N. Market St., PO Box 249, Lincoln, MO 65338 / 660-547-3334; FAX: 660-547-2881 gustock@wenig.com www.wenig.com

Werth, T. W., 1203 Woodlawn Rd., Lincoln, IL 62656 / 217-732-1300

Wescombe, Bill (See North Star West)

Wessinger Custom Guns & Engraving, 268 Limestone Rd., Chapin, SC 29036 / 803-345-5677

West, Jack L., 1220 W. Fifth, P.O. Box 427, Arlington, OR 97812

Western Cutlery (See Camillus Cutlery Co.)

Western Design (See Alpha Gunsmith Division)

Western Mfg. Co., 550 Valencia School Rd., Aptos, CA 95003 / 831-688-5884 lotsabears@eathlink.net

Western Missouri Shooters Alliance, PO Box 11144, Kansas City, MO 64119 / 816-597-3950; FAX: 816-229-7350

Western Nevada West Coast Bullets, PO BOX 2270, DAYTON, NV 89403-2270 / 702-246-3941; FAX: 702-246-0836

Westley Richards & Co., 40 Grange Rd., Birmingham, ENGLAND / 010-214722953

Westley Richards Agency USA (See U.S. Importer for

Westwind Rifles, Inc., David S. Sullivan, P.O. Box 261, 640 Briggs St., Erie, CO 80516 / 303-828-3823

Weyer International, 2740 Nebraska Ave., Toledo, OH 43607 / 419-534-2020; FAX: 419-534-2697

Whildin & Sons Ltd, E.H., RR 2 Box 119, Tamaqua, PA 18252 / 717-668-6743; FAX: 717-668-6745

Whinnery, Walt (See Walt's Custom Leather)

Whiscombe (See U.S. Importer-Pelaire Products)

White Barn Wor, 431 County Road, Broadlands, IL 61816

White Pine Photographic Services, Hwy. 60, General Delivery, Wilno, ON K0J 2N0 CANADA / 613-756-3452

White Rifles, Inc., 1464 W. 40 South, Linden, UT 84042 / 801-932-7950 www.whiterifles.com

White Rock Tool & Die, 6400 N. Brighton Ave., Kansas City, MO 64119 / 816-454-0478

Whitestone Lumber Corp., 148-02 14th Ave., Whitestone, NY 11357 / 718-746-4400; FAX: 718-767-1748

MANUFACTURER'S DIRECTORY

Wichita Arms, Inc., 923 E. Gilbert, P.O. Box 11371, Wichita, KS 67211 / 316-265-0661; FAX: 316-265-0760

Wick, David E., 1504 Michigan Ave., Columbus, IN 47201 / 812-376-6960

Widener's Reloading & Shooting Supply, Inc., P.O. Box 3009 CRS, Johnson City, TN 37602 / 615-282-6786; FAX: 615-282-6651

Wideview Scope Mount Corp., 13535 S. Hwy. 16, Rapid City, SD 57701 / 605-341-3220; FAX: 605-341-9142 wvdon@rapidnet.com www.jii.to

Wiebe, Duane, 5300 Merchant Cir. #2, Placerville, CA 95667 / 530-344-1357; FAX: 530-344-1357 wiebe@d-wdb.com

Wiest, Marie. See: GUNCRAFT SPORTS, INC.

Wilcox All-Pro Tools & Supply, 4880 147th St., Montezuma, IA 50171 / 515-623-3138; FAX: 515-623-3104

Wilcox Industries Corp., Robert F Guarasi, 53 Durham St., Portsmouth, NH 03801 / 603-431-1331; FAX: 603-431-1221

Wild Bill's Originals, P.O. Box 13037, Burton, WA 98013 / 206-463-5738; FAX: 206-465-5925 wildbill@haleyon.com

Wild West Guns, 7521 Old Seward Hwy., Unit A, Anchorage, AK 99518 / 800-992-4570 or 907-344-4500; FAX: 907-344-4005 wwguns@ak.net www.wildwestguns.com

Wilderness Sound Products Ltd., 4015 Main St. A, Springfield, OR 97478 / 800-47-0006; FAX: 541-741-0263

Wildey, Inc., 45 Angevine Rd, Warren, CT 06754-1818 / 203-355-9000; FAX: 203-354-7759

Wildlife Research Center, Inc., 1050 McKinley St., Anoka, MN 55303 / 612-427-3350; or 800-USE-LURE; FAX: 612-427-8354

Will-Burt Co., 169 S. Main, Orrville, OH 44667

William Fagan & Co., 22952 15 Mile Rd., Clinton Township, MI 48035 / 810-465-4637; FAX: 810-792-6996

William E. Phillips Firearms, 38 Avondale Rd., Wigston, Leicester, ENGLAND / 0116 2886334; FAX: 0116 2810644 wephillips@aol.com

William Powell & Son (Gunmakers) Ltd., 35-37 Carrs Lane, Birmingham, B4 7SX ENGLAND / 121-643-0689; FAX: 121-631-3504

William Powell Agency, 22 Circle Dr., Bellmore, NY 11710 / 516-679-1158

Williams Gun Sight Co., 7389 Lapeer Rd., Box 329, Davison, MI 48423 / 810-653-2131 or 800-530-9028; FAX: 810-658-2140 williamsgunsight.com

Williams Mfg. of Oregon, 110 East B St., Drain, OR 97435 / 503-836-7461; FAX: 503-836-7245

Williams Shootin' Iron Service, The Lynx-Line, Rt. 2 Box 223A, Mountain Grove, MO 65711 / 417-948-0902; FAX: 417-948-0902

Williamson Precision Gunsmithing, 117 W. Pipeline, Hurst, TX 76053 / 817-285-0064; FAX: 817-280-0044

Willow Bend, P.O. Box 203, Chelmsford, MA 01824 / 978-256-8508; FAX: 978-256-8508

Wilsom Combat, 2234 CR 719, Berryville, AR 72616-4573 / 800-955-4856; FAX: 870-545-3310

Wilson Case, Inc., PO Box 1106, Hastings, NE 68902-1106 / 800-322-5493; FAX:

402-463-5276 sales@wilsoncase.com www.wilsoncase.com

Wilson Combat, 2234 CR 719, Berryville, AR 72616-4573 / 800-955-4856

Winchester Div. Olin Corp., 427 N. Shamrock, E. Alton, IL 62024 / 618-258-3566; FAX: 618-258-3599

Winchester Sutler, Inc., The, 270 Shadow Brook Lane, Winchester, VA 22603 / 540-888-3595; FAX: 540-888-4632

Windish, Jim, 2510 Dawn Dr., Alexandria, VA 22306 / 703-765-1994

Wingshooting Adventures, 0-1845 W. Leonard, Grand Rapids, MI 49544 / 616-677-1980; FAX: 616-677-1986

Winkle Bullets, R.R. 1, Box 316, Heyworth, IL 61745

Winter, Robert M., P.O. Box 484, 42975-287th St., Menno, SD 57045 / 605-387-5322

Wise Custom Guns, 1402 Blanco Rd., San Antonio, TX 78212-2716 / 210-828-3388

Wise Guns, Dale, 1402 Blanco Rd., San Antonio, TX 78212 / 210-734-9999

Wiseman and Co., Bill, PO Box 3427, Bryan, TX 77805 / 409-690-3456; FAX: 409-690-0156

Wisners Inc/Twin Pine Armory, P.O. Box 58, Hwy. 6, Adna, WA 98522 / 360-748-4590; FAX: 360-748-1802

Wolf (See J.R. Distributing)

Wolf Performance Ammunition, 2201 E. Winston Rd. Ste. K, Anaheim, CA 92806-5537 / 702-837-8506; FAX: 702-837-9250

Wolfe Publishing Co., 6471 Airpark Dr., Prescott, AZ 86301 / 520-445-7810 or 800-899-7810; FAX: 520-778-5124

Wolf's Western Traders, 1250 Santa Cora Ave. #613, Chula Vista, CA 91913 / 619-482-1701 patwolf4570book@aol.com

Wolverine Footwear Group, 9341 Courtland Dr. NE, Rockford, MI 49351 / 616-866-5500; FAX: 616-866-5658

Wood, Frank (See Classic Guns, Inc.), 5305 Peachtree Ind. Blvd., Norcross, GA 30092 / 404-242-7944

Woodleigh (See Huntington Die Specialties)

Woods Wise Products, P.O. Box 681552, Franklin, TN 37068 / 800-735-8182; FAX: 615-726-2637

Woodstream, P.O. Box 327, Lititz, PA 17543 / 717-626-2125; FAX: 717-626-1912

Woodworker's Supply, 1108 North Glenn Rd., Casper, WY 82601 / 307-237-5354

Woolrich, Inc., Mill St., Woolrich, PA 17701 / 800-995-1299; FAX: 717-769-6234/6259

Working Guns, Jim Coffin, 1224 NW Fernwood Cir., Corvallis, OR 97330-2909 / 541-928-4391

World of Targets (See Birchwood Casey)

World Trek, Inc., 7170 Turkey Creek Rd., Pueblo, CO 81007-1046 / 719-546-2121; FAX: 719-543-6886

Worthy Products, Inc., RR 1, P.O. Box 213, Martville, NY 13111 / 315-324-5298

Wostenholm (See Ibberson [Sheffield] Ltd., George)

Wright's Gunstock Blanks, 8540 SE Kane Rd., Gresham, OR 97080 / 503-666-1705 doyal@wrightsguns.com www.wrightsguns.com

WTA Manufacturing, P.O. Box 164, Kit Carson, CO 80825 / 800-700-3054; FAX:

719-962-3570 wta@rebeltec.net http://www.members.aol.com/ductman249/wta.html

Wyant Bullets, Gen. Del., Swan Lake, MT 59911

Wyant's Outdoor Products, Inc., PO Box 9, Broadway, VA 22815

Wyoming Custom Bullets, 1626 21st St., Cody, WY 82414

Wyoming Knife Corp., 101 Commerce Dr., Ft. Collins, CO 80524 / 303-224-3454

X

X-Spand Target Systems, 26-10th St. SE, Medicine Hat, AB T1A 1P7 CANADA / 403-526-7997; FAX: 403-528-2362

Y

Yankee Gunsmith "Just Glocks", 2901 Deer Flat Dr., Copperas Cove, TX 76522 / 817-547-8433; FAX: 254-547-8887 ed@justglocks.com www.justglocks.com

Yavapai College, 1100 E. Sheldon St., Prescott, AZ 86301 / 520-776-2353; FAX: 520-776-2355

Yavapai Firearms Academy Ltd., P.O. Box 27290 Prescott Valley, AZ 86312 / 928-772-8262; FAX: 928-772-0062 info@yfainc.corn www.yfainc.com

Yearout, Lewis E. (See Montana Outfitters), 308 Riverview Dr E, Great Falls, MT 59404 / 406-761-0859

Yee, Mike. See: CUSTOM STOCKING

Yellowstone Wilderness Supply, P.O. Box 129, W Yellowstone, MT 59758 / 406-646-7613

Yesteryear Armory & Supply, P.O. Box 408, Carthage, TN 37030

York M-1 Conversions, 12145 Mill Creek Run, Plantersville, TX 77363 / 936-894-2397; FAX 936-894-2397

Young Country Arms, William, 1409 Kuehner Dr. #13, Simi Valley, CA 93063-4478

Z

Zabala Hermanos S.A., P.O. Box 97, 20600 Elbar Elgueta, Guipuzcoa, 20600 SPAIN / 943-768076; FAX: 943-768201

Zander's Sporting Goods, 7525 Hwy 154 West, Baldwin, IL 62217-9706 / 800-851-4373; FAX 618-785-2320

Zanotti Armor, Inc., 123 W. Lone Tree Rd., Ceda Falls, IA 50613 / 319-232-9650

Zeeryp, Russ, 1601 Foard Dr., Lynn Ross Manor Morristown, TN 37814 / 615-586-2357

Zero Ammunition Co., Inc., 1601 22nd St. SE, PC Box 1188, Cullman, AL 35056-1188 / 800-545-9376; FAX: 205-739-4683

Ziegel Engineering, 1390 E. Bunnett St. #I, Signa Hill, CA 90755 / 562-596-9481; FAX: 562-598-4734 ziegel@aol.com www.ziegeleng.com

Zim's, Inc., 4370 S. 3rd West, Salt Lake City, UT 84107 / 801-268-2505

Z-M Weapons, 203 South St., Bernardston, MA 01337 / 413-648-9501; FAX: 413-648-0219

Zufall, Joseph F., P.O. Box 304, Golden, CO 80402-0304

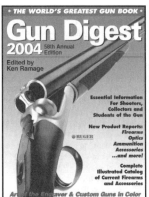
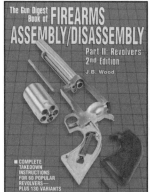

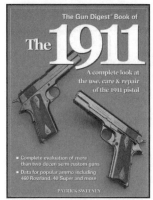
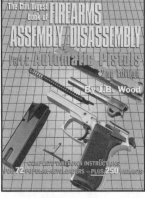
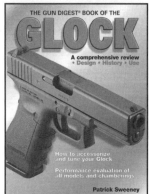

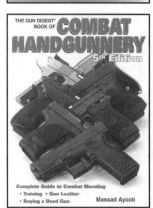

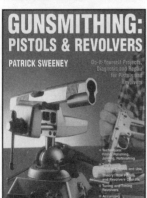
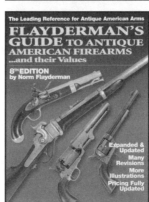
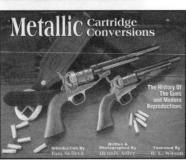
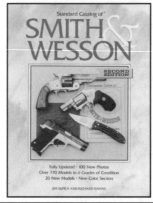